THE STRUGGLE FOR DEMOCRACY

THE STRUGGLE FOR DEMOCRACY

THIRD EDITION

Edward S. Greenberg
University of Colorado

Benjamin I. Page
Northwestern University

An Imprint of Addison Wesley Longman, Inc.

New York • Reading, Massachusetts • Menlo Park, California • Harlow, England
Don Mills, Ontario • Sydney • Mexico City • Madrid • Amsterdam

Acquisitions Editor: Peter Glovin
Developmental Manager: Elissa M. Pinto
Supplements Editor: Tom Kulesa
Project Editor: Marina Vaynshteyn
Text Designer: Alice Fernandes-Brown
Cover Designer: Kay Petronio
Cover Photo: Jeff Speilman/The Image Bank
Art Studio: Electragraphics
Photo Researcher: Mira Schachne
Electronic Production Manager: Alexandra Odulak
Desktop Project Administrator: Sarah Johnson
Manufacturing Manager: Hilda Koparanian
Electronic Page Makeup: Sarah Johnson
Printer and Binder: Courier/Kendallville, Inc.
Cover Printer: The Lehigh Press, Inc.
Background images in part openers, chapter openers, and boxes: courtesy of Images © 1996 PhotoDisc, Inc.

For permission to use copyrighted material, grateful acknowledgment is made to the copyright holders on pp. C1–C3, which are hereby made part of this copyright page.

Library of Congress Cataloging-in-Publication Data

Greenberg, Edward S., (date)–
The struggle for democracy / Edward S. Greenberg, Benjamin Page.—3rd ed.
p. cm.
Includes bibliographical references and index.
ISBN 0-673-98089-8
1. United States—Politics and government. 2. Democracy—United States.
I. Page, Benjamin I. II. Title.
IN PROCESS
320.973—dc20 96-41899
CIP

ISBN 0–673–98089–8

12345678910—CRK—99989796

Brief Contents

Contents

CHAPTER 4 The Evolving Structure of the United States

III Political Linkage

CHAPTER 5 Public Opinion

CHAPTER 8 Political Parties

CHAPTER 9 Voting and Elections

CHAPTER 10 Social Movements

List of Boxes

The Struggle for Democracy

Resource Feature

What Role for Government?

Politics and Film

Preface

Our goal in this textbook is to provide a teaching and learning tool that enables students to think clearly and critically about American democracy, gives a clear and interesting presentation, and helps readers to understand and appreciate the fascinating and complex operations of American government and politics. The enthusiastic reception of the first two editions of the text by instructors and students suggests that we have largely been on target in meeting this goal. Nothing is perfect, however, so we have made some changes in this edition that we believe will make the text even more effective for teaching and learning.

Hallmarks of the Text

We organize the materials in this text around two main concepts: *democracy* and the story of how people have struggled to achieve it; and *tools for understanding* American government and politics, with special emphasis on the influence of structural factors like the economy, social change, cultural ideas, and the international system.

- **Democracy**

  For many years now, we have been impressed and excited by the growing demand of people all over the world for democracy, that is, for individual freedom and the right for people to rule themselves. We think it is timely and important in light of the struggles for democracy going on in places like South Africa, China, and Eastern Europe, to reexamine and reevaluate the health and vitality of democracy in the United States, the original home of liberal democracy and the inspiration for much that is happening in the world today.

  Thinking critically about democracy In order to properly examine and evaluate the health and vitality of democracy, we must first understand the meaning of democracy and learn how to use this definition to measure the relative distance of real-world institutions and practices from the ideal. In the first chapter, we carefully define democracy and suggest key factors that indicate the degree to which any society can be said to be democratic. In each subsequent chapter, we invite readers to use this definition and these indicators to think about the quality of democracy in the United States, to judge the degree to which this country is becoming more or less democratic, and to assess which institutions hinder or encourage the full development of democracy. For example, in Chapter 8, we ask students to evaluate the degree to which American political parties help or hinder citizens' ability to control the actions of public officials. By using this approach, we hope to engage the critical thinking faculties of undergraduate students in a way that has not been done well in introductory textbooks.

The struggle for democracy An overarching theme that we call "the struggle for democracy" ties the various parts of the text together and gives the narrative a dramatic quality that makes learning about American politics and government more interesting for students. In using this theme to tell the story of democracy in America, we hope to share with students some of the excitement and high moral purpose that often infuse politics and governing, and to provide a counterweight to some of the cynicism and political apathy that seem to prevail today. We use the struggle for democracy theme as a way to suggest that the United States is a far more democratic place than it was at the beginning, and that the main reason why this is so has been because of the determination of Americans over the years to fight for democracy. We make the additional point that the United States is less democratic than it might be, and that further progress will depend mainly on the continuing struggle for democracy. This theme is woven throughout the book and is the subject of a special boxed feature.

Tools for Understanding Politics and Government

We believe that government and politics can only be understood when they are analyzed in the larger environment in which they are embedded. This larger environment, we suggest, is defined by the nature of American society and its economy, by the unique American political culture, and by the international system. In each chapter, we endeavor to show how these multiple factors shape the way citizens and political leaders act and the policies government adopts. For instance, in Chapter 4, we show how changes in the global economy have shaped the political agenda in the United States and how our political culture, with its strong emphasis on individualism and distrust of strong government, has influenced the kinds of policies we have adopted in response to global change.

To help students come to grips with this rich environment of social, economic, cultural, and international influences, we present a powerful yet simple analytical framework in Chapter 1 to help students keep track of these multiple influences and identify how they interact with political and governmental institutions and actors. By doing so, we hope that students will begin to understand the American political system in a holistic and integrated fashion so that seemingly unconnected and random information about political actors, government institutions, and structural factors can be seen to be operating together in readily understandable ways.

Organization and Coverage

For the most part, the text is organized like the typical course in American government and politics. Part I is the introduction to the text and focuses on the issues of democracy and tools for understanding. Part II is about the structural foundations of American government and politics and addresses, in addition to subjects like the economy, culture, and international system, the constitutional framework of the American political system and the development of the federal system. Part III focuses on what we call *political linkage* institutions, like parties, elections, public opinion, social movements, and interest groups, that serve to convey the wants, needs, and demands of individuals and groups to public officials. Part IV concentrates on the central institutions of the national government, including the presidency, Congress, and the Supreme Court. Part V includes chapters that describe the kinds of policies that the national government produces and attempt to analyze how effective government is in solving pressing problems.

Although all of the usual topics in the introductory course are covered in the text, our focus on democracy and the struggle for democracy, as well as our focus on tools for understanding that emphasize the larger environment within which American politics and government operate, allows us to talk about the traditional topics in a fresh way and to pay attention to topics that are not well covered in other texts.

- We pay much more attention than other texts to *structural* factors, including the American economy, social change in the United States, the American political culture, and changes in the global system, and examine their impact on politics, government, and public policy. These factors are first described in Chapter 4—a chapter that is unique among introductory texts—and brought to bear on a wide range of issues throughout subsequent chapters. For example, our discussion of interest group politics includes relevant information about how the distribution of income and wealth affects the ability of different groups to form effective lobbying organizations.
- We attend very carefully to issues of *democratic political theory*. This follows from our critical thinking objective, which asks students to assess the progress and prospects for democracy in the United States, and from our desire to present American history as the history of the struggle for democracy.
- We also include more *historical* information than is common among introductory texts, because the struggle for democracy theme and the attention we pay to evaluating the progress of democracy in the United States require historical perspective. Our focus on the political impact of economic, social, and global change also requires a historical perspective.
- We also include substantial *comparative* information, because we believe that a full understanding of government and politics and of the impact of structural factors on them is only possible after developments, practices, and institutions in the United States are compared to those in other nations. Comparative materials are highlighted in the body of the text by a small globe that appears in the margin.

- Our approach also means that the subjects of *civil liberties* and *civil rights* are not treated in conjunction with the Constitution in Part II, which is the case with many introductory texts, but in Part V on public policy. This is because we believe that the real-world status of civil liberties and civil rights, while partially determined by specific provisions of the Constitution, is better understood as a product of the interaction of structural, political, and governmental factors. Thus, the status of civil rights for gays and lesbians depends not only on constitutional provisions but on the state of public opinion, degrees of support from elected political leaders, and the decisions of the Supreme Court.

We realize, however, that many instructors prefer to introduce their students to the subjects of civil liberties and civil rights immediately after consideration of the Constitution. Those instructors who feel more comfortable presenting the materials in this way can simply assign the liberties and rights chapters out of order. No harm will occur by doing so.

What's New in This Edition

A number of important changes have been made in this edition. They include the following:

- Information has been updated throughout. There is not a single page in the text without fresh information. Timely subjects, such as the affirmative action controversy, changing party alignments, and the impact of global change, are given greater attention.
- Civil liberties and civil rights are treated in separate chapters in this edition rather than in a single chapter as in the first two editions. Additionally, the chapters now appear at the beginning of Part V as a way to emphasize the particular importance of rights and liberties in American democracy.
- We have made the text more user friendly for students by paying more attention to the layout of text and the highlighting of key points, better defining technical terms, presenting more detailed captions that explain tables and graphs, and providing more information in photo captions.
- We have placed our analytical framework further into the background. While the framework is still there—it determines the entire argument of the book as well the organization of the chapters—we no longer make it as prominent a feature as it was in the first two editions. A smaller portion of Chapter 1 is devoted to its presentation, for instance, and we no longer ask students to master the framework. We hope and expect that students will come to think about American government and politics in a holistic fashion, with special emphasis on the impact of structural factors like the economy and the global system, in the natural course of absorbing and thinking about materials presented in the text. Those instructors who found the analytical framework useful in their teaching will find that the framework is still here, though more subtly presented, and they can continue to emphasize it in their classes. Those instructors who are not interested in the framework per se, or who think it too complicated for their students, will find that this edition of *The Struggle for Democracy* will enhance their teaching because the analytical framework, though in the background, helps to organize course materials in such a coherent fashion that students can more easily understand the complexities of American government and politics.

Features

We have incorporated a number of features intended to make learning more interesting and effective. The following features are found in each chapter:

- *The Struggle for Democracy* is a boxed feature that highlights political struggles throughout our history to enhance popular sovereignty, political equality, and liberty. Examples include the struggle to add the Bill of Rights to the Constitution (Chapter 2), attempts to reform our present system of campaign finance (Chapter 7), the fight to make "one-person, one-vote" the law of the land (Chapter 14), the on-going effort by women to increase representation and power in governmental institutions (Chapter 15), and Thurgood Marshall's courageous defense of black civil rights in the deep South in the 1950s (Chapter 17).
- *In This Chapter* opens each chapter and lists the major topics to be addressed.
- An *opening vignette* highlights the major themes of the chapter by describing an important event or development that continues to affect contemporary American politics. Examples include the welfare reform movement in the states (Chapter 3), corporate downsizing and the rise of income inequality in the United States (Chapter 4), the collapse of the Democratic Party's New Deal coalition (Chapter 8), the Reagan Revolution (Chapter 12), the Oklahoma City bombing and the rise of militant anti-federal government sentiments (Chapter 13), and the budget deadlock in the 104th Congress and the partial closures of the federal government (Chapter 19). There are also new chapter-opening vignettes on the 1996 presidential and congressional elections.
- Boldfaced terms are tied to *definitions in the margins* and to a *glossary* at the end of the text.
- *Comparative* materials are highlighted in the margin by a globe, drawing students' attention to the discussion.

- Discussions of *democracy* are highlighted by an icon that serves to draw students' attention to the topic.

- A chapter *summary* helps students review important chapter materials.
- A list of annotated *Suggested Readings,* appearing at the end of each chapter, helps students delve deeper into subjects that interest them.
- An important new feature for this edition is an annotated *World Wide Web* list (of *Internet Sources*), with Internet addresses that links students to a wealth of information on the Web about politics and government, as well as information about the economy, social conditions, cultural trends, and global military, diplomatic, and economic developments. Web site materials are provided by government agencies, universities and research institutes, mass media outlets (newspapers and news magazines, networks, wire services, and the like), interest groups, and private individuals.

The following features appear frequently throughout the text:

What Role for Government? is a new boxed feature that addresses the ongoing controversies over the proper role of the national government in American life. Examples include the role of government in job creation in the economy (Chapter 4), in censoring the content of the Internet (Chapter 16), and in providing racial remedies such as affirmative action and minority "set asides" (Chapter 17).

Politics and Film boxes examine how Hollywood portrays various aspects of American politics. Examples include boxes on how the women's movement has influenced films (Chapter 10), on the changing treatment of African-Americans in films (Chapter 17), and how the Vietnam War was presented in cinema. Unique in introductory textbooks, this feature reflects the importance we attribute to popular culture in shaping American political life.

Resource Feature boxes provide additional information, often of a technical nature.

We also provide several appendixes, to which students may refer frequently:

- The Declaration of Independence
- The Constitution
- *The Federalist Papers,* Nos. 10, 51, and 78
- A complete listing of United States Presidents and Congresses

Supplements

Longman provides an impressive array of text supplements to aid instructors in teaching and students in learning. Each item in this extensive package works together to create a fully integrated learning system. Great care was taken to provide both students and professors with a supportive supplements package that accurately reflects the unique spirit of *The Struggle for Democracy.*

For the Instructor

Instructor's Manual Written by Mary L. Carns of Stephen F. Austin State University, the *Instructor's Manual* will help instructors prepare stimulating lectures, classroom activities, and assignments. The manual features chapter outlines and summaries, a broad range of teaching suggestions, ideas for student research, and suggestions for discussions that complement the themes in the text. For each text chapter, the *Instructor's Manual* provides a detailed list of all pedagogical features found in the book as well as a useful cross-referencing guide to help instructors integrate all of the supplements available from Longman. The manual also includes a new multimedia section containing annotated descriptions of a wide variety of films, videos, and software.

Test Bank Robert England of Oklahoma State University wrote and revised approximately 4,000 multiple-choice, short-answer, true-false, matching, and essay questions expressly designed to reinforce and test students' knowledge of the *concepts* and *themes* presented in the third edition of *The Struggle for Democracy.* Each question is cross-referenced to the corresponding text topic and page number. To promote greater testing flexibility, about 15 percent of the multiple-choice questions appear in the *Study Guide* or the *SuperShell* computerized tutorial. Each question is also accompanied by a descriptor indicating the required skill level, whether a question is new or revised, or whether it appears in the *Study Guide* or on *SuperShell.* The *Test Bank* is available in both print and electronic formats.

TestMaster The *Test Bank* is available on *TestMaster* software, allowing instructors to edit existing questions and add new questions. *TestMaster* is available for IBM PCs and compatibles and for Macintosh.

QuizMaster Coordinated with the *TestMaster* program, *QuizMaster* allows instructors to give students timed or untimed tests on line; on completing the tests, students can see their scores and view or print diagnostic reports listing topics or objectives that have been mastered or topics requiring further review. When *QuizMaster* is installed on a network, students' scores are saved so instructors can view students', class, or course progress. *QuizMaster* is available for IBM PCs and compatibles and for Macintosh.

E-mail Instructors and students can address their questions and comments about *The Struggle for Democracy* directly to Ed Greenberg, one of the book's authors, at the University of Colorado through E-mail. Greenberg can be reached via the Internet at **Edward.Greenberg@colorado.edu**

Transparency Resource Package John C. Domino of Sam Houston State University has selected more than 80 full-color transparencies that reinforce the information and themes presented in *The Struggle for Democracy, 3/e.*

***Struggle for Democracy* Home Page** Designed and maintained by Michael Martinez of the University of Florida, the site features chapter-by-chapter summaries and topic links, updated analysis of current events by the authors, and student activities. The Internet address is **http://www.awl.com/longman/amgov/struggle/struggle.html**

Laser Disc

Multimedia

Politics in Action *Laser Disc* Eleven "Lecture Launchers," covering broad subjects such as social movements, conducting a campaign, and the passage of a bill, are examined through narrated videos, interviews, edited documentaries, original footage, and political ads. *Politics in Action* is available as an easy-to-use laser disc or videotape, and is accompanied by an extensive *User's Manual,* which provides background on the segments, links to topics in textbooks, discussion questions, and bar codes (for easy access when using the laser disc version).

For the Student

Study Guide Written by Mary L. Carns of Stephen F. Austin State University, the *Study Guide* reinforces text discussions to guide students in their understanding of American government and politics. Written in a straightforward, student-friendly manner, the guide features an introduction, chapter summaries, key concepts, crossword puzzles, suggested assignment topics, and research questions and resources. Sample tests, including a mix of conceptual and factual questions, help students evaluate their own understanding of each chapter in *The Struggle for Democracy, 3/e.*

The HarperCollins Political Pamphleteer To help instructors and students incorporate the expertise of others into lectures and reading, HarperCollins asked specialists in various areas of political science to write essays appropriate for 50-minute classes. Each pamphlet in the series complements or elaborates on the themes raised in *The Struggle for Democracy.* Pamphlet titles include "Women and Politics"; "The Environment and Politics"; "Urban Politics"; "Latinos and Politics"; "National Health Care"; "Bill of Rights"; "Blacks and Politics"; "Landmark Supreme Court Decisions"; and "Affirmative Action and the Supreme Court."

SuperShell Student Tutorial Software Prepared by Robert England of Oklahoma State University (the author of the *Test Bank*), *SuperShell* helps students retain key concepts and ideas from *The Struggle for Democracy, 3/e* through a versatile drill-and-practice format. Each chapter features chapter outlines for the text, glossary terms and their definitions in a flash-card format, and 40 multiple-choice, 20 true-false, and 20 short-answer questions that are not found in the *Study Guide. SuperShell* provides immediate correct answers and page references, maintains a running score of each student's performance, and is available for IBM PCs and compatibles.

Acknowledgments

Writing and producing an introductory textbook is an incredibly complex, cooperative enterprise in which many people besides the authors play roles. We would like to take the opportunity to thank them, one and all. We start with the many wonderful people at Addison Wesley Longman and HarperCollins. We owe a special debt to our first executive editor, Lauren Silverman, whose guidance, attention, affection, and intelligence led us from the beginning to the end of the project. Every author team should be blessed with such an editor at least once in its career. Leo Wiegman, Lauren's successor, brought great knowledge and love of the discipline to the second and third editions. Special thanks also go to Susan Katz, who believed in and supported this book from the beginning, and to Marcus Boggs, who showed his support in many ways. Arthur Pomponio, the development editor for the first edition and the managing editor for the second and third, helped us keep our argument straight and our eye on the prize. Joe Budd helped pull all the pieces of the project together for the second edition while Ann Kirby did the same for this edition. Project editors Donna DeBenedictis, Melonie Parnes, and Marina Vaynshteyn did incredible work on the three editions, as design managers Jill Yutkowitz, Lucy Krikorian, and Alice Fernandes-Brown did in coordinating an award-winning design and striking art program. Photo researchers Leslie Coopersmith, Carol Parden, and Mira Schachne unearthed the dazzling array of photographs found in the three editions. And senior marketing manager Suzanne Daghlian successfully conveyed our vision to the Longman sales force.

There are many colleagues we want to thank. Ken Kollman, an assistant professor at the University of Michigan, provided immensely valuable contributions to both the first and second editions. William Haltom of the University of Puget Sound wrote the first draft of the chapter on civil rights and liberties for the first edition and helped revise that chapter for the second edition. Ed Greenberg offers special thanks to Mike Lynn and Vicki Ash for their hours of research assistance, to Illana Gallon who saved him from many errors of fact and interpretation, and to the students in his introductory American Government and Politics course at the University of Colorado for revealing, in no uncertain terms, what worked and what didn't work in the text. Ben Page would particularly like to thank Aaron Bicknese, Noelle Gonzales, Heajeong Lee, Richard Powell, and David Wrobel for their help with the first and second editions, and Richard Powell, Jason Tannenbaum, and Heajeong Lee for their help on the third.

Addison Wesley Longman enlisted the help of many political scientists on various aspects of this project. Their advice was invaluable, and the final version of the book is far different (and no doubt better) than it would have been without their help. We would like to extend our appreciation to the following political scientists, who advised, consulted, and guided us through the first, second, or third editions of *The Struggle for Democracy* and its supplements:

Gordon Alexandre, Glendale Community College
John Ambacher, Framingham State College
Ross K. Baker, Rutgers University
Ryan Barrilleaux, University of Miami
Stephen Bennett, University of Cincinnati
Bill Bianco, Duke University
Melanie J. Blumberg, University of Akron
Joseph P. Boyle, Cypress College
Evelyn Brodkin, University of Chicago
James Bromeland, Winona State University
Barbara Brown, Southern Illinois University–Carbondale
Joseph S. Brown, Baylor University
David E. Camacho, Northern Arizona University
Mary Carns, Stephen F. Austin State University
Jim Carter, Sam Houston State University
Gregory Casey, University of Missouri
Paul Chardoul, Grand Rapids Community College
Alan J. Cigler, University of Kansas
David Cingranelli, State University of New York at Binghamton
John Coleman, University of Wisconsin
Ken Collier, University of Kansas
Edward Collins, Jr., University of Maine
Lee Collins, Monmouth College
Richard W. Crockett, Western Illinois University
Lane Crothers, Illinois State University
Landon Curry, University of Texas
Christine Day, University of New Orleans
Alan Draper, St. Lawrence University
Euel Elliott, University of Texas
Robert S. Erikson, University of Houston
Thomas Ferguson, University of Massachusetts, Boston
M. Lauren Ficaro, Chapman University
John Geer, Arizona State University
Scott D. Gerber, College of William and Mary
Thomas Gillespie, Seton Hall University
Doris A. Graber, The University of Illinois
John Green, University of Akron
Daniel P. Gregory, El Camino Community College
Eric E. Grier, Georgia State University
Bruce E. Gronbeck, University of Iowa
Maria Guido, Bentley College
Russell L. Hanson, Indiana University
Richard Herrera, Arizona State University
Roberta Herzberg, Indiana University
Seth Hirshorn, University of Michigan
Eugene Hogan, Western Washington University
Marilyn Howard, Cols State Community College
Ronald J. Hrebnar, University of Utah
David Hunt, Triton College
Jon Hurwitz, University of Pittsburgh
James Hutter, Iowa State University
Gary C. Jacobson, University of California at San Diego
William Jacoby, University of South Carolina
Willoughby Jarrell, Kennesaw State College
Christopher B. Jones, Eastern Oregon State University
William Kelly, Auburn University
Fred Kramer, University of Massachusetts
Richard Lehne, Rutgers University
Jan E. Leighley, Texas A & M University
Joel Lieske, Cleveland State University
Stan Luger, University of Northern Colorado
Michael W. McCann, University of Washington
Carroll R. McKibbin, California Polytechnic State University
Dean E. Mann, University of California
Joseph R. Marbach, Seton Hall University
Michael D. Martinez, University of Florida
Louise Mayo, County College of Morris
Neil Milner, University of Hawaii
Kristen R. Monroe, Princeton University
Mike Munger, University of Texas
Laurel A. Myer, Sinclair Community College
Albert Nelson, University of Wisconsin–La Crosse

David Nice, Washington State University
Charles Noble, California State University–Long Beach
Colleen M. O'Connor, San Diego Mesa College
Daniel J. O'Connor, California State University–Long Beach
John Orman, Fairfield University
Marvin Overby, University of Mississippi
Kenneth Palmer, University of Maine
Toby Paone, St. Charles Community College
Arthur Paulson, Southern Connecticut State University
Mark P. Petracca, University of California
Joseph Peschek, Hamline University
Larry Pool, Mountain View College
John D. Redifer, Mesa State College
Richard Reitano, Dutchess Community College
Curtis G. Reithel, University of Wisconsin–La Crosse
Russell D. Renka, Southeast Missouri State University
Richard C. Rich, Virginia Tech
Leroy N. Rieselbach, Indiana University
Sue Tolleson Rinehart, Texas Tech University
Phyllis F. Rippey, Western Illinois University
David Robinson, University of Houston–Downtown
David W. Romero, University of California
Francis E. Rourke, Johns Hopkins University
David C. Saffell, Ohio Northern University
Donald L. Scruggs, Stephens College
Jim Seroka, University of North Florida
L. Earl Shaw, Northern Arizona University
John M. Shebb, University of Tennessee
Mark Silverstein, Boston University
Morton Sipress, University of Wisconsin–Eau Claire
Henry B. Sirgo, McNeese State University
David A. Smeltzer, Portland State University
C. Neal Tate, University of North Texas
Robert Thomas, University of Houston
Richard J. Timpone, State University of New York–Stony Brook
Eric Uslaner, University of Maryland
Elliot Vittes, University of Central Florida
Charles Walcott, University of Minnesota
Susan Weissman, St. Mary's College of California
Nelson Wikstrom, Virginia Commonwealth University
Daniel Wirls, University of California
Eugene R. Wittkopf, Louisiana State University
Jay Zarowitz, Muskegon Community College

And finally, we thank you, the instructors and students who use this book. May it bring you success!

Edward S. Greenberg
Benjamin I. Page

PART I

Introduction: Main Themes

In Part I, we explain the overall plan of the book, describe the main themes that will recur throughout its pages, and suggest why the topics that will be explored are important to know. We introduce the central dramatic thread that ties the book together: the struggle for democracy. We tell how the book will go about making the point that American political life has always involved a struggle among individuals, groups, classes, and institutions over the meaning, extent, and practice of democracy. We suggest that, while democracy has made great progress over the years in the United States, it remains only imperfectly realized and is threatened by new problems that only vigilant and active citizens can solve.

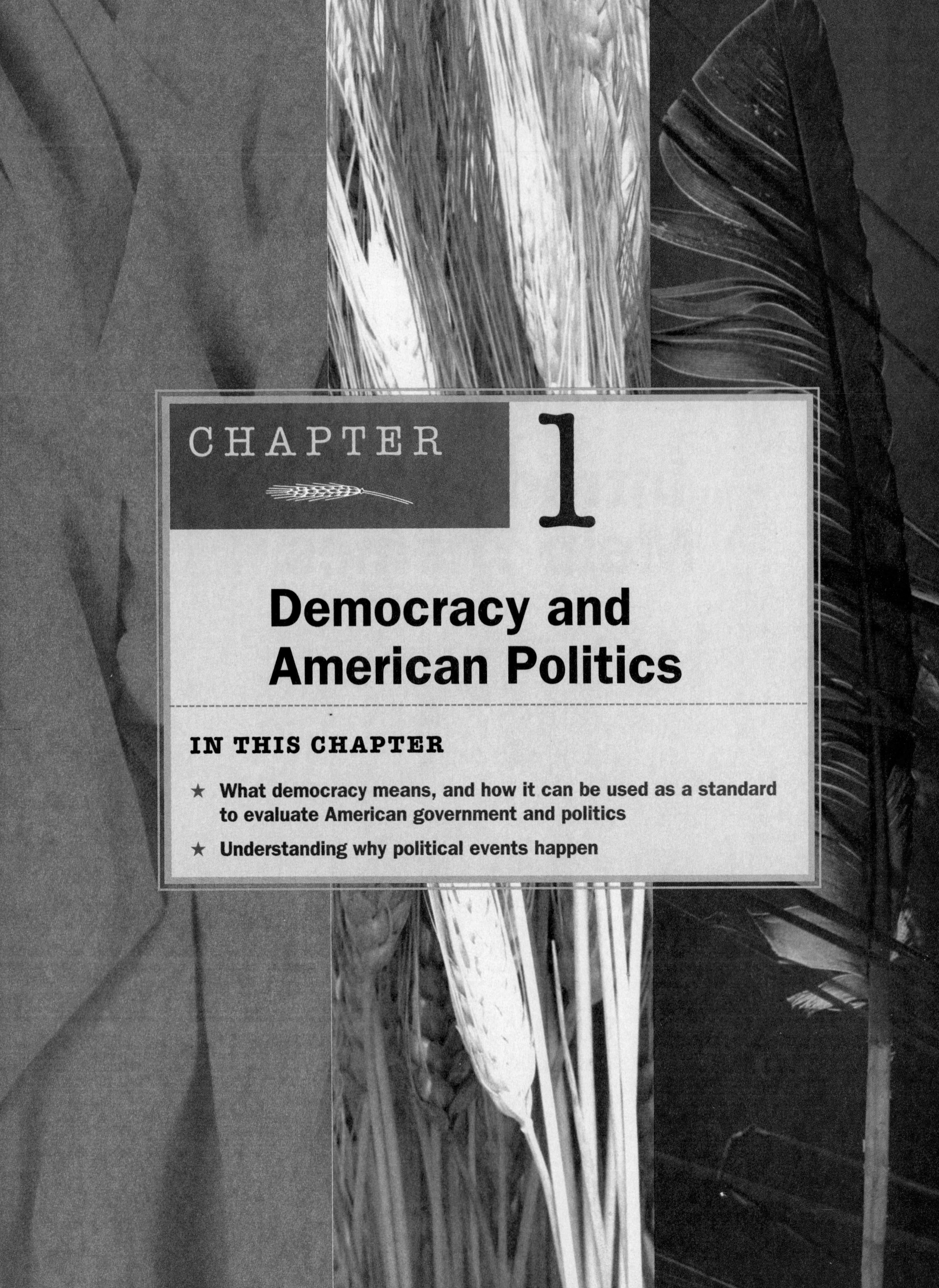

CHAPTER 1

Democracy and American Politics

IN THIS CHAPTER

- ★ What democracy means, and how it can be used as a standard to evaluate American government and politics
- ★ Understanding why political events happen

Robert Moses and the Struggle for Voting Rights

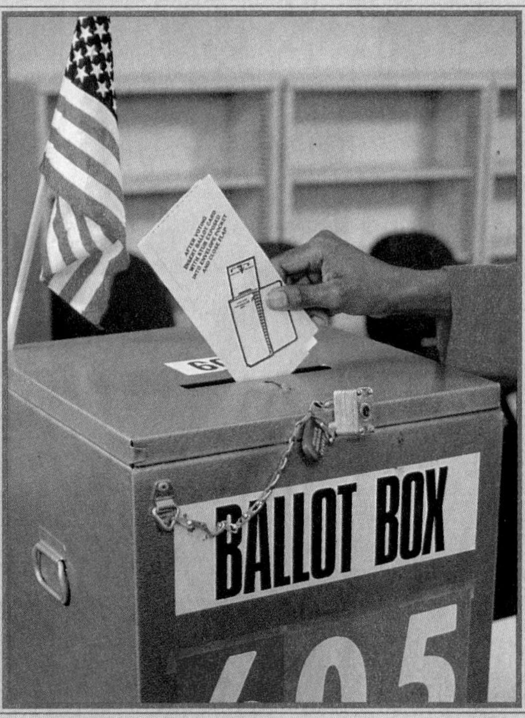

The right to vote in elections is fundamental to democracy. But many Americans have won the right to vote only after long struggles. It took more than 30 years from the adoption of the Constitution, for instance, for most states to allow people without property to vote. Women gained the right to vote in all U.S. elections only in 1920, and young people aged 18 to 20 did so only beginning in 1971. As the following story indicates, most African Americans in the United States did not have an effective right to vote until after 1965.

The Civil Rights Acts of 1957 and 1960 were intended, in part, to guarantee that African-Americans living in the southern states would be allowed to vote in local, state, and national elections. In the early 1960s, these laws had little effect in rigidly segregated states like Mississippi. There, only 5 percent of African-Americans were registered to vote, and none held elective office, though they accounted for 43 percent of the population. In Amite County, Mississippi, only one African-American was registered to vote out of approximately 5,000 eligible voters; in Walthall County, not a single black was registered, though roughly 3,000 were eligible to vote.[1] What kept them away from the polls was a combination of arcane and biased voting registration rules, economic pressures, and physical intimidation and violence directed against those brave enough to defy the prevailing political and social order. In Ruleville, Mississippi, Mrs. Fannie Lou Hamer was forced out of the house she was renting on a large plantation, fired from her job, and arrested, jailed, and beaten by police after she tried to register to vote. In Mileston, after an unsuccessful attempt to register, Hartman Turnbow lost his house to a Molotov cocktail. He was later arrested for arson.[2]

The Student Non-Violent Coordinating Committee (widely known by its initials, SNCC) launched its Voter Education Project in 1961 with the aim of ending black political isolation and powerlessness in the Deep South. Composed primarily of African-American college students from both the North and the South, SNCC aimed to increase black voter registration and to challenge exclusionary rules like the poll tax, which required people to pay a tax in order to vote, and the literacy test, which required people to prove their literacy before they could register. SNCC also wanted to enter African-American candidates in local elections. Their first step was to create "freedom schools" in some of the most segregated counties in Mississippi, Alabama, and Georgia to teach black citizens about their rights under the law and to encourage them to register to vote. Needless to say, SNCC volunteers tended to attract the malevolent attentions of police, local officials, and vigilantes.

The first of the freedom schools was founded in McComb, Mississippi, by a remarkable young man named Robert Parris Moses. Raised in Harlem, educated at Hamilton College and Harvard, and familiar with the South through frequent visits to relatives there, Moses was moved deeply by the first signs of the emerging civil rights struggle and quit his teaching job in order to work with other young people in SNCC. Despite repeated threats to his life and more than a few physical attacks, Moses traveled the back roads of Amite and Walthall counties, meeting with small groups of black farmers and encouraging them to attend the SNCC freedom school. At the school, he showed them not only how to fill out the registration forms but how to read and interpret the constitution of Mississippi, for the "literacy test" required potential voters to interpret to the satisfaction of the county registrar any of the constitution's 285 sections

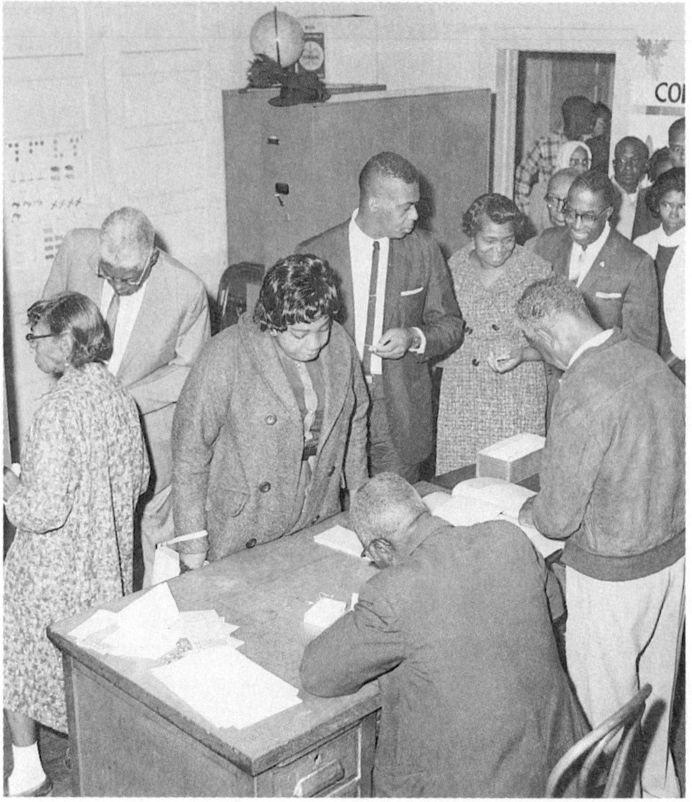

Discriminatory registration restrictions and intimidation heavily curbed African-American voting in the deep South for almost 100 years after the end of slavery. It was not until the passage of the 1965 Voting Rights Act that literacy tests, poll taxes, and other devices designed to keep Blacks away from the polls were outlawed, and African-Americans were able to turn out at the polls in record numbers.

(generally, only blacks failed the test, even lawyers and teachers). Once people in the school gathered the courage to journey to the county seat to try to register, Moses went along with them to lend support and encouragement.

Moses suffered for his activities. Over a period of a few months, he was arrested several times for purported traffic violations; attacked on the main street of Liberty, Mississippi, and beaten with the butt end of a knife by the cousin of the county sheriff; assaulted by a mob behind the McComb County courthouse; hit by police and dragged into the station house while standing in line at the voting registrar's office with one of his students; and jailed for not paying fines connected with his participation in civil rights demonstrations.

Despite the efforts of Bob Moses and other SNCC volunteers and the bravery of African-Americans who dared to defy the rules of black political exclusion in Mississippi, African-American voting registration increased hardly at all in that state in the early 1960s. Black political participation there would have to await passage by Congress of the 1965 Voting Rights Act, whose powerful tools of federal government enforcement guaranteed the voting rights of all citizens. The Voter Education Project, however, was one of the key building blocks of a powerful civil rights movement (see Chapter 10) that would eventually force federal action in the 1960s to support the citizenship rights (or **civil rights**) of African-Americans in the South.

civil rights Guarantees of equal citizenship to all social groups.

Robert Moses and the black citizens of Mississippi were willing to risk life and limb to gain full and equal citizenship in the United States. Likewise, throughout our history, Americans from all walks of life have joined the struggle to make the United States a more democratic place. The same thing is happening in many parts of the world today. We live in an age of democratic aspiration and upsurge; people the world over are demanding the right to govern themselves and control their own destiny. And more and more of them are realizing their dream. Americans are participants in this drama, not only because American political ideas and institutions have often provided inspiration for democratic movements in other countries, but also because the struggle for democracy continues in our own society. In the United States, where it is honored and celebrated, democracy remains an unfinished product. This continuing struggle for democracy, to expand and complete it, is a major feature of American history and a defining characteristic of our politics today. It is, moreover, the central theme of this book.

Democracy

> **Why should there not be a patient confidence in the ultimate justice of the people? Is there any better, or equal, hope in the world?**
>
> **—Abraham Lincoln, First Inaugural Address**

The extraordinary attractiveness of democracy's central idea—that ordinary people want to rule themselves and are capable of doing so—is only one reason why democracy has become so popular here and abroad. Political thinkers have suggested a number of reasons why democracy is superior to other forms of political organization. Some have argued, for instance, that democracy is the form of government that best protects human rights because it is the only one based on a recognition of the intrinsic worth and equality of human beings. Others believe that democracy is the form of government most likely to reach rational decisions because it can count on the cooperation and expertise of a

The struggle for democracy has become a global phenomenon. Here, newly enfranchised black citizens in South Africa demonstrate for their favorite candidate.

Democracy requires broad participation of citizens in public affairs. Recognizing that young voters are the least likely to vote, MTV's "Rock the Vote" campaign has been trying to draw more members of this group into political affairs. Here, MTV News' Tabitha Soren interviews Republican presidential candidate Bob Dole.

society's entire population. Other thinkers have claimed that democracies are more stable and long-lasting because their leaders, having been elected, enjoy a strong sense of legitimacy among their citizens. Still others suggest that democracy is the form of government most conducive to economic growth and well-being, a claim that is strongly supported by research findings. Others, finally, believe that democracy is the form of government under which human beings, because they are free, are best able to develop their natural capacities and talents.[3] There are many compelling reasons, then, why democracy has been preferred by so many.

We suggest that Americans prefer democracy over other forms of government. We further suggest that democracy has made enormous advances over the course of American history. Nevertheless, democracy remains incomplete in the United States, an aspiration rather than a finished product. Our goal in this book is to help students think carefully about the quality and progress of democracy in the United States. We want to help students reach their own independent judgments about the degree to which politics and government in the United States make our country more or less democratic. We want to help students draw their own conclusions about which political practices and institutions in the United States encourage and sustain democracy, and which ones discourage and undermine it.

In order to draw reasonable conclusions about how democratic we are and how democratic we are likely to become, and in order to understand why so many people have struggled so hard to attain it, we first need to be clear about the meaning of democracy. Not everyone uses the term in the same way or means the same thing by it. Because democracy has become so popular, the term has come to be associated with every conceivable type of political arrangement or regime, no matter how undemocratic they might be; the now-collapsed Soviet-style regimes of Eastern Europe once called themselves "people's democracies," for instance. So, considerable clarification is required before democracy can be used as a measuring rod to assess American government and politics.

The Democratic Idea

Many of our ideas about democracy originated with the ancient Greeks. The Greek roots of the word *democracy* are *demos,* meaning "the people," and *kratein* meaning "to rule." **Democracy,** then, is "rule by the people" or, to put it another way, self-government by the *many,* as opposed to the *few* or the *one.* This is similar to Lincoln's definition in his Gettysburg Address: "Government of the people, by the people, and for the people."

democracy A system of rule by the people, defined by the existence of popular sovereignty, political equality, and political liberty.

Most Western philosophers and rulers before the eighteenth century were not friendly to the idea of rule by the *many.* Most believed that governing was a difficult art, requiring the greatest sophistication, intelligence, character, and training, and not the province of ordinary people. Most preferred rule by a select *few* (such as an aristocracy, in which a hereditary nobility rules) or by an enlightened *one* (such as a sovereign or a military chieftain). In practice, most governments were quite undemocratic.

The idea that ordinary people might rule themselves represents an important departure from such beliefs. At the heart of democratic theory is a faith in the capacity of ordinary human beings to govern themselves wisely. As the American philosopher John Dewey put it,

> The foundation of democracy is faith in the capacities of human nature; faith in human intelligence and in the power of pooled and cooperative experience. It is not belief that these things are complete but that if given a show they will grow and be able to generate progressively the knowledge and wisdom needed to guide collective action.[4]

Also crucial to the concept of democracy is the idea that it is the purpose of a government to serve *all* of its people and that, ultimately, none but the people themselves can be relied on to know and to act in accord with their own values and interests. Power in any other hands will eventually lead to **tyranny.**

tyranny The abuse of power by a ruler or government.

Direct Versus Representative Democracy

To the ancient Greeks, democracy meant rule by the common people exercised *directly* in open assemblies. They believed that democracy implied face-to-face deliberation and decision making about the public business. Direct participatory democracy requires, however, that all citizens be able to meet together regularly to debate and decide the issues of the day. Such a thing was possible in fifth century B.C. Athens, which was small enough to allow all citizens to gather together in one place. In Athens, moreover, citizens had time to meet and to deliberate because much of the productive work of society was done by slaves.

Because direct, participatory democracy is possible only in small communities where citizens with abundant leisure time can meet often face-to-face, it seems an unworkable arrangement for a society like the United States, which is large and populous, and where most people do not have time for continuous involvement in public meetings.[5] Although Thomas Jefferson advocated "direct action of the citizens" as the ideal form of democracy, he lamented that "such a government is evidently restrained to very narrow limits of space and population."[6] He recognized, as we must, that democracy in large societies must take the representative form, since millions of citizens cannot meet in open assembly. By **representative democracy** we mean a system in which the people select others, called *representatives,* to act in their place.

representative democracy Indirect democracy, in which the people rule through elected representatives.

The essence of the classical Greek idea of democracy was face-to-face deliberations among citizens in open assemblies. This is difficult to achieve in societies with large populations where democracy depends, instead, on the election of representatives.

Though representative (indirect) democracy seems to be the only form of democracy possible in large-scale societies, some political commentators argue that the participatory aspects of direct democracy are worth preserving as an ideal, and that certain domains of everyday life—workplaces and schools, for instance—could be enriched by more direct democratic practices.[7] It is worth pointing out, moreover, that direct democracy can and does flourish in some local communities today. In many New England towns, for example, citizens make decisions directly at town meetings.

Fundamental Principles of Representative Democracy

In large societies like our own, then, democracy means *rule by the people, exercised indirectly through elected representatives.* Still, this definition is not sufficiently precise to use as a standard by which to evaluate the American political system. To help further clarify the definition of democracy, we add three additional benchmarks drawn from the scholarly literature and current understanding about democracy. These benchmarks are *popular sovereignty, political equality,* and *political liberty.* A society in which all three flourish, we argue, is a healthy representative democracy. A society in which any of the three is absent or impaired falls short of the representative democratic ideal. Let us see what each of them means.

popular sovereignty A basic principle of democracy; means that the people ultimately rule.

Popular Sovereignty **Popular sovereignty** means that the ultimate source of all public authority in a democracy is the people and that government does the people's bidding. If ultimate authority resides not in the hands of the *many,* but in the hands of the *few* (as in an aristocratic order) or of the *one* (whether a benevolent sovereign or a ruthless dictator), then democracy does not exist.

How can we recognize popular sovereignty when we see it? Four observable conditions are especially important: (1) Government policies reflect the popular will; (2) people participate in the political process; (3) high-quality information and debate are available; and (4) the majority rules.

Government Policies Reflect What the People Want One sign of popular sovereignty is a close correspondence between what government does and what the people want it to do. It is hard to imagine a situation in which the people rule but government officials make policy contrary to the people's wishes.

This much seems obvious. However, does the democratic ideal require that government always do exactly what the people want, right away, responding to every whim and passing fancy of the people? This question has troubled many democratic theorists, and most have answered that democracy is best served when public officials and representatives respond to what might be called the "deliberative will" of the people: what the people want after they have deliberated about an issue with others. We might, then, want to speak of democracy as a system in which government policies conform to what the people want over some period of time (though not too long).

People Participate in the Political Process How can the popular will be known, and what makes the people's representatives respect it? Though public opinion polls may convey to political leaders what the public thinks and wants, it is through widespread participation in politics that the popular will is formed, expressed, and enforced. Without widespread participation, what the people want can only be guessed at or approximated. And without participation, nothing guarantees that officials will respond to what the people want. Widespread popular participation—at least in voting in elections—is necessary to ensure that responsive representatives will be chosen and that they will have continuous incentives to pay attention to the people. Because widespread participation is so central to popular sovereignty, we can say that the less political participation there is in a society, the weaker is the democracy.

High-Quality Information and Debate Are Available Fashioning an authentic popular will requires that people have available to them accurate political information, insightful interpretations, and vigorous debate. These are the responsibility of government officials, opposition parties, opinion leaders, and the mass media. If false or biased information is provided, if policies are not challenged and debated, or if misleading interpretations of the political world (or none at all) are offered, then the people cannot form opinions in accord with their values and interests, and popular sovereignty cannot be said to exist.

The Majority Rules How can the opinions and preferences of many individual citizens be combined into a single binding decision? Since unanimity is unlikely (and an insistence on unanimous agreement for policy changes would enshrine the status quo), reaching a decision requires a decision rule. If the actions of government are to respond to all citizens, each citizen being counted equally, the only decision rule that makes sense is **majority rule.**[8] The only alternative to majority rule is minority rule, which would unacceptably elevate the *few* over the *many.* In practical terms, what this means is that the popular will, formed in the best circumstances after careful deliberation, is discovered by ascertaining the positions on public issues of the majority of citizens.

majority rule The form of political decision making in which policies are decided on the basis of what a majority of the people want.

Majority rule has additional virtues. For instance, it is the only way to make decisions that recognize the intrinsic worth and equality of human beings; any other way of making decisions puts a minority of one sort or another at the head of the line and weights the preferences of some people more heavily than those of others. It is, then, the only way to make decisions that are consistent with political equality. Moreover, majority rule maximizes the number of people involved in decision making, enhancing participation, which is important to popular sovereignty. Also, majority rule may be more likely (though it is far from certain) to reach correct decisions, because it relies on "pooled judgments"—judgments that take into account a broader range of information, opinions, and expertise than any other way of making decisions. Finally, because more people are involved in making decisions under majority rule, policies that result from such a process are more likely to be accepted by the people than decisions made in other ways.

political equality The principle that says that each person in a democracy must carry equal weight in the conduct of the public business.

Political Equality The second fundamental principle of democracy, following popular sovereignty and closely intertwined with it, is **political equality,** meaning that each person carries the same weight in voting and other political decision making.

Imagine, if you will, a society in which one person could cast 100 votes in an election, another person 50 votes, and still another 25 votes, while many unlucky folks had only 1 vote each—or none at all. We would surely find such an arrangement a curious one, especially if that society described itself as democratic. We would react in this way because equality of citizenship has always been central to the democratic ideal. Democracy is a way of making decisions in which each person has one and only one voice. It means that people deliberate about their common problems and concerns as equals. Any other arrangement would violate our belief in the intrinsic worth of the individual and would fail to ensure that the government would pay equal attention to the values and interests of all citizens.

Most people know this intuitively. Our sense of what is proper is offended, for instance, when some class of people is denied the right to vote in a society that boasts the outer trappings of democracy. The denial of citizenship rights to African-Americans in the South before the passage of the 1965 Voting Rights Act is an example. We count it a victory for democracy when previously excluded groups are enfranchised.

Does democracy require substantial equality in the distribution of income and wealth? Thinkers as diverse as Aristotle, Rousseau, and Jefferson all thought so, because they believed that great inequalities in economic circumstances eventually turn into political inequality. Political scientist Robert Dahl describes the problem in the following way:

> If citizens are unequal in economic resources, so are they likely to be unequal in political resources; and political equality will be impossible to achieve. In the extreme case, a minority of rich will possess so much greater political resources than other citizens that they will control the state, dominate the majority of citizens, and empty the democratic process of all content.[9]

The ideal society for the practice of democracy, according to both Aristotle and Jefferson, is one with a large middle class built on a wide dispersion of private property, without an arrogant and overbearing wealthy class, and without a discontented and dangerous poverty-stricken class.

In later chapters, we will see that income and wealth are distributed highly unequally in the United States, and that this inequality is often translated into great inequalities among people and groups in the political arena.

While political equality is a cornerstone of American democracy, the nation's understanding of who is entitled to equal status has changed over the years. Just as African-Americans had to struggle for the right to vote, so, too, did women in the 1920s and 18- to 20-year-olds in more recent times. The right to vote was granted to all men regardless of race in 1870, although stringent registration rules made it very difficult for nonwhites to exercise this right. It wasn't until 1920 that the Nineteenth Amendment extended the right to vote to women; in 1971, a constitutional amendment lowered the voting age from 21 to 18.

Particularly important in this regard is unequal influence in the control of information, financial contributions to electoral campaigns, and access to interest groups. This unequal influence may represent a serious problem for American democracy.

Political Liberty The third basic element of democracy is **political liberty.** Political liberty refers to basic freedoms essential to the formation and expression of the popular will and its translation into policy. These essential liberties include the freedoms of speech, of conscience, of the press, and of assembly and association, embodied in the First Amendment to the U.S. Constitution.

political liberty The principle that citizens in a democracy are protected from government interference in the exercise of a range of basic freedoms, such as the freedoms of speech, association, and conscience.

Without these liberties (and a few more, including freedom from arbitrary arrest and the right to run for public office), the other fundamental principles of democracy could not exist. Popular sovereignty cannot be guaranteed if people are prevented from participating in politics or if opposition to the government is crushed. Popular sovereignty cannot prevail if the voice of the people is silenced, if citizens are not free to argue and debate, and to form and express their political opinions.[10] Political equality is violated if some people but not others can speak out.

For most people, democracy and liberty are inseparable. The concept of *self-government* implies not only the right to vote and to run for public office but also the right to speak one's mind, to petition the government, and to join with others in political parties, interest groups, or social movements. For example, the democratic upsurge that swept through Eastern Europe during the early

1990s generated demands not only for elected governments but also for an environment of political freedom that would make such elections meaningful.

Over the years, a number of political philosophers and practitioners have viewed liberty as *threatened* by democracy, rather than as essential to it. We will have more to say about this subject later, as we consider several possible objections to democracy. But it is our position that self-government and political liberty are inseparable, in the sense that the former is impossible without the latter. It follows that a majority cannot deprive an individual or a minority of its political liberty without violating democracy itself.

Objections to Majoritarian Representative Democracy

Not everyone is persuaded that democracy is the best form of government. Here are the main criticisms that have been leveled against democracy as we have defined it.

Democracy Leads to Bad Decisions Majoritarian, representative democracy is not perfect. There is no guarantee that it will always lead to good decisions. A majority, like a minority, can be unwise; it can be cruel and uncaring; it can be carried away by fads and fashions; and it can be misled by unscrupulous or incompetent leaders. Democratic theorist Robert Dahl points out, however, that no other form of decision making can be shown to lead consistently to better and wiser decisions.[11] The historical record on the results of rule by aristocrats, kings, princes, civil servants, or experts is not encouraging. Given its many other virtues, we would probably do best to stick with majority-rule representative democracy, despite its faults.

"Majority Tyranny" Threatens Liberty James Madison and other Founders of the American republic feared that majority rule was bound to undermine freedom and threaten the rights of the individual. They created a constitutional system (as you will see in Chapter 2), in fact, that was designed to protect certain liberties against the unwelcome intrusions of the majority. The fears of the Founders were not without basis. What they called the "popular passions" have sometimes stifled the freedoms of groups and individuals who have dared to be different. Until quite recently, for instance, a majority of Americans were unwilling to allow atheists or Communists the same rights of free speech that they allowed others, and conscientious objectors were harshly treated during World War I and World War II.

majority tyranny Suppression of the rights and liberties of a minority by the majority.

Though there have been instances during our history of **majority tyranny,** in which the majority violated the citizenship rights of a minority, there is no evidence that the *many* consistently threaten liberty more than the *few* or the *one.* Or to put it another way, the majority does not seem to be a special or unique threat to liberty. Violations of freedom seem as likely to come from powerful individuals and groups or from government officials as from the majority. Here are some important examples.

There were three periods in the history of the United States when liberty was most endangered, and the majority does not figure as the main culprit in any of them:

- In the late 1790s, criticism of public officials was made a crime under the Alien and Sedition Acts.
- After World War I, a "red scare" swept the nation, highlighted by the infamous antiradical, anti-immigrant, and antiunion raids of Attorney General A. Mitchell Palmer.

- In the late 1940s and early 1950s, another "red scare," conventionally known as *McCarthyism* (after Senator Joseph McCarthy, who led the assault), was unleashed.

The first two assaults on liberty were initiated by high government officials who acted without any discernible sign of majority pressure to do so. The third, while eventually supported by the majority, at least for a short time, seems to have been initiated by conservative leaders in an effort to discredit and roll back the liberal policies of the New Deal.[12]

Liberty is essential to self-government, and threats to liberty, whatever their origin, must be guarded against by those who love democracy.[13] But we must firmly reject the view that majority rule inevitably or uniquely threatens liberty. Majority rule is unthinkable, in fact, without the existence of basic political liberties.

The People Are Irrational and Incompetent Political scientists have spent decades studying the attitudes and behavior of citizens in the United States, and some of the findings are not encouraging. For the most part, the evidence shows that individual Americans do not care a great deal about politics and are rather poorly informed, unstable in their views, and not much interested in participating in the political process. These findings have led some observers to assert that citizens are ill equipped for the responsibility of self-governance and that public opinion (i.e., the will of the majority) should not be the ultimate determinant of what government does.

In Chapter 5, we will see, however, that this evidence about individuals has often been misinterpreted and that the American public taken collectively is more informed, sophisticated, and stable in its views than it is generally given credit for.

Majoritarian Democracy Threatens Minorities We have suggested that, when rendering a decision in a democracy, the majority must prevail. In most cases, the minority on the losing side of an issue need not worry unduly about its well-being because many of its members are likely to be on the winning side in future decisions. Thus, many people on the minority and losing side of an issue like welfare reform may be part of the majority and winning side on an issue like educational spending. What prevents majority tyranny over a minority in most policy decisions in a democracy is that the composition of the majority and the minority is always shifting.

What happens, however, in cases that involve race, ethnicity, or religion, for example, where minority status is fixed? Does the majority pose a threat to such minorities? Many people worry about such a possibility. The worry is that unbridled majority rule leaves no room for the claims of minorities. This worry has some historical foundations, for majorities have trampled on the rights of minorities with depressing frequency. Majorities long held, for instance, that African-Americans were inferior to whites and undeserving of full citizenship rights. Irish, Eastern European, Asian, and Latin American immigrants to our shores, among others, have all been subjected to periods of intolerance on the part of the majority, as have Catholics and Jews.

Nevertheless, the threat of majority tyranny may be exaggerated. As Robert Dahl points out, there is no evidence to support the belief that the rights of racial, ethnic, and religious minorities are better protected under alternative forms of political decision making, whether rule by the *few* or by the *one.*[14]

Moreover, it is not clear that a minority can ever feel entirely secure unless it has the full power of decision over all matters that directly or indirectly af-

Political hysteria has periodically blemished the record of American democracy. Fear of domestic communism, captured in this editorial cartoon, has been particularly potent in the twentieth century, and has led to the suppression of political groups deemed threatening by the authorities.

fect it. In extreme cases, this may require (and justify) the formation of a separate, independent country. But within a single nation like the United States, any broad minority power would raise the specter of minority tyranny—in which a minority dominates the majority—which is certainly not preferable to majority rule.

In any case, democracy, as we have defined it, requires the protection of crucial minority rights. Recall that majority rule is only one of the defining conditions of popular sovereignty and that popular sovereignty is only one of the three basic attributes of democracy, the others being *political equality* and *political liberty*. The position of minorities is protected in a fully developed democracy, in our view, by the requirements of equal citizenship (the right to vote, to hold public office, to be protected against violence, and to enjoy the equal protection of the law) and access to the full range of civil liberties (speech, press, conscience, and association). To the extent that a majority violates the citizenship rights and liberties of minorities, society falls short of the democratic ideal.

Democracy as an Evaluative Standard: How Democratic Are We?

After this discussion, it should be easy to see how and why the democratic ideal can be used as a measuring rod with which to evaluate American politics. It is important to remember, of course, that democracy is not the only available measuring rod. Each of us has a set of values or cherished goals by which we can also judge government policies: efficiency, community, national strength, law and order, equality, and more. The advantage of using democracy as the main evaluative standard in this book derives from its peculiar relevance for judging the adequacy of the political process and from its exalted position among the values held by most Americans.

We have learned that the fundamental attributes of democracy are popular sovereignty, political equality, and political liberty. Each suggests a set of questions that will be raised throughout this book to think critically about American political life.

Questions About Popular Sovereignty Does government do what citizens want it to do? Do citizens participate in politics? Can citizens be involved when they choose to be, and are political leaders responsive? Do political linkage institutions, such as political parties, elections, interest groups, and social movements, effectively transmit citizens' preferences to political leaders? What is the quality of the public deliberation on the major public policy issues of the day? Do the media and political leaders provide accurate and complete information?

Questions About Political Equality Do some individuals and groups have persistent and substantial advantages over other individuals and groups in the political process? Or is the political game open to all equally? Do government decisions and policies benefit some individuals and groups more than others?

Questions About Political Liberty Are citizens' rights and liberties universally available, protected, and used? Are people free to vote? Can they speak freely and freely form groups to petition their government? Do public authorities, private groups, or the majority threaten liberty or the rights of minorities?

These questions will help us assess where we are and where we are going as a democracy. We do not believe that popular sovereignty, political equality, and political liberty are attainable in perfect form. They are, rather, ideals to which our nation can aspire and standards against which we can measure reality. They can help us identify where democracy may be in jeopardy and where it may be becoming more vigorous.

Understanding How American Politics Works

In addition to helping you raise questions about the quality of democracy in the United States, our goal in this textbook is to help you understand how American government and politics work. This is not as straightforward a goal as it may seem. Understanding is not simply a matter of gathering the facts; insight does not necessarily come from just gathering and digesting information. After all, there is no shortage of information around us. Daily, we probably learn more than we will ever need to know about government decisions, political maneuvering and conflict, social and economic developments, and U.S. relations with other nations from newspapers, magazines, and television; but, because this information comes to us in unconnected bits and pieces, jumbled and out of context, making sense of it is no easy task. In fact, for many Americans, our nation's political life seems hopelessly confused and confusing.

This need not be the case. Things are not as disconnected and random as they appear. There are regular tendencies and patterns in our political life, if only we know how to organize this flood of information. In the remainder of this chapter, we describe a simple way to organize information and to think about how our political system works. Here we set out the basic guidelines that structure how we will talk about and understand government and politics in the United States.

The Main Factors of Political Life Are Interconnected

If we are to understand why things happen in government and politics, we begin with the actors and institutions most immediately involved in an event or decision. To understand why the 1965 Voting Rights Act happened—to use the example that appears in the story that opens this chapter, for instance—we would begin with an examination of Congress and its members, President Lyndon Johnson (who was the most vigorous proponent of the voting rights legislation) and his advisers in the White House and the executive branch, and the Supreme Court, which was becoming increasingly supportive of civil rights claims in the mid–1960s.

Knowing about these things, however, does not tell us all that we need to know. In order to understand why Congress, the president, and the Court behaved as they did in 1965, we would want to pay attention to the pressures brought to bear on them by public opinion (increasingly supportive of civil rights), the growing electoral power of African-Americans in the states outside the South, and, most important, the moral and disruptive power of the civil rights movement inspired by people like Robert Moses.

Even knowing these things, however, would not tell us all that we need to know about why the 1965 Voting Rights Act happened. Our inquiry would have to go deeper. Additional factors, such as economic and social change, the culture, the constitutional rules and the international position of the United States, also mattered. Economic changes in the nation over the course of many decades, for instance, triggered the "great migration" of African-Americans from the rural South to the urban North. Over the long run, this population shift to states with large blocks of **electoral college** votes, critical to the election of presidents, enhanced the political power of African-Americans. Changing ideas about black equality, first triggered by the rich cultural life of what was called the Harlem Renaissance in the 1920s, were also important in the story of why the 1965 Voting Rights happened, because they served to increase the number of Americans who were bothered by the second-class citizenship of African-Americans and willing to support changes in their status. The U.S. involvement in World War II and the Korean War, in which African-Americans served with distinction, was also important in the story of voting rights because it helped change the views of the white majority about black citizenship. For their part, black Americans began to think differently about themselves and what they were owed because of their involvement in these wars. Finally, the **Cold War** struggle of the United States against the Soviet Union played a role in the voting rights story. The struggle between the two superpowers took place in the Third World, populated mainly by people of color, and American leaders found themselves continually embarrassed and their efforts undermined by the second-class citizenship of African-Americans in the United States. This circumstance convinced most national leaders to seek the end of the system of official **segregation** in the South (called **Jim Crow**).

We see, then, that a full explanation of why the 1965 Voting Rights Act happened requires that we move beyond a narrow focus on government officials and the political affairs that are the stuff of everyday news broadcasts. We do not want to leave matters here, however. To say simply that many factors are involved in explaining why political events or government actions happen still does not tell us how these factors are organized in understandable patterns.

electoral college Representatives of the states who formally elect the president; the number of electors in each state is equal to its total number of its senators and representatives.

Cold War A term used for the period of tense relations between the United States and the Soviet Union, stretching from the late 1940s to the late 1980s.

segregation A social order characterized by the legal separation of the races; common in the southern states from the late nineteenth century until the 1960s.

Jim Crow Popular term for the system of legal racial segregation that existed in the American South until the middle of the twentieth century.

The Main Factors of Political Life Can Be Organized into Categories

To see better how explanatory factors are interconnected, we believe it is helpful to organize each and every actor, institution, and process that affects our political life—whether public officials, voters, interest groups, political parties, the mass media, Congress, the courts, or economic change—into three categories or levels. We call these the structural, the political linkage, and the governmental levels. Here is what we include in each level:

- The *governmental level* includes all public officials and institutions (Congress, the president, the executive branch, and the Supreme Court) that have formal, legal responsibilities for making public policy.
- The *political linkage level* includes those political actors, institutions, and processes that are involved in transmitting the wants and demands of individuals and groups to government officials and in affecting the policies that the government pursues. These include public opinion, political parties, interest groups, the mass media, and elections.
- The *structural level* includes more fundamental and enduring factors that influence government and politics, including the U.S. economy and society, the constitutional rules, the political culture, and the international system.

This textbook is organized around these three categories. The chapters in Part II focus on factors at the structural level. The chapters in Part III are about political linkage processes and institutions. The chapters in Part IV attend to government institutions and leaders.

Structural Level Factors Are Particularly Important

Very often, we shall find that the most powerful explanations of why things happen in American political life are located at the structural level, and that the lines of influence flow from the structural level to the political linkage and governmental levels. This is so because it is structural factors that largely determine what issues become important in American politics (often called the **political agenda**), shape the distribution of resources and power in American society, and influence the wants, needs, and perceptions of the American people. And it is the constitutional rules that structure how political conflict takes place and how government behaves.

political agenda The menu of issues of peak concern to citizens and public officials.

We note the special place of structural factors by devoting an entire chapter to issues of society, economy, culture, and the international system (Chapter 4) and two to the constitutional rules (Chapters 2 and 3). Throughout the book, we ask how these many structural factors influence American politics and government.

American Politics Should Be Understood Holistically

All of these organizing principles can be drawn together by seeing American politics and government as an ordered whole. This is the best way to answer "why-things-happen" questions about American politics. You will see, for ex-

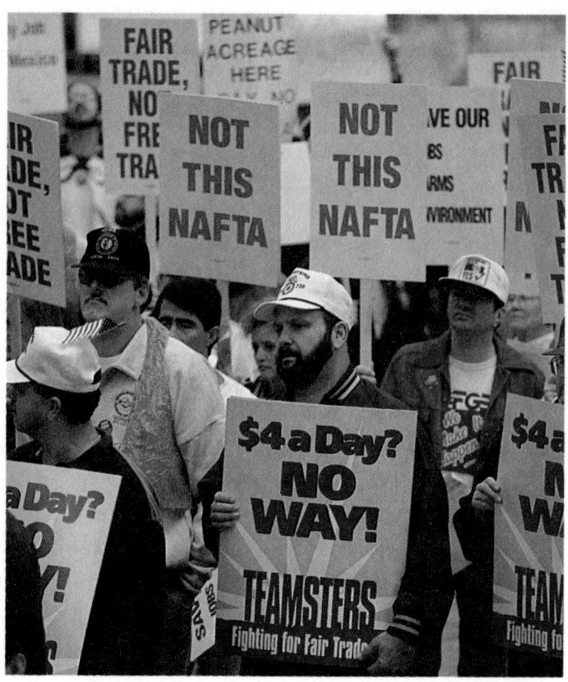

Changes in the economy almost always affect the lives of ordinary people and the nature of issues that become important in American politics. The globalization of the economy has affected many aspects of American life, including jobs and the cost of products and services. Here, anti-NAFTA (the North American Free Trade Agreement) demonstrators voice their concern about the possible export of jobs under the free trade arrangements between the United States, Canada, and Mexico.

ample, that it is seldom a sufficient explanation of a political event to say that "President Clinton wanted it." What the president wants and does may be very important, but we also need to ask why he wanted it and why he was able to get it. The answers will usually require a look at other *governmental* institutions: Why did Congress go along? Why did the executive branch follow the president's instructions? Why didn't the Supreme Court interfere? It will also require a consideration of *political linkage* institutions and processes: Was the president responding to public opinion or to organized interest groups? Why was a president who wanted this policy elected in the first place? Often, a full explanation will require a consideration of *structural* factors: Did the state of the U.S. economy make this policy necessary? Did international trade or the military balance of world power make a difference? How about the age, health, and occupational characteristics of the American population?

We believe, then, that American political life must be understood as an integrated, ordered whole, and that what goes on in government can be understood only through a consideration of all three levels of analysis. Action by public officials is the product not simply of their personal desires (though these are important), but also of the influences and pressures brought to bear by other governmental institutions and by individuals, groups, and classes at work in the political linkage sphere. Political linkage institutions and processes, in turn, can often be understood only when we see how they are shaped by the larger structural context, including such things as the economy and the political culture. (See Figure 1.1.)

It should also be kept in mind that feedback occurs as well. That is to say, influences sometimes flow in the opposite direction, from the governmental level to the other levels. For instance, federal tax laws influence the distribution of income and wealth in society, government regulations affect the operations of business, and decisions by the courts may determine what interest

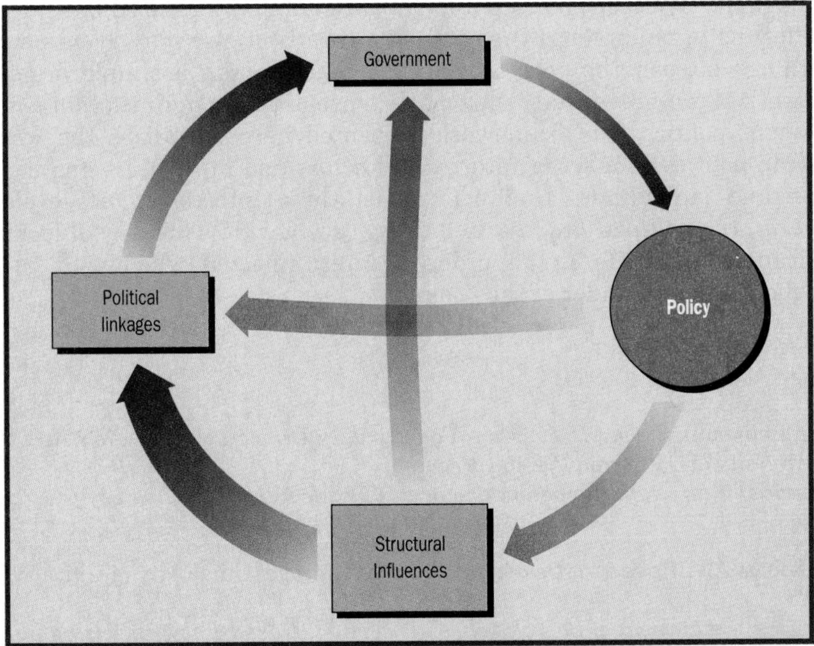

Figure 1.1 ■ **A Framework for Understanding American Government and Politics**

Various actors, institutions, and processes interact to influence what government does in the United States. Events at the structural level, such as the economy, the culture, and the Constitution, play a strong role in political events. They may influence the government directly or, as is more often the case, through political linkages such as elections, parties, and interest groups. In a democratic society, the policies created by the government should reflect these influences. These policies then go on to influence the structural and linkage levels, repeating the process.

groups and political parties are able to do. We will want to pay attention, then, to these sorts of influences in our effort to understand how the American political system works.

You need not worry about remembering exactly which actors and influences belong to which of the three levels. That will become obvious because the chapters of the book are organized into sections corresponding to them. Nor do you need to worry about exactly how the people and institutions at the different levels interact with each other. This will become clear as materials are presented and learned, and as you become more familiar with the American political process.

Summary

The struggle for democracy has played an important role in American history and remains an important theme in our country today, as well as in many other parts of the world. The struggle has involved the effort to make popular sovereignty, political equality, and political liberty more widely available and practiced. Because democracy holds a very special place in Americans' pantheon of values and is particularly relevant to judging political processes, it is the standard used throughout this text to evaluate the quality of our politics and government.

The materials about politics and government are organized in a way that will allow us to understand the confusing details of everyday events and see *why* things happen the way they do. In this chapter, a simple organizing framework is presented that helps make sense of the sometimes confusing details about politics. The framework presented here visualizes the world of American politics as a set of interrelated *actors* and *influences*—institutions, groups, and individuals—that operate on three interconnected levels: the *structural,* the *political linkage,* and the *governmental.* This way of looking at American political life as an ordered, interconnected whole will be used throughout the remainder of the book.

Suggested Readings

Barber, Benjamin. *Strong Democracy: Participatory Democracy for a New Age.* Berkeley: University of California Press, 1984.
The case for direct, participatory democracy by a leading contemporary political theorist.

Dahl, Robert A. *A Preface to Democratic Theory.* Chicago: University of Chicago Press, 1956.
The classic statement of the "pluralist" conception of democracy, criticizing pure majority rule.

———. *Democracy and Its Critics.* New Haven: Yale University Press, 1989.
A sweeping defense of democracy against its critics by one of the most brilliant political theorists of our time.

Held, David. *Models of Democracy.* Stanford, CA: Stanford University Press, 1987.
A highly accessible review of the many possible meanings of democracy.

Putnam, Robert D. *Making Democracy Work: Civic Traditions in Modern Italy.* Princeton: Princeton University Press, 1993.
A brilliant and controversial argument that the success of democratic government depends on the vitality of a participatory and tolerant civic culture.

Spitz, Elaine. *Majority Rule.* Chatham, NJ: Chatham House, 1984.
A provocative and richly detailed defense of majority rule democracy.

Wittman, Donald. *The Myth of Democratic Failure: Why Political Institutions Are Efficient.* Chicago: University of Chicago Press, 1995.
Using economic models of reasoning, the author argues that democratic institutions are as efficient as economic markets.

Internet Sources

There are a number of sites on the World Wide Web that serve as gateways to a vast collections of materials on American government and politics. In subsequent chapters, we will indicate the location of sites on the Web to begin searches on the specific subject matter of the chapters. Here we concentrate on the general "gateways," the starting points for wide-ranging journeys through cyberspace, geared to subjects governmental and political.

For most students, connections to the Internet will be through systems already in operation at most colleges and universities. For some students, connections will be through one of the commercial services such as America On-Line, Compuserve, Prodigy, or Microsoft Network. As part of its service, each has a Net navigator, a tool used to get around the Internet and find what one wants. University and college systems are likely to have the Netscape navigator. Whichever navigator one uses, it is quite simple to type in the addresses of the "gateways" listed below. The navigator will do the rest. Once at the gateway, a simple click on highlighted words and phrases will take users to a particular body of information. Good hunting.

The "gateways" are listed in order of usefulness, in the opinion of the authors:

1. The Jefferson Project http://www.stardot.com/jefferson/
2. Political Science Resources http://www.keele.ac.uk/depts/po/psr.htm
3. The Internet Public Library http://ipl.sils.umich.edu/
4. Yahoo/Government http://www.yahoo.com/Government/
5. Politics Now http://www.politicsnow.com/
6. Doug Ingram's News and Politics Page http://www.astro.washington.edu/ingram/politics.html

Primary documents on democracy and other ideologies may be found on the "Political Thought" page of Political Science Resources. Simply follow the path from the Political Science Resources home page.

Notes

1. William H. Chafe, *The Unfinished Journey: America Since World War II* (New York: Oxford University Press, 1986), p. 304; Howard Zinn, *SNCC: The New Abolitionists* (Boston: Beacon Press, 1964), p. 64.
2. Chafe, *Unfinished Journey,* p. 305.
3. Robert Dahl, *Democracy and Its Critics* (New Haven: Yale University Press, 1989).
4. John Dewey, *The Public and Its Problems* (New York: Holt, 1927), p. 211.
5. See Robert A. Dahl, *After the Revolution: Authority in the Good Society* (New Haven: Yale University Press, 1970); Dahl, *Democracy and Its Critics;* Jane Mansbridge, *Beyond Adversary Democracy* (New York: Basic Books, 1980).
6. From "To John Taylor," May 28, 1816, *The Living Thoughts of Thomas Jefferson,* ed. by John Dewey (New York: Longmans, Green, 1940).
7. See Benjamin Barber, *Strong Democracy: Participatory Democracy for a New Age* (Berkeley: University of California Press, 1984); Peter Bachrach, *The Theory of Democratic Elitism* (Boston: Little, Brown, 1967); Robert A. Dahl, *A Preface to Economic Democracy* (Berkeley: University of California Press, 1985); C. B. MacPherson, *Democratic Theory: Essays in Retrieval* (Oxford, U.K.: Clarendon, 1973); Carole Pateman, *Participation and Democratic Theory* (London: Cambridge University Press, 1970).
8. Kenneth May, "A Set of Independent, Necessary, and Sufficient Conditions for Simple Majority Decision," *Econometrica,* Vol. 20 (1952), pp. 680–684, shows that only majority rule can guarantee popular sovereignty, political equality, and neutrality among policy alternatives. See also Douglas W. Rae, "Decision Rules and Individual Values in Constitutional Choice," *American Political Science Review,* Vol. 63 (1969), pp. 40–53; Phillip D. Straffin, Jr., "Majority Rule and General Decision Rules," *Theory and Decision,* Vol. 8 (1977), pp. 351–360.
9. Dahl, *Preface to Economic Democracy,* p. 68.
10. Robert Dahl, "On Removing Certain Impediments to Democracy in the United States," *Political Science Quarterly,* Vol. 92, No. 1 (Spring 1977), p. 14; Elaine Spitz, *Majority Rule* (Chatham, NJ: Chatham House, 1984), p. 83; Dahl, *Democracy and Its Critics,* p. 170.

11. Dahl, *Democracy and Its Critics,* p. 156.

12. David Caute, *The Great Fear* (New York: Simon & Schuster, 1978); Victor Navasky, *Naming Names* (New York: Viking, 1980); Michael Rogin, *The Intellectuals and McCarthy* (Cambridge: MIT Press, 1967).

13. See Bernard Berelson, Paul F. Lazarsfeld, and William McPhee, *Voting* (Chicago: University of Chicago Press, 1954); V. O. Key, *Public Opinion and American Democracy* (New York: Knopf, 1961); Herbert McClosky and Alida Brill, *Dimensions of Tolerance* (New York: Sage, 1983). But see, in rebuttal, James L. Gibson, "Political Intolerance and Political Repression During the McCarthy Red Scare," *American Political Science Review,* Vol. 82 (1988), pp. 511–529; Benjamin I. Page and Robert Y. Shapiro, *The Rational Public* (Chicago: University of Chicago Press, 1992).

14. Dahl, *Democracy and Its Critics,* p. 161.

PART II

Structure

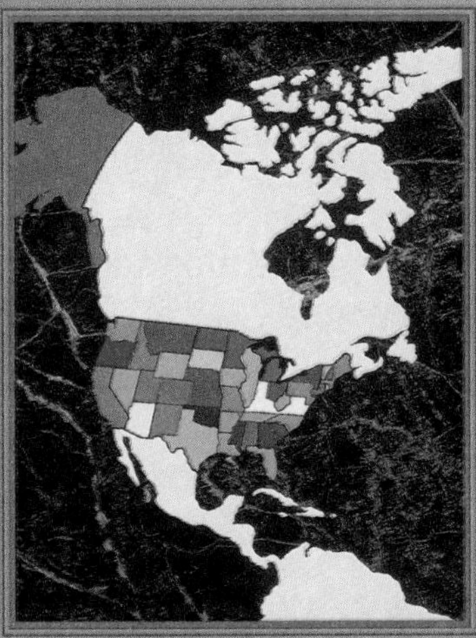

The chapters in Part II focus on structural influences on American government and politics. Structural influences are enduring features of American life that play key roles in determining what issues become important in politics and government, how political power is distributed in the population, and what attitudes and beliefs guide the behavior of citizens and public officials.

The constitutional rules are a particularly important part of the structural context of American political life. These rules are the subject matter of two of this part's chapters. Chapter 2 tells the story of the Constitution: why a constitutional convention was convened in Philadelphia in 1787, what the Founders intended to accomplish at the convention, and how specific provisions of the document have shaped our political life since the nation's founding. Chapter 3 examines federalism, asking what the framers intended the federal system to be and how it has changed over the years. Both chapters explore the relationship of the constitutional rules and the practice of democracy in the United States.

The basic characteristics of American society also influence the workings of our political and governmental institutions, as well as the attitudes and behaviors of citizens and public officials. Chapter 4 looks in detail at the American economy, society, and political culture, as well as this country's place in the world, showing how they structure much of what goes on in our political life. Together, the chapters in this part serve to show the structural underpinnings of American politics and government and set the stage for the chapters that follow.

The Constitution

IN THIS CHAPTER

- ★ The enduring legacies of the American Revolution and the Declaration of Independence
- ★ Our first constitution: The Articles of Confederation
- ★ The constitutional convention
- ★ What the framers created
- ★ How the Constitution structures the rules of American politics

Shays's Rebellion

Artemas Ward, commander of American forces at Bunker Hill, a Revolutionary War hero, and a state judge, could not convince the crowd of several hundred armed farmers to allow him to enter the Worcester, Massachusetts, courthouse. For nearly two hours, he pleaded and threatened, but to no avail. Though most admired him for his achievements, they were determined that he not hold court that day in September 1786, when he was to begin legal proceedings to seize farms for nonpayment of taxes. He left Worcester in a fury, unable to convince the local militia to come to his assistance, and carried word of the rebellion to Boston. Other judges trying to hold court in western Massachusetts in the summer and fall of 1786 had no better luck.[1]

The farmers of western Massachusetts were probably not a rebellious lot by nature, but desperate times pushed many of them to desperate actions. All over the new nation, the end of the Revolutionary War in 1783 had brought economic readjustment, the collapse of prices for agricultural products, and widespread economic distress and poverty among farmers. Poor farmers sought relief from their troubles from state governments, and for the most part, political leaders responded. Several states lent money (in the form of scrip, or paper money) to farmers to pay their taxes and debts. Other states passed stay laws, which postponed tax and mortgage payments for hard-pressed farmers.

In Massachusetts, however, the state legislature refused to help. Worse yet, the legislature and the governor decided that all state debts were to be paid off in full in order to establish the creditworthiness of the state. The state's debt, accumulated to pay the costs of the Revolutionary War, was owed primarily to a handful of the wealthiest citizens of the state, who had bought up outstanding notes for pennies on the dollar. To make good on this debt, the legislature levied heavy taxes that fell disproportionately on farmers, especially those in the western part of the state. When taxes could not be paid, which was distressingly common, money could be raised by the state only through foreclosure proceedings: the public sale of farmers' lands, buildings, and livestock. Tax foreclosures and imprisonment under harsh conditions for those who could not pay their debts became quite common. Responding to these dire circumstances, many western Massachusetts farmers took up arms to prevent courts from sitting.

By September 1786, Governor James Bowdoin had seen enough. He issued a proclamation against unlawful assembly and called out the militia to enforce it. Six hundred soldiers were sent to Springfield to ensure that the state supreme court could meet and issue the expected indictments against the leaders of the insurrection. The soldiers were met there by 500 or 600 armed farmers led by a former Revolutionary War officer, Captain Daniel Shays. After a long standoff, the militia withdrew, leaving the rebels in charge and the court unable to meet.

These events only hardened the resolve of the governor to break the rebellion. The armed forces he sent from Boston proved too much for the hastily organized and ill-equipped force under Daniel Shays. By the spring of 1787, the Boston militia had defeated the rebels in two pitched battles—one at Springfield and the other at Petersham—and Shays's Rebellion (as it was soon called) was at an end.

Though the insurrection was put down rather handily, most of the new nation's leading citizens were alarmed by the apparent inability of state governments under the Articles of Confederation to maintain public order. Under the Articles, our first constitution (in effect from 1781 to 1788) the national government in Philadelphia was virtually powerless. Responsibility for civil order was mainly in the hands of the states. Shays's Rebellion realized the worst fears of national leaders about the dangers of ineffective state governments and popular democracy out of control, unchecked by a strong national government. George Washington worried, "If government cannot check these disorders, what security has a man?"[2] It was in this climate of crisis that a call was issued for a constitutional convention to meet in Philadelphia in order to correct the flaws in our first constitution. Rather than amend the Articles of Confederation, however, the men who met in Philadelphia in the summer of 1787 wrote an entirely new constitution.

This chapter is about the founding of the United States and the formulation of the constitutional rules that structure American politics today. We will examine why particular constitutional rules were selected and how they influence what happens at all levels of government and politics in the United States. In this chapter, we will also pay significant attention to conflicts over the meaning of democracy and its place in the Constitution. We will see that the *struggle for democracy* has been a feature of political life in the United States from the very beginning.

The Political Theory and Practices of the Revolutionary Era

Initially, the American Revolution (1775–1783) was waged more to preserve an existing way of life than to create something new. By and large, American colonists in the 1760s and 1770s were proud to be affiliated with Great Britain and satisfied with the general prosperity that came with participation in the British commercial empire.[3] When the revolution broke out, the colonists at first wanted only to preserve the English constitution and their own rights as English subjects. These traditional rights of life, liberty, and property seemed to be threatened by British policies on trade and taxation. Rather than allowing the American colonists to trade freely with whomever they pleased and to produce whatever goods they wanted, for instance, England was restricting the colonists' freedom to do either in order to protect its own manufacturers. To pay for the military protection of the colonies against raids by Native Americans and their French allies, England imposed taxes on a number of items, including sugar, tea, and stamps (required for legal documents, pamphlets, and newspapers). The imposition of these taxes without the consent of the colonists seemed an act of tyranny to many English subjects in America.

Though the initial aims of the Revolution were quite modest, the American Revolution, like most revolutions, did not stay on the track planned by its leaders. Though it was sparked by a concern for liberty—understood as the preservation of traditional rights against the intrusions of government—it also stimulated the development of sentiments for popular sovereignty and political equality (recall the definitions of *popular sovereignty* and *political equality* presented in Chapter 1). As these sentiments grew, so did the likelihood that the American colonies would split from their British parent and form a system of government more to the liking of the colonists.

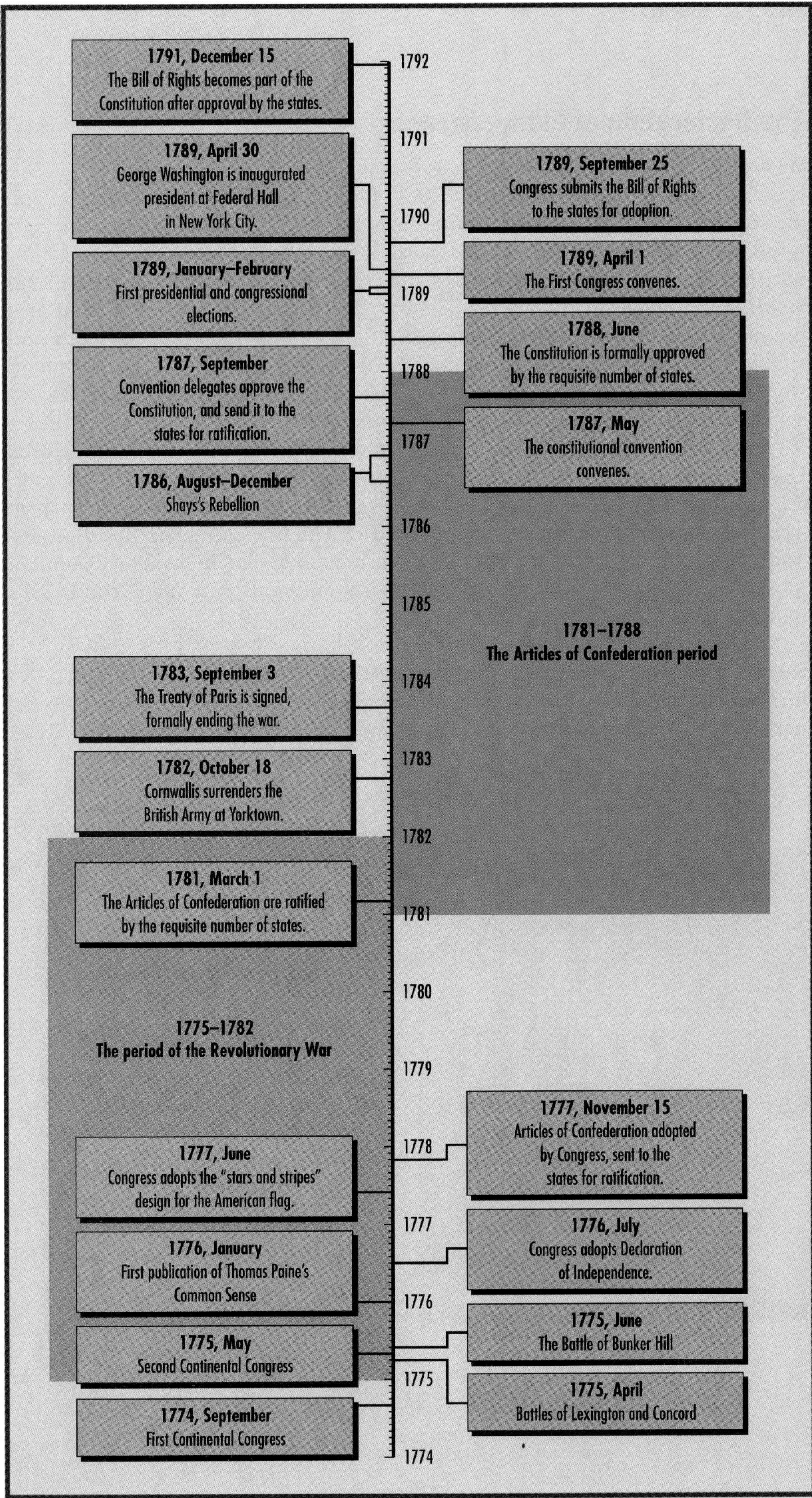

Figure 2.1 ■ Timeline of the Founding of the United States, 1774–1791

The Declaration of Independence

When the Second Continental Congress began its session on May 10, 1775—the First had met only briefly in 1774 to formulate a list of grievances to submit to the British Parliament—the delegates did not have independence in mind, even though armed conflict with Britain had already begun with the battles of Lexington and Concord. Pushed by the logic of armed conflict, an unyielding British government, and Thomas Paine's incendiary call for American independence in his wildly popular pamphlet *Common Sense,* however, the delegates had concluded by the spring of 1776 that separation and independence were inescapable. South Carolina took the first step when it adopted its own constitution and declared itself free from British control. The legislature of Virginia followed suit, its delegates boldly proclaiming that "the United Colonies are, and of right ought to be, free and independent States." In early June, spurred by the examples of these two states, the Continental Congress appointed a special committee, composed of Thomas Jefferson, John Adams, and Benjamin Franklin, to draft a declaration of independence. The document, mostly Jefferson's handiwork, was adopted unanimously by the Second Continental Congress on July 4, 1776.

Key Ideas in the Declaration of Independence The ideas in Jefferson's Declaration are so familiar to us that we may easily miss their revolutionary importance. In the late eighteenth century, most societies in the world were ruled

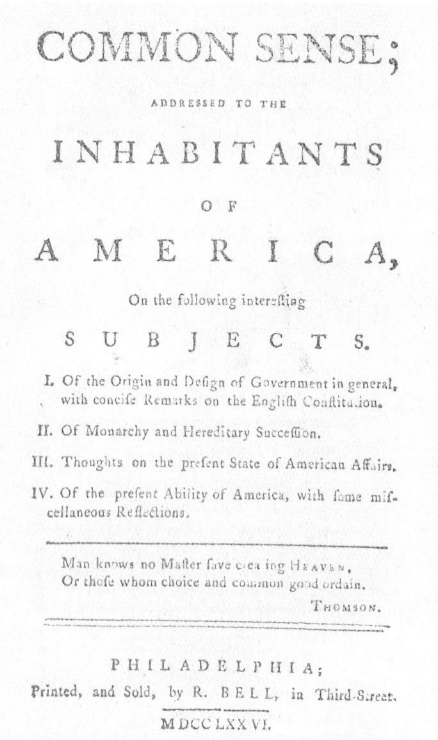

COMMON SENSE;

ADDRESSED TO THE

INHABITANTS

OF

AMERICA,

On the following interesting

SUBJECTS.

I. Of the Origin and Design of Government in general, with concise Remarks on the English Constitution.

II. Of Monarchy and Hereditary Succession.

III. Thoughts on the present State of American Affairs.

IV. Of the present Ability of America, with some miscellaneous Reflections.

Man knows no Master save creating HEAVEN,
Or those whom choice and common good ordain.

THOMSON.

PHILADELPHIA;

Printed, and Sold, by R. BELL, in Third-Street.

MDCCLXXVI.

American leaders were reluctant at first to declare independence from Great Britain. One of the things that helped change their minds was Thomas Paine's wildly popular and incendiary pamphlet *Common Sense,* which mercilessly mocked the institution of monarchy.

Here the members of the Second Continental Congress sign the Declaration of Independence. Its main author, Thomas Jefferson, is prominently featured in this rendering of what has been called the *fateful step.*

by kings with authority purportedly derived from God, subject to little or no control by their subjects. Closely following John Locke's ideas in *The Second Treatise on Government,* Jefferson's argument that legitimate government can be established only by the people and can govern only with their consent seemed outrageous at the time. However, these ideas sparked a very responsive chord in peoples everywhere when they were first presented, and they remain extremely popular all over the world today, more than 200 years later. The argument as presented in the Declaration of Independence goes as follows:

- *Human beings possess rights that cannot be legitimately given away or taken from them:* "We hold these truths to be self-evident, that all men are created equal, that they are endowed by their Creator with certain unalienable Rights, that among these are Life, Liberty, and the Pursuit of Happiness."
- *People create government to protect these rights:* "That to secure these rights, Governments are instituted among Men, deriving their just powers from the consent of the governed."
- *If government fails to protect people's rights or itself becomes a threat to them, then people can withdraw their consent from that government and create a new one:* "That whenever any Form of Government becomes destructive of these ends, it is the Right of the People to alter or to abolish it, and to institute new Government, laying its foundation on such principles, and organizing its powers in such form, as to them shall seem most likely to effect their Safety and Happiness."

Omissions in the Declaration The Declaration of Independence left several issues unsettled, however, including what to do about slavery in light of the Declaration's spirited defense of inalienable rights and the claim that "all men are created equal." It was also silent on the important issue of whether the colonies were declaring for independence as a single new nation or as 13 separate nations. And it said nothing about the political status of women, Native Americans, or African-Americans who were not slaves.

Theory in Practice: Early State Constitutions

During the Revolutionary War, when Great Britain was unable to exercise control in very many places in the American colonies, 11 of the 13 colonies wrote constitutions and created their own governments. By looking at what was common to the constitutions of these new governments, we can begin to understand the nature of the prevailing political ideas of the period.

- *Bills of rights.* Most of the state constitutions, following Virginia's lead in June 1776, incorporated bills of rights: listings of those rights that could not be violated by governments, even governments based on popular consent. Freedom of speech is an example.
- *Restrictions on the powers of the executive.* It was widely believed that all rulers are tempted by the attractions of power and are prone to tyranny. As one delegate to the Delaware constitutional convention put it, "The executive power is ever restless, ambitious, and ever grasping at increase of power."[4] Such abuses of power were familiar to the colonists; in the troubled period leading up to the outbreak of the Revolutionary War, several colonial governors appointed by the British crown had suspended elected colonial legislatures and exercised near-dictatorial powers. The constitution makers wanted their chief executives to be administrators rather than rulers. The states took various steps to put this sentiment into action, including election of the chief executive by the legislature, limitations on terms of office, limited powers of appointment, and no veto power over legislation.
- *Legislative supremacy.* The new state constitutions sought to make the **legislative branch,** the elected lawmaking part of government, supreme and to protect it from the intrusions of the **executive branch.** Most of the state constitutions gave a broad range of powers to the legislative branch, including many that had traditionally been the prerogative of the executive in Britain, for example, declaring war and peace, granting pardons, and conducting foreign policy.

legislative branch The elected lawmaking part of government.

executive branch The part of government responsible for executing or carrying out the laws passed by a legislative body or the decisions rendered by a court.

- *Frequent elections.* Almost without exception, the new state constitutions required annual legislative elections. Those who drew up these constitutions apparently believed that even an elected legislature can become tyrannical if its members remain in office too long.
- *Restrictions on the right to vote and hold elective office.* While the new state constitutions were far more democratic than anything else existing in the world at that time, the retention of property qualifications for voting and office holding made these constitutions less democratic than we expect today. Large numbers of white males (roughly 30 to 40 percent)[5] were excluded from political life in the states because they did not own the requisite amount of land (25 settled acres or 500 unsettled

acres in Virginia, for instance), could not afford to pay the poll tax, or did not pay the minimum level of property tax. Women were also excluded from voting and office holding, as were slaves and most "free blacks" (blacks who were not slaves). The terms *the people* and *popular consent,* then, implied a much narrower conception of *people* and *popular consent* than we hold today.

The Articles of Confederation: The First Constitution

The leaders of the American Revolution almost certainly did not envision as a goal the creation of a single, unified nation. At most, they envisioned a loose **confederation** among the states, a form of government in which the states are virtually independent and hold most governmental powers, while the central government holds almost none. This stance should not be surprising. Most Americans in the late eighteenth century believed that a government based on popular consent and committed to the protection of individual rights was possible only in small, homogeneous republics, where government was close to the people and where fundamental conflicts of interest among the people did not exist. Given the great geographical expanse of the colonies, as well as the varied ways of life and economic interests of the colonies, a single unified republic seemed unlikely.

confederation A loose association of states or units bound together for limited purposes.

Provisions of the Articles

Our first constitution, passed by the Second Continental Congress in the midst of the Revolutionary War in 1777, but not ratified by the requisite number of states until 1781, created a nation that was hardly a nation at all. The Articles of Confederation created in law what had existed in practice from the time of the Declaration of Independence: a loose confederation of independent states, with little power in the central government, much like the United Nations today. Under the Articles, most important decisions were made in state legislatures.

The main provisions of the Articles carried out this overall objective. While there was a central government of sorts—there was a national Congress, for instance—it had few responsibilities and virtually no power. It could make war or peace, but it had no power to levy taxes (even customs duties) to pursue either goal. It could not regulate commerce between the states, nor could it deny the states the right to collect customs duties. It had no independent chief executive to ensure that the laws passed by Congress would be enforced, nor had it a national court system to settle disputes between the states. The few areas of responsibility assigned to the central government—to establish a postal service, to set uniform standards of weights and measures, and to manage affairs with Native Americans—were almost impossible to legislate because of the rule that all congressional legislation had to be approved by 9 of the 13 states. Finally, any defects in the new constitution were difficult to remedy because amending the Articles required the unanimous approval of the states.

Shortcomings of the Articles of Confederation

The Articles did what their authors wanted them to do: to preserve the power, independence, and sovereignty of the states, and to ensure that the central government would not encroach on the liberty of the people. Unfortunately, there were also many problems that the confederation was ill equipped to handle.

For instance, the new central government was unable to finance its activities. The government was forced to rely on each state's willingness to pay its annual tax assessment. Few states were eager to cooperate. As a result, the bonds and notes of the confederate government became almost worthless (giving rise to the saying "not worth a Continental"), and the government's attempts to borrow were stymied.

The central government was also unable to defend American interests in foreign affairs. Without a chief executive, with veto power over actions of the central government in the hands of the states, and devoid of a standing military, the confederation lacked the capacity to reach binding agreements with other nations or to deal with a wide range of problems. These included the continuing presence of British troops in western lands ceded to the new nation by Britain at the end of the Revolutionary War, violent clashes with the Native Americans on the western frontier, and piracy on the high seas.

The government was also unable to prevent the outbreak of commercial warfare between the states. As virtually independent nations, with the power to levy customs duties, many states became intense commercial rivals of their neighbors and sought to gain every possible advantage against the products of other states. New York and New Jersey, for instance, imposed high tariffs on goods that crossed their borders from other states.

The Calling of the Constitutional Convention

It is now conventional wisdom among historians that the failures of the Articles of Confederation just described led most of the leading citizens of the confederation to, believe that a new constitution was desperately needed for the fledgling nation. What is left out of many accounts of the convening of the Constitutional Convention in Philadelphia, however, is the story of the growing concern among many of the most influential men in the confederation that the passions for democracy and equality among the common people set loose by the American Revolution were getting out of hand. Recall that the initial objectives of the American War for Independence were freedom of trade, lower taxes, and the protection of traditional English liberties. War and revolution always demand popular participation and sacrifice, however. People must be willing to pay taxes and to volunteer for the fighting; they must be willing to risk their lives and property. To get them to do so, revolutionary leaders generally tend to describe their struggle in universal terms, applicable to all. During the American Revolution, appeals to the people for the defense of freedom and for the spread of the blessings of liberty were often translated by the people to mean their right to better access to the means of government and to the means of livelihood.[6] The common people were convinced that success would bring substantial improvements in their lives.[7]

This fever for popular participation and greater equality is not what most of the leaders of the American Revolution had in mind. As historian Richard Hofstadter puts it, "As the revolution took away the restraining hand of the British government, old colonial grievances of farmers, debtors, and squatters against merchants, investors, and large landholders had flared up anew; the lower orders took advantage of new democratic constitutions in several states, and the possessing classes were frightened."[8]

The Constitution is preserved and on display at the National Archives in Washington, DC.

The Republican Beliefs of the Founders

A society with substantial popular participation and equality was not an admirable society from the point of view of the Founders, who were believers in the republican theory of government. Eighteenth-century republicans (today's Republican party is named after this doctrine, but they are not one and the same) advocated a form of government that, while based on popular consent, limits office holding and the right to vote, places obstacles in the path of popular democracy, and limits the purposes and powers of the government.

Though republican doctrine held that legitimate government must be based on the consent of the governed, an overriding fear of tyranny caused it to limit the role of the common people. Republican writers believed that **tyranny,** defined as the abuse of power by the ruler and the destruction of the liberty of his or her subjects, can be imposed by the *one,* the *few,* or the *many.* That is, tyranny can derive from the misrule of a sovereign, a hereditary aristocratic class, or the common people as a whole. Republicans believed that the only way to gain the consent of the governed, and to prevent tyranny at the same time, was to elect government leaders and limit the power of government. The election of representatives would keep tyrannical kings and others from power, while ensuring popular consent. Limiting the power of government, either by stating what government could and could not do in a written constitution, or by fragmenting governmental power in the very way government is organized, would prevent tyranny no matter who gained leadership posts.

tyranny The abuse of power by a ruler or government.

Though eighteenth-century republicans believed in representative government—a government whose political leaders are elected *by the people*—they were quite unsympathetic to democracy and defined *the people* in the above formulation in an extremely narrow way. Eighteenth-century republicans did not believe that every person ought to be eligible to vote and to hold office. For the most part, they believed that public affairs ought to be left to men, and that these men ought to be from among the "better" elements of society: the conduct of the public business was, in their view, the province of those with wisdom and experience, capacities mainly associated with people of social standing, substantial financial resources, and high levels of education. One of Madison's complaints, stated in *The Federalist,* No. 62, was that the states under the Articles of Confederation were allowing government "to fall into the Hands of those whose ability or situation in Life does not entitle them to it."

Nor did eighteenth-century republicans believe that elected representatives should be too responsive to public opinion. Once in office, representatives were to exercise independent judgment, taking into account the needs and interests of society rather than the moods and opinions of the people.

Eighteenth-century republicans, then, did not believe in democracy as defined in Chapter 1. Though republican doctrine allowed the common people a larger role in public life than existed in other political systems of the day, the role of the people was to be far more limited than we expect today (the differences between republican and democratic doctrines are highlighted in Table 2.1). The view of the republican Founders is captured in the following remarks by prominent delegates to the constitutional convention:

> Jeremy Belknap: "Let it stand as a principle that government originates from the people; but let the people be taught that . . . they are not able to govern themselves."[9]

> Fisher Ames: "A republic is that structure of an elective government, in which the administration necessarily prescribe to themselves the general good as the object of all their measures; a democracy is that, in which the present popular passions, independent of the public good, become a guide to the rulers. In the first, the reason and interests of society govern; in the second, their prejudices and passions."[10]

Table 2.1

Comparing Eighteenth-Century Republicanism and the Democratic Ideal

Republicanism	Democracy
Government is based on popular consent.	Government is based on popular consent.
Rule by the people is indirect, through representatives.	Rule by the people may be direct or indirect.
The term *people* is narrowly defined (by education, property holding, social standing).	The term *people* is broadly defined.
Elected representatives act as "trustees" (act on their own to discover the public good).	Elected representatives act as "delegates" (instructed by the people; accurately reflect their wishes).
Barriers to majority rule exist.	Majority rule prevails.
Government is strictly limited in function.	Government does what the people want it to do.
Government safeguards rights and liberties, with a special emphasis on property rights.	Government safeguards rights and liberties, with no special emphasis on property rights.

James Madison: "[Democracies] have ever been spectacles of turbulence and contention; have ever been found incompatible with personal security or the rights of property; and have in general been as short in their lives as they have been violent in their deaths" (from *The Federalist,* No. 10).

Why the Founders Were Worried

An Excess of Democracy in the States Worries that untamed democracy was on the rise were not unfounded.[11] Launched in the name of other goals, the American Revolution soon began to take on a more democratic character as it engaged the common people. In the mid–1780s, for instance, popular conventions were created in several states to keep tabs on state legislatures and issue instructions to them on legislation. Both conventions and instructions struck directly at the heart of the republican conception of the legislature as a deliberative body shielded from popular opinion.[12]

The constitution of the state of Pennsylvania under the Articles of Confederation was also an affront to republican principles. Benjamin Rush, a signatory to the Declaration of Independence, described it as "too much upon the democratic order."[13] This constitution replaced the property qualification to vote with a very small tax (thus allowing many more people to vote), created a single-house legislative body whose members were to be elected in annual elections, mandated that legislative deliberations be open to the public, and required that proposed legislation be widely publicized and voted on only after a general election had been held (making the canvassing of public opinion easier).

To many advocates of popular democracy, including Tom Paine, the Pennsylvania constitution was the most perfect instrument of popular sovereignty. To others, like James Madison, the Pennsylvania case was a perfect example of popular tyranny exercised through the legislative branch of government.[14] Because we are generally more favorable to democracy today than were the Founders, we are likely to see their worries as somewhat overwrought. Nevertheless, we must note the seriousness of their concerns.

The Threat to Property Rights in the States One of the freedoms that republicans wanted to protect against the intrusions of a tyrannical government was the right of the people to acquire and enjoy private property. Developments toward the end of the 1770s and the beginning of the 1780s seemed to put this freedom in jeopardy. For one thing, the popular culture was growing increasingly hostile to privilege of any kind, whether of social standing, education, or wealth. Writers derided aristocratic airs; expressed their preference for unlettered, plain-speaking leaders; and pointed out how wealth undermined equal rights.[15] Legislatures were increasingly inclined, moreover, to pass laws protecting debtors. Rhode Island and North Carolina issued cheap paper money, which note holders were forced to accept in payment of debts; other states enacted **"stay" acts,** which forbade farm foreclosures for nonpayment of debts. Popular opinion, while strongly in favor of property rights (after all, most of the debtors in question were owners of small farms), also sympathized with farmers, who were hard-pressed to pay their debts with increasingly tight money, and believed—with some reason—that many creditors had accumulated notes speculatively or unfairly and were not entitled to full repayment. There was, third and finally, Shays's Rebellion in western Massachusetts, where armed rebels tried to prevent the state courts from seizing farms for the nonpayment of debts. This rebellion greatly alarmed American notables.

"stay" acts Enactments postponing the collection of taxes and/or mortgage payments.

The Constitutional Convention

By 1787, most of America's economic, social, and political leaders were convinced that the new nation and the experiment in self-government were in great peril. First, under the Articles of Confederation, the central government could not protect or advance the national interest in the world, pay its debts, guarantee domestic tranquillity, or establish a unified national economy. Second, democratic tendencies were threatening to undermine the republican principles of the new nation. These concerns helped convince leaders in the states to select 73 delegates to attend the Constitutional Convention in Philadelphia (only 55 actually showed up for its deliberations). The goal was to create a new government capable of providing both energy and stability.

The convention officially convened in Philadelphia on May 25, 1787, with George Washington presiding. It met in secret for a period of almost four months. By the end of their deliberations, the delegates had hammered out a constitutional framework that has served as one of the structural foundations of American government and politics to the present day.

Who Were the Founders?

The delegates were not common folk. There were no common laborers, skilled craftspeople, small farmers, women, or racial minorities in attendance. Most delegates were wealthy men: holders of government bonds, real estate investors, successful merchants, bankers, lawyers, and owners of large plantations worked by slaves. They were, for the most part, far better educated than the average American and solidly steeped in the classics. The journal of the convention debates kept by James Madison of Virginia shows that the delegates were conversant with the great works of Western philosophy and political science; with great facility and frequency, they quoted Aristotle, Plato, Locke, Montesquieu, and scores of other thinkers. They were also a surprisingly young group, averaging barely over 40 years of age. Finally, they were a group with very broad experience in American politics; almost all of them had been active in the Revolution and in the postwar state governments. More than half of them had served in Congress.

Ever since the publication in 1913 of historian Charles Beard's provocative book, *An Economic Interpretation of the Constitution,*[16] debate has raged among scholars about the intentions of the framers. Beard boldly claimed that the framers were engaged in a conspiracy to protect their immediate and personal economic interests. Those who controlled the convention and the ratification process after the convention, he suggested, were owners of public securities who were interested in a government that could pay its debts, merchants interested in protections of commerce, and land speculators interested in the protection of property rights.

Beard has his defenders and detractors.[17] It is generally agreed that Beard overemphasized the degree to which the framers were driven by the immediate need to "line their own pockets," failed to give credit to other more noble motivations, and even got many of his facts wrong. A simple "self-interest" analysis is not supportable. On the other hand, Beard was probably right on the mark in suggesting that broad economic and social-class motives were at work in shaping the actions of the framers. This is not to suggest that they were not concerned about the national interest, economic stability, or the preservation of liberty. It is to suggest, however, that the ways in which they understood the national interest, economic stability, and the preservation of liberty were fully compatible with their own positions of economic and social eminence.

It is fair to say that the Constitutional Convention was the work of American notables deeply concerned about the instability and the economic chaos of the confederation and about a rising democracy's threat to the kind of society in which they held a favored position. As one historian has put the issue, "What was at stake for [the framers] was more than speculative windfalls in securities; it was the question of what kind of society would emerge from the revolution when the dust had settled." The kind of society they hoped for was one in which private property was protected and their own considerable financial and social standing was maintained. To argue, as some do, that social class motives did not exist because political and ideological issues were also at stake is not convincing.

Consensus and Conflict at the Convention

The delegates to the convention agreed with one another on many fundamental points. They agreed, for instance, that the Articles of Confederation had to be scrapped and a new constitution put in their place. In deciding on this course as one of their first official acts, the delegates went far beyond their instructions from Congress.

The delegates also agreed that a substantially strengthened national government was needed to protect American interests in the world, provide for social order, and regulate interstate commerce. Such a government would diminish the power and sovereignty of the states. Supporters of the idea of a strong, centralized national government, such as Alexander Hamilton, had long argued this position. By the time of the convention, even such traditional opponents of centralized governmental power as James Madison had changed their minds. As Madison put it, some way must be found "which will at once support a due supremacy of the national authority, and leave in force the local authorities so far as they can be subordinately useful."[19]

But the delegates also believed that a strong national government was potentially tyrannical and should not be allowed to fall into the hands of any particular interest or set of interests, particularly what Madison referred to as "the majority faction," by which he meant the majority of the people. The delegates' most important task became that of finding a formula for instituting republican government—one based on popular consent but not unduly swayed by public opinion and popular democracy. As Benjamin Franklin put it, "We have been guarding against an evil that old states are most liable to, excess of power in the rulers, but our present danger seems to be defect of obedience in the subjects."[20]

Instituting republican government, however, would be no easy task, because the raw material for republican government—a virtuous people, one that put the common good above self-interest—did not seem to exist in America. As the framers saw it, their task was to try to arrange governmental institutions in a way that would preserve the essentials of **republicanism** in a society composed of an "immoderate and unvirtuous" people—to find, as James Madison put it, "a republican remedy for the diseases most incident to republican government."[21]

republicanism A political doctrine advocating limited government based on popular consent, protected against majority tyranny.

Despite this general consensus, the delegates disagreed on a sufficient number of details to take up 115 days of sometimes heated debate. The most important debates involved the conflict between large and small states over the issue of representation in the national government, the status of slavery, and the selection of the president.

Virginia Plan Proposal by the large states at the Constitutional Convention to create a strong central government with power apportioned to the states on the basis of population.

New Jersey Plan Proposal of the smaller states at the Constitutional Convention to create a government based on the equal representation of the states in a unicameral legislature.

The Great Compromise By far the most intense debate concerned the relative power of large and small states in the new nation. The debate centered on the so-called **Virginia Plan,** drafted by James Madison. The plan proposed the creation of a strong central government controlled by the most populous states: Virginia, Massachusetts, and Pennsylvania. The Virginians wanted a national legislature with seats apportioned to the states on the basis of population size, and with the power to appoint the executive and the judiciary and to veto state laws. The smaller states countered with a set of proposals drafted by William Paterson of New Jersey (thereafter known as the **New Jersey Plan**), whose central feature was a single-house national legislature whose seats were apportioned equally among the states. The New Jersey Plan envisioned a slightly more powerful national government than the one that existed under the Articles of Confederation, but one that was to be organized on representational lines not unlike those in the Articles, in which each of the states remained sovereign. The Virginia Plan, on the other hand, with its strong national government run by a popularly elected legislature, represented a fundamentally different kind of national union: one in which national sovereignty was superior to state sovereignty.

Debate over this issue was so intense that no decision could be reached on the floor of the convention. As a way out of this impasse, the convention appointed a committee to hammer out a compromise. The Committee of Eleven met over the Fourth of July holidays while the convention was adjourned. It presented its report, sometimes called the Great Compromise, and sometimes called the **Connecticut Compromise** (because it was drafted by Roger Sherman of that state), on July 5, 1787. Its key feature was a two-house national legislature, in which each state's representation in the House of Representatives was to be based on population (thus favoring the large states), while representation in the Senate was to be equal for each of the states (thus favoring the small states). The compromise, adopted on July 16, broke the deadlock at the convention and allowed the delegates to turn their attention to other matters.

Connecticut Compromise Also called the *Great Compromise;* the compromise between the New Jersey and Virginia Plans put forth by the Connecticut delegates at the constitutional convention; called for a lower legislative house based on population and an upper house based on equal representation of the states.

Slavery The delegates also grappled with the issue of slavery, no easy matter in a society where slavery was institutionalized, and a revolution had just been fought in support of the proposition that "all men are created equal." While there was great distaste for the institution of slavery among many nonsouthern delegates, and some attempt to outlaw its practice, the delegates ultimately recognized that most of the southern states (where close to one-half of the total population of the confederation lived) would not agree to a provision abolishing the institution. Southern bargaining power was so substantial, in fact, that the delegates adopted several provisions that explicitly recognized the legal standing of slavery (without mentioning it by name). First, it counted three-fifths of a state's slave population (referred to as ". . . three-fifths of all other Persons") in the calculation of how many representatives a state was entitled to in the House of Representatives (Article I, Section 2, paragraph 3). Second, it forbade enactments against the slave trade until the year 1808 (Article I, Section 9). Third, it required nonslave states to return runaway slaves to their owners in slave states (Article IV, Section 2, paragraph 3).

One of the great shortcomings of the framers was their inability or unwillingness to abolish slavery in the Constitution. It would take a great and terrible civil war to rectify their mistake.

It would finally take a terrible civil war to abolish slavery in the United States. At the convention, Virginia delegate George Mason had a foreboding of such an outcome when he observed about slavery that "providence punishes national sins by national calamities."[22]

The Presidency The Virginia Plan called for a single executive, while the New Jersey Plan called for a plural executive. In the spirit of cooperation that pervaded the convention after the Great Compromise, the delegates quickly settled on the idea of a single executive. They could not agree, however, on how this executive should be chosen. Both sides rejected a direct election by the people of the chief executive, of course, because this would be "too much upon the democratic order," but they locked horns over the Virginia Plan's method of selection: by the vote of state legislatures. The compromise that was eventually struck involved a provision for an **electoral college** that would select the president. In the electoral college, each state would have a total of votes equal to its total number of representatives and senators in Congress. Members of the electoral college would then cast their votes for president. Should the electoral college fail to give a majority to any person, which most framers assumed would usually happen, then the House of Representatives would choose the president, with each state having one vote (see Article II, Section 1, paragraphs 2 and 3). As we shall see, the system of presidential election did not work out as expected and became far more democratic over the course of our history.

electoral college Representatives of the states who formally elect the president; the number of electors in each state is equal to the total number of its senators and representatives.

What the Framers Wrought

In order to understand American politics today, it is extremely important to know and understand the Constitution of the United States. To be sure, the document has been formally amended 27 times, and some very important things have changed in it because of judicial interpretations and political practices: in particular, democratic control of government and the scope of federal governmental authority have both greatly increased. But the major outlines of our present-day government are expressed in, and substantially determined by, the Constitution that was written in Philadelphia. The U.S. Constitution, in fact, can be considered one of the major *structural* factors that has influenced the evolution of American government and continues to shape politics today. Advice on how to read the Constitution is offered in the Resource Feature box on page 42.

What kind of government was created by the framers? In this section, we examine the fundamental design for government found in the Constitution.

The Framers Created a Republican Form of Government Recall that republican doctrine advocated a form of government that, while based on popular consent and some popular participation, limits office holding and the right to vote, places obstacles in the path of majoritarian democracy, and limits the purposes and powers of the government. All of these principles are expressed in the U.S. Constitution.

federalism A system in which significant governmental powers are divided between a central government and smaller units, such as states.

Federalism The Articles of Confederation envisioned a nation structured as a loose union of politically independent units with little power in the hands of the central government. The Constitution fashioned a **federal** system, in which some powers are left to the states, some powers are shared by the component units and the central government, and some powers are granted to the central government alone. As Madison put it in *The Federalist,* No. 46, the state and national governments "are but different agents and trustees of the people, constituted with different powers."

The powers in the Constitution tilt slightly toward the center, however[23] (see Table 2.2). This recasting of the union from a loose confederation to a more centralized federal system is boldly stated in Article VI, Section 2, commonly called the **supremacy clause:**

supremacy clause The provision in Article VI of the Constitution that the Constitution itself and the laws and treaties of the United States are the supreme law of the land, taking precedence over state laws and constitutions.

> This Constitution and the Laws of the United States which shall be made in Pursuance thereof; and all Treaties made, or which shall be made, under the Authority of the United States, shall be the supreme Law of the Land; and the Judges in every State shall be bound thereby, any Thing in the Constitution or Laws of any State to the Contrary notwithstanding.

We shall see in later chapters that, when the national and state governments have been in conflict in cases before it the U.S. Supreme Court has used the supremacy clause to increase the power of the national government.

The tilt toward national power was also enhanced by assigning important powers and responsibilities to the national government: to regulate commerce, to provide a uniform currency, to provide uniform laws on bankruptcy, to raise and support an army and a navy, to declare war, to collect taxes and customs duties, to provide for the common defense of the United States, and more (for these provisions, see Article I, Section 8). Especially important for later constitutional history is the last of the clauses in Section 8, which states that Congress has the power to "make all laws which shall be necessary and proper" to

Table 2.2

Two Systems of Government in the United States

	Articles of Confederation	U.S. Constitution
Basic Theory	A loose confederation of independent states, with a weak central government.	A federation of states, with powers divided between states and a central government.
Central Government	No chief executive or national judiciary. Legislature has no power to levy taxes, to regulate commerce between states, or to enforce national policy.	Powers are divided between executive, judicial, and legislative branches, each with certain powers over one another. Central government can levy taxes, regulate commerce and currency, enforce national laws, and raise a military.
State Governments	Sovereign states have veto power over constitutional change, independent power over militia and over commerce between states.	States are represented in the national government in Congress and through electoral votes in presidential elections; approval of three-fourths of the states needed to amend the Constitution.

carry out its specific powers and responsibilities. We shall see later how this **elastic clause** became one of the foundations for the growth of the federal government in the twentieth century. An example is the draft. Although a draft is not mentioned in the Constitution, Congress has instituted a draft several times as a way to carry out its duties to raise an army and a navy.

elastic clause Article I, Section 8; also called the "necessary and proper" clause; gives Congress the authority to make whatever laws are necessary and proper to carry out its enumerated responsibilities.

The framers did not render the states powerless, however, as you will see in the next chapter. In our system, the states remain important actors. But there is no denying the scale of the change in the power and responsibility of the national government, a matter that remains controversial (see the box "What Role for Government?" on pp. 46–47).

Limited Government The basic purpose of the U.S. Constitution, like any written constitution, is to define the purposes and powers of the government. Such a definition of purposes and powers automatically places a boundary between what is permissible and what is impermissible. By listing the specific powers (as in Article I, Section 8) of the national government and specifically denying others to the national government (as in Article I, Section 9, and in the first ten amendments to the Constitution, known as the **Bill of Rights**), the Constitution carefully limited what government may legitimately do.

Bill of Rights The first ten amendments to the Constitution, concerned with basic liberties.

Checks on Majority Rule Being sorely afraid of unbridled democracy, the framers created a constitution by which the people rule only indirectly, barriers are placed in the path of majorities (see Figure 2.2), and deliberation is prized over conformity to the popular will. As political philosopher Robert Dahl puts it, "In order to achieve their goal of preserving a set of inalienable rights superior to the majority principle . . . the framers deliberately created a framework of government that was carefully designed to impede and even prevent

RESOURCE FEATURE

Reading the Constitution

The Constitution of the United States deserves a slow and careful reading. Every word counts. Each word or phrase tells something important about how American government works. If you keep in mind how the document is organized, it will help you understand the structure of the Constitution as a whole and will make it much easier to locate specific provisions.

The Constitution begins with a Preamble, which declares that "we the people" (not just the separate states) establish the Constitution and lists its purposes.

Article I concerns the legislative branch. It provides for a House of Representatives, elected by the people and apportioned according to population; and then a Senate, with equal representation for each state. After discussing various rules and procedures, including the presidential veto (Sections 4–7), it goes on in Section 8 to enumerate the specific powers of Congress, concluding with the "necessary and proper" clause. It then limits Congress's powers (Section 9) and those of the states (Section 10).

Article II deals with the executive branch. It vests the executive power in a single president of the United States. After describing the complex electoral college scheme for electing presidents indirectly (changed, in effect, by the development of a party system) and dealing with qualifications, removal, compensation, and the oath of office, it describes the presidential powers and duties (Sections 2 and 3) and provides for impeachment.

Article III concerns the judicial branch. It vests the judicial power in a Supreme Court, letting Congress establish other courts if desired. It provides for a limited original jurisdiction and (subject to congressional regulation) for broader appellate jurisdiction (i.e., jurisdiction to review lower court decisions). It specifies a right to jury trials and then (Section 3) defines treason, ruling out certain punishments for it.

Article IV deals with interstate relations, requiring that full faith and credit be given other states' acts and that fugitives (slaves) be delivered up. Section 3 provides for the admission of new states and the regulation of U.S. territories. Section 4 guarantees a republican form of government to the states.

Article V provides for two ways of proposing constitutional amendments and for two ways of ratifying them; it forbids amendments changing equal state suffrage in the Senate or (before 1808) prohibiting the slave trade or changing the apportionment of taxes.

Article VI assumes the debts of the confederation; makes the Constitution, laws, and treaties of the United States the supreme law of the land; and requires an oath of U.S. and state officials.

Article VII provides that the Constitution will be established when ratified by nine state conventions.

Members of the convention sign their names to the Constitution on September 17, 1787. The Constitution did not become the law of the land, however, until the ninth state, New Hampshire, ratified it nine months later.

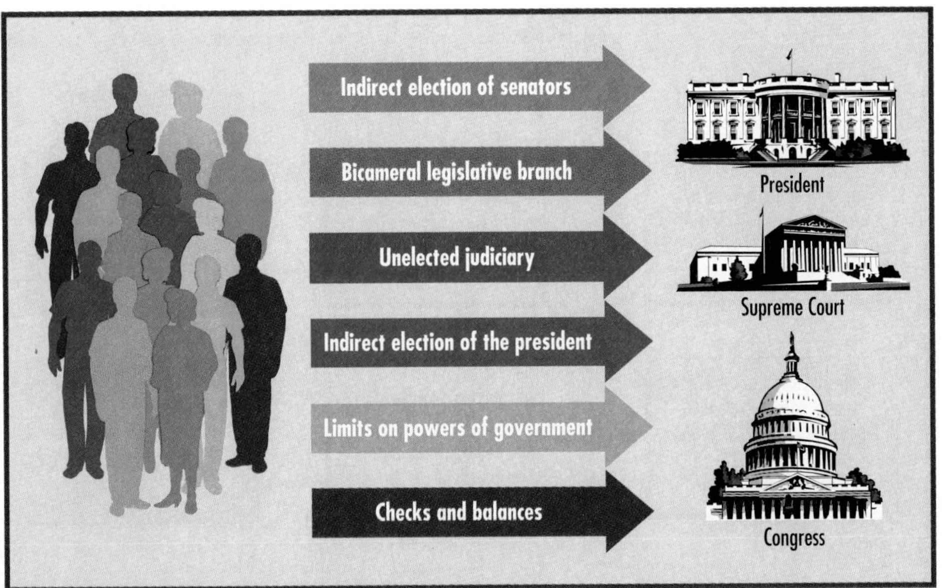

Figure 2.2 ▪ Limiting the Power of the Majority

The framers were concerned that the unreflective and unstable opinions of the majority might overwhelm the considered judgments of government leaders and lead to tyranny. One antidote was to create mechanisms in the Constitution which, while preserving "the consent of the governed," ensured that the voice of the people would be muted in the councils of government.

the operation of majority rule."[24] Let us see how the framers planned to constrain the majority.

Of the three branches of government, only a part of one of them was to be selected by the direct vote of the people: the House of Representatives (Article I, Section 2, paragraph 1). As for the rest of the national government, the president was to be elected by the electoral college; the members of the Senate were to be elected by the state legislatures; and judges were to be appointed by the president and confirmed by the Senate. Representatives, senators, and presidents were to be elected, moreover, for different terms (two years for representatives, four years for presidents, and six years for senators), from different constituencies, and (often) at different times. These noncongruencies in elections were intended to ensure that popular majorities, at least in the short run, would be unlikely to overwhelm those who governed. Finally, the framers rejected the advice of radical democrats, such as Thomas Paine, Samuel Adams, and Thomas Jefferson, to allow the Constitution to be easily amended. Instead, they created an amending process that is exceedingly cumbersome and difficult (see Figure 2.3).

Thus, the framers designed a system in which the popular will, while given some play (more than anywhere in the world at the time), was largely deflected and slowed, allowing somewhat insulated political leaders to deliberate at their pleasure.

Fragmented Government During the American Revolution, American leaders worried mainly about the misrule of executives (kings and governors) and judges. As an antidote, they substituted legislative supremacy, thinking

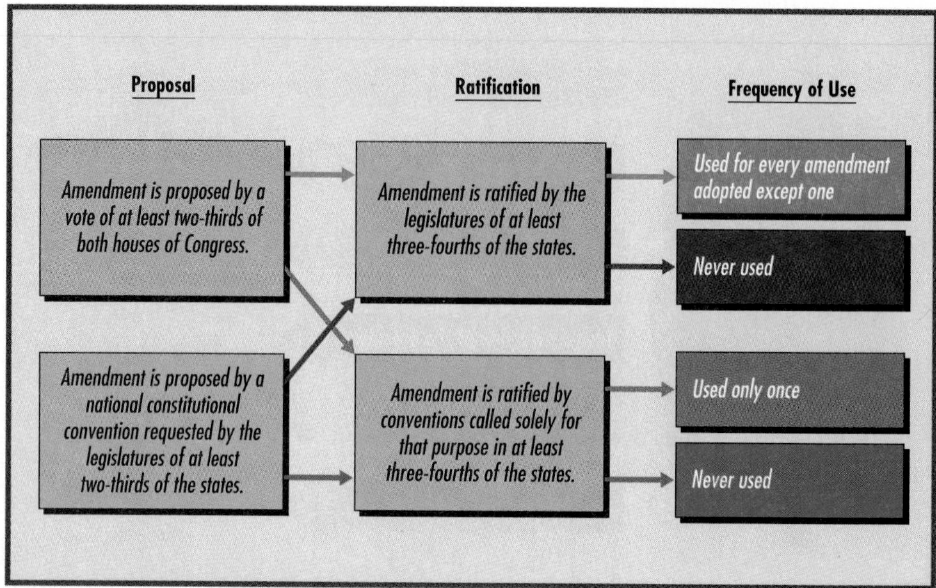

Figure 2.3 ▪ Amending the Constitution

With two ways of proposing a constitutional amendment, and two ways of ratifying one, there are four routes to changing the Constitution. In all but one case (the Twenty-First Amendment, which repealed prohibition), constitutional amendments have been proposed by Congress and then ratified by the state legislatures.

that placing power in an elected representative body would make government effective and nontyrannical. (We described legislative supremacy above in the section on theory and practice in the early state constitutions.) The men who drafted the Constitution, however, while still leery of executive and judicial power, were more afraid by 1887 of the danger of legislative tyranny. To deal with this problem, the framers turned to the ancient notion of mixed or balanced government, popularized by the French philosopher Montesquieu. The central idea of balanced government is that concentrated power of any kind is dangerous and that the way to prevent tyranny is first to fragment governmental power into its constituent parts—executive, legislative, and judicial—and place each one into a separate and independent branch. (In parliamentary systems, on the other hand, these powers are combined in a single body.) In the U.S. Constitution, Article I (on the legislative power), Article II (on the executive power), and Article III (on the judicial power) designate separate spheres of responsibility and enumerate specific powers for each branch. We call this the **separation of powers.**

separation of powers The distribution of government legislative, executive, and judicial powers to separate branches of government.

To further ensure that power would not be exercised tyrannically, the framers arranged for the legislative, executive, and judicial powers to check one another in such a way that "ambition . . . be made to counteract ambition."[25] They did this by ensuring that no branch of the national government would be able to act entirely on its own without the cooperation of the others. To put it another way, each branch has ways of blocking the actions of the others. For instance, Congress is given the chief lawmaking power under the Constitution, but a bill can become a law only if the president signs it. The

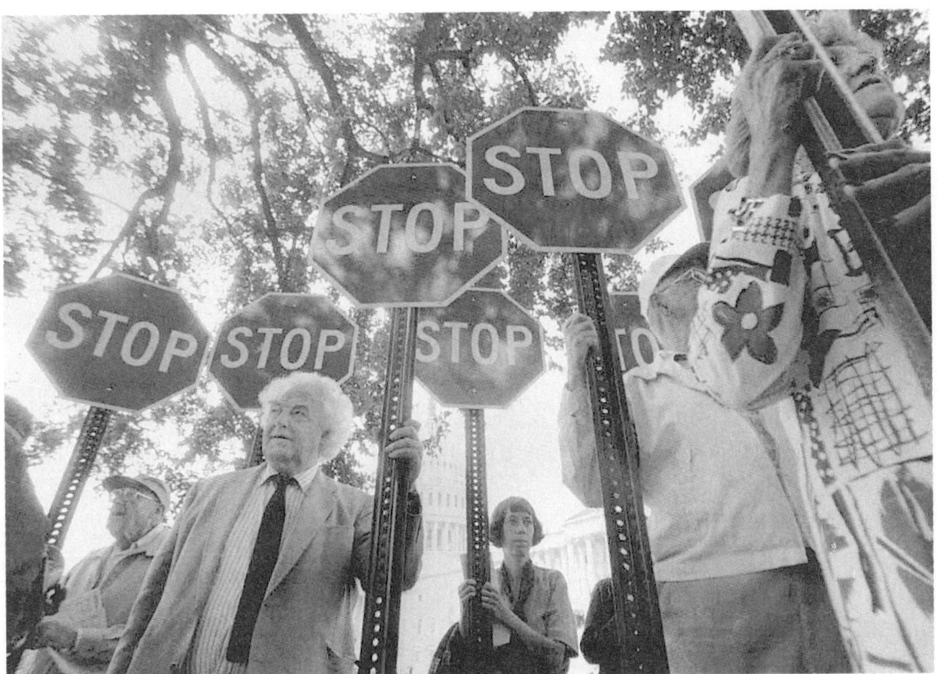

Because the legislative branch plays such a prominent role in fashioning the national budget, budget-related protests are frequently aimed at Congress. Here, outside the Capitol, a group of elderly voters protests proposed Medicare cuts.

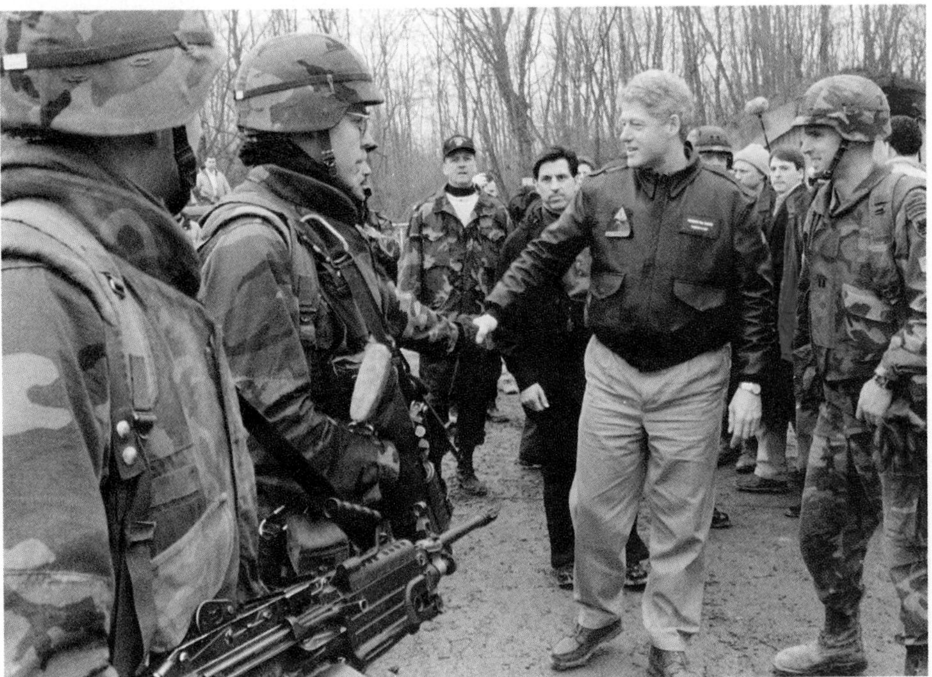

The President is the Commander in Chief of the nation's armed forces under the Constitution's separation-of-powers arrangements. Here, President Clinton acting in his capacity as Commander in Chief, visits American troops deployed in Bosnia to keep the peace in former Yugoslavia.

WHAT ROLE FOR GOVERNMENT?

An Activist or a Minimal Federal Government?

Should we have an activist national government with a broad range of responsibilities, or a minimal national government confined to those responsibilities specified in the Constitution? In this box, eminent historian Arthur Schlesinger, Jr., makes the case for an expansive government; Cato Institute director Stephen Moore makes the case against.

Arthur Schlesinger, Jr., Makes the Case for an Activist National Government[a]

Recent months have witnessed an attack of unprecedented passion and ferocity against the national government. The Republic Party has apparently embarked on a crusade to destroy national standards, national projects, and national regulations and to transfer domestic governing authority from the national government to the states. A near majority of the Supreme Court even seems to want to replace the Constitution by the Articles of Confederation. There has not been so basic an assault on the national government since the Civil War.

. . .

Oklahoma City, according to the polls, has led the general public to reconsider the clichés and to decide that the national government is not such a monster after all. But it has not deterred the anti-government wrecking crew on Capitol Hill in their mania for devolution and deregulation—that is, for dismantling the national government, shifting its functions to the states and repealing or eviscerating national laws that protect the consumer, the investor, the worker, the minorities, the poor, and the dispossessed; or that benefit scientific research and development, education, the environment, and the arts.

. . .

The assault on the national government is represented as a disinterested movement to "return" power to the people. But the withdrawal of the national government does not transfer power to the people. It transfers power to the historical rival of the national government and the prime cause of its enlargement—the great corporate interests.

Theodore Roosevelt, a Republican, was the father of "big government." As he observed of the greedy trusts of his day, "If this irresponsible outside power is to be controlled in the interest of the general public, it can be controlled in only one way—by giving adequate power of control to the National Government." The fight against government regulation of corporate privilege, TR added, "is chiefly done under cover; and especially under the cover of an appeal to State's rights."

Getting the government off the back of business really means putting business on the back of government. It is a delusion to say that because State government is closer to the people it is therefore more responsive to their needs and concerns. Local government is the government of the locally powerful. Historically it has been the national government that has served as the protector of the powerless—workers, farmers, minorities, children, disabled, old folks—against local exploitation or neglect. Had the State Rights creed triumphed, we would still have slavery in the U.S.

. . .

The know-nothing crusade against government springs from a conviction that, if we get government off our backs, our problems will solve themselves. But, far from solving problems, the old unregulated *laissez-faire* economy of the Nineteenth Century generated the problems that produced class war and the *Communist Manifesto.* What rescued capitalism from Marxist prophecy in the Twentieth Century was the work of reformers like the two Roosevelts who used the national government to humanize the industrial order, to cushion the operations of the economic system, to strengthen the bargaining position of workers and farmers and consumers, to reduce the economic gap between the classes, to ensure against recurrent depression by built-in economic stabilizers; above all, to combine individual opportunity with social responsibility.

[a]*The National Times* (October–November 1995), pp. 36–37. Reprinted with permission of *The Wall Street Journal* ©1995 Dow Jones & Company, Inc. All rights reserved.

Stephen Moore Makes the Case Against an Activist National Government[b]

The U.S. Constitution is fundamentally a rulebook for government. Its guiding principle is the idea that the state is a source of corruptive power and ultimate tyranny. Washington's responsibilities were confined to a select few enumerated powers, involving mainly protecting the national security of the nation and preserving public safety. In the realm of domestic affairs, the Founders foresaw limited federal interference in the daily lives of its citizens. The minimal government involvement in the domestic economy that was envisioned by the drafters of the Constitution would be financed and delivered at the state and local levels.

. . .

No matter how long one searches through the Constitution, it is impossible to find any language that authorizes at least 90 percent of the civilian programs that Congress crams into the federal budget today.

There is no granting of authority for the federal government to pay money to farmers, run the health-care industry, impose wage and price controls, give welfare to the poor and unemployed, provide job training, subsidize electricity and telephone service, lend money to businesses or foreign governments, or build parking garages, tennis courts, and swimming pools. The Founders did not create a Department of Commerce, a Department of Education, or a Department of Housing and Urban Development. This was no oversight: they simply never imagined that government would take an active role in such activities.

Recognizing the propensity of governments to expand, and, as Jefferson put it, for "liberty to yield," the Framers added the Bill of Rights as an extra layer of protection of the rights of individuals against the state. The Bill of Rights was inserted to ensure that government would never grow so large that it could trample on the individual and economic liberties of American citizens. The 10th Amendment to the Constitution states the Founders' intentions quite clearly and unambiguously: "The powers not delegated to the United States by the Constitution . . . are reserved to the States respectively, or to the people." Such plain language would not seem to be easy to misinterpret. Put simply, if the Constitution doesn't specifically permit the federal government to do something, then it doesn't have the right to do it.

. . .

The . . . major event that weakened constitutional protections against big government was the ascendancy of Franklin Roosevelt and his New Deal agenda to the White House during the Great Depression. During this era, one after another constitutional safeguards against excessive government were [*sic*] either wholly ignored or spectacularly misinterpreted by the Congress and the courts. Most notable and tragic has been the perversion of the "general welfare" clause of the Constitution. Article I, Section 8 of the Constitution says:

> The Congress shall have power to lay and collect taxes, duties, imposts, and excises to pay the debts, provide for the common defense, and promote the general welfare of the United States.

Since the 1930s, the courts have interpreted this phrase to mean that Congress may spend money for any purpose, whether an enumerated power of government or not, as long as legislators deem it to be in "the general welfare of the United States." That is, this innocent clause has become the equivalent of carte blanche spending authority for Congress.

This was exactly the opposite of what the drafters of the Constitution intended. It is almost beyond dispute that the Founders meant the general-welfare clause to be a limiting provision on government. They meant that the government's spending and taxing powers could only be used for purposes that were in the general welfare of the nation and its citizens collectively, not of particular groups of citizens—farmers, students, welfare recipients, minorities, the disabled. Jefferson was forever concerned that the general-welfare clause might be perverted. To clarify its meaning, in 1798 he wrote: "Congress has not unlimited powers to provide for the general welfare, but only those specifically enumerated."

[b]Stephen Moore, "The Unconstitutional Congress," *The Policy Review,* No. 75 (Spring 1995). Internet: http://www.townhall.com/heritage/p_review/spring95/tablth.html

Supreme Court, moreover, has the power (though it is not specifically mentioned) to reject a law formulated by Congress and signed by the president if it is contrary to the Constitution. What is at work here was described nicely by Thomas Jefferson: "The powers of government should be so divided and balanced among several bodies of magistracy, as that no one could transcend their legal limits, without being effectually checked and constrained by the others."[26] We call the provisions that accomplish this objective **checks and balances.** Figure 2.4 shows in detail how each separate branch of the federal government can be checked by the other two. In this constitutional scheme, each branch has power, but none is able to exercise all of its powers on its own.

checks and balances The constitutional principle that government power shall be divided, and that the fragments should balance or check one another to prevent tyranny.

The Framers Created the Foundations for a National Free Enterprise Economy

Recall that the framers were concerned that a system "too much upon the democratic order" would eventually threaten private property. They believed, following John Locke, that the right to accumulate, use, and transfer property was one of the fundamental, inalienable rights that governments were instituted to defend, so they looked for ways to protect property. Recall, also, that the men who wrote the Constitution were concerned that the obstacles to trade that had appeared under the Articles of Confederation were threatening to block the emergence of a vibrant national economy in which most of them were involved.

Property rights are protected in several places in the Constitution. Article I, Section 10, forbids the states to impair the obligation of contracts, to coin money, or to make anything but gold and silver coin a tender in payment of debts. In other words, the states could no longer help debtors by printing inflated money, forgiving debts, or otherwise infringing on the property of creditors, as had happened in such places as Rhode Island under the Articles of Confederation. Article IV, Section 1, further guarantees contracts by establish-

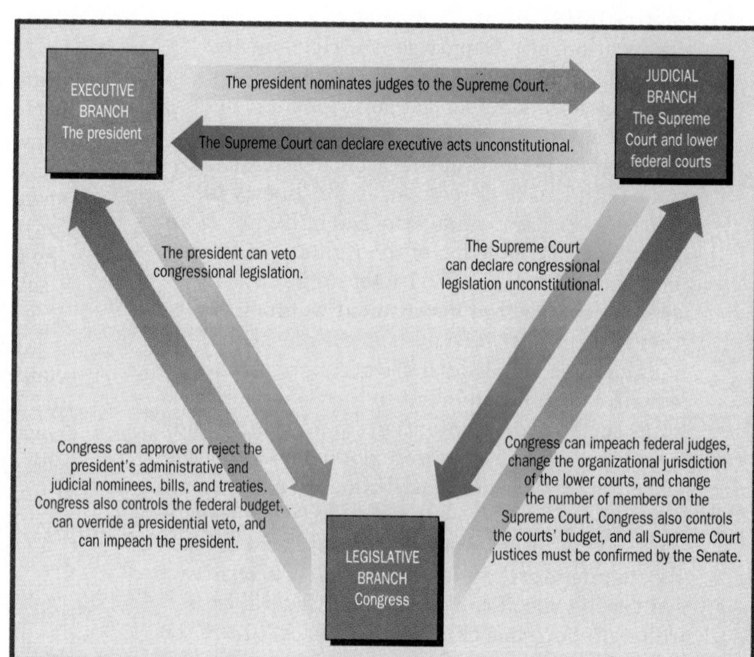

Figure 2.4 ■ Checks and Balances

The framers believed that tyranny might be avoided if the power of government were fragmented into its executive, legislative, and judicial components, and if each component were made the responsibility of a separate branch of government. To further protect against tyranny, they created mechanisms by which the actions of any single branch could be blocked by either or both of the other branches. This system of checks and balances is highlighted in this drawing.

ing that the states must give "full faith and credit" to the public acts, records, and judicial proceedings of every other state, which meant that one could no longer escape legal and financial obligations in one state by moving to another. In addition, the Constitution guaranteed that the U.S. government would pay all debts contracted under the Articles of Confederation (Article VI, Section 1). Article IV, Section 2, paragraph 3, even protected private property in slaves by requiring states to deliver escaped slaves back to their owners.

Besides protecting private property, the framers took additional steps to encourage the emergence of a national free enterprise economy. Article I, Section 8, grants Congress the power to regulate interstate commerce (thus ending the chaos of individual states' regulations); to coin money and regulate its value (thus establishing a uniform national currency); to establish uniform laws of bankruptcy; and to protect the financial fruits of invention by establishing patent and copyright laws. At the same time, Article I, Sections 9 and 10, broke down barriers to trade by forbidding the states to impose taxes or duties on other states' exports, to enter into foreign treaties, to coin money, or to lay any imposts or duties on imports or exports.

The Battle to Ratify the Constitution

One of the truly remarkable things about the story of the Constitution is how the delegates to the convention proposed that it be ratified. Congress had instructed the delegates to the convention to propose changes to the Articles of Confederation. Under the provisions of the Articles of Confederation, such alterations would have required the unanimous consent of the 13 states. To follow such a course would have meant instant rejection of the new constitution, because Rhode Island, never friendly to the deliberations in Philadelphia, surely would have voted against it, and one or two additional states may well have joined Rhode Island. Acting boldly, the framers simply stated that ratification would be based on guidelines specified in Article VII of the unratified document they had just written, namely, approval by nine states meeting in special constitutional conventions. Congress agreed to this procedure, voting on September 28, 1787, to transmit the Constitution to the states for their consideration.

The battle over ratification was heated, and the outcome was far from certain. That the Constitution eventually carried the day may be partly attributed to the fact that the **Federalists** (those who supported the Constitution) did a better job of making their case than the **Anti-Federalists** (those who opposed the Constitution). Their intellectual advantages were nowhere more obvious than in the 85 articles written in defense of the Constitution for New York newspapers, under the name "Publius," by Alexander Hamilton (who wrote the most), James Madison (who wrote the best), and John Jay (who wrote only three). Collected later and published as *The Federalist Papers,* these articles strongly influenced the debate over ratification and remain the most impressive commentaries ever written about the U.S. Constitution (see Numbers 10 and 51 by Madison in the Appendix).

Federalists Proponents of the Constitution during the ratification fight; also the political party of Hamilton, Washington, and Adams.

Anti-Federalists Opponents of the Constitution during the fight over ratification.

The struggle over ratification mainly pitted the wealthy and town interests, which favored ratification, against the less wealthy and rural interests, which opposed ratification. It also pitted advocates of small-scale, decentralized republican government against advocates of a more centralized republican system.[27]

Opposition to the Constitution also came from those who were concerned about the absence of a bill of rights. Though the Federalists firmly believed that a bill of rights was unnecessary because of the protection of rights in the state constitutions and the many safeguards against tyranny in the federal constitution, they promised to add a bill of rights during the first session of Congress. They kept their promise. The First Congress passed a bill of rights in the form of the first ten amendments to the Constitution (see Table 2.3 and Appendix), and the amendments were eventually ratified by the required number of states. We will explore the Bill of Rights at various places throughout the text, but especially in chapters on civil rights and civil liberties (also see The Struggle for Democracy box "The Struggle for the Bill of Rights").

Ratification of the Constitution was a very close call. Most of the small states quickly approved, attracted by the formula of equal representation in the Senate. Federalists organized a victory in Pennsylvania before the Anti-Federalists realized what had happened. After that, the ratification struggle was very hard. Rhode Island voted no. North Carolina abstained because of the absence of a bill of rights and did not vote its approval until 1790. In the largest and most important states, the vote was exceedingly close. Massachusetts approved by a vote of 187–168; Virginia by 89–79; and New York by 30–27. The struggle was especially intense in Virginia, where prominent, articulate, and influential men were involved on both sides of the question. The Federalists could call on George Washington, James Madison, John Marshall, and Edmund Randolph. The Anti-Federalists countered with George Mason, Richard Henry Lee, and Patrick Henry. Patrick Henry was particularly passionate, saying that the Constitution "squints towards monarchy." Though New Hampshire technically put the Constitution over the top, being the ninth state to vote approval, the proponents did not rest easily until approval was narrowly voted by Virginia and New York.

Table 2.3

The Bill of Rights[a]

Amendment I	Freedom of religion, speech, press, and assembly
Amendment II	The right to bear arms
Amendment III	Prohibition against quartering of troops in private homes
Amendment IV	Prohibition against unreasonable searches and seizures
Amendment V	Rights guaranteed to the accused: requirement for grand jury indictment; protections against double jeopardy, self-incrimination; guarantee of due process
Amendment VI	Right to a speedy and public trial before an impartial jury, to cross-examine witnesses, and to have counsel
Amendment VII	Right to a trial by jury in civil suits
Amendment VIII	Prohibition against excessive bail and fines, and against cruel and unusual punishment
Amendment IX	Rights not listed in Constitution that are retained by the people
Amendment X	The retaining by the states of those powers not denied to them by the Constitution or delegated to the national government

[a]See Appendix for a full enumeration.

Despite the passions that were unleashed during the debate over the refashioning of the nation's fundamental law, Americans very quickly accepted the new order. It is not entirely clear why this happened. Perhaps it was simple weariness from the long effort to win independence and to create a new nation. Perhaps it was because George Washington was elected the nation's first president under the new Constitution, lending great legitimacy to the new venture. Perhaps it was because most of the prominent political figures involved in the struggle for independence and in the ratification fight, even those in the Anti-Federalist camp, quickly came to accept and support the new government.

The Changing Constitution, Democracy, and American Politics

The constitution is the basic rule book for the game of American politics. Constitutional rules apportion power and responsibility among governmental branches, define the fundamental nature of the relationships between governmental institutions, specify how individuals are to be selected for office, and tell how the rules themselves may be changed. Every aspiring politician who wants to attain office, every citizen who wants to influence what government does, and every group that wants to advance its interests in the political arena must know the rules and how to use them to best advantage. Because the Constitution has this character, we understand it to be a fundamental structural factor influencing all of American political life.

The Constitution and Democracy

It is important to ask how the Constitution relates to democracy, remembering that instituting democratic government was not the aim of the framers. Recall that the framers believed liberty and popular sovereignty to be contradictory. Because they especially valued liberty, they tried in a variety of ways to control the play of popular democracy in American political life, using constitutional mechanisms to do so. We believe that they did not fully appreciate the extent to which liberty, popular sovereignty, and political equality are compatible. We made the case in Chapter 1 that most people today include political liberty as a basic attribute of democracy itself; they believe—quite correctly in our view—that democracy is possible only where popular sovereignty, political equality, and political liberty coexist. The framers' contribution to the advance of democracy is, then, ambiguous, for while they tried to control popular sovereignty and political equality, they made an important contribution by strengthening and protecting political liberty.

The efforts of the framers to limit democracy were not entirely successful. Popular democracy proved to be an idea of such power that our political life has become considerably more democratic than the framers imagined or wanted. This democratization of American politics, as well as the ongoing historical "struggle for democracy" that caused it, will be recounted at various points in this book. Fortunately for us, the framers created a constitutional system capable of accommodating the yearning among Americans for more popular sovereignty, political equality, and political liberty.

"The Struggle for the Bill of Rights"

The Struggle for Democracy

Most Americans rightly see the Bill of Rights—the first ten amendments to the Constitution—as the legal foundation of American freedom. Its simple but evocative listing of the fundamental individual liberties to be protected against government intrusion, though sometimes violated during our history, has served to inspire and animate the political activities of many people over the years. The struggle to expand the reach of these liberties is a part of the story of the struggle for democracy in the United States. It may come as a surprise, then, that the Bill of Rights almost did not happen.

The farmers did not include liberties like the freedoms of speech, assembly, press, and conscience in the Constitution, nor were there very many protections familiar to us today for individuals accused of crimes (trial by jury, the prohibition of excessive bail, and the like). There are two primary reasons why the framers failed to act on a bill of rights. First, they pointed to the fact that bills of rights existed already in most state constitutions, and that the new central government they had invented had no power to contravene them. Second, they believed they had created a republican government whose power was so fragmented and constrained by features like the separation of powers, checks and balances, and federalism that it posed no threat to freedom.

Many Americans remained unconvinced by these reassurances, and their voices were so strong and insistent that the framers were forced to listen. The main proponents of an explicit statement in the Constitution of a bill of rights were those who have come to be known as the Anti-Federalists. Though the Anti-Federalists opposed ratification of the Constitution created in Philadelphia on several grounds, and though a number of Anti-Federalists would not be satisfied unless the entire Constitution were rejected, most in the Anti-Federalist camp opposed ratification on the grounds that the Constitution did not contain provisions for the protection of individual liberties against government intrusions. In the view of one of their number, Marcy Otis Warren, "The rights of individuals ought to be the primary object of all government, and cannot be too securely guarded by the most explicit declarations in their favor."[a] Luther Martin, another Anti-Federalist and author of the Virginia Declaration of Rights, observed, "There is no declaration of rights; and the laws of the general government being paramount to the laws and constitutions of the several states, the declarations of rights in the separate states are no security."[b] Thomas Jefferson (who did not openly identify with the Anti-Federalist camp) also initially opposed ratification on the grounds that, in his words in a letter to James Madison, "A bill of rights is what the people are entitled to against every government on earth . . . and what no just government should refuse."[c]

Using the issue of the absence of a bill of rights in the Constitution, the Anti-Federalists began to gain ground in their fight against ratification. After eight states had ratified, momentum slowed down in several states which had not yet voted. Especially important because of their size and economic prominence were Virginia, Massachusetts, and New York. The new Constitution was in very real jeopardy, and the vote would prove to be extremely close in each of these states. What apparently turned the tide and pushed ratification over the top was the promise by James Madison and other Federalists (those in favor of the new Constitution) that the First Congress would amend the

How the Constitution Changes

The story of the gradual spread of democracy in the United States should remind us that constitutional rules, like all rules, can and do change over time. Their tendency to change with the times is why we sometimes use the term the *living Constitution.* The Constitution changes in a number of ways:

- *Formal amendment.* The Constitution may be formally amended by use of the procedures outlined in Article V of the Constitution (see

Constitution to include a bill of rights. The promise convinced Jefferson, then serving as American ambassador in Paris, to support ratification. It also convinced a number of prominent Anti-Federalists such as John Hancock and Samuel Adams to vote for ratification. And it convinced just enough other waiverers to support ratification so that the Constitution managed (though just barely) to gain approval in the requisite number of states.

One of the remarkable aspects of this story is that the Federalists, made up of the most prominent (including George Washington), wealthy, and politically connected people in the nation, were forced to make a promise that many of them did not necessarily favor.[d] A bill of rights would not have happened had not the Anti-Federalists so successfully pressed their case.

[a]Quoted in Scott Douglas Gerber, *To Secure These Rights: The Declaration of Independence and Constitutional Interpretation* (New York: New York University Press, 1995), p. 66.

[b]Ibid.

[c]Ibid., p. 67.

[d]James MacGregor Burns and Stewart Burns, *A People's Charter: The Pursuit of Rights in America* (New York: Knopf, 1991); Main, *The Anti-Federalists.*

Figure 2.3 on how the Constitution is formally amended). This method has resulted in the addition of 27 amendments since the founding, 10 of which (the Bill of Rights) were added within three years of ratification. That only 17 have been added in the roughly 200 years since suggests that this method of changing the Constitution is extremely difficult. Nevertheless, formal amendments have played an important role in expanding democracy in the United States by ending slavery; extending voting rights to African-Americans, women,

The Constitution's full faith and credit provision says that the states must acknowledge and obey contracts agreed to in other states. If some states begin to allow marriages between gay and lesbian couples, other states which do not recognize such unions may be forced to do so because of this constitutional provision. Several states have undertaken steps to try to prevent this from happening.

and young people 18 to 20; and making the Senate subject to popular vote.

judicial review The power of the Supreme Court to declare actions of the other branches and levels of government to be unconstitutional.

- *Judicial interpretation* The Constitution is also changed by decisions and interpretations of the U.S. Supreme Court. For instance, in *Marbury v. Madison* (1803), the Court claimed the power of **judicial review**—the right to declare the actions of the other branches of government null and void if they are contrary to the Constitution— even though such a power is not specifically enumerated in the Constitution. In *Griswold v. Connecticut* (1965), and later in *Roe v. Wade* (1973), the Court supported a fundamental right of privacy even though such a right is nowhere explicitly mentioned in the Constitution.
- *Political practices* The meaning of the Constitution also changes through changing political practices. Political parties and nominating conventions are not cited in the Constitution, but it would be hard to think about American politics today without them. It is also fair to say that the framers would not recognize the modern presidency, which is now a far more important office than they envisioned, a change that has been brought about largely by the political and military involvement of the United States in world affairs.

In the remainder of the text, the story of how formal amendments, judicial interpretations, and political practices have changed the constitutional rules in the United States will be told in more detail.

Summary

The first constitution joining the American states was the Articles of Confederation. Under its terms, the states were organized into a loose confederation in which the states retained full sovereignty and the central government had little power. Because of a wide range of defects in the Articles of Confederation and fears among many American leaders that democratic and egalitarian tendencies were beginning to spin out of control, a gathering was called in

Philadelphia to amend the Articles of Confederation. The delegates chose, instead, to formulate an entirely new constitution, based on the principles of republicanism (federalism, limited government, the separation of powers, checks and balances, and limitations on majority rule).

The Constitution was ratified in an extremely close vote of the states after a hard-fought struggle between the Federalists and the Anti-Federalists. The Federalists were supported primarily by the economically better-off, urban interests, and believers in a more centralized republicanism; the Anti-Federalists were supported primarily by the economically less well-off, rural interests, and believers in small-scale republicanism. Despite its "close shave," the Constitution became very popular among the American people within only a few years of the ratification fight. Because of the struggle for democracy by the American people, the Constitution has become far more democratic over the years than was originally intended by the framers.

Suggested Readings

Beard, Charles A. *An Economic Interpretation of the Constitution.* New York: Macmillan, 1913.
The classic and controversial work by the progressive historian, which sparked decades of debate among historians about the motivations of the Founders.

Bernstein, Richard B. *Are We to Be a Nation?* Cambridge: Harvard University Press, 1987.
An accessible, comprehensive, and balanced account of the making of the U.S. Constitution. Includes an extensive collection of documents, drawings, and paintings.

Brown, Robert. *Charles Beard and the Constitution.* Princeton: Princeton University Press, 1956.
The most influential refutation of the Beardian thesis on the motivations of the Founders.

The Federalist Papers. Clinton Rossiter, ed. New York: New American Library, 1961.
Classic commentaries on the Constitution and its key provisions, written by Alexander Hamilton, John Jay, and James Madison.

Storing, Herbert J. *What the Anti-Federalists Were For.* Chicago: University of Chicago Press, 1981.
The most complete collection available on the published views of the Anti-Federalists. Includes convincing commentary by Storing.

Wills, Gary. *Inventing America: Jefferson's Declaration of Independence.* New York: Random House, 1978.
A different and controversial look at the intellectual origins of the American experiment.

———. *Explaining America: The Federalist.* New York: Doubleday, 1981.
A fresh look at the writing of the Constitution by one of America's most provocative intellectuals.

Wood, Gordon. *The Creation of the American Republic.* New York: Norton, 1972.
The most exhaustive and respected source on America's changing ideas during the period 1776–1787, or from the start of the American Revolution to the writing of the Constitution.

———. *The Radicalism of the American Revolution.* New York: Knopf, 1992.
Examines and rejects the argument that the American Revolution was merely a political and not a social and economic revolution.

Internet Sources

Constitution Resources http://www.santacruz.k12.ca.us/vft/constitution.html
The Constitution on-line, The Federalist Papers, *historical speeches on constitutional issues, sources on civil rights and civil liberties, and constitutions from around the world are a few of the highlights of this site.*

The Cornell University Law School http://www.law.edu/
Pathways to the full text of U.S. Supreme Court decisions and opinions, articles on constitutional issues, and much more.

Political Science Resources: Political Thought http://www.keele.ac.uk/depts/po/psr.htm
A vast collection of documents on democracy, liberty, and constitutionalism.

Notes

1. Page Smith, *A People's History of the Young Republic: vol. 3. The Shaping of America* (New York: McGraw-Hill, 1980), p. 25.
2. Quoted in Jackson Turner Main, *The Anti-Federalists* (Chapel Hill: University of North Carolina Press, 1961), p. 62.
3. Richard Bushman, "Revolution," in Eric Foner and John A. Garraty, eds., *The Reader's Companion to American History* (Boston: Houghton Mifflin, 1991), p. 936; Gordon S. Wood, *The Creation of the American Republic* (New York: Norton, 1972), p. 12.
4. Quoted in Wood, *Creation of the American Republic,* p. 135.
5. James A. Morone, *The Democratic Wish* (New York: Basic Books, 1990), p. 36.
6. See Hannah Arendt, *On Revolution* (New York: Viking, 1965).
7. Smith, *Shaping of America,* pp. 8–9.
8. Richard Hofstadter, *The American Political Tradition* (New York: Vintage Books, 1948), p. 4.
9. Quoted in Main, *The Anti-Federalists,* p. 163.
10. Gordon Wood, *The Creation of the American Republic* (New York: Norton, 1972), ch. 8.
11. See Gordon S. Wood, *The Radicalism of the American Revolution* (New York: Knopf, 1992).
12. Wood, *Creation of the American Republic,* pp. 311–318.
13. Ibid., ch. 8.
14. Samuel Elliot Morison, *The Oxford History of the American People* (New York: Oxford University Press, 1965), p. 274.
15. See Wood, *Creation of the American Republic,* p. 400.
16. Charles Beard, *An Economic Interpretation of the Constitution* (New York: Macmillan, 1913).
17. See Robert Brown, *Charles Beard and the Constitution* (Princeton: Princeton University Press, 1956); Hofstader, *The American Political Tradition;* Leonard Levy, *Constitutional Opinions* (New York: Oxford University Press, 1986); Robert A. McGuire and Robert L. Ohsfeldt, "An Economic Model of Voting Behavior over

Specific Issues at the Constitutional Convention of 1787," *Journal of Economic History,* Vol. 66 (March 1986), pp. 79–111; Morone, *The Democratic Wish;* Forrest McDonald, *We the People: The Economic Origins of the Constitution* (Chicago: University of Chicago Press, 1958); Gordon Wood, *The Convention and the Constitution* (New York: St. Martin's Press, 1965); Wood, *Creation of the American Republic.*

18. Staughton Lynd, *Class Conflict, Slavery, and the United States Constitution* (Indianapolis: Bobbs-Merrill, 1967), p. 70.

19. Wood, *Creation of the American Republic,* p. 473.

20. Benjamin Franklin, quoted in Wood, *Creation of the American Republic,* p. 432.

21. *The Federalist,* ed. by Clinton Rossiter (New York: New American Library, 1961), Nos. 10 and 39.

22. Max Farrand, *The Records of the Federal Convention of 1787* (New Haven: Yale University Press, 1937).

23. "The Invention of Centralized Federalism," in William Riker, ed., *The Development of Centralized Federalism* (Boston: Kluwer Academic, 1987).

24. Robert A. Dahl, "On Removing the Impediments to Democracy in the United States," *Political Science Quarterly,* Vol. 92, No. 1 (Spring 1977), p. 5.

25. *The Federalist,* No. 51.

26. Thomas Jefferson, *Notes on the State of Virginia,* ed. by Thomas Perkins Abernathy (New York: Harper & Row, 1964), p. 120.

27. See Main, *The Anti-Federalists;* Wood, *Creation of the American Republic;* Smith, *Shaping of America,* p. 99; Herbert Storing, *What the Anti-Federalists Were For* (Chicago: University of Chicago Press, 1981), p. 71.

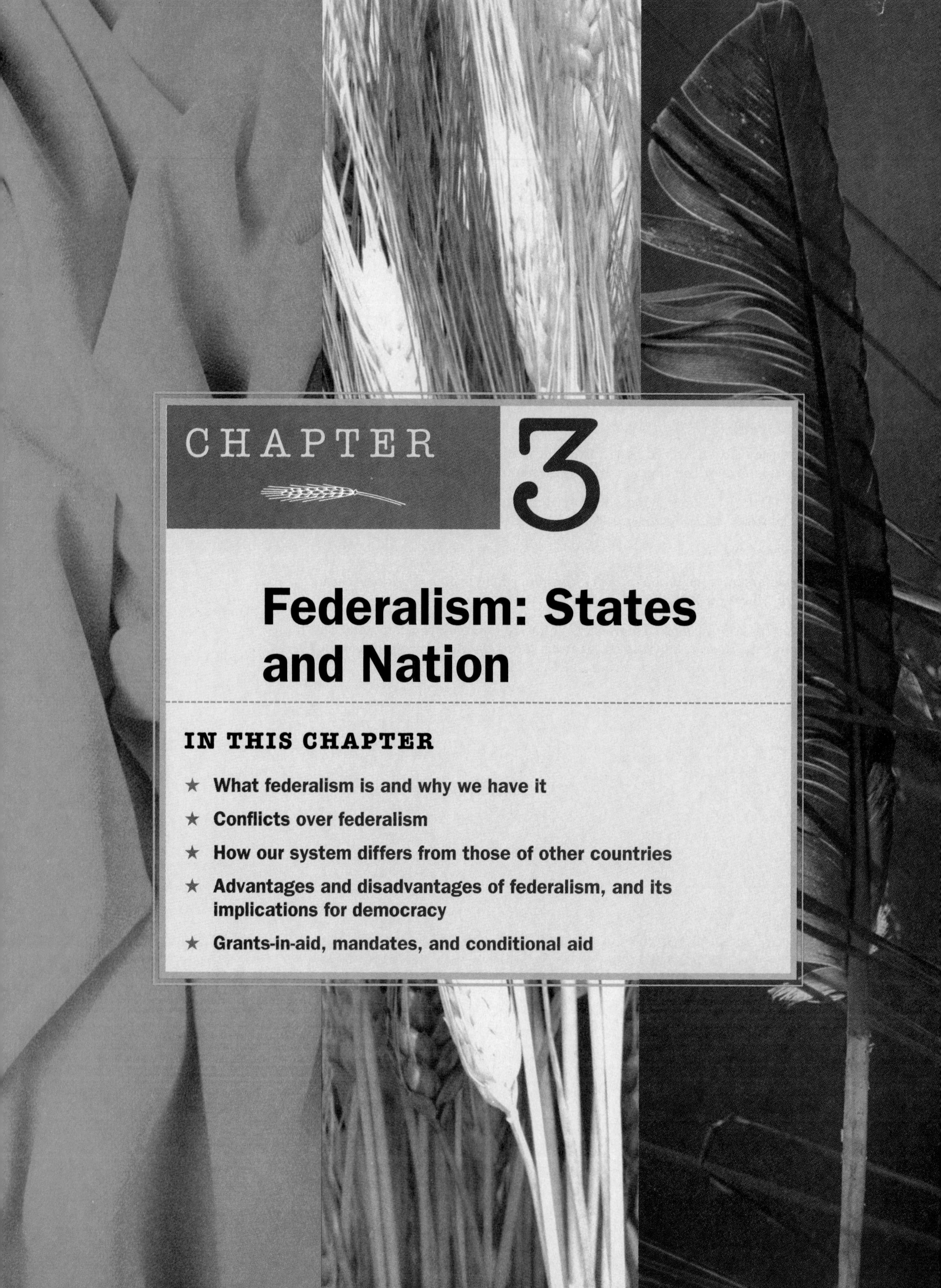

CHAPTER 3

Federalism: States and Nation

IN THIS CHAPTER

- ★ What federalism is and why we have it
- ★ Conflicts over federalism
- ★ How our system differs from those of other countries
- ★ Advantages and disadvantages of federalism, and its implications for democracy
- ★ Grants-in-aid, mandates, and conditional aid

Welfare Reform and the States

Bill Clinton and many Republican and Democratic members of Congress promised to "end welfare as we know it." Long before Congress and the president could agree on a specific plan, however, many state governments—with special permission from Washington—took the lead in trying out their own welfare reforms. This interplay between national and state governments illustrates the dispersion of power in our federal system.

Under the Social Security Act of 1935, the U.S. government established Aid to Families with Dependent Children (AFDC) as an entitlement program for children in poor, mostly female-headed, families. The states administered the program, offering different levels of benefits from one state to another. But the national government, which provided most of the money, also made the rules about who was eligible, for how long, and under what circumstances. It guaranteed that any eligible family in the country would be entitled to benefits.

That pattern of national rule setting began to change around the beginning of the 1990s. New, mostly Republican, state governors and legislatures were elected, promising to reform welfare by encouraging work and parental responsibility. Pioneers like Republican governor Tommy G. Thompson of Wisconsin, who took office in 1987, came up with many different ideas: requiring efforts to find work; putting time limits on benefits; easing benefit reductions when recipients earned some money working; helping with training, day care, job placement, and community service jobs; requiring young mothers to live with their parents or other adults; paying bonuses for staying in school; and restricting payments for new children born to mothers on welfare.[1]

The Bush administration and especially the Clinton administration granted many "waivers," exceptions to the national rules, so that states could experiment with these ideas. By 1995, 32 states had waivers, affecting about half the nation's 14 million welfare recipients. More than 30 states let recipients earn more and keep assets without losing benefits; 25 states required teen-age mothers to live with adults; and more than 20 got waivers to require and/or help welfare recipients find work.

Some of the results were impressive. In Wisconsin, for example, after Thompson took office and persuaded Washington to give him 179 waivers, the welfare rolls dropped by 27 percent, and spending was cut by $210 million per year. The money that was poured into child care and job training seemed to pay off, saving about $2 in welfare costs for each $1 spent. Michigan, under Republican Governor John Engler, cut caseloads to the lowest point in 21 years, led the nation by steering 30 percent of its 190,000 welfare recipients into work, and saved about $100 million a year.[2] Thompson's next goal was to end welfare altogether, sending people to a job center instead, and guaranteeing placement in private employment (with training and subsidies if needed) or in community service.[3]

Finally, in 1996, the president and Congress ended national rules and benefit guarantees altogether, so that Washington now has no role except to provide money. Some advocates of the poor fear that without entitlements federal money will later dry up, and that without national standards some states will be unable or unwilling to provide adequate jobs, day care, or other benefits. The results remain to be seen.

The mixture of state and national action on this issue, and the state experimentation that affected policymaking in the nation as a whole, is characteristic of American federalism. So is the conflict between national standards and local flexibility.

President Clinton meets with governors at the White House.

Federalism as a System of Government

The United States is full of governments. We have not only a "federal" government in Washington, D.C. (which, in order to avoid confusion, we will refer to in this chapter as the *national* or *central* government), but also governments in each of 50 states and in each of thousands of smaller governmental units, such as counties (about 3,000 of them), cities, towns and townships, school districts, and special districts that deal with such matters as parks and sanitation. According to one estimate, there are about 83,000 local governments in the United States, including school districts[4] (see Figure 3.1).

All these governments are organized and related to each other in a particular way. The small governments—those of counties, cities, towns, and special districts—are legal creatures of state governments. They can be created, changed, or abolished by state laws, at the state's convenience. But state governments themselves have much more independence. Together with the national government in Washington, D.C., they form what is known as a federal system. The *federal system* is part of the basic structure of U.S. government, deeply rooted in our Constitution and history. It is one of the most important features of American politics, since it affects practically everything else.

The Nature of Federalism

federalism A system in which significant governmental powers are divided between a central government and smaller units, such as states.

confederation A loose association of states or units bound together for limited purposes.

Federalism is a system under which significant government powers are divided between the central government and smaller governmental units. Neither one completely controls the other; each has some room for independent action. A federal system can be contrasted with two other types of government: a confederation and a unitary government. In a **confederation,** the constituent states get together for certain common purposes but retain ultimate individual authority and can veto major central governmental actions. The present-day United Nations and our revolutionary government under the Articles of Con-

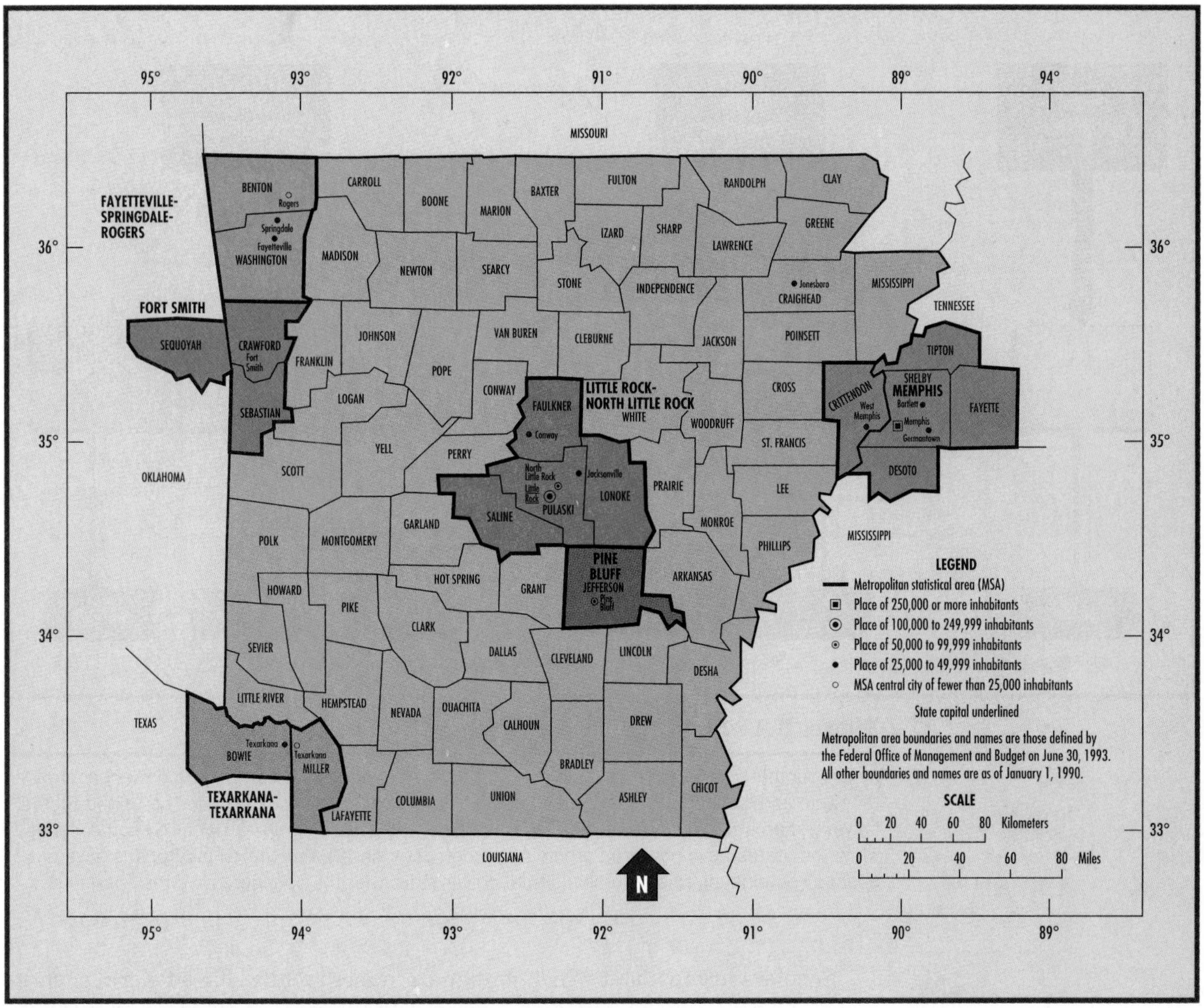

Figure 3.1 ■ **Multiple Governments in the Federal System**

Arkansas, like other states, includes many county, city, and town governments. Each of these is subordinate to the state government, which, in turn, shares powers with the national government in Washington. Some metropolitan areas lap over into adjoining states.

Source: U.S. Department of Commerce, Bureau of the Census, *City and County Data Book* (Washington, D.C.: U.S. Government Printing Office, 1994, p. C4).

federation are examples. In a **unitary system,** the central government has all the power and can change its constituent units or tell them what to do. Most governments in the world today are unitary systems. These three different types of governmental systems are contrasted in Figure 3.2.

unitary system A system in which a central government has complete power over its constituent units or states.

Federalism is not a common way of organizing governments around the world. At the beginning of the 1990s, according to their formal structure, 140 (88 percent) of the 159 member countries in the United Nations had unitary rather than federal governments. In the years since the founding of the United States, however, a number of important countries—mostly large and diverse ones—have also established federal systems, often modeling them on the U.S. system.

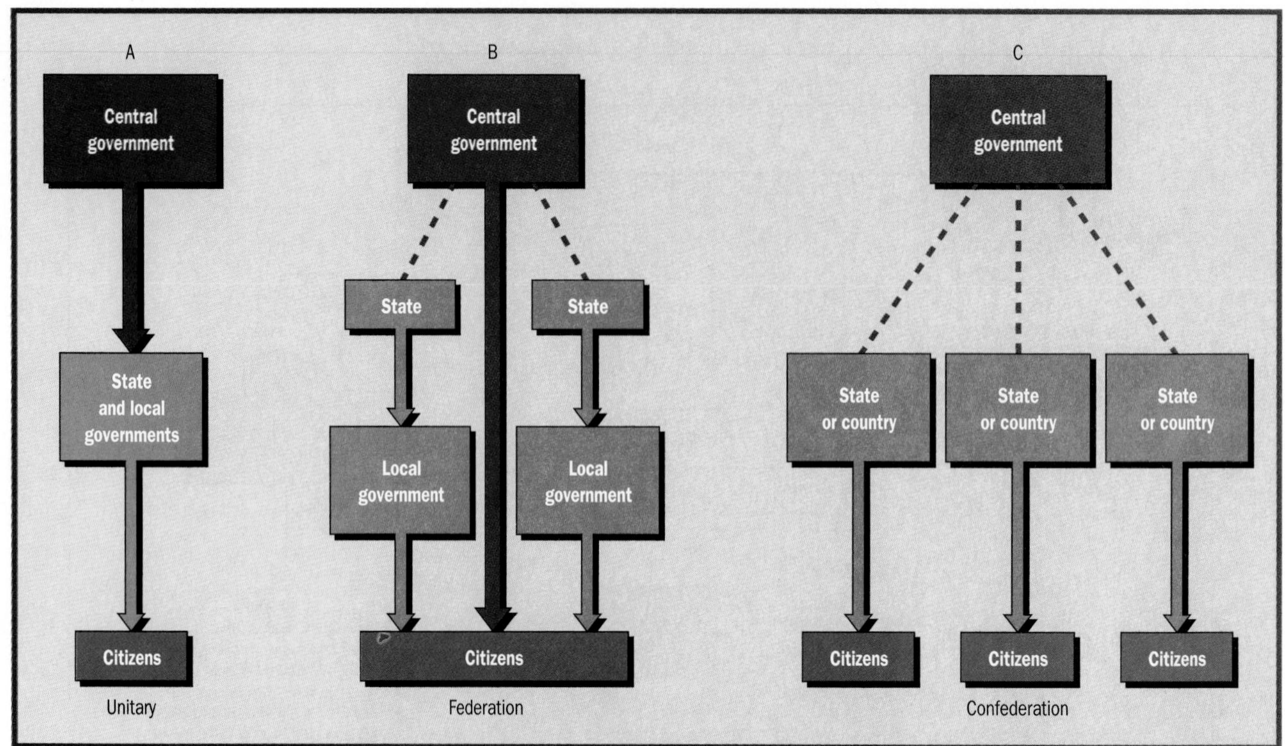

Figure 3.2 ■ **Types of Political Systems**

Most countries of the world have unitary systems (A), in which the central government controls the state and local governments, which in turn exert power over the citizens. The United States, however, has a federal system (B), in which the central government has power on some issues, while the states have power on others. In a confederation (C), the central institutions have only a loose coordinating role, and all ultimate power stays with the constituent states or countries.

Scholars argue about which foreign countries "really" have federal governments. Federalism is a matter of degree. There are 19 countries with formally federalist constitutions, but they vary significantly. For example, German *Länder* and Mexican states do not have exactly the same independent powers as American states do. Among the many unitary countries, some (such as the United Kingdom and Italy) have subunits with a certain amount of autonomy, while others (such as France and Japan) are more completely dominated by the central government. There are no neat boundaries; scholars have suggested that there is a continuum from "unitary" to "formally federal," "quasi-federal," "federal," and "confederal" polities.[5]

Moreover, countries change their systems—or even disintegrate—from time to time, especially when ethnic minorities demand self-rule. Federalism in the old Soviet Union was mostly a constitutional fiction, but in 1991 the Soviet republics—Ukraine, Kazakhstan, and many others—declared their independence, leaving Russia as a smaller but still diverse federation. The former Yugoslavia broke up into a number of separate countries, including Slovenia, Croatia, Bosnia, and Serbia. In 1995, Quebec voters very nearly endorsed separation from Canada, rejecting the idea by only 50.4 percent to 49.5 percent. In contrast, the separate countries of Western Europe have been moving slowly toward union. Still, at any given moment, we can observe patterns in the types of countries that have federal systems.

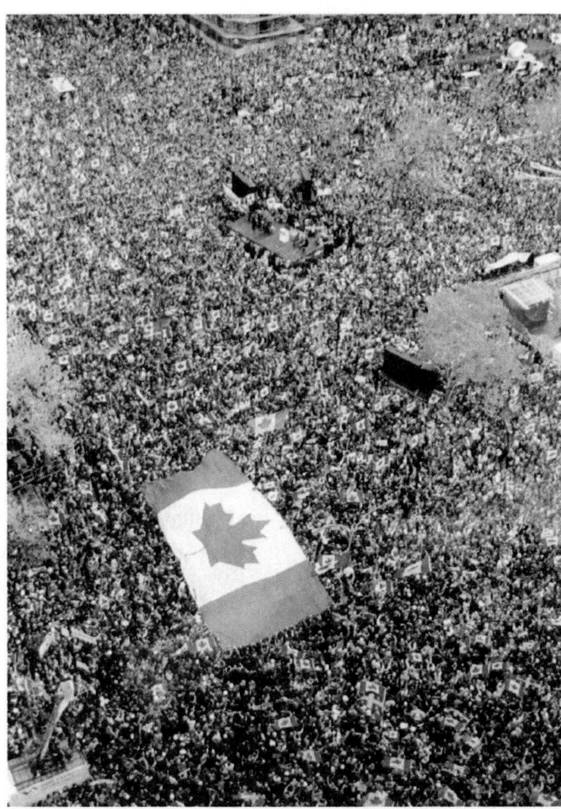

Countries change their systems—or even disintegrate—from time to time for a variety of reasons. In 1995, voters in Quebec, Canada, elected to remain part of Canada by a slim margin of less than one-tenth of 1 percent.

The Roots of Federalism

Some of the elements of federalism go back in history at least as far as the Union of Utrecht in the Netherlands in 1579, but federalism as it exists today is largely an American invention.[6]

Historical Origins American federalism emerged from the particular way in which the states declared independence from Britain—becoming, in effect, separate countries—and then joined together to form a confederation and then a single nation, as discussed in the previous chapter. But we can gain further insight into *why* the United States adopted and has continued a federal system if we look at what other countries with similar systems have in common (see Table 3.1).

The Role of Size and Diversity Most federal systems around the world are found in countries that are geographically large and have regions that differ in economic activity, religion, ethnicity, and language. In Germany, for example, the conservative Catholics of the south have traditionally been different from the liberal Protestants of the north and east. In Canada, the farmers of the central plains are not much like the fishers of Nova Scotia, and the French-speaking (and primarily Catholic) residents of Quebec differ markedly from the mostly English-speaking Protestants of the rest of the country. German, French, and Italian are dominant languages in different parts of Switzerland. India consists of many dramatically different ethnic and religious groups, living far apart in different climates and speaking different languages. Such

Table 3.1

Selected Federal and Unitary Countries

Most federal systems, like those at the top of the table, are large and diverse. Unitary governments, which are much more common, are usually found in smaller and more homogeneous countries like those at the bottom of the table.

Name	Land Area (Sq. Miles)	Population	Major Languages	Major Religions (at Least 1% of Population)	Comments
I. Federal					
Canada	3,849,672	28,434,545	English, French	Roman Catholic, Protestant, Eastern Orthodox, Jewish	Regionally diverse economy
Germany	137,820	81,337,541	German	Roman Catholic, Protestant, Muslim	Regionally diverse economy and religious cleavages
India	1,222,559	936,545,814	Hindi, Telugu, Bengali, Marathi, Tamil, Urdu, English, at least 350 others	Hindu, Muslim, Christian, Sikh	Extremely diverse ethnically, religiously, and economically
Russia	6,592,800	149,909,089	Russian, Ukrainian, Belorussian, Tatar	Orthodox Christian, Muslim, Protestant, Roman Catholic	Extremely diverse ethnically, religiously, and economically
USA	3,679,192	263,814,032	English, Spanish	Protestant, Roman Catholic, Jewish, Muslim	Regionally diverse economy
II. Unitary					
France	210,026	58,109,160	French	Roman Catholic, Protestant, Muslim	Relatively homogeneous
Denmark	16,638	5,199,437	Danish	Lutheran	Relatively homogeneous
Hungary	35,920	10,318,838	Hungarian	Roman Catholic, Protestant	Relatively homogeneous
Japan	145,883	125,506,492	Japanese	Shinto, Buddhist, Christian	Relatively homogeneous

diverse groups often want the local independence that federalism allows, rather than submitting to a unified central government.

The United States, too, is large and diverse, though it is certainly less diverse than India or Russia. From the early days of the Republic, the slave-holding and agriculture-oriented South was quite distinct from the merchant Northeast, and some important differences persist today. Illinois is not Louisiana; the farmers of Iowa differ from defense and electronics workers in California. In *The Federalist Papers,* the Founders argued that this size and diversity made federalism especially appropriate for the new United States.

U.S. Federalism: Pro and Con

Federalism is a key *structural* characteristic of American government, affecting many aspects of politics. For example, federalism tends to prevent the emergence of fully unified or disciplined political parties, since politicians have separate power bases in separate states or localities. It limits what the Congress and the president can do, by reserving some powers to the states. It allows for a patchwork of different policies to be pursued in different parts of the country. Federalism also may have important effects on how well democracy works.

Over the years, from the framing of the U.S. Constitution to the present day, people have offered a number of strong arguments for and against federalism, in contrast to a more unitary system. Let us consider some of these arguments.

Pro: A Diversity of Needs The oldest and most important argument in favor of decentralized government is that, in a large and diverse country, needs and wants and conditions differ from one place to another. Why not let different states enact different policies to meet their own needs? Federalism may enhance popular sovereignty and majority rule democracy, in the sense that distinct majorities in different states can legislate specific policies that they want instead of being subordinated to a single national majority.

Con: The Importance of National Standards On the other hand, the "needs" or desires that different states pursue may not be worthy ones. William Riker has pointed out that, historically, one of the main effects of federalism was to let white majorities in the southern states enslave and then discriminate against black people, without interference from the North.[7] In attempting to block the registration of a black student at the University of Alabama in 1963, Governor George C. Wallace spoke of the "right of state authority in the operation of the public schools, colleges, and universities"; he refused to submit to "illegal usurpation of power" by the central government. Perhaps it is better, in some cases, to insist on national standards that apply everywhere.

Pro: Closeness to the People It is sometimes claimed that state and local governments are closer to the ordinary citizens, who have a better chance to know their officials, to be aware of what they are doing, to contact them, and to hold them responsible for what they do. Thus, President Ronald Reagan, in his 1982 State of the Union address, declared, "[My New Federalism] will be designed and administered closer to the grassroots and the people it serves . . . the programs will be more responsive to both the people they are meant to help and the people who pay for them."[8] "Isn't it time we got Washington off our backs?" asked the 1994 Contract with America.[9]

Con: Low Visibility and Lack of Popular Control However, others respond that geographical closeness may not be the real issue. More Americans are better informed about the *national* government than they are about state and local governments (only about 28 percent can name their state senator),[10] and more people participate in national than in state or local elections. When more people know what the government is doing and more people vote, they are better able to insist that the government do what they want. For that reason, responsiveness to ordinary citizens may actually be greater in national government. In that sense, the government in Washington, D.C., may possibly be "closer" to most citizens than their nearby state capital is.

Pro: Innovation and Experimentation When the states have independent power, they can try out new ideas. Individual states can be "laboratories." If the experiments work, other states or the nation as a whole can adopt their ideas, as has happened on such issues as allowing women and 18-year-olds to vote, fighting air pollution, and dealing with water pollution. Early research by political scientist Jack Walker showed that certain states, especially New York, California, and Massachusetts, regularly took the lead in policy innovation.[11] More recently, health policies in several states, such as Hawaii and Oregon (which have extended medical care to most of their populations) and Tennessee (which shifted from state-run Medicare to private plans), have inspired proposals for the whole country. As we saw in the opening story, Wisconsin and Michigan have been innovative in welfare reform.

Likewise, when the national government is controlled by one political party, federalism allows the states with majorities favoring a different party to compensate by enacting different policies. This aspect of diversity in policymaking is related to the Founders' contention that tyranny is less likely when government's power is dispersed. Multiple governments reduce the risks of bad policy or the blockage of the popular will; if things go wrong at one governmental level, they may go right at another.

Con: Spillover Effects and Competition Diversity and experimentation in policies, however, may not always be good. Divergent regulations can cause bad effects that spill over from one state to another. If New Jersey imposed severe restrictions on the size and weight of trucks traveling on its highways, shipments to New York might be blocked. If cities around the country set different limits on noise at airports, as they used to do, airplane manufacturers and airlines would be under conflicting pressures about what sorts of planes to build and use. (In 1990, Congress set uniform airplane noise standards for the whole country.) When factories in the Midwest spew out oxides of nitrogen and sulfur that fall as acid rain in the Northeast, the northeastern states can do nothing about it. The Midwestern states have refused to pay what it would cost to help the northeasterners. Only nationwide rules can solve such problems.

Similarly, it is very difficult for cities or local communities to do much about poverty or other social problems. If a city raises taxes to pay for social programs, businesses and the wealthy may move out of town, and the poor may move in, impoverishing the city.[12] In recent years, many factories have moved from the northern Frost Belt to the southern Sun Belt, partly in search of low taxes and a good "business climate," where wages are lower and organized labor is kept at bay by "right-to-work" laws. A newspaper ad once proclaimed, "When the old corporate tax bite eats away profits, CUT OUT FOR TEXAS."[13]

Thus, innovation by local governments may be undercut by competition among communities for wealth and resources. Perhaps only the national government can deal with the aspects of taxes and spending that affect people across state boundaries or that would cause destructive competition among the states.

What Sort of Federalism?

As the above arguments indicate, a lot is at stake. It is not likely, however, that Americans will ever have a chance to vote yes or no on the federal system, or to choose a unitary government instead. What we can decide is exactly *what sort* of federalism we will have, that is, how much power will go to the states as compared to the national government. Indeed, we may want a fluid system in which the balance of power varies from one kind of policy to another.

The balance of power between states and nation has become a very hot issue in recent years, particularly after Republican congressional candidates in 1994 campaigned on the Contract with America, which emphasized reducing the national government's role. (Recall the discussion in Chapter 2.) Shortly after the Republicans captured control of the House and Senate that year, Congress passed and President Clinton signed a bill restricting "unfunded mandates." The Republicans went on to propose sweeping changes to turn over to the states the responsibility for Medicaid (medical care for the poor), AFDC (welfare), and other longtime national government programs.

At about the same time, the U.S. Supreme Court showed signs of shifting power from the national to the state governments, giving new force to the Tenth Amendment. For example, a Court majority led by Chief Justice William Rehnquist ruled that the Gun-Free School Zones Act of 1990 was unconstitutional because, in trying to ban guns from schools, the national government had exceeded its powers under the commerce clause. Dissenting justice Stephen Breyer called this reversal of broad federal powers "extraordinary," and Yale law professor Bruce Ackerman referred to a "constitutional moment," an epochal shift in political philosophy.[14]

It is important to keep in mind that arguments about federalism do not concern just abstract theories; they affect who wins and who loses valuable benefits. People's opinions about federalism often depend on their interests, their ideologies, and the kinds of things they want government to do.

The Constitution and Shared Powers

Federalism is embodied in the U.S. Constitution in two main ways: (1) power is expressly given to the states, as well as to the national government, and (2) the states have important roles in shaping, and choosing officials for, the national government itself.

Independent State Powers

While the Constitution makes the central government supreme in certain matters, it also makes clear that the state governments have independent powers. The **supremacy clause** in Article VI declares that the Constitution, laws, and treaties of the United States shall be the "supreme law of the land," but Article I, Section 8, enumerates what kinds of laws Congress has the power to pass, and the Tenth Amendment declares that the powers not delegated to the central government by the Constitution, nor prohibited by the Constitution to the states, are "*reserved to the states* [emphasis added] respectively, or to the people." This provision is known as the **reservation clause.**

supremacy clause The provision in Article VI of the Constitution that the Constitution itself and the laws and treaties of the United States are the supreme law of the land, taking precedence over state laws.

reservation clause The Tenth Amendment to the Constitution, reserving powers to the states or the people.

The U.S. Constitution, in other words, specifically lists what the national government can do: lay taxes, regulate commerce, establish post offices, declare war, and the like, plus make laws "necessary and proper" for carrying out those powers. The Constitution then provides that all other legitimate government functions may be performed by the states, except for a few things, such as coining money or conducting foreign policy, which are forbidden by Article I, Section 10.

The reservation clause is unique to the United States. Other federal systems, like Canada's and Germany's, reserve to the national government all functions not explicitly given to the states.

The States' Roles in National Government

Moreover, the Constitution's provisions about the formation of the national government recognize a special position for the states. The Constitution declared in Article VII that it was "done in Convention by the unanimous consent of the *states* present" (emphasis added) and provided that it would go into effect, not when a majority of all Americans voted for it, but when the conventions of nine *states* ratified it. Article V provides that the Constitution can be amended only when conventions in or the legislatures of three-quarters of the states ratify an amendment. Article IV, Section 3, makes clear that no states can be combined or divided into new states without the consent of the state legislatures concerned. Thus, the state governments have charge of ratifying and amending the Constitution, and the states control their own boundaries.

The Constitution also provides special roles for the states in the selection of national government officials. The states decide who can vote for members of the U.S. House of Representatives, by deciding who votes for their own legislatures (Article I, Section 2). Each state is given two senators, who cannot be taken away even by constitutional amendment (Article V), and who, until 1913, were chosen by the state legislatures rather than by the voters (Article I, Section 3; but see the Seventeenth Amendment). And the states play a key part in the complicated system of choosing a president (Article II, Section 1). The Struggle for Democracy box on page 70 shows how federalism affected the campaign of young people to win the right to vote.

Relations Among the States

Our federal system includes a few national provisions (in Article IV of the Constitution) that regulate relations among the states. For example, each state is required to give "full faith and credit" to the public acts, records, and judicial proceedings of every other state, and the citizens of each state are entitled to all the "privileges and immunities" of the citizens in the several states. Also,

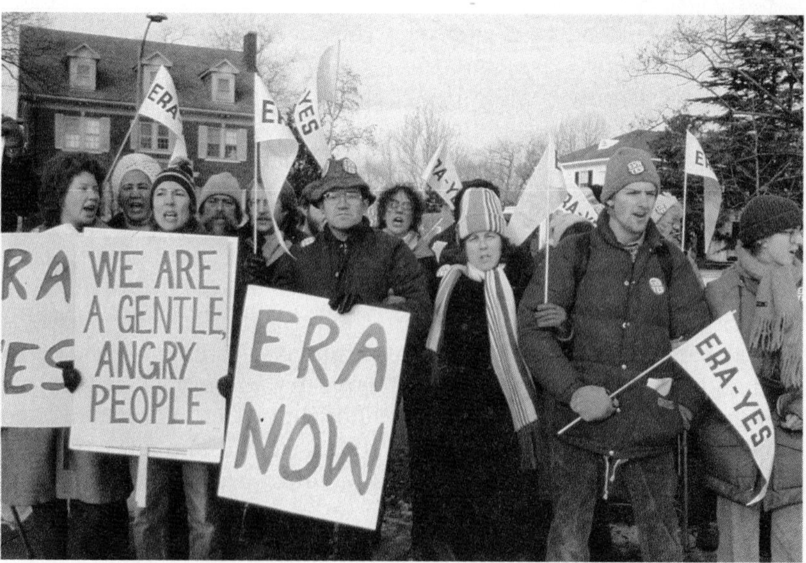

State governments play a central part in amending the Constitution. The Equal Rights Amendment for women did not quite win ratification by the necessary three-quarters of the states.

fugitives from justice have to be delivered up to a state demanding them back. The constitutional provisions underlying the federal system are summarized in Table 3.2.

The Evolution of Federalism

It took a long time after the adoption of the Constitution for the present federal system to emerge. There were ebbs and flows in the relative power of the states and the federal government. Eventually, however, the national government gained ground. This increase in its power partly reflected trends discussed in the next chapter: increased industrialization, economic growth, and increasing foreign policy involvement. In addition, bitter and divisive conflicts over a series of issues, especially slavery, race, and regional economic interests, changed the shape of American federalism, moving us toward the stronger, more unified national government that we have today.

Table 3.2

Constitutional Underpinnings of Federalism

Provisions	Where to Find Them in the Constitution	What They Mean
Supremacy of the national government in its own sphere	• The supremacy clause: Article VI	The supremacy clause establishes that federal laws take precedence over state laws.
Limitations on national government powers and reservation of powers to the states	• Enumerated national powers: Article I, Section 8 • Limits on national powers: Article I, Section 9; Article IV, Section 3; Eleventh Amendment • Bill of Rights: First through Tenth Amendments • Reservation clause: Tenth Amendment	The powers of the federal government are laid out specifically in the Constitution, as are strict limitations on the power of the federal government. Powers not specifically spelled out are reserved to the states or the people.
Limitations on state powers	• Original restrictions: Article I, Section 10 • Civil War amendments: Thirteenth through Fifteenth Amendments	The Constitution places strict limitations on the power of the states in particular areas.
State role in national government	• Ratification of Constitution: Article VII • Amendment of Constitution: Article V • Election of representatives: Article I, Section 2 and Section 4 • Two senators from each state: Article I, Section 3 • No deprivation of state suffrage in Senate: Article V • Choice of senators: Article I, Section 3 (however, see Seventeenth Amendment) • Election of president: Article II, Section 1 (however, see Twelfth Amendment)	The states' role in national affairs is clearly laid out. Rules for voting and electing representatives, senators, and the president are defined so that state governments play a part.
Regulation of relations among states	• Full faith and credit: Article IV, Section 1 • Privileges and immunities: Article IV, Section 2	Constitutional rules ensure that the states must respect each others' legal actions.

Young People Win the Right to Vote

The Struggle for Democracy

On June 19, 1968, students at University of the Pacific in Stockton, California, formed a group called LUV (Let Us Vote) and began a national campaign to lower the voting age from 21 to 18.[a]

In 1971, LUV won: the Twenty-Sixth Amendment to the U.S. Constitution established the right of 18- to 20-year-olds to vote in all federal, state, and local elections, overriding contrary state laws and adding about 11 million young people to the electorate. How this important expansion of democracy came about illustrates certain complexities of our federal system.

At the structural level, international events—especially the Vietnam War—and changing demographics helped fuel the drive for the new amendment. That thousands of young men were mature enough to fight and die for their country provided an overwhelming moral argument in favor of letting them vote. Getting young people to "work within the system," rather than protesting outside it (as thousands of antiwar demonstrators were then doing), provided a strong practical argument. Moreover, evidence that young people were better educated than their elders —more of them were completing high school and going on to college—undermined the old argument that ignorant youths were incapable of making intelligent political decisions.

Political support was widespread. Student groups like LUV and public-interest lobbies like Common Cause put their energy into the amendment and won support from such diverse groups as the American Legion, the Junior Chamber of Commerce, and the American Federation of Labor and Congress of Industrial Organizations (AFL-CIO). Democrats saw the registration of millions of young voters as an opportunity to move the electorate in their own liberal direction. When surveys showed young people to be little different in their political affiliations from anyone else, however, and when it became clear that radical student protestors were a small minority, Republicans jumped on the bandwagon and supported the amendment as well.

The Twenty-Sixth Amendment also gained impetus from the need to cure a peculiar new problem of American federalism: dual systems of voter registration. Beginning in 1970, by congressional legislation, national elections for Congress and the presidency included 18- to 20-year-old participants, but many state and local elections did not. The U.S. Supreme Court had upheld the constitutional power of the states to set the voting age for their own elections. The result was a mess. Different groups of voters had to be registered separately for the two kinds of elections, even when both were held at the same time and in the same place.

After Congress overwhelmingly voted for the Twenty-Sixth Amendment in March 1971, it took only two months and seven days—the shortest time ever for a constitutional amendment to be ratified—for it to be approved by the required 38 states. (One 64-year-

Early Conflicts Between the States and the Nation

In the late 1790s, during the administration of John Adams, Thomas Jefferson's Republicans deeply resented the Alien and Sedition Acts, which the Federalists used to punish political dissent. The Virginia and Kentucky Resolutions (secretly authored by Madison and Jefferson) declared that the states did not have to obey unconstitutional national laws, and indicated that the states could decide what was unconstitutional. In this case, the Republicans, representing the more agrarian, democratic, and liberal South, were advocating states' rights against a national government run by the more merchant-oriented, conservative Federalists of the Northeast.

About a decade later, the merchants of New England turned the southerners' own arguments against them when they strongly opposed Democratic-Re-

old state representative in Alabama, trying to stop it with a filibuster, despaired: "I'm physically unable to stand here any longer.") After Ohio became the thirty-eighth and decisive state to ratify the amendment, President Nixon said, "Some 11 million young men and women who have participated in the life of our nation through their work, their studies, and their sacrifices for its defense now are to be fully included in the electoral process of our country. I urge them to honor this right by exercising it, by registering and voting in each election."[b]

[a]"Collegians Open Voting-Age Drive," *New York Times* (December 20, 1968), p. 51.
[b]"States Ratify Full 18-Year-Old Vote," *New York Times* (July 1, 1971), p. 1.

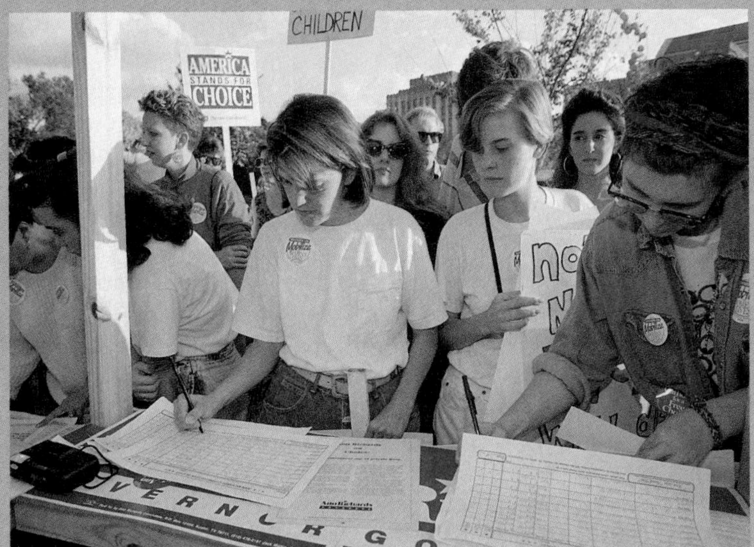

Eighteen-year-olds register to vote. Their right to vote in all states was established in 1971 by the Twenty-Sixth Amendment to the Constitution.

publican president Madison's War of 1812 against Britain, which interfered with their trade; at the Hartford Convention, they resolved that unconstitutional actions by the national government (namely, the embargo on trade with Britain) could be declared null and void by the states. Neither of these efforts at **nullification** prevailed, however. Nor did the later attempt by John C. Calhoun and other southern agriculturalists to declare null and void the "tariff of abominations," the high 1833 tariff (which raised the prices of imports and hurt southern agricultural exports).

nullification An attempt by states to declare national laws or actions null and void.

These early conflicts demonstrate that the exact shape of federalism matters: it affects such things as wars, civil liberties, and trade, which have an impact on many people's lives. These conflicts also show that people's positions on matters of high "principle," such as the proper nature of federalism, have a way of shifting, depending on the immediate issues at stake. The advocates of states' rights have sometimes been northerners and sometimes southerners, sometimes liberals and sometimes conservatives, depending on exactly who would gain or lose. Self-interest continues to affect people's attitudes about federalism today.

The early conflicts helped establish that the states could not simply nullify, or disregard, national government actions. The ultimate shape of federalism in the United States, however, was even more strongly affected by U.S. Supreme Court decisions and by the Civil War.

The Role of the Supreme Court

One crucial question about federalism in the early years of the United States concerned who, if anyone, would enforce the supremacy clause. Who would make sure that the U.S. laws and Constitution were actually the "supreme law of the land," controlling state laws? The answer turned out to be the U.S. Supreme Court, but this answer emerged only gradually and haltingly as the Court established its power within the federal system.

Judicial Review of State Actions In an early case, *Chisholm v. Georgia* (1793), the Supreme Court heard a lawsuit brought by two citizens of South Carolina against the State of Georgia, over a debt they said the state owed them. Georgia refused to appear in court, arguing that the federal courts had no power to hear suits against sovereign states. The Supreme Court, rejecting that argument, ordered payment of the money to the Carolinians. But what one scholar calls a "gale of opposition" from states' rights advocates led to the adoption of the Eleventh Amendment to the Constitution, taking away any U.S. judicial power over suits commenced against a state.[15]

Only after the strong-willed and subtle John Marshall became chief justice and (in 1803) established the Supreme Court's authority to declare *national* laws unconstitutional, did the Supreme Court return to the question of power over the states. In *Fletcher v. Peck* (1810), it established the power of **judicial review** over the states, holding a state law unconstitutional under the U.S. Constitution.[16]

judicial review The power of the U.S. Supreme Court to declare actions of the other branches and levels of government to be unconstitutional.

Fletcher v. Peck resulted from the sale of a huge tract of land—including most of what is now Mississippi and Alabama—at bargain prices by the corrupt Georgia legislature. Amid scandal and public outrage, a new Georgia legislature voted to rescind the sale, but meanwhile, millions of acres had been resold to more-or-less innocent third parties. After a complicated series of events, the Supreme Court ruled that the third-party titles to the land were valid because the rescinding act violated the U.S. Constitution. Exactly what provision of the Constitution (if any) had been violated was left murky. What is most significant about *Fletcher v. Peck* is that, for the first time, the Court clearly exercised the power to hold state laws unconstitutional. Chief Justice Marshall cleverly avoided explicit discussion of the Court's power. He simply took it for granted and used it.

Shortly afterward, in 1816, the Supreme Court further solidified its position in relation to the states by explicitly upholding as constitutional the Court's use of a "writ of error" to review (and overturn) state court decisions that denied a claim made under the Constitution or laws or treaties of the United States. In language important to the interpretation of federalism, Justice Joseph Story declared that the Constitution was the creation of "the people of the United States," not of the individual states, and that the people could—and did—decide to modify state sovereignty.[17]

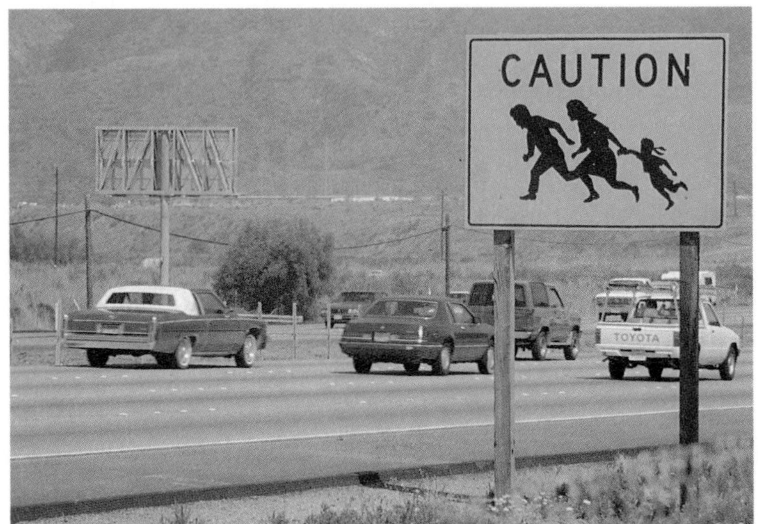

Motorists on California Interstate 5 near San Diego are cautioned to look out for illegal immigrants trying to cross the highway. How to control the entry of illegal immigrants and how to pay for services for them have become issues of contention between several states and the federal government.

However, although the Supreme Court had clearly established its power to declare state laws unconstitutional, it hardly ever used that power until many years later, after the Civil War. Moreover, the Court made clear that the Bill of Rights protected citizens only against *national* government action; the Court would not enforce citizens' property rights or other liberties against the states.[18] This stance too, changed, but only after the Civil War.

The Necessary and Proper Clause The Supreme Court did, however, provide crucial legal justification for the expansion of national government power in the important case of *McCulloch v. Maryland* (1819). The *McCulloch* case arose because the State of Maryland had imposed a tax on notes issued by the Bank of the United States, which had been incorporated by Congress in 1816. The U.S. government argued that such a tax on a federal entity was invalid. Maryland replied that the incorporation of the bank had been unconstitutional, exceeding the powers of Congress, and that, in any case, the states could tax whatever they wanted to within their own borders. But Chief Justice Marshall upheld the constitutionality of the bank's incorporation and its immunity from taxation, and he made a major statement justifying extensive national authority.[19]

In the Court's decision, Marshall declared that the Constitution emanated from the sovereign people. The people had made their national government supreme over all rivals within the sphere of its powers, and those powers must be construed generously if they were to be sufficient for the "various crises" of the age to come. Congress had the power to incorporate the bank under the clause of Article I, Section 8, authorizing Congress to make all laws "necessary and proper" for carrying into execution its named powers. Moreover, Maryland's tax was invalid, because "the power to tax involves the power to destroy," which would defeat the national government's supremacy within its sphere. Justice Marshall's broad reading of the **necessary and proper clause** (also known as the *elastic clause*) laid the foundation for an expansion of what the national government could do in the years ahead. He made clear that states would not be allowed to interfere.

necessary and proper clause Article I, Section 8, of the Constitution: "The Congress shall have Power . . . To make all Laws which shall be necessary and proper for carrying into Execution the foregoing powers." Also known as the *elastic clause.*

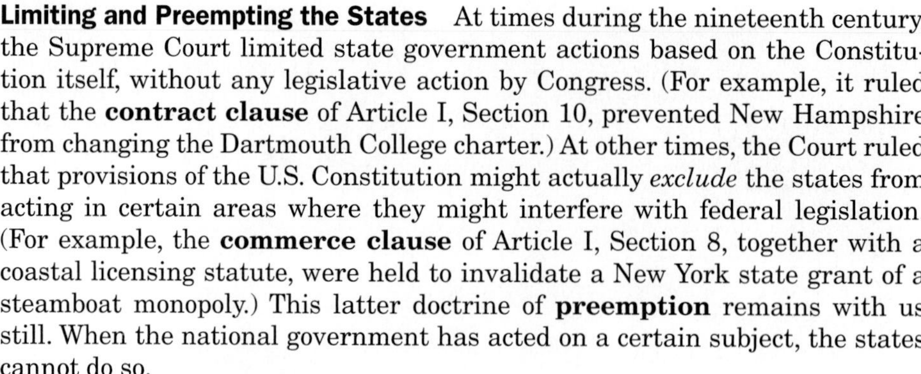

Limiting and Preempting the States At times during the nineteenth century, the Supreme Court limited state government actions based on the Constitution itself, without any legislative action by Congress. (For example, it ruled that the **contract clause** of Article I, Section 10, prevented New Hampshire from changing the Dartmouth College charter.) At other times, the Court ruled that provisions of the U.S. Constitution might actually *exclude* the states from acting in certain areas where they might interfere with federal legislation. (For example, the **commerce clause** of Article I, Section 8, together with a coastal licensing statute, were held to invalidate a New York state grant of a steamboat monopoly.) This latter doctrine of **preemption** remains with us still. When the national government has acted on a certain subject, the states cannot do so.

contract clause In Article I, Section 10, of the Constitution: No state shall pass any "Law impairing the Obligation of Contracts."

commerce clause The section of Article I, Section 8, of the Constitution which says "Congress shall have the power . . . To regulate Commerce with foreign Nations, and among the several States."

preemption Exclusion of the states from actions that might interfere with federal legislation.

The Slavery Issue

In the second decade of the nineteenth century, the issue of slavery in the western territories began to dominate disputes about the nature of federalism. As new, nonslave states were settled and sought to join the Union, white southerners feared that their political power in Washington, D.C. (especially in the Senate)—and therefore their ability to protect their own slave system—was slipping away.

The Missouri Compromise of 1820 established an equal number of slave and free states and banned slavery in the territories above a line running westward to the Rockies from Missouri's southern border. But the acquisition of vast new territories in the Southwest through the Mexican War reopened the question of whether new states would be slave or free. The Compromise of 1850 admitted California as a free state and temporarily balanced matters (in white southerners' eyes) by enacting the Fugitive Slave Act, which compelled private citizens in the North to help return runaway slaves—legislation that many northerners bitterly resented. The 1854 decision to organize Kansas and Nebraska as territories and let them decide for themselves whether to become slave or free states (even though they were above the Missouri Compromise line and therefore supposed to be free) led to violence between pro- and antislavery forces in "bleeding Kansas."

In 1860, the northern and southern wings of the Democratic party split apart over the slavery issue. The old Whig party was destroyed by the issue, and the candidate of the newly formed Republican party, Abraham Lincoln (who opposed slavery in the western territories), was elected president. South Carolina seceded from the Union, soon followed by the other six states of the Deep South, which created the Confederate States of America. President Lincoln decided to relieve the besieged U.S. garrison at Fort Sumter, South Carolina, and the devastating Civil War (or "War Between the States") began.

Expansion of National Power

After the Civil War, the nature of American federalism changed significantly, and the power of the national government expanded relative to that of the states.

Crucial Effects of the Civil War

The war itself brought about some changes.

CAUTION!!

COLORED PEOPLE

OF BOSTON, ONE & ALL,

You are hereby respectfully CAUTIONED and advised, to avoid conversing with the

Watchmen and Police Officers of Boston,

For since the recent ORDER OF THE MAYOR & ALDERMEN, they are empowered to act as

KIDNAPPERS

AND

Slave Catchers,

And they have already been actually employed in KIDNAPPING, CATCHING, AND KEEPING SLAVES. Therefore, if you value your LIBERTY, and the *Welfare of the Fugitives* among you, *Shun* them in every possible manner, as so many *HOUNDS* on the track of the most unfortunate of your race.

Keep a Sharp Look Out for KIDNAPPERS, and have TOP EYE open.

APRIL 24, 1851.

THEODORE PARKER'S PLACARD

Placard written by Theodore Parker and printed and posted by the Vigilance Committee of Boston after the rendition of Thomas Sims to slavery in April, 1851.

The Fugitive Slave Act of 1850, which required that runaway slaves be captured and returned to their owners in the South, inflamed tensions between North and South and helped lead to the greatest crisis of U.S. federalism: the Civil War. This poster was made by abolitionist opponents of the act.

Indissoluble Union The complete northern victory and unconditional southern surrender in the Civil War decisively established that the Union was indissoluble; states could not withdraw or secede. Hardly any American now questions the permanence of the union, though it is interesting to compare this attitude with our present-day support for the right of new countries to secede from existing countries, as Croatia and Bosnia did from Yugoslavia.

Constitutional Amendments The Civil War also resulted in constitutional changes that subordinated the states to certain new national standards, enforced by the central government. The Thirteenth Amendment abolished slavery, and the Fifteenth gave (male) former slaves a constitutional right to vote. (This right was enforced by the national government for a short time after the Civil War; it was then widely ignored until the 1965 Voting Rights Act.)

The Fourteenth Amendment (1868) included broad language going well beyond the slave issue: it declared that *no state* shall "deprive any person of life, liberty, or property, without due process of law; nor deny to any person within its jurisdiction the equal protection of the laws." The **due process clause** eventually became the vehicle by which the Supreme Court ruled that many civil liberties in the Bill of Rights, which originally protected people only against the national government, also provided protections against the states. And the **equal protection clause** was eventually made the foundation for protecting the rights of blacks, women, and other categories of people against discrimination by state or local governments. (These matters are discussed in Chapters 16 and 17.)

due process clause The section of the Fourteenth Amendment that reads "nor shall any State deprive any person of life, liberty, or property, without due process of law"; a guarantee against arbitrary or unfair government action.

equal protection clause The section of the Fourteenth Amendment that reads "nor deny to any person within its jurisdiction the equal protection of the laws"; a guarantee that citizens are to be treated equally.

Emergency Powers Still another effect of the Civil War was to set precedents for an enormous expansion of the federal government's power, especially in wartime. President Lincoln exerted extraordinary emergency powers, spending government money without congressional authorization, suspending the writ of habeas corpus (the right of prisoners to demand that reasons be given for their imprisonment) in war zones, and freeing slaves in occupied southern territories. The huge military and industrial effort of waging the war established patterns for future national government action of many sorts.

Expanded National Activity Since the Civil War

Since the Civil War, the activities of the national government have expanded greatly, so that they now touch on almost every aspect of daily life and are thoroughly entangled with state government activities. During the late nineteenth century, the national government was increasingly active in administering western lands, subsidizing economic development (granting railroads enormous tracts of land along their transcontinental lines), helping farmers, and beginning to regulate business, particularly through the Interstate Commerce Act of 1887 and the Sherman Antitrust Act of 1890. The national government became still more active with Woodrow Wilson's "New Freedom" domestic legislation in 1913–1914, and with the great economic and military effort of World War I.

The New Deal and World War II Still more important, however, was Franklin Roosevelt's New Deal of the 1930s. In response to the Great Depression, the New Deal created many new national regulatory agencies to supervise various aspects of business, including communications (the Federal Communications Commission, or FCC), airlines (the Civil Aeronautics Board, or CAB), financial markets (the Securities and Exchange Commission, or SEC), utilities (the Federal Power Commission, or FPC), and labor-management relations (the National Labor Relations Board, or NLRB). The New Deal also brought national government spending in such areas as welfare and relief, which had previously been reserved almost entirely to the states, and established the Social Security pension system. National government spending on domestic matters continued to grow in subsequent decades, particularly during and after Lyndon Johnson's Great Society of the 1960s.

Wars were also crucial in the expansion of national government power. The federal government did not spend as much as the states and localities combined until two years of World War I (temporarily) and then during World War II, which involved a total economic and military mobilization to fight Germany and Japan.

Ever since World War II, the federal government has spent *nearly twice as much* per year as all of the states and localities put together, much of the money going in direct payments to individuals (through such items as Social Security benefits). Increasingly, though, the states—and especially local governments—have had many more civilian *employees,* so that there is some ambiguity about which level of government is actually "bigger."[20] (See Figure 3.3.)

The Supreme Court's Role For several decades, beginning in the late nineteenth century, the U.S. Supreme Court resisted the growth in national government power to regulate business. In 1895, for example, it said that the Sherman Antitrust Act could not forbid monopolies in manufacturing, since

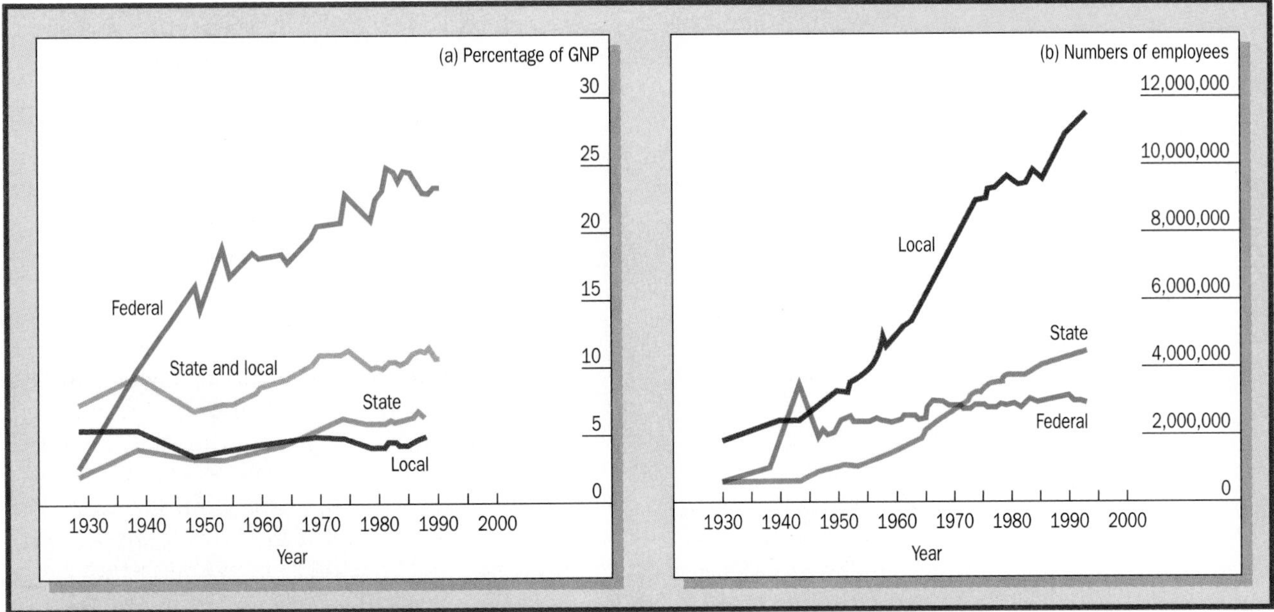

Figure 3.3 ▪ The Size of Federal, State, and Local Governments

The federal (national) government is now much larger than all the state and local governments put together in terms of the money it spends (a), but it is much smaller than local government in terms of number of employees (b).

Sources: Harold Stanley and Richard G. Niemi, *Vital Statistics of American Politics,* 4th ed. (Washington, D.C.: Congressional Quarterly Press, 1990), p. 334; U.S. Department of Labor, Bureau of Labor Statistics, *Monthly Labor Review* (December 1987), p. 72; (December 1989), p. 78; (December 1991), p. 84; (August 1993), p. 76.

manufacturing affected interstate commerce only "indirectly." In 1918, the Court struck down as unconstitutional a national law regulating child labor. During the 1930s, the Supreme Court declared unconstitutional such important New Deal measures as the National Recovery Act and the Agricultural Adjustment Act.[21]

More recently, however, the Supreme Court has been a nationalizing force. It has interpreted the Constitution more and more broadly, to permit or ratify ever-expanding national government authority. After 1937, warding off President Roosevelt's plan to enlarge the Supreme Court and appoint more friendly justices, the Court upheld the essential elements of the New Deal, including the Social Security Act and the National Labor Relations Act. Since that time, the Court has upheld virtually every piece of national legislation that has come before it.

An important example is the Civil Rights Act of 1964, which rests on a very broad interpretation of the commerce clause. In the 1964 act, the national government asserted a power to forbid discrimination at lunch counters and other public accommodations on the grounds that they are engaged in interstate commerce: they serve food imported from out of state. State economies are so closely tied to each other that, by this standard, practically every economic transaction everywhere affects interstate commerce and is subject to national legislative power. (It remains to be seen whether a new trend is represented by the 1995 Court decision overturning gun control around schools as too broad a use of the commerce power.)

Lyndon Johnson visits Job Corps sites. The Job Corps was part of Johnson's Great Society of the 1960s, which relied heavily on categorical grants to state and local governments.

"Marble Cake" Today, federalism is very different from what it was in the 1790s or early 1800s. One major difference is that the national government is dominant in many policy areas; it calls many shots for the states. (Only very recently has some of this dominance been challenged.) Another difference is that state and national government powers and activities have become deeply intertwined and entangled. An old, simple metaphor for federalism was a "layer cake": a system of **dual federalism** in which state and national powers were neatly divided into separate layers. If we stay with bakery images, a much more accurate metaphor for today's federalism is a "marble cake": a **cooperative federalism** in which elements of national and state influence swirl around each other, without any clear boundaries.[22] Much of this intertwining is due to financial links among the national and the state and local governments.

dual federalism Federalism in which the powers of the states and the national government are neatly separated like the sections of a layer cake.

cooperative federalism Federalism in which the powers of the states and the national government are intertwined like the swirls in a marble cake.

The Rise of National Grants-in-Aid to the States

One of the most important elements in modern American federalism is the grant of money from the national government to state and local governments, which have been used to increase national government influence over what the states and localities do. These grants have grown from small beginnings to form a substantial part of government budgets.

The Origin and Growth of Grants

National government grants to the states began at least as early as the 1787 Northwest Ordinance. The U.S. government granted land for government buildings, schools, and colleges in the Northwest Territory and imposed various regulations, such as forbidding the importation of any new slaves. During the early nineteenth century, the national government provided some land grants to the states for roads, canals, and railroads, as well as a little cash for militias; after 1862, it helped establish agricultural colleges.

Some small cash-grant programs were begun around 1900 for agriculture, vocational education, and highways. At the beginning of the twentieth century, annual national grants to the states totaled only some $6 million; they grew to about $100 million in the early 1920s and to nearly $300 million toward the end of the 1930s.[23]

However, it was during the 1950s, 1960s, and 1970s, under both Republican and Democratic administrations, that by far the biggest growth occurred. Such programs as President Dwight Eisenhower's interstate highway system and President Lyndon Johnson's Great Society poured money into the states. The annual amount of national grants-in-aid had reached $91.5 billion by 1980: close to $500 for each person in the country.[24] (See Figure 3.4 for the trend in constant dollars.)

Reasons for Grants

National grant money to the states increased because Congress sought to deal with many nationwide problems—especially interstate highways, poverty, crime, and pollution—by setting policy at the national level and by providing money from national tax revenues, while having state and local officials carry the policies out. There were three main reasons for doing things this way.

Spillovers First, the states refused to take responsibility on their own for many of these problems, mainly because of **spillover effects,** sometimes called *externalities,* affecting people outside their borders. The states would not spend their own money if much of the benefit would go to people elsewhere. For example, Milwaukee, Wisconsin, did not want to pay to clean up its pollution of Lake Michigan, when a cleanup would mostly benefit Chicago, Illinois. Thinly populated states like Nevada did not want to pay for interstate highways so the residents of other states could drive through. Also, states were reluctant to spend money to fight poverty, if that spending would raise taxes, scare away business investment, and perhaps attract more poor people. Spillovers made national government involvement seem necessary.

spillover effects Policy effects that go outside the boundaries of the governmental unit making the policy.

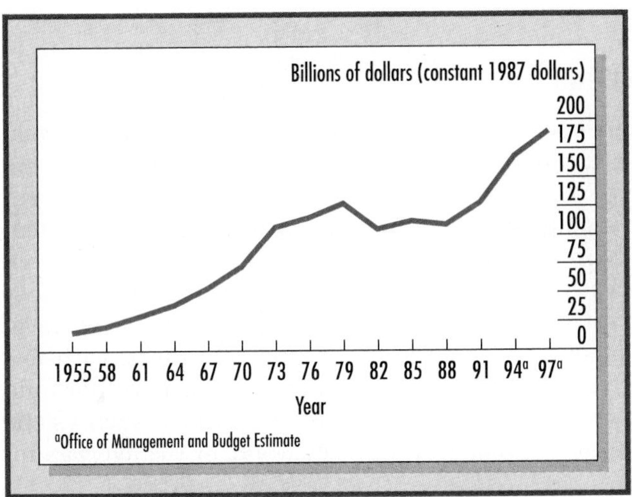

Figure 3.4 ■ **The Growth of Federal Grants-in-Aid**

Federal grants-in-aid to state and local governments grew sharply during the 1960s and peaked at the end of the 1970s. They then declined in the early 1980s and increased more gradually afterward.

Sources: Advisory Commission on Intergovernmental Relations, *Significant Features of Fiscal Federalism* (Washington, D.C.: ACIR, 1992), Vol. 2, p. 60; David B. Walker, *The Rebirth of Federalism* (Chatham, N.J.: Chatham House, 1995), Table INT–1.

Abundant National Government Resources Second, in the 1960s, when many of these programs were begun, national government tax revenues seemed abundant. The federal government had a large budget to work with. Moreover, the money came mostly from the federal income tax, which was rather **progressive;** that is, people with high incomes paid a higher percentage of what they earned than did people with low incomes. The federal income tax seemed an especially appropriate source of money for combating poverty.

progressive taxes Taxes that take the largest percentage share of income from those at the upper end of the income scale.

Local Provision Third, however, these new programs involved complicated goods and services that required management at the local level. Unlike Social Security benefits, which can be administered nationwide from Washington, D.C., with relative ease, the new programs involved the building of new facilities (such as clinics and sewage treatment plants) and the development of new programs (such as preschool education, special education, and job training) that the federal government could not efficiently oversee. Even if the national government was needed to provide money and direction, local officials on the scene seemed to be the appropriate people to actually carry out the programs.

Categorical Grants

categorical grants Federal aid to states and localities clearly specifying what the money can be used for.

Many of the new programs were established through **categorical grants,** which give the states money but clearly specify the category of activity for which the money has to be spent and often define rather precisely how the program should work. For example, the Medicaid program of 1965 and the Clean Air Act of 1970 provided large amounts of money along with specific instructions on how to use it.

As the new programs were developed and enacted, there was much talk about a new system of "cooperative" federalism. Soon, however, conflicts between the national and the state governments emerged. In some cases, when national rules and guidelines were vague, state and local governments used the money for purposes different from those Congress intended. When the rules were tightened up, some state and local governments complained about "red tape." And if state and local governments were bypassed, they complained that their authority had been undermined. The Community Action program, for example, designed to fund local organizations and to empower poor people, was abolished when it aroused vehement objections by mayors and others whose authority was threatened.[25]

Block Grants and Revenue Sharing

block grants Federal grants to the states to be used for general types of activities.

general revenue sharing Federal aid to the states without any controls on how the money is spent.

The Republican Nixon and Ford administrations tended to loosen national control, moving more toward **block grants,** which give money for more general purposes and with fewer rules than categorical grant programs. **General revenue sharing** went a step further, offering the states money with no federal controls at all. Already in the 1960s, five block grant programs had been established, for such purposes as community development, law enforcement assistance, and employment training and assistance. President Nixon spoke of a "New Federalism" and pushed to increase these kinds of grants, with few strings attached. They often provided money under an automatic formula related to the statistical characteristics of each state or locality, such as the number of needy residents, the total size of the population, or the average income level.

Disputes frequently arise when these formulas benefit one state or region rather than another. Cities and states from the northern Frost Belt, for example, have fought some bitter battles with those from the southern Sun Belt over how much more money would come with future population growth. In 1995 and 1996, northeastern states with high Medicaid benefit levels sought large block grants to keep those benefits up, while southwestern states, despite their lower benefits, insisted on an equal share of grants.

Since statistical counts by the census affect how much money the states and localities get, census counts themselves have become the subject of political conflict. Illinois, New York, and Chicago sued the Census Bureau for allegedly undercounting their populations, especially the urban poor, in the 1990 Census; court battles went on for years.

Block grants—and especially revenue sharing—reached a peak at the end of the 1970s, when they constituted about one-quarter of the total grants-in-aid. But then they fell out of favor. Increasing numbers of strings were attached to the money, and general revenue sharing was completely ended in 1987.

One reason for the decline in block grants and revenue sharing was that the strongest backers of the grant programs all tended to distrust state and local governments. The advocates of antipoverty and environmental programs, for example, feared that special interests at the local level would divert money away from its original purposes. So the program backers insisted that the national government impose tight regulations on how the money could be spent.

Thus, the Democrats in Congress defeated most of President Reagan's 1981 effort to consolidate 57 programs into a few block grants. So many restrictions were imposed that the nine new block grants resembled categorical grants. Similar struggles continue in the 1990s, as Democrats resist Republican efforts to transform categorical programs like Medicaid into block grants.

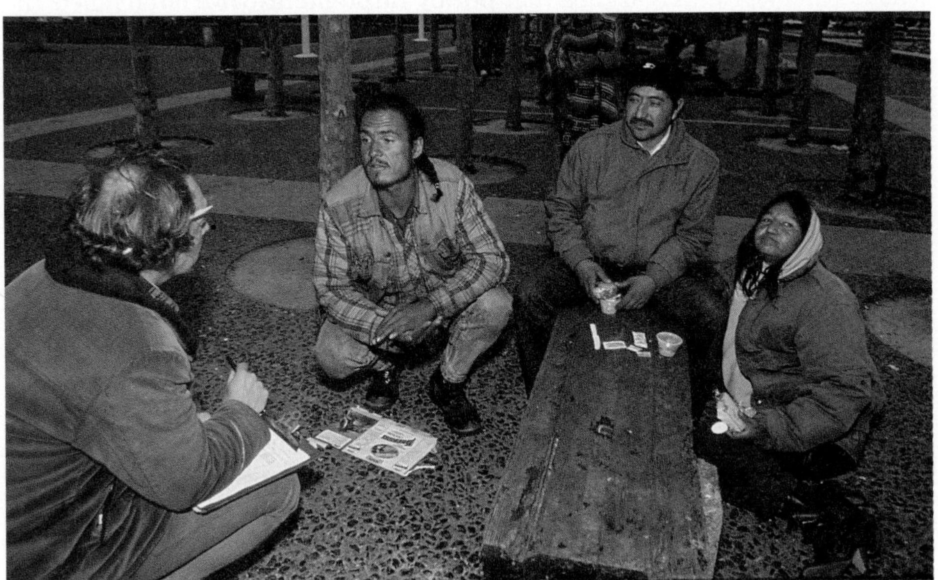

The states depend on federal aid to help them take care of the homeless. But when 1990 census takers failed to count a large number of homeless people, cities received less money in national grants.

The Slowdown in National Money

At the same time that block grants were falling out of favor, the flow of federal money to state and local governments began to slow down. In terms of constant purchasing power, federal grants-in-aid declined from $131.4 billion in 1978 to just $106.5 billion in 1982. (Look back at Figure 3.4.) As a proportion of the whole economy (the gross domestic product, or GDP), grants dropped from a peak of 3.6 percent in 1978 to just 2.6 percent in 1984.[26]

By 1984, the states were getting only about 30 percent as much revenue from the federal government as from their own sources, compared to the heftier 39 percent of 1976. Localities, especially big cities, were pinched even harder. Their federal grants, which had amounted to 17.5 percent of their own revenues in 1978, dropped steadily to only 6.3 percent in 1988.[27]

Reasons for the Slowdown

The reasons for this slowdown, which continues today, include certain *structural* factors—the general decline in the growth rate of the U.S. economy and increasing pressure on national tax revenues—together with major political changes, such as increased interest-group pressure to cut domestic spending, which contributed to the arrival of more conservative political leaders in the 1980s and 1990s.

Breakup of Support Block grants and revenue sharing lost support among liberals in Congress when some money went to beautify suburban shopping malls and to buy heavy weaponry for police, rather than to rebuild poor inner-city neighborhoods. At the same time, many conservatives were objecting to the more closely targeted and regulated categorical grant programs, citing red tape and lack of responsiveness to local needs.

policy implementation The execution, or actual carrying out, of policy.

The Question of Effectiveness Reinforcing these objections, a number of scholars and journalists argued that **policy implementation** often failed: the relationships between the state and national governments were too complicated; too many different, uncoordinated agencies were involved; and the rules were too rigid. Perhaps there was simply no hope of attaining the objectives of national legislation.[28] Other research has indicated that many federal grants-in-aid have had good effects and have been administered efficiently and effectively; some federal programs have redistributive purposes that the states would not undertake on their own.[29] But an image of failure haunted federal grants through much of the 1980s.

Economic Pressure After the oil crisis of 1973–1974, the American economy sank into a period of "stagflation": simultaneous inflation (rising prices) and stagnation (low growth and high unemployment). At the same time, international economic competition was getting rough. Japanese electronic goods and automobiles took over more and more of the U.S. market; U.S. firms had a harder and harder time selling their products abroad. (See the next chapter.) Then, after the second oil price shock in 1979, the United States suffered through its worst recession since World War II, with high unemployment accompanied by inflation.

A New Conservative Climate With these structural forces at work, the political response was very conservative, opposed to government spending or regulation. Business firms fought to reduce their costs by eliminating expensive regulations, lowering wages, and cutting their taxes. Business invested money in think tanks, publications, and political action committees (PACs) to promote these conservative causes and to assist conservative political candidates.[30]

Together with discontent about stagflation and Carter administration foreign-policy failures, the outpouring of conservative money in 1980 helped to elect as president Ronald Reagan, who was committed to cutting domestic spending, cutting taxes, and increasing military spending. When the Reagan administration took office in 1981, with many more Republicans in Congress and with the still-majority Democrats weakened and apprehensive, it did exactly what it said it would do. Reagan's dramatic 1981 success in cutting taxes is described in Chapter 12. Another important part of Reagan's program involved cutting back federal grants to the states and especially to cities.

Continuing Financial Stringency

During the late 1980s and the early 1990s, grants-in-aid stabilized and then began to rise once again (see Figure 3.4.). But state populations and state needs are growing, too. The national government's contribution, as a proportion of the nation's economy, has not returned to the old peak of 3.6 percent of the gross domestic product; the figure settled at just 3.0 percent in the mid–1990s. Federal grants to states as a proportion of their own revenue have stayed near the low point of 30 percent, and the federal share of local revenues has dropped below 6 percent.[31]

Thus, the Clinton presidency did not appreciably reverse this situation of tight resources, and the Republican-dominated One Hundred and Fourth Congress accentuated it. Congress offered even less money to the states, as Republicans delivered on the provision in their "Contract with America" to cut federal spending. They made many state governors happy by trying to turn power over to the states—again shifting from categorical to block grants in such areas such as welfare, Medicaid, and child nutrition. But the congressional Republicans also cut the overall amount of spending directed to the states. Some state governments, their tax rates already high, face great difficulty in finding new revenue to match their new responsibilities.

"Sorry, but all my power's been turned back to the states."
By Lorenz; © The New Yorker Magazine, Inc.

The Balance of Power and Control

Most contemporary conflicts about federalism concern not just money, but also control. The national government exerts a strong influence over many state-administered programs, using a variety of different means, such as mandates and conditions.

Mandates

mandate A demand; for example, a demand that the states carry out certain policies.

The government in Washington, D.C., often imposes a **mandate,** or demand, that the states carry out certain policies even when little or no national government aid is offered. (An "unfunded" mandate involves no aid at all, or less aid than compliance will cost.) Mandates have been especially important in the areas of civil rights and the environment. Most civil rights policies flow from the equal protection clause of the Fourteenth Amendment to the U.S. Constitution, or from national legislation that imposes uniform national standards. Most environmental regulations also come from the national government, since problems of dirty air, polluted water, and acid rain spill across state boundaries. Many civil rights and environmental regulations, therefore, are enforced by the federal courts.

Since the 1954 Supreme Court decision in *Brown v. Board of Education,* for example, the federal (i.e., national) courts have required that many local school districts admit black children to previously all-white schools. They have required local governments to redraw attendance boundaries so that schools will not stay segregated because of segregated housing patterns. And in some places (such as Boston), the courts have appointed special federal "masters" with the authority to administer the schools themselves.

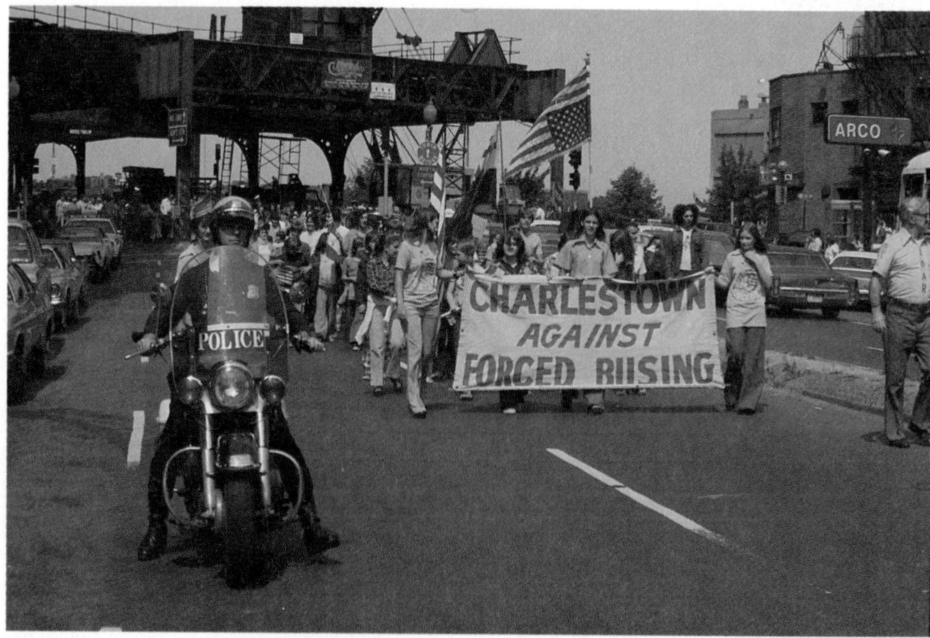

Opposition to federal court-ordered busing—like this demonstration in Charlestown, Massachusetts—formed one element in a conservative turn in U.S. politics at the end of the 1970s.

Federal courts have also forced local fire departments to end discrimination against minorities in their hiring decisions; have insisted on scattered (rather than concentrated and segregated) locations for public housing; and have ordered communities to end police brutality against minorities.

The courts also have mandated expensive reforms of overcrowded state prisons, most notably in Texas. National legislation and regulations have required state governments to provide costly special facilities for the disabled, to set up environmental protection agencies, and to limit the kinds and amounts of pollutants that can be discharged. The states often complain bitterly about federal mandates that require state spending without providing the money.

Cutting back on these "unfunded mandates" was one of the main promises in the Republicans' 1994 Contract with America.[32] The congressional Republicans delivered on their promise early in 1995 with a bill that had bipartisan support in Congress and that President Clinton signed into law. Because it does not apply to past mandates, however, and because it does not ban unfunded mandates but only regulates them (requiring cost-benefit analyses, for example), it is not yet clear how much impact the legislation will have.

Conditions on Aid

As we have seen, many categorical grant-in-aid programs require that the states spend federal money only in certain restricted ways. Increasingly, even general block grants have carried **conditions.** In theory, these conditions are "voluntary," because the states could refuse to accept the aid. But in practice, there is no clear line between incentives and coercion. Since the states cannot generally afford to give up federal money, they have to accept the conditions.

conditions Provisions in federal assistance requiring that state and local governments follow certain policies in order to obtain the money.

Some of the most important provisions of the 1964 Civil Rights Act, for example, are those which declare that no federal aid of any kind can be used in ways that discriminate against people on grounds of race, gender, religion, or national origin. Thus, the enormous program of national aid for elementary and secondary education, which began in 1965, became a powerful lever for forcing schools to desegregate. Likewise, the national money that goes to universities to help pay for teaching and research would be cut off if the universities discriminated in admissions or hiring.

The national government uses its money to influence many diverse kinds of policies. During the energy crisis of the 1970s, all states were required to impose a 55-mile-per-hour speed limit or lose a portion of their highway assistance funds. All states did so (the requirement was finally repealed in 1995). Similarly, in 1984, all states were required to set a minimum drinking age of 21 or have their highway aid cut by 15 percent.

Often, the national government entirely "preempts" state government action concerning some policy area—that is, it sets up laws and standards that override any state rules—but relies on state enforcement of the national standards. Examples include clean air standards, occupational health and safety rules, and environmental restrictions on surface mining. National versus state regulation of nursing homes was one of the most contested issues of the 1995 and 1996 budget battles.

Increased Responsibilities and Increased Burdens on the States

In recent years, state governments have become more active in many areas. Some of these have been regulatory, not involving a lot of new spending.

California and New York innovated with environmental protection policies, for example, moving ahead of the more cautious Reagan and Bush administrations. Some states took the lead in requiring that women be paid according to the "comparable worth" of their jobs. After the U.S. Supreme Court's 1989 *Webster* decision, which gave the states more leeway to regulate abortion, several states liberalized their abortion laws, while others made them more restrictive.

Other state innovations, however, require substantial government spending. Many states, for example, increased their Medicaid programs to help the poor and elderly with medical expenses. The more generous programs, like those of Hawaii and Oregon, turned out to be quite expensive. Such programs often require new taxes, especially when national government grants-in-aid are harder to get. Many states have raised sales taxes and excise taxes on gasoline, cigarettes, alcohol, and the like, all of which hit low- and middle-income people particularly hard. These taxes hurt. But the alternatives are also painful: to cut popular programs or to face deficits and budget crises.

By the early 1990s, therefore, state politics had become hazardous to the health of incumbent officials. Voters were angry and tended to throw state governors out of office, often after their first term. In 1990, for example, the party in power lost a stunning 14 of the 36 gubernatorial elections. Incumbent Democrats, who tended to defend state spending programs, were especially hard hit in 1993 and 1994, losing the mayoralties of New York City and Los Angeles and many state representatives and governors.

Many new Republican governors and mayors were elected, pledging to make government more efficient and, in some cases, to cut taxes as well. Governor Christine Todd Whitman of New Jersey, for example, took office promising sharp cuts in the state income tax; she amazed everyone by keeping her promise ahead of schedule. Whitman gained further national visibility when she delivered the Republican response to President Clinton's 1995 State of the Union address.

Mayor Rudolph Guliani of New York City took on employee unions and cut city employment and spending. Republican governors Tommy G. Thompson (Wisconsin), John Engler (Michigan), and William F. Weld (Massachusetts) all tackled their welfare systems, using federal waivers to try various ideas for getting recipients off the welfare rolls and into jobs (recall our opening story). Tennessee swiftly privatized its Medicaid system, shifting beneficiaries into health maintenance organizations (HMOs) and other managed-care plans.

devolution The delegation of power by the central government to state or local bodies.

In Washington, the trend toward the **devolution** of policymaking to the states culminated in the great budget battle of 1995–1996. As part of its drive for a balanced budget, the Republican majority in Congress passed a comprehensive Budget Reconciliation Act which would have abolished the national programs for Medicaid and for welfare (AFDC), turning these matters over to the states along with new block grants of national money. But President Clinton vetoed the bill (objecting to cuts in Medicare, education, and environmental programs), and negotiations over possible compromises broke down. Later Clinton signed a separate bill abolishing welfare entitlements.

The block grants included in devolution proposals are generally smaller than the amounts the federal government spent under previous legislation. Thus, pressure is put on the states to save money by increased efficiency, or to cut benefits, or to come up with new resources of their own. If they cannot do so, it is possible that they will turn back to the national government for expanded aid, and the question of conditions may arise once again. Struggles between state and national authority are likely to continue.

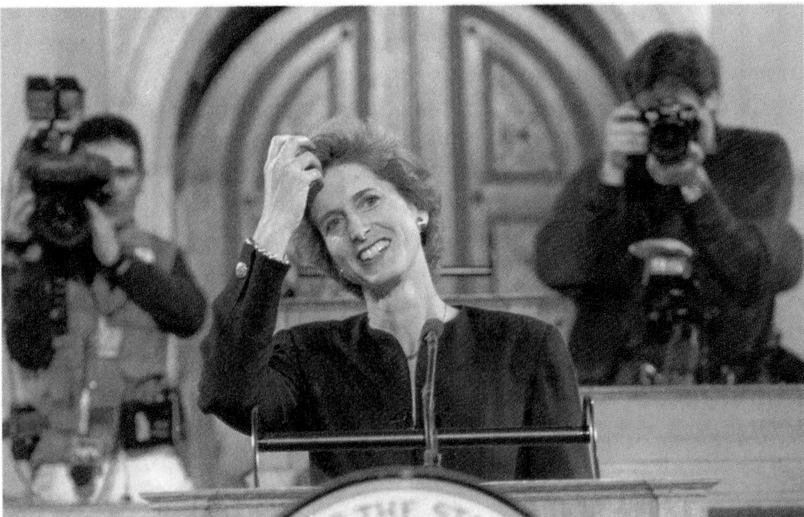

Governor Christine Todd Whitman of New Jersey gained widespread notice for her sharp cuts in state income taxes; she delivered the Republican response to President Clinton's 1995 State of the Union message.

The Consequences of Federalism

Our federal system has many consequences. One is a high degree of complexity in policymaking and policy implementation. The involvement of many different state, local, and national agencies in the same policy areas means possible inefficiency and confusion about who is responsible. Federalism does, however, permit a diversity of responses to diverse situations, and it allows for experimentation and for trying out policies different from those of the particular party that is running things in Washington, D.C.

At the same time, federalism leads to substantial inequalities of certain kinds across the states. The levels of benefits under the Aid to Families with Dependent Children (AFDC) welfare program, for example, have varied widely. In the same year that Connecticut gave a maximum of $680 per month to a poor family of three, Mississippi provided only $120, which—even together with food stamps—came to less than half the poverty threshhold.[33] Unemployment insurance benefits vary from only one-fifth of former wages to close to one-half. Similarly, local control of law enforcement, together with the Supreme Court's reliance on "community standards" to define "obscenity," means that a rap group's performances may be declared illegal and punished in one town but may be perfectly legal in another.

Certain kinds of policies may be inherently difficult or impossible to carry out at state or local levels. If we want redistributive programs, for example, which transfer resources from the rich to the poor, or if we want to protect the environment across city and county and state lines, it may be necessary to prevent competition among the states and to impose uniform national standards.

How Democratic Is Federalism?

In terms of our evaluative theme, it is not easy to judge whether federalism is a help or a hindrance to democracy. On the one hand, retaining some political power in the states does promote democracy by permitting the state governments to counterbalance unpopular actions by the national government. It also promotes democracy by allowing the people in each community to do what their own majorities prefer, rather than their all having to conform to a single national majority.

On the other hand, federalism may interfere with democracy by blurring responsibility and making it hard for voters to assign credit or blame. Moreover, democratic processes may not work as well at the state level as they do at the national level. In state politics, popular participation tends to be lower, politics tends to be less visible, and interest groups may have an easier time getting their way. If the well-organized and the affluent have extra influence, political equality is impaired. The national government, and especially popular presidents, may be better able to mobilize the public, to make politics visible, and to ensure that the government responds to what the ordinary citizens want. To the extent that this is true, a federal system that gives power over important political decisions to the states may dilute democratic control.

Summary

Federalism, a system under which political powers are divided between the state and national governments, is a key structural aspect of American politics. Federalism is unusual in the world today; it is most frequently found in large, diverse countries. Arguments in favor of federalism have to do with diversity of needs, closeness to the people, experimentation, and innovation. Arguments against federalism involve national standards, popular control, and needs for uniformity.

The U.S. Constitution specifies the powers of the national government and reserves all others (except a few that are specifically forbidden) to the states. The Constitution also provides special roles for the states in adopting and amending the Constitution and in choosing national officials. The precise bal-

Low voting turnout in state and local elections may mean that a shift of power and responsibility from the federal level to the state level will decrease the quality of American democracy.

ance of federalism has evolved over time, the national government gaining ground as a result of U.S. Supreme Court decisions, the Civil War, expanding national domestic programs, and two world wars.

Contemporary federalism involves complex "marble-cake" relations among the national and state governments, in which federal grants-in-aid play an important part. Grants for many purposes grew rapidly but have now slowed down, putting the states under great financial pressure. The national government also influences or controls many state policies through mandates and through conditions placed on aid. The recent trend has been toward a substantial devolution of powers and responsibilities to the states. Federalism has mixed implications for democracy.

Suggested Readings

Grodzins, Morton. *The American System.* New Brunswick, NJ: Transaction Books, 1983.
Describes and approves of a complex intermingling of national, state, and local government functions.

Peterson, Paul E. *The Price of Federalism.* Washington, DC: Brookings Institution, 1995.
Describes modern federalism and argues that the national government does best at redistributive programs, while the states and localities do best at economic development.

Peterson, Paul E., Barry G. Rabe, and Kenneth Wong. *When Federalism Works.* Washington, DC: Brookings Institution, 1986.
Analyzes the workings of several national programs that are implemented at the state and local levels.

Pressman, Jeffrey L., and Aaron Wildavsky. *Implementation*, 3rd ed. Berkeley: University of California Press, 1984.
A classic account of the difficulties in carrying out a federal program.

Riker, William H. *The Development of American Federalism.* Boston: Kluwer Academic, 1987.
A leading discussion of what American federalism is and how it came about.

Walker, David B. *The Rebirth of Federalism.* Chatham, NJ: Chatham House, 1995.

Internet Sources

The Budget of the United States http://www.doc.gov/inquery/BudgetFY96/BudgetFY96.html
Much information about how modern federalism works can be found in the annual budget of the federal government.

The Jefferson Project: Political Thought http://www.stardot.com/jefferson/po/thought.htm
Primary and secondary documents on the meaning of federalism.

The National Center for State Courts http://www.ncsc.dni.us/ncsc.htm
Linkages to the home pages of the court systems of each of the states.

The National Conference of State Legislatures http://www.ncsl.org/statfed/afipolicy.htm
Articles and reports on how federal government policies and the budget affect, or are likely to affect, the states.

State Constitutions http://www.iwc.com/entropy/marks/stcon.html
A site where the constitutions of all the states may be found.

Notes

1. "A Welfare Revolution Hits Home, But Quietly," *New York Times* (August 13, 1995), Sec. 4, pp. 1, 5; "States Are Already Providing Glimpse at Welfare's Future," *New York Times* (September 21, 1995), pp. 1, 11.
2. "Michigan's Welfare System: Praise amid Warning Signs," *New York Times* (October 24, 1995), pp. 1, 12; "Steps Taken on Michigan Welfare," *New York Times* (November 1, 1995), p. 11.
3. "Truly Amazing Budget Tricks," *Chicago Tribune* (August 11, 1995), p. 27.
4. Harold Stanley and Richard Niemi, *Vital Statistics on American Politics,* 4th ed. (Washington, DC: CQ Press, 1994), p. 316.
5. Gabriel Almond and G. Bingham Powell, Jr., *Comparative Politics Today: A World View,* 5th ed. (New York: HarperCollins, 1991).
6. William H. Riker, *The Development of American Federalism* (Boston: Kluwer Academic, 1987), pp. 56–60.
7. William H. Riker, *Federalism: Origin, Operation, Significance* (Boston: Little, Brown, 1964), ch. 6.
8. Quoted in Robert Jay Dilger, ed., *American Intergovernmental Relations Today* (Englewood Cliffs, NJ: Prentice-Hall, 1986), p. 188.
9. Ed Gillespie and Bob Schellhas, eds., *Contract with America: The Bold Plan by Rep. Newt Gingrich, Rep. Dick Armey and the House Republicans to Change the Nation* (New York: Random House, 1994), p. 125.
10. Robert S. Erikson, Norman R. Luttbeg, and Kent L. Tedin, *American Public Opinion: Its Origins, Content and Impact,* 3rd ed. (New York: Macmillan, 1988), p. 42.
11. Jack Walker, "The Diffusion of Innovations Among the American States," *American Political Science Review,* Vol. 63 (1969), p. 883.
12. Paul E. Peterson, *City Limits* (Chicago: University of Chicago Press, 1981); Peterson, *The Price of Federalism* (Washington, DC: Brookings Institution, 1995).
13. Jeffrey Henig, *Public Policy and Federalism* (New York: St. Martin's Press, 1985), p. 155.
14. "A Gun Ban Is Shot Down," *Time Magazine* (May 8, 1995), p. 85.
15. Robert G. McCloskey, *The American Supreme Court,* 2nd ed., ed. by Sanford Levinson (Chicago: University of Chicago Press, 1994), pp. 21–23.
16. McCloskey, *American Supreme Court,* pp. 31–34.
17. *Martin v. Hunter's Lessee* (1816); see McCloskey, *American Supreme Court,* pp. 39–42.
18. *Barron v. Baltimore* (1833); see McCloskey, *American Supreme Court,* pp. 77–79.
19. McCloskey, *American Supreme Court,* pp. 43–45.
20. Stanley and Niemi, *Vital Statistics,* pp. 317, 334.
21. McCloskey, *American Supreme Court,* pp. 97–100, 111–112.
22. Morton Grodzins, *The American System* (New Brunswick, NJ: Transaction Books, 1983).
23. David B. Walker, *Towards a Functioning Federalism* (Cambridge, MA: Winthrop, 1981), pp. 60–63; U.S. Bureau of the Census, *Statistical History of the U.S.* (1963), pp. 484–516.

24. Paul E. Peterson, Barry G. Rabe, and Kenneth Wong, *When Federalism Works* (Washington, DC: Brookings Institution, 1986), p. 2.
25. Daniel Patrick Moynihan, *Maximum Feasible Misunderstanding* (New York: Free Press, 1970).
26. David B. Walker, *The Rebirth of Federalism* (Chatham, NJ: Chatham House, 1995), Table INT–1.
27. Stanley and Niemi, *Vital Statistics,* p. 324.
28. Jeffrey L. Pressman and Aaron Wildavsky, *Implementation,* 3rd ed. (Berkeley: University of California Press, 1984); Martha Derthick, *New Towns in Town: Why a Federal Program Failed* (Washington, DC: Brookings Institution, 1977); Eugene Bardach, *The Implementation Game,* 4th ed. (Cambridge: MIT Press, 1982).
29. Peterson, Rabe, and Wong, *When Federalism Works.*
30. Thomas Ferguson and Joel Rogers, *Right Turn: The Decline of the Democrats and the Future of American Politics* (New York: Farrar, Straus & Giroux, 1986); Thomas Byrne Edsall, *The New Politics of Inequality* (New York: Norton, 1984).
31. Walker, *Rebirth of Federalism,* Table INT–1; Stanley and Niemi, *Vital Statistics,* p. 324.
32. Gillespie and Schellhas, *Contract with America,* p. 125.
33. Stanley and Niemi, *Vital Statistics,* p. 338.

CHAPTER

4

The Evolving Structure of the United States

IN THIS CHAPTER

- ★ How population size, location, and diversity affect American politics
- ★ How the free enterprise economy shapes American political life
- ★ Income and wealth distribution, and why they matter
- ★ The impact of the nation's changing place in the world
- ★ What Americans believe about people, politics, government, and the economy

Stagnant Wages; Political Anger

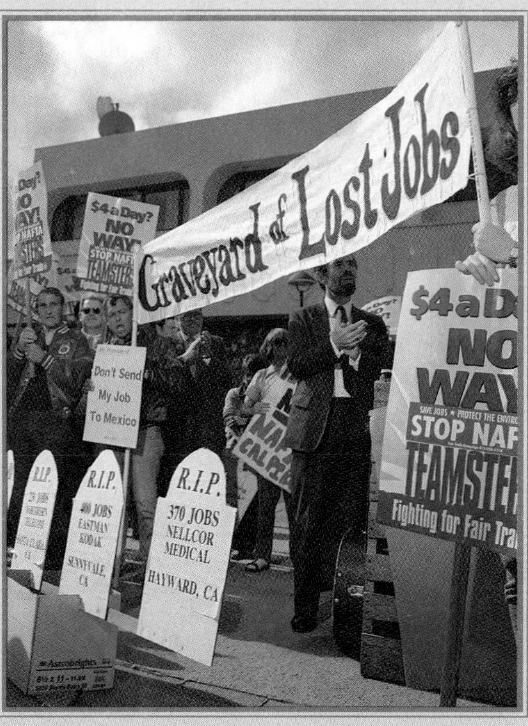

Nancy Budd worked for 11 years as a ticket agent for American Airlines. She lost her job when American subcontracted its ticketing operations to another company. Nancy Budd was offered a job by the subcontractor for $16,000, considerably less than the $40,000 she had been receiving before American "downsized" its operations. Gloria Zajackowski, after 17 years on the job, was laid off when her company, Briggs and Stratton, facing fierce competition from Japanese small-engine manufacturers, moved 2,000 jobs from Milwaukee to Kentucky and Missouri. Briggs and Stratton pointed to the 50 percent reduction in its wage and benefit costs that would result from the move. After a long job search, Tabitha Silva, laid off from her bookkeeper job in a large accounting firm, found employment with a temporary-help agency. She is doing the same work as before, but at one-third her former hourly wage, and she is without retirement or health benefits. Computer programmer Jessie Lindsay lost her job when her company, CSX Corporation, decided to contract out (or "outsource") many of its computing operations to lower-priced programmers in India and the Philippines.[1]

These stories have become all too familiar to Americans, long accustomed to well-paid and relatively secure jobs. A growing number of people are facing the prospect of job loss, stagnant or decreasing wages and salaries, and shrinking benefit packages. Oddly enough, this trend is developing at a time when the economy is growing and when American corporations are becoming very competitive in world markets, enjoying near-record profits, and paying out healthy salaries to their top executives and substantial dividends to their stockholders.

It has been a staple of economic theory and the business press that workers' wages and salaries are (and ought to be) tied to trends in productivity. That is, falling or stagnant worker compensation, it is said, is caused by falling or stagnant productivity. Rising compensation, on the other hand, is caused by rising productivity. If workers produce more goods and services more cheaply, the result will eventually appear in their paychecks. In this way, it is said, both business and labor share the fruits of improving economic performance. By this way of reasoning, the growth of the American economy in recent years, the increased competitiveness and profitability of American corporations, and gains in productivity ought to have translated into improved wages and salaries. While this has been true in the United States and other rich countries for much of the twentieth century, it no longer seems to be the case. According to recent reports from the U.S. Department of Labor, workers' wages and benefits are no longer tracking changes in productivity in the economy, and median family incomes are lagging behind overall economic growth (see Figure 4.1). While workers have consistently taken home about two-thirds of the nation's economic output, they took home only about 50 percent in 1995, even as productivity increased. The principal gains from the growth in productivity in recent years have gone primarily to dividends and investment.[2]

Economists do not agree about whether this is a short-term development or the portent of things to come. There are at least a few reasons to worry that it may be the latter. Each involves persistent downward pressures on wages and salaries.

- First, new technologies, especially in information and communications, have made it possible for companies to produce more goods and services with fewer workers. Neither switching telephone calls nor manufacturing cars, for instance, requires nearly as many workers as it did only a decade ago.

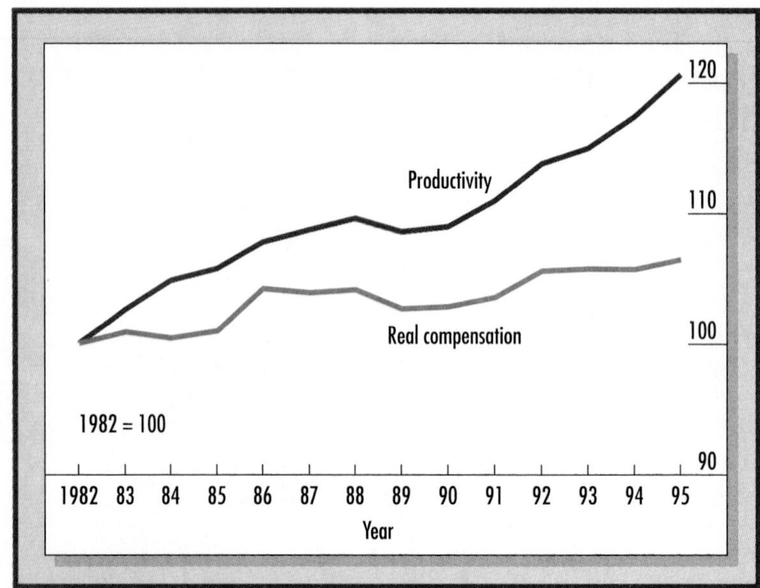

Figure 4.1 ▪ Productivity Versus Real Worker Compensation in the United States

Historically, the wages and benefits of American workers have tracked changes in worker productivity in the economy as a whole. That is, as workers have produced more, their wages and benefits have increased accordingly. Starting in the 1980s, and accelerating in the 1990s, however, the historical link between worker compensation and worker productivity has been broken. In this new context, the economy is doing well, but working Americans are not.

Source: Morgan Stanley, based on Government Statistics. Reported in *The New York Times,* January 2, 1996, p. C20.

- Second, companies in highly competitive markets are increasingly trying to identify aspects of their operations that might be better handled by subcontractors or temporary workers. Notably, most subcontractors and temporary-help firms pay lower wages and provide few benefits.
- Third, many companies are relocating substantial parts of their operations to overseas locations where labor costs are much lower than in the United States. This trend began in basic manufacturing, but it now includes high-tech sectors like computer software. The end result of these developments is both job loss and, for those with jobs, pressure on many workers to restrain their wage, salary, and benefit demands for fear of putting themselves on the street.

It is inevitable that these changes in the living standards of Americans will have political repercussions. According to many observers, it is the stagnation and even decline in the economic prospects of many Americans that are at the heart of the widespread political alienation we see today, including declining trust and confidence in political leaders, political parties, and government. It may explain anti-incumbent attitudes and the appeal of independent candidates. It may have something to do, as well, with the rise in hostility toward immigrants, both legal and illegal, who are perceived by many to be (incorrectly, in our view) at the root of our economic troubles. It may also have something to do with the decreasing willingness of Americans to support welfare and other antipoverty programs at a time when many taxpayers themselves feel financially strapped.

This story points to several of the many *structural* factors that shape American politics and what government does. It highlights the fact that many developments that occur in the world, in the economy, and in society—well away from the White House, the halls of Congress, and the chambers of the Supreme Court—matter a great deal in the substance and conduct of politics and the quality of democracy in the United States.

In this chapter, we complete our examination of the structural factors that affect the American political agenda, the distribution of power in American politics, and the perceptions and outlooks of the American people. In Chapters 2 and 3, we described the constitutional rules that shape how American government and politics work. However, understanding the constitutional rules is not sufficient for understanding how our system works. After all, several other countries have constitutions that look much like our own, but their political systems work much differently from ours. Clearly, other influences must be at work. We believe that the most important of these influences are found in society, the economy, the political culture, and the international system. These are the subject matter of this chapter.

American Society: How It Has Changed, and Why It Matters

The "typical" American today is very different from the "typical" American of 1950, let alone 1790, when the first census was conducted. Where we live, how we work, our racial and ethnic composition, and our average age and standard of living have all changed substantially. Each change has influenced our political life. This section examines how the American people have changed and why the change matters.

Growing Diversity

Ours is an ethnically, religiously, and racially diverse society. The white European Protestants, black slaves, and Native Americans who made up the bulk of the U.S. population when the first census was taken in 1790 were joined by Catholic immigrants from Ireland and Germany in the 1840s and 1850s (see Figure 4.2). In the 1870s, Chinese migrated to America, drawn by jobs in railroad construction. Around the turn of the century, most immigration was from eastern, central, and southern Europe, with its many ethnic, language, and religious groups. Today, most immigration is from Asia and Latin America. The result of this history is substantial diversity in the American population (see Figure 4.3).

The rate of migration to the United States has accelerated in recent years. If illegal entrants are included in the total, over 10 million people immigrated to the United States during the 1980s, the highest total in any decade in American history (though the number of immigrants as a percentage of total U.S. population comes nowhere near the figures for the decades around the turn of the century). As a result, the percentage of foreign-born people in the United States rose from 4.4 percent in 1980 to 8.7 percent in 1994 (but compare these numbers to 13.5 percent in 1910), out of a total population of approximately 264 million. In California, one-fourth of the population today is foreign-born.[3]

The most recent wave of immigration, like all the previous ones, has added to our rich language, cultural, and religious traditions, but it has also created significant political and social tensions. The arrival of immigrants who are dif-

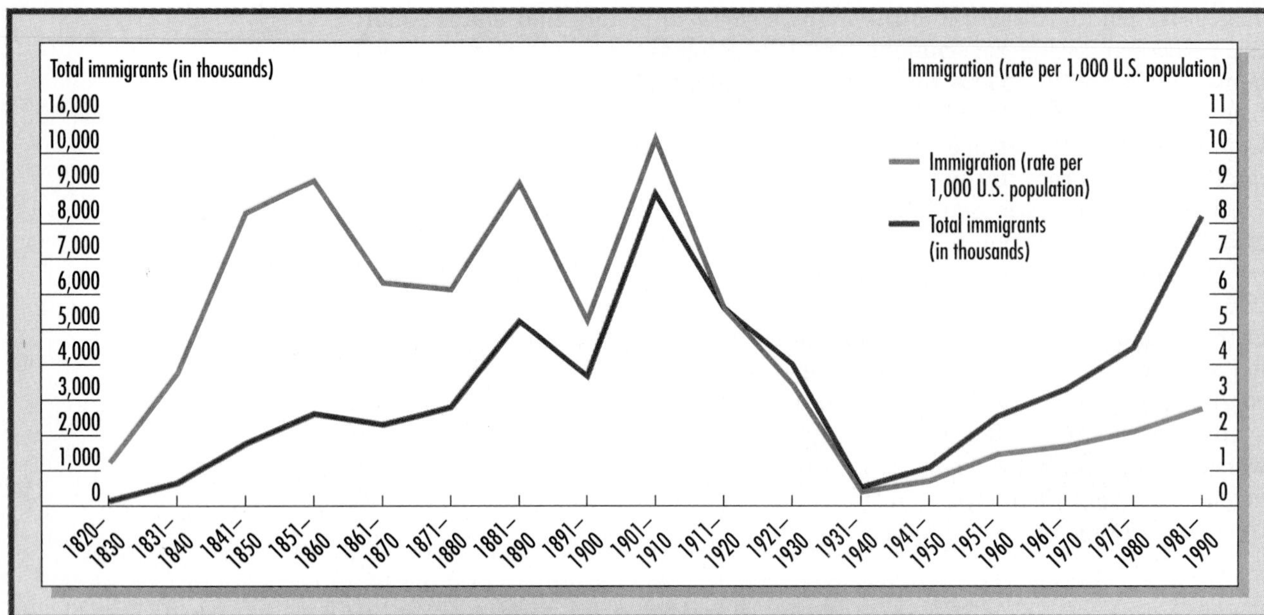

Figure 4.2 ■ **Immigration to the United States, by Decade**

Measuring immigration to the United States in different ways gives rise to quite different interpretations of its scale. Measured in total numbers, the high points of immigration were the 1880s, the decade and a half after 1900, and the 1980s. Measured in terms of the total U.S. population, however, it is clear that immigration was an important factor in population change for much of the nineteenth century and the early part of this century, but not much after that. Recent increases in immigration, relative to the total U.S. population, moreover, remain historically low.

Source: *Statistical Abstracts of the United States, 1991* (Washington, DC: U.S. Census Bureau, 1991), Table 5.

nativist Antiforeign; referring to political movements active in the nineteenth century.

ferent from the majority population in significant ways has often sparked anti-immigration agitation and demands that public officials stem the tide. **Nativist,** or antiforeign, reactions to Irish Catholic migrants were common throughout the nineteenth century. Anti-Chinese agitation swept the western states in the 1870s and 1880s. Alarm at the arrival of waves of immigrants from eastern, southern, and central Europe in the early part of this century led

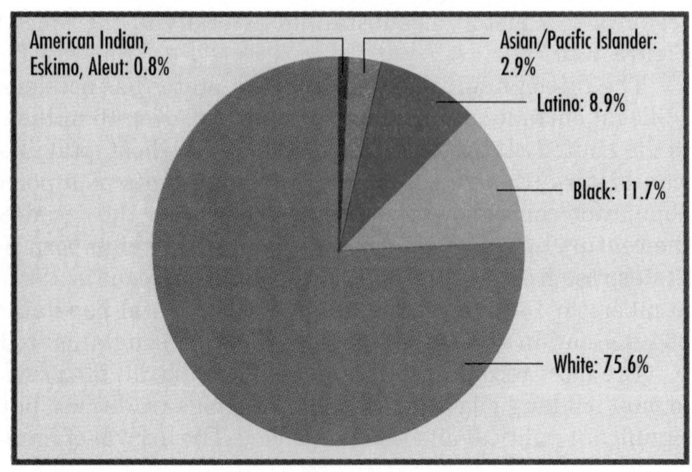

Figure 4.3 ■ **Racial Composition of the United States**

The United States is a racially diverse society and is becoming more so every year. Whites remain a majority by a substantial margin, however.

Source: *Washington Post* (September 23, 1991), p. 7, based on data from the U.S. Census Bureau.

S. Kelly © 1995 *San Diego Union–Tribune,* Copley News Service.

Congress virtually to close the doors of the United States in 1921 and to keep them closed until the 1950s.

The current wave of Spanish-speaking immigration has led to similar unease. Many Americans seem worried about the rising tide of immigration. A *Time* magazine poll in the fall of 1993 reported that 73 percent of Americans want strict limits imposed on immigration to the United States. In early 1994, the General Social Survey poll showed that 61 percent of Americans favored making English the "official language" of the United States. Politicians have responded to this public mood. Legislation has been passed in several states to make English the official language, and Robert Dole endorsed a proposal to make English the official language in the United States during his 1996 campaign for the White House. In 1994, Californians approved Proposition 187, which barred welfare, health, and education benefits to illegal immigrants, and efforts to pass similar propositions in other states are advancing in spite of the adverse response of the courts. Congress passed a bill in 1996 cutting the number of legal immigrants, denying government benefits to illegal immigrants, and beefing up the protection of U.S. borders against illegal entrants.

The ethnic, racial, and religious diversity of the United States has many other important consequences for American politics. For instance, it may help explain the relatively low level of social class identification and labor union membership in the United States. Diversity multiplies interests and makes it difficult for people from different backgrounds to organize parties and unions along social-class lines, weakening the social basis for the welfare state (see Chapter 20). Countries such as Sweden, Norway, Denmark, the Netherlands, and Austria, where politics tend to divide along social class lines, have relatively homogeneous populations and highly developed welfare states.

Racial division between blacks and whites has been an especially important feature of American society and, consequently, of its politics. Because African-Americans are, on average, much worse off economically than white Americans and have suffered discrimination on many fronts (especially in housing and jobs), for instance, they have been much more supportive of an activist role for government in providing jobs, public services, and protection against discrimination. Many other Americans, perhaps feeling the pinch of tough economic times (discussed in the opening story and in further detail below), have grown increasingly resistant to government programs whose benefits are targeted at specific minority groups.

Changing Location

Where the growing population of the United States is located also matters. While we began as a country made up of rural and small-town people, we very rapidly became an urban people. By 1910, 50 cities had populations of more than 100,000, including 3 with more than 1 million (New York, Philadelphia, and Chicago). Urbanization, caused mainly by the industrialization of the nation (the rise of large manufacturing firms required many industrial workers, while the mechanization of farming meant that fewer agricultural workers were needed) continued unabated until the mid–1940s. After World War II, a massive federal and state road-building program and government-guaranteed home loans for veterans (part of the G.I. bill) started the process by which the United States became an overwhelmingly suburban nation (see Figure 4.4).

This shift in the location of the American population has had important political ramifications. The continued drain of population from rural areas, for instance, has diminished the power of the rural voice in state and national politics. For their part, central cities, burdened with populations of the poor and the less well-to-do and a shrinking tax base, find it increasingly difficult to provide the level of public services considered normal only a few years ago. Heavily dependent on the assistance of the federal government, moreover, central-city populations have become even more consistently Democratic in their voting preferences than in the past. On the other hand, those living in the dis-

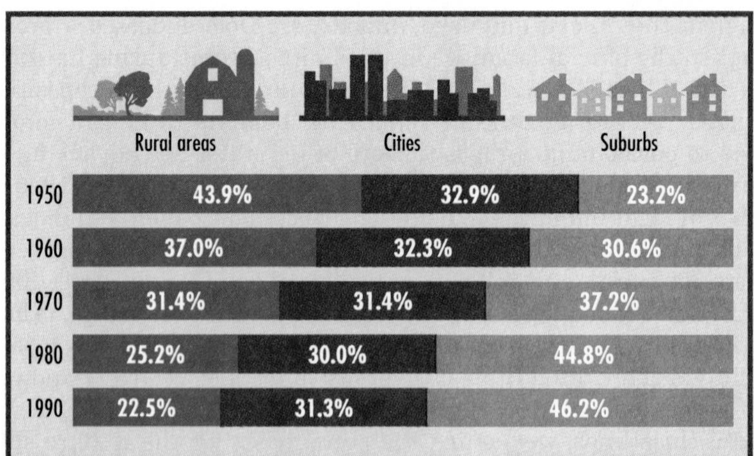

Figure 4.4 ▪ **Population Shift: From Rural to Urban to Suburban**

In a relatively short period of time, the United States has changed from a society in which the largest percentage of the population lived in rural areas to one in which the largest percentage lives in suburbs. This development has produced several important changes in American politics and in the fortunes of our political parties.

Source: U.S. Census Bureau, 1991.

After World War II, federal government spending on highways and mortgage loan guarantees helped fuel the explosive growth of the suburbs.

tant suburbs, mainly middle-class and working-class homeowners, have become less willing to support programs for central-city populations. Voters in these areas have grown decidedly unfriendly to politicians who promise substantial governmental aid to solve urban problems and have become considerably more Republican in recent elections.

The U.S. population has also moved west and south over the course of American history. The shift accelerated after World War II as people followed manufacturing jobs to these regions (many companies were attracted to the western and southern states because of their low taxes and antiunion policies). This population shift has led to changes in the relative political power of the states. Following each census from 1950 to 1990, states in the East and the upper Midwest—often referred to as the **Rust Belt** because of their loss of manufacturing jobs—lost congressional seats and presidential electoral votes. States in the West and the South—often referred to as the **Sun Belt** because of their generally pleasant weather—gained at their expense. Figure 4.5 shows the extent of change during the 1980s. Because the Sun Belt states are generally more conservative than other states, their conservativeness may have contributed to Republican party gains.

Rust Belt States of the upper Midwest that have lost manufacturing jobs.

Sun Belt States of the lower South, Southwest, and West where sunny weather and often conservative politics prevail.

Changing Jobs and Occupations

At the time of the first census in 1790, almost three-quarters of all Americans worked in agriculture. Most of the rest of the population worked in the retail trade, transportation, and skilled trades closely connected to agriculture. About 80 percent of the working, male, nonslave population was self-employed, owning small farms, stores, wagons and horses, and workshops.[4]

The American occupational structure was radically transformed by the industrialization of the United States that took off in the late nineteenth century (often called the **Industrial Revolution**). By 1910, the proportion of the labor

Industrial Revolution The period of transition from predominantly agricultural to predominantly industrial societies in the Western nations in the nineteenth century.

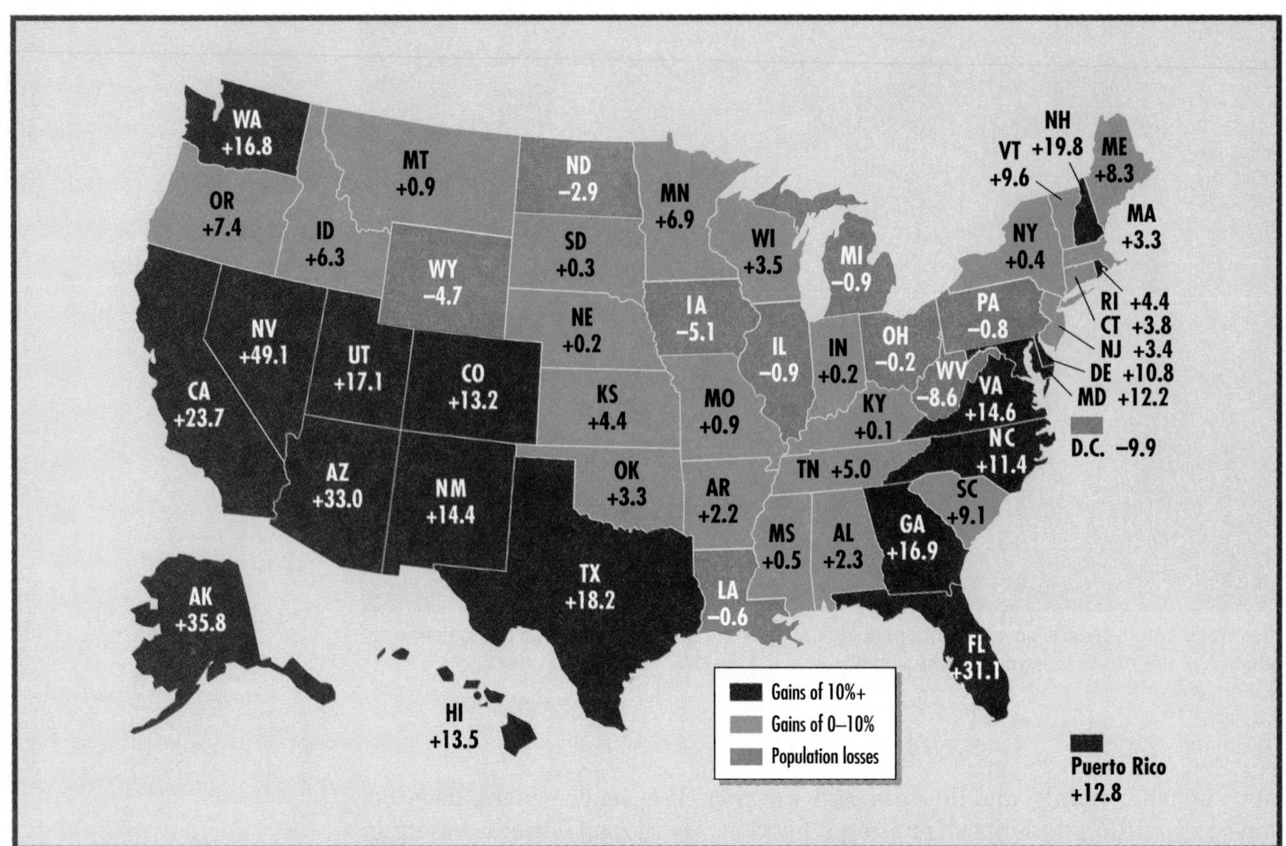

Figure 4.5 ■ **Population Change in the States, 1980–1990**

The 1990 U.S. Census showed that the relative population sizes of the states changed substantially in the 1980s. For the most part, it was the Sun Belt states of the South and the West that gained population (and the state of Washington) and the Rust Belt states of the upper Midwest and East that lost population. One political outcome of this change is that the Sun Belt states gained representatives in the U.S. House of Representatives, while the Rust Belt states lost representatives.

Source: U.S. Census Bureau, 1991.

blue-collar workers Industrial workers; may be skilled, semiskilled, or unskilled.

white-collar workers Those who work in service, sales, and office jobs.

force in agriculture had dropped to only 32 percent, and those working for others for wages and salaries had swelled to over 69 percent.[5] By 1940, the "typical" American wore a **blue collar** and worked in manufacturing as a skilled, semiskilled, or unskilled worker.

In 1950, the United States became the first nation in the world where **white-collar workers** (clerical, technical, professional, managerial, services, and sales) were in the majority. The decline of certain manufacturing industries, the disappearance of the small family farm, and the rapid rise of the high-technology and information sector have accelerated the shift of employment from factory and farm to the office. Figure 4.6 shows how the American occupational structure has changed over the years.

Occupational change matters a great deal in our politics. Displaced workers, for instance, often ask government to expand welfare benefits, job retraining, and programs that encourage economic development.

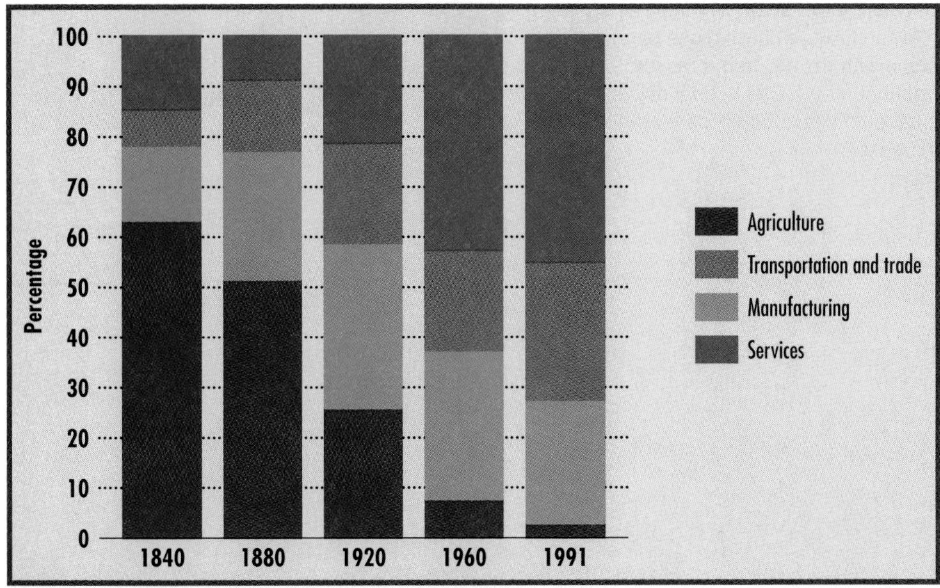

Figure 4.6 ■ Changes in U.S. Occupational Structure

The United States has been undergoing a long-term transformation in its occupational structure. Most notable has been the rapid decline in the number of Americans working in agriculture, as well as the expansion in the number of those working in service occupations, ranging from sales clerks to financial analysts. Also notable have been the rise and decline in the proportion of Americans in manufacturing occupations.

Source: U.S. Bureau of Labor Statistics, *Employment and Earnings* (January 1992).

The shift from manufacturing to service occupations also affects the fortunes of labor unions. As heavy industry has become less important in the American economy, the proportion of Americans who belong to labor unions has declined sharply, from approximately 33 percent in the early 1950s to less than 16 percent today. Since unions have always been a strong voice for liberalism, support for liberal economic and social policies has grown weaker.

The expansion of service, clerical, technical, and other kinds of white-collar jobs has coincided, moreover, with a substantial expansion in the number of female workers. The participation of women in the paid workforce has passed 75 percent and is rapidly approaching the participation rate of men. In fact, fully 60 percent of all new jobs in the 1980s went to women, mostly in the white-collar and service sectors. This massive entry by women into working life outside the home has had enormous political consequences. For one thing, paid work has improved women's income (though women still earn only about three-quarters of what men earn) and has increased their influence and self-confidence in many spheres, including politics. These developments very likely contributed to the formation of the women's movement (see Chapter 10). Moreover, because women with young children are now working outside the home in unprecedented numbers, we are likely to see strong pressures for government-funded child care and early education, and for the extension of the school day. Women's workforce participation was surely a factor in the passage of the Family Leave Act in 1993, which allows employees to take unpaid leave from their jobs if they must take care of sick children.

Because fewer and fewer families can afford the luxury of having one parent stay home with the children, pressures on government for a longer school day and increased funding for day care are likely to increase.

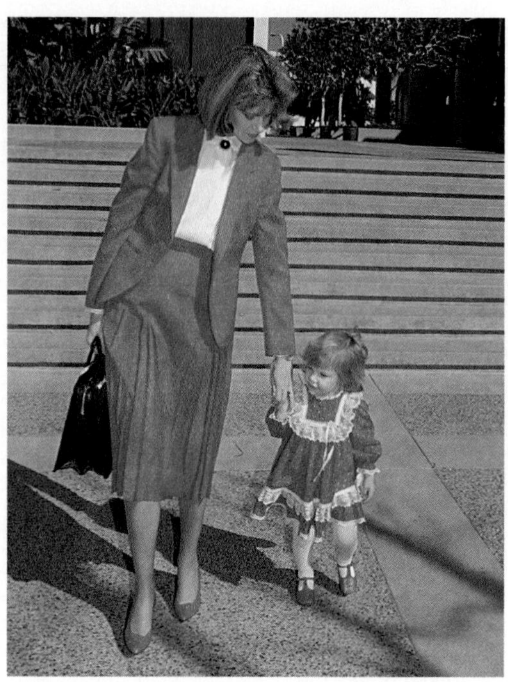

The Aging of the American Population

One of the most significant trends in the United States and in other industrialized countries is the aging of the population. In 1800, the median age in the United States was just under 16; today it is 33. By 2030, it will be about 38. The proportion of the population over age 65 has been growing, while the proportion between the ages of 18 and 64 has been shrinking. Today, 12.6 percent of Americans (about 30 million) are elderly. By 2030, it is likely to be about 20 percent. Meanwhile, the proportion of the population in the prime working years is likely to fall from 61.4 percent today to about 56.5 percent in 2030 (see Figure 4.7). Moreover, the number of the very old—those over 85—is the fastest growing age segment of all. Thus, a growing proportion is likely to be dependent and in need of services, and a shrinking proportion is likely to be taxpaying wage or salary earners.

Because the population is aging, the financing of Social Security and Medicare is likely to remain an important political question for the foreseeable future. The voting power of the elderly is likely to make it difficult for elected officials to substantially reduce social insurance programs for those over 65. Meanwhile, the tax load on those still in the workforce may feel increasingly burdensome. How this issue will play out in the near future will be interesting to follow.

The American Standard of Living

The United States enjoys one of the highest standards of living in the world. In per capita gross domestic product (GDP), the usual measure of standard of living, the United States leads the world (see Figure 4.8). But on the United Nations Human Development Index, which combines life expectancy, adult literacy, and per capita income, the United States ranked only nineteenth in 1994

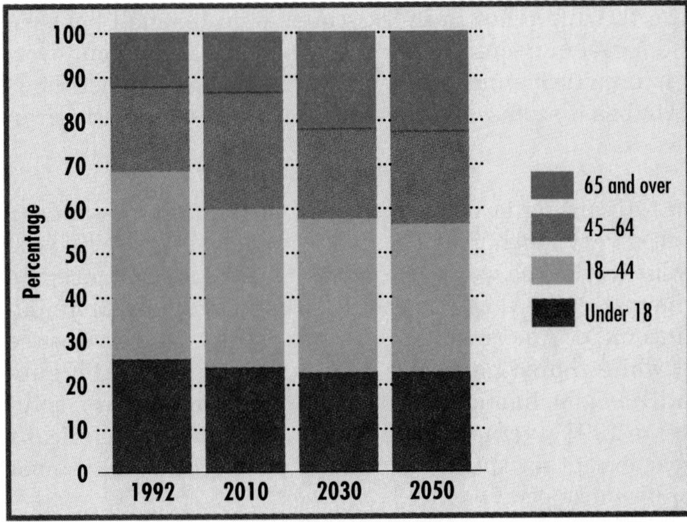

Figure 4.7 ▪ **Projected Distribution of U.S. Population by Age, 1992–2050**

The American population is gradually aging. The proportion of Americans under the age of 18 has been shrinking, while the proportion over 65 has been growing. Population experts believe the trend will continue.

Source: U.S. Census Bureau, *Current Population Reports, Special Studies,* Series P–23, No. 184 (February 1993), p. 1.

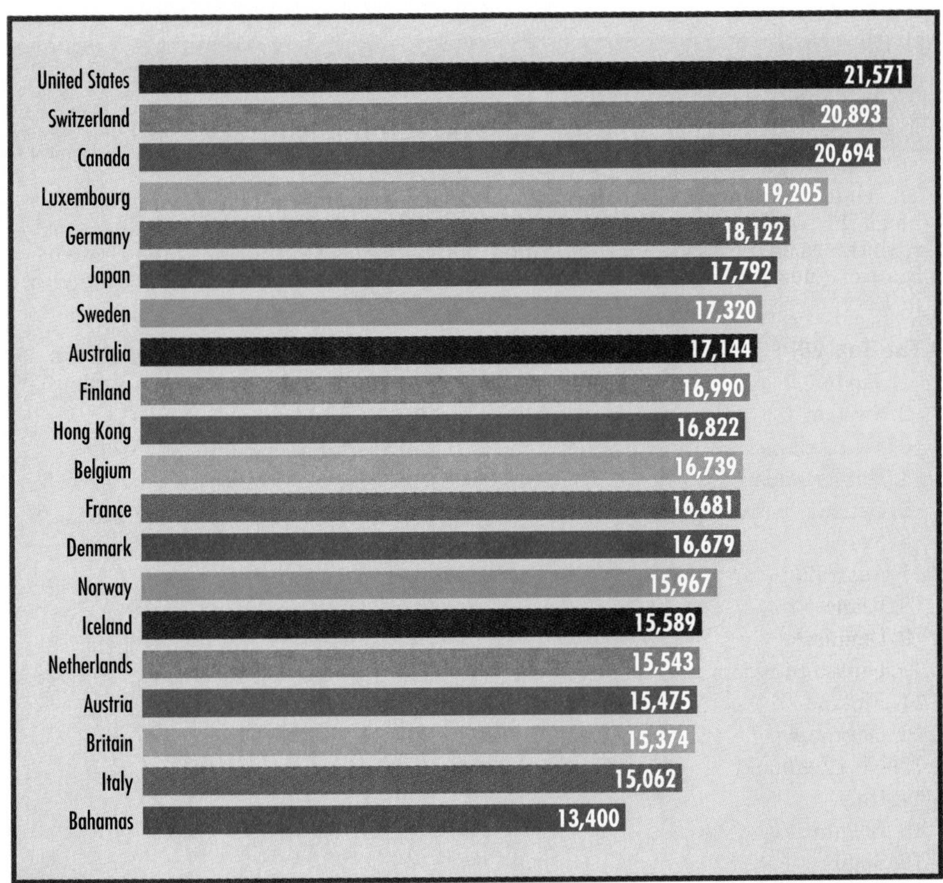

Figure 4.8 ▪ **Per Capita GDP of Selected Countries, Corrected for Purchasing Power (in 1990 U.S. Dollars)**

The United States remains the world's richest country measured on a per capita basis. Its lead over other rich countries has grown very small, however.

Source: *Fortune* (July 26, 1993), p. 96.

(see Table 4.1). Because the difference in index scores is quite small between Japan in first place and Israel in twentieth place, it is safe to say that our overall standard of living is impressive indeed. There is mounting evidence, however, that all is not as well as it seems, and this fact may be affecting American politics in important ways.

Persistent Stagnation According to most measures, the American standard of living has not improved very much, if at all, since the early 1970s. While the United States still ranks first in the world in GDP per capita, for instance, the size of our lead over the rest of the world has been shrinking rapidly. More important, the median income of American families has hardly improved since the early 1970s, even while the economy has continued to grow (see Figure 4.9). Between 1989 and 1995, median family income (in constant dollars) actually fell. And from 1988 to 1993, average weekly wages declined for Americans at all educational levels, except for those with advanced degrees, and the net worth of American families dropped.[6]

Stagnation in overall living standards is politically important because the American people have come to expect steady improvement in how well they

Table 4.1

United Nations Human Development Index for 1994

The United Nations Human Development Index is one measure of the quality of life of the people in society. Rather than depending on income alone, it includes such things as life expectancy, education, and nutrition. On this index the United States standard of living, while quite high, trailed behind that of 18 other countries in 1994.

The Top 20	Index Score	The Bottom 5	Index Score
1. Japan	0.996	126. Chad	0.157
2. Sweden		127. Sierra Leone	
3. Switzerland		128. Burkina Faso	
4. Netherlands		129. Mali	
5. Canada		130. Niger	0.116
6. Norway			
7. Australia			
8. France			
9. Denmark			
10. United Kingdom			
11. Finland			
12. Germany			
13. New Zealand			
14. Italy			
15. Belgium			
16. Spain			
17. Ireland			
18. Austria			
19. United States			
20. Israel	0.957		

Source: United Nations Development Program, The United Nations, New York, 1995.

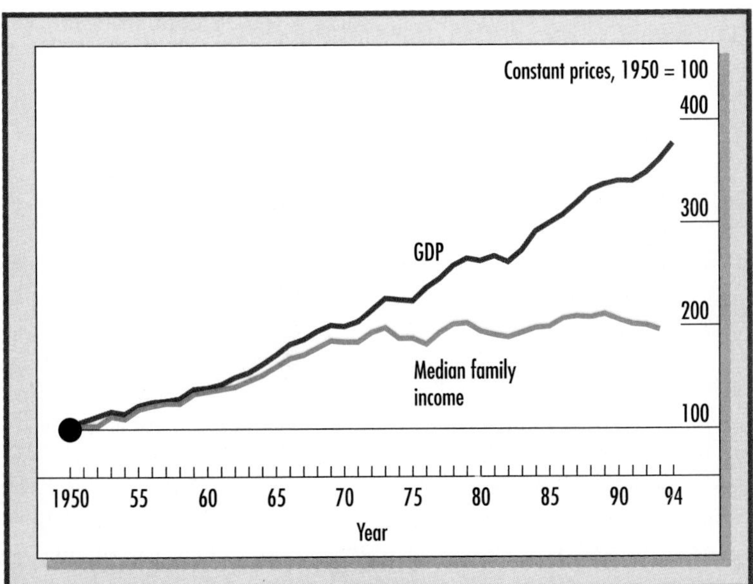

Figure 4.9 ■ **Trends in U.S. Median Family Income**

Median family income, controlled for inflation, has hardly grown since the early 1970s, even though more family members are working today than in the past.

Source: *The Economist* (September 16, 1995), p. 47.

live. And they expect their children to be even better off. This expectation may be what lies behind the rising anger among many Americans about taxes, new immigrants, and welfare recipients, as well as the growing discontent with government and political leaders.

The resurgence of the American economy and significant advances in productivity may eventually raise the mean income of Americans, but it is still too early to tell. For this to happen, economic growth would have to be translated into jobs paying good wages, something that is not inevitable in light of downsizing (see the chapter opening story) and downward pressures on employee compensation.

Income and Wealth Inequality Inequality in the distribution of income and wealth among Americans has been high for a long time and is becoming even more pronounced. Figure 4.10 shows the proportion of the total national income received by each fifth (or "quintile") of the population over the past several decades. Several things are apparent. First, unequal distribution has always been pronounced; the top fifth of all families has received at least seven times more income than the bottom fifth throughout the post–World War II era. Second, income inequality has become much more pronounced during the 1980s and 1990s, with the top group increasing its advantage and the bottom two quintiles falling further behind. Indeed, the 48.5 percent share of income enjoyed by the top fifth of families in 1995 is the highest ever recorded.

Income inequality is greater in the United States than in any other Western democratic nation. Figure 4.11 shows how selected countries compare on what is called the GINI Index, where a score of 0.0 means perfect equality in a population and 1.0 means perfect inequality (one person has all of the income). The United States has the highest (most unequal) score.

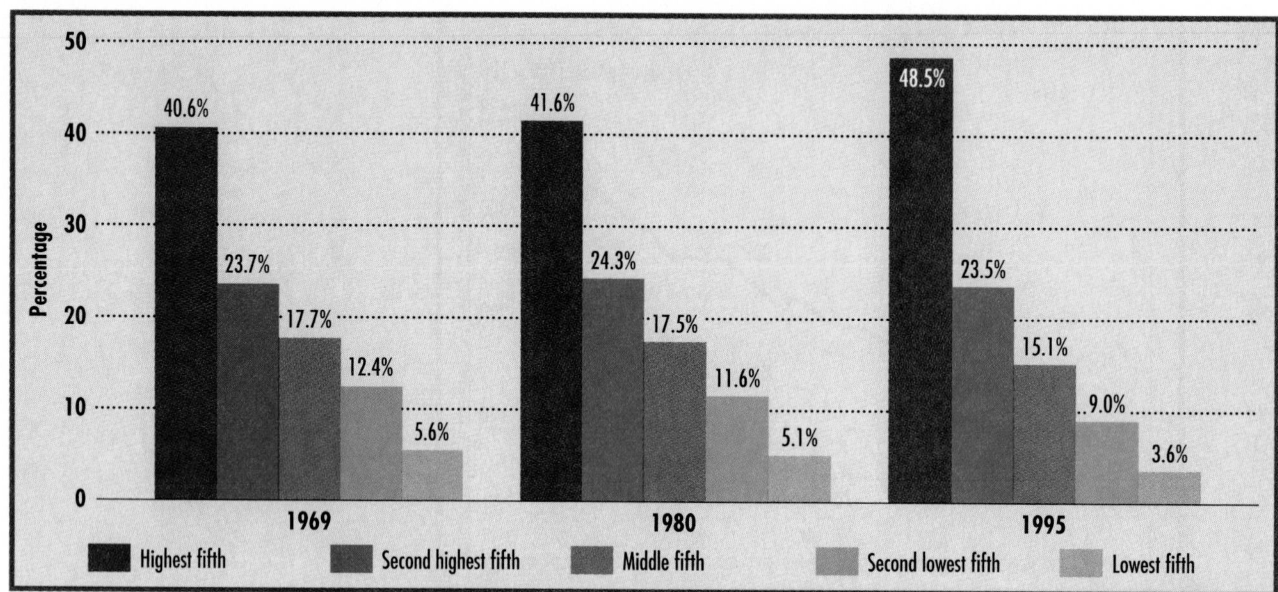

Figure 4.10 ■ Income Distribution in the United States, by Quintiles, 1969–1995

Income inequality has been increasing in the United States, reaching levels not seen since the 1920s. A standard way to measure income inequality is to compare the proportion of national income going to each 20 percent (called *quintiles*) of the population. Especially striking is the shrinking share of the bottom 20 percent and the increasing share of the top 20 percent.

Source: U.S. Bureau of the Census, *Current Population Reports, 1995,* Series P–60.

Among Americans, wealth is even more unequally distributed than income. According to a major new study by Edward Wolff for the Twentieth Century Fund, the top 1 percent of households—with a net worth of at least $2.3 million—owns nearly 40 percent of the nation's wealth, up from 20 percent in 1975.[7] Some researchers suggest that this level of wealth inequality was last seen in the 1920s.[8]

The Troubled Middle Class While mean family income stagnated and declined during the 1980s, then, the income situation of the very richest Americans improved substantially. Indeed, three-quarters of all *income* gains during

Figure 4.11 ■ Comparative Income Distribution

The GINI Index is a standard measure of income inequality used by economists. A GINI Index of 1.00 is equal to perfect inequality, where a single person has everything, and all others have nothing. A score of 0.00 is perfect equality, where the income share of every person is the same. The higher the score, the greater the level of income inequality. Note that the GINI score for the United States is higher than those of other highly developed capitalist societies.

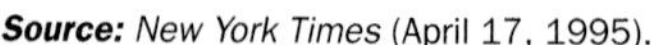
Source: *New York Times* (April 17, 1995).

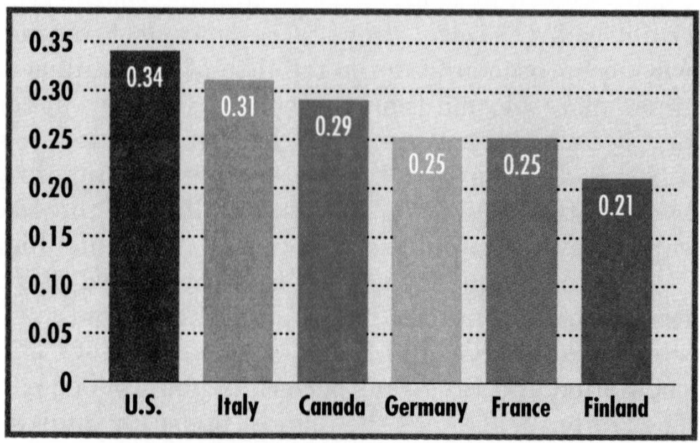

the 1980s went to the top 20 percent of families; 100 percent of increased *wealth* went to the same families.[9] By implication, those who are not rich could not have seen improvement in their economic situation. Figures on declining wages and salaries among all Americans without advanced degrees, as well as among workers in manufacturing, imply that the middle class is finding it ever more difficult to participate in what many have called the American dream. The Panel Study of Income Dynamics, an annual survey that follows 5,000 representative American families, reports that the middle class shrank by 20 percent from the late 1970s to the late 1980s.[10] The situation may be even worse than it seems for the middle class, because income figures do not take into account the rapidly increased burdens of payroll and real estate taxes, medical and housing costs, and college education, or the decline in public services that is evident almost everywhere.[11]

The mood of the broad American middle class is becoming extremely dark. A 1995 poll by Peter Horst and Robert Teeter revealed that 55 percent of Americans with college degrees believe that their children will be less well off than they are. Only one in three believes that the American dream can be achieved by hard work. As one respondent put it, "I am not optimistic about the future. The world has changed in ways I find to be extremely frightening. . . . My children are not going to have the opportunities I have had."[12]

The middle class, angered by its economic circumstances and bewildered by the behavior of the main political parties (Democrats seem to many of them to speak for higher taxes, special interests, and racial minorities, while Republicans seem to many of them to speak for big business and the wealthy[13]), may well seek alternative political solutions. This search is likely to have important long-term implications for American politics. Middle-class anger was surely a factor in the defeat of incumbent president George Bush in the 1992 election (he received only 38 percent of the vote); much of the middle-class vote went to the candidates who promised change (together, Democrat Clinton and Independent Perot garnered 62 percent of the vote). A similar middle-class anger was aimed at congressional Democrats in 1994 and gave the GOP (Republicans) control of Congress for the first time in 40 years.

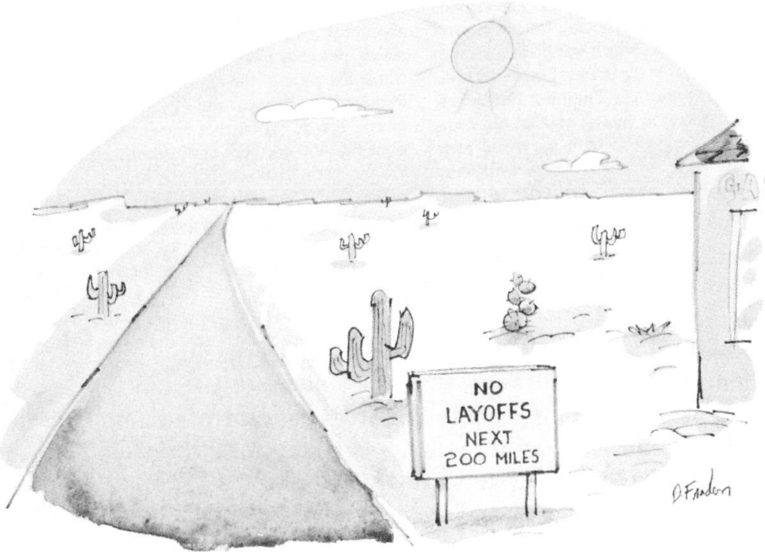

Drawing by D. Fradon; © 1993 The New Yorker Magazine, Inc.

WHAT ROLE FOR GOVERNMENT?

Can Government Help Create an Economy with Plentiful Jobs and Decent Wages? Comparing Europe and the United States

What policies should we adopt to help us address the problems caused by a rapidly changing economy in which the demand for unskilled and semiskilled labor has been sharply reduced? In the following excerpt, Stanford University economist Paul Krugman argues that both the quasi-free market approach of the United States and the welfare state approach of Europe pose problems. Is there a third way? Can governments help create jobs with decent wages?

> For a generation after World War II, the economies of the West offered both [jobs and wages]—that is, there were jobs for the great bulk of those who wanted them, and those jobs paid wages whose purchasing power rose steadily for just about everyone. Since the early 1970s, however, the economies of North America and Western Europe have not delivered that kind of broad prosperity. In the United States, the problem is essentially one of wages: Most people who seek jobs still get them, but an increasing fraction of our workers receive wages that both they and the rest of us regard as poverty-level. In Europe, wages at the bottom have declined less, but in their place long-term unemployment has consistently risen.
>
> . . .
>
> Modern technology in effect mandates much wider disparities in earnings among workers than we have experienced in the past. In the United States, where markets are left relatively untrammeled by concerns about justice or fairness, the result has been a startling polarization of the earnings distribution. In Europe, where collective bargaining and the much heavier hand of the welfare state have limited income inequality, the same forces have manifested themselves instead in growing unemployment.
>
> . . .
>
> The labor market in the United States is very different from that of any other advanced country in that it resembles much more closely the economist's ideal of a freely competitive matching of supply and demand. Only 12 per cent of U.S. private-sector workers belong to unions; thus, collective bargaining plays a minor role in wage determination. The U.S. minimum wage is low compared with average wages and has failed to keep up with inflation. Unemployment compensation in the United States is ungenerous both in size and duration. Workers are under far more pressure to seek jobs,

poverty line The federal government's calculation of the amount of income families of various sizes need to stay out of poverty.

The Fall and Rise of Poverty A sizable number of Americans are poor, and after years of progress in reducing poverty, an increasing number are again dropping into this category. In 1955, almost 25 percent of Americans fell below the federal government's official **poverty line.** By 1973, the figure had declined to 11.6 percent. Beginning in the late 1970s, however, the percentage of Americans classified as poor began to inch upward. It receded a bit in the mid–1980s and started to rise again in the early 1990s, reaching 15.1 percent in 1993 (see Figure 4.12).

The distribution of poverty is not random. It is concentrated among racial minorities, single-parent, female-headed households, and children. One in three African-Americans lives in poverty, as do three in ten Latinos. Over one in three poor people live in single-parent, female-headed households, and one in five are children (22 percent). The poverty rate among children in 1993 was

at whatever wages are offered, than their European or Canadian counterparts.

. . .

It is an unhappy picture, though with one bright spot: There are still jobs, if not good jobs, for most people who want them. Whatever else may have gone wrong with the U.S. economy, over the past 20 years it has been an impressive engine of job creation. There has, in particular, been no long-term trend towards higher unemployment rates. That stands in great contrast to the dismal employment performance on the other side of the Atlantic

. . .

In the early 1980s the problem of European unemployment became an obsession with many European economists, and several of them—notably Sweden's Assar Lindbeck and Germany's Herbert Giersch—converged on a basic diagnosis, which Giersch memorably dubbed "Eurosclerosis." According to that view, high European unemployment was the unintended byproduct of the European welfare state, which reduced the incentives both for firms to offer jobs and for workers to accept them.

The point was not difficult to understand. In virtually all European countries, unemployed workers are assured of a minimal income, no matter how long it has been since they last worked (in contrast to the time-limited U.S. system of unemployment insurance). Further, medical care is a universal right and housing is often subsidized as well. The result is that an unemployed European does not need to search for employment with the desperation of his [*sic*] American counterpart. Meanwhile, all benefits are paid for by a system of contributions from employers that considerably raises the cost of providing employment.

. . .

There is no perfect solution to this dilemma. Nobody has yet found a way to raise taxes or provide benefits without reducing incentives. The best that we can hope for is a society that shows more sense of community than the United States, but that does so in ways that exact less toll on incentives than the European welfare states.

Source: Paul Krugman, "Europe Jobless, America Penniless," *Foreign Policy* 95 (Summer, 1994), pp. 19–34.

the highest since 1964, before President Lyndon Johnson declared his War on Poverty. One report claims that 5.5 million children under the age of 12 go hungry every day in the United States.[14]

Inequality and poverty have important implications for American politics. For one thing, inequalities in living standards contribute to many of the social problems that eventually demand the attention of government. Crime, drug use, and family disintegration are tied to economic distress. A society with significant levels of inequality and widespread poverty must eventually pay attention to the discontent and disruption that are its natural outcome. Policing and social welfare programs are two of several possible public-policy responses.

Inequality is also important in how democracy works. Extensive *material inequality,* as we suggested in Chapter 1, may undermine the possibilities for

Figure 4.12 ■ Percentage of the U.S. Population Below the Poverty Line, 1960–1993

The proportion of Americans living in poverty decreased throughout the 1960s, leveled off for most of the 1970s, and has been increasing ever since. Poverty among African-Americans followed the general trend, but at higher levels of poverty.

Source: U.S. Census Bureau, *Current Population Reports*, "Money Income and Poverty Status in the United States," Series P-60.

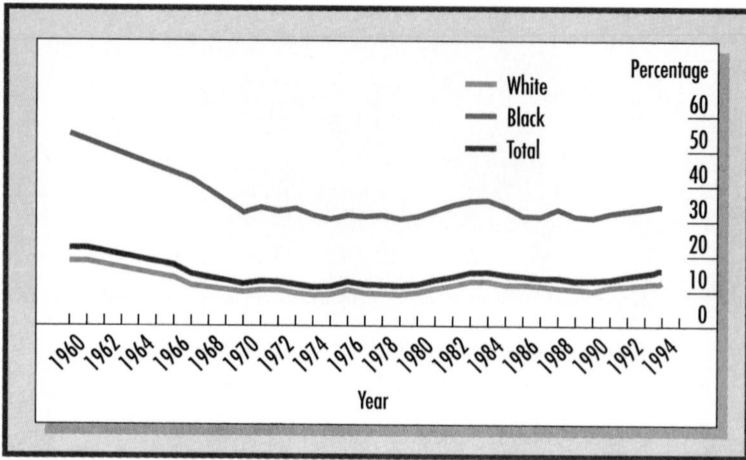

political equality, one of the foundations of democracy. Those with access to financial resources can use their resources to enhance their political voice and their ease of access to public officials. Poorer Americans are less likely to exercise their right to vote. Those without money are unlikely to make contributions to political campaigns or to groups that will fight for their interests. Those worried about putting food on the table are unlikely to be able to buy television time or advertising space to address the issues that concern them. That is why, as we pointed out in Chapter 1, Thomas Jefferson feared that democracy would be at risk in a highly unequal society.

The proportion of Americans living in poverty and suffering homelessness has increased significantly since the 1980s, at the same time that the proportion of very wealthy Americans has also increased. The contrast between rich and poor is evident on the streets of most large American cities.

The American Economy

Virtually everything we have discussed so far in this chapter is shaped by the American economy. The growth, diversification, and geographical dispersion of the American population, for instance, can be traced to economic changes. Occupations, standards of living, and inequality of income and wealth are closely connected to the operations of our economic institutions. Even important elements of the American political culture, as we shall soon see, are associated with our economy and how it works.

The kind of economic system we have in the United States is known by a number of names: **capitalism,** market economy, and free enterprise are the most common. Such an economy has two defining features: private ownership of economic instruments like factories, machinery, resources, land, and investment capital, and the existence of markets to coordinate most economic activity. Even while retaining these basic characteristics, American capitalism has changed a great deal over the years. We look now at how it has changed and why economic change is politically important.

capitalism An economic system characterized by private ownership and the existence of markets that coordinate most economic activities.

The Industrial Revolution and the Rise of the Corporation

Until the Civil War, American capitalism (except in the slave South) was highly competitive, with many small enterprises, first tied to agriculture and then increasingly to industry. After the Civil War, and partly as a result of it, the economy became increasingly industrialized and concentrated in giant enterprises.[15] The Civil War helped spur the Industrial Revolution: factories and shipyards were built, technological breakthroughs occurred, thousands of miles of rail lines were laid, and fortunes were made on government contracts for war materials. It also temporarily eliminated the South as a significant political power in Washington, D.C., and allowed the North to enact government policies that favored free enterprise: the Homestead Act of 1862 to open the West to the family farm, a high protective tariff to protect new industries, and subsidies for railroad construction. By the turn of the century, only 35 years after Lee's surrender at Appomattox Courthouse, the United States was the world's leading industrial power, accounting for almost 24 percent of the world's total manufacturing output.

Industrial enterprises grew to unprecedented size in the late nineteenth and early twentieth centuries. Workers were gathered together into workplaces that were of enormous size, requiring coordination by an army of managers. Partly, this change in scale was related to technology: the steam engine, electrical power, and the assembly line provided the means of gathering together thousands of working people for industrial production. Partly, this change in scale was tied to cost: most of the new industrial technologies required unheard-of levels of investment capital. Large enterprises were also encouraged by changes in the laws of incorporation, which allowed competing corporations to merge into single, giant enterprises. A wave of mergers between 1896 and 1904 fashioned the corporate-dominated economy familiar to us today.[16]

The Post–World War II Boom

The steady growth in the size, health, and economic importance of the American corporation continued virtually unabated (with a brief but painful pause during the Great Depression) until the early 1970s. By 1973, the 500 largest corporations (as compiled by *Fortune*) accounted for 42 percent of total U.S. assets and over 35 percent of total U.S. revenues. The enormous growth in the wealth of the American economy after World War II, fueled by the activities of the major corporations, was the foundation of the rapid improvements in the American standard of living and the burgeoning middle class discussed above. Many economists and politicians worried, however, that the sheer size and domination of markets by large corporations were making the economy less competitive than it ought to be. Many also worried that this much-concentrated economic power could be, and often was, translated into political power (see Chapter 7).

After World War II, the largest American corporations increasingly looked abroad for sources of raw materials and markets for their finished products. This turn of affairs was not entirely new; American oil companies, for instance, had scoured the world for petroleum reserves and markets in the early part of the twentieth century. But in the postwar period, many other corporations joined the game. Most corporations began by simply selling abroad those products they made in the United States. Over time, however, they gradually internationalized portions of their other activities, including product design, advertising, financing, and manufacturing.[17] (**Globalization** is the term that is most often used for this internationalization of a broad range of corporate activities.) American corporations dominated world markets in this period. As late as 1975, 11 of the largest 15 corporations in the world were American; as recently as 1981, 40 percent of the world's total foreign direct investment was still accounted for by the United States.[18] The globalization of corporate activities inevitably affected U.S. foreign policy. With worldwide economic interests at stake, American political leaders came under great pressure to pay attention to developments and events in the far corners of the world.

globalization The decentralization of corporate design, production, marketing, and sales activities around the world.

Global Competition: Transformation and Uncertainty

A transformation of the American economy is now under way. This transformation, and the problems and opportunities it produces, will affect American politics profoundly.

The American economy is becoming more integrated into the global economy and, therefore, more subject to its rise and fall. Both exports and imports account for a larger proportion of total U.S. economic activity than at any time in our history. And U.S. corporations are more closely tied to the corporations of other countries in joint ventures and partnerships. It is not yet clear whether these developments will help or hurt the American people. What is clear, however, is that, in a transnational, integrated global economy, the destiny of any single nation, no matter how powerful, is not entirely in its own hands; it is also affected by the decisions of people, organizations, and governments in other nations. Potentially, this globalization places many economic enterprises out of the reach of the instruments of American democracy.

Since the early 1970s, moreover, the United States has lost its position as the world's preeminent and unchallenged economic power. Between the early 1970s and the early 1990s, the U.S. share of world manufacturing declined. A large part of the reason was the lower share of its GDP that the United States devoted to fixed investment in plant, equipment, and research and development compared to Europe, Japan, and the so-called newly industrializing economies (NIEs) of Asia (see Figure 4.13). Though America's manufacturing sector has staged a comeback in recent years (especially in autos, computer

The largest American corporations are also global corporations in the sense that they produce and market their products all over the world.

chips, and telecommunications), it is unlikely that the United States will ever again be as dominant as in the past.

The relative decline in America's manufacturing position has had a devastating impact on workers' wages, has raised "protectionist" sentiments, and has spurred proposals to shield American industry from foreign competition.

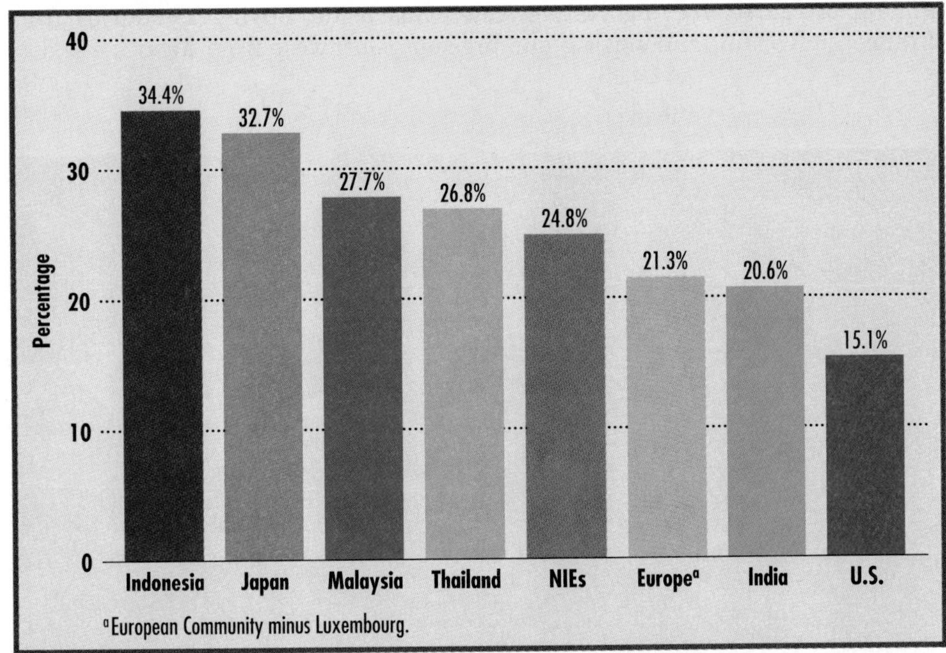

Figure 4.13 ■ **Fixed Investment as a Percentage of GDP, 1988–1992**

One of the reasons the newly industrializing economies (NIEs) of Asia have been growing at such impressive rates is their propensity to save and invest. The United States has lagged significantly behind, leading many economists to worry about the long-term performance of the American economy.

Source: *International Monetary Fund, 1993.*

The intensity of the fight over the North American Free Trade Agreement (NAFTA) and the General Agreement on Tariffs and Trade (GATT) shows how America's changing position in the world has generated a set of important issues in American politics.

The United States is finally no longer the undisputed power in world finance. The United States became the leading creditor nation in the world after World War I and dominated international finance for many years. By 1987, however, it had become the leading debtor nation in the world. United States banking institutions, for a long time the largest and most influential in the world, now rank, as a group, well below the banks of the new financial colossus, Japan. By 1988, only 1 of the top 15 banks in the world was American-owned. By 1993, Japanese banks held 44 percent of total world bank deposits, while the U.S. share had dropped to 8 percent.

The uncertainty and periodic hardships caused by changes in America's place in the international economy were eventually expressed in our politics. They became grist for the mill of presidents, Congress, and voters, affecting public policies that range from federal taxes to education, social welfare, national defense, and business regulation, to mention only a few of the most obvious.

The United States in the International System

For most of the nineteenth century, the attention of most Americans and their leaders was focused on the North American continent. Their energies were devoted primarily to filling in a vast, continental-scale nation-state—which required, of course, moving Native Americans aside, buying territories from France and Spain, and seizing our present Southwest from Mexico—and to

With the end of the Cold War, the role of the United States has changed significantly in a new world order that places economic concerns before military ones. Here President Clinton meets with other world leaders to talk about trade issues.

building an industrial economy. The great expanse of the Atlantic Ocean allowed our domestic growth and development to move forward, unhindered by the European powers. Our foreign policy was **isolationist;** that is, American policy leaders believed in attending to our own affairs and staying out of world affairs, unless directly threatened. By the late nineteenth and early twentieth centuries, however, our attentions began to turn abroad (note the Spanish-American War, President Theodore Roosevelt's arbitration of the Russo-Japanese War, interventions in Cuba and Central America, and World War I), and our growing economic power inevitably provided a seat at the table of the world's most important nations. It was World War II, however, that propelled the United States into its position as the world's most important power.

isolationism The policy of avoiding involvement in foreign affairs.

The United States as a Superpower

World War II thrust the United States into the leadership position that its economic position in the world had portended since 1900. The war stimulated a massive expansion of the entire industrial economy. At the same time, the financial and manufacturing infrastructures of our prewar economic rivals—Britain, France, Japan, and Germany—were devastated by the war. By the end of the war, the United States accounted for one-half of the total manufacturing, shipping, and exporting of the entire world.[19]

World War II also solidified the position of the United States as the leading financial nation in the world. By the end of the war, the United States held two-thirds of the gold reserves of the world in its vaults, and the American dollar became the principal currency of world trade.

The United States emerged from the war with a large military establishment and military superiority in most areas in which it counted. There was also a new belief among both the population and the nation's leaders that isolationism was dangerous and contrary to our long-term national interests.

Within a decade of the end of World War II, the United States stood as the unchallenged economic, political, and military power among the Western nations. For the first time in its history, the United States was willing and able to exercise leadership on the world level. It was the United States that pulled the major capitalist nations together for the first time in their history into a political and economic alliance. It provided funds for rebuilding Europe and for development projects in the Third World. It successfully pushed for free international trade and provided a stable dollar to serve as the basis of the international monetary system. And it organized and largely paid for the joint military defenses of them all. Is it any wonder, then, that *Life* magazine editor Henry Luce was moved to label the period the "American Century"?

The fly in the ointment, of course, was the Soviet Union. Although badly crippled by the war (it is said that 20 million of its citizens died in the conflict), the Soviet Union entered the postwar era with the world's largest land army, superpower ambitions of its own, and a strong desire to keep the nations on its periphery in eastern and southern Europe in hands it considered friendly. In the ensuing **Cold War,** which began in the late 1940s and lasted for four decades, the two superpowers faced each other as leaders of conflicting political, economic, and ideological alliances; became engaged in a nuclear arms race; and fought surrogate wars with each other in various locations in the Third World, from the Belgian Congo, to Central America, to Afghanistan.

Cold War A term used for the period of tense relations between the United States and the Soviet Union, stretching from the late 1940s to the late 1980s.

America's superpower status had many political implications. For one thing, superpower status required a large military establishment and tilted government spending priorities toward national defense. For another thing, as we will see in later chapters, it enhanced the role of the president in policymaking and diminished that of Congress. Finally, superpower status and the struggle with the Soviet Union contributed to a climate of opinion favoring secrecy in the name of "national security," with unfortunate consequences for the practice of democracy.

A Multipower-Centered World?

The 1980s and 1990s saw startling changes in the world political, military, and economic systems. Communism collapsed in Eastern Europe. The Soviet Union ceased to exist. China switched to a market economy.

Though the collapse of the Soviet Union left the United States as the world's only military superpower, American presidents have sometimes had difficulty translating this position into diplomatic preeminence. Because of the collapse of the USSR, friends and former adversaries feel freer to go their own way. Germany, France, and Japan have their own ideas about the proper directions for world economic and trade policies, for instance. The increasing autonomy of our allies became evident in the debate over ending the civil war in Bosnia, where the United States and its European allies were often at loggerheads over the proper course of action. After several years, of course, they agreed to deploy forces to police the peace agreement reached by the warring parties.

bipolar system An international system with two great powers.

multipolar system An international system with more than two great powers.

In some sense, the **bipolar** world (the United States and the USSR) of the post–World War II years has given way to a **multipolar** world with multiple centers of power—a pluralistic world with the United States as the most powerful nation, important but not able to dictate to allies or enemies. Whether a safer and more humane world order will emerge from this transformation remains to be seen. What is clear is that this new world order will offer many challenges for American politics and government. Issues such as U.S. policy on

With the collapse of Communism in the Soviet Union and Eastern Europe, the United States–USSR bipolar world ceased to exist, giving way to a world with multiple centers of power.

national and ethnic aspirations in Eastern Europe, foreign aid to the fragments of the former Soviet Union, peacekeeping roles in places like Bosnia and Haiti, and the improvement of American economic competitiveness will demand attention from American leaders and citizens for a long time to come.

The Foundation Beliefs of American Political Culture

The kinds of choices Americans make in meeting these challenges will depend a great deal on the kinds of values and beliefs Americans have about human nature, society, economic relations, and the role of government. Government policies tend to reflect our ideas and beliefs as a people. The fundamental values and beliefs that have political consequences make up the American *political culture.* The general outlines of the American political culture are discussed in this section. Many of the details on how these beliefs are expressed in everyday politics can be found in Chapter 5.

There is a great deal of evidence that Americans share a political culture.[20] To be sure, we are a vast, polyglot mixture of races, religions, ethnicities, occupations, and lifestyles. Nevertheless, one of the things that has always struck observers of the American scene is the degree to which a broad consensus seems to exist on many of the fundamental beliefs that shape our political life. We focus here not on transitory ideas about particular issues that are in the headlines at the moment, but on what might be called *foundation beliefs,* that is, beliefs that shape how people classify, think about, and resolve particular issues that arise in the headlines or in their local communities.

Competitive Individualism

Americans tend to believe that an individual's fate is, and ought to be, tied to his or her own efforts. Those with talent, grit, and the willingness to work hard are more likely than not to end up on top, it is believed; those without at least some of these qualities are more likely than not to wind up on the bottom of the heap. Americans tend to assume that people generally get what they deserve, even as they acknowledge occasional exceptions.

Americans also tend to believe that people are naturally competitive, always striving to better themselves in relation to others. Popular literature in America has always conveyed this theme, ranging from the Horatio Alger books of the late nineteenth century to the many guidebooks to "getting ahead," "making it," and "getting rich" of our own time.

The belief in competitive individualism affects how Americans think about many issues, including inequality. Americans overwhelmingly endorse the idea of "equality of opportunity" (the idea that people ought to have an equal shot in the competitive game of life), for instance, yet they overwhelmingly reject the idea that people should have equal rewards. Not surprisingly, Americans tend to look favorably on government programs that try to equalize opportunity—Head Start, education programs of various kinds, school lunch programs, and the like—but are generally against programs such as welfare, which seem to redistribute income from the hardworking middle class to those who are considered "undeserving." Figure 4.14 shows that "equal opportunity" is broadly supported by Americans but that "equal outcomes" are not.

Since it is assumed that people get different rewards based on their own efforts, a belief in equality of opportunity seems consistent with highly unequal outcomes; that is, Americans find inequality of income and wealth

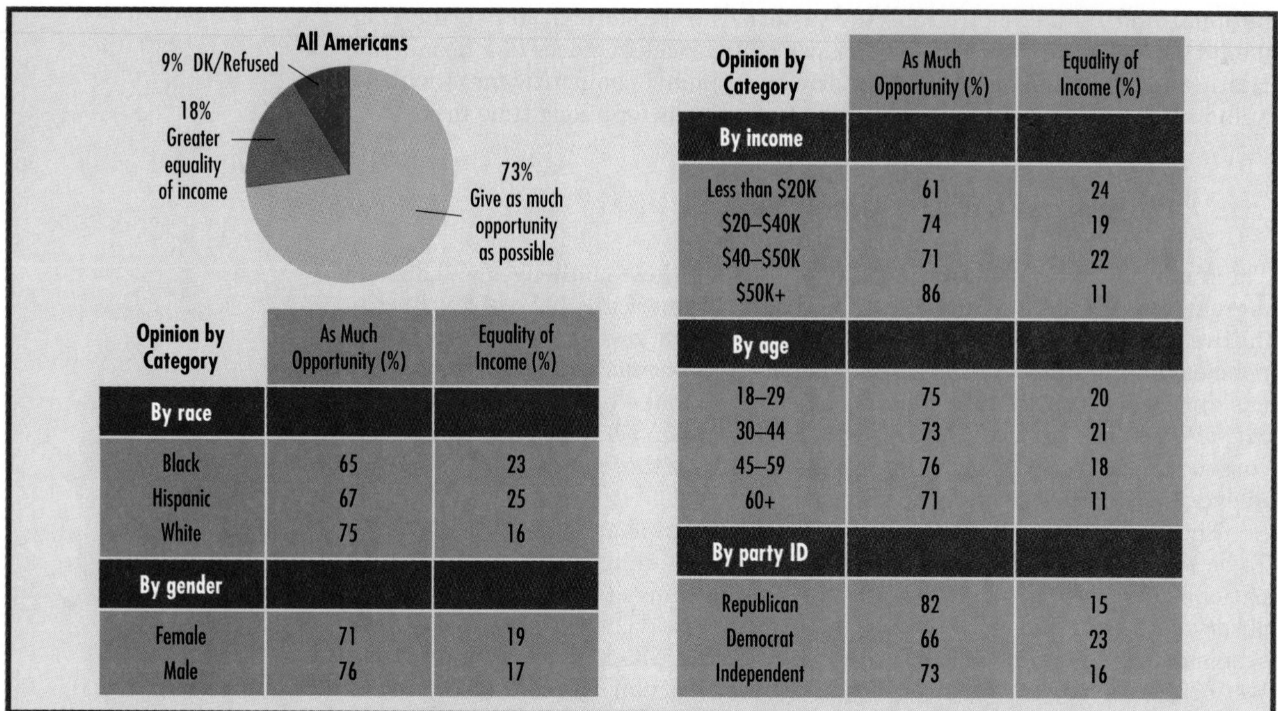

Figure 4.14 ■ **Should Government Make Americans More Equal?**

A substantial majority of Americans believe that the role of government is to help create more opportunities for individual improvement rather than to ensure greater income equality. Though more African-Americans, Hispanics, and the poor want the government to play an income-equalizing role, a majority of these groups still favor the "equal opportunity" option.

Source: Roper Center for Reader's Digest, August–September, 1994. Reported in *The Public Perspective,* April–May 1995, p. 19.

acceptable, as long as it is the outcome of a process in which individuals fairly compete with each other.[21] In Sweden, on the other hand, citizens generally believe that equality of condition is an important value and support government policies that redistribute income.[22]

Competitive individualism, so central to the American political culture, is not common in most other modern capitalist nations. In Japan, for instance, commitment to the work team, to the company, and to the community is more highly regarded than commitment to personal advancement. In Sweden, people are less likely to talk about their individual rights and more about their social obligations.[23]

Limited Government

Closely associated with the idea of individualism is the belief that government must be limited in its power and responsibilities, for, taken too far, a powerful government is likely to threaten individual rights and to get in the way of economic efficiency. This idea, drawn from Adam Smith and John Locke, our early history, and the words of the Declaration of Independence, remains attractive to most Americans even today, when we expect government to do far more than the framers ever imagined. This belief is not universally shared. In such countries as Japan, Sweden, Germany, and France, where governments have al-

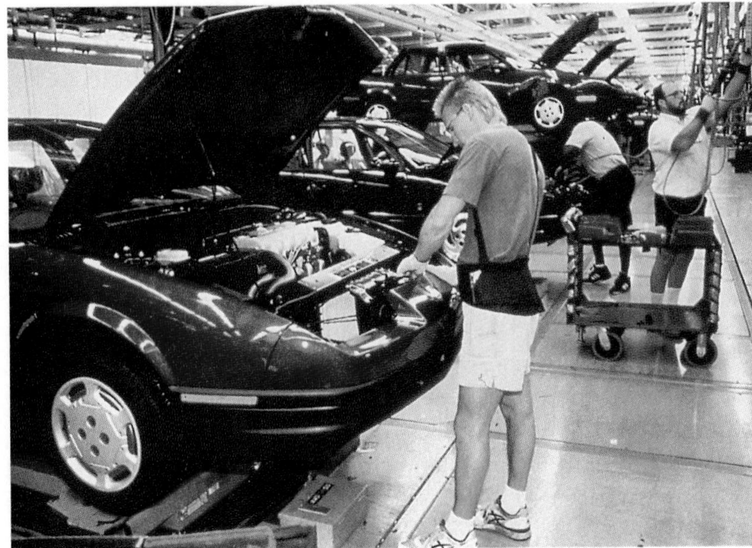

In Japan, commitment to the work team and to the company is a more important cultural value than it is in the United States. Some companies, such as Saturn Autos, have adapted the Japanese team approach by focusing on the individual's contribution to the team and the product, appealing to individualism, a cherished American value.

ways been powerful and have played an important role in directing society and the economy, limited government has little attraction for either the political leaders or the public. Figure 4.15 shows some of these national differences.

Free Enterprise

Americans tend to support the basic precepts of free enterprise capitalism: private property and the efficiencies of the free market. Private property notions,

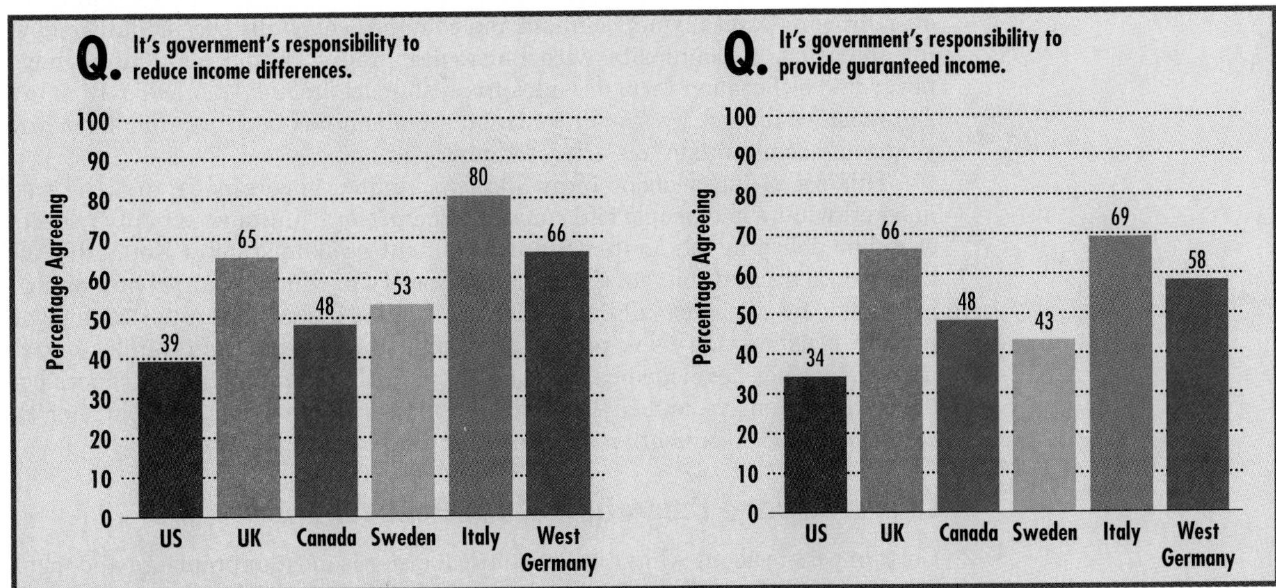

Figure 4.15 ▪ **Government and Equality: Comparing Americans to Others**

Compared to people in other capitalist democracies, Americans do not believe that government is responsible for making incomes more equal.

Source: ISSP Surveys, 1992. Reported in *The American Perspective* (April–May 1995), p. 20.

articulated by the philosopher John Locke, have been reinforced by the experience of fairly widespread property ownership in the United States compared to that in many other countries,[24] and are strongly associated with the belief in individualism. Locke argued that, while God gave the earth and its resources in common to human beings, He also gave human beings a set of abilities—industry (the willingness to work hard) and creativity, for example—which they have a right and an obligation to use. When they use these abilities, people turn common property into private property. By mixing their labor with the naturally occurring abundance of the earth (the land, forests, rivers, and so on), people are justified in taking the product of that effort for their own as private property. Because people are different in their abilities and their willingness to work, this process will always result in inequality. Inevitably, some will end up with more property than others.

The basic theory of the free market was worked out by Adam Smith in his classic work, *The Wealth of Nations*.[25] Smith taught that, if the market were left alone to operate naturally, following the laws of supply and demand, it would coordinate economic life in a nearly perfect fashion. The market works best if people are free to pursue their own interests. Since the market is efficient and effective if left alone, government should not interfere with its operations. Though few Americans now accept this "pure" free-market ideal, most Americans today, as in the past, believe that the private sector is usually more effective and efficient than the public sector.

Given the esteem in which competitive individualism, private property, and the market are held, as well as the historical success of the American economy, it is entirely understandable that Americans tend to hold the business system (though not large corporations) in very high regard. As President Calvin Coolidge put it, "The business of America is business." Most Americans agree.

One indicator of the high regard in which the economic system is held by Americans is the almost complete absence of support for movements that favor overthrowing capitalism. Socialism and communism, while occasionally enjoying moments of popularity with particular groups in the population, have never had either long-term or widespread support among Americans. In many European countries, by way of contrast, socialism has been popular for many years, and communism has attracted many others.

This set of ideas about individualism, limited government, and the free market (what some people call *classical liberalism*)[26] influences many aspects of public policy in the United States. Eminent economist John Kenneth Galbraith once decried the fact that ours is a society in which great private wealth exists side by side with public squalor. By that, he meant that Americans favor private consumption over public provision, and private over public initiatives.[27] In other developed capitalist nations, citizens and political leaders believe that extensive and high-quality public services in mass transit, health care, housing, and education are part and parcel of the good society.

Citizenship and the Nature of the Political Order

Certain beliefs about what kind of political order is most appropriate and what role citizens should play shape the actual daily behavior of citizens and political decision makers alike.

Democracy At the time of its founding, democracy was not highly regarded by elites in the United States. During our history, however, the practice of

Walt Whitman: Poet of Democracy

The Struggle for Democracy

The democratic process requires a political culture that respects ordinary people and believes in their ability to govern themselves. Walt Whitman was one of the giants of American letters who helped fashion the transformation of the American political culture from its aristocratic roots. Whitman was a rugged outdoorsman, a printer, and a crusading newspaper editor, best known, then and now, as a poet whose celebration of the common people earned him the title "the poet of democracy."

During the Civil War, Whitman chronicled the experience of soldiers, citizens, and even President Lincoln in his poetry. When his brother was wounded, he went to see him and stayed on to help in the hospital. His personal contact with wounded soldiers deeply affected him and reaffirmed his democratic sentiments.

Whitman's celebration of the dignity of common people and the character of their everyday lives is captured in these selections from his most famous work, *Leaves of Grass* (1855):

(15) The pure contralto sings in the organloft,
The carpenter dresses his plank. . . . the tongue of his foreplane whistles its wild ascending lisp,
The married and unmarried children ride home to their thanksgiving dinner,
The pilot seizes the king-pin, he heaves down with a strong arm,
The mate stands braced in the whaleboat, lance and harpoon are ready,
The duck-shooter walks by silent and cautious stretches,
The deacons are ordained with crossed hands at the altar,
The spinning-girl retreats and advances to the hum of the big wheel,
The farmer stops by the bars of a Sunday and looks at the oats and rye, . . .
The machinist rolls up his sleeves. . . . the policeman travels his beat. . . . the gate-keeper marks who pass,
The young fellow drives the express-wagon. . . . I love him though I do not know him; . . .
(24) Whoever degrades another degrades me. . . . and whatever is done or said returns at last to me,
And whatever I do or say I also return.
I speak the password primeval. . . . I give the sign of democracy;
By God! I will accept nothing which all cannot have their counterpart of on the same terms.

democracy has been enriched and expanded, and the term *democracy* has become an honored one.[28] While regard for democracy is one of the bedrocks of the American belief system today, Americans have not necessarily always behaved democratically. After all, African-Americans were denied the vote and other citizenship rights in many parts of the nation until the 1960s. It is fair to say, nevertheless, that most Americans believe in democracy as a general principle and take seriously any claim that their behavior is not consistent with it.

Freedom and Liberty Foreign visitors have always been fascinated by the American obsession with individual "rights," the belief that, in the good society, government leaves people alone in their private pursuits. Studies show that freedom (also called *liberty*) is at the very top of the list of American beliefs and that it is more strongly honored here than elsewhere.[29] From the very beginning, what attracted most people to the United States was the promise of freedom in the New World. Many came for other reasons, to be sure: a great many came for strictly economic reasons; some came as convict labor; and some came in chains as slaves. But many who came to these shores seem to have done so to taste the freedom to speak and think as they chose, to worship as they pleased, to read what they might, and to assemble and petition the government if they had a mind to.

As in many cases, however, to believe in something is not necessarily to act consistently with that belief. There have been many intrusions on basic rights during our history. Later chapters address this issue in more detail.

Populism

The term *populism* refers to the hostility of the common person to power and the powerful. While public policy is not often driven by populist sentiments (for the powerful, by definition, exercise considerable political influence), populism has always been part of the American belief system and has sometimes been expressed in visible ways in American politics (as well as in our films; see the Politics and Film box).

One of the most common targets of populist sentiment has been concentrated economic power and those who exercise it. Andrew Jackson mobilized this sentiment in his fight against the Bank of the United States in the 1830s. The bank was seen by many as an instrument of wealthy financial interests. The Populist movement of the 1890s directed its political and legislative efforts against the new corporations of their day, especially the banks and the railroads, whose actions were adversely affecting ordinary farmers. Corporations were the target of popular hostility during the dark days of the Great Depression and also in the 1970s, when consumer groups made the lives of some corporate executives extremely uncomfortable. Contemporary public opinion polls find strong popular support for free enterprise existing side by side with negative feelings about corporations and corporate leaders.

Populism is also hostile to the concentration of power in government. Alabama's segregationist governor George Wallace successfully tapped into this sentiment in his run for the Democratic presidential nomination in 1968, when he complained about the "pointy-headed intellectuals in Washington." The populist sentiment may be seen today in the rising discontent of portions of the middle class, a phenomenon reviewed earlier. A sense that a distant government has forgotten the common person has probably fueled a drift away from the Democratic and Republican parties and the rise of alternatives, such as Ross Perot and other independent candidates.

Piety

The United States is, by any measure, a strikingly religious society.[30] Polls conducted since the mid–1970s consistently show that about 40 percent of the American people claim to have had a personal experience with God. The Amer-

There are more churchgoers in the United States than in any other highly industrialized nation.

ican people are clearly more religious than people in any other Western society (see Figure 4.16). One recent poll, for instance, shows that 94 percent of Americans, but only 37 percent of Japanese, say they believe in God.[31]

Religious faith affects politics in important ways. Churches and religious believers have often found themselves on the liberal side of the political divide

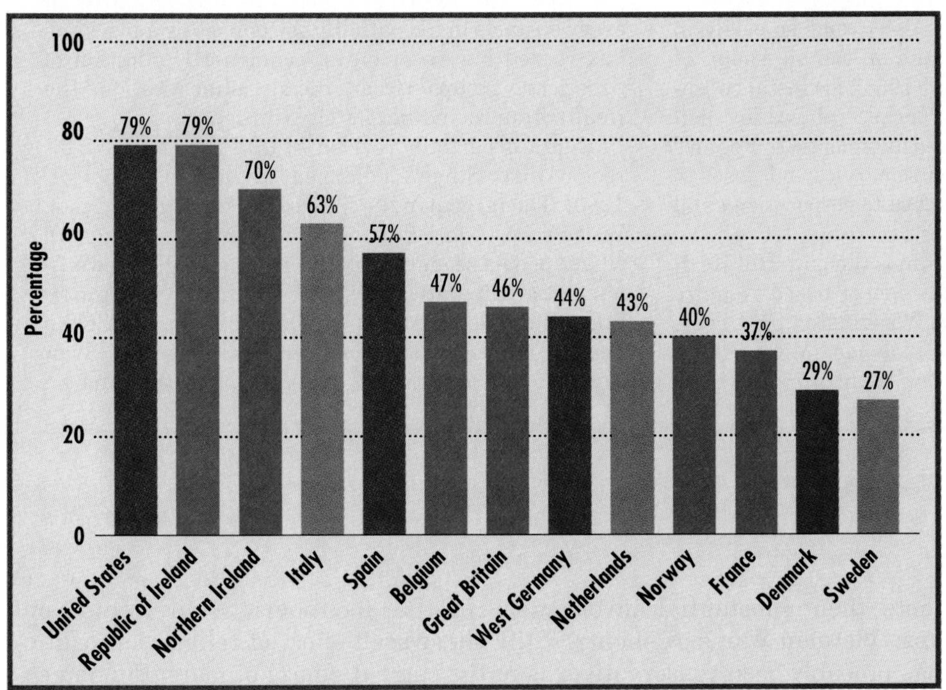

Figure 4.16 ▪ **Comparing Nations on Strength of Religious Beliefs**

This shows the percentage of people who say they draw comfort and strength from religion, by country. Note that the United States is at the top of the list, tied with Ireland.

Source: Social Surveys, The Gallup Organization, 1981.

POLITICS AND FILM

The Common Man (and Woman) Takes on the Big Guys

The populist strain in the American political culture is commonly featured in Hollywood films. Hollywood often presents stories of the common person's struggle against the economically and politically powerful, given the appeal of this theme at the box office. Frank Capra's classic films of the 1930s and 1940s are the most well known of this genre.

> In Capra's most admired movies, members of the snootier classes were greedy or black-hearted swine. In Capra's America, good, upright, innocent Mr. Deeds, Mr. Smith, John Doe, and George Bailey were all at the mercy of vile capitalists, lawyers, and politicians who infested society. . . . In *Mr. Deeds Goes to Town, Mr. Smith Goes to Washington, Meet John Doe,* and *It's a Wonderful Life,* the nastiness of society's pillars is drawn in harsh caricature strokes.[a]

In Capra's films, the common people always overcome the odds, the powerful are vanquished, and the values of hard work, simplicity, honesty, and self-reliance are rewarded. Victories don't come so easily in today's films for those who take on the big shots. In Francis Ford Coppola's *Tucker* (1988), for instance, automobile visionary Preston Tucker (played by Jeff Bridges) takes on the Big Three automobile companies in the late 1940s with a revolutionary car but loses to an unholy alliance of the giant auto corporations and their political allies in Congress.

In *Silkwood* (1983), the villain is the powerful Kerr-McGee Corporation, whose energy-based empire wielded imposing influence in Washington, D.C. (personalized by Senator Kerr of Oklahoma). Meryl Streep plays Karen Silkwood, a nuclear plant worker who is radicalized by the corporation's lax attention to worker safety and goes public with her fears. For her trouble, she is purposely contaminated by plutonium, though it is never clear whether the culprit is a fellow worker or the company. Just like the real Karen Silkwood, the heroine dies in a car crash on her way to meet a *New York Times* reporter with her story and supporting evidence. The film implies, with its menacing headlights glaring through the rear window of Silkwood's car, that she was murdered—a view held to this day by many unionists, feminists, and friends of Silkwood.

The common man is bewildered, depressed, and angry in *Falling Down* (1993). Michael Douglas (pictured) plays an aerospace engineer who has lost his job in a corporate restructuring and has lost his wife and child to divorce. Feeling trapped and put upon at every turn, his life in shambles, he lashes out at every group he imagines to be at fault. Leaving his car in the middle of a Los Angeles freeway traffic jam, he starts a journey across the city in which he wreaks havoc on every obstacle in his path. By the end of his journey, he has vented his anger on an ecumenical collection of American groups, from racial minorities to the wealthy, and to indifferent city workers.

Capra is partially revived in *Wall Street* (1987), director Oliver Stone's indictment of the Reagan "go-go" 1980s. The targets in the film are, as the title suggests, Wall Street (a familiar target of American populism), where people seem to make money through shrewd financial manipulations without making anything useful, and its most visible manifestation, Gordon Gekko (loosely modeled on convicted inside trader Ivan Boesky). The protagonist, Bud Fox (played by Charlie

(note their substantial involvement in the abolitionist, civil rights, and anti–Vietnam War movements). Still, the overall effect of religion on politics has probably been conservative, as in the current efforts of many Fundamentalists. This is another reason that socialist and social democratic parties have had little success in America. Most established churches, whether Catholic or Protestant, have issued pronouncements against communism, Marxism, and socialism. Also, the highest levels of piety are found in the United States

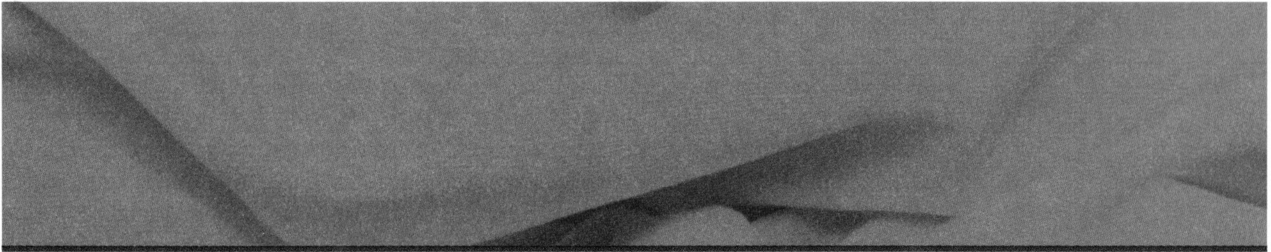

Sheen), an ambitious son of a working-class father, has fallen in with Gekko, attracted by the glamour and riches of his life, and has forgotten the fundamental values of his airplane mechanic father (played by Martin Sheen).

Bud sees the light, however, when Gekko's machinations threaten to destroy the company that his father works for and the jobs that his father and his friends depend on. He then cooperates with the authorities to bring Gekko down, in return for a reduced prison sentence. Bud returns to his fundamental values and is reunited with his family, however, only through a circuitous and morally ambiguous route that would never have occurred in Capra's films.

The Capra spirit is fully revived in the 1993 hit film *Dave,* in which Kevin Kline plays the role of an ordinary citizen who masquerades as the president of the United States. Filling in for the dead president, he brings the common touch to his role, bettering the corrupt advisers that surround the office, forging a bond with the American people, winning the love of the real president's estranged wife, and solving seemingly unsolvable problems (for instance, the budget deficit) with simple common sense. The implication is that our system would work if only we let regular people run the show. If only things were that easy.

[a]Russell Baker, "Capra Beats the Game," *New York Times* (September 9, 1991), p. E1.

among nonwhites, people with the least formal education, and those at the lower end of the income scale—precisely the strongest supporters of leftist political parties in Europe. Finally, polls generally show that the most religious among the American population are also the most politically conservative. It is not surprising, then, to learn that the Christian Coalition, which has gained prominence and influence in American politics in recent years, almost always supports conservative causes and Republican candidates.

Structural Influences on American Politics

We have now examined a number of structural factors that influence American politics. In Chapters 2 and 3, we examined the constitutional rules; in this chapter, we considered the main features of American society, economy, political culture, and the international system, and how each influences important aspects of politics and government in the United States. These structural factors are interrelated. The kind of constitutional rules we have are, to a substantial degree, shaped by our beliefs about the nature of the individual, society, and government that make up our political culture. The political culture, in turn, with its ideas celebrating the market, competitive individualism, and private property, is perfectly attuned to a free enterprise economy. How the economy operates and develops has a lot to do with the life of the American people (where people live, what kind of work they do, etc.) and the nation's place in the world. The characteristics of the American population trigger their own effects; their level of education and skill has a lot to do with American economic performance, for instance.

One of the recurring themes that appears throughout this book is the substantial growth in the size, reach, and responsibilities of the federal government. Much of this growth, we will see, is related to changes in the structural factors described in this chapter.

Summary

How politics and government work in practice is shaped by such structural factors as the nature of society, the economy, the nation's place in the world, and the political culture.

The most important changes in the American population are its growth; its diversification along ethnic, religious, and racial lines; its relocation from rural to urban and suburban areas and to the Sun Belt; and its gradual aging. The population is also marked by the existence of substantial inequalities in income and wealth, a growing unease in large portions of the middle class about its future prospects, and a surprisingly high level of poverty. These factors affect the agenda of American politics and the distribution of political power.

The American economy is a capitalist, or free enterprise, economy. American capitalism has changed from a highly competitive, small-enterprise form to a highly concentrated, corporate-dominated one with a global reach. Economic change has had important reverberations in American politics.

The emergence of the United States as a superpower in the twentieth century changed the content of foreign policy, the balance of power between the president and Congress, the size of the federal government, and the priorities of the government's budget. The collapse of socialism in Eastern Europe and the Persian Gulf War affirmed the position of the United States as the world's most important military power, but relative economic decline has forced the United States to share power in the political and economic arenas with Western Europe and Japan. This new situation is filled with uncertainties that will affect U.S. foreign and domestic policy.

Americans believe strongly in individualism, limited government, and free enterprise. Beliefs about democracy, liberty, and the primacy of the common people also help define the political culture, as does a strong religious commitment. The political culture shapes American ideas about what the good society should look like, the appropriate role for government, and the possibilities of self-government.

Suggested Readings

Bellah, Robert N., R. Madsen, W. M. Sullivan, A. Swidler, and S. M. Tipton. *Habits of the Heart.* Berkeley: University of California Press, 1985.
A convincing description of competitive individualism and its effects.

Chafe, William H. *The Unfinished Journey,* 2nd ed. New York: Oxford University Press, 1995.
A history of postwar America, with special attention to how structural transformations have shaped American political life.

Dicken, Peter. *Global Shift: The Internationalization of Economic Activity.* New York: Guilford Press, 1992.
A comprehensive look at the scope, causes, and consequences of economic globalization.

Hanson, Russell. *The Democratic Imagination in America.* Princeton: Princeton University Press, 1985.
A history of the democratic idea in America; stresses its changing character.

Hochschild, Jennifer L. *Facing Up to the American Dream.* Princeton: Princeton University Press, 1995.
A brilliant examination of the ideology of the American dream and how race and social class affect its interpretation and possibilities.

Phillips, Kevin. *Boiling Point: Democrats, Republicans, and the Decline of Middle Class Prosperity.* New York: Random House, 1993.
Makes the argument that the middle class is in trouble economically and socially and that the resulting middle-class anger will transform American politics.

Roberts, Samuel. *Who We Are.* New York: Times Books, 1993.
A portrait of the American population based on the 1990 U.S. Census.

Wills, Gary. *Under God: Religion and American Politics.* New York: Simon & Schuster, 1991.
The best recent interpretation of the centrality of religion in American political life.

Internet Sources

The Economic Bulletin Board telnet ebb.stat-usa.gov
Current economic information from federal agencies.

The Economist Magazine http://www.economist.com/index.html
The home page of one of the world's leading publications on the United States and the international economy.

Statistical Abstracts of the United States http://www.census.gov:80/stat_abstract/
A vast compendium of statistical information on the government, the economy, and the society.

STAT-USA http://www.STAT-USA.gov/
Business and economic information supplied by federal agencies.

Yahoo/Economics and Business http://www.yahoo.com/Business_and_Economy/
A gateway to a wealth of information about business and the economy.

Yahoo/Society and Culture http://www.yahoo.com/Society_and_Culture/
A gateway to a wealth of information about society and cultural issues.

Notes

1. All of these cases are from "The Wage Squeeze," *Business Week* (July 17, 1995), p. 21.

2. Keith Bradsher, "Productivity Is All, but It Doesn't Pay Well," *New York Times* (June 25, 1995), p. E4.

3. Spencer Rich, "A 20-Year High Tide of Immigration," *Washington Post,* National Edition (September 7, 1995), p. 16.

4. Michael Reich, "The Proletarianization of the Workforce," in Richard Edwards, Michael Reich, and Thomas A. Weisskopf, eds., *The Capitalist System* (Englewood Cliffs, NJ: Prentice Hall, 1966), p. 125.

5. These two figures are from Stanley Lebergott, "The American Labor Force," in Lance E. Davis, ed., *American Economic Growth* (New York: Harper & Row, 1972), p. 187; Reich, "The Proletarianization," p. 124.

6. Kevin Phillips, *Boiling Point: Democrats, Republicans, and the Decline of Middle-Class Prosperity* (New York: Random House, 1993), p. 23.

7. Edward N. Wolff, *Top Heavy: A Study of Increasing Inequality of Wealth in America* (New York: Twentieth Century Fund, 1995).

8. See Paul R. Krugman, "The Right, the Rich, and the Facts," *The American Prospect* (Fall 1992), pp. 24–25; Kevin Phillips, *The Politics of Rich and Poor* (New York: Random House, 1990).

9. Phillips, *The Politics of Rich and Poor,* p. 102.

10. Greg J. Duncan, Timothy Smeeding, and Roger Willard, "The Incredible Shrinking Middle Class," *American Demographics,* Vol. 14 (May 1992), pp. 34–38.

11. Phillips, *Boiling Point.*

12. Michael Shanahan and Miles Benson, "Americans Lose Their Rose-Colored Glasses," *Times-Picayune* (May 4, 1995), p. 1.

13. Thomas Byrne Edsall and Mary D. Edsall, *Chain Reaction: The Impact of Race, Rights, and Taxes on American Politics* (New York: Norton, 1991); Katherine S. Newman, *Declining Fortunes* (New York: Basic Books, 1993); Phillips, *Boiling Point.*

14. Robert Pear, "5.5 Million Children in U.S. Are Hungry," *New York Times* (March 15, 1991), p. 18.

15. See Edward S. Greenberg, *Capitalism and the American Political Ideal* (Armonk, NY: M. E. Sharpe, 1985), ch. 4.

16. On this history, see Thomas C. Cochran and William Miller, *The Age of Enterprise* (New York: Harper & Row, 1961); Greenberg, *Capitalism and the American Political Ideal;* Louis M. Hacker, *American Economic Growth and Development* (New York: Wiley, 1970); Robert Wiebe, *The Search for Order* (New York: Hill & Wang, 1967).

17. On the globalization process see Peter Dicken, *Global Shift: The Internationalization of Economic Activity* (New York: Guilford Press, 1992).

18. U.S. Department of Commerce, *International Direct Investment* (Washington, DC: U.S. Government Printing Office, 1984), p. 1.

19. Paul Kennedy, *The Rise and Fall of the Great Powers* (New York: Random House, 1987), p. 358.

20. Jennifer Hochschild, *Facing Up to the American Dream* (Princeton: Princeton University Press, 1995), ch. 1.

21. See Jennifer Hochschild, *What's Fair? American Beliefs About Distributive Justice* (Cambridge: Harvard University Press, 1981); Herbert McClosky and John Zaller,

The American Ethos: Public Attitudes Toward Capitalism and Democracy (Cambridge: Harvard University Press, 1984); Sidney Verba and Gary R. Orren, *Equality in America* (Cambridge: Harvard University Press, 1985).

22. Verba and Orren, *Equality in America,* p. 255.

23. M. Donald Hancock, *Sweden: The Politics of Post-Industrial Change* (Hinsdale, IL: Dryden Press, 1972); Kay Schlozman and Sidney Verba, *Insult to Injury* (Cambridge: Harvard University Press, 1979).

24. Alexis de Tocqueville, *Democracy in America,* vol. 2 (New York: Langley Press, 1845).

25. Adam Smith, *The Wealth of Nations* (New York: Modern Library, 1937), originally published in 1776.

26. On the domination of classical liberalism in America, see Louis Hartz, *The Liberal Tradition in America* (New York: Harcourt, Brace, 1955). But also see Rogers M. Smith, "Beyond Tocqueville, Myrdal, and Hartz: The Multiple Traditions of America," *The American Political Science Review,* Vol. 87, No. 3 (September 1993), pp. 549–566.

27. John Kenneth Galbraith, *American Capitalism* (New York: Houghton Mifflin, 1956); also see McClosky and Zaller, *The American Ethos,* pp. 270–271.

28. Russell Hanson, *The Democratic Imagination in America* (Princeton: Princeton University Press, 1985).

29. McClosky and Zaller, *The American Ethos,* p. 18.

30. Gary Wills, *Under God: Religion and American Politics* (New York: Simon & Schuster, 1991).

31. "Religious Beliefs and Practices," *Public Perspective* (August–September 1995), p. 30.

PART III

Political Linkage

In Part II, we discussed a number of fundamental *structural* factors that affect how American politics works: the Constitution, our federal system, the nature of the American society and economy, the political culture, and the international system. Throughout the remainder of the book, you will discover the pervasive effects that these factors have on political processes, governmental institutions, and public policies.

In this section, we turn to the *political linkage* level of analysis, discussing in separate chapters public opinion, the mass media, organized interest groups, political parties, elections, and social movements. These people and institutions are affected in many ways by the structural factors already discussed. They, in turn, strongly affect the governmental institutions that will be the subject of the next section of the book. They are not a formal part of government, but they directly influence what sorts of people are chosen to be government officials—who is elected president and who goes to Congress, for example. They also affect what these officials do when they are in office and what sorts of public policies result.

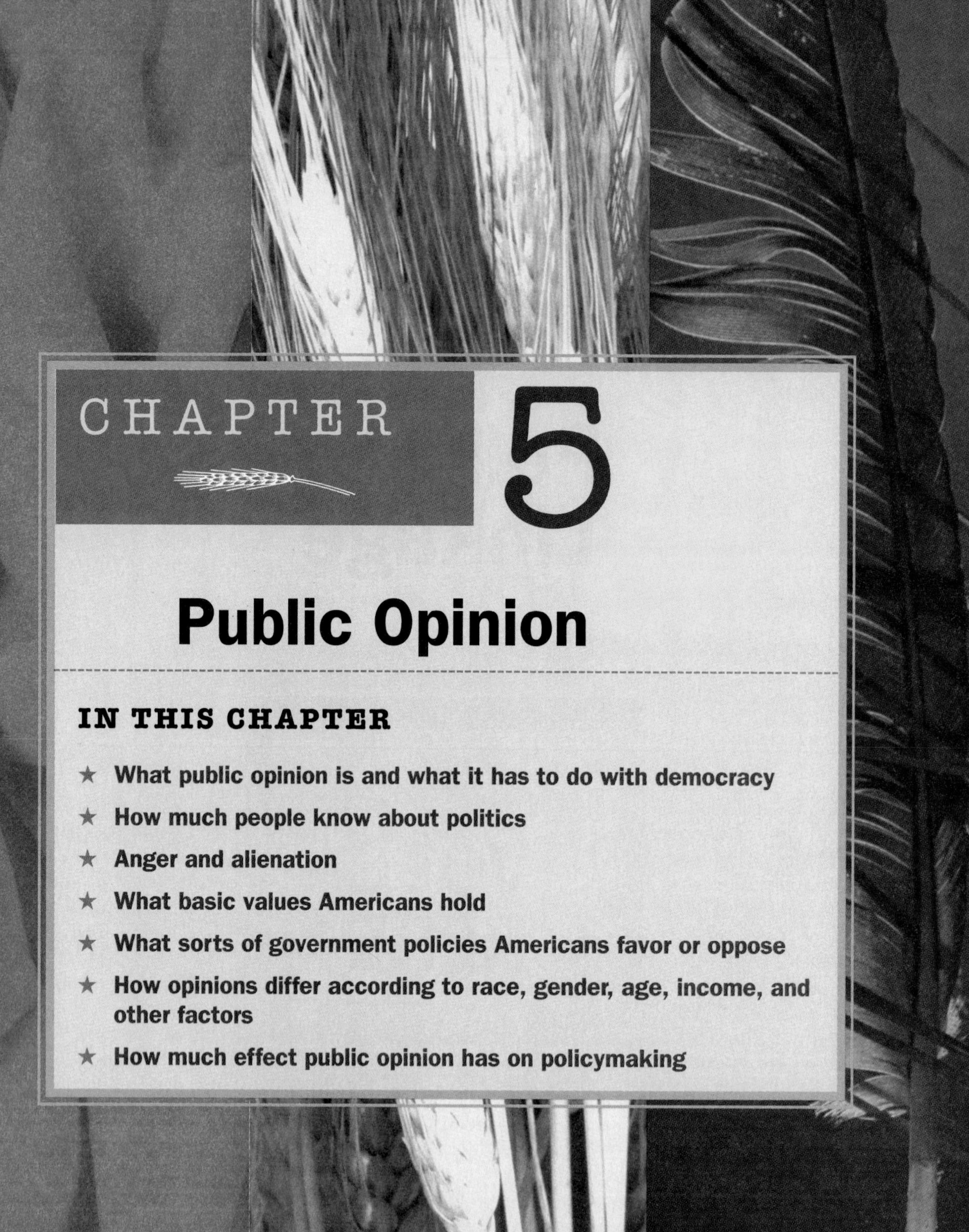

CHAPTER 5

Public Opinion

IN THIS CHAPTER

- ★ What public opinion is and what it has to do with democracy
- ★ How much people know about politics
- ★ Anger and alienation
- ★ What basic values Americans hold
- ★ What sorts of government policies Americans favor or oppose
- ★ How opinions differ according to race, gender, age, income, and other factors
- ★ How much effect public opinion has on policymaking

The Vietnam War and the Public

On August 2, 1964, the U.S. Department of Defense announced that the U.S. destroyer *Maddox,* while on "routine patrol" in international waters in the Gulf of Tonkin near Vietnam, had undergone an "unprovoked attack" by three communist North Vietnamese PT boats. Two days later, the Defense Department reported a "second deliberate attack" on the *Maddox* and its companion destroyer, the *C. Turner Joy.* At 11:37 p.m. that night, in a nationwide television broadcast, President Lyndon Johnson referred to "open aggression on the high seas" and declared that these hostile actions required that he use military force in reply. Air attacks were launched against four North Vietnamese PT boat bases and an oil storage depot.[1]

Years later, the *Pentagon Papers,* a secret Defense Department study, revealed that the American people had been deceived. The *Maddox* had not been on an innocent cruise: sailing past South Vietnamese gunboats that—with U.S. planning and support—had just raided a North Vietnamese island, it had steamed near the coastline, deliberately provoking North Vietnamese radar defenses. The second "attack" apparently never occurred; it was imagined by an inexperienced sonar man in dark and stormy seas. At the time, however, few skeptics raised questions. On August 7, 1964, by a vote of 88–2, the Senate passed the Tonkin Resolution, which approved the president's taking "all necessary measures," including the use of armed force, to repel any armed attack and to assist any ally in the region. A legal basis for full U.S. involvement in the Vietnam War had been established.

For more than a decade, the United States had been giving large-scale military aid to the French colonialists, and then to the American-installed South Vietnamese government, in order to fight nationalists and communists in Vietnam. More than 23,000 U.S. military advisers were there by the end of 1964, occasionally engaging in combat. But the American public knew and cared little about the guerrilla war. Few knew exactly where Vietnam was. People were willing to go along when their leaders told them that action was essential in order to resist communist aggression. In May 1964, among the only 37 percent of Americans who offered any opinion, three times as many wanted to maintain the present policy or get tougher (12 percent) as wanted to get out of Vietnam (4 percent).[2]

After the Tonkin incident, people paid more attention. Public support for the war increased. When asked in August what should be done next in Vietnam, 48 percent said to keep troops there, get tougher, or take definite military action; only 14 percent said negotiate or get out. Through the fall of 1964, more people wanted to step up the war than wanted to pull out, and many endorsed the current policy. In 1965, after the United States had begun the heavy "Rolling Thunder" bombing of North Vietnam, and after large numbers of U.S. troops had gradually engaged in combat in South Vietnam, public support of the war continued. Month after month, pollsters found that only small minorities wanted to withdraw from Vietnam; as many or more wanted to escalate further, and the center of gravity favored continuing the current policy.

But the number of U.S. troops in Vietnam rose rapidly, from 184,300 at the end of 1965 to 536,100 at the end of 1968, and casualties increased correspondingly. A total of 1,369 Americans were killed in 1965; 5,008 in 1966; 9,377 in 1967; and 14,589 in 1968. Many thousands more were wounded, and others were captured or missing.[3] Television news began to display weekly casualty counts in the hundreds, with pictures of dead American soldiers going home in body bags. The war became expensive, as politicians put it, in "American blood and treasure." Senate hearings aired antiwar testimony. Peace marches and demonstrations, although resented by much of the public, nonetheless increased pressure to end the war.

By December 1967, about as many people (45 percent) agreed as disagreed with the proposition that it had been a "mistake" to send troops to fight in Vietnam. A large majority said they favored "Vietnamization," that is, bringing U.S. troops home as South Vietnamese replaced them.

Then, catastrophe struck. In January 1968, during Vietnam's Tet holidays, the North Vietnamese army launched what became known as the *Tet offensive:* massive attacks throughout South Vietnam, including an assault on the U.S. embassy in Saigon. The American public was shocked by televised scenes of urban destruction and bloody corpses, of U.S. soldiers destroying Ben Tre village "in order to save it," of marines bogged down in the rubble of the ancient city Hue, and of a 77-day siege of Khe Sanh. The chief lesson seemed to be that a U.S. victory in Vietnam, if feasible at all, was going to be very costly.

The initial public reaction was to fight back. The proportion of Americans describing themselves as "hawks," who wanted to step up the military effort, rose from 52 percent in December 1967 to 61 percent in early February 1968, while the number of "doves," who wanted to withdraw from Vietnam, fell. But criticism of the war by politicians, newspaper editorials, television commentators such as Walter Cronkite, and others mushroomed. President Johnson—staggered by a surprisingly strong vote for antiwar candidate Eugene McCarthy in the New Hampshire primary—announced that he would limit the bombing of North Vietnam, seek a negotiated settlement, and withdraw as a candidate for reelection. In March 1968, only 41 percent of Americans described themselves as "hawks," a very sharp drop from the 61 percent of early February (see Figure 5.1). Anger over Vietnam contributed to the election defeat of the Democrats the following November.

By January 1969, when the new Nixon administration took office, a substantial majority of the public favored monthly reductions in the number of U.S. soldiers in Vietnam: 57 percent approved the idea, while only 28 percent disapproved. In June, Nixon announced the withdrawal of 25,000 troops, followed by announcements of 35,000 more in September, another 50,000 in December, and 150,000 during the following year. Large majorities of the public approved the withdrawals. Most said they wanted to continue them even if the South Vietnamese government collapsed. There can be little doubt that public opinion influenced U.S. disengagement from the war.

This did not mean that a majority of Americans wanted to get out of Vietnam immediately; most disliked the idea of a communist victory. But antiwar marches and demonstrations continued during 1970 and 1971, and many people wanted a faster pace of withdrawal. Gradually, U.S. troops came out of Vietnam; in January 1973, after the intensive Christmas bombing of North Vietnam, a peace agreement was finally signed. Two years later, the North Vietnamese army took control of Saigon and unified Vietnam.

The Vietnam story illustrates several important points about public opinion. Government officials can sometimes lead or manipulate opinion (as in the misrepresented Gulf of Tonkin incident), especially when it concerns obscure matters in faraway lands. Also, opinion is affected by events and circumstances, and by reports in the mass media. And public opinion, even on foreign policy matters, may have a strong impact on policymaking. In this chapter, we will explore the nature, sources, and effects of public opinion, as well as its relation to ideas about democracy.

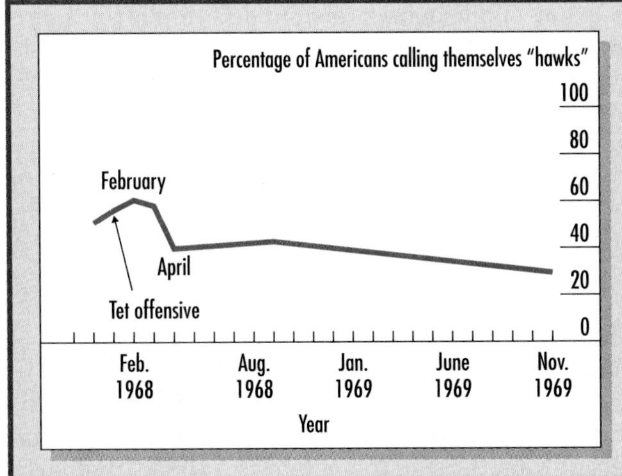

Figure 5.1 ▪ **"Hawks" Versus "Doves," 1967–1969**

The Vietnam War: After the Tet offensive of January–February 1968, the number of self-proclaimed "hawks," who wanted stronger military action in Vietnam, first rose a bit and then declined sharply. The number of "doves," who wanted a U.S. withdrawal, rose correspondingly.

Source: Gallup Surveys.

Democratic Theory and Public Opinion

The political attitudes and beliefs expressed by ordinary citizens are known collectively as **public opinion.** If democracy is, as Abraham Lincoln put it, "government of the people, by the people, and for the people," then, clearly, public opinion—especially the collective policy preferences of ordinary citizens—plays a crucial part in democratic government. In a perfect democracy, based on popular sovereignty and majority rule, the government would do exactly what its citizens wanted.

public opinion Political attitudes and beliefs expressed by ordinary citizens.

An important test of how well democracy is working, then, is how closely government policy corresponds to the expressed wishes of its citizens. To what extent does the government respond to public opinion, as opposed, say, to the demands of organized interest groups?

Curiously, however, many leading political theorists, including some who say they believe in democracy, have expressed grave doubts about the wisdom of the public. James Madison, Alexander Hamilton, and other Founders of our national government worried that the public's "passions" would infringe on liberty, and that public opinion would be susceptible to radical and frequent shifts.[4] Walter Lippmann declared that most people do not know what goes on in the world; they have only vague, media-provided pictures in their heads. Lippmann approvingly quoted Sir Robert Peel's reference to "that great compound of folly, weakness, prejudice, wrong feeling, right feeling, obstinacy and newspaper paragraphs which is called public opinion."[5]

Modern survey researchers have not been much kinder. The first voting studies, carried out during the 1940s and 1950s, turned up what scholars considered appalling evidence of public ignorance, lack of interest in politics, and reliance on group or party loyalties rather than judgments about the issues of the day. Repeated surveys of the same individuals found that their responses seemed to change randomly from one interview to another. Philip Converse, a leading student of political behavior, coined the term "nonattitudes": on many issues of public policy, many or most Americans seemed to have no real views at all but simply offered "doorstep opinions" to satisfy interviewers.[6]

What should we make of this? If ordinary citizens are poorly informed and capricious in their views, or if they have no real opinions at all, it hardly seems desirable—or even possible—that public opinion should determine what governments do. Both the feasibility and the attractiveness of democracy seem to be thrown into doubt. When we examine exactly what sorts of opinions ordinary Americans have, however, and how those opinions are formed and changed, we will see that such fears about public opinion have been greatly exaggerated.

What People Know About Politics

Years ago, those who wanted to find out anything about public opinion had to guess, based on what their barbers or taxi drivers said, or on what appeared in letters to newspaper editors, or on what sorts of one-liners won cheers at political rallies. But the views of personal acquaintances, letter writers, or rally audiences are often quite different from those of the public as a whole. Similarly, the angry people who called in to radio talk shows at the beginning of the Clinton administration tended to be more conservative and anti-Clinton than most Americans.[7] Listeners could easily get a mistaken impression of what was on their fellow citizens' minds. To figure out what the average American thinks, we cannot rely on unrepresentative groups or noisy minorities.

Gauging What People Think

sample survey An interview study asking questions of a set of people who are chosen as representative of the whole population.

A clever invention, the opinion poll or **sample survey,** now eliminates most of the guesswork in measuring public opinion. A survey consists of systematic interviews conducted by trained professional interviewers, who ask a standardized set of questions of a rather small number of randomly chosen Americans—usually about 1,000 or 1,500 of them. Such a survey can reveal with remarkable accuracy what all 260 million or so of us are thinking.

The secret of success is to make sure that the sample of people interviewed is representative of the whole population, that is, that the proportions of people in the sample who are young, old, female, college-educated, black, rural, Catholic, southern, western, and so forth are all about the same as in the U.S. population as a whole. This representativeness is achieved best when the people being interviewed are chosen through **random sampling,** which ensures that each member of the population has an equal chance of being chosen. Then, survey researchers can add up all the responses to a given question and compute the percentages of people answering one way or another. Statisticians can use probability theory to tell how close the survey's results are likely to be to what the whole population would say if asked the same questions. Findings from a random sample of 1,500 people have a 95 percent chance of accurately reflecting the whole population within about 3 or 4 percentage points.[8]

random sampling The selection of survey respondents by chance, with equal probability, in order to ensure their representativeness of the whole population.

Perfectly random sampling is not feasible. Personal interviews have to be clustered geographically so that interviewers can easily get from one respondent to another. Telephone interviews—the cheapest and most common kind—are clustered within particular telephone exchanges. Still, the samples that survey organizations use are sufficiently representative so that survey results closely reflect how the whole population would have responded if everyone in the United States had been asked the same questions at the moment the survey was carried out. (The results may apply only at that moment, however; see the Resource feature.)

When you are interpreting surveys, you need to pay close attention to the precise wording of the questions. It often makes a big difference exactly how

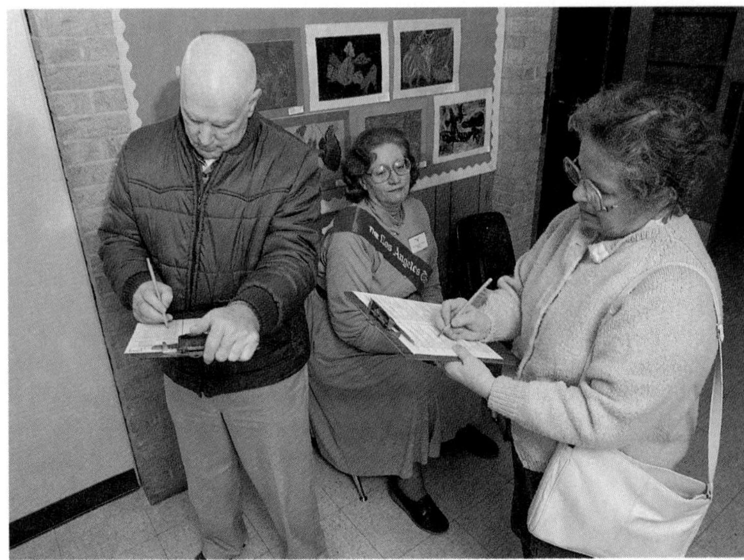

Exit polls, which survey the opinions of people as they leave the polling place after voting, are a major source of information on who votes and how they make voting decisions.

questions are asked. In one survey, for example, support for a constitutional amendment requiring a balanced budget dropped from 70 percent to 31 percent when the question specified that Medicare would be cut.[9] Moreover, "closed-ended" or "forced-choice" questions, which ask the respondents to choose among preformulated answers, do not always reveal what people are thinking on their own or what they would come up with after a few minutes of thought or discussion. For that reason, "open-ended" questions are sometimes asked to yield more spontaneous answers, and small discussion groups or "focus groups" are brought together to show what emerges when people talk among themselves about the topics a moderator introduces.

Individuals' Ignorance

Several decades of polling have shown that most ordinary Americans do not know or care a lot about politics. Nearly everyone knows some basic facts, such as the name of the capital of the United States and the length of the president's term of office. But only about two-thirds of adults know which party has the most members in the House of Representatives. Only about one-half know that there are two U.S. senators from their state, and fewer can name their representative in the House. And only about 30 percent know that the term of a U.S. House member is two years.[10]

People have particular trouble with technical terms, geography, and abbreviations. In the 1960s, only 38 percent knew that Russia was not a member of "NATO" (the North Atlantic Treaty Organization), an alliance directed against the Soviet Union. In the 1980s, very few could identify the important "SALT" negotiations (the Strategic Arms Limitation Talks) between the United States and the Soviet Union. Today, many are fuzzy about the location of such places as Bosnia, Iraq, and Haiti.

The things that most Americans don't know may not be vital, however. If citizens are aware that there is a military alliance of Western countries, for example, or that arms control talks went on between the United States and the Soviet Union, is it crucial that they recognize the acronyms *NATO* and *SALT*?

RESOURCE FEATURE

Polls and Election Results

Modern methods of polling, initially developed for market research, won political prominence with the 1936 presidential election, when George Gallup, Elmo Roper, and Archibald Crossley used sophisticated sampling and interviewing techniques to ask Americans how they were going to vote.

In previous elections, the *Literary Digest* magazine had conducted national "straw votes" by sending ballots to people listed in telephone and car-ownership directories. Those lists were quite unrepresentative of the population in the 1930s: many people did not have telephones or cars, so many lower-income citizens were left out of the straw vote. The *Literary Digest* had been lucky and had predicted several election outcomes correctly, because low-income people had been voting about the same way as everyone else. In 1936, however, poor people voted overwhelmingly for President Franklin D. Roosevelt and his New Deal, while wealthier people tended to vote against them. *Literary Digest,* underrepresenting poor people, predicted that the Republican challenger, Alf Landon, would defeat Roosevelt. But Gallup, Roper, and Crossley, with their more representative samples, all predicted victory for Roosevelt. When Roosevelt won by a landslide, scientific polling methods became the standard, and straw votes fell out of favor.

Pollsters have not entirely escaped trouble since then. In 1948, early surveys showed Republican Thomas E. Dewey so far ahead of President Harry Truman that nearly everyone became certain of a Dewey victory. Several newspapers even printed early editions declaring that Dewey had been elected. But the polling had stopped too soon and had missed a last-minute Truman surge; Truman won by a narrow margin. Since then, polls have generally kept asking questions right up to Election Day and have warned that the results hold only for the time of a poll, not necessarily for the future.

In recent decades, the polls' record of accuracy has been quite impressive. Gallup's election predictions have averaged only 1.4 percentage points off the actual results, for example. Professionally designed polls and surveys are also usually quite accurate in telling what policies Americans prefer and what values they hold, though careful attention must be paid to the wording of questions.

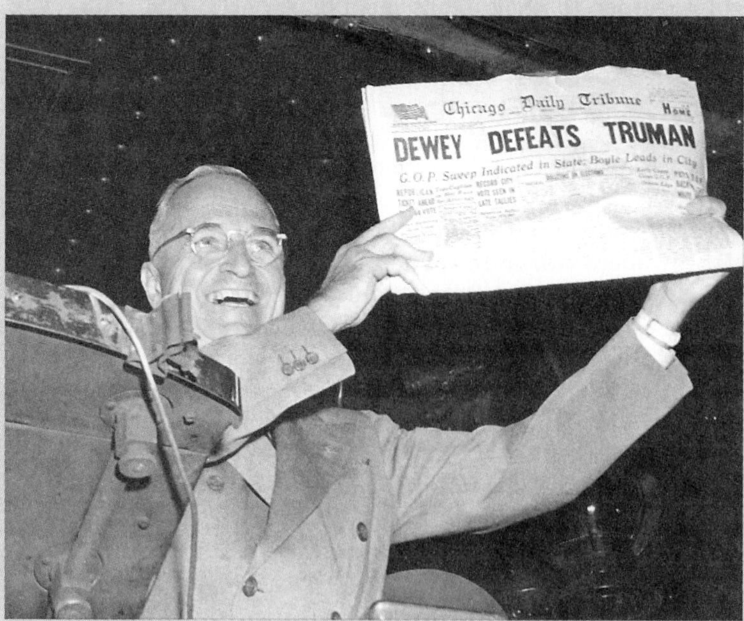

Harry Truman mocks an edition of the *Chicago Tribune* proclaiming his Republican challenger, Thomas Dewey, president. Opinion polls stopped asking questions too early in the 1948 election campaign, missing Truman's last-minute surge.

How important is it for people to know about the two-year term of office for the U.S. House of Representatives, as long as they are aware of the opportunity to vote each time it comes along? Perhaps most people know as much as they need to know in order to be good citizens, particularly if they can form opinions with the help of better-informed cue givers (experts and political leaders) whom they trust, or by means of simple rules of thumb.[11]

In any case, the lack of knowledge does not represent just stupidity or laziness. There are good reasons for it. Most people are busy with their jobs and families. They don't have much time or energy left for politics. Unless following politics happens to give them pleasure, there is little reason for them to invest much effort in it. Scholars remind us that a single citizen has only a minuscule chance of determining the outcome of an election in which thousands or millions vote; from a purely selfish point of view, it is not worth a lot of trouble to decide how to vote. The real surprise may be that people know as much as they do.[12]

We do not mean to minimize the consequences of people's lack of political knowledge. It has some extremely important implications. As we will see in Chapter 7, for example, when policy decisions are made in the dark, out of public view, interest groups may influence policies that an informed public would oppose. Nor do we mean to encourage complacency, fatalism, or ignorance. Individuals should take the personal responsibility to be good citizens, and organized efforts to alert and to educate the public are very valuable. But low levels of information are a reality that must be taken into account. It is unrealistic to expect everyone to have a detailed knowledge of a wide range of political matters.

By the same token, we should not expect the average American to have an elaborately worked out **ideology,** or system of interlocking attitudes and beliefs. You yourself may be a consistent liberal or conservative (or populist, socialist, libertarian, or something else), with many opinions that hang together in a coherent structure. (We will discuss ideologies further, below.) But surveys show that most people's attitudes are only loosely connected to each other. Most people have opinions that vary from one issue to another: conservative on some issues, liberal on others. Surveys and in-depth interviews indicate that these are often linked by underlying themes and values, but not necessarily in the neat ways that the ideologies of leading political thinkers would dictate.[13]

ideology A system of interrelated attitudes and beliefs.

For the same reasons, we should not be surprised that most individuals' expressed opinions on issues tend to be unstable. Many people give different answers when the same survey question is repeated four years, or two years, or even a few weeks after their first response. Scholars have disagreed about what these unstable responses mean, but uncertainty and lack of information very likely play a part.

Collective Knowledge and Stability

None of this, however, means that the opinions of the public, taken as a whole, are unreal, unstable, or irrelevant. The collective whole is greater than its individual parts.

Even if there is some randomness in the average individual's expressions of political opinions—even if people often say things off the top of their heads to survey interviewers—the responses of thousands or millions of people tend to average out this randomness and reveal a very stable **collective public opinion.** Americans' collective policy preferences are actually very stable over time. That is, the percentage of Americans that favors a particular policy

collective public opinion The political attitudes and beliefs of the public as a whole, expressed as averages, percentages, or other summaries of many individuals' opinions.

usually stays about the same, unless circumstances change in important ways. Year after year, for instance, very high and steady majorities of the public have said that they want to spend more on Social Security, health, aid to education, and protection of the environment. Other examples of stability in collective public opinion will be mentioned later in this chapter.

Moreover, even if most people form many of their specific opinions by deferring to those they trust (party leaders, television commentators, and the like) rather than by compiling their own mass of political information, the resulting public opinion need not be ignorant or unwise, because the trusted leaders may themselves take account of the best available information. Some recent research has indicated that Americans' collective policy preferences react rather sensibly to events, to changing circumstances, and to new information, so that we can speak of a "rational public."[14]

Not all scholars are convinced that public opinion acts rationally, but the evidence is clear, at least, that the American public as a collective whole has real opinions, not just "nonattitudes," and that many of the Founders' fears of capriciousness or fluctuations in public opinion are no longer justified, if they ever were.

How People Feel About Politics

Americans have feelings and opinions about many different political matters, including specific policies, basic values, the Republican and Democratic parties, and government itself.

Anger and Alienation

An especially important aspect of public opinion concerns general confidence or trust in government institutions. In recent years, trust and confidence have been low; many Americans have felt angry and alienated.

Since the late 1960s, more and more members of the public have expressed disillusionment with the federal government, seeing it as imposing too high taxes and wasting a lot of money. In 1992, fully 70 percent of Americans said they were "dissatisfied" with the overall performance of the national government, a feeling that contributed to the independent candidacy of Ross Perot and the defeat of President George Bush in that year. In the spring of 1993, only 25 percent of Americans said they had confidence that the federal government could be trusted to "do what is right" most of the time, compared to the 75 percent who had this confidence in 1958.[15] This sour mood contributed to the ousting of many Democratic members of Congress in 1994. Again in 1996, large majorities expressed dissatisfaction and distrust.

political efficacy The sense that one can affect what government does.

Similarly, citizens' sense of **political efficacy**—their feeling that they can make a difference, and that government will respond to their concerns—has dropped markedly. By the beginning of the 1990s, large numbers of Americans were saying that elected officials do not care what "people like me" think (66 percent said so in 1994, up from 49 percent in 1987), that government is "run for a few big interests" (75 percent), and that voting does no good.[16] Figure 5.2 shows that more and more Americans have come to believe that officials are not interested in the average person.

These feelings of anger, alienation, and mistrust may have a variety of sources, including the negative treatment of politics and politicians in the

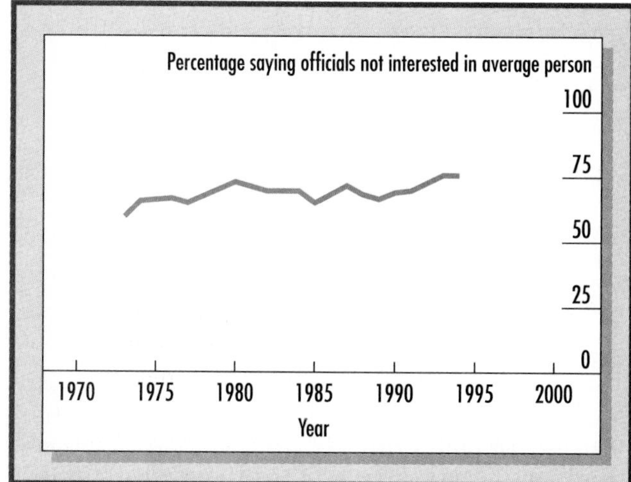

Figure 5.2 ▪ **Decline in Political Efficacy**

In recent years, high and growing numbers of Americans have said that public officials are not interested in the average person.

Source: General Social Survey data, 1973–1996.

mass media (see the next chapter). They are closely related to many people's judgments that Congress, the presidency, and the other institutions of government have simply not been performing well.

Dissatisfaction with Government Performance

One important aspect of unhappiness with politics is a judgment that the president has not been doing a good job. For many decades, pollsters have been asking people whether they approve or disapprove of "President XXX's handling of his job." The percentage of people saying that they approve—the **presidential approval rating**—is taken as a crucial indicator of a president's popularity. Trends in presidential popularity are often displayed in a sort of rising and falling "fever chart." Approval tends to fluctuate up and down with particular events, but in recent years, most presidents have come on hard times.

presidential approval rating A president's standing with the public, indicated by the percentage of Americans who tell survey interviewers that they approve a president's "handling of his job."

George Bush, for instance, maintained a fairly stable and high popularity rating of about 65 percent approval during his first two years in office; then, the Persian Gulf War boosted him to a record 89 percent approval in March 1991. But Bush's approval rating declined rather steadily and rapidly in response to economic recession, falling below 30 percent in the summer of 1992. This was one of the biggest declines in polling history. Bill Clinton began in office with an approval rating in the 50–60 percent range, but after a series of troubles, it dropped into the 40s, and by October 1994, it had fallen into the 30s. This was the largest drop ever registered in the first two years of a presidency. Only in 1995 and 1996, amidst disillusionment with the new Republican Congress, did Clinton's popularity recover somewhat.

We will see in later chapters that a president's popularity has very important consequences. It is a good predictor of whether he will win reelection and whether his party will win or lose congressional seats. Clinton's low popularity at the time of the 1994 midterm elections was an important factor in the devastating defeat of the Democratic party, which lost control of both houses of Congress for the first time in 40 years. Presidential popularity may also affect how much influence the president has in Congress and how effectively he can persuade the public to agree with his policy stands. A president who is very

POLITICS AND FILM

Government as Villain

Years before Republicans drew up their Contract with America, Hollywood scripted its own contract, which took weak and corrupt government as its target. From the compromises politicians inevitably made in their pursuit of power in *The Candidate* (1972) and the cynical view of politics in *Nashville* (1975) to Hollywood's tale about Watergate in *All the President's Men* (1976), film reflected the shifting mood of a country that was increasingly disillusioned by the Vietnam War and the Watergate scandal. The government once capable of winning World War II and ending the Great Depression seemed to have been cruelly replaced by feckless leaders who routinely lied to the people.

Today, as people's faith in politicians—as well as most institutions—plummets, the seed of antigovernment fervor reflected in the films of the 1970s has grown to an unremitting attack in the 1990s. Now antigovernment films go well beyond the implications of the earlier era to accusations of gross incompetence, treachery, and even murder.

Most recently, in *Bad Company,* a former CIA agent lists his job skills as "blackmail, bribery, subversion and the odd kidnapping," reinforcing the movie's theme that there's little distinction between an underground criminal organization and the U.S. intelligence agency. In *Murder in the First,* a young attorney discovers a government conspiracy supported by J. Edgar Hoover, the head of the FBI, to stop him from exposing the atrocities of Alcatraz.

Even comedies seem to reflect deep American anger toward government and the belief that the term *public servant* is an oxymoron. *Speechless,* a recent film about two speechwriters (reminiscent of James Carville and Mary Matalin) for opposing candidates for the U.S. Senate, shows politicians without convictions whose hands are always open to bribes.

In these movies, there's no check on the balance of evil. In *Clear and Present Danger* the National Security Adviser orders the death of Jack Ryan (Harrison Ford), the deputy director of the CIA, because Ryan gets in his way. In *Dave* the White House Chief of Staff hides the comatose president (Kevin Kline) and finds a look-alike (Mr. Kline) to serve as the puppet head of his government. The counsel in *No Way Out* defines power as the ability to shoot staff members in cold blood.

Long gone are films like *The F.B.I. Story* (1959), in which heroic agents brave the odds to defeat Public Enemy No. 1, or *Notorious* (1946), directed by Alfred Hitchcock, with Cary Grant as a federal agent willing to risk his life to fight the Nazis. Occasionally, a remake of an earlier story, like the 1987 film *The Untouchables,* starring Kevin Costner, portrays a heroic federal agent like Eliot Ness. But even he must fight a corrupt Chicago police department. Today, it's much more common to find an FBI or CIA agent in film who is responsible for the deaths of innocent children or American soldiers. A good agent, like Mr. Ford's Jack Ryan, wages a life-and-death battle against the worst public enemy of all, his own government.

Years ago, a director who suggested that corruption existed in government paid a heavy price. Frank Capra was relentlessly attacked by a Washington

popular with the public can be a political powerhouse; an unpopular president is in serious trouble.

The public's evaluations of presidents' handling of their jobs depend on how well things are actually going. The state of the economy is especially important: when the country is prosperous and ordinary Americans are doing well and feeling confident about the future, the president tends to be popular; when there is high inflation or unemployment, or when general living standards remain stagnant, the president's popularity falls. International crises may lead the public to "rally 'round the flag" and support the president (providing that leaders in both parties are doing so), but that solidarity lasts only a little while unless the crisis works out well. If bad news keeps coming, people

press corps sympathetic to the government (a quaint notion today) after the 1939 release of *Mr. Smith Goes to Washington.* The portrayal of scheming senators who lined their own pockets prompted Joseph P. Kennedy, then the U.S. ambassador to Britain, to urge the head of Columbia Pictures, Harry Cohn, to stop the release of the movie in Europe.

While filmmakers these days don't share Mr. Capra's censorship worries, they hear the message of his picture: It's up to the little guy to fight the powers that be. In *Dave,* the acting president, who used to run a temporary-employment agency, believes that good, hardworking people like him can fix a country that has been sorely misled. When Dave asks an accountant friend to help him cut the federal budget, the friend reduces the complexities of the federal budget to a simple question: "Who does these books? I mean, if I ran my business this way, I'd be out of business."

Source: Marie Laurino, "Hollywood Presents: Government as Villain," *New York Times* (February 12, 1995), p. H13.

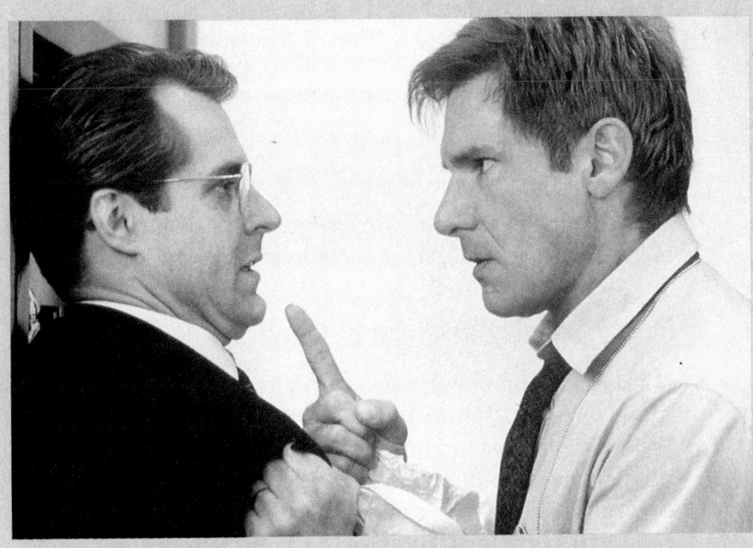

begin to disapprove of the president's performance.[17] In recent years, with economic stagnation and anxiety, the news has often been bad.

Evaluations of Congress have not been surveyed as regularly as those of the president, but it appears that Congress has often been highly unpopular. The Democratic-controlled Congress of the 1980s and early 1990s, for example, was thoroughly disliked by the time the Democrats were ousted from control in 1994. The Republican-controlled 104th Congress that took office after the 1994 elections initially won solid public support: in December 1994, 52 percent of Americans approved, while only 41 percent disapproved.[18] But this enthusiasm quickly faded; even by the spring of 1995, 57 percent disapproved of the performance of Congress, while only 34 percent approved. The 1995–1996 budget

Public opinion about the president is influenced heavily by structural factors and events. Here, George Bush and General Norman Schwarzkopf exult during a victory parade after the Persian Gulf War. As often happens in times of international crisis, Bush's popularity was boosted by the war. However, his popularity fell sharply soon after the war ended, as people turned their attention to a domestic economy mired in recession.

battles with President Clinton—especially over proposals to cut back the growth of Medicare and Medicaid—led to still further drops in the approval of Congress.

Party Loyalty and Party Decline

party identification The sense of belonging to one or another political party.

Historically, one of the most important political attitudes in the United States has been loyalty to a political party. Many Americans still feel such a loyalty. When survey researchers ask people whether, generally speaking, they consider themselves Republicans, Democrats, independents, or what, more than 60 percent pick one of the two major parties. That sense of belonging to a party is called **party identification.** Among the roughly one-third of Americans who identify themselves as independents, many say they "lean" toward one party or the other and are sometimes included among those who identify with that party.

Many people begin to identify with a party when they are rather young. Usually they adopt the same party as their parents and tend to stick with it through the rest of their lives, though the extent and strength of party identification have slipped in recent years. People use the party label to help organize their thinking about politics: to guide them in voting, in judging new policy proposals, and so on. For example, people who consider themselves Republicans are much more likely than Democrats to vote for Republican candidates and to approve of Republican presidents; they tend to belong to different social and economic groups; and they are somewhat more likely to favor policies associated with the Republican party.

For most of the time since the highly popular New Deal of the 1930s, more Americans have identified themselves as Democrats than as Republicans. The Democrats have been the majority party, with a recent peak in 1965, when 52 percent of those surveyed said they considered themselves Democrats, and only 24 percent considered themselves Republicans. But the big Democratic advantage of the 1950s and 1960s declined substantially during the 1970s, 1980s, and 1990s, when the numbers of adherents of each party began to be about even. In fact, the Republicans have sometimes had a slight lead in recent years.[19] You can see these trends in Figure 5.3.

The party balance among voters has important effects on who rules in Washington, D.C., especially on which party controls Congress.

In recent decades, along with a decline in the proportion of people who identify with one of the two parties, there has been a rise in the number of broadly defined independents (including "leaners"), from around 20 percent to nearly 40 percent of eligible voters. Although some scholars maintain that these figures exaggerate the rise of independents, because many "leaners" behave just the way people do who say they consider themselves Republicans or Democrats,[20] there has clearly been a decline in the proportion of Americans who identify strongly with either of the two major parties.

While the reasons for this decline are not completely clear, they seem to have to do with urban unrest, Watergate, hard economic times (reviewed in Chapter 4) and the disappointments of the Vietnam War, plus general alienation and doubts that either party stands for what voters want.[21] We will discuss this topic further in Chapter 8.

Basic Values and Beliefs

Of fundamental importance in politics are Americans' basic beliefs and values. Often, there is a high degree of consensus about such matters. As we saw in Chapter 4, this is especially true of certain values involving freedom, democracy, capitalism, and equal opportunity that have become part of the political culture.

Freedom It has been written that "no value in the American ethos is more revered than freedom. The rights of individuals to speak, write, assemble and

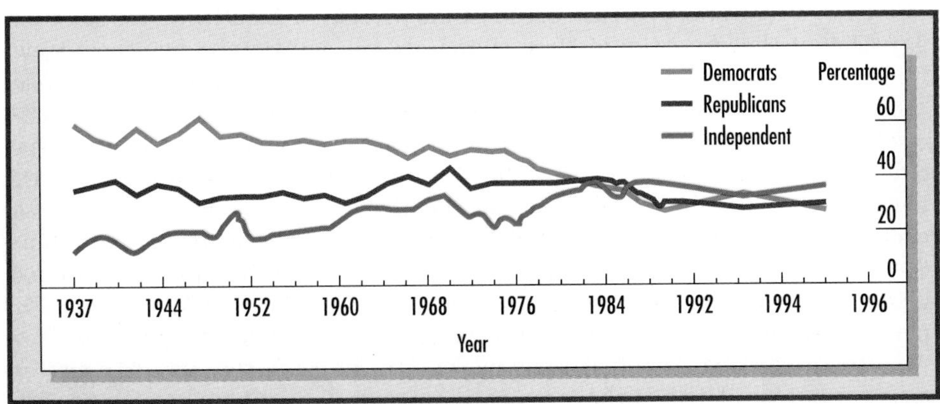

Figure 5.3 ▪ **Trends in Party Identification**

Over the years, the proportion of people calling themselves Republicans has increased, while the proportion of Democrats has decreased; the two are now roughly equal. More and more Americans call themselves independents.

Sources: The Gallup Organization, "The Gallup Poll Party ID Trend to 1937," no date; *The Gallup Report,* May 1987, pp. 16–17; January–February 1985, p. 21; *Gallup Opinion Index,* July 1979, p. 34; October 1967, p. 6; and unpublished data from the Gallup Poll.

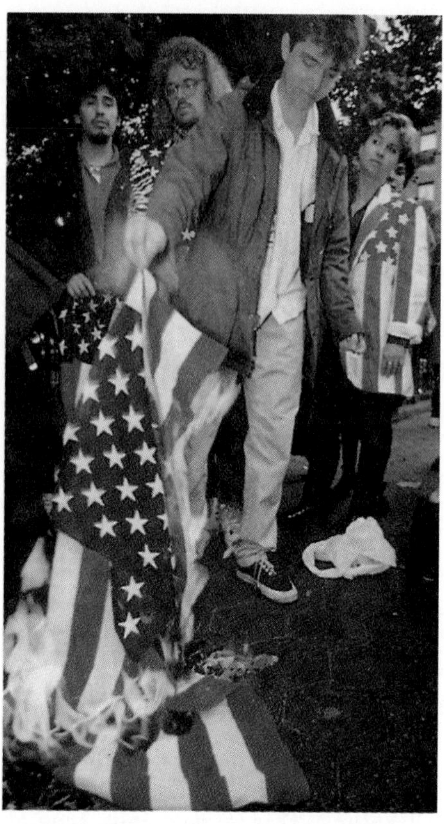

Most Americans revere the flag and oppose the liberty of others to destroy it, as these Minnesota anarchists did during a demonstration in Washington, D.C.

worship freely, to engage in occupations and pastimes of their own choosing, and to be secure from arbitrary restraints on their conduct are central to the nation's democratic tradition."[22]

A number of surveys over the years have documented this enthusiasm for liberty, at least in the abstract. Eighty-nine percent of Americans, for example, agreed that they believed in "free speech for all no matter what their views might be." Large majorities have said that freedom to worship as one pleases "applies to all religious groups, regardless of how extreme their beliefs are."[23]

This high regard for liberty in the abstract sometimes falls apart in specific cases, however, especially when it comes to extreme or threatening minorities. Many people in the 1950s opposed allowing Communists or Nazis—or even Socialists or atheists—to hold meetings, to teach school, or even to have their books in public libraries. While intolerance of those groups has lessened, many Americans favor repressing newer kinds of radicals.[24] Most people (83 percent in one survey) want flag-burning protests to be illegal. And most Americans favor censoring obscene books. The majority supports free expression but opposes letting atheists speak in a civic auditorium (see Figure 5.4). Thus, many Americans are willing to sacrifice certain people's liberty for the sake of morality and order. This attitude may pose a problem for political liberty, one of the key elements of democracy.

Economic Liberty The public is generally enthusiastic about *economic* liberty. Private ownership of property, for example, is strongly supported: 84 percent of Americans have said that it is "necessary for economic progress," and 87

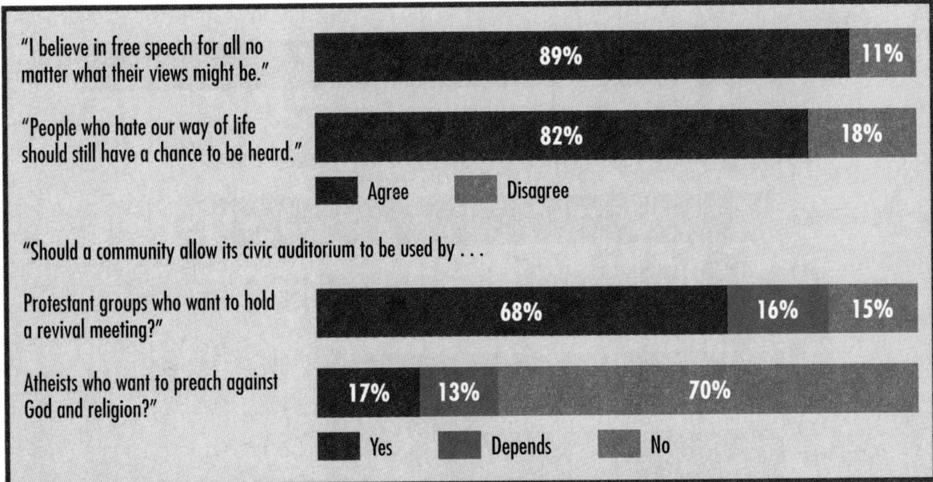

Figure 5.4 ▪ **Americans' Ambivalence About Freedom of Speech**

Overwhelming majorities say they believe in free speech, but very few would allow atheists to preach against God and religion in a civic auditorium.

Source: Herbert McClosky and John Zaller, *The American Ethos: Public Attitudes Toward Capitalism and Democracy* (Cambridge: Harvard University Press, 1984), pp. 25, 37.

percent have said that it is "as important to a good society as freedom." There is overwhelming rejection of communism or socialism. Americans so obviously believe in freedom to choose their jobs, to spend their money as they wish, and to own whatever they can afford to buy, that surveys do not even bother to ask questions about such matters.

Capitalism The word **capitalism** is not particularly popular in the United States, but the substance of it—free markets and the private ownership of the means of production—has strong support. Surveys have found that large majorities agree that "the free enterprise system [is] necessary for free government" (80 percent) and that, on the whole, our economic system is "just and wise" (77 percent). Most say that the private enterprise system is "generally a fair and efficient system," that it "gives everyone a fair chance," and that freedom depends on it. Most Americans say they believe in the idea of working hard. They think it is fair to tie economic rewards to work and that it is necessary to do so in order to get people to work.[25]

capitalism An economic system based on the private ownership of property and the existence of markets to coordinate most economic activities.

Equality Americans favor equality of opportunity, but they are not much interested in equality of result. There is not much public support for a substantial redistribution of wealth or income, especially as compared with the attitudes of citizens in other advanced industrial countries. In one survey, only 13 percent of Americans said that reducing income inequality was an "essential" government responsibility, compared to 25 percent of Britons and 29 percent of West Germans. Only 34 percent of Americans, compared to 55 percent of Britons and 60 percent of West Germans, said the same about guaranteeing jobs.[26] As Figure 5.5 indicates, even in countries like Italy, Germany, Britain, Sweden, and Canada—which already have less unequal incomes than the United States—there is more public support than in the United States for reducing income inequality further. Most Americans tend to think that people

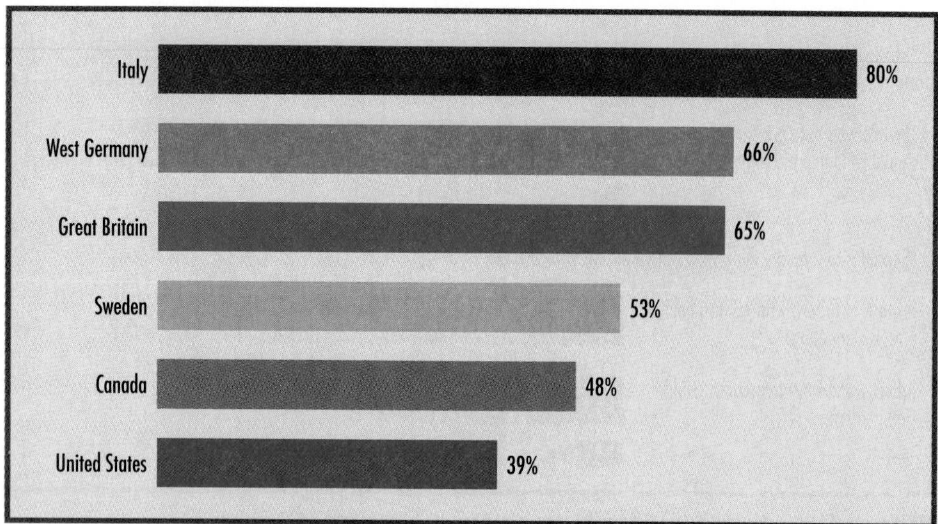

Figure 5.5 ▪ Support for Reducing Income Inequality, by Country

More people in other countries favor reducing income inequality than do in the United States.
Source: ISSP surveys, 1992. Reported in *Public Perspective,* April–May 1995.

should generally be left to get ahead on their own, as long as they have a fair start.

equality of opportunity An equal chance to get ahead economically and socially.

This does not mean that people want unrestrained private enterprise, however. For one thing, there is an overwhelming sentiment in favor of **equality of opportunity:** most Americans think that everyone should have an equal chance to do well and that government should help make sure that they can. In one survey, fully 98 percent agreed that "everyone in America should have equal opportunities to get ahead," and 98 percent also agreed that "children should have equal education opportunities."

Moreover, most Americans believe in some sort of safety net for those who fall behind in the competitive race and who cannot help themselves. For decades, most Americans have favored a whole series of government social programs, such as old-age pensions and help with education, medical care, and jobs, that depart from a pure free enterprise system. "Big business" is unpopular, too. Most of the public favors various kinds of government regulation of business, in the public interest, especially for protection of the environment.

conservatives Those who favor private enterprise and oppose government regulations or spending; the term sometimes also refers to those who favor military strength or the enforcement of traditional social values.

liberals Those who favor government regulation of business and government spending for social programs; the term sometimes also refers to those who favor international cooperation or favor civil liberties and diverse lifestyles.

Conflicts Among Values The ideas of equal opportunity, regulation, and safety nets may conflict with the ideas of economic liberty and capitalism. How, for example, can the poor be helped without the taxation of people who have higher incomes and thus, perhaps, limitations on their liberty? How can the children of the poor get opportunities that are equal to those of the children of the rich without a redistribution of income or restrictions on the freedom of the rich to spend money on their own children? On the other hand, how free can people be if they are desperately poor?

Some Americans (those who call themselves economic **conservatives**) tend to put more emphasis on economic liberty and freedom from government interference. Others (known as **liberals**) stress equality of opportunity and the need for government regulation and safety nets. Government regulation of the economy and spending to help the disadvantaged are two of the main sources of political disputes in America; they make up a big part of the difference between the ideologies of liberalism and of conservatism.

Confusingly, however, the terms *liberalism* and *conservatism* are also used to refer to positions on other issues, such as foreign policy ("hawks" who favor interventionism and the use of military force are sometimes called *conservatives*), and—most important—such social issues as abortion, prayer in the schools, homosexuality, pornography, crime, and political dissent. Those who favor free choices and the rights of the accused are often said to be liberals, while those preferring government enforcement of order and traditional values are called conservatives. This may be why more Americans identify themselves as "conservatives" than as "liberals" (37 percent vs. 27 percent in one recent survey), even though large majorities favor many liberal economic policies.[27]

Opinions on economic and social issues do not necessarily go together, however. Many people are liberal in some ways but conservative in others. Additional terms, such as **populist** (economically liberal but socially conservative) and **libertarian** (economically conservative but socially liberal), are sometimes useful.

populists Those who are liberal on economic issues but conservative on social issues.

libertarians Those who are conservative on economic issues but liberal on social issues.

Democracy The American public strongly believes in democracy—especially in popular sovereignty, political equality, and majority rule. According to one early survey, 95 percent agreed that "every citizen should have an equal chance to influence government policy."[28] Overwhelming majorities of Americans say that public officials should be chosen by majority vote (95 percent); that everyone is entitled to the same legal rights and protections no matter what their political beliefs are (93 percent); and that people in the minority should be free to try to win majority support for their opinions (89 percent).[29]

Support for majority rule and popular control of government is rock solid, as is evident in the strong public opposition to any arrangements that are thought to dilute democracy, even the electoral college (which can elect presidents with only a minority of the nationwide vote) or proposals for longer presidential terms (which would tend to insulate presidents from control by the voters). In past surveys, for example, 67 percent have approved of getting rid of the electoral college, and 70 percent have opposed a six-year presidential term.[30]

Policy Preferences

According to democratic theory, one of the chief determinants of what governments do should be what the citizens *want* them to do, that is, citizens' **policy preferences.** We can learn a lot about Americans' policy preferences from graphs that show what percentages of the public have favored various government policies at different times. Besides showing which sorts of policies have been favored and which have been opposed, these graphs indicate that collective public opinion is generally stable, and that the public often distinguishes sharply among different policy alternatives.

policy preferences Citizens' preferences concerning what policies they want government to pursue.

Spending Programs As Figure 5.6 indicates, for example, large and rather stable majorities of Americans (60 or 70 percent in recent years) have thought that we are spending "too little" on fighting crime and on education. These are very popular programs. The public has given similarly high and stable support to Social Security (in one recent survey, 49 percent said we were spending "too little" on Social Security, while only 7 percent said "too much"[31]), and to

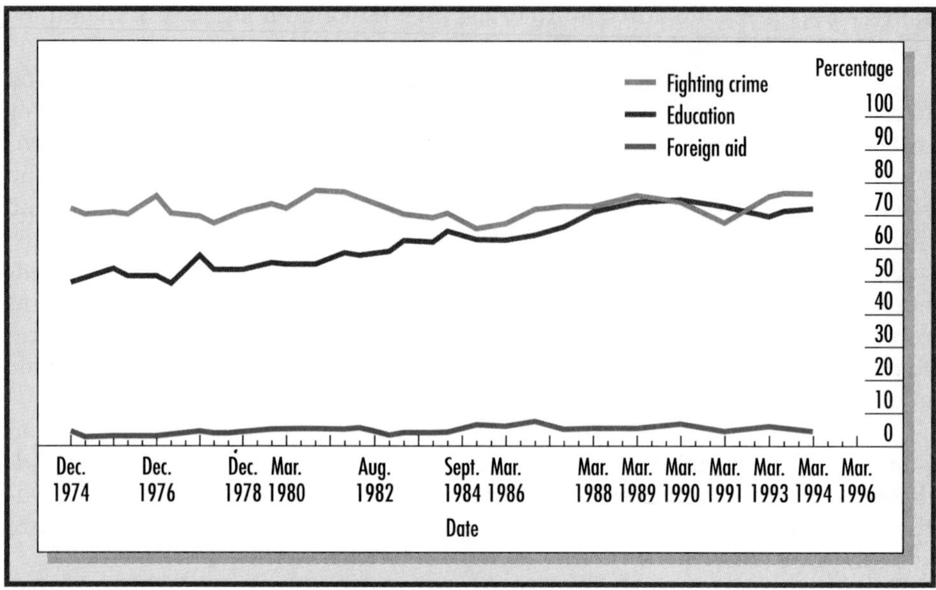

Figure 5.6 ▪ Public Support for Spending Programs

Large, fairly stable majorities of Americans have favored increased spending for fighting crime and aiding education, but very few have favored increased foreign aid.

Source: Data from NORC GSS surveys.

environmental programs and government help with medical expenses. This was true even while major cuts in domestic programs were being proposed by the Republican 104th Congress. Large majorities favor guaranteeing universal access to health care and having the government in Washington "see to it that people have help in paying for doctors and hospital bills."[32]

By contrast, very few people—only about 5 percent—have thought too little was being spent on foreign aid; many more think too much is being spent. Except for disaster relief, foreign aid is generally unpopular. (The reason may be, in part, that few realize how little is spent on foreign aid: only about 1 percent of the budget. When this is made clear, support for economic aid rises sharply.[33]) Large majorities of the public oppose military aid or arms sales abroad. The space program wins only a little more support.

Defense spending has had high public approval during wars and crises, but in recent years—especially after the end of the Cold War—more people have wanted to cut than to increase military spending.[34] Most Americans would prefer to shift financial resources from the military to domestic problems.

Some observers have claimed to see a recent conservative shift in public opinion. No substantial shift of this sort can be discerned in most survey questions about spending policies, although there are signs of less enthusiasm for spending specifically to help the poor, and of extensive support for shifting policy responsibilities from the federal government to the states. Large majorities also favor deficit reduction, at least in general terms (in one survey, for example, 81 percent favored a balanced budget amendment to the Constitution, and only 12 percent were opposed), but most of this support disappears if it is suggested that Social Security, Medicare, or education spending would be cut.[35]

Social Issues As Figure 5.7 shows, Americans make sharp distinctions among different circumstances when deciding whether they favor permitting abortions. During most of the 1980s and into the 1990s, about 90 percent of Americans have favored allowing legal abortion if a woman's health is endangered. About 80 percent would permit abortion in cases of serious birth defects. But only about 40 or 50 percent approve of abortion if a woman is poor or simply wants no more children.

This same graph indicates how approval of abortion under each of the different circumstances rose markedly between 1965 and the early 1970s. Since no surveys were conducted for several years in between, we cannot tell exactly when public opinion changed or how smoothly it did so, but nearly all of the change occurred before the U.S. Supreme Court's *Roe v. Wade* decision in January 1973, which declared that the Constitution protects a woman's right to have an abortion. Changing public attitudes may have affected the Court's decision; they did not result from it.

Other surveys have revealed strong liberalizing trends, over many years, concerning civil rights and civil liberties. Beginning in the 1940s or 1950s, more and more Americans have favored having black and white children go to the same schools and integrating work, housing, and public accommodations. (At the same time, however, there is considerable opposition to busing and affirmative action.[36]) More and more members of the public have also favored letting various dissenting groups (Communists, Socialists, atheists, and others) teach school, speak in public, and have their books in libraries. These trends are discussed further in Chapter 17.

Attitudes about the rights of homosexuals are more complicated. Although large majorities of the public, on the order of 70 percent, have long declared homosexuality to be "always wrong," increasing majorities have opposed having homosexual relations declared illegal or keeping homosexual men and women out of most kinds of jobs. But many people have said gays should not be

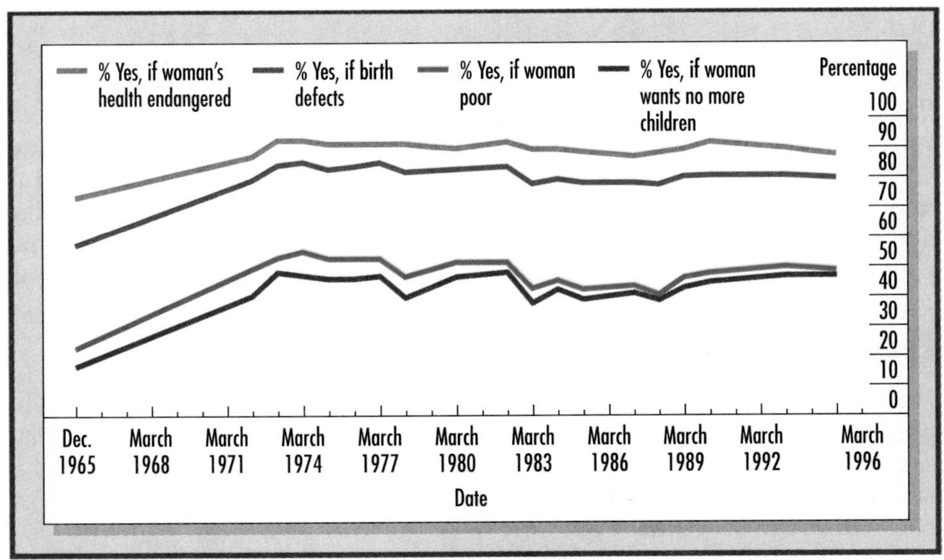

Figure 5.7 ■ Public Approval for Allowing Abortions

Public opinion about abortion varies greatly with the circumstances. Large majorities favor allowing abortions if the woman's health is endangered or in the case of serious birth defects, but only about half the public would allow abortions in cases of poverty or simply wanting no more children.

Source: Data from NORC GSS surveys.

schoolteachers or members of the clergy, and after the uproar at the beginning of the Clinton administration, small majorities have opposed allowing openly gay men and women to serve in the military.[37]

On a number of issues, Americans are socially conservative. Large majorities, for example, favor allowing organized prayer in the public schools, banning pornography, preventing flag burning, penalizing drug use, punishing crimes severely, and imposing capital punishment for murder. On the other hand, large majorities favor various kinds of gun regulation, which are thought of as liberal measures.

Foreign Policy In the realm of foreign policy, public opinion sometimes changes rapidly. Major international events affect opinions, as we saw in the case of "hawks" and "doves" after the Tet offensive during the Vietnam War. But often, foreign policy opinions are quite stable. Since World War II, for example, two-thirds or more of those giving an opinion have usually said that the United States should take an "active part" in world affairs. The exact percentage favoring an active role has varied somewhat, rising to a peak of about 83 percent in 1965, near the onset of the Vietnam War; dropping to about 62 percent after the failure of that war; and recovering a bit in later years. But the percentage has remained consistently high, not fluctuating much with alleged public "moods."[38]

As we have seen, however, general support for internationalism does not imply support for foreign aid (opposition to military aid is especially high), and the public has been quite hesitant to use U.S. troops abroad. Just before U.S. troops were sent as peacekeepers to Bosnia, for example, 78 percent of the public opposed the idea, and only 17 percent were in favor.[39] Opposition faded as the operation began to look less risky, but any substantial casualties abroad arouse large-scale public disapproval.

Sources of Political Attitudes

political socialization Teaching and learning about politics.

Where do all of these political attitudes and opinions come from? Political learning, sometimes called **political socialization,** begins when people are very young. Their families and schools play a key role as agents of socialization. However, people continue to form and to change their political attitudes and beliefs throughout their lives, as they are exposed to new experiences and political events.

Family

Most children get their first ideas about politics from their parents and siblings. Very early, perhaps by the age of 5 or 6, they learn that they are Americans, living in a free country. They begin to hear about the existence of a government headed by a distant but powerful president, who is often seen as paternal and benevolent.

Before long, by about the second or third grade, many children begin to learn that "we" (our family) are Republicans or Democrats, just as "we" are Baptists or Jews or Catholics. At first, this idea doesn't have much content; the two parties are regarded as being rather like two sports teams, and we root for ours against the opposition. But gradually, children learn that the parties stand for somewhat different things. "We" believe that government should do some things and not do others.

"My grandson, needless to say, is also pro-Reagan."

Children often inherit their political party affiliations from their families and friends.
By Lorenz; © The New Yorker Magazine, Inc.

Most children—though certainly not all—adopt their parents' party identification and keep it the rest of their lives. One leading study, based on interviews with high school students and their parents, found that 59 percent of the young people identified with the same party as their parents.[40]

It was once thought that this identification represented a blind "habit," and that people mindlessly carried on their parents' party tradition, even if it made no sense in their own lives. But people inherit more than a party label from their parents; party loyalty tends to come along with ethnicity, religion, and the values, beliefs, and practices that form a person's identity. Moreover, people's life circumstances—their levels of education, types of occupation, places of residence, and so on—often resemble those of their parents, so that a party affiliation that makes sense for the parents may make sense for them, too. Finally, it has become clear that, when people's circumstances or opinions change, they *do* often change party loyalty; this loyalty is not a rigid habit. The recent defections of southern whites from the Democratic to the Republican party, as well as the widespread decline of party identification in the face of escalating political dissatisfaction and alienation, show that party loyalties are not set in concrete.

Schools

When children go to school, they are exposed both to classroom teaching and to interaction with other students. In class, they salute the American flag and talk about "liberty and justice for all." The president and the U.S. government become more familiar. The idea of democracy is introduced, often through voting for class officers and straw votes for presidential candidates. Ideas about order and authority are conveyed by the system of classroom discipline.

Schools play an important role in shaping Americans' political opinions and values. Patriotism is encouraged from the early grades, when students learn the traditional Pledge of Allegiance.

From their peers, grade-schoolers learn a bit more about "us" and "them": Republicans and Democrats. A national election may come along, stimulating discussion of what the parties stand for. A few policy issues are mentioned. Environmental concerns, for example, which fit well with young children's interest in plants and animals, are often emphasized in class and on the playground.

In later grades and in high school, the political lessons become more explicit. Social studies, history, and civics classes describe the structure of the U.S. government and often argue the virtues of liberty, democracy, and equal opportunity. Slightly different lessons are taught in different communities: middle- and upper-middle-class children, for example, may be encouraged more often than working-class children to get out and make the system work for them. Compared with white children, black children are less likely to say that the government is "very helpful," but black high school students seem to respond more than white students to civics instruction.[41] All are taught the duty to vote. A few get involved in protests and demonstrations.

Of course, political learning does not stop in high school; experiences in college and throughout life make a difference, too. But by the time they reach their 20s, most Americans have a reasonably well-formed set of basic values, a sense of belonging to a political party, some evaluations of government performance, and some policy preferences. In one survey, for example, fully 88 percent of first-year college students said that the government was not doing enough to control pollution.[42]

Workplace and Home

When young adults go to work for the first time, economic realities suddenly become more pressing, and government policies concerning taxes, job creation, unemployment insurance, pensions, and the like begin to have personal relevance. Some people adjust their party loyalties, even their worldviews and ideologies. Liberal idealists may begin to worry more about economic efficiency, keeping taxes low, and meeting a payroll. Conservative enthusiasts of free enterprise, finding themselves at the mercy of market forces (perhaps being laid off or losing their health insurance), may begin to hanker for government protection. Working-class and poor people generally develop more sympathy for the underdog than do those who are making a lot of money. The unemployed sometimes become less enthusiastic about the American dream.[43]

There are also indications that the organization of the workplace makes a difference. Assembly line workers, used to taking orders, tend not to participate actively in politics unless a strong labor union mobilizes them—as few now do. Workers in cooperatively owned and operated businesses, like the plywood plants of the Northwest, tend to participate more.[44] Owners of small businesses, on their own against a sometimes hostile world, learn to push government to get what they want. Corporate executives take for granted that politicians will pay attention when they call.

As people establish homes and families, they begin to worry about property taxes, schools for their children, protection against crime, and efficient garbage collection. They tend to get more involved in politics.

Events and the Media

What happens in the political world often changes people's attitudes and beliefs. This is especially true of the young, who tend to solidify their policy preferences and party loyalties in response to historical events at the time they come of age, be it the Great Society, the Vietnam War, the Reagan years, or the turmoil of the 1990s. But it is true of adults, too. People change their evaluations of presidents quickly when surprisingly good or bad things happen. They also adjust their policy preferences to new circumstances, as in the case of Vietnam, the end of the Cold War, and other issues we have mentioned. Party loyalties, once thought to be virtually immune to change, are now known to adjust to the parties' performances in war and peace and to their management of the economy.[45]

Of course, political events do not always speak for themselves; often, they become known to the public only through the mass media, which may bring particular biases or points of view to bear. As we will discuss further in Chapter 6, when the mass media report experts', commentators', and political leaders' interpretations of what is going on, these have significant effects on public opinion. Public debate and discussion, even by protestors and holders of minority views, may play a critical role in helping the public to change its opinions; hence the importance of protecting the right of free speech, the subject of the Struggle for Democracy feature.

Economic and Social Structure

The various sources of political learning (or "agents of socialization") sometimes affect different people in different ways, but often, millions of Americans learn the *same* ideas and attitudes, based on a common history and shared experiences with the American economy, culture, and society. These *structural* factors have profound effects on American public opinion and make it different in important ways from public opinion in other countries.

Americans' deep commitment to democracy, for example, undoubtedly stems from more than 200 years of generally successful experience with democratic

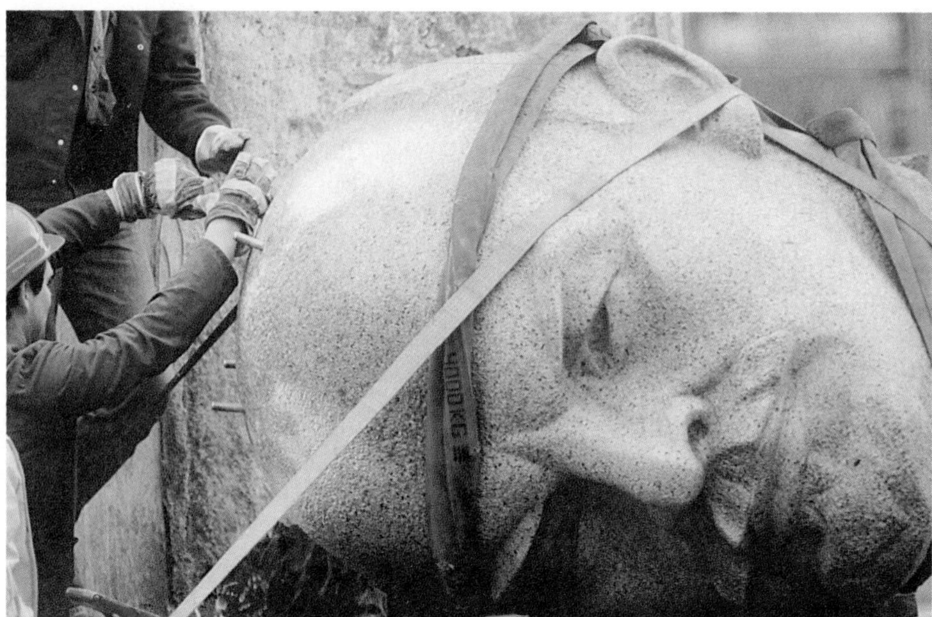

Major domestic or international events have a strong influence on public opinion, and media coverage plays a role in the degree to which public opinion is swayed. The collapse of Communism and the end of the Cold War—symbolized to many Americans by the destruction of the Berlin Wall and demolition of Communist statues—diverted the public's attention from international security issues and toward domestic problems such as the economy.

institutions, and from social conditions that help make democracy work: economic affluence (for most people) and high levels of education. People in Russia, China, Angola, or El Salvador, with different histories and different social conditions, do not so universally support democratic procedures.

Similarly, the American public's enthusiasm for political and economic liberty, as well as its embrace of the idea of private property and a free enterprise system, has a lot to do with the existence of a free enterprise economy in the United States and with its success in producing abundant consumer goods and high standards of living. The particular vision of equal opportunity found in the United States also has roots in American history, particularly in the successful absorption of diverse immigrant groups.

The economic and social structures that have shaped our basic values of democracy, liberty, equality, and the like have also affected many of our policy preferences, such as the reluctance to have government interfere with the economy and (at the same time) the desire for social policies that soften the impact of the market. Similarly, the shape of the international system, the U.S. position as a superpower, and the friendly or unfriendly acts of other nations all affect what kinds of foreign policy we favor.

Structural changes bring about changes in policy preferences. The end of the Cold War and the breakup of the Soviet Union, for example, led people to favor arms control and cuts in military spending. The rise of international economic competition since the 1970s, and the hard economic times it has brought, has had widespread consequences that may include political anger and alienation, the decline of the political parties, lowered support for government spending, opposition to immigration, a resentment of minorities, and an upswing in religious faith.

Abrams and Free Speech

The Struggle for Democracy

Informed public opinion requires vigorous public debate. The freedom of speech that we enjoy today has emerged through a series of political struggles and U.S. Supreme Court cases, including *Abrams et al. v. United States* (1919).

In August 1918, five Russian-born immigrants in New York City printed and distributed 5,000 leaflets that attacked the "hypocrisy" of the "coward" President Woodrow Wilson for sending U.S. troops to intervene in the Russian Revolution. They denounced capitalism as the "enemy of the workers of the world"; asserted that ammunition factories were producing bullets, bayonets, and cannon "to murder not only the Germans, but also your dearest, best, who are in Russia and are fighting for freedom"; and called for a general strike.

The five were tried, convicted, and sentenced to 20 years in prison under the Espionage Act of 1918, for conspiring, while the United States was at war with Germany, to publish "disloyal, scurrilous and abusive language about the form of Government of the United States" and language intended to encourage resistance to the war and the curtailment of war production. The five appealed their conviction on the grounds that the First Amendment to the Constitution protects freedom of speech and the press. The Supreme Court ruled against them.

The five immigrants went to jail, but what is remembered from *Abrams* is the eloquent defense of free speech in Justice Oliver Wendell Holmes's dissenting opinion. Holmes, while expressing no agreement with the "creed of ignorance and immaturity" in the leaflets, denied that the defendants had actually attacked the U.S. form of government or specifically intended to cripple the prosecution of the war. Even if they had, no harm had been done, and no more than nominal punishment should be inflicted. Holmes declared that "we should be eternally vigilant against attempts to check the expression of opinions that we loathe and believe to be fraught with death, unless they so imminently threaten immediate interference with the lawful and pressing purposes of the law that an immediate check is required to save the country." (This statement resembles the "clear and present danger" test that Holmes enunciated in *Schenck v. United States,* also in 1919.)

Persecution for the expression of ideas, Holmes acknowledged, is tempting: "But when men have realized that time has upset many fighting faiths, they may come to believe that . . . the ultimate good desired is better reached by free trade in ideas—that the best test of truth is the power of the thought to get itself accepted in the competition of the market."

Our present constitutional protections of free speech, which have advanced a great deal since the time of *Abrams,* are discussed in Chapter 17.

Supreme Court Justice Oliver Wendell Holmes, Jr.

When we think about public opinion as a source of influence on policymaking, it is important to remember that public opinion is itself shaped by structural factors. This is one of the ways in which the economic and social structure of the United States and the shape of the international system affect U.S. government policy.

How People Differ

In talking about American public opinion as a collective whole, we should not ignore important distinctions among different sorts of people in different circumstances. Black people and white people; Catholics, Jews, and Protestants; southerners and northeasterners; poor people and rich people; women and men—all tend to differ in their political attitudes.

Race and Ethnicity

Among the biggest differences are those between white and black Americans. Hispanics and Asian-Americans also have some distinctive political opinions. Many white ethnic groups, however, are no longer much different from other members of the population.

African-Americans Blacks, who stayed loyal to the Republican party (the party of Lincoln) long after the Civil War, became Democrats in large proportions with the New Deal of the 1930s. Most black Americans have remained Democrats, especially since the civil rights struggles of the 1960s.[46] Today, African-Americans are the most solidly Democratic of any group in the population: some 70 percent call themselves Democrats, while only about 6 percent call themselves Republicans (see Figure 5.9). In the 1994 congressional elections, 88 percent of African-Americans cast their votes for Democratic candidates, compared to only 42 percent of whites.[47]

Black Americans also tend to be much more liberal than whites on economic issues, especially those involving aid to minorities or help with jobs, housing, medical care, education, and so on, as indicated in Figure 5.8. This liberalism reflects African-Americans' economically disadvantaged position in American society and the still-real effects of slavery and discrimination. On

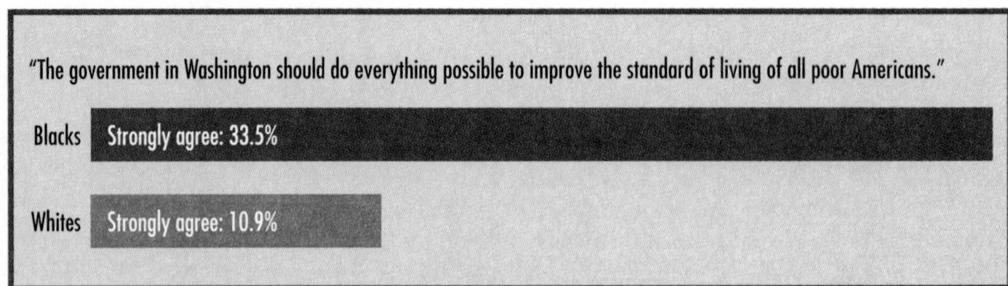

Figure 5.8 ▪ Government Help for the Poor

Many more black than white Americans feel that the government should improve the standard of living of poor people.

Source: NORC General Social Survey Cumulative Data Set, 1991–1994.

some social issues, however, blacks tend to hold strong religious values and to be rather conservative: more are opposed to abortion, for example, than are whites. Overall, many more blacks consider themselves "liberal" (36 percent in 1994) as consider themselves "conservative" (24 percent, the rest being "moderate"), while the proportions among white voters are almost exactly reversed.[48]

Hispanics Hispanics or Latinos—people of Spanish-speaking background—represent the fastest-growing ethnic group in America, numbering more than 23 million, or 9 percent of the population.[49] However, the Hispanic population itself is quite diverse. Cuban-Americans, many of them refugees from the Castro regime, tend to be conservative, Republican, strongly anti-Communist, and skeptical of government programs. The much more numerous Americans of Mexican or Puerto Rican ancestry, on the other hand, are mostly Democrats and quite liberal on economic matters, though rather traditional on social questions—reflecting their predominant Roman Catholicism.

Hispanics are one of the least politically active groups in the United States. Only about 29 percent of eligible Hispanics vote in presidential elections, compared with about 64 percent of non-Latino whites and 54 percent of blacks.[50] Low incomes, suspicion of the authorities, and lack of facility with the English language discourage participation. The Hispanic community's low participation rate and its internal divisions make it a sleeping giant in American politics, capable of great influence—especially in such key states as Texas, California, and Florida—but not yet making its weight fully felt.

Asian-Americans Asian-Americans, a small but growing part of the U.S. population, come from quite diverse backgrounds in Japan, Korea, Vietnam, China, and elsewhere. As a group, Asian-Americans have tended to be successful educationally and economically, to participate fairly actively in politics, and to be conservative and Republican.

White Ethnics Other ethnic groups are not so distinctive in their political opinions. Irish-Americans and people of Italian, Polish, and other southern or eastern European ancestry, for example, became strong Democrats as part of the New Deal coalition. But as they achieved success economically, their economic liberalism faded, and their social conservatism prevailed. By the 1980s, these groups were not much different from average Americans.

Religion

Ethnic differences are often interwoven with differences in religious faith and values.

Catholics Roman Catholics, who constitute about 26 percent of the U.S. population, were heavily Democratic after the New Deal but now resemble other Americans in their party affiliations. Catholics' economic liberalism has faded somewhat with rises in their income, though this liberalism remains substantial. Catholics have tended to be especially concerned with family issues and to espouse measures to promote morality (e.g., antipornography laws) and law and order. But most American Catholics disagree with many church teachings: they support birth control and the right to have abortions in about the same proportions as do other Americans. Two-thirds favor allowing priests to marry and allowing women to be priests.[51]

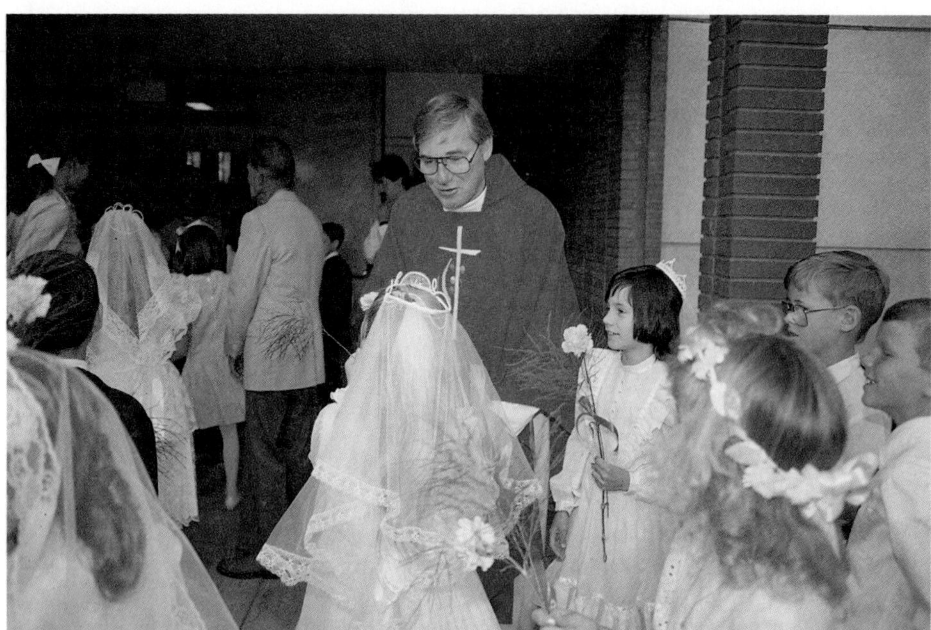

First communion at a Roman Catholic church in Tarzana, California. Catholics, who constitute about one-fourth of the U.S. population, tend to be economically liberal and socially conservative.

Jews American Jews (only about 2 percent of the U.S. population) began to join the Democratic party in the 1920s and did so overwhelmingly in the 1930s, in response to Franklin D. Roosevelt's New Deal social policies and his foreign policy of resisting Hitler. Most Jews have stayed with the party. Next to African-Americans, they remain the most Democratic group in the United States: about 47 percent identify themselves as Democrats, and only 23 percent as Republicans.[52] In the 1994 congressional elections, Jews cast 78 percent of their vote for Democratic House candidates, and only 22 percent for Republicans.[53]

Jews are exceptionally liberal on such social issues as civil liberties and abortion. They also tend to be staunch supporters of civil rights, despite tensions with blacks over such matters as U.S. policy toward Israel and the Palestinians, and anti-Semitic remarks by some black leaders. Rising incomes have somewhat undercut Jews' economic liberalism, but they remain substantially more supportive of social welfare policies than other groups.

Mormons The 4 million or so Mormons, members of the fast-growing Church of Jesus Christ of Latter-day Saints, are distinguished by being the most staunchly conservative and most solidly Republican of any major religious denomination. A survey at the beginning of the 1990s found that Mormons were 51 percent Republican and only 23 percent Democrat, whereas Presbyterians were 44 percent Republican (28 percent Democrat), Episcopalians 41 percent Republican (25 percent Democrat), and Lutherans 37 percent Republican (26 percent Democrat).[54]

Protestants Protestants, who constitute a large majority of Americans, do not differ much from the U.S. average in most respects. But Protestants come in many varieties, from the relatively high-income (socially liberal, economically conservative) Episcopalians and Presbyterians, to the generally liberal Universalist-Unitarians and middle-class northern Baptists, to the lower-income and quite conservative Southern Baptists and evangelicals of various denominations.

In the early 1980s, evangelical Christians played an important part in the "new right" segment of Ronald Reagan's conservative movement, working hard against abortion, against pornography, for law and order, and for their version of family values. Some, disappointed by failures to achieve their national goals at that time, turned toward local and state politics and had considerable success in picketing and disrupting abortion clinics, changing public school curricula, and pushing anti-gay-rights referenda. The Christian Coalition provided much energy and activism for the Republicans' 1994 congressional election victory. Fully 76 percent of white born-again Christians voted for Republican House candidates in that year, while only 24 percent voted for Democrats.[55]

Region

It is still true that "the South is different." Regional differences have been reduced because of years of migration by southern blacks to northern cities, the movement of industrial plants and northern whites to the Sun Belt, and economic growth catching up with that of the North. But the large black population and the primarily agricultural economy of the South have put their stamp on southern politics to the present day.

Even now, white southerners tend to be somewhat less enthusiastic about civil rights than northerners; only people from the Rocky Mountain West are nearly as conservative on racial issues.[56] Southerners also tend to be conservative on social issues, such as school prayer, crime, women's rights, and abortion, and supportive of military spending and a strong foreign policy (though fairly liberal on economic issues, such as job guarantees and health insurance).

These distinctive policy preferences have undercut southern whites' traditionally strong identification with the Democratic party, especially since the 1960s and 1970s, when the national Democrats became identified with liberal social policies and antiwar foreign policy. The switch to the Republican party of the white South in the 1994 elections, in fact, is one of the major reasons Republicans were able to win control of Congress. Figure 5.9 shows differences in party loyalties among regional and other social groups.

On many issues northeasterners tend to be the most different from southerners, with midwesterners, appropriately, in the middle. Pacific Coast residents resemble northeasterners in many respects, but people from the Rocky Mountain states tend to be quite conservative; between the 1950s and the 1980s, they moved strongly against government job guarantees and health insurance assistance, for example.[57] The mountain states' traditions of game hunting in wide-open spaces have led them, like southerners, to cherish the right to bear firearms and to resist gun controls. As Figure 5.10 indicates, there are substantial regional differences on social issues like free speech. Taken as a whole, westerners may now be the most Republican of regional groups.[58]

City and Country

Whatever region they live in, urban, rural, and suburban residents tend to differ from each other in understandable ways. City dwellers are especially conscious of poverty, unemployment, and urban problems; many of them want the federal

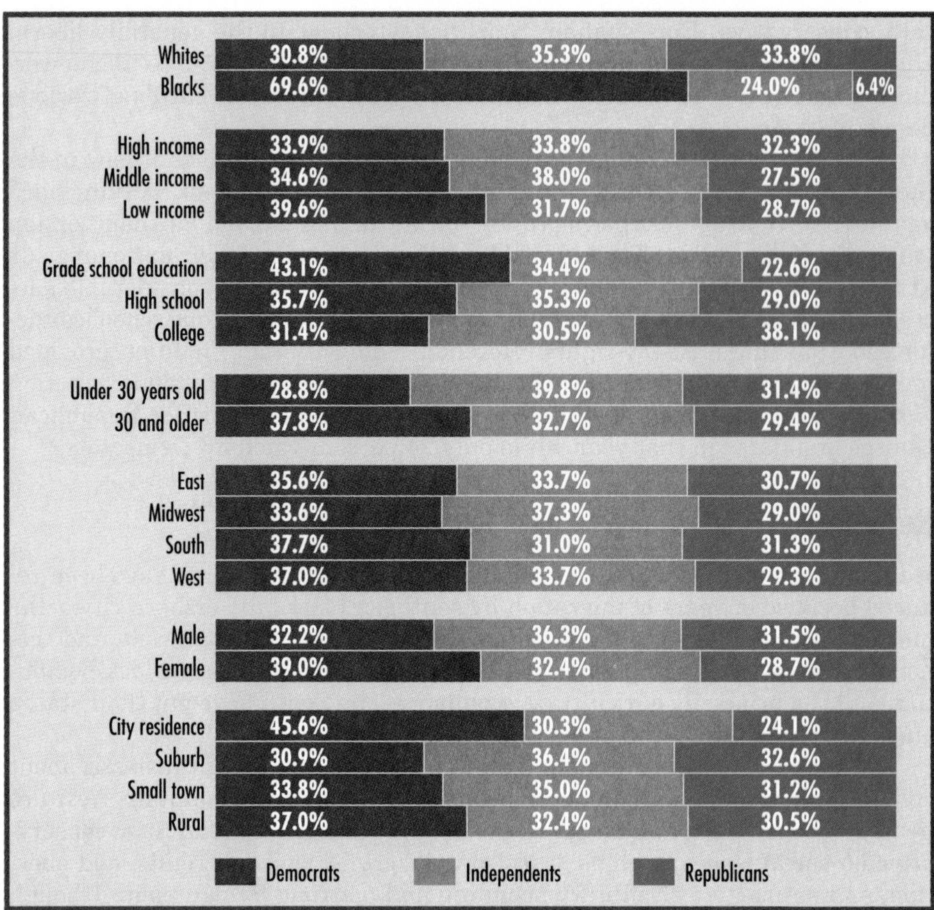

Figure 5.9 ■ **Party Loyalties Among Various Social Groups**

Blacks, city dwellers, women, and people of lower income and educational levels tend to be Democrats, while whites, suburbanites, men, the college-educated, and those with high incomes tend to be more Republican.

Source: General Social Survey Cumulative Data Set, 1991–1994.

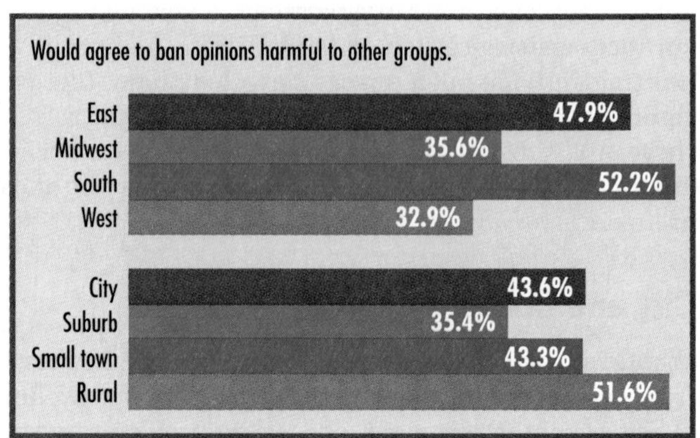

Figure 5.10 ■ **Opinions on Restricting Free Speech, by Region and Type of Community**

More southerners than westerners or midwesterners, and more rural Americans than suburbanites, would ban opinions harmful to other groups.

Source: General Social Survey Cumulative Data Set, 1991–1994.

The skyline of New York City, where political attitudes on such issues as the environment differ from those of people living in the Sawtooth Mountains in Stanley, Idaho.

government to help. Suburbanites, who are more comfortably off, are somewhat less eager to fight poverty and are more resistant to high taxes, though they tend to be highly concerned about the environment and to be socially liberal, strongly favoring free choice in matters of sex, religion, and lifestyle.

Country dwellers tend, on the average, to be conservative, both economically and socially (see Figure 5.10); to favor military strength; and to support law and order and conventional morality, while opposing stringent gun controls.

Social Class

Compared with much of the world, the United States has had rather little political conflict among people of different income or occupational groupings; in fact, rather few Americans think of themselves as members of a social "class" at all. The label of "working class," which in Europe has been a badge of pride for members of powerful organized labor movements and social democratic parties, is often rejected by Americans; nearly half the population consider themselves "middle class."[59]

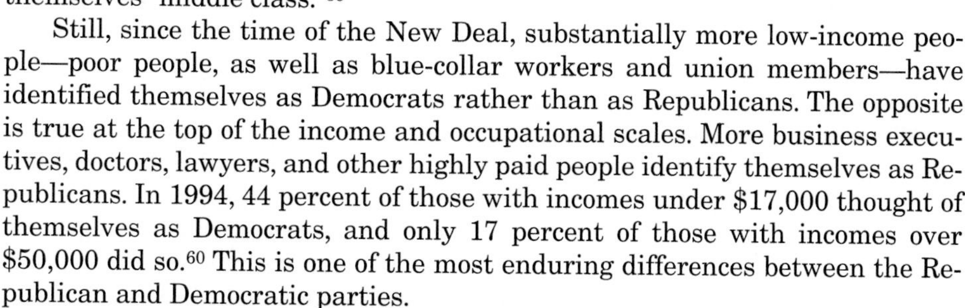

Still, since the time of the New Deal, substantially more low-income people—poor people, as well as blue-collar workers and union members—have identified themselves as Democrats rather than as Republicans. The opposite is true at the top of the income and occupational scales. More business executives, doctors, lawyers, and other highly paid people identify themselves as Republicans. In 1994, 44 percent of those with incomes under $17,000 thought of themselves as Democrats, and only 17 percent of those with incomes over $50,000 did so.[60] This is one of the most enduring differences between the Republican and Democratic parties.

Lower-income people also have some distinctive policy preferences. Not surprisingly, they tend to favor much more government help with jobs, education, housing, medical care, and the like, whereas the highest-income people, who would presumably pay more and benefit less from such programs, tend to oppose them. Although all groups in the population have moved away from wanting to aid the poor, those of low income are somewhat more willing to help them (see Figure 5.11). To complicate matters, however, some groups of high-income people—especially highly educated professionals—tend to be very liberal on social issues involving sexual behavior, abortion rights, free speech, and civil rights. They also tend to be especially eager for government action to protect the environment. Once again, no simple "liberal" *versus* "conservative" distinction can accurately sum up all differences in opinions.

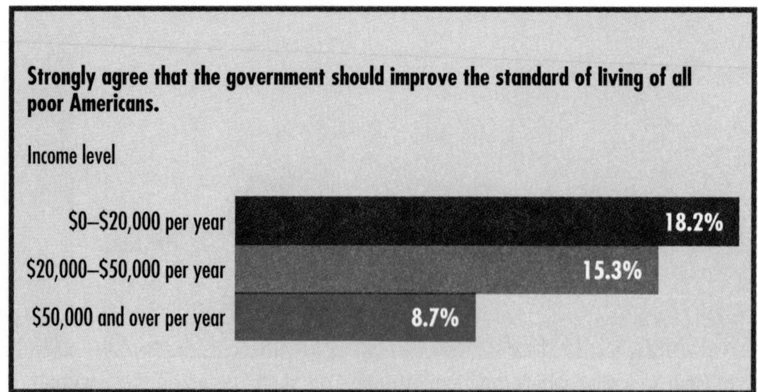

Figure 5.11 ■ **Attitudes Toward Government Help for the Poor, by Income Level**

Few Americans are now very eager to aid the poor, but low-income people are somewhat more supportive than others.

Source: General Social Survey Cumulative Data Set, 1989–1991.

Educational Level

The level of formal education that people reach is closely related to their income level, because education helps people earn more and also because the wealthy can pay for more and better schooling for their children. But education has some distinct political effects of its own.

As we will see in Chapter 9, education is generally considered the strongest single predictor of participation in politics. College-educated people are much more likely to say that they vote, talk about politics, go to meetings, sign petitions, and write letters to officials than are people who have attained only an elementary or a high school education. (There is some evidence, however, that they only *say* they vote more; the well-educated may be embarrassed to admit not doing so.) The highly educated know more about politics. They know what they want and how to go about getting it, joining groups and writing letters and faxes to public officials.

Those with more schooling also have some distinctive policy preferences. As we have indicated, they are especially protective of the civil rights, civil liberties, and individual freedom of atheists, homosexuals, protestors, and dissenters (see Figure 5.12). Education may contribute to tolerance by exposing people to diverse ideas or by training them in elite-backed norms of tolerance.

The most highly educated people tend to be the most tuned in to news and commentary in the media, and to change their opinions somewhat more quickly than do others. This is unusual; most of the groups that we have discussed, even those with rather distinctive policy preferences, tend to change opinion together, in the same direction, at about the same times.[61]

Gender

Women and men are moderately different in certain political respects. A moderate and apparently growing "gender gap" in party loyalties exists: in 1994, 39 percent of women, but only 33 percent of men, considered themselves Democrats.[62]

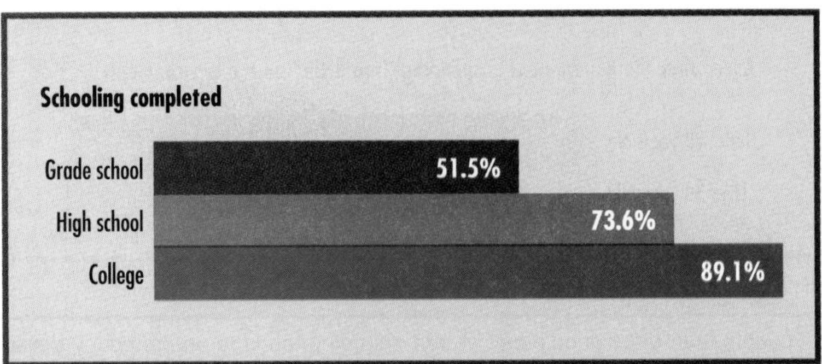

Figure 5.12 ■ **Tolerance of Atheists' Speaking Publicly, by Education Level**

Many more college-educated than grade-school-educated people favor letting atheists speak in public auditoriums.

Source: General Social Survey Cumulative Data Set, 1991–1994.

Women were prevented from participating in politics for a large part of our history; they got the vote, by constitutional amendment, only in 1920. Not all of them immediately took advantage of this new opportunity. For many years, women voted and participated in politics at lower rates than men: about 10 or 15 percent lower in the elections of the 1950s, for example. Only after the women's movement gained force during the 1970s did substantial numbers of female candidates begin to run for high office. Though an office-holding gap remains, the participation gap has virtually disappeared.[63]

Women do differ somewhat from men in certain policy preferences. Women tend to be more opposed to violence, whether by criminals or by the state. More of them oppose capital punishment and the use of military force abroad. More favor arms control and peace agreements. Women also tend to be somewhat more supportive of protective policies for the poor, the elderly, and the disabled.[64]

Contrary to the common impression, as a group, women have not been particularly more supportive than men of women's rights or abortion choice. This is another case, like that of Catholic Americans and the Catholic church, in which the opinions of ordinary members of social groups are not necessarily the same as those of the organizations that claim to represent them. Women do differ among themselves, however; professionals and others working outside the home are much more liberal on these issues than are homemakers.

Age

The young and the old differ on certain matters that touch their particular interests: the draft in wartime, the drinking age, and, to some extent, Social Security and Medicare. But the chief difference is that young people are more attuned to the particular times in which they are growing up. Those who were young during the 1960s were especially quick to favor civil rights for blacks, for example. In recent years, young people have been especially concerned about environmental issues (see Figure 5.13). Often, social change occurs by generational replacement. Old ideas, like the Depression–era notion that women should stay at home and "not take jobs away from men," die off with old people.

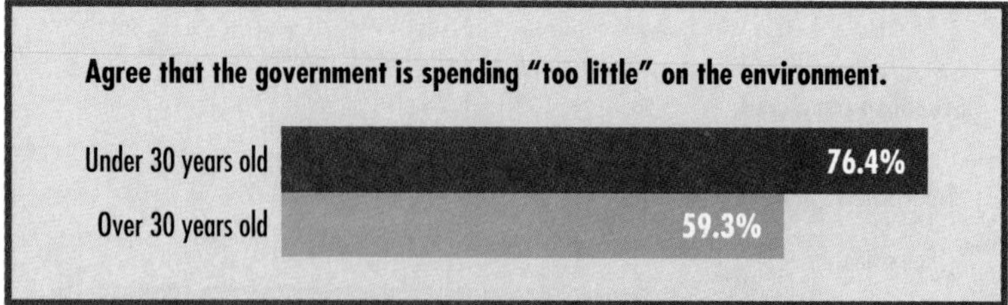

Figure 5.13 ▪ Support for Environmental Spending, by Age

More young people than older people say we are spending too little on protecting the environment.

Source: General Social Survey Cumulative Data Set, 1991–1994.

Public Opinion and Policy

We have argued that one crucial test of how well democracy is working is how closely a government's policies correspond to the expressed wishes of its citizens. How close, then, is the relationship between what American citizens want—that is, collective public opinion in the whole nation—and what the U.S. government actually does?

The Effects of Public Opinion on Policy

Our opening story about the Vietnam War suggests that, at least under some circumstances, public opinion does affect policymaking. Other evidence also indicates that it often does so, though not always.

One striking example of government responsiveness to the public occurred in the early 1990s, when Senate Republicans abandoned their filibuster against the Brady Bill to impose a five-day waiting period for handgun purchases, after angry constituents called and wrote. Polls showed that more than 90 percent of Americans supported the bill.[65] Similarly, in 1995 and 1996, congressional Republicans gradually backed off from their proposals to cut projected spending on Medicare, education, and the environment, as letters, phone calls, and opinion surveys revealed heavy public opposition.

Usually, public opinion influences policymaking in less dramatic ways. Looking at many different policy issues—foreign and domestic—one scholar found that, about two-thirds of the time, U.S. government policy corresponds with what opinion surveys say the public wants. The same two-thirds correspondence has appeared when other scholars investigated how *changes* in public opinion relate to changes in federal, state, and local policy. Moreover, when public opinion changes by a substantial and enduring amount and the issue is prominent, government policy has moved in the same direction *87 percent* of the time within a year or so afterward.[66]

According to still another study, the policies enacted in particular *states* correspond rather closely to the opinions of the states' citizens; that is, the states with mostly liberal citizens tend to have mostly liberal policies, whereas the states with mostly conservative citizens have mostly conservative policies.[67] Using sophisticated research methods, this study largely dismissed the possibility that policy differences cause the opinion differences (i.e., that citizens go along with whatever their government is doing). Public opinion seems to be a significant influence on government policy. Changes in opinion really do bring about changes in policy.

Opinion Manipulation This evidence does not completely settle the matter. For one thing, even if public opinion is a "proximate" influence on policy—that is, even if opinion "stands next to" policymaking and directly affects it—we still need to know what factors affect public opinion itself. If public opinion can be manufactured by the media or easily manipulated by interest groups or political leaders (as in the Tonkin Gulf example), then it would not make much sense to talk about democratic policymaking. It would be the media and the elites that really controlled policy, with public opinion simply acting as a transmission belt.

We have, however, already mentioned reasons for being skeptical of the idea that public opinion can be pushed around at will. Usually, personal experiences, objective events, and structural realities, rather than politicians' rhetoric, have the most to do with the shape of public opinion. Of course, some exceptions, like Tonkin, stand out; they may be most common in foreign affairs, where the government can sometimes control what information is made available. We need to discuss opinion manipulation further in later chapters. For now, however, the main point is that public opinion is a substantial and important proximate influence on policymaking.

Summary

Public opinion consists of the political attitudes and beliefs expressed by ordinary citizens; it can be measured rather accurately through polls and surveys. The democratic ideals of popular sovereignty and majority rule imply that government policy should respond to the wishes of the citizens. An important test of how well democracy is working, therefore, is how closely government policy corresponds to public opinion.

Most people do not know a lot of facts about politics and do not have well-worked-out ideologies or highly stable policy preferences. Contrary to the fears of the Founders and others, however, the *collective* public opinion of Americans is real and stable, and it takes account of the available information.

Many Americans feel angered by and alienated from politics and disapprove of the performance of political leaders. Party loyalty, though still widely held, has declined in strength. Most Americans strongly believe in freedom, economic liberty, capitalism, equality of opportunity, and democracy. Liberals and conservatives disagree about economic regulation and safety nets for the unfortunate. Majorities of the public favor government action on crime, education, medical care, and the environment. Support is lower for defense and the space program, and much lower for foreign aid. Support for civil rights, civil liberties, and the right to have an abortion has increased, but the public is conservative about patriotism, crime, prayer, and obscenity.

People learn their political attitudes and beliefs from their families, peers, schools, and workplaces; they also respond to political events and the mass media. Structural factors in the society, the economy, and the international system strongly affect public opinion. Opinions and party loyalties differ according to race, religion, region, urban or rural residence, social class, education level, gender, and age. Blacks, Jews, city dwellers, women, and low-income people tend to be particularly liberal and Democratic; white Protestants, suburbanites, males, and the wealthy tend to be conservative and Republican.

Public opinion has substantial effects on what federal, state, and local governments do, but responsiveness to public opinion is incomplete.

Suggested Readings

Erikson, Robert S. *American Public Opinion: Its Origins, Content, and Impact,* 5th ed. New York: Allyn & Bacon, 1995.
A comprehensive textbook, with abundant data and citations.

Hochschild, Jennifer L. *What's Fair? American Beliefs About Distributive Justice.* Cambridge: Harvard University Press, 1986.
Explores public opinion through in-depth interviews with a small number of people.

McClosky, Herbert, and John Zaller. *The American Ethos: Public Attitudes Toward Capitalism and Democracy.* Cambridge: Harvard University Press, 1984.
A major study of some of Americans' most important beliefs and values.

Page, Benjamin I., and Robert Y. Shapiro. *The Rational Public: Fifty Years of Trends in Americans' Policy Preferences.* Chicago: University of Chicago Press, 1992.
Extensive description of opinion trends, arguing that the public is rational.

Sussman, Barry. *What Americans Really Think and Why Our Politicians Pay No Attention.* New York: Pantheon, 1988.
A brief and lively account of public opinion, by a leading journalistic analyst of polls.

Internet Sources

The Gallup Organization http://www.gallup.com/
Access to recent Gallup polls as well as to the Gallup archives.

The Right Side of the Web http://www.clark.net/pub/jeffd/index.html
The gateway to conservative organizations, parties, candidates, and commentators.

The Roper Center http://www.lib.uconn.edu/RoperCenter/
The Roper Center is the main repository in the United States of public opinion polls on government and politics.

Social Science Data Collection http://ssdc.ucsd.edu/ssdc/pubopin.html
Here is where you will find articles and books about polling, published public opinion polls, and raw polling data.

Turn Left http://www.idir.net/~cubsfan/liberal.html
The gateway to liberal organizations, parties, candidates, and commentators.

Notes

1. Joseph C. Goulden, *Truth Is the First Casualty: The Gulf of Tonkin Affair—Illusion and Reality* (Chicago: Rand McNally, 1969).
2. John E. Mueller, *War, Presidents and Public Opinion* (New York: Wiley, 1973), p. 81.
3. U.S. Department of Defense, OASD (Comptroller), *Selected Manpower Statistics* (Washington, DC: Government Publications, June 1976), pp. 59, 60.
4. Alexander Hamilton, James Madison, and John Jay, *The Federalist Papers,* ed. by Clinton Rossiter (New York: New American Library, 1961 [1787–1788]). See Benjamin I. Page and Robert Y. Shapiro, *The Rational Public: Fifty Years of Trends in Americans' Policy Preferences* (Chicago: University of Chicago Press, 1992), chaps. 1, 2.
5. Walter Lippmann, *Public Opinion* (New York: Macmillan, 1922), p. 127.
6. Philip E. Converse, "The Nature of Belief Systems in Mass Publics," in David Apter, ed., *Ideology and Discontent* (New York: Free Press, 1964), pp. 206–261; Converse,

"Attitudes and Non-attitudes: Continuation of a Dialogue," in Edward R. Tufte, ed., *The Quantitative Analysis of Social Problems* (Reading, MA: Addison-Wesley, 1970), pp. 168–189.

7. Times Mirror Center for the People and the Press, "The Vocal Minority in American Politics," press release, July 16, 1993.
8. Robert S. Erikson, *American Public Opinion: Its Origins, Content, and Impact,* 5th ed. (New York: Macmillan, 1995), tells much more about the techniques and the results of polling. See also Herbert Asher, *Polling and the Public,* 3rd ed. (Washington, DC: Congressional Quarterly Press, 1995).
9. Elizabeth Kolber, "Public Opinion Polls Swerve with the Turns of a Phrase," *New York Times* (June 5, 1995), pp. A1, C11.
10. Erikson, *American Public Opinion;* Page and Shapiro, *The Rational Public,* pp. 9–14. We also calculated some percentages from the General Social Survey for this book.
11. Paul M. Sniderman, Richard A. Brody, and Philip E. Tetlock, *Reasoning and Choice: Explorations in Political Psychology* (New York: Cambridge University Press, 1991); see also Michael X. Delli Carpini and Scott Keeter, *Information and Empowerment: What Americans Know About Politics and Why It Matters* (New Haven: Yale University Press, 1996).
12. See Anthony Downs, *An Economic Theory of Democracy* (New York: Harper, 1957), chaps. 11–13.
13. Robert E. Lane, *Political Ideology: Why the American Common Man Believes What He Does* (New York: Free Press, 1962); Jennifer L. Hochschild, *What's Fair? American Beliefs About Distributive Justice* (Cambridge: Harvard University Press, 1986).
14. Page and Shapiro, *The Rational Public.*
15. *Public Perspective* (March–April 1994), p. 3.
16. Times Mirror Center for the People and the Press, reported in *Public Perspective* (November–December 1994), p. 4.
17. Samuel Kernell, "Explaining Presidential Popularity," *American Political Science Review,* Vol. 72 (June 1978), pp. 506–522; Richard A. Brody, *Assessing the President: The Media, Elite Opinion, and Public Support* (Stanford, CA: Stanford University Press, 1991).
18. Gallup surveys, December 1994 and May 11–14, 1995.
19. *Public Perspective,* (September–October 1993), p. 11; Gallup survey, April 5–6, 1995.
20. Bruce E. Keith, David B. Magleby, Candice J. Nelson, Elizabeth Orr, Mark C. Westlye, and Raymond E. Wolfinger, *The Myth of the Independent Voter* (Berkeley: University of California Press, 1992).
21. Walter Dean Burnham, "The Appearance and Disappearance of the American Voter," in Richard Rose, ed., *Electoral Participation: A Comparative Analysis* (Beverly Hills, CA: Sage, 1980), pp. 35–73; Michael B. MacKuen, Robert S. Erikson, and James A. Stimson, "Macropartisanship," *American Political Science Review,* Vol. 83, No. 4 (1989), pp. 1125–1143.
22. Herbert McClosky and John Zaller, *The American Ethos: Public Attitudes Toward Capitalism and Democracy* (Cambridge: Harvard University Press, 1984).
23. McClosky and Zaller, *The American Ethos,* pp. 32, 37.
24. Samuel A. Stouffer and James A. Davis, *Communism, Conformity, and Civil Liberties* (New York: Transaction, 1992); John L. Sullivan, James Piereson, and George

E. Marcus, *Political Tolerance and American Democracy* (Chicago: University of Chicago Press, 1993).

25. McClosky and Zaller, *The American Ethos,* pp. 108, 133, 135, 140.
26. Russell Dalton, *Citizen Politics in Western Democracies* (Chatham, NJ: Chatham House, 1988), p. 100.
27. General Social Survey, 1994 (36 percent called themselves "moderate"); Fay Lomax Cook and Edith J. Barrett, *Support for the American Welfare State* (New York: Columbia University Press, 1992).
28. James W. Prothro and Charles M. Grigg, "Fundamental Principles of Democracy: Bases of Agreement and Disagreement," *Journal of Politics,* Vol. 22 (1960), pp. 276–294.
29. Robert S. Erikson, Norman R. Luttbeg, and Kent L. Tedin, *American Public Opinion: Its Origins, Content, and Impact,* 4th ed. (New York: Macmillan, 1991), p. 108.
30. George Gallup, Jr., *The Gallup Poll* (Wilmington, DE: Scholarly Resources, 1980), p. 258; 1986, p. 217.
31. General Social Survey, 1994, reported in *Public Perspective* (April–May 1995).
32. Humphrey Taylor, Lawrence R. Jacobs, and Robert Y. Shapiro, "Polling and Opinion on Health Care Reform," *Public Perspective* (May–June 1993), especially p. 26.
33. Steven Kull, *Americans and Foreign Aid: A Study of American Public Attitudes* (Washington, DC: Program on International Policy Attitudes, University of Maryland, March 1, 1995).
34. John E. Rielly, ed., *American Public Opinion and U.S. Foreign Policy 1995* (Chicago: Chicago Council on Foreign Relations, 1995), p. 12.
35. *New York Times*/CBS survey, December 9, 1994.
36. Donald R. Kinder and Lynn M. Sanders, *Divided by Color* (Chicago: University of Chicago Press, 1996).
37. Page and Shapiro, *The Rational Public,* pp. 98–100; "Views About Homosexuality," *Public Perspective* (March–April 1993), pp. 82–83.
38. William Caspary, "The 'Mood Theory': A Study of Public Opinion and Foreign Policy," *American Political Science Review,* Vol. 64 (1970), pp. 536–547; Rielly, *American Public Opinion and U.S. Foreign Policy 1995,* p. 13.
39. *Time*/CNN survey, December 7, 1994.
40. Calculated from M. Kent Jennings and Richard Niemi, *The Political Character of Adolescence* (Princeton: Princeton University Press, 1974), p. 41. See also Jennings and Niemi, *Generations and Politics* (Princeton, NJ: Princeton University Press, 1981).
41. Edward S. Greenberg, "Black Children and the Political System," *Public Opinion Quarterly,* Vol. 34 (1970), pp. 333–345; Jennings and Niemi, *Political Character* pp. 205–206.
42. *New York Times* (January 29, 1991), p. A18.
43. Kay Lehman Schlozman and Sidney Verba, *Injury to Insult: Unemployment, Class, and Political Response* (Cambridge: Harvard University Press, 1981), p. 141.
44. Edward S. Greenberg, *Workplace Democracy: The Political Effects of Participation* (Ithaca, NY: Cornell University Press, 1986).
45. Morris P. Fiorina, *Retrospective Voting in American National Elections* (New Haven: Yale University Press, 1981).
46. John R. Petrocik, *Party Coalitions: Realignments and the Decline of the New Deal Party System* (Chicago: University of Chicago Press, 1981), p. 38.

47. "Portrait of the Electorate," *New York Times* (November 13, 1994), p. 15.

48. GSS data, 1994.

49. U.S. Department of Commerce, *Current Population Reports,* Series P20–475, *The Hispanic Population in the U.S.* (Washington, DC: U.S. Government Printing Office, March 1993).

50. U.S. Department of Commerce, *Current Population Report,* Series P20–466, *Voting and Registration in the Election of November 1988* (Washington, DC: U.S. Government Printing Office, 1989), p. v.

51. Ari L. Goldman, "Catholics Are at Odds with Bishops," *New York Times* (June 19, 1992), p. A8; *Time*/CNN poll, December 12, 1994.

52. *Public Perspective* (September–October 1993), p. 10.

53. "Portrait of the Electorate," *New York Times* (November 13, 1994), p. 15.

54. *New York Times* (April 10, 1991), p. A11.

55. "Portrait of the Electorate," *New York Times* (November 13, 1994), p. 15.

56. Peter F. Galderisi et al., eds., *The Politics of Realignment* (Boulder, CO: Westview Press, 1987), pp. 91–97.

57. Galderisi et al., *The Politics of Realignment,* pp. 94–95.

58. *Public Perspective* (September–October 1993), p. 10.

59. In 1994, 5 percent of Americans called themselves "lower-class," 46 percent said "working-class," 46 percent "middle-class," and 3 percent "upper-class" (1994 NES).

60. 1994 NES data.

61. John R. Zaller, *The Nature and Origins of Mass Opinion* (New York: Cambridge University Press, 1992); Page and Shapiro, *The Rational Public,* ch. 7.

62. 1994 NES data.

63. M. Margaret Conway, *Political Participation in the United States* (Washington, DC: Congressional Quarterly Press, 1985), p. 27.

64. Robert Y. Shapiro and Harpreet Mahajan, "Gender Differences in Policy Preferences: A Summary of Trends from the 1960s to the 1980s," *Public Opinion Quarterly,* Vol. 50 (1986), pp. 42–61.

65. Linda M. Harrington, "Senate Approves Brady Bill: GOP Relents on Gun Control; NAFTA OK'd," *Chicago Tribune* (November 21, 1992) pp. A1, A17.

66. Alan D. Monroe, "Consistency Between Public Preferences and National Policy Decisions," *American Politics Quarterly,* Vol. 7 (January 1979), pp. 3–19; Benjamin I. Page and Robert Y. Shapiro, "Effects of Public Opinion on Policy," *American Political Science Review,* Vol. 77 (March 1983), pp. 175–190.

67. Gerald C. Wright, Jr., Robert S. Erikson, and John P. McIver, "Public Opinion and Policy Liberalism in the American States," *American Journal of Political Science,* Vol. 31 (November 1987), pp. 980–1001. See also Robert A. Erikson, Gerald Wright, and John McIver, *Statehouse Democracy: Public Opinion and Democracy in the American States* (New York: Cambridge University Press, 1994).

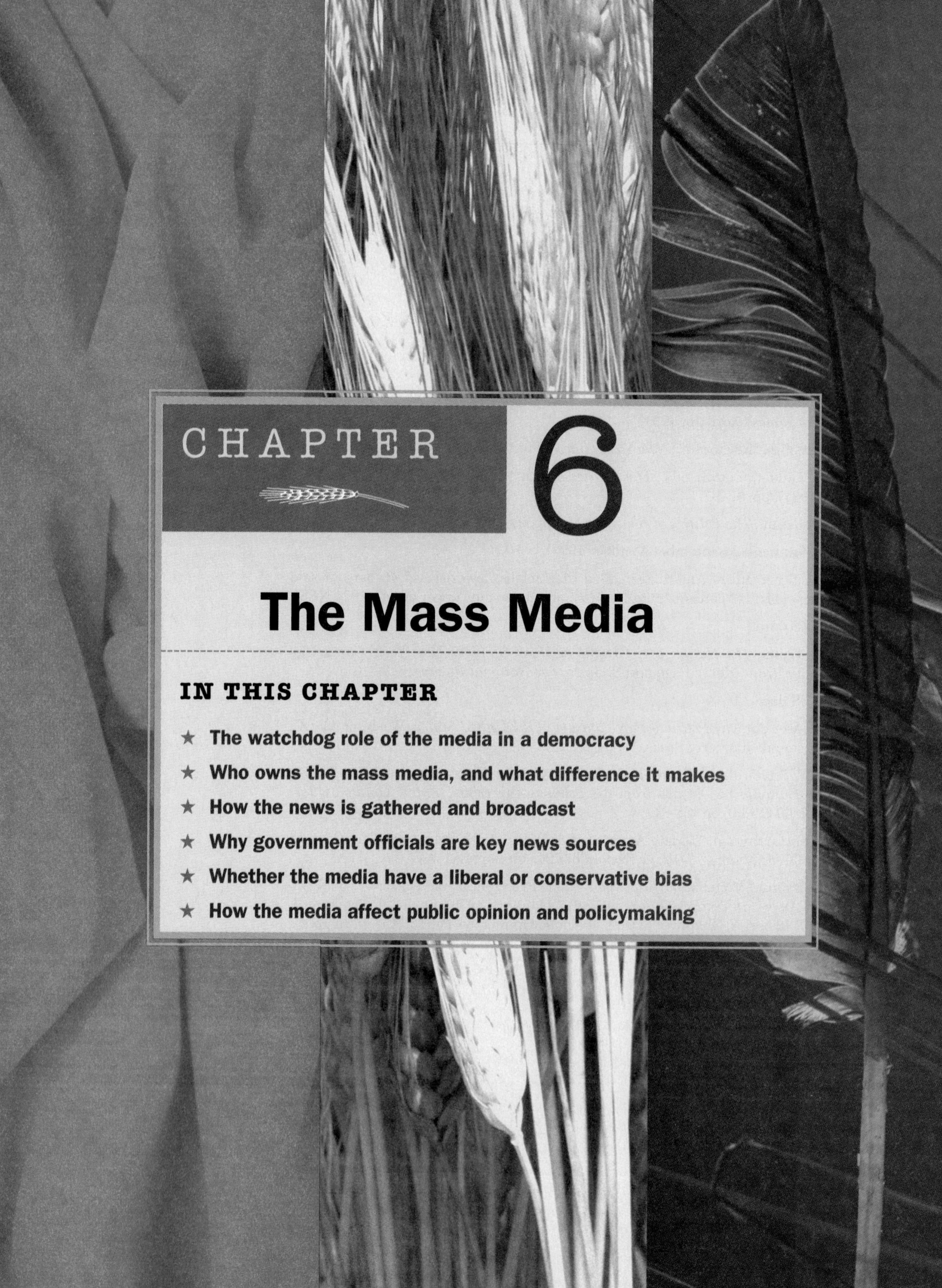

CHAPTER 6

The Mass Media

IN THIS CHAPTER

- ★ The watchdog role of the media in a democracy
- ★ Who owns the mass media, and what difference it makes
- ★ How the news is gathered and broadcast
- ★ Why government officials are key news sources
- ★ Whether the media have a liberal or conservative bias
- ★ How the media affect public opinion and policymaking

Covering the Watergate Scandal

A ringing telephone woke 29-year-old *Washington Post* reporter Bob Woodward on Saturday morning, June 17, 1972. Could he come to the office? Five men had been arrested for burglary at the headquarters of the Democratic National Committee in the opulent Watergate apartment/office complex; they were carrying photographic equipment and electronic gear.[1]

In the *Post's* newsroom, Woodward learned the details that had been phoned in by a veteran police reporter. The five men, arrested at 2:30 a.m., had been wearing business suits and surgical gloves and carrying a walkie-talkie, 40 rolls of film, cameras, lock picks, pen-size tear gas guns, bugging devices, and many sequentially numbered $100 bills.

The Yale-educated Woodward also learned that hard-driving college dropout Carl Bernstein (only 28 years old but with 12 years of newspaper experience) was working on the same story for the *Post.* The collaboration between Woodward and Bernstein started uneasily but eventually produced one of the most remarkable stories in the history of American journalism.

At the preliminary hearing in court that afternoon, Woodward heard accused burglar James McCord describe his profession as "security consultant," recently retired from government: "CIA," he whispered to the judge. Meanwhile, Bernstein learned from Miami contacts that the four other accused burglars had anti-Castro Cuban backgrounds and possible CIA (Central Intelligence Agency) connections. The *Post* ran a front-page story on Sunday about the attempt to bug the Democrats, leaving the burglars' motives a mystery.

The Associated Press wire service revealed that McCord was the security coordinator for the Committee to Reelect the President (CREEP), the chief Republican campaign organization in 1972. John Mitchell, President Nixon's campaign manager and former attorney general, denied that the burglars had been acting for the campaign. A police source told the *Post,* however, that the burglars' address books and papers referred to E. Howard Hunt, "W. House" or "W.H." With a few phone calls, Woodward was able to establish that Hunt was a consultant working for Charles W. Colson, special counsel to the president of the United States. "White House Consultant Linked to Bugging Suspects," Woodward's story was headlined.

Presidential press secretary Ronald Ziegler described the incident as a "third-rate burglary attempt," not worthy of further White House comment; President Nixon flatly said that "the White House has had no involvement whatever." But *Newsday* and the *New York Times* established that the CREEP office of G. Gordon Liddy, a former White House aide, had received many phone calls from one of the burglars. The *Times* reported that $100,000 in that burglar's bank account had come from a Mexico City lawyer. Bernstein traced $25,000 of the money to the head of Nixon's 1968 Midwest campaign, who told Woodward that it consisted of contributions that he had personally turned over to the finance chairman of CREEP.

Throughout the summer and fall of 1972, the "Woodstein" pair pursued leads from scores—eventually hundreds—of sources, including the mysterious "Deep Throat," an administration insider or insiders whom Woodward says he often met after midnight in an underground parking garage.[2]

The *Post* reporters discovered that the Watergate break-in was just the tip of an iceberg. CREEP had kept hundreds of thousands of dollars in a secret fund, controlled by top White House and campaign officials, which they had used to carry out extensive espionage, sabotage, and dirty tricks against Democratic candidates. They had provided psychiatric records that caused Thomas Eagleton to resign as George McGovern's vice-presidential running mate; they had disrupted schedules and harassed candidates' families. The October 10 "Woodstein" story put the picture together: "FBI Finds Nixon Aides Sabotaged Democrats." Over the next few

All the President's Men, Woodward and Bernstein's best-selling account of their investigation into Watergate, was adapted for the screen and starred Robert Redford and Dustin Hoffman in the lead roles. The success of both the novel and the film signified a new era in American journalism, as the media began to take a more critical look at the government and glorified investigative reporters like Woodward and Bernstein as heroes.

days, the *Post, Time* magazine, and the *New York Times* reported several direct links to the White House, including some through Chief of Staff H. R. Haldeman.

The White House, however, cried "hearsay," "innuendo," and partisan politics; no one "presently employed" in the White House had been involved. Senator Robert Dole called the *Post* a "partner in mudslinging" of the McGovern campaign. A grand jury indicted only Hunt, Liddy, and the five burglars, and Watergate was not much of an issue in the 1972 presidential election, in which Nixon overwhelmingly defeated McGovern.[3] Only later revelations provoked the series of trials, congressional investigations, and impeachment hearings that eventually drove Nixon from office and convicted his attorney general, his chief of staff, and others of crimes.

But Bernstein's and Woodward's tenacious investigative reporting set those events in motion. In May 1973, the *Post* won the Pulitzer Prize for distinguished public service in journalism. Some observers complained that the *Post* had unfairly hounded the Nixon administration, but most concluded that it had shown how a free press can serve democracy well by digging out important facts for the American people.

Roles of the Mass Media in Democracy

Journalist and scholar Walter Lippmann once declared that "a free press is not a privilege, but an organic necessity in a great society. Without criticism and reliable and intelligent reporting, the government cannot govern."[4]

The central idea of democracy is that ordinary citizens should control what their government does. However, citizens cannot hope to control officials, to choose candidates, to speak intelligently with others about public affairs, or even to make up their minds about what policies they favor unless they have good information about politics. Most of that information must come through the mass media. How well democracy works, then, depends partly on how good a job the mass media are doing.

Watchdog over Government

watchdog The role of the media in scrutinizing the actions of government officials.

One role of the media in a democracy is that of **watchdog** over government. The idea is that the press—acting as a better protector than the voyeuristic pet in the cartoon—should dig up facts and warn the public when officials are doing something wrong. Only if they know about errors and wrongdoing can citizens hold officials accountable for setting things right.

The First Amendment to the Constitution ("Congress shall make no law . . . abridging the freedom . . . of the press") helps ensure that the media will be able to expose officials' misbehavior without fear of censorship or prosecution. This is a treasured American right that is not available in many other countries. Under dictatorships and other authoritarian regimes, the media are usually tightly controlled. Even in a democratic country like Great Britain, strict secrecy laws limit what the press can say. (The scandal-exposing book *Spycatcher,* for example, was banned in Britain even after it was published in the United States.) In many countries, including France, Israel, and Sweden, the government owns and operates major television channels, and makes sure that the programs are not too critical.[5]

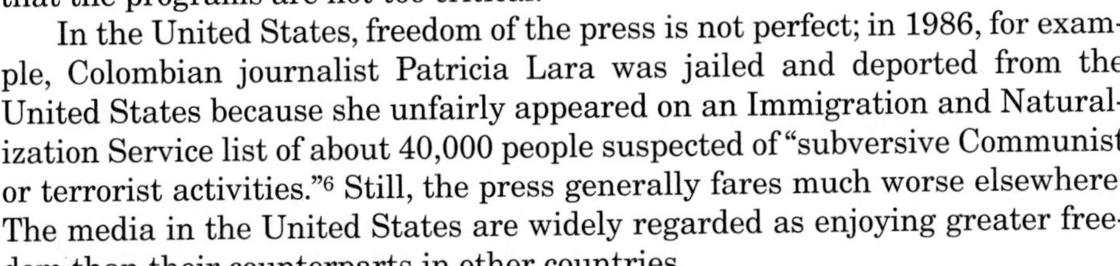

In the United States, freedom of the press is not perfect; in 1986, for example, Colombian journalist Patricia Lara was jailed and deported from the United States because she unfairly appeared on an Immigration and Naturalization Service list of about 40,000 people suspected of "subversive Communist or terrorist activities."[6] Still, the press generally fares much worse elsewhere. The media in the United States are widely regarded as enjoying greater freedom than their counterparts in other countries.

While some Americans saw the *Post's* pursuit of the Watergate story as a partisan vendetta against the Nixon administration, more probably considered it a great achievement of investigative journalism. Polls showed that public confidence in the media rose significantly after the Watergate affair, and many young men and women were inspired to go to journalism schools and to take up careers as reporters.

But how common is such a watchdog role? Even without formal censorship or government ownership of the media, various factors, including the way in which the mass media are organized and their routines of news gathering, may limit how willing or able the media are to be critical of government policies.

Of course, there is a fine line between vigorous investigation and misleading or unfair pursuit of scandal. Is the press *too* critical on trivial matters, too

PUBLIC WATCHDOG

Reprinted by permission Tribune Media Services.

quick to blow scandals out of proportion and to destroy political leaders' careers?[7]

Clarifying Electoral Choices

A second role of the mass media in a democracy is to make clear what electoral choices the public has: what the political parties stand for, and how the candidates shape up in terms of personal character, knowledge, experience, and positions on the issues. Without such information, it is difficult for voters to make intelligent choices.

How much or little attention do the media pay to candidates' stands on public policies? Do they devote too much coverage to the horse race aspect of campaigns instead? In scrutinizing the character and personality of candidates, do the media go overboard in digging up dirt and reporting negative material even when it is very minor?

Providing Policy Information

A third role of the mass media is to present a diverse, full, and enlightening set of facts and ideas about public policy. Citizens need to know how well current policies are working, as well as the pros and cons of the alternative policies that might be tried, to formulate sensible preferences. In a democracy, government should respond to public opinion, but that opinion should be well informed.

How much policy information do the U.S. media actually convey, and how accessible is it? How diverse and how accurate is that information? Is it biased—toward liberalism, for example, or toward conservatism? Are some voices heard and others ignored? We will address such questions in this chapter.

Whether or not they fulfill these three ideal roles, the mass media clearly play important parts in the political system. They act as amplifiers for speaking to citizens and trying to persuade them. The media also serve as channels of communication among political and governmental institutions, helping Congress, the president, and members of the executive branch to figure out what the others are doing. And finally, the media may themselves be political actors, with their own goals and interests, trying to influence politics just as other interest groups do. Thus, the mass media serve as a critical link among political and governmental institutions, and they also act as political institutions in their own right.

Structure: The Development of Journalism in America

The media have changed greatly over our history and continue to change rapidly. But many of their important characteristics are rooted in how they first developed.

When the country was founded, communication was difficult. It ordinarily took several days for news to travel from Boston to New York by horseback. A few small, expensive newspapers existed in the cities to tell affluent merchants and tradespeople about shipping schedules and the prices of goods; other papers emerged as organs of political parties (Federalist, Republican, or Democratic), arguing issues in a fiercely partisan fashion. But such limited media could not carry out the watchdog role very successfully or convey full information about electoral choices or public policy.

Newspapers

Modern newspapers were made possible by technological innovations and economic growth. Key technological breakthroughs in the early 1800s included the invention of the "cylinder" press, powered by steam; machines for typecasting; a machine for large-scale papermaking; and, by the middle of the century, the rotary press. Meanwhile, the population grew, and public education spread, creating a large, literate audience. Improvements in home lighting made nighttime reading easier.[8]

The Penny Press In 1833, the first "penny paper," the *New York Sun,* was founded. It and its successors, especially James Gordon Bennett's *New York Herald,* reached mass audiences of ordinary working people by means of low prices and human interest stories, written in a breezy and often sensational style that is still with us today. Bennett pioneered society news, exposés of upper-class scandals, and spectacular coverage of bizarre murder trials, along with financial news.

Then, the invention of the telegraph revolutionized news gathering and transmission. The first wire story was sent from Washington, D.C., to Baltimore in 1844. Soon, six New York papers formed the Associated Press, a cooperative that spread across the country, pooling news and distributing it almost instantly among many cities. Thus, it was possible to reach hundreds of thousands, or even millions, of people with fast-breaking national news, in a fashion that we now take for granted.

THE SUN.

NUMBER 1.] NEW YORK, TUESDAY, SEPTEMBER 3, 1833. [PRICE ONE PENNY.

PUBLISHED DAILY,

AT 222 WILLIAM ST.

The object of this paper is to lay before the public, at a price within the means of every one, ALL THE NEWS OF THE DAY, and at the same time afford an advantageous medium for advertising. The sheet will be enlarged as soon as the increase of advertisements requires it—the price remaining the same.

Yearly advertisers, (without the paper,) Thirty Dollars per annum—Casual advertising, at the usual prices charged by the city papers.

Subscriptions will be received, if paid in advance, at the rate of three dollars per annum.

FOR ALBANY—PASSAGE ONLY $1.

The large and commodious steamboat COMMERCE, Capt. R. H. Fitch, will leave the foot of Courtlandt street on Friday, at five o'clock, P. M. for Albany, stopping at the usual landing places to land and receive passengers. Passage $1. For particulars apply to the Captain on board.

From New York, Mondays, Wednesdays, Fridays
From Albany, Tuesdays, Thursdays, Saturdays.

FOR NEWPORT AND PROVIDENCE.

The splendid steamboat BENJAMIN FRANKLIN, Capt. E. S. Bunker, and the PRESIDENT, Capt. R. S. Bunker, will leave New York at 5 o'clock, P. M. and Providence at 12 o'clock M. every Monday, Wednesday and Friday. For further information apply to the Captain on board, foot of Courtlandt-st. or at the office, 11 Broad st.

FOR HARTFORD—PASSAGE 1 DOLLAR.

THROUGH BY DAYLIGHT.

AN IRISH CAPTAIN.

"These are as sweet a pair of pistols as any in the three kingdoms;" said an officer, showing a pair to a young student of his acquaintance, "and have done execution before now; at the slightest touch, off they go, as sweet as honey, without either recoiling or dipping. I never travel without them."

"I never heard of highwaymen in this part of the country."

"Nor I," replied the officer, "and if I had I should not trouble myself to carry the pistols on their account—Highwaymen are a species of sharks who are not fond of attacking us lobsters; they know we are a little too hard to crack. No, my dear sir, highwaymen know that soldiers have not much money, and what they have they fight for."

"Since that is the case, how come you to travel always with pistols?"

"Because," answered the officer, "I find them very useful in accommodating any little difference I may accidentally have with a friend, or which one friend may chance to have with another."

"Do you often settle differences in that way?"

"Why, I was twice out before I arrived at your age.—The first time was with a relation of my own, who said he would see my courage tried before he would contribute with the others towards the purchase of my first commission; so I sent him word that I would be happy to give him one proof the very next morning, and when we met, I touched him so smartly in the leg, that he has halted ever since. But all his doubts being now removed, he cheerfully contributed his quota with the rest of my relations...

The Sun, first published in New York in 1833, was the original "penny paper." Despite its dull format and small headlines, *The Sun* gained popularity with human interest stories like the one reported in this edition about a pistol-packing Irish police captain.

yellow journalism Sensational newspaper stories with large headlines and, in some cases, color cartoons.

Yellow Journalism Sensational treatment of the news mushroomed at the end of the nineteenth century. Joseph Pulitzer of the *New York World* (1883) and William Randolph Hearst, the strong-willed publisher of the *New York Journal* (1885)—on whose career the film *Citizen Kane* is based—combined sensationalism and political crusades, creating **yellow journalism,** with oversized headlines and full-color illustrations and comics. (The term *yellow journalism* is still used today; it came from a front-page cartoon character called "The Yellow Kid.")

Hearst's crusades included, in 1898, helping to provoke war against Spain over Spanish control of Cuba, a key step in the emergence of the United States as a world power. Hearst's headlines proclaimed that the Spanish had blown up the U.S. battleship *Maine* in a Cuban harbor, though Spanish involvement was never proved and most historians believe the explosion was an accident. According to legend, Hearst cabled to artist Frederic Remington in Cuba, "You furnish the pictures and I'll furnish the war."

Today's tabloids, like the New York *Post,* are less likely to start wars, but their journalistic techniques still resemble those of Hearst's papers.

objective news News reported with no evaluative language and with any opinions quoted or attributed to a specific source.

Objective News The growth of telegraphed national news and large-circulation newspapers also led to a new sort of news, however: bland, **objective news** stories that relied heavily on interviews and scrupulously attributed all opinions to named sources. Such stories could be wired all over the country and used by many different sorts of publications without offending their diverse audiences. The Associated Press (AP) employed its own reporters as well as gathering reports from member papers, and it sent stories to hundreds of newspapers. The International News Service, Scripps-Howard Service, and other wire services soon did the same. Today, the AP stands as the chief source of national and international news for most newspapers and as a major source for television networks. Many small papers simply print AP stories intact.

,000 REWARD.—WHO DESTROYED THE MAINE?—$50,000 REWARD

NEW YORK JOURNAL

AND ADVERTISER. FIRST EDITION.

NEW YORK, THURSDAY, FEBRUARY 17, 1898.—16 PAGES. PRICE ONE CENT

DESTRUCTION OF THE WAR SHIP MAINE WAS THE WORK OF AN ENEMY

$50,000!

$50,000 REWARD! For the Detection of the Perpetrator of the Maine Outrage!

Assistant Secretary Roosevelt Convinced the Explosion of the War Ship Was Not an Accident.

The Journal Offers $50,000 Reward for the Conviction of the Criminals Who Sent 258 American Sailors to Their Death. Naval Officers Unanimous That the Ship Was Destroyed on Purpose.

$50,000!

$50,000 REWARD! For the Detection of the Perpetrator of the Maine Outrage!

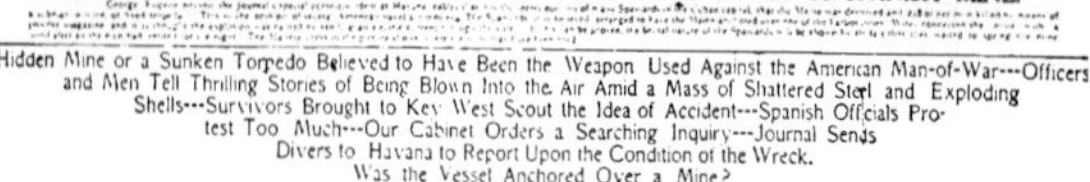

NAVAL OFFICERS THINK THE MAINE WAS DESTROYED BY A SPANISH MINE.

Hidden Mine or a Sunken Torpedo Believed to Have Been the Weapon Used Against the American Man-of-War---Officers and Men Tell Thrilling Stories of Being Blown Into the Air Amid a Mass of Shattered Steel and Exploding Shells---Survivors Brought to Key West Scout the Idea of Accident---Spanish Officials Protest Too Much---Our Cabinet Orders a Searching Inquiry---Journal Sends Divers to Havana to Report Upon the Condition of the Wreck. Was the Vessel Anchored Over a Mine?

William Randolph Hearst's *New York Journal* stirred war fever in 1898 with unsubstantiated charges that the Spanish had destroyed the U.S. battleship *Maine* in Cuba.

The development of wire services meant that more political news could be spread much more quickly, to much bigger audiences, and in a much more nationally uniform way than ever before. This trend was accentuated by the development of large "chains" of newspapers, owned by the same company and pursuing uniform editorial policies. Thus, the changing *structural* factors of industrialization and technology changed the shape of political communication and the shape of politics. The increasing objectivity and widening circulation of the media had major advantages for democracy, but also some disadvantages, which we will discuss.

Objective news came to be exemplified by the *New York Times,* which Adolph S. Ochs began to revitalize in 1896. The *Times,* claiming to publish "All the News That's Fit to Print" and aspiring to be America's "newspaper of record," specialized in thoroughness rather than liveliness or cleverness. It remains the preeminent U.S. newspaper for reporting on international affairs. It is rivaled only by the *Washington Post* for the extent of its domestic political reporting, and by the *Wall Street Journal* for business and financial news.

Magazines and Electronic Media

Newspapers have been joined, as sources of political news, by increasing numbers of magazines; then, by radio and television; and most recently, by new, interactive media like fax machines and the Internet, which permit instant communication among citizens and public officials.

Magazines Several journals of opinion and analysis were founded in the nineteenth century. Some of these, such as *The Nation* and the *Atlantic Monthly,* continue to be published; a wide range of other journals—liberal, conservative, radical and reactionary—have entered the political debate.

Beginning in the 1920s, Henry Luce's *Time,* the weekly newsmagazine, brought analysis and interpretation of the week's news, written in a quick and colorful style, to hundreds of thousands and then millions of readers; it later drew competition from *Newsweek* and *U.S. News & World Report.* Large-circulation magazines like the *Saturday Evening Post, Life,* and especially *Readers' Digest* gained circulations in the millions. Countless specialized journals appeared, providing information and entertainment of diverse sorts. By the 1970s and 1980s, national editions of several newspapers—for example, the *New York Times,* the *Wall Street Journal,* and *USA Today*—became, in effect, daily newsmagazines for a national audience. Sensational weekly tabloids, such as the *National Inquirer,* the *Globe,* and the *Star* sprouted on supermarket shelves.

Radio Radio significantly changed the face of the mass media. Commercial radio stations with broad audiences were established during the 1920s and were soon organized into networks that shared news and other programs. By 1938, the three radio networks had 97 percent of the nighttime broadcasting power of all U.S. radio stations.[9] In the depths of the Great Depression of the 1930s, millions of Americans could hear the reassuring voice of President Franklin Roosevelt giving "fireside chats." Later, millions could hear the latest news about the battles with Japan and Nazi Germany during World War II, which they could also see in dramatic movie newsreels and in the glossy pictures of the new *Life* magazine, which offered a grab bag of photos of movie stars, royalty, nature, art, and daily life.

Figure 6.1 ▪ **The Rise and Rise of Television**

The number of households with television sets rose sharply in the 1950s and has kept increasing since. During the 1980s, subscriptions to cable televisions soared.

Source: Jerry L. Salvaggio and Jennings Bryant, eds., *Media Use in the Information Age* (Hillsdale, NJ: Erlbaum, 1989); *U.S. Statistical Abstract,* 1992, p. 551.

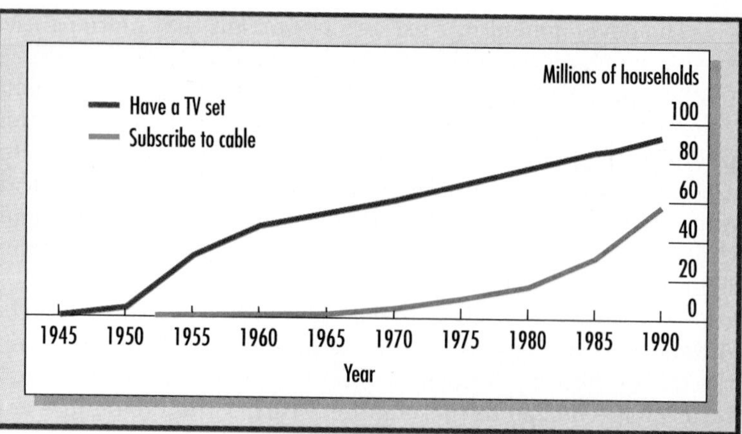

Television The television revolution transformed American media yet again. Television was invented just before World War II; it was developed commercially in the late 1940s and invaded American households on a large scale in the 1950s. In 1950, only 12 percent of American households had a television set, but by 1960, 87 percent did (see Figure 6.1 for the growing number of households). Scores and then hundreds of television stations were established around the country. Most channels were affiliated with one of the three major networks—ABC, CBS, and NBC—which provided the bulk of prime-time programming. The networks also produced and distributed national news programs, which in 1963 were expanded from 15 minutes to 30 minutes of early evening time, and which became *the* major source of national news for most Americans. Since then, polls have regularly shown that most people name television as their most important source of news, and most say they trust television a great deal.

Now practically all American families (98 percent of them) have at least one television set. Most have more than one. Nearly two-thirds of U.S. families now have cable service, which gives them a wide and expanding range of channels.[10] These often include CNN (Cable News Network), broadcasting news 24 hours a day, and C-SPAN, the ultimate fare for political junkies, serving up, for the truly dedicated, live coverage of Congress and other political institutions. Most Americans can, in their own living rooms, see and hear the president of

During the Persian Gulf War, television networks were saturated with war footage released by the U.S. Defense Department, as well as with live coverage of the destruction in Baghdad and Tel Aviv.

Talk radio has become a very influential—and decidedly conservative—voice in American politics. Right-wing personality Rush Limbaugh, who often criticizes the mass media as being too liberal, draws a large and loyal audience on radio and in syndicated television.

the United States and catch glimpses of events in Eastern Europe, China, South Africa, and other places of interest around the world, if they are so inclined.

Radio, once thought dead, has been reborn, especially for commuters, joggers, and people who work at home. Besides music, AM and FM stations offer frequent news bulletins and lengthy call-in talk shows, on which all manner of political opinions, including the cranky and the outrageous, are voiced. Nationally syndicated talk show hosts like Rush Limbaugh have become a political force, able to generate a flood of mail to Congress or the White House. Public Broadcasting System (PBS) stations provide extended news analysis and commentary, often thoughtful and occasionally unorthodox.

New Media Facsimile ("fax") machines have made it easy to bombard politicians with instant opinions and requests. Personal computers and modems in many homes create opportunities to gather information from a host of sources, including politicians' own home pages on the World Wide Web; to discuss politics with other citizens in chat groups; and to talk back to politicians—registering public opinion on-line. Information technology keeps advancing, opening up possibilities like custom feeds of television news for local mixing, two-way video communication, and instant electronic referendum voting.

The actual gathering of news now sometimes involves a broader set of participants. People with their own video recorders have become do-it-yourself electronic journalists, passing on videotapes of hot news stories to television news shows. In 1991, for example, a bystander on an apartment balcony recorded Los Angeles police officers beating and kicking black motorist Rodney King after his arrest for speeding; broadcasts of the videotape created a nationwide furor about police brutality and set the stage for the riots that followed the initial acquittals of the accused police officers.

These new media have the potential to revolutionize politics. They contribute to democracy by giving citizens fuller and easier access to information and opinions about government performance, electoral choices, and policy options. But they may also pose certain dangers to democracy. They make it easier for talk show hosts or organized groups to mobilize narrow segments of

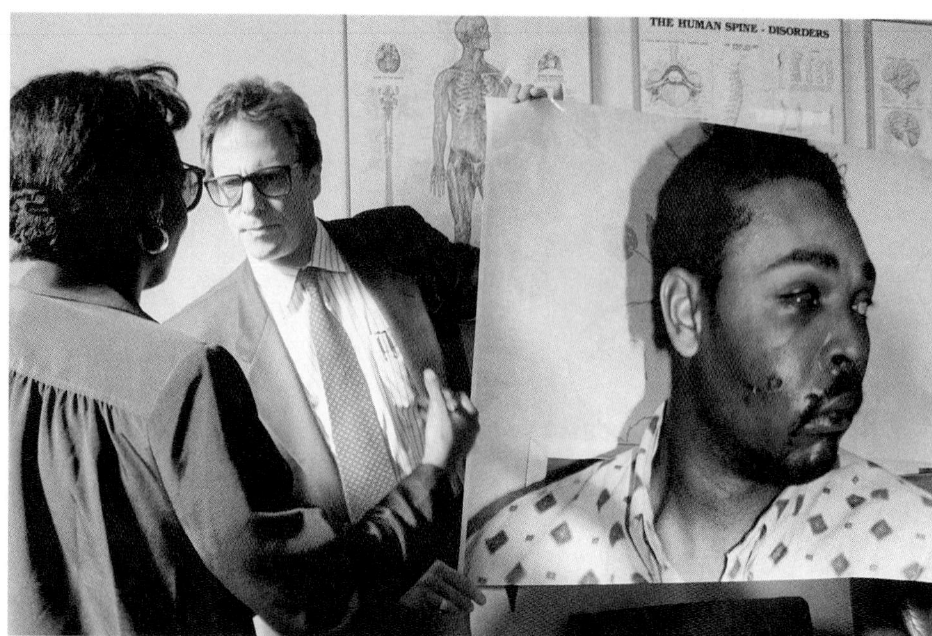

The 1991 beating of motorist Rodney King by Los Angeles police officers was captured on videotape by a bystander with a home video recorder. The footage shocked the American public, raising questions about racially motivated police brutality.

the population and bury Washington under blizzards of electronic messages that may not represent the views of the citizenry as a whole.

We have seen, then, that transformations of the mass media in the United States have been shaped by structural changes in the U.S. economy and society. These include economic development, population expansion and dispersion, technological innovation, and new forms of corporate business organization. The result is a vast and pervasive mass media industry that has enormous effects on politics.

How the Media Work

The precise ways in which the media are organized and function affect whether citizens get the kinds of information they need for democracy to work properly.

Organization of the Mass Media

In the United States, nearly all media are privately owned businesses. Usually, very large businesses, U.S. radio and television broadcasters in the early 1990s had total operating revenues of about $29 *billion;* cable and other pay television services brought in an additional $23 billion.[11] Many more billions of dollars were earned by newspapers and magazines.

Corporate Ownership Some television stations and newspapers—especially the smaller ones—are still owned locally, by families or by groups of investors.

Many of the biggest stations and papers, however, as well as the television networks, are owned by large media corporations, some of which, in turn, are subsidiaries of enormous conglomerates. General Electric bought RCA and its subsidiary NBC in 1986. Gulf + Western has a strong position in book publishing and films. In a wave of mergers and acquisitions in the middle and late 1990s, the Disney company bought ABC, Time Warner acquired Turner Broadcasting, and Westinghouse Electric bought CBS. A few giant corporations now have widespread holdings in the news and entertainment media and in telecommunications. Rupert Murdoch's News Corporation, for example, owns newspapers, magazines, television, motion pictures, and book publishers (see Table 6.1).

Table 6.1

Media Giants

Company and Top Executive (Age)	Key Properties
Walt Disney Michael Eisner (53)	• ABC Television Network • Walt Disney Pictures • Touchstone Pictures • Miramax • The Disney Channel • ESPN2 (controlling interest) • A & E (partial ownership) • Lifetime (partial ownership) • Fairchild Publications
Time Warner Gerald M. Levine (56)	• Time Inc. Magazines • Warner Books • Turner Broadcasting • Warner Music Group • Warner Bros. Pictures • Warner Bros. Television • Time Warner Cable • Home Box Office • Various newspapers and magazines
Viacom Summer M. Redstone, chairman (72) Frank J. Biondi, president (52)	• Paramount Motion Picture Group • United Paramount Network • MTV Networks • Showtime • Simon & Schuster Publishing • Blockbuster Video • North American Paramount theme parks
News Corporation Rupert Murdoch (54)	• Fox Broadcasting Co. • Star TV • 20th Century Fox • TV Guide • HarperCollins Publishers • Delphi Internet Services • Various newspapers and magazines

A few large corporations now dominate the news and entertainment media. Changes come rapidly; in 1995 Westinghouse corporation joined the pack, acquiring CBS Television.

Source: *Wall Street Journal (August 1, 1995)*, p. B1.

As these mergers and acquisitions indicate, the concentration of media ownership has been increasing. In 1981, 46 corporations controlled most of the activity (that is, more than half the circulation and revenues) of daily newspapers, magazines, television, books, and motion pictures. The 46 had shrunk to 29 by 1986, and then to 17 by 1990, the most recent year for which comprehensive figures are available.[12]

Fourteen companies, headed by Gannett (*USA Today* and 92 other dailies), Knight-Ridder, and Newhouse, dominate the newspaper business. In fact, by 1990, the ten largest chains accounted for nearly half the total daily newspaper circulation in the United States. Three corporations—Time Warner (with 40 percent of all magazine revenues), Murdoch's News Corp, and Gannett—control most magazine publishing. The owners of the major television networks (General Electric—NBC; Westinghouse—CBS; and Disney—Capital Cities/ABC; now joined by Time Warner with TBS and CNN) dominate television. Six corporations receive more than half of the $10 billion in book-publishing revenues. And four firms (Warner Communications, Gulf + Western, Universal-MCA, and Columbia Pictures) get more than half the gross box office revenues from movies.

There has been a strong tendency for newspapers to merge. The vast majority of towns and cities that have any newspaper at all have only one. In about two dozen cities, including San Francisco, Seattle, Detroit, and Cincinnati, two newspapers appear, but they are owned by the same people and share printing and other facilities.[13] "Alternative" weeklies in major cities, though popular with many younger readers, have a relatively small circulation and do not provide the full range of political news.

Scholars disagree about the impact of corporate ownership and increased competition. A few see efficiency gains and no problems; they argue that owners don't interfere with what the media print or broadcast. But some critics maintain that the owners and managers of these media corporations are mostly wealthy and conservative, happy with the American free enterprise system within which they have done so well, and unlikely to present critical views. They point to the fact that, shortly after ABC was acquired by Disney (whose president promised to make ABC reflect "what this country stands for"), it abruptly dropped liberal talk show host Jim Hightower, who had boasted 2 million listeners in 150 markets on ABC radio.[14] Many scholars worry that increased concentration of ownership may lead to less diversity of news and opinion.

Uniformity and Diversity Whoever owns them, most newspapers and television stations depend largely on the same sources for news. The AP wire service is now subscribed to by almost all major newspapers in the country. The AP supplies most of the main national and international news stories—even those that are rewritten to carry a local reporter's byline. Most of what appears on network television news, too, is inspired by the AP wire. As we will see, much news comes from public officials.

Along with the centralization and unification of the mass media, however, there is also quite a lot of diversity, for those who make the effort to seek it out. People who are especially interested in politics can find special publications that look at the world in a way that they find compatible or interesting, whether it is the *Weekly Standard* or *National Review* (conservative), *The Nation* (liberal), *Commentary* (neoconservative), *Mother Jones* (irreverent), The *New York Review of Books* (intellectual and critical), the *New Yorker, Rolling Stone,* or dozens of others with small circulations—even the tiny, sometimes

Diverse media are readily available to those who seek them out. In addition to the countless magazines and newspapers available on newsstands and in public libraries, cable television and the rapidly expanding Internet are allowing a greater number of voices to be heard.

one-person 'zines listed in *Factsheet 5.* Cable channels and on-line computer services add still more diversity; the World Wide Web provides a wealth of information uncontrolled by government or corporations.

Profit Motives But media corporations, like other corporations, are in business primarily to make a profit. This fact has important consequences. It means, for example, that the major mass media must appeal to large audiences and get many people to buy their publications or the products they advertise. If most people are mainly interested in entertainment and want their news short, snappy, and sensational, that is what they will get, on network television news and in *USA Today.*

The profit motive also means that the biggest mass media tend to avoid controversial material that might seem "extreme" or offensive to substantial groups of viewers. Examples are legion. General Motors once canceled its sponsorship of an Easter program on the life of Jesus because evangelical groups objected. A number of public television stations refused to air a program on Palestinian grievances because of strong objections by Jewish groups. Despite some outstanding specials, therefore, most viewers of the mass media are not exposed to a lot of controversial ideas.

Audience Power and Democracy The power of the audience to determine what appears in newspapers and on television might be seen as a force for democracy, enabling as many people as possible to see and hear what they want, while those with different tastes can turn to specialized media outlets. But there are at least three possible problems with this idea.

First, even if most people are not eager to get a lot of political information, it might be a good idea to provide it anyhow, in order to help society as a whole by encouraging citizens to form reasonable political opinions and to make sound decisions. Second, consumer sovereignty over the media is not really the same as one-person–one-vote, majority rule democracy. The media are less concerned with average citizens than with those who will buy the most from advertisers—a more affluent, middle- to upper-middle-class group. Further, when the media respond to protests, it is usually to those that are the noisiest and best organized, not to ordinary citizens. (CBS, for example, long delayed airing an interview on *60 Minutes,* with a whistleblower on the tobacco industry, fearing lawsuits from Brown & Williamson.) Third, and perhaps most important, advertisers and media owners do not have to maximize the size of their audiences or their advertising revenues on each story or broadcast; they can give up some immediate income for the sake of other aspects of profit making or for causes in which they strongly believe. Advertisers may, for example, pressure the media not to expose environmentally damaging activities by their own companies. Television stations may go easy on the businesses owned by their own corporations and on politicians who regulate them.

News Making

The kind of news that the media present is affected by the organization and technology of news gathering and news production. Much depends on where reporters are, what sources they talk to, and what sorts of video pictures are available.

Where the News Comes From For national news, most reporters are located in Washington, D.C., site of the main federal government institutions, or in New York City, the biggest U.S. urban area and the center of most media operations. Thus, the national news has a strong Washington–New York orientation.

The major television networks and most newspapers cannot afford to station many reporters outside Washington or New York. The networks usually add just Chicago, Los Angeles, Miami, and Houston or Dallas. Some significant stories from outside the main media centers simply do not make it into the national news. CNN and other news-only channels have a big advantage on fast-breaking news, which they are ready to cover (through their own reporters or the purchase of local footage) and to use immediately on their continuous newscasts.

While some newspapers have strong regional bureaus, the majority print mostly wire service reports of news from elsewhere around the country. The television networks' assignment editors also rely on the wire services to decide what stories to cover; during one month that was studied, NBC got the idea for 70 percent of its domestic film stories from the wire services.[15]

Since it takes a long time (about six hours) to shoot pictures, transport them back to the studio, and process and edit them, most television news stories are assigned to predictable events—news conferences and the like—long before they happen, usually in one of the cities with a permanent television crew. For such spontaneous news as riots, accidents, and battles, special video camera crews can be rushed to the location, but they usually arrive after the main events occur and have to rely on "reaction" interviews or aftermath stories. If action pictures are obtained, they usually do not get to the studio until well after the event has happened (during the Vietnam War, most films came days late) and are edited into a generic story line so that they won't seem dated. Only a few major, ongoing crises (like the Persian Gulf war and the Los Angeles riots) or events of exceptional viewer interest (the O. J. Simpson trial) are covered with live action footage beamed everywhere by satellite.

Only events of immediate importance or extreme viewer interest are reported with live satellite feeds. Coverage of O. J. Simpson's murder trial was carried live to satisfy the public's curiosity about the goings-on. Even the most important political events rarely receive such attention from the media.

Episodic Foreign Coverage Very few newspapers other than the *New York Times* can afford to station reporters abroad. Even the *Times* and the networks and wire services cannot regularly cover most nations of the world. They keep reporters in the countries of greatest interest to Americans—those that have big effects on American interests or enjoy close economic or cultural ties with the United States, such as Great Britain, Germany, Japan, Israel, Russia, and China—and they have regional bureaus in Africa and Latin America. In many countries, however, they depend on "stringers" (local journalists who file occasional reports). During major crises or big events, the media send in temporary news teams, like the armies of reporters who swarmed to Saudi Arabia during the Persian Gulf War. The result is that most media devote most of their attention to limited areas of the world, dropping in only occasionally on others.

Foreign news, therefore, tends to be episodic. An unfamiliar country, such as Rwanda or Haiti, suddenly jumps into the headlines with a spectacular story of a coup, an invasion, or a famine, which comes as a surprise to most people because they have not been prepared by background reports. For a few days or weeks, the story dominates the news, with intensive coverage through pictures, interviews, and commentaries. Then, if nothing new and exciting happens, the story grows stale and disappears from the media. Most viewers are left with little more understanding of the country than they began with. Thus, they find it difficult to form judgments about U.S. foreign policy.

Official Sources

Most political news is based on what public officials say. This fact has important consequences for how well the media serve democracy.

beat The assigned location where a reporter regularly gathers news stories.

Beats and Routines A newspaper or television reporter's work is usually organized around a particular **beat,** which he or she checks every day for new stories. Most political beats center on some official government institution that regularly produces news, such as a local police station or city council, the White House, Congress, the Pentagon, an American embassy abroad, or a country's foreign ministry.

In fact, many news reports are created or originated by officials, not by reporters. Investigative reporting of the sort that Bernstein and Woodward did on Watergate is rare, because it is so time-consuming and expensive. Most reporters get most of their stories quickly and efficiently from press conferences and the press releases that officials write, along with comments solicited from other officials.

One pioneering study found that government officials, domestic or foreign, were the sources of nearly three-quarters of all news in the *New York Times* and the *Washington Post.* Moreover, the vast majority—70 to 90 percent—of all news stories were drawn from situations over which the newsmakers had substantial control, such as press conferences (24.5 percent), interviews (24.7 percent), press releases (17.5 percent), and official proceedings (13 percent).[16] An exhaustive study of *CBS Evening News, NBC Nightly News, Newsweek,* and *Time* found much the same thing. Most stories concerned "knowns" (famous people, especially officials) and their conflicts, decisions, and personnel changes; most stories came from official sources.[17] The same is true of wire service reports and local newspapers.

Mutual Needs Reporters and officials work with each other every day. They need each other. Reporters want stories; they have to cultivate access to people who can provide stories with quotes or anonymous leaks. Officials want favorable publicity and want to avoid or counteract unfavorable publicity. Thus, a comfortable relationship tends to develop. For example, when President Clinton flew to Bosnia in 1995 on *Air Force One* to witness the signing of the Bosnian peace accord, ABC News anchor Peter Jennings was invited to join him on the plane and was given an exclusive interview. Even when reporters put on a show of aggressive questioning at White House press conferences, they usually work hard to stay on good terms with officials and to avoid fundamental challenges of their positions.

The pattern of cozy relationships between reporters and their sources may be one reason the local reporters Woodward and Bernstein made more progress on the Watergate story than the large White House press corps did. White House reporters eventually began to suspect that the president's press secretary and even the president himself were lying, but they were slow to confront them. Remember, too, that Woodward and Bernstein themselves relied mostly on officials; they were fortunate to find middle-level officials who were estranged or guilt-ridden and would talk against the president. Interesting news often comes from angry or disenchanted officials.

The media's heavy reliance on official sources means that government officials are sometimes able to control what journalists report and how they report it. The Reagan administration was particularly successful at picking a "story of the day" and having many officials feed that story to reporters, with a unified interpretation.[18] Reliance on officials also means that, when officials of both parties agree on something, debate tends to be constricted. After President Clinton and congressional Republicans agreed that the federal budget should be balanced in seven years, for example, very few voices were heard in the media arguing that ten years would be soon enough or that precise balance was not important.

Pressure on the Media

Occasionally, high officials resort to direct pressure or intimidation to affect how news is reported. In 1983, for example, a young *New York Times* reporter in El Salvador named Ray Bonner was replaced by a reporter less critical of U.S. policy after an intense lobbying campaign by the Reagan administration.[19]

Pressure may also come from media owners and advertisers. The Anchorage (Alaska) *Times,* which was purchased by Veco International, a company hired by Exxon to work on the enormous Exxon *Valdez* oil spill, illustrated stories of the cleanup with before-and-after pictures provided by, but not attributed to, Exxon.[20] In response to a study, 89.8 percent of all editors reported that advertisers had attempted to influence story content; many admitted that they had succeeded.[21]

Controlling Journalists More often, however, advertisers, media owners, and high government officials exert influence over media coverage quietly and inconspicuously, through the editors and producers who are hired and fired by media owners. Newspaper and magazine editors and television producers hire reporters, assign them to stories, review and edit their work, and decide what to print or put on the air. They exert control over journalists not just by assigning, accepting or rejecting, and altering their stories, but also by administering praise, criticism, promotions, and advice. Successful reporters quickly learn what sorts of stories please their bosses and what sorts of stories don't, so that direct pressure is usually unnecessary.[22]

Newsworthiness Decisions about what kinds of news to print or to televise depend largely on professional judgments about what is **newsworthy.** Exactly what makes a story newsworthy is difficult to spell out, but experienced editors make quick and confident judgments of what their audiences (and their employers) want. If they were consistently wrong, they would probably not remain editors for very long.

newsworthy Worth printing or broadcasting as news, according to editors' judgments.

In practice, newsworthiness seems to depend on such factors as novelty (man bites dog, not dog bites man); drama and human interest; relevance to the lives of Americans; high stakes (e.g., physical violence or conflict); and comprehensibility. Some trivial topics are judged newsworthy, like the hair styles of O. J. Simpson trial stars Marcia Clark and Kato Kaelin. As the term *news story* implies, news works best when it can be framed as a familiar kind of narrative: an exposé of greed or corruption, conflict between politicians, or a foreign affairs crisis. On television, of course, dramatic or startling film footage helps to make a story gripping.

Objectivity

Political news does not make much sense without an interpretation of what it means and whether the news is good or bad. Under the informal rules of "objective" journalism, however, explicit interpretations by journalists are avoided, except for commentary or editorials that are labeled as such. In news stories, most interpretations are left implicit (so that they are hard to detect and hard to argue with) or are given by so-called experts who are interviewed for comments.

The Experts Experts are selected partly for reasons of convenience and audience appeal: scholars who live close to New York City or Washington, D.C., who like to speak in public, and who are skillful in coming up with colorful quotations on a variety of subjects are contacted again and again. They often show up on television to comment on the news of the day, even on issues that are far from the area of their special expertise.

The experts and commentators featured in the media are often ex-officials. Their views are usually in harmony with the political currents of the day; that is, they tend to reflect a fairly narrow spectrum of opinion close to that of the party in power in Washington, D.C., especially the party of the president. During the 1980s and early 1990s, for example, the experts most frequently quoted on television were a handful of former Reagan or Bush administration officials and others associated with conservative think tanks, such as the American Enterprise Institute and the Center for Strategic and International Studies. The commentator "punditocracy" was also quite conservative.[23]

At other times, with different politicians in power, different kinds of experts have been favored. Antipoverty warriors got a lot of media attention during the Lyndon Johnson administration, for example, and some liberal and centrist voices began to reappear in the media when President Clinton replaced Bush. But radical independent thinkers like I. F. Stone, whose *Weekly* became influential for a time during the Vietnam War, or Noam Chomsky, a fierce critic of media reporting on U.S. foreign policy, have rarely penetrated the mainstream media at all.

Think Tanks Research centers and think tanks like the American Enterprise Institute, the Heritage Foundation, and the Brookings Institution, which publish policy-oriented books and articles and get media exposure for their experts, are an important source of ideas and analyses that eventually work

Antiestablishment journalist I. F. Stone's *Weekly* gained much attention for its criticism of the Vietnam War. Most news printed and broadcast by the mainstream U.S. media, however, comes from official sources.

their way through the media to affect public opinion and policymaking. These think tanks popularize academic scholars' ideas and apply them to policy problems.

Think tanks also serve as a channel through which corporations, foundations, and other large donors may affect the course of public opinion and public policy. The funding of think tanks comes heavily from domestic and foreign corporate sources, which may influence what they study and how they study it. During the 1980s, for example, the Heritage Foundation, which issued a series of reports favorable to Taiwan, received more than $3 million from Taiwan companies coordinated by the Taiwanese government.[24]

Is the News Biased?

Few topics arouse more disagreement than the question of whether the mass media in the United States have a liberal or conservative **bias**—or any bias at all. For years, a number of journalists and scholars have maintained that the media tend to be a proestablishment, conservative force, reflecting their corporate ownership and their dependence on official sources for news. Conservative critics have counterattacked, arguing that liberal media elites regularly publish and broadcast antiestablishment, antiauthority news with a liberal bias.

bias Deviation from some ideal standard, such as representativeness or objectivity.

Liberal Reporters Surveys of reporters' and journalists' opinions suggest that they tend to be somewhat more liberal than the average American—though by no means radical—on certain matters, including the environment and such social issues as civil rights and liberties, abortion, and women's rights.[25] This is especially true of those employed by certain elite media organizations, including the *New York Times,* the *Washington Post,* and PBS. It is likely that reporters' liberalism has been reflected in the treatment of some stories about such issues as nuclear energy, the greenhouse effect, and toxic waste. In 1990, for example, an exhaustive three-volume government report that found that damage from acid rain had been greatly overestimated was ignored by virtually all the major media, except *60 Minutes* and the *Wall Street Journal.*[26]

But there is little or no systematic evidence that reporters' personal values regularly affect what appears in the media. Journalists' commitment to the idea of objectivity helps them resist temptation, as do critical scrutiny and rewriting by editors. And in any case, the liberalism of journalists may be offset by their need to rely on official sources and by conservatism among media owners and publishers. This may be particularly true on economic issues, such as fighting inflation and cutting government spending rather than creating jobs and raising wages.

Conservative Owners The owners and top managers of most media corporations tend to be very conservative. The shareholders and executives of multibillion-dollar corporations are not very interested in undermining capitalism or, for that matter, in increasing their own taxes, raising labor costs, or offending their advertisers. These owners and managers ultimately decide which reporters, newscasters, and editors to hire or fire, to promote or discourage. Journalists who want to get ahead, therefore, may have to come to terms with the policies of those who own and run media businesses.

One sign of conservatism in the media is newspapers' endorsements of presidential candidates, which are mostly decided on by owners and publishers. In all six presidential elections from 1968 through 1988, more newspapers—usually many more—backed the Republican than the Democratic candidate. In 1988, for example, one week before the election, 195 dailies had endorsed George Bush, whereas just 51 had endorsed Michael Dukakis.[27] Only in 1992 was the picture different: the "new," friendly-to-business Democrat, Bill Clinton, won a majority of endorsements.[28]

What Is Bias? One reason observers keep arguing about the question of bias is that it is not easy to define or measure. Some scholars have simply counted what proportion of references to some political figure or policy (e.g., presidential candidate Richard Nixon or the Vietnam War) seemed to be positive or negative. However, negative coverage may reflect objectively bad news—for example, Vietnam War casualties or the Watergate revelations—rather than bias, or the media may just be quoting what leading news sources are saying, whether the sources are right or wrong.

A more sophisticated concept of bias involves a deviation from some perfect representation of objective reality. Yet there is lots of room for argument about which aspects of reality are worth reporting and about what the facts are; what is true and what is false. Is the truth whatever our best experts say it is? If so, who gets to decide who the best experts are?

A different concept of bias involves slanted or evaluative language. *Time* magazine at one time referred to "mossback" Republicans, as opposed to the progressive variety it favored; newspapers sometimes tag views they dislike as "radical" or "controversial," while annointing certain experts as "highly regarded." But that sort of bias, too, is hard to measure and depends on the eye of the beholder. One person's terrorist is another's freedom fighter. In the 1996 presidential primaries, some media judged Pat Buchanan's stands to be "extreme"; others called them "populist," tapping broad discontent among citizens.

Dominant Points of View

Even if we cannot be sure whether or how the media are biased, it is easy to identify certain tendencies in media coverage, certain beliefs that are assumed, and certain values and points of view that are emphasized.

Patriotism Most news about foreign affairs, for example, takes a definitely pro-American, patriotic point of view, usually putting the United States in a good light and its opponents in a bad light. It is also ethnocentric, focusing on things that interest and concern ordinary Americans. For example, U.S. newspapers and television devoted intensive, year-long coverage to the fate of 49 Americans held hostage in the U.S. embassy in Tehran, Iran; more recently, they exhaustively covered a U.S. pilot, Scott O'Grady, who had been shot down over Bosnia. But much less attention has been paid to the slaughter of millions of people in Indonesia, Nigeria, East Timor, Cambodia, and Rwanda.

This patriotic and ethnocentric perspective, together with heavy reliance on U.S. government news sources, means that coverage of foreign news generally harmonizes well with official U.S. foreign policy. Studies show that, historically, the media have tended to go easy on such right-wing dictators as the shah of Iran, Ferdinand Marcos of the Philippines, and Anastasio Somoza of Nicaragua, even though they oppressed their own people, because they were firm anticommunist allies of the United States.[29] Similarly, the U.S. media stuck with ally Boris Yeltsin long after he became highly unpopular in Russia. By the same token, the media tend to go along with the U.S. government in assuming the worst about official "enemies." During the Cold War, for example, the media publicized unsubstantiated accusations that the Soviet Union had tried to kill Pope John Paul II, had used germ warfare in Cambodia, and had deliberately shot down a civilian Korean airliner.[30] More recently, the media have demonized Saddam Hussein and other official foes of the United States.

In foreign policy crisis situations, the reliance on official news sources means that the media sometimes propagate government statements that are false or misleading, as in the announcement of unprovoked attacks on U.S. destroyers in the Gulf of Tonkin at the beginning of the Vietnam War (recall the story in Chapter 5). Secret information can also be controlled by the government. The widely publicized "missile gap" that led to a big arms buildup during the Kennedy years and the "window of vulnerability" that preceded the Reagan defense budget increases both turned out to be illusions.[31]

Approval of Free Enterprise Another tendency of the media is to run stories generally approving of free enterprise, free international trade, and minimal regulation. Our economic system wins approval, while variant or alternative systems, like European social democracies with comprehensive social welfare programs, are generally disapproved. Individual U.S. corporations are criticized for errors and misdeeds, but the economic system itself is rarely challenged. This stance is hardly surprising, since most Americans like the U.S. system, but it discourages the consideration of alternatives.

Deference to Public Officials Public officials are essential news sources, whom the media are reluctant to alienate; in day-to-day coverage, most **incumbents** are treated with considerable respect and deference. This treatment limits the media's watchdog function. Press coverage of popular presidents has tended to be especially favorable, while that of Congress has generally been skimpier and more negative.[32] For the same reasons, the views of the incumbent political party in Washington, D.C., tend to receive a lot of attention: the officials, experts, and commentators quoted in the media tend to come mostly from whichever party is in power. Thus, conservative Republican viewpoints gained much more favorable treatment in the media after the Republican takeover of Congress in the 1994 elections.[33]

incumbent One who holds office.

Negativity and Scandal In recent years, however, political candidates and officials have been subjected to a relentless barrage of negative material. Some of this coverage starts with negative advertisements by opponents, which are then sometimes echoed in media reporting. At the beginning of the 1996 campaign, for example, Iowa, New Hampshire, and other states were saturated with ads by Steve Forbes, Bob Dole, and Phil Gramm attacking each other as old and tired, lacking ideas, or favoring the rich. Research has shown that negative ads increase citizens' anger and alienation and discourage them from voting.[34] News stories often picked up and amplified these negative themes.

Incumbent officials, too, now get plenty of negative publicity when they are weakened and unpopular or when there is evidence of scandal in their personal or financial lives, which creates dramatic human interest stories. Publicity about charges that Senator Robert Packwood sexually harassed a number of women staff members eventually forced him to resign. The "Whitewater" allegations against President Clinton and First Lady Hillary Rodham Clinton—that they had dealt improperly with a real estate investment and a bank's campaign contributions while Clinton was governor of Arkansas and had obstructed justice while in the White House—were doggedly pursued by the

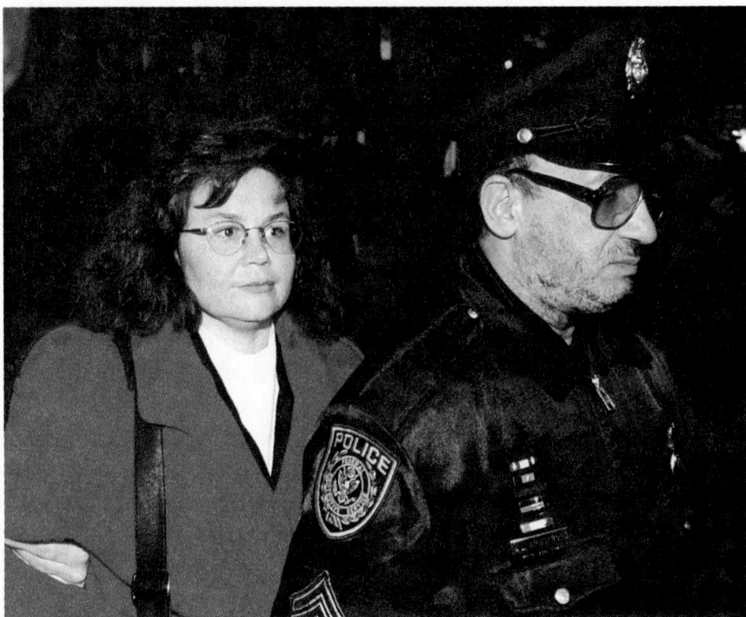

The media tend to be kinder to sitting presidents than to candidates or lower-level officials. Bill Clinton's alleged extramarital affair made major headlines during his first campaign for the presidency, but the fervor subsided once he took office. Lower-level elected officials are less immune to scandals. Congresswoman Enid Waldholz, pictured here, resigned from office after revelations that her husband mismanaged and defrauded her campaign.

American Spectator, the *New York Times,* and other media for more than three years leading up to the 1996 election.

Structural Influences and Limited Political Information To say that the media have these tendencies is to say that the media are influenced by the major structural and political forces in the United States. The position of the United States in the international system and the nature of the U.S. economic and social systems deeply affect every individual and institution in the country, including the media. The political forces that are dominant in the country at a given time also tend to dominate the media.

At the same time, most communications scholars agree that the media coverage of political news has certain distinctive features that result from characteristics of the mass media themselves, including the prevailing technology and organization of news gathering, corporate ownership, and the profit-making drive to appeal to mass audiences. These characteristics of the media mean that news, especially on television, tends to be episodic, fragmented, personalized, and dramatic rather than sustained, analytical, or dispassionate.[35] As a result, the media provide less useful or enlightening political information to citizens than they might. The public's capacity to form intelligent opinions is weakened, and popular sovereignty and democracy suffer.

Effects of the Media on Politics

The old idea that the mass media have only "minimal effects" on politics is now discredited. The contents of the media do make a difference; they affect public opinion and policymaking in a number of ways.

Agenda Setting

Several studies, for example, have demonstrated **agenda-setting** effects. The topics that get the most coverage in the media are the same ones that most people tell pollsters are the most important problems facing the country. This correlation does not result just from the media's printing what people are most interested in; it is a real effect of what appears in the media. In controlled experiments, people who are shown doctored television news broadcasts emphasizing a particular problem (e.g., national defense) mention that problem as being important more often than people who see un-tampered-with broadcasts.[36]

agenda setting Influencing what people consider important.

Of course, media managers do not arbitrarily decide what news to emphasize; their decisions reflect what is happening in the world and what American audiences care about. If there is a war or an economic depression, the media report it. But some research has indicated that what the media cover sometimes diverges from actual trends in problems. Publicity about crime, for example, may reflect editors' fears or a few dramatic incidents rather than a rising crime rate. When the two diverge, it seems to be the media's emphasis rather than real trends that affects public opinion.[37] Other examples include periodic surges and declines in the number of stories about the AIDS epidemic or about illegal drug use.

Framing and Effects on Policy Preferences

Experiments also indicate that the media's **framing**, or interpretation of stories, affects how people think about political problems and how they assign blame. Whether citizens ascribe poverty to laziness of the poor or to the nature of the economy, for example, depends partly on whether the media run stories about poor individuals (implying that they are responsible for their own plight) or stories about overall economic trends like wage stagnation and unemployment.[38]

framing Providing a context for interpreting, for example, in news stories.

What appears in the media affects people's policy preferences as well. One study found that changes in the percentages of the public that favored various policies could be predicted rather accurately by what sorts of stories appeared on network television news shows between one opinion survey and the next. News from experts, commentators, and popular presidents had especially strong effects, while news openly attributed to interest groups had no impact or even a negative effect.[39]

Impact on Policymaking

By affecting what ordinary Americans think is important, how they understand problems, and what policies they want, the media indirectly affect what government does, because the government responds to public opinion. Heavy support for NAFTA (the North American Free Trade Agreement) by the *New York Times* and other media, for example, probably helped counteract public opposition due to fears of job losses. In addition, the media affect who is elected to office. As we will see in Chapter 9, media stories about the character of presidential and other candidates have enormous effects on fund-raising and on citizens' judgments of who would make a good leader. And media-reported rumors can destroy the careers of public officials.

Moreover, what appears in the media has a direct effect on policymaking. Policymakers learn about the world and about each other's activities from the

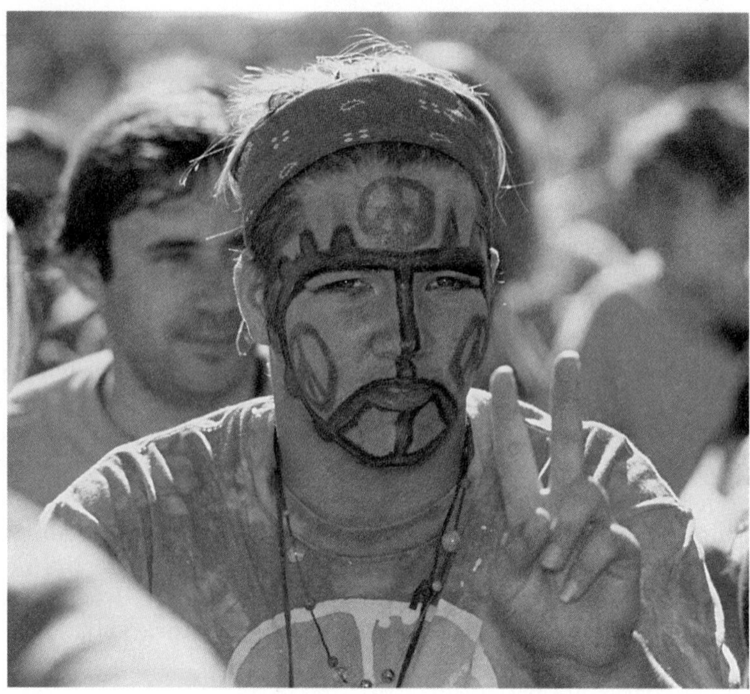

In portraying dissenters, such as this peace protester, the media tend to emphasize the unusual, the violent, or the bizarre.

media. Investigative journalism that exposes problems, for example, often leads local, state, or federal officials to act. Sometimes, journalists and politicians actively work together: the journalists expose problems that the politicians want to solve, and then the politicians' statements, hearings, and bills prolong the story for journalists to continue reporting.[40]

Censorship and Government Regulation

Our Constitution protects freedom of the press, and the U.S. government has less legal control over the media than the government of most other countries do. But our government has the authority to make various technical and substantive regulations on the electronic media, if it wishes.

Constitutional Protection

Early in American history, government sometimes interfered with the press in a heavy-handed way. Under the Alien and Sedition Acts of 1798, for example, several Anti-Federalist newspaper editors were jailed for criticizing John Adams's administration.

In recent years, however, the Constitution has been interpreted as forbidding government from preventing the publication of most kinds of political information, or from punishing its publication afterward. The main exceptions involve national security, especially in wartime.

Prior Restraint Several U.S. Supreme Court decisions, beginning in the 1920s and 1930s, have ensured the press a great deal of constitutional protection. The First Amendment provision that Congress shall make no law "abridging freedom of speech, or of the press" has been held by the Supreme Court to prevent the federal censorship of newspapers or magazines. Only under the most pressing circumstances of danger to national security can the government engage in **prior restraint** and prevent the publication of material to which it objects. (See the chapter on civil liberties.)

prior restraint The government's power to prevent publication, as opposed to punishment afterward.

On June 30, 1971, for example, the Supreme Court denied a request by the Nixon administration to restrain the *New York Times* and the *Washington Post* from publishing excerpts from the "Pentagon Papers," a secret Defense Department history of the U.S. involvement in Vietnam. The Court declared that "the Government 'thus carries a heavy burden of showing justification for the enforcement of such a restraint.' . . . The Government had not met that burden." Justice Hugo Black's concurring opinion has become an important statement on freedom of the press (see the Struggle for Democracy box).

Wartime Controls In a sense, however, the "Pentagon Papers" case was an easy one, because it concerned the right to publish a two-year-old history and analysis of past government policy, not information about current military or foreign policy actions that could jeopardize American lives. During wartime, the government has almost always asserted broad powers to control what reporters can see and what they can print.

During the Civil War, the War Department required newspapers to clear all telegraphed information with the department; when that measure failed, they harassed reporters. During World War I, the Post Office Department refused to deliver 44 newspapers and magazines through the mail because of alleged pro-German or prosocialist content. During World War II, the Office of Censorship monitored all news entering and leaving the country, but it focused mainly on news about casualties and troop and ship movements rather than on political matters.[41]

Relatively free media access to the Vietnam War eventually brought a flood of negative stories.[42] U.S. officials, having learned their lesson, kept the media away from the invasions of Grenada and Panama and tightly restricted access to the 1991 war with Iraq. During that war the military imposed an elaborate system of control and censorship, requiring reporters to work only in escorted pools, limiting their access to U.S. troops, and censoring their stories. The media went along with these restrictions at the time, and large majorities of the public approved of it, but the result was incomplete and misleading coverage.[43]

Coverage of the Persian Gulf War, even more than that of previous wars, was carefully controlled and censored by the U.S. military.

The Pentagon Papers and Freedom of the Press

The Struggle for Democracy

In 1967, when the Vietnam War was going badly for the United States, Secretary of Defense Robert MacNamara commissioned a top-secret historical study to see exactly what had gone wrong. The Pentagon researchers spent 18 months and compiled 47 volumes of material on U.S. involvement in Southeast Asia. Their final report, submitted in January 1969, was a devastating account of misrepresentations, falsehoods, civilian bungling, military blunders, and deception by American officials.[a]

Two years later, in March 1971, Daniel Ellsberg (one of the Pentagon researchers) provided a copy of the report to the *New York Times.* The *Times* then spent three months agonizing over whether or not to publish it; editors said yes, but business and legal people said no. Finally, on June 13, 1971, the *Times* published six solid pages of excerpts from the report (which came to be known as the "Pentagon Papers") and promised nine more installments.

Outraged at what he considered a breach of national security, President Nixon had Attorney General John Mitchell ask the *Times* to cease publication; when they refused, the government obtained a restraining order in federal district court and stopped the *Times* from publishing anything beyond the third installment. This was the first time since the Alien and Sedition Acts of 1798 that the federal government had tried in advance to get a court to prevent a newspaper from publishing news or commentary.

But the *Washington Post,* after a brief internal struggle, took up where the *Times* had left off. When the attorney general went back to court and stopped the *Post,* 19 other newspapers in rapid succession continued publication. Furthermore, the newspapers that had been stopped appealed their restraining orders to the circuit court of appeal and finally to the U.S. Supreme Court.

On June 30, in *New York Times Co. v. United States,* the Supreme Court ruled, by a vote of 6 to 3, in favor of the newspapers. The justices wrote nine separate opinions; two of the six that favored the newspapers did so on narrow grounds. The concurring opinion by Justice Hugo Black made the most eloquent case for absolute First Amendment protection of freedom of the press, so that the media can serve as watchdogs:

> Paramount among the responsibilities of a free press is the duty to prevent any part of the Government from deceiving the people and sending them off to distant lands to die of foreign fever and foreign shot and shell. . . . The *New York Times* and the *Washington Post* and other newspapers should be commended for serving the purpose that the Founding Fathers saw so clearly. In revealing the workings of government that led to the Vietnam War, the newspapers nobly did precisely that which the founders hoped and trusted they would do.

[a]James Aronson, *The Press and the Cold War,* new and expanded ed. (New York: Monthly Review, 1990), pp. 292–295.

Punishment Besides the constitutional limits on censorship, newspapers and magazines are also protected against most kinds of punishment after they have printed something. Punishable obscenity, for example, has been narrowly defined. The Constitution has also been interpreted as preventing libel laws from being used against publications that print criticisms of public figures, as long as they take reasonable care not to spread damaging falsehoods.

Although the government has many informal ways of influencing the press, then, there is little formal regulation of newspapers or magazines in the United States.

The Electronic Media

The electronic media are theoretically much more susceptible to direct government regulation, though such regulation is now very limited.

Government Licensing of the Airwaves The federal government has broad powers to regulate the use of the airwaves, which are considered public property. Ever since the passage of the Radio Act of 1927 and the Communications Act of 1934, which established the Federal Communications Commission (FCC), the government has licensed radio and television stations and has required them to observe certain rules as a condition for obtaining licenses.

FCC rules specify the frequencies on which stations can broadcast and the amount of power that they can use, in order to prevent interference among broadcasters of the sort that had brought chaos to radio during the 1920s. Government regulations divide the VHF television band into 12 channels and allocate them in such a way that most major cities have three VHF stations—the main reason for the early emergence of just three major networks. The development of scores of UHF (high-numbered) channels and their transmission by cable to remote locations have greatly opened up variety and competition.

For a long time, in order to prevent monopolies of scarce channels, federal rules prohibited networks or anyone else from owning more than 5 VHF stations around the country. As UHF competition grew, however, the VHF limit was loosened to 12 stations in 1989 and was further deregulated in 1990 and 1996, so that one company's stations can now cover up to 35 percent of U.S. households. FCC rules have also insisted on local control of programming, giving local affiliate stations considerable influence over the networks through their "clearance" of national programs.

The Telecommunications Act of 1996, which revolutionized the industry by allowing telephone companies, cable companies and broadcasters all to compete with each other, also provided that new frequencies should be given to broadcasters free of charge, in order to provide high-definition TV. Critics called this a "giveaway" of public airwaves worth some $10 billion to $70 billion and called for requiring new public services or auctioning the frequencies off in order to get government revenue.

Public Service Broadcasting The FCC was mandated by Congress to regulate the airwaves for the "public interest, convenience, or necessity." This vague phrase has been interpreted as including "the development of an informed public opinion through the public dissemination of news and ideas concerning the vital public issues of the day," with ideas coming from "diverse and antagonistic sources," and with an emphasis on service to the local community.

In practice, this requirement has mainly meant FCC pressure (backed up by the threat of not renewing stations' licenses) to provide a certain number of hours of news and "public service" broadcasting. Thus, government regulation created an artificial demand for news programming, before it became profitable, and contributed to the rise of network news and its expansion from 15 to 30 minutes in 1963, as well as to the development of documentaries and specials. As one network executive observed, "News, for most stations, is the price of the license."[44] In that way, government regulation presumably contributed to informed public opinion and to democracy.

Recently, however, this public service requirement has been eroded. According to one study, after the deregulation of the 1980s, public interest programming dropped from an average of 19 minutes a day to less than 5 minutes a day.[45]

Subsidies for Public Broadcasting The federal government provides some modest subsidies for public broadcasting: about $275 million in 1996, constituting just 14 percent of the budgets of the several hundred U.S. public radio and television stations. Leading congressional Republicans initially proposed to "zero out" this support; after protests from viewers and listeners, the subsidies were kept in place, but at lower levels.[46]

fairness doctrine A past requirement that television stations present contrasting points of view.

Fairness For many years, the **fairness doctrine** of 1949 required that licensees present contrasting viewpoints on any controversial issue of public importance that was discussed. This requirement led to efforts at balance—presenting two sides on any issue that was mentioned—and sometimes to the avoidance of controversial issues altogether. It was left mostly up to broadcasters, however, to decide what was important or controversial and what constituted a fair reply and a fair amount of time to give it.

Fairness is not easy to define: Which of the unlimited number of possible opinions deserve a hearing? The FCC itself long ago made clear that it did not intend to make time available to "Communist viewpoints," and both of the "two sides" that the media air are usually quite mainstream. As the Reagan-appointed FCC moved in a conservative direction during the 1980s and criticized the "fairness doctrine," the Democrat-dominated Congress attempted to enact the doctrine into law, but President Reagan vetoed the bill. The FCC subsequently abolished the doctrine, arguing that it was unconstitutional.

equal time provision A past requirement that television stations give or sell the same amount of time to all competing candidates.

Equal Time Similarly, the **equal time provision** of the 1934 Communications Act required that, except for news programs, stations that granted (or sold) air time to any one candidate for public office had to grant (or sell) other candidates equal time. This requirement threatened to cause the media great expense when minor party candidates insisted on their share of air time or when opponents wanted to reply to political speeches by incumbent presidents in election years. Contrary to its intent, therefore, this requirement led to some curtailment of political programming.

Equal time provisions were suspended in 1960 to allow televised debates between candidates John F. Kennedy and Richard M. Nixon, and in 1976 and 1980 the FCC permitted the staging of the Ford-Carter and Carter-Reagan debates as "public meetings," sponsored by the League of Women Voters, to get around the provision. Then, in 1983, the FCC declared that radio and television broadcasters were free to stage debates at all political levels among candidates of their own choosing.[47]

Rate Regulation Federal and local regulation of the rates charged by cable TV firms (many of them monopoly providers in local areas) has been imposed, removed, and imposed once again. Most recently, with the Telecommunications Act of 1996, cable rate regulation is scheduled to be ended by 1999, by which time it is thought that competition from the telephone companies may keep cable rates down.

Taken as a whole, then, government regulation of the media does not now amount to much. The trend has been toward a free market system with little government interference.

The only new regulations recently imposed have been the 1996 provision requiring that television manufacturers include a "V-chip" that can shut off

Election year debates, such as this 1992 debate among presidential candidates George Bush, Ross Perot, and Bill Clinton, have become a regular television feature and may have a profound effect on elections.

programs that broadcasters rate as obscene or violent and a provision banning obscenity on the Internet. The Internet ban has provoked protests and court challenges on the grounds that it violates freedom of speech. Proposals to control campaign attack advertising (perhaps by outlawing short spot ads, or by paying for longer, issue-oriented discussions with public money) have not got very far.

Do the Media Serve Democracy?

The media help promote democracy by providing access to political information. At the same time, however, the information they provide may often be incomplete or biased.

Access to Information

The mass media are essential to the workings of democracy in a large modern nation. Without the media, ordinary citizens would have little hope of learning what is happening abroad; they could not begin to think about what sorts of policies the United States should pursue in foreign affairs. Nor, without media, could most Americans learn what their government is doing domestically or what sorts of candidates are running for office.

In these respects, the spread of the mass media in the United States, and the penetration of millions of homes by newspapers, radio, television, and computers, has undoubtedly helped democracy. It has made it much easier for ordinary citizens to form policy preferences, to judge the actions of government, and to figure out whom they want to govern them. Mass media thus tend to broaden the scope of conflict and contribute to political equality. When citizens, rather than just political leaders or special-interest groups, know what is going on, they can have a voice in politics. Moreover, interactive media and media-published polls help politicians hear that voice.

Criticisms of the Media

At the same time, many advocates of democracy are very critical of the media. We have seen that there are some grounds for criticism. Scholars who want the media to be highly informative, analytical, and issue-oriented are appalled by the personalized, episodic, dramatic, and fragmented character of most news stories, which do not provide sustained and coherent explanations of what is going on.

Others worry about ideological biases that they think arise from a leftist media elite, or from a corporate-owned and fundamentally conservative media industry. Some criticize the media's patriotic and ethnocentric tendencies to support official U.S. foreign policy and even to pass along deliberate untruths stated by government officials. If the media regularly present one-sided or false pictures of politics, then people may form mistaken policy preferences. Government responsiveness to manipulated preferences would not be truly democratic.

We have pointed out several examples of media coverage that may have misled citizens, but we have also mentioned the great difficulty of defining or measuring bias systematically, as well as the strong differences of opinion that exist on this subject. You should form your own judgment, by reading and watching the media with a keen, critical eye, alert to possible omissions or distortions (see the Resource Feature).

Still other critics worry that constant media exposés of alleged official wrongdoing or government inefficiency, and the mocking tone aimed at virtually all political leaders by talk radio hosts, have fueled the growing political cynicism of the public.

How to Judge the Media

How you judge the media may depend on exactly what standards you apply. Some see it as a major flaw if the mass media fail to present informative, analytical, sophisticated coverage of political issues; they argue that extensive public deliberation and discussion are essential to democracy, and that a shortage of good information makes it difficult for citizens to form intelligent political judgments.

On the other hand, some observers argue that citizens do not need a lot of detailed information; they just need to know what the issues are and which policies are advocated by the leaders or the groups they trust. Perhaps a skimpy presentation of news is enough, as long as it is not terribly biased and as long as diverse elite interpretations are offered.[48] If so, the crucial question is whether political competition is vigorous enough to provide diverse, reliable cues to the public. You must decide for yourself whether it is.

Summary

The shape of the mass media in the United States has been determined largely by structural factors: technological developments (the invention of printing presses, wire services, radio, television, computers, and satellites); the growth

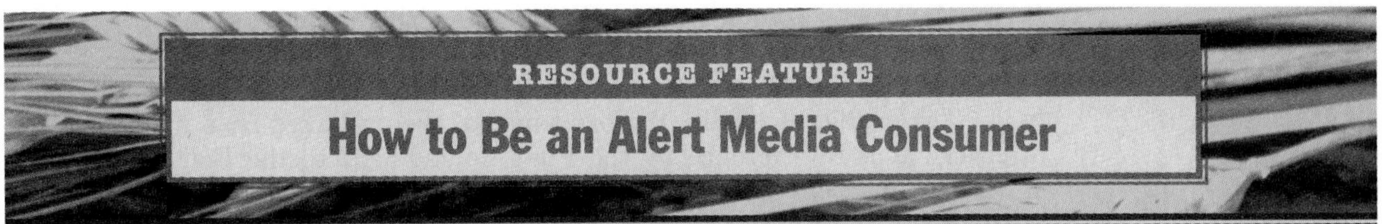

RESOURCE FEATURE
How to Be an Alert Media Consumer

Noam Chomsky, a famous linguist and one of the sharpest critics of the U.S. mass media, once wrote that he was mystified about why his teeth were wearing down, until his wife pointed out that he ground them in rage every time he read the *New York Times*.[a] But Chomsky and other careful observers manage to ferret out useful bits of information from the *Times* and other media, even when they think most news stories are parroting the official line. If you want to get the most you can from the media, we offer the following suggestions:

1. *Go beyond TV news.* Compare its coverage of issues with that in documentaries, newspapers, and magazines. Do TV news programs leave important things out? What? Why?
2. *Expand the points of view to which you are exposed.* Take a look at magazines or programs with which you think you disagree, and question your own beliefs. What kinds of viewpoints are presented in the mainstream media, and what kinds are not?
3. *Analyze news stories.* Watch out for stereotypes or simple plot lines. What concrete facts and evidence are offered? Who are the sources, and why? Whose interests might the story serve? Whose viewpoint is left out?
4. *Read between the lines.* Watch for hints that the reporter does not really believe what a news source is saying. Watch for omissions, or contradictions, or stray facts that don't fit the story line but may be crucial.
5. *Challenge what you read or see.* Ask what is assumed to be true (perhaps because "everybody believes it"). Are you sure it is really so? What has been left out? How would a person from another country, or from another planet, interpret the story?

[a] "All the News That Fits: Noam Chomsky on the *New York Times*," *Utne Reader* (February–March 1986), pp. 50–55.

of the American population and economy; and the development of a privately owned, corporation-dominated media industry.

The profit motive leads the major media to appeal to large audiences by limiting the quantity and depth of political news, by appealing to patriotism and other mainstream political values, and by emphasizing dramatic stories with visual impact and human interest. Media owners and advertisers sometimes shape the news to help their own businesses, or to express values supportive of free enterprise and the existing social system.

News gathering is organized around New York City, Washington, D.C., and a handful of major cities in the United States and abroad. Most foreign countries are ignored unless there are transient crises or other big stories to communicate. Most news comes from government officials, who cultivate friendly relations with the press and provide accessible press conferences and handouts, as well as sometimes applying pressure.

Observers disagree about whether the media are biased in a liberal or a conservative direction. Reporters tend to be liberal, especially on social issues, but this tendency may be balanced or reversed by conservative owners and editors. The U.S. media tend to reflect ethnocentrism, support for U.S. foreign policy, support for American-style capitalism, and generally favorable treatment of the politicians in power. But they broadcast negative campaign ads, publicize personal scandals, and sharply criticize officials who have lost popularity.

Media stories have substantial effects on the public's perceptions of problems, its interpretations of events, its evaluations of political candidates, and its policy preferences.

The media, especially the print media, are protected from many kinds of government interference by the First Amendment to the Constitution. But censorship occurs during wars and crises, and officials have indirect ways of influencing the news. The electronic media are legally open to direct regulation, but such regulation, including the fairness doctrine and equal time provisions, has mostly lapsed.

There is disagreement about how well the media act as public watchdogs and how well they provide information about public policy and electoral choices. The media provide citizens with political information that is essential to the working of democracy. At the same time, however, many observers criticize them for not being sufficiently informative or analytical. Others worry about possible liberal or conservative biases, or about excessive negativism, or about tendencies to support official policy.

Suggested Readings

Alterman, Eric. *Sound and Fury: The Washington Punditocracy and the Collapse of American Politics.* New York: HarperCollins, 1992.
A scathing critique of columnists and commentators.

Bagdikian, Ben. *The Media Monopoly,* 4th ed. Boston: Beacon Press, 1992.
Analyzes the corporate structure of the media and its consequences.

Bennett, W. Lance. *News: Politics of Illusion,* 3rd ed. New York: Longman, 1995.
A critique of the news as trivial and uninformative. See also Bennett, The Governing Crisis. *New York: St. Martin's Press, 1992.*

Graber, Doris. *Mass Media and American Politics,* 4th ed. Washington, DC: Congressional Quarterly Press, 1993.
A basic textbook on the subject.

Page, Benjamin I. *Who Deliberates? Mass Media in Modern Democracy.* Chicago: University of Chicago Press, 1996.
A discussion of how the media do or do not serve democracy well, with illustrative case studies.

Patterson, Thomas E. *Out of Order.* New York: Knopf, 1993.
An analysis and critique of the media coverage of elections.

Internet Sources

CNN Interactive http://www.cnn.com/
Up-to-the-minute news from CNN.

Mass Media Article Index http://www.mannlib.cornell.edu/cgibin/description.cgi?669.html
The largest collection of information on-line about the mass media.

Mass Media Resources http://128.227.230.15/commres/
Articles and reports on the mass media.

NBC News http://www.nbc.com/index.html
Up-to-the-minute news from the NBC news division.

The *New York Times* http://www.nytimes.com/
Selected articles from the newspaper of record.

Time Warner's Pathfinder http://pathfinder.com/@@7oPdTUFjQwAAQD5w/pathfinder/explore.html
Time *magazine articles and daily news updates.*

Tribune Company http://www1.trib.com/NEWS/APwire.html
Direct connections to the Reuters and Associated Press wire services.

USA Today http://www.usatoday.com/usafront.htm
Articles from the national newspaper.

Notes

1. Carl Bernstein and Bob Woodward, *All the President's Men* (New York: Simon & Schuster, 1974), tells the reporters' own story of their pursuit of the Watergate story.
2. Woodward's background in Naval Intelligence and his past association with Alexander Haig have led to speculation that "Deep Throat" may have been Haig and/or other military men disillusioned with Nixon. Len Colodny and Robert Gettlin, *Silent Coup* (New York: St. Martin's Press, 1991).
3. Gladys Engel Lang and Kurt Lang, *The Battle for Public Opinion: The President, the Press, and the Polls During Watergate* (New York: Columbia University Press, 1983), Chap. 3 and p. 51.
4. Walter Lippmann, address in London, May 27, 1965.
5. Doris Graber, *Mass Media and American Politics,* 4th ed. (Washington, DC: Congressional Quarterly Press, 1992), p. 35.
6. *New York Times* (October 17, 1986), p. B2.
7. See Suzanne Garment, *Scandal: The Crisis of Mistrust in American Politics* (New York: Random House, 1991).
8. Bernard Roshco, *Newsmaking* (Chicago: University of Chicago Press, 1975), Chap. 3, gives a good, brief history of the daily press in America.
9. Edward Jay Epstein, *News from Nowhere: Television and the News* (New York: Vantage, 1973), p. 51.
10. *Statistical Abstract of the United States, 1994,* p. 567; Funk & Wagnalls, *World Almanac and Book of Facts, 1995,* p. 310.
11. United States, *Statistical Abstract, 1994,* p. 571.
12. Ben Bagdikian, *The Media Monopoly,* 4th ed. (Boston: Beacon Press, 1993), pp. 18–26; Graber, *Mass Media,* p. 44.
13. Bagdikian, *Media Monopoly,* p. 124.
14. Eric Alterman, "Radio Squelch," *The Nation* (October 16, 1995), p. 410.
15. Epstein, *News from Nowhere,* p. 142.
16. Leon V. Sigal, *Reporters and Officials: The Organization and Politics of News Reporting* (Lexington, MA: D. C. Heath, 1973), p. 124.

17. Herbert J. Gans, *Deciding What's News: A Study of CBS Evening News, NBC Nightly News,* Newsweek, *and* Time (New York: Random House, 1979), pp. 9, 10, 16, Chap. 4.
18. Mark Hertsgaard, *On Bended Knee* (New York: Farrar, Straus & Giroux, 1988), p. 5.
19. Michael Massing, "About-Face on El Salvador," *Columbia Journalism Review* (November–December 1983), pp. 42–49.
20. *Washington Monthly* (July–August 1990), p. 48.
21. "Many Editors Report Advertiser Pressure," *Advertising Age* (January 11, 1993), p. 22.
22. Warren Breed, "Social Control in the Newsroom," *Social Forces,* Vol. 33 (May 1955).
23. Lawrence C. Soley, *The News Shapers: The Sources Who Explain the News* (New York: Praeger, 1992); Eric Alterman, *Sound and Fury: The Washington Punditocracy and the Collapse of American Politics* (New York: HarperCollins, 1992).
24. Jim Mann, "Donations Add to Influence in U.S.: Taiwan a Big Contributor to Think Tanks," *Los Angeles Times* (September 5, 1988), p. 23.
25. William Schneider and I. A. Lewis, "Views on the News," *Public Opinion,* Vol. 8 (August–September 1985), p. 7; Karlyn Keene et al., "Monitoring Media Attitudes," *American Enterprise* (July–August 1990), p. 95; S. Robert Lichter, Stanley Rothman, and L. S. Lichter, *The Media Elite* (Bethesda, MD: Adler & Adler, 1986).
26. Howard Kurtz, "Acid Rain on the Media Parade; A Big Report Pooh-Poohing the Danger Gets Scant Press," *Washington Post Weekly Edition* (January 21–27, 1991), p. 38.
27. *Editorials on File,* Vol. 19, No. 21 (November 1–15, 1988), p. 1272.
28. *Editor and Publisher* (October 24, 1992), pp. 9–10, 44; (November 7, 1992).
29. William A. Dorman and Mansour Farhang, *The U.S. Press and Iran: Foreign Policy and the Journalism of Deference* (Berkeley: University of California Press, 1987); Raymond Bonner, *Waltzing with a Dictator: The Marcoses and the Making of American Policy* (New York: Times Books, 1987).
30. Edward S. Herman and Noam Chomsky, *Manufacturing Consent: The Political Economy of the Mass Media* (New York: Pantheon, 1988).
31. Fred Kaplan, *The Wizards of Armageddon* (New York: Simon & Schuster, 1983); Tom Gervasi, *The Myth of Soviet Military Supremacy* (New York: Harper & Row, 1986).
32. Graber, *Mass Media,* p. 290; Timothy E. Cook, *Making Laws and Making News: Media Strategies in the U.S. House of Representatives* (Washington, DC: Brookings Institution, 1989).
33. Katharine Q. Seelye, "Clinton Edges Congress in Amount of Television Coverage, Study Says," *New York Times* (April 4, 1995), p. 24 D.
34. Thomas E. Patterson, *Out of Order* (New York: Knopf, 1993); Steven Ansolabehere and Shanto Iyengar, *Going Negative: How Attack Ads Shrink and Polarize the Electorate* (New York: Free Press, 1996).
35. W. Lance Bennett, *News: Politics of Illusion,* 3rd ed. (New York: Longman, 1996).
36. Shanto Iyengar and Donald R. Kinder, *News That Matters* (Chicago: University of Chicago Press, 1987).
37. G. Ray Funkhauser, "The Issues of the Sixties: An Exploratory Study in the Dynamics of Public Opinion," *Public Opinion Quarterly,* Vol. 37 (Spring 1973), pp. 62–75.

38. Shanto Iyengar, *Is Anyone Responsible? How Television News Frames Political Issues* (Chicago: University of Chicago Press, 1991).

39. Benjamin I. Page, Robert Y. Shapiro, and Glenn R. Dempsey, "What Moves Public Opinion?" *American Political Science Review,* Vol. 81 (1987), pp. 23–43.

40. David L. Protess, Fay Lomax Cook, Jack C. Doppelt, James S. Ettema, Margaret T. Gordon, Donna R. Leff, and Peter Miller, *The Journalism of Outrage: Investigative Reporting and Agenda Building in America* (New York: Guilford Press, 1991).

41. Jean Folkerts and Dwight C. Teeter, *Voices of a Nation: A History of the Media in the U.S.* (New York: Macmillan, 1989), pp. 214, 348–349, 456–457.

42. Daniel C. Hallin, *The "Uncensored War": The Media and Vietnam* (Berkeley: University of California Press, 1989).

43. W. Lance Bennett and David L. Paletz, eds., *Taken by Storm: The Media, Public Opinion, and U.S. Foreign Policy in the Gulf War* (Chicago: University of Chicago Press, 1994).

44. Epstein, *News from Nowhere,* pp. 48, 60.

45. *Atlanta Journal and Constitution* (May 16, 1991).

46. Lawrie Mifflin, "Reprieve for PBS but Hunt for Funds Continues," *New York Times* (January 2, 1996), p. 9.

47. Graber, *Mass Media,* pp. 67–68.

48. John A. Ferejohn and James H. Kuklinski, eds., *Information and Democratic Processes* (Urbana: University of Illinois Press, 1990); Benjamin I. Page, *Who Deliberates? Mass Media in Modern Democracy* (Chicago: University of Chicago Press, 1996).

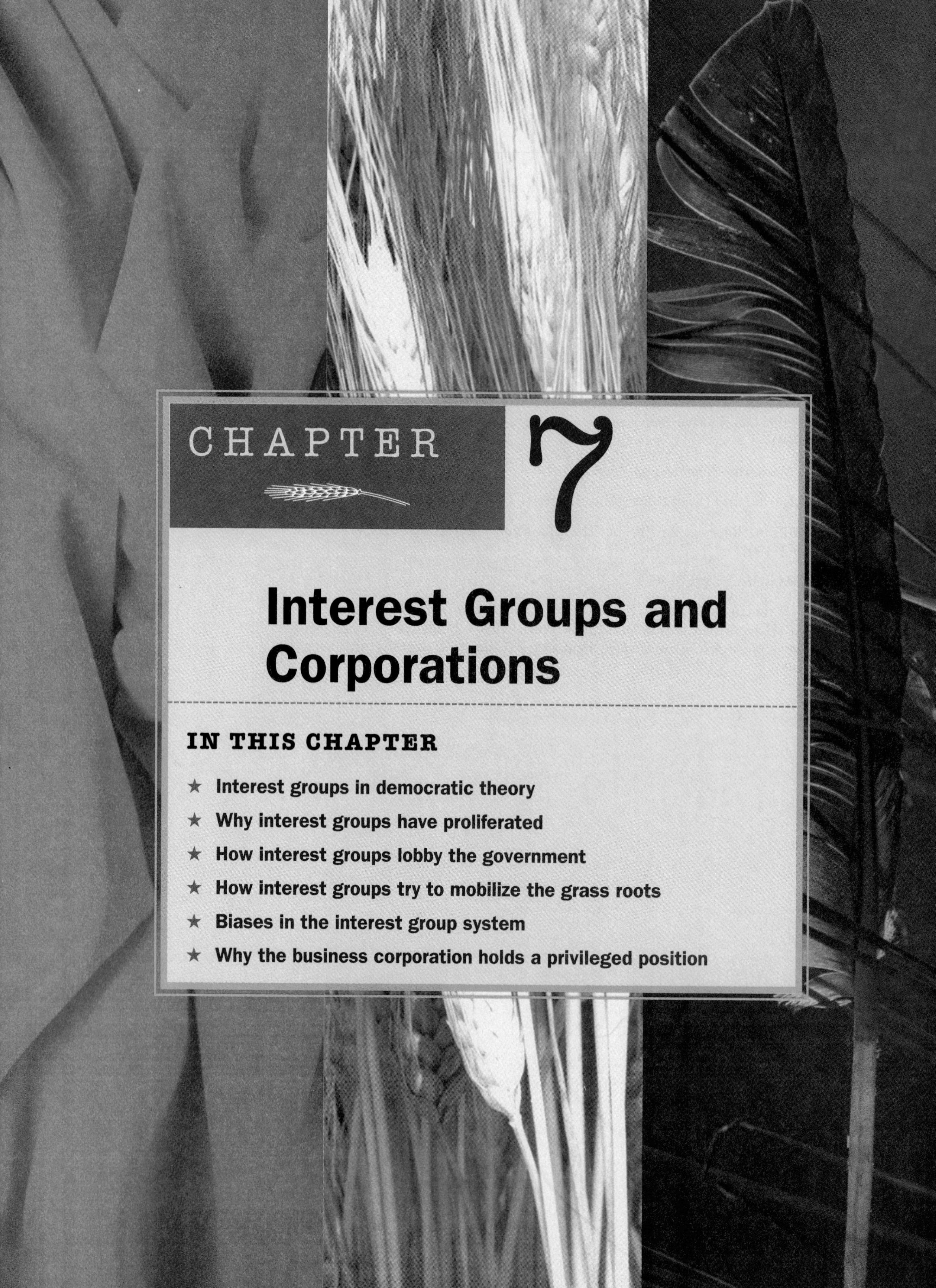

CHAPTER 7

Interest Groups and Corporations

IN THIS CHAPTER

- ★ Interest groups in democratic theory
- ★ Why interest groups have proliferated
- ★ How interest groups lobby the government
- ★ How interest groups try to mobilize the grass roots
- ★ Biases in the interest group system
- ★ Why the business corporation holds a privileged position

Killing Health Care Reform[1]

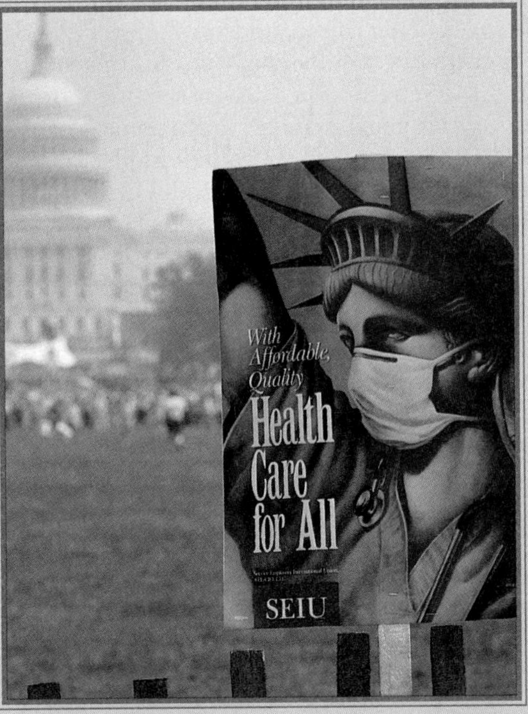

When President Clinton addressed a joint session of Congress in September 1993 to outline his plan for refashioning the nation's health care system, the prospects for passage seemed quite good. After all, 56 percent of Americans supported the proposal, according to the Gallup Poll, and only 24 percent were opposed. The proposal was also favored by the congressional leadership, Democratic majorities in both houses, the labor unions, the American Association of Retired People (AARP), and many large corporations faced with mounting health insurance costs for their employees. First Lady Hillary Rodham Clinton was placed at the helm of this effort, dramatizing the importance the administration put on seeing the health care reform succeed. By the fall of 1994, however, the Clinton plan lay in shambles. Most major corporations had withdrawn their support, and a substantial majority of Americans were now opposed. Unable to build a majority for passage in either chamber, congressional leaders withdrew the legislation rather than bring it to a vote.

The Clinton health care proposal fell victim to one of the most effective, extensive, and expensive grassroots lobbying campaigns in American history. Several groups were particularly important in this effort: the Health Insurance Association of American (HIAA), the National Federation of Independent Businesses (NFIB), the Pharmaceutical Manufacturers Association (PMA), and the American Medical Association (AMA).

The HIAA received the most attention for its advertising campaign. The HIAA represented health insurance companies concerned that the Clinton plan's provisions for managed care and control of health care costs would have serious adverse consequences for them. A series of "Harry and Louise" ads featured a middle-class couple, already covered by company-provided health insurance and strapped by household bills, worrying aloud about the complexity of the Clinton plan, the loss of their free choice of doctors, the increase in their taxes, and the creation of a "billion-dollar government bureaucracy."

The "Harry and Louise" campaign was incredibly effective. Over 50 percent of Americans reported that they could recall the ads and relate details about them. The media gave the ads a great deal of attention on news and discussion programs, and President and Mrs. Clinton felt it necessary to denounce them. The Clintons' complaints about "Harry and Louise" had the inevitable effect, of course, of focusing even more attention on the ads.

The 600,000-member National Federation of Independent Businesses (NFIB), with members in every congressional district in the nation, was especially concerned about employer mandates in the health care reform bill, the provision that would require small businesses to pay much of the cost of employee health insurance premiums. Rather than use a national ad campaign strategy like the HIAA, the NFIB focused on mobilizing its large membership, especially those located in the congressional districts of senators and representatives serving on the committees considering the legislation. A steady stream of informative literature, phone calls, advice on how to contact their senators and representatives, and fund-raising appeals went out to members. Newspaper ads in key congressional districts and targeted campaign contributions were also a major part of the campaign. One particularly pointed newspaper ad featured controversial Surgeon General Joycelyn Elders (who favored divisive ideas like condom distribution in schools) and ended with the tag line "President Clinton picked this doctor. Now he wants to pick your doctor."

The pharmaceutical manufacturers focused on two strategies: first, a letter-writing campaign against price controls on drugs, directed at members of the tax-writing committees in Congress, and second, timely campaign contributions to key members of Congress, especially House and Senate leaders and committee chairs. The PMA also joined forces with other interests opposed to cost containment in an organization called the Health Care Leadership Council (HCLC). The HCLC contributed $26 million to the campaign chests of members of Congress and hired a grassroots campaign consulting firm for $2 million to stir up people in "swing" congressional districts.

The AMA joined in the attack on the Clinton plan, spending over $2 million on a series of newspaper and magazine ads. The AMA's campaign focused on fears of bureaucratic medicine and the move toward managed care, asking readers, "Would you trust your life to an M.D. or an M.B.A.?" The AMA also dramatically boosted its campaign contributions to members of Congress opposed to the bill or wavering on it, and encouraged its doctor-members to do the same. The American Dental Association, the American Hospital Association, and the American Nurses Association joined the AMA in its campaign contribution strategy.

The AARP, labor unions, and health reformers tried to fight back with their own advertising campaigns in favor of the Clinton plan, but to little avail. By the time proponents had swung into gear in the early spring of 1994, public opinion had already shifted decisively against the plan. As one political consultant concluded,

> Not only did the anti-reform forces outspend the other side, they outorganized them. They used direct mail, telemarketing, they kept their members informed and they made sure these members sent letters and phone calls to Washington. Overall, what impressed me the most was the anti-reform movement's sheer persistence. It was "take-no-prisoners."[2]

There are many reasons why the Clinton health care plan never made it through the legislative labyrinth of Congress. It may well have been true that the plan was deeply flawed, being far more complex and internally contradictory than it needed to be. Moreover, the plan may have been far too ambitious, trying, in effect, to transform the financing and delivery of services of the entire American health care system. Finally, perhaps the proponents of the plan, including the Clintons, failed to mount an effective campaign for it until it was too late. While each and every one of these reasons is important, what cannot be ignored is the massive campaign waged against the plan by private interest groups.

This story highlights the important role played by interest groups and businesses in American politics and the many tools of influence they use. It touches on the main issues that will be addressed in this chapter. In particular, the chapter looks at the debate about how much influence interest groups and businesses wield. Our goal is to understand better the relationship among interest groups, business, and democracy. We want to know whether popular sovereignty, political equality, and political liberty are enriched or diminished by the activities of interest groups and businesses. To answer these questions, however, we must first understand how structural, political linkage, and governmental factors shape interest groups and what they do.

Interest Groups in a Democratic Society: Contrasting Views

Interest groups are private organizations that try to shape public policy. They are made up of people who share an interest that they are trying to protect or advance with the help of government. To do this, interest groups try to influence the behavior of public officials, such as presidents, members of Congress, bureaucrats, or judges. These efforts are often perceived by officials as constituting pressure on them, so interest groups are often called **pressure groups.** The term **lobbies** is also commonly used—because of the practice of interest group representatives' talking to representatives and senators in the lobbies outside committee rooms—as in references to the "dairy lobby," or the "gun lobby."

interest group Private organizations and associations that try to influence public policy as a way to protect or advance some interest.

pressure group Another name for *interest group* or *lobby;* implies a group that brings pressure to bear on government decision makers.

lobbies Another name for interest or pressure groups; also, acts of conveying groups' interest to government decision makers.

The Evils of Faction

The danger to good government and the public interest from interest groups is a familiar theme in American politics. They are usually regarded as narrowly self-interested, out for themselves, and without regard for the public good.

This theme is prominent in *The Federalist,* No. 10, in which James Madison defined **factions** (his term for interest groups and narrow parties, which he thought were dangerous to good government) in the following manner: "a number of citizens, whether amounting to a majority or a minority of the whole, who are united and actuated by some common impulse of passion, or of interest, adverse to the rights of other citizens or to the permanent and aggregate interests of the community."[3]

faction Madison's term for groups or parties that try to advance their own interests at the expense of the public good.

The "evils-of-faction" theme recurs throughout our history. President Andrew Jackson attacked the Bank of the United States and its supporters as a selfish special-interest group during the presidential campaign of 1832. During the Progressive Era at the turn of the century, "muckraking" journalists such as Ida Tarbell, Lincoln Steffens, Upton Sinclair, and Frank Norris uncovered corrupt alliances between government and huge corporate conglomerates, or trusts, that exercised enormous influence over the nation's banking, railroad, oil, and steel industries.

In our own day, consumer advocates, such as Ralph Nader, have revived the theme of selfish interests as one of the central ideas in their efforts to increase the regulatory role of government. The cozy relationship between the folks in Washington and the special interests continues to play a prominent role in elections, as evidenced by Ross Perot's championing of this theme during his runs for the presidency in 1992 and 1996.

Interest Group Democracy: The Pluralist Argument

According to many political scientists, however, interest groups do not hurt democracy and the public interest but are an important instrument in attaining both. The argument of these **pluralist** political scientists is shown in Figure 7.1 and goes as follows:[4]

pluralist A political scientist who views American politics as best understood in terms of the interaction, conflict, and bargaining of groups.

- Free elections, while essential to a democracy, do not adequately communicate the wants and interests of the people to political leaders.

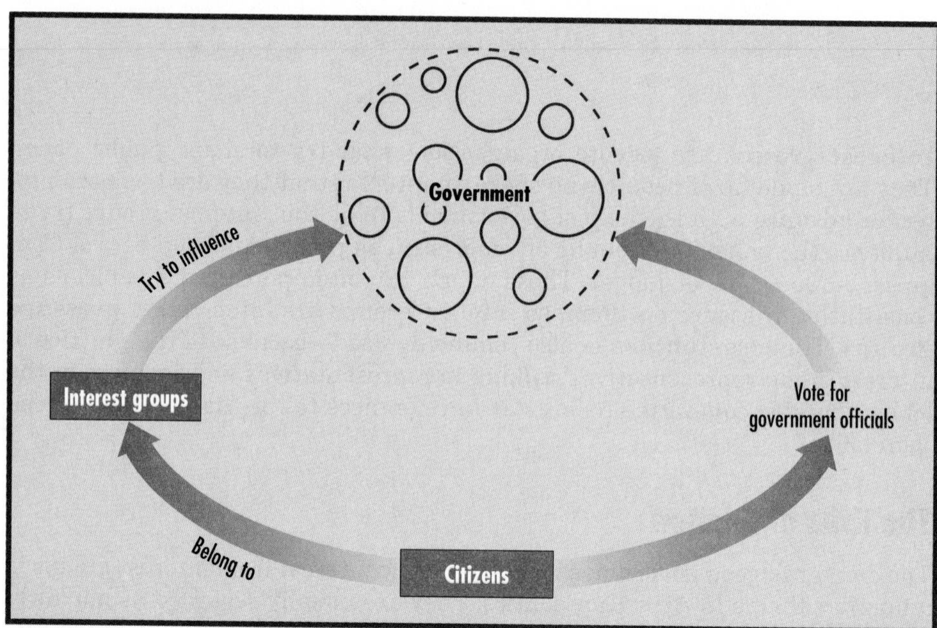

Figure 7.1 ■ **The Pluralist View of American Politics**

In the "pluralist" understanding of the way American democracy works, citizens have several ways to influence government leaders. In addition to voting, citizens also have the opportunity to belong to organizations that convey member views to officials. Because of weak political parties, federalism, checks and balances, and the separation of powers, access to such leaders is relatively easy.

Source: Edward S. Greenberg, *The American Political System,* 5th ed. (Glenview, IL: Scott, Foresman, 1989).

In the late nineteenth century, most Americans thought of the Senate as the captive of large corporate trusts and other special interest groups, as depicted in this popular cartoon, "Bosses of the Senate."

These are better conveyed to political leaders on a day-to-day basis by the many groups and organizations to which people belong.

- Interest groups are easy to create; people in the United States are free to join or to organize groups that reflect their interests.
- Because of federalism, checks and balances, and the separation of powers, government power in the United States is broadly dispersed, so that governmental institutions are remarkably porous and open to the entreaties of the many and diverse groups that exist in society.
- Because of the ease of group formation and the accessibility of government, all interests in society can have their views taken into account by some public official. Thus, the system is highly democratic.

Pluralists see interest groups, then, not as a problem but as an additional tool of democratic representation, similar to other democratic instruments like public opinion and elections. We shall explore the degree to which this position is valid in this and other chapters.

Interest Group Formation: Structural, Political Linkage, and Governmental Factors

Nobody knows exactly how many interest groups exist in the United States, but there is wide agreement that the number began to escalate in the late 1960s and has grown steadily ever since. We have a more precise count, however, of the number of paid lobbyists who work for interest groups in Washington and try to affect government policies. In 1991, more than 14,000 lobbyists worked there, up from 4,000 in 1977.[5] There are now so many Washington representatives, in fact, that they have created a new lobbying organization to protect their interests as lobbyists: the American League of Lobbyists.[6]

Much of the increase in the number of interest groups is accounted for by the growing number of public interest or citizen groups organized around some cause or idea, rather than an economic or occupational interest, the traditional basis for forming interest groups. These include environmental, consumer, civil rights, prolife, and women's organizations, as well as ideological organizations. Nevertheless, business, producer, and occupational groups still dominate by their sheer numbers: one study done during the Reagan years showed that corporations made up 52 percent of all organizations having Washington, D.C. representatives, that trade and other business associations accounted for another 20 percent, and that professional associations accounted for an additional 8 percent, for a total of 80 percent of the organizations.[7] And there is no evidence that these proportions have changed very much since this study was done.

Structural factors account for most of what the interest group system looks like. Interest groups seem to flourish where there are many interests, where the political culture supports the pursuit of private interests, where the rules make it easy to organize such interests, and where government is sufficiently active for its policies to affect private parties.

Diverse Interests

The United States is a diverse and complex society of many races, religions, and ethnic groups distributed across a vast continent. Work and occupations have become more complex as agriculture and crafts have been augmented by factory, office, and laboratory work. The economy has changed from one of small, competitive firms and substantial income and wealth equality to one characterized by national and global corporations and substantial distances between the rich and the poor. Technological and scientific developments have produced a host of new products, problems, ways of life, and occupations. These trends have contributed to diversification and complexity, and to an inevitable multiplication of interests. For example, the rise of the computer is associated with not only computer manufacturers, but software companies, software engineers, computer magazines, technical information providers, computer component jobbers, and others too numerous to mention. Each sector has particular interests to defend or advance, and each has formed an association to try to do so.

The Rules of the Game

The rules of the political game in the United States encourage the formation of interest groups. The First Amendment to the Constitution, for instance, guarantees citizens the right to speak freely, to assemble, and to petition the government, all of which are essential to citizens' ability to form organizations to advance their interests before government. Moreover, the government is organized in such a way that officials are relatively accessible to interest groups. Because of federalism, checks and balances, and the separation of powers, there is no dominant center of decision making, as there is in such unitary states as Great Britain and France. There, most important policy decisions are made in parliamentary bodies. In the United States, important decisions are made by many officials, on many matters, in many jurisdictions. Consequently, there are many more places where interest group pressure can be effective. Finally, there are no strong, centralized political parties in the United States that might serve to overcome the decentralized, fragmented quality of the policymaking process in the United States, as there are in the European democracies. The upshot is easy group access to public officials in the United States.

The Growth in Government

Government does far more today than it did during the early years of the Republic. As government takes on more responsibilities, it quite naturally comes to have a greater impact on virtually all aspects of economic, social, and personal life. People, groups, and organizations are increasingly affected by the actions of government, so the decisions made by presidents, members of Congress, bureaucrats, and judges are increasingly important. It would be surprising indeed if, in response, people, groups, and organizations did not try harder to influence the public officials' decisions that affect them.

Disturbances

The existence of diverse interests, the rules of the game, and the importance of government decisions and policies enable and encourage the formation of interest groups, but formation seems to happen only when interests are threat-

Discontent among American farmers in the late nineteenth century led to the formation of protest organizations and, eventually, the Populist party. One predecessor of the Populist party was the Grange, which fought for social and cultural benefits for isolated rural communities.

ened, usually by some change in the social and economic environment, or by some change in government policy. This is known as the **disturbance theory** of interest group formation.[8] Examples are many. Thus, farmers formed the Grange in the late nineteenth century when their way of life was threatened by the policies of banks and railroads. The successes of the consumer and environmental protection movements in the late 1960s and the early 1970s were an important reason why threatened corporations created scores of **political action committees (PACs)** to protect their interests in Washington.[9] The Christian Coalition was created at a time when many Fundamentalist Christians felt threatened by family breakdown, crime, inadequate schools, and the growing voice of gays and lesbians.

disturbance theory A theory that locates the origins of interest groups in changes in the economic, social, or political environment that threaten the well-being of some segment of the population.

political action committee (PAC) A private organization whose purpose is to raise and distribute funds to candidates in political campaigns.

Incentives

Some social scientists argue, however, that people are not inclined to form groups, even when their common interests are threatened, unless the group can offer a selective, material benefit to them.[10] A selective, material benefit is something tangible that is available to the members of an interest group but not to nonmembers. If someone can get the benefit without joining the group, then joining makes no sense; he or she can obtain the same benefit without contributing. Such "**free riding**" generally comes into play when a group is interested in a collective good, that is, a governmental program that will assist all the members of some category whether they belong to a formal organization or not. All wheat farmers, for instance, benefit from governmental price supports for wheat and need not join the National Wheat Growers Association to get the benefit. People do join when an association has benefits that are

free rider One who gains a benefit without contributing; a term used to explain why it is so difficult to form social movements and noneconomic interest groups.

available only to its members, for example, discounted life and health insurance programs for the members of the Wheat Growers Association.

This theory emphasizes how difficult and unlikely it is that interest groups will form at all. It cannot account very well, therefore, for the upsurge in group formation during the 1960s and 1970s, especially of the public interest and ideological variety.[11] The proliferation of such groups suggests that groups form not only around selective, material incentives, but also around "purposive," or ideological, issue-oriented incentives, and around "solidaristic" (in the sense of being part of something that one values) ones. People often join groups, for instance, because they believe in a particular cause (nuclear disarmament, civil rights, prayer in the public schools, or an end to legal abortion, for example) or because they enjoy the companionship afforded by belonging to a group.

What Interests Are Represented

What kinds of interests find a voice in American politics? A useful place to start is with political scientist E. E. Schattschneider's distinction between "private" and "public" interests. Although the boundaries between the two are sometimes fuzzy, the distinction remains important: public interests are those that are connected in one way or another to the general welfare of the community; private interests, on the other hand, are associated with benefits for some fraction of the community.[12] The latter are mainly economic interests, groups with some tangible stake they wish to protect or to advance by means of government action. The former are mainly noneconomic groups motivated by some ideology, by the desire to advance a general cause—civil rights or environmental protection—or by the commitment to some public policy—gun control or an end to abortion. Private interest groups mainly provide selective benefits to their members; public interest groups mainly provide solidaristic and purposive incentives.

Private Interest Groups

There is a wide range of private interest groups active in American politics.

Producers Producer groups represent enterprises that produce some good or service. In this group, we would include business and agriculture. Because of the vast resources at their disposal and because of their strategic role in the health of the economy, these groups wield enormous power in Washington, D.C. Agriculture has more than held its own over the years through such organizations as the American Farm Bureau Federation and scores of commodity groups, for example, the American Dairy Association and the American Wheat Growers Association. Business has always been a powerful player in national politics and seems to have enhanced its influence considerably in recent years.

Professionals Professional groups represent the interests of professionals, such as doctors, lawyers, and dentists. Because of the prominent social position of professionals in local communities and their ability to make substantial campaign contributions, such organizations are very influential in the policy-making process on matters related to their professional expertise and concerns. The American Medical Association and the American Dental Association, for instance, lobbied strongly against the Clinton health care proposal and helped kill it in the 103rd Congress.

Unions Though labor unions are sometimes involved in what might be called public interest activities (such as supporting civil rights legislation), their main role in the United States has been to protect the jobs of their members and to gain maximum wages and benefits for them. Unlike labor unions in many parts of the world, which are as much political and ideological organizations as economic ones, American labor unions focus primarily on "bread-and-butter" issues. Their lobbying activities tend to revolve around legislation, judicial interpretations, and administrative rulings that affect their ability to protect the jobs, wages, and benefits of their members and to maintain or increase the size of the union membership rolls.

Most observers believe that the political power of labor unions has eroded in dramatic ways over the past several decades.[13] In 1993, organized labor pulled out all of the stops in a campaign to kill the North American Free Trade Agreement (NAFTA) but was unsuccessful even though Democrat Bill Clinton was president and a Democratic majority sat in both houses of Congress. Nor did strong union support of President Clinton's health care bill help stave off its defeat.

The long-term decline of labor unions' political influence may be chiefly a matter of declining membership. Labor union membership has always been low in the United States compared with other Western nations (see Figure 7.2), and it has been declining at a brisk pace in recent years, from a high point of 33 percent of the workforce in 1955 to about 16 percent today.

Americans have long been ambivalent about the role of labor unions in American life, as seen in the treatment of unions in Hollywood films (see the Politics and Film box on page 220). This ambivalence has probably diminished the influence of unions in American politics.

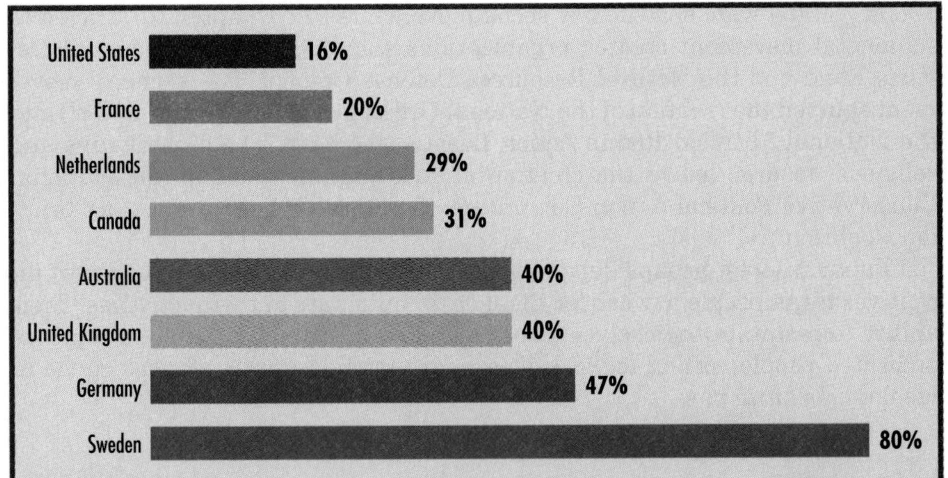

Figure 7.2 ▪ **Union Membership as a Percentage of the Total Labor Force, 1993**

Labor union membership as a percentage of the total workforce is lower in the United States than in other capitalist democracies. This fact has important implications for American politics.

Source: Central Intelligence Agency, *World Fact Book* (Washington, DC: CIA, 1994).

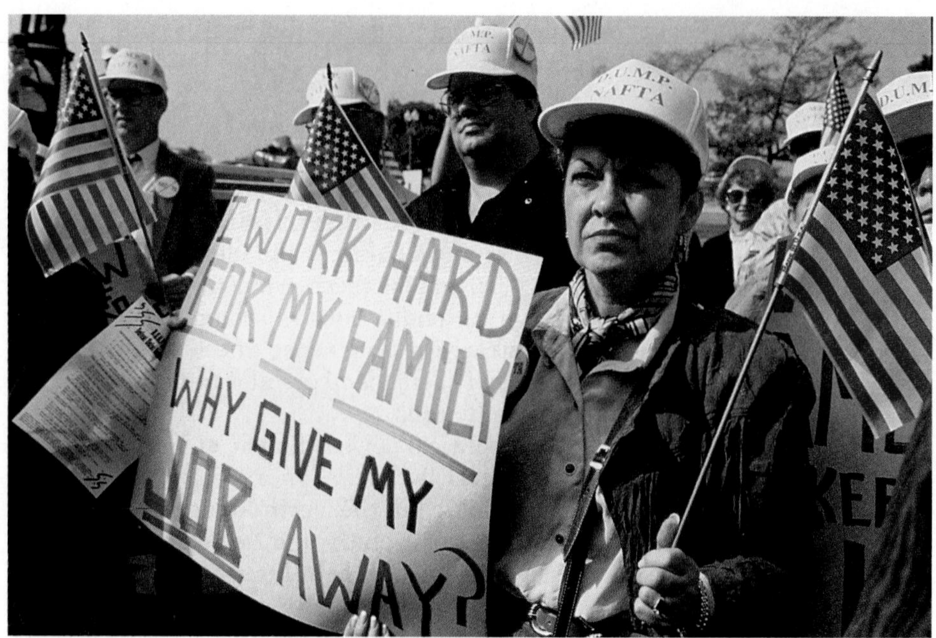

Organized labor suffered a devastating political loss when Bill Clinton convinced Congress to pass the North American Free Trade Agreement over its strong objections.

Public Interest Groups

Public interest groups, sometimes called *citizens' groups,* try to get government to do things that will serve the general public—according to their own views, of course—rather than the direct material interests of their own members.[14] People active in such groups tend to be motivated by ideological concerns or a belief in some cause.

Public interest groups of one kind or another have always been around, but a great upsurge in their number and influence has taken place since the late 1960s.[15] Many were spawned by social movements (see Chapter 10). The environmental movement created organizations such as the Environmental Defense Fund and the Natural Resources Defense Council. The women's movement spurred the creation of the National Organization for Women (NOW) and the National Abortion Rights Action League (NARAL). The conservative and religious upsurge led to the creation of such organizations as the National Conservative Political Action Committee, the Moral Majority, and the Christian Coalition.

Public interest groups depend primarily on solidaristic and purposive incentives to get people to work for them or to contribute to their activities. Their ability to maintain themselves as organizations seems to depend on a mix of dedicated people willing to work long hours in the interest of some cause or ideology, for little pay.

What Interest Groups Do

Interest groups are in the business of conveying the views and defending the interests of individuals and groups to public officials. The scope of interest group activities, then, is as wide as the reach of government officials; the activities are aimed at wherever decisions are made, whether in the legislative, executive, or judicial branch of the federal government, or in the states or cities.

There are two basic types of interest group activity.[16] The inside game involves the direct contact of interest group representatives and government officials. This is the kind of activity that has been around the longest and is the most familiar. The outside game involves interest group mobilization of public opinion, voters, and important contributors in order to bring pressure to bear on elected officials. It is an indirect form of influence and is becoming increasingly common.

The Inside Game

The term *lobbying* conjures up visions of a cigar-chomping interest group representative, his arm around the shoulder of an important senator or representative, advising him on how he ought to vote on some obscure provision of the tax code, and slipping an envelope, fat with currency, into his suit pocket. Or it conjures up images of favors given: paid vacations to exotic locations, honorarium payments for brief speeches at association meetings, and other unsavory exchanges verging on bribery.

The images both reveal and confuse. These things surely happened in the past; some continue to happen today; some will surely happen in the future. In general, however, the images do not enable us to understand fully the intricacies of the inside game. This game does not involve bribes. Rather, it is more the politics of insiders and the "old-boy" network (though, increasingly, women

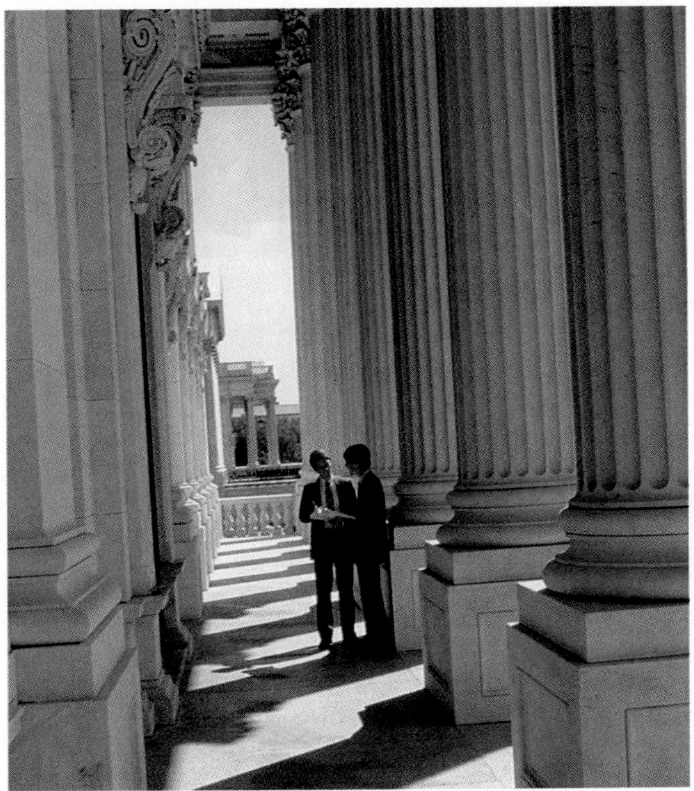

An important part of the job of the lobbyist is to convey the views and concerns of interest group members to representatives and senators. The ability to hire and deploy lobbyists, however, is not randomly distributed among Americans. Those with the greatest economic resources tend to dominate the "inside game" of interest group politics.

POLITICS AND FILM

Are Labor Unions the Good Guys or the Bad Guys?

Americans have always been uncertain about labor unions. Most recognize that unions have done things to help workers, yet many also worry that unions have become powerful and sometimes corrupt special-interest groups. This ambiguity is reflected in films about labor unions.

Filmmaker John Sayles makes the case for unions in *Matewan* (1987), a film about the labor wars in the West Virginia coalfields in the 1920s. Sayles paints a grim picture of the lives of miners and their families' life. In Matewan, as in the other coalfield towns, life is short, nasty, and virtually devoid of hope. Finally pushed to revolt by their misery, the miners go on strike. The company tries to foment interethnic and interracial strife that will leave the miners disunited and weak by using immigrant Italian and black strikebreakers (such tactics were commonly used during this period). Joe Kenehan, the labor union organizer, tries to keep the miners unified, brings blacks and Italians into the union, and slowly shapes a successful resistance to the coal company. The company responds by sending in its "goons" to break the strike. The film ends with a deadly gun battle in the streets of the town, a preview of the violence that was to hit West Virginia in subsequent years.

Martin Ritt's *Norma Rae* (1979) is a celebration of the promise of labor unions to workers who are at the very bottom of the heap. Sally Field plays the title role in this film about one woman's successful effort to organize southern textile workers. Ritt shows us why the workers needed unions by dramatizing the dangerous and unhealthy conditions in the mill and the miserable living conditions of these low-wage workers. Norma Rae, a mother and a widow who has finally had it with the company, joins forces with a union organizer and begins to fight back. She is a resilient, spunky, wisecracking, and courageous woman who manages to bring her fellow workers, at first afraid or apathetic, over to the union side. The movie hit the theaters just as real textile workers began their nationwide boycott of J. P. Stevens. The union won in the movie and in the J. P. Stevens campaign, too.

Director Paul Schrader shows us the dark side of organized labor in his grim film about the automobile industry, *Blue Collar* (1978). Richard Pryor, Harvey Keitel, and Yaphet Kotto play three buddies who work in an automobile plant and concoct a scheme to steal money from their union local. They are driven to this desperate act by the almost hopeless quality of their lives, which Schrader shows in graphic detail: the noise and repetitive boredom of their assembly line jobs, the financial trap that each of them is in, and the empty quality of their lives off the job. These three small-time operators find only $600 in the union treasury but discover a notebook that documents union officials' involvement in loan-sharking operations. This is the jackpot that they've been looking for, a ticket to escape from their dead-end jobs, for they intend to use the notebook to blackmail the culprits. The attempt is doomed from the start, however, for the union is much stronger than they are. In the end, the three friends are destroyed. The picture of the union painted by Schrader is unrelentingly negative: both uncaring and corrupt, and, when need be, evil.

In *F.I.S.T.* (1978), director Norman Jewison tells the tale of a union that begins in the 1930s as a protector

are part of the network). It is the politics of "one-on-one" persuasion, in which the skilled lobbyist tries to get a decision maker to understand and sympathize with the interest group's point of view. Access is critical if one is to be successful at this game, as is an intimate understanding of the game itself: its rules, the key players, and the flow of the action.

Many of the most successful lobbyists are recruited from the ranks of retired members of the House, the Senate, and high levels of the bureaucracy. The promise of lucrative employment based on their skills—and especially on their many contacts—is what keeps so many of them around Washington, D.C., after they leave office. Few return from whence they came. The very best of them have been in and out of one office or another in one administration or

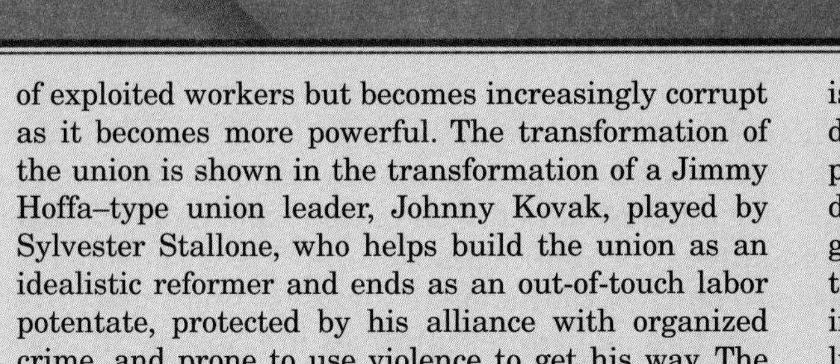

of exploited workers but becomes increasingly corrupt as it becomes more powerful. The transformation of the union is shown in the transformation of a Jimmy Hoffa–type union leader, Johnny Kovak, played by Sylvester Stallone, who helps build the union as an idealistic reformer and ends as an out-of-touch labor potentate, protected by his alliance with organized crime, and prone to use violence to get his way. The message of the film is not only that power corrupts but also that labor unions are no better at protecting and caring for their members than are the giant corporations for which they work.

A more sympathetic interpretation of Jimmy Hoffa is found in *Hoffa* (1992), written by David Mamet and directed by Danny DeVito. The title character is played by Jack Nicholson. The film is an effective dramatization of Hoffa's famous line "I gotta do what I gotta do!" It's a tough and unforgiving world out there, the film says, and the niceties of the civilized world are ineffective against powerful corporations and their police and political allies. In fact, following the niceties can get you killed. The film seems to suggest that intimidation, violence, and even an alliance with organized crime, though regrettable, were part and parcel of building one of the most powerful and effective labor unions in American history.

another for many years, know the Washington, D.C., scene as a wine connoisseur knows wine, and are compensated very well for their services. What works at key moments in the policy process may be a phone call to the right person, an important piece of intelligence picked up during a lunch conversation, or an introduction made at a diplomatic reception. These kinds of contact are not something done very easily by an outsider. Commenting on how closely he worked with members of Congress on the 1986 Tax Reform Act, one lobbyist pointed out, "All of us have just come off the Hill. We worked with the people we lobby. They're our friends."[17]

The inside game seems to work best when the issues are narrow and technical, do not command much media attention or public passion, and do not stir up counteractivity by other interest groups. This is not to say that interest groups play a role only on unimportant matters. Great benefit can come to an interest group or a large corporation from a small change in a single provision of the tax code or in a slight change in the wording or timing of an administrative ruling. The Electronics Industry Association was at the center of the action that created a 10 percent research-and-development write-off in the 1981 tax bill, for instance.

Lobbying Congress The essence of the inside game in Congress is the cultivation of personal relationships with those who matter, whether they be Senate and House leaders, other influential and well-placed legislators, chairpersons of important committees or subcommittees, or key members of congressional staffs. Because much of the action in Congress takes place in the committees, and because senators and representatives are busy with a wide range of responsibilities, cultivating relationships with important staff members is especially important for successful lobbyists. As one lobbyist put it, "If you have a staff member on your side, it might be a hell of a lot better than talking to the member."[18]

Nothing beats the personal contact: passing along a useful piece of information, presenting research results, conveying the viewpoint of interests that are important in the district, helping craft detailed legislation, and drafting speeches. The good lobbyist cultivates such contacts and shows how he or she can be helpful.

Interest group representatives sometimes testify at committee or subcommittee hearings. The hearing is less important in shaping legislation than the direct forms of contact we have described. However, testifying at a committee hearing has its political uses. It can be used by the lobbyist to make a case to the public on a pending piece of legislation, or it can be used to show members of the interest group or the chief executive officer (CEO) of the corporation that the lobbyist is doing his or her job. Interest group testimony can be used by the legislator to build public support for something that he or she wants to do.

Sometimes the relationship between an interest group and the majority party on a committee becomes so close that the interest group becomes quasi-governmental in nature. The National Rifle Association, for instance, did much of the investigative legwork and provided many of the questions for majority Republican members of the House Government Reform and Oversight Committee in 1995 when it conducted hearings on the federal government's raid of David Koresh's Branch Davidian Compound in Waco, Texas.

Lobbying the Executive Branch Career civil servants and political appointees in the executive branch have a great deal of discretionary authority, because Congress often legislates broad policies, leaving it to bureaucratic agencies to fill in the details. The Environmental Protection Agency (EPA), for instance, is charged with setting the standards for air- and waterborne pollutants, and these standards have a major impact on how various industries conduct their business.

Interest groups try to establish stable and friendly relationships with those agencies of the executive branch that are most relevant to their interests. Pharmaceutical companies, for example, stay in touch with the relevant people at the Food and Drug Administration (FDA).

The key to success in lobbying the executive branch is similar to that in lobbying Congress: personal contact and cooperative long-term relationships. Interest group representatives can convey technical information, present the results of their research, help a public official deflect criticism, and show how what the group wants is compatible with good public policy and the political needs of the official. In a pinch, and as a last resort, these representatives can leave the impression that, for noncooperation, there will be future opposition and adverse publicity or, for cooperation, a job or a lucrative consulting contract after retirement from public service.

The payoffs of attentiveness to the bureaucracy can be considerable. The tobacco industry was able to convince the Environmental Protection Agency (EPA) in 1990, for instance, to "blackball" scientists with strong antismoking views as candidates for a scientific advisory panel on the potential dangers of secondary cigarette smoke.[19]

Lobbying the Courts Interest groups also lobby the courts, though not in the same way they lobby the other two branches. A group may find that neither Congress nor the White House is favorably disposed to its interests, and that the courts may be an alternate route to meeting its needs. For example, realizing that the improvement of the lot of black people was very low on the agenda of presidents and members of Congress during the 1940s and 1950s, the National Association for the Advancement of Colored People (NAACP) turned to the courts for satisfaction. The effort eventually paid off in the landmark *Brown v. Board of Education* (1954) decision.

Going to court is a secondary strategy for most groups, because they must have what is called **standing;** that is, the group must be a party to a case and able to demonstrate a direct injury. Going to court, moreover, is very expensive and beyond the means of many groups. Rich interest groups and corporations mostly play this part of the lobbying game. Industrial corporations take the EPA to court on roughly 85 percent of the agency's rulings, for instance, delaying the implementation of EPA rulings from two to four years in most cases.[20]

standing A legal term meaning that one may bring legal action because one is affected by the issues raised.

Interest groups sometimes lobby the courts by filing amicus curiae (friends-of-the-court) briefs in cases involving other parties. In this kind of brief, a person or an organization that is not a party in the suit may file an argument in support of one side or the other in the hope of swaying the views of the judge or judges. Major controversies before the Supreme Court on such issues as abortion, free speech, or civil rights attract scores of amicus curiae briefs.

Interest groups also involve themselves in the appointment and approval of federal judges. Particularly controversial appointments, such as the Supreme Court nominations of Louis Brandeis (whom corporate interests considered too liberal) in 1916, Robert Bork (whom many women's and civil rights interests considered too conservative) in 1987, and Clarence Thomas (who was opposed by liberal and women's groups) in 1992, have drawn interest group attention and strenuous efforts for or against the nominee.

The Outside Game

Elected officials are more likely to listen to groups that can demonstrate grassroots support for their positions and power at the polls. The outside game is a form of interest group activity in which popular support for interest group concerns is identified, created, mobilized, and brought to bear on policymakers in government.

Mobilizing Membership When a bill relevant to an interest group comes before Congress, the efforts of the group's lobbyists are greatly enhanced if members of Congress know that the folks back home care about their actions. Interest groups with a large membership base try to persuade their members to send letters and to make telephone calls to the appropriate officials. This kind of campaign is especially effective if there are many group members in the congressional district or state. The opposition of the AMA (which represents most doctors in private practice) and the National Federation of Independent Business (which represents small business) to key aspects of the Clinton health care initiative helped persuade members of Congress to scuttle the legislation.

Interest group leaders generally do not wait for their members to react spontaneously; they use direct mailings to sound the alarm. Mailings define the threat to members, suggest a way to respond to the threat, and supply the addresses and phone numbers of the people to contact in Washington. Members are grouped by congressional district and state and are given the addresses of their own representatives or senators. Often, groups include a preprinted postcard or letter for the member to sign and mail. The National Rifle Association mobilizes its members whenever the threat of federal gun control rears its head. Environmental organizations sound the alarm whenever Congress threatens to loosen environmental protections.

Organizing the District Members of Congress are most attuned to those in their state or district who can affect their reelection prospects. The smart interest group, therefore, not only will convince its own members in the state and district to put pressure on the senator or congressional representative, but will also make every effort to be in touch with the most important campaign contributors and opinion leaders there. When the Public Securities Association (which represents major banks and Wall Street investment houses) wanted to save the tax exemption for "tax-free" municipal bonds in the 1986 Tax Reform bill, it hired a firm to organize politically influential people and groups in the districts of key members of the House Ways and Means Committee (which is responsible for writing tax legislation). Realizing that "tax-free" municipal bonds are the main source of the money borrowed by various governments to pay for things from stadiums, to hospitals, to sewage treatment plants, to university buildings, to business and industrial parks, the firm concentrated on building a coalition of local government officials, small-business owners, newspaper publishers, construction firms, labor unions, and other interested parties to bring pressure on Ways and Means Committee members.

Shaping Public Opinion "Educating" the public on issues that are important to the interest group is one of the central features of new-style lobbying. The idea is to shape opinion in such a way that government officials will be favorably disposed to the views of the interest group. These attempts to shape public and elite opinion come in many forms.

Publication of Research Results Almost every interest organization has a research staff or access to professionals who will do research for it. When the organization believes it has research results that will bolster its position, it calls a press conference to present a summary and mails the research report to influential people in government, the media, and education. The Tobacco Institute, for example, regularly reports on the alleged failure of scientists to establish a direct link between smoking and cancer.

Advertising Interest groups often conduct national and regional advertising campaigns to impress their views on government policy. Sometimes this advertising takes the form of pressing a position on a particular issue, such as NARAL's advertising against the nomination of Robert Bork to the Supreme Court or Northrop Corporation's touting the B-2 Stealth bomber in 1989 when the future of its funding was in doubt. Sometimes it is "image" advertising, in which some company or industry portrays its positive contribution to American life.[21] The Chemical Manufacturers Association, for instance, sponsored a full-page ad in the *Washington Post* on Earth Day announcing its concern for the environment even though its members are, according to the EPA, among the worst polluters in the nation.[22]

Maintaining Working Relations with the Media The well-heeled interest group regularly prepares materials that will be of use to radio and television broadcasters and to newspaper and magazine editors. Many produce opinion pieces, magazine articles, television and radio "bites," and even television documentaries. Many interest-group media campaigns involve "staged" events to be covered as news. The environmentalist group Greenpeace puts the news media on full alert, for instance, when it tries to disrupt a whaling operation or a nuclear weapons test.

Direct Marketing Advances in computer and communications technology have made the direct marketing of products and services a common feature of modern life. Interest groups have borrowed many of the techniques of direct marketing to get their message to the public and to channel responses to public officials. With computerized mailing and telephone lists, for instance, it has become quite easy to identify target groups to receive information on particular issues. Groups pushing for cuts in the capital-gains-tax rate, for instance, will direct their mail and telephone banks to holders of the American Express card or to ZIP code addresses identified as upper-income neighborhoods. People for the American Way, a group opposed to censorship and the rise of the radical right, focuses its mailings on likely liberal-oriented people such as readers of the *New Republic, The Nation,* and the *New York Times* and members of the American Civil Liberties Union.

Involvement in Campaigns and Elections Interest groups are key players in American electoral politics. The range of their activities is very wide.

Many interest groups rate members of Congress on their support for the interest group's position on a selection of key votes in the House and Senate. This practice is most common among public interest and ideological groups, though labor unions and business organizations are involved as well. These ratings are distributed to the members of the interest group and other interested parties in the hope that the ratings will influence their voting behavior.

Interest groups also encourage their members to get involved in the electoral campaigns of candidates who are favorable to their interests. Groups often assist campaigns in more tangible ways: allowing the use of their telephone banks, mailing lists, FAX and photocopy machines, computers, and the like. Some interest groups help with fund-raising events or ask members to make financial contributions.

Some interest groups encourage their members to run for public office and provide most of the financing and campaign infrastructure. In recent years, the Christian Coalition has been very active and very successful in this way,

The Christian Coalition, founded by televangelist Pat Robertson, has been very important in Republican nomination politics in recent years. Here, the Christian Coalition's Executive Director, Ralph Reed, joins House Speaker Newt Gingrich at a press conference announcing the Coalition's "Contract for American Families."

running its members as Republican candidates in races stretching from school boards to Congress.

A few interest groups, mostly of the public interest or citizens' group variety, endorse particular candidates for public office. The strategy may backfire and is somewhat risky, for to endorse a losing candidate is to risk losing access to the winner. Nevertheless, it is fairly common now for labor unions, environmental organizations, religious groups, and ideological groups to make such endorsements.

Interest groups sometimes sponsor ballot initiatives at the state and local level. Coloradans for Family Values, a Christian profamily group, sponsored and won an initiative in Colorado (since declared unconstitutional by the Supreme Court) that forbids any local community to pass ordinances that protect gay and lesbian rights.

Interest groups are also an increasingly important part of campaign fundraising. We will say more about this in the next section.

The Interest Group System and Democracy

The political scientist E. E. Schattschneider once observed that the flaw in the pluralist (or interest group) heaven is "that the heavenly chorus sings with a strong upper class accent."[23] (He might reasonably have added corporate, professional, and trade association accents.) If Schattschneider was correct, the norm of political equality is violated by the interest group system, and democracy is less fully developed than it might be. In this section, we look at possible inequalities and evaluate their effects.

Representational Inequalities

Not all segments of society are equally represented in the interest group system. For the most part, the interest group game in Washington, D.C., is dominated, in sheer numbers and weight of activity, by corporations, business trade associations, and professional associations. To be sure, these three do not entirely monopolize the game (see Table 7.1). Labor unions, citizens' groups and civil rights organizations, religious organizations, and groups advancing the interests of women, the elderly, and the poor are in the game. Nevertheless, the disproportion is striking: business, trade, and professional associations account for over two-thirds of all associations that have a lobbying presence in Washington, D.C. Moreover, the representational advantage of business and the professions is increasing, and there is evidence that business and professional groups have more permanency than others. Public interest groups tend to come and go. Business, professional, and trade associations stay.[24]

Resource Inequalities

Business corporations and professionals (doctors, lawyers, dentists, accountants, and so on) are in the most economically well-off sectors of American society. It is hardly surprising that interest groups representing them enjoy a

Table 7.1

Organizations Having Washington Representation

This table shows that not all segments of the American people are equally represented in Washington politics. Corporations enjoy a distinct advantage in having a lobbying presence there.

	Percentage
Corporations	45.7
Trade and other business associations	17.9
Foreign commerce and corporations	6.5
Professional associations	6.9
Unions	1.7
Citizens' groups	4.1
Civil rights groups/Minority organizations	1.3
Social welfare and the poor	0.6
New entrants (elderly, women, handicapped)	1.1
Governmental units—United States	4.2
Other foreign	2.0
Other unknown	8.2
	100.2%[a]
	(N = 6601)

[a]Totals more than 100 percent because of rounding.

Sources: Based on information taken from Arthur C. Close, ed., *Washington Representatives—1981,* 5th ed. (Washington, DC: Columbia Books, 1981); and Denise S. Akey, ed., *The Encyclopedia of Associations,* 16th ed. (Detroit: Gale Research Company, 1981). From Kay Lehman Schlozman and John T. Tierney, *Organized Interests and American Democracy* (New York: Harper & Row, 1986), p. 67.

substantial resource advantage over others. Interest groups representing business and the professions can afford to spend far more than other groups to hire professional lobbying firms, form their own Washington, D.C., "liaison" office, place advertising in the media, conduct targeted mailings, mobilize their members to contact government officials, and pursue all of the other activities of old- and new-style lobbying. Not many other groups can match the routine lobbying presence of business and the professions. The resource advantages and political weight of the insurance industry, hospital associations, and the AMA are so high that members of the Clinton administration, though convinced of the superiority of the "single-payer" (government), Canadian-style national health care system, introduced an entirely different plan in 1993 because of fear that the "single-payer" system could not buck the combined power of these interest groups.[25]

Corporate, trade, and professional associations are also the major players in PAC fund-raising and spending[26] (see Figures 7.3 and 7.4), though large and committed membership organizations like the National Rifle Association also play a big role. During the 1994 congressional elections, political action committees representing business and the professions accounted for 62 percent of all PACs and 64 percent of all PAC contributions to congressional candidates. In 1996, business and professional PACs played a similar role. PACs representing the least-privileged sectors of American society are notable for their absence. As Republican Senator Robert Dole of Kansas once put it, "There aren't any poor PACs or food stamp PACs or nutrition PACs or Medicare PACs."[27]

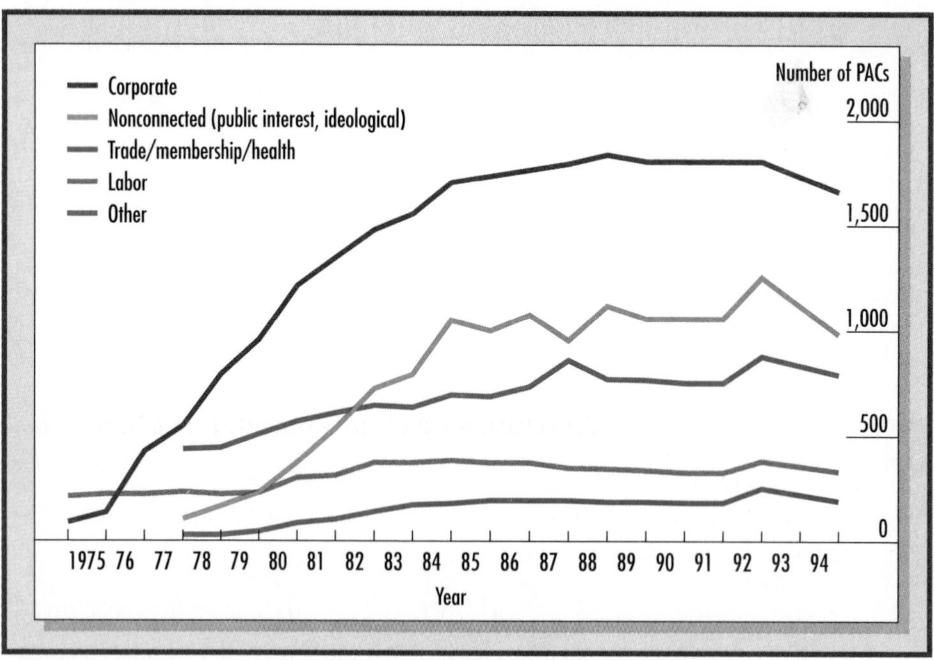

Figure 7.3 ■ **PAC Growth in the United States, 1974–1994**

Political action committees are playing an increasingly important role in financing congressional elections. The growth in the share provided by corporate, nonconnected (ideological), and trade groups is particularly striking, as is the small share accounted for by organized labor. Note, however, the recent slight decline in the number of PACs.

Source: Federal Election Commission, Washington, DC, *1995 Annual Report.*

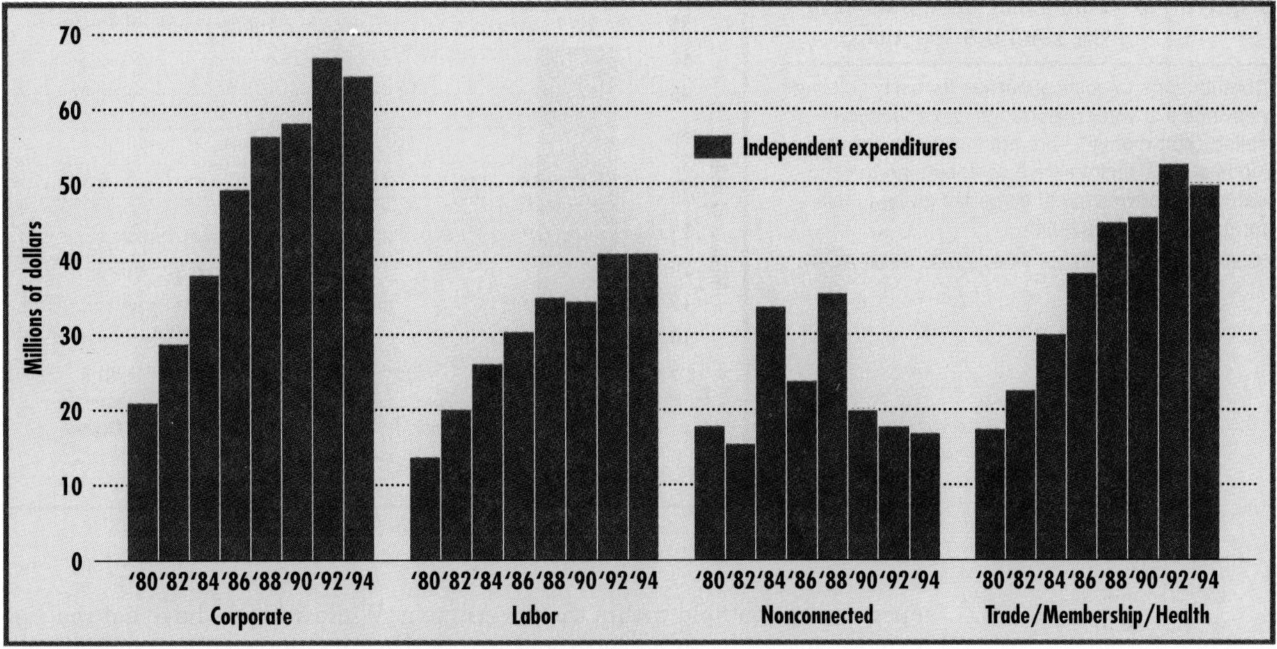

Figure 7.4 ▪ PAC Support of Candidates in the United States

The steady election-by-election growth in PAC giving is shown in this graph. Note the consistent rise in corporate, labor, and trade-group giving, and the rather unsteady history of giving by non-connected groups.

Source: Federal Election Commission, *1995 Annual Report.*

Business and the professions also dominate contributions to the political parties for their campaign activities. These are called **soft-money** contributions. The advantage of such soft-money contributions is the absence of limits on how much can be contributed. Corporations are also allowed to make direct soft-money contributions from their own coffers without the requirement that the money be raised from individual corporate employees or stockholders (which is true of PAC contributions to candidates). Figure 7.5 shows the great advantage that business and the professions enjoy in this kind of campaign giving.

soft money Expenditures by political parties on general public education, voter registration, and voter mobilization.

Interest groups don't contribute money to campaigns and to candidates without some expectation of a return on their investment. It has been argued that there are so many interest groups around that they tend to neutralize each other, that is, that contributions don't really matter. This may, in fact, sometimes be true on high-visibility issues in which the public and an array of interest groups are engaged. Where interest groups seem to matter the most is in the small details of legislation, forged mainly in the committees and subcommittees of Congress: a small subsidy in a defense spending bill, a waiver for a particular industry or company in an environmental bill, or a tax loophole written for a particular corporation in an 800-page tax law.

Access Inequality

Inequalities of representation and resources are further exaggerated by the ability of some groups, especially those representing large corporations, to gain

Figure 7.5 ▪ Soft-Money Contributions in the 1994 U.S. Elections

Contributions to political parties for party building activities like voter registration and education—called "soft money"—are not subject to the same kinds of legal limits as are contributions to candidates. The advantage of corporate giving in this form is clear in this graph.

Source: Federal Election Commission, *1995 Annual Report.*

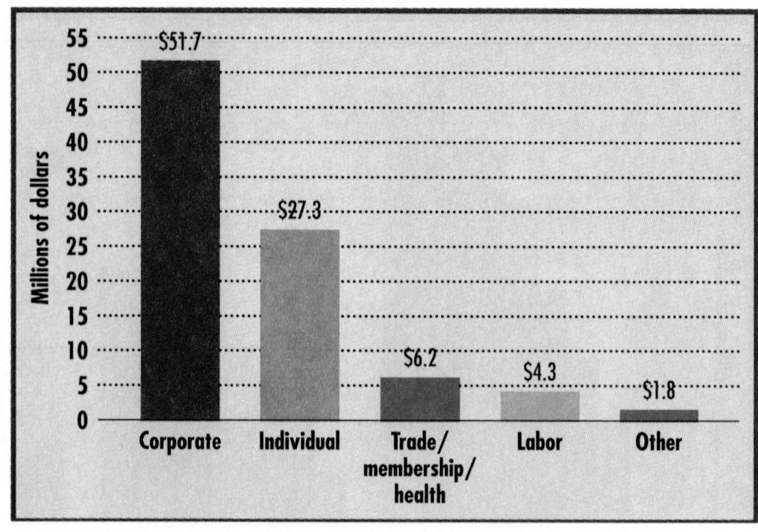

a permanent foothold within the government. While scholars have not reached a consensus on its exact form and extent, they have identified several basic forms that this phenomenon takes.

capture A situation in which a regulated industry exercises substantial influence on the government agency regulating it.

What some scholars call **capture** is the form of government-business partnership that has been most common in regulated industries. Because regulatory agencies and regulated industries must live with each other for many

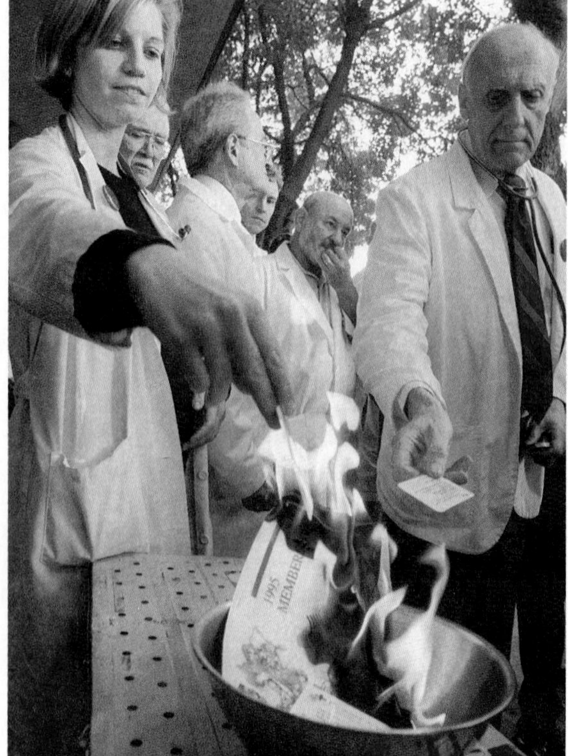

The American Medical Association was strongly opposed to President Clinton's health care proposal, and its lobbying activities and campaign contributions played a significant role in its defeat. Here, doctors opposed to the stance of the AMA on the health care issue burn their association membership cards.

Trying to Break the Link Between Money and Politics[a]

The Struggle for Democracy

John Bonifaz, a young Boston lawyer, is on a crusade to break the link between wealth and politics. Because Congress and state legislatures are slow to make major changes in how campaigns are financed, Bonifaz is trying to get the courts to accept his argument that the present system is unconstitutional because it limits access to the political arena to those who have considerable amounts of money. Such a system, he believes, is no more acceptable than other unconstitutional practices limiting free and equal access to participation in public life; such as poll taxes and excessive filing fees. Instead of the current system, he suggests, we should have a system of publicly financed campaigns. "It's a public process," he says, "so it makes no sense to have it privately financed."

Bonifaz has made his argument in a series of articles appearing in newspapers and prestigious law reviews. The focus of his attack is *Buckley v. Valeo* (1976), in which the Supreme Court ruled that laws that limit the amount of money a private individual can use to support political ideas or to pay for his or her own political campaign violate the First Amendment's free speech protections. Bonifaz is trying to convince the courts to overturn *Buckley* on two grounds: first, that the existing interpretation protects the First Amendment rights of only the wealthy, denying such protections to those without money, and second, that the existing ruling violates the "equal protection" guarantees of the Fourteenth Amendment. Only a nationwide system of public financing for campaigns can break the link between private money and politics, while meeting the requirements of the First and Fourteenth Amendments.

To test these theories, Bonifaz has filed suit in federal district court on behalf of a defeated Democratic candidate for the House of Representatives, Sal Albanese, who was outspent by his opponent, Republican Susan Molinari, by a 2 to 1 margin in the 1992 election. In the suit, brought in October 1994, Bonifaz asked the court to order Congress to create a public financing system for elections that would redress the inequities in fund-raising between incumbents and challengers and between rich and not-so-rich candidates.

Few give the suit much chance of succeeding, not only because it takes on long-settled constitutional law, but because the evidence shows that those with the most money don't always win contested elections. Notwithstanding his prospects, Bonifaz presses on, hoping for an unexpected victory in court, and for a change in public opinion that may at long last force Congress to action on campaign finance reform.

[a]See Todd Purdum, "Trying a Constitutional Task to Curb Campaign Financing," *New York Times* (October 21, 1994).

years, must depend on each other for technical information, and tend to trade top personnel, regulatory agencies became allies and protectors of and advocates for the industries they regulate. Often cited is the case of the Interstate Commerce Commission (ICC), which was created to regulate the railroad industry in the late nineteenth century, but which, over time, came to be its protector.[28] The demise of several regulatory agencies in recent years, including the ICC, has probably decreased the incidence of capture, though capture has not disappeared.

Political scientist Theodore Lowi has described a system of interest group–government partnership which he has termed **"interest group liberalism."**[29] He argues that much of federal government policymaking is actually turned over to interest groups. Many (though not all) of the most important of these arrangements involve business corporations. Thus, the private medical community is involved in deciding local payment guidelines in the Medicare

interest group liberalism A political regime in which interest groups help formulate and carry out government policies.

program, and the Rivers and Harbors Commission (a trade association of construction companies) works closely with the Army Corps of Engineers.

iron triangle An enduring alliance of common interest between an interest group, a congressional committees, and a bureaucratic agency.

Scholars and journalists have also identified subgovernments in particular areas of policymaking called **iron triangles.** In this three-way arrangement (see Figure 7.6), an alliance is formed among a private interest group (usually, but not always, a business corporation or business trade association), a bureaucratic agency, and some committee or subcommittee of Congress. The goal of the iron triangle is to advance and protect government programs that work to the mutual benefit of its members. One commonly cited iron triangle is the alliance among the Pentagon, defense contractors, and the armed services committees of Congress. In this case, a defense contractor such as Lockheed gains when Congress appropriates money for additional missiles, as do the U.S. Air Force and the member of Congress whose district contains the missile plant. That is, all three have a common interest in pushing for such an appropriation and may be quite influential when they join together.

Such semipermanent interest-group footholds in the government have been more common in the United States, where central government power is fragmented and where the legislative branch plays an important role in policymaking, than in countries with parliamentary systems. In Great Britain, the Cabinet, the prime minister, and the ministries are the principal policymakers, and the government and the political parties are highly centralized. Ordinary members of the House of Commons (called *backbenchers*) play almost no policy role, and the committees of the House are relatively unimpor-

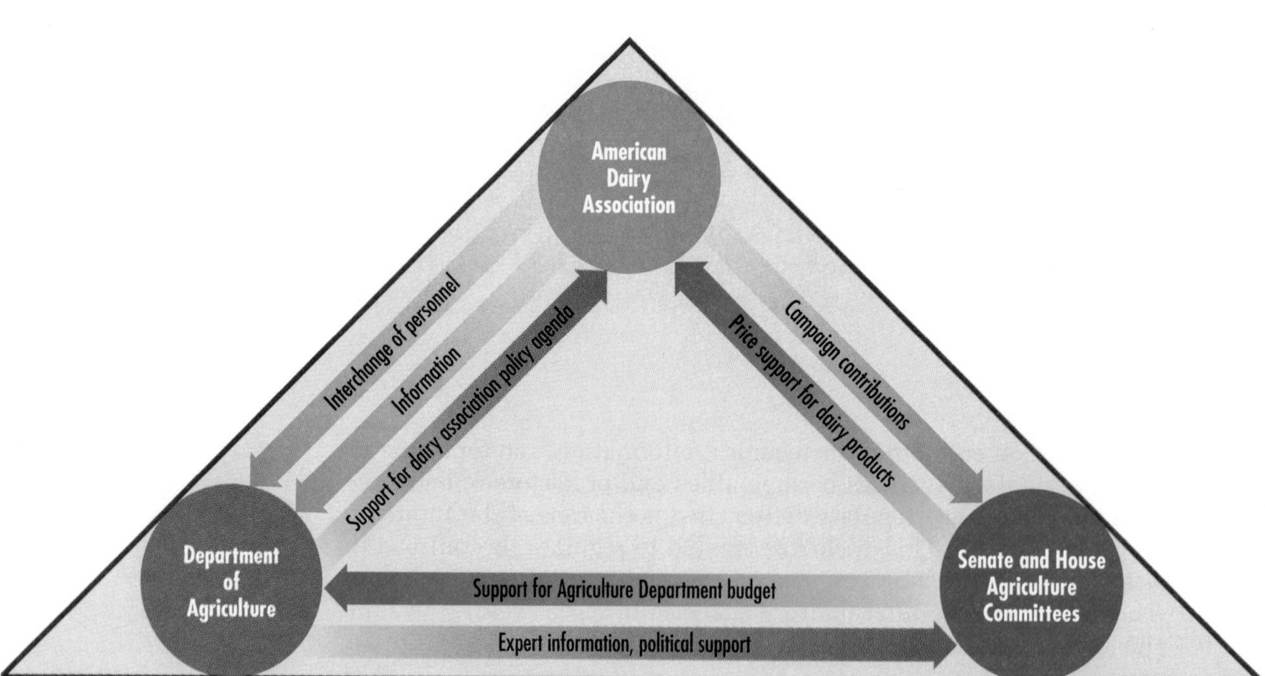

Figure 7.6 ▪ Iron Triangle

In an iron triangle, an alliance based on common interests is formed among a powerful corporation or interest group, an agency of the executive branch, and congressional committees or subcommittees. In this example from the dairy industry, an alliance is formed among parties that share an interest in the existence and expansion of dairy price supports.

tant. As a consequence, interest groups in Great Britain concentrate their attention on the parties, cabinet ministers, and the permanent civil service. In most continental European countries, interest groups tend to be organized into large peak associations, representing business, labor, and agriculture, which are regularly consulted by the ministries involved in planning. Again, relationships between parliamentary committees and narrow interest groups are uncommon.

Political scientists argue that the capture and iron triangle arrangements are no longer as common as they once were.[30] Policy, they suggest, is no longer formed in the dark, out of public sight. Political scientists are more apt to talk today about "issue networks," in which each major policy arena attracts its own broad and diverse set of actors.[31] A set of corporations, bureaucratic agencies, and congressional committees are still involved, to be sure, but so, too, are a broad range of interest groups (including public interest groups) and policy experts. The 1994 debate on the Clinton health care proposal, for instance, involved not only the American Medical Association, the U.S. Department of Health and Human Services, and congressional committees, but many public interest groups, labor unions, medical policy experts, state government representatives, and more. Even so, each of these models of the policy process in Washington are still characterized by the existence of privileged access for some, the frequent exclusion of the public, and the violation of the principle of political equality. Even if the process is marginally more open, it is still those interest groups representing the most privileged groups and sectors of American society that dominate the game.

The Special Place of Business Corporations

Economist and political scientist Charles Lindblom argues that corporations wield such disproportionate power in American politics that they undermine democracy. He closed his widely read book *Politics and Markets* with this observation: "The large private corporation fits oddly into democratic theory. Indeed, it does not fit."[32] Let's see why he reached this somber conclusion.

We have already learned about many of the advantages that business corporations and business trade associations representing groups of corporations enjoy over others in the policy process. The largest corporations are way ahead of their competitors in the number of interest organizations that represent them, the number of lobbyists they employ, the level of resources that are available to them and that they use for political purposes, the ease of access they have to government officials, and their ability to shape public perceptions and opinions.

An additional source of corporate power is the general regard in which business is held in American society and the central and honored place of business values in our culture. Belief in the virtues of individualism, the free market, and private property puts business in a special place in the hearts of its compatriots; faith in free enterprise gives special advantages to the central institution of free enterprise: the business corporation (see Chapter 4). Any political leader contemplating hostile action against corporations must contend with business's special place of honor in the American political culture.

Business corporations are also unusually influential because the health of the American economy—and, thus, the standard of living of the people—is tied closely to the economic well-being of large corporations. It is widely and not entirely unreasonably believed that what is good for business is good for

Because the well-being of many Americans depends on the well-being of American corporations, political leaders often equate the interests of business with the interests of the nation. Here, President George Bush celebrates the opening of a Toys R Us store during a trip to Japan to promote U.S. exports.

America. The result, according to Lindblom, is that government officials tend to defer to the needs of the corporations. Because of their vital role in the economy, government officials tend to interpret business corporations not as "special interests," but as the voice of the national or general interest, and to listen more attentively to their demands and entreaties than they do to those of other sectors of American society. In this sense, corporations enjoy a "privileged position" in American politics. No other interest or set of interests in American society can lay claim to such a powerful political resource.

Business corporations are also powerful because of the mobility of capital in an increasingly open and competitive world economy. Because large corporations can move their operations to many other places on the globe, political leaders are increasingly of a mind to maintain a friendly and supportive investment climate for them.

Large corporations do not, of course, entirely run the show, as in Marxist accounts. Though they have the most resources, for instance, these resources do not translate automatically into real political influence. One interest group may have enormous resource advantages over other interest groups, for instance, but may use its resources ineffectively. Or an interest group with great resources may find itself opposed by other interest groups that together are able to mobilize impressive resources of their own. A powerful interest group may also find that an elected politician is not cooperative because the voters in his or her district are of a different mind from the interest group. So, even with this immense set of resources, business power is not automatically and inevitably translated into political power (though it often is).

Nor does business always get its way in Washington, D.C. There are many issues of great importance on which business in general, or one corporation in particular, loses in the give-and-take of politics. There are times when business finds itself squared off against powerful coalitions of other interest groups (labor, consumer, and environmentalist groups, let us say). On occasion, corporations also find themselves at odds with one another on public policy issues. The trucking, railroad, and airline industries, for instance, may have a common stance on labor unions but have important conflicts of interest about federal transportation policy.

Most important, corporate political power is not a constant in American politics; it waxes and wanes over time.[33] Corporate political power was most impressive during the 1920s, the Reagan 1980s, and in the 104th Congress after the 1994 elections, for instance. Corporations were less able to get their way during other periods, such as the early 1970s, when the power of corporations was almost matched by that of the consumer and environmental movements, and some business leaders began to complain that they were politically helpless.

Corporate power seems to reach its apex under certain conditions.[34] During bad economic times, for instance, Americans are more interested in getting the economy going again than in undertaking reforms that might cut into corporate profits. Politicians in bad times are more solicitous of corporate interests. In good economic times (the late 1960s, for example), politicians are less worried about corporate profits' drying up if tax money is used for social purposes.

Corporations are most powerful when they can build alliances among themselves. Most of the time, corporations are in competition with one another; they do not form a unified political bloc capable of moving government to action on their behalf. On those few occasions when corporations feel that their collective interests are at stake, however, they are capable of coming together to form powerful political coalitions. As political scientist David Vogel has put it, "When business is both mobilized and unified, its political power can be formidable."[35] During the mid–1970s, corporations felt that they were under assault, and they responded by building broad political coalitions that proved irresistible. These became the foundation of the movement for deregulation, tax cuts, and curtailment of domestic programs, an important part of the conservative trend in American politics that led to the election of Ronald Reagan in 1980.

In our view, the best way to think about corporations in American politics is to see their power waxing and waning within what Charles Lindblom called their overall "privileged position."[36] That is, corporations enjoy substantial built-in advantages over competing groups as a matter of course. Within this generally "privileged position," corporate power may be greater at certain times and smaller at other times, but only within the boundaries of a game in which corporations enjoy advantages over other groups. When corporations feel that their collective interests are at stake—when labor unions are particularly aggressive or when government's regulatory burden is perceived to be too heavy—and when they are able to present a united front, they are simply unbeatable. This cannot be said about any other sector of American society.

Curing the Mischief of Factions

James Madison was thinking mainly about the tyranny of "majority factions" when he referred to the "mischief of factions." We have learned, however, that the politics of faction is usually the province not of majorities, but of narrow,

particularistic, and privileged interests. This is a problem in two respects. First, it undermines political equality, which is vital to a functioning democracy (see Chapter 1). Second, it makes it difficult for the United States to formulate broad and coherent national policies. Policy tends to be, instead, a glued-together patchwork of agreements made between narrow factions, each with its own ends in mind.[37]

Here, then, is a dilemma. We are saddled with a politics of faction that significantly undermines political equality and the likelihood of making coherent national policy, yet the right of the people to form organizations for the purpose of petitioning the government is one of our most fundamental and cherished rights. Can we alleviate some of the most pressing "mischiefs of faction" without diminishing our freedom?

Americans have been worried about the politics of faction for a long time, and more than a few efforts have been made to solve some of the most glaring problems. Disclosure has been the principal tool of regulation. The Public Utilities Act of 1935 required that lobbyists for that industry register with Congress. Registration requirements were added for lobbyists for the shipping and maritime industries under the Merchant Marine Act of 1938. In 1946, Congress imposed a requirement that all lobbyists working in Congress be registered (the Federal Regulation of Lobbying Act). In 1993, Congress passed a Clinton administration proposal requiring that lobbyists report on virtually all of their activities, including what policies they have been trying to influence, which federal agencies and congressional committees they have been in contact with, who their employers are, and how much money they have spent on lobbying campaigns. It remains to be seen whether this new legislation will make a difference.

Reformers have also tried to regulate some of the most troublesome abuses of the politics of faction. Sections of the Ethics in Government Act (1978), for instance, try to regulate abuses of the so-called revolving door, in which former government officials become lobbyists for those interests with which they formerly dealt in their official capacity. The act forbids ex-officials to lobby their former agency for a year, or to lobby at all (with no time limit) on any issue in which the official was substantially involved. Bill Clinton instituted the most stringent ethics rules for top officials in the nation's history, requiring that senior executive-branch appointees refrain from lobbying their former agencies for five years after leaving public service, and from ever representing foreign governments. However, Clinton's proposal to prevent members of Congress from accepting gifts and other perks from private organizations—free lunches, vacations, and the like—was defeated by a Republican filibuster in the Senate in 1994 (a watered-down version passed in 1995).

Another effort to alleviate some of the mischiefs of faction is the attempt to control some of the campaign practices of PACs. The evidence seems to suggest that PAC money in campaigns has become very important in American politics and is dominated by narrow segments of American society. Not much progress has been made on this front, however.

While disclosure of lobbying activity and the regulation of some of the worst abuses of the interest group system are to be applauded, many worry that these reforms have not got to the heart of the main problems. Recognizing this worry, some political scientists have suggested that we focus our efforts on strengthening the institutions of majoritarian democracy. The key institution of majoritarian democracy, at least in theory (as we shall see in the next chapter), is the political party. Parties can, as political scientist Walter Dean Burnham put it, "generate countervailing collective power on behalf of the many individually powerless against the relatively few who are individually—or organizationally—powerful."[38] Others believe that the narrowness of interest group politics might be tempered by strengthening the presidency, our only nationally elected office.[39]

Efforts to reform the interest group system in the service of majoritarian democracy may be frustrated in the end, however, by the inescapable fact that highly unequal resources inevitably find their way into our political life. Those with the most resources and interests to protect will usually discover how to influence government officials in ways and to an extent beyond the capacities of most other Americans. It is for this reason that Thomas Jefferson and Abraham Lincoln worried about the possibilities of democracy in a society marked by great inequalities in wealth and income (see Chapter 4). Whether there is a way to decrease inequalities without seriously eroding our liberties remains to be seen, though the experience of capitalist democracies in Western Europe suggests that such a thing may be possible.

Summary

Americans have long denigrated special interests as contrary to the public good. Some political scientists, however, see interest groups as an important addition to the representative process in a democracy.

The United States provides a rich environment for interest groups because of our constitutional system, our political culture, and the broad responsibilities of our government.

A number of interests are accommodated in our interest group system. The most important private interests include business, agriculture, labor, and the professions. Public interest or citizens' groups try to advance some issue or ideological interest that is not connected to the direct material benefit of their own members. There has been a significant expansion in the number of such groups since 1968.

Interest groups attempt to influence the shape of public policy in a number of ways. In the inside game, interest group representatives are in direct contact with government officials and try to build influence on the basis of personal relationships. In the outside game, interest groups attempt to apply indirect pressure to officials by mobilizing other groups, the members of their own group, public opinion, elite opinion, and the electorate to support their positions on policy matters.

Business, trade, and professional associations dominate the interest group system. They enjoy clear advantages over other groups in terms of resources and access to public officials. The business corporation holds an especially privileged place in the interest group system because of the support of business values in our culture and the perceived importance of the corporation to the economic well-being of Americans.

In its present form, the interest group system makes political equality less likely and thus helps to diminish democracy in the United States. Most reforms have failed to get to the root of the problem.

Suggested Readings

Cigler, Allan J., and Burdett A. Loomis (eds.). *Interest Group Politics.* Washington, DC: CQ Press, 1995.

A collection of essays that report the most significant recent research findings about interest groups.

Clawson, Dan, Alan Deustadtl, and Denise Scott. *Money Talks: Corporate PACs and Political Influence.* New York: Basic Books, 1992.
A careful examination of how corporate PACs work based on interviews with corporate leaders.

Dahl, Robert A. *A Preface to Democratic Theory.* Chicago: University of Chicago Press, 1956.
The leading theoretical statement of the pluralist position and the democratic role of the interest group.

Lindblom, Charles. *Politics and Markets.* New York: Basic Books, 1977.
A controversial and widely commented-on book, in which one of the leading pluralist theorists concludes that the modern corporation is incompatible with democracy.

Olson, Mancur. *The Logic of Collective Action.* Cambridge: Harvard University Press, 1965.
A "rational-choice" argument on the place of material and selective benefits in the formation and maintenance of groups, and on the difficulty of forming groups based on values and ideology.

Petracca, Mark P. (ed.). *The Politics of Interests.* Boulder, CO: Westview Press, 1992.
A collection of articles by leading political scientists that summarizes the state of knowledge about interest groups and their impact on American politics.

Rauch, Jonathan. *Demosclerosis: The Silent Killer of American Government.* New York: Random House/Times Books, 1994.
A passionate and detailed description of how the proliferation of interest groups has led to bad public policies.

Vogel, David. *Fluctuating Fortunes: The Political Power of Business in America.* New York: Basic Books, 1989.
A look at the political power of large corporations during the 1970s and 1980s; useful for its wealth of information, even though the author sometimes underestimates the extent of the political power of business.

Internet Sources

The Capital Source http://politicsusa.com/PoliticsUSA/CapSource/Source_1.html.cgi
An extensive listing of lobbying and interest group organizations and how to reach them. Searches can be done by the organization or the individuals one is trying to locate.

The Jefferson Project http://www.stardot.com/jefferson/
Links to the home pages of activist groups, liberal and conservative.

Labor Net http://www.igc.apc.org/labornet/
Access to labor unions and information on labor issues.

Yahoo/Public Interest Groups http://www.yahoo.com/Economy/Organizations/Public_Interest_Group
Direct links to the home pages of scores of public interest groups.

Notes

1. This story is based on information from Thomas Scarlett, "Killing Health Care Reform," *Campaigns and Elections* (October, 1994), Muriel Bee, "Heavy Stakes in

Health Reform," *Sacramento Bee* (August 22, 1994), p. 3; Barbara Sinclair, "Trying to Govern Positively in a Negative Era," in Colin Campbell and Bert A. Rockman, eds. *The Clinton Presidency* (Chatham, NJ: Chatham House, 1996).

2. Scarlett, "Killing Health Care Reform."

3. *The Federalist Papers,* ed. by Clinton Rossiter (New York: New American Library, 1961).

4. Arthur F. Bentley, *The Process of Government* (Chicago: University of Chicago Press, 1908); David Truman, *The Governmental Process* (New York: Knopf, 1951); V. O. Key, *Politics, Parties, and Pressure Groups* (New York: Thomas Y. Crowell, 1952); Robert Dahl, *A Preface to Democratic Theory* (Chicago: University of Chicago Press, 1956); Robert Dahl, *Who Governs?* (New Haven: Yale University Press, 1961).

5. Arthur C. Close, ed., *Washington Representatives, 1977–1991* (Washington, DC: Columbia Books, 1991).

6. Mark P. Petracca, "The Rediscovery of Interest Group Politics," in Mark P. Petracca, ed., *The Politics of Interests: Interest Groups Transformed* (Boulder, CO: Westview Press, 1992), p. 13.

7. Kay Lehman Schlozman and John T. Tierney, *Organized Interests and American Democracy* (New York: Harper & Row, 1986), pp. 77–78.

8. Truman, *Governmental Process.*

9. David Vogel, *Fluctuating Fortunes: The Political Power of Business in America* (New York: Basic Books, 1989), ch. 8.

10. Mancur Olson, *The Logic of Collective Action* (Cambridge: Harvard University Press, 1965).

11. On Olson's theory see Brian Barry and Russell Hardin, eds., *Rational Man and Irrational Society?* (Newbury Park, CA: Sage, 1982); Dennis Chong, *Collective Action and the Civil Rights Movement* (Chicago: University of Chicago Press, 1991); Russell Hardin, *Collective Action* (Baltimore: Johns Hopkins University Press); Terry Moe, *The Organization of Interests* (Chicago: University of Chicago Press, 1980).

12. E. E. Schattschneider, *The Semi-Sovereign People* (Glenview, IL: Holt, Rinehart & Winston, 1960).

13. Thomas Edsall, *The New Politics of Inequality* (New York: Norton, 1984); Michael Goldfield, *The Decline of Organized Labor in the United States* (Chicago: University of Chicago Press, 1987); Edward S. Greenberg, *Capitalism and the American Political Ideal* (Armonk, NY: M. E. Sharpe, 1985); Vogel, *Fluctuating Fortunes.*

14. Jeffrey M. Berry, *Lobbying for the People* (Princeton, NJ: Princeton University Press, 1977), p. 7.

15. Berry, *Lobbying for the People;* David Broder, *Changing the Guard* (New York: Simon & Schuster, 1980); Hugh Heclo, "Issue Networks and the Executive Establishment," in Anthony King, ed., *The New American Political System* (Washington, DC: American Enterprise Institute, 1978); Schlozman and Tierney, *Organized Interests;* Jack L. Walker, "The Origins and Maintenance of Interest Groups in America," *American Political Science Review,* Vol. 77, No. 2 (June 1983), pp. 390–406; G. K. Wilson, *Interest Groups in the United States* (New York: Oxford University Press, 1981).

16. Jack L. Walker, Jr., *Mobilizing Interest Groups in America* (Ann Arbor: University of Michigan Press, 1991).

17. Jeffrey H. Birnbaum and Alan S. Murray, *Showdown at Gucci Gulch* (New York: Vintage Books, 1988), p. 178.

18. Jeffrey M. Berry, *The Interest Group Society* (Glenview, IL: Scott, Foresman/Little, Brown, 1989), p. 141.

19. "Tobacco Group Lobbies EPA on Study Panel," *New York Times,* National Edition (October 22, 1990), p. A11.

20. William Greider, *Who Will Tell the People* (New York: Simon and Schuster, 1992), p. 110.

21. Schlozman and Tierney, *Organized Interests,* p. 175.

22. Dan Clawson, Alan Neustadt, and Denise Scott, *Money Talks: Corporate PACs and Political Influence* (New York: Basic Books, 1992), p. 3.

23. Schattschneider, *Semisovereign People,* p. 35.

24. Schlozman and Tierney, *Organized Interests,* pp. 77, 79.

25. Tom Hamburger and Ted Marmor, "Dead on Arrival: Why in Washington Single Payer Doesn't Have a Single Prayer," *Washington Monthly* (September 1993), pp. 27–32.

26. Frank J. Sorauf, *Inside Campaign Finance* (New Haven: Yale University Press, 1992), p. 100.

27. "Money Talks, Congress Listens," *Boston Globe* (December 12, 1982), p. A24.

28. Marver Bernstein, *Regulating Business by Independent Commission* (Princeton: Princeton University Press, 1955).

29. Theodore Lowi, *The End of Liberalism* (New York: Norton, 1969).

30. Allan J. Cigler, "Interest Groups," in William Crotty, ed., *Political Science: Looking to the Future,* vol. 4 (Evanston, IL: Northwestern University Press, 1991); Robert H. Salisbury et al., "Who Works with Whom? Interest Group Alliances and Opposition," *American Political Science Review,* Vol. 81 (1987), pp. 1217–1234.

31. Jeffrey M. Berry, "Citizen Groups and the Changing Nature of Interest Group Politics in America," *The Annals,* Vol. 528 (July 1993), pp. 16–23; Hugh Heclo, "Issue Networks and the Executive Establishment," in Anthony King, ed., *The New American Political System* (Washington, DC: American Enterprise Institute, 1978); Robert H. Salisbury, John P. Heinz, Edward O. Laumann, and Robert L. Nelson, "Triangles, Networks, and Hollow Cores," and Mark P. Petracca, "The Rediscovery of Interest Group Politics," in Petracca (ed.), *The Politics of Interests.*

32. Charles Lindblom, *Politics and Markets* (New York: Basic Books, 1977), p. 356. For criticisms of Dahl and Lindblom from the left, see John Manley, "Neo-Pluralism: A Class Analysis of Pluralism I and Pluralism II," *American Political Science Review,* Vol. 77 (June 1983), pp. 368–383. For criticisms from the right, see Irving Kristol, *Two Cheers for Capitalism* (New York: Basic Books, 1977); James Q. Wilson, "Democracy and the Corporation," in Robert Sessen, ed., *Does Big Business Rule America?* (Washington, DC: Ethics and Public Policy Center, 1987).

33. David Vogel, *Fluctuating Fortunes: The Political Power of Business in America* (New York: Basic Books, 1989).

34. Ibid.

35. Vogel, *Fluctuating Fortunes,* p. 291.

36. Lindblom, *Politics and Markets,* ch. 13.

37. Jonathan Rauch, *Demosclerosis: The Silent Killer of American Government* (New York: Random House, 1994).

38. Walter Dean Burnham, *Critical Elections and the Mainsprings of American Politics* (New York: Norton, 1970), p. 133.

39. John E. Chubb and Paul E. Peterson, "American Political Institutions and the Problem of Governance," in John E. Chubb and Paul E. Peterson, eds., *Can the Government Govern?* (Washington, DC: Brookings Institution, 1989).

CHAPTER 8

Political Parties

IN THIS CHAPTER

- ★ Why political parties are important in a democracy
- ★ How American political parties are different from parties elsewhere
- ★ Why we have a two-party system
- ★ How our party system has changed over the years
- ★ What role third parties play
- ★ How the Republican and Democratic parties are different

The Decline and Fall of the New Deal Coalition

Steve White, a flange-turner at the Puget Sound naval shipyard, a Catholic and a lifelong liberal Democrat, not only voted Republican in the 1994 congressional and state elections but became a campaign worker for the successful Republican congressional candidate in his district.[1] Steve White was not alone. So many working-class Catholic men (as well as other Americans) joined him in 1994, in fact, that they brought to an end the clear dominance the Democratic party had enjoyed in American politics since the 1930s.

The election tidal wave swept away Democrats high and low. The scale of the Democrats' defeat has been matched only a few times in the history of the United States. Republicans won control of both houses of Congress for the first time in 40 years. In the House of Representatives, the Republicans increased their total by 52 seats, handing the Democrats the worst defeat for an incumbent president's party since Truman's Democratic party lost 55 in 1946. In the Senate, Republicans won 24 of 36 races, picking up 8 seats. Going down to defeat were many Democratic party stalwarts, including the Speaker of the House, Tom Foley of Washington.

The scale of the Republican victory in the South was noteworthy. A Democratic party stronghold for most of the time since the end of the Civil War in 1865, the South became a Republican party stronghold in 1994 when the party won 62 of 125 House seats, 14 of 22 Senate seats, and 6 of 11 governorships in the states of the old Confederacy. Not even Vice-President Al Gore could stem the tide. In his home state of Tennessee, where he campaigned hard, Republicans won two Senate seats (one to fill Gore's vacated seat), a majority in the state's delegation to the House of Representatives, and the governorship.

The purported anti-incumbent mood in the country mainly proved to be an anti-Democratic-incumbent phenomenon. The only incumbents who lost were Democrats, 30 of them in the House. Republicans, on the other hand, batted 1.000; not a single Republican incumbent lost in the House or Senate. Republicans were also successful in gubernatorial races, where they increased their number to 30 across the nation and gained control of the statehouse in 8 of the 9 largest states.

More important for the long-term prospects of the Democrats was evidence that the New Deal coalition—the voting bloc and interest group alliance that was the foundation of the party's long-term success—had finally been shattered. The voting blocs and groups of the New Deal coalition first came together to elect Franklin Roosevelt president in the 1930s and remained largely intact into the 1970s. The coalition was made up of a number of groups whose votes went overwhelmingly to Democrats for over four decades: Jews, African-Americans, labor union members and their families, blue-collar workers, white ethnics, Catholics, white southerners, Evangelical Protestants, and urban dwellers in general. With the exception of Jews, African-Americans, and labor union households, voters in each of these groups slowly drifted away from the Democrats in the 1980s and made a definitive break in 1994.

In the 1994 congressional elections, a number of groups decisively switched to the GOP after drifting that way for many years.[2] For instance, 58 percent of white Americans voted Republican, as did 66 percent of Protestants and 53 percent of white Catholics (who had voted overwhelmingly Democratic from the 1920s until the 1980s). Long a part of the coalition, 75 percent of white evangelicals voted Republican. Most important, given its late-nineteenth- and twentieth-century role as the geographic foundation of the Democratic party, the South gave 55 percent of its vote to the GOP, whites in the region voting Republican at a 65 percent clip. While the poor and the economically marginal gave their votes to the Democrats, the large middle class (those with family incomes between $30,000 and $50,000) voted for their opponents. White downscale Americans—those with less than a college degree—increased their GOP vote by 13 percentage points. While Democratic and Republican party identifiers naturally voted for their favorite party, 54 percent of independents voted for the Republicans. Democrats continued to hold the loyalties of urban voters and of union households, but both represent a declining share of the American electorate. The suburban vote (strongly Republican), for instance, had become the largest segment of the electorate in the 1992 presidential election, even while union membership has fallen to its lowest point (only 16 percent of employed Americans) since the early 1950s. Democrats also continued to receive strong support from Jews (78 percent), African-Americans (88 percent), and Hispanics (70 percent), but the members of the latter two groups tend to vote at lower rates than other Americans.

Despite their impressive victory in 1994, it is unlikely that the Republicans will replace the Democrats as the nation's dominant party. For them to do so will require not only a string of victories in presidential and congressional elections but also the ability to build an electoral coalition that is as broad and as enduring as the New Deal Coalition. The 1996 elections suggest that this has not happened. Though Republicans captured both houses of Congress, Democrats not only won the presidency but made important gains in governorships and control of state legislatures.

In this chapter, we will examine American political parties in depth. We not only will address historical changes in party dominance in American politics but will ask what difference such swings in party fortunes make for government policies and the lives of Americans. We also will ask why American political parties are the way they are and what implications the answer has for the workings of democracy in the United States. We will see that such structural factors as our constitutional rules, our culture, and our economy are important in determining the kinds of parties we have.

The Role of Political Parties in a Democracy

Political parties are organizations that try to win control of government by getting people elected to public office who carry the party label. In representative democracies, parties are the principal organizations that recruit candidates for public office, that run their candidates against the candidates of other political parties in competitive elections, and that try to organize and coordinate the activities of government officials under party banners and programs.

Many political scientists believe that political parties are essential to democracy. They agree with E. E. Schattschneider that "political parties created democracy and . . . modern democracy is unthinkable save in terms of the parties."[3] What Schattschneider and others see in the political party is the main instrument of popular sovereignty and especially, majority rule: "The parties are the special form of political organization adapted to the mobilization of majorities. How else can the majority get organized? If democracy means anything at all it means that the majority has the right to organize for the purpose of taking over the government."[4]

In theory, political parties can do a number of things to make popular sovereignty possible.[5]

Keeping Elected Officials Responsive For one thing, they can provide a way for the people to keep elected officials responsive through competitive elections. Unified, coherent parties that compete in elections can help voters choose between alternative policy directions for the future, for instance. Competitive party elections, moreover, allow voters to judge the past performance of a governing party and to decide whether to allow that party to continue in office. Or parties can adjust their **party platforms** to reflect the preferences of the public as a way to win elections (these three ways in which elections relate to democracy are discussed in Chapter 9).

platform A party's statement of its positions on the issues of the day.

Including a Broad Range of Groups Political parties are also important for popular sovereignty because they generally try to include as many groups in the population as they possibly can. Parties are by nature inclusive, as they must be if they are to create a winning majority coalition in elections. It is customary for parties in the United States to recruit candidates for public office from many ethnic and racial groups and to include language in their platforms to placate and attract a diversity of groups.

Stimulating Political Interest When they are working properly, moreover, political parties stimulate interest in politics and public affairs and increase

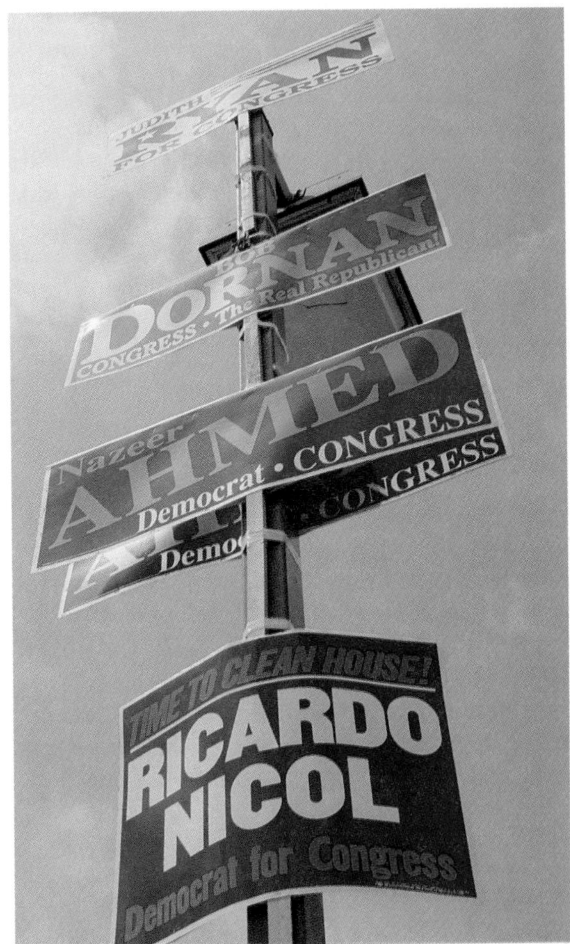

Political parties generally try to broaden their appeal by running candidates from a wide range of ethnic, racial, and religious groups.

participation.[6] They do this as a natural by-product of their effort to win or retain power in government; they mobilize voters, bring issues to public attention, and educate on the issues that are of interest to the party. Competition between political parties increases public awareness of, and interest in, candidates and issues. Party competition, by "expanding the scope of conflict," attracts attention and gets people involved.[7]

Ensuring Accountability Finally, parties can help make officeholders more accountable. When things go wrong or promises are not kept, it is important in a democracy for citizens to know who is responsible. Where there are many offices and branches of government, however, it is hard to pinpoint responsibility. Officials tend to blame others. Citizens find it difficult to unravel the details. Political parties can simplify this difficult task by allowing for collective responsibility. Citizens can pass judgment on the governing ability of a party as a whole and decide whether to retain the incumbent party or to throw it out of office in favor of an alternative party.

In theory, then, political parties can be tools of popular sovereignty. Whether or not our own political parties fulfill these responsibilities to democracy is the question we explore in the remainder of this chapter as well as in Chapter 9. We begin by describing the most important characteristics of the American party system.

The Two-Party System

The United States comes closer to having a "pure" two-party system than any other nation in the world. Most nations have either one-party systems or multiparty systems. Most Western democracies have multiparty systems (see Table 8.1). In the United States, however, two parties have dominated the political scene since 1836, and the Democrats and the Republicans have controlled the presidency and Congress since 1860. Minor or third parties have rarely polled a significant percentage of the popular vote in either presidential or congressional elections (more will be said later about third parties and independent candidates).

A History of the Two-Party System

Although the United States has had a two-party system for most of its history, it would be a mistake to assume that this system has been static. The party system has, in fact, changed a great deal, both mirroring and playing a central role in the dynamic and sometimes chaotic story of the development of the United States, as described in Chapter 4.

The First Party System: Federalists Versus Democratic Republicans Though the Founders were hostile to parties in theory, they created them almost immediately. The first was formed in the 1790s by George Washington's energetic secretary of the treasury, Alexander Hamilton. In a successful effort to push through the administration's ambitious legislative program, Hamilton persuaded sympathetic members of Congress to form a loosely organized party that eventually took the name Federalist.

Thomas Jefferson, James Madison, and others formed a party in Congress to oppose the Hamilton domestic program of protective tariffs, a national bank,

Table 8.1

Party Systems in Other Democratic Nations

Parliamentary democracies, where electoral rules and traditions favor the existence of small parties, tend to be multiparty systems in contrast to the American two-party system. This table shows the many parties that hold seats in the parliaments of other Western democracies.

Nation	Parties with Parliamentary Seats in 1994	Nation	Parties with Parliamentary Seats in 1994
Australia	Labor Liberal National Democrat Green	Japan	Liberal Democratic Japan Socialist Clean Government Communist Democratic Socialist
Canada	Progressive Conservative Liberal New Democratic Québécois Bloc Reform	Germany	Christian Democratic Union Christian Social Union Social Democratic Free Democratic Green
France	Socialist Rally for the Republic Union for French Democracy Centrists Communists	Spain	Socialist Workers Popular Convergence and Unity Social Democratic Center Basque Popular Basque National
Italy	Christian Democratic Communist Renewal Socialist Social Democratic Italian Social Movement Radicals Green Liberal	Sweden	Social Democratic Moderate Liberal Center Communist Left Christian Democratic New Democracy
		Britain	Conservative Labour Liberal Democratic

Source: Central Intelligence Agency, *World Fact Book* (Washington, DC: CIA, 1995).

and federal assumption of Revolutionary War debts, which they believed hurt the economic interests of many groups in American society.[8] They also opposed Federalist foreign policy. They called their faction Republican, though the Federalists tried to discredit them by calling them Democratic Republicans (the term *democratic* was a term of derision, not praise, in those days).

In full control of the federal government after the 1796 election, the Federalists passed the notorious Alien and Sedition Acts to stop Republican criticism of Federalist policies. Ten Republican editors and printers were imprisoned and fined. Not intimidated, the Republican party used the Alien and Sedition Acts to rally opposition to the Federalists and won a decisive victory in the election of 1800. Jefferson's victory was only the prelude to a string of spectacular successes by Democratic Republican presidential candidates.

The Federalist party gradually disappeared, tainted by its pro-British sympathies during the War of 1812 and its image as a party of the wealthy and the aristocratic in an increasingly democratic America. By 1816, the first two-party system had evolved into a one-party or no-party system, generally known (because of the absence of party competition) as the Era of Good Feelings.

The Second Party System: Democrats Versus Whigs The Era of Good Feelings of the 1820s gave way in the 1830s to a strong two-party system. The Democrats (the former Democratic Republicans) and a new political party, the Whigs, were parties of a very different sort from those in the first party system. Instead of being loosely organized groups of local dignitaries and public officials, they were well organized, with sharply contrasting programs tied to a highly partisan electorate. The changes seem to have been caused by a significant democratization of American life. By the late 1820s and 1830s, the legal barriers to voting by adult white males had disappeared. In addition, most states had passed laws requiring the direct popular election of presidential electors, taking the process out of the hands of state legislatures. With the extension of the right to vote and the popular election of presidents, power in American politics gravitated to organizations capable of reaching, organizing, and mobilizing millions of voters. In these changed circumstances, loosely organized parties of local dignitaries would no longer do.

Neither national party was able to withstand the drift of the country toward civil war. The northern and southern wings of each party mirrored the split in the nation. The Whig party simply disintegrated and disappeared. Several of its fragments came together with *free-soilers* (who opposed the expansion of slavery into the western territories) and antislavery Democrats to form a new Republican party—the ancestor of the present-day Republicans—which ran its first presidential candidate, John Frémont, in the election of 1856. The Democrats survived but could not agree on a single candidate to run against Republican Abraham Lincoln in 1860, so each wing of the party nominated its own candidate.

The second party system was characterized by well-organized parties, skilled in the use of methods (like this parade) to mobilize the "common man" to participate in electoral politics.

From the Civil War to 1896: Republicans and Democrats in Balance Once the southern states had reentered the Union after Reconstruction, the Republicans and the Democrats found themselves roughly balanced in national politics. Between 1876 and 1896, the Democrats managed to control the presidency for 8 of 20 years, the Senate for 6 years, and the House of Representatives for 14 years. Each party had a strong regional flavor. The Democratic party was primarily a white southern party, though Catholics and many workers in northern urban areas also supported it. The GOP (the "Grand Old Party," another name for the Republican party) became a party of business, the middle class, and newly enfranchised African-Americans.

The Party System of 1896: Republican Dominance Beneath the apparent calm of a balanced two-party system, however, a storm was brewing. The late nineteenth century was a time of rapid economic and social change and disruption, one effect of which was to spawn a host of protest movements and third parties. The Populist party, the most important of them, garnered 8.5 percent of the total vote in the 1892 election. It won four states in the electoral college, running on the slogan "Wealth belongs to him who creates it." During the 1890s, Populist party candidates also won governorships in eight states and control of at least as many state legislatures. Most significantly, the party proved to be popular not only with farmers in the West and the South, but also with unions and workers in industrial cities. It also managed to create an alliance of poor black and white farmers in many of the states of the Deep South, posing a threat to the area's traditional leadership.

In 1896, the Populist party joined with the Democratic party to nominate a single candidate for the presidency, the charismatic orator William Jennings Bryan, who urged "free coinage of silver" to help debtors with cheaper currency. The threat of a radical agrarian party, joining blacks and whites, and farmers and labor unionists, proved to be too much for many Americans and contributed to one of the most bitter electoral campaigns in U.S. history. Conservative Democrats deserted their party to join the Republicans. Businesses warned each other and their workers in no uncertain terms about the dangers of a Populist-Democratic victory. Newly formed business organizations, like the National Association of Manufacturers, spread the alarm about a possible Democratic victory. In the South, efforts to intimidate potential black voters increased dramatically.[9] Mark Hanna, the "boss" of the GOP and president of the Hanna Steel Company, raised the enormous sum (for that era) of $3.3 million to back William McKinley's run for the presidency.[10]

The Republicans won handily and dominated American politics until the Great Depression and the election of 1932. Between 1896 and 1932, the Republicans won control of both houses of Congress in 15 out of 18 elections, and of the presidency in 7 out of 9. Democrats won the presidency in 1912 and 1916 only because the Republicans were split between the old guard, led by William Howard Taft, and the "Bull Moose" faction of former Republican president Teddy Roosevelt.

The New Deal Party System: Democratic Party Dominance The Great Depression, the **New Deal,** and the leadership of President Franklin D. Roosevelt fundamentally changed the conception of the proper role of the federal government. These developments also ushered in a long period of Democratic party dominance.

New Deal The programs of the administration of President Franklin D. Roosevelt.

Election returns make clear the fundamental shift in party dominance. From 1932 through 1972, the Democrats won 7 out of 11 presidential elections, enjoyed control of the Senate and the House of Representatives for all but four years, and prevailed in a substantial majority of governorships and state legislatures across the nation.

The Democrats also enjoyed a substantial lead over the Republicans in party identification among the electorate (as the newly developed opinion polls and surveys showed) and were supported by a broad coalition of groups. By the middle of the 1930s, the **New Deal coalition**—a strong, but informal alliance of workers, Catholics, Jews, unionists, small- and medium-sized farmers, urban dwellers, white ethnics, southerners, and blacks—were firmly in the Democratic party camp. Several scholars have suggested, moreover, that a number of large multinational corporations and major investment banks were an integral part of the coalition as well, supplying personnel, ideas, and campaign money throughout the period.[11]

New Deal Coalition The informal electoral alliance of working-class ethnic groups, Catholics, urban dwellers, Jews, racial minorities, and the South that was the basis of the Democratic party dominance of American politics from the New Deal to the early 1970s.

The Post–New Deal Party System As we suggested in the story opening this chapter, the electoral coalition that formed the basis of the New Deal party system seems to have disappeared. The 1994 elections, we argued, represented its final demise, though the death struggle had been going on for some time. A number of factors were responsible: the defection of white blue-collar workers and their families, the white South, and religious conservatives; a decline in the number of Democratic party identifiers in the population; and a general loss of confidence in the Democrat-dominated Congress and many of its policies. This decline in support for the Democrats took well over a decade and a half to reach full lethal flower. What is to take its place, however, is unclear.

Realignment A case can be made that the American party system is being realigned. By **realignment,** political scientists mean the emergence of a new party system in which one political party displaces another (in this case, Republicans displace Democrats) and becomes dominant. In a realigned system, Republicans would win a disproportionate share of federal and state offices, build a lead in party identifiers in the population, have their ideas dominate the national agenda, and move government policies in new directions. They would enjoy these advantages over several decades.[12]

realignment The process by which one party supplants another as the dominant party in a political system.

There is some evidence that realignment may be taking place. First, in the 1994 electoral landslide, voters seemed to be making a clear choice between the parties when they swept away only Democrats, leaving Republicans unscathed. Second, there is the apparent transformation of the South from a bastion of the Democratic party to a bastion of the Republican party, with little prospect that the region will move back to the Democratic side anytime soon. Third, there is the loss of the long-term Democratic party lead in party identifiers in the population. Finally, there is the perceptible shift in the terms of political debate in the nation toward Republican positions. For example, Democrats increasingly speak of balanced budgets and family values while President Clinton declared the "end of big government" in his 1996 State of the Union address.

Dealignment An even stronger case can be made, perhaps, for what political scientists call **dealignment.**[13] Dealignment may be thought of as a transformation in the party system in which a previously dominant party loses preeminence (the Democrats) but no new party takes its place on a long-term basis. This new party system is characterized by the relative parity of the major parties in a context where the population not only identifies less with either party but becomes increasingly alienated from them and less confident that they can solve the nation's problems.

dealignment A process by which the superiority of a dominant political party diminishes without another party supplanting it.

Governor Mario Cuomo of New York concedes defeat on election night, 1994. In this election, many Democratic Party icons like Cuomo fell before the Republican electoral landslide.

There is evidence to support the dealignment interpretation. Polls show a decline in strong party identifiers in the American population, a rise in the number who claim to be independents, and a decrease of trust in the capacities and intentions of both parties and those who lead them.[14] We also have witnessed a proliferation of independent candidates and third-party efforts in the 1990s. And voting participation is dropping, down to 49 percent in 1996.

Despite appearances to the contrary, moreover, Americans did not support a conservative shift in national policies in 1994, a shift required in the realignment interpretation. While Americans were increasingly conservative at the abstract, ideological level—that is, more distrustful of and less confident in government, and more opposed to taxes and regulation—substantial majorities continued to want the federal government to spend money to protect the environment, educate children, support the elderly with Social Security and Medicare, and alleviate poverty.[15] Bill Clinton focused on these themes and their contrast with the Republican "Contract with America" in fashioning his landslide reelection in 1996.

Though Americans seem less tied to and less supportive of the major parties, the dealignment thesis neither requires nor implies that party organizations are moribund or that parties are unimportant in American politics. Indeed, the American parties are well funded and increasingly technologically sophisticated as campaign organizations, and they are most certainly important in organizing and energizing the government.

There have been five relatively stable periods in the history of the two-party system in the United States, each stretching over 30 or 40 years, linked to one another by much shorter periods of transformation or realignment (Figure 8.1 shows this history in graphic form). Realignments seem to be triggered by structural factors. They occur when the old party system is unable to accommodate or solve the problems that develop during periods of rapid social,

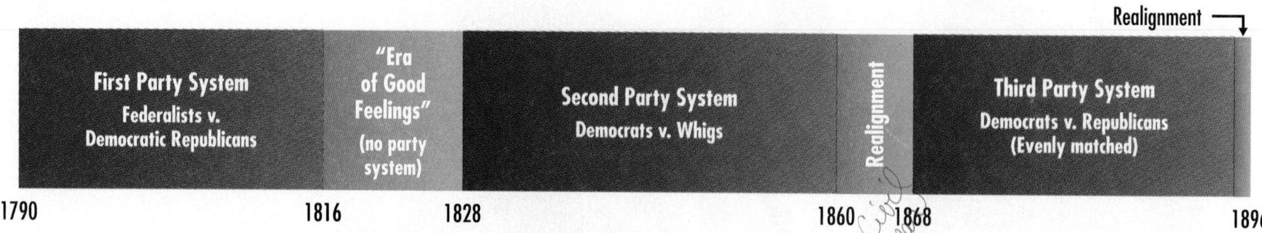

Figure 8.1 ▪ Party Systems and Realignment
American history may be divided into a series of stable-political-party eras, punctuated by brief periods of transitions from one party era to another. Our present period of uncertainty in American politics is highlighted in this graph of party eras.

economic, and cultural change. The New Deal party system, for instance, was triggered by the crisis of the Great Depression and favorable public reactions to government efforts to deal with the economic collapse. Our current transformation may have been triggered by changes in the economy and the consequent stagnation of living standards for many Americans (see Chapter 4).

It is too early to tell whether the American party system is being realigned or dealigned. The answer can be found only in the results of future elections and the actions of the federal government. Here is what to look for: If realignment has taken place, the Republicans will prevail in national and state elections for the near future, and their ideas will determine the main outlines of government policy. If dealignment has taken place, volatility will become the hallmark of American politics. Democrats and Republicans will take turns being swept from office, independent and third-party candidates will continually appear, and public policy will lurch from one direction to another. Because little changed in 1996—the Democrats retained the presidency and the Republicans the Congress—we must still wait for an answer to the realignment question.

Why a Two-Party System?

Most Western democracies have multiparty systems. Why are we so different from other countries? There are several possible answers.

Electoral Rules

The kinds of rules that organize elections help determine what kind of party system exists. Which rules are chosen, then, has important consequences for a nation's politics.

proportional representation A type of electoral system in which legislative seats are apportioned to political parties in proportion to the popular vote that each party receives.

Proportional Representation Most other democratic nations use some form of **proportional representation** (PR) to elect their representatives.[16] In PR systems, each party is represented in the legislature in rough proportion to the percentage of the popular vote it receives in an election. In a perfect PR system, a party winning 40 percent of the vote would get 40 seats in a 100-seat legislative body, a party winning 22 percent of the vote would get 22 seats, and so on. In such a system, even very small parties would have a reason to maintain their separate identities, for no matter how narrow their appeal, they would win seats as long as they could win a proportion of the popular vote. Voters with strong views on an issue or with strong ideological outlooks could vote for a party that closely represented their views. A vote for a small party would not be wasted, for it would ultimately be translated into legislative seats and, perhaps, a place in the governing coalition.

Israel and the Netherlands come closest to having a pure PR system, organized on a national basis; most Western European nations have departures of varying significance from the pure form. Most, for instance, vote on slates of party candidates within multimember electoral districts, apportioning seats in each district according to each party's percentage of the vote. Most also have a minimum threshold (often 5 percent) below which no seats are awarded.

Winner-Take-All, Single-Member Districts Elections in the United States are organized on a "winner-take-all," single-member-district basis. Each electoral district in the United States, whether it is an urban ward, a county, a congressional district, or a state, generally elects only one person to a given office and does so on the basis of whoever wins the *most* votes (not necessarily a majority of 50 percent plus 1). This arrangement creates a powerful incentive for parties to coalesce and for voters to concentrate their attention on big parties. Let's see why.

From the vantage point of party organizations, this type of election discourages minor-party efforts, because failure to come in first in the voting leaves such a party with no representation at all. Leaders of such parties are tempted to merge with a major party. By the same token, a disaffected faction or group within a party is unlikely to leave the party and go out on its own in an electoral system like ours, because the probability of gaining political office is very low.

From the voter's point of view, a single-member, winner-take-all election means that a vote for a minor party is wasted. Those who vote for a minor party may feel good, but most voters have few illusions that such votes will translate into representation and are not inclined to cast them.

Note that the most important office in the American government, the presidency, is elected in what is, in effect, a single-district (the nation), winner-take-all election. In parliamentary systems, the executive power is lodged in a cabinet, where several parties may be represented. It is not uncommon in parliamentary systems for the prime minister to come from one of the lesser parties (former Italian prime minister Giovanni Spadolini came from a party with only 3 percent of the parliamentary seats). In such systems, parties have an incentive to maintain their separate identities. In the United States, only one party candidate can win a majority of the electoral votes in the contest for the presidency. Minor parties are really not in the game for the main prize. Note that Ross Perot won 19 percent of the popular vote in the 1992 presidential election but failed to win a single electoral vote.

Restrictions on Minor Parties

Once a party system is in place, the dominant parties often establish rules that make it difficult for other parties to get on the ballot. A number of formidable legal obstacles stand in the way of third parties and independent candidates in the United States. While many of these restrictions have been eased because of successful court challenges by recent minor-party and independent presidential candidates, the path to the ballot remains a difficult one in many states (see Table 8.2). In 1992, however, with the help of a strong volunteer movement and a great deal of money, Ross Perot was able to gain a place on the ballot in all 50 states. His reform party did the same thing in 1996.

The federal government's partial funding of presidential campaigns has made the situation of third parties even more difficult. Major-party candidates automatically qualify for federal funding once they are nominated. Minor-party candidates must attract a minimum of 5 percent of the votes cast in the general election to be eligible for public funding, and they are not reimbursed until after the election. Moreover, federal funding is given to the Democrats

Table 8.2

State Requirements for Ballot Access (with Party Affiliation)

It is not easy for a new political party to get its name on the ballot. This table shows the number of signatures on petitions required in each of the states.

	Number of Signatures Required	Percentage of Registered Voters		Number of Signatures Required	Percentage of Registered Voters
Alabama	35,973	1.62	Missouri	10,000	0.34
Alaska	2,586	0.77	Montana	10,471	2.04
Arizona	15,062	0.73	Nebraska	5,741	0.62
Arkansas	0[b]	0.00	Nevada	3,761	0.60
California	89,006	0.60%	New Hampshire	3,000	0.45
Colorado	0[a]	0.00	New Jersey	800	0.02
Connecticut	7,500	0.40	New Mexico	2,339	0.33
Delaware	180[d]	0.06	New York	15,000	0.17
District of Columbia	3,500[d]	0.97	North Carolina	51,904	1.43
			North Dakota	7,000	1.51
Florida	65,596	1.00	Ohio	33,463	0.54
Georgia	30,036	1.00	Oklahoma	41,711	2.04
Hawaii	3,829	0.78	Oregon	18,316	1.02
Idaho	9,644	1.54	Pennsylvania	30,000[d]	0.51
Illinois	25,000	0.41	Rhode Island	1,000	0.18
Indiana	29,822	0.97	South Carolina	10,000	0.67
Iowa	1,500	0.09	South Dakota	7,792	0.72
Kansas	16,418	1.25	Tennessee	37,179	1.39
Kentucky	5,000	0.23	Texas	43,963	0.51
Louisiana	0[a]	0.00	Utah	300	0.03
Maine	4,000	0.44	Vermont	1,000	0.27
Maryland	10,000	0.42	Virginia	16,000[d]	0.53
Massachusetts	10,000	0.32	Washington	200	0.01
Michigan	30,891	0.50	West Virginia	6,837	0.77
Minnesota	2,000	0.07	Wisconsin	2,000	0.06
Mississippi	0[c]	0.00	Wyoming	8,000	3.36

[a]No signatures required. Must pay $500 to get on ballot.

[b]Just hold a meeting.

[c]Just be organized.

[d]Estimate.

Source: *New York Times* (September 28, 1995), p. A7. Based on information from *Ballot Access News.*

The rules for getting independent and third-party candidates on the ballot are highly restrictive, and the limitations on funding and media air time make running a successful independent campaign exceedingly difficult. With billions of dollars at his disposal and an army of volunteers to support him, Ross Perot was able to get on the ballot in all 50 states in 1992 and was invited to join Clinton and Bush in presidential debates. Although Perot did not win any states in the general election, he did make a major impact, capturing almost 20 percent of the popular vote.

and the Republicans to run their conventions; minor parties receive no convention funding. Because Ross Perot was able to finance his 1992 independent campaign mainly on his own, he had no need of federal funding and was not hurt by these features of our system of campaign finance—but few independent candidates are billionaires. Other independent candidates and minor parties, then, must somehow get over the financing hurdle.

Finally, the television networks are no longer obliged to give equal time to parties other than the Republicans and the Democrats. Congress took special action to suspend the Federal Communications Commission's equal-time and fairness-doctrine requirements to allow televised debates among presidential aspirants within each of the major parties, and between the major-party nominees in the general election campaign.[17] Perot joined the debates in 1992 after Clinton and Bush invited him, but they were not required by law to do so. In 1996, however, Perot was not invited to join the Clinton–Dole debates.

Popular Attitudes

The attitudes of the American people are also an important factor in maintaining a two-party system. Once a party system is in place, it comes to seem natural—the only possible kind of party system. This attitude is passed on to children by families, schools, and the media. Children learn that there are only Democrats and Republicans and that their family is one or the other. We have discovered, however, that these ties to the two parties have been unraveling.

This situation may account for the flurry of independent candidacies and third-party efforts in the 1992 and 1996 presidential races.

The Absence of a Strong Labor Movement

The relative weakness of the American labor movement has already been noted in several places in this book. In the Western European countries, the organized labor movement was instrumental in the creation of Socialist and Labor political parties that challenged classical liberal (free enterprise, small government) and traditional conservative (monarchist, Catholic, and aristocratic) parties. The British Labour party, for instance, was created by trade union officials and Socialists in 1906. Strong Socialist and Labor parties in Europe did not replace traditional Liberal and Conservative parties (except in Great Britain) but spurred them on to more spirited organizing and electioneering of their own. The result has been the creation of a basic three-party system in many European countries—Conservative, Liberal, and Labor or Socialist—with a number of small satellite parties (encouraged by PR electoral systems) clustered about them.

The Role of Minor Parties in the Two-Party System[18]

Minor parties have played a less important role in the United States than in virtually any other democratic nation. In our entire history, only a single minor party (the Republican) has managed to replace one of the major parties. Only six (not including the Republicans) have been able to win even 10 percent of the popular vote in a presidential election, and only seven have managed to win a single state in a presidential election. In 1992, Ross Perot, running as an independent candidate, garnered 19 percent of the vote under the United We Stand America label (which was not, strictly speaking, a political party), the highest total ever for a pure "outsider."

Minor parties have come in a number of forms:

- *Protest parties* sometimes arise as part of a protest movement. The People's or Populist party, for instance, grew out of the western and southern farm protest movement against practices in the railroad and banking industries in the late nineteenth century.
- There have also been *ideological parties* organized around coherent sets of ideas. The several socialist parties have been of this sort, as has the Libertarian party, with its program advocating the "complete privatization of society."
- *Single-issue parties* are barely distinguishable from interest groups. What makes them different is their decision to run candidates for office. The Prohibition party and the Free Soil party fall into this category.
- *Splinter parties* form when a faction in one of the two major parties bolts to run its own candidate or candidates. An example is the Bull Moose Progressive party of Teddy Roosevelt, formed after Roosevelt split with the Republican party regulars in 1912.

Minor parties do a number of things in American politics. Sometimes, they articulate new ideas that are eventually taken over by one or both major parties. The Free Soil party advocated policies on the admission of new states that became part of the Republican party agenda in 1856. The Socialist party under

Norman Thomas advocated public works projects as a way to battle unemployment during the Great Depression, an idea that became part of the Democrats' New Deal legislative package. The tremendous attention that the balanced-budget issue has received recently is surely related to its centrality in Ross Perot's 1992 presidential campaign.

Sometimes, minor parties allow those with grievances to express themselves in a way that is not possible within the major parties. More cynical scholars suggest that unhappy groups are thus able to "blow off steam" without seriously disturbing the normal political process or threatening those holding public office. Less cynical scholars believe that expressions of discontent and the threat that major-party voters will defect keep the major parties responsive.

Because minor parties, by definition, are unlikely to win national elections, they are usually not as cautious as the major parties. They tend to be loud, unambiguous about policies, and ideologically committed. Thus, they probably expand the scope of conflict in American politics, increase interest and attention in at least some segments of the public, and bring a few more Americans into the political process. The Perot campaign, for instance, helped reverse a long decline in voter turnout in 1992.

The Parties as Organizations

I don't belong to an organized political party. I'm a Democrat.

—WILL ROGERS

American parties don't look much like the parties in other democratic countries. In most democratic countries, the political parties are fairly well-structured organizations, led by party professionals, and committed to a set of policies and principles. They also tend to have clearly defined membership requirements, centralized control over party nominations and electoral financing, and disciplinary authority over party members holding political office. None of this is true of our own major parties. We look at each of these items in this section.

The Insubstantial Nature of American Political Parties

The classic boss-led political machines of American folklore—so long identified with such names as Tammany Hall, "Boss Tweed" of New York, Richard Daley of Chicago, and Huey Long of Louisiana—have disappeared from the cities and states where they once existed, mainly because of reforms that ended party control over government contracts and jobs. Political machines have never existed at the national level. There has never been a "boss" of any of our major political parties. There have been leaders with clout, reputation, and vision, to be sure, but never a "boss" who could issue commands and be reasonably certain that such commands would be obeyed. Newt Gingrich exercised strong leadership over Republican House members in the 104th Congress, but his influence did not extend to Senate Republicans, let alone to Republican governors and mayors. Even popular, charismatic, and skillful presidents, including George Washington, Abraham Lincoln, Woodrow Wilson, Franklin D. Roosevelt, Harry Truman, John F. Kennedy, and Ronald Reagan, have had nearly as much trouble controlling the many diverse and independent groups and individuals within their own parties as they have had dealing with the opposition.

The vagueness of party membership is a good indicator of the insubstantial nature of our parties. Think about what it means to be a Republican or a Democrat in the United States. Americans do not join parties in the sense of paying dues and receiving a membership card. To Americans, being a member of a party may mean voting most of the time for the candidate of a party or choosing to become a candidate of one of them. Or it may mean voting in a party primary. Or it may mean contributing money to, or otherwise helping in, a local, state, or national campaign of one of the party candidates. Or it may just mean that one generally prefers one party to another most of the time. These are loose criteria for membership, to say the least—looser than for virtually any other organization that one might imagine.

The Formal Organization of American Political Parties

The Republican and Democratic parties, it is often said, are not organizations in the usual sense of the term, but loose collections of local and state parties, candidates and officeholders, and associated interest groups that get together every four years to nominate a presidential candidate. There is more to the national parties than this stereotype suggests, but not much.

Unlike in a corporation, a bureaucratic agency, a military organization, or even a political party in most other countries, the official leaders of the major American parties cannot issue orders that get passed along a chain of command to those at the bottom. Each level of the party is relatively independent and acts in concert with the others—on occasion—not on the basis of orders, but on the basis of common interests, sentiment, and the desire to win elections. There are few resources or devices within either of the two parties to compel a lower level of the party organization to follow a particular policy. Most important, the national party is unable to control its most vital activity—the nomination of candidates running under its party label—or the flow of money that funds electoral campaigns, or the behavior of its officeholders.

Party Conventions This is not to suggest that the parties are entirely devoid of tools to encourage coordination and cooperation among their various levels. The national party conventions are the governing bodies of the parties (see Chapter 9 for more on the conventions). Convention delegates meet every four years not only to nominate presidential and vice-presidential candidates, but also to write a party platform and to revise party rules. (The proceedings are often contentious, as "The Struggle for Democracy" box on the Mississippi Freedom Democratic Party shows.)

Though the national convention is the formal governing body of each of the parties, it cannot dictate to party candidates or party organizations at other levels of jurisdiction. The presidential nominee need not adhere to either the letter or the spirit of the party platform, for instance, though most nominees stay fairly close to the platform most of the time (usually because the winning candidate's supporters control the platform-writing committee). State and local party organizations may nominate whomever they choose to run for public office and may or may not support key planks in the party platform. The all-white Mississippi delegation to the 1964 Democratic convention even refused to endorse Lyndon Johnson, the Democratic presidential candidate.

National Party Committees The Democrats and Republicans each have a national committee,[19] the purpose of which is to conduct the business of the party during the four years between national conventions. While the national com-

National party conventions serve several purposes for American political parties. At the quadrennial gatherings, delegates choose presidential and vice-presidential candidates, settle party rules, write the party platform, repair or build political coalitions, and, as shown here, attempt to whip up enthusiasm for their nominees.

mittees have little power, they provide valuable services for local and state parties, and for party candidates at all levels. These include campaign training materials, assistance on creating audiovisual materials and campaign literature, research on the opposition, and even limited campaign funds. The Republican National Committee's $1.7-million studio in Washington, for instance, produces daily 15-minute news feeds for 750 television affiliates and news services around the country.[20]

The national committees are made up of elected committeemen and committeewomen from each of the states, a sizable staff, and a chairperson. The national committees rarely meet. The real business of the committee is run by the party chairperson, assisted by the committee staff. The chairperson exercises little power when a president from his or her party is in office, as he or she is compelled to take direction from the White House. When the opposition controls the presidency, the party chairperson exercises more influence in party affairs, though the extent of that power should not be exaggerated.

Congressional Campaign Committees Almost as old as the national party committees, but entirely independent of them, are the congressional campaign committees that aid members of Congress in their campaigns for reelection. They help raise money, provide media services (making short videotapes of the members of Congress for local television news shows, for instance), conduct research, and do whatever else the party members in Congress deem appropriate. These committees are controlled by the party members in Congress, not the party chairperson, the national committees, or even the president.

Political action committees (PACs) run by prominent members of Congress further decentralize the party structure. Newt Gingrich used his—called GOPAC—to assist House candidates who were loyal to his vision of the

Fannie Lou Hamer and the Mississippi Freedom Democratic Party

The Struggle for Democracy

Fannie Lou Hamer's story electrified the nation and threatened to ruin Lyndon Johnson's party. Testifying in 1964 before the Credentials Committee of the Democratic National Convention and a national television audience, Hamer, a 40-year-old black sharecropper from Mississippi, described what had happened to her when she tried to register to vote:

> They beat me and they beat me with a long, flat blackjack. I screamed to God in my mind. My dress worked itself up. I tried to pull it down. They beat my arms until I had no feeling in them.

The 1964 Democratic convention in Atlantic City was meant to be a celebration of President Lyndon Johnson and a launching pad for the fall presidential campaign against Republican Barry Goldwater. The idea was to downplay intraparty conflicts, convey a message of unity and purpose to the country, and focus on defeating the Republicans. The appeal of the Mississippi Freedom Democratic Party (MFDP) to the Credentials Committee to be seated in place of the state's official Democratic party delegation in the racially charged atmosphere of 1964 threatened to throw a monkey wrench into the party works.

The MFDP had been created by black and white Mississippians in 1963 as a vehicle to encourage black political participation in the most segregated state in the Union. Only 5 percent of blacks in the state were registered to vote. Efforts by blacks to register were typically met with firings, threats, mortgage foreclosures, and violence. Hamer and the others who had founded the MFDP thought that they had a good chance to be seated at the convention. The regular Mississippi Democratic party remained lily-white (precinct and county party meetings were closed to blacks) at a time when the national party had embraced the civil rights cause, and it openly supported the Republican candidate Barry Goldwater. The insurgents believed that a new party organization, open to all Mississippians and committed to supporting the Democratic party nominee and platform in Atlantic City, could not fail to win the fight to be seated as the official delegation. Many Mississippians, black and white, put their reputations, fortunes, and lives on the line to change the political climate of their state. Eventually, over 80,000 citizens of the state participated in MFDP delegate selection meetings—far more than participated in the affairs of the regular party.

Lyndon Johnson would have none of it. He was angry that the credentials fight was detracting from his nomination, and he feared that replacing the official delegation would lead to the wholesale defection of the South in the November elections. He rejected a compromise offer by several leading Democrats to seat both delegations. All he was willing to deliver were two at-large seats to the MFDP and a pledge that no segregated delegations would be seated at future Democratic conventions. The pledge was made official party policy and eventually made American politics more democratic by lowering racial barriers to participation in party affairs in all of the states. It was a bitter pill to swallow, however, for those who had risked so much to be there and who had expected so much. Hamer and the other MFDP delegates left Atlantic City in anger and disgust.

Sources: William H. Chafe, *The Unfinished Journey* (New York: Oxford University Press, 1986), pp. 311–314; Godfrey Hodgson, *America in Our Time* (New York: Vintage, 1978), pp. 213–215; Taylor Branch, *Parting the Waters: America in the King Years, 1954–63* (New York: Simon & Schuster, 1988), pp. 819–820.

Republican party. Observers estimate that GOPAC was instrumental in the election of 33 of the 53 first-term Republicans in the 104th Congress.[21]

The Primacy of Candidates[22]

In Germany, individual candidates for the Bundestag (the equivalent of the House of Representatives) are less important than the political parties. Candidates are nominated by local party committees dominated by party regulars. Party lists for the general election are drawn up by state (*Länder*) party organizations, which are also dominated by party regulars. Independent candidates cannot force themselves on the party through primaries or caucuses open to the public, as in the United States, because such extraparty devices do not exist. Money for conducting electoral campaigns, moreover, is mostly raised and spent by the party organizations, not individual candidates (much free television and radio time is also provided to the parties, and substantial government money helps to run campaigns and other party affairs). The state and federal party organizations also run virtually every aspect of Bundestag campaigns. Finally, the campaign is waged between the parties and their alternative programs, not between individual candidates, and the electorate tends to make its choices based on feelings about the parties rather than about the candidates.

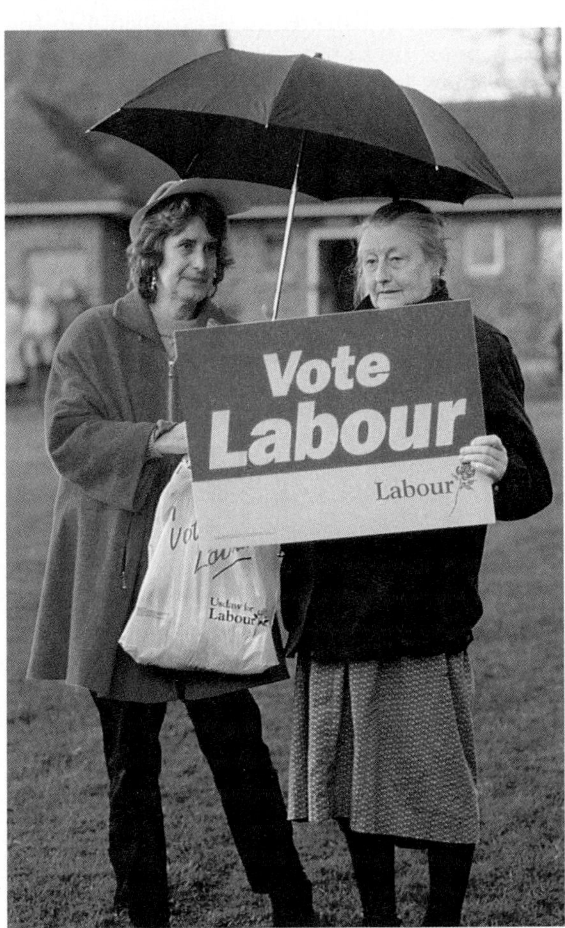

In most European countries, people vote for parties rather than individual candidates. These party activists are urging British voters to cast their ballots for the Labour Party, for instance, rather than for the rival Conservative Party.

American politics is "candidate-centered." Here, candidates are primary and the parties are secondary; party activities are shaped by the electoral needs of their candidates. Candidates have independent sources of campaign financing, their own campaign organizations, and their own campaign themes and priorities.

Once in office, though they may be influenced by a degree of party loyalty, politicians are largely free to go their own way, influenced only by considerations concerning winning the next election. If people in office refuse to toe the "party line," as vague as that line usually is, the party can do little about it. President Franklin D. Roosevelt could not even get his vice-president, John Garner, to support many of his New Deal programs.

Our parties may be becoming even more candidate-centered. In the past, party candidates were usually nominated in district, state, and national conventions, where party regulars played a major role. They are now almost exclusively nominated in primaries or grassroots caucuses, where the party organizations are almost invisible. Nomination comes to those who are best able to raise money, gain access to the media, form their own electoral organizations, and win the support of powerful interest groups (like the Christian Coalition and the National Rifle Association). Nominations are increasingly slipping out of the grasp of party regulars and officials. Republican leaders could do little to prevent Steve Forbes and Pat Buchanan from becoming major forces early in the fight for the party's 1996 presidential nomination.

Nominees are so independent that they sometimes oppose party leaders and reject traditional party policies. Republicans were embarrassed when David Duke, former Grand Wizard of the Ku Klux Klan, was elected to the Louisiana State Legislature in 1988 under the Republican banner and ran for the governorship as a Republican in 1990, despite the opposition of state and national Republican officials. Democratic congressional candidates were advised by pollster Stanley Greenberg to distance themselves from Democratic president Bill Clinton and to downplay the party label in the 1994 campaign. Ironically, Clinton's pollster Richard Morris advised the president to distance himself from congressional Democrats in 1996.

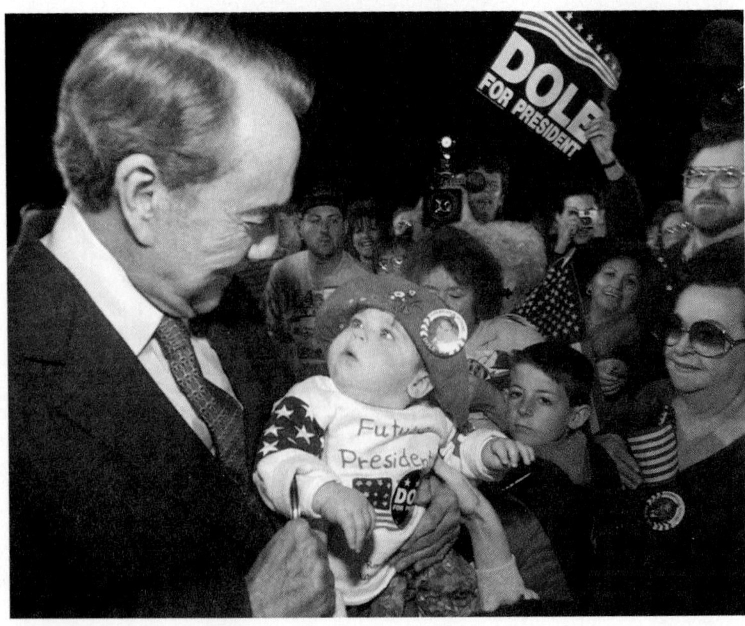

During the fight for the Republican presidential nomination in 1996, Robert Dole stressed his conservative views on abortion, affirmative action, the environment, and his history of party loyalty. During the general election, however, seeking to reach a broader audience, he downplayed his conservative ideological ideas and his Republican Party credentials in an effort to win the broad center of the electorate.

Party Goals

Obviously, parties want to win elections and put their people in office. But for what purpose? That question is not as easy to answer as it may seem, given the fragmentation and complexity of the party organizations. Each party component tends to have its own goals.

The Goals of Party Activists Party activists, the people who do the most important organizational work of the parties—those who work for candidates, raise money for the party, hold party offices, and serve as delegates to party conventions—can be divided into two main subgroups, each with somewhat different goals.[23] *Party professionals* are the traditional party workers whose first commitment is to the party itself. They tend to be pragmatic, oriented to winning elections. Issues and ideology are less important to them than finding candidates who will appeal to as many voters as possible. *Party amateurs* tend to be motivated by ideological or issue concerns. To them, the party is an instrument for advancing an ideological agenda (usually liberalism in the Democratic party and conservatism in the Republican party) or a particular issue, such as civil rights or opposition to abortion. Party amateurs, while interested in finding a winning candidate, often want candidates to conform to their ideological or issue agenda.

The Goals of Party Officeholders First and foremost, party officeholders want to retain their position or gain higher office—whether to satisfy personal ambition or to make good public policy, or both—and they mold most of their behavior with an eye on the next election. Even officeholders who came to office on ideological or issue-oriented grounds tend to moderate their position in order to ensure reelection.

The Goals of Party Voters Party voters are not as easy to pigeonhole. They are a diverse lot, only loosely connected to the party organization. Some want ideological and issue purity from the party. Others seek party victory, even if it means only the lesser of two evils.

The Goals of Party Contributors Financial contributors are also diverse in their goals. Many are interested in ideological or policy issues. Substantial National Rifle Association contributions to Republican candidates, for instance, virtually guaranteed that no new gun-control laws would be passed in the Republican-dominated 104th Congress. Many are attracted to a particular candidate. Others give out of loyalty to the party. The biggest corporate and PAC contributors, it is probably safe to say, are trying either to guarantee access to officeholders or to encourage or discourage the enactment of policies relevant to their interests.

Ideology and Program

Because the Republican and Democratic parties are both broad coalitions, seeking to attract as many people as possible in order to prevail in winner-take-all, single-member-district elections, there are strong pressures on them to be ideologically ambiguous. On the other hand, each party has a core of supporters, like delegates to the party convention and caucus attenders, who are more ideologically oriented than the general public. The result is a party system composed of parties far less ideologically focused and identifiable than the parties in other democratic countries, but with significant ideological and policy differences between them, nevertheless. And the parties seem to be getting more ideological.

Ideology may be understood as an organized set of beliefs about the fundamental nature of the good society and the role government ought to play in achieving it. In other Western democracies, it is common for the major parties to be quite closely connected with an ideology, in the sense that their activists, members, and officeholders identify with it, campaign with themes based on its ideas, and are guided by it in their governmental actions. Socialist and Labor parties often line up in elections against Liberal and Conservative or Catholic parties, with Marxist, Christian Socialist, Monarchist, Neo-Fascist, Nationalist, and other parties entering into the contest as well.

Ideological contests in the European manner are not the norm in U.S. elections, for the parties believe in many of the same fundamentals: free enterprise, individualism, the Constitution, the Bill of Rights, and so on. On the other hand, the differences between Democrats and Republicans on many issues are real, important, and enduring and are becoming more distinctive. Let us examine how the parties are different.

Public Perceptions of Party Ideologies For one thing, the Democratic and Republican parties differ in the electorate's perceptions of them. According to studies by the Center for Political Studies of the University of Michigan, over 60 percent of the American people report that they see the parties as different on a whole range of issues. Most see the Democrats as the more liberal party (in the sense of favoring "an active federal government, helping citizens with jobs, education, medical care, and the like"[24]) and the Republicans as the more conservative (opposing such government activism). The parties also differ in terms of *who supports them.* Americans who classify themselves as liberals overwhelmingly support Democratic candidates; self-described conservatives overwhelmingly support Republicans. This alignment is not surprising.

Ideology in Party Platforms Our parties also tend to write different political platforms. Scholars have discovered persistent differences in the platforms of the two parties in terms of rhetoric (Republicans tend to talk more about opportunity and freedom), issues (Democrats worry more about poverty and social welfare), the public policies advocated, and the pledges made.[25]

William Kristol, here addressing the annual convention of the Christian Coalition, has become one of the leading voices for conservatism in the United States and an influential actor within the Republican Party.

The Ideologies of Party Activists The activists of one party are quite different in their views from activists and voters in the other party. Of the delegates to the 1992 Republican National Convention, 63 percent called themselves conservative and 1 percent called themselves liberal, for instance, while delegates to the Democratic convention split 47 percent liberal and 5 percent conservative.[26] Republican delegates are usually more conservative than Republican voters and much more conservative than the general public. Democratic National Convention delegates are usually more liberal than Democratic voters and much more liberal than the general public. The same is true of those who take part in primaries and grassroots caucuses when compared to the average voter.

Party Ideologies in Action Finally, the parties differ in what they do when they win. Republican members of Congress tend to vote differently from Democrats, the former being considerably more conservative on domestic issues. This difference translates into public policy. Republicans and Democrats produce different policies on taxes, corporate regulation, and welfare when they are in power.[27] This became especially clear in the 104th Congress, where the Republicans waged a unified campaign against spending, taxing, regulatory, and entitlement programs.

Are the Parties Becoming More Ideological? The Republican party has become a much more consistently conservative party since the middle 1970s, advocating free markets and less regulation, low taxes, a halt to most abortions, diminished social spending, opposition to affirmative action, and a hard line on "law and order." The party seems to have settled on a vision in which government helps create a society where individuals are free to pursue their own happiness and to take the consequences if they fail, without the government's providing a minimum standard of living below which people cannot fall. Newt Gingrich's "Contract with America," which virtually all Republican House candidates signed before the 1994 elections, vividly demonstrates this point. This growing conservatism is a product of the increasing influence on the party of the business community, antitax groups, the white South, the Christian Coalition, and conservative former Democrats (like Senator Phil Gramm of Texas), and of the decline in influence of its moderate wing (represented in the past by such figures as Nelson Rockefeller).[28] The voluntary retirement of Republican moderates such as Senator William Cohen (Maine) and Senator Nancy Kassebaum (Kansas) exemplifies the latter trend. It is worth pointing out, however, that the Republicans remain deeply divided on social issues such as abortion, school prayer, and regulation to protect the environment.

The Democratic party is less ideologically coherent than the Republican party. It is split between a moderate wing (represented by the Democratic Leadership Council) that opposes racial remedies like affirmative action and advocates lower taxes, deregulation, and a crackdown on crime, among other things, and a more liberal wing that advocates traditional Democratic party programs, in which government plays a central role in societal improvement, racial and gender justice, economic growth, and the protection of civil liberties. In Congress, the Democrats are becoming a more consistently liberal party as southern conservative Democrats increasingly join the Republican party or are defeated in elections, leaving the liberal wing in control. President Clinton, on the other hand, took centrist positions during the 104th Congress on issues such as the budget and welfare reform, much to the discomfort of many liberal congressional Democrats, and ran as a centrist candidate in the 1996 election (e.g., stressing "law and order," deficit reduction, and family values).

The overwhelming support of Newt Gingrich's Contract with America by Republican candidates for the House of Representatives in 1994 shows how strongly conservative the party has become in recent years.

The Parties in Government

Fearful of the tyrannical possibilities of a vigorous government, the framers designed a system of government in which power is so fragmented and competitive that effectiveness is unlikely. One of the roles that political parties can play is to overcome this "deadlock" by persuading officials of the same party in the different branches of government to cooperate with one another on the basis of party loyalty.[29] The constitutionally designed conflict between president and Congress can be bridged when a single party controls both branches, for instance.

The problem of governing presented by fragmented and separated powers in the United States is almost unique among the Western democracies. In parliamentary systems such as those of Great Britain, Germany, and Japan, there is no separation of powers between the branches of the national government. The executive and the legislative branches are combined; the prime minister is the leader of the majority party in the parliament and is elected by and from that body. Members of the cabinet, the heads of the executive departments of government, are themselves members of the parliament.

We will learn in considerable detail what parties do in government in later chapters on Congress (Chapter 11), the president (Chapter 12), the executive branch (Chapter 13), and the courts (Chapter 14). In general, we will see that the parties only partially improve the coherence and responsiveness of our government. The parties seem to be the best institutions we have for making government work in a cohesive and responsive fashion, but they do not consistently do the job very well. Because they are unable to command the complete loyalty and attention of their adherents or to direct the behavior of their officeholders much, American parties are tremendously handicapped in playing this important role.

Though the parties are rarely able to overcome the deadlock of American politics, they sometimes do. There have been brief periods in our history when the ties of party among presidents, members of Congress, and the heads of the executive branch agencies have been strong, resembling something like the party government in Great Britain. These few occasions—between 1933 and 1936, when Franklin D. Roosevelt fashioned the first New Deal; after the 1964 election, when Lyndon Johnson created the Great Society; and in 1981 and 1982, when Ronald Reagan led a tax and budget revolution—are notable for their infrequent occurrence.

The Problem of Divided Party Government

For much of the past three decades, Republicans controlled the presidency, while Democrats controlled one or both houses of Congress. After the 1994 election, the situation reversed, with Republicans gaining control of Congress and Democrats winning the presidency (see Figure 8.2). After the 1996 election,

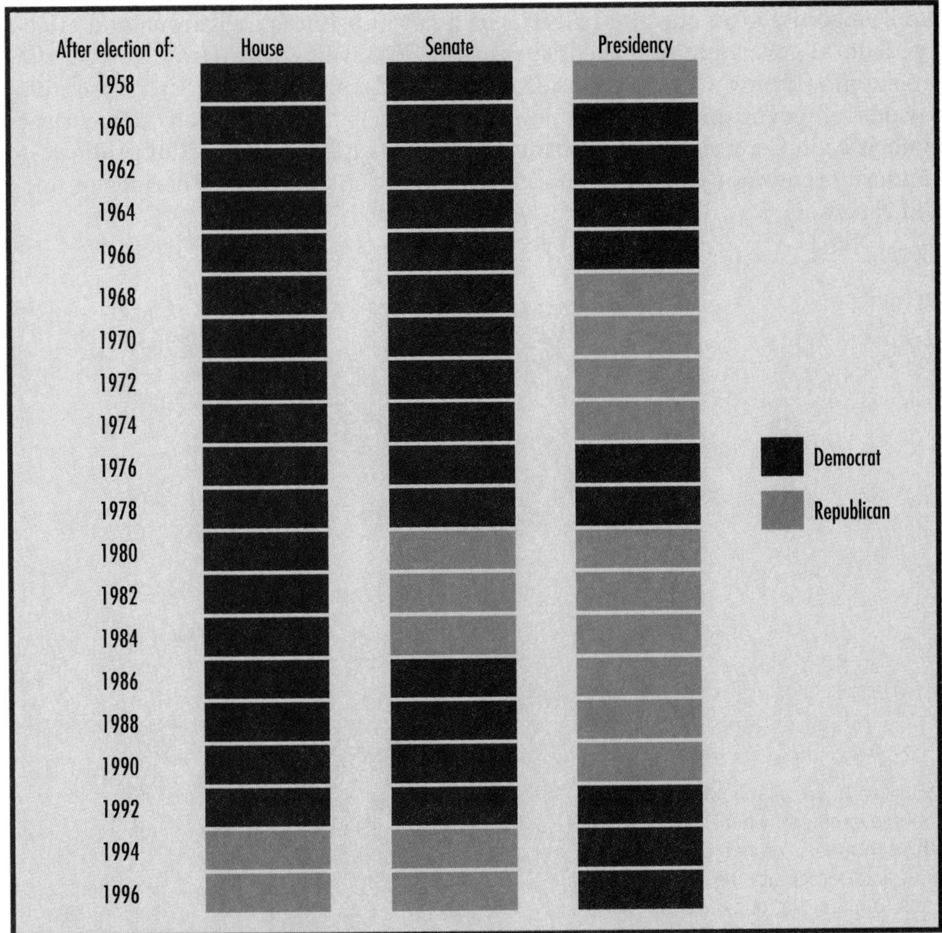

Figure 8.2 ▪ **Party Control of Congress and the Presidency**

One of the most striking things about our recent political history is the persistence of split party control of the presidency and Congress. Scholars disagree about the effects of this development: some believe it has crippled the federal government; others say split party control makes no difference.

Republicans continued their control of both houses of Congress and the Democrats continued their hold on the White House.

Divided party control of the federal government has worried scholars and journalists for many years and has produced a substantial literature that examines its causes and assesses its affects.[30] Many scholars and journalists believe the effects to be pernicious. At best, they suggest, divided party control adds to the gridlock and paralysis that are built into the constitutional design of our system of government.[31] At worst, they suggest, divided party control gives rise to a state of near civil war between the two branches, in which each tries to damage the other in the interests of advancing the fortunes of its party.[32] In the 104th Congress, Republican investigations into the Clintons' involvement in the Whitewater affair, the First Lady's role in the firing of White House travel office personnel, the federal government's handling of the Branch Davidian tragedy at Waco, and FBI actions in the Randy Weaver affair in Idaho are good examples.

Some scholars have begun to argue, however, that divided party control may not be very important. They point to cases in which unified party control did not have good results and cases in which divided control did not prevent the fashioning of coherent policy. Unified party control of government under the Democrats after the 1936 election did not guarantee a vigorous and effective federal government in the last years of Roosevelt's New Deal. Democratic presidents Jimmy Carter and Bill Clinton did not produce very impressive periods of government performance even when both enjoyed Democratic majorities in Congress. Some recent evidence suggests, in fact, that gridlock is no more prominent in periods of divided party control than in periods of unified control.[33]

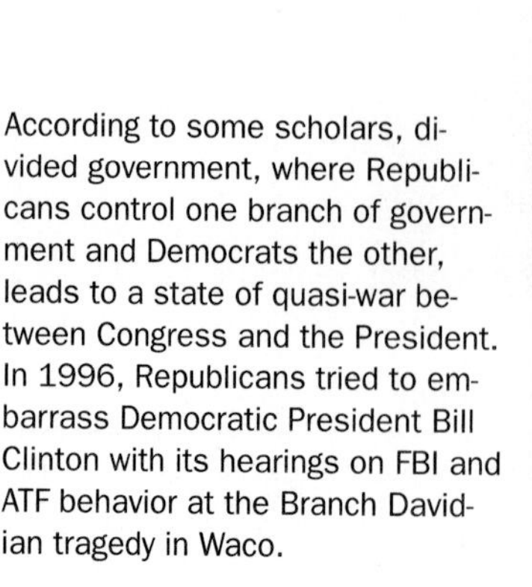

According to some scholars, divided government, where Republicans control one branch of government and Democrats the other, leads to a state of quasi-war between Congress and the President. In 1996, Republicans tried to embarrass Democratic President Bill Clinton with its hearings on FBI and ATF behavior at the Branch Davidian tragedy in Waco.

Parties in the Electorate

Parties are not only organizations and officeholders but also images in the minds of voters and potential voters, mental cues that affect the behavior of the electorate. This aspect of the parties was discussed in Chapter 5 and will be considered in greater detail in the next chapter. We have also noted the loosening ties of the electorate to the two major parties in the earlier discussions in this chapter of the collapse of the New Deal coalition and dealignment. For now, we simply state the point that partisanship has been declining in the American electorate for a number of years.

If the parties were not important to the practices of democracy, the decline of stable partisanship would not be a cause for concern. Given the centrality of the parties to popular sovereignty, however, the decline of partisanship in the electorate is important.

Party Decline, Reform, and Democracy

Though several scholars remain unconvinced that the parties have declined—witness their increased capacities in fund-raising, campaign assistance, and the like[34]—the evidence presented so far suggests otherwise. We have seen a noticeable decline in party identification, confidence, popular regard, and willingness to vote a straight-party ticket. Each of these factors suggests that the two major parties are no longer as central as they once were in tying people's everyday concerns to their choices in the political system. We have also seen that the parties have lost much control over what had long been understood to be central party functions: nominating candidates and organizing campaigns. The parties must share the former function with individual candidates and primary voters, and the latter with candidates' electoral organizations, pollsters, direct mail companies, and campaign consulting firms. Local grassroots party organizations wither and lose vitality as more and more attention and resources are given to television and other media campaigns.[35]

Party Decline and Political Volatility

Frank Sorauf and Lewis Allen Beck, two leading scholars on American political parties, suggest that weaker parties will lead to greater political volatility and uncertainty:

> What seems likely . . . is a politics of greater fluidity and instability, carried on by a wider range of political organizations. . . . The erosion of the one, stable, long-run loyalty in American politics will contribute to a politics more often dominated by the short-term influences of the charismatic candidate or the very salient issue. In its volatility, its lack of continuity, and its lack of predictability, the new electoral politics may increasingly resemble that of the one-party factional and personal politics in the American South in the 1930s and 1940s.[36]

Party Decline and Interest Group Influence

Weaker parties also mean that interest groups have greater freedom of action. This is a large problem for American democracy and rational public policy. First, to the degree that national policy mainly reflects conflicting interest group demands, it will lack coherence and rationality. Second, since the interest group system is particularly well suited to those with substantial resources, the decline of the parties will probably push the worst-off members of society even further outside the policymaking process. If this should happen, political equality will be further eroded.

Party Decline and Policy Coherence

Political parties are the closest thing we have to an institution capable of fashioning policy coherence out of interest group politics, while bringing broad elements of the public into the political arena. The relative decline of the political parties ought to be of concern, then, to those Americans who care about the coherence, rationality, and effectiveness of public policy, and about the democratic character of our political life.

If political parties are important to the practice of democracy and the effectiveness of government but are declining in their effectiveness, what can be done about it? Can the parties be revitalized as democratic instruments?[37]

Party Reform

Many party-strengthening reform proposals seem politically achievable. One proposal calls for changes in federal and state laws that would deemphasize primaries in the presidential nominating process, giving power back to the party convention. Another calls for the guaranteed representation of party professionals and officeholders at the nominating conventions, returning a measure of power to those working directly for the parties. Some have proposed increased public funding for party activities, as well as the provision of free radio and television time to the parties, as ways to decrease the influence of private-interest money in American elections. Another proposal is to remove the spending limits on the parties in electoral campaigns—on the condition that the parties not be allowed to solicit or use "soft money" from PACs—so that our politics becomes less "candidate-centered." Finally, a return to the balloting system by which voters may, in effect, pull a single party lever instead of voting for each office would be welcomed by advocates of strong parties.

It is conceivable that reforms like these could be instituted and might stop the decline of the parties and enhance their role in American politics and governing. Such changes might represent a net gain in the ability of the American people to participate in politics and to keep their representatives responsible and responsive. This gain would represent an increase in popular sovereignty and political equality, especially if wider involvement in party affairs were somehow encouraged. This would be no small achievement.

Summary

The American party system is unique among the Western democracies in several respects. First, ours is a relatively pure two-party system and has been so since the 1830s. Second, our major parties are fragmented, decentralized, and candidate-centered, having very little power in their national party organizations to affect the behavior of individual candidates, officeholders, or state and local party organizations. Thus, it is difficult for the parties to provide governance that is coherent, consistent, and effective. The American parties are less ideological than the parties in other democracies, but the differences between Democrats and Republicans are both enduring and important, and they are becoming more evident.

Though made up of the same two parties for well over a century, the two-party system has not been stagnant. It has undergone a series of realignments, spurred by structural changes in society and the economy, in which the relative power of the parties has shifted, as have the voting alignments of the public, the dominant political coalitions, and public policy. We now seem to be in a period of dealignment.

Recognizing that the parties are inescapably linked to the practice of democracy, yet aware that the American political parties are unable to fulfill their democratic promise properly, many scholars, journalists, and practitioners have advocated a variety of reforms to strengthen them. The reforms address party candidate selection, campaign finance, and increasing party control over officeholders.

Suggested Readings

Aldrich, John. *Why Parties?* Chicago: University of Chicago Press, 1995.
Uses a rational-choice perspective from economics to show how the parties we have are the product of the rational pursuit of the goals of officeseekers and officeholders.

Burnham, Walter Dean. *Critical Elections and the Mainsprings of American Politics.* New York: Norton, 1970.
The classic analysis of the realignment process in the American party system.

Greenberg, Stanley B. *Middle Class Dreams.* New York: Times Books, 1994.
An imaginative analysis by Bill Clinton's leading pollster of the "failed" party realignments of the 1960s and 1980s.

Key, V. O., Jr., *Southern Politics.* New York: Knopf, 1949.
Though somewhat dated, a penetrating and entertaining look at politics in a region devoid of real parties, and a model, perhaps, of what politics might look like in the United States if so-called dealignment continues.

Mayhew, David R. *Divided We Govern: Party Control, Lawmaking, and Investigations, 1946–1990.* New Haven: Yale University Press, 1991.
A sophisticated attempt to assess the impact of divided government. Argues that the alarm about divided government has been overstated.

Reichley, A. James. *The Life of the Parties: A History of American Political Parties.* New York: Macmillan, 1992.
The leading history of the American party system, with special attention paid to the question of party decline in the modern era and what might be done about it.

Sundquist, James L. *Dynamics of the Party System.* Washington, DC: Brookings Institution, 1983.
A history of the party system and its transformations, rich in detail and theoretically sophisticated.

Internet Sources

Democratic National Committee http://www.democrats.org/

The Jefferson Project/Parties http://www.stardot.com/jefferson/parties/
Access to the home pages of national, state, and local parties, including fringe parties of the left and the right.

Pathfinder, Campaign 96 http://pathfinder.com/@@7oPdTUFjQwAAQD5w/pathfinder/politics/1999
A complete compendium on the parties and the candidates in the 1996 national elections, including election results and public opinion on candidates and issues.

Political Science Resources/Parties http://www.keefe.ac.uk/depts/po/parties.htm
Documents, candidates, manifestos, and platforms of American and foreign political parties.

Republican National Committee http://www.rnc.org/

Notes

1. David Broder, "The Abandoned Constituency," *Washington Post National Edition* (January 13–20, 1995), p. 3.
2. The following numbers are from exit polls conducted by and reported in the *New York Times* on November 13, 1994; the Mikkofsky International Exit Poll reported in Lyman A. Kellstedt et al., "Has Godot Finally Arrived?" *Public Perspective* (June–July, 1995), pp. 18–22; Stanley Greenberg, "After the Republican Surge," *Public Perspective* (Fall 1995), pp. 66–72.
3. E. E. Schattschneider, *Party Government* (New York: Holt, Rinehart & Winston, 1942), p. 208.
4. Ibid., p. 208.
5. See A. James Reichley, *The Life of the Parties: A History of American Parties* (New York: Free Press, 1992), chap. 1.
6. Steven J. Rosenstone and John Mark Hansen, *Mobilization, Participation, and Democracy in America* (New York: MacMillan, 1993).
7. E. E. Schattschneider, *The Semi-Sovereign People* (New York: Holt, Rinehart & Winston, 1960).
8. Thomas Ferguson, "Party Realignment and American Industrial Structure: The Investment Theory of Political Parties in Historical Perspective," in Paul Zarembka et al., eds., *Research in Political Economy,* Vol. 6 (Greenwich, CT: JAI Press, 1983), pp. 31–35.
9. C. Vann Woodward, *The Strange Career of Jim Crow* (New York: Oxford University Press, 1966).
10. Herbert Alexander, *Financing Politics* (Washington, DC: Congressional Quarterly Press, 1980), p. 5.
11. Ferguson, "Party Realignment"; Edward S. Greenberg, *Capitalism and the American Political Ideal* (Armonk, NY: M. E. Sharpe, 1985).
12. On realignment, see Walter Dean Burnham, *Critical Elections and the Mainsprings of American Politics* (New York: Norton, 1970); Walter Dean Burnham, "Critical Realignment Lives: The 1994 Earthquake," in Colin Campbell and Bert A. Rockman eds., *The Clinton Presidency* (Chatham, NJ: Chatham House Publishers, 1996); William Nisbet Chambers and Walter Dean Burnham, eds., *The American Party Systems* (New York: Oxford University Press, 1967); Jerome Clubb, William H. Flanigan, and Nancy H. Zingale, *Partisan Realignment* (Newbury Park, CA: Sage, 1980); V. O. Key, Jr., "A Theory of Critical Elections," *Journal of Politics,* Vol. 17 (1955), pp. 3–18; James L. Sundquist, *Dynamics of the Party System* (Washington, DC: Brookings, 1973).
13. Helmut Norpoth and Jerrold Rusk, "Partisan Dealignment in the American Electorate," *American Political Science Review,* Vol. 76 (September 1982). Also see Sabato, *The Party's Just Begun;* Sundquist, *Dynamics of the Party System;* Martin P. Wattenberg, *The Decline of American Political Parties* (Cambridge: Harvard University Press, 1994); Stanley B. Greenberg, *Middle Class Dreams* (New York: Times Books, 1995); Everett C. Ladd, "The 1994 Congressional Elections," *Political Science Quarterly,* Vol. 110, pp. 1–23.
14. Ladd, "The 1994 Congressional Elections"; Wattenberg, *The Decline of American Political Parties.*
15. Ladd, "The 1994 Congressional Elections"; Ferguson, *Golden Rule.*
16. The classic statement on the impact of electoral rules is found in Maurice Duverger, *Political Parties* (New York: Wiley, 1954).
17. Nelson W. Polsby, *The Consequences of Party Reform* (New York: Oxford University Press, 1983), p. 83.

18. Steven J. Rosenstone, Roy L. Behr, and Edward H. Lazarus, *Third Parties in America* (Princeton: Princeton University Press, 1984).
19. See Cornelius P. Cotter and Bernard Hennessy, *Politics Without Power: The National Party Committees* (New York: Atherton, 1964).
20. R. H. Melton, "Forget the Hustings," *Washington Post National Education* (May 1–7, 1995), p. 13.
21. Stephen Engelberg and Katherine Q. Seelye, "Gingrich: Man in Spotlight and Organization in Shadow," *New York Times* (December 18, 1994), p. 1.
22. Colin Campbell et al., *Politics and Government in Europe Today* (Orlando, FL: Harcourt Brace Jovanovich, 1990), pp. 304–310.
23. Austin Ranney, *Curing the Mischiefs of Faction* (Berkeley: University of California Press, 1974); James Q. Wilson, *The Amateur Democrat* (Chicago: University of Chicago Press, 1962).
24. Benjamin I. Page, *Choices and Echoes in Presidential Elections* (Chicago: University of Chicago Press, 1978), p. 63.
25. Alan D. Monroe, "American Party Platforms and Public Opinion," *American Journal of Political Science,* Vol. 27 (February 1983), p. 35; Gerald Pomper, *Elections in America* (New York: Longman, 1980), p. 169.
26. Harold W. Stanley and Richard G. Niemi, *Vital Statistics on American Politics* (Washington, DC: Congressional Quarterly Press, 1993), Table 4–10.
27. Douglas Hibbs, *The American Political Economy* (Cambridge: Harvard University Press, 1987); Dennis P. Quinn and Robert Shapiro, "Business Political Power: The Case of Taxation," *American Political Science Review,* Vol. 85 (September 1991), pp. 851–874.
28. Thomas Byrne Edsall, *The New Politics of Inequality* (New York: Norton, 1984); Kevin Phillips, *Boiling Point* (New York: Random House, 1993); David Vogel, *Fluctuating Fortunes* (New York: Basic Books, 1989).
29. James MacGregor Burns, *Deadlock of Democracy* (Englewood Cliffs, NJ: Prentice Hall, 1967).
30. Morris Fiorina, *Divided Government* (New York: Macmillan, 1992); Gary Jacobson, *The Electoral Origins of Divided Government: Competition in U.S. House Elections* (Boulder, CO: Westview Press, 1990); David Mayhew, *Divided We Govern: Party Control, Lawmaking, and Investigations* (New Haven: Yale University Press, 1991).
31. Hedrick Smith, *The Power Game* (New York: Random House, 1988), p. 652.
32. Benjamin Ginsberg and Martin Shefter, *Politics by Other Means: The Declining Significance of Elections in America* (New York: Basic Books, 1990).
33. Mayhew, *Divided We Govern.*
34. Xandra Kayden and Eddie Mahe, Jr., *The Party Goes On: The Persistence of the Two-Party System in the United States* (New York: Basic Books, 1985); Bruce E. Keith, David B. Magleby, Candice J. Nelson, and Raymond E. Wolfinger, *The Myth of the Independent Voter* (Berkeley: University of California Press, 1992); Gerald M. Pomper, *Party Renewal in America* (New York: Praeger, 1981); Sabato, *The Party's Just Begun.*
35. Wattenberg, *The Decline of American Political Parties,* chap. 10.
36. Sorauf and Beck, *Party Politics in America,* p. 493.
37. These reforms are discussed in James Reichley, *The Life of the Parties,* chap. 21 (New York: The Free Press, 1992); Larry Sabato, *The Party's Just Begun,* chaps. 6 and 7 (Glenview, Ill.: Scott Foresman, 1988).

Voting and Elections

IN THIS CHAPTER

- ★ The role of elections in a democracy
- ★ How African-Americans, women, and young people won the right to vote
- ★ Why many Americans don't go to the polls
- ★ How to run for the presidency
- ★ What part money plays in elections
- ★ How voters decide to vote
- ★ Why elections matter

Bill Clinton's Electoral Reward

In 1992, when the United States was suffering from high unemployment and a weak economy, incumbent President George Bush was punished at the polls and defeated for reelection, getting only 38 percent of the popular vote against Bill Clinton and Ross Perot. Four years later, by contrast, when the economy was growing again and Americans' incomes were rising, incumbent President Clinton was rewarded with a decisive reelection victory. Clinton won 49 percent of the popular vote against Bob Dole's 41 percent and Perot's 9 percent. He swept the electoral college, winning 379 out of the 538 electoral votes and taking nearly every state outside the Great Plains, the Rocky Mountains, and the old South (see Figure 9.1).

Presidential elections often reflect the state of the American economy. When times are good, the incumbent party generally wins; when the economy goes bad, the incumbent president or his party loses. In fact, political scientists have found that they can predict vote percentages and election outcomes quite accurately, long before anyone votes, simply by knowing whether (and by how much) the average American's income has risen or fallen in the year or two before election day.

The outcome of the 1996 election, then, was largely decided by the end of 1995, when Clinton began to recover from the missteps, confusions, and unpopularity of his first two years. A key element in that recovery was the economy. The budget deficit dropped to half the size it had been in 1992; inflation slowed; unemployment fell from 7.7 percent to 5.2 percent; and—most important—after years of wage stagnation, the average American's wages finally began to creep upward. At last, recovering from three years in the doldrums, President Clinton's approval rating climbed above the 50 percent mark.

Also helping Clinton was the widespread perception that the efforts at "revolution" by Newt Gingrich and the Republican Congress had gone too far, trying to impose cuts on Medicare, Medicaid, and environmental and other programs by forcing temporary shutdowns of the federal government. Still another factor was Clinton's strategy, beginning in the summer of 1995, of seizing the Republican position on many issues—toughness on crime, balancing the budget, reforming welfare, and the like. (After the election, some people joked that the Republicans had won both Congress and the presidency; the New York Times business section was headlined, "Business Was a Big Winner, Too.")

The 1996 campaign itself was not very exciting. Clinton faced no challenge at all within his own party; all potential rivals were deterred by his increased popularity and by the "new," pro-business Democrat Clinton's awesome success at campaign fund-raising. The Republicans sparked a little more interest when conservative Senator Phil Gramm amassed some $20 million to challenge front-runner Bob Dole, and when right-wing populist Pat Buchanan and millionaire libertarian Steve Forbes jumped in as well, fiercely attacking Dole. But Gramm and Forbes got nowhere with rank-and-file Republican voters. Buchanan, fanning fears of job insecurity, foreign economic competition, illegal immigration, and moral decay , gave Dole a scare by winning the New Hampshire primary. But after New Hampshire, far outspent and out-organized, Buchanan quickly faded.

By March, therefore, the major party nominations (not officially decided until August) were effectively locked up: it would be Clinton, the bruised but newly popular incumbent, versus Dole, the former Senate majority leader, who was famous for his taciturnity, his sharp wit, and his skill at negotiating legislative compromises, but not for oratorical eloquence, executive ability, or visions of the future. Ross Perot's Reform Party also qualified for

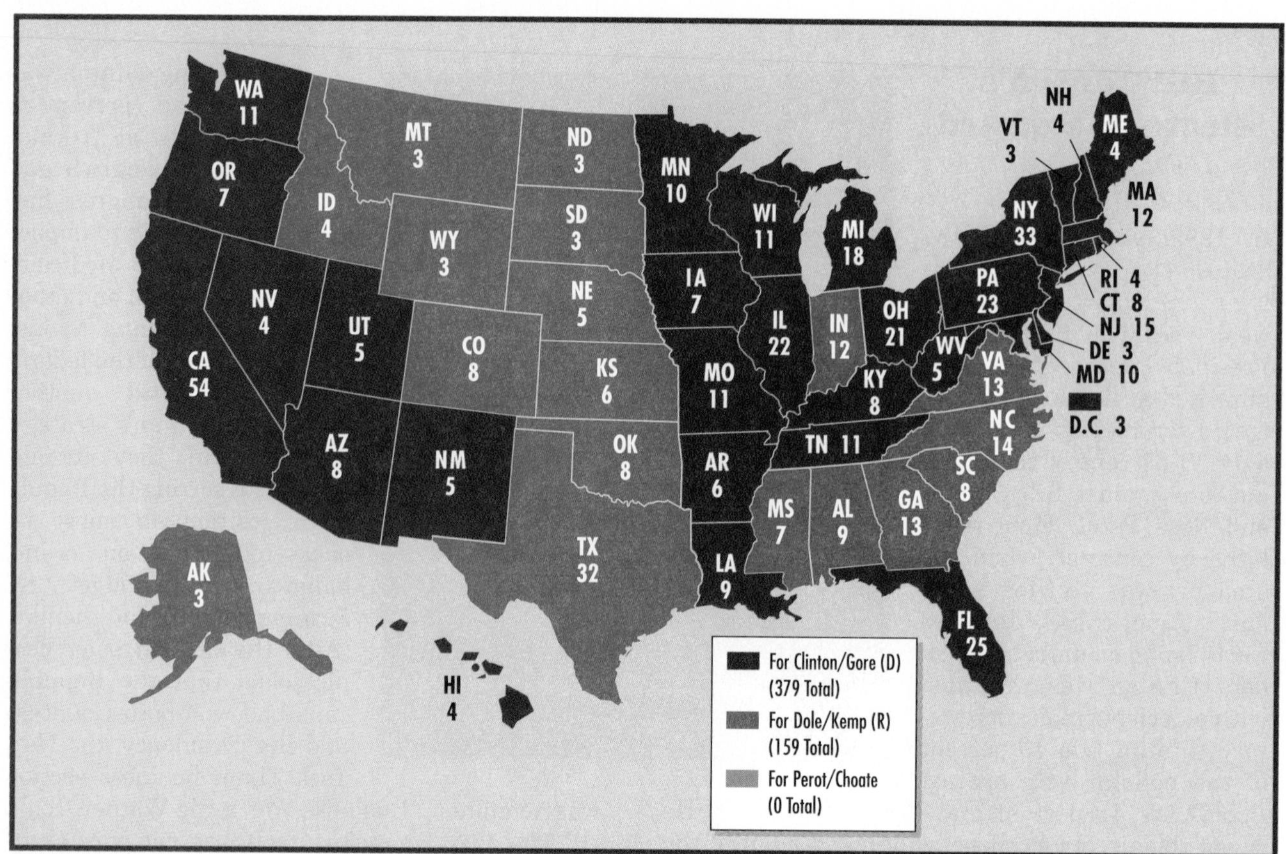

Figure 9.1 ▪ **Electoral Votes, 1996 Presidential Election**

Source: "How the Parties Fared," *New York Times*, November 7, 1996, p. B–1.

the ballot in every state, but Perot—deflated by years of negative media coverage and voter scrutiny—had less appeal than four years before.

Early polls showed a solid Clinton lead. Dole tried to shake up the race with a number of bold gestures. He resigned from the Senate, which had been his beloved professional home for decades, in order to campaign as an "outsider." Ignoring the very conservative Republican platform (which proposed 13 constitutional amendments, including a ban on abortion under any circumstances), Dole constructed a party convention in San Diego that featured fresh and moderate Republican faces like those of former military chief Colin Powell and New Jersey Governor Christine Whitman. He picked energetic supply-sider Jack Kemp as his running mate, and shelved his lifetime record as a deficit hawk, proposing a huge 15 percent across-the-board tax cut.

But—except for a temporary postconvention bounce in the polls—none of these moves, nor Dole's sharp attacks on Clinton's ethics and character, generated significant headway. Amidst an outpouring of negative TV ads by both parties, funded by unprecedented hundreds of millions of dollars in unregulated "soft money" and supposedly independent expenditures, Clinton sailed along, touting modest ideas for the future, and maintained a 12 to 15 percentage point lead in polls of likely voters all the way from June to November.

On election day, it became clear that the public was not enthusiastic about its choices. Turnout fell to a record low unmatched since 1924, with only about 49% of eligible voters going to the polls. (Only union members and Hispanics, energized by union organizers and anti-immigrant campaign rhetoric, voted in higher proportions than before; as usual, people with low incomes or little formal education voted at the lowest rates.) Much of Perot's vote reflected anti-Clinton and anti-Dole protest rather than eagerness to elect Perot.

The vote split along the usual lines. Most people voted for the presidential candidate of their own party. Blacks voted heavily Democratic (84 percent for Clinton and only 12 percent for Dole); so did Jews (78 percent for Clinton), Hispanics (72 percent), and—less overwhelmingly—members of union households (59 percent for Clinton), people with incomes below $15,000 (59 percent), and those with less than high school education (59 percent). The gender gap was wide: 54 percent of women, but only 43 percent of men, voted for Clinton. High proportions of white Protestants (especially evangelicals), upper-income people, and college graduates voted for Dole.

Exit polls confirmed the main message of the election: most voters thought that economic times were relatively good and saw no reason to throw out the incumbent; instead, they rewarded him. The issues mentioned as most important were the economy and jobs, followed by Medicare and Social Security. Most voters (57 percent) called the condition of the economy "excellent" or "good," and about 70 percent of those voted for Clinton. Most people said the country was "moving in the right direction," and nearly 80 percent said their family finances were the same or better than four years before. Large majorities of them, too, voted for Clinton.

Just beneath the surface of Clinton's reelection victory, however, were some ominous signs about the future. The low turnout, the Perot protest, and Clinton's failure to win even 50 percent of the popular vote all signaled lack of enthusiasm, as did the exit poll findings that more than half of voters did not consider Clinton honest or trustworthy. During the campaign, investigations into various scandals—especially the "Whitewater" financial deals and campaign contributions back in Arkansas and charges of a White House coverup—had only temporarily quieted, with special prosecutors and Republican congressmen all set to revive them. In the week or two before election day, Dole, Perot, and others had hammered away at charges of questionable or illegal Democratic fund-raising from foreign business interests in Indonesia, Taiwan, and elsewhere.

Clinton would have to work with a Republican House and Senate, and predictions of bipartisan cooperation were questionable at best. The economy, perhaps near the peak of a long upswing, showed signs of slowing down; a new recession would be especially painful since the current upswing had barely begun to break the wage stagnation of two previous decades. Around the world, in Russia, China, the Balkans, the Middle East, and elsewhere, bubbled hints of potential foreign policy crises. When a country's fortunes turn bad, electoral reward can be followed quickly by electoral punishment. As 1997 began, therefore, it was far too early to call Vice President Al Gore a shoo-in for election in the year 2000.

Elections and Democracy

Elections are fundamental to democratic politics. They are supposed to be the chief means by which citizens control what their government does, through popular sovereignty and majority rule. Many important struggles for democracy in the United States have involved conflicts over the right to vote.

But can elections actually ensure that governments will do what their people want? How? In a small, participatory democracy such as a town meeting, the answer is easy: People simply vote directly on what to do. A new road is built, or the town library is expanded, only if a majority of citizens votes for the action. In a large, complicated society like the entire United States, however, it is not generally feasible to have everyone vote directly on policies. That would take too much time and energy and would unreasonably ask citizens to become experts on everything. As we indicated in Chapter 1, probably the best that can be done is to have a representative democracy, in which the people choose representatives to do the policymaking.

The Problem of Democratic Control

In a representative democracy, however, it is not so obvious how the people can control their representatives. How can ordinary citizens make certain that elected officials will respond to them, that these officials will work for what the people want rather than pursue their own ends or cater to special interests?

Democratic theorists have suggested several different processes by which two-party elections of representatives, like those we have in the United States, can bring about the democratic control of government. We will briefly discuss three of these processes, indicating how they might work in theory and what could go wrong in practice.[1] The rest of this chapter is concerned with what actually happens in American elections and whether elections really bring about democratic control.

Responsible-Party Government

responsible party A political party that takes clear, distinct, stands on the issues and enacts them as policy.

The idea of **responsible-party** government is based on the old commonsense notion that elections should present a "real choice": political parties should stand for different policies, the voters should choose between them, and the winning party should carry out its mandate.

The Theory For this system to work perfectly, each of the two parties must be cohesive and unified; each must take clear policy positions that differ significantly from the other party's positions; the citizens must accurately perceive these positions and vote on the basis of them; and the winning party, when it takes office, must do exactly what it said it would do. If all these conditions are met, then obviously the party with the more popular policy positions will win and enact its program. Government will do what the majority of the voters want. Moreover, in the course of defending their distinctive platforms, the parties may help educate the citizens about public policy and mobilize them to take part in politics.[2]

Problems Even if an election were to work exactly as the responsible-party ideal dictates, however, a serious problem arises: There is no actual guarantee that either party would take policy positions that pleased the voters, only that the winning party's stand is less *un*popular than the loser's, which may not be particularly popular at all! Crucial decisions about what the parties stand for and what choices they present to the voters would be made by someone other than ordinary citizens: by party leaders or perhaps by interest groups.

Moreover, the conditions under which responsible-party government is supposed to work are not fully met—and are not ever likely to be met—in the United States. As we saw in the last chapter, the Republican and Democratic parties are *not* very unified or cohesive, for reasons deeply rooted in our Constitution and our political structure. The parties do *not* always take clear stands and are sometimes deliberately ambiguous. Nor do the parties necessarily take stands that are distinctly different from each other. Sometimes, avoiding unpopular or extreme positions, both parties say very nearly the same things. Furthermore, the voters do not vote solely on the issues. And the parties do not always keep their promises.

Clearly, then, the responsible-party idea does not correspond exactly to what happens in American elections. But we will see that it comes close enough to the truth to describe at least a part of reality. Also, theories about responsible parties provide some useful standards for judging what may be wrong with U.S. elections and how they might be improved, particularly with respect to the clarity of stands on issues, the unity of the parties, and the mobilization of voters.

Electoral Competition

A very different, and less obvious, sort of democratic control might come about through a process of **electoral competition** over issues. Here, unified parties compete for votes by taking the *most popular* positions they can. Both parties are therefore likely to end up standing for the *same* policies: those favored by the most voters. Whoever wins does what the voters want.

electoral competition A process by which parties seeking votes move toward the center of the political spectrum.

The Theory Scholars have proved mathematically that, if citizens' preferences are organized along a single dimension (such as the liberal-conservative continuum shown in Figure 9.2), if parties purely seek votes, and if various other conditions are met, then both parties will take positions exactly at the *median* of public opinion, that is, at the point where exactly one-half the voters are more liberal and one-half are more conservative. If either party took a position even a bit away from the median, the other party could easily win more votes by taking a position closer to the median.[3]

If electoral competition drives parties together in this way, and if they keep their promises, then, in theory, it should not matter which party wins; the winner enacts the platform that the most voters want. Democracy is ensured by

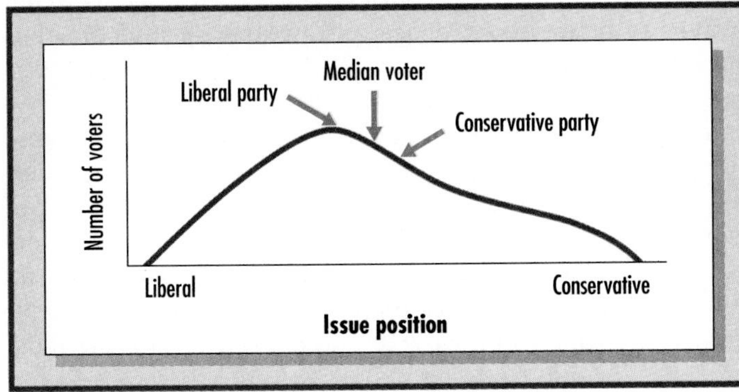

Figure 9.2 ▪ **Electoral Competition**

Electoral competition pushes the two parties to take positions near the middle of the distribution of voters.

the hidden hand of competition. According to this economics-style way of thinking, selfish, vote-seeking parties do what the voters want, in just the same way that selfish, money-seeking business firms are forced to produce what consumers want.

To be sure, electoral competition processes cannot ensure that the parties will educate or mobilize voters, as in a responsible-party process. But they have the advantage (from a cynical point of view) of depending only on selfish, vote-seeking motives, rather than requiring idealism from politicians. Most important, they hold out the promise that popular sovereignty and a perfectly democratic outcome—rather than just the lesser of two evils—may result from elections.

Problems Again, however, the conditions needed for electoral competition to work perfectly are not likely to be met in the real world. Electoral competition ensures democratic control only if the parties are unified and take clear stands, for purely and directly vote-seeking reasons; it can break down if the parties are fragmented or ambiguous, care about policies, or seek contributors' dollars rather than citizens' votes. In order for democratic control to be complete, everyone has to vote. Moreover, the voters must consider nothing but the issues (not being distracted by candidates' personalities or images, for example) and must know exactly where the parties stand. And the parties have to keep their promises. There are reasons to doubt that any of these things will happen flawlessly.

Still, we will see that these conditions are *close enough* to the truth so that electoral competition does work, to a significant extent, in real elections. Indeed, electoral competition is probably one of the main reasons that government policy is significantly influenced by public opinion. Moreover, by looking at how actual elections deviate from the theoretical ideal of electoral competition (e.g., how money and campaign contributions sometimes push parties away from popular policies), we can see specific ways in which American elections might be improved as instruments of democracy.

Electoral Reward and Punishment

A third process by which elections might bring about democratic control of government is **electoral reward and punishment.**

electoral reward and punishment A process in which people vote for the incumbents when times are good and against them when times are bad.

The Theory Here, the idea is that the voters simply make retrospective, backward-looking judgments about how well incumbent officials have done in the past, rewarding success with reelection and punishing failure by throwing the incumbents out. The result, in theory, is that politicians who want to stay in office have strong incentives to bring about peace and prosperity and to solve problems that the American people want solved. Politicians' ambitions force them to anticipate what the public wants and to accomplish it.[4]

The reward-and-punishment process of democratic control has the advantage of simplicity. It requires very little of voters: no elaborate policy preferences, no study of campaign platforms, just judgments of how well or how badly things have been going. Also, like electoral competition, it relies on politicians' selfishness rather than their altruism. It allows time for deliberation, and it lets leaders try out experimental or temporarily unpopular policies, as long as the results work out well and please the public in time for the next election.

Problems On the other hand, reward and punishment may be a rather blunt instrument. It gets rid of bad political leaders only after (not before) disasters happen, without guaranteeing that the next group of leaders will be any better. It relies on politicians' *anticipating* the effects of future policies, which they cannot always do successfully. Moreover, the reward-and-punishment process focuses only on the most crucial issues and may leave room for unpopular policies on matters that are less visible. It may also encourage politicians to produce deceptively happy but temporary results that arrive just in time for Election Day and then fade away.

Imperfect Electoral Democracy

We will see that each of the three processes of democratic control we have discussed works, to some extent, in American elections. But none of them works well enough to guarantee perfectly democratic outcomes. In certain respects, they conflict with each other: responsible parties and electoral competition, for example, tend to push in opposite directions. In other respects, all three processes require similar conditions that are not met in reality.

All three, in order to pin down politicians' responsibility clearly, require more unified political parties than we actually have. Similarly, they cannot ensure government responsiveness to all citizens unless *all* citizens have the right to vote and everyone exercises that right. However, millions of Americans cannot or do not go to the polls. Their voices are not clearly heard; political equality is not achieved. Even after two centuries of struggle to expand the right to vote, nonparticipation remains a major problem in American democracy.

Another problem for all three processes is that money, organizational resources, and active campaigning—not just citizens' policy preferences and votes—may influence the stands that parties take and the outcomes of elections. Thus, money givers, activists, and the leaders of organized groups have more influence than ordinary citizens do; again, political equality is not realized.

Still another problem (a rather subtle one) is that citizens' policy preferences and goals may themselves be manipulated, so that government responsiveness to them does not necessarily ensure authentic democracy. We will touch on several of these problems in the remainder of the chapter.

Political Participation

Political **participation** is political activity by individual citizens. It includes **unconventional participation,** in demonstrations, boycotts, and the like, of the sort that will be discussed in Chapter 10, and also **conventional participation,** which we focus on here, such as writing letters, contacting officials, going to meetings, working in campaigns, and giving money.

The most basic form of conventional political participation, the one that plays the most central part in theories of democratic control through elections, is the act of voting.

participation Political activity, including voting, campaign activity, contacting officials, and demonstrating.

unconventional participation Political activity through demonstrations or protests, rather than taking part in elections or contacting officials.

conventional participation Political activity related to elections (voting, persuading, and campaigning) or to contacting public officials.

The Expansion of the Franchise

In the early years of the United States, the **franchise,** the legal right to vote, was quite restricted. Most people could not vote at all. Slaves, Native Americans,

franchise The right to vote.

Early U.S. elections were poorly organized and hard to get to. Only a small proportion of the population was eligible to vote.

and—in most places—women were excluded altogether. In most states, people without a substantial amount of property were not allowed to vote. In some states, people with the "wrong" religious beliefs were excluded.

Furthermore, it was not always easy to get to the polls. The first federal election (1788–1789) was an especially messy affair. Voting days were different everywhere: House elections were held on December 22 in Connecticut, on January 7–10 in Maryland, and anywhere from February 11 to April 27 in New Jersey. Voters had to go to their county seats, which in Virginia sometimes meant traveling nearly 50 miles over mountains and watercourses. On their arrival, the polls might be open or they might not, depending on the sheriff's whim. The whole process was so restricted, difficult, and confusing that only 11 percent of the minority eligible to vote, or about *1 American in 40,* actually voted in the first presidential election.[5] A modern human-rights-monitoring group would not have been pleased.

One of the most important developments in the political history of the United States, an essential part of the struggle for democracy, has been the expansion of the right to vote. The extension of the franchise has been a lengthy process, lasting some 200 years. It has not been smooth or simple; surges of democratization have sometimes been followed by setbacks, and victories have been achieved only through vigorous political struggle.

White Male Suffrage The first barriers to fall were those concerning property and religion. So strong were the democratic currents during Thomas Jefferson's presidency (1801–1809) and in the years leading up to the election of Andrew Jackson in 1828 that, by 1829, property and religious requirements had been dropped in all states except North Carolina and Virginia. (Virginia finally went along in 1852.) That left universal **suffrage,** or the ability to vote, firmly in place for adult white males in the United States. The idea was so well established by the 1830s that the aristocratic French visitor Alexis de Tocqueville reported that opponents of suffrage "hide their heads."[6]

suffrage The right to vote.

In Europe, by contrast, only Switzerland (1848) had attained universal white male suffrage and meaningful control of government by the middle of the nineteenth century; only France (1877) and Norway (1898) had done so even by the end of the century. Most of Europe, including Britain, did not achieve that degree of democracy until after World War I, pushed by strong working-class movements organized into socialist parties and trade unions.[7]

Blacks, Women, and Young People Despite this head start for the United States compared to the rest of the world, however, the struggle to expand the suffrage to include African-Americans, women, and young people proved to be very difficult and painful. Ironically, universal white male suffrage was often accompanied by the withdrawal of voting rights from black freedmen, even in states that did not permit slavery.[8] It took the bloody Civil War to free the slaves, and the Fifteenth Amendment to the U.S. Constitution (1870) to formally extend the right to vote to all blacks, in both North and South. Even so, most blacks were effectively disenfranchised in the South by the end of the nineteenth century and mostly remained so until the 1960s civil rights movement and the Voting Rights Act of 1965.

Women won the right to vote with the Nineteenth Amendment to the Constitution (1920), after a long political battle (see the Struggle for Democracy feature). Residents of the District of Columbia were allowed to vote in presidential—though not congressional—elections after 1961, and 18- to 20-year-olds gained the franchise only in 1971 (recall the story in Chapter 3).

The result of these changes at the state and national levels was an enormous increase in the proportion of Americans who were legally eligible to vote: from about 23 percent of the adult population in 1788–1789, to nearly 100 percent—practically all citizens except convicted felons and people in mental institutions—by the beginning of the 1970s.

Direct Partisan Elections A related trend has involved the more direct election of government officials, replacing the old indirect methods that insulated officials from the public. At the same time, the development of a two-party system has clarified choices by focusing citizens' attention on just two alternatives for each office.

By the time of the Jefferson-Adams presidential campaign of 1800, which pitted the new Republican and Federalist parties against each other, most state legislatures had stopped picking the presidential electors themselves (as the Constitution permits). Instead, the legislatures allowed a popular vote for electors, most of whom were pledged to support the presidential candidate of one party or the other.

This is the same system we use today: in practically every state, there is a winner-take-all popular vote for a slate of electors, who are pledged ahead of time to a particular candidate. In fact, only the name of the candidate and the party to whom the electors are pledged, not the names of the electors we are actually voting for, appears on the ballot. Thus, when the winning electors meet as the **electoral college** in their respective states and cast ballots to elect the president, their actions are generally controlled by the popular vote

electoral college Representatives of the states who formally elect the president; the number of electors in each state is equal to the total number of its senators and representatives.

Women Win the Right to Vote

The Struggle for Democracy

The struggle for women's suffrage was long and difficult. What began as a radical idea at the Seneca Falls Convention in 1848 became law in 1920, through the efforts of a powerful social movement.

Women's suffrage organizations were formed soon after the Civil War. For more than two decades, though, the radical National Woman Suffrage Association (NWSA) and the more conservative American Woman Suffrage Association (AWSA) feuded over how to pressure male politicians. Women like Susan B. Anthony (with the NWSA) and Lucy Stone (with the AWSA) were divided by temperament and ideology. Anthony favored dramatic action to expose men's hypocrisy. At an 1876 centennial celebration of the United States in Philadelphia, Anthony and several other women marched onto the platform, where the emperor of Brazil and other dignitaries sat, and handed over a declaration of women's rights. They then marched off the platform and read the declaration aloud. Stone favored quieter methods of persuasion.

Then, in 1890, the two main organizations joined together to form the National American Woman Suffrage Association (NAWSA). They dropped such controversial demands as divorce reform and legalized prostitution in favor of one order of business: women's suffrage. The movement was now focused, mostly united, and growing more powerful every year. One major boost was the endorsement of women's suffrage by the Women's Christian Temperance Union (WCTU), a vigorous organization whose primary goal was the abolition of the liquor trade. The NAWSA and the WCTU joined other women's groups to form an umbrella group, the General Federation of Women's Clubs (GFWC), which boasted 2 million members by 1910.

In 1912, the NAWSA organized a march to support a constitutional amendment for suffrage. Over 5,000 zealous women dressed in white, some on horseback, paraded through the streets of Washington before Woodrow Wilson's inauguration. The police offered the marchers no protection from antagonistic spectators, despite the legal parade permit they had obtained. This lack of protection outraged the public and attracted media attention to the suffrage movement. The NAWSA took advantage of the favorable publicity, launching a petition drive and sending regular delegations to press President Wilson for a national solution.

Women's groups worked state by state, senator by senator, pressuring male politicians to support women's suffrage. After two prominent senators from New England were defeated in 1918 primarily because of the efforts of suffragists and prohibitionists, the political clout of the women's groups reached an all-time high.

that chose them. This system, odd and cumbersome as it is, ensures that American citizens choose their president more-or-less directly. (Later in the chapter, we will discuss the electoral college system more fully.)

Subsequently (by 1840), the parties started nominating presidential candidates in national conventions instead of congressional caucuses. Later still (especially after reform upsurges in the early 1900s and the 1970s), the parties began letting voters elect many convention delegates directly, in primaries, instead of having party activists choose them through state caucuses or state conventions. These innovations probably increased the democratic control of government, though we will see that each of them has antidemocratic features, too.

The direct popular election of U.S. senators did not replace their being chosen by state legislatures until 1913, with the Seventeenth Amendment to the Constitution. Since 1913, all members of the Senate have been subject to direct

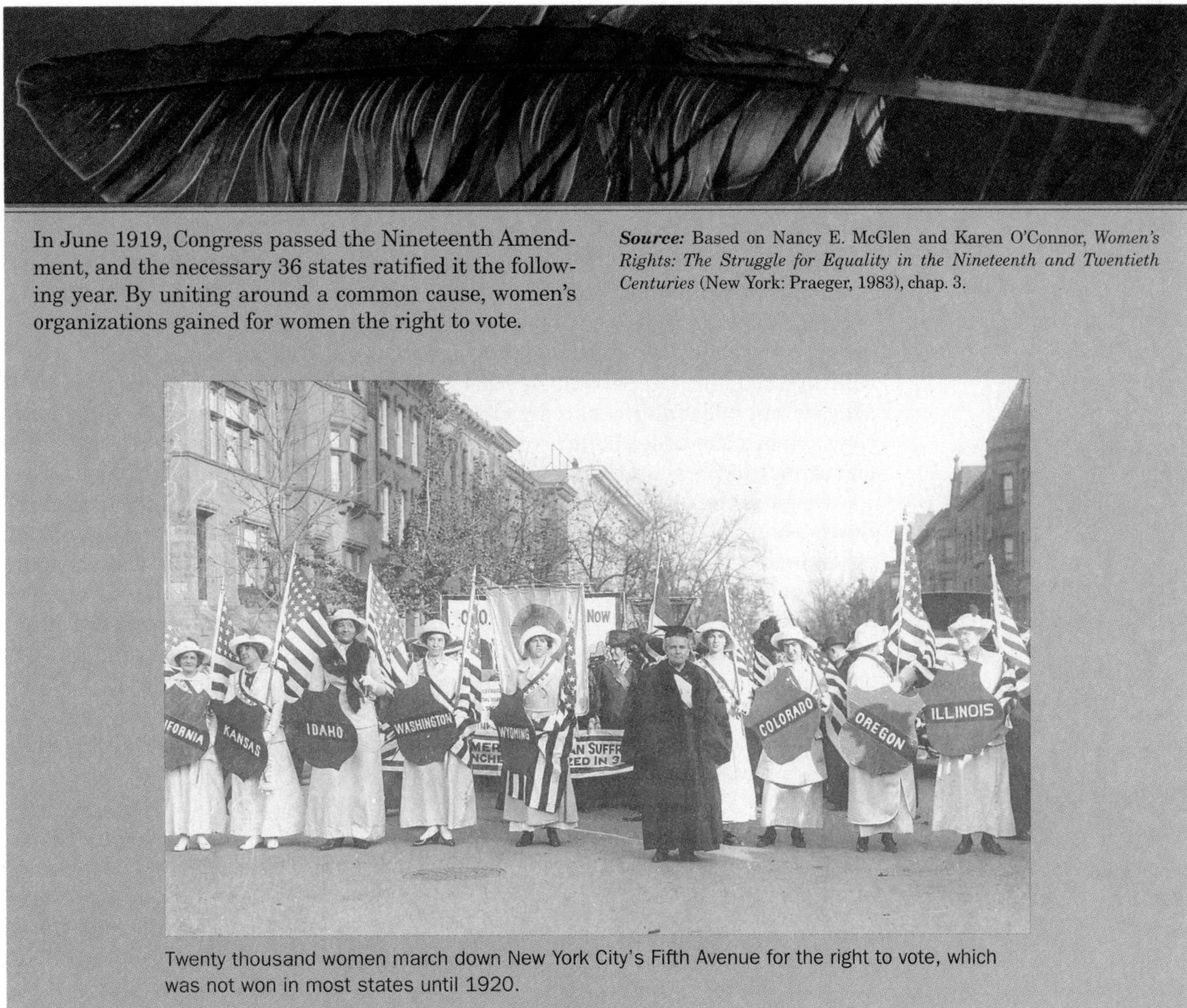

In June 1919, Congress passed the Nineteenth Amendment, and the necessary 36 states ratified it the following year. By uniting around a common cause, women's organizations gained for women the right to vote.

Source: Based on Nancy E. McGlen and Karen O'Connor, *Women's Rights: The Struggle for Equality in the Nineteenth and Twentieth Centuries* (New York: Praeger, 1983), chap. 3.

Twenty thousand women march down New York City's Fifth Avenue for the right to vote, which was not won in most states until 1920.

choice by the voters, just as members of the House of Representatives have been from the country's beginnings.

Taken together, the expansion of the franchise and the development of direct, two-party elections have represented major successes in the struggle for democracy. But victory is not yet complete.

The Vanishing Electorate

Early increases in voting participation have given way, in the twentieth century, to serious declines.

During the first hundred years or so of the United States, not only did more and more people gain the right to vote, but also higher and higher proportions of eligible voters actually "turned out" on Election Day and voted. It is not easy to be sure of the exact **turnout** percentages because of data

turnout The proportion of eligible people who vote.

inaccuracies and voting fraud, but in presidential elections, the figure of roughly 11 percent of eligible voters who turned out in 1788–1789 jumped to about 31 percent in 1800 (when Thomas Jefferson was first elected) and to about 57 percent in 1828 (Andrew Jackson's first victory). By 1840, the figure had reached *80 percent,* and it stayed at about that level until 1896.[9]

The disturbing fact is that, today, a much smaller proportion of people participate in politics than did during most of the nineteenth century. Since 1912, only about 55 to 65 percent of eligible Americans have voted in presidential elections, and still fewer in other elections: 40 to 50 percent in off-year (non-presidential-year) congressional elections, and as few as 10 to 20 percent in primaries and minor local elections. In recent years, the turnout rate has dropped to the low end of those ranges. It was only 36 percent in 1986, 37 percent in 1990, and 39 percent in 1994; in those off-years, little more than *one-third* of eligible Americans participated in electing congressional representatives. Hence the talk about a vanishing electorate. (Take a look at Figure 9.3 on turnout in presidential elections.)

Despite the early development of broad suffrage rights in the United States, our voting turnout rate is exceptionally low compared with that of other modern industrialized countries, where 80 percent rates are common (see Figure 9.4). Most observers consider this a serious problem for democracy in America, particularly since (as we will see) those who vote tend to be different from those who do not. Nonvoters do not get an equal voice in political choices. Political equality, one of the key elements of democracy, is violated.

Causes of Low Turnout Why do so few Americans participate in elections? Scholars have identified several possible factors.

Barriers to Voting In the United States, only those who take the initiative to register before an election are permitted to vote. Sometimes, registration is made difficult by limited locations, limited office hours, and requirements to register long before the election. This is especially hard on people who move

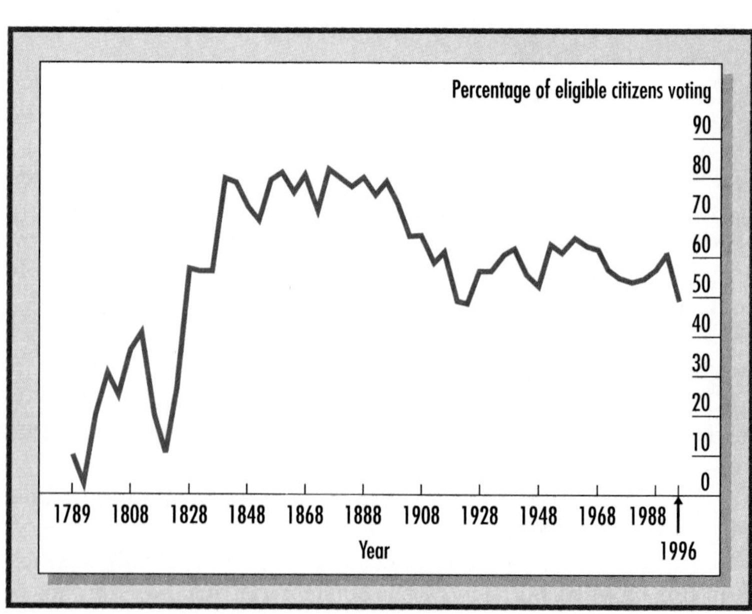

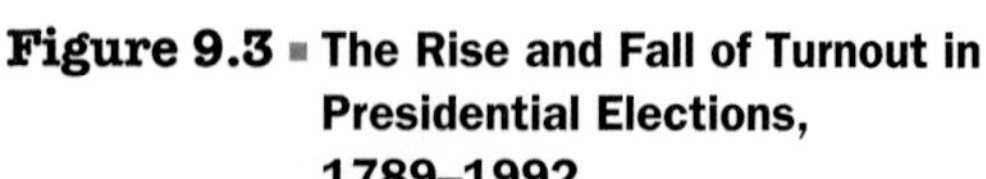

Figure 9.3 ■ The Rise and Fall of Turnout in Presidential Elections, 1789–1992

Turnout in presidential elections rose sharply during the nineteenth century but has declined in the twentieth century.

Sources: Walter Dean Burnham, "The Turnout Problem," in A. James Reichley, ed., *Elections American Style* (Washington, D.C.: Brookings Institution, 1987), pp. 113–114; U.S. Census, Bureau, *Current Population Survey.*

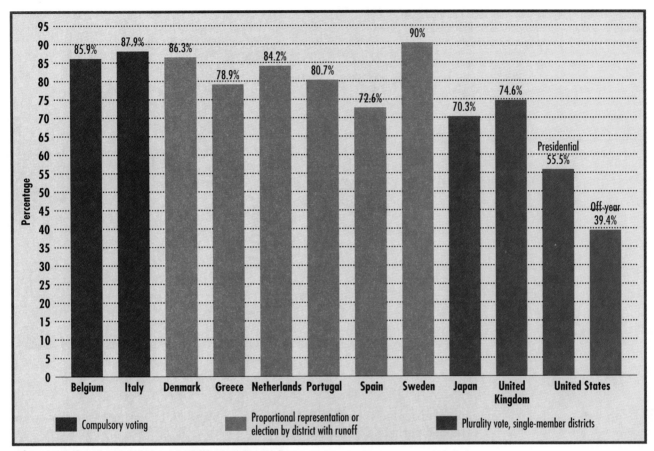

Figure 9.4 ■ **Voting Turnout in Different Countries**

Turnout is substantially lower in the United States than in other advanced industrial countries.

Source: Walter Dean Burnham, "The Turnout Problem," in A. James Reichley, ed., *Elections American Style* (Washington, D.C.: Brookings Institution, 1987), p. 107.

from one community to another. In one presidential election, about 35 percent of the nonvoters, and only 16 percent of voters, said that they had moved in the past two years.[10]

In most European countries with high turnout rates, the government, rather than individual citizens, is responsible for deciding who is listed as eligible to vote. In fact, in some countries, such as Belgium and Luxembourg, citizens are *required* to vote and may have to pay a fine if they don't. Moreover, in most countries, all election days are holidays; unlike Americans, Europeans do not have to vote very early or late in the day or get special permission to leave their jobs in order to go to the polls.

The United States could certainly increase political equality and popular sovereignty by making voting easier. One way to do so would be to ease registration requirements, perhaps allowing registration by postcard or same-day registration at polling places. The federal "motor voter" law passed in 1993, providing for registration in motor vehicle bureaus and other government offices, was a step in this direction. Another way would be to ease the voting act itself, by making every election day a holiday, or by allowing an extended voting period like the two-and-a-half weeks tried in Texas, or by broadening the

In Oregon, voting entirely by mail (or by dropping off ballots in convenient collection boxes) has saved the state money and increased turnout.

right of absentee voting as in California, or by allowing voting by mail over an extended period as in Oregon.

Lack of Attractive Choices Some scholars believe that the nature of the political parties and the choices that they offer also affect turnout. As Figure 9.4 indicates, countries with proportional representation and multiparty systems—that is, with diverse parties from which to choose—have averaged an 83 percent turnout rate, whereas single-district, plurality-vote countries (which usually have just two parties) have had a voter turnout rate that is closer to 70 percent. Many American citizens may not like the candidates of either of the major parties well enough to bother voting for them.

Also, unlike most European countries, the United States does not have a workers' party to mobilize blue-collar workers and poor people. Political scientist and historian Walter Dean Burnham argues that the crushing defeat of the Populists and the radical Democrats in 1896 led to a conservative realignment that excluded many citizens from the electoral process and discouraged people from voting. Subsequent "reforms," such as personal registration requirements, reduced participation especially sharply among immigrants and workers in the big cities—perhaps deliberately, in order to cut back the political power of working people.[11] According to this point of view, some upper-middle-class people and organized business interests are happy with low turnout, especially among lower-income citizens, and try to discourage broader participation.

Changes in Eligibility Rules Changes in eligibility rules have also affected turnout rates, at least temporarily. As Figure 9.3 indicates, turnout as a proportion of eligible voters dropped just after women were enfranchised in 1920, because, at first, women were less likely to vote than men. But that difference gradually disappeared. In fact, in some recent elections (1988 and 1992, though not 1994), women voted at rates slightly higher than men. Similarly, turnout percentages dropped a bit after 18-year-olds won the vote in 1971, because young people do not participate as much; they are less firmly established in their local communities.

Alienation The apathy about and alienation from politics that many Americans feel have undoubtedly contributed to declines in turnout. In 1994, 82 percent of nonvoters said that government "is run by a few big interests" looking out for themselves, and 67 percent said that people in government "waste a lot of money paid in taxes."[12] Some of this alienation results from well-publicized attacks on government and from recent economic problems, including recessions and job insecurity. But much of it can be traced back as far as the 1960s, to the assassination of popular leaders (e.g., John F. Kennedy, Robert Kennedy, and Martin Luther King, Jr.) and to the Vietnam war, urban unrest, and the Watergate and Iran-Contra scandals.[13] Perhaps the most fundamental causes are long-lasting economic troubles like wage stagnation, which neither party seems to remedy.

Lack of Voter Mobilization by Parties A related factor may be the failure of the political parties to register low-income citizens, especially African-Americans and Latinos. In recent years, neither the Republican nor the Democratic party has seemed very eager to increase the number of voters among the poor, possibly because of worries that they would support candidates like Jesse Jackson who are more liberal than most party officials.[14]

Campaigning and Contacting Despite the low voter-turnout levels in the United States, however, Americans are actually more likely than people in other countries to participate actively in campaigns.[15] During the 1992 presidential campaign, some 18 percent of adults said they gave money, a remarkable 29 percent said they had attended meetings, 8 percent had attended a political rally, and 5 percent had worked actively in a campaign organization.[16]

Much the same thing is true of contacting public officials; in about one-third (34 percent) of Americans say they have done so during the past year, most often with local elected officials.[17] Exactly why Americans vote less, but campaign for candidates and contact officials more, than citizens elsewhere is something of a puzzle.

Who Participates?

Political participation varies a great deal according to people's income, education, age, and ethnicity.

Income and Education For the most part, politically active people are those with higher-than-average incomes and more formal education.[18] These people are also more likely to vote. This difference has important effects on the working of democracy, because it undermines political equality; some kinds of people have more representation and more influence than others.

There is a class bias in both political participation and voting. In 1992, for example, 81 percent of adults with four or more years of college reported that they had voted, but only 58 percent of high school graduates and 35 percent of those who had not graduated from high school had done so (see Figure 9.5). In 1994, 82 percent of those with incomes of $90,000 or above said they had voted,

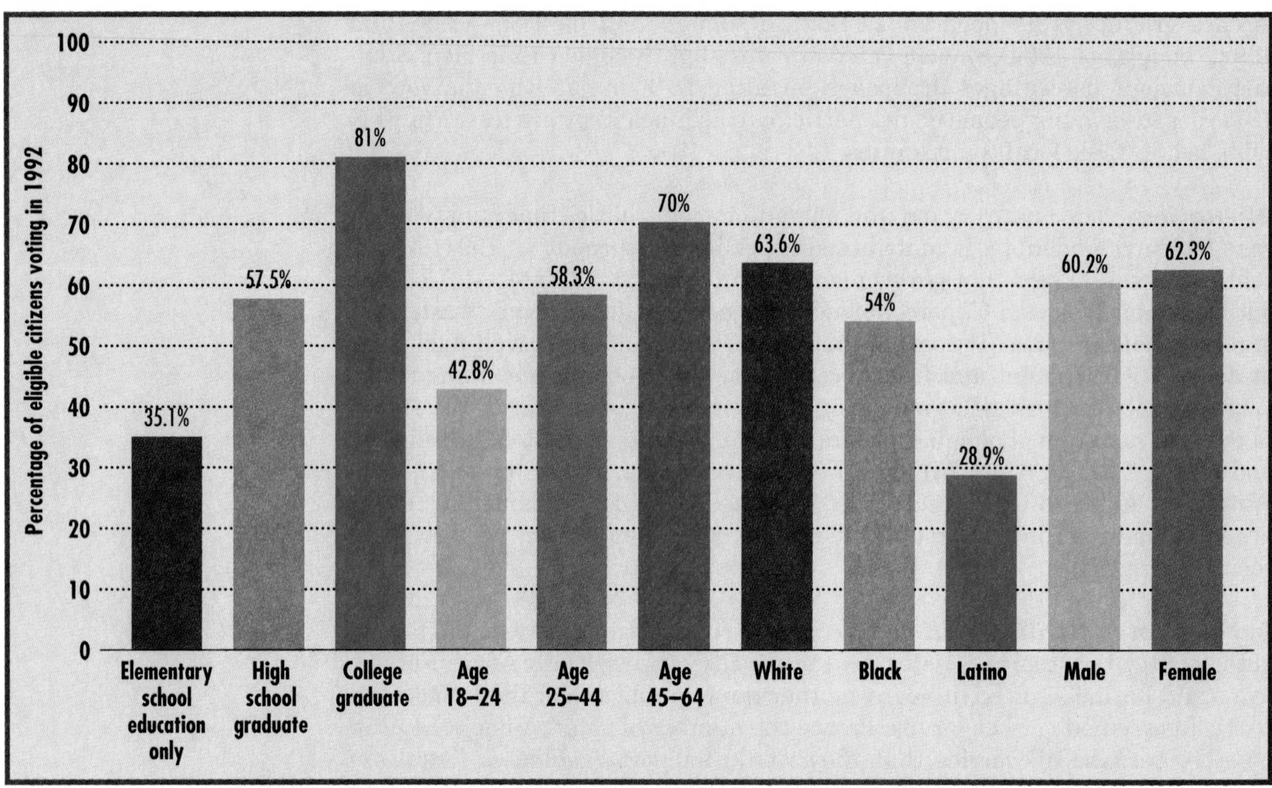

Figure 9.5 ■ **Presidential Election Turnout in 1992, by Social Group**

Education, age, race, ethnicity, and gender all effect voting habits. Members of certain social groups are more likely to vote in elections than others.

Source: U.S. Census Bureau, "Voting and Registration in the Election of November 1992."

but only 49 percent of those with incomes under $20,000 said they had done so. Only 37 percent of the unemployed said they had voted.[19]

Some statistical analyses have indicated that the crucial factor in voter turnout is level of formal education. When other factors are controlled for, college-educated people are much more likely to tell interviewers that they have voted than are the grade-school- or high-school-educated.[20] There are several possible reasons: People with more education learn more about politics, are less troubled by registration requirements, and are more confident in their ability to affect political life.

On the other hand, some "vote validation" studies have indicated that some highly educated people just *say* they have voted because they think they should vote. Income level may be more important than education in affecting who actually votes.

Citizens with lower incomes also tend to participate less by working in campaigns, giving money, contacting officials, and the like. Wealthier Americans, who have more time, more money, and more knowledge of how to get things done, tend to be much more active politically. As a result, they may have more political clout than their fellow citizens. This class bias in political participation is much greater in the United States than in most other advanced countries.

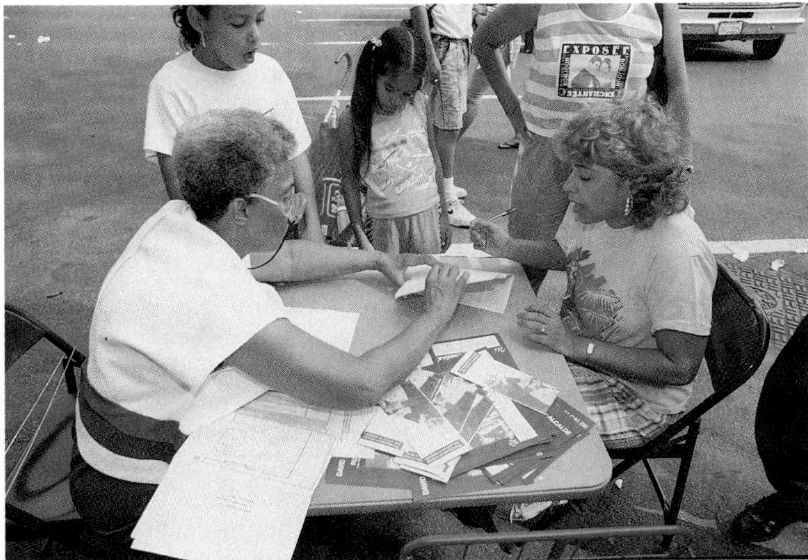

Latinos have the potential to be an important force in American politics, but low registration and voting rates have limited their influence.

Race and Ethnicity In the past, fewer black people than whites voted, but now the proportions are more nearly equal: 64 percent of whites and 54 percent of blacks voted in 1992 (see Figure 9.5). The remaining differences result from blacks' lower average levels of income and education. Blacks are at least equally likely to vote, and sometimes more likely, than whites of similar background.

Hispanics, however, have very low participation rates; only 29 percent voted in 1992. Many Hispanics are discouraged from participating by low incomes, language problems, or suspicion of government authorities. Asian-Americans, on the other hand, show growing levels of participation, especially in money giving.

Age and Gender The very young are less likely than their elders to vote: only 43 percent of 18- to 20-year-olds did so in 1992, compared with 73 percent of 65- to 74-year-olds. Young people tend to be less rooted in communities, less familiar with registration and voting procedures, and less clear about what stake they have in elections.[21]

The gender gap in participation, however, has almost entirely disappeared (see Figure 9.5).

Does It Matter Who Votes? How much difference do participation biases make? Some observers have argued that it doesn't matter if many people don't vote, because their preferences aren't much different from those who do; the results would be about the same if everyone voted. In some elections, nonvoters have shown support for the same candidate who won, so that their votes would apparently have changed nothing,[22] and some surveys have indicated that nonvoters' policy preferences are little different from those of voters. A few scholars have even claimed that low voter turnout is a positive benefit, on the supposition that less-educated people are ignorant anyway, and that nonvoting increases the stability of the system and discourages demagoguery.[23]

However, we should not be too quick to accept these arguments, just as few now accept the nineteenth-century view that there was no need for women to vote because their husbands could protect their interests. For one thing, the preferences of voters and nonvoters are often substantially different. In the congressional elections of 1994, for example, 52 percent of voters, but only 44 percent of nonvoters, disapproved of President Clinton's handling of his job.[24] Those who voted the new Republican majorities into the House and Senate were more anti-Clinton and more pro-Republican than the U.S. citizenry as a whole.

For another thing, even when the expressed preferences of nonvoters or nonparticipators do not look very distinctive, their objective circumstances, and therefore their needs for government services, may differ markedly.[25] Latinos, the young, and citizens with low incomes might benefit from government programs that are of less interest to other citizens. A political system that included and mobilized these people vigorously might produce quite different policies, perhaps more like those of the European social democracies.[26] Of course, we cannot be sure that they would do so, but one sign of what a difference participation can make is that, when black Americans won effective voting rights, the number of elected black officials rose sharply and nonblack politicians and officials paid much more attention to black constituents (see Chapters 1 and 10).

In any case, broader participation in U.S. elections would increase popular sovereignty and political equality and would thus contribute to democracy. The recent appeal of third-party candidates and protest movements signals that something is wrong. The limited number of Americans who vote is one major respect in which the struggle for democracy has not fully succeeded.

Campaigning for Office

The ideas we discussed about how elections might ensure democratic policymaking all depend in various ways on what sorts of choices are presented to the voters. It makes a difference what kind of people run for office, whether they take clear policy stands, whether those stands differ from each other, and whether they stand for what the average voter wants. In evaluating how democratic our elections are, therefore, we need to examine what kinds of alternatives are put before the voters in campaigns.

Running for a Presidential Nomination

The major party candidates for president of the United States are chosen well before the November election, and they are often effectively chosen even before the parties hold nominating conventions. They are drawn from a rather small pool of potential candidates. Despite what some parents tell their children, not every American has a significant chance of becoming president.

Who Has a Chance In any given election, in fact, only a handful of candidates are serious possibilities. So far in American history, these have virtually always been middle-aged or elderly white men, with extensive formal education, fairly high income, and substantial experience as public figures—usually as government officials (especially governors or senators) or military heroes. Movie stars, media commentators, business executives, and others who would be president almost always have to perform lesser government service before they are seriously considered for the presidency. Ronald Reagan, for example, most of whose career was spent acting in motion pictures and on television, served as governor of California before being elected president.

In recent years, the presidency has been practically monopolized by former governors (who have demonstrated executive ability), vice-presidents (who have had a close look at how the job is done), and U.S. senators (who have been exposed to a wide range of U.S. foreign and domestic policies). Since 1936, 39 percent of all presidential nominees have been governors, 33 percent vice-presidents, and 17 percent senators.[27] The best single stepping-stone to become president is clearly the vice-presidency, itself usually filled by former senators or governors. Since 1900, 5 of the 18 presidents have succeeded from the vice-presidency after the president's death or resignation, and two others—Nixon and Bush—have been former vice-presidents elected in their own right.

Serious candidates for president almost invariably represent mainstream American values and policy preferences. Seldom does an "extreme" candidate get very far. Serious candidates are also generally acceptable to the business community and have enthusiastic support from at least some sectors of industry or finance. The reasons are that the parties want to nominate winners and that a filtering process is involved in gaining previous offices: those who have previously won elections to Congress and governorships, enabling them to emerge as presidential candidates, have already demonstrated popular appeal to voters and an ability to raise money and motivate party activists.

Getting Started A person who wants to run for the presidency usually begins at least two or three years before the election by testing the waters, asking friends and financial backers if they will support a run, and observing how people react to the mythical "Great Mentioner." A friendly journalist may write that Senator Blathers "has been mentioned" as a smart, attractive, strong candidate; Blathers waits to see whether anyone agrees. The precandidate may commission a national survey to check for name recognition and a positive image. He may put together an exploratory committee to round up private endorsements, commitments, and financial contributions, perhaps setting up private PACs (political action committees) to gather money.

Many potential candidates, even prominent ones, drop out before getting started. In 1996, for example, Republicans Dan Quayle, William Bennett, Jack Kemp, Richard Cheney, and (at the last minute) Colin Powell all decided not to run, because of weak poll results, difficulties in fund-raising, the likely unpleasantness of campaigning, or other reasons.

If all goes well in the early stages, the presidential aspirant becomes more serious, assembling a group of close advisers, formulating strategy, officially announcing his candidacy, raising large amounts of money, and putting together organizations ("Draft Blathers" or "Citizens for Blathers" committees) in key states. Early money is crucial, to finance organization and advertising, and to qualify for federal matching funds later. By December 1995, for example, Senators Bob Dole and Phil Gramm had each gathered more than $20 million for pursuit of the 1996 Republican nomination; Steve Forbes had set aside an equal amount from his private fortune. (For the Hollywood view of campaigning, see the Politics and Film box.)

One important early decision concerns how to pitch the campaign: As an outsider getting rid of the mess in Washington, D.C. (Forbes)? As the most competent and most centrist standard-bearer for the party (Dole)? As the voice for a particular program (austere economic conservative Gramm or social conservative and economic populist Pat Buchanan)? Another major decision involves

Colin Powell, highly popular as chairman of the Joint Chiefs of Staff under presidents Bush and (briefly) Clinton, was much discussed as a possible presidential or vice-presidential candidate on the Republican ticket in 1996. But he declined to run and instead campaigned for Bob Dole.

which state primaries, caucuses, and straw votes to enter. Each entry takes a lot of money, energy, and organization, and any loss is damaging; many candidates drop out after just a few early defeats, as Gramm did in 1996—even before the New Hampshire primary—when he was upset in the Louisiana and Iowa caucuses. To win the nomination, it is generally necessary to put together a string of primary victories.

conventions Gatherings of delegates who nominate a party's presidential candidate.

primary elections State elections in which delegates to national presidential nominating conventions are chosen.

caucuses Meetings of party activists to choose delegates to national presidential nominating conventions.

Primaries and Caucuses Party nominees for president are chosen every four years at national party **conventions,** made up of state delegations from around the country. Since the 1970s, most of the delegates to the conventions—currently about 67 percent of the Democratic delegates and 55 percent of the Republican delegates—have been chosen in state **primary elections,** with direct voting by citizens.[28] (Some primaries are "open" to all voters; others are "closed," that is, reserved for those who register with the party whose primary election it is.) The Democrats' popularly elected delegates are supplemented by "superdelegates," usually members of Congress or local officials. A few states use **caucuses,** where active party members and officials choose delegates to state conventions, which, in turn, select the delegates to the national convention.

Since the states and the parties—not the federal government—control this nominating process, the system is a disorganized, even chaotic one, and it changes from one election to the next.

The "smoke-filled rooms" and deal making among party leaders that once characterized national conventions (it took ten ballots for the Republicans to nominate Warren Harding in 1920, for example) are mostly a thing of the past.

POLITICS AND FILM

Campaigns on Film

Election campaigns are highly entertaining dramas. Yet they have not drawn much attention from Hollywood. There are a few exceptions, however.

The Last Hurrah (1958) is John Ford's portrayal of the decline of old-style politics and the birth of a new style, and a statement about what has been lost in the transition. Spencer Tracy plays Frank Skeffington, mayor and machine boss of an small, unnamed eastern city, who is running for reelection. He is opposed by a mediocre but photogenic candidate supported by the city's wealthy, who put their money behind him, focusing on the relatively new medium of television. Skeffington campaigns as he always has: meeting people face-to-face. Much to his surprise, he loses the election. His campaign strategy of personal contact is no match for the new media-style campaign. He promises his followers that he will run for the governorship, but Ford leaves the viewer with the impression that politicians like Skeffington will be as extinct as dinosaurs in the coming media age.

The media campaign has arrived with a vengeance in the Michael Ritchie film *The Candidate* (1972). Robert Redford plays an idealistic candidate for the U.S. Senate from California (modeled, apparently, on a real candidate and senator, John Tunney), whose campaign of "talking about the issues" is in a near-terminal state, with little media attention and declining poll numbers. Enter Peter Boyle, playing a hard-nosed professional campaign consultant, who fashions a modern campaign based on the sound bite, advertising, and staged television events. In the end, the change in strategy works, and Redford wins the election in a close race. In the process, however, the man who began the campaign is swallowed whole by the process and is unrecognizable in the end. Ritchie seems to suggest that the juggernaut of modern campaigns inevitably overwhelms even the best candidates.

Two other films also focus on the role of the increasingly important campaign consultant. Sidney Lumet's *Power* (1986) features Richard Gere as a consultant willing and able to package anyone who wants to pay for his services. Other consultants believe in their candidates and are tied to particular parties. We see them at work in the brilliant documentary *The War Room,* which follows the work of Bill Clinton's campaign staff in 1992.

Tim Robbins wrote, directed, and stars in *Bob Roberts* (1992), an eerily prescient film about a wealthy businessman who spends lavishly on a campaign to win a U.S. Senate seat. Robbins's film is a none-too-subtle warning about the dangers to a free society of the volatile combination of right-wing populism (with its dominant themes of patriotism, racism, antigovernmentism, and antifeminism), big money, and the modern mass media. Although it is meant to be a satire—which exaggerates to make a point—the movie viewer cannot help but feel that *Bob Roberts* fails in this regard, because it simply cannot keep up with actual developments in American politics, where wealthy candidates buy media attention, and radio and TV talk show hosts help set the American political agenda.

Socially conservative, nationalist, and economically populist media commentator Pat Buchanan shook up the Republican Party with early caucus and primary victories in 1996. Although he was overwhelmingly defeated for the nomination by Bob Dole, Buchanan, with support from many party activists, continued to pressure Dole to take conservative stands on abortion and other issues.

Now the trick is to win delegates in primaries and caucuses and among party officials.[29]

Momentum It is especially important for a candidate to establish *momentum* by winning early primaries and caucuses. Early winners get press attention, financial contributions, and better standings in the polls, as voters and contributors decide they are viable candidates and must have some merit if people in other states have supported them. All these factors—attention from the media, money, and increased popular support—help the candidates who win early contests to go on and win more and more contests.[30]

Even before the beginning of each presidential election year, therefore, a number of candidates descend on the sites of the early contests. These early contests include the Iowa caucuses, where thorough organization is the key; the New Hampshire primary, considered crucial because it comes first, though the state is atypical of the country as a whole; the very big New York and California primaries (which used to occur later in the nomination season but are now near the beginning); and the big primaries in Texas and Florida. Many states, seeking to gain influence, have scheduled their primaries earlier in the year (see Table 9.1), so that many of them now cluster together in March—putting an even heavier burden on the candidates to be organized everywhere and to campaign everywhere at once.

Iowa and New Hampshire have long-established traditions of "retail politics": candidates make speeches, meet for coffee or supper with potential supporters and money givers, and press the flesh at farmhouses, malls, and factory gates. Reporters and camera crews follow along, capturing each gaffe or coup, filming sound bites for TV news, and making their own judgments about who is "viable" or not and who has "character." Campaign workers go door to door, talking up their candidates, passing out literature, and getting people to the polls. Increasingly, however, expensive paid advertisements blanket the airwaves (e.g., Steve Forbes's advocacy of a "flat tax" and his attacks on opponents). Some

Table 9.1

1996 Primary Calendar

Date	State	System	Date	State	System
Feb. 6	Louisiana	Caucus (R)	March 17	Puerto Rico	Primary (R)
Feb. 12	Iowa	Caucus	March 19	Illinois	Primary
Feb. 20	New Hampshire	Primary		Michigan	Primary
Feb. 24	Delaware	Primary		Ohio	Primary
Feb. 27	Arizona	Primary (R)		Wisconsin	Primary
	North Dakota	Primary (R)	March 23	Wyoming	Caucus (D)
	South Dakota	Primary	March 25	Utah	Caucus (D)
March 2	South Carolina	Primary (R)	March 26	California	Primary
March 5	Colorado	Primary		Connecticut	Primary
	Georgia	Primary		Vermont	Caucus (D)
	Idaho	Caucus (D)	March 30	Virgin Islands	Caucus (D)
	Maryland	Primary	April 2	Kansas	Primary
	Minnesota	Caucus (D)		Minnesota	Primary (R)
	Vermont	Primary (R)	April 4	Alaska	Caucus (D)
	Washington	Caucus (D)	April 7	Puerto Rico	Primary (D)
	American Samoa	Caucus (D)	April 13	Virginia	Caucus (D)
March 7	Missouri	Caucus (D)	April 23	Pennsylvania	Primary
	New York	Primary	May 5	Guam	Caucus (D)
	North Dakota	Caucus (D) (through March 21)	May 7	District of Columbia	Primary
				Indiana	Primary
March 9	Arizona	Caucus (D)		North Carolina	Primary
	South Carolina	Primary (D)	May 14	Nebraska	Primary
	Democrats Abroad	Caucus (D) (through March 11)		West Virginia	Primary
			May 21	Arkansas	Primary
March 10	Nevada	Caucus (D)		Oregon	Primary
March 12	Florida	Primary	May 28	Idaho	Primary (R)
	Hawaii	Caucus (D)		Kentucky	Primary
	Louisiana	Primary		Washington	Primary (R)
	Maine	Primary (D)	June 4	Alabama	Primary
	Massachusetts	Primary		Montana	Primary
	Mississippi	Primary		New Jersey	Primary
	Oklahoma	Primary		New Mexico	Primary
	Rhode Island	Primary			
	Tennessee	Primary			
	Texas	Primary/Caucus (D)			

Competition among states to have an early influence on the nominating process has caused primaries and caucuses to be bunched together at the beginning of the election year. This calendar shows the dates for planned primaries and caucuses for the 1996 election.

Source: *Congressional Quarterly Weekly Report* (April 29, 1995), p. 39.

lower-budget candidates, like Pat Buchanan, have figured out how to dominate radio talk shows with multiple call-ins from their hotel rooms.

Winners in the early primaries and caucuses move on to the next; others drop out. In 1996, for example, after Bob Dole began to defeat all his opponents in early primaries, most of them called it quits. Dole went on to win later primaries without significant opposition, even though Pat Buchanan officially remained in the race for a while.

How to Win Four main factors affect candidates' success in gathering delegates.

1. *The general attractiveness of the candidate,* especially the personal image conveyed by television, but also the candidate's stands on issues and his connections in the public mind with the good or bad times that the country is enjoying.
2. *Viability,* as judged by the media and as reflected in the polls. Citizens are reluctant to nominate or vote for someone who has no chance.
3. *Organizational strength,* particularly the number of hardworking activists who will pack the caucuses, stuff envelopes, go door-to-door, and get voters to the polls.
4. *Money* to pay for the television ads, organizing, and travel that a campaign requires. Money can help make candidates to look more attractive, to win votes, to seem more viable, and to build strong organizations. Even abundant ready money, which Phil Gramm called "a politician's best friend," cannot compensate for a candidate's lack of attractiveness to voters, as Gramm himself discovered. But *lack* of money can destroy a campaign entirely.

In recent years, most successful presidential nominees have won primary after primary, gathering in the supporters of losing candidates who have bowed out, and they have gone on to the convention with a substantial plurality of delegates. Michael Dukakis, for example, entered the 1988 Democratic convention with about 70 percent of the delegates committed to him; Jesse Jackson, Dukakis's nearest competitor, had only 1,218 delegates. In 1992, Bill Clinton had by far the biggest bloc of delegates going into the convention, as did Dole in 1996.

The Convention When there is a foreordained front-runner, the national convention generally becomes a coronation ceremony, in which prepledged delegates ratify the selection of the leading candidate, accept that candidate's choice for the vice-presidency, and put on a colorful show for the media and the country. Speeches and videos explain why "our" party, with vision, experience, and heart, is far better than "theirs." Enthusiasm and unity are staged for the national television audience; it is a disaster if serious conflicts break out or the timing goes wrong. (In 1992, George Bush's reelection campaign was set back when convention speaker Pat Buchanan declared a "religious war.")

Republican and Democratic convention delegates tend to be quite different from each other, reflecting the different nature of their party coalitions. They tend to disagree markedly on certain political issues, Democratic delegates being much more liberal, Republican delegates being much more conservative, and the average American citizen being somewhere in the middle (see Chapter 8 and Figure 9.6). Delegates to both parties' conventions are predominately white and financially well off, but the Democrats typically have many more African-American, Latino, female, and working-class delegates. Democratic delegates sometimes also seem to be rowdier and more excited about politics.

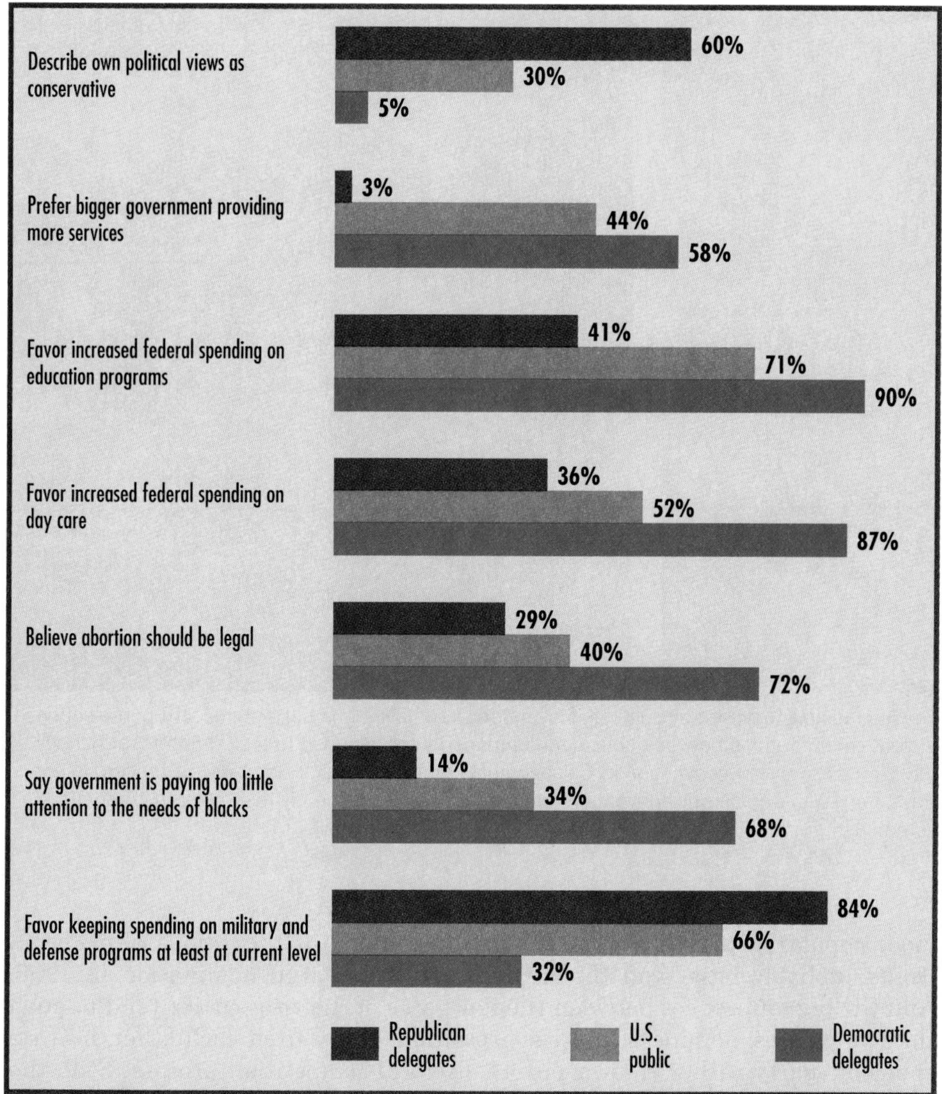

Figure 9.6 ▪ Opinions and Views: Convention Delegates Versus the Public

Republican convention delegates tend to be more conservative, and Democratic delegates more liberal, than the general population.

Source: *New York Times* (August 14, 1988), p. A32.

Rarely nowadays is there a real contest at the national convention, in which delegates actually require repeated balloting to make a choice. Rarely, for example, do they have to decide between their "professional" heads and their "purist" hearts: whether to nominate a likely winner or one who stands for ideas that they hold dear (as when the Republicans renominated President Ford rather than their favorite, Ronald Reagan, in 1976).

The evidence from polls indicates that, at virtually all recent national conventions, the party nominee has been the surviving candidate who has had the most support from rank-and-file party identifiers in the nation as a whole. The candidates who have survived the hurdles of raising money, mobilizing activists, and winning primary votes do not, of course, necessarily include the

The impression conveyed by political conventions can have an important impact upon elections. Violent confrontations between police and demonstrators opposed to the Vietnam War during the 1968 Democratic convention in Chicago hurt nominee Hubert Humphrey's chances. In contrast, the 1996 Democratic convention (also in Chicago) more nearly resembled a coronation ceremony.

most popular potential presidents in the country; if they did, Colin Powell would probably have won the Republican presidential nomination in 1996. And the big differences between the delegates of the two parties tend to push the two parties' nominees and issue positions away from each other, in a responsible-party rather than a purely electoral-competition process. Still, the parties do try to appeal to the voters.

Nomination Politics and Democracy What does all this have to do with democratic control of government? Several things. One, as we have indicated, is that the nomination process has some success in coming up with candidates who are personally attractive to voters and who take stands with wide popular appeal, much as electoral competition theories dictate. On the other hand, as the sharp differences between Republican and Democratic convention delegates suggest, Republican and Democratic nominees tend to differ in certain systematic ways, in responsible-party fashion. Party **platforms**—the parties' official statements of their stand on issues—tend to include appeals to average voters but also distinctive appeals to each party's constituencies.

platform A party's statement of its positions on the issues of the day.

Both these tendencies might be considered good for democracy. However, the crucial role of party activists and money givers in selecting candidates means that nominees and their policy stands are chosen partly to appeal to the party elites and financial contributors, rather than to ordinary voters. Thus, neither party's nominee may stand for what ordinary citizens want, the result being voter dissatisfaction (even disgust) and no ideal democratic outcome.

Like most incumbents, President Clinton in 1996 took advantage of the office and campaigned largely in a "nonpolitical fashion." He even avoided formally declaring that he was a candidate for the Democratic Party nomination.

Incumbents and Independents We have been focusing on how outsiders and political challengers try to win party nominations. Things are very different for incumbent presidents seeking reelection, like Bill Clinton in 1996 or George Bush in 1992, or even for an heir-apparent vice-president, like Bush in 1988. These candidates must also enter and win primaries, but they have the machinery of government working for them and, if times are reasonably good, a unified party behind them. They campaign on the job, taking credit for policy successes while discounting failures. Sometimes, they can plead the press of business and conduct a "Rose Garden" campaign without leaving the White House, as even embattled Jimmy Carter did in defeating Edward Kennedy for the Democratic nomination in 1980. Winning renomination is usually easy, except in cases of disaster like the 1968 Vietnam war debacle for Lyndon Johnson (see Chapter 5).

Independent candidates are different, as well, since they do not need to win a major party nomination. In 1992, for example, Ross Perot—emphasizing budget balancing, political reforms, and opposition to international trade agreements—spent many millions of dollars of his own money, qualified for the ballot in all 50 states, and won a substantial 19 percent of the popular vote against Bush and Clinton. Clearly, millions of Americans were dissatisfied with both major party candidates. In 1996, discontent with the Republicans and Democrats and disgust with the flood of unregulated campaign money got Perot 9 percent of the vote.

The Autumn Campaign

Incumbents and challengers alike, having won a party nomination, must face the autumn campaign, which traditionally began in early September (on Labor Day) but now tends to start right after the conventions or even earlier. In 1996, for example, Clinton and Dole were already aiming fire at each other by March and April.

In 1988, a Republican group used the case of Willie Horton, a convicted murderer who raped a woman while on furlough from a Massachusetts prison, to imply that Democratic presidential candidate Michael Dukakis (then Massachusetts governor) was soft on crime.

For the general election, if not before, the candidates set up a campaign organization in each state, sending aides to coordinate backers and local party leaders. Intense money raising continues, and a new round of public financing kicks in. Candidates plan itineraries to make three or four speeches in different media markets each day, concentrating on big states but also touching the whole country.

A new media blitz begins, with many brief spot commercials on television, including "attack" ads like the famous Willie Horton spot in 1988, in which Republicans used photographs of a paroled rapist to raise racial fears and to portray Democratic candidate Michael Dukakis as soft on crime. Political consultants use voter focus groups to identify "hot-button" emotional appeals. Negative advertising has been heavily criticized as simplistic and misleading, but it has often proved effective and is difficult to control or counteract.

Another element of strategy is to get potential supporters registered and to the polls. Organized labor (now under revitalized leadership) often energizes turnout campaigns for the Democrats, and conservative Christian groups do so for the Republicans. As we have noted, low-income and minority citizens have sometimes been ignored by both major parties; the Nation of Islam and various Hispanic groups now show signs of trying to mobilize them. Asian-Americans are also becoming more active.

Informing Voters What kinds of information do voters get in campaigns?

Issues Some of this information concerns issues. In accord with electoral competition theories, both the Republican and the Democratic candidates usually try to appeal to the average voter by taking similar, popular stands on policy, especially foreign policy. Bill Clinton and Bob Dole both stayed close to the center in 1996, as did Clinton and Bush in 1992. On the other hand, as responsible-party theories suggest, Republican and Democratic candidates usually do differ somewhat on a number of issues, such as medical care, federal aid to education, social welfare, civil rights, the environment, and abortion. On these issues, the Democratic candidate tends to take a more liberal stand than the Republican, just as Democratic party identifiers, activists, money givers, and convention delegates tend to be more liberal than their Republican counterparts.

Presidential candidates usually do not say a great deal about specific policies; they tend to be vague and ambiguous, in order to avoid offending voters who disagree with them. No one could object to George Bush's 1988 promises to be an "education president" and an "environmental president," or to Clinton's 1992 promise of "change." What did they mean? Candidates often emphasize symbolic matters that appeal to virtually everyone, such as Bush's invocation of the American flag and the pledge of allegiance.

Past Performance Often, candidates talk about past performance and future goals. The "outs" blame the "ins" for wars, recessions, and other calamities. Perot and Clinton both emphasized the weak state of the economy in 1992, just as Reagan in 1980 had bemoaned the high "misery index" of inflation and unemployment. The "in" party brags about how it has brought peace and prosperity, and it paints a warm picture of a glorious future, without saying exactly how it will come about.

Incumbent presidents, of course, can do things that accurately or inaccurately suggest successful performance. They can try to schedule recessions for off years, pumping up the economy in time for reelection. Or they can make dramatic foreign policy moves just before Election Day, like Nixon's 1972 trips to Russia and China.

Personal Characteristics Most of all, however, voters get a chance to learn about the real or alleged personal characteristics of the candidates. Even when the candidates are talking about something else, they give an impression of either competence or incompetence. Jimmy Carter, for example, emphasized his expertise as a "nuclear engineer," whereas Gerald Ford was haunted by films of him stumbling on airplane ramps. Both Dole and Clinton in 1996 could claim extensive skill and experience in governing.

Candidates also come across as warm or cold. Dwight D. Eisenhower's radiant grin appeared everywhere in 1952 and 1956, as did Reagan's in 1984, but Richard Nixon was perceived as cold and aloof in 1968, despite clever efforts at selling his personality. Warmth was not Dole's strongest selling point in 1996.

Still another dimension of candidates' personality is strength or weakness. George Bush overcame the so-called wimp factor in 1988 with his tough talk about crime and the flag. Merely by surviving many personal attacks in 1992, Clinton appeared strong and resilient.

The sparse and ambiguous treatment of policy issues in campaigns, as well as the emphasis on past performance and personal competence, fits better with ideas about electoral reward and punishment than with responsible parties or issue-oriented electoral competition. Candidate personalities are not irrelevant to the democratic control of government. Obviously, it is useful for voters to pick presidents who possess competence, warmth, and strength. And citizens may be more skillful in judging people than in figuring out complicated policy issues.

On the other hand, perhaps voters can be fooled by dirty tricks or slick advertising that sells presidential candidates' personalities and tears down the opponent. Moreover, the focus on personal imagery may distract attention from policy stands. If candidates who favor unpopular policies are elected on the basis of attractive personal images, democratic control of policymaking is weakened. By the purchase of advertising and the hiring of smart consultants, money may, in effect, overcome the popular will.

Money and Elections

Most observers agree that money creates problems in U.S. elections. The main problem is probably not that too much money is spent, but that the money comes from private sources that may influence policymaking.

The Cost of Presidential Campaigns Presidential campaigns do cost a great deal of money. In 1992, for example, prenomination spending by all candidates totaled $153.2 million; the cost of the conventions was $59.6 million; and general election expenses amounted to $310.5 million. When some miscellaneous expenses are added in, the grand total cost of the 1992 presidential election was around $550 million.[31] In addition, the political parties spend a lot of unregulated (and often unreported) **soft money,** some of which helps presidential candidates.

soft money Expenditures by political parties on general public education, voter registration, and voter mobilization.

There is no question that these expenses, especially of advertising, have increased substantially over the years. In 1984, for example, when the presidential candidates ran 166 minutes of national television ads in the last 10 days of the election, the candidates spent a total of $154 million on spot advertising: *100 times* the amount spent in 1952, when television had just begun.[32] Figures that ignore inflation (as these do) also give the appearance of a huge increase in total presidential election spending: from a mere $30 million in 1960, to $138 million in 1972, $325 million in 1984, and $550 million in 1992.[33]

There is actually room for argument, however, about whether we should think of these sums as a lot of money or not so much. The $550 million in prenomination direct spending on all presidential candidates in 1992, for example, translates to about $2 (two dollars) for each person in the country—hardly a great burden, and very little compared to the cost of advertising commercial products. Moreover, contrary to many people's impression, the trend of rising expenditures does not look so very steep when it is put in terms of constant dollars, adjusted for inflation (see Figure 9.7). Perhaps the main problem is not the absolute amount of expenditures, but the system of raising most of the money from private sources, which discourages some prospective candidates and raises questions about whether money buys political influence.

Where Does the Money Come from? Since 1971, part of the money for presidential election campaigns has come from the federal treasury, paid by the

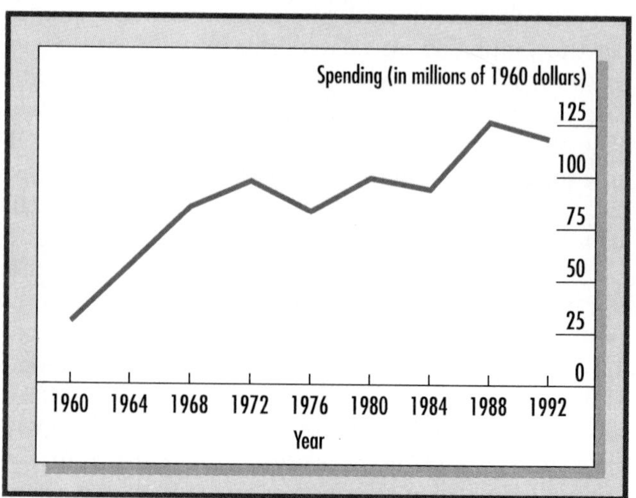

Figure 9.7 ▪ **The Total Cost of Presidential Elections, Adjusted for Inflation**

The cost of presidential elections has risen substantially since 1960, largely as a result of television advertising, but the increase does not look very dramatic in recent years when amounts are adjusted for inflation.

Source: Citizen's Research Foundation, *Financing the 1992 Election,* p. 21.

taxpayers—about $55 million each to Clinton and Bush in 1992. (Perot did not get any that year, though he did in 1996.) Taxpayers can check off a box on their tax returns to authorize a $3 contribution from public funds (not from themselves). The government "matches" small contributions to candidates during the primaries and finances the party nominees who agree to spending limits. Public financing, though not popular with all citizens, has the advantage of eliminating any question of bribery or buying of favors.

However, public money accounted for only about 36 percent of Clinton's and Bush's resources in 1992. The rest had to come from contributions by individuals, businesses, labor unions, or special-interest groups. The same "reforms" of 1974 and later that required candidates to report the sources of their funds and that prohibited any individual from contributing more than $1,000 directly to a candidate also left very large loopholes. For example, political action committees were legalized, even for business and unions, which had previously been prohibited from making political contributions. PACs are now allowed to contribute up to $5,000 per candidate per election; furthermore, people are permitted to contribute $5,000 to each of as many PACs as they like, so that big interests (e.g., major corporations) just have to create multiple PACs or bundle contributions from individual members and employees.

Most important, people and organizations can contribute unlimited amounts of soft money to state and local political parties. And they can spend unlimited amounts of money in support of any candidate as long as the spending is independent of the candidate. The "fat cats" are back, if they ever left; anyone who wants to invest a lot of money in politics can figure out a way to do it (see the Resource Feature).

RESOURCE FEATURE

What Is Allowed in Campaign Finance

The rules concerning campaign money change from time to time; here is how things stood in preparation for the 1996 elections.

- *Individuals'* contributions in one electoral cycle were limited to $1,000 directly to any one candidate, $5,000 to a multicandidate committee, and $20,000 to national party committees; one person's total contributions to these recipients could not exceed $25,000 in a single calendar year. But there were no limitations on contributions to state and local parties, or on "independent" expenditures on behalf of a candidate or a party, or on a person's contributions to his own candidacy.
- *PACs* were limited to a $5,000 contribution per candidate per election, but there was no limit on the number of PACs that an interest group could form or to which an individual could contribute—a big loophole.
- *Party committees'* contributions to candidates could not exceed 2 cents for each member of the U.S. voting-age population. But "party-building" activities, such as registration and turnout drives at the state and local levels, had no limits. Money spent in this way, called *soft money,* has become increasingly important.
- *Candidates* had to report to the Federal Election Commission (FEC) any contributions over $100. Candidates who received public funding (as nearly all except Ross Perot and Steve Forbes have done) had to report all expenditures and identify all contributors, and their expenditures were subject to limits tied to inflation. Presidential primary candidates could receive federal matching funds for any contribution up to $250.

Source: Federal Election Commission regulations, 1995

Much of the election money comes from people who want something from government, such as tax benefits, regulatory relief, or military contracts. For example, Common Cause found that the 249 people who provided $100,000 each (a total of almost $25 million) to the Republican party for 1988 as part of "Team 100" included Eastern Airlines chairman Frank Lorenzo, who early in 1989 received a favorable decision from the president not to mediate Eastern's labor strike. Team 100 also included Ronald Perelman, William Belzberg, Henry Kravis, George Roberts, T. Boone Pickens, Meshulam Riklis, and other prominent figures involved in takeovers and leveraged buyouts, which generally require government approval. Oil companies and their executives gave at least $1.7 million to Team 100. Several of them, including Occidental, were interested in opening up offshore drilling in California and Florida, or in opening the Arctic National Wildlife Refuge for drilling.[34]

Such patterns are not confined to the Republicans. In 1992, Democrat Bill Clinton got much of his crucial early money from Arkansas businesses like Tyson Foods, Murphy Oil, Wal-Mart, and the Stephens family enterprises. For the general election, he received large amounts of money from investment bankers eager for deficit cutting; from banks and multinational corporations interested in the North American Free Trade Agreement; and from hospitals, insurance companies, and pharmaceutical firms fearful of the shape of medical care reform. Robert Rubin and Roger Altman, leading figures in the Goldman, Sachs and Blackstone investment banking firms, ended up with top economic jobs in the Clinton administration.[35]

In 1996, the Center for Public Integrity found that the main candidates for the Republican and Democratic presidential nominations had all relied, throughout their careers, on certain big money backers. Bill Clinton's biggest career funders, for example, included Goldman Sachs, the New York Teachers Union, a Washington law firm, and the Gallo wine family. Bob Dole relied heavily on the Gallos, a New York holding company, the Koch oil firm, and the Archer, Daniel Midlands agribusiness. Pat Buchanan's big money came from several wealthy families and from textile firms that wanted high protective tariffs. Phil Gramm depended on the National Rifle Association, the American Medical Association, Boone Pickens's oil company, and the First City bank corporation of Houston.[36]

Does Money Talk? It is widely believed, though difficult to prove, that those who contribute money often get something back. The point is not that many politicians take outright bribes, or that it is easy to buy elections. Indeed, exchanges between politicians and money givers are complex and varied, sometimes yielding little benefit to contributors; in some cases, these exchanges come closer to extortion by politicians than to bribery of them.

Undeniably, however, cozy relationships do tend to develop between politicians and major money givers. Contributors gain access to, and a friendly hearing from, those whom they help to win office. Also, though scholars differ on the exact extent of the effect, contributors' money certainly does tend to increase the chances of victory of like-minded politicians, who can be counted on to do what the contributors want without any need for pressure. Furthermore, although the candidates with the most money do not always win, those without a substantial amount of money nearly always lose.

It is clear that money givers are different from average citizens. They have special interests of their own. As our discussion of contributors in 1988, 1992, and 1996 indicated, much campaign money comes from large corporations, investment banking firms, wealthy families, labor unions, professional associations (e.g., of doctors, lawyers, or realtors), and issue-oriented groups like the National Rifle Association. The big contributors generally do not represent ordinary workers, consumers or taxpayers, let alone minorities or the poor. Surveys show that the individuals who give money tend to have much higher incomes and more conservative views on economic issues than the average American.[37]

The result is political inequality. Those who are well organized or have a lot of money to spend on politics have a better chance of influencing policy than ordinary citizens do, and they tend to influence it in directions different from those the general public would want. This is one way in which the interest groups described in Chapter 7 can turn their economic power into political power, overcoming the legal equality embodied in the idea of one-person–one-vote. Business interests, with their vast resources, have particular advantages in influencing both parties. The role of money in elections is a major problem for the working of democracy in the United States.

Election Outcomes

After the parties and candidates have presented their campaigns, the voters decide. Presidential elections are held on the first Tuesday after the first Monday in November of each year that is divisible by four; off-year congressional elections come during the other even-numbered years. Exactly how people make their voting decisions affects how well or how poorly elections contribute to the democratic control of government.

How Voters Decide

Years of scholarly research have made it clear that feelings about the parties, the candidates, and the issues have substantial effects on how people vote.[38]

Social Characteristics People's socioeconomic status, religion, and ethnic background are significantly related to how they vote. Since the 1930s, for example, African-Americans, Jews, and lower-income citizens have tended to vote heavily for Democrats, while white Protestants and upper-income Americans have voted mostly for Republicans: in 1992, 82 percent of blacks, but only 39 percent of whites, voted for Clinton against Bush and Perot; 59 percent of people with family incomes under $15,000, but only 36 percent of those with incomes over $75,000, voted for Clinton; and 78 percent of Jews, but only 23 percent of white born-again Christians, voted for Clinton.[39] (See Figure 9.8.)

Similar patterns show up in congressional elections. In 1994, 62 percent of those with family incomes under $15,000 voted for Democratic congressional candidates, while only 45 percent of those with incomes over $100,000 did so. Fully 78 percent of Jews, but only 24 percent of white born-again Christians, voted Democratic; 88 percent of blacks, but only 42 percent of whites, voted for the Democrats.[40]

Party Loyalties To some extent, these social patterns work through long-term attachments to, or identification with, political parties. As we saw in previous chapters, many or most Americans still say they consider themselves Republicans or Democrats. Party loyalties vary among different groups of the population, often because of past or present differences between the parties on

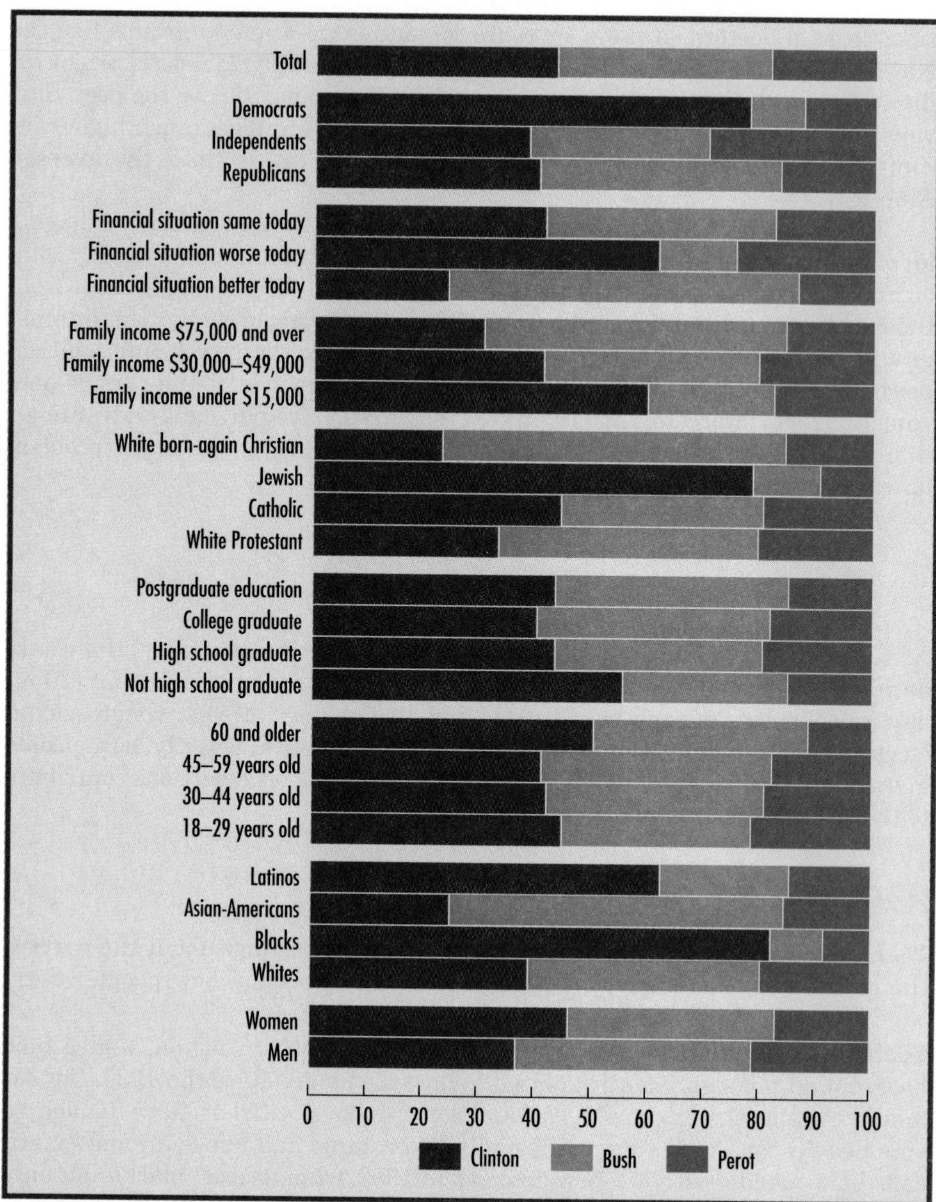

Figure 9.8 ▪ **How Groups Voted in the 1992 Presidential Election**

Minorities and lower-income voters tended to vote for Bill Clinton in the 1992 election, while white Protestants and higher-income people tended to favor Bush.

Source: *New York Times* (November 5, 1992), p. B9.

policy issues, especially economic and social issues. For this reason, party cues help many people vote for candidates who are close to them on the issues.

Party loyalties are good predictors of how people will vote. Those who say they consider themselves Republicans tend to vote for Republican candidates in one election after another, and those who consider themselves Democrats vote for Democratic candidates. This is especially true in congressional elections and in state and local races, where most voters know little more about the candidates than their party labels (in 1994, for example, 90 percent of people who considered themselves Democrats voted for Democratic candidates for the House of Representatives, and 93 percent of Republicans voted for Republicans[41]). But it is also true of presidential elections. In every election since 1952, 90 percent or more of self-identified "strong" Republicans have voted for the Republican candidate—except in 1992, when 86 percent did so. In all those elections (except for 1972, when many abandoned McGovern), 84 percent or more of "strong" Democrats voted for the Democratic candidate—as 93 percent did in 1992.[42]

Because party loyalties are so important, some scholars speak of a **normal vote:** a proportion of the votes that each party would win if only party affected voting decisions and if independents split evenly. Since party loyalties are rather stable over time (changing in large numbers only during **realignment** periods, such as those of 1896 or 1932; see Chapter 8), the normal vote stays about the same from one election to another. If nothing else were going on, the majority party—for example, the Democrats between 1932 and 1992—would win every election. In fact, this has been very nearly true of congressional elections, in which the Democrats nearly always won majorities in the House of Representatives and the Senate during this period.

normal vote The proportion of the votes that each party would win if party identification and nothing else affected voting decisions.

But the results of presidential elections indicate that something else has been going on. In fact, of the 11 presidential elections from 1952 to 1992, the Democrats won only 4, or 37 percent! This is hardly an imposing winning streak for the majority party. Many recent presidential elections have been **deviating elections,** in which the minority party has won without a realignment of party loyalties.

deviating elections Elections in which the party with only a minority of identifiers wins.

We know part of the reason: party loyalties have been weakening. Even though strong party identifiers have continued to vote for their party, there have been fewer strong party identifiers since about 1968; many people consider themselves independents and just lean toward one party.

Candidates Another reason why presidential election outcomes have not simply reflected the party balance, and why the Democrats have lost so often, is that voters pay a lot of attention to their perceptions of the personal characteristics of candidates. They vote heavily for candidates who have experience, appear strong and decisive, and seem to display personal warmth. The Republican candidate in 1952 and 1956, Dwight D. Eisenhower, had a tremendous advantage in these respects over his Democratic opponent, Adlai Stevenson;[43] so did the Republican Richard Nixon over George McGovern in 1972, and the Republicans Ronald Reagan over Walter Mondale in 1984 and George Bush over Michael Dukakis in 1988. Only in 1964 did the Democratic candidate (Lyndon Johnson) appeal to voters substantially more than the Republican candidate (Barry Goldwater). In elections between 1952 and 1972, the contrast between Republican and Democratic candidates typically gained the Republicans 4 or 5 percentage points—just enough to overcome the Democrats' advantage in the normal vote.

Issues Voters also pay attention to issues, even beyond the party-cleavage issues that are reflected in party loyalties. Sometimes, this means choosing between different policy proposals for the future, such as Reagan's 1980 promises to cut back federal government activity or Clinton's 1992 pledges of jobs and a middle-class tax cut. More often, however, issue voting has meant **retrospective voting,** that is, making judgments about the past, especially on major questions about war or peace and the state of the economy. The voters tend to

retrospective voting Voting on the basis of the past performance of a government.

Dwight Eisenhower, popularly known as "Ike," was one of the most popular American politicians of the twentieth century.

reward the incumbent party for what they see as good times and to punish it for what they see as bad times.[44]

Foreign Policy Foreign policy can be important. Bitter disillusionment over the Korean War hurt the Democrats in 1952, just as the Vietnam War cost them in 1968, and unhappiness about American hostages in Iran and the Soviet intervention in Afghanistan hurt Jimmy Carter in 1980. During nearly all

of the last 45 or 50 years, in fact, Republican candidates have been seen as better at providing foreign policy strength and at keeping us out of war.

The Economy The economy also matters a great deal. After severe economic downturns, Americans tend to vote the incumbent party out of office, as they did the Republicans during the Great Depression in 1932. Since that time, the Democrats have generally been seen as the party of prosperity. This advantage disappeared for a while, after a combined onslaught of inflation and recession hurt Democrat Jimmy Carter in the 1980 election. But in 1992, the electorate punished Republican George Bush for the poor state of the economy; he received only 38 percent of the popular vote against Clinton and Perot. The economic pressures brought by international competition and U.S. corporate downsizing threaten to cause electoral punishment of incumbents, whichever party they belong to, for some time to come.

Social Issues and the Environment In recent years, new issues have also become important to voters. These include deficit cutting, free trade, and the role of money in politics, which energized Perot's candidacies. They also include concern about the environment, which hurt the Republicans in 1996, and conflicting views about crime, pornography, and especially abortion.

The Electoral College

The outcome of presidential elections does not purely reflect the number of popular votes cast for each candidate; it depends on the votes in the electoral college.

When American voters think they are voting for a presidential candidate whose name appears on the ballot, they are actually voting for a slate of **electors**—equal in number to the number of U.S. senators and representatives from their state—who have promised to support the candidate. (Very rarely have electors reneged on their promises and cast ballots for someone else.) Nearly all states now have **winner-take-all** systems, which select the entire slate of electors for the candidate who won the most popular votes; Maine and Nebraska, in slight variations, choose electors by congressional district rather than statewide.

electors Those who are elected in the states to formally choose the U.S. president.

winner-take-all An electoral system in which the party or candidate winning the most votes gets all the representatives.

The whole "college" of electors from different states never actually meets; instead, the electors meet in their respective states and send to Washington, D.C., lists of how they have voted (see the Twelfth Amendment to the Constitution). If a candidate gets a majority of all the electoral votes in the country, he is elected president. Never since 1824 has it been necessary to resort to the odd constitutional provisions that apply when no one gets a majority of electoral votes: then, the House of Representatives chooses among the top three candidates, by majority vote among state delegations.

For most practical purposes, this peculiar electoral college system works about the same way as if Americans chose their presidents by direct popular vote. The old idea that electors would exercise their independent judgments is long gone. But the system does have certain consequences:

1. *Magnifying the popular support of winners.* A candidate who wins in many states, by a narrow margin in each, can win a "landslide" in the electoral college. In 1992, for example, Bill Clinton's bare 43 percent of the popular vote (to George Bush's 38 percent) translated into 370 electoral votes, to Bush's 168.

plurality More votes than other candidates, but not necessarily a majority.

Ordinarily, this magnification just adds legitimacy to the democratic choice, especially when the winner has only a **plurality** of the popular vote, that is, more than anybody else but less than a majority of all votes. Many of our presidents have been elected with less than 50 percent of the popular vote—most recently, Clinton, Richard Nixon (1968), John Kennedy (1960), and Harry Truman (1948).

2. *Letting the less popular candidate win.* In theory, however, a president could be elected who had *fewer* votes than an opponent, if those votes happened to produce narrow margins in many states. Such an undemocratic result actually occurred in 1876, when Rutherford Hayes defeated Samuel Tilden, and in 1888, when Benjamin Harrison beat the more popular Grover Cleveland. Several early nineteenth-century presidents were probably chosen with only small fractions of the popular vote, though we cannot be sure because some of the statistics are unreliable. Most notably, in 1824 John Quincy Adams defeated the very popular Andrew Jackson in the House of Representatives.

3. *Discouraging third parties.* Our constitutional arrangements for a single president and single-member congressional districts (rather than proportional representation) already discourage third parties; if candidates cannot win a plurality, they get nothing. The electoral college adds symbolically to this discouragement: a third party with substantial support may get no electoral votes at all, if its support is scattered among many states. In 1992, for example, Ross Perot's impressive 19 percent of the popular vote translated into *zero* electoral votes, because he failed to win a plurality in any state.

Those who would like to abolish the electoral college point to its narrowing of choices and the possibility of undemocratic outcomes. Those who like it claim that it discourages fraud by limiting the votes that any one state can cast, that the two-party system it encourages is good, and that the added legitimacy of electoral college "landslides" is helpful—or at least harmless.

Do Elections Matter?

When we ask whether elections make a difference, we are likely to look for dramatic cases in which big issues were at stake between the two parties and the election ushered in a new era of policymaking and party realignment. Such cases exist, but elections matter in other ways as well.

Party Realignments Realigning elections include the Republican wins of 1860 (leading to the Civil War and the end of slavery) and 1896 (defeating agrarian radicals and consolidating the forces of industrialization) and the Democratic victory of 1932, which inaugurated the New Deal and many of our contemporary social welfare programs. The 1980 Reagan victory, as well as the 1994 congressional Republican win, had major policy effects, though they did not bring a large-scale realignment of party loyalties.

Such decisive elections are rare, however; it does not usually make a dramatic difference whether the Republicans or the Democrats win. Still, even when the final choice is less critical, elections do matter in several different ways related to the democratic control of government.

Democratic Control In terms of the responsible-party idea, for example, the fact that Republicans tend to be more conservative than Democrats on a number of economic and social issues provides voters with a measure of democratic control by enabling them to detect differences and make choices. Alternatively, through electoral punishment, voters can exercise control by reelecting successful incumbents and throwing failures out of office, thus making incumbents think ahead. Finally, electoral competition forces the parties to compete by nominating centrist candidates and by taking similar issue stands close to what most Americans want. This, in fact, may be the chief way in which citizens' policy preferences affect what their government does.

Clearly, then, U.S. elections help make the public's voice heard, but they do not bring about perfect democracy. Two key reasons are the limited and biased participation of citizens and the crucial effects of money and activists on election outcomes. Uneven participation and the role of money and activists both impair political equality by giving some people more political influence than others.

In later chapters, we will see how these features of elections carry through into the post-election political process to allow various people and organizations other than the general public—especially interest groups, corporations, and elite party coalitions—to exert influence on policymaking. Elections serve as a major conduit by which many people and institutions influence the governmental officials who make policy.

Summary

Elections are the most important means by which citizens can exert democratic control over their government. Voters can choose *responsible parties* to carry out their distinctive programs. *Electoral competition* forces vote-seeking parties and candidates to appeal to the center of public opinion. *Electoral reward and punishment* give officials incentives to carry out policies that will win public approval. However, none of these processes guarantees a perfectly democratic outcome.

Political participation can be conventional (voting, helping in campaigns, and contacting officials) or unconventional (protesting or demonstrating). The right to vote, originally quite limited, was expanded in various historical surges to include nearly all adults and to apply to most major offices. Turnout has declined, however, and in recent years, only about half the eligible voters have cast ballots for the presidency.

Candidates for president start by testing the waters, raising money, and forming campaign organizations; in a series of state primaries and caucuses, they seek delegates to the national nominating conventions, which generally choose a clear front-runner or the incumbent president. During the campaign, the candidates are generally vague about issues: they build personal images and emphasize past performance.

About one-third of the cost of presidential campaigns is paid from public funds; the rest of the money comes from individuals and organizations, many of which seek self-benefiting policies. Contributions probably subvert democracy by leading to a degree of political inequality.

Voters' decisions depend heavily on party loyalties, the personal characteristics of the candidates, and the issues, especially the state of the economy and of U.S. foreign policy. After recessions and unsuccessful wars, the incumbent party generally loses. The electoral college does not always accurately reflect popular votes. Elections "matter" not only when there is a clear choice, but also when electoral reward or punishment occurs, or when electoral competition forces both parties to take similar, popular stands.

Suggested Readings

Anonymous. *Primary Colors: A Novel of Politics.* New York: Random House, 1996.
Thinly disguised as fiction, a lively and sometimes ribald account of Bill Clinton's campaign for the 1992 Democratic presidential nomination.

Burnham, Walter Dean. *Critical Elections and the Mainsprings of American Politics.* New York: Norton, 1970.
The classic discussion of realigning elections and historical patterns in U.S. voting behavior.

Ferguson, Thomas. *Golden Rule.* Chicago: University of Chicago Press, 1995.
A highly critical account of the role of money in recent elections. See also Thomas Ferguson and Joel Rogers. Right Turn: The Decline of the Democrats and the Future of American Politics. *New York: Farrar, Straus & Giroux, 1986.*

Fiorina, Morris. *Retrospective Voting in American National Elections.* Cambridge: Harvard University Press, 1981.
A sophisticated statistical analysis of voting on the basis of party loyalty and past- and future-oriented issues.

Polsby, Nelson. *Presidential Elections,* 9th ed. New York: Free Press, 1996.
A thorough textbook on the nomination process, campaigning, and voting.

Sidney Verba, Kay Lehman Schlozman, and Henry E. Brady. *Voice and Equality: Civic Volunteerism in American Politics.* Cambridge: Harvard University Press, 1995.
A comprehensive analysis of political participation and its relation to democratic theory.

Internet Sources

Allpolitics http://allpolitics.com/
Election news and features, public opinion polls on candidates and issues, and election quizzes from CNN and Time *magazine.*

Campaign Central http://www.clark.net/central/
Weekly updates on national and state campaigns, top political stories of the day, and a directory of campaign consultants.

Campaign96 http://politicsUSA.com/PoliticsUSA/campaign96/
Candidate profiles, opinion polls, candidate appearance schedules, and text of speeches by the leading national candidates.

Election America http://electionamerica.com/
Information on national and state candidates; campaign news.

HumanServe http://www.essential.org/human_serve/
Home page for the main citizen watchdog for the National Voter Registration Act of 1993 (the Motor Voter Act); reports, documents, commentary, and statistics on registration under the act.

Pathfinder, Campaign http://pathfinder.com/@@7oPdTUFjQWAAQD5w/pathfinder/politics/1999
Everything for the campaign junkie in one location: for example, materials from major and minor political parties, profiles of the candidates, the latest polling and election results, news and features on the major campaigns, and candidate position papers.

PoliticsNow http://www.politicsnow.com/
Up-to-the-minute campaign news and features from ABC News, The National Journal, The LA Times, Newsweek *magazine, and the* Washington Post.

Notes

1. For further discussion, see Benjamin I. Page, *Choices and Echoes in Presidential Elections: Rational Man and Electoral Democracy* (Chicago: University of Chicago Press, 1978), Chap. 2; Robert A. Dahl, *Democracy and Its Critics* (New Haven: Yale University Press, 1989).
2. See Austin Ranney, *The Doctrine of Responsible Party Government: Its Origins and Present State* (Urbana: University of Illinois Press, 1962); E. E. Schattschneider, *Party Government* (New York: Holt, Rinehart & Winston, 1942).
3. Anthony Downs, *An Economic Theory of Democracy* (New York: Harper & Row, 1957); Otto Davis, Melvin Hinich, and Peter Ordeshook, "An Expository Development of a Mathematical Model of the Electoral Process," *American Political Science Review,* Vol. 64 (June 1970), pp. 426–448.
4. See V. O. Key, Jr., *Public Opinion and American Democracy* (New York: Knopf, 1961); Morris P. Fiorina, *Retrospective Voting in American National Elections* (Cambridge: Harvard University Press, 1981).
5. Neil Spitzer, "The First Election," *The Atlantic,* Vol. 262, No. 5 (November 1988), pp. 18–20.
6. Chilton Williamson, *American Suffrage* (Princeton, NJ: Princeton University Press, 1960), pp. 223, 241, 260. More precisely, there was universal suffrage for white male taxpayers.
7. Dietrich Rueschemeyer, Evelyne Huber Stephens, and John D. Stephens, *Capitalist Development and Democracy* (Chicago: University of Chicago Press, 1992), Chap. 4.
8. See John Hope Franklin, *From Slavery to Freedom* (New York: Knopf, 1967); Leon Litwack, *North of Slavery* (Chicago: University of Chicago Press, 1961).
9. Walter Dean Burnham, "The Turnout Problem," in James Reichley, ed., *Elections American Style* (Washington, DC: Brookings Institution, 1987), pp. 113–114.
10. *New York Times* (November 21, 1988), p. B16.
11. Walter Dean Burnham, "The System of 1896," in Paul Kleppner et al., *The Evolution of American Electoral Systems* (Westport, CT: Greenwood Press, 1981), p. 148.
12. Data analyzed by the authors from 1994 National Election Study.
13. Paul R. Abramson and John H. Aldrich, "The Decline of Electoral Participation in America," *American Political Science Review,* Vol. 76 (September 1982), pp. 502–521.
14. Walter Dean Burnham, "The Class Gap," *New Republic,* Vol. 198 (May 9, 1988), pp. 30–34.
15. Russell Dalton, *Citizen Politics in Western Democracies* (Chatham, NJ: Chatham House, 1988), p. 42.
16. *Public Perspective* (March–April, 1994), p. 85.
17. Sidney Verba, Kay Lehman Schlozman, and Henry E. Brady, *Voice and Equality: Civic Volunteerism in American Politics* (Cambridge: Harvard University Press, 1995), pp. 51, 56.
18. Verba et al., *Voice and Equality,* Chap. 7; Sidney Verba and Norman H. Nie, *Participation in America* (New York: Harper & Row, 1972).
19. 1994 National Election Study.

20. Raymond E. Wolfinger and Steven J. Rosenstone, *Who Votes?* (New Haven: Yale University Press, 1980).

21. Susan A. MacManus, *Young v. Old* (Boulder, CO: Westview Press, 1996), Chap. 2.

22. E. J. Dionne, "If Nonvoters Had Voted: Same Winner, but Bigger," *New York Times* (November 21, 1988), p. B16.

23. Bernard R. Berelson, Paul F. Lazarsfeld, and William N. McPhee, *Voting* (Chicago: University of Chicago Press, 1954).

24. 1994 National Election Study.

25. Sidney Verba, Kay Lehman Schlozman, Henry Brady, and Norman H. Nie, "Citizen Activity: Who Participates? What Do They Say?" *American Political Science Review,* Vol. 87 (June 1993), pp. 303–318.

26. See John Stephens, *The Transition from Capitalism to Socialism* (London: Macmillan, 1979).

27. Harold Stanley and Richard Niemi, *Vital Statistics on American Politics* (Washington, DC: Congressional Quarterly Press, 1988), p. 213; updated.

28. Harold Stanley and Richard G. Niemi, *Vital Statistics on American Politics* (Washington, DC: Congressional Quarterly Press, 1991), pp. 53–55.

29. Stephen J. Wayne, *The Road to the White House 1992* (New York: St. Martin's Press, 1992).

30. Larry Bartels, *Presidential Primaries and the Dynamics of Public Choice* (Princeton: Princeton University Press, 1988); John Aldrich, *Before the Convention* (Chicago: University of Chicago Press, 1980).

31. Herbert E. Alexander and Anthony Corrado, *Financing the 1992 Election* (New York: M. E. Sharpe, 1995), p. 20.

32. Sig Mickelson, *Whistle Stop to Sound Bite* (New York: Praeger, 1989), p. 155.

33. Alexander and Corrado, *Financing,* p. 21.

34. Jean Cobb and Jeffrey Denny, "The Fat-Cat Club: Membership Has Its Privileges," *Washington Post National Weekly Edition* (April 28, 1990), p. 25.

35. Thomas Ferguson, *Golden Rule* (Chicago: University of Chicago Press, 1995), Chap. 6.

36. Jane Fritsch, "Who's Who of Money Moguls in '96 Race," *New York Times* (January 12, 1996), p. A7; Charles Lewis and the Center for Public Integrity, *The Buying of the President* (New York: Avon Books, 1996).

37. See Verba et al., *Voice and Equality.*

38. Efforts to sort out their relative contributions include Benjamin I. Page and Calvin Jones, "Reciprocal Effects of Policy Preferences, Party Loyalties, and the Vote," *American Political Science Review,* Vol. 73 (December 1979), pp. 1071–1089, and Gregory B. Markus and Philip E. Converse, "A Dynamic Simultaneous Equation Model of Public Choice," *American Political Science Review,* Vol. 73 (December 1979), pp. 1066–1070.

39. Exit poll, Voter Research and Surveys, reported in the *New York Times* (November 5, 1992), p. B9.

40. "Portrait of the Electorate," *New York Times* (November 13, 1994), p. 15.

41. Ibid.

42. Herbert B. Asher, *Presidential Elections and American Politics: Voters, Candidates, and Campaigns Since 1952,* 4th ed. (Chicago: Dorsey, 1988), pp. 88–89, updated with NES data.

43. Donald E. Stokes, "Some Dynamic Elements of Contests for the Presidency," *American Political Science Review,* Vol. 60 (March 1966), pp. 19–28.

44. Fiorina, *Retrospective Voting.*

CHAPTER 10

Social Movements

IN THIS CHAPTER

- ★ Why social movements happen
- ★ How social movements fit in a democratic society
- ★ What social movements do in politics
- ★ How social movements influence what government does

Christian Conservatives Reshape the Republican Party

The religious right hasn't even touched the tip of the iceberg compared to what the religious left has done. Now it's our turn.

PARTICIPANT AT A CHRISTIAN COALITION ORGANIZATION MEETING, 1994[1]

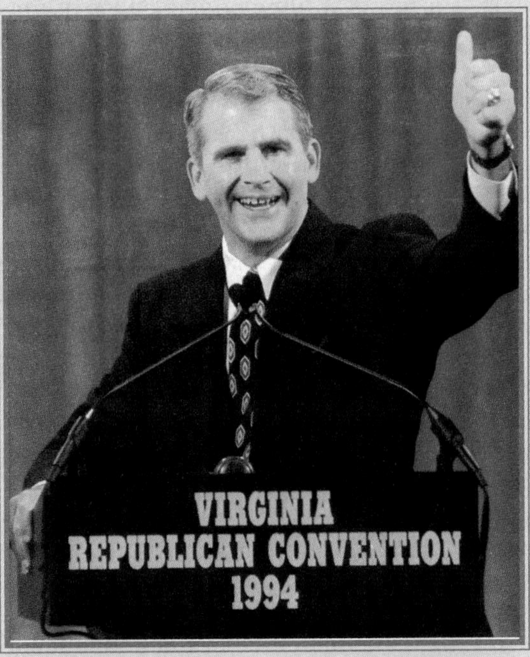

Fourteen thousand delegates packed the convention hall in Richmond, Virginia. They were gathered to select the Republican candidate for the U.S. Senate to run against Democrat Charles Robb in the 1994 elections. The convention opened with a dramatic flourish. The lights dimmed, and a giant screen began to show pictures of political figures bound to arouse the ire of the party faithful. Each was enthusiastically booed in turn: first Jane Fonda, then Jesse Jackson, then Dan Rather, and then, finally, President Bill Clinton. And then the screen began to show a film about the person almost all of them had come to nominate: Oliver North. In the film, the former marine talked of patriotism, bravery, resolve, and fidelity, but most important, about family and traditional religious values. At the film's conclusion, the hall erupted into cheers of "Ollie, Ollie," and North himself appeared onstage highlighted by a single spotlight, prepared to claim his prize. The nomination was his for the asking; the outcome was never in doubt.[2]

When the prospect of North's nomination first surfaced, mainstream Republican party leaders were horrified. Here was a candidate, after all, who had been deeply implicated in the Iran-Contra affair and who had been convicted of lying to Congress (though his conviction was eventually overturned on a technicality) running for membership in the very body to which he had lied and for which he had poured out his contempt. Now he might be running under the party label. The denunciations and warnings began to sound. Ronald Reagan let it be known that he was unhappy with the prospect of a North nomination. Conservative former attorney general Edwin Meese joined the naysayers. Former defense secretary Casper Weinberger, conservative jurist Robert Bork, and columnist George Will added their concerned voices. John Warner, the Republican senator from Virginia, was especially incensed by the North candidacy, and most Republican party officials in the state expressed their worries. None of it mattered; a vast majority of the 14,000 delegates at the convention had been committed to North before they arrived in Richmond on June 3.

Though North would eventually lose in the general election in November to Democrat Robb (and became one of the very few Republican casualties in the 1994 national elections), his nomination was a clear indication that a new day was dawning in the GOP, one in which the influence of a vigorous Christian conservative movement would play a very influential role. Christian conservatives, working caucus by caucus, with dedicated volunteers and abundant resources, had gradually taken over the grassroots organizational structure of the Republican party in Virginia. In 1994, they achieved similar success in Texas, Minnesota, Oregon, Iowa, Washington, and South Carolina. In Iowa, for instance, Christian conservatives won control of the Republican party's central committee, ousted party moderates, and wrote a platform which included a provision requiring that public schools teach "creationism" and eliminate all materials that might support or acknowledge lesbian or gay lifestyles. In Minnesota, Christian conservatives persuaded the Republican state convention not to renominate its own incumbent governor and to select, instead, an antiabortion activist.

A number of factors seem to have played a role in the formation and growth of the Christian conservative movement, which has come to play such an important role in American politics. Like all social movements, it had to start with a group of

Americans who shared a strong sense of grievance. For many conservative religious Americans, a number of changes in American life since the early 1970s seemed to threaten the values they held most dear, their expectations about what kind of society they wanted for their children and themselves, and their expectations about the appropriate role of government in these matters. What most worried them was the rise in the number of abortions (legitimized by the Supreme Court decision *Roe v. Wade* in 1973), the challenge of gay and lesbian rights to what they considered traditional family values, and the banning of prayer in the public schools. To many, the moral foundations of the nation were crumbling, with devastating implications for crime, drug use, and family stability. Their ire eventually targeted the Democrats, who seemed to them responsible for most of the policies to which they objected.

Concerned religious conservatives were drawn into political activity by a range of organizations tied to evangelical churches. When the Internal Revenue Service denied tax-exempt status to Christian academies (private schools) in 1978 (during the Democratic administration of Jimmy Carter) because their policies created segregated schools, an element of the clergy began to organize and exhort their congregations to political action against the Democrats. Out of these first stirrings came the Moral Majority, led by Jerry Falwell, and the Religious Roundtable, which endorsed Ronald Reagan for the presidency in 1980.

In 1992, TV evangelist Pat Robertson made a bid for the Republican presidential nomination. Though he lost, his candidacy drew many Christian conservatives into politics for the first time. His campaign also created the organizational infrastructure for a sophisticated political operation, as well as a treasury to match. After his failed bid, he formed an organization called the Christian Coalition, selected a young and highly skilled political operative, Ralph Reed, as its executive director, and turned over his 2-million-person mailing list to Reed. Unlike other conservative religious organizations, the Christian Coalition did not focus its energies on television and radio shows. It concentrated instead on raising money for political campaigns, energizing its **grassroots** supporters, and showing them how to gain control of the nomination and convention machinery of the Republican party in the states. The rest, as they say, is history.

grassroots Referring to constituents, voters, or the rank and file of a party.

The Christian Coalition is only one organization—though the most powerful one, to be sure—in a large and influential conservative religious movement in the United States that includes "schools, institutes, newspapers, magazines, radio and television stations, thousands of politically mobilized churches."[3] It is a movement that is almost unanimously hostile to the Democratic party and its candidates, and that is the most vocal and active and largest part of the Republican party electoral base. The Christian Coalition has become a central player in the dramatic reorientation of American public policy in the mid–1990s. Seasoned political observers give credit to the Christian Coalition, for instance, for helping to elect a substantial majority of the new Republican members of Congress in the 1994 elections, enabling the party to take control of both houses of Congress for the first time in 40 years.

Though social movements with this kind of clout are the exception rather than the rule in American politics, others also have played an important role in American political life. This chapter is about what social movements are, how and why they form, what tactics they use, and how they affect American political life and what government does. Social movements receive less attention from political scientists than do elections, parties, and interest groups, but they are important. Many social movements have influenced what government does. This chapter is also about the role social movements play in the struggle for democracy.

What Are Social Movements?

Social movements are loosely organized collections of people and organizations who act over time, outside established institutions, to promote or resist social change. The Christian conservative movement described in the chapter opening story, for instance, is a broad collection of people, churches, and other organizations that have come together to resist the **secularization** of American society and to promote religious values in American life. The sole aim of social movements is not to elect their own members to public office, like political parties, though they may sometimes try to do so. Their sole aim, like that of interest groups, is not to lobby political decision makers, though they may sometimes try to do this as well. What sets social movements apart from parties and interest groups is their focus on broad, societywide issues and trends and their tendency to act outside the normal channels of government and politics, using unconventional and often disruptive tactics.[4]

secularization The spread of nonreligious values and outlooks.

This general definition of social movements requires further elaboration if we are to understand their role in American politics. Here, we highlight some important things to know about them.

Social Movements Are Generally the Political Instruments of Political Outsiders

Movements often help those who are outside the mainstream to gain a hearing from the public and from political decision makers. Insiders don't need social movements; they can rely, instead, on interest groups, political action committees (PACs), lobbyists, campaign contributions, and the like to have their voices heard.

Social Movements Are Mass Grassroots Phenomena

Since outsiders and excluded groups often lack the financial and political resources of insiders, they must take advantage of what they have: numbers, energy, and commitment. In order to gain attention, moreover, social movements often use unconventional tactics, such as demonstrations and sit-ins. Officials and citizens almost always complain that social movements are ill-mannered and disruptive. For social movements, that is precisely the point.

Social Movements Are Populated by Those with a Shared Sense of Grievance

People would not take on the considerable risks involved in joining others in a social movement unless they felt a strong, shared sense of grievance against the status quo and a desire to bring about social change. Social movements tend to form when a significant number of people come to define their own troubles and problems not in personal terms, but in more general social terms (the belief that there is a common cause of all of their troubles), and when they believe that the government can be moved to take action on their behalf. Because this is a rare combination, social movements are very difficult to organize and sustain.

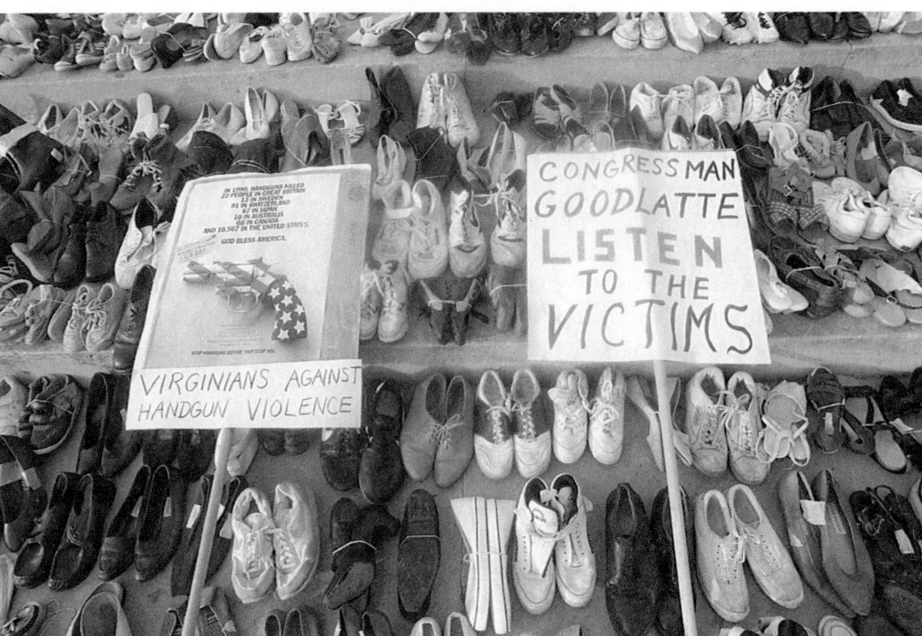

Social movements are generally made up of political and/or social outsiders with a shared sense of grievance. In order to gain the support of people who do not share their grievances, activists rely on dramatic actions. Symbolic gestures such as these shoes of people killed by hand guns are an effective way of gaining the attention of those not directly affected by gun violence, and of alerting them to the great number of people who are.

Major Social Movements in the United States

Many social movements have left their mark on American political life and have shaped what government does in the United States. Here, we describe some of the most important.

- The *abolitionists* aimed to end slavery in the United States. They were active in the northern states in the three decades before the outbreak of the Civil War. Their harsh condemnation of the slave system helped bring on the war that ended slavery.
- The *anti–Vietnam War* movement was active in the United States in the late 1960s and early 1970s. Its aim was to end the war in Vietnam. It used a wide variety of tactics in this effort, from mass demonstrations to voting registration and civil disobedience. Scholars are divided over the issue of whether the movement shortened or prolonged the war.
- The *civil rights* movement began in the late 1950s, reached the peak of its activity in the mid–1960s, and gradually lost steam after that. The movement is one of the most influential on record, having pressed successfully for the end of formal segregation in the South and discriminatory practices across the nation (see Chapter 1). The main weapons of the movement were civil disobedience and mass demonstrations.
- The *environmental* movement has been active in the United States since the early 1970s. Its aim has been to encourage government regu-

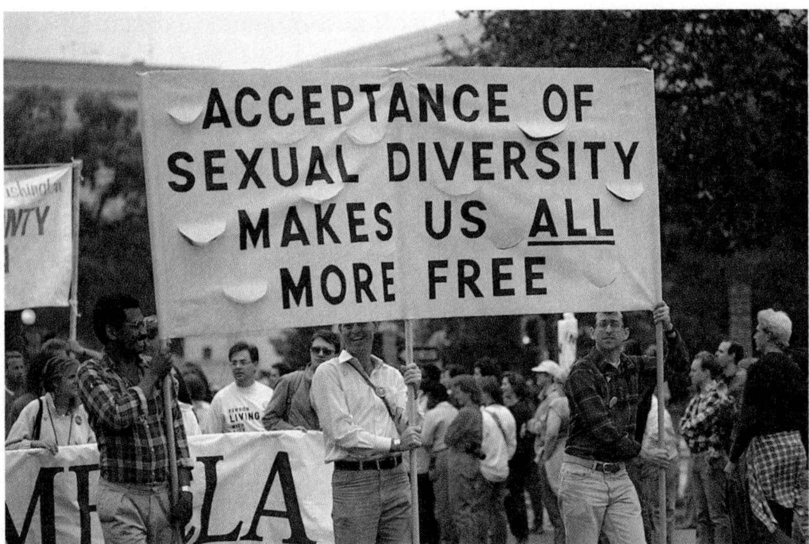

Demonstrators march in Washington, D.C., to demand government action to combat the AIDS epidemic. New social problems often generate new social movements.

lation of damaging environmental practices and to raise the environmental sympathies of the public. While the vitality of the movement has waxed and waned over the years, the strongly proenvironmental regulation views of the public suggest that it has been unusually successful. Though disruptive tactics have sometimes been used, the movement has depended more on legal challenges to business practices and the creation of lobbying organizations.

- The *gay and lesbian* movement began in earnest in the late 1960s. Its aim was to gain the same civil rights protections under the law enjoyed by African-Americans and other minority groups, and to gain respect from the public. Ranging from patient lobbying and voting to mass demonstrations, the movement's efforts have been partially successful but have also sparked strong counterattacks by groups like the Christian Coalition that are opposed to their objectives.

- The *labor* movement represents efforts by working people over the years to protect jobs, ensure decent wages and benefits, and guarantee safe and wholesome workplaces. The periods of greatest militancy—when working people took to the streets and the factory floors to demand recognition of their unions—were in the 1880s, the 1890s, and the 1930s. The labor movement eventually forced the federal government to recognize the right of working people to form labor unions to represent them in negotiations with management.

- A *peace* movement in one form or another has been around since the time of World War I, when it tried to encourage resistance to the draft. Its strategy of encouraging Americans to refuse service on religious or moral grounds—known as *conscientious objection*—was carried over to World War II, the Korean War, and the Vietnam War. The movement also focused on the threat of nuclear war, taking shape as "ban-the-bomb" protests in the 1950s, "nuclear-freeze" demonstrations in the 1980s, and attempts in the 1980s to force local governments to declare their localities "nuclear-free zones," where no nuclear weapons could be manufactured or stored.

- The *Populist* movement was made up of disaffected farmers of the American South and West in the 1880s and 1890s who were angry with business practices and developments in the American economy that were adversely affecting them. Their aim was to force public ownership or regulation of the banks, grain storage companies, and the railroads. For a short time, they were quite successful, winning control of several state legislatures, sending members to Congress, helping to nominate William Jennings Bryan as the Democratic candidate for president in 1896, and forcing the federal regulation of corporations (e.g., in the Interstate Commerce Commission Act).
- *Religious Fundamentalist* movements have occurred at several different moments in American history and have been very influential. These movements have brought together strongly religious people trying to infuse American society and public policies with their values. These movements were particularly vital during the decades preceding the American Revolution and the Civil War; in the late nineteenth and early twentieth centuries, when religious revivals swept across the country; and in our own day. The contemporary movement of Christian conservatives falls within this tradition and has become very important in American politics, especially on the issue of abortion.
- The Prolife (anti-abortion) movement is part of the current larger religious Fundamentalist movement. Its main objective is to end the practice of abortion in the United States.
- The *women's suffrage* movement, active in the late nineteenth and early twentieth centuries, had a limited objective: to win for women the right to vote. The movement used a wide variety of tactics, including civil disobedience, mass demonstrations, and hunger strikes, as well as quiet lobbying. It won its objective when the Nineteenth Amendment to the Constitution was ratified in 1920.
- The *women's* movement has been important in American life since the late 1960s. Its aim has been to win civil rights protections for women and to broaden the participation of women in all aspects of American society, economy, and politics. Though it did not win one of its main objectives—passage of the Equal Rights Amendment to the U.S. Constitution—the broad advance of women on virtually all fronts in the United States attests to its overall effectiveness.

Where Social Movements May Fit in a Majoritarian Democracy

At first glance, social movements do not seem to fit very well in a democracy. First, social movements usually start out as minority phenomena, whereas democracy requires majority rule. Second, social movements often use disruptive tactics, when it seems that many channels already exist (e.g., voting, petitioning and writing to policymakers, and writing letters to newspapers) for people to express their grievances. In this section, we talk about how social movements can (and often do) help make American politics more democratic.

Encouraging Participation

Social movements may increase the level of popular involvement and interest in politics. In one sense, this is true simply by definition: Social movements are the instruments of outsiders. Thus, the civil rights movement encouraged the involvement of southern African-Americans who had long been barred from the political life of their communities. The Christian conservative movement spurred the political involvement of previously politically apathetic evangelicals.

Social movements also encourage popular participation by dramatizing and bringing to public attention a range of issues that have been ignored or have been dealt with behind closed doors. The reason is that their tactics make these movements' members highly visible. They offer irresistible fare for the television camera. This ability to make politics more visible—called broadening the **scope of conflict**[5] by political scientist E. E. Schattschneider—makes politics the province of the many rather than the few.

scope of conflict Referring to the number of groups involved in a political conflict; few groups mean a narrow scope of conflict, and many groups mean a wide scope of conflict.

Overcoming Political Inequality

Social movements also sometimes allow those without substantial resources to enter the game of politics. Many social movements are made up of people who do not have access to the money, time, contacts, or organizational resources that fuel normal politics.[6] The unsettling tactics associated with such **mass mobilizations** may serve as a substitute for the missing political resources of such groups and thus help increase political equality.

mass mobilization The process of involving large numbers of people in a social movement.

Fashioning New Majorities

Social movements may also help fashion new majorities in society. Social movements are the province of minorities, of course, and in a democracy, minorities should have their way only if they can convince enough of their fellow citizens that what they want is reasonable. Before the 1930s, for instance, only a minority of Americans may have been convinced that labor unions were a good idea. The **Great Depression** and a vigorous, militant labor movement changed the opinion climate in the nation and created the basis for federal laws protecting the right of working people to form labor unions. Such issues as gender-based job discrimination and pay inequity were not important to the general public until they were brought center stage by the women's movement. The anti–Vietnam War movements began with only a few, like Mary Beth Tinker (see The Struggle for Democracy), but eventually won over the majority.

Great Depression The period of economic crisis in the United States stretching from the stock market crash of 1929 to the entry of America into World War II.

Overcoming Gridlock

Sometimes, it takes the energy of a social movement to overcome the antimajoritarian aspects of our constitutional system and get anything done at all. As political scientists Theodore Lowi has described the issue:

> Our political system is almost perfectly designed to maintain an existing state of affairs. . . . Our system is so designed that only a determined and undoubted

Mary Beth Tinker Protests the War

The Struggle for Democracy

In 1965, the war in Vietnam was just beginning to escalate, and widespread opposition had not yet appeared. Taking an open antiwar stand against prevailing opinion was not easy at that time, and few took the risk. One who did was Mary Beth Tinker, a 13-year-old eighth-grader in Des Moines, Iowa, who felt strongly that the war was wrong. To express her feelings, she chose to wear a black armband to school. As she described it:

> I went to school and I wore the armband all morning. The kids were kind of talking, but it was all friendly, nothing hostile. Then I got to my algebra class, right after lunch, and sat down. The teacher came in, and everybody was kind of whispering; they didn't know what was going to happen. Then this guy came to the door of the class and he said, Mary Tinker, you're wanted out here in the hall. Then they called me down to the principal's office.

Mary was suspended from school by the principal, a decision that was eventually upheld by the school board. She and her parents insisted that Mary had the right to wear an armband as long as it did not disrupt classes or bother her classmates, but school officials were adamant. Mary held her ground, even in the face of several attempts to intimidate her.

> People threw red paint at our house, and we got lots of calls. We got all kinds of threats to our family, even death threats. They even threatened my little brothers and sisters, which was really sick. People called our house on Christmas Eve and said the house would be blown up by morning. There was a radio talk-show host . . . who started in on our family, the Tinker family. . . . One night he said that if anyone wanted to use a shotgun on my father he would pay court costs if anything happened.

Mary's right to wear an armband to protest the war in Vietnam was eventually upheld by the U.S. Supreme Court. By the time the Court ruled on the case, many other Americans had joined Mary in her opposition to the government's Vietnam policy.

Source: Peter Irons, *The Courage of Their Convictions* (New York: Free Press, 1988), pp. 231–253.

> majority could make it move. This is why our history is replete with social movements. It takes that kind of energy to get anything like a majority. . . . Change comes neither from the genius of the system nor from the liberality or wisdom of its supporters and of the organized groups. It comes from new groups or nascent groups—social movements—when the situation is most dramatic.[7]

It is important to note that many of the social reforms of which most Americans are most proud—the right of women to vote, equal citizenship rights for African-Americans, Social Security, collective bargaining, and environmental protection—have been less the result of "normal" politics than of social movements started by determined minorities.

Factors That Encourage the Creation of Social Movements

A certain combination of factors, mainly structural in nature, is apparently necessary for a social movement to develop.[8] We review the most important ones here.

The Existence of Social Distress

Those who are safe, prosperous, and unthreatened generally have no need of social movements. Those whose lives are difficult and unsafe, or whose way of life or values are threatened, on the other hand, often find social movements an attractive means of calling attention to their plight and of pressing for changes in the status quo.[9]

Social distress caused by economic and social change helped create the conditions for the rise of most of the major social movements in American history. For example, the Populist movement occurred after western and southern farmers suffered great economic reverses during the latter part of the nineteenth century. The labor movement during the 1930s was spurred by the virtual collapse of the industrial sector of the American economy, historically unprecedented levels of unemployment, and widespread destitution. The rise of the Christian conservative movement seems to be associated with the perceived threat of the apparent decline in religious and family values in American life. For many women, distress caused by discriminatory hiring, blocked career advancement, and unequal pay at a time when they were entering the job market in increasing numbers during the 1960s and 1970s made the option of a women's movement an attractive one.[10]

The Availability of Resources for Mobilization

Social strain and distress are almost always present in society. But social movements occur, it seems, only when the aggrieved group has the resources (including skilled leaders) sufficient to organize those who are suffering strain and distress.[11] The grievances expressed by the labor movement had existed

Social movements are a response to a real, immediate social distress or injustice. When women began to enter the job market in increasing numbers during the 1960s and 1970s, discriminatory hiring, sexist barriers to career advancement, and unequal pay were unspoken realities of the business world. As more and more women refused to accept these injustices, the women's movement emerged.

for a long time in the United States, but it was not until a few unions developed, generating talented leaders, a very active labor press, and widespread media attention, that the movement began to take off. The women's movement's assets included a sizable population of educated and skilled women, a lively women's press, and a broad network of meetings to talk about common problems[12] (generally called *consciousness-raising groups*). The Christian conservative movement could build on a base of skilled clergy (for instance, Jerry Falwell and Pat Robertson), an expanding evangelical church membership, religious television and radio networks, and highly developed fund-raising technologies. Gay and lesbian activists could depend on a rich assortment of organizations, an active press, and the financial support of gay- and lesbian-owned businesses.

For its part, the 1960s civil rights movement could count on organizationally skilled clergy and close-knit congregations, black-owned newspapers and radio stations, an expanding pool of African-American college-educated youth, and blocs of African-American voters located in electorally important states. The existence of such experienced, tested, and effective organizations as the Congress of Racial Equality (CORE), the Urban League, and the National Association for the Advancement of Colored People (NAACP) was invaluable.

A Supportive Environment

The rise of social movements requires more than the existence of resources for mobilization among aggrieved groups. The times must also be right, in the sense that a degree of support and tolerance must exist for the movement among the public and society's leaders.[13] The Populist upsurge took place, for instance, at a time when many Americans other than farmers were also concerned about the rising power of corporations. Christian conservatives mobilized in an environment in which many other Americans were also worried about changes in social values and practices, and when the Republican party was looking for a way to detach traditional Democratic voters from their party. The labor movement's upsurge during the 1930s coincided with the electoral needs of the Democratic party.[14] The women's movement surged at a time when public opinion was becoming much more favorable toward women's equality.[15]

We see the same thing at work with regard to the 1960s civil rights movement. It made its demands at a time when overt racism of the public was in decline outside the South and when national leaders were becoming increasingly concerned about the effects of segregation in the South on American foreign policy and the economy. Sympathy for black demands by political leaders was further encouraged by the rising electoral power of black Americans in some large northern states.

The Existence of a Sense of Efficacy Among Participants

Some scholars believe that if they are to develop an effective social movement, those who are on the outside looking in must come to believe that their actions can make a difference, that other citizens and political leaders will listen and respond to their grievances. A *sense of efficacy* is what political scientists call this "I-can-make-a-difference-in-politics" attitude. Without a sense of **political efficacy,** grievances might explode into brief demonstrations or riots, but they would not support a long-term effort requiring time, commitment, and risk.

political efficacy The sense that one can affect what government does.

It may well be that the highly decentralized and fragmented character of our political system helps to sustain a sense of efficacy, since movements often find places in the system where they will be heard by officials. Christian conservative social movements have had little impact on school curricula in unitary political systems like that of Great Britain, for instance, where educational policy is made in London, so few try to do anything about it. Here, Christian conservatives know they can gain the ear of local school boards and state officials in regions where religious belief is strong. Gays and lesbians have been able to convince public officials and local voters to pass antidiscrimination ordinances in accepting communities, such as San Francisco and Boulder, Colorado.

A Spark to Set Off the Flames

Social movements require, as we have seen, a set of grievances among a group of people, the resources to form and sustain organization, a supportive environment, and a sense of political efficacy among the potential participants in the movement. But they also seem to require something to set off the mix, some dramatic precipitating event (or series of events), sometimes called a *catalyst,* to set them in motion. The gay and lesbian movement seems to have been sparked by the 1969 "Stonewall rebellion," a riot set off by police harassment of the patrons of a gay bar in New York City. The most important catalyst for the civil rights movement was Rosa Parks's simple refusal to give up her seat on a Montgomery, Alabama, bus in 1957 (described in Chapter 1).

A number of catalytic events also galvanized the women's movement. There was the 1963 publication of Betty Friedan's *Feminine Mystique,* in which she spoke to women's discontent ("a problem that has no name," as she put it) as no one had done before. The example set by the civil rights movement showed many women that outsiders could gain a hearing in American politics if they were willing to use collective-action tactics. There was also the failure of the federal government to enforce Title VII of the 1964 Civil Rights

Social problems often simmer quietly until a catalytic event brings about a social movement. In 1955, Rosa Parks refused to give up her seat to a white person on a Montgomery city bus as required by law. Her arrest sparked a year-long bus boycott that signaled the beginning of the American civil rights movement.

The sit-down strike was invented by labor movement activists in the American auto industry in the 1930s. Here union members strike but stay put on the job site, daring management to use violence to end it.

Act, which guaranteed women protections in the area of equal employment. Finally, younger women active in the civil rights and anti–Vietnam War movements discovered that they were not well treated within these movements, despite the movements' rhetoric of equality, and concluded that women's problems could be addressed only if women took their own political initiative.

The Tactics of Social Movements

sit-down strike A form of labor action in which workers stop production but do not leave their job site.

civil disobedience The act of purposely breaking a law and accepting the consequences of the action, as a way to publicize its unjust nature.

Social movements tend to use collective action and unconventional tactics to make themselves heard. Such tactics depend on the dramatic gesture and are often disruptive. The women's suffrage movement used mass demonstrations and hunger strikes to great effect. The labor movement invented **sit-down strikes** and plant takeovers as its most effective weapons in the 1930s. Prolife activists added to the protest repertoire clinic blockades and the harassment of clinic doctors and employees and their families. More extreme elements even added violence against clinics and doctors, including murder.

The most effective tool of the civil rights movement was nonviolent **civil disobedience,** which is a conscious refusal to obey a law that a group considers unfair, unjust, and/or unconstitutional. A particularly dramatic and effective use of this tactic took place in Greensboro, North Carolina. Four black students from North Carolina Agricultural and Technical State University sat down at a "whites-only" lunch counter in a Woolworth's store on February 1, 1960, and politely asked to be served. When requested to leave, they refused. They stayed put and remained calm even as a mob of young white men screamed at them, covered them with ketchup and mustard, and threatened to lynch them. Each day, more students from the college joined them. By the end of the week, over 1,000 black students had joined the sit-in to demand an end to segregation. These actions ignited the South. Within two months, similar sit-ins had taken place in nearly 60 cities across nine states; almost 4,000 young people had tasted a night in jail for their actions. Their bravery galvanized other blacks across the nation and generated sympathy among many whites. The student sit-in movement also spawned a new and more impatient civil rights organization, the Student Nonviolent Coordinating Committee (SNCC). (See the story of the SNCC in the Struggle for Democracy box in Chapter 1.)

Another particularly effective use of nonviolent civil disobedience was organized in Birmingham, Alabama, by the spiritual leader of the civil rights movement, Dr. Martin Luther King, Jr., who led a series of massive nonviolent demonstrations to demand the **integration** of schools and public transportation. Nonviolent demonstrators, most of whom were schoolchildren, were assaulted by snarling police dogs, electric cattle prods, and high-pressure fire hoses that sent demonstrators sprawling. Police Commissioner Eugene "Bull" Connor filled his jails to overflowing with hundreds of young marchers, who resisted only passively, alternately praying and singing civil rights songs, including "We Shall Overcome." The quiet bravery of the demonstrators and the palpable sense among public officials and private-sector leaders in the nation that matters were quickly spinning out of control convinced President John Kennedy on June 11, 1963, to introduce his historic civil rights bill for congressional consideration.

integration Policies encouraging the interaction of different races, as in schools or public facilities.

Nonviolent civil disobedience proved to be the most effective tool of the civil rights movement. By violating unjust laws quietly and nonviolently, protesters alerted outsiders to the injustice of their situation. The sit-in at a "whites-only" lunch counter in Greensboro, North Carolina, sparked similar protests all over the country, and the arrests of the protesters generated sympathetic interest among previously apathetic whites.

Why Social Movements Decline

Even strong and influential social movements are very difficult to sustain. Let's consider why.

The Unexpected Problem of Success

Success may undermine a social movement as surely as failure. Unless it can find other issues around which to organize, a social movement will find that achieving its central goal destroys its very reason for being. The abolitionist movement became irrelevant with the passage of the Thirteenth Amendment ending slavery. The women's suffrage movement disappeared after the ratification of the Nineteenth Amendment, which granted women the right to vote. The passage of major civil rights bills in 1964 and 1965, which met the main goals of the civil rights movement (an end to official segregation in the South and guarantees of full citizen rights for all black Americans), caused significant declines in grassroots activity among the black population and in the influence of traditional civil rights organizations like the NAACP and CORE.[16]

The Danger of Factionalism

A social movement must successfully address three different audiences: the movement's activists, the general public, and political decision makers. More specifically, it must maintain the enthusiasm of activists, attract more activists and support from the aggrieved group, gain sympathy from the general public, and force a positive response from public officials. These often contradictory objectives may lead to internal fragmentation over strategy, tactics, and ideology. These divisions may become quite heated, since movements attract people who feel passionately about some problem, who have risked a great deal to get involved, and who are attempting to change an entrenched status quo. In such a context, it is difficult to keep disputes at a low temperature. The Populists split over the issue of whether to include African-American farmers in their movement. The Students for a Democratic Society (SDS), one of the main organizations of the anti–Vietnam War movement of the late 1960s, split over the use of violence as a tactic after the destructive rampage of its most militant faction (called the Weathermen) along Chicago's fashionable Michigan Avenue. The women's movement was split by the often acrimonious disagreements of mainstream feminists and the radical and socialist wings of the movement.[17] The antiabortion Prolife movement is showing deep fissures because of the increasing willingness of its most extreme elements to use violence against clinics and clinic doctors and staff.

The civil rights movement was fragmented by the radicalization of portions of the black community and the rise of the ideology of black pride and empowerment (termed *black power*) as the reigning ideology among many blacks, especially the young. Frustrated by the lack of progress on many fronts, and taking pride in black identity, many in the movement rejected the gradualist and integrationist orientation for a radical and separatist one. The commitment to nonviolence, while retained by Rev. King's Southern Christian Leadership Conference (SCLC) and the NAACP, was renounced by SNCC, by the Black Muslims and their popular spokesman Malcolm X, and by the new Black Panther party, led by Hewey Newton and Bobby Seale. The movement never recovered from this split.

The Erosion of Public Support

Social movements also decline when popular support of their goals begins to erode. Less public support usually translates into fund-raising difficulties, less responsiveness on the part of public officials, and greater tolerance of groups that oppose the goals of the social movement. Public support may be eroded for any number of reasons. The public may perceive that enough has been done already to meet the grievances of the members of the movement, or that the movement has gone too far, asking too much of other Americans. Or the public may simply get bored and move on to other issues. All of these factors were in play as the civil rights movement became decreasingly relevant to political decision makers after the mid–1960s.

The Declining Commitment of Movement Activists

Additionally, activists may simply grow weary of the struggle. Because social movements ask so much of their activists in terms of time, financial sacrifice, and risk (of injury, job loss, jail sentences, etc.), and because they depend on nonmaterial inducements to encourage participation (ideology, an attractive goal, a sense of solidarity, etc.), it is difficult to sustain high levels of active involvement for very long.

The Rise of Opposition

Finally, successful social movements almost always spark a reaction from groups that oppose their gains. The size, commitment, and resources of opposition groups may match or even exceed those of the protest movement itself.[18] For instance, during the 1970s and 1980s, the civil rights movement sparked a backlash against the federal government among white southerners that

Successful social movements such as the civil rights movement often generate countermovements opposed to their main goals and aspirations. Here, the Ku Klux Klan marches to protest the Martin Luther King holiday.

contributed to the success of such politicians as George Wallace and the rise of Republican party fortunes in the South.[19] The women's and the gay and lesbian rights movements sparked a powerful backlash among Christian conservatives. The successes of the environmental movement during the 1970s energized a powerful, well-funded, and well-organized counteroffensive by America's leading corporations and business organizations, which succeeded eventually in rolling back federal environmental regulations.[20]

Why Some Social Movements Succeed and Others Do Not

Social movements have had a significant impact on American politics and on what government does. Not all social movements are equally successful, however. What makes some more successful than others seems to be the proximity of the movement's goals to American values, its capacity to win public attention and support, and its ability to affect the political fortunes of elected leaders.

Low-Impact Social Movements

A social movement will have little impact if it has few followers or activists, has little support among the general public, and is unable to disrupt everyday life significantly or to affect the electoral prospects of politicians. The poor people's movement, which tried to convince Americans to enact policies that would end poverty in the United States, failed to make much of a mark in the late 1960s. Some people tried to form a movement to oppose the Gulf War with mass demonstrations but failed to attract many adherents.

A social movement is particularly unlikely to have an impact on policy when it stimulates the formation of a powerful countermovement. The rational politician may find it prudent to take no action at all when he or she has difficulty calculating the relative weight of the two sides in a dispute between movements. This is one of several things that happened to the proposed **Equal Rights Amendment (ERA)** to the Constitution, banning discrimination on the grounds of sex. The ERA failed to receive the approval of the necessary three-fourths of the states after anti-ERA forces (mainly Christian conservatives) rallied to block action during the 1970s.[21]

Equal Rights Amendment (ERA) Proposed amendment to the U.S. Constitution stating that equality of rights shall not be abridged or denied on account of sex.

Repressed Social Movements

Social movements committed to a radical change in the society and the economy tend to threaten widely shared values and the interests of powerful individuals, groups, and institutions. As a result, they rarely gain widespread popular support and almost always arouse the hostility of political leaders. Such movements very often face repression of one kind or another.[22] In the late nineteenth and early twentieth centuries, for instance, the labor movement was hindered by court injunctions, laws against the formation of labor unions, violence by employer-hired armed gangs, and strikebreaking by the National Guard and the U.S. armed forces. In 1877, 60,000 National Guardsmen were mobilized in ten states to break the first national railroad strike. The strike against Carnegie Steel in 1892 in Homestead, Pennsylvania, brought the mobilization of 10,000 militiamen, the arrest of 16 strike leaders on conspiracy charges, and the indictment of 27 labor leaders for treason. The Pullman strike of 1894 was abruptly ended by the use of federal troops and by the arrest and indictment of union leaders.

Other troublesome social movements have stimulated similar responses. Thus, the radical branch of the anti–Vietnam War movement was crippled during the late 1960s and early 1970s by widespread infiltration by the Federal Bureau of Investigation (FBI) and other federal, state, and local police agencies; by arrests for minor infractions; and by the frequent use of conspiracy trials.

Partially Successful Social Movements

Some social movements have enough power and public support to generate a favorable response from public officials but not enough to force them to go very far. In these situations, government may respond in a partial or half-hearted way. President Franklin D. Roosevelt responded to the social movements pressing for strong antipoverty measures during the Great Depression by proposing the passage of the Social Security Act, which fell far short of movement expectations.[23] The Prolife movement discovered that President Reagan was willing to use movement rhetoric and to appoint sympathetic judges but was unwilling to submit antiabortion legislation to Congress. Bill Clinton promulgated a "don't ask, don't tell" policy, a change in past policy, but one falling short of his promise to end the ban on gays' and lesbians' entering the military.

Successful Social Movements

Those social movements that have many supporters, win wide public sympathy, do not challenge the basics of the economic and social order, and wield some clout in the electoral arena are likely to achieve a substantial number of their goals. The civil rights movement is the best example. After years of struggle, the movement forced action on the Civil Rights Act of 1964 and the Voting Rights Act of 1965. These enactments helped sound the death knell of the "separate-but-equal" doctrine enunciated in the infamous *Plessy* decision (1896), engineered the collapse of legal segregation in the South, and made the guarantee of full citizenship rights for African-Americans a reality. The Voting Rights Act was particularly important in transforming the politics of the South. Black registration and voting turnout increased dramatically all over the region during the late 1960s and the 1970s. Elected black officials filled legislative seats, city council seats, the mayors' offices in large and small cities, and sheriff's offices. Between 1970 and 1989, the number of elected black officials increased fivefold, from 1,472 to over 7,000. In 1989, voters in Virginia elected the first African-American governor in the nation's history, Douglas Wilder, a man who had once worked his way through college as a waiter in a segregated private club.

Elected white officials, tacking with the new winds of change, soon began to court the black vote. George Wallace, who first became famous by "standing in the schoolhouse door" to prevent the integration of the University of Alabama and who once kicked off a political campaign with the slogan "Segregation Today, Segregation Tomorrow, Segregation Forever," actively pursued the black vote in his last run for public office.

Movements can be successful even if new laws are not passed. Other measures of success include increased respect for members of the movement, changes in fundamental underlying values, and increased representation of the group in decision-making bodies. The women's movement has had this kind of success. Though the Equal Rights Amendment failed to be approved (the movement's main goal), women's issues came to the forefront during these years, and to a very substantial degree, the demands of the movement for equal treatment and respect made great headway in many areas of American life[24] (see the Politics and Film box as an example). Gays and lesbians have also found greater acceptance in many areas of American life, ranging from theater and film (note the success of *Angels in America* and *Philadelphia*) to corporate practices (note the recent inclusion of domestic partners in health insurance benefits at large corporations like Coors and Disney).

POLITICS AND FILM

The Women's Movement Hits Hollywood

The women's movement was a long time coming to Hollywood, but it seems to have arrived with a bang. *Thelma and Louise* was the breakthrough film; it is hard to imagine that this "buddy-road-outlaw" movie, with two women as the protagonists, could have been made before the modern women's movement, or that a paying audience would have flocked to see it. Hollywood has traditionally preferred its women subordinate: objects of men's desires, or bimbos, or victims, or avenging angels. While Hollywood can still be counted on to produce films with women in such roles—witness *Disclosure* with Demi Moore as the male's worst affirmative-action nightmare, or *Showgirls,* little more than a high-priced stag show—things have changed since *Thelma and Louise* showed us two lively "good old girls" who depend on themselves, take their own pleasures, and make their own way in a man's world.

Two things seem to explain the change. First, the women's movement has apparently altered the opinions of filmmakers in general. Mostly male producers and directors are again willing to believe that films about women's issues and films that treat women sympathetically, and as full and complex people, are artistically and financially worth doing, very much like the films featuring Bette Davis, Joan Crawford, and Katherine Hepburn during the 1930s, 1940s, and 1950s. Note the recent spate of films based on the novels of Jane Austen—*Persuasion, Sense and Sensibility, Emma,* and *Clueless* (the amusing takeoff on *Emma*)—with their full, complex, intelligent, and politely assertive women. Note as well, *What's Love Got to Do With It,* the film biography of singer Tina Turner, in which a long-abused woman takes control of her life and goes on to make her way in the world. And there is the surprise hit *Waiting to Exhale* Forest Whitaker's film of Terry MacMillan's novel. Told from a female perspective, *Waiting to Exhale* is about four African-American women grappling with their lives and their relationships with their men. The complex relationships between mothers and daughters are portrayed in *The Joy Luck Club* which is based on the novel by Amy Tan and was directed by Wayne Wang.

Perhaps more important for women's equality in Hollywood over the long haul is the increasing presence of women in Hollywood as producers, directors, and writers, as Lisa Henson, president of Columbia Pictures has noted.[a] Penny Marshall is one of the most successful of these directors (*Big,* 1988, and *Awakenings,* 1990). Her film *A League of Their Own* (1992), based on a true story, portrayed the lives of professional women baseball players during World War II. Unique among Hollywood films, it portrays young women as skilled athletes, friends, and colleagues. Academy Award–winning actress Jodie Foster produced *Nell* and directed *Home for the Holiday* which explored aspects of women's lives. Joycelyn Moorhouse examined female bonding in *How to Make an American Quilt* while Nicole Kidman used her star power to push for the production of *To Die For,* a wickedly funny satire on ambition and women's careers. In *I Like it like That* director-writer Darnell Martin examined the hardships and joys of financially strapped Puerto Rican women in the South Bronx. The transformation of Lisette, the story's main character, from an abused and poverty-stricken mother to a self-confident and economically independent person is convincing and moving.

A Special Note on the Success of the Civil Rights Movement

It is unlikely that any social movement can be entirely successful. Though some achieve their initial goals, few have been able to alter significantly the fundamental structural conditions that caused the distress and gave rise to the grievances in the first place. This is especially apparent when we consider the civil rights movement.

Despite the important gains represented by the civil rights laws passed in the 1960s, the movement did not enjoy much success in changing forms of

The movie industry has changed so much, in fact, that it has even begun to treat homosexual women more sympathetically. To be sure, there remain films like *Basic Instinct* (1992) that treat lesbians as pathological demons. But there are also films, like Rose Troche's *Go Fish* and Maria Maggenti's *The Incredibly True Adventures of Two Girls in Love* that offer the general public sympathetic and discerning insights into this nearly invisible community.

Hollywood has surely changed, and the women's movement has had a great deal to do with it. The film industry has long made movies in which men are portrayed with all of the rich and diverse characteristics of the human experience, ranging from heroes and saints to cowards and predators. It appears that women are beginning to get the same treatment.

Source: Bernard Weinraub, "Finally, Enough Actresses to Nominate for Oscars," *New York Times* (December 12, 1995), p. B1.

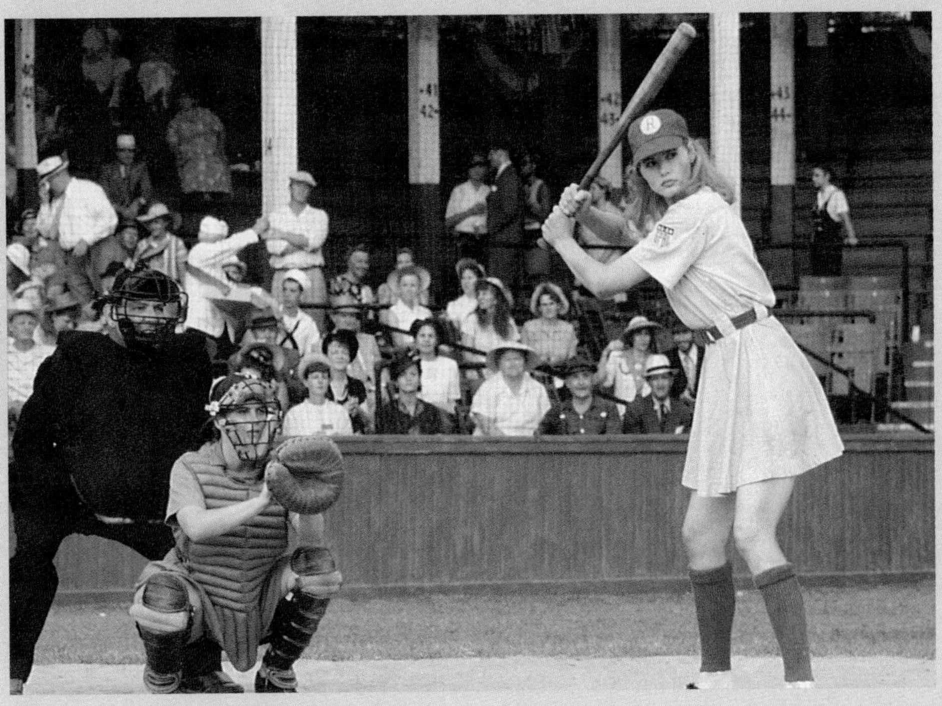

racial disadvantage based on social practices rather than law. Housing segregation remains very much a part of the American landscape, for instance, and the resulting ghettoization is strongly associated with economic and political isolation and weakness.[25] One recent study reports that African-Americans find it more difficult than any other racial or ethnic group to buy suburban homes because of the practices of real estate agents and lending institutions.[26] A recent National Research Council report also shows that blacks rank significantly behind whites in their access to quality health care and education. The report concludes that integration of blacks into a "color blind society is unlikely in any foreseeable future."[27] The Harvard Project on School Desegregation reports that 66 percent of all black students today attend schools that are predominantly minority in their makeup, the highest percentage since 1968.[28]

Nor did the civil rights movement have much of an impact on the overall economic standing of African-Americans, despite the emergence of a substantial black middle class; taken as a whole, African-Americans still lag behind white Americans on most economic indicators (see Figure 10.1). In recent years, the relative economic standing of African-Americans has actually declined.[29]

The results of the economic disparity between black and white Americans, as well as of that between middle-class and lower-class blacks, are seen most dramatically in the desperate situation of the black residents of urban ghettos such as South Central Los Angeles and the South Bronx in New York City. In the nation's ghettos, a deadly combination of poverty, violence, and deteriorating social services has produced a substantial decline in life expectancy.[30]

Nor have the civil rights laws minimized the psychological and social divide that exists between the races. A majority of white Americans believe, for instance, that the situation of African-Americans has improved, that the federal government has gone about as far as it can to rectify racial injustice, and that policies like **affirmative action** are no longer necessary. A majority of African-

affirmative action Programs of private and public institutions meant to overcome the effects of and to compensate for past discrimination.

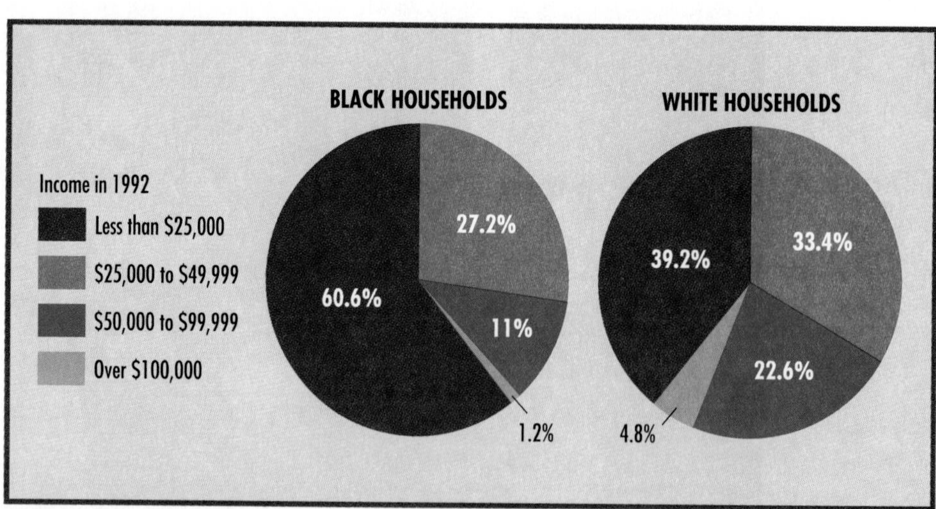

Figure 10.1 ■ **Black and White Household Income Compared, 1993**

Although the size of the black middle class has grown over the past two decades, black household income still lags substantially behind that of whites. In this graph we see that a smaller proportion of African-American than white households falls within the top two income categories, and that a much larger proportion falls into the lowest.

Source: U.S. Census Bureau, *Current Population Reports, 1993.*

While the civil rights movement was successful in ending legal segregation and broadening the opportunities available to black Americans, it has not been able to mend the social and psychological rift between different racial groups. Reactions to O. J. Simpson's acquittal on murder charges were strongly divided along racial lines and dramatically illustrated the degree to which blacks and whites are disconnected.

Americans take the opposite view on each of these points.[31] The startlingly different reactions of whites and blacks to the verdict in the O. J. Simpson trial showed the existence of this racial divide in a particularly dramatic fashion.

Social Movements and American Democracy

Social movements have made important gains for democracy in the United States. Without them, our politics would be dominated by an electoral system in which the less advantaged play a smaller role than other Americans, and by an interest group system that heavily overrepresents the interests of business and upper-income people. Social movements are one of the most effective means by which outsiders enter the game of American politics and make the playing field a little more level. While they tend to be noisy, impolite, and disruptive, they make our political process more democratic than it might otherwise be.

Summary

Social movements emphasize rather dramatically the point that the struggle for democracy is a recurring feature of our political life. They are mainly the instruments of political outsiders who want to gain a hearing in American politics. Social movements often contribute to democracy by increasing the visibility of important issues, by encouraging wider participation in public affairs, and (sometimes) by providing the energy to overcome the many antimajoritarian features of our constitutional system.

Social movements try to bring about social change through collective action. Their rise is tied to the availability of organizational and leadership resources to a group of people who have a strong sense of grievance. Successful social movements happen, moreover, only if the political environment is supportive, in the sense that at least portions of the general population and some public officials are sympathetic to the movement's goals. The decline of social movements is associated with a number of things, including goal attainment, factional splits, the exhaustion of movement activists, and the replacement of grassroots activity by formal organizations.

Social movements have had an important impact on our political life and in determining what our government does. Some of our most important legislative landmarks can be attributed to them. However, social movements do not always get what they want. They seem to be most successful when their goals are consistent with the central values of the society, have wide popular support, and fit the needs of political leaders.

Suggested Readings

Branch, Taylor. *Parting the Waters: America in the King Years, 1954–1963.* New York: Simon & Schuster, 1988.

A detailed and compelling description of the civil rights movement, with a particular focus on Martin Luther King, Jr. Winner of the National Book Award and the Pulitzer Prize.

Bruce, Steve. *The Rise and Fall of the New Christian Right.* New York: Clarendon Press, 1990.

The most complete analysis of the Christian conservative movement and its impact on American politics.

Chafe, William. *The Unfinished Journey,* 2nd ed. New York: Oxford University Press, 1995.

A justly celebrated history of America since the end of World War II, with a particular focus on the civil rights and women's movements.

Hochschild, Jennifer L. *Facing Up to the American Dream.* Princeton: Princeton University Press, 1995.

A sensitive and compelling analysis of the nature of the racial divide in the United States, why it exists, and how it may affect American politics.

Klein, Ethel. *Gender Politics.* Cambridge: Harvard University Press, 1984.

An analytically sophisticated and empirically detailed examination of the emergence of the women's movement and feminist politics.

Mansbridge, Jane J. *Why We Lost the ERA.* Chicago: University of Chicago Press, 1986.

Argues that the strong ideological inducements necessary to retain the involvement of movement activists worked against the attempt by the women's movement to push through the Equal Rights Amendment.

Miller, James. *Democracy Is in the Streets.* New York: Simon & Schuster, 1987.

A sophisticated account of the student antiwar movement and its roots in a particular strand of participatory democratic theory.

Piven, Frances Fox, and Richard A. Cloward. *Poor People's Movements.* New York: Vintage, 1979.

A controversial treatment of poor people's movements that argues that they are successful only as long as, and to the extent that, they remain grassroots, disruptive insurgencies.

Internet Sources

Afronet http://www.afronet.com/
A web site devoted to materials on African-American political, social, economic, and cultural life.

Directory of Grassroots Organizations http://www.ai.mit.edu/projects/ppp/groups.html
Full descriptions of grassroots organizations and their activities, as well as how to get in touch with them.

Human Rights Source http://www.gatech.edu/amnesty/source.html
Links to groups involved with the women's, Native American, and gay and lesbian rights movements.

The Jefferson Project/Issues http://www.stardot.com/jefferson/issues/
Links to information about activist groups from all locations on the political spectrum.

Prolife News http://www.pitt.edu/~stfst/AboutPLN.html
Information about the Prolife movement

Notes

1. Dan Balz, "Christian Conservatives Are Organizing to Make Change," *Washington Post National Edition* (August 14, 1994), p. 14.
2. On the Virginia convention, see Sidney Blumenthal, "Christian Soldiers," *New Yorker* (September 12, 1994), pp. 31–37.
3. Ibid., p. 36.
4. Joyce Gelb, *Feminism and Politics: A Comparative Perspective* (Berkeley: University of California Press, 1989), pp. 14, 30. Also see Doug McAdams, *Political Process and the Development of Black Insurgency* (Chicago: University of Chicago Press, 1982); David Plotke, "Citizenship and Social Movements," paper delivered at the annual meetings of the American Political Science Association, Washington, DC, September 2–5, 1993.
5. E. E. Schattschneider, *The Semi-Sovereign People* (New York: Holt, Rinehart & Winston, 1960), p. 142.
6. Richard Polenberg, *One Nation Divisible* (New York: Penguin, 1980), p. 268.
7. Theodore J. Lowi, *The Politics of Disorder* (New York: Basic Books, 1971), p. 54.
8. Doug McAdam, John D. McCarthy, and Mayer N. Zald, "Social Movements," in Neil J. Smelser, ed., *Handbook of Sociology* (Newbury Park, CA: Sage, 1994); Sidney Tarrow, *Social Movements, Collective Action, and Politics* (New York: Cambridge University Press, 1994).
9. Neil J. Smelser, *Theory of Collective Behavior* (New York: Free Press, 1962).
10. Barbara Sinclair Deckard, *The Women's Movement* (New York: Harper & Row, 1983); Ethel Klein, *Gender Politics: From Consciousness to Mass Politics* (Cambridge: Harvard University Press, 1984), chap. 2.
11. William Gamson, *The Strategy of Social Protest* (Homewood, IL: Dorsey, 1975); John D. McCarthy and Mayer N. Zald, "Resource Mobilization and Social Movements: A Partial Theory," *American Journal of Sociology,* Vol. 82, No. 6 (1977), pp. 1212–1241.
12. Jo Freeman, *The Politics of Women's Liberation* (New York: David McKay, 1975).

13. McAdams, *Political Process and the Development of Black Insurgency;* Peter K. Eisenger, "The Conditions of Protest Behavior in American Cities," *American Political Science Review,* Vol. 67 (1973), pp. 11–28.
14. Frances Fox Piven and Richard A. Cloward, *Poor People's Movements* (New York: Vintage, 1979), chap. 3.
15. Klein, *Gender Politics,* pp. 90–91.
16. See Dennis Chong, *Collective Action and the Civil Rights Movement* (Chicago: University of Chicago Press, 1991).
17. Freeman, *Politics of Women's Liberation;* Susan M. Hartmann, *From Margin to Mainstream: American Women and Politics Since 1960* (Philadelphia: Temple University Press, 1989), chap. 3; Jane Mansbridge, *Why We Lost the ERA* (Chicago: University of Chicago Press, 1986).
18. L. Marvin Overby and Sarah Ritchie, "Mobilized Masses and Strategic Opponents: A Resource Mobilization Analysis of the Nuclear Freeze and Clean Air Movements," *Western Political Quarterly,* Vol. 44 (June 1991), pp. 329–351.
19. See Kevin P. Phillips, *Post-Conservative America* (New York: Random House, 1982).
20. See Thomas Byrne Edsall, *The New Politics of Inequality* (New York: Norton, 1984); Edward S. Greenberg, *Capitalism and the American Political Ideal* (Armonk, N.Y.: M.E. Sharpe, 1985).
21. Jane Mansbridge, *Why We Lost the ERA.*
22. See David Caute, *The Great Fear* (New York: Simon & Schuster, 1978); Robert Justin Goldstein, *Political Repression in Modern America* (Cambridge, MA: Schenkman, 1978); Alan Wolfe, *The Seamy Side of Democracy* (New York: David McKay, 1978).
23. Greenberg, *Capitalism and the American Political Ideal.*
24. William Chafe, *The Unfinished Journey* (New York: Oxford University Press, 1986); Barbara Sinclair Deckard, *The Women's Movement* (New York: Harper & Row, 1983); Ethel Klein, *Gender Politics: From Consciousness to Mass Politics* (Cambridge, MA: Harvard University Press, 1984), ch. 2; Jo Freeman, *The Politics of Women's Liberation* (New York: David McKay, 1975).
25. Cathy J. Cohen and Michael C. Dawson, "Neighborhood Poverty and African American Politics," *American Political Science Review,* Vol. 87 (June 1993), pp. 303–318; Douglas S. Massey and Nancy A. Denton, *American Apartheid: Segregation and the Making of the Underclass* (Cambridge: Harvard University Press, 1993).
26. Constance Hays, "Study Says Blacks, More Than Other Groups, Face Segregation," *New York Times* (March 14, 1989), p. A1.
27. Julie Johnson, "Blacks Found Lagging Despite Gains," *New York Times* (July 28, 1989), p. A5.
28. William Celis, "Study Finds Rising Concentration of Black and Hispanic Students," *New York Times* (December 14, 1993), p. 1.
29. Jeremiah Cotton, "Opening the Gap: The Decline in Black Economic Indicators in the 1980s," *Social Science Quarterly,* Vol. 70, No. 4 (December 1988), pp. 803–819.
30. Philip Hilts, "Life Expectancy for Blacks in U.S. Shows Sharp Decline," *New York Times* (November 29, 1990), p. 11.
31. Jennifer Hochschild, *Facing Up to the American Dream* (Princeton: Princeton University Press, 1995).

PART IV

Government and Governing

The chapters in Part IV examine how federal government institutions operate and how and why public officials, both elected and appointed, behave as they do while in office. Part IV includes chapters on Congress, the presidency, the executive branch, the Supreme Court, and state and local government.

The chapters in this part assume that government institutions and public officials can be understood only in their structural and political contexts. What government does is influenced strongly by structural factors such as the constitutional rules, the economy, the political culture, society, and the nation's place in the world. In addition to these structural factors, the actions of government are also shaped by political linkage institutions such as elections, parties, interest groups, public opinion, and social movements, which transmit the preferences of individuals and groups to public officials.

Democracy is the evaluative thread that runs through each chapter. We ask about the degree to which federal government institutions and public officials advance or retard the practice of democracy in the United States. We conclude that democratic practices have gradually improved over the years at the governmental level, but that significant barriers to the full realization of democracy still exist.

CHAPTER 11

Congress

IN THIS CHAPTER

- ★ How the Constitution shapes Congress
- ★ How Congress has changed over the years
- ★ How the members of Congress represent their constituents
- ★ The role of money and interest groups in congressional elections
- ★ What leaders, political parties, and committees do in Congress
- ★ How a bill becomes a law

Republicans Retain Control of Congress

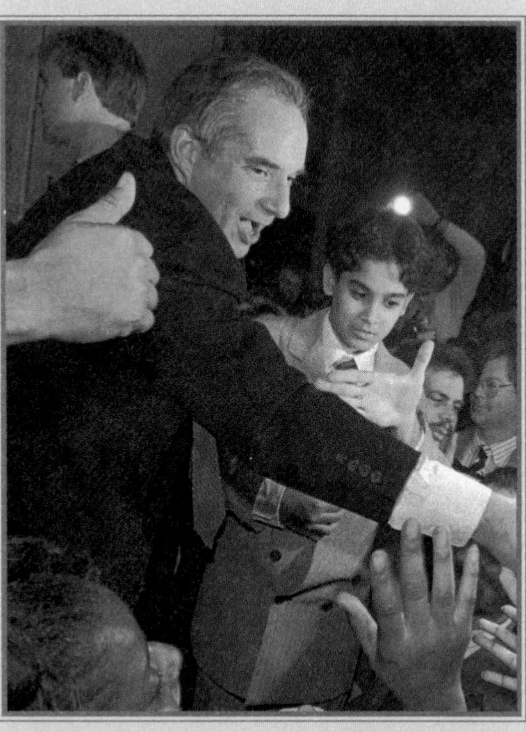

Phil English of Pennsylvania was one of 73 conservative Republican freshmen who entered the House of Representatives after the 1994 elections eager to transform the direction of American government. Like most of the other 70 GOP freshmen seeking reelection in 1996, English found himself in a bruising electoral battle, tarnished by ties to Speaker of the House Newt Gingrich and by the federal government shutdowns forced by Republicans during the budget fight with President Clinton.

Phil English's house district was one of 30 "swing districts" across the nation—places where the race between the candidates was so close that the outcome could not be predicted with any degree of confidence—where the election results would determine which political party ended up controlling the House of Representatives in the 105th Congress. Because of this, the election in Pennsylvania's 21st district attracted the attention of both political parties and a wide range of interest groups, as well as a great deal of campaign money.

English and his Democratic opponent Ron DiNicola raised unprecedented amounts of money for their campaigns from individuals, PACs, and party organizations. But direct contributions to each candidate's campaign were but the tip of the money iceberg. Like in most other congressional races, the bulk of campaign dollars in the English–DiNicola contest was of the "soft money" and "parallel campaign" variety. Interest groups keen to help one side or the other, for instance, are legally permitted to give whatever amount they wish to political parties for party "educational" activities. This form of fundraising and spending goes under the heading of "soft money." Interest groups are also allowed to run their own television, radio, and print advertising campaigns on the issues so long as such issue campaigns are not directly linked to the campaigns of particular partisan candidates. Such campaigns are known as "parallel campaigns." In the end, the English–DiNicola race became an expensive radio, television, and print advertising battle between a Republican coalition made up of groups like the U.S. Chamber of Commerce, the National Rifle Association, tobacco companies, and the Christian Coalition, and a Democratic coalition made up of the AFL-CIO labor federation, environmental organizations, and prochoice groups. English won reelection by a narrow margin even though Democrat Bill Clinton comfortably won the state of Pennsylvania.

In many ways, the Phil English–Ron DiNicola race in Pennsylvania's 21st district mirrored what happened nationally in 1996. Most importantly, perhaps, was the scale and pattern of campaign finance. Congressional candidates raised a record $400 million, a 27 percent increase over 1994, according to the Federal Election Commission. Being the majority party in both houses of Congress, and, therefore, a tempting target for interest groups seeking access to those who make important policy decisions, Republicans raised and spent the most. In some races, the disproportionalities were quite dramatic. In Texas, for instance, Democratic challenger Victor Morales raised but $750,000 in his unsuccessful campaign to unseat Senator Phil Gramm, blessed with a war chest of $10.6 million.

The $400 million in the campaign coffers of the candidates does not begin to approach the actual amount of money spent on congressional races in 1996. To that amount must be added money raised and spent by parties on "soft-money" educational campaigns and by interest groups on their own educational advertising featuring attacks on Bill Clinton's character and "tax-and-spend" liberalism on one side and on a Newt Gingrich–led party of radical fanatics on the other. Because neither the Christian Coalition nor the Sierra Club considered their advertising "partisan," neither felt obligated

Table 11.1

Results of the 1996 Congressional Elections

	Senate	House
Partisan alignment in the 105th Congress*	55 R; 45 D	228 R; 206 D; 1 I
Net change from 104th Congress	+2 R	+8 D
Percent incumbents reelected	97	94
Percent turnover in membership	16	20
Percent of total congressional votes cast for each party nationally**		50 D; 50 R

*The alignment in the House is an approximate figure because several special elections have yet to be held and a number of vote recounts are still to be done as of this writing.

**Exit polls by Voter News Service, November 5, 1996, reported in the *New York Times,* November 7, 1996, p. B3.

to report such expenditures. Though the AFL-CIO received the most attention for its campaign expenditures (estimated at about $70 million for candidate and party contributions, and for its own advertising), business as a whole outspent labor unions by a three-to-one margin, according to the nonpartisan Center for Responsive Politics.

Like Phil English, a majority of the GOP freshman class in the 104th Congress won reelection despite being targeted for extinction by the Democratic Party and labor, environmental, and women's groups. Only 12 of their number lost their seats, though another 22 won by the skins of their teeth with margins of 2 percentage points or less. Though Democrats picked up seats in the 1996 House elections (see Table 11.1), the staying power of their 1994 class allowed Republicans to retain control of the House of Representatives.

Republicans enjoyed more success in Senate races where they picked up 2 additional seats, bringing their majority to 55–45. Though short of a "veto-proof" majority—60 votes would be required to break any "filibuster" mounted by the Democrats—Republicans are in a position to exercise considerable power on a number of fronts in the 105th Congress, including investigations of Bill and Hillary Clinton and close scrutiny of Bill Clinton's judicial and executive branch appointments. Because many of the 21 newly elected Republican Senators replaced Southern Democrats and retired Republican moderates like Bill Cohen of Maine and Nancy Kassebaum and Bob Dole of Kansas, the Senate in the 105th Congress is certain to be more conservative than it was in the 104th.

In winning control of Congress in two consecutive elections, Republicans achieved what they had not been able to do since 1928. They accomplished this feat even while Democrat Bill Clinton fashioned an easy victory over Republican Bob Dole in the presidential election. How could such a thing happen? A number of possibilities exist. Some commentators have suggested that many Clinton supporters who would otherwise have voted for Democrats in congressional races simply stayed home with the presidential race a foregone conclusion. Others have suggested that a last-minute surge by Ross Perot brought to the polls voters who generally favor Republicans in congressional elections. It is also the case that the Democrats were more vulnerable from the start because Democrats made up a substantial majority of representatives and senators who retired prior to the elections. Finally, others have suggested that Americans consciously and rationally voted to continue "divided government," trusting neither party with unchecked power. Knowing that Bill Clinton would be elected president, the argument goes, a substantial number of Americans responded to the message delivered by the Republican Party in the last week of the campaign to maintain GOP control in Congress to ensure a balance of power in Washington. Opinion polls conducted in the final days of the campaign showed that many Americans were indeed worried about a government in Washington under the control of a single party.

The 1996 congressional elections also showed that the Republican and Democratic parties are now evenly balanced nationally, with the popular vote for the House across the country split 50–50. And, there is every reason to believe that the two parties will remain competitive for the foreseeable future. This apparent balance between the parties speaks to the issue of partisan realignment raised in Chapter 8. It is now becoming clear that while Democratic dominance has ended in American politics, Republicans have not replaced them at the top.

The 1996 elections also continued the shift in the geographic foundations of the parties. The GOP added most of its new seats in the House and the Senate in the South and in the mountain states, areas where it has now become overwhelmingly dominant (for instance, Republicans hold nearly 6 in 10 House seats in what was once the solidly Democratic South), while the Democrats solidified their hold on the Northeast and the West Coast.

Incumbents in both parties and in both houses of Congress made a very strong showing in the 1996 elections. In the Senate, Larry Pressler of South Dakota was the only incumbent to lose. There was, nevertheless, substantial turnover in the Senate because of a record number of retirements. Of the 34 seats up for election, 15 were open-seat (no incumbent running) elections. New to the Senate in 1997, then, were the winners of these seats and Tim Johnson of South Dakota who defeated Pressler, for a total of 16 new senators. In the House, incumbents also did well, winning 94 percent of their races. Again, however, this does not tell the turnover story. Adding those who did not return to the House because of voluntary retirement or defeat at the party nomination stage (53 in total) to those who were rejected by the voters in November, only 80 percent of House members returned for the 105th Congress. Coupled with the high turnover of membership in 1992 and 1994, fresh faces are the order of the day in the House of Representatives.

Finally, it appears as if advances made by women in recent elections has slowed considerably. Despite a record number of women candidates in the party primaries and in the general election, voters added only two women members to the House, bringing their total to 49 there, and one additional senator, bringing the total of women senators to 10.

In this chapter, we turn our attention to the United States Congress, examining in particular how Congress works as a representative and as a governing institution. We will learn how the ability and willingness of the members of Congress to meet their complex responsibilities is affected by other government institutions and actors, political linkage institutions such as interest groups, public opinion and elections, and structural factors such as constitutional rules and economic and social change. In the course of this examination, we will address the question of the democratic character of Congress and how the struggle for democracy has affected its development.

Sources: *The New York Times Special Election Edition,* Thursday, November 7, 1996, Section B; "Decision '96," MSNBC News, http://www.msnbc.com, November 6, 7, and 8, 1996; "Campaign '96," Politics Now, http://www.politicsnow.com, November 6, 7, and 8, 1996.

The Structural Foundations of the Modern Congress

A number of structural factors have strongly shaped how the modern Congress works. The most important of these factors are reviewed in this section.

Constitutional Design

As we saw in Chapter 2, the framers of the Constitution were ambivalent about democracy and concerned about the possibility of government tyranny. Yet they also wanted an energetic government capable of accomplishing its assigned tasks. These multiple objectives and concerns are reflected in the constitutional design of Congress.

Empowering Congress The framers began by empowering Congress, making the legislative branch the center of lawmaking in the federal government. In Article I, Section 1, of the Constitution, they gave Congress the power to make the laws: "All legislative power herein granted shall be vested in a Congress of the United States."

For the framers, Congress was the main bearer of federal governmental powers. In listing the powers and responsibilities of Congress in Article I, Section 8, they were largely defining the powers and responsibilities of the national government itself.[1] Among the most significant of these **enumerated powers** are the powers to tax and spend; to borrow money; to regulate commerce between the states and with foreign countries; to raise, support, and maintain an army and a navy; to provide for a uniform system of weights and measures; to provide a monetary system; to set up federal courts; to establish post offices and post roads; to declare war; and to make rules for the conduct of government. There is also a provision, known as the **elastic clause,** that gives Congress broad powers to legislate beyond its enumerated powers and that has been the basis for much of the expansion of the federal government's role in our national life. It reads: Congress shall have power "to make all laws which shall be necessary and proper for carrying into execution" all of its other powers. In addition to the grants of power to Congress as a whole, the Constitution also defines particular responsibilities of the House of Representatives and of the Senate. These are summarized in Table 11.2.

enumerated powers Powers of the federal government specifically mentioned in the Constitution.

elastic clause Article I, Section 8; also called the necessary and proper clause; gives Congress the authority to make whatever laws are necessary and proper to carry out its enumerated responsibilities.

Constraining Congress The framers wanted to create an energetic government with a strong legislative branch, but fearing tyranny, they also specifically wanted to limit congressional power. Making Congress a **bicameral** body served this purpose. The framers divided the legislative branch into two houses. This system followed the precedent of the British Parliament, which is organized into the House of Commons and the House of Lords, and that of the colonial legislatures in America. This way of organizing the legislative branch was consistent with the republican idea that laws should be made only after patient deliberation. Single-house legislative bodies, they believed, would be prone to rash action.

The Constitution contains other features that constrain the power of Congress. Article I, Section 9, prohibits **bills of attainder, ex post facto laws,** the granting of titles of nobility, and the suspension of the right of **habeas corpus.** Other prohibitions are found in the Bill of Rights. Note that the First Amendment, perhaps the most important constitutional proviso protecting political liberty, begins with the words "Congress shall make no law."

bicameral A legislative body made up of two houses.

bill of attainder A governmental decree or announcement that a person is guilty of a crime that carries the death penalty, rendered without benefit of a trial.

ex post facto law A law that retroactively declares some action illegal.

habeas corpus The legal doctrine which holds that those who are arrested must have a timely hearing before a judge.

Table 11.2

Constitutional Differences Between the House and the Senate

Though the two chambers of Congress share the responsibility of making the nation's laws, the constitutional design of each is unique; each has a set of specified powers and responsibilities and a different basis of representation, term of office for its members, and size.

Senate	House of Representatives
Six-year term	Two-year term
Two senators per state	Number based on population size (minimum of one per state)
100 members	435 members (total determined by Congress)
Minimum age 30 years	Minimum age 25 years
One-third elected each election cycle	Entire membership elected each election cycle
Power of advice and consent for judicial and upper-level executive-branch appointments	Originates revenue bills
Power of advice and consent for treaties	
Power to try impeachment	Power to bring impeachment charges

We also learned in Chapter 2 that the national government was organized on the basis of a "separation of powers" and "checks and balances," so that "ambition might check ambition" and protect the country from tyranny (see *The Federalist,* No. 51, in the Appendix). This means that, while the framers saw the legislative branch as the vital center of a vigorous national government, they wanted to make sure that Congress would be surrounded by competing centers of government power. We will see in this and other chapters that this fragmentation of governmental power in the United States affects how Congress works and often makes it difficult to fashion coherent and effective public policies.

Representation in Congress The most heated and lengthy debates during the Constitutional Convention concerned representation in Congress. The "Great Compromise" apportioned the House of Representatives on the basis of population and the Senate on the basis of equal representation of the states (refer to Chapter 2 for details). This arrangement significantly increased the clout in Congress of states of small population.

The terms of office of the members of the House of Representatives were set at two years. The terms of the members of the Senate, on the other hand, were set at six years, with only one-third of the seats up for election in each two-year election cycle. By this arrangement, the framers hoped to prevent the takeover of Congress by transitory popular majorities.

The Constitution called for the election of senators by state legislatures, not by the people. Again, the objective seems to have been to insulate one house of Congress from popular pressures and to make it a seat of deliberation and reflection. As James Madison put it, "The use of the Senate is to consist in its

The Direct Election of Senators

The Struggle for Democracy

By the end of the nineteenth century, the selection of senators by state legislatures, in addition to being out of step with the strong democratic sentiments of the time, had become riddled with corruption and inefficiency. Outright bribery of state legislators by prospective senatorial candidates had become widespread. To be successful at bribery required, of course, access to funds that allowed one to outspend rivals. This, in turn, required that prospective senators be personally wealthy—thus, the popular designation of the Senate in the late nineteenth century as the "millionaires' club"—or tied to powerful economic interests. In one notorious case, William Lorimer of Illinois was elected to the Senate in 1909, despite widely publicized evidence that he was being paid by several large corporations (yet had no apparent duties) and had paid off key Illinois legislators to secure his election.

Another problem was that party competition in the states made it difficult for state legislatures to agree easily on a selection. Things became especially difficult when one party controlled the state house of representatives and the other party controlled the state senate, or when party competition was close and each took turns in power. In the first type of situation, deadlocks would develop that would deprive states of representation in the Senate. During the 1890s, several states were without one of their senators for more than two years. In 1895, the Delaware legislature took 217 ballots over a period of three months without being able to make a decision. In the second type of situation, winning parties in the legislature would throw out the senators of the other party, substituting their own people as quickly as possible. Sometimes, the U.S. Senate would refuse to seat these new people, further confusing the situation and diminishing the representation of the state in Washington, D.C.

The call for the direct election of senators was first made by labor and farmers' groups in the last third of the nineteenth century, mainly on the grounds of democracy and the need to separate the U.S. Senate from the "grip of the plutocrats." Progressive reformers added their own voices, mainly on the grounds of efficiency and good government. By the turn of the century, as far as we are able to tell in the absence of polling, most Americans favored the direct election of senators. Both parties endorsed the idea. The House of Representatives passed resolutions in favor of a constitutional amendment changing the Senate selection process in every Congress after 1900. But the constitutional proposal, not surprisingly, died in the Senate each time.

Frustrated in the Senate, reformers did an end run, concentrating on the states. They enacted laws mandating popular referendums on potential Senate candidates and compelling state legislatures to follow the referendum results when choosing senators. By 1912, 29 states had instituted these electoral reforms, effectively placing the selection of senators in the hands of the people in a majority of the states. The method passed an important test in 1910 in the State of Nevada, when a Democrat-controlled state legislature elected Republican George Nixon to the Senate because he had won a popular referendum over his Democratic rival.

The U.S. Senate, seeing the proverbial handwriting on the wall, finally gave in and approved a proposal for a constitutional amendment for the direct election of senators in 1912. The requisite number of states had approved the Seventeenth Amendment by 1913.

Source: Bob Dole, *Historical Almanac of the United States Senate* (Washington, DC: U.S. Government Printing Office, 1989), pp. 180–184; J. W. Peltason, *Understanding the Constitution* (New York: Holt, Rinehart & Winston, 1988), p. 254.

proceeding with more coolness . . . and with more wisdom than the popular branch."[2] The election of senators by the state legislatures could not survive the democratizing tendencies in the country, however. The Seventeenth Amendment, passed in 1913, gave the people the power to elect senators directly.

Federalism Congress is also greatly affected by the federal design of the Constitution. In our federal system, some powers and responsibilities are granted to the national government, some are shared, and some are reserved for the states. It is inevitable in such a system that conflicts will occur between state governments and the national government and its legislative branch. Such conflicts sometimes reach the Supreme Court for resolution. In *United States v. Lopez* (1995), for instance, the Court ruled that Congress had gone too far in the use of its commerce clause powers when it passed a law banning firearms in and around public schools. While the goal was worthy, perhaps, such a matter was the business of the states, not of Congress, in the opinion of the Court.

Federalism also infuses "localism" into congressional affairs.[3] Though Congress is charged with making national policies, we should remember that the members of the Senate and the House come to Washington as the representatives of states and districts. They inevitably consider local concerns when making national policies.

The Historical Development of Congress

The many economic and social changes that have occurred in the United States (described in Chapter 4) have also influenced how Congress works today.[4]

The First Congress The First Congress convened on March 4, 1789, in the Federal Hall in New York City. Because both the House and the Senate were small bodies, neither needed strong leadership or committees to manage its business. Each house considered bills as a "committee of the whole" in which all members participated. The flow of business was manageable because the federal government did not play a very large role in American life. Few members saw service in Congress as a lifelong career. Most expected to return to private life or to politics in their home states. All of this has changed.

Increase in Size The most obvious change since 1789 has been the growth in the size of Congress. Because the Senate is made up of two senators from each state, it naturally grows as the number of states in the nation increases. The Senate in the 1st Congress had 26 members, representing the 13 states; today the Senate has 100 members, representing 50 states.

Membership in the House of Representatives is apportioned to each state on the basis of its population size. Rapid population increase in the nineteenth

When the first U.S. Congress convened in New York City in 1789, the entire legislative body consisted of only 81 members, 59 in the House and 22 in the Senate (two states had not yet ratified the Constitution) so that all members could participate in all decisions. As the nation—and consequently the Congress—grew, the direct consideration of bills by the entire legislature became cumbersome. Today, bills must first pass through committees before they are voted on by the entire body.

century brought the number of representatives in the House from 65 in 1789 to 435 in 1912. Believing they had reached the limit of a functioning legislative body, the House members froze the upper limit at 435, where it has remained. Since the American population continued to grow after 1912, while the size of the House has remained fixed, the average population size of each congressional district has increased dramatically, from a little over 200,000 in 1912 to almost 600,000 today.

Increase in the Volume of Congressional Business The federal government now plays a larger role in American life than the framers envisioned because of structural changes in the United States. Urbanization, population growth, industrialization, economic change and instability, and our emergence as a superpower have generated a wide range of problems and opportunities that have led to the growth of a vigorous and interventionist government. As government has taken on more responsibilities, the sheer volume of congressional business has expanded accordingly.

We can see this progression in a number of ways. More bills are introduced today than in the past. In the 1st Congress, 144 bills were introduced. Today, 9,000 to 10,000 are normal. Far more staff members work in Congress than in the past, to help with the institution's expanded legislative business (see Figure 11.1); the total peaked at about 18,000 in 1994 before the new Republican majorities in the House and Senate substantially cut back the numbers of committee staff (by one-third) in the 104th Congress. Congress also stays in session for many more hours per year than it did in the past, increasing from about 800 hours for the House in 1955 to almost 1,600 today.[5]

Institutionalization and Professionalization[6] As Congress grew in size and considered ever more complex issues, it became more *structured, organized,*

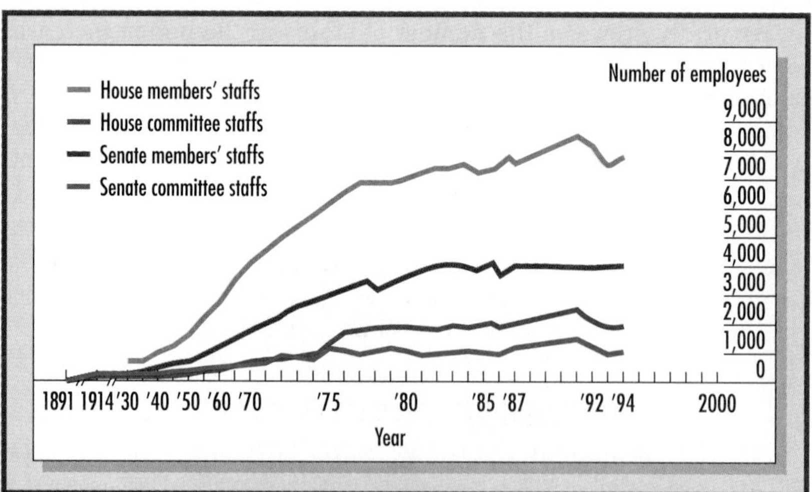

Figure 11.1 ■ **Size of House and Senate Staffs**

One indicator of the substantial growth in the responsibilities and activities of Congress is the increase in the number of staff members who work for senators, representatives, and the committees in the two houses. Note that the increase in staff is mainly a post–World War II phenomenon.

Sources: Norman J. Ornstein, Thomas E. Mann, and Michael J. Malbin, *Vital Statistics on Congress 1989–1990* (Washington, DC: Congressional Quarterly Press, 1990), p. 130; the Clerk of the U.S. House of Representatives and the General Accounting Office for 1991; *Congressional Record Service Report* (October 24, 1994).

regularized, and *rule-bound,* especially the House of Representatives (because it is so much bigger than the Senate). Formal ways of doing things replaced many informal arrangements. Legislative business today is done mainly in specialized committees and subcommittees, by subject-matter specialists and professional staff. Much of the coordination is accomplished by elaborate rules of procedure (particularly in the House of Representatives) and well-understood precedents. Today's system is very different from that of the First Congress.

Congress has also become more "professionalized," in the sense that more members today think of their jobs as careers than they did in the past. Until the late nineteenth century, members of Congress came and went frequently. From the late nineteenth century to the end of the 1980s, however, there was a trend toward lower turnover and much longer average terms in office. There was somewhat of a change in the 1990s, because the 1992 and 1994 elections resulted in substantial membership turnover. Though incumbents did well in 1996, a record number of retirements meant that turnover continued to be significant.

Sharing Power with the President Another historical trend has been the increasing power of the presidency in fashioning national policies. With the exception of foreign and military affairs, where they expected the president to take the lead, the framers gave Congress the main responsibility for national policymaking. In the twentieth century, however, presidents have taken a much more central role in fashioning the nation's legislative agenda. Franklin Roosevelt's New Deal, Lyndon Johnson's Great Society, and Ronald Reagan's conservative "revolution" (described in the opening story in Chapter 12) come to mind as particularly significant examples of presidential initiative on the domestic legislative front, but all modern presidents have tried to take the lead on domestic issues. The agenda of the 103rd Congress, for instance, was dominated by President Clinton's proposals for deficit reduction, economic stimulation, gays in the military, and national health insurance.

This is not to say that Congress has become a weak branch. It remains formidable and independent, less powerful than in the nineteenth century perhaps, but able to go head to head with the president on most issues. The powerful role of congress becomes apparent when it is compared to the role of legislatures in other democratic countries. In England, important bills are written in the ministries, approved by the Cabinet, and debated in the House of Commons. Members are allowed only 12 days during a session to introduce bills (always minor ones) and 10 days to make motions. Party discipline ensures that the members of Parliament will rarely amend legislation and that the fate of legislation will never be in doubt.

Congress may well experience a growth in power as the nation turns its attention from the Cold War with the Soviet Union to the task of solving domestic problems, an arena in which Congress feels no need to defer to the president, as President Bill Clinton discovered. For instance, the Republican 104th Congress, led by House Speaker Newt Gingrich, set the nation's legislative agenda in the 104th Congress after the GOP's stunning victory in 1994.

Representation and Democracy

Ours is a representative democracy in which the members of Congress serve as our legislative representatives. We want to ask in this section whether they carry out this representative responsibility in a way that can be considered democratic. To answer this question, we need to look at several aspects of representation.

Styles of Representation

delegate The doctrine, best articulated by Edmund Burke, that elected representatives ought to act in perfect accord with the wishes of their constituents.

trustee Edmund Burke's term for representatives who believe they ought to use their best judgment, rather than instructions from their constituents, in making legislative decisions.

In a letter to his constituents written in 1774, English politician and philosopher Edmund Burke described two principal styles of representation. As a **delegate,** the representative tries to mirror perfectly the views of his or her constituents. As a **trustee,** the representative acts independently, trusting to his or her own best judgment of the issues. Burke preferred the trustee approach: "Your representative owes you, not his industry only, but his judgment; and he betrays you, instead of serving you, if he sacrifices it to your opinion."[7]

Campaigning for Congress in Illinois several decades later, Abraham Lincoln argued otherwise: "While acting as [your] representative, I shall be governed by [your] will, on all subjects upon which I have the means of knowing what [your] will is."[8]

The members of Congress choose between these two styles of representation probably less according to their personal tastes than according to judgments about the relative safety of their seats. Representatives and senators without real electoral competition can better afford to choose the trustee style. Senators with six-year terms face the electorate less often than members of the House, so they are freer than representatives to assume the trustee style.

Who Are the Members of Congress?

One way to represent is to be similar to those one is representing. If we want a political system in which the views of women are taken into account, for instance, we might want a significant number of women in Congress. From this perspective, a perfectly representative legislative body would be similar to the general population in race, sex, ethnicity, occupation, religion, age, and the like. In this sense, the U.S. Congress is highly *unrepresentative.*

Gender and Race Both women and racial minorities are significantly underrepresented in Congress, particularly in the Senate, despite recent gains. We can see this in Figure 11.2, which compares the distribution of women and minorities in the 104th Congress (1995–1996) with their distribution in the country as a whole.

Black representation reached its peak during the post–Civil War Reconstruction period, when blacks played an important political role in several southern states. They disappeared from Congress for many years after the reimposition of white supremacy in the South at the end of the nineteenth century. Though a handful of black representatives from northern cities served during the first half of the twentieth century—Oscar DePriest from Chicago's predominantly black South Side and Adam Clayton Powell from New York City's Harlem, for instance—no significant numbers of black legislators entered Congress until the late 1960s. Even though their number increased from 26 to 39 between the 102nd (1991–1992) and 104th Congresses (1995–1996), their numbers are still well below what one might expect, given the proportion of blacks in the American population.

Nine additional Latinos were elected to the House in the 1992 congressional elections, but the loss of one seat in 1994, left their total at eighteen. Though Latinos are even more poorly represented than African-Americans,

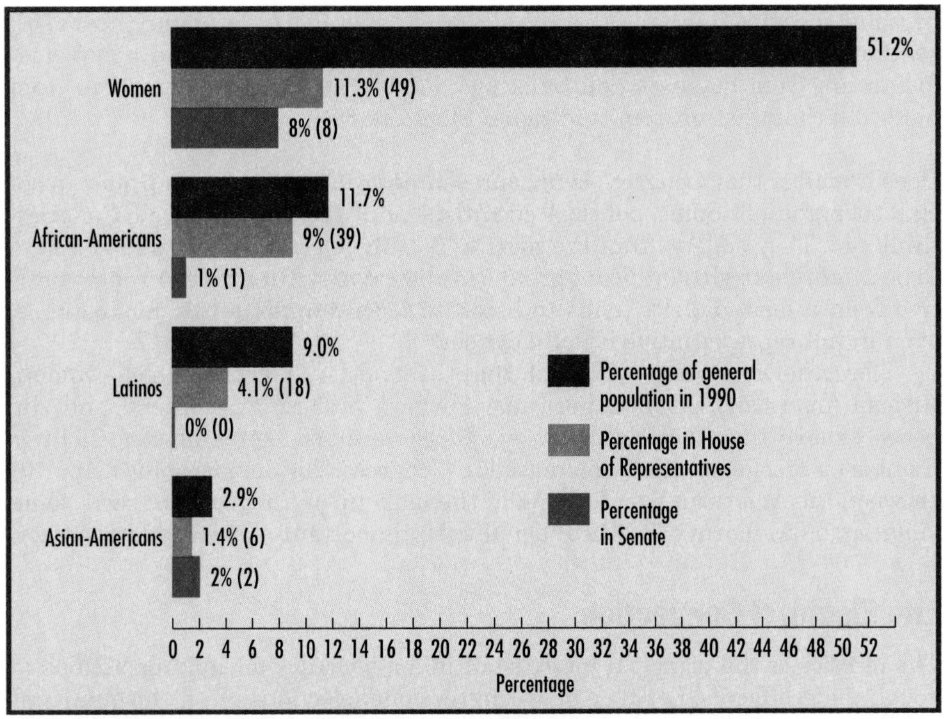

Figure 11.2 ▪ Women and Minorities in Congress

Though their numbers in Congress have increased in recent years, women and racial minorities are still substantially underrepresented compared with their proportion in the American population. This figure compares the percentages of women and racial minorities in each house of the 104th Congress with their percentages in the population. Please refer to the opening story for information on the 105th Congress elected in 1996.

the increase in their numbers will probably give the Latino caucus a greater voice in legislative affairs than in the past. Asian-Americans have also seen their numbers increase in recent years, with 6 representatives and 2 senators in the 104th Congress. One Native American, Ben Nighthorse Campbell (Republican of Colorado), holds a seat in the U.S. Senate.

The first woman to sit in Congress was Jeannette Rankin of Montana, elected in 1916. The number of women has slowly increased, reaching a total of 48 in the House and 7 in the Senate in the 103rd Congress, a dramatic jump from 29 and 2 in the 102nd, justifying the designation of 1992 as the "year of the woman." In 1992, Carol Moseley-Braun (Democrat of Illinois) became the first African-American woman to be elected to the Senate. Proportionally, however, female representation in Congress is still only about one-half the average for legislative bodies around the world and nowhere near the more than 50 percent of women represent in the U.S. population. Moreover, women have not yet reached the top leadership posts in either chamber; only three chair standing committees in the House and Senate.

The 1996 elections affected the gender and racial makeup of Congress. The numbers are reviewed in the story on the elections that opens this chapter.

Social Class Members of Congress are far better educated than the rest of the population. They tend to come from very high-income families and to have personal incomes that are substantially above average. At least one-third of all senators are millionaires.[9] More than one-half are lawyers, and about one-fourth are from business and banking. Notably absent are lawmakers from blue-collar families or from traditional blue-collar jobs.

Does it matter that Congress is unrepresentative of the American people in social background? Some political scientists and close observers of Congress think not. They suggest that the need to face the electorate forces lawmakers to be attentive to all significant groups in their **constituencies.** A representative from a farm district tends to listen to farm **constituents,** for instance, even if that representative is not a farmer.

constituency The district of a legislator.

constituent One who lives in the district of an elected official.

Nevertheless, many who feel they are not well represented—women, African-Americans, Asian-Americans, Latinos, blue-collar workers, and the poor—believe that their interests would get a much better hearing if their numbers were substantially increased in Congress. The demographic disparity between the American population and the makeup of Congress suggests some violation of the norm of political equality, an important element of democracy.

The Electoral Connection

The election is the principal instrument in a democracy for linking citizens to government officials. Let's see how congressional elections affect the quality of representation in the United States.

Electoral Districts Each state is entitled to two senators. Remember, that the agreement among the framers to grant equal representation to the states as part of the Great Compromise (see Chapter 2) was one of the key decisions

Members of Congress must spend a considerable amount of their time staying in touch with their constituents. Here Democratic Senator Dianne Feinstein of California greets a potential voter.

made at the Constitutional Convention. Equal representation, however, gives extraordinary power in the Senate to states with small populations. Alaska, for instance, has exactly the same number of senators as California, though it has only one-fiftieth of California's population. This arrangement can substantially distort popular sentiment and thus diminish democracy. The degree to which the Senate is unrepresentative of the United States can be seen in the following fact: Fifty-four senators (a majority large enough to pass legislation) in the 104th Congress came from states which together made up only 20 percent of the American population.

Representation in the House of Representatives is determined by a state's population. **Reapportionment,** or redistribution of the 435 House seats among the states, occurs every ten years, after the national census (see Figure 11.3 for the most recent changes). After the census, some states keep the same number of seats; others gain or lose them. States gaining or losing seats must then redraw the boundary lines of their congressional districts. In the past, this reapportionment was left entirely to the state legislatures. Very often, the result was congressional districts of vastly different population size—in New

reapportionment The redrawing of congressional district lines to account for population change.

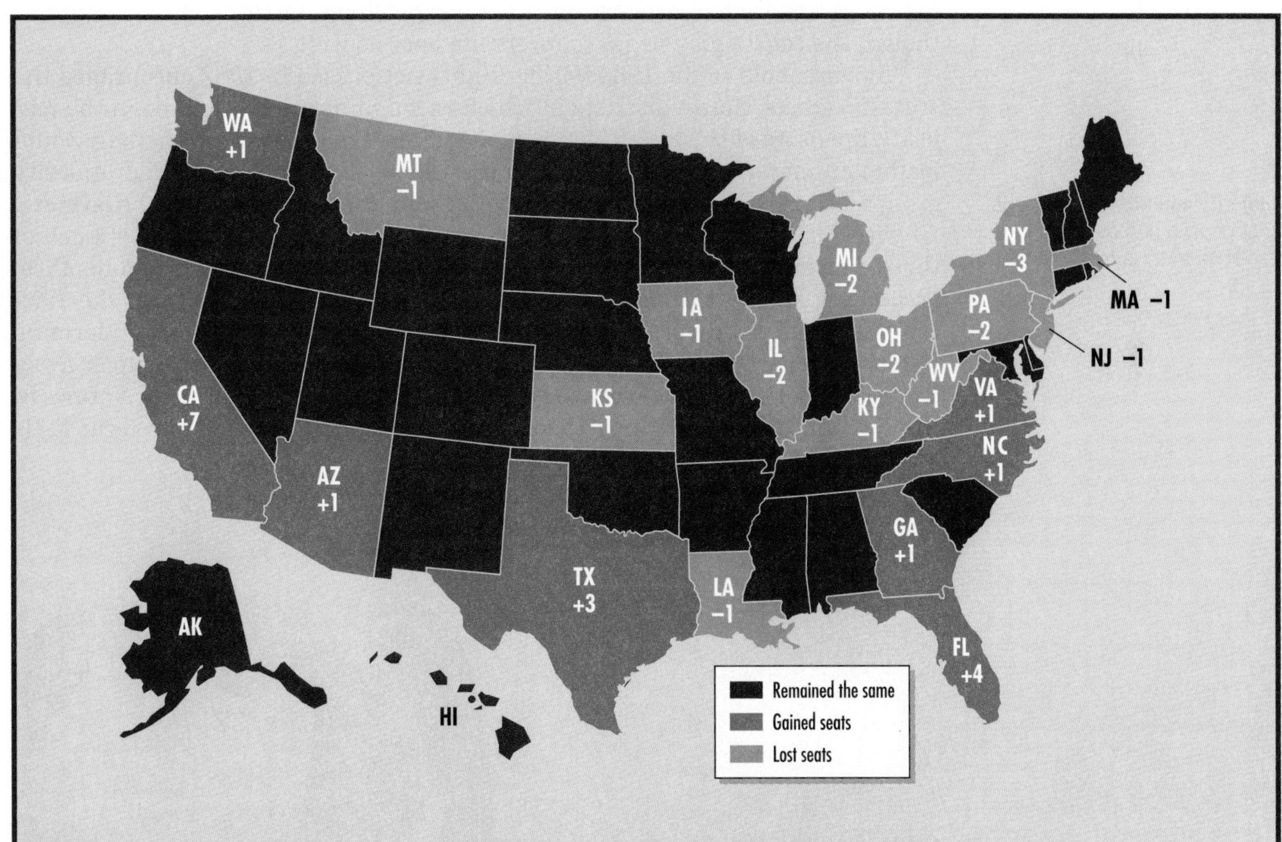

Figure 11.3 ▪ States Gaining and Losing Congressional Seats Following the 1990 Census

The number of representatives for each state in the House of Representatives is based on the size of its population. Because the relative sizes of the states changes over time, the number of representatives from each state is recalculated after each census. This graph shows which states gained and lost representatives between the 1980 and 1990 censuses.

York in the 1930s, some congressional districts were ten times larger than others—and a significantly overrepresented rural population. The Supreme Court ruled in *Wesberry v. Sanders* (1964), however, that the principle of one-person–one-vote applies to congressional districts. Today, all congressional districts are of roughly equal population size.

While congressional districts must be approximately the same size in population, state legislatures are still relatively free to draw district lines where they choose. The party that controls the state legislature usually tries to draw the lines in a way that will help its candidates win elections. The results are often strange indeed. Rather than creating compact and coherent districts, neighborhoods, towns, and counties can be strung together in odd-looking ways in order to take full partisan advantage of the redistricting process. At its extreme, such a process is called **gerrymandering,** after Governor Elbridge Gerry of Massachusetts, who signed a bill in 1811, that created a district that looked like a salamander. It made wonderful raw material for editorial cartoonists.

gerrymander Redrawing electoral district lines to give an advantage to a particular party or candidate.

The Supreme Court has tried to prevent the most flagrant abuses, especially when some identifiable group of voters (for example, racial minorities) is disadvantaged, but redistricting is a practice that is difficult to regulate. Parties in power continue to try to draw district lines to their own advantage, though the courts may begin to intervene here as well.

Amendments to the 1965 Voting Rights Act passed in 1982 encouraged the states to create House districts in which racial minorities would be in the majority. Sponsors of the legislation hoped and expected that these changes would lead to an increase in the election to the House of members of racial minority groups. The result was the formation of 24 new **majority-minority districts,** 15 with African-American majorities, and 9 with Latino majorities.[10] Each of these districts did, in fact, elect a member of a racial minority group to office, accounting for most of the increase in minority representation after the 1992 congressional elections. The creation of such districts tended to undermine Democratic party strength in other districts, however, because it took away traditionally Democratic-oriented minority-group voters from them. Naturally, the Republicans were happy to support minority group efforts to form their own districts.

majority-minority districts Districts drawn purposely so that a racial minority is in the majority.

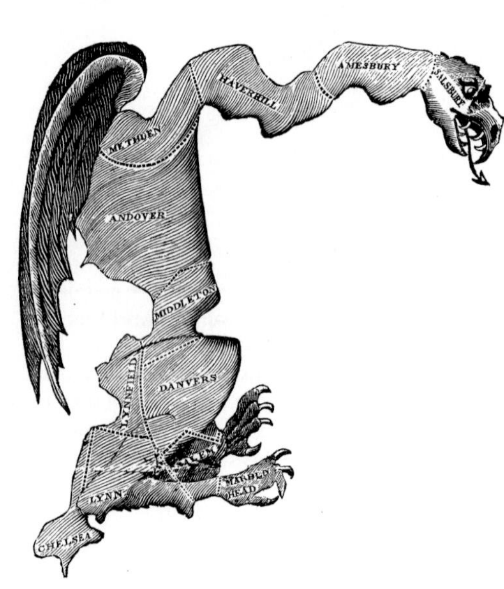

The term *gerrymander* is derived from this 1812 Elkanah Tinsdale cartoon, which lampoons a Massachusetts district drawn to ensure the election of a Republican candidate. The "Gerry-mander" was named after Massachusetts Governor Elbridge Gerry, who signed the bill that created the salamander-shaped district.

The creation of some of these districts took great imagination. North Carolina's Twelfth District, for instance, created after the 1990 census, linked a narrow strip of African-American communities along 160 miles of Interstate 85 connecting Durham and Charlotte. After first encouraging the creation of majority-minority districts, the Supreme Court, is having second thoughts about districts that are highly irregular in form, noncontiguous, unconnected to traditional political jurisdictions (*Shaw v. Reno,* 1993), or drawn solely to aid one race (*Miller v. Johnson,* 1995). Because these rulings put majority-minority districts at risk, it is likely that the representation of racial minorities in Congress will decrease. A portent of what may be coming are recent decisions by federal district courts to scrap two of three majority-minority districts in Georgia, and to redraw 13 congressional districts in Texas.

Money and Congressional Elections Running for the House or the Senate is a very expensive proposition, and it keeps getting more expensive. In the 1994 congressional elections, candidates for the House and the Senate spent over $690 million, up over 53 percent from 1990 and about 200 percent since 1972. Senate races were the most expensive. In California, Michael Huffington and Dianne Feinstein spent the most in 1994 (nearly $44 million), followed by Virginia, where Oliver North and Charles Robb spent almost $26 million. Incumbents, as usual, attracted and spent the most money (see Figure 11.4). For statistics on congressional spending in the 1996 elections, see the story that opens this chapter.

There is nothing particularly surprising about the increased costs of political campaigns. Inflation has played a part, as has the ever greater reliance on

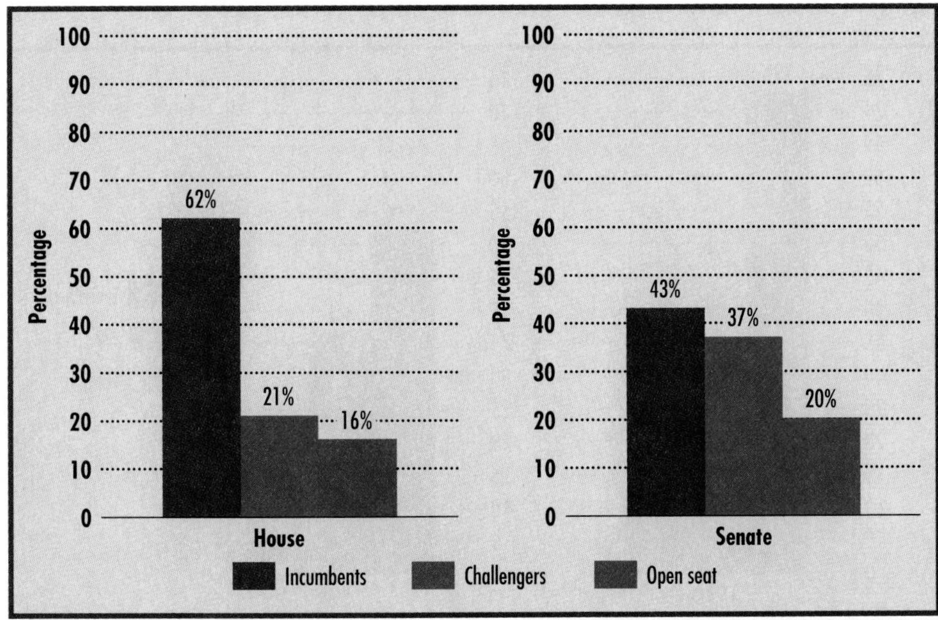

Figure 11.4 ▪ Campaign Money Spent by Incumbents, Challengers, and Open Seat Candidates, 1994

Because campaign contributors want to have access to important decision makers in Congress, they tend to give a disproportionate share to incumbents rather than to challengers. This is one of the most important electoral advantages of incumbents. Please refer to the opening story for information on the 105th Congress elected in 1996.

expensive campaign technologies, such as mass and targeted mailings; polling; focus groups; television, radio, and print advertising; and phone banks. So, too, has the decline of party loyalty in the electorate, which compels each candidate to try to reach each and every potential voter on his or her own.

Spending matters. Though candidates who spend the most money do not always win, they do most of the time. This is especially true in those elections in which an incumbent is not involved (called **open seat elections**), where Republicans have enjoyed big spending advantages in recent elections.[11]

open seat election An election in which there is no incumbent officeholder.

PAC (political action committee) A private organization whose purpose is to raise and distribute funds to candidates in political campaigns.

Congressional campaign money comes from four main sources: individuals, **PACs,** parties, and the candidates themselves (see Figure 11.5). The largest share comes from individual contributors, though the size of the share has declined substantially since 1974, with PACs picking up most of the slack. Not surprisingly, individual contributors are significantly more affluent than the average citizen.

PACs are the fastest-growing part of the campaign financing system, accounting for more than twice the proportion of campaign funding they did in 1974. PACs can contribute up to $5,000 per candidate per election, and they can give to as many candidates as they wish. They are also free to spend without limit when publicizing their positions on public issues. Such issue campaigns are often thinly veiled efforts to help a particular candidate or party (thus, their common designation, **parallel campaigns**). The National Conservative Political Action Committee (NICPAC), a conservative ideological PAC, was, for all intents and purposes, a part of the 1980 and 1984 Reagan campaigns.

parallel campaign A device used to bypass campaign-spending-limits laws; a campaign that helps a particular candidate without mentioning the name of the candidate.

Many people believe that the increased role of PACs in congressional campaigns increases the influence of interest groups in general, and of business in-

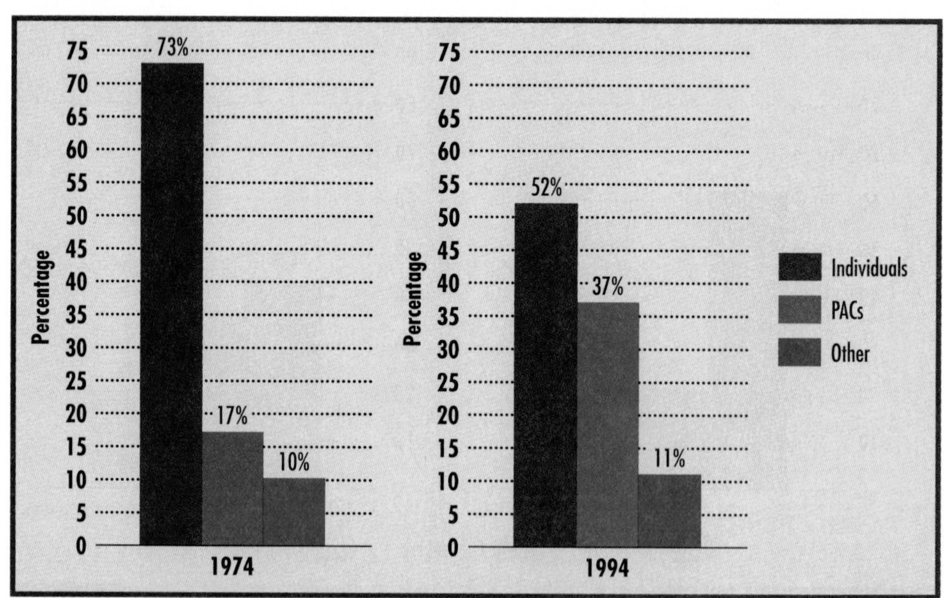

Figure 11.5 ▪ Where Congressional Campaign Money Comes from, Comparing 1974 and 1994

Though the largest share of campaign contributions still comes from individuals, the share contributed by political action committees (PACs) is growing rapidly. This is shown by a comparison of the sources of campaign giving in 1974 and 1994.

Source: Based on Roger H. Davidson and Walter J. Oleszek, *Congress and Its Members,* 4th ed. (Washington, DC:

terests in particular. Corporate, trade, and professional groups together account for over 60 percent of all PAC expenditures in congressional races (see the more detailed discussion in Chapter 7).

Many candidates support their election campaigns out of their own pockets. Obviously, a substantial number of them must be wealthier than the average American, though few are as wealthy or as free with their money as Michael Huffington. In the 1994 elections, he spent $28 million out of his own pocket in a failed effort to get elected to the Senate from California.

Congressional candidates also receive campaign money from their political parties. Party organizations are allowed to make a $5,000 contribution per campaign to each candidate. Though this portion of campaign spending has remained relatively constant in House elections, the parties are now playing a slightly more important role than in the past in Senate elections.

There are no legal limits on **soft-money** contributions, money that individuals, groups, and corporations give to political parties for general education, registration, and "get-out-the-vote" campaigns. Nor are there limits on how much soft money the parties can spend, even though such spending obviously benefits individual candidates. According to most experts, soft money has become the principal means by which large corporations and wealthy individual contributors have been able to circumvent the stringent legal limits on contributions.[12] The Midland Corporation and its owner, for instance, contributed over $600,000 to the Republican party during the 1992 election cycle.[13]

soft money Expenditures by the political parties on general public education, voter registration, and voter mobilization.

The Incumbency Factor Incumbents—those already holding elected office—win at much higher rates in the House today than they did in the last century or the first half of this one. The ability of House incumbents to get reelected improved especially from the late 1940s into the 1990s (see Figure 11.6), allowing the Democratic party to maintain control over the House of Representatives for four decades (from 1955 to 1994), even as Republicans like Dwight Eisenhower, Richard Nixon, Ronald Reagan, and George Bush were winning presidential elections. In spite of mounting discontent with Congress and the anti-incumbent talk of recent years, members of the House of Representatives who choose to run for reelection are still almost always successful. In the 1992 and 1994 elections, when anti-incumbent feelings seemed to be running extraordinarily high, incumbency reelection rates in the House were 88 percent and 92 percent, respectively. In 1996, House and Senate incumbents were even more successful.

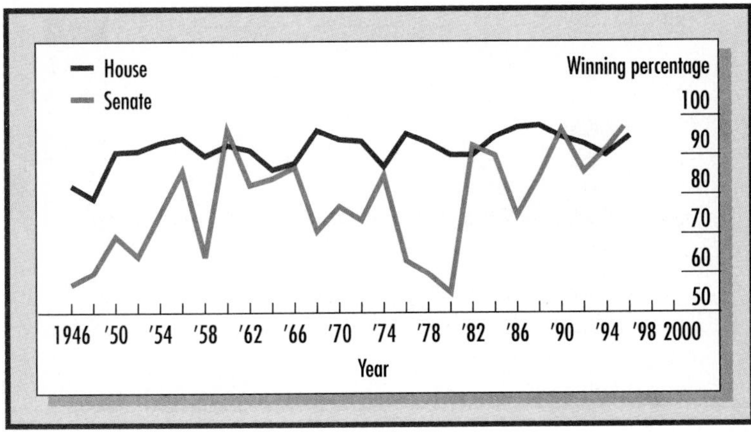

Figure 11.6 ▪ Rates of Incumbent Reelection in Congress

The probability that incumbents will be reelected remains at historic highs. This does not mean, however, that the membership of Congress is stagnant. Turnover in membership is substantial because of retirements and the defeat of incumbents in primary elections.

Source: *Congressional Quarterly Weekly Report* (November 12, 1994), p. 3237 and calculations by the authors for 1996.

Discontent with Congress has helped fuel a sometimes bitter national campaign to limit the number of terms that may be served by senators and representatives. Many believe, as does the cartoonist David Horsey, that such measures are antidemocratic.

Despite what looks like business as usual, however, something quite extraordinary has been going on beneath the surface in recent elections. Lots of fresh faces have begun to appear in Congress (see Figure 11.7). If we look at the percentage of incumbents who actually return to Congress after an election rather than at the percentage reelected, we see evidence of a high turnover. In the four House elections spanning the years 1984 to 1990, the return rate was at or near 90 percent. In 1992, it fell to 75 percent, rising to only 81 percent in 1994. In 1996, the return rate was 80 percent. Turnover occurred because many incumbents either retired (perhaps not confident about their renomination or reelection) or were defeated at the nomination stage by opponents within their own party. Democratic members quit their positions in unprecedented numbers during the Republican ascendancy in the 104th Congress. Eight Democratic Senators, including widely respected Senators Bill Bradley of New Jersey and Sam Nunn of Georgia, announced in 1995 that they would not seek reelection. Several Republican moderates, such as Nancy Kassebaum of Kansas, William Cohen of Maine, and Hank Brown of Colorado,

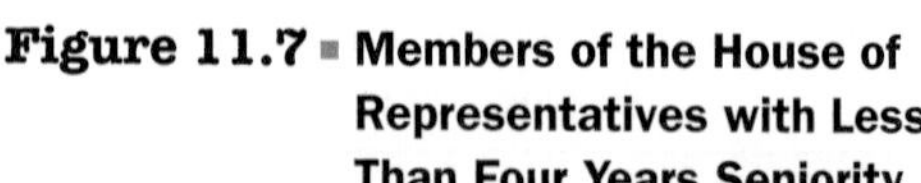

Figure 11.7 ▪ Members of the House of Representatives with Less Than Four Years Seniority

The turnover in Congress in recent years has been surprisingly high. This figure shows that almost half of the members of the House of Representatives have served fewer than four years.

Source: *Congressional Quarterly Weekly Report* (November 12, 1994), p. 3238.

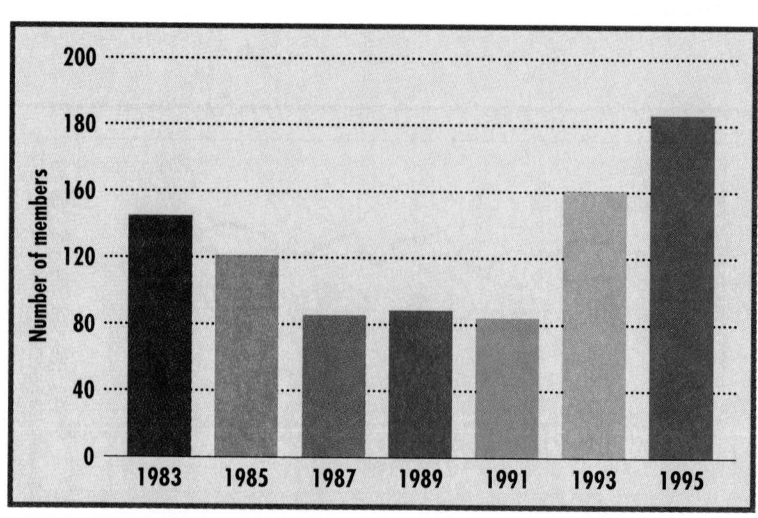

perhaps feeling vulnerable because of the strong conservative turn of their party, also decided to retire rather than seek reelection.

Why Incumbents Still Have Some Advantages For those members of Congress who have not retired or been defeated at the nomination stage, incumbency continues to be a valuable resource, despite the growing popular disillusionment with Congress (see Figure 11.8). For one thing, incumbents attract more money than their rivals, by a 2:1 ratio in the Senate and a 3:1 ratio in the House. PACs, interest groups, and corporations want access to key decision makers in the House and the Senate. They look at campaign contributions as an "investment," a way to guarantee that their phone calls will be answered, that they will be allowed to make their case, and that their interests will be taken into account.[14] To contribute to a challenger is to jeopardize access if the challenger loses.

The flow of money is particularly heavy to those incumbents who sit on key committees or hold important leadership posts. During consideration of the 1986 tax reform bill, for instance, PACs gave one-third of their total $66.8 million in contributions to members of the two tax-writing committees of Congress. The American Medical Association and the American Hospital Association contributed considerable sums to House Speaker Newt Gingrich and Majority Leader Richard Armey during the debate over Medicare reform in 1995.

Incumbents also use the congressional machinery to help their reelection chances.[15] Already well known to voters, members of Congress have many ways to advertise their accomplishments and keep their names before the public. For instance, the **franking privilege** allows them to mail newsletters, legislative updates, surveys, and other self-promoting literature free of charge. The House and the Senate also provide travel budgets for lawmakers to make periodic visits to their states or districts. Because members believe that time spent in their districts helps their electoral chances—a belief supported by a great deal of research[16]—they spend lots of time back home. Some manage to spend three or four days per week in their districts or states, meeting constituents, giving speeches, raising money, and so on. The congressional leadership helps by trying to schedule important legislative business for the Tuesday-to-Thursday period.

franking, franking privilege Public subsidization of mail from the members of Congress to their constituents.

Incumbents also use their offices to "service the district." One way is through **casework:** helping constituents cut through the red tape of the federal bureaucracy, whether it be by speeding up the arrival of a late Social Security check or expediting the issuance of a permit for grazing on public land.[17]

casework Services performed by members of Congress for constituents.

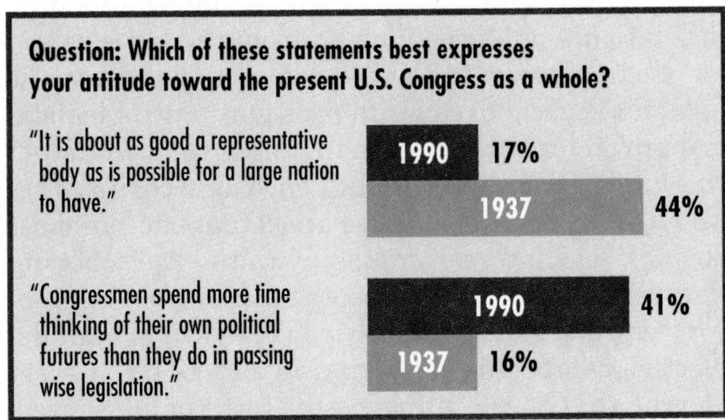
Question: Which of these statements best expresses your attitude toward the present U.S. Congress as a whole?
"It is about as good a representative body as is possible for a large nation to have."
1990 17%
1937 44%
"Congressmen spend more time thinking of their own political futures than they do in passing wise legislation."
1990 41%
1937 16%

Figure 11.8 ▪ **Regard for Congress, Then and Now**

Americans show much lower regard for Congress today than they did in the past.

Source: *The Public Perspective* (March–April 1994), p. 5.

Federal projects awarded to districts are part of what is commonly called the legislative *pork barrel.* Pork has long been an important reelection resource for congressional incumbents since they claim credit for its being awarded.

pork Also called pork barrel; projects designed to bring to the constituency jobs and public money for which the members of Congress can claim credit.

Generous budgets for establishing and staffing offices in the constituency help representatives and senators do casework. Another way to "service the district" is to provide **pork:** federal dollars for various projects in the district or state. In his first three years as chairman of the Appropriations Committee, Senator Robert Byrd of West Virginia managed to steer $750 million in federal contracts and grants to his state, along with 3,000 federal jobs. Speaker Newt Gingrich's Georgia district ranked first among all House districts in federal defense dollars spent in 1996. Challengers can promise to deliver more pork, but incumbents can point to tangible accomplishments.

These resources are considerable, and they give incumbents certain advantages over challengers. On the other hand, if negative attitudes about Congress and anti-incumbent feelings stay at their present levels, incumbency may become a burden for many members of Congress seeking reelection. Challengers can always charge the incumbent with being part of the "mess in Washington," a theme with surprising staying power in American politics.

How Democratic? Representatives and senators pay a great deal of attention to the interests and the preferences of people in their districts and states. Because they are worried about being reelected, they try to see as many people as they can during their frequent visits home, and they pay attention to their mail and the public opinion polls. To a considerable degree, moreover, they vote and pass laws in accordance with public opinion. Research shows that members of Congress vote in a manner that is consistent with public opinion in their districts about two-thirds of the time.[18] As a whole, Congress produces laws that are consistent with national public opinion at about the same rate.[19]

In a substantial number of cases, however, Congress does *not* follow public opinion. Congressional refusal for several decades to pass gun control legislation, in spite of high public approval for such legislation, comes to mind. Moreover, on many issues of high complexity or low visibility, such as securities regulation, the public may have no opinions. It is in these areas that one can most fully see the influence of money and interest groups at work. The lobbying community, we have learned, overwhelmingly represents business and the professions. Moreover, legislators who are almost entirely on their own in organizing and financing their reelection campaigns are tempting targets for interest groups and PACs. To the degree that these influences distort popular sovereignty and undermine political equality, democracy is impaired.

How Congress Works

Congress is a vital center of decision making and policymaking in our national government. It has not become a place where the executive's bills are simply rubber-stamped, as legislative bodies have become in many parliamentary systems. In Great Britain, for instance, roughly 97 percent of the government's (the Cabinet's) bills are approved by the House of Commons.[20] By all accounts, Congress remains the most influential legislative body among the Western democratic nations. It has power; it must be attended to by other political actors; and it plays an important part in making national policy. In this section, we turn our attention to how Congress is organized and functions as a working legislative body.

Among the important things you will learn about how Congress is organized and works are the following:

- It is less hierarchical than collegial.
- It is highly fragmented and decentralized.
- It is very sensitive to outside influences.
- It more easily stops than passes legislation.
- It is becoming increasingly partisan in its deliberations.
- The Senate and the House of Representatives are different in many ways.

Where the Congressional Agenda Comes From

Congress is embedded in a rich structural, political, and governmental environment that influences what it pays attention to. For instance, the other branches of government are a constant influence on the congressional agenda. Supreme Court rulings often spark a legislative reaction. After the Court ruled that the states were free to regulate abortions in the *Webster* case (1989), for instance, Congress reacted by expanding the public funding of abortions in Washington, D.C. as a way to send a message about its support of abortion rights to the court and to the states.

The president and the executive branch are also important in shaping the legislative agenda. Many of the bills that are introduced by lawmakers in the House and the Senate are actually drafted in such places as the Department of Agriculture and the Commerce Department and come to Congress after being cleared by the Office of Management and Budget. Much of what Congress does by way of lawmaking is in response to the legislative program of the president, usually presented in conjunction with his annual State of the Union, economic, and budget messages. Congress must also monitor how the president and the federal bureaucracy carry out the laws, and the Senate is responsible for approving or disapproving presidential nominations to the federal courts and executive branch leadership positions, as well as treaties.

The congressional agenda is also shaped by the many groups and individuals who put pressure on it and its members. Because of their important role in campaign finance, interest groups play a particularly important role in defining the issues before the House and the Senate. Lawmakers must balance the needs and demands of interest groups against those of the public as expressed in public opinion polls and elections. Thus, the 1994 elections, which resulted in an overwhelming Republican victory, made the agenda of the 104th

Congress much more conservative than those of its immediate predecessors. The media are also continuous players in shaping what issues are attended to in the legislative branch. Social movements also sometimes try to impose their own needs.

At a more fundamental level, structural change mobilizes political and governmental institutions, groups, and individuals. Economic dislocations, for instance, may trigger demands for congressional action from voters, interest groups, and other government officials. Population change, including the effects of immigration and aging, adds a range of new issues to the congressional menu, as do changes in the U.S. economic and military position in the world.

Congressional Committees

Most of the work of Congress takes place in its many committees and subcommittees. Committees are where many of the details of legislation are hammered out, and where much of the oversight of executive branch agencies takes place. In general, committees are not central to the activities of legislative bodies in other democratic countries. In the British House of Commons, for instance, committees cannot offer amendments that alter the substance or general principles of bills.

Why Congress Has Committees Committees serve several useful purposes. For one thing, they allow Congress to process the huge flow of business that comes before it. The committees serve as screening devices, allowing only a small percentage of those bills put forward to take up the time of the House and the Senate.

Committees are also islands of specialization, where members and staff develop the expertise to handle complex issues and to meet executive branch experts on equal terms. The Ways and Means Committee of the House can go toe-to-toe with the Treasury Department, for instance; the House and Senate Armed Services Committees can generate expertise equal to that of the Department of Defense. Committee expertise is one of the reasons Congress remains a vital lawmaking body.

Members of Congress also use their committee positions to enhance their chances for reelection. Rational lawmakers usually try to secure committee assignments that will allow them to channel benefits to their constituents.

The Types of Committees in Congress There are several kinds of committees, each of which serves a special function in the legislative process.

standing committees Relatively permanent congressional committees that address specific areas of legislation. Examples are the House Appropriations, Budget, Rules, and Ways and Means Committees.

A **standing committee** is a permanent committee, specified in the House and Senate rules (see Table 11.3). Standing committees are the first stop for House and Senate bills. The size of the standing committees and their subject-matter jurisdictions in today's Congress were set in the Legislative Reorganization Act of 1946 and have been slightly altered several times since. The ratio of Democrats to Republicans on each committee is set for each house through a process of negotiation between the majority and minority party leaders. The majority party naturally enjoys a majority on each of the committees and controls the chair, as well as an extraheavy majority on the most important committees, such as the Budget and Finance Committee in the Senate and the Rules Committee, and Ways and Means Committee in the House. Not surprisingly, the decision about the ratio of Democrats and Republicans on committees is a point of considerable contention between the two parties.

Table 11.3

Standing Committees of the House and the Senate, 104th Congress

Committee	Size; Party Ratio	Subcommittees
House		
Agriculture	47 (26R; 21D)	5
Appropriations	52 (31R; 21D)	13
Banking and Financial Services (*formerly Banking, Finance, and Urban Affairs—jurisdiction expanded*)	46 (25R; 21D)	5
Budget	44 (24R; 20D)	—
Commerce (*formerly Energy and Commerce—jurisdiction narrowed*)	46 (25R; 21D)	5
Economic and Educational Opportunity (*formerly Education and Labor*)	35 (19R; 16D)	5
Government Reform and Oversight (*formerly Government Operations—jurisdiction expanded*)	38 (21R; 17D)	7
House Oversight (*formerly House Administration*)	8 (5R; 3D)	—
International Relations (*formerly Foreign Affairs*)	39 (21R; 18D)	5
Judiciary	35 (20R; 15D)	5
National Security (*formerly Armed Services—jurisdiction expanded*)	50 (27R; 23D)	5
Public Lands and Resources (*formerly Natural Resources—jurisdiction expanded*)	35 (19R; 16D)	5
Rules	13 (9R; 4D)	2
Select Intelligence	14 (8R; 6D)	2
Small Business	35 (19R; 16D)	4
Standards of Official Conduct	14 (7R; 7D)	
Technology and Competitiveness (*formerly Science, Space, and Technology—jurisdiction expanded*)	50 (27R; 23D)	4
Transportation and Infrastructure (*formerly Public Works and Transportation—jurisdiction expanded*)	58 (31R; 27D)	6
Veterans' Affairs	31 (17R; 14D)	3
Ways and Means	35 (21R; 14D)	5
Senate		
Agriculture, Nutrition, and Forestry	17 (9R; 8D)	4
Appropriations	28 (15R; 13D)	13
Armed Services	21 (11R; 10D)	6
Banking, Housing, and Urban Affairs	16 (9R; 7D)	4
Budget	22 (12R; 10D)	—
Commerce, Science, and Transportation	19 (10R; 9D)	6
Energy and Natural Resources	18 (10R; 8D)	4
Environment and Public Works	16 (9R; 7D)	4
Finance	20 (11R; 9D)	8
Foreign Relations	18 (10R; 8D)	7
Government Affairs	15 (8R; 7D)	5
Indian Affairs	17 (9R; 8D)	—
Judiciary	18 (10R; 8D)	6
Labor and Human Resources	16 (9R; 7D)	4
Rules and Administration	16 (9R; 7D)	—
Small Business	19 (10R; 9D)	—
Veterans' Affairs	19 (10R; 9D)	—

Source: *Congressional Quarterly Weekly Report* (January 21, 1995), pp. 217, 217–240.

The avalanche of legislative business cannot be managed and given the necessary specialized attention in the full House and Senate standing committees. For most bills, **hearings,** negotiations, and **markup** take place in subcommittees. It is in the subcommittees, moreover, that most oversight of the Execution branch (to be explained below) takes place. The number of subcommittees multiplied in the House under Democratic party leadership, starting in the early 1970s, eventually reaching 150 in number. The Democrats also strengthened the subcommittees by giving each of them a budget and a professional staff, free of control by the chair of the standing committee, as well as a fixed jurisdiction. Subcommittee chairs were also given additional authority over the conduct of subcommittee business, budget, and staff.

hearings The process of a congressional committee or subcommittee's taking testimony from witnesses.

markup The process of revising a bill in committee.

These changes substantially decentralized power in the House, giving rise to what some congressional scholars call "subcommittee government." While the proliferation of subcommittees has a good legislative rationale—managing the flow of business and bringing specialized knowledge to bear—it mainly provided members of the majority party with an important base from which to advertise themselves and serve their districts and has made it more difficult to fashion coherent public policy.[21]

The tide has now turned. The trend for several years now has been partially to recentralize power in the hands of House, Senate, and party leaders. When the Democrats were in control in the early 1990s, they cut the number of subcommittees by 15 and placed limits on the number of subcommittees on which members could serve. During the same period, there was, a gravitation of power toward a new and more centralized committee hierarchy in the House, with Appropriations, Budget, Ways and Means, and Rules at the top, a development caused by tight budget constraints and the desire of members of the House to try to regain control of the federal budget.[22]

The Republican capture of both houses of Congress after the 1994 elections increased the momentum of these changes. In control of the House machinery for the first time in 40 years, Republicans cut the number of committees and subcommittees from 146 to 116 (it was as high as 192 in 1988), slashed the number of committee staff by almost a third, and granted more power to Speaker of the House Newt Gingrich. The Senate pared its total number of committees and subcommittees from 111 to 99.

select committees Temporary committees in Congress created to conduct studies or investigations. They have no power to report bills.

Select committees are temporary committees created to conduct studies or investigations. They have no power to report bills. They exist because there are sometimes matters that standing committees and subcommittees cannot handle or do not wish to handle. Often, the issues before select committees are highly visible and gain a great deal of public attention for their members. Select committees investigated the Watergate scandal, the Iran-Contra affair, and the assassination of President Kennedy.

joint committees Congressional committees with members from the House and the Senate.

Joint committees, with members from both houses, are organized to facilitate the flow of legislation. The Joint Budget Committee, for instance, helps to speed up the normally slow legislative process of considering the annual federal budget.

conference committees Ad hoc committees, made up of members of both the Senate and the House of Representatives, set up to reconcile differences in the provisions of bills.

Before a bill can go to the president for signature, it must pass in identical form in each chamber. The committee that irons out the differences between House and Senate versions is called a **conference committee,** and one is created anew for each piece of major legislation. While it is probably an exaggeration to call conference committees the "third house of Congress," as some political observers do, there is no denying their central role in the march of bills through the legislative labyrinth. Although they are supposed to "split the difference" between versions of bills coming out of the House and the Senate, conference committees sometimes add, subtract, or amend provisions that are of great consequence. Much of the power of conference committees comes from the fact that bills reported by them to the House and Senate must be voted up or down; no new amendments are allowed.

How Members of Congress Get on Committees Because committees are so central to the legislative process, getting on the right one is important for reelection and for achieving policy goals. Committee assignments are determined by the political parties, guided by the members' **seniority** and preferences. Each party in each chamber goes about the assignment process in a slightly different way. House Democrats use their Steering and Policy Committee to make assignments. House Republicans use a Committee on Committees, on which strong Republican states are most heavily represented. In the Senate, both parties use small steering committees made up of party veterans and leaders to make assignments. For Republicans, the key player in the appointment of this committee is the chairperson of the Republican Conference (all Republican senators); for Democrats, the key player is the Floor Leader.

seniority Length of service, on which most assignments are based.

Lawmakers generally try to land positions on committees that will help them serve their constituencies and better their prospects for reelection. Thus they will try to join a committee that directly serves their constituency—Agriculture if the member is from a farm district or state, or Interior if the member is from a mining or oil district—or one of the elite committees, for instance, Ways and Means, Finance, or Appropriations. Appointment to an elite committee gives a lawmaker not only high visibility and a central role in policymaking, but also a strategic vantage point from which to help the constituency and one's own reelection prospects. There is a long waiting list for assignments to the most powerful committees, so new members are unlikely to be appointed to them. For these assignments, members have to wait their turn. In terms of nonelite standing committees, parties and congressional leaders try to defer to the wishes of their members, within the constraints of the seniority system.[23] House Speaker Newt Gingrich and Majority Leader Richard Armey broke these long-standing traditions after the 1994 elections, however, engineering the appointment of seven first-term Republicans to the House Appropriations Committee and three to Ways and Means. In this case, ideology and commitment to the Contract with America by the newcomers trumped seniority.

The seniority principle usually prevails in the appointment of committee and subcommittee chairs. For most of this century before the 1970s, appointment by seniority was an unbreakable rule. The most senior committee member of the majority party automatically became chair of the committee; the most senior member of the minority party automatically became the **ranking minority member.** Both Republicans and Democrats in the House instituted the secret ballot among party members for the election of chairs after 1974, however, and seniority was occasionally ignored. Once again, Speaker Gingrich broke long traditions in the 104th Congress, frequently bypassing the most senior committee members in favor of appointment or chairs who would support his conservative legislative program. Senate Republicans followed seniority traditions more closely, refusing to pass over Jesse Helms for the chairmanship of the Foreign Relations Committee in 1995, for instance, even after he had made controversial and widely criticized remarks about President Clinton (e.g., "If he comes to North Carolina, he'd better bring a bodyguard").

ranking minority member The minority party member with the greatest seniority on a committee.

The Role of Committee Chairs Not so long ago, chairs of committees were the absolute masters of all they surveyed. From 1910, when substantial power was stripped from the Speaker of the House and distributed to committee chairs, until the early 1970s, when the Democrats reined in the autocratic chairs they had created, those who headed congressional committees were their unchallenged masters. Committee chairs hired and assigned staff, controlled the budget, created or abolished subcommittees at will, controlled the agenda, scheduled meetings, and reported (or refused to report) bills to the floor.

In both houses since the mid–1970s, the power of committee chairs has migrated first, from the chair to the subcommittees and, eventually, to the party and house leadership (as we shall see later). Decisions that were entirely the province of the chair in the past are now entirely in other hands or are shared with others.

Still, committee chairs remain the most influential and active members of their committees. They cannot command obedience, but they are at the center of all of the lines of communication, retain the power to schedule meetings and control the agenda, control the committee staff, manage committee funds, appoint members to conference committees, and are usually the most senior and experienced members of their committees, to whom some deference is owed. Thus, most senators tended to defer to the views of Sam Nunn of Georgia on matters of national defense and military organization when he was the chair of the Senate Armed Services Committee. His opposition to President Clinton's plan to drop the ban on gays and lesbians in the military forced the president to adopt a "don't ask, don't tell" policy.

Political Parties in Congress

Political parties have a very strong presence in Congress. Its members come to Washington, D.C. as elected candidates of a political party. At the opening of

Former Senate Armed Services Committee chair Sam Nunn (right) and committee member Senator John Warner speak to a sailor aboard the aircraft carrier USS *John F. Kennedy* as part of the committee's hearings on gays in the military. Nunn used his powerful position to successfully oppose Bill Clinton's proposal to end the military's ban on gays.

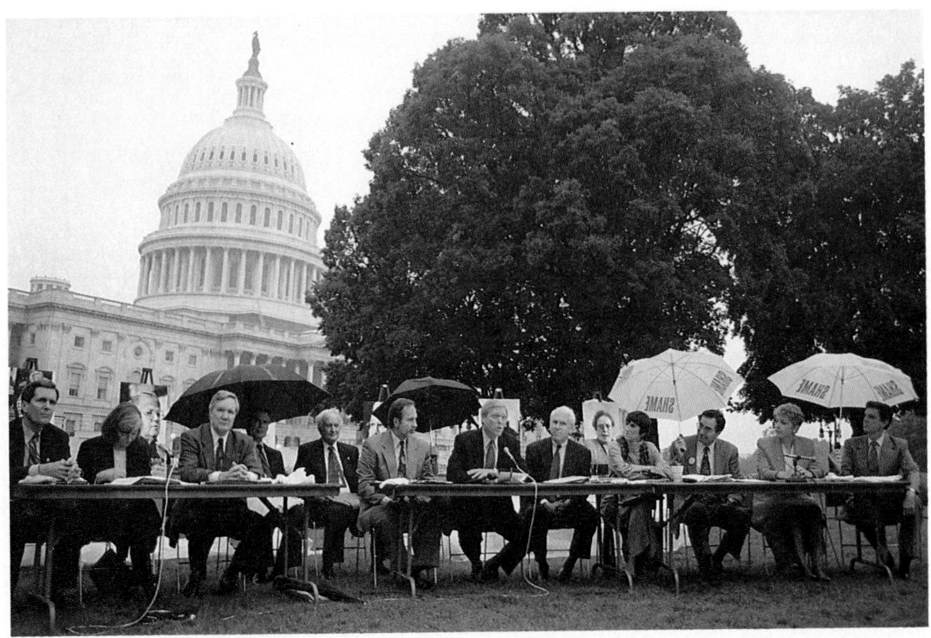

The majority party organizes the House at the beginning of each session of Congress and generally has its way if its members remain disciplined. Here the leadership of the minority Democrats in the 104th Congress protest their exclusion from House deliberations by holding mock sessions outside on the capitol lawn.

each session, they organize their legislative business along political party lines. At the opening of each new Congress, each **party caucus** meets to select party committees and officers. The majority party in the House selects the Speaker of the House, while the majority party in the Senate selects the president pro tempore (usually its most senior member) and the Majority Leader. The majority party in each house also selects committees the chairs of the and subcommittees and decides the party ratios on them. Technically, the majority party only nominates and introduces motions to the full House and Senate to effect all of the above, but it always wins on a straight party-line vote.

party caucus (caucus system) A meeting of party activists to choose delegates to presidential nominating conventions.

The Party Composition of Congress The Democratic party dominated the modern Congress until the 1994 elections (see Figure 11.9). It was the majority party in the House of Representatives for all but four years between 1933 and 1994. The Democratic domination of House elections remained solid even in the face of GOP landslide wins in the presidential elections of 1980 (Reagan), 1984 (Reagan), and 1988 (Bush). In the Senate, Republicans were in the majority for only ten years during this same period. Democratic party domination ended with the 1994 elections, however, when Republicans won the control of both houses of Congress for the first time in 40 years.

The Republicans repeated their feat in 1996. Their back-to-back sweeps of both houses of Congress had not happened for the GOP since 1928.

Party Voting in Congress The political parties provide important glue for the decentralized fragments of Congress and legislative process. Party labels are important cues for members of Congress as they decide how to vote on issues before the committees and on the floor of the House and the Senate. We know

Figure 11.9 ▪ Democrat Representation in Congress

Democrats were in the majority in both houses of Congress for most of the years between the early 1930s and 1994. Democratic dominance ended with the 1994 elections when the Republicans won the majority control of both houses for the first time in 40 years. They repeated their victory in 1996.

Sources: Harold W. Stanley and Richard G. Niemi, *Vital Statistics on American Politics* (Washington, D.C.: Congressional Quarterly Press, 1994), Table 3.16; *New York Times* (November 9, 1994), p. 1; 1996 calculated by the authors.

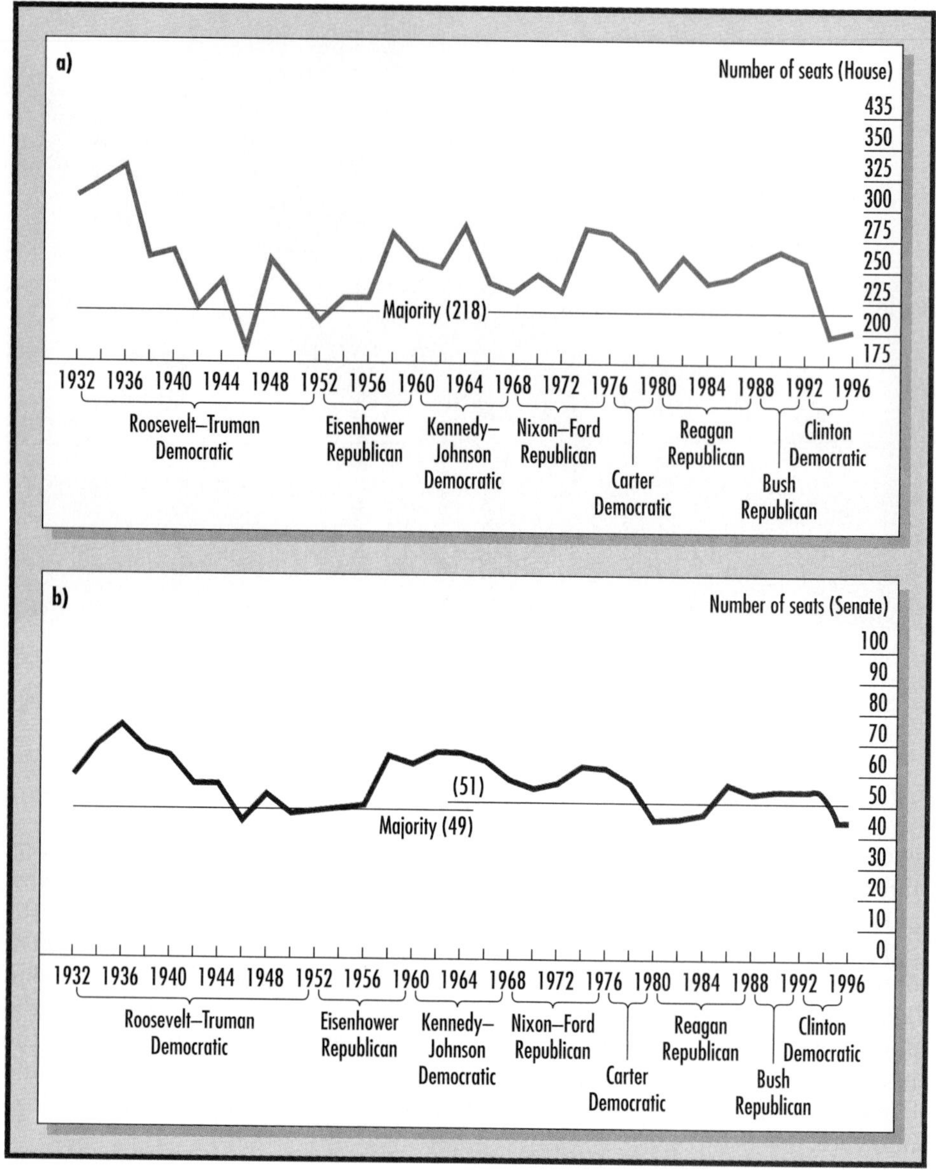

this from a long tradition of research on party divisions in roll call voting. This research tells us that party affiliation is the best predictor of the voting behavior of members of the Congress.

Figure 11.10 shows how often a majority of Democrats opposed a majority of Republicans in recent Congresses. We see that party cohesion is fairly substantial in both chambers and has been steadily increasing since the early 1980s, especially in the House. The party unity of Republicans skyrocketed in the 104th Congress, reaching its highest level since the measurement of this statistic began in 1954. Congress is clearly becoming more partisan than has traditionally been the case in the United States.

There are a number of reasons why party unity is increasing. For one thing, southern conservative Democrats—frequent allies of Republicans in Congress in the past—are fast disappearing, as many politicians and voters have switched over to the Republican party in the rapidly realigning South. The defeat in the 1994 elections of influential Democratic Representative Jim

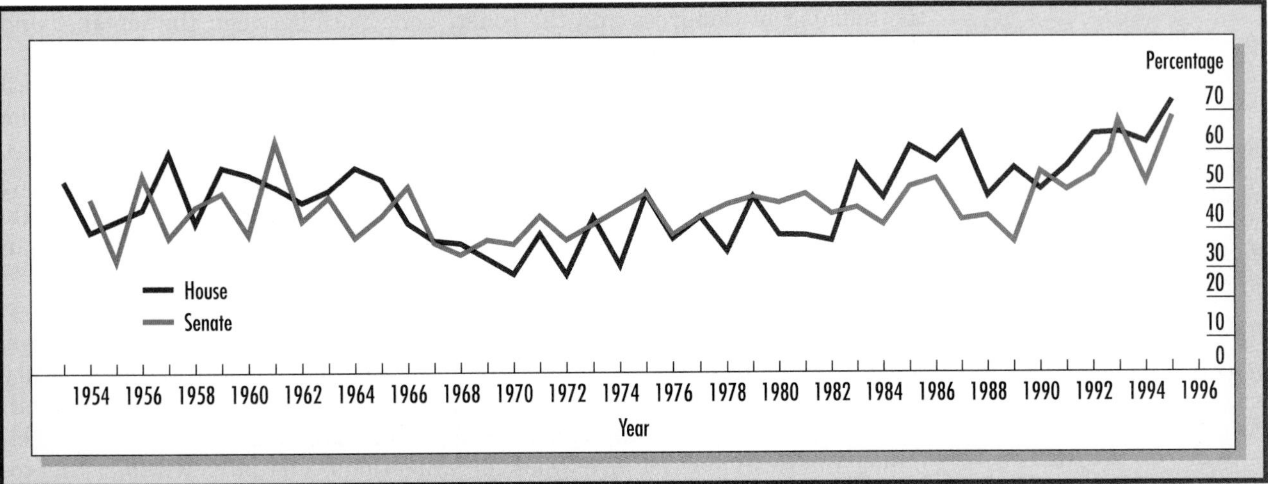

Figure 11.10 ▪ Partisan Roll Call Votes in Congress

Partisanship has been growing in Congress. One indicator is the increase in the number of recorded roll call votes in which a majority of Democrats voted against a majority of Republicans. This graph plots this statistic for both the House of Representatives and the Senate. Note that in recent years, the House has been more partisan than the Senate.

Source: *Congressional Quarterly Weekly Report* (January 27, 1996), p. 199.

Sasser of Tennessee, the subsequent switch to the Republican party of Senator Richard Shelby of Alabama, and the retirement of Democratic senator Sam Nunn of Georgia are examples of what is happening throughout the region. Another reason is that there are fewer moderate Republicans in Congress after a tidal wave of conservative Republicans was elected in 1994, making the congressional Republicans more ideologically cohesive. The strong leadership of conservative Speaker Newt Gingrich has made Republicans in the House even more united. On bills from the Contract with America, House Republicans voted as a near-unanimous bloc. Indeed, the ability of House Republicans to prevail on virtually every major issue in the contract with only 53 percent of the House membership is unprecedented in American history.

Although party label remains the best predictor of the voting behavior of members of Congress and is becoming ever more important, the party is not as important as it is in parliamentary systems like that of Great Britain. There, not just simple majorities, but at least 90 percent of the members of one party oppose at least 90 percent of the members of the main opposition party on virtually every major vote.[24] In the German Bundestag, party line votes have averaged close to 98 percent in recent years. On major issues like the budget, typically 100 percent of one party opposes 100 percent of the other party (or parties) in both Great Britain and Germany.

It's not entirely clear whether party voting differences are caused directly by party affiliation or indirectly by the character of constituencies or ideology. Some scholars have found strong independent party effects irrespective of constituency or ideology. Others argue that the tendency of people in the same party to vote together is a reflection of the fact that Democratic lawmakers come from districts and states that are similar to each other and that Republican lawmakers come from places that are different from the constituencies of Democrats. Republicans generally come from higher-income districts than Democrats. Democratic districts, in turn, tend to contain more union members and racial minorities. The strongest tie, in this line of argument, is between the member of Congress and the constituency, not between the member and the party.[25]

Increasingly, differences in party voting seem attributable to ideological differences between the two parties. Both in the electorate and among the members of Congress, Democrats are becoming more consistently **liberal,** while Republicans are becoming more consistently **conservative.** People who see the world in liberal terms tend to drift toward the Democratic party, while those who see the world in conservative terms find their way to the Republican party. Ideology thus strengthens the glue provided by the party label.

liberal The political position that holds that the federal government has a substantial role to play in economic regulation, social welfare, and overcoming racial inequality.

conservative The political position that holds that the federal government ought to play a very small role in economic regulation, social welfare, and overcoming racial inequality.

Party Discipline in Congress The increase in party unity in Congress, though substantial, is unlikely to bring American parties to the level of unity found in most parliamentary systems, however. The reason is that American parties, unlike their counterparts in Europe, have few tools of party discipline. American parties are weak organizations, virtually without the resources to impose discipline on their legislative representatives. Members of Congress are essentially independent operators who mount their own campaigns. Their reelection prospects depend on their own ability to service their districts and to maintain good relationships with their constituents. They do not depend on the party.

Our parties, moreover, have no power to compel compliance with party positions or to discipline recalcitrant members who stray from the party line, assuming that a party line can be discerned. Party caucuses have no authority to strip lawmakers of their party label, no matter how egregious their behavior. At most, they sometimes remove a renegade party member from an important committee. The Democrats did this to Representative Phil Gramm of Texas in 1983, removing him from his post on the Budget Committee after he led the fight for the Reagan budget proposal against his own party. He then switched parties and became a prominent Republican senator.

Congressional Leadership[26]

The political parties also work through the leadership structure of Congress, since the leaders of the majority political party are, at the same time, the leaders of the House and the Senate.

Leadership in the House The leader in the House of Representatives is the Speaker of the House. This position is recognized in the Constitution and stands in the line of succession to the presidency, right after the vice-presidency. The Speaker is treated by his colleagues, the president, and the media as the spokesperson for the House in general and for the majority party in Congress in particular. During the long period of divided party government from 1981 to 1992—with a Republican president and a Democratic House—the Speaker received the kind of attention usually given to the leader of the opposition in parliamentary systems. Speakers such as "Tip" O'Neill and Thomas Foley were among the most recognizable congressional figures of their day. Newt Gingrich was arguably the nation's most recognizable figure in 1995 when his legislative agenda (the Contract with America), rather than President Clinton's, dominated the nation's attention.

Until 1910, the Speaker exercised great power over the House legislative process. The bases of his power were his right to appoint committees and their chairs and his position as chair of the Rules Committee. The revolt of the rank and file against Speaker "Uncle Joe" Cannon in 1910 resulted in the Speaker's

As Speaker, Newt Gingrich exercised power in the 104th Congress to a degree not seen in the House of Representatives in modern times. His power came from his high standing among House Republicans, especially freshman members, and new powers granted to him by the majority Republicans.

removal from the Rules Committee and the elimination of the Speaker's power to appoint committees and their chairs.

From 1910 until the early 1970s, the weakened Speaker competed with a handful of powerful committee chairs for leadership of the House. A few Speakers, such as Sam Rayburn of Texas, were able to lead by sheer dint of their personalities and legislative skills, but power tilted toward the chairs most of the time.

The Democratic Caucus staged a revolt against the committee system after 1974 and restored some of the powers of the Speaker, especially in making committee assignments. The Democratic Caucus also gave the Speaker more power to refer bills to committee, control the House agenda, appoint members to select committees, and direct floor debate. This change gave Speakers O'Neill, Jim Wright, and Foley considerable leadership resources. The Republican Caucus gave even more power to control the House legislative process to their first Speaker since 1954, Newt Gingrich. He quickly put his stamp on the House, appointing committee chairs who supported his conservative Contract with America, often ignored seniority, and limited the tenure of committee chairs to six years. Some scholars suggest that Gingrich's speakership is the most powerful one since Cannon's.[27] Ironically, his power and visibility led to a precipitous decline in his public standing in 1996 when Americans turned against most elements of the Gingrich agenda.

Personality and style make a difference in how these leadership resources are used. Jim Wright tended toward partisan conflict and a touch of autocracy, as does Speaker Gingrich; Tom Foley relied more on bipartisanship and accommodation.

The majority party in the House also selects a majority floor leader to help the Speaker plan strategy and manage the legislative business of the House. Neither House nor party rules spell out the responsibilities of this office. The nature of the job depends very much on what the Speaker wants and on the incumbent's talents and energy. In recent years, the majority floor leader position has been a way station on the road to the Speakership for Democrats; Jim Wright and Tom Foley both held the job. The Speaker is also assisted by a party **whip,** who acts as a liaison between the leaders and the rank and file. The whip (helped by deputy whips) counts heads on important bills, explains leadership positions, tries to persuade, gathers legislative intelligence, and makes sure that the faithful get to the floor to cast their votes.

whip A political party member in Congress charged with keeping members informed of the plans of the party leadership, counting votes before action on important issues, and rounding up party members for votes on bills.

The minority party elects a minority floor leader, who acts as the chief spokesperson and legislative strategist for the opposition. The minority leader not only tries to keep the forces together but also seeks out members of the majority party who might be won over against the House leadership on key issues. Minority leader styles differ greatly. Republican Robert Michel of Illinois tried to cooperate with the Democratic party majority, believing that this was the only way to win approval for portions of the GOP agenda. This style was heartily rejected by minority whip (and eventually Speaker) Newt Gingrich of Georgia, whose style was to attack and to expose the shortcomings of the Democrats as part of an overall strategy to win an eventual Republican majority in elections for the House. His strategy paid off in 1994 to the amazement of many skeptics.

Leadership in the Senate Leadership in the Senate is less visible. Those with the formal leadership titles exercise little influence. The presiding officer of the Senate is the vice-president of the United States, but he is rarely in evidence and has no power other than the right to vote to break a tie (as Vice-President Al Gore did in order to pass President Clinton's budget in 1993) should one occur on the Senate floor. The majority party also elects a president pro tempore (always the member with the most seniority) to preside in the absence of the vice-president. Presiding is such an unrewarding chore that even the president pro tempore rarely acts as the presiding officer, so senators from the majority party take turns wielding the gavel.

The Senate majority leader is as close as one comes to a leader in this body, but the powers of the office pale before those of the Speaker of the House. The Senator majority leader has some influence in committee assignments, office space designation, and control of access to the floor of the Senate. The majority leader is also important in the scheduling of the business of the Senate. The degree of actual influence is based less on formal powers, however, than on skills of personal persuasion, the respect of colleagues, visibility in the media as majority party spokesperson, and a role at the center of many of the various communications networks.

The power of the position is thus personal and not institutional; it cannot be passed on to the next leader. Acknowledged as the most effective majority leader in this century, Lyndon Johnson could not transfer his power to his successor after he resigned his seat to join John F. Kennedy on the Democratic party's presidential ticket. The majority party in the Senate remains a body of independent, relatively equal members tied together very loosely by the thin threads of party loyalty, ideology, and mutual concern about the next election. It is not an environment conducive to decisive leadership.

Late president of the United States, Lyndon B. Johnson of Texas was one of the most effective majority leaders in the history of the Senate. Here he urges senators Humphrey, Kennedy, Proxmire, and Symington to vote for an important civil rights bill.

The Senate minority leader exercises even less power than the majority leader. A skilled politician can use the position, however, to articulate the minority legislative program, to rally the troops for partisan battle when necessary, and to force concessions from the majority. Robert Dole of Kansas (Majority leader in the 104th Congress and Republican presidential candidate in 1996) was extremely effective, as was Everett Dirksen of Illinois in the early 1960s.

Caucuses

Caucuses (in addition to the Republican and Democratic **party caucuses** already mentioned) also exercise some influence in Congress. A caucus is a group formed by lawmakers who share a particular set of policy or ideological interests that are not otherwise recognized in the formal organization of the House or the Senate. Over 130 existed in the 103rd Congress. Caucuses serve as a basis for the formation of political coalitions that cross the boundaries between committees, parties, and even chambers. The Congressional Caucus for Women's Issues, for instance, played an important role in legislation that enforces child support payments and in the passage of the Family Leave Act. The 1992 elections added new members to the black and Latino caucuses, which added to their influence in Congress. Under the direction of House Speaker Gingrich, however, staff and budget support for caucuses was cut in 1995, leaving them far less influential than in the past.

caucus, congressional party Members of a single party in one of the houses of Congress who meet to elect leaders, approve committee assignments, and debate party positions on policies.

Rules and Norms in the House and Senate

Like all organizations, Congress is guided by both formal rules and informal norms of behavior.[28] Rules specify precisely how things should be done and what is not allowed. Norms are generally accepted expectations about how people ought to behave and how business ought to proceed. While the Constitution mandates each chamber to create its own rules, and thus, their formal rules differ considerably, some norms of behavior are common to both houses of Congress.

reciprocity A congressional norm in which members of Congress defer to the judgment of subject-matter specialists, mainly on minor technical bills.

Members of the House are expected to become specialists in some area or areas of policy and to defer to the judgment of the specialists on most bills. This mutual deference is known as **reciprocity.** The norm of reciprocity is much less evident in the Senate. Because there are fewer members, because they are elected on a statewide basis, and because the Senate has been the breeding ground for many presidential candidacies, a senator has more prestige and power than a representative. As a result, senators generally are unwilling to sit quietly for a term or two, waiting their turn. It is not unusual for a first-term senator to introduce major bills and make important speeches. In the House, such a thing was very unusual in the past. There, the old rule held sway: "To get along, go along." However, things may be changing in the House, where Republican freshmen played a very visible role in the 104th Congress's conservative revolution.

It is expected in both chambers that lawmakers will respect, or at least tolerate, the reelection motivations of their colleagues. They are expected, for instance, to support a legislative schedule that allows for abundant visits back to the constituency, and to vote funding for campaign-related activities such as the frank and budgets for district offices. They must learn, moreover, to put up with activities that have no specific legislative purpose but which allow their fellow lawmakers to advertise, take credit, and take positions; the insertion of materials into the *Congressional Record,* and speeches on the floor tailored to the evening news back home are good examples.

At one time, senators and representatives were expected to act with courtesy and civility toward one other, even if they detested one another—hence, the informal prohibition against the use of names and the elaborate references to the "honorable gentleman from Wisconsin" or the "senior senator" from California. This expectation of civility has largely disappeared in recent years, especially in the House, as Congress has become a more partisan and ideological place. The nastiness surrounding the Senate hearings on the nominations of Robert Bork and Clarence Thomas for the Supreme Court is a good example of this mood change, as was the successful effort, led by then minority whip Newt Gingrich, to topple Speaker Wright in the House. Partisan warfare over most of President Clinton's legislative initiatives in 1993 and 1994 continued this trend, as did Newt Gingrich's vigorous partisan leadership in the House and the pointedly partisan Democratic response to it.[29]

Legislative life is much more rule-bound in the House of Representatives, because of its large size, than in the Senate; it tends to be more organized and hierarchical (see Table 11.4) on the differences between the two chambers). Leaders in the House have more power, the majority party exercises more control over legislative affairs, the procedures are more structured, and the individual members have a harder time making their mark. The Senate tends to be a more open and fluid place, and it lodges less power in its leaders than does the House. Each senator is more of an independent operator than his or her House colleagues. The Senate is a much more relaxed place, one that accommodates mavericks, tolerates the foibles of its members, and pays more attention to the minority party.

unanimous consent Legislative action taken "without objection" as a way to expedite business; used to conduct much of the business of the Senate.

Differences between the House and the Senate are especially apparent in floor debate. Bills are scheduled for floor debate in the Senate, for instance, not by a powerful Rules Committee, but by **unanimous consent,** so that

Table 11.4

Differences Between the House and Senate: Rules and Norms

Senate	House
Informal, open, nonhierarchical	Rule-bound, hierarchical
Leaders have few formal powers	Leaders have many formal powers
Members may serve on two or more major committees	Members restricted to one major committee
Less specialized	More specialized
Unrestricted floor debate	Restricted floor debate
Unlimited amendments possible	Limited amendments
Amendments need not be germane	Amendments must be germane
Unlimited time for debate unless shortened by unanimous consent or halted by invocation of cloture	Limited time for debate
More prestige	Less prestige
More reliance on staff	Less reliance on staff
Minority party plays a larger role	Minority party plays a smaller role
Less partisan	More partisan

business can be blocked by a single dissenter. Unlike in the House, where debate on a bill is strictly regulated as to amendments and time limit, the Senate's tradition allows for unlimited numbers of amendments and unlimited debate. Senators in the minority have periodically used this tolerance of unlimited amendments and debate to good effect. Because limiting debate is so difficult in the Senate, the opponents of a bill can tie up legislative business by refusing to stop debating its merits. This practice is known as the **filibuster.** During a filibuster, senators opposing a bill have been known to talk for hour upon hour, often working in shifts. The only requirement is that they say something; they cannot hold the floor without speaking. During a filibuster, senators need not even talk about the bill itself; Senate rules do not require remarks to be germane. Senators have read from novels or quoted verse, have told stories about their children, and have quoted long lists of sports statistics. The purpose is to force the majority to give up the fight and to move on to other business. The filibuster record for a single senator belongs to Strom Thurmond of South Carolina, who held the floor for over 24 hours opposing the 1957 Civil Rights bill.

filibuster A parliamentary device used in the Senate to prevent a bill from coming to a vote by "talking it to death"; made possible by the norm of unlimited debate.

When a very strong majority favors a bill or when a bill that has great national import and visibility is before the body, the Senate can close debate by invoking **cloture.** Cloture requires support by three-fifths of those present and voting. It is very rarely tried; it very rarely succeeds. A Republican filibuster in 1993 forced President Clinton to abandon his economic stimulus plan after Democrats failed to convince any Republicans to join them in a vote to invoke cloture. Another Republican filibuster in 1994 killed campaign reform legislation. Cloture is so difficult to invoke that the mere threat of a filibuster by a determined minority party, a growing trend in the Senate, often forces the majority to comply with the wishes of the minority. Many believe that the

cloture A vote to end a filibuster or a debate; requires the votes of three-fifths of the membership of the Senate.

increasing use of the filibuster threat undermines majority rule and therefore undermines democracy.

Legislative Responsibilities: How a Bill Becomes a Law

We can put much of what we have learned to work by seeing how a bill wends its way through the legislative labyrinth to become a law. The path by which a bill becomes a law is so strewn with obstacles that few survive; only about 6 percent of all bills that are introduced are enacted. To make law is exceedingly difficult; to block bills from becoming laws is relatively easy. At each step along the way (see Figure 11.11), a "no" decision can stop the passage of a bill in its tracks. As one account puts it:

> A United States Congressman [and Senator] has two principal functions: to make laws and to keep laws from being made. The first of these he and his colleagues perform only with sweat, patience, and a remarkable skill in the handling of creaking machinery; but the second they perform daily, with ease and infinite variety.[30]

Introducing a Bill A bill can be introduced only by a member of Congress. In reality, bills are often written in the executive branch. The initial draft of the bill that became the Tax Reform Act of 1986, for instance, was fashioned in the Treasury Department by a committee headed by then secretary James Baker. After their 1994 electoral landslide victory, however, congressional Republicans largely ignored legislative proposals from the Clinton administration, focusing instead on the promises in their Contract with America.

Bills are often written by interest groups. Industry trade groups, for instance, wrote substantial parts of bills designed to roll back timber and mining regulation in 1995. With the exception of tax bills (which must originate in the House), a bill may be introduced in either the House or the Senate. In the House, a member introduces a bill by putting it into the **hopper** (a box watched over by one of the House clerks). In the Senate, a member must announce a bill to the body after being recognized by the presiding officer. The bill is then assigned a number, with the prefix *H.R.* in the House or *S.* in the Senate.

hopper The box in the House of Representatives in which proposed bills are placed.

The lawmaker who introduces the bill (or resolution; see Table 11.5) is its sponsor. Lawmakers try to build support by signing on as many cosponsors as possible; it is even better for the bill if its cosponsors cross party and ideological lines.

Committee Action on a Bill The presiding officer in the Senate or the Speaker in the House refers the bill to the appropriate standing committee. In about 80 percent of cases, referral to committee is routine; the subject matter of the bill clearly indicates the appropriate committee. Revenue bills go automatically to the Ways and Means Committee in the House and to the Finance Committee in the Senate, for instance. In the other 20 percent of cases, the relevant committee is not so obvious because of overlapping committee jurisdictions. For instance, the House Committee on International Relations is in charge of "international policy," whereas the Commerce Committee is in charge of "foreign commerce generally." In such cases, House leaders can exercise some discretion or send a bill (or parts of a bill) to more than one committee. The practice of multiple referral usually involves the most complex and important bills and has increased substantially since the mid–1970s.[31] The more committee

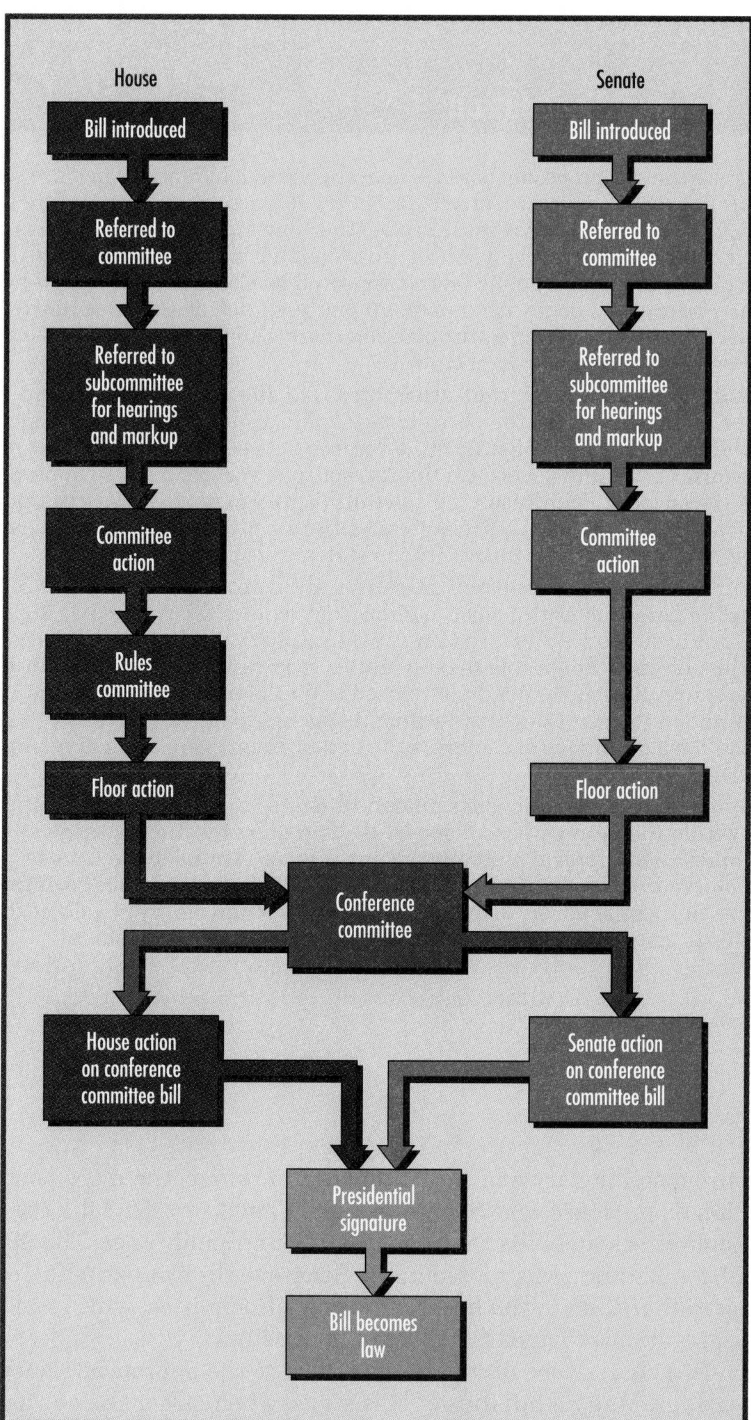

Figure 11.11 ■ How a Bill Becomes a Law

This diagram shows the path by which most bills introduced in Congress become law. You will learn in the accompanying text that the road bills must travel is a complex and difficult one, and that few survive. A bill can be derailed at any stop in the above passage. A subcommittee can refuse to report a bill; a bill may be defeated on the floor of each chamber; a conference committee may fail to reach an agreement on a compromise; the conference bill may be defeated in either chamber; or the president may veto the bill.

Table 11.5

Types of Legislation

Bill: Most legislative proposals before Congress are in a bill form. They are designated *H.R.* (House of Representatives) or *S.* (Senate) according to where they originate, followed by a number assigned in the order in which they were introduced, from the beginning of each two-year congressional term. *Public bills* deal with general questions and become public laws if approved by Congress and signed by the president. *Private bills* deal with individual matters, such as claims against the government, immigration and naturalization cases, and land titles. They become private laws if approved and signed.

Joint resolution: A joint resolution, designated *H. J. Res.* or *S. J. Res.,* requires the approval of both houses and the president's signature, just as a bill does, and has the force of law. There is no significant difference between a bill and a joint resolution. The latter generally deals with limited matters, such as a single appropriation for a specific purpose. Joint resolutions are also urged to propose constitutional amendments, which do not require a presidential signature, but become a part of the Constitution when three-fourths of the states have ratified them.

Concurrent resolution: A concurrent resolution, designated *H. Con. Res.* or *S. Con. Res.,* must be passed by both houses but does not require the president's signature and does not have the force of law. Concurrent resolutions are generally used to make or amend rules applicable to both houses or to express their joint sentiment. A concurrent resolution, for example, is used to fix the time of adjournment of a Congress and to express Congress's annual budgeting plan. It may also be used to convey the congratulations of Congress to another country on the anniversary of its independence.

Resolution: A simple resolution, designated *H. Res.* or *S. Res.,* deals with matters entirely within the prerogatives of one house. It requires neither passage by the other chamber nor approval by the president and does not have the force of law. Most resolutions deal with the rules of one house. They are also used to express the sentiments of a single house, to extend condolences to the family of a deceased member, or to give "advice" on foreign policy or other executive business.

Source: Roger H. Davidson and Walter J. Oleszek, *Congress and Its Members* (Washington, D.C.: Congressional Quarterly Press, 1994), p. 325.

referrals are discretionary and not automatic, of course, the more power there is in the hands of House and Senate leaders. They can refer bills they like to friendly committees and bills they don't like to unfriendly ones. The 1964 Civil Rights bill, for instance, was routed in the Senate to the sympathetic Commerce Committee rather than to the hostile Judiciary Committee, which was chaired by arch-segregationist James Eastland of Mississippi.

Committee chairs normally pass the bill on to the appropriate subcommittee for hearings. Many a bill dies at this stage, when either the subcommittee or the full committee declines to consider it further. A bill quietly killed in committee can reach the floor only by a device called a **discharge petition,** which is rarely successful.

discharge petition A bill before a committee for at least 30 days while the House is in session may be forced out of the committee and brought to the floor for consideration if a petition with the signatures of 218 House members is secured.

If a bill is accepted for consideration, the subcommittee generally holds hearings, taking testimony from people for and against it. Subcommittee staff not only help prepare representatives and senators for the questioning but also often take part in the questioning themselves. The subcommittee may then forward the bill as rewritten by the staff and subcommittee members to the full committee, or it can decide to allow the bill to go no further.

Congressional staff assist members of Congress carry out their many legislative responsibilities. Here representative Connie Marelli meets with members of her staff to plan the day's activities.

Rewriting the bill in committee is called the **markup**, which usually occurs amid very intense of bargaining and deal making, with an eye toward fashioning a bill that will muster majority support in the full committee and on the floor of the House and the Senate, and that will gain the support of the president. The staff plays a central role in the markup. Lawmakers and staff are also usually in contact with relevant interest groups and executive branch policymakers.

markup The process of amending and rewriting a bill in committee.

The subcommittee reports its action to the full committee. The committee chair, in consultation with other important members of his or her committee, may opt for the committee to hold its own hearings and markup sessions, may decide to kill the bill outright, or may simply accept the action of the subcommittee. If the subcommittee has done its job well and has consulted with the most important players on the full committee (especially the chair), the committee will simply rubber-stamp the bill and move it along for floor action.

Floor Action on a Bill If a bill is favorably reported from committee, congressional leaders schedule it for floor debate. In the House, a bill must first go to the Rules Committee, which must issue a rule under whose terms the bill will be considered. A rule specifies such things as the amount of time for debate and the number (if any) and nature of amendments allowed. The Rules Committee may choose not to issue a rule at all or to drag its feet, as it did with civil rights bills until the mid–1960s. This has happened less often in recent years because both Democratic and Republican Speakers have had more power over Rules Committee appointments. The committee can also grant a "closed rule," allowing only an up or down vote without amendments, as it generally does with tax bills.

Floor debate in the Senate, where rules do not limit debate, is much more freewheeling. Floor debate is also more important in the Senate in determining the final form a bill will take because Senate committees are less influential than House committees. Senators are also less likely to defer to committee judgments.

After floor debate, the entire membership of the chamber votes on the bill, either as reported by the committee or (more often) after amendments have been added. If the bill receives a favorable vote, it then goes through the same obstacle course in the other chamber or awaits action by the other house if the bill was introduced there at the same time.

Conference Committee Even if the bill makes it through both houses, its journey is not yet over. Bills passed by the House and the Senate are almost always different from one another, sometimes in minor ways and sometimes in quite substantial ways. Before the bill goes to the president, its conflicting versions must be rewritten so that a single bill gains the approval of both chambers of Congress. This compromise bill is fashioned in a conference committee made up of members from both the House and the Senate, customarily from the relevant committees.

There are ways to avoid "going to conference," and each is used frequently. First, one house may simply adopt the bill from the other house, word for word. Second, members of the two houses may confer throughout, sending bills back and forth, so that the differences are ironed out before final passage.[32]

A bill from a conference committee must be voted up or down on the floors of the House and the Senate; no amendments or further changes are allowed. If, and only if, both houses approve it, the bill is forwarded to the president for consideration.

Presidential Action Because the president plays an important constitutional role in turning a bill into a law, he or his assistants and advisers are usually consulted throughout the legislative process. If the president approves the bill, he signs it and it becomes law. If he is not particularly favorable but does not want to block the bill, it becomes law after ten days if he takes no action. He can also **veto** the bill and return it to Congress. A bill can still become law by a two-thirds vote of each house, which will override the president's veto. A president can also kill a bill at the end of a congressional session if he takes no action and Congress adjourns before ten days pass. This is known as a **pocket veto.**

veto The presidential power to disapprove a bill that has been passed by both houses of Congress. The president's veto can be overridden by a two-thirds vote in each house.

pocket veto A bill is vetoed if the president does not act on it before 10 days have passed and, in the meantime, Congress adjourns.

Legislative Oversight of the Executive Branch

Oversight is another important responsibility of Congress. Oversight involves keeping an eye on how the executive branch carries out the provisions of the laws that Congress has passed, and on possible abuses of power by executive branch officials, including the president. Oversight is primarily the province of the committees and subcommittees of Congress, and it is among Congress's most visible and dramatic roles. Dramatic examples of legislative probes of alleged administrative misconduct include Watergate, the Iran-Contra affair, Whitewater, the savings-and-loan collapse and bailout, and the Branch Davidian tragedy in Waco.

Hearings are an important part of the oversight process. Testimony is taken from agency officials, outside experts, and such congressional investigatory institutions as the Government Accounting Office (GAO) and the Office of Technology Assessment (OTA). The hearings are not simply information-gathering exercises, however. As often as not, they are designed to send signals from committee members to the relevant part of the bureaucracy. Hearings that focus on the overly aggressive efforts of Internal Revenue Service (IRS) agents to collect taxes, for instance, are a clear signal to IRS officials that they had better rein in their agents before the next round of hearings on the budget. In another familiar example, hearings that focus on abuses in the awarding of defense contracts are designed to force more stringent contracting behavior by the Pentagon.

Congress spends an increasing amount of its time on oversight. Given the scale of federal government activities, however, it can pay attention to only the small tip of the iceberg that is the executive branch. For the most part, members of Congress pay attention to matters brought to them by others, mainly by constituents, the media, and interest groups.[33] This ensures not only that important problems will be attended to, but also that the representatives and senators who are involved can claim credit and stockpile goodwill (and contributions) for the next election cycle. One problem with this "fire alarm" model of oversight, however, is the favored attention it gives to the concerns of organized interest groups. The National Rifle Association was particularly influential in persuading Congress to investigate the actions of the Alcohol, Tobacco, and Firearms Agency after Waco.

Congressional Ethics

To many Americans, the term *congressional ethics* is an oxymoron, that is, a contradiction in terms. While most Americans would probably not go as far as Mark Twain, who once described Congress as the only "distinctively native American criminal class,"[34] it is widely believed that things are not as they should be in Congress regarding ethical behavior. While there is no evidence that the members of Congress are any less honest than any other group of professionals—being in the public eye and under constant press scrutiny, in fact, probably keeps the number of lawbreakers among them comparatively low—the number of highly publicized ethics cases in recent years has not helped their collective reputation. Jim Wright was forced to quit the Speakership in 1989, for instance, after the House Ethics Committee supported charges of fund-raising improprieties. An FBI "sting" operation in the early 1980s, called Abscam, netted six House members who had agreed to accept bribes from agents posing as representatives of oil-rich Middle Eastern countries pushing for special legislative treatment. Speaker Newt Gingrich created a firestorm when it was learned that he had accepted a $4.3-million book advance (later returned) from HarperCollins, owned by publishing tycoon Rupert Murdoch, who had business pending before Congress.

Other Americans worry about what seem to be undue and excessive privileges paid for by taxpayers: discounted meals, haircuts, medical care, and electronic goods; protection against parking tickets and bounced checks; and periodic "junkets" to exotic locations, purportedly on legislative business. Still others believe that the main ethical problem of Congress is the close relationship members enjoy with interest groups and their dependence on those who give them large contributions and other perks.[35]

The growing public outcry over these concerns forced Congress to create codes of ethics and other rules for its members and to establish ethics committees in both houses in order to oversee them. The codes of ethics concentrate primarily on the disclosure of personal finances, restrictions on the amount of outside income that a member can earn, regulation of the personal use of taxpayer-provided services, such as staff and the frank, and recent restrictions on gifts. The purview of the Senate Ethics Committee expanded in 1993 to include an investigation of sexual harassment charges against Robert Packwood

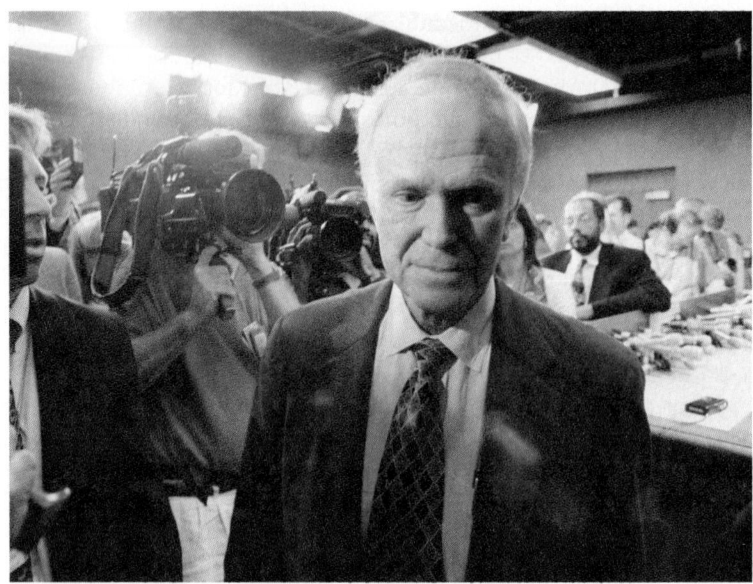

Senator Robert Packwood was forced to defend himself before the Senate Ethics Committee against sexual harassment charges. After the Committee found against him, intense public and media pressure convinced him to resign his seat.

(Republican of Oregon). It recommended that he be expelled, but Packwood resigned instead. Most observers and many lawmakers do not believe, however, that ethics reforms have gone very far in restricting practices that undermine public confidence in the ethical conduct of the members of Congress. Many Americans have responded by supporting proposals to limit the terms of the members of Congress and by an increasing willingness to vote against incumbents.

Congress, Public Policy, and Democracy

The way Congress is organized and operates greatly influences the kinds of public policies we have and the quality of democracy in the United States.

Democracy

Now that we know more about what representatives and senators do and how Congress operates, we can turn our attention to the central theme of this text: how our political institutions contribute to, or detract from, democracy.

One of the main dramas of congressional life is the struggle between majority public opinion and interest groups as the engine of the legislative process. Each and every member of Congress, as we have seen, faces both kinds of pressure from her or his constituencies. The evidence we have presented suggests that, when the public is aware of issues and expresses its opinion, Congress is quite responsive to it. This connection between majority opinion and congressional behavior operates through a number of mechanisms, reviewed in this and earlier chapters, including public opinion polls, mail from constituents, electoral competition, and the party system.

While Congress responds to popular preferences to an impressive degree, it is far from perfect in doing so. There is not only the one time in three that it acts *contrary* to public opinion, but also the many occasions when it must grapple with issues of which the public is either unaware or on which has no opinion at all. It is here that interest groups become especially important. The fundamental changes in telecommunications policies made by the 104th Congress—ranging from cable television and phone systems to radio station ownership—were enacted with very little public attention. The policies were largely the outcome of clashes and agreements between major telecommunication companies and trade groups and their congressional allies.

When the issues before Congress are technical and obscure, and public attention is low, Congress responds to narrow, particularistic, and privileged interests. At such times, lawmakers tend to parcel out government benefits to the well organized in their districts and states. This response is significantly related to the prominent role played by interest groups, large contributors, and PACs. While it is hard to prove the existence of quid pro quo's—trading campaign contributions for legislative favors—the suspicion of such arrangements is widespread among citizens and professional Congress-watchers alike.

At the least, lawmakers hear more frequently and effectively from the organized. The general public may not know the details of a congressionally mandated action in the Interior Department, for instance, but mining and oil interests will surely be in touch. Interest groups, as we have seen, "sing with a strong upper-class accent"; they seriously overrepresent the privileged. Thus, they pose serious problems for the principle of political equality. Since the few are heard at the expense of the many, moreover, popular sovereignty is not well served in this aspect of congressional functioning.

The relationship between Congress and democracy, then, is a complicated one. Our suggestion is that Congress is frequently, but not always, an effective instrument of democracy. The principles of popular sovereignty and political equality are especially at risk when Congress responds to organized and privileged groups rather than to the public. To the degree that this is a problem, however, the blame should probably not be on the shoulders of Congress but on a party system that does not work as well as it might as a democratic instrument. When the party and electoral systems accurately transmit popular preferences to Congress, lawmakers respond.

Congress as Policymaker

A frequently heard criticism of Congress is that it is so parochial and fragmented that it cannot fashion coherent national policy.[36] The argument goes this way. First, Congress is filled with members who are judged by the voters on the basis of their individual attributes and service to the district and to interest groups, not on the basis of the performance of Congress as a whole. One result is that lawmakers worry more about themselves than about the standing and effectiveness of their institution or its collective national policymaking responsibilities.[37]

Second, because lawmakers are responsive to organized interests, serve the constituency as their first order of business, and try to avoid difficult decisions that might put their reelection at risk (or so it is claimed), Congress cannot easily tackle the nation's most difficult problems or think about solutions in general terms. Congress would rather practice "distributive" politics, in which benefits are parceled out to a wide range of constituency and interest group claimants. While this pattern conforms to the self-interested electoral calculations of the individual member, it is, according to many, the basis for the overall ineffectiveness and decline of Congress as a national policymaking institution.

It is hard to assess the validity of these criticisms. The evidence is mixed. Congress has, at times, fashioned broad and coherent national policies in response to tangible problems and strong majority opinions. We have also seen that Congress retains a far greater policymaking role than legislative bodies in parliamentary systems, and that, on domestic issues, it is becoming ever more forceful. Nevertheless, historically, Congress has functioned best as a policymaker when the president, supported by the existence of a national majority in favor of a particular course of action, is able to provide strong leadership. Franklin Roosevelt's New Deal legislative program, Lyndon Johnson's Great Society, and Ronald Reagan's conservative triumphs in 1981 come to mind. For a time, during Newt Gingrich's leadership of the conservative revolution in the House of Representatives in the 104th Congress, it appeared that a major legislative program could be passed without (or against) presidential leadership. Once most bills from the Contract with America failed to become law, however, it became apparent again that the creation of broad and coherent national policies requires presidential leadership.

Summary

The framers of the Constitution wanted to fashion a legislative branch that was both energetic and limited. They granted Congress legislative power, gave it an existence independent of the executive branch, and enumerated an impressive range of powers. They also gave the other branches powers to check legislative excesses, created a bicameral body, and strictly denied certain powers to Congress.

Structural change in the nation has shaped Congress, influencing it to increase in size, expand the volume and complexity of its business, and become more institutionalized and professional.

Congress is a representative institution. Its members are constantly balancing the preferences of the people in their constituencies and important interest groups and contributors. Because elections are the most important mechanism for representation, and because they are the way in which members attain office, elections dominate the time and energy of lawmakers and shape how Congress organizes itself and goes about its business.

To conduct its business, Congress depends on an elaborate set of norms and rules, a web of committees and subcommittees, political parties, legislative leaders, and an extensive staff. Several of these elements encourage fragmentation, decentralization, and occasional gridlock, but also the development of the specialized expertise that allows Congress to meet the executive branch on equal terms. Other tools help the members coordinate and expedite legislative business.

Congress is highly responsive to majority opinion when the issues are visible to the American people and when the people have formed clear preferences about them. Much of the time, however, Congress responds mainly to interest groups and those who make large contributions, putting the principles of popular sovereignty and political equality at risk. A stronger party system would probably make Congress a more consistent instrument of democracy.

Suggested Readings

Birnbaum, Jeffrey H., and Alan S. Murray. *Showdown at Gucci Gulch: Lawmakers, Lobbyists, and the Unlikely Triumph of Tax Reform.* New York: Vintage Books, 1988.

A wonderfully revealing and entertaining account of the passage of the 1986 Tax Reform Act; filled with memorable characters and details of legislative life.

Caro, Robert. *The Years of Lyndon Johnson.* New York: Knopf, 1982.
This classic and award-winning biography of Lyndon Baines Johnson of Texas reveals more about how Congress worked in the "old days" than virtually any academic treatise.

Davidson, Roger H., and Walter J. Oleszek. *Congress and Its Members,* 5th ed. Washington, DC: Congressional Quarterly Press, 1996.
A detailed summary of the prevailing scholarly and journalistic literature on the U.S. Congress.

Dodd, Lawrence C., and Bruce I. Oppenheimer, eds., *Congress Reconsidered,* 6th ed. Washington, DC: Congressional Quarterly Press, 1997.
Original articles summarizing research on virtually every aspect of Congress by leading congressional scholars.

Fenno, Richard F., Jr. *Home Style: House Members in Their Districts.* Boston: Little, Brown, 1978.
A modern classic that examines what members do in their districts and why they do it.

Fiorina, Morris P. *Congress: Keystone of the Washington Establishment,* 2nd ed. New Haven: Yale University Press, 1989.
A very influential book that worries about how the individualistic, rational calculations of members of Congress may hurt collective responsibility and institutional effectiveness.

Oleszek, Walter J. *Congressional Procedures and the Policy Process.* Washington, DC: CQ Press, 1996.
The most comprehensive compilation yet published of the rules and operations of the legislative process in Congress, written by a scholar who served as the policy director of the Joint Committee on the Organization of Congress.

Internet Sources

Almanac of American Politics http://www.PoliticsUSA.com/PoliticsUSA/resources/almanac/mas1.htm
In-depth information about U.S. senators and representatives.

Capitol Watch http://www.capitolwatch.com
Politics and policies in Congress with links to other government agencies and news sites on the Web.

Federal Election Commission gopher://c-span.org:70/11/Resource/fec/1994
Detailed information on congressional campaign fund-raising and spending.

Thomas http://thomas.loc.gov/
Expansive repository of information on the House of Representatives, including the full text and progress of bills, the Congressional Record, *legislative procedures and rules, committee actions, and more.*

U.S. House of Representatives Home Page http://www.house.gov/
House schedule, House organization and procedures, links to House committees, information on contacting representatives, and historical documents on the House of Representatives.

U.S. Senate Home Page http://www.senate.gov/
Similar to the House of Representatives Home Page, focused on the Senate.

Notes

1. Roger H. Davidson and Walter J. Oleszek, *Congress and Its Members,* 4th ed. (Washington, DC: Congressional Quarterly Press, 1994), pp. 17–18.

2. Quoted in Charles Warren, *The Supreme Court in U.S. History* (Boston: Little, Brown, 1919), p. 195.

3. Walter J. Oleszek, *Congressional Procedures and the Policy Process* (Washington, D: CQ Press, 1996), p. 4.

4. See David W. Brady and Elaine K. Swift, "Out of the Past: Theoretical and Methodological Contributions of Congressional History," *P.S.: Political Science and Politics* (March 1991), pp. 61–64; Davidson and Oleszek, *Congress and Its Members,* chap. 2.

5. Davidson and Oleszek, *Congress and Its Members,* p. 31.

6. Nelson Polsby, "The Institutionalization of the U.S. House of Representatives," *American Political Science Review,* Vol. 62, No. 2 (March 1968), pp. 144–168.

7. Quoted in Charles Henning, *The Wit and Wisdom of Politics* (Golden, CO: Fulcrum, 1989), p. 235.

8. Abraham Lincoln, Announcement in the *Sagamo Journal,* New Salem, Illinois (June 13, 1836).

9. Davidson and Oleszek, *Congress and Its Members,* p. 122.

10. Ibid., pp. 57–59.

11. Gary C. Jacobson, *Politics of Congressional Elections,* 2nd edition (Boston: Little Brown, 1987), p. 49.

12. Thomas Ferguson, *Golden Rule* (Chicago: University of Chicago Press, 1995).

13. Neil A. Lewis, "Limits on Donating to Candidates Aren't Deterring the Big Spenders," *New York Times* (May 16, 1992), pp. 1, 7.

14. Richard Hall and Frank W. Wayman, "Buying Time: Moneyed Interests and the Mobilization of Bias in Congressional Committees," *American Political Science Review,* Vol. 84, No. 3 (September 1990), pp. 797–820.

15. David R. Mayhew, *Congress: The Electoral Connection* (New Haven: Yale University Press, 1974).

16. Malcolm Jewell, "Legislators and Their Districts," *Legislative Studies Quarterly,* Vol. 13, No. 3 (August 1988), pp. 403–412.

17. Bruce Cain, John Ferejohn, and Morris Fiorina, *The Personal Vote: Constituency Service and Electoral Independence* (Cambridge: Harvard University Press, 1987); Glenn Parker, *Homeward Bound: Explaining Change in Congressional Behavior* (Pittsburgh: University of Pittsburgh Press, 1986).

18. R. S. Erikson, "Constituency Opinion and Congressional Behavior," *American Journal of Political Science,* Vol. 22 (1978), pp. 511–535; Robert S. Erikson and Gerald C. Wright, "Voters, Candidates, and Issues in Congressional Elections," in Lawrence C. Dodd and Bruce I. Oppenheimer, eds., *Congress Reconsidered,* 4th ed. (Washington, DC: Congressional Quarterly Press, 1989), pp. 91–116.

19. Alan Monroe, "Consistency Between Public Preferences and National Policy Decisions," *American Politics Quarterly,* Vol. 7 (1979), pp. 3–19; Benjamin I. Page and Robert Y. Shapiro, "Effects of Public Opinion on Policy," *American Political Science Review,* Vol. 77 (1983), pp. 175–190.

20. Richard Rose, "Politics in England," in Gabriel A. Almond and G. Bingham Powell, Jr., eds., *Comparative Politics Today* (Glenview, IL: Scott, Foresman/Little, Brown, 1988), p. 162.

21. Morris P. Fiorina, *Congress: Keystone of the Washington Establishment,* 2nd ed. (New Haven: Yale University Press, 1989); Mayhew, *Congress: The Electoral Connection.*

22. Lawrence C. Dodd and Bruce I. Oppenheimer, "Maintaining Order in the House: The Struggle for Institutional Equilibrium," in Dodd and Oppenheimer (eds.), *Congress Reconsidered,* 5th ed. (Washington, DC: Congressional Quarterly Press, 1993), p. 51.

23. David A. Rhode and Kenneth A. Shepsle, "Democratic Committee Assignments in the House of Representatives: Strategic Aspects of a Social Choice Process," in Matthew D. McCubbins and Terry Sullivan, eds., *Congress: Structure and Policy* (New York: Cambridge University Press, 1987).

24. Frank J. Sorauf and Paul Allen Beck, *Political Parties in America* (Glenview, IL: Scott, Foresman/Little, Brown, 1988), p. 410.

25. Davidson and Oleszek, *Congress and Its Members,* pp. 366–368.

26. See John J. Kornacki, ed., *Leading Congress: New Styles, New Strategies* (Washington, DC: Congressional Quarterly Press, 1990); David W. Rohde, *Parties and Leaders in the Postreform Congress* (Chicago: University of Chicago Press, 1991).

27. Walter J. Oleszek, *Congressional Procedures and the Policy Process,* 4th ed. (Washington, DC: Congressional Quarterly Press, 1996), p. 33.

28. Davidson and Oleszek, *Congress and Its Members,* pp. 128–133; Donald R. Mathews, *U.S. Senators and Their World* (Chapel Hill: University of North Carolina Press, 1960).

29. Eric M. Uslaner, *The Decline of Comity in Congress* (Ann Arbor: University of Michigan Press, 1996).

30. Robert Bendiner, *Obstacle Course on Capitol Hill* (New York: McGraw-Hill, 1964), p. 15.

31. Gary Young and Joseph Cooper, "Multiple Referral and the Transformation of House Decision Making," in Dodd and Oppenheimer, *Congress Reconsidered,* 5th ed.

32. Oleszek, *Congressional Procedures,* p. 273.

33. Matthew D. McCubbins and John Schwartz, "Congressional Oversight Overlooked: Police Patrols and Fire Alarms," in Matthew D. McCubbins and Terry Sullivan, eds., *Congress: Structure and Policy* (Cambridge: Cambridge University Press, 1987).

34. Henning, *The Wit and Wisdom of Politics,* p. 38.

35. Philip M. Stern, *The Best Congress Money Can Buy* (New York: Pantheon, 1988).

36. Fiorina, *Congress: Keystone of the Washington Establishment;* Mayhew, *Congress: The Electoral Connection;* Jacobson, *Politics of Congressional Elections.*

37. Morris P. Fiorina, "The Decline of Collective Responsibility," *Daedalus,* Vol. 109, No. 3 (Summer 1980); Cain, Ferejohn, and Fiorina, *The Personal Vote.*

CHAPTER 12

The President

IN THIS CHAPTER

- ★ Why the presidency expanded into a powerful office
- ★ The many roles of presidents
- ★ Why presidents often disagree with Congress
- ★ How democratic the presidency is: whether presidents listen and respond to the public
- ★ Why different presidents often pursue similar policies

The Reagan Revolution

Ronald Reagan took office in 1981 after a landslide election victory, promising a "new American revolution" that would change the size, reach, and responsibilities of the federal government. In order to "get government off the backs of the people," he proposed the largest tax cut in American history ($750 billion over six years), mainly for upper-income groups and corporations; sharp cutbacks in regulations; and major reductions in domestic social programs, entirely eliminating some of them, such as job training and public service employment. Promising to regain respect and influence for the United States around the world, he proposed the steepest rise in defense spending in peacetime American history (20 percent per year).

The Reagan program was breathtaking in scope. Most observers were skeptical about its chances in Congress, because the Republicans had only a slim majority in the Senate and the Democrats still controlled the House of Representatives, with 243 seats to the Republicans' 192. Surely, the Reagan Revolution would be buried in committees, or compromised, and business would go on as usual.

President Reagan thought otherwise. He brought all his formidable personal skills, energy, and resources to bear on the task of passing his program. Reagan cultivated friendly relations with members of Congress, inviting them to White House breakfasts and passing out presidential cuff links and tickets for the presidential box at the Kennedy Center for the Performing Arts. He offered shrewd deals to those who would back his tax and budget package: sugar price supports for representatives from Louisiana; Amtrak and Conrail funding increases for "gypsy moth" moderate Republicans from the Northeast; natural gas deregulation for representatives from the energy states.

Besides carrots, Reagan also used the stick. Democrats from conservative areas in the South, where a majority of voters had supported Reagan, found the White House turning up the heat in their own districts, mobilizing influential groups like the National Conservative Political Action Committee and the Moral Majority, sending in Vice-President Bush and Representative Jack Kemp, and getting major campaign contributors to urge cooperation with Reagan.[1]

Aiming to put further pressure on Congress, Reagan worked to build up his popularity with the general public. Like most new presidents, Reagan began with a fairly high level of popular approval. He sustained and increased it with his genial and winning public personality, the emotional patriotism that swelled among Americans on the return of U.S. hostages from Iran in January, and the successful launch of the space shuttle *Columbia*. In April, Reagan turned his survival of an assassination attempt into a public relations triumph, displaying courage and humor. While still recovering, he made a dramatic televised appearance before Congress to plead for his programs. As Representative Dan Rostenkowski, leader of the Democrats on the tax issue, put it, "The President can gear up his army with just one television appearance. That's fighting the Army, Navy, Marines and Air Force."[2]

Although polls showed continuing public support for many domestic social programs that Reagan opposed, the politicians were awed by the scale of Reagan's electoral victory and by the height of his popularity. The administration's budget sailed through the Senate by a vote of 72 to 20, with hardly a change. Budget aide David Stockman later gloated, "The politicians had flinched. They had rubber-stamped the Reagan Revolution."[3]

Even in the Democrat-controlled House of Representatives, Reagan got his way at every critical juncture, mainly because of support from southern conservative Democrats, nicknamed "boll weevils."

Hoarse and tired after a last-minute speech, Reagan telephoned final, late-night appeals to 16 House members. (Reagan's arch foe, House Speaker "Tip" O'Neill, later lamented, "The members adored it when he called . . . they can go back to their districts and say, 'I was talking to the President the other day.'"[4] The next day, Reagan won the crucial budget "reconciliation" vote.

The president also worked tirelessly for his tax cut bill. Using the same mix of personal charm and popularity, judicious compromises, winning rhetoric, and hints of retribution for those who failed to cooperate, he had his way here as well. The Economic Recovery Tax Act was passed on July 29, 1981.

The Reagan Revolution would prove to have profound effects that lasted on into the 1990s and beyond. The military buildup may have contributed to the collapse of the Soviet Union, which squandered vast resources trying to catch up. Social programs, though not cut as drastically as Reagan wanted, remained under severe pressure in later years because less tax revenue was available. The tax cuts probably contributed to the substantial economic growth of the 1980s, but also to a massive increase in the size of the national debt (which *tripled* in the Reagan years) and to dramatic increases in income and wealth inequality. Wealthy people got most of the gains, while the middle class and the poor made little or no progress.[5] Nevertheless, the Reagan Revolution was a huge political success. It provided much of the inspiration for the 1994 "Contract with America" and for renewed Republican efforts to cut spending and taxes in 1995 and 1996.

What accounts for Reagan's victory? It was a big surprise to those who had been talking about the weak, "imperiled" presidency during Jimmy Carter's term of office. If we take things at face value, it appears that Ronald Reagan was a heroic figure, able single-handedly to shake America from its lethargy and reinvigorate the presidential office.

Without doubt, Reagan's personal skills and energy played an important part. We will see in this chapter, however, that presidential will, determination, and personality represent only part of the story. The president always acts in a context defined by the Constitution and the evolution of the office, a particular governmental and political environment, and a larger economic, social, cultural, and international structure. Moreover, what sort of president we have, and what he wants and tries to accomplish, is itself influenced by political and structural factors.

In Reagan's case, the times were ripe for his brand of leadership. The nation had experienced dramatic drops in its international economic and military standing, in its confidence, and in corporate profits and people's standards of living. People were ready, even desperate, for change. Media, business, and academic leaders began calling for a reorientation of public policy. Conservative political action committees, think tanks, and interest groups, fueled by massive corporate funding, mounted a campaign for a conservative policy renewal in Washington and for the election of Reagan and other Republicans.[6] Congress, itself under pressure from financial contributors and unsure how to escape the downward spiral, looked for presidential leadership and ultimately responded when Reagan provided it.

The Reagan Revolution, from this viewpoint, involved much more than Ronald Reagan; to understand it requires that we understand not just the personality, style, and effectiveness of Reagan as president but also the governmental, political, and structural contexts within which he operated. The same is true of other presidents.

The Expanding Presidency

The American presidency has grown considerably over the years. The increase in presidential responsibilities, burdens, power, and impact since our nation's beginnings is obvious if we compare the presidencies of Bill Clinton and George Washington—a little more than 200 years apart.

Bill Clinton Versus George Washington

In 1996, Clinton presided over a federal budget involving more than $1.5 *trillion* ($1,500 billion) in annual expenditures and a federal establishment with approximately 2.9 million civilian employees. He made decisions concerning laws, regulations, and spending that touched every aspect of the society and the economy. He was commander in chief of the armed forces, with about 1.6 million men and women in uniform; hundreds of military bases at home and scattered throughout the world; and perhaps 20,000 deliverable nuclear warheads, enough to obliterate every medium-sized or large city in the world many times over. Clinton's United States in 1996 had a population of about 263 million diverse people, living in cities, suburbs, and countryside, and working in offices, factories, shops, and fields; a gross national product of more than $6.7 trillion, or about $25,500 for each person in the country; and a land area of some 3.8 million square miles, stretching from Alaska to Florida and from Hawaii to Maine.[7]

By contrast, when George Washington took office as the first president, he had a total budget (from 1789 through 1791) of just over $4 million. Washington had only a handful of federal employees. Even by 1801, there were only about 300 federal officeholders in the capital. Washington's cabinet consisted of just five officials: the secretaries of state, war, and the treasury, a postmaster general, and an attorney general (who acted as the president's personal

The office of the presidency has grown in scale and in responsibility. As commander in chief of the armed forces, Washington commanded an army of just over 700 soldiers and had little to do with affairs outside the United States. Bill Clinton, in comparison, controls over 1.5 million troops all over the world.

attorney, rather than as head of a full-fledged Justice Department). The entire Department of State consisted of just one secretary, one chief clerk, six minor clerks, and one messenger.

In 1790, only about 700 Americans were in uniform, and they had no way to project force around the world. Federal government functions were few. The entire United States consisted of just the 13 original eastern and southeastern states, with only 864,746 square miles of land area; the population was only about 4 million persons, most living on small farms.[8]

The Founders' Conception of the Office of President

The Founders certainly had in mind a presidency more like Washington's than Clinton's. As we discussed in Chapter 2, Article II of the Constitution provided for a single executive who would be strong, compared to his role in the Congress-dominated Articles of Confederation, but the Constitution's sparse language barely hinted at the range of things twentieth-century presidents would do. The Constitution made the president "commander in chief" of the armed forces, for example, without any suggestion that there would be a vast standing army that presidents could send abroad to fight, without a declaration of war. It empowered presidents to appoint and to "require the opinion in writing" of executive department heads, without indicating that a huge federal bureaucracy would evolve. The Constitution provided that presidents could from time to time "recommend . . . measures" to Congress, without specifying that these proposals would come to dominate the legislative agenda. Still, the vague language of the Constitution proved flexible enough to encompass the great expansion of the presidency.

The Dormant Presidency

In Chapter 4, we described some of the great structural changes in the economy, society, and territory of the United States that led to an enormous expansion in the federal government. Certain presidents played important parts in these trends, and the office of the presidency changed, along with the country.

From the time of George Washington's inauguration at Federal Hall in New York City to the end of the nineteenth century, the presidency, for the most part, conformed to the designs of the Founders. The presidency did not, by and large, dominate the political life of the nation. Presidents saw their responsibility as primarily involving the execution of policies decided by Congress. Congress was a fully equal branch of government, or perhaps more than equal.

Structural Factors Why does the early presidency seem so weak in comparison with the contemporary presidency? Surely, it is not because early presidents were less intelligent, vigorous, or ambitious; some were and some were not. A more satisfying answer is that the nation did not often require a very strong presidency before the twentieth century, particularly in the key area of foreign policy and military leadership. Only in the twentieth century did the United States become a world power, involved in military, diplomatic, and economic activities around the globe. With that *structural* development came a simultaneous increase in the power and responsibility of the president.

It was not until the late nineteenth century, moreover, that the economy of the United States was transformed from a simple free market economy of farmers and small firms to a corporate-dominated economy, with units so large that their every action had social consequences. This transformation eventually led to demands for more government supervision of the American economic system. As this role of government grew, so, too, did that of the president.

Though the presidency was largely dormant during the late eighteenth and most of the nineteenth centuries, events and the actions of several presidents during this period anticipated what was to happen to the office in our own time. Precedents were set; expectations were formed; rules were changed.

Important Early Presidents For example, the war hero George Washington solidified the prestige of the presidency at a time when executive leadership was mistrusted. Washington also affirmed the primacy of the president in foreign affairs and (with help from Treasury Secretary Alexander Hamilton) set a precedent for fashioning a domestic legislative program. Thomas Jefferson, though initially hostile to the idea of a vigorous central government, boldly made the Louisiana Purchase from France, which roughly doubled the size of the United States and opened the continent for Americans all the way to the Pacific Ocean. Rough-hewn frontiersman Andrew Jackson, elected with broader popular participation than ever before, helped transform the presidency into a popular institution, as symbolized by his vigorous opposition to the Bank of the United States (which was seen by many ordinary Americans as a tool of the wealthy.)

James Polk, though often ignored in textbook accounts of "great" presidents, energetically exercised his powers as commander in chief of the armed forces; he provoked a war with Mexico and acquired most of what is now the southwestern United States and California. Abraham Lincoln, in order to win the Civil War, invoked emergency powers based on his broad reading of the Constitution: he raised and spent money and deployed troops on his own, with Congress acquiescing only afterward; he temporarily suspended the right of habeas corpus and allowed civilians to be tried in military courts; he freed

Andrew Jackson was hailed as a hero for opposing the "monster" bank of the United States.

Abraham Lincoln (shown here with Union General George Brinton McClellan at the Antietam battlefield during the Civil War) was the first president to invoke emergency powers; his liberal interpretation of the Constitution set precedents for later use.

slaves in the confederate states by issuing the Emancipation Proclamation. Temporarily, during the Civil War, government tax revenues escalated, expenditures increased to unprecedented levels, and the number of civilian federal employees exploded.

The Twentieth-Century Transformation

The more enduring changes in the presidency, however, came only in the twentieth century, when new structural conditions made an expanded presidency both possible and necessary.

Theodore Roosevelt When Theodore Roosevelt took office after William McKinley was assassinated in 1901, he enunciated a "stewardship" theory of the presidency, vigorously pushing the prerogatives and enhancing the powers of the office as no president had done since Lincoln. Roosevelt was happiest when he was deploying the troops as commander in chief or serving as the nation's chief diplomat. Against Congress's wishes he sent the "Great White Fleet" of navy steamships around the world to demonstrate American power; he intervened in Central America to establish the Panama Canal Zone and to protect American economic and political interests; and he successfully mediated disputes between Japan and Russia, for which he won the Nobel Peace Prize.

trusts Popular term used around the turn of the century to refer to large combinations of business corporations.

On the domestic front, Roosevelt pushed for regulation of the new and frightening business corporations, especially by busting **trusts,** and he established many national parks. In "Teddy" Roosevelt, we see the coming together of an energetic and ambitious political leader and a new set of structural factors in the United States, particularly the U.S. emergence as a world power and an industrialized economy.

Woodrow Wilson Woodrow Wilson's presidency marked further important steps in the expansion of the federal government and the presidency. Wilson's "New Freedom" domestic program built on the Progressive Era measures of Theodore Roosevelt, including further regulation of the economy by establishment of the Federal Reserve Board (1913) and the Federal Trade Commission (1914). Wilson was a great admirer of the British parliamentary system, in which the prime minister formulates the nation's legislative agenda. He was able to do much the same sort of thing himself, because the climate was ripe for the regulation of American business and because (as we will see) he established direct connections with the general public.

Even more important were foreign affairs. The United States had already emerged on the world stage at the turn of the century, with the Spanish-American War and the Great White Fleet. Under Wilson, World War I brought an enormous increase in activity: a huge mobilization of military personnel and a large, new civilian bureaucracy to oversee the production and distribution of food, fuel, and armaments by the American "arsenal of democracy." Although these temporary agencies were dismantled at the end of the war, the federal government and the presidency never returned to their earlier modest scale.

Franklin Roosevelt It was Franklin D. Roosevelt, however, who presided over the most significant expansion of presidential functions and activities in American history. In a very real sense, the founding of the modern American presidency occurred during Roosevelt's administration, in response to the Great Depression and World War II. In 1931, there were some 600,000 federal employees; a decade later, the number topped 1.4 million.

By staying in touch with and responding to the people during the crisis of the Great Depression, Franklin Delano Roosevelt helped define the modern presidency.

The depression had devastated the American economy: at the beginning of 1933, more than one-third (37.6 percent) of nonfarm workers were unemployed.[9] Many companies went bankrupt, and countless farmers lost their land. In its first 100 days, the Roosevelt administration and the Democratic majority in Congress pushed into law a series of measures for economic relief that grew into vast programs of conservation and public works, farm credit, business loans, and relief payments to the destitute.

Besides these temporary antidepression measures, Roosevelt's New Deal permanently established a number of independent regulatory commissions to regulate aspects of business (the stock market, telephones, utilities, airlines) and enacted programs like Social Security, to insure workers and their families against disability and retirement, and the Wagner Act, to help workers join unions and bargain collectively with their employers. Each of these measures required an administrative apparatus; each brought the president into more intimate involvement in the U.S. economy. By the end of the 1930s, a whole new structure was in place to coordinate the new agencies. In 1939, the Executive Office of the President was established to help the president oversee the federal bureaucracy.

The Impact of World War II Even bigger changes, however, resulted from World War II. The government again mobilized the entire population and the whole economy for the war effort. In 1941, there were 1.8 million men and women on active military duty; by 1945, 12 million were in uniform. Most were demobilized at the end of the war, but the armed forces remained much larger than in the 1930s and were quickly built up once again for the Cold War and the Korean War. With the end of World War II, the United States was established as a military superpower, unrivaled by any other country but the Soviet Union. Since the time of Franklin Roosevelt, all U.S. presidents have administered a huge national-security state with large standing armed forces, nuclear weapons, and bases all around the world.

Similarly, World War II brought unprecedented governmental involvement in the economy, with temporary war agencies regulating prices, rationing necessities, monitoring and stimulating industrial output, and helping to develop human resources for domestic production. These agencies were dismantled after the war, but they trained a large cadre of officials in an activist view of what the federal government could and should do, and they set precedents for presidential and governmental actions that continue to the present day. All presidents since Roosevelt have presided over a huge government apparatus that has been active in domestic policy as well as in foreign policy.

How Important Are Individual Presidents?

We cannot be sure to what extent presidents themselves caused this great expansion of the scope of their office. Clearly, they played a part. Lincoln, Wilson, and Franklin Roosevelt, for example, not only reacted vigorously to events but also helped to create events; each had something to do with the coming of the wars that were so crucial in adding to their activities and powers. Similarly, we cannot assume that every president would have made the Louisiana Purchase, as Jefferson did, or would have fought the Great Depression so actively—and transformed the shape of the presidency so thoroughly—as Franklin Roosevelt did. Yet these great presidents (see Table 12.1) were also the product of great times; they stepped into situations that had deep historical roots and dynamics of their own.

Table 12.1

Presidential Greatness

In 1982, a sample of 953 professors of American history rated the presidents as they are listed here.

Great	1. Lincoln	*Average*	18. McKinley
	2. F. Roosevelt		19. Taft
	3. Washington		20. Van Buren
	4. Jefferson		21. Hoover
Near Great	5. T. Roosevelt		22. Hayes
	6. Wilson		23. Arthur
	7. Jackson		24. Ford
	8. Truman		25. Carter
Above Average	9. J. Adams		26. B. Harrison
	10. L. Johnson	*Below Average*	27. Taylor
	11. Eisenhower		28. Tyler
	12. Polk		29. Fillmore
	13. Kennedy		30. Coolidge
	14. Madison		31. Pierce
	15. Monroe	*Failure*	32. A. Johnson
	16. J. Q. Adams		33. Buchanan
	17. Cleveland		34. Nixon
			35. Grant
			36. Harding

Source: Robert K. Murray and Tim H. Blessing, *Journal of American History* (December 1983).

Lincoln found a nation that was in bitter conflict over the relative economic and political power of North and South, and that was focused on the question of slavery in the western territories; war was a likely, if not inevitable, outcome. Wilson and Roosevelt each faced a world in which German expansion threatened the perceived economic and cultural interests of the United States, and in which U.S. industrial power permitted a strong response. The Great Depression, resistant to Herbert Hoover's more traditional, voluntaristic, free market remedies, fairly cried out for a new kind of presidential activism. Thus, the great upsurges in presidential power and activity were, at least in part, a result of forces at the *structural* level, that is, the result of developments in the economy, American society, and the international system.

Presidential Personality and Style

The American presidency looks like a highly personal office, seeming to change drastically with the personality and style of the person who occupies that office.[10] In actuality, the presidency is not just an individual; it is an institution, shaped by forces both inside and outside government. Nevertheless, the personalities and styles of presidents do make a difference and are worth some attention.

The Styles of Recent Presidents

A quick look at post–World War II presidents indicates how personality and style matter, and how they differ from one president to another.

Harry Truman (1945–1953) Truman's style was feisty and combative, whether he was taking on Congress, the Republicans, the Soviets, or the media. Truman's "give 'em hell" style in his 1948 come-from-behind election victory seemed in harmony with his decisions to challenge the Soviets in Europe and to send U.S. troops to Korea.[11]

Dwight Eisenhower (1953–1961) Eisenhower was a commanding personality who radiated warmth and won great popularity. Much like our first war hero president, George Washington, Eisenhower's public persona was that of a father figure who stayed above the political fray. Eisenhower seemed to preside loosely over the executive branch, yet scholars have argued that he exerted firm control through hidden-hand techniques.[12]

John Kennedy (1961–1963) Kennedy was a glamorous president—handsome, young, energetic, stylish, and blessed with a winning sense of humor. (Once a high school boy asked President Kennedy how he had become a war hero. Kennedy replied, "It was absolutely involuntary. They sank my [PT] boat."[13]) Trying to "get America moving again" after the quiet Eisenhower years, Kennedy pursued anti-Communist activism abroad but bumped into a conservative coalition of congressional Republicans and southern Democrats when he tried to pass domestic programs. Years later, average Americans (though not so many historians; see Table 12.1) rated Kennedy as one of the great presidents and celebrated the Kennedy days as "Camelot" in books and films.[14]

Lyndon Johnson (1963–1969) Johnson, who assumed the presidency after Kennedy was assassinated, was spectacularly successful in enacting civil rights, Medicare, and other Great Society domestic programs, but he was eventually overwhelmed by the Vietnam War and urban unrest. At his best, Johnson seemed to be a giant of a man, physically large, bursting with superhuman energy ("He has extra glands," one aide remarked), working his will on Congress; his powerful personal presence overawed those he could grasp in his hands. But Johnson's style was better suited to the floor of the Senate, where he had been majority leader, than to the world stage or television; there he appeared to be stiff and sober and even a purveyor of deception ("My granddaddy fought at the Alamo," he fibbed).[15]

Richard Nixon (1969–1974) Nixon was seen by many Americans as a cold, awkward, and perhaps ruthless personality, but also as a striving common man and an experienced, shrewd, hard-driving professional, especially adept at foreign policy. A Republican, Nixon deemphasized domestic matters, though he signed some significant legislation (much of it Democrat-sponsored). The same secretive style that had helped him negotiate an end to the Vietnam War and a diplomatic opening to China probably contributed to the cover-up of Watergate crimes and misdeeds (recall Chapter 6) that led to his resignation in disgrace.[16]

Gerald Ford (1974–1977) Ford, who ascended to the presidency when Nixon resigned and served only briefly, was widely perceived as solid but unexciting,

POLITICS AND FILM

Oliver Stone Raises More Hackles

If we are to believe the cries of outrage from the nation's historians and journalists, Oliver Stone's *Nixon* is the worst threat to American civilization since "Beavis and Butthead." . . . The rhetoric of its detractors has already escalated to the point where one Sunday-morning ABC News talking head . . . likened Mr. Stone to Leni Riefenstahl.

Such innuendo surely merits the adjective Nixonesque. Leni Riefenstahl's 1934 *Triumph of the Will* was a documentary featuring the real-life Hitler and fashioned to advance the Nazi cause. Mr. Stone's *Nixon* is a historical drama, clearly labeled as such and starring an English actor (Sir Anthony Hopkins, pictured) who doesn't remotely resemble its title character, about a lost cause—a man who has not only been out of power for 20 years but is dead. Yet Riefenstahl and Stone were equated anyway, by a journalist who was faulting Mr. Stone for monkeying with history!

What's going on here? Of course *Nixon* is a mixture of fact and fantasy—just like every historical drama before it. In *Past Imperfect,* a new book put out by the Society of American Historians, our best historians, including some *Nixon* critics like Stephen Ambrose and Richard Reeves, challenge the factual accuracy or thematic validity of virtually every historical epic in cinematic history. And not just movies that deal with distant or Shakespearean history (*A Man for All Seasons, Spartacus, Henry V*) but relatively contemporary films like *The Longest Day, Patton, Gandhi, Malcolm X* and, yes, both *JFK* and *All the President's Men.*

. . .

Mr. Stone's movie is less simple-minded than most. The one Nixon expert who applauds it for its emotional truth, Bob Woodward, argues persuasively that "about half the movie is based on facts" with the other half ranging "from sound speculation to borderline slander." This .500-plus batting average is in the league of *Schindler's List* and far higher than that of *The Alamo* and *The Green Berets,* to pick just two John Wayne potboilers inflicted on me and the rest of America's youth during the Nixon era. What's more, *Nixon* is so nakedly subjective—employing hallucinatory camera work, a fractured time scheme and deliberately operatic dramatic overstatement—that far from masquerading as docudrama, it flaunts its fantasies.

So why single out *Nixon* for disfavor? Its critics say they only want to protect "young people"—but what really seems to get under their skin is the director's political slant, which is unreconstructed 60's leftist. Mr. Stone sees America in the grip of a "system" or "beast"—his terms for what used to be vilified as the military-industrial complex—that's as implacably evil as the Indians were in the westerns of another Hollywood era. Because Mr. Stone is as powerful a film maker in his way as a conservative like John Ford was in his, he draws you into his conspiratorial case, at least while you're sitting in the theater.

Source: Frank Rich, "The Stoning of Stone," *New York Times* (December 7, 1995), p. A11.

Richard Nixon scored a number of foreign policy successes during his presidency, including reestablishing friendly U.S. relations with mainland China after a 23-year break.

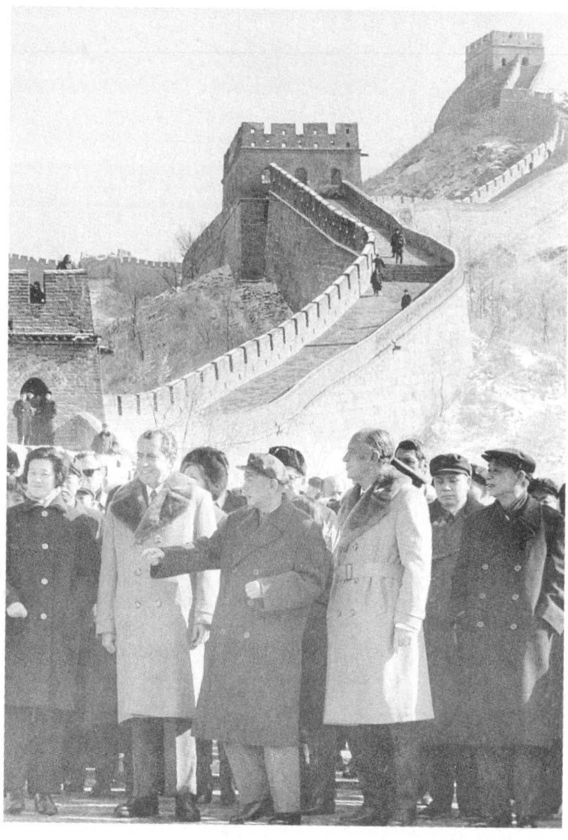

a former college football center unused to playing quarterback. The reassuring effect of Ford's honest manner was undercut by his pardon of Nixon for any crimes committed in the Watergate affair (even before Nixon had been formally charged with any), and his apparent propensity for stumbling and pratfalls made him the butt of jokes about physical clumsiness. More important, Ford had the misfortune to occupy the presidency during a period of deep economic recession and rapid inflation, which began just after the first oil price rise of 1973–1974, instituted by the Organization of Petroleum Exporting Countries (OPEC).[17]

Jimmy Carter (1977–1981) Carter was an outsider (a peanut farmer, governor of Georgia, and "nuclear engineer") who projected an image of moral rectitude, frequently criticizing the Washington establishment. Carter's relaxed, open, and unassuming down-home style, as well as his deeply held Southern Baptist values, initially reassured a nation troubled by Vietnam and Watergate.[18] Soon, however, the media depicted a disorganized administration and anguished or vacillating decision making, not up to the challenges of the second big OPEC oil price rise (1979), **stagflation** in the economy, the introduction of Soviet troops into Afghanistan, or the taking of American hostages in Iran. Defeated after one term, Carter later established a reputation as an outstanding ex-president, working vigorously for human rights and international peace.[19]

stagflation A combination of economic stagnation and inflation.

Ronald Reagan (1981–1989) Reagan, like Carter, was an outsider who attacked the government in Washington, D.C., but he projected warmth and bub-

Jimmy Carter won points from the public for his industriousness and informality, but he was voted out of office after domestic and foreign policy troubles.

bling optimism. Reagan, a long-time movie and TV actor, charmed the public with self-deprecating humor and roused public passions with dramatic appeals and emotion-laden anecdotes. Although seeming to hold rather loose reins on the executive branch (leaving specifics to others, displaying fuzziness about facts, and occasionally dozing off in cabinet meetings), Reagan nearly always knew what he wanted and often got it (recall our opening story). He had the good fortune to serve as president at a time when the U.S. economy was ready to recover from the oil price shocks and when the Soviet Union was becoming weaker and more conciliatory.[20]

George Bush (1989–1993) Bush promised a "kinder, gentler" presidency but delivered a less charismatic one than Reagan's. Still, while awkward at speaking and occasionally called a "wimp," Bush was no pushover. Born to a wealthy and prominent family in Connecticut, Bush had headed west, making his own mark in the rough-and-tumble Texas oil business. He had served in Congress and as chair of the Republican party, then as ambassador to the United Nations, liaison to China, and director of the Central Intelligence Agency (CIA), before being elected Reagan's vice-president. As president, Bush kept a firm hand on foreign affairs; he navigated through the collapse of communism in Eastern Europe and triumphed over Saddam Hussein in the Persian Gulf War. But he paid less attention to domestic policies, and when the U.S. economy declined, he suffered electoral punishment.

Bill Clinton Former Arkansas governor Clinton entered office with fewer than half the votes in a three-way race, burdened by questions about marital infidelity, his avoidance of Vietnam War service, and the finances of the Whitewater real estate venture. As president, Clinton came across as boyish, eager to please, energetic, hardworking, and immersed in policy details, but also as indecisive and not always trustworthy. Lacking Washington experience and facing opposition within his own congressional party, he suffered early setbacks in appointments and policies; Clinton seemed better at listening and talking than at deciding or commanding.

After the Republicans' 1994 congressional victory, the policy initiative passed largely to Congress. Clinton reacted partly by adopting Republican ideas (e.g., a balanced budget in seven years) and partly by resisting unpopular parts of the Republican "revolution," such as extensive cuts in Medicare or educational and environmental programs. This resistance enabled him to recapture substantial public favor as he headed toward the 1996 election.

Presidential Character

Which aspects of presidential style and personality are most important, and how do they interact with the institution of the presidency? A theory concerning these matters has been proposed by political scientist James David Barber.[21]

Barber's Theory According to Barber, much depends on the president's *character,* his enduring orientation toward life and toward himself, which is mainly formed in childhood. One crucial dimension of character involves whether a president is *active* or *passive:* full of energy, like the human cyclone Lyndon Johnson, or inactive, like the nap-taking Calvin Coolidge. Another key dimension concerns whether a person is *positive* or *negative,* whether he feels good or bad about life, about the job of the presidency, and about himself.

When these two dimensions are combined, they suggest four fundamental types of character. Barber most admires the *active-positive* type: healthy, full of energy and enthusiasm for the job, and a "doer." He places such presidents as Franklin Roosevelt and Kennedy in this category, along with Carter, Ford, and Truman.

Active-negative personalities, on the other hand, are said to be dangerous. Their activity has a compulsive, aggressive quality, as if they are trying to compensate for something; this quality leads to rigid, inflexible behavior, with disastrous results. Woodrow Wilson, for example, may have suffered damaged self-esteem as a child because of his domineering father, a strict preacher and scholar who humiliated young "Tommy" Wilson in public and forced him to produce perfect translations from Greek and Latin. Wilson subsequently resented authority figures and resisted compromise, even to save his beloved League of Nations treaty.[22] Barber also judges as active-negative personalities Richard Nixon and Lyndon Johnson, both of whom—in the Watergate scandal and the Vietnam War—seemed stubbornly to pursue a course of action after it had failed disastrously.

According to Barber, a *passive-positive* personality like William Howard Taft, Warren Harding, or perhaps Ronald Reagan, deprived of love in childhood, seeks love and affection by being agreeable and cooperative rather than assertive. (Bill Clinton, with an alcoholic and sometimes abusive stepfather, might also fit this pattern.) Passive-positive presidents don't usually accomplish much. A *passive-negative* personality, such as Calvin Coolidge or perhaps Dwight Eisenhower, compensates for low self-esteem and a feeling of uselessness by doing dutiful service—doing little and enjoying it less, withdrawing from conflict by emphasizing vague principles and standing for rectitude.

Assessing the Barber Theory Barber's theory has provoked much criticism. Some scholars argue that character comes in many more than four types. Some say it is difficult or impossible to categorize individual presidents. (Was Reagan, who reshaped American politics, really passive?) Others suggest that ideology may be more important than character. (Perhaps Herbert Hoover resisted government action against the Great Depression because of his conservative worldview, not because of a negative character or the student-manager style he had learned at Stanford University.) Still others suggest that presidents are less affected by their character than by events and circumstances; the situation may make the person, rather than vice versa. (Perhaps it was the failure of the Vietnam War, rather than a character flaw, that made Lyndon Johnson's outlook so negative at the end of his presidency.)[23]

Beyond Character Most political scientists put less emphasis on character and more emphasis on a president's situation and surroundings, as we do in this book. In discussing recent presidents, for example, we have noted several events (oil price rises, recessions, and wars) that seemed more important than personalities and styles in affecting what presidents did and how they fared. The limited role of presidents' personal characteristics is also suggested by the way that changes in political party control of government constrain presidents and help bring forth different sorts of presidents at different times, and by enduring *trends* in the presidency, that is, major changes that have occurred over many years, regardless of who was president, as a result of fundamental historical processes. Such trends include the tremendous increase in the power, responsibilities, burdens, and impact of the presidency, in both foreign and domestic policy, and (to be discussed further, below) a significant increase in the closeness of presidents to the general public, as leaders and as democratic representatives of the people.

These trends in the presidency are closely related to the *structural* trends in American political development that we outlined in Chapter 4: the great expansion in the size of the United States; the political, military, and economic interactions of the United States with the rest of the world; industrialization; the revolution in mass communications; and the growth of democracy throughout the U.S. political system. Presidents have taken part in each of these trends, sometimes affecting them, but often just reflecting or symbolizing them.

The Many Roles of the President

Since Franklin Roosevelt's day, the American presidency has involved powers and duties, unimaginable to the Founders, that touch the daily lives of everyone in the United States and indeed everyone in the world. Political scientist Clinton Rossiter's writings introduced generations of students to the many different "hats" that presidents wear.[24]

Chief of State

The president is a symbol of national authority and unity. In contrast to European parliamentary nations like Great Britain or Norway, where a monarch acts as chief of state while a prime minister serves as head of the government, in the United States the two functions are combined. It is the president who performs many ceremonial duties (e.g., attendance at funerals, the proclamation of official "days," and the celebration of heroes and anniversaries) that are carried out by members of royal families in other nations. Jimmy Breslin, an irreverent New York newspaper columnist, once wrote, "The office of President is such a bastardized thing, half royalty and half democracy, that nobody knows whether to genuflect or spit."[25]

Commander in Chief

The Constitution explicitly lodges command over the American armed forces in the office of president. The development of so-called war powers has grown enormously over the years, to the point where President Bush, in 1990, was quickly able to put more than 500,000 U.S. troops in the Persian Gulf area, poised to strike against Iraq. Despite substantial congressional opposition, President Clinton claimed the power in 1995 to send several thousand American troops as peacekeepers to Bosnia.

Chief Legislator

While constitutional responsibility for the legislative agenda seems at first glance clearly given to Congress, over the years the initiative for public policy has partly shifted to the president and the executive branch. Now Congress often awaits and responds to presidential State of the Union addresses, budgets, and legislative proposals. The twentieth century is dotted with presidential labels on legislation: Wilson's New Freedom, Roosevelt's New Deal, Truman's Fair Deal, Kennedy's New Frontier, and Johnson's Great Society. Ronald Reagan pushed through major changes in 1981 and remained a dominant legislative force during much of the 1980s.

Divided party control of government can make a difference, however: Bill Clinton took the initiative during his first two years, on taxes and spending, national service, the North American Free Trade Agreement (NAFTA), health care, crime, and other matters, but then Clinton found himself reacting to proposals from the Republican-controlled 104th Congress.

Manager of the Economy

We now expect presidents to worry about, and do something about, the economy. The Great Depression convinced most Americans that the federal government has a role to play in fighting economic downturns, and the example of Franklin Roosevelt convinced most Americans that the main actor in this drama ought to be the president. The Employment Act of 1946 mandates that the president report on the state of the economy and recommend actions to maintain employment and to control inflation. The role is now so well established that even conservative presidents, such as Ronald Reagan and George Bush, have felt compelled to encourage the involvement of the federal government in the prevention of bank failures, the stimulation of economic growth, and the promotion of exports abroad.

Chief Diplomat

The Constitution, by specifying that the president "shall have the power . . . to make Treaties" and to appoint and receive ambassadors, lodges the main diplomatic responsibility of the United States with the presidency. It is in this

Bill Clinton encourages the famous handshake between the late Israeli prime minister Yitzhak Rabin and Palestine Liberation Organization chairman Yasser Arafat. The president is the chief diplomat of the United States.

role, perhaps, that American presidents are most visible: traveling abroad, meeting with foreign leaders, and negotiating and signing treaties. President Bush's successful arms control negotiations with Soviet leaders and his extraordinary efforts to assemble and hold together the multinational coalition against Iraq made the diplomatic function especially prominent in his presidency. President Clinton, though focused mainly on domestic matters, helped try to bring Israelis and Palestinians together, brokered peace talks over Bosnia, and repeatedly met with foreign leaders to open markets for American trade.

Several other "hats" could be mentioned. For example, the president serves as head of his political party and as leader and representative of the general public—topics that we will discuss further. Each of these presidential functions is demanding; together, they are overwhelming. "Passive" presidents may well be a vanishing breed.

The President's Staff and Cabinet

Of course, presidents do not face their burdens alone; they have gradually acquired many advisers and helpers.

The White House Staff

The White House Staff, for example, which is specially shaped to fit the particular needs of each president, includes a number of close advisers.

chief of staff A top adviser to the president who also manages the White House staff.

Chief of Staff One top adviser, usually designated **chief of staff,** tends to serve as the president's right hand, supervising other staff members and organizing much of what the presidency does. For most of George Bush's term, conservative former New Hampshire governor John Sununu had a firm hand on domestic and foreign policy. Bill Clinton brought his old friend from Arkansas, Thomas "Mack" McLarty, a utility executive who took a while to learn the ways of Washington politics. He was later replaced by a low-key, consummate insider: former member of Congress Leon Panetta.

Presidents use their chiefs of staff in different ways. Franklin Roosevelt kept a tight rein on things himself, granting equal but limited power and access to several close advisers in a *competitive* system. Dwight Eisenhower, used to the *hierarchical* army staff system, gave overall responsibility to his chief of staff, Sherman Adams. Richard Nixon similarly relied on the tough Robert Haldeman. In the early Reagan White House, however, James Baker shared power *collegially* with Assistant to the President Michael Deaver and Counselor to the President Edwin Meese. Clinton set up a similar troika, in which McLarty shared power with campaign official and former press secretary George Stephanopoulos and with Republican troubleshooter David Gergen. When this arrangement proved ineffective, Clinton switched to a more centralized operation under Panetta.

national security adviser A top foreign policy and defense adviser to the president who heads the National Security Council.

National Security Adviser Another important staff member in most presidencies is the **national security adviser,** who is also head of the president's National Security Council, operating out of the White House basement. The national security adviser generally meets with the president every day in order to brief him on the latest events and to offer advice on what to do. Some recent national security advisers, such as Henry Kissinger (under Nixon) and Zbigniew Brzezinski (under Carter), have been strong foreign policy managers and active, world-hopping diplomats, who sometimes clashed with the secretaries of state and defense. The most recent presidents, however, have appointed such team players as Robert "Bud" MacFarlane and John Poindexter (Reagan), Brent Scowcroft (Bush), and Anthony Lake (Clinton), who have closely reflected the president's wishes and quietly coordinated policy among the various executive departments.

Leon Panetta (center), here discussing the budget with administration officials and members of Congress, centralized White House operations as President Clinton's Chief of Staff.

Other Advisers Most presidents also have a top domestic policy adviser, like Clinton's Bruce Reed, who coordinates plans for new domestic laws, regulations, and spending, though this role is often subordinate to that of the chief of staff and is not usually very visible. Close political advisers, often old comrades of the president from past campaigns, may be found in a number of different White House or other government posts (James Baker served as Bush's secretary of state, for example) or may have no official position at all, like Republican consultant Dick Morris, who crafted Clinton's 1996 reelection strategy of "triangulating" positions partway between those of congressional Democrats and Republicans before Morris's downfall in a scandal.

Prominent in every administration is the press secretary, who holds press conferences, briefs the media, and becomes a major administration voice in the media. This may or may not be the same person who is director of communications and generally manages how the president and his activities are presented to the public. George Stephanopoulos initially tried to do both jobs for Bill Clinton but wound up in shouting matches with the media and was replaced as spokesperson by Dee Dee Myers and then by the unflappable Michael McCurry. These communications and media positions, along with that of in-house pollster or public opinion surveyor, have become increasingly important as the president's connections with the public have grown closer.

Nearly all presidents have a legal counsel (a hotseat for Whitewater inquiries in the Clinton administration), a special assistant to act as a liaison with Congress, another to deal with interest groups, another for political matters, and still another for intergovernmental relations. However, the exact shape of the White House staff changes greatly from one presidency to another.

Power and Accountability White House staff members are people the president talks to every day; they are the ones who do their best to see that he gets his way. They and their deputies leave "the White House wants . . ." messages all around Washington and are treated with deference, if not affection. Indeed, chiefs of staff often make enemies, and several have been felled by scandals. Aides often jockey for position and bicker among themselves. In the second Reagan administration, Chief of Staff Donald Regan offended other staffers with his imperious manner and was eventually deposed—apparently with a push from First Lady Nancy Reagan.[26]

One thing is certain: Staff members have to speak accurately for the president. They must do what the president wants, or what he *would* want if he knew the details. The ideal staffer knows exactly what the boss wants and does it, with or without being told; otherwise, he or she won't last long. Of course, it can be useful for a president to create the *impression* that staff members are acting on their own, particularly when they are doing something unpopular or even illegal. One of Eisenhower's favorite hidden-hand techniques was to have Sherman Adams take the heat for tough decisions.

The Executive Office of the President

One step removed from the White House staff, mostly housed in its own building nearby, is a set of organizations that forms the **Executive Office of the President (EOP)**

Most important of these organizations is the **Office of Management and Budget (OMB).** The OMB is in charge of "the numbers." Acting on agency requests, it advises the president on how much the administration should

Executive Office of the President (EOP) A group of organizations that advise the president on a wide range of issues; includes the Office of Management and Budget, the National Security Council, and the Council of Economic Advisers.

Office of Management and Budget (OMB) An organization within the Executive Office of the President that advises on the federal budget, domestic legislation, and regulations.

RESOURCE FEATURE

Hillary Rodham Clinton and the Role of the President's Spouse

Eleanor Roosevelt championed the poor and downtrodden; Jacqueline Kennedy brought French cuisine and style to the White House; Lady Bird Johnson promoted highway beautification. Many presidential spouses have whispered advice and pursued special causes, but most have focused on a "First Lady" role that emphasized decorating and entertaining. Hillary Rodham Clinton for the first time tried to play an active, public, full-time role in national policymaking, with mixed results.

Rodham Clinton had a law degree from Yale and extensive legal experience. She had headed task forces on education and medical reform in Arkansas and had served nationally as president of the Children's Defense Fund. While campaigning, Bill Clinton suggested that he and his wife would be partners in office, and that voters would get "two for one."

Some Americans were delighted by this prospect. Others, concerned about the question of accountability, were not so sure. Some who favor traditional homemaker roles for women were troubled when Rodham Clinton made an offhand, dismissive comment about how she could have stayed home and baked cookies instead of pursuing her legal career.

When Bill Clinton took office in January 1993, he appointed his wife to chair his task force on health care reform, the most momentous and difficult issue facing his administration. The task force, which included six cabinet secretaries and several White House officials, organized a large staff of working groups that worked long hours (often in secret) for many months to thrash out a proposal. In September 1993, Rodham Clinton went to Capitol Hill to testify about the plan. She dazzled the legislators with her grasp of detail (explaining highly technical matters without consulting notes), warmed them with references to her mother and her daughter, and flattered them a bit in standard congressional style. In a virtually unprecedented tribute, the Ways and Means Committee applauded as Rodham Clinton left the hearing. Newspapers headlined, "Hillary . . . Wins Raves . . . Captivates Lawmakers." "This is as big as it comes," an aide commented. "This is Eleanor Roosevelt time."[a]

But the triumph did not last. The health care proposal bogged down for a year and was eventually withdrawn without a vote. After the 1994 elections, the new Republican Congress voiced sharp criticism of Rodham Clinton's role as an unelected official, her allegedly liberal influence on the president, and her earlier involvement in questionable financial dealings back in Arkansas. With a few exceptions (including a weekly newspaper column, a trip to the international women's conference in China, and a tour promoting her book on children), Rodham Clinton withdrew into the background and returned to traditional "First Lady" activities. Elizabeth Hanford Dole promised that, if her husband was elected president, she would stay out of governmental matters and head the American Red Cross.

Americans remain ambivalent and divided about Rodham Clinton herself and about the proper role of a presidential spouse.

[a]Adam Clymer, "Hillary Clinton, on Capitol Hill, Wins Raves, If Not a Health Plan," *New York Times* (September 29, 1993), p. A1.

propose to spend for each government program and where the money will come from. The OMB also exercises legislative clearance; that is, it examines the budgetary implications of any proposed legislation and sometimes kills proposals as being too expensive or as being inconsistent with the president's philosophy or goals.

The director of the OMB is occasionally a major figure in the administration—as was David Stockman, the chief architect of Reagan's 1981 budget and tax proposals—but more often is quietly influential, like Alice Rivlin, a "deficit hawk" who sought to cut budget deficits for President Clinton. (Rivlin was replaced by Franklin Delano Raines when she moved to the Federal Reserve Board.)

Another unit in the Executive Office of the President is the **Council of Economic Advisers (CEA),** a small group of economists that advises the president on economic policy. Occasionally, the head of the council exercises great influence, as Walter Heller did during the Kennedy administration. More often, the head of the CEA is inconspicuous (like Clinton's Laura D'Andrea Tyson) or downright invisible, as was the case when President Reagan did not want economist "doomsayers" to protest large budget deficits.

Council of Economic Advisers (CEA) An organization in the Executive Office of the President made up of a small group of economists who advise on economic policy.

The Executive Office of the President also includes the **National Security Council (NSC),** a body of leading officials from the State and Defense Departments, the Central Intelligence Agency (CIA), the military, and elsewhere who advise the president on foreign affairs. The NSC has been particularly active in crisis situations and covert operations. The NSC staff, charged with various analytical and coordinating tasks, is headed by the president's national security adviser. At times, the NSC staff has gone beyond analysis to conduct actual operations, the most famous of which was the Iran-Contra affair, under the direction of Lieutenant Colonel Oliver North, when weapons were secretly sold to Iran in the hope of freeing U.S. hostages and some of the proceeds were illegally diverted to the Nicaraguan Contra rebels.

National Security Council (NSC) An organization in the Executive Office of the President made up of officials from the State and Defense Departments, the CIA, and the military, advising on foreign and security affairs.

In recent years, the Executive Office of the President has also included the Office of Science and Technology Policy, the Council on Environmental Quality, and the Office of U.S. Trade Representative. Again, however, the makeup of the EOP changes from one administration to another, depending on which national problems seem most pressing and on the preferences and operating styles of individual presidents. For instance, the Office of the U.S. Trade Representative became prominent under Clinton, because of his interest in trade problems with Japan, China, and other countries. One recent arrangement of the EOP is shown in Figure 12.1.

The Executive Office of the President has a measure of independence. Its employees cannot be considered personal arms of the president in quite the same way that the White House staff is, and they do not meet with him as frequently. Still, they are generally loyal and responsive to the president and assist him in establishing central authority over the wider bureaucracy of the executive branch. Much of that bureaucracy is more distant and more independent, sometimes responding to constituency pressures that conflict with the president's program. Federal agencies outside the immediate reach of the president and his staff are more likely to go their own way. We will have more to say about this phenomenon later in this chapter and in Chapter 13.

The Vice-Presidency

Vice-presidents find themselves in an awkward position, because their main job is to be available in case something happens to the president. They play

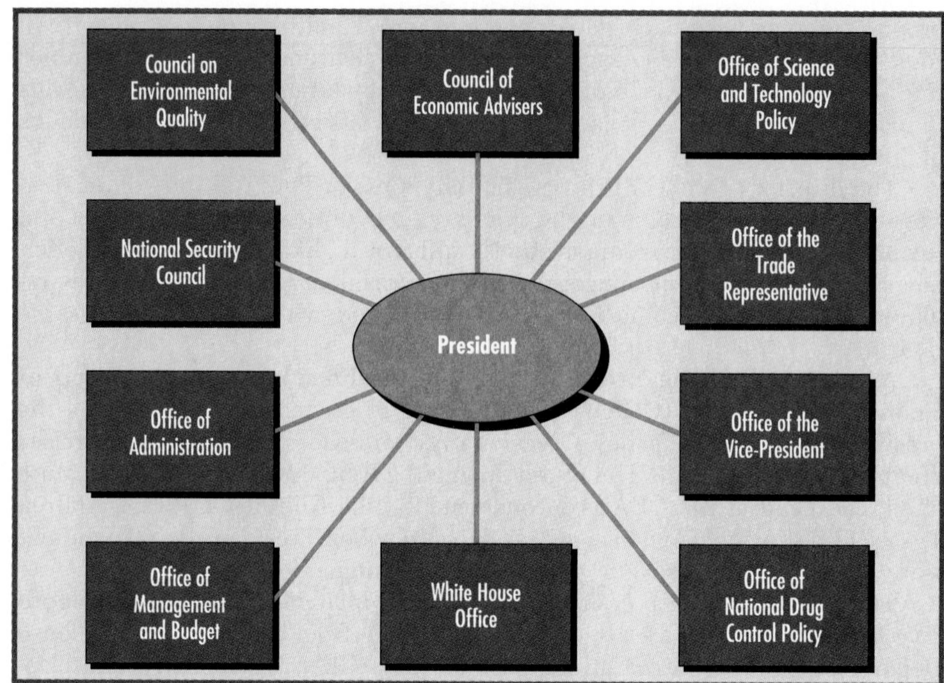

Figure 12.1 ■ The Executive Office of the President in the Clinton Administration

The Executive Office of the President assists the president in establishing central authority over the wider bureaucracy of the executive branch.

Source: *U.S. Government Manual, 1995,* pp. 91–109.

what has been called "American roulette," fearing (or hoping) to take over the presidency in case of disaster. All too often, disaster does strike. In the twentieth century, more than one quarter of all our presidents—Theodore Roosevelt, Calvin Coolidge, Harry Truman, Lyndon Johnson, and Gerald Ford—stepped up from the vice-presidency after the death or resignation of the president. Moreover, two others, Richard Nixon and George Bush, were elected to the presidency on their own after serving as vice-president. The two-term limit on presidents (imposed in 1951 by the Twenty-Second Amendment to the Constitution) makes such succession easier.

A Once-Insignificant Office The vice-presidency itself, however, has not always been highly regarded. John Nance Garner, Franklin Roosevelt's first vice-president, has been quoted as saying in his earthy Texan way that the office was "not worth a pitcher of warm piss."[27] When Harry Truman was informed that Franklin Roosevelt wanted him on the 1944 ticket as vice-president, Truman complained, "I don't want to be Vice-President. I bet I can go down the street and stop the first ten men I see and that they can't tell me the names of two of the last ten Vice-Presidents of the United States."[28]

Within administrations, vice-presidents used to be fifth wheels, not fully trusted (since they could not be fired) and not personally or politically close to the president (since they were frequently chosen to be different from the president, in order to "balance the ticket" and win over a different set of voters). The Constitution mentions nothing about what vice-presidents should do except preside over the Senate, a largely ceremonial duty (except for rare tie-breaking votes) which is usually left to senators who act as president "pro tempore." Vice-presidents used to spend much of their time running minor errands of state, attending funerals of foreign leaders not important enough to demand presidential attention, or carrying out limited diplomatic missions.

Some vice-presidents were virtually frozen out of the policymaking process. Eisenhower cruelly told the press that he might be able to cite something important that Vice-President Nixon had done, if he had a week to think about it. Harry Truman was never informed of the existence of the Manhattan Project that built the atomic bomb, and he felt "the moon, the stars, and all the planets had fallen on me" when he suddenly had to assume the presidency.[29]

Increasing Importance of the Vice-Presidency In recent years, however, presidents have realized that it is a favor to the country to give their potential successors some training before they take over the job. Ronald Reagan included George Bush in major policy meetings and put him in charge of antidrug efforts. In turn, Bush involved Dan Quayle in the space program and had him head a commission to oversee government deregulation. For Clinton, Al Gore took on a number of important assignments, including the formulation of environmental policy, coping with Ross Perot's opposition to NAFTA, and the ambitious effort to "reinvent government."[30]

Indeed, Al Gore may have become the most active and influential vice-president in American history. In a dramatic exception to "ticket balancing," Gore was chosen not because he was different from Clinton but because he was very similar: a fellow centrist Democrat from the border South. In office, Gore and Clinton became very close. Gore played a part in virtually all decisions, and Clinton rarely overruled him.[31]

Presidential Succession In 1804, the Twelfth Amendment fixed the flaw in the original Constitution under which Aaron Burr, Thomas Jefferson's running

Al Gore got the assignment to debate Ross Perot over the North American Free Trade Agreement.

mate in 1800, had tied Jefferson in electoral votes and tried, in the House of Representatives, to grab the presidency for himself. Since then, vice-presidents have been elected specifically to that office on a party ticket with their president. But now there is also another way to become vice-president. The Twenty-Fifth Amendment (ratified in 1967) provides for the succession in case of the temporary or permanent inability of a president to discharge his office. It also states that if the vice-presidency becomes vacant, the president can nominate a new vice-president, who takes office on confirmation by both houses of Congress. This is how Gerald Ford became vice-president in 1973, when Spiro Agnew was forced to resign because of a scandal, and how Nelson Rockefeller became vice-president in 1974, when Ford replaced Richard Nixon as president (see Table 12.2).

The Cabinet

The president's cabinet is not mentioned in the Constitution. No legislation designates the composition of the cabinet, its duties, or its rules of operation. Nevertheless, all presidents since George Washington have had one. It was Washington who established the practice of meeting with his top executive officials as a group to discuss policy matters. Later presidents continued the practice, some meeting with the cabinet as often as twice a week—as James Polk and Andrew Johnson did—and others paying it less attention. Andrew Jackson, for example, depended much more on a "kitchen cabinet" of informal advisers than on one composed of the heads of the executive departments.[32]

In recent times, the cabinet has consisted of the heads of the major executive departments, plus the vice-president, the director of the CIA, and whichever other officials the president deems appropriate. Often, these have included the ambassador to the United Nations. The cabinet is a highly visible symbol of the executive branch of the U.S. government.

Limited Role Rarely, if ever, though, have presidents actually relied on the cabinet as a decision-making body. Presidents know that they alone will be

Table 12.2

Presidential Succession and the Twenty-Fifth Amendment

Under the Twenty-Fifth Amendment to the U.S. Constitution, if the president is removed from office, dies, or resigns, the vice-president becomes president.

Whenever the office of vice-president is vacant, the president nominates a new vice-president, who takes office when he has been confirmed by majority vote of both houses of Congress.

If the president (*or* the vice-president and a majority of the cabinet) submits to Congress a written declaration that the president is unable to discharge the powers and duties of his office, the vice-president becomes acting president.

If the president later submits a written declaration that no inability exists, he resumes the powers and duties of his office, *unless* the vice-president, a majority of the cabinet, and a two-thirds vote in both houses of Congress declare that he is unable to do so.

held responsible for decisions, and they alone keep the power to make them. According to legend, when Abraham Lincoln once disagreed with the entire cabinet, he declared, "Eight votes for and one against; the nays have it!"

Most recent presidents have convened the cabinet infrequently and have done serious business with it rarely. Ronald Reagan held only a few cabinet meetings each year, and those were so dull and unimportant that Reagan was said to doze off from time to time. Bill Clinton, with his "policy wonk" mastery of details, thoroughly dominated cabinet discussions.

Why the Weak Cabinet? One reason for the weakness of the cabinet, especially in recent years, is simply that government has grown large and specialized. Most department heads are experts in their own areas, with little to contribute elsewhere. It could be a waste of everyone's time to engage the secretary of housing and urban development in discussions of military strategy.

Another reason is that cabinet members occupy an ambiguous position: they are advisers to the president but also represent their own constituencies, including the permanent civil servants in their departments and the organized interests that their departments serve. They may have substantial political stature of their own, somewhat independent of the president's.[33]

Most presidents deliberately appoint some department heads with independent power bases in order to reward parts of their electoral coalitions and to sell their programs to particular interest groups. Often, the secretary of commerce has ties with business (Clinton's Ron Brown, for example, was close to multinational corporations and New York investment bankers). The secretary of agriculture generally has links with farmers. The secretary of labor often stands close to unions, especially under the Democrats, who have had strong ties with the AFL-CIO—though Clinton chose an independent policy intellectual, Robert Reich. Treasury secretaries tend to get on well with bankers, and interior secretaries relate to western ranchers (or, like Clinton's Bruce Babbitt, to environmentalists). These relationships sometimes lead to tension between the president and the department heads, and they make the cabinet an awkward body for doing business.

Close Confidants Most presidents also try to include in the cabinet some people with whom they have close personal and political ties: former campaign managers, advisors, and so on. Thus, John Kennedy appointed his brother Robert attorney general. When criticized, Kennedy replied (tongue in cheek): "I can't see that it's wrong to give him a little legal experience before he goes out to practice law."[34] Likewise, Richard Nixon appointed his campaign manager and former law partner John Mitchell to that same post, as Ronald Reagan did with Edwin Meese. George Bush named his longtime friend and adviser James Baker secretary of state. Bill Clinton, on the other hand, generally ignored close associates and tried to appoint a cabinet that "look[ed] like America" in terms of race and gender (if not income level), with three women (including the attorney general, Janet Reno), four African-Americans, and two Latinos.

In any case, whether they are symbols of diversity, representatives of interest groups, nonpartisan administrators, or close presidential confidants, cabinet members acquire importance from their own talents and characteristics and from their relationships with the president or with their own departments and constituencies, not from their membership in the cabinet as a collective body.

The President and the Bureaucracy

Many people assume that the president has firm control over the executive branch of government, that he can simply order departments and agencies to do something, and they will do it. But Richard Neustadt, in his important book *Presidential Power,* showed that that is far from the whole truth.[35]

Giving Orders

Yes, presidents can issue orders, as Harry Truman did in 1951, when he fired General Douglas MacArthur as commander of U.S. forces in Korea for defying Truman's policies and threatening to take the war into China. But such actions may be very costly. MacArthur arrived home a hero, welcomed by ticker-tape parades in New York City and allowed to address a joint session of Congress. Truman lost political support and never regained the momentum of his presidency. Such a drastic use of power ordinarily makes sense only as a last resort, after all other methods have failed.

Moreover, in the day-to-day operation of government, direct command is seldom feasible. Too much is going on. Presidents cannot keep personal track of each one of the millions of government officials and employees. The President can only issue general guidelines and pass them down the chain of subordinates, hoping that his wishes will be followed faithfully. But lower-level officials, protected by civil service status from being fired, may have their own interests, their own institutional norms and practices, that lead them to do something different. It is said that President Kennedy was painfully reminded of this during the Cuban Missile Crisis of 1962, when Soviet Premier Khrushchev demanded that U.S. missiles be removed from Turkey in return for the removal of Soviet missiles from Cuba: Kennedy was surprised to learn that the missiles had not already been taken out of Turkey, for he had ordered them removed a year earlier. Those responsible for carrying out this directive had not followed through.[36]

Presidential Persuasion

To a large extent, a president must *persuade* other executive branch officials to do things: He must bargain, compromise, and convince others that what he wants is in the country's best interest and in their own interest as well. Neustadt put it very strongly: "Presidential power is the power to persuade."[37]

Of course, presidents can do many things besides persuade: appoint top officials who share the president's goals; put White House observers in second-level department positions; reshuffle, reorganize, or even—with the consent of Congress—abolish agencies that are not responsive; influence agency budgets and programs through OMB review; and stimulate pressure on departments by Congress and the public.

Still, the president's ability to gain bureaucratic acquiescence is limited. The federal bureaucracy is not merely a creature of the president but is itself a partly independent governmental actor. It is also subject to influences from the political linkage level—especially by public opinion and organized interests, often working through Congress. Congress, after all, appropriates the money. This constrains what presidents can do and helps ensure that the executive branch will respond to broad forces in society rather than simply to the wishes of one leader.

The President and Congress: Perpetual Tug of War

The president and Congress are often at odds. This is a *structural* fact of American politics, deliberately intended by the Founders when they wrote the Constitution.

Conflict by Constitutional Design

The Founders created a system of checks and balances between Congress and the president, setting "ambition to counter ambition" in order to prevent tyranny. Since virtually all constitutional powers are shared, there is a potential for conflict over virtually all aspects of government policy.

Shared Powers Under the Constitution, presidents may propose legislation and can sign or veto bills passed by Congress, but both houses of Congress must pass any laws and can override presidential vetoes. Presidents can appoint ambassadors and high officials and make treaties with foreign countries, but the Senate must approve them. Presidents nominate federal judges, including U.S. Supreme Court justices, but the Senate must approve the nominations. Presidents administer the executive branch, but Congress appropriates funds for it to operate, writes the legislation that defines what it is to do, and oversees its activities.

Presidents cannot always count on the members of Congress—even their fellow partisans—to agree with them. As Oklahoma Republican representative Mickey Edwards said in 1990, when he was upset by George Bush's reversal of his "no new taxes" pledge; "We admire the President, and we support the President, but we don't work for the President."[38]

The potential conflict written into the Constitution becomes real because the president and the Congress often disagree about national goals, especially when there is **divided government,** that is, when the president and the majority in Congress belong to different parties. During the last four decades, the voters have frequently elected Republican presidents along with congresses controlled by large majorities of Democrats; in 1994, the voters put a Republican-controlled Congress in place, with a Democratic president in office. There is some evidence that voters may do this on purpose, to avoid giving either party complete control of government.[39]

divided government Control of the executive and the legislative branches by different political parties.

Separate Elections In other countries' parliamentary systems, the national legislatures choose the chief executives, so that unified party control is ensured. But in the United States, there are separate elections for the president and the members of Congress. Moreover, our elections do not all come at the same time. In presidential election years, two-thirds of the senators do not have to run and are insulated from new political forces that may affect the choice of a president. In nonpresidential, "off" years, all members of the House and one-third of the senators face the voters, who sometimes elect a Congress with views quite different from those of the president chosen two years earlier. In 1986, for example, halfway through Reagan's second term, the Democrats recaptured control of the Senate and caused Reagan great difficulty with Supreme Court appointments and other matters. The Republicans did the same thing to Clinton in 1994.

In all these ways, our constitutional structure ensures that presidents are limited and affected in what they can do by another governmental institution—

namely, Congress, which, in turn, reflects various political forces that may differ from those affecting the president. Scholars disagree about the precise effects of divided government. It may not actually cause serious "gridlock," since about as much legislation is passed when government control is divided as when it is unified.[40] But divided government almost certainly does cause increased conflict, like the budget battles between Clinton and Congress that involved nasty rhetoric and temporary government shutdowns in 1995–1996.

And the Winner Is . . .

It is difficult to be precise about the relative influence of Congress and the president, but most observers agree that each branch has probably come out on top at different times. In fact, the uneven expansion of the presidency throughout American history can be interpreted in terms of its shifting relationship with Congress. After the highly visible and successful presidencies of Washington and Jefferson, for example, Congress dominated an "Era of Good Feelings." After the lively Jackson presidency, the Whig presidents were mostly weak, and Congress, rather than the president, dealt with economic expansion and the slavery issue. Lincoln's strong wartime presidency was followed by a long period of legislative ascendancy, as Congress came to be the dominant federal voice in the Reconstruction of the South and in the probusiness, laissez-faire policies of the late nineteenth and early twentieth centuries.

From this point of view, the presidencies of Theodore Roosevelt (1901–1909) and Woodrow Wilson (1913–1921) represent brief interludes of presidential upsurge during a half century of congressional domination. With the Great Depression, the New Deal, World War II, and the powerful example of Franklin Roosevelt, the presidency gained ascendancy for over a half century.[41] With the end of the Cold War and the diminution of a credible military threat to the United States, however, presidential dominance over Congress may have faded.

Cycles of Congressional Resurgence This pattern suggests that presidents tend to emerge as dominant during times of great national crisis (especially war or depression), when Americans will unite under strong leadership. Then, when the crisis is over, there is a reaction against the strains of crisis management, a reduction in federal government activity, and a return to a more relaxed system of congressional government. It may be that the character and personality of the presidents we choose—and the amount of latitude we allow them once they are in office—partly reflect the different expectations of the public in these different situations.

Since World War II, with the increased international role of the United States, all presidents have been active in foreign affairs; none has accepted subordination to Congress in the fashion of the nineteenth century or even the 1920s. Yet some indications remain of a cycle in presidential-congressional relations. After Lyndon Johnson's successes in enacting his Great Society programs of the 1960s, for example, and after his assertive foreign policy moves in Vietnam and elsewhere, followed by the secretive and equally assertive Nixon administration, complaints were heard of an "imperial presidency." Then Congress fought back.[42]

During the 1970s, Congress cut off U.S. aid to South Vietnam and halted the bombing of Cambodia. Overriding a presidential veto, it passed the War Powers Resolution—an effort to control the future use of U.S. troops abroad. Congress tried to increase its role in the budgetary process by restricting presidents' **impoundment** of congressionally appropriated money and by setting up the Congressional Budget Office and a system of budget resolutions and reconciliations. (This system later occupied center stage in the budget battles of 1981, 1990, and 1995–1996.) Congress also reduced presidents' emergency powers, restricted executive agreements and arms sales abroad, and generally played a more active part in foreign policy. After investigating and publicizing assassination plots against foreign leaders, mind-altering drug experiments, and illegal spying on American citizens, it also increased the congressional oversight of CIA covert operations.

impoundment Refusal by the president to spend money appropriated by Congress.

From Reagan to Clinton This period of congressional resurgence did not last long. After the crises and traumas of the late 1970s, Ronald Reagan took office and reasserted presidential authority. He initiated covert operations abroad in places like Nicaragua and Afghanistan, and he used U.S. military force in Grenada and Libya. His 1981 tax and budget success was another dramatic sign of change.

For nearly eight years, Reagan thoroughly dominated American politics. Yet signs of a new revival in Congress could be seen as early as 1982 and 1983, when some of the tax cuts were reversed and when pressure began to mount to slow the military buildup and try harder to negotiate with the Soviets. By 1987, after the election of a Democratic majority in the Senate, Reagan was unable to prevail on many new initiatives; his nomination of the highly conservative Robert Bork to the Supreme Court, for example, was defeated.

When George Bush took office in 1989, facing an even stronger Democratic Congress than Reagan had, he continued to assert presidential authority in foreign affairs, most notably in coping with the collapse of communism in Eastern Europe and rolling back Iraq's attack on Kuwait. But Bush could succeed on the domestic front only by vetoes or deference to the congressional branch. Bush's 1990 budget negotiations led to an embarrassing revolt in his own party, and few of his limited legislative proposals got anywhere.

Bill Clinton did a little better, with a few hard-fought victories during his first two years (on family leave, national service, deficit cutting, NAFTA, and gun control), but he sustained a bitter defeat on his health care proposal. Clinton's troubles mounted after that, as the new Republican Congress assertively pushed a broad agenda of deregulation and cuts in spending and taxes. Congress was in the saddle again, even trying to define U.S. foreign policy. Only Clinton's dogged resistance to the Republicans' budget proposals, in which much of the public took Clinton's side, restored some presidential clout.

What Makes a President Successful with Congress?

A number of political scientists have studied presidents' successes and failures in getting measures that they favor enacted into law by Congress and have suggested reasons why some presidents on some issues do much better than others.

Party and Ideology The most important factor is a simple one: the number of people in Congress who agree with the president in ideology and party affiliation. When the same political party controls both the presidency and the Congress, presidents tend to get their way. When the opposite party controls Congress, presidents tend to be frustrated. The bigger majority a president's party has, the better the president does (see Figure 12.2).[43]

This success not necessarily mean that presidents actively whip their fellow partisans into line. As we have seen, the parties are rather weakly

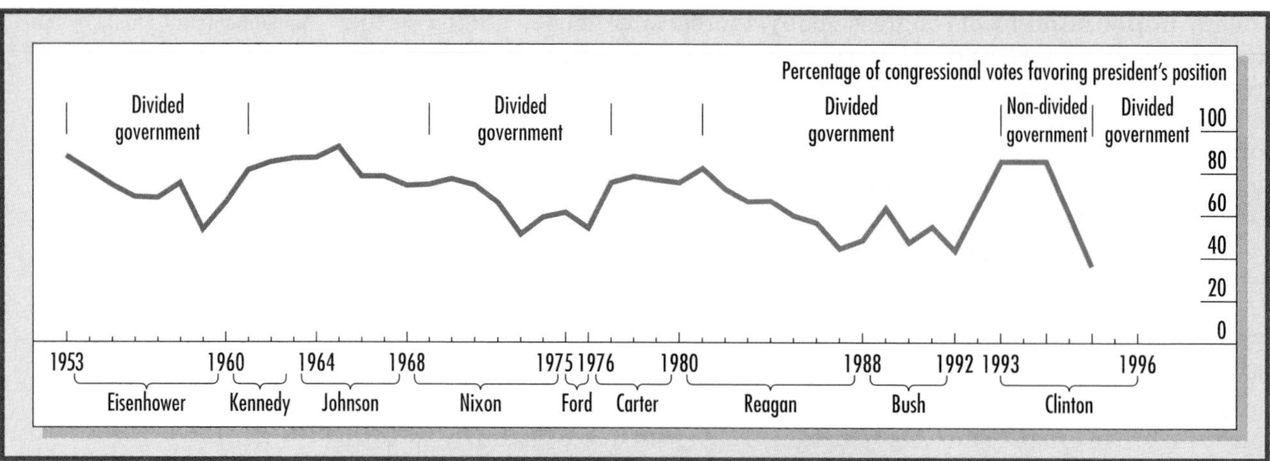

Figure 12.2 ▪ Presidential Success in Congress

Who controls the Congress can have a strong impact on a president's success. In periods of divided government, when the opposing party has a majority in Congress, policies favoring the president's position receive fewer votes.

Sources: Congressional Role Call, 1992 (Washington, DC: Congressional Quarterly Press, 1993), p. 9-B; CQ *Weekly Report* (January 27, 1996), p. 194.

organized in Congress and do not often enforce discipline. But party members do tend to be like-minded; they tend to vote together because they share the same values, and, for the same reason, they tend to go along with a president of their own party.[44] So, when Congress is full of members of the president's party, it tends to pass legislation that the president likes; when it is not, it does

President Clinton, by using his veto power, generally prevailed in the 1995–1996 budget battles with then–Senate Majority Leader Bob Dole and House Speaker Newt Gingrich.

not. Republican presidents Nixon, Reagan, and Bush eventually ran up against assertive Democratic Congresses; Democratic President Bill Clinton had to deal with very energetic Republicans.

Foreign Policy Issues Presidents tend to do better on foreign policy issues than on domestic ones. Political scientist Aaron Wildavsky went so far as to refer to "two presidencies," the president being much more dominant on foreign matters. Wildavsky found that during the 1948–1964 period, 59 percent of presidents' proposals on foreign policy were passed, but only 40 percent of their domestic proposals were passed.[45]

This difference may have decreased somewhat since the Vietnam War, but it remains significant. Congressional Democrats, at least, have tended to defer to Republican presidents on foreign policy.[46] The congressional vote in January 1991, authorizing Bush to use force against Iraq, once again illustrated presidential primacy in foreign affairs. Sometimes, of course, presidents do not seek legislative approval at all in foreign affairs: they simply act. But this course may be less common since the end of the Cold War.

Appointments On certain special kinds of issues, presidents nearly always get their way. The Senate, for example, confirms some 99 percent of the presidential appointments of officials. Battles over confirmation are uncommon, and presidential losses, such as the defeat of Reagan's nominee Robert Bork, are even more rare; they generally happen only when a president is severely weakened and the Senate is controlled by the opposition.

On the other hand, presidents are not all-powerful on appointments; they must take account of what Congress wants when they are deciding whom to appoint in the first place. **Senatorial courtesy** allows the senior senator of the president's party to blackball potential nominees from his state. And nominations in trouble are generally withdrawn before a vote. A number of Clinton's nominations were withdrawn, including those of Zoë Baird and Kimba Wood (accused of tax or immigration improprieties with domestic helpers) for attorney general, Lani Guinier (committed to increasing minority voting power) for assistant attorney general for civil rights, and Henry Foster (a obstetrician who had performed some abortions) for surgeon general.

senatorial courtesy The tradition which holds that the president's nominations must be cleared with the senior senator of the president's party from the appointee's state.

Vetoes When the issue is a presidential veto of legislation, the president is again very likely to prevail. As Figure 12.3 shows, vetoes have not been used often, except by certain "veto-happy" presidents, such as Franklin Roosevelt, Truman, Ford, and (at an earlier time) Grover Cleveland. But when vetoes have been used, they have seldom been overridden—only 5 percent of the time for Truman and only 1.5 percent for Roosevelt. The Democrats' moderate success in overriding Reagan's vetoes (12 percent of the time) was unusual and did not extend to Bush's term. For a long time, Bush had a perfect record of sustaining vetoes (22 in a row) on civil rights, the extension of unemployment benefits, and a number of other issues. Bill Clinton did not use the veto at all during his first two years in office, when he had a Democratic party majority in Congress, but then wielded the veto fiercely, and with substantial success, on the budget and in other confrontations with the Republican Congress.

These percentages of veto success may be misleadingly high, because presidents like to preserve an image of impregnability; they generally avoid casting vetoes that might be overridden. On the other hand, the mere *threat* of a

Figure 12.3 ■ Presidential Vetoes (Average per Year)

While some presidents have wielded veto power often, most have used it fairly conservatively. One key reason that vetoes are rarely necessary is that Congress is unlikely to pass a bill that the president will not approve.

Source: Calculated by the authors from Harold Stanley and Richard Niemi, *Vital Statistics on American Politics* (Washington, DC: Congressional Quarterly Press, 1990), p. 252; 1992 *Congressional Quarterly Almanac,* p. 6; Congressional Index, 1995–96, p. 9701.

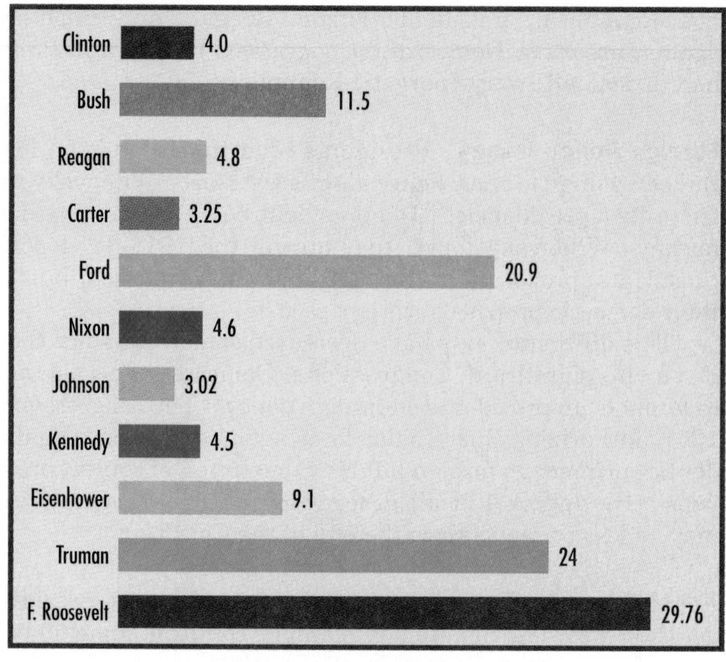

veto—without any need to carry it out—is often enough to discourage Congress from doing something the president will not approve.

Popularity One might assume that presidents are more successful when their own popularity is high and less successful when it is low, since the members of Congress may fear that a popular president's electoral **coattails** will defeat them in the next election if they don't go along. But statistical studies disagree about this, and some find no effect of presidential popularity at all.[47] The reason may be that coattails have not been very strong in recent years. Also, presidents rarely succeed in defeating the congressional mavericks of their own party, who are usually entrenched in friendly districts.

coattails The ability of a popular, high-level official to win votes for lower-level officials of the same party.

Legislative Skills Statistical studies of large sets of roll call votes reveal little or no discernible effect of presidents' legislative skills. On crucial pieces of legislation, however, where presidents make a major effort, there can be little doubt that their legislative skills make a big difference. Lyndon Johnson's famous "treatment" and his wheeling and dealing surely picked up votes, as did Ronald Reagan's efforts on the 1981 tax and budget measures. In 1993, Bill Clinton won his fight for NAFTA only after months of cajoling and badgering congressional representatives, plus making a flurry of last-minute deals (promising to protect Florida citrus growers, for example, from cheaper Mexican imports). Afterward, Clinton's chief congressional liaison, Howard Paster, quit in exhaustion.

Some presidents, such as Johnson, Kennedy, Ford, Reagan, and Clinton, have paid a lot of attention to legislative relations, carefully organizing their liaison staffs, doing head counts of voting intentions, and passing out favors and compromises in order to win. Others, such as Eisenhower, Nixon, Carter, and Bush, have been more detached and less skillful.

Lyndon Johnson was famous for exerting strong personal pressure on legislators.

The President and the People: An Evolving Relationship

The complicated relationships among the president, the executive branch as a whole, and Congress have a lot to do with the different political forces that act on them at different times, that is, with the different effects of public opinion, the political parties, and organized interests on what they do. Particularly important is the special relationship between the president and the general public, which has evolved over many years.

Getting Closer to the People

The Founders thought of the president as an elite leader, relatively distant from the people, interacting with Congress often but with the people only rarely. Most nineteenth-century presidents and presidential candidates thought the same. They seldom made speeches directly to the public, for example, generally averaging no more than ten such speeches per year.[48]

In the earliest years of the American Republic (as we have seen in Chapters 2 and 9), presidents were not even chosen directly by the voters, but by electors chosen by state legislators or, in case no one got an electoral college majority, by the House of Representatives. The Constitution thus envisioned very indirect democratic control of the presidency. The president, in the view of the Founders, was definitely not to be a direct agent of the people.

More Democratic Elections As we have also seen, however, this system quickly evolved into a more democratic one in which the people played a more direct part. The two-party system developed, with parties nominating candidates and running pledged electors, and the state legislators allowing ordinary citizens to vote on the electors. Presidential candidates began to win clear-cut victories in the electoral college, taking the House of Representatives out of the process. Voting rights were broadened, as well. Property and religious qualifications were dropped early in the nineteenth century. Later, slaves were freed and given the right to vote; still later, women, Native Americans, and 18-year-olds won the franchise.

Going Public By the beginning of the twentieth century, presidents began to speak directly to the public. Theodore Roosevelt embarked on a series of speech-making tours in order to win passage of legislation to regulate the railroads. Woodrow Wilson made appeals to the public a central part of his presidency and created an entirely new constitutional theory advocating close connections between the president and the public. Wilson saw the desires of the public as the wellspring of democratic government: "As is the majority, so ought the government to be."[49] He argued that presidents are unique because only they are chosen by the entire nation. Presidents, he said, should help educate the citizens about government, should interpret their true will, and should faithfully respond to it. (See the Struggle for Democracy box.)

Wilson's theory of the presidency has been followed more and more fully in twentieth-century thought and practice. All presidents, especially since Franklin Roosevelt, have attempted to respond to public opinion; all, to one degree or another, have attempted to speak directly to the people about policy. The extent of change is striking. In the nineteenth century, for example, fewer than 1 percent of presidents' official statements and messages were oral; nearly all were written. Only about 7 percent were addressed to the people; the bulk went to Congress. In the twentieth century, by contrast, nearly one-half of official statements (42 percent) have been oral, and nearly one-half (41 percent) have been addressed directly to the people.[50]

Using the Media More and more frequently, presidents go public, using television to bypass the print media and speak to the public directly about policy. They have held fewer news conferences with White House correspondents (where awkward questions cannot be excluded), dropping from Hoover's and Roosevelt's averages of six or seven per month to Carter's and Reagan's average of fewer than one per month. (Bush increased the number somewhat, but Clinton, to the great annoyance of the press, cut them back again.) Instead, since Hoover's administration, all presidents have used radio and television to make major addresses to the national public: an average of about ten per year, with a slight increase over time. There has also been a huge increase in minor addresses to special audiences, from Hoover's mere 10 per year to Eisenhower's 30, Kennedy's 50, Carter's and Reagan's 70, and Bush's more than 100 per year.[51]

Kennedy appeared on television more frequently than any president before or since, and he established a reputation for style and wit in live, daytime press conferences. Richard Nixon pioneered prime-time television addresses, at which Ronald Reagan later excelled. Bush displayed less rhetorical polish but spoke often to national TV audiences. Bill Clinton was more interactive with citizens, appearing on radio and TV talk shows and holding informal "town hall meetings" on such subjects as health care; he also emulated Reagan's weekly radio addresses.

More and more, presidents have traveled outside the White House to make public appearances. Often, the settings convey a visual message: Nixon wearing

Woodrow Wilson and Presidential Democracy

The Struggle for Democracy

The struggle for democracy sometimes involves officials as well as citizens, and it sometimes concerns ideas and theories as well as actions. Thomas Woodrow Wilson, a Democratic president in the midst of a Republican era, was elected in 1912 only because William Howard Taft and the independent "Bull Moose" party candidate, Theodore Roosevelt, split the Republican vote. Yet Wilson embodied the strongly Progressive sentiment of his time and played a crucial part in the democratization of the American presidency.

Even after the franchise was broadened and citizens won the right to vote directly for pledged presidential electors, presidents had remained rather remote from the citizenry and from what the Founders had feared as the public's passions. Throughout the nineteenth century, presidential candidates conducted election campaigns coyly, not appealing directly for votes and refusing to say where they stood on the issues. Once in office, they dealt with Congress and the executive branch but declined to discuss the merits of public policy with ordinary citizens. Wilson, scholar and politician, changed that. He argued that presidents are special because they, alone among government officers, are elected by a national electorate and can claim a national mandate. Presidents, therefore, should both lead and respond to the public, interpreting the true desires of the citizenry, mobilizing public support for policies in accord with those desires, and providing energetic leadership; when necessary, they should overcome obstruction by Congress. In short, the president should give much greater weight to public opinion than the Founders had intended.

Wilson acted on his vision. He gave many public speeches directly to the people, rather than just written communiqués to government agencies and Congress. He revived the practice, which Jefferson had abandoned, of delivering the State of the Union address in person rather than in writing. And he declared in his first address that the people, not just Congress, were his true audience. Finally, he appealed directly to the public (although unsuccessfully) to pressure their senators into supporting the League of Nations treaty.

We now take it for granted that presidents will follow Wilson's practice of going public. But Wilson forged the crucial connection between the presidency and the people. He once declared of the president:

> The nation as a whole has chosen him, and is conscious that it has no other political spokesman. His is the only national voice in affairs. Let him once win the confidence of the country, and no other single force can withstand him, no combination of forces will easily overpower him. . . . He is the representative of no constituency, but of the whole people. When he speaks in his true character, he speaks for no special interest. If he rightly interprets the national thought and boldly insists on it, he is irresistible.[a]

[a]Woodrow Wilson, *Constitutional Government in the United States,* quoted in James M. Burns, *Presidential Government* (Boston: Houghton Mifflin, 1965), p. 96.

Source: Based on Jeffrey K. Tulis, *The Rhetorical Presidency* (Princeton: Princeton University Press, 1987).

a hard hat and waving to cheering construction workers in order to show his support for the conservative "silent majority," or Bush visiting a flag factory just after the 1988 election. Most spectacular is travel abroad, which displays the chief executive as *presidential,* as the head of state, and highlights his foreign policy achievements: Kennedy speaking at the Berlin Wall in 1963; Nixon raising his glass in toast at the Great Hall of the People in Beijing in 1972; or Reagan strolling through Red Square in Moscow with Mikhail Gorbachev in 1988.

Leading Public Opinion

Especially since the rise of television, modern presidents have enhanced their power to shape public opinion, as Reagan did in mobilizing support for his tax and budget cuts in 1981, and as Bush did in building support for the Persian Gulf War. Some studies have indicated that, when a popular president takes a stand in favor of a particular policy, the public's support for that policy tends to rise. A determined president, delivering many speeches and messages over a period of several weeks or months, may be able to gain 5 to 10 percentage points in support of that policy in the polls.[52] This is not an enormous effect, but it tends to confirm Theodore Roosevelt's claim that the presidency is a "bully pulpit." And presidents undoubtedly have a much greater *indirect* impact, influencing what others say and helping to shape the terms of public discourse.

The power to lead the public also implies a power to *manipulate* public opinion, if a president is so inclined—that is, to deceive or mislead the public so that it will approve policies that it might oppose if it were fully informed. Es-

John F. Kennedy, protesting the wall that divided East and West Berlin, delivers his famous "Ich bin ein Berliner" speech before a crowd of over 250,000 people. Travel abroad, like Kennedy's 1964 visit to West Berlin, is often a spectacular way for the chief executive to display his "presidential" stature.

pecially in foreign affairs, presidents can sometimes control what information the public gets. Lyndon Johnson purposely misstated the facts about the Gulf of Tonkin incident at the beginning of the Vietnam War (recall the story in Chapter 5); during and after the confrontation with Iraq, President Bush concealed the U.S. role in building up Saddam Hussein and the ambiguous events leading up to Iraq's invasion of Kuwait.

Those who seek energetic presidential leadership must face the possibility that that leadership will go wrong and result in demagoguery or manipulation.[53] The dilemma cannot be resolved. The power to do good is power to do evil as well. But some safeguards may exist, including the capacity of the public to judge character when it is choosing a president, as well as the ability of other national leaders to counteract a deceitful president. Johnson and Nixon learned this bitter lesson: the former declined to run for a second term; the latter resigned. The most serious threats to democracy may come when the leaders of both parties are united and no one challenges falsehood.

Responding to the Public

In any case, the relationship between presidents and the public is very much a two-way street. Besides trying to lead the people, presidents definitely tend to respond to public opinion. Presidents are elected, and a candidate (like Barry Goldwater in 1964) whose goals are far out of line with what the public favors does not usually win office in the first place. Electoral competition produces presidents who tend to share the public's policy preferences. Moreover, most presidents want to be reelected or to win a favorable place in history, and they know that they are unlikely to do so if they defy public opinion on many major issues. Usually, they try to anticipate what the public will want, in order to win electoral reward and avoid electoral punishment.

Quiet Influence For the most part, this influence of public opinion is so unobtrusive as to be almost invisible. What presidents *want* to do closely resembles what the public wants—that is one reason they were elected—so that there is often no conflict to observe. Only occasionally does a modern president get so badly out of touch with the public that the full power of public opinion is revealed. When the Reagan administration hinted at cuts in Social Security, for example, in 1981 and again in 1982, the storm of protest led to very hasty retreats.

More often, in day-to-day politics, it simply turns out that what the president does is largely in harmony with what the general public wants. When the public during the late 1960s and early 1970s wanted more "law and order," President Nixon appointed conservative judges to the Supreme Court and arranged for federal aid for local law enforcement. When public opinion moved (temporarily) toward favoring a buildup of defense during the late 1970s, Carter and Reagan followed suit. As a general matter, when polls show that public opinion has changed, presidents have tended to shift policy in the same direction: this has been true about 84 percent of the time.[54]

Listening to the Public There is plenty of evidence that presidents pay attention to what the public is thinking. At least since the Kennedy administration, presidents and their staffs have carefully read the available public opinion surveys and have often conducted their own polls.[55] Ronald Reagan, the "Great Communicator," was also a "Great Listener"; his chief pollster, Richard Wirthlin, developed the most thorough and intensive polling operation yet devised,

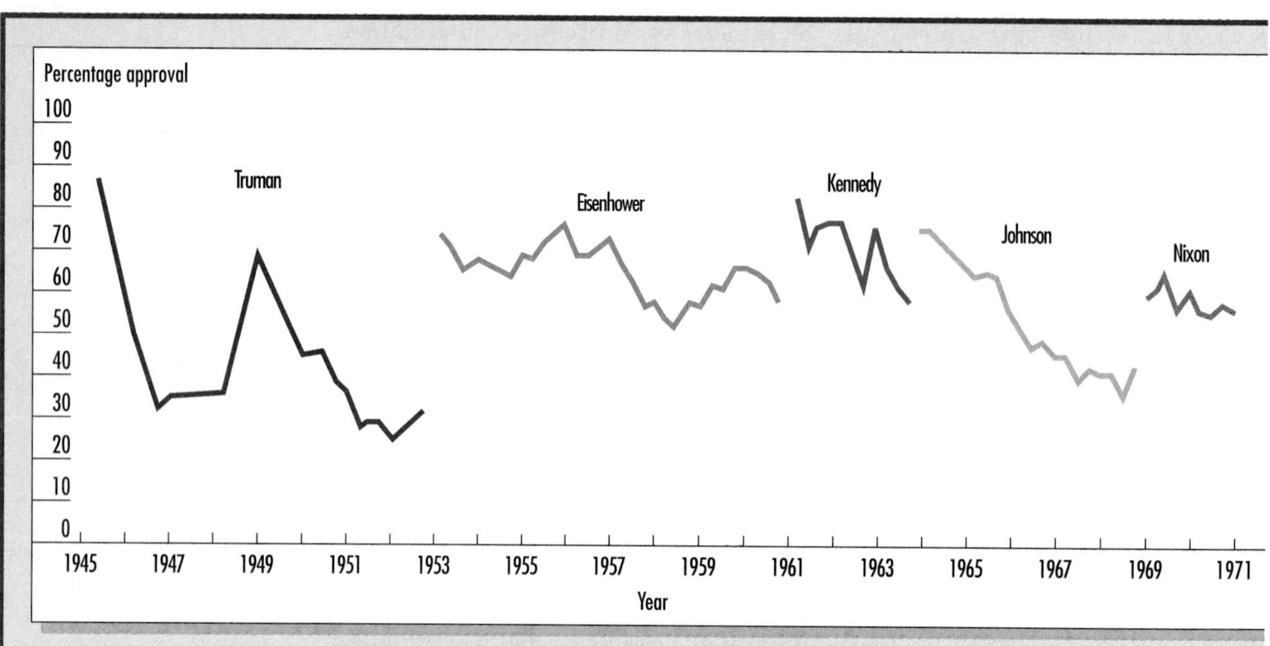

Figure 12.4 ▪ Trends in Presidential Popularity, 1945–1996

Popularity ratings of presidents rise and sink in response to political, social, and economic events.

Sources: Gallup surveys, reported in Harold Stanley and Richard Niemi, *Vital Statistics on American Politics,* (Washington, DC: Congressional Quarterly Press, 1990), p. 256; CBS/*New York Times* surveys reported in the *New York times* (November 26, 1991), p. A1; *Gallup Poll Monthly* (December 1992), pp. 38–39; (July 1993); (July 1995); (February 1996).

spending about $1.1 million per year and carrying out more than 500 surveys on a monthly schedule.[56] Wirthlin's information helped the administration package and sell its programs. More important, from the point of view of democracy, it helped the president to choose policies that the American public favored and to change or discard those (like the sending of troops to Lebanon) that proved unpopular.

President Bush kept track of opinion polls, too, but apparently not systematically enough—or not responsively enough—to avoid domestic policy troubles. Clinton relied on a number of pollsters, including Stanley Greenberg (whose polls and focus groups steered Clinton through the rapids of the 1992 election) and Doug Schoen, who worked with Dick Morris to chart Clinton's centrist 1996 reelection strategy.

The Role of Presidential Popularity

presidential popularity Conventionally indicated by the percentage of Americans who approve a president's "handling" of the job.

The public also influences presidents through its judgments about presidential performance: that is, through **presidential popularity** or unpopularity. Since the 1930s, Gallup and others have regularly asked Americans whether they approve or disapprove of President X's "handling" of the job. The percentage of people who approve varies from month to month and year to year, and as time passes, these varying percentages can be graphed in a sort of fever chart of how the public has thought the president was doing (see Figure 12.4).

The president cares a great deal about these approval percentages, because they have a lot to do with how his party will fare in midterm elections, whether he himself will win reelection, and (perhaps) how much clout he will

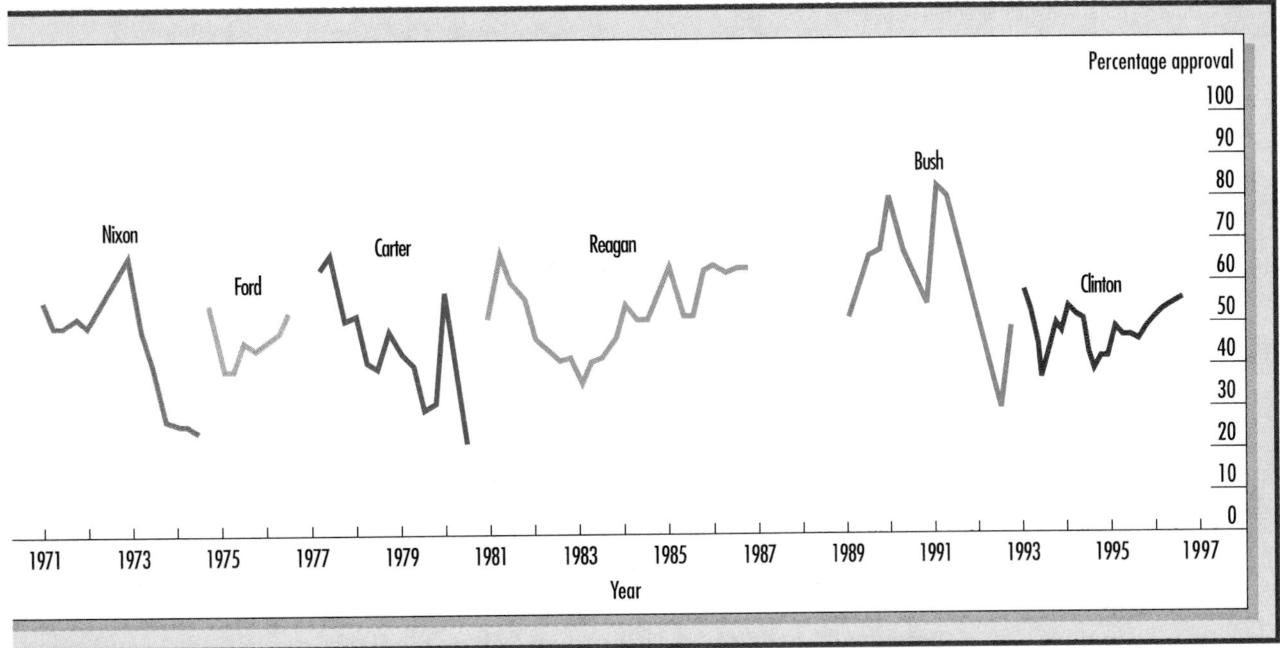

have in Congress. A president approved by 70 percent of Americans is in far better shape than one approved by only 30 percent. Presidents try to figure out what makes their popularity to go up or down, and try to do something about it. What does cause presidential popularity to rise or fall?

Time Historically, most presidents have begun their terms of office with a majority of Americans—usually 60 percent or more—approving of how they are handling their job. Most presidents have tended to lose popularity as time passed. But this loss of popularity does not represent an inexorable working of time; Eisenhower and Reagan actually gained popularity during their second terms. Those who lose popularity do so in response to bad news. Good news generally makes presidents more popular.[57]

The Economy One of the most serious kinds of bad news involves economic recession. When the economy goes sour, fewer Americans approve of the president. This happened to Reagan from late 1981 to early 1983, during the worst recession of the postwar period, when his popularity dropped from a high of 68 percent to a low of only 35 percent. It happened to Bush in mid–1990 (before Operation Desert Storm) and again in mid–1991, as the economy faltered. During Bill Clinton's first year, the lingering recession—along with his troubles about appointments, gays in the military, and Bosnia, Somalia, and Haiti—kept his approval rating mostly a bit below 50 percent. It remained in the doldrums even as the economy recovered, perhaps because of continued corporate downsizing and stagnant wages; only in 1996 did Clinton's ratings rise as the economic news improved.

War Another important kind of bad news concerns an unsuccessful war, especially a limited war that drags on with high casualty rates, like the Korean War (which detracted from Truman's already low popularity in 1950 and 1951) or the Vietnam War (which badly eroded Johnson's popularity from 1965 to 1968). On the other hand, of course, peace and prosperity tend to send

George Bush's popularity fell dramatically during the 1991–1992 recession; his only hope for reelection was that the economy would recover in time, but it did not.
The Record, New Jersey/Jimmy Margulies.

presidents' popularity ratings upward, as economic recovery did for Reagan. Bush's approval rating soared on the successful conclusion of the war with Iraq, before falling sharply with the recession.

rally 'round the flag A temporary rise in presidential popularity due to solidarity during a crisis.

Rallies Certain kinds of symbolic events or crises in which patriotism is invoked can produce a **rally 'round the flag,** a temporary surge in presidential popularity. Bush's immense gain in popularity following Operation Desert Storm was only temporary, as messy aftereffects of the war became apparent and as the public turned its attention to domestic problems. The switch from wartime euphoria to domestic economic pain brought one of the sharpest drops in presidential popularity ever recorded, from a high of 89 percent approval in March 1991, to a low of just *29 percent* approval in August 1992.[58]

Presidents are generally aware of what helps or hurts them with the public; they know that they will win electoral rewards if things go well but will face electoral punishment if things go badly. They have strong incentives, therefore, to anticipate public reaction and to do things that will please the public.

Presidents as Tribunes

Taken together, then, the evidence indicates that there is some truth to the idea that presidents are tribunes of the people, protecting and defending ordinary citizens. Presidents are close to the public, both leading public opinion and responding to it.

It is important not to carry this idea too far, however. We have seen that presidents have occasionally misled the public and have manipulated public opinion. Sometimes, too, they ignore public opinion or defy it, responding instead to organized interest groups or to the activists and money givers in their own political parties. Public opinion is not the only political factor affecting presidents.

Interest Groups, Political Parties, and Social Movements

Presidents are also influenced by organized interest groups, by political parties, and, sometimes, by social movements.

Interest Groups

Interest groups' relationships with presidents, like other aspects of interest group politics, form a sort of unexplored continent. Much of what goes on is probably kept hidden from scholars and observers. (Some presidential meetings with corporate CEOs, for example, are apparently omitted from the official White House log.) But we can be reasonably sure, from various hints and fragments of evidence, that organized groups exert important kinds of influence.[59]

Interest group money helps candidates win presidential nominations and elections, so that those who take office do not simply reflect the preferences of ordinary citizens; they tend to share, or at least sympathize with, the goals of their benefactors. At the least, presidents give special access to those who helped get them into office, such as the "Team 100" contributors of $100,000 each to Bush's campaign, described in Chapter 9. Moreover, in some policy areas, it is impossible for the president to govern without the cooperation of interest groups; this is especially true of businesspeople and the heads of large corporations, who occupy a privileged position as spokespersons for what economic and foreign policies must be carried out if a free enterprise economy is to flourish.[60]

Precisely which interest groups have the most influence on policy depends partly on which party controls the presidency, because some groups are much more closely allied with one party than with the other. Since the 1930s, for example, organized labor and certain business firms (particularly multinational, capital-intensive firms) have been closely tied to the Democratic party; more recently, civil rights, women's, and environmental groups have joined this alliance as well. The Republican party, on the other hand, has had much closer ties to most manufacturing corporations, small businesses, agribusiness, and organizations of well-to-do professionals, such as doctors and lawyers.[61] The policies of the parties in office tend to reflect these differences.

These ties, of course, do not mean that interest groups get everything they want from presidents. The very diversity of money givers makes it impossible. When Clinton, for example, went along with his Wall Street and multinational corporate backers on budget cutting and NAFTA, he acted against other big contributors, such as the United Steelworkers of America, the National Education Association, and the Sheet Metal Workers. To some extent, presidents can pick and choose among groups. Sometimes, presidents can mobilize groups to help achieve their own goals.[62]

Political Parties

Republican presidents tend to do different things from Democratic presidents. Changes in party control of the presidency produce significant changes in policy.

Despite the pressure that electoral competition puts on political parties to win votes by moving to the center, the parties also maintain some real differences, as the responsible-party model indicates. As we saw in Chapters 8 and 9, the parties consist of activists and financiers with distinctive policy goals, and of ordinary voters who differ, though less sharply, in the same sorts of ways.

As a result of party influence, there tend to be partisan cycles of presidential action, with different policies depending on which party holds office. Democratic presidents tend to fight unemployment,[63] to favor civil rights and environmental measures, and to promote domestic social welfare programs; Republicans tend to worry about inflation, to cut taxes and domestic expenditures, and to take conservative stands on social issues such as abortion.

Such cycles may relate to the preferences of the general public. At each election, the program of the winning party tends to represent what the public wants—at least, to represent it somewhat better than the other party does. There can be little doubt, for example, that in 1992, as in 1960, many Americans were ready for more activist government, or that, in 1980, many voters wanted to whittle down certain domestic programs, cut their tax burden, and build up the military. But party victories also carry the seeds of their own destruction, because each party tends to go further in its favored direction than the public wants. Thus, Johnson's Great Society led to a desire for retrenchment; Reagan's attacks on domestic social programs and the massive military buildup led to a desire for peace, arms control, and the renewal of domestic programs. There may be oversteering, first in one direction and then in another.

Social Movements

Social movements occasionally provide yet another political-level influence on presidents. They do so in at least two different ways. Mass demonstrations and protests cause disruptions that are inconvenient or dangerous to ignore, forcing presidents to take action in order to defuse them. Or mass movements may produce changes in general public opinion that, in turn, affect presidents. Either way, presidents and other political leaders have to pay attention. As we have seen, the civil rights movement affected President Kennedy's and President Johnson's espousal of the civil rights legislation of 1964 and 1965; the antiwar movement affected President Johnson's and President Nixon's decisions to diminish U.S. involvement in the Vietnam War.

Thus, the president is only partly a tribune of the people: he also responds to interest groups, political parties and party coalitions, the media, and mass movements, which sometimes push him in different directions from those the ordinary citizens want.

Structural Influences on the Presidency

Some of the political influences on presidents that we have discussed—especially public opinion—provide substantial continuity from one president to the next. Thus, we can speak of an *enduring* presidency, a presidency that does not merely fluctuate with the whims of whoever holds office, but that also reflects the goals and preferences of the people, groups, and institutions that make up American society.

But the enduring presidency goes beyond that. Both continuities and changes in what presidents do tend to reflect *structural* influences, basic features of the United States and the world that influence (1) what kinds of problems and issues come before presidents; (2) how people think about these problems and what they want presidents to do about them; and (3) who has the political resources and power to insist on a hearing from the president. A full understanding of American politics must take into account what goes on in the economy, in society, and in the international system.

The International System

From the end of World War II to the end of the Cold War, all presidents, Republican and Democrat alike, pursued a broadly similar set of foreign policies. While postwar presidents differed in their means, they fundamentally agreed on the ends: the containment of the influence of the Soviet Union, the solidification of the Western alliance, the encouragement of open economies in which American business might compete, and opposition to leftist or nationalist movements in the developing world. The reason for this continuity is that U.S. foreign policies reflected the basic features of the international system (particularly its **bipolarity,** with two superpowers), the U.S. position in that system as the dominant superpower, and the nature of U.S. economic interests in markets, raw materials, and investment opportunities.

bipolar system An international system with two great powers.

When the international system changes, presidential policy tends to change, no matter who is president. Thus, when it became painfully evident by the 1970s that the United States had declined in international economic competitiveness and relative economic strength, Presidents Carter and Reagan introduced measures to reduce taxes, to lighten the burden of regulation, to subsidize high-technology industries, and to encourage exports. When the Soviet Union began to move in conciliatory directions and then collapsed, Reagan and Bush responded in friendly fashion, despite their history of fierce anticommunism. The end of the Cold War left President Clinton more free to focus on domestic issues, while still pursuing free trade and other foreign economic policy aims.

The Economy

Similarly, all presidents, whether Republican or Democrat, must work to help the economy grow and flourish, with low levels of unemployment and inflation. A healthy economy is essential to a president's popularity and continuation in office, to tax receipts that fund government programs, and to the maintenance of social peace and stability. A healthy economy, in turn, requires that the main investors in the American economy—wealthy individuals, banks (both foreign and domestic), and corporations—continue to have confidence in the future. This has tended to create a set of presidential policies that favor such investors.

The presidency, then, like all other institutions of our national government, reflects influences at the political level—interest groups, political parties, and especially public opinion—and also structural influences, especially from the international system and the U.S. economy.

Summary

The American presidency began small; only a few nineteenth-century presidents (e.g., Jefferson, Jackson, Polk, and Lincoln) made much of a mark. In the twentieth century, however, as a result of industrialization, two world wars, and the Great Depression, presidential powers and resources expanded greatly. The presidency largely attained its modern shape under Franklin Roosevelt.

Presidents have varied in personality and style, with significant consequences. Despite the enormous resources and large staffs available to presidents, they are constrained in what they can do, especially concerning domestic policy. Presidents cannot always control their own executive branch. They engage in tugs-of-war with Congress, pushing their programs with varying success, depending on their party's strength in the legislature and the nature of the issue.

The presidency has become a far more democratic office than the Founders envisioned. Presidents listen to public opinion and respond to it, as well as leading (and sometimes manipulating) the public. But presidents are not therefore pure tribunes of the people, because they are also influenced by interest groups, party activists, and financial contributors in ways that may diverge from what the public wants. Further, presidents are affected by such structural factors as the nature of the American economic and social systems and the U.S. position in the world.

Suggested Readings

Barber, James David. *The Presidential Character: Predicting Performance in the White House,* 4th ed. Englewood Cliffs, NJ: Prentice Hall, 1992.
A fascinating, though controversial, analysis of the nature and impact of presidential personalities.

Bond, Jon R., and Richard Fleischer. *The President in the Legislative Arena.* Chicago: University of Chicago Press, 1990.
A thorough, quantitative look at presidents' relations with Congress.

Brody, Richard A. *Assessing the President.* Stanford, CA: Stanford University Press, 1991.
A thorough analysis of what affects presidents' popularity.

Campbell, Colin, and Bert A. Rockman, eds. *The Clinton Presidency: First Appraisals.* Chatham, NJ: Chatham House, 1996.
A critical but balanced set of essays offering insights into the first two years of the Clinton administration.

Cannon, Lou. *President Reagan: The Role of a Lifetime.* New York: Simon & Schuster, 1991.
A close, critical look at Ronald Reagan and his presidency.

Neustadt, Richard E. *Presidential Power and the Modern Presidents: The Politics of Leadership from Roosevelt to Reagan.* New York: Free Press, 1990.
The classic study of how presidents do or do not get their way, updated to include recent presidencies.

Tulis, Jeffrey K. *The Rhetorical Presidency.* Princeton: Princeton University Press, 1987.
Tells how presidents have moved from the Founders' conception of a distant relationship with the public to the modern closeness.

Internet Sources

The White House Home Page http://www.whitehouse.gov/
Information on the First Family, recent presidential addresses and orders, text from news conferences, official presidential documents, and ways to contact the White House.

U.S. Presidents http://oeonline.com/~willfs/govt.html
Biographies of the American presidents.

Also refer to the several general political information Internet sites listed at the end of Chapter 1:

Associated Press Searchable News Feed
Doug Ingrams' News and Politics Page
Fedworld
The Internet Public Library
The Jefferson Project
Political Science Resources
Time Warner's Pathfinder

Notes

1. Hedrick Smith, "The President as Coalition Builder: Reagan's First Year," in Thomas E. Cronin, ed., *Rethinking the Presidency* (Boston: Little, Brown, 1982), pp. 277–281.

2. Smith, "The President as Coalition Builder," p. 278.

3. David A. Stockman, *The Triumph of Politics: How the Reagan Revolution Failed* (New York: Harper & Row, 1986), p. 169.

4. Tip O'Neil (with William Novak), *Man of the House* (New York: Random House, 1987), pp. 341–341.

5. Kevin Phillips, *The Politics of Rich and Poor: Wealth and the American Electorate in the Reagan Aftermath* (New York: Random House, 1990).

6. Thomas Byrne Edsall, *The New Politics of Inequality* (New York: Norton, 1984); Thomas Ferguson and Joel Rogers, *Right Turn: The Decline of the Democrats and the Future of American Politics* (New York: Farrar, Straus & Giroux, 1986).

7. *The World Almanac 1996* (Mahwah, NJ: Funk & Wagnalls, 1995); *Information Please Almanac, 1996* (Boston: Houghton Mifflin, 1995).

8. *Historical Statistics of the United States: Colonial Times to 1970* (U.S. Department of Commerce), pp. 8, 1143.

9. *Historical Statistics,* Part I, p. 126.

10. Norman C. Thomas, Joseph A. Pika, and Richard A. Watson, *The Politics of the Presidency,* 3rd ed. (Washington, DC: Congressional Quarterly Press, 1994).

11. David G. McCullough, *Truman* (New York: Simon & Schuster, 1992).

12. Fred I. Greenstein, *The Hidden-Hand Presidency: Eisenhower as Leader* (New York: Basic Books, 1982).

13. Paul F. Boller, Jr., *Presidential Anecdotes* (New York: Oxford University Press, 1981), pp. 299, 302.

14. Arthur M. Schlesinger, Jr., *A Thousand Days* (Boston: Houghton-Mifflin, 1965), gives a friendly account of the Kennedy administration; Henry Fairlie, *The Kennedy Promise* (1972), makes a scathing assessment.

15. Doris Kearns Goodwin, *Lyndon Johnson and the American Dream* (New York: Harper & Row, 1976); Robert Dallek, *Lone Star Rising* (New York: Oxford University Press, 1991); Joseph A. Califano, *The Triumph and Tragedy of Lyndon Johnson* (New York: Simon & Schuster, 1991).

16. Stephen E. Ambrose, *Nixon* (New York: Simon & Schuster, 1987).

17. John Robert Greene, *The Presidency of Gerald R. Ford* (Lawrence: University of Kansas Press, 1995).

18. Bruce Miroff, "The Presidency and the Public: Leadership as Spectacle," in Michael Nelson, ed., *The Presidency and the Political System,* 4th ed. (Washington, DC: Congressional Quarterly Press, 1995), pp. 273–296.

19. Herbert D. Rosenbaum and Alexej Ugrinsky, eds., *Jimmy Carter: Foreign Policy and Post-Presidential Years* (Westport, CT: Greenwood Press, 1994).

20. Lou Cannon, *President Reagan: The Role of a Lifetime* (New York: Simon & Schuster, 1991).

21. James David Barber, *The Presidential Character: Predicting Performance in the White House,* 4th ed. (Englewood Cliffs, NJ: Prentice Hall, 1992).

22. See Alexander L. George and Juliette L. George, *Woodrow Wilson and Colonel House* (New York: John Day, 1956).

23. See Alexander George, "Assessing Presidential Character," *World Politics* (January 1974), pp. 234–282; Jeffrey Tulis, "On Presidential Character," in Jeffrey Tulis and

Joseph M. Bessettee, eds., *Presidency in the Constitutional Order* (Baton Rouge: Louisiana State University Press, 1981); Michael Nelson, "The Psychological Presidency," in Michael Nelson, ed., *The Presidency and the Political System,* 2nd ed. (Washington, DC: Congressional Quarterly Press, 1988), p. 185.

24. Clinton Rossiter, *The American Presidency,* rev. ed. (New York: Harcourt, Brace & World, 1960).

25. Quoted in Laurence J. Peter, *Peter's Quotations* (New York: Morrow, 1977), p. 405.

26. Donald Regan, *For the Record* (San Diego: Harcourt Brace Jovanovich, 1988); Kitty Kelley, *Nancy Reagan: The Unauthorized Biography* (New York: Simon & Schuster, 1991).

27. Nathan Miller, *FDR: An Intimate History* (Lanham, MD: Madison Books, 1983), p. 276.

28. Jonathan Daniels, *The Man of Independence* (Philadelphia: Lippincott, 1950), p. 232.

29. Samuel Gallu, *Give 'Em Hell Harry* (New York: Viking Press, 1975), p. 17.

30. Joseph A. Pika, "The Vice-Presidency: New Opportunities, Old Constraints," in Michael Nelson, ed., *The Presidency and the Political System,* 4th ed. (Washington, DC: Congressional Quarterly Press, 1995), pp. 496–528.

31. Elizabeth Drew, *On the Edge: The Clinton Presidency* (New York: Simon & Schuster, 1994), p. 227.

32. Richard Fenno, *The President's Cabinet* (Cambridge: Harvard University Press, 1959).

33. Fenno, *The President's Cabinet,* pp. 239–244.

34. Benjamin Bradlee, *Conversations with Kennedy* (New York: Norton, 1975), p. 38.

35. Richard E. Neustadt, *Presidential Power and the Modern Presidents: The Politics of Leadership from Roosevelt to Reagan* (New York: Macmillan, 1990).

36. Graham T. Allison, *Essence of Decision: Explaining the Cuban Missile Crisis* (Boston: Little, Brown, 1971), pp. 141–142.

37. Neustadt, *Presidential Power,* chap. 2.

38. *New York Times* (July 19, 1990), p. A2.

39. Morris Fiorina, *Divided Government* (New York: Macmillan, 1992).

40. See David R. Mayhew, *Divided We Govern: Party Control, Lawmaking, and Investigations, 1946–1990* (New Haven: Yale University Press, 1991); Mark Peterson, *Legislating Together* (Cambridge: Harvard University Press, 1990).

41. Arthur M. Schlesinger, Jr., *The Imperial Presidency,* 2nd ed. (Boston: Houghton Mifflin, 1989).

42. See James L. Sundquist, *The Decline and Resurgence of Congress* (Washington, DC: Brookings Institution, 1981).

43. George C. Edwards III, *Presidential Influence in Congress* (San Francisco: Freeman, 1980); Jon R. Bond and Richard Fleischer, *The President in the Legislative Arena* (Chicago: University of Chicago Press, 1990); Peterson, *Legislating Together.*

44. Terry Sullivan, "Headcounts, Expectations and Presidential Coalitions in Congress," *American Journal of Political Science* (1988), Vol. 32, pp. 657–689.

45. Aaron Wildavsky, "The Two Presidencies," in Aaron Wildavsky, ed., *Perspectives on the Presidency* (Boston: Little, Brown, 1975), pp. 448–461.

46. Steven Shull, *The Two Presidencies: A Quarter-Century Assessment* (Chicago: Nelson Hall, 1991); Bond and Fleischer, *The President in the Legislative Arena;* Terry Sullivan, "A Matter of Fact: The 'Two Presidencies' Thesis Revitalized," in Shull, *The Two Presidencies,* pp. 143–157.

47. Edwards, *Presidential Influence,* pp. 90–100; Bond and Fleischer, *The President in the Legislative Arena.*

48. Jeffrey K. Tulis, *The Rhetorical Presidency* (Princeton, NJ: Princeton University Press, 1987), Chaps. 2–3, esp. p. 64.

49. Woodrow Wilson, *Leaders of Men,* T. H. Vail Motter, ed. (Princeton: Princeton University Press, 1952), p. 39; quoted in Tulis, *The Rhetorical Presidency,* Chap. 4, which analyzes Wilson's theory at length and expresses some skepticism about it.

50. Tulis, *The Rhetorical Presidency,* pp. 138, 140.

51. Samuel Kernell, *Going Public: Strategies of Presidential Leadership,* 2nd ed. (Washington, DC: Congressional Quarterly Press, 1993), p. 92 and Chap. 4.

52. Benjamin I. Page and Robert Y. Shapiro, "Presidents as Opinion Leaders: Some New Evidence," *Policy Studies Journal,* Vol. 12 (June 1984), pp. 649–661; Benjamin I. Page, Robert Y. Shapiro, and Glenn R. Dempsey, "What Moves Public Opinion," *American Political Science Review,* Vol. 81 (March 1987), pp. 23–43; but see Donald L. Jordan, "Newspaper Effects on Policy Preferences," *Public Opinion Quarterly,* Vol. 57 (Summer 1993), pp. 191–204.

53. Tulis, *The Rhetorical Presidency.*

54. Benjamin I. Page and Mark P. Petracca, *The American Presidency* (New York: McGraw-Hill, 1983), p. 122. See Benjamin I. Page and Robert Y. Shapiro, "Effects of Public Opinion on Policy," *American Political Science Review,* Vol. 77 (March 1983), pp. 175–190.

55. Lawrence Jacobs and Robert Shapiro, "The Rise of Presidential Polling: The Nixon White House in Historical Perspective," *Public Opinion Quarterly,* Vol. 59, No. 2 (Summer 1995), pp. 163–195.

56. Jack J. Honomichl, "How Reagan Took America's Pulse," *Advertising Age* (January 23, 1989), pp. 1, 25, 32.

57. Richard A. Brody, *Assessing the President* (Stanford, CA: Stanford University Press, 1991). See also John E. Mueller, "Presidential Popularity from Truman to Johnson," *American Political Science Review,* Vol. 64 (March 1970), pp. 18–34; Samuel Kernell, "Explaining Presidential Popularity," *American Political Science Review,* Vol. 72 (June 1978), pp. 506–522.

58. *The Gallup Poll Monthly,* No. 328 (January 1993).

59. See Mark P. Petracca, ed., *The Politics of Interests* (Boulder, CO: Westview Press, 1992).

60. Charles E. Lindblom, *Politics and Markets* (New York: Basic Books, 1977).

61. Alexander Heard, *The Costs of Democracy* (Chapel Hill: University of North Carolina Press, 1960); Thomas Ferguson and Joel Rogers, *Right Turn* (New York: Hill & Wang, 1986); Thomas Ferguson, *Golden Rule* (Chicago: University of Chicago Press, 1995).

62. Mark A. Peterson, "Interest Mobilization and the Presidency," in Petracca, ed., *The Politics of Interests,* pp. 221–241.

63. Douglas A. Hibbs, Jr., "Partisan Theory After Fifteen Years," *European Journal of Political Economy,* Vol. 8 (1992), pp. 361–373.

CHAPTER 13

The Executive Branch

IN THIS CHAPTER

- ★ Is the federal bureaucracy compatible with democracy
- ★ Who bureaucrats are and what they do
- ★ How the executive branch is organized
- ★ What's wrong and what's right with the federal bureaucracy
- ★ Myths about the federal bureaucracy

The Federal Bureaucracy Under Siege

When news of the terrorist bombing of the Federal Center in Oklahoma City hit the airwaves on April 19, 1995, retired Sheriff Howard Stewart of Meadville, Pennsylvania, immediately dismissed the speculation of the experts that it was somehow connected to the troubled politics of the Middle East:

> "When I realized the date, and I thought about all the anger and fear that's out there," Stewart says, "I said to my wife, I don't think it was Arabs that did this."[1]

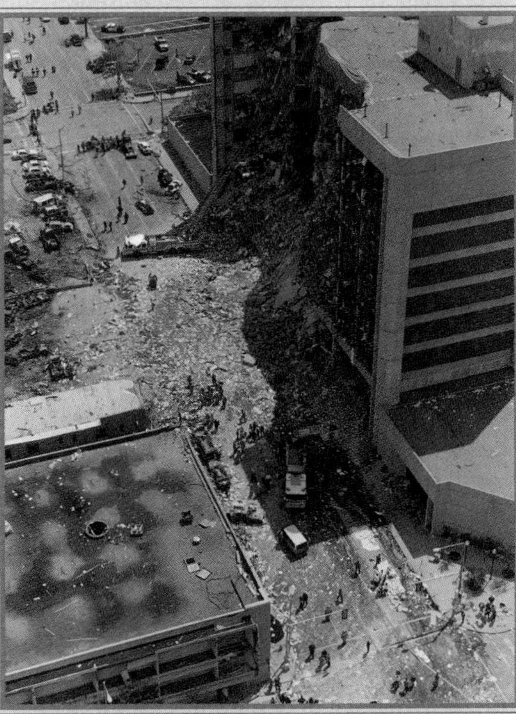

Stewart had reason to suspect a homegrown origin for the attack on a government center; he had been hearing some strange antigovernment rumblings in his quiet, conservative rural community, coming not from extremists but from many of its leading citizens. In the coffee shops on Main Street, talk was of a government conspiracy to enslave Americans to the United Nations. Color-coded highway signs, it was being said, were guideposts for foreign invaders. Meadville citizens were particularly exercised by federal gun-control laws, the 1993 siege in Waco of the Branch Davidians, and restrictive environmental regulations.

Several Meadville residents rejected the Oklahoma City bombing, as the act of a madman, but said they understood how the rising anger with the federal government might trigger something like it:

> "I don't want anything to do with them, but I think I understand their attitude," says Daniel J. Leech, president of Leech Carbide, a local manufacturer. "If you ran a small business, you'd understand, too. People are being squeezed more and more all the time. The government makes it almost impossible for small business to stay in business. Pressure just builds over time."

Leech's remark unleashes a torrent of anger at government among his companions. Doug Lodge, a roofer who lives in farm country, says farmers around him can't drain land because "if a cattail grows, it's wetland; if a beaver moves, it's a habitat."

Anti-federal- government anger is a staple of American political history. Many *Anti-Federalists* believed that the Constitution gave undue power to the central government. Buttressed by the theories of John C. Calhoun, the State of South Carolina passed a resolution in 1830 suggesting that the states had the right to nullify federal laws. Several of the New England states thought about seceding from the union in 1812 to remove themselves from federal authority, and the South did so in 1860, bringing on the Civil War. Many conservatives, including a majority on the Supreme Court for a few years, believed that the expansion of federal authority during the Great Depression in the 1930s was unconstitutional. Many whites in the South grew angry with the federal government in the 1960s and 1970s because of its championing of civil rights. Antiwar activists during the years of the Vietnam War were unhappy with the Defense Department for waging the war, and with the Central Intelligence Agency and the FBI for interfering with legitimate protest activities. Much of the corporate community turned against the federal government in the 1980s and 1990s for what seemed like undue zeal on the part of government officials for environmental and consumer protection. The chorus of anti-federal-government complaints has ebbed and flowed throughout our history.

The current anti-federal-government mood has had a profound impact on public policy, with many historically federal responsibilities now transferred or being considered for transfer, to the states. The mood has also helped focus critical attention on the executive branch, that part of the government that carries out federal policy.

Complaints about the size, cost, inefficiency, and excessive interference of the "bureaucracy in Washington" are common, as is unhappiness about particular parts of the executive branch, such as the Internal Revenue Service, the Postal Service, and the Bureau of Alcohol, Tobacco, and Firearms. Members of the U.S. Forest Service report that they do not wear their uniforms in town in several western communities because of the negative reactions the uniform provokes.

One result of the anti-federal-government mood in the country, according to some scholars,[2] is that the executive branch is becoming increasingly crippled in its ability to carry out its duties: American citizens and businesses are less cooperative, the morale of federal government workers is dropping, talented people are leaving the federal government, and fewer talented people are looking to careers in the public service.

In this chapter, we look in detail at the executive branch, also known as the *federal bureaucracy*. We will examine how the executive branch is organized and what it does. We will learn that the executive branch is not simply a bureaucratic extension of the president's will, operating at his beck and call. Political and governmental influences, such as interest groups, Congress, the media, and public opinion, shape the kind of bureaucracy we have. So do such structural factors as the Constitution, the economy, and the political culture. So do the backgrounds and training of the people who work in government.

Ultimately, this chapter is about how the federal bureaucracy affects the health and vitality of democracy in the United States. As we look at this question, we will also try to dispel some of the prevailing myths about bureaucracy.

The American Bureaucracy Compared

The American bureaucracy is different from bureaucracies in other democratic nations. Such structural influences as the American political culture and the constitutional rules of the game have a great deal to do with these differences.

A Hostile Political Culture

Americans do not trust government; nor do they think it can accomplish most of the tasks assigned to it. They believe, on the whole, that the private sector can usually do a better job.

civil service Federal government civilian employees, excluding political appointees.

civil servants Government workers employed under the merit system; not political appointees.

This hostile environment influences the bureaucracy in several ways. For one thing, our public bureaucracy is surrounded by more legal restrictions and is subject to more intense legislative oversight than bureaucracies in other countries. Because **civil servants** have so little prestige, moreover, many of the most talented people in our society tend to stay away; they do not aspire to be civil servants. This is not true in many other democratic countries. In France, Great Britain, and Germany, for instance, the higher **civil service** is filled by the best graduates of the countries' elite universities and are accorded enormous prestige. Finally, the highest policymaking positions in the U.S. executive branch are closed to civil servants; they are reserved for presidential political appointees. This is not true in other democracies.

Incoherent Organization

Our bureaucracy is an organizational hodgepodge. It does not take the standard pyramidal form, as do bureaucracies elsewhere. There are few clear lines of control, responsibility, and accountability. Some bureaucratic units have no relationship at all to other agencies and departments. As one of the leading students of the federal bureaucracy once put it, other societies have "a more orderly and symmetrical, a more prudent, a more cohesive and more powerful bureaucracy . . . [whereas] we have a more internally competitive, a more experimental, a noisier and less coherent, a less powerful bureaucracy."[3] Our bureaucracy was built piece by piece over the years in a political system without a strong central government. Bureaucracies in other democratic nations were often created at a single point in time, by powerful political leaders, such as Frederick the Great in Prussia and Napoleon in France.[4]

Divided Control

Adding to the organizational incoherence of our federal bureaucracy is the fact that it has two bosses—the president and Congress—which are constantly vying for control. In addition, the federal courts keep an eye on it. This situation derives from the separation of powers and checks and balances in our Constitution, which gives each branch a role in the principal activities and responsibilities of the other branches. No other democratic nation has opted for this arrangement. Most prefer a parliamentary system in which legislative and executive powers are combined in a single body, dominated by a cabinet and a prime minister. In parliamentary systems, moreover, the courts play a limited role in bureaucratic oversight. Bureaucrats in parliamentary systems have a single boss, a minister appointed by the prime minister.

Accessibility

Because of incoherent organization, the lack of a chain of command with clear lines of authority and accountability, and divided control at the top, ours is an extremely open and porous bureaucracy. Individuals and groups can get a hearing and a response from bureaucrats without necessarily starting at the top, as one would have to do in France, Japan, or Germany. In one sense, this is potentially a very democratic arrangement, encouraging citizen participation in bureaucratic affairs. In practice, however, it provides a very fertile environment for interest groups that know exactly where to go to get what they want, while the general public is usually unaware. **Iron triangles** and other forms of privileged access abound, as related in Chapter 7.

Iron triangle An enduring alliance of common interest between an interest group, a congressional committee, and an executive branch department or agency.

Transformation of the Executive Branch: The Structural Context

Executive departments and officers are mentioned in the Constitution only in an indirect, offhand way. The Constitution neither specifies the number and kinds of departments to be established nor describes other executive agencies. The framers apparently wanted to leave these questions to the wisdom of Congress and the president.

We saw in the last chapter that the executive branch grew from very modest beginnings in President Washington's administration to a very large bureaucracy in our own day of about 3 million civilian employees working in 14 departments, a White House minibureaucracy, and literally hundreds of bureaus, agencies, commissions, services, and boards. Figure 13.1 depicts the overall organization of the federal government and suggests the extraordinarily wide range of its responsibilities.

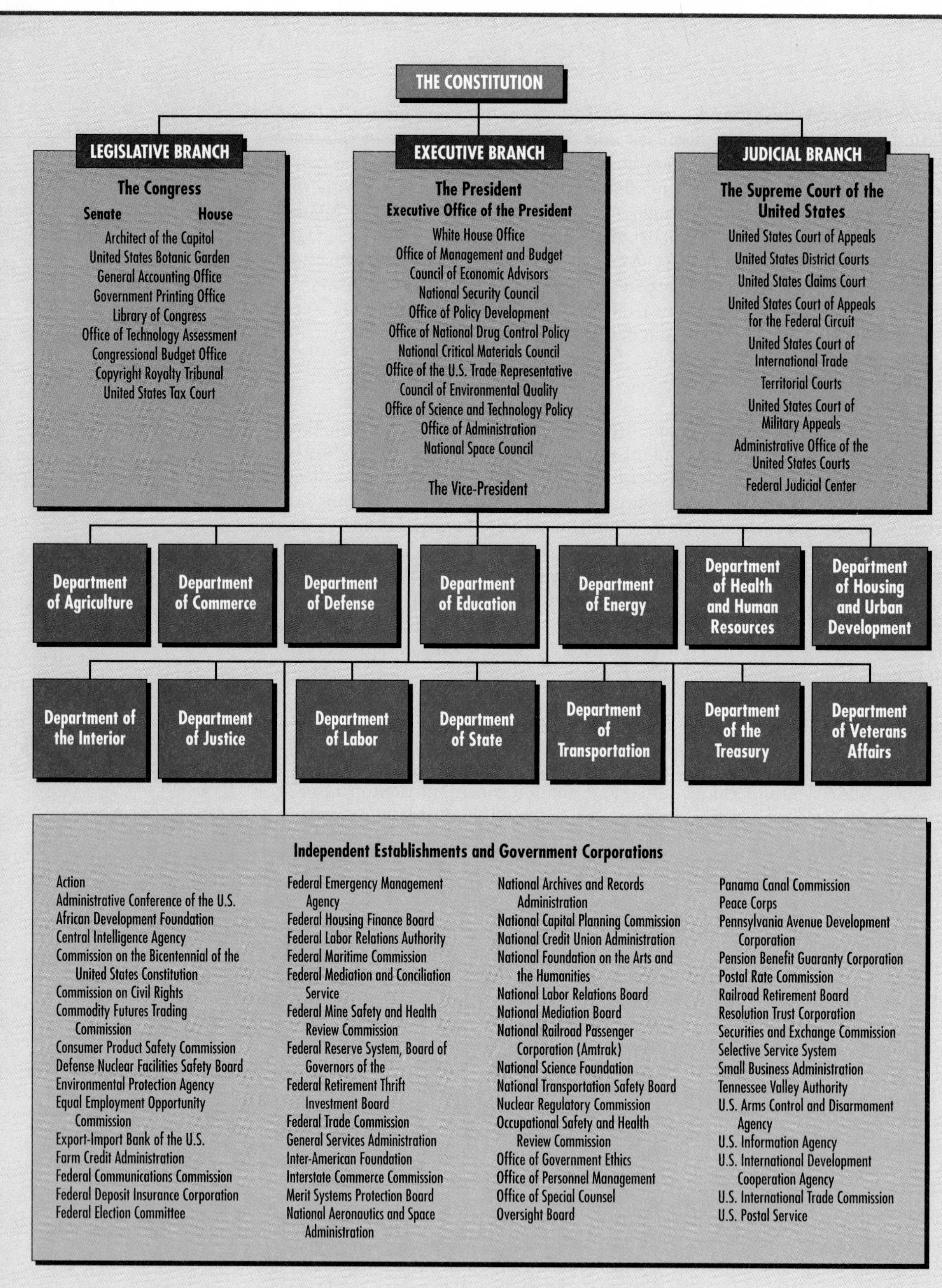

Figure 13.1 ▪ **The Government of the United States**

Source: *U.S. Government Organization Manual, 1996.*

A Brief Administrative History of the United States

The most immediate causes for the transformation of the role of the federal government and the scale of the bureaucracy are political linkage-level pressures—from public opinion, voters, parties, interest groups, and social movements—on government decision makers. The more fundamental causes are changes in such structural factors as the U.S. economy, its population, and the role of the United States in the world.

Nineteenth-Century Changes Until the Civil War, the federal government had few responsibilities, and the administrative apparatus of the executive branch was relatively undeveloped. Alexis de Tocqueville, the perceptive French observer of the fledgling American democracy, could hardly find a government at all: "[In America], society governs itself for itself."[5]

The problems and opportunities created by rapid population growth, westward expansion, the Industrial Revolution, and economic uncertainty in the last quarter of the nineteenth century gradually changed people's thinking about the appropriate responsibilities of government and the size of the bureaucracy.[6] The Department of the Interior, created in 1849, was given responsibility for Indian affairs, the census, and the regulation of public lands and mining. The Department of Justice was created in 1870 to handle the federal government's growing legal burden in the fields of civil and criminal, antitrust, tax, and natural resources law. The Department of Agriculture became a full-fledged cabinet department in 1889 in response to the economic crisis in the farm economy and the demands of farm groups. The Department of Labor was created in 1913 in an effort to ease the rising tensions between workers and owners. The Department of Commerce was created in the same year to foster technological development, standardization, and business cooperation.

The Corporation and the Progressives The rise to prominence of the large corporations in the late nineteenth and early twentieth centuries, and the problems caused by them, also contributed to a rethinking of the role of the federal government. Monopoly practices in the railroad, manufacturing, oil, and banking industries triggered reform movements that resulted in new federal regulatory laws, of which the most important were the Interstate Commerce Act (1887) and the Sherman Antitrust Act (1890). Progressive reformers and farsighted business leaders who were worried about the growing public hostility to big business helped convince Congress to pass such landmark legislation as the Federal Reserve Act (passed in 1914 to stabilize the banking industry), the Pure Food and Drug Act (1906), the Meat Inspection Act (passed in 1906 in response to the horrors reported in Upton Sinclair's book *The Jungle*), and the Federal Trade Commission Act (1914).[7] Each piece of legislation was a response to a set of problems, each expanded the federal government's responsibilities, and each created a new executive branch agency to carry out the law.

The Great Depression It was the Great Depression that forever changed how Americans thought about government. President Franklin Roosevelt and Congress responded to economic collapse, widespread social distress, and serious threats of violence and social conflict with a range of new programs: work programs for the unemployed, relief for the poor, Social Security, regulation of the banks and the securities industry, agricultural subsidy programs, collective bargaining, and programs to encourage business expansion. Each program carried with it the addition of new bureaucratic agencies to the executive branch.

World War II and Its Aftermath World War II, America's new role as a superpower, and the long Cold War with the Soviet Union, also brought a substantial increase in the federal government's responsibilities and in the size of the executive branch. Some old-line departments, such as the Department of State, grew substantially after World War II. The Department of Defense was created by merging the old Army and Navy Departments and adding an Air Force component. New administrative units such as the Central Intelligence Agency, the National Security Agency, the National Security Council, the Agency for International Development, and the U.S. Arms Control and Disarmament Agency were created to fill new needs and missions. The Atomic Energy Commission was created both to regulate and to encourage atomic power and weapons production. The Internal Revenue Service expanded its operations so that it could collect the revenues to pay for these new responsibilities. By 1950, a federal bureaucracy of substantial size and impact was firmly in place.[8]

The Regulatory State During the 1960s and 1970s, successful social reform movements and important changes in public opinion convinced political leaders to take on new responsibilities in the areas of civil rights, urban affairs, environmental and consumer protection, workplace safety, and education. Important among these initiatives was the formation of the Department of Health, Education, and Welfare (now split into the Department of Health and Human Services and the Department of Education). The Environmental Protection Agency was created to monitor compliance with federal environmental laws and to regulate business activities that might add pollutants to the nation's air and water. The Occupational Safety and Health Administration keeps its regulatory eye on potentially dangerous workplace practices. Each expansion of responsibility, as in the past, brought an expansion in the size of the executive

During World War II and the Cold War that followed, the increased responsibilities of a superpower were thrust on the U.S. federal government. The executive branch grew so rapidly during the war that temporary buildings were constructed along the mall in Washington, D.C., to house such new bureaucratic components as the Atomic Energy Commission.

branch. Though the Reagan revolution slowed the growth in the federal government's responsibilities, it was unable to roll back most of the programs and agencies created since the Great Depression.

Devolution and Rollback On taking control of Congress after their 1994 landslide electoral victory, Republicans began to pare down the size of the federal government, roll back many of its regulatory responsibilities, and shift a number of functions to the states. For instance, Congress made it more difficult to identify and protect wetlands. It also shifted much of the responsibility for providing public assistance to the states (see Chapter 3). Finally, Congress made deep slashes in the federal budget, which forced substantial "downsizing" in a broad range of executive branch agencies. Increasingly, Republicans especially, but many Democrats as well, are asking what essential services the federal government should provide. This "devolution and rollback" theme was echoed by Bill Clinton in his 1996 State of the Union address, in which he announced the "end of big government." Nevertheless, the federal government's size and reach remain quite substantial in historical terms.

Bureaucracy

bureaucracy A form of large organization characterized by a chain of command, a hierarchy of offices with specified missions, formal rules of behavior, and appointment on the basis of merit and specialized knowledge.

bureaucrat One who works in a bureaucratic organization.

Bureaucracy has always been an unsavory word in American politics, and it remains so today. The word implies red tape, inefficiency, and nonresponsiveness. Politicians are always promising to "clean up the bureaucratic mess in Washington." To social scientists, however, *bureaucracy* and **bureaucrat** are neutral terms that describe a type of social organization and the people who work in it. Bureaucracies are *large organizations* in which people with *specialized knowledge* are organized into a clearly defined *hierarchy* of bureaus or offices, each of which has a specified *mission.* There is a clear *chain of command,* in which each person has one and only one boss or supervisor, and a set of *formal rules* to guide behavior. Appointment and advancement, moreover, are based on *merit* rather than on social connections or election to office. This description is, of course, a model or an ideal type; in the real world, there are many deviations from it.[9]

One advantage of a bureaucratic organization is its ability to organize large tasks.[10] Hierarchical organizations with clear chains of command are able to mobilize and to coordinate the efforts of thousands of people. Bureaucratic organization enabled the Defense Department to deploy over 500,000 troops and 11 million tons of weapons and equipment to the Saudi Arabian desert in a matter of months, for instance, in preparation for the Persian Gulf War against Iraq.

Another advantage of bureaucracies is the concentration of specialized talent that is found in them. People enter bureaucratic organizations on the basis of merit. They either pass an examination that determines if they are qualified or bring to their jobs the kind of experience or training that the bureaucratic organization needs. Thus, the Public Health Service recruits doctors, nurses, and medical technicians. The National Weather Service wants talented meteorological scientists. People in bureaucratic organizations also tend to remain in the same agencies or bureaus for years, where they hone their narrow specializations and become very good at what they do. These specialists can be rapidly mobilized when a president or a congressional committee needs information that will enable it to make national policy. To combat AIDS, for instance, they can turn for help to the scientists and doctors at the National Centers for Disease Control or the National Institutes of Health.

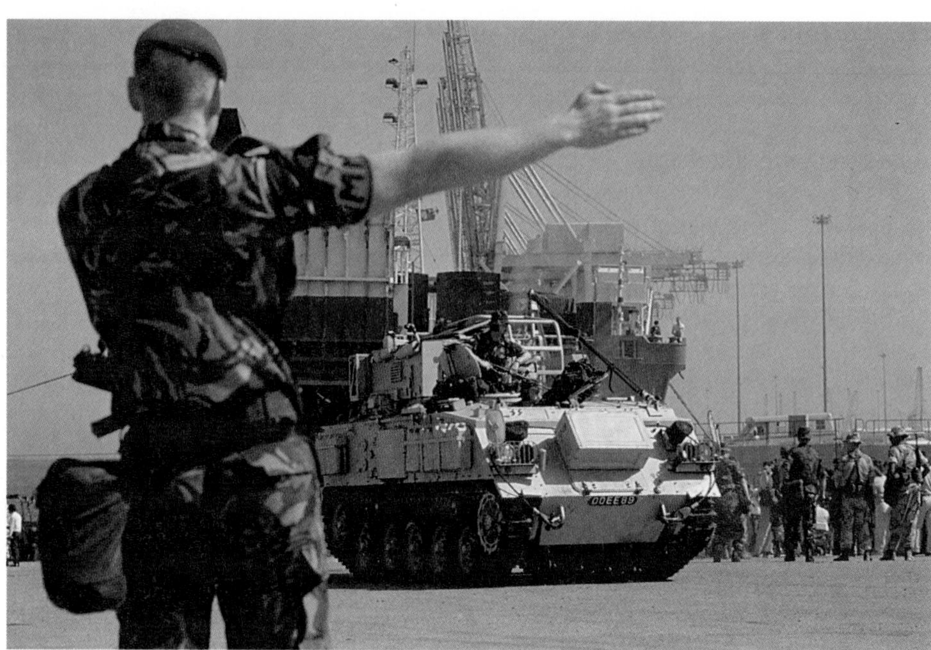

Massive tasks often require the kind of specialized knowledge and hierarchical command that can be provided only by a fairly large bureaucracy. In preparation for the Gulf War, for example, the Defense Department was able, in a matter of months, to deploy over 500,000 troops and 11 million tons of equipment to the Saudi Arabian desert.

Despite the complaints and jokes about bureaucracy, then, it has considerable advantages as a form of organization. This is not to say, of course, that bureaucracy is without problems. Nor is it to say that bureaucracy is the best form of organization; in the business world, for instance, flatter, less hierarchical forms are being introduced. It is only to say that the American rhetorical distaste for bureaucracy tends to hide some of its benefits.

How the Executive Branch Is Organized

The executive branch is made up of several different kinds of administrative units, which make the federal bureaucracy a very complicated entity.

The most familiar are *departments,* which are headed by cabinet-level secretaries, appointed by the president and approved by the Senate (see Table 13.1). Departments are meant to carry out the most essential government functions. The first three were War, State, and Treasury.

Over the years, departments (and employees) were added as the need arose, as powerful groups demanded them, or as presidents and members of Congress wished to signal a new national need or to cement political alliances with important constituencies. Powerful interest groups were behind the creation of the Departments of Agriculture and Commerce, for instance. Jimmy Carter highlighted his concerns in the midst of the OPEC (Organization of Petroleum Exporting Countries) oil crisis by persuading Congress to create the Department of Energy. He supported the creation of the Department of Education, separating it from the original Department of Health Education, and Welfare, to acknowledge the political backing of the National Education Association.

Table 13.1

Employees of Executive Branch Departments, 1995

Department	Number of Civilian Employees (in thousands)
Agriculture	109
Commerce	36
Defense	834
Education	5
Energy	21
Health and Human Services	62
Housing and Urban Development	13
Interior	76
Justice	102
Labor	18
State	25
Transportation	65
Treasury	161
Veterans Affairs	224

Source: The Budget of the United States Government, Fiscal 1996, Table s–21 (estimated figures).

Subdivisions within cabinet departments are known as *bureaus* and *agencies.* In some departments, such as Housing and Urban Development, these subdivisions are closely controlled by the department leadership, and the entire department works very much like a textbook hierarchical model. In other cases, where the bureaus or agencies have fashioned their own relationships with interest groups and powerful congressional committees, the departments are little more than holding companies for powerful bureaucratic subunits.[11] During the long reign of J. Edgar Hoover, for instance, the FBI did virtually as it pleased, even though it was (and remains) a unit within the Justice Department.

Independent executive agencies report directly to the president rather than to a department cabinet-level secretary. They are usually created to give greater control to the president in carrying out some executive function or to highlight some particular public problem or issue that policymakers wish to address. The General Services Administration (which builds and maintains federal facilities, orders supplies, and the like) and the Office of Personnel Management, for instance, serve all of the executive departments; it would make no sense to locate them in any single department.[12] The Environmental Protection Agency (EPA) was given independent status to focus government and public attention on environmental issues and to give the federal government more flexibility in solving environmental problems.

Government corporations are agencies that operate very much like a private company. They can sell stock, retain and reinvest earnings, and borrow money, for instance. They are usually created to perform some crucial economic activity that private investors are unwilling or unable to perform. Amtrak, for instance, was created to provide passenger rail service after the virtual collapse of the private passenger-rail industry. The U.S. Postal Service was transformed from an executive department to a government corporation in 1970 to increase efficiency. The Resolution Trust Corporation was created to coordinate the bailout of the savings-and-loan industry.

Independent regulatory commissions, such as the Securities and Exchange Commission and the Consumer Product Safety Commission, are responsible for regulating those sectors of the economy where it is judged that the free market does not work properly to protect the public interest. The commissions are "independent" in the sense that they stand outside the departmental structure and are protected against direct presidential or congressional control. A commission is run by commissioners with long, overlapping terms, and many require a balance between Republicans and Democrats.

Foundations are units that are separated from the rest of government to protect them from political interference with science and the arts. Most prominent are the foundations for the Arts and for the Humanities and the National Science Foundation.

What Do Bureaucrats Do?

Bureaucrats engage in a wide range of activities that are relevant to the quality of democracy in the United States and affect how laws and regulations work.

Executing the Law

The term *executive branch* suggests the branch of the federal government that executes or carries out the law. The framers of the Constitution assumed that Congress would be the principal national policymaker and that the president and those he appointed to administrative positions in the executive branch "shall take care that the laws be faithfully executed" (Article II, Section 2). For the most part, this responsibility is carried out routinely; mail is delivered, troops are trained, and Social Security checks are mailed on time.

Sometimes, executing the law is not so easy, however, because it is not always clear what the law means. Often (all too often, according to some critics[13]), Congress passes laws that are vague about goals and short on procedural guidelines. It may do so because its members believe that something should be done about a particular social problem but are short on specifics about how to solve it, or because its members have definite ideas but disagree

The Immigration and Naturalization Service is now being called on to do more about slowing the flow of illegal immigration, but it must operate within guidelines and budgets determined by Congress.

among themselves. The Office of Economic Opportunity, for example, was created in 1965 as part of Lyndon Johnson's War on Poverty, with a mandate to eliminate poverty, but it received virtually no guidance about what time frame was contemplated or what specific things it ought to do. Vaguely written statutes and directives, then, leave a great deal of discretion to bureaucrats.

Regulating (Rule Making)

Congress often gives bureaucratic agencies the power to write specific rules. Because of the complexity of the problems that government must face, Congress tends to create agencies and to specify the job or mission that it wants done and then charges the agency with using its expertise to do the job. Congress created the EPA, for instance, and gave it a mission—to help coordinate the cleanup of the nation's air and water—but it left to the EPA the power to set the specific standards that communities and businesses must meet. The standards set by the EPA have the force of law unless they are rescinded by Congress or overruled by the courts. The Food and Drug Administration (FDA) writes rules about the introduction of new drugs that researchers and pharmaceutical companies are obliged to follow. New and proposed rules from all sources of the federal government are published daily in the *Federal Register,* a truly formidable document.

Some critics believe that Congress delegates entirely too much lawmaking to the executive branch, but it's difficult to see what alternative Congress has. It cannot micromanage every issue. And in the end, Congress retains control; it can change the rules written by bureaucrats if they drift too far from congressional intent or constituent desires. The ability of several agencies (like the

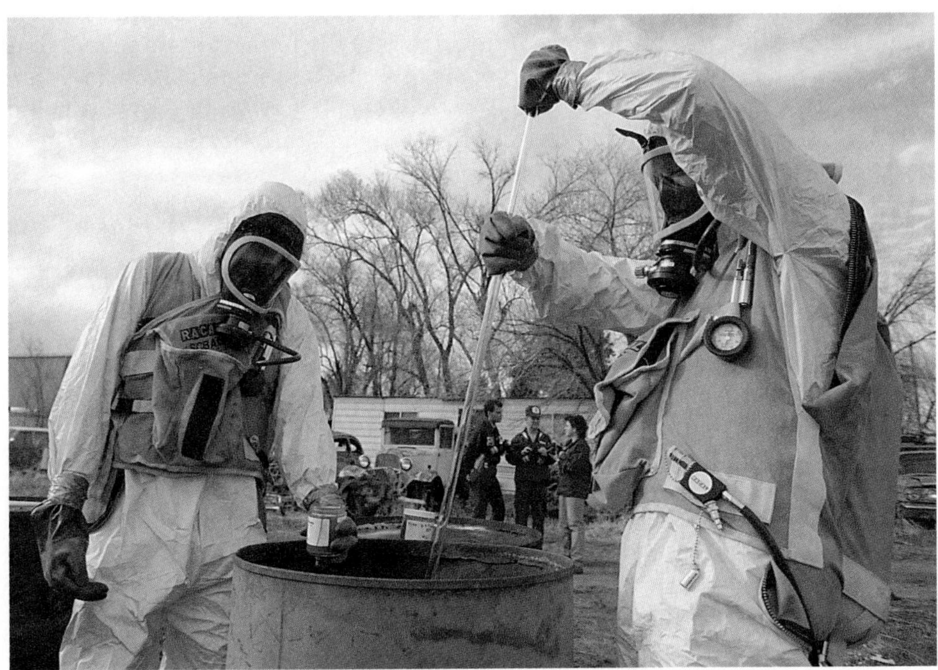

Congress identifies tasks and creates agencies to complete them using their own expertise. For example, the Environmental Protection Agency was created by Congress to clean up and prevent pollution in the nation's air and water; the EPA creates and implements environmental standards without much direct congressional involvement.

EPA) to write rules was sharply curtailed by the Republican-dominated Congress in 1995, for instance. Bureaucratic rule making is also carefully watched by presidents and (increasingly) by the courts. The Administrative Procedures Act, moreover, requires that interested citizens and groups be allowed to comment on new rules before they can be issued.

Other critics simply believe that there are too many rules and regulations. When candidates promise to "get government off our backs," the reference is to the purported burdens of regulation. Several attempts have been made to roll back executive-branch rule making. Under Ronald Reagan, required **cost-benefit analysis** was introduced as a way to slow the rule-making process. President Bush created the Competitiveness Council under Vice-President Dan Quayle to review and make exceptions to regulations deemed unfriendly to business. All recent presidents have used the Office of Management and Budget to review "excessive" rule making.

cost-benefit analysis A method of evaluating rules and regulations which weighs their potential costs against their potential benefits to society.

Adjudicating

Congress has given some executive branch agencies the power to conduct quasi-judicial proceedings in which disputes are resolved. Much as in a court of law, the decisions of an administrative law judge have the force of law, unless appealed to a higher panel. The National Labor Relations Board, for instance, adjudicates disputes between labor and management on matters concerning federal labor laws. Disputes may involve claims of unfair labor practices, for instance—firing a labor organizer falls into this category—or disagreements about whether proper procedures were followed in filing for a union certification election.

Bureaucrats exercise a great deal of discretion. They do not simply follow a set of orders from Congress or the president but find many opportunities to exercise their own judgment. Because bureaucrats make important decisions that have consequences for many other people, groups, and organizations, we can say that they are policymakers. They are *unelected policymakers,* however, and this fact should immediately alert us to some potential problems with regard to the practice of democracy.

Who Are the Bureaucrats?

Because bureaucrats exercise substantial discretion as policymakers, we want to know who they are. How representative are they of the American people? In a democracy, one would probably want to see a pretty close correspondence between the people and bureaucrats.

The Merit Services

There are three different personnel systems in the executive branch: the career civil service, separate merit services in specific agencies, and political appointees.

The Career Civil Service From the election of Andrew Jackson in 1828 until the late nineteenth century, the executive branch was staffed through what is commonly called the **spoils** system. It was generally accepted that the "spoils of victory" belonged to the winning party. Winners were expected to clear out

spoils The practice of distributing government offices and contracts to the supporters of the winning party; same as patronage.

people who were loyal to the previous administration and to replace them with their own people. Also known as *patronage,* this system of appointment occasioned no great alarm in the beginning because of the small and relatively unimportant role of the federal government in American society. The shortcomings of the War Department and other bureaucratic agencies during the Civil War, however, convinced many people that reform of the federal personnel system was required. Rampant corruption and favoritism in the government service during the years after the Civil War gave an additional boost to the reform effort, as did the realization that the growing role of the federal government required more skilled and less partisan personnel. The final catalyst for change was the assassination in 1881 of President James Garfield by a person who (it is said) badly wanted a government job but could not get one.

The Civil Service Act of 1883, also known as the Pendleton Act, created a bipartisan Civil Service Commission to oversee a system of appointments to certain executive branch posts on the basis of merit. Competitive examinations were to be used to determine merit. In the beginning, the competitive civil service system included only about 10 percent of federal positions. Congress has gradually extended the reach of the career civil service; today, it covers about 60 percent of federal employees. In 1978, Congress abolished the Civil Service Commission and replaced it with two separate agencies: the Office of Personnel Management and the Merit Systems Protection Board. The former administers the civil service laws, advertises positions, writes examinations, and acts as a clearinghouse for agencies that are looking for workers. The latter settles disputes concerning employee rights and obligations, hears employee grievances, and orders corrective action when needed.

Agency Merit Services Many federal agencies require personnel with the particular kinds of training and experience appropriate to their special missions. For such agencies, Congress has established separate merit systems administered by each agency itself. The Public Health Service, for instance, recruits its own doctors. The State Department has its own examinations and procedures for recruiting foreign service officers. NASA (the National Aeronautics and Space Administration) recruits scientists and engineers without the help of the Office of Personnel Management. About 35 percent of all federal civilian employees fall under these agency-specific merit systems.

Declining Status of the Civil Service American civil servants have never enjoyed the high status of the civil servants in the Western European nations, because of the traditional antigovernment attitudes in the United States and the American preference for the private sector over the public sector (see Chapter 4). The recent increase in anti-federal-government feelings in the country (see the opening story in this chapter) has made the lives of civil servants even less enviable than before. Elected officials constantly denigrate government workers, and candidates promise to downsize the bureaucracy if elected. Many policymaking responsibilities have been taken from their hands and shifted to political appointees or to the states. Pay and benefits have not kept up with the rise in the cost of living. In some job classifications, for instance, salaries in 1991 were only 75 percent of what they were in 1970 in real dollar terms.[14]

Needless to say, morale among civil servants is low and declining. Many of the most talented are leaving federal service. For instance, approximately 40 percent of the members of the Senior Executive Service, the highest ranks of the civil service, have quit in recent years.[15]

How Different Are Civil Servants? Civil servants are very much like other Americans.[16] Their educational levels, regional origins, average income, and age distribution match almost exactly those of the general population. Civil servants' political beliefs and opinions also match almost exactly those of the general American public (see Table 13.2), though they tend to favor the Democrats a bit more than the general public and are *slightly* more liberal on social issues than the national average.[17] Women and minorities are very well represented (the latter are actually overrepresented). In addition, the demographic representativeness of the bureaucracy is far greater in the United States than in virtually any other democratic nation.[18]

Table 13.2

Political Attitudes of the American Public and Public Employees

	The Public (%)	Public Employees (%)
Government spends too little on		
Halting crime	65	67
Improving education	65	61
Improving health	62	64
Dealing with drug addiction	62	63
Improving the environment	61	63
Welfare	39	40
Problems of cities	39	40
Condition of blacks	32	31
The military	21	25
Space exploration	14	17
Foreign aid	5	4
Own taxes too high	66	62
Would favor law		
Legalizing abortion	38	42
Making divorce harder	54	48
Making pornography illegal	42	37
Keeping marijuana illegal	80	80
Requiring gun permits	73	70
Would allow public speech		
By a homosexual	70	80
Against all churches	68	80
Claiming blacks inferior	60	67
By admitted communist	60	72
Advocating military rule	57	65
Dealing with crime		
Approve death penalty	77	77
Courts too lenient	87	84
Approve wiretapping	21	30
Police shouldn't strike citizens	24	20

Source: Gregory B. Lewis, "In Search of the Machiavelian Milquetoasts: Comparing Attitudes of Bureaucrats and Ordinary People," *Public Administration Review*, Vol. 50 (March–April 1990), pp. 220–227.

It is worth noting, however, that women and minorities are overrepresented in the very lowest civil service grades and are underrepresented in the highest. They also are far less evident in the special-agency merit systems (such as the Foreign Service and the FBI) and in the professional categories (scientists at the National Institutes of Health; doctors in the Public Health Service).

The representative character of the merit services here contrasts sharply with the situation in Great Britain and France. Those of aristocratic background have long dominated the upper levels of the civil service in the former; graduates of the elite *grandes écoles,* like the École National d'Administration, dominate in the latter.

Political Appointees

The highest policymaking positions in the federal bureaucracy (e.g., department secretaries, assistants to the president, and leading officials in the agencies) enter government service not by way of competitive merit examinations but by presidential appointment. There are about 1,200 of these top appointments that require Senate confirmation, and about 2,000 more that do not. These patronage positions, in theory at least, allow the president to translate his electoral mandate into public policy by permitting him to put his people in place in key policymaking jobs.

Most presidents use patronage not only to build support for their programs, but also to firm up their political coalition by being sensitive to the needs of important party factions and interest groups. Ronald Reagan used his appointments to advance a conservative agenda for America and made conservative beliefs a "must" for high bureaucratic appointments.[19] President Bill Clinton, on the other hand, promised to make government "look more like America," and he did so by appointing many women (see Figure 13.2) and minorities to top posts in his administration, including Attorney General Janet Reno, Secretary of Energy Hazel O'Leary, Secretary of Commerce Ron Brown, and Secretary of Housing and Urban Development Henry Cisneros.

Top political appointees are not very representative of the American people. They tend to be much better educated and wealthier than other Americans. They also tend to be professionals, independent businesspeople, or executives from large corporations and financial institutions.[20] This narrow and

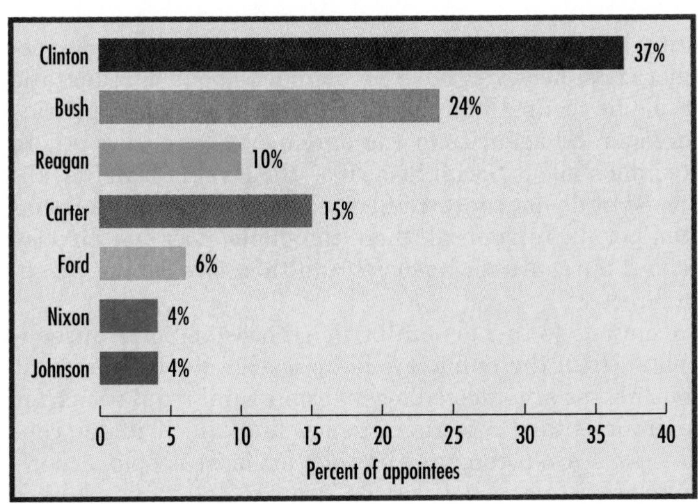

Figure 13.2 ■ **Percentage of Women and Minorities Appointed by the Presidents to the Executive Branch**

Presidents have appointed women and minorities to top posts in the federal government with increasing frequency. President Clinton has had a particularly notable record in this regard.

Source: *The Boulder Daily Camera,* Knight-Ridder Newspapers, February 13, 1996, p. 1.

privileged pool of appointees has important ramifications for the practice of democracy, because it is these officials who exercise the most discretion and make the most important policy decisions. To be sure, background is not everything in the determination of the outlook and behavior of political appointees, but it cannot be discounted either.

Top political appointees do not last very long on the job. On average, they stay in office only 22 months; political scientist Hugh Heclo called them "birds of passage."[21] They leave for many reasons. Most are accomplished people from the private sector who see government service as only a short-term commitment. Most make financial sacrifices to become top bureaucratic officials. Many don't find the notoriety appealing. Finally, many become frustrated by how difficult it is to change public policy and to implement it.

The Federal Bureaucracy and Democracy

In this section, we turn to the problem of the relationship between the bureaucracy and democracy. We use the definition of *democracy* set out in Chapter 1: a system of government characterized by popular sovereignty, political equality, and political liberty.

Popular Sovereignty

The term *popular sovereignty* refers to the fit between what the people want and what the government does. It requires that the bureaucracy be accountable to the people. Strangely enough, the framers gave very little thought to the accountability of the executive branch, assuming, perhaps, that once policy was made by Congress or the president, implementation would follow automatically.[22]

It should be understood that maximizing democratic accountability in the bureaucracy may conflict with other things we care about. Accountability assumes a close control of bureaucratic behavior, either directly by the people or indirectly by the people through Congress and the president. It implies limitations on bureaucratic discretion. Decreasing the scope of discretion may have the effect, however, of reducing the efficiency and effectiveness of bureaucratic institutions because it decreases the free play of bureaucratic expertise. Balancing the two goals is hard. Nevertheless, it is a choice American citizens must make.

Public Opinion Scrutiny by the public is an important instrument of democratic control. Most Americans, however, have no opinions about bureaucratic agencies as such. The public focuses mainly on the *content* of public policies rather than on the bureaucratic agencies or the bureaucrats who carry them out. Americans have opinions about Social Security—the level of benefits, eligibility, taxes, and so on—but do not concern themselves much with the Social Security Administration per se. In general, then, the public does not directly know or think much about bureaucratic agencies and therefore cannot be expected to control them directly.

There are many exceptions to this generalization, however. Some bureaucratic agencies are constantly in the public eye and occasion the development of opinions. So many businesses are affected by environmental regulations, for instance, that the Environmental Protection Agency finds itself under constant scrutiny. Because taxes are a constant irritant for most people, Americans tend to have opinions—not very favorable, to be sure—about the Internal Revenue Service and its agents. The conservative antitax tide was so strong in the country and in the 104th Congress in 1995, in fact, that the IRS felt it prudent to drop its very unpopular random audit program.

A disaster or a string of disasters can focus public attention on an agency, as NASA discovered to its discomfort with the *Challenger* explosion, the Hubble telescope (defective, but later repaired), the lost Mars probe, and aborted missions. The Branch Davidian tragedy in Waco focused a harsh light on the Bureau of Alcohol, Tobacco, and Firearms.

The prize for favorable opinion goes to the FBI during the years when it was headed by J. Edgar Hoover. Hoover carefully crafted the bureau's reputation as a great crime fighter through such public relations gimmicks as the "Ten Most Wanted List"; encouragement of, and technical support for, favored radio and television programs; and well-publicized staged arrests of easily apprehended bank robbers and kidnappers. More difficult problems, such as organized and white-collar crime, received a lower priority. None of the directors who followed Hoover have been able to play the public relations game with his skill. One result is that the FBI is no longer immune from growing hostility to the federal government.

For the most part, public opinion controls the federal bureaucracy only indirectly and intermittently. For popular sovereignty to be effective, it must usually work through elected officials, such as the president and the members of Congress, who are themselves accountable to the people.

The President and the Federal Bureaucracy The president, being the nation's chief executive, is the formal head of the executive branch. The president's leadership position is recognized in the Constitution's grant of executive power, its designation of the president as commander in chief of the armed forces, and its charge that he ensure that the laws will be faithfully executed. In reality, however, he has only limited abilities to control the executive branch. Virtually every modern president has been frustrated by the discovery that he cannot assume that bureaucrats will do what he wants them to do.[23]

Richard Nixon was so frustrated by his inability to move the federal bureaucracy that he came to think of it as an alien institution filled with his Democratic party enemies. His strategy was to intimidate bureaucrats or

Executive branch agencies often come to public attention after a highly visible disaster. Here, federal investigators try to determine the cause of an airline crash. While the airlines are private, nongovernmental entities, the National Transportation Safety Board investigates crashes.

bypass them. He created the notorious "plumbers" unit in the White House to act as his personal domestic surveillance and espionage unit. Revelation of its activities was one of the factors leading the House Judiciary Committee to recommend approval of three articles of impeachment in the Watergate scandal. Ronald Reagan, also distrustful of the regular bureaucracy and frustrated by what he considered its unwillingness to support his foreign policy program, allowed Oliver North to use the National Security Council to sell arms to Iran illegally and to funnel the money to the anti-Communist Contra rebels in Nicaragua.

Why Presidents Are Often Stymied by the Bureaucracy Why are presidents so frustrated by the bureaucracy? If a president is the chief executive, why can't he simply issue orders?

The sheer size and complexity of the executive branch is important. There is so much going on, in so many agencies, involving the activity of tens of thousands of people, that simply keeping abreast of what's going on is no easy task. Moreover, because of civil service regulations, presidents have no say about the tenure or salary of most bureaucrats. When presidents want something to happen, they are unlikely to get instantaneous acquiescence from bureaucrats who do not fear them as they would fear a private employer. Presidents also find that they are not the only ones trying to control the actions of bureaucrats; they must always share executive functions with Congress and sometimes with the courts. Finally, bureaucratic agencies are heavily insulated against presidential efforts to control them because of agency alliances with powerful interest groups.

Tools of Presidential Leadership Presidents are not entirely helpless, of course. They have a number of ways to encourage bureaucratic compliance.[24] Occasionally, because of a crisis or a widely shared national commitment, decisive bureaucratic action is possible, as during Roosevelt's New Deal era, Lyndon Johnson's first years as president, and Ronald Reagan's first administration.

Even during ordinary times, however, the president is not helpless. First, although it is difficult to measure precisely, the president's prestige as our only nationally elected political leader makes his wishes hard to ignore. Teddy Roosevelt once called the presidency a "bully pulpit." What he meant was that it is the president and only the president who can speak for the nation, set the tone for the government, and call the American people to some great national purpose. A popular president, willing and able to play this role, is hard to resist. Bureaucrats are citizens and respond like other Americans to presidential leadership. When a president chooses to become directly involved in some bureaucratic matter—for example, with a phone call to a reluctant agency head or a comment about some bureaucratic shortcoming during a press conference most—bureaucrats respond.

The power of appointment is also an important tool of presidential leadership. If a president is very careful to fill the top administrative posts with people who support him and his programs, he greatly increases his ability to have his way. Though the Senate must advise on and consent to many of his choices, it rarely interferes, recognizing, perhaps, that a coherent administration requires that a president have his own people in place.

The president's power as chief budget officer of the federal government is also a formidable tool of administration. No agency of the federal bureaucracy, for instance, can make its own budget request directly to Congress. The president's main budgetary instrument, the Office of Management and Budget (OMB), also has the statutory authority to block proposed legislation coming from any executive branch agency if it deems it contrary to the president's budget or program. Under Ronald Reagan, the OMB became a required review point for all new regulatory rules promulgated by the executive branch.

From the presidential point of view, the bureaucracy always seems on the verge of spinning out of control. In the years since World War II, a sizable bureaucracy (the White House office and the Executive Office of the President, described in Chapter 12) has developed to help the president stay on top of the far-flung executive branch. The aim is to reach the point at where there is a reasonable probability that things will happen when the president says, "Do this! Do that!" The development of the legislative, rule-making, and budget coordination responsibilities of the OMB under recent presidents is the most important example.[25]

Even with these tools, however, the president is limited in his ability to act as chief executive. This arrangement is very different from that in parliamentary regimes, in which the head of government exercises more direct and decisive control. A British prime minister, for instance, can appoint, transfer, or dismiss cabinet ministers at will; can reorganize the ministries; and can alter personnel policies, including the duties and pay of civil servants.

Congress and the Federal Bureaucracy Congress also exercises considerable influence over the federal bureaucracy.

Legislating Behavior The president and Congress share control over the executive branch. The congressional tools of control, in fact, are at least as formidable as those of the president.[26] Congress legislates the mission of bureaucratic agencies and the details of their organization and can change either one. Congress can also alter agency policy or behavior. It prevented the Federal Trade Commission for many years from requiring health warnings on cigarette packages, for example, because of pressure from the tobacco industry.

Controlling the Budget Congress can also use its control over agency budgets to influence agency behavior. In theory, Congress uses the budget process to assess the performance of each agency each year, closely scrutinizing its activities before determining its next **appropriation.** Congress has neither the time nor the resources actually to do such a thing and usually gives each agency some small increment over what it had in the previous year.[27] Of course, if a particular agency displeases Congress, its budget may be cut; if a new set of responsibilities is given to an agency, its budget is usually increased. Sometimes, these agency budget actions are taken with the full concurrence of the president; often, they are not. Congress sometimes lends a sympathetic ear and increases the budgets of agencies that are not favored by the president. Congress consistently gave more money than President Reagan wanted given to the EPA, the National Institutes of Health, and the National Science Foundation.

appropriation Legal authority for a federal agency to spend money from the U.S. Treasury.

Oversight Hearings Oversight hearings are an important instrument for conveying the views of the members of Congress to bureaucrats. There is a great deal of evidence that agency heads listen when the message is delivered clearly.[28] Congress does not always speak with a single voice, however. Congress is a highly fragmented and decentralized institution, and its power is dispersed among scores of subcommittees. Often, the activities of a particular bureaucratic agency are the province of more than a single committee or subcommittee, and the probability of receiving mixed signals from them is very high. A skilled administrator can often play off these competing forces against each other and gain a degree of autonomy for his or her agency.

Popular Sovereignty Reconsidered Popular sovereignty requires that government do what the people want it to do. What the people want is conveyed to the executive branch directly by public opinion and indirectly through Congress and the president. The materials we have reviewed in these pages suggests, however, that popular sovereignty over bureaucracy is less effective than we might like it to be in a democracy. The voice of public opinion is muted, while directions from the elected branches often are garbled and confused (see Figure 13.3).

Political Equality

In several respects, the bureaucracy meets the standard of political equality. There is no reason to believe that federal agencies treat classes of citizens unequally on a regular basis, for instance, though there are occasional incidents in which some—racial minorities and women, in particular—have been treated unfairly. We also know that the American people are fairly well represented among federal workers, both in a demographic sense and in terms of their outlooks, except with regard to political appointees. In another important respect, however, the standard of political equality is not met, namely, in the overrepresentation of interest groups. We have seen throughout this text that the interest group system is a major source of inequality in American politics.

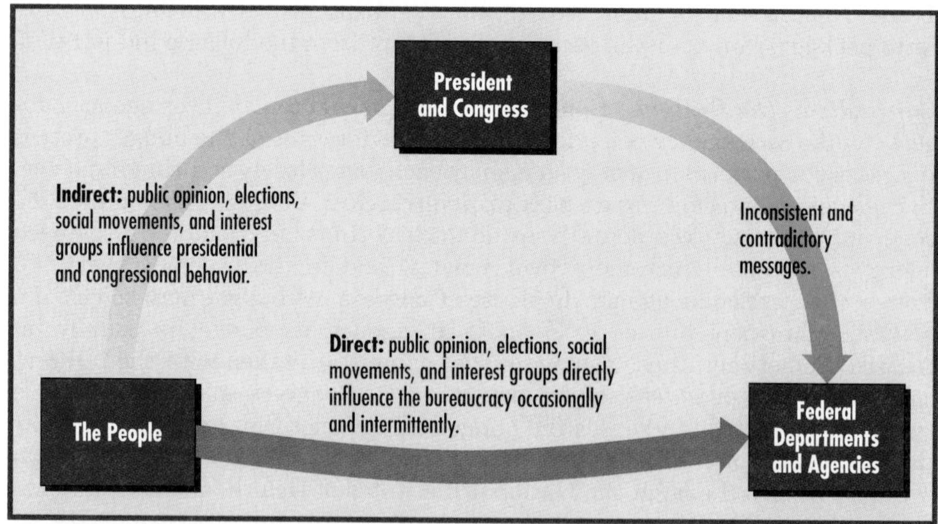

Figure 13.3 ■ **Popular Control of the Bureaucracy: Imperfect Popular Sovereignty**

Popular control of the federal bureaucracy is complex, indirect, and only partially effective. The public does not elect government bureaucrats, and public opinion has little direct impact on their behavior. However, the members of Congress and the president, all of whom are answerable to the electorate and attentive to public opinion, exercise an important influence on bureaucratic behavior. Because elected officials often send mixed signals, however, some of the effectiveness of such controls is diminished.

It should come as no surprise to learn that this inequality is re-created in many of the actions of the federal bureaucracy.

As we saw in Chapter 7, the federal bureaucracy is permeated by networks of government interest group alliances. In most cases, the interests that are disproportionately represented are business interests. Bureaucratic agencies often act as the supporters and protectors of these interest groups against other government bodies, other interests, and the public. Sometimes, the symbiotic relationship becomes so pronounced that the private interest group comes to make its own public policies and regulations, with the federal agency serving to legitimize its actions. Thus, bankers closely advise the Treasury Department on rules and regulations pertinent to bank policy. Political scientist Grant McConnell once described this situation in the following way: "The existence of an array of narrow-interest-centered power structures within the open framework of American political life is no secret. It is not a hidden government, it is highly visible to anyone who spends time in Washington or who reads news beyond the headlines."[29]

Interest groups are able to penetrate the federal bureaucracy and play an important role in its activities partly because of the absence of central administrative direction. With no clear leadership at the top, each agency must fashion its own political alliances in order to protect itself. Agencies fashion their alliances where they can: with other executive branch agencies when there are common interests, with congressional committees and subcommittees, and with interest groups. When the Reagan administration wanted to cut the annual appropriation for the National Science Foundation in the early 1980s, for instance, the foundation's leaders mobilized friendly members of Congress and university and scientific associations in its defense.

Another reason that agencies welcome interest group alliances is to help in their skirmishes with other federal agencies. The Defense Department and NASA annually disagree about how much of the space program ought to be devoted to military projects. In their struggle before the White House staff, the OMB, and Congress, each throws allied interest groups—defense contractors, scientific organizations, patriotic groups, and so on—into the breach.

Political Liberty

It is difficult to reach a firm conclusion about the role of the federal bureaucracy in protecting and sustaining political liberty because it is made up of so many agencies. For the most part, these agencies go about their business—delivering the mail, advising farmers, funding scientific research, collecting taxes, providing disaster relief, publishing statistical reports, issuing Social Security checks, and so on—without affecting political liberty one way or the other.

However, while federal agencies do not normally intrude on the liberty of Americans, enough of them have done so to cause concern among those who cherish freedom. During the post–World War I "Red Scare," the Immigration and Naturalization Service and the Justice Department harassed dissident organizations and individuals. During the early 1970s, the Justice Department funded "Red Squads" in local police departments to spy on and disrupt legal political organizations opposed to U.S. policy in Vietnam. Antiwar organizations were also the targets of infiltration by the Central Intelligence Agency (which is forbidden by law to engage in activities within U.S. borders), mail openings by the Postal Service, and international telephone intercepts by the National Security Agency. The Internal Revenue Service allowed itself to be used by presidents to harass their political opponents: Franklin Roosevelt and Richard Nixon were the most frequent abusers of this service.[30] Many NRA members worry that the Bureau of Alcohol, Tobacco, and Firearms has been guilty of violating the Fourth Amendment.

The agency that most often violated the freedoms of the American people, however, was the Federal Bureau of Investigation during the long tenure of Director J. Edgar Hoover. During the McCarthy hysteria in the 1950s, Hoover set up a program for Americans to report the suspicious behavior of their neighbors to the FBI. Under a program called Cointelpro, the bureau engaged in a campaign to harass and discredit civil rights leaders and to disrupt the legal activities of civil rights organizations. The vendetta against Martin Luther King, Jr., was particularly ugly. Apparently appalled by King's "I Have a Dream" speech at the Lincoln Memorial in 1963 (for it established him in Hoover's eyes as the "most dangerous and effective Negro leader in the country"), Hoover decided to "take him off his pedestal [and] reduce him completely in influence." To this end, the FBI tapped King's phones, spied on his activities, leaked incriminating information about his private life to the press, mailed anonymous letters to King's wife implying improprieties on the part of her husband, and directed threats at him, including a bizarre note suggesting that he commit suicide.[31]

It may be that the behavior of the FBI and other agencies damaging to civil liberties are the proverbial exceptions that prove the rule. There is no way to know for sure. These examples suggest, however, that Americans cannot afford to be complacent about the state of their liberties. Their preservation is part of the continuing struggle for democracy.

Longtime FBI Director J. Edgar Hoover too often used the powers of his office to violate the rights and liberties of people and groups he disliked.

Common Criticisms of the Federal Bureaucracy

Bureaucrats are often portrayed in popular culture as lazy paper shufflers or as indifferent, unresponsive, inhumane clerks denying us the benefits or services to which we are entitled. Occupational-prestige polls always find civil servants near the bottom (close to politicians and used-car salespeople, we might add). Politicians feed on this popular culture when they "run against Washington," promising to pare the bureaucracy down to size and to get it off the backs of the American people.

Let's look at the most common criticisms of the federal bureaucracy and see how much merit they have.

Criticism Number 1: The Federal Bureaucracy Is Always Expanding

Surprisingly, this complaint has no basis in fact. While the number of federal civilian employees expanded dramatically in the twentieth century, it has remained relatively stable since the mid–1960s, at roughly 3 million. Since the early 1990s it has actually been dropping (see Figure 3.3), though federal regulations and mandates have required states and localities to hire more people. Government does more and spends more money today than it did in 1950, but it does so with about the same number of employees. Nor is it the case that all bureaucratic agencies grow without stopping. Even important ones decrease in size, as have the Departments of Defense and State since 1970.

Criticism Number 2: The Federal Bureaucracy Is Ineffective

By effective, we mean "able to carry out missions and reach goals." The record of the federal bureaucracy with respect to effectiveness is mixed. NASA landed a man on the moon in less than a decade, fulfilling President Kennedy's promise to the American people. But by the same token, NASA has suffered repeated problems in its shuttle program over the years.

Those who worry about government effectiveness must contend with the fact that the framers did not necessarily want government to be effective, because they were worried first and foremost about tyranny. They created a system in which power would be fragmented. They were willing to trade some efficiency for inoculation against an overbearing and threatening government. Remember, also, that the federal bureaucracy was not designed as a rational machine with a clear chain of command, as in most democratic nations. It is, instead, an architectural hodgepodge, with parts added on as the political process demanded.

Finally, one must ask, "Compared to what?" While most of us feel absolutely certain that the federal bureaucracy cannot be as effective in meeting its goals as private organizations, evidence that supports such a belief is not overwhelming. Many studies on productivity, costs, and innovation show no public-private differences.[32] Large organizations, public or private, may be quite similar. It took private American automakers at least two decades to formulate an effective response to the challenge of foreign imports, for example. More research needs to be done on this issue, to be sure, but one would do well to be skeptical of the conventional wisdom about government bureaucratic ineptitude.

Criticism Number 3: The Federal Bureaucracy Is Wasteful and Inefficient

Waste in government is such an enduring theme in American politics that it is hard to imagine a political campaign without it. Once again, however, the matter is more complex than it may seem.

In actuality, the opportunity for agencies to waste money is quite limited, since the bureaucracy has discretionary control over only about 5 percent of the total federal budget. Ninety-five percent is **earmarked** for specific purposes or is distributed to beneficiaries by formula, or **entitlements.** Almost all of the federal budget goes to pay the interest on the national debt, to direct payments to individuals (e.g., military pensions and Social Security benefits), and to grants-in-aid to states and localities. The small discretionary pot that remains is closely monitored and is encumbered with strict rules on its use. None of this suggests that there isn't waste or inefficient use of taxpayers' money in bureaucratic agencies. It is to say, however, that the charges are probably exaggerated. Of course, if what we mean by "waste of taxpayers' money" is spending on programs that we don't like (for some, it may be welfare; for others, it may be a new strategic bomber), then our complaint is not with the bureaucracy but with the policymaking branches of the federal government: the president and Congress. Government can seldom please everyone.

earmarked A budget expenditure tied to a particular program or purpose.

entitlements Government benefits that are distributed automatically to citizens who qualify on the basis of a set of guidelines set by law. Americans over the age of 65 are entitled to Medicare coverage, for instance.

Perhaps more important, there are certain things we want government to do that are hard to assess in terms of economic costs and benefits, but that most Americans consider worth doing: pollution control, first-class airports and harbors, national defense, and scientific research come to mind. These things involve "public goods" that the private market does not price efficiently or provide adequately.

Where there is inefficiency and waste, of course, the president and Congress should insist that the bureaucracy do better.

Criticism Number 4: The Federal Bureaucracy Is Mired in Red Tape

Americans complain incessantly about bureaucratic rules, regulations, formal procedures, and forms. Our discontent is summarized by the term **red tape.** At one time or another, we have all felt stymied by rules and procedures, irritated by delays, and frustrated by forms and have cried out, "Red tape!" But how valid is the complaint?

red tape Popular term for overbearing bureaucratic rules and procedures.

Again, we run into the problem of measurement. How can we be sure that there is more red tape in the federal bureaucracy than there is in other large institutions? Surely, there are miles of red tape (forms, procedures, permissions, and the like) in universities and large, private corporations. Moreover, red tape is often in the eye of the beholder. What is a waste of time and an inconvenience to one person may represent good public policy to another. The charge of "red tape" is almost always hurled at agencies that are carrying out policies we don't like. For example, following federal procedures for the disposal of dangerous chemicals may not be what chemical companies would want to do on their own, but Americans have shown that they want strong environmental protection laws. Monitoring disposal is part of what protects us.

To be sure, there is some truth to many of the stereotypes about the federal bureaucracy. It is large; there are programs that do not work; there is waste and inefficiency; there is a great deal of red tape. We would suggest, however, that the stereotypes greatly exaggerate the extent of the problem, for our measuring instruments are very imprecise. Nor do we have reason to believe that the pathologies are unique to the federal bureaucracy. Finally, we must recognize that many of the pathologies, to the extent that they do exist, do not necessarily originate in the bureaucracy but are imposed by other governmental bodies and the provisions in the Constitution.

Reforming the Federal Bureaucracy

How should we fix what's wrong with the federal bureaucracy? It depends on what we think is wrong.

Scaling Back the Size of the Bureaucracy

"Cutting the Fat" For those who worry that the federal bureaucracy is simply too big and costly, what might be called the "meat axe" approach is the preferred strategy. Virtually every candidate worth his or her salt promises to "cut the fat" if elected. Bill Clinton made such a promise during the 1992 presidential campaign, and he carried through after his election. In the early weeks of his administration, he ordered that 100,000 federal jobs be eliminated within four years, that freezes be placed on the salaries of government workers, that cost-of-living pay adjustments be reduced, and that the use of government vehicles and planes be sharply restricted.[33]

The stalement between President Clinton and Congress on the 1996 budget resulted in two partial shutdowns of the federal government. Negative popular reactions to this action showed that Americans were not as anxious to cut back the size of government as many believed.

The Republicans came to power in Congress in 1995 promising the wholesale elimination of government agencies and departments. House Republicans managed to pass bills to abolish the Departments of Education and Energy, but the proposals languished in the Senate.

privatization The process of turning over certain government functions to the private sector.

Privatizing An increasingly popular strategy for scaling back the federal bureaucracy is to turn over several of its functions and responsibilities to the private sector. The **privatization**[34] approach is based on two beliefs: (1) that private business can almost always do things better than the government, and (2) that competitive pressure from the private sector will force government agencies to be more efficient. Many states and local communities have "contracted out" to private companies public services like trash collecting, the management of jails and prisons, and even the schools. For many years, the federal government has contracted out some activities; the defense contracting system by which the Department of Defense buys fighter planes, submarines, and missiles from private corporations is a good example. Advocates of privatizing simply want the process to go further, turning over to private companies things such as the postal system, the federal prisons, and air traffic control.

Critics worry that privatizing government carries two significant costs.[35] First, private business might not provide services that do not turn a profit. Delivery of mail to remote locations is something that the Postal Service does, for instance, but that a private company might decide not to do. Second, a private business under government contract is several steps removed from political control, and the normal instruments of democratic accountability, however imperfect, might not be as effective as they are in controlling government agencies. The voice of the public, that is to say, whether voiced in public opinion polls or elections, might not be heard with much clarity by private companies.

One strong argument against the privatization of government agencies is that private corporations might discontinue—or at least increase the price of—services that are costly and less profitable. For example, the U.S. Postal Service provides mail delivery to remote and less populous areas, such as the Alaskan outback, for the same cost as it does for the rest of the country. A private, profit-motivated company might be less inclined to do so.

Reinventing Government

President Clinton turned over the responsibility for "reinventing government" to Vice-President Al Gore at the beginning of his administration. The term *reinventing government* comes from a popular and influential book of the same name written by David Osborne and Ted Gaebler.[36] Their proposal for transforming the federal government involves not only cutting the fat and privatizing (as discussed in the previous section), but introducing business principles into the executive branch. Their idea is that government agencies will provide better public services if they are run like private businesses. Forcing agencies to compete for customers, for instance, would motivate government employees to be more attentive to their customers (citizens). Paying employees on the basis of their performance rather than by pay grade (the present system) would make them work harder and better. Giving government managers the authority to assign and reassign tasks, like managers in private businesses, they argue, would increase the efficiency of the agency. Allowing agency heads more freedom to experiment—to allowing them to be more entrepreneurial, if you will—might lead to innovative solutions to pressing social problems.

Gore's *National Performance Review* report followed closely the proposals made by Osborne and Gaebler. Though a few of his proposals have been put into effect by executive order, most await action by Congress.

President Clinton and Vice-President Al Gore cut "red tape" as a dramatic way to introduce Gore's plan to reinvent government by introducing business principles into the operations of the Executive Branch. Congress approved only a few of the plan's provisions.

Lani Guinier's Quiet Dignity

The Struggle for Democracy

Representing the NAACP's Legal Defense and Education Fund, University of Pennsylvania law professor Lani Guinier had been fighting the Republican-dominated Civil Rights Division of the Justice Department for years. Now, she was President Bill Clinton's nominee to head the Civil Rights Division as assistant attorney general. Little did she or President Clinton know what lay in store after he nominated her in 1993.

Lani Guinier had argued in court and in her scholarly publications that means had to be found to address the problem of the powerlessness of permanent minorities (such as African-Americans) living in majoritarian democratic societies. She suggested that, despite their right to vote, African-Americans would always be outvoted in the United States, even on matters of vital interest to them, because of their inescapable minority status. None of the existing voting rights laws (such as the Voting Rights Act of 1965) can overcome this problem, even though they do an excellent job of protecting the right of members of minority groups to vote and run for public office.

In her scholarly writings, Guinier examined how various voting mechanisms might better serve to account for and represent minority interests. Most of the mechanisms are commonly used in other democratic countries. At various times she explored the usefulness of proportional representation (see Chapter 8), weighted voting schemes that would encourage white lawmakers to be more responsive to black concerns, and the reservation of certain vital issues to determination by the African-American community alone. Another mechanism she examined was cumulative voting, widely used in the corporate world. In this scheme, a voter has the same number of votes as there are seats to fill (say, five votes to fill five seats in a state's congressional delegation); the voter can cast all these votes for a single candidate or divide them among several. Under such a voting arrangement, minority group members might concentrate their votes on one or two candidates, ensuring the election of at least a few of their choices. Under conventional voting arrangements, a minority cannot be successful in the election of a candidate to any of the five seats.

Guinier's nomination set off a firestorm. Even friendly critics were concerned about what seemed a "we-they" view of race relations in which an African-American minority was always at the mercy of a white majority. (To be fair to Guinier, she supported similar protections for the white minority in South Africa.) For Republican conservatives still smarting over the Democratic Senate majority's treatment of Ronald Reagan's Supreme Court nominee Robert Bork (who was rejected by the Senate Judiciary Committee) and of George Bush's nominee Clarence Thomas (who was

Protecting Against Bureaucratic Abuses of Power

There are many who believe that a bureaucracy of the size and shape of our present one, while necessary in a modern society, is potentially dangerous. Closer control over the bureaucracy by elected political bodies and by clear legislative constraints has been the preferred solution. There are many legislative enactments that try to keep bureaucratic activity within narrow boundaries. The Legislative Reorganization Act of 1970 was partially designed to improve congressional subcommittee oversight capabilities. The Budget and Impoundment Control Act of 1974 was designed to enhance the ability of Congress to shape the federal budget and to monitor agency use of federal monies. The Freedom of Information Act of 1966 was designed to enhance the ability of the press and private citizens to obtain information about bureaucratic policies and activities. The Ethics in Government Act of 1978 strengthened requirements of financial disclosure by officials and prohibitions against conflicts of interest.

barely confirmed after accusations of sexual harassment were brought by Anita Hill), the Guinier nomination was a golden opportunity to turn the tables. Clint Bolick, a conservative activist and close friend of Justice Thomas, led the charge with an op-ed piece in the *Wall Street Journal,* in which he claimed that "she demands equal legislative outcomes, requiring abandonment not only of the 'one person, one vote' principle, but majority rule itself." The *Journal* chose as its headline for the piece, "Clinton's Quota Queen."

From then on, in increasingly acrimonious attacks, politicians, journalists, and pundits almost always referred to her as the "quota queen." Attacks came, predictably, from conservatives: Minority Leader Robert Dole, PBS commentator Paul Gigot, Senator Alan Simpson, columnist George Will, and Bolick were the most prominent. Inaccuracies poured from the mainstream press: the Associated Press wire service reported that Guinier favored giving African-Americans the power to veto legislation (which she firmly opposed); the *Columbia Journalism Review* found that most reporters had not read her work and had depended on sources firmly opposed to her views.

The drumbeat of criticism became so loud and persistent that even Democratic liberals began to abandon Guinier. Senator Joseph Biden, chair of the Judiciary Committee, relayed his concerns to President Clinton. So did Senator Ted Kennedy. The first African-American woman senator, Carol Mosely Braun of Illinois, refused to meet with her. Finally, President Clinton, caving in to the criticism and claiming that he had not read her scholarly work, withdrew the nomination.

In retrospect, almost everyone involved agreed that she had been treated shabbily: she was not allowed by the White House to answer her critics, was not granted a hearing before Congress to explain her views, and was dropped without warning by the president. As conservative thinker William Bennett put it, "I think she was given a raw deal." Yet, throughout, Lani Guinier maintained a quiet dignity, never lashing out at unfaithful friends or unfair critics. In the weeks and months after her nomination had been withdrawn, Guinier was free to explain her ideas on national news and interview programs. Many Americans began to see her as an articulate, sensitive, and insightful analyst of the enduring problem of racial division in America and of what might be done to overcome it. Ironically, as the racial divide in the United States became glaringly evident after the O. J. Simpson trial and Louis Farrakhan's Million Man March, many saw a painfully lost opportunity in the failed appointment. The only one who seemed to come out of the episode with dignity and enhanced stature was Lani Guinier.

This story is based on materials from Neil A. Lewis, "Woman in the News: Carol Lani Guinier," *New York Times* (May 5, 1993), p. A5; Bob Dart, "Ex-nominee Goes Easy on Clinton," *Atlanta Constitution* (June 5, 1993), p. A8; Stephen L. Carter, "Foreword," in Lani Guinier, *The Tyranny of the Majority* (New York: Free Press, 1994).

Some reformers would like to see greater protection provided for **whistleblowers,** those bureaucrats who report corruption, financial mismanagement, abuses of power, or other official malfeasance. All too often, these courageous people, acting in the public interest, are fired or harassed on the job. This happened to Ernest Fitzgerald, a civilian cost accountant at the Pentagon, who lost his job after he revealed $2-billion cost overruns on the C5A military transport plane (he eventually won reinstatement from the courts, but it took 14 years to do so). The Merit Systems Protection Board is supposed to offer protection against such actions, but most observers do not believe that it has been entirely effective.

whistleblowers People who bring official misconduct in their agencies to public attention.

Increasing Popular Participation

Many people worry that federal bureaucrats go about their business without the public having much say in what they do. Without citizen input, it is argued, bureaucrats lose touch with the people they are supposed to serve—a situation

The Pentagon, said to be the world's largest building, houses the government's largest agency, the Department of Defense.

that leads to irrational policies and citizen alienation from the bureaucracy. Citizen participation in agency affairs has been pushed by some reformers as a solution.[37] The antipoverty program of Lyndon Johnson's Great Society required the "maximum feasible participation" of the poor in its design and implementation. President Bush's housing secretary Jack Kemp introduced tenant councils to help administer federal housing programs at the neighborhood level.

Enhancing Democracy

There are, finally, proposals to enhance democracy and accountability in bureaucratic affairs. For the people to rule, popular sovereignty, political equality, and political liberty must flourish.

Popular sovereignty requires that the elected representatives of the people closely control the bureaucracy. Popular sovereignty implies that administrative discretion should be narrowed as much as possible and that clear directions and unambiguous policies should be communicated by elected officials to bureaucratic agencies. (Note that this is a very different goal from the one envisioned by the advocates of privatization and "reinventing government.") How might such a thing be achieved?

Some have argued that the only public official who has an interest in seeing that the bureaucracy *as a whole* is well run and coherently organized is the president. Accordingly, one suggestion for reform is to increase the powers of the president so that he can be the chief executive, in fact and not just in name.[38] Another way to enhance the ability of elected leaders to issue clear directives and coherent policies is to have them speak with a more unified voice. But this, we have seen, is unlikely to happen in our constitutional system of separation of powers and divided government. Short of a fundamental constitutional reform that would change the United States into a parliamentary democracy—which is not about to happen—the only instrument that is available for overcoming the separation of powers is the political party. Political party reform would seem to be at the very top of the agenda, then, for those who care about the state of popular sovereignty in the United States.

We have learned throughout this book that the interest group system is a major factor in American political life that works to undermine political

POLITICS AND FILM

The FBI Takes Credit

During the summer of 1964, three civil rights workers involved in a campaign to help black citizens register to vote (in a project known as Mississippi Freedom Summer) disappeared after being arrested for a minor traffic violation in Philadelphia, Mississippi. The bodies of the three young people (one black and two white) were later found by FBI agents, buried in an earthen dam. The perpetrators turned out to be local members of the Ku Klux Klans and their allies in the Philadelphia sheriff's office. Director Alan Parker's *Mississippi Burning* (1988) is a powerful fictionalized account of the investigation that brought the murderers to justice. The film is wrenchingly graphic, showing, as no other film has, the terror under which blacks lived in the Deep South during this period. Lynchings, beatings, and church burnings are portrayed in moving detail.

Willem Dafoe and Gene Hackman portray two FBI agents sent to Philadelphia to investigate the disappearances. The Dafoe character, who has comes to the FBI by way of Harvard Law School and the Justice Department, plays by the book and makes no progress in cracking the case. The Hackman character, a native Mississippian and former small-town sheriff, is familiar with towns like Philadelphia, and his contacts with the townspeople slowly help him uncover the conspiracy. When the investigation reaches a dead end because of Dafoe's earnest but ineffectual methods, and the violence against blacks reaches a fever pitch, Hackman decides to use his own brutal methods. The Klan is fought with Klan methods, and justice is achieved by vigilante means.

In addition to its call for vigilante justice as the only way to get results, a common theme in Hollywood films, there are several other troubling aspects of *Mississippi Burning.* First, the film seriously misrepresents the role of African-Americans in their own liberation. Parker shows them only as helpless victims, sheeplike and unprepared for what befalls them, turning to white outsiders (like the FBI) for help and protection. Nowhere to be seen on the screen are the courageous efforts to transform Mississippi by African-Americans themselves. The activists of the Southern Christian Leadership Conference, the Congress of Racial Equality, and the Student Nonviolent Coordinating Committee (which conceived of and ran the Mississippi Freedom Summer project) are absent. So, too, are the many ordinary Mississippi African-Americans who were brave enough to join rallies, protests, and demonstrations.

Second, Parker seriously misrepresents the role of the FBI. While it is true that the Bureau broke the case, it must be pointed out that the FBI was no friend of the civil rights movement during the long tenure of J. Edgar Hoover. Indeed, Hoover was actively hostile to the movement and its leadership. He believed that the movement was communist at its core and spent much of his time trying to discredit it and its leaders. His vendetta against Martin Luther King, Jr., is well known, and the Bureau's unwillingness to protect civil rights workers throughout the South is almost legendary. The Bureau was particularly remiss in not protecting the Freedom Riders and activists trying to register voters in Mississippi. Parker's error in showing a black FBI agent in his film is particularly glaring, for the Bureau was lily-white at the time. Hoover was literally pushed into the Philadelphia investigation by public pressure and began to integrate the Bureau only when he could no longer hold out. To turn the tragedy of Chaney, Goodman, and Schwerner (the three civil rights workers who had disappeared) into a celebration of the FBI may strike some people as odd indeed.

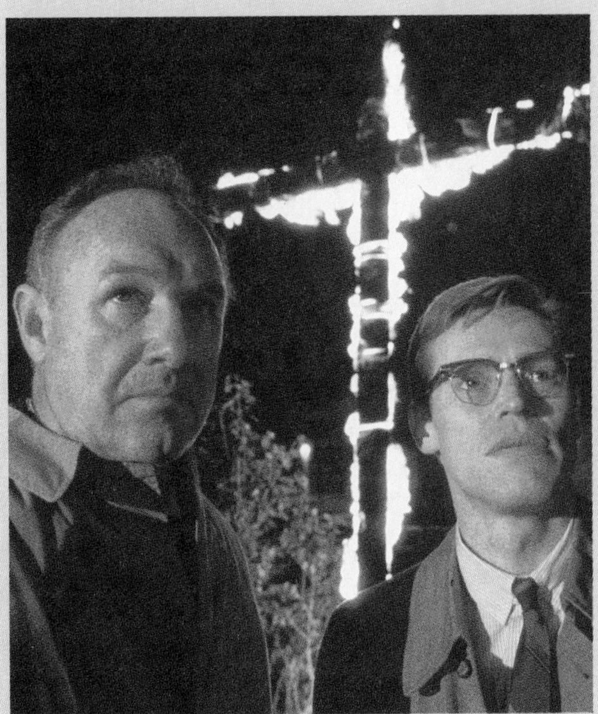

Gene Hackman and Willem Dafoe portray FBI agents who battle the KKK in Mississippi in the mid-1960s.

equality. We have seen how interest groups have carved out privileged positions at various places in the federal bureaucracy, made all the worse by their alliances with assorted congressional committees and subcommittees. The most significant reform to enhance political equality would involve diminishing the power and influence of interest groups.

To the extent that bureaucratic intrusions on political liberty involve autonomous agencies' following their own agenda—such as the FBI under Hoover—enhancing the control of elected officials over them would represent important safeguards of liberty. To the extent that bureaucratic intrusions on political liberty involve actions carried out at the request of elected officials—like the presidential use of the IRS against opponents—improving the degree of popular control over elected political officials would represent an additional safeguard. Such reforms would not, however, completely guarantee the protection of liberty from bureaucratic action. What remains to us in the face of violations of our rights is our constitutional tradition, our willingness to stand up for our rights and the rights of others, and the courts.

Summary

The executive branch has grown in size and responsibility. This growth is a consequence of a transformation in the conception of the proper role of government because of structural changes in the economy and the society. While *bureaucracy* is not a popular term in the American political tradition, we have created a sizable one. The reason is partly, that bureaucratic organizations have certain strengths that make them attractive for accomplishing large-scale tasks.

Bureaucrats are involved in three major kinds of activities: executing the law, regulating, and adjudicating disputes. In each of these, they exercise a great deal of discretion. Because they are unelected policymakers, democratic theory demands that we be concerned about who the bureaucrats are. In the merit services, they are very much like other Americans in terms of background and attitudes. Political appointees, however, the most important bureaucratic decision makers, are very different from their fellow citizens. Democracy also requires that the federal bureaucracy be under popular control, that political equality be the context of bureaucratic behavior, and that the executive branch enhance, rather than endanger, freedom. The evidence on whether these goals have been achieved is mixed. The executive branch is fairly responsive to the popular will, but popular control is undermined by incoherent organization and divided control between the president and Congress. Bureaucratic operations depart substantially from the norm of political equality because of the significant influence of interest groups. Political liberty has occasionally been threatened by such agencies as the FBI.

Bureaucratic pathologies, while real, are either exaggerated or the result of political forces outside the bureaucracy itself: the constitutional rules and the struggle between the president and Congress.

Proposals to reform the executive branch are related to what reformers believe is wrong with the federal bureaucracy. Those who worry most about size and inefficiency propose budget and personnel cuts, privatization, and the introduction of business principles into government. Those who want to make democracy more of a reality propose strengthening our political parties, giving more control over the bureaucracy to the president, and diminishing the role of interest groups.

Suggested Readings

Goodsell, Charles T. *The Case for Bureaucracy,* 3rd ed. Chatham, NJ: Chatham House, 1994.
A well-written polemic that gives the other side of the bureaucratic story.

Gruber, Judith E. *Controlling Bureaucracies: Dilemmas in Democratic Governance.* Berkeley: University of California Press, 1987.
An exploration of the practical and philosophical problems inherent in different ways of controlling the bureaucracy.

Heclo, Hugh. *A Government of Strangers.* Washington, DC: Brookings Institution, 1977.
A look at political appointees and how they attempt to gain control of the agencies they head.

Osborne, David and Ted Gaebler, *Reinventing Government* (Reading, MA: Addison-Wesley, 1992).
The bible for "reinventing government" advocates.

Skowronek, Stephen. *Building a New American State: The Expansion of National Administrative Capacities, 1877–1920.* New York: Cambridge University Press, 1982.
A careful historical analysis of the first budding of an expanded federal bureaucracy.

The Washington Monthly.
Washington's leading journal of "bureaucracy bashing"; filled with outrageous, and sometimes illuminating, stories.

Wilson, James Q. *Bureaucracy: What Government Agencies Do and Why They Do It.* New York: Basic Books, 1991.
A look at the federal bureaucracy by one of the nation's leading conservative academics.

Internet Sources

Fedworld http://www.fedworld.gov/
The gateway to the federal government's numerous web sites and gophers; connections to virtually every federal department, bureau, commission, and foundation, as well as access to government statistics and reports.

Jefferson Project http://www.stardot.com/jefferson/government/
Access to Fedworld and other government web sites and gophers, as well as to academic and journalistic accounts and analyses of the federal government.

Yahoo: Executive Branch http://www.yahoo.com/Government/ExecutiveBranch_Branch/
Similar to Jefferson Project above. Which one to use depends on personal taste.

Notes

1. Dale Russakoff, "Panic in Middle America," *Washington Post Weekly Edition* (May 15–21, 1995), p. 10. All remaining quotes in this section are from the story by Russakoff.

2. Charles T. Goodsell, *The Case for Bureaucracy* (Chatham, NJ: Chatham House Publishers, 1994); B. Guy Peters, *American Public Policy,* 4th ed. (Chatham, NJ: Chatham House Publishers, 1996).

3. Wallace Sayre, "Bureaucracies: Some Contrasts in Systems," *Indian Journal of Public Administration,* Vol. 10, No. 2 (1964), p. 223.

4. Richard J. Stillman II, *The American Bureaucracy* (Chicago: Nelson-Hall, 1987), p. 18.

5. Alexis de Tocqueville, *Democracy in America,* Vol. 1 (New York: Vintage Books, 1945), p. 59.

6. Stephen Skowronek, *Building a New American State: The Expansion of National Administrative Capacities, 1877–1920* (New York: Cambridge University Press, 1982), pp. 19–46.

7. See Edward S. Greenberg, *Capitalism and the American Political Ideal* (Armonk, NY: M. E. Sharpe, 1985); Samuel P. Hays, *The Response to Industrialization* (Chicago: University of Chicago Press, 1957); Gabriel Kolko, *The Triumph of Conservatism* (Chicago: Quadrangle, 1967); Robert Wiebe, *The Search for Order: 1877–1920* (New York: Hill & Wang, 1967); James Weinstein, *The Corporate Ideal in the Liberal State* (Boston: Beacon Press, 1968).

8. Matthew A. Crenson and Francis E. Rourke, "American Bureaucracy Since World War II," in Louis Galambos, ed., *The New American State* (Baltimore: Johns Hopkins University Press, 1987).

9. See Michel Crozier, *The Bureaucratic Phenomenon* (Chicago: University of Chicago Press, 1964); Anthony Downs, *Inside Bureaucracy* (Santa Monica, CA: Rand, 1964); Alvin W. Gouldner, *Patterns of Industrial Bureaucracy* (New York: Free Press, 1954); James G. March and Herbert Simon, *Organizations* (New York: Wiley, 1958); Robert Michels, *Political Parties* (New York: Free Press, 1962, originally published in 1915); Max Weber, *Economy and Society* edited by Guenther Roth and Claus Wittich, based on the 4th German edition, University of California Press, Berkeley 1978.

10. Kenneth J. Meier, *Politics and the Bureaucracy: Policymaking in the Fourth Branch of Government* (Boston: Duxbury Press, 1979), p. 52.

11. B. Guy Peters, *American Public Policy: Promise and Performance* (Chatham, NJ: Chatham House Publishers, 1996), p. 100.

12. Peters, *American Public Policy,* p. 103.

13. Theodore J. Lowi, *The End of Liberalism,* 2nd ed. (New York: Norton, 1979).

14. G. Guy Peters, "Searching for a Role: The Civil Service in American Democracy," *International Political Science Review,* Vol. 14, (1993), p. 376.

15. Ibid., p. 375.

16. See Samuel Krislov and David H. Rosenbloom, *Representative Bureaucracy and the American Political System* (New York: Praeger, 1981); Charles T. Goodsell, *The Case for Bureaucracy,* 3rd ed. (Chatham, NJ: Chatham House, 1994).

17. Kenneth John Meier, "Representative Bureaucracy: An Empirical Analysis," *American Political Science Review,* Vol. 69 (June 1975), p. 532; Stanley Rothman and S. Robert Lichter, "How Liberal Are Bureaucrats," *Regulation* (November–December 1983), pp. 35–47.

18. See Goodsell, *The Case for Bureaucracy,* chap. 5; Meier, "Representative Bureaucracy," pp. 537–539.

19. Richard P. Nathan, *The Administrative Presidency* (New York: Wiley, 1983).

20. Beth Mintz, "The President's Cabinet, 1897–1973," *Insurgent Sociologist,* Vol. 5, No. 3 (Spring 1975), pp. 1–13.

21. Hugh Heclo, *A Government of Strangers* (Washington, DC: Brookings Institution, 1977), p. 103.

22. Judith E. Gruber, *Controlling Bureaucracies: Dilemmas in Democratic Governance* (Berkeley: University of California Press, 1987), p. 7.

23. Richard Neustadt, *Presidential Power* (New York: Wiley, 1960).

24. Terry M. Moe, "Control and Feedback in Economic Regulation," *American Political Science Review,* Vol. 79 (1985), pp. 1094–1116; Richard W. Waterman, *Presidential Influence and the Administrative State* (Knoxville: University of Tennessee Press, 1989).

25. Francis E. Rourke, "Bureaucracy in the American Constitutional Order," *Political Science Quarterly,* Vol. 102, No. 2 (Summer 1987), pp. 217–232.

26. Matthew D. McCubbins, "The Legislative Design of Regulatory Structure," *American Journal of Political Science,* Vol. 29 (1985), pp. 421–438.

27. Richard Fenno, *The Power of the Purse* (Boston: Little, Brown, 1966); Aaron Wildavsky, *The Politics of the Budgetary Process* (Boston: Little, Brown, 1964).

28. John A. Ferejohn and Charles R. Shipan, "Congressional Influence on Administrative Agencies: A Case Study of Telecommunications Policy," in Lawrence C. Dodd and Bruce I. Oppenheimer, eds., *Congress Reconsidered,* 4th ed. (Washington, DC: Congressional Quarterly Press, 1989).

29. Grant McConnell, *Private Power and American Democracy* (New York: Knopf, 1967), p. 339.

30. David Burnham, *A Law unto Itself: Power, Politics, and the IRS* (New York: Random House, 1989).

31. Quotes are from the *New York Times* (April 16, 1976), p. 1. On the campaign against King, see Taylor Branch, *Parting the Waters: America in the King Years* (New York: Simon & Schuster, 1988); Noam Chomsky, *Cointelpro* (New York: Monad Press, 1975); David Garrow, *The FBI and Martin Luther King* (New York: Norton, 1981); Kenneth O'Reilly, *Racial Matters: The FBI's Secret File on Black America, 1960–1972* (New York: Free Press, 1989).

32. See Goodsell, *The Case for Bureaucracy,* pp. 61–69.

33. Ibid., p. 177.

34. See Emanuel S. Savas, *Privatization: The Key to Better Government* (Chatham, NJ: Chatham House, 1987); Sheila B. Kamerman and Alfred J. Kahn, eds., *Privatization and the Welfare State* (Princeton: Princeton University Press, 1989).

35. Roberta Lynch and Ann Markusen, "Can Markets Govern?" *American Prospect* (Winter 1994), pp. 125–134.

36. David Osborne and Ted Gaebler, *Reinventing Government* (Reading, MA: Addison-Wesley, 1992).

37. Milton Kotler, *Neighborhood Government* (Indianapolis: Bobbs-Merrill, 1969); Marilyn Gittell, *Participants and Participation* (New York: Praeger, 1967).

38. Terry M. Moe, "The Politics of Bureaucratic Structure," in John E. Chubb and Paul E. Peterson, *Can the Government Govern?* (Washington, DC: Brookings Institution, 1989), p. 280; John E. Chubb and Paul E. Peterson, eds., "American Political Institutions and the Problem of Governance," in Chubb and Peterson, eds., *Can the Government Govern?* (Washington, DC: Brookings Institution, 1989), p. 41; James Sundquist, *Constitutional Reform and Effective Government* (Washington, DC: Brookings Institution, 1986).

CHAPTER 14

The Courts

IN THIS CHAPTER

- ★ How the federal court system is organized and how it operates
- ★ What judicial review is and how it came to be
- ★ How the Supreme Court works
- ★ How and why judicial interpretations of the Constitution have changed
- ★ The role of the Supreme Court in a democratic society

The Court Changes Course on *Roe v. Wade*

On January 22, 1973, the U.S. Supreme Court made abortion legal in the United States. Writing for a 7–2 majority in the case of *Roe v. Wade,* Justice Harry Blackmun argued that a state's interest in regulating abortion to protect the life of a fetus can override a woman's fundamental right to privacy only after the second trimester of pregnancy, when the fetus becomes viable. Before *Roe,* the availability of abortion was entirely up to state legislatures, and few were willing to allow the practice.

Sixteen years later, in the case of *Webster v. Reproductive Health Services* (1989), the Supreme Court retreated from *Roe*'s prohibition against government interference with a woman's right to choose in the first six months of her pregnancy. Speaking for a 5–4 majority, Chief Justice William Rehnquist upheld a Missouri law that barred the use of public money and facilities to perform abortions at any time and required physicians to test for fetal viability at 20 weeks. Significantly, the language in the Court's written opinion invited other states to legislate various limits on abortions. Guam, Louisiana, Utah, and Pennsylvania did so in very short order.

Why did the Supreme Court change its mind? The Constitution had not been amended in the years between *Roe* and *Webster,* yet the Court's interpretation of the constitutional standing of privacy and the right of the states to regulate abortions had changed substantially. To understand this transformation, it is important to understand that judicial decisions are influenced by changes in the political and governmental environment within which the Supreme Court operates. There is no doubt that major transformations had occurred in American politics in the decade and a half following *Roe.* Most important was the rising tide of conservatism in American politics and the resurgence of the fortunes of the Republican party, and the decline of liberalism and the fortunes of the Democratic party. This transformation affected each of the branches of the federal government, including the Supreme Court.

The *Roe* decision was a product of its time. It was decided by a Court in 1973 that could sometimes still muster a liberal majority. Moreover, the decision was rendered at a time when the women's movement, then at the height of its political influence (see Chapter 10), was pushing unrestricted access to abortions as a major objective.

However, the *Roe* decision also was a catalyst for the formation of the Prolife movement, which is committed to ending abortion in the United States. This movement would become an important part of the conservative Republican coalition that dominated American politics in the 1980s. One student of the Prolife movement has described the important place of the abortion issue in this political transformation:

> Abortion suddenly became the right issue, and what an issue it was. As the bottom-line demand of the women's movement, it was a quick and easy symbol for sexual permissiveness and feminism, and opposition to it signaled an uneasiness about the whole feminist agenda. It was a Catholic issue, theoretically mobilizing those millions of voters. It was a moral issue, giving conservatives that human dimension they so often seemed to lack. It had a fanatic following who had already demonstrated their capacity to work tirelessly. It was the kind of issue that people could rally around.[1]

The conservative movement, with the antiabortion issue at its core, managed to break away significant numbers of Catholics and southern white Protestants from the New Deal coalition (see Chapter 8), which had dominated American politics for so long, and helped to refashion the public agenda in the nation. It also contributed mightily to the election of Ronald Reagan and a Republican Senate in 1980, and to the reelection of Reagan in 1984.

A string of retirements from the Supreme Court gave President Reagan the opportunity to refashion the Court in his own conservative image. Though he lost in his attempt to appoint Robert Bork to the Court, Reagan gained Senate approval for the appointment of other conservatives: Sandra Day O'Connor, Antonin Scalia, and Anthony Kennedy. He also succeeded in elevating Justice William Rehnquist to the position of chief justice. The shift in the nation's politics and the appointive powers of a popular president led to the formation of a new and formidable Supreme Court conservative majority that was willing to reconsider its earlier abortion decision.

This story tells us many things about the Supreme Court that will be elaborated on in this chapter. Like the president and the Congress, the Court makes decisions that have important consequences for the American people. Unlike the president and the Congress, it does not pass new laws; it interprets the meaning of the law, especially the Constitution. In doing so, however, the Court cannot help but make law. In this sense, the Court is a national policymaker.

This story also shows that the Court is embedded in a rich governmental, political linkage and structural environment that shapes its behavior. The other branches of government impinge on its deliberations; political linkage institutions such as elections, interest groups, and social movements matter; and structural factors such as economic and social change influence its agenda and decisions.

Finally, because the story shows that an unelected Court makes important decisions about public policies, it raises fundamental questions about our democracy, the central theme of this book. In this chapter, we consider the ambiguous relationship of the Court and democracy.

The Structural Context of Court Behavior

Constitutional Powers

> **The judicial Power of the United States shall be vested in one supreme Court, and in such inferior Courts as the Congress may from time to time ordain and establish.**
>
> **THE U.S. CONSTITUTION, ARTICLE III, SECTION 1**

> **We are under a Constitution, but the Constitution is what the judges say it is, and the judiciary is the safeguard of our liberty and our property under the Constitution.**
>
> **—CHIEF JUSTICE CHARLES EVANS HUGHES, SPEECH, 1907[2]**

The Constitution speaks only briefly about the judicial branch and doesn't provide much guidance about what it is supposed to do or how it is supposed to go about its job. It says little about its powers in relationship to the other two federal branches or about its responsibilities in the area of constitutional interpretation. Article III is considerably shorter than Articles I and II on the Congress and the president. It creates a federal judicial branch; it states that judges shall serve life terms; it specifies the categories of cases the Court may or must hear (to be explained later); and it grants Congress the power to create additional federal courts as needed. Article III of the Constitution is virtually devoid of detail.

The Concept of Judicial Review

Extremely interesting is the Constitution's silence about **judicial review,** the power of the Supreme Court to declare state and federal laws and actions null and void when they conflict with the Constitution. Debate has raged for many years over the question of whether the framers intended that the Court should have this power.[3]

judicial review The power of the Supreme Court to declare unconstitutional the actions of other branches and levels of government.

The framers surely believed that the Constitution ought to prevail when other laws were in conflict with it. But did they expect the Court to make the decisions in this matter? Jefferson and Madison thought that Congress and the president were capable of rendering their own judgments about the constitutionality of their actions. Alexander Hamilton, on the other hand, believed that the power of judicial review was inherent in the notion of the separation of powers and was essential to balanced government. As he put it in *The Federalist,* No. 78 (see Appendix), the very purpose of constitutions is to place limitations on the powers of government, and it is only the Court that can ensure such limits in the United States. The legislative branch, in particular, is unlikely to restrain itself without the helping hand of the judiciary. In Hamilton's words,

> The interpretation of the laws is the proper and peculiar province of the courts. A constitution is, in fact, and must be regarded by the judges as a fundamental law. It must therefore belong to them to ascertain its meaning, as well as the meaning of any particular act proceeding from the legislative body. If there should happen to be an irreconcilable variance between the two, that which has the superior obligation and validity ought, of course, to be preferred: in other words, the constitution ought to be preferred to the statute; the intention of the people to the intention of their agents.[4]

While the Constitution is silent on the issue of judicial review, most of the Founders probably agreed with Alexander Hamilton (left), who argued that the Supreme Court's power to interpret the Constitution and declare state and federal laws and actions unconstitutional is inherent in the notion of the separation of powers. However, it was not until the Supreme Court's 1803 *Marbury v. Madison* decision that Chief Justice John Marshall (right) affirmed the Court's power of judicial review.

Hamilton's view was undoubtedly the prevailing one among the framers. They were firm believers, for instance, in the idea that there was a "higher law" to which governments and nations must conform. Their enthusiasm for written constitutions was based on their belief that governments must be limited in what they could do in the service of some higher or more fundamental law, such as that pertaining to individual rights. The attitudes of the time strongly supported the idea that judges, being free of popular pressures and conversant with the legal tradition, were best able to decide when statutory and administrative law were in conflict with fundamental law.[5] (See Table 14.1 on the varieties of law.) It still remains something of a mystery, however, why the framers said nothing explicitly about such an important power.

Marbury v. Madison Chief Justice John Marshall boldly claimed the power of judicial review for the U.S. Supreme Court in the case of *Marbury v. Madison* in 1803.[6] The case began with a flurry of judicial appointments by President John Adams in the final days of his presidency, after his Federalist party had suffered a resounding defeat in the election of 1800. The apparent aim of these so-called midnight appointments was to establish the federal courts as an outpost of Federalist party power (federal judges are appointed for life) in the midst of Jeffersonian control of the presidency and the Congress.

William Marbury was one of the midnight appointments, but he was less lucky than most. Though his commission was signed and sealed, it had not

Table 14.1

The Varieties of Law

Law in the United States has four possible sources: a constitution, a legislature, an administrative agency, or a court.

The Constitution	*Constitutional law* is the most basic form of law in that it sets the rules of the game for the entire governing process and requires that no other law or regulation may violate it. In our federal system, the U.S. Constitution is not only superior to all statutes and regulations made by the other branches of government, but also is superior to state constitutions.
The legislature	*Statutes* are the laws made by legislative bodies, including the Congress of the United States. They are usually more detailed than constitutional provisions.
Administrative agencies	*Administrative rules and regulations* are issued by officials of the executive branch when authorized to do so by Congress. When the Occupational Safety and Health Administration issues a regulation requiring shields on band saws in lumber mills, it is making administrative law.
The courts	*Court-made law* is fashioned in the course of deciding cases that come before the courts. The interpretations that courts make of all other kinds of law—constitutional, statute, and administrative—are binding on every person and institution that falls within the jurisdiction of the particular court. Supreme Court interpretations (known as opinions) of constitutional issues, such as the unacceptability of segregated education in *Brown v. Board of Education,* are the most far-reaching examples of this kind of lawmaking.

been delivered to him before the new administration took office. Jefferson's secretary of state, James Madison, refused to deliver the commission, sensing what the Federalists were up to. Marbury sued Madison, claiming that the secretary of state was obligated to deliver the commission, and asked the Supreme Court to issue a **writ of mandamus** (a court order compelling a public official to act) to force Madison to do so.

writ of mandamus A court order that forces an official to act.

Marshall faced a quandary. If the Court decided in favor of Marbury, Madison would almost surely refuse to obey, opening the Court to ridicule for its weakness. The fact that Marshall was a prominent Federalist political figure might even provoke the Jeffersonians to take more extreme measures against the Court. On the other hand, if the Court ruled in favor of Madison, it would suggest that an executive official could defy without penalty the clear provisions of the law.

Marshall's solution was worthy of Solomon. The Court ruled that William Marbury was entitled to his commission and that James Madison had broken the law in failing to deliver it. By this ruling, the Court rebuked Madison. However, the Court said it could not compel Madison to comply with the law, because that part of the Judiciary Act of 1789 that granted the Court the power to issue writs of mandamus was unconstitutional. It was unconstitutional because it expanded the **original jurisdiction** of the Supreme Court as defined in Article III, which could not be done except by constitutional amendment.

original jurisdiction The location where a particular kind of case is initially heard in court.

On the surface, the decision was an act of great modesty. It suggested that the Court could not force the action of an executive branch official. It suggested that Congress had erred in the Judiciary Act of 1789 by trying to give the Supreme Court too much power. Beneath the surface, however, was a less modest act: the claim that judicial review was the province of the judicial branch alone. In Marshall's words, in his written opinion, "It is emphatically the province and duty of the judicial department to say what the law is." In making this claim, he was following closely Hamilton's argument in *The Federalist,* No. 78.

The Supreme Court used the power of judicial review with great restraint, perhaps recognizing that its regular use would invite retaliation by the other branches of government. Judicial review was not exercised again until 1857, 54 years after *Marbury,* and has been used to declare acts of Congress unconstitutional only about a hundred times since then. The Court has been much less reluctant to overrule the laws of the states and localities, however; it has done so over a thousand times (see Table 14.2).

Judicial Review Abroad Judicial review does not exist in all democratic countries. In Great Britain, where there is no written constitution or bill of rights, and no separation of powers or checks and balances, the fundamental law is simply the body of laws passed by Parliament. No court can declare a parliamentary action null and void. In Switzerland, the high court can exercise judicial review over the actions of the cantons (similar to our states), but not over those of the national assembly. As in the United States, however, judicial review exists in Australia, Japan, Germany, and Canada.

Judicial Review and Democracy Judicial review raises questions about democracy. It involves the right of a body shielded from direct accountability to the people—federal judges are appointed, not elected, and serve for good behavior (meaning for life)—to set aside the actions of government bodies whose members are directly elected. Some believe that this is the only way to protect

Table 14.2

Supreme Court Decisions Involving Judicial Review, 1789–1991

Year	Previous Supreme Court Decisions Overruled	Acts of Congress Held Unconstitutional	State and Local Laws Overturned
1789–1800 (Pre-Marshall)	0	0	0
1801–1835 (Marshall Court)	3	1	18
1836–1864 (Taney Court)	4	1	21
1865–1873 (Chase Court)	4	10	33
1874–1888 (Waite Court)	13	9	7
1889–1910 (Fuller Court)	4	14	92
1910–1921 (White Court)	5	12	125
1921–1930 (Taft Court)	6	12	143
1930–1940 (Hughes Court)	21	14	83
1941–1946 (Stone Court)	15	2	32
1947–1952 (Vinson Court)	13	1	45
1953–1969 (Warren Court)	45	25	166
1969–1986 (Burger Court)	52	34	207
1986– (Rehnquist Court)	21	7	56

Source: Adapted from David O'Brien, *Storm Center: The Supreme Court in American Politics,* 3rd ed. (New York: Norton, 1993), p. 209.

the rights of political and racial minorities, to check the potential excesses of the other two government branches and the states, and to preserve the rules of the democratic process. Others believe that judicial review has no place in a democratic society. We will come back to this issue later in this chapter.

The Federal Court System: Organization and Jurisdiction

Ours is a federal court system. There is one system for the national government (the federal courts) and one in each of the states. Each state has its own system of courts, which adjudicate cases on the basis of its own constitution, statutes, and administrative rules. In total, the great bulk of laws, legal disputes, and court decisions (roughly 99 percent) are located in the states. The most important political and constitutional issues, however, eventually reach the federal courts. In this chapter, our focus is on the federal courts.

Constitutional Provisions

The only court specifically mentioned in the Constitution's Article III is the U.S. Supreme Court. The framers left to Congress the tasks of designing the details of the Supreme Court and establishing "such inferior courts as may from time to time ordain and establish." Beginning with the Judiciary Act of 1789, Congress has periodically reorganized the federal court system. The end result is a three-tiered pyramidal system (see Figure 14.1). At the bottom are 94 federal district courts, with at least one district in each state. In the middle

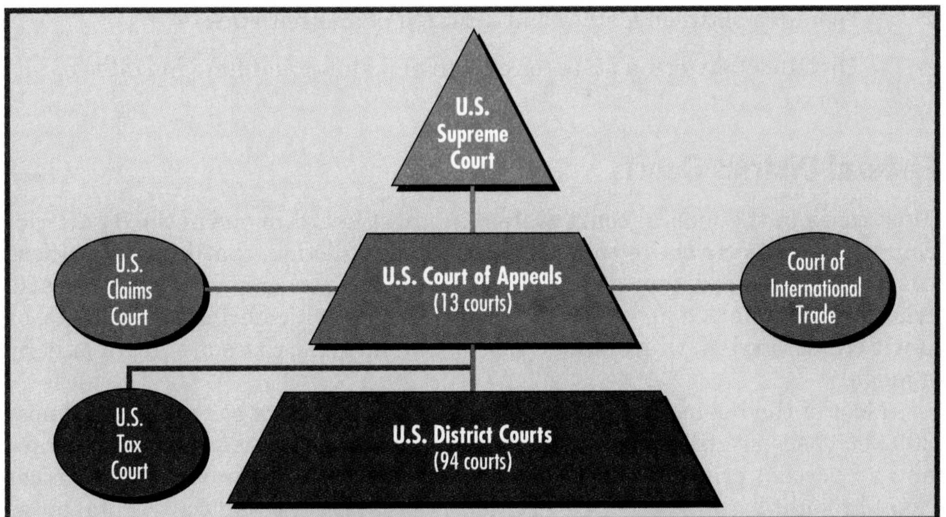

Figure 14.1 ■ **The U.S. Federal Court System**

The federal court system is a three-tiered pyramidal system, with the Supreme Court at the top. Below it are 13 federal courts of appeal and 94 district courts, with at least one district in each state. Additional courts exist to hear cases in highly specialized areas, such as taxes and international trade.

Source: Administration Office of the U.S. Courts, Washington, D.C.: 1995.

are 13 courts of appeal. At the top of the pyramid is the Supreme Court. These courts are called **constitutional courts** because they were created by Congress under Article III, which discusses the judicial branch. Congress has also created a number of courts to adjudicate cases in highly specialized areas of concern, such as taxes and maritime law. These were established under Article I, which specifies the duties and powers of Congress, and are called **legislative courts.**

constitutional courts Federal courts created by Congress under the authority of Article III of the Constitution.

legislative courts Highly specialized federal courts created by Congress under the authority of Article I of the Constitution.

Article III does not offer many guidelines for the federal court system, but the few requirements that exist are very important. The Constitution requires, for instance, that federal judges serve "during good behavior," which, in practice, means for life. Since impeachment by Congress is the only way to remove federal judges, the decision about who will be a judge is an important one. Article III also states that Congress cannot reduce the salaries of judges once they are in office. This provision was designed to maintain the independence of the judiciary by protecting it from legislative intimidation.

Article III also specifies the kinds of cases that are solely the province of the federal courts:

- The Constitution—disputes involving the First Amendment or the commerce clause, for example.
- Federal statutes and treaties—including disputes involving ambassadors and other diplomats
- Admiralty and maritime issues
- Controversies in which the U.S. government is a party
- Disputes between the states

- Disputes between a state and a citizen of another state
- Disputes between a state (or citizen of a state) and foreign states or citizens

Federal District Courts

grand juries Groups of citizens who decide whether there is sufficient evidence to bring an indictment against accused persons.

petit (trial) juries Trial juries; they hear evidence and sit in judgment on charges brought in civil or criminal cases.

Most cases in the federal court system are first heard in one of the 94 district courts. District courts are courts of original jurisdiction, that is, courts where cases are first heard; they do not hear appeals from other courts. They are also trial courts; some use juries (either **grand juries,** which bring indictments, or **petit (trial) juries,** which decide cases), and in some, cases are heard only by a judge.

Most of the business of the federal courts takes place at this level. Almost 300,000 cases are filed annually, roughly 80 percent of them being civil cases and 20 percent criminal cases. The former include everything from antitrust cases brought by the federal government, to commercial and contract disputes between citizens (or businesses) of two or more states. The latter include violations of federal criminal laws, such as bank robbery, interstate drug trafficking, and kidnapping.

Most civil and criminal cases are concluded at this level. In a relatively small number of cases, however, one of the parties to the case may feel that a mistake has been made in trial procedure or in the law that was brought to bear in the trial. Or one of the parties may feel that a legal or constitutional issue is at stake that was not taken into account at the trial stage or was wrongly interpreted. In such cases, one of the parties may appeal to a higher court.

U.S. Courts of Appeal

circuits The 11 geographical jurisdictions and 2 special courts that hear appeals from the federal district courts.

appellate courts Courts that hear cases on appeal from other courts.

briefs Documents prepared by attorneys and presented to courts; these documents set out the arguments in cases.

opinion (of the court) The majority opinion that accompanies a Supreme Court decision.

precedents Rulings by courts that guide judicial reasoning in subsequent cases.

stare decisis The legal doctrine that says precedent should guide judicial decision making.

The United States is divided into 12 geographic jurisdictions (see the map in Figure 14.2), called **circuits,** to hear appeals from the district courts. There is also a thirteenth appeals court, called the U.S. Court of Appeals for the Federal Circuit, located in Washington, D.C., which hears cases on patents and government contracts. Almost 40,000 cases are filed annually in the federal appeals courts, though only about 5,000 reach the formal-hearing stage. Cases cannot originate in these courts but must come to them from other courts. Because they exist only to hear appeals, they are referred to as **appellate courts.** New factual evidence cannot be introduced before such courts; no witnesses are called or cross-examined. Lawyers for each side argue with each other and make their case for the judges not by the examination of witnesses or documents, but by the submission of **briefs** that set out the legal issues at stake. Judges usually convene as panels of three (though, on important cases, there are more—sometimes seven members) to hear oral arguments from the lawyers on each side of the case and to cross-examine them on points of law. Weeks or even months later, after considerable study, writing, and discussion among the judges, the panel issues a verdict. In important cases, the verdict is usually accompanied by an **opinion** that sets forth the reasoning behind the decision.

Once appellate decisions are published, they become **precedents,** which guide the decisions of other judges. While judges do not slavishly follow precedents, they tend to move away from them only when necessary and only in very small steps. This doctrine of closely following precedents as the basis for legal reasoning is known as **stare decisis.**

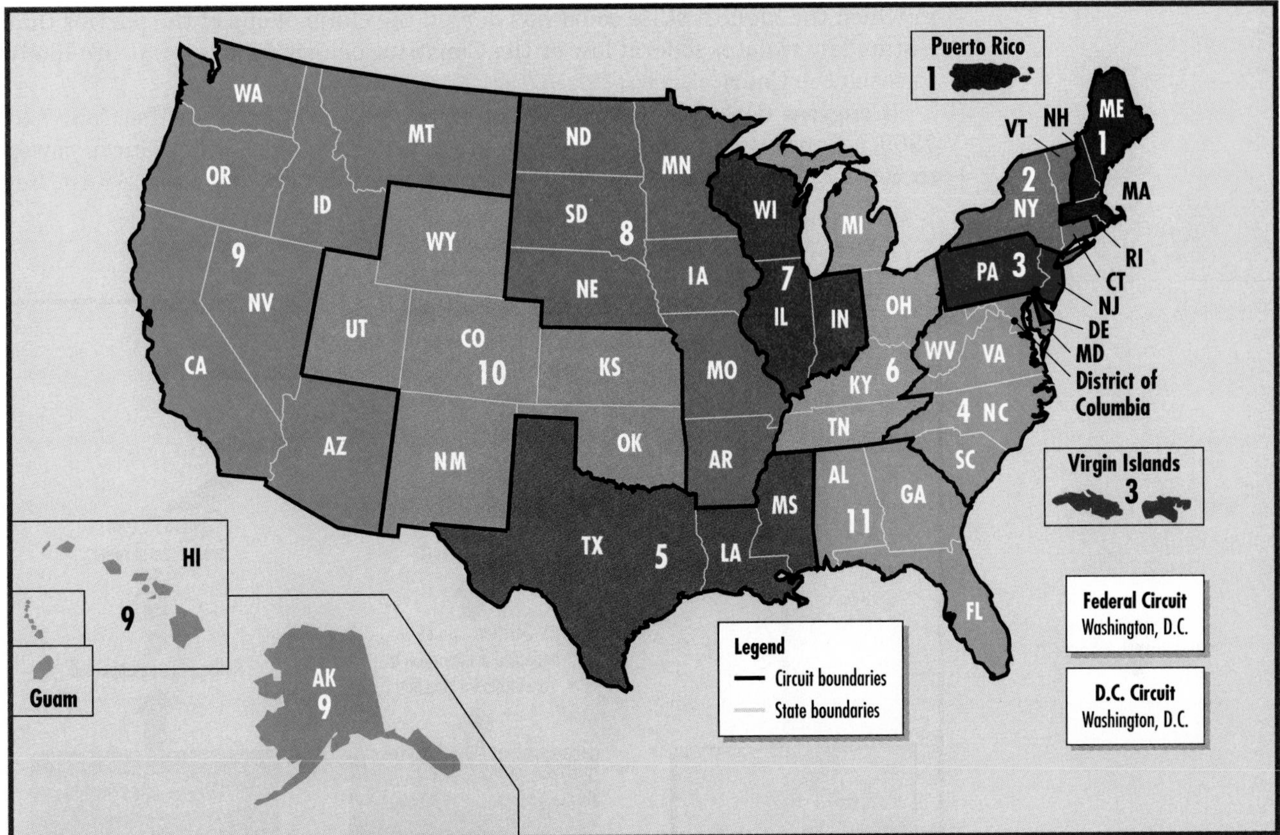

Figure 14.2 ▪ **U.S. Federal Circuit Courts**

The United States is divided into 11 geographic regions, each housing a federal circuit court of appeals; there are also 94 U.S. district courts, where most cases originate. Two additional circuit courts of appeal, the D.C. Circuit Court and the Federal Circuit Court, are located in Washington, D.C.

Source: Administrative Office of the U.S. Courts, January 1983.

The Supreme Court

Congress decides how many judges sit on the Supreme Court. The first Court had 6 members. The Federalists reduced the number to 5 in 1801 to prevent newly elected president Thomas Jefferson from filling a vacancy. In 1869, Congress set the number at its present 9 members (8 associate justices and a chief justice). It has remained this way ever since, weathering the failed effort by President Franklin Roosevelt to "pack" the Court with more politically congenial justices by expanding its size to 15.

The Supreme Court is both a court of original jurisdiction and an appellate court. That is, some cases must first be heard in the Supreme Court. Disputes involving ambassadors and other diplomatic personnel, two or more states, the federal government and a state, or a state and a citizen from another state start in the Supreme Court rather than in some other court.

The Supreme Court also, and most importantly, serves as an appellate court for the federal appeals courts and for the highest courts of each of the states. Cases in which a state or a federal law has been declared unconstitutional, or in which the highest state court has denied the claim of one of the parties that a state law violates federal law or the Constitution (see Figure 14.3), are likely to reach the Court.

Congress determines much of the appellate jurisdiction of the Court. In 1869, a Congress controlled by radical Republicans removed the Court's power to review cases falling under the Reconstruction program for the South. Re-

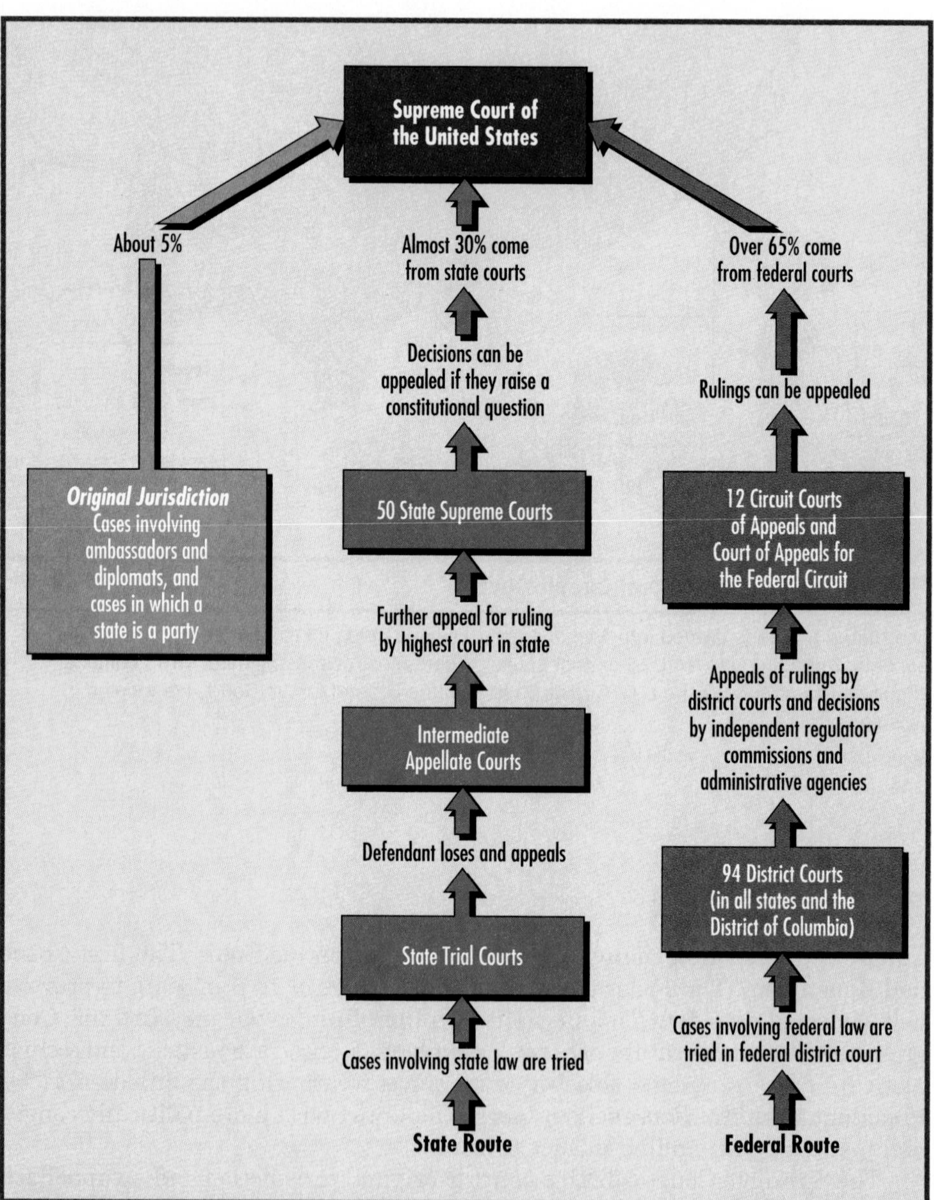

Figure 14.3 ■ How Cases Get to the Supreme Court

The vast majority of cases that reach the Supreme Court come to it from the federal court system. Most of the others come on appeal from the highest state courts. A handful originate in the Supreme Court itself.

Source: Adapted from David O'Brien, *Storm Center: The Supreme Court in American Politics,* 3rd ed. (New York: Norton, 1993).

sponding to a plea from Chief Justice Rehnquist to lighten the Court's caseload, Congress dropped the requirement that the Supreme Court *must* hear cases in which a state court declares a federal statute unconstitutional. It can choose, but is not obligated, to do so.

Because it is the highest appellate court in the federal court system, the decisions and opinions of the Supreme Court become the main precedents on federal and constitutional questions for courts at all other levels of jurisdiction. It is for this reason that Supreme Court decisions receive so much attention from other political actors, the media, and the public.

Appointment to the Federal Bench

Because federal judges are appointed for life and make important decisions, it matters in a democratic society who they are and how they get to the bench. If they are isolated from popular influence, then democracy is at risk. We will see that the courts are not divorced from or above the political process but are an integral part of the political interplay of American life. The voice of the people affects judges. Whether that voice is strong enough to sustain democracy, however, is a subject that we will address throughout the remainder of this chapter.

Who Are the Appointees?

Appointees to the federal bench must be (by custom, not law) lawyers, but they need not have judicial experience. Almost one-half of all Supreme Court justices during this century have had no prior experience as judges. Among the ranks of the "inexperienced" are some of the most prominent and influential justices in our history, including John Marshall, Louis Brandeis, Harlan Stone, Charles Evans Hughes, Felix Frankfurter, and Earl Warren, as well as the present chief justice, William Rehnquist.[7]

Because federal judges are lawyers, they tend to come from privileged backgrounds. Moreover, federal judges, and particularly Supreme Court justices, come from the most elite parts of the legal profession. For the most part, they are white male Protestants from upper-income or upper-middle-class backgrounds, who attended the most selective and expensive undergraduate and graduate institutions.[8] There have been only two African-American justices (Thurgood Marshall and Clarence Thomas), two women (Sandra Day O'-Connor and Ruth Bader Ginsburg), seven Jews, and seven Catholics on the High Court during its history, through 1996. The representativeness of judicial appointees at the circuit and district court levels is better, but still a long way from reflecting the composition of the legal profession, much less the American people as a whole. If you believe, as most observers of the courts do, that judges bring their personal outlook to bear when they are deciding cases, then this significantly unrepresentative composition of the federal judiciary may be cause for concern.

The Appointment Process

Federal judges assume office after they have been nominated by the president and approved by the Senate. Presidents pay special attention to judicial appointments, since they are a way for presidents to affect public policy long after they leave office.

In some respects, all presidents approach the appointment process in the same way. After defining the kind of person in whom he is interested in general terms, the president delegates the task of identifying judicial candidates to one or more senior White House staff members and the attorney general. Lists of potential candidates are drawn up after wide consultation with influential senators (who must eventually approve the nominee), party luminaries, state and local bar associations, legal scholars, and leaders of important interest groups. The FBI conducts background checks of the leading candidates, and the American Bar Association is asked to evaluate them. Presidents tend to consider only those who have been active in their own party, for they are the most likely to share the presidents' policy and ideological commitments.[9] Some Supreme Court nominees have even been close advisers to the president before their appointment: Felix Frankfurter to Roosevelt; Arthur Goldberg to Kennedy; Abe Fortas to Johnson; and Warren Burger to Nixon.

Presidents take many things into consideration besides merit. No president wants a nomination rejected by the Senate, so he and his advisers consult with key senators, especially those on the Judiciary Committee, before nominations are forwarded. Nominations for district court judgeships are subject to what is called **senatorial courtesy,** the right of the senior senator from the president's party in the state where the district court is located to approve the nominee. In the past, senatorial courtesy was so strong that the appointment process was reversed in practice: senators simply forwarded the name of the person whom they wanted nominated, and the White House concurred. Senatorial courtesy does not operate, however, in appointments to the circuit courts, whose jurisdictions span more than a single state, or to the Supreme Court, whose jurisdiction is the entire nation. Nevertheless, presidents must be extremely attentive to the views of key senators.

senatorial courtesy The tradition which holds that judicial nominations for federal district court appointments must be cleared by the senior senator of the president's party from the relevant state.

On occasion, despite presidential efforts to placate it, the Senate has refused to give its "advice and consent." Of the 143 nominees for the Supreme Court since the founding of the Republic, the Senate has refused to approve 28 of them, only 5 in this century. There have also been several near defeats; Bush's nominee Clarence Thomas was confirmed by only a margin of four votes after questions were raised about his legal qualifications and about sexual harassment charges brought by Anita Hill. Rejection of nominees has usually happened when the president was weak or when the other party was in control of the Senate, especially when the president was trying to make **lame-duck appointments**—appointments made as the president was known to be leaving office. Several recent presidential defeats—Nixon's nominees G. Harold Carswell and Clement Haynsworth, and Reagan's nominee Robert Bork—were the product of deep ideological differences between the president and a Senate controlled by the other political party.

lame-duck Ones who serve out terms after being defeated in an election or after deciding not to run again.

Though presidents must be concerned about the merit of their candidates and their acceptability to the Senate, they also try by their appointments to make their mark on the future. Presidents go about this in different ways.

President John F. Kennedy, worried about the fate of his legislative program and foreign policy initiatives in a Congress that was dominated by powerful southern committee chairmen, nominated judges who would be acceptable to the South. Many of these prosegregation judges eventually frustrated Kennedy and his brother, Attorney General Robert Kennedy, when the administration later pushed its civil rights agenda.

Jimmy Carter wanted to be remembered as the president who opened public service and the courts to women and minorities. He appointed more women, blacks, and Latinos to the federal bench than any president before him.

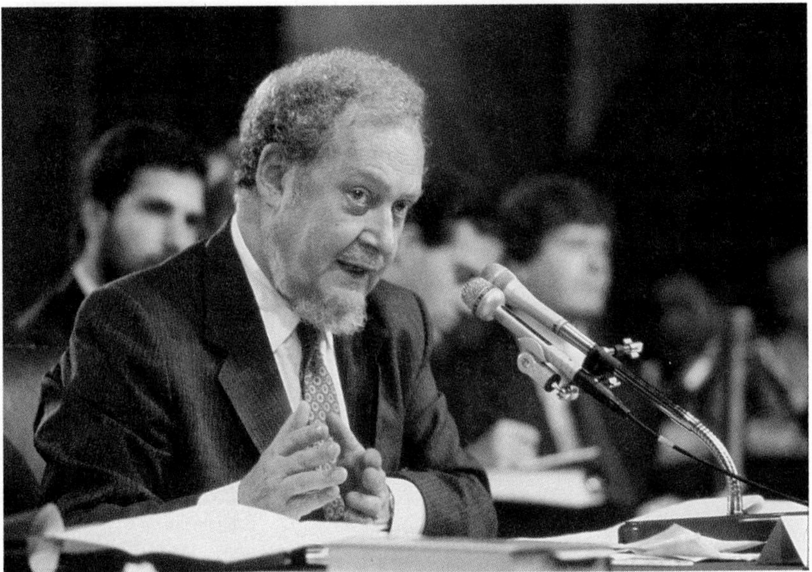

Robert Bork, one of Ronald Reagan's nominees for the Supreme Court, was turned down by a historic margin after lengthy committee hearings and a bruising debate on the floor of the Senate. Many Americans and a majority of senators considered his views too extreme.

Other presidents have been more interested in nominating judges who shared their ideological and program commitments. John Adams nominated John Marshall and a number of other judges to protect Federalist principles during the ascendancy of the Jeffersonians. Franklin Roosevelt tried to fill the courts with judges who favored the New Deal. Ronald Reagan favored conservatives who were committed to rolling back affirmative action and other civil rights claims, abortion rights, protections for criminal defendants, and broad claims of standing in environmental cases. George Bush continued this conservative drift with his nomination of Clarence Thomas.

Bill Clinton, eager to avoid a bitter ideological fight in the Senate, where he was trying to forge a bipartisan coalition to support the North American Free Trade Agreement and a national crime bill, nominated two moderates for the High Court—Ruth Bader Ginsburg and Stephen Breyer—in the first years of his administration. The Ginsburg nomination was also indicative of Clinton's apparent commitment to diversifying the federal court system. Over one-half of federal court nominees during the first two years of his administration were women and minorities (see Figure 14.4).

Presidents are often disappointed in how their nominees behave once they reach the Court. Dwight Eisenhower was dumbfounded when his friend and nominee, Earl Warren, became the leader of a Court that transformed constitutional law with regard to civil rights and criminal procedure. Nixon was puzzled when Chief Justice Warren Burger voted with a unanimous Court to override the president's claim of **executive privilege** and forced him to give up the documents that would seal his fate in the Watergate affair. George Bush was surprised when his nominee, David Souter, refused to vote for the overturn of *Roe* in *Planned Parenthood v. Casey* (1992). Despite these dramatic examples, the past political and ideological positions of federal court nominees are a pretty good guide to their later behavior on the bench.[10]

executive privilege A presidential claim that certain communications with subordinates may be withheld from Congress and the courts.

Figure 14.4 ■ Presidential Appointments of Female and Minority Judges, 1976–1996

Presidents Carter and Clinton fashioned impressive records of nominating women and minorities to the federal courts.

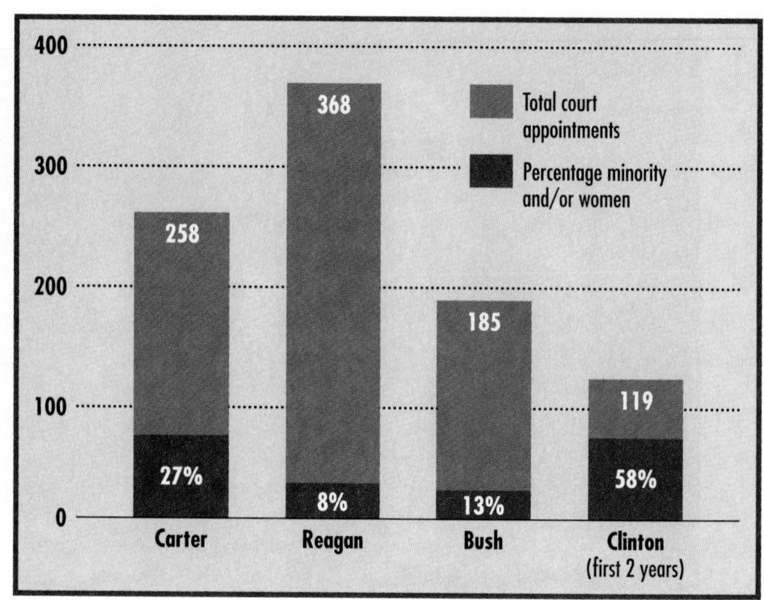

The Supreme Court in Action

The Supreme Court meets from the first Monday in October until late June or early July, depending on the press of business. Let's see how it goes about deciding cases.

Norms of Operation

A set of unwritten but clearly understood rules of behavior—called *norms*—shapes how the Court does things. One norm is *secrecy,* which keeps the con-

Presidents usually nominate people for the Supreme Court who agree with them on ideological and policy grounds. Moderate liberal justice Stephen Breyer was nominated by Bill Clinton.

flicts between justices out of the public eye and elevates the stature of the Court. Justices do not grant interviews very often. Reporters are not allowed to stalk the corridors for a story. Law clerks are expected to keep all memos, draft opinions, and conversations with the justices they work for confidential. Justices are not commonly seen on the frantic Washington, D.C., cocktail party circuit. When meeting in conference to argue and decide cases, the justices meet alone, without secretaries or clerks. While breaches of secrecy have occurred on occasion, allowing "insider" books, such as *The Brethren,* to be published, they are the exceptions. As a result, we know less about the inner workings of the Court than about any other branch of government. *Courtesy* is another norm. Though justices may sometimes express their displeasure and distaste for each other in private, in public they treat each other with great formality and respect. The justices shake hands before court sessions and conferences. They refer to each other as "my brother" or my "dissenting sister." Differences of opinion are usually respected (Justice Scalia, with his acerbic views on the positions of several of his colleagues, seems to be the current exception); justices are allowed every opportunity to make their case to their fellow justices.

Seniority is another important norm. Seniority determines the assignment of office space, the seating arrangements in open court (the most junior are at the ends), the order of speaking in conference (the chief justice, then the most senior, and so on down the line), and the order of voting (the most junior goes first). Speaking first helps senior members set the tone for discussion; voting last gives them the power to prevail in close decisions.

The Supreme Court operates in a different realm from other branches of government. While senators argue vehemently in front of cameras and viewers and are usually stalked by reporters outside Senate sessions, Supreme Court justices are bound to unwritten rules of courtesy and secrecy; their arguments are not made public, and they rarely speak to reporters. Here, Chief Justice William Rehnquist and Justice Ruth Bader Ginsburg leave court with little interference from the press or the public.

Finally, the justices are expected to stick very closely to *precedent* when they are reaching a decision. When the Court departs from a precedent, it is essentially overruling its own past actions, exercising judicial review of itself. In most cases, departures from precedent come in only very small steps over many years. For example, several decisions chipped away at the "**separate but equal**" doctrine of *Plessy v. Ferguson* before it was decisively reversed in *Brown v. Board of Education.* If there is a significant ideological turnover on the Court, however, change may come more quickly. The current Rehnquist Court has been particularly aggressive in overturning precedents on criminal justice and civil rights.

separate but equal The constitutional doctrine articulated in *Plessy v. Ferguson* (1896) that laws separating the races is permissible if equal public facilities and services are provided.

Controlling the Agenda

The Court has a number of screening mechanisms to control what cases it will hear, so that it can focus on cases that involve important federal or constitutional questions.

Several technical rules help keep down the numbers: Cases must be **real and adverse;** that is, they must involve a real dispute between two parties. The disputants in a case must have **standing;** that is, they must have a real and direct interest in the issues that are raised. The Court sometimes changes the definition of *standing* to make access for **plaintiffs** easier or more difficult. The Warren Court favored an expansive definition; the Rehnquist Court, a restricted one. Cases must also be **ripe;** that is, all other avenues of appeal must have been exhausted, and the injury must already have taken place (the Court will not accept hypothetical cases). Appeals must also be filed within a specified time limit, the paperwork must be correct and complete, and a filing fee of $200 must be paid. The fee may be waived if a petitioner is poor and files an affidavit **in forma pauperis** ("in the manner of a pauper"). One of the most famous cases in American history, *Gideon v. Wainwright* (1963), which established the right of all defendants to have lawyers in criminal cases, was submitted in forma pauperis on a few pieces of lined paper by a Florida State Penitentiary inmate named Clarence Earl Gideon. The Rehnquist Court has been less friendly to indigent petitions than previous Courts and has taken several steps to cut down what the chief justice calls "frivolous" suits by "jailhouse lawyers."

The most powerful tool that the Court has for controlling its own agenda is the power to grant or not to grant a **writ of certiorari.** A grant of "cert" is a decision of the Court that an appellate case raises an important federal or constitutional issue that it is prepared to consider.[11] Under the **rule of four,** petitions are granted cert if at least four justices vote in favor. There are several reasons why a petition may not command four votes, even if the case involves important constitutional issues: it may involve a particularly controversial issue that the Court would like to avoid, or the Court may not yet have developed a solid majority and may wish to avoid a split decision. Few petitions survive all of these hurdles. Of the almost 8,000 cases that are filed in each session, the Court grants cert for only about 100 (a few years ago, it averaged about 270). In cases denied cert, the decision of the lower court stands.

Deciding how freely to grant cert is a tricky business for the Court. Used too often, it threatens to inundate the Court with cases. Used too sparingly, it leaves in place the decisions of 13 different federal appeals courts on substantial federal and constitutional questions, as well as the decisions of state supreme courts.

real and adverse A Supreme Court rule stating that cases must involve a genuine dispute between two parties. This requirement helps the Court screen out a number of requests for appeal, thus reducing the number of cases it will consider hearing.

standing A legal term meaning that one may bring legal action because one is affected by the issues raised.

plaintiff One who brings suit in a court.

ripeness A condition a case must meet before the Supreme Court will hear it; the condition is that all other avenues of appeal have been exhausted and the injury has already occurred.

in forma pauperis Describing a process by which indigents may file a suit with the Supreme Court, free of charge.

writ of certiorari An announcement that the Supreme Court will hear a case on appeal from a lower court; its issuance requires the vote of four of the nine justices.

rule of four An *unwritten* practice that requires at least four justices of the Supreme Court to agree that a case warrants review by the Court before it will hear the case.

Deciding Cases

Cases granted cert are scheduled for oral argument. Lawyers on each side are alerted to the key issues that the justices wish to consider, and new briefs are invited. Briefs are also submitted on most important cases by other parties who may be interested in the disputes. These "friend-of-the-court," or **amicus curiae,** briefs may be submitted by individuals, interest groups, or some agency of the federal government, including the Justice Department or even the president.

amicus curiae Literally, a friend of the court; describing a brief in which those not directly a party to a suit may have their views heard.

Each case is argued for one hour: one-half hour is given to each side in the dispute. Oral argument is not so much a presentation of arguments, however, as it is a give-and-take between the lawyers and the justices, and among the justices themselves. When the federal government is a party to the case, the solicitor general or one of his deputies presents the oral arguments. Some justices—Antonin Scalia, for instance—are famous for their close grilling of lawyers. Clarence Thomas tends to pose broad hypothetical questions, while Chief Justice Rehnquist becomes irritated when lawyers wander from the main issues. Sandra Day O'Connor is prone to start her questioning by reproaching lawyers for some error in their argument. Ruth Bader Ginsburg often asks that lawyers skip abstract legal fine points and put the issues in terms of their impact on ordinary people.

After hearing oral arguments and reading the briefs in the case, the justices meet in conference to reach a decision. The custom is for each justice to state his or her position, starting with the chief justice and moving through the ranks in order of seniority. Chief justices of great stature and intellect, such as John Marshall and Charles Evans Hughes, used the opportunity to speak first as a way of structuring the case and of swaying votes. Those who did not command much respect from the other justices (for example, Warren Burger) were less able to shape the decision process. In most cases, the statement of each justice makes it clear how the Court is divided on the issues, so a vote is usually unnecessary.

Political scientists have tried to determine what factors are most important in predicting how the justices will vote. One approach looks at the ideological predilections of the justices and manages to explain a great deal about their voting behavior.[12] Another approach focuses on the diaries and personal papers of retired justices and shows that a great deal of negotiating and "horse-trading" goes on, with justices trading votes on different cases and joining opinions they do not like so that they can have a hand in modifying them.[13] Another approach tries to link voting behavior to social background, types of previous judicial experience, and the political environment of family upbringing.[14] None of these approaches has been totally successful, mainly because much of what the Court does in conference is secret and can be only imperfectly reconstructed. About all that one can say is that the justices tend to form relatively stable voting blocs that make Court decisions relatively predictable on a wide range of issues. Thus, many scholars attribute the change of direction of the Court on civil rights and church-state issues in the 1995 session to the emergence of a strong conservative block (Scalia, Thomas, Rehnquist, Kennedy, and O'Connor).

The vote in conference is not final. As Justice John Harlan once explained it, "The books on voting are never closed until the decision finally comes down."[15] The justices have an opportunity to change their votes in response to the opinion supporting the majority decision. An opinion is a statement of the legal reasoning that supports the decision of the Court. There are three kinds

concurring opinion The opinion of a judge or judges who vote with the majority on a case but wish to set out different reasons for their decision from those of the majority.

dissenting opinion The opinion of the judges who are in the minority in any particular case before the Supreme Court.

of opinions. The opinion of the Court is the written opinion of the majority. A **concurring opinion** is the opinion of a justice or justices who support the majority decision but have different legal reasons for doing so. A **dissenting opinion** presents the reasoning of the minority. Dissenting opinions sometimes become the basis for future Court majorities.

If he votes with the majority in conference, the chief justice assigns the opinion. He can assign it to any justice in the majority, often to himself. Some jurists and scholars believe that this power to assign is the most important role of the chief justice, and it is guarded jealously. Warren Burger was so eager to play a role in opinion assignments that, much to the distress of his colleagues, he would often delay announcing his vote so that he could place himself with the majority. Justice William Douglas angrily charged that Burger voted with the majority in *Roe* only so he could assign the case to a justice who was closer to the minority view.[16] If the chief justice's opinion is with the minority, the opinion is assigned by the most senior member of the majority.

The justice assigned to write the opinion does not work in isolation. He or she is assisted not only by law clerks, but also by other justices, who helpfully provide memoranda suggesting wording and reasoning. Most opinions go through numerous revisions and are subject to a considerable amount of bargaining among the justices goes on.

It is only when an opinion is completed that a final vote is taken in conference. The justices are free to change their earlier votes: they may join the majority if they are now persuaded by its reasoning, or a concurring opinion may be so compelling that the majority may decide to replace the original majority opinion with it.

Key Personnel

A number of key actors help manage the flow of the Court's business.

The Chief Justice The formal powers of the office of chief justice are not impressive. Whatever power a chief justice has is a mix of his own leadership abilities; the prestige of the office derived from the actions of past chief justices, such as Marshall, Hughes, and Warren; and a set of norms that make him "first among equals."

The chief justice also has certain administrative responsibilities. He is in charge of the management of the Supreme Court building and the personnel who work there, from guards and cooks to maintenance workers. He also serves as chair of the U.S. Judicial Conference, which coordinates many of the activities of the federal court system (budgets, procedures, and the like) and of the Federal Judicial Center, which does research and trains personnel for the administration of the federal courts. Former chief justice Warren Burger estimated that about one-third of his time was spent on these various administrative activities. Chief Justice William Rehnquist is less interested in this aspect of his job. (Table 14.3 lists all chief justices.)

The Solicitor General The solicitor general is appointed by the president to serve as the representative of the U.S. government before the Supreme Court. He and his staff decide which cases to appeal from the lower courts and which cases between private parties or the states to join on an amicus curiae basis. He and his staff prepare new briefs or revise briefs written by the Justice Department or other federal agencies on all of the relevant cases, and he serves as the government's representative in oral argument.

Table 14.3
Chief Justices of the Supreme Court

Chief Justice	Appointing President	Dates of Service
John Jay	Washington	1789–1795
John Rutledge	Washington	1795–1795
Oliver Ellsworth	Washington	1796–1800
John Marshall	J. Adams	1801–1835
Roger Brooke Taney	Jackson	1836–1864
Salmon Portland Chase	Lincoln	1864–1873
Morrison Remick Waite	Grant	1874–1888
Melville Weston Fuller	Cleveland	1888–1910
Edward Douglass White	Taft	1910–1921
William Howard Taft	Harding	1921–1930
Charles Evans Hughes	Hoover	1930–1941
Harlan Fiske Stone	F. Roosevelt	1941–1946
Frederick Moore Vinson	Truman	1946–1953
Earl Warren	Eisenhower	1953–1969
Warren Earl Burger	Nixon	1969–1986
William Hubbs Rehnquist	Reagan	1986–

Although the office is hardly visible to the public, it is very important in the relationship between the judicial and executive branches of the federal government. The solicitor general screens cases from around the country and submits only those that he considers to be of the greatest constitutional moment. There is evidence that the Court pays close attention to what he submits when it is deciding whether or not to grant certiorari because, being the representative of the president, he signals what the administration considers most important.[17]

Law Clerks Supreme Court clerks are a very select group of young lawyers recruited from among recent graduates of the most prestigious law schools in the United States. Most of them go on to distinguished legal careers; many become law school professors; and a few—William Rehnquist, for instance—become Supreme Court justices. The clerks' main role is to assist the justice to whom they are assigned in the preparation of cases. Clerks prepare memoranda on cases being considered for certiorari, screen petitions for in forma pauperis filings, do legal research, and increasingly write initial drafts of opinions for their justices. Their particular duties or the time they spend on each duty varies widely, because each justice decides how to use his or her clerks. Some justices are close to their clerks, treat them very much as colleagues, and give them important responsibilities in writing opinions and in negotiating revisions with the clerks of the other justices. Other justices like to keep their clerks on a shorter lead, giving them less independence. The trend over recent decades has been for clerks to assume more and more responsibility for drafting and revising opinions, though each justice has the final word. This trend

Chief Justice Rehnquist meets with his law clerks to discuss pending cases.

represents a dramatic change from the early twentieth century, when justices like Oliver Wendell Holmes and Louis Brandeis used their clerks mainly as research assistants.[18]

The Supreme Court as a National Policymaker

People often say that the Court should not make policy but should only settle disputes. But because the disputes it settles involve contentious public issues (such as abortion rights and affirmative action) and fundamental questions about the meaning of our constitutional rules, the Court cannot help but make public policy. We have already seen examples in this chapter of Court decisions that have shaped important aspects of our national policies. To be sure, there are certain restrictions on the Court's power to make policy; it must, for instance, wait for cases to reach it, and it must stay close to precedent. Being without enforcement powers, moreover, the Court must also worry about the problem of compliance (see below). Nevertheless, in the course of settling disputes, it makes decisions that are legally binding on other political actors and citizens on matters of public policy.

It seems likely that the Court recognizes and cultivates its policymaking role. In the main, the Court does not see itself as a court of last resort, simply righting routine errors in the lower courts or settling minor private disputes. It sees itself, instead, as the "highest judicial tribunal for settling policy [and constitutional] conflicts" and chooses its cases accordingly.[19] The fact that decisions are not simply handed down but come with an opinion attached for the purpose of guiding the actions of other courts, litigants, and public officials is another demonstration that the Court recognizes its policymaking role.

Structural Change and Constitutional Interpretation

Scholars generally identify three periods in the history of constitutional interpretation by the Supreme Court in the United States.[20] We will see how changes in constitutional law have been influenced by structural factors, particularly economic change.

Period I: From Marshall to the Civil War We saw in Chapter 4 that the United States experienced significant growth and change during the first 75 years of its existence. This growth was accompanied by changes in constitutional law. Chief Justice John Marshall, who presided over the Supreme Court from 1801 to 1835, was the key judicial figure during this important period in our history.[21] Marshall was a follower of the doctrines of Alexander Hamilton, who believed that American greatness depended on a strong national government, a partnership between government and business in which industry and commerce were encouraged, and a national market economy free of the regulatory restraints of state and local governments. In a string of opinions that have shaped the fundamentals of American constitutional law, Marshall interpreted the Constitution to mean "maximum protection to property rights and maximum support for the idea of nationalism."[22]

Federal Supremacy and National Power The framers created a system of "centralized federalism." A number of decisions by the Marshall Court, such as *Fletcher v. Peck* (1810) and *McCulloch v. Maryland* (1819), emphasized the "centralized" part of the formulation and significantly enhanced national power over the states. These cases are discussed in Chapter 3.

A National Economy *Gibbons v. Ogden* (1824) helped create the foundations of a national economy in which commerce could flow freely between the states. According to the Court, power over interstate commerce was entirely in the hands of the national government, and no state could interfere with it by imposing taxes or tariffs. Historian Charles Warren called the *Gibbons* decision "the emancipation proclamation of American commerce."[23] In *Dartmouth College v. Woodward* (1819), the Court ruled that a corporation was considered "a person under the law" and that, like any other citizen, the terms of its contract (in this case, to form and operate as a corporation) could not be impaired or changed by the state. The decision reassured business leaders that corporations would be largely free of state regulation.

Period II: Government and the Economy The Civil War and the Industrial Revolution triggered the development of a mass-production industrial economy dominated by the business corporation. Determining the role to be played by government in such an economy was a central theme of late nineteenth- and early twentieth-century American political life. The courts were involved deeply in this rethinking. At the beginning of this period, the Supreme Court took the position that the corporation was to be protected against regulation by both the state and federal governments; by the end, it had caved in to the desire of the people and the political branches for the expansion of government regulation and management of the economy during the crisis of the Great Depression.

The main protection for the corporation against regulation was the Fourteenth Amendment. This amendment was passed in the wake of the Civil War to guarantee the citizenship rights of freed slaves. In one of the great ironies of American history, this expansion of federal power over the states to protect rights—the operative phrase was from Section 1: "nor shall any state deprive any person of life, liberty, or property without due process of law"—was gradually translated by the Court to mean the protection of corporations (which

Under the leadership of Chief Justice John Marshall, the Supreme Court weakened the power of the states to regulate interstate commerce, encouraging the emergence of a vital national economy.

were considered "persons" under the law) and other forms of business from state regulation.

This reading of laissez-faire economic theory into constitutional law made the Supreme Court the principal ally of business in the late nineteenth and early twentieth centuries. The Court overturned efforts by both the state and federal governments to provide welfare for the poor; to regulate manufacturing monopolies; to initiate an income tax; to regulate interstate railroad rates; to provide scholarships to students; to regulate wages, hours, and working conditions; and to protect consumers against unsafe or unhealthy products. The Court also supported the use of judicial injunctions to halt strikes.

The business–Supreme Court alliance lasted until the Great Depression. Roosevelt's New Deal reflected a new national consensus on the need for a greatly expanded federal government with a new set of responsibilities: to manage the economy; to provide a safety net for the poor, the unemployed, and the elderly; to protect workers' right to form labor unions; and to regulate business in the public interest. The Supreme Court, however, was opposed. Filled with justices born in the nineteenth century and committed to the unshakable link between the Constitution and laissez-faire economic doctrine, the Court dealt a series of stunning reversals to the New Deal in 1935 and 1936. It declared unconstitutional the Agricultural Adjustment Act, the National Industrial Recovery Act, the Bituminous Coal Act (which regulated wages and working conditions in the mining industry), and a New York State minimum wage law. Waiting in the wings for Court scrutiny were the Wagner Labor Relations

During the crisis of the Great Depression, the federal government took on greater responsibilities for protecting the welfare of the American people. The Supreme Court was slow to endorse the change, but eventually did so under intense political pressure.

Act and the Social Security Act, and their prospects for survival did not look good.

In an extraordinary turn of events, the Supreme Court reversed itself in 1937, finding the Social Security Act, the Labor Relations Act, and state minimum wage laws acceptable. It is not entirely clear why the so-called "switch-in-time-that-saved-nine" occurred, but surely Roosevelt's landslide election in 1936, the heightening of public hostility toward the Court, and Roosevelt's plan to "pack the Court"—that is, to expand the court by up to six in order to appoint additional justices friendly to the New Deal—all played a role. Whatever the reason, the Court abandoned its effort to prevent the government from playing a central role in the management of the economy and the regulation of business, and it came to defer to the political linkage branches of government on such issues by the end of the 1930s. In doing so, it brought another constitutional era to a close.

Period III: Individual Rights and Liberties Three fundamental issues of American constitutional law—the relationship of the states to the nation, the nature of private property and the national economy, and the role of government in the management of the economy—were essentially settled by the time World War II occurred. Since then, the Court has turned its main attention to the relationship between the individual and government.[24]

Most of this story is told in the chapters on civil rights and civil liberties. For now, it is sufficient to point out that the Court, especially during the tenure of Chief Justice Earl Warren, decided cases that expanded protections for free expression and association, religious expression, fair trials, and civil rights for minorities. In another series of cases dealing with the apportionment of electoral districts, the Court declared for political equality, based on the principle of "one person, one vote." In many of its landmark decisions, the Court applied the Bill of Rights to the states. Though the Court's record was not without blemishes during and after World War II, it made significant strides in expanding the realm of individual freedom.

Constitutional law and the Court do not stand still, however. Like all political institutions, both are responsive in the long run to changes in the world around them. A new conservative majority has emerged on the Supreme Court, fashioned out of the conservative mood of the country and the judicial nominations of Presidents Reagan and Bush (75 percent of all sitting federal judges when Bill Clinton came into office had been appointed by his two Republican predecessors). This new majority has moved the Court to reconsider many of its earlier decisions on rights and liberties.

The Debate over Judicial Activism

Has the Court become too involved in national policymaking? Many people think so; others think not. Let us examine several of the ways in which what is called **judicial activism** is expressed.

judicial activism Actions by the courts which, according to critics, go beyond the role of the judiciary as interpreter of the law and adjudicator of disputes.

Judicial Review We have already seen how the Court, under John Marshall's leadership, claimed the right of judicial review in the case of *Marbury v. Madison* (1803). The power was not exercised by the Court to any great extent until the late nineteenth century. The rate of judicial review has picked up during the twentieth century, however, with most of the Court's adverse attention being paid to the states. The trend suggests that the Court has become more willing in modern times to monitor the activities of other governmental entities. Many conservatives were particularly unhappy about the Warren Court's willingness to overturn state laws on racial segregation and criminal procedure. Now that conservatives enjoy a majority on the Court, their criticism of judicial review has diminished.

Reversing the Decisions of Past Supreme Courts We have seen that adherence to precedent is one of the traditional norms that guides judicial decision making. The Warren, Burger, and Rehnquist Courts, however, have not been reluctant to overturn previous Court decisions. The most dramatic instance, of course, was the reversal of *Plessy* by *Brown,* though there have been many others, including the *Roe* to *Webster* change reviewed in the opening story of this chapter, as well as the rapid overturns of precedents involving the rights of criminal defendants. Critics claim that the too-frequent reversal of Court opinion creates instability and uncertainty on the meaning of the law and an inappropriate assertion of power. Others claim that the Court must be able to fit the law with the times and changing circumstances.

Deciding "Political" Issues Critics claim that the Court is taking on too many matters that are best left to the other, elected branches of government (*Baker v. Carr* was an important case addressing this issue; see the Struggle for Democracy feature). An often-cited example is the Court's willingness to become increasingly involved in the process of drawing congressional electoral district boundaries in the states. Defenders of the Court argue that, when such basic constitutional rights as equality of citizenship are at peril, the Court is obligated to protect these rights, no matter what other government bodies may choose to do.

Remedies The most criticized aspect of judicial activism is the tendency for federal judges to impose broad remedies on states and localities. A **remedy** is what a court determines must be done to rectify a wrong. Since the 1960s, the Court has been more willing than in the past to impose remedies that require other governmental bodies to take action. Some of the most controversial of these remedies include court orders requiring states to build more prison space and mandating that school districts bus students to achieve racial balance. Such remedies often require that governments spend public funds for things they do not necessarily want to do. Critics claim that the Court's legitimate role is to prevent government actions that threaten rights and liberties, not to compel government to take action to meet some policy goal.

remedy An action that a court determines must be taken to rectify a wrong.

Original Intention Much of the debate about the role of the Court centers on the issue of **original intention.** Advocates of original intention and its twin, **strict construction,** believe that the Court must be guided by the original intentions of the framers and the words found in the Constitution. They believe that the expansion of rights that has occurred since the mid–1960s—such as the right to privacy that formed the basis of the *Roe v. Wade* decision and new rights for criminal defendants—are illegitimate, having no foundation in the framers' intentions or the text of the Constitution.

Opponents of original intention believe that the intentions of the Founders are not only impossible to determine, but unduly constricting. In this view, jurists, must try to reconcile the fundamental principles of the Constitution with changing conditions in the United States.

original intention The doctrine that the courts must interpret the Constitution in ways consistent with the intentions of the framers rather than in light of contemporary conditions and needs.

strict construction Associated with *original intention;* the doctrine that the provisions of the Constitution have a clear meaning and that judges must stick closely to this meaning when rendering decisions.

The modern Court is more activist than it was in the past; most justices today hold a more expansive view of the role of the Court in forging national policy than their predecessors did. Despite all of the debate about whether this stance is proper, the Court is likely to remain activist for a long time to come. First, belief in judicial activism, whether it is admitted or not, is shared by liberals and conservatives alike. As one scholar put it, "The ideologically conservative Burger and Rehnquist Courts . . . have been as activist as the liberal Warren Court. Their differences lie in the directions in which they have pushed constitutional law and politics."[25] Second, it is unlikely that the justices, once having tasted political power, will give it up easily and take a back seat to the president and the Congress. Because the Court is likely to remain activist, the debate about judicial activism is not likely to disappear from American politics.

The Courts and Democracy: The Political Linkage and Governmental Contexts

The courts make public policy and will continue to do so. Fears of an "imperial judiciary," however, are somewhat exaggerated. Rather than a federal court system in which judges are free to make public policy on their own, ours is a system in which judges are constrained by the actions and preferences of many other political and governmental actors, including, to some degree, the people. The degree to which the people play a role in influencing the actions of the courts is, of course, a key determinant of the quality of American democracy.

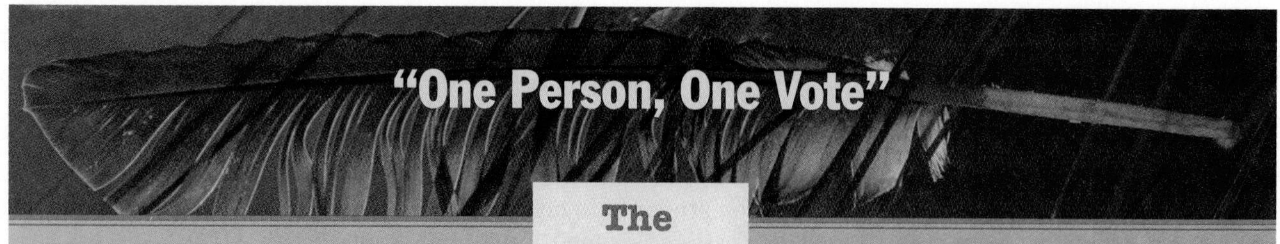

"One Person, One Vote"

The Struggle for Democracy

Political equality is one of the defining characteristics of democracy (see Chapter 1), yet the principle of "one person, one vote," by which the vote of one person carries the same weight as the vote of every other person, was not guaranteed by the Supreme Court until the 1960s. The case that opened the door to the transformation of constitutional law in this area was *Baker v. Carr* (1962). The Court decided in this case that the federal courts could hear challenges to legislative malapportionment under the equal protection clause of the Fourteenth Amendment. In rendering this decision, the Court reversed long-settled constitutional doctrine and encouraged challenges to malapportionment in the states. By doing so, the Court enriched democracy in the United States.

Malapportionment means drawing legislative district lines in such a way that the resulting districts (whether state legislative or congressional districts) vary substantially in population. Legislative district lines are generally redrawn after each census to take account of the shifting population in the states. In many cases, however, state legislatures had failed for a very long time to redraw district lines even as the populations of their states were becoming more urban and suburban. The result was that rural legislative districts, with sparse populations, had the same number of representatives as urban and suburban districts with dense populations. That is, rural populations had more representation than they deserved, based on a one-person–one vote standard, and urban and suburban populations had less. This arrangement was especially disadvantageous to racial minorities and the poor living in central cities.

In Tennessee, though the state constitution required that the legislature reapportion legislative districts after each census, the legislature had not redrawn legislative district lines since 1901 and showed no signs of doing so after the 1960 census. One legislative district in Memphis had a population 19 times the size of one of the state's rural districts, so that the citizens of the Memphis district enjoyed only one-nineteenth the representation of the rural district in the state legislature. Finding no redress in the Tennessee legislature or the state courts, a group of plaintiffs from Memphis requested that the federal district court put a halt to legislative elections in the state until the situation was rectified. The district court turned down their request, saying that apportionment cases

Governmental-Level Influence on the Supreme Court

The Supreme Court must coexist with other governmental bodies that have their own powers, interests, constituencies, and visions of the public good. Recognizing this, the Court usually tries to stay somewhere near the boundaries of what is acceptable to other political actors. It does so for a number of reasons.

Being without "purse or sword," as Hamilton put it in *The Federalist,* No. 78, the Court cannot force others to obey its decisions. It can only hope that respect for the law and the Court will be enough to cause government officials to do what it has mandated in a decision. If the Court fails to gain voluntary compliance, it risks a serious erosion of its influence, for it then appears weak and ineffectual.

Presidential Influence The president, being the chief executive, is supposed to carry out the Court's decrees. However, presidents who have opposed or have been lukewarm to particular decisions have been known to drag their

were not the province of the federal courts. The plaintiffs then appealed to the Supreme Court. Much to the surprise of long-time observers of the Court, it accepted the case and eventually ruled in favor of a reexamination of constitutional doctrine on apportionment.

The Supreme Court had long avoided involvement in apportionment controversies, defining them as "political" in nature, meaning they involved issues which judges thought were best left to the political branches (executive and legislative). The doctrine distinguishing "political" matters from "judicial" matters was first articulated by Chief Justice John Marshall in *Marbury v. Madison* (1803) and had been refined by Chief Justice Roger Taney in *Luther v. Borden* (1849). It was applied to the legislative apportionment issue in *Colegrove v. Green* (1946), in which justice Felix Frankfurter (still on the Court for the *Baker* case) wrote that the "Court ought not to enter this "political thicket."

Frankfurter remained strongly opposed on doctrinal grounds to Supreme Court involvement in apportionment cases, so he opposed the Tennessee plaintiffs, but he was also worried that a ruling on the issue would bring a storm of criticism from elected state officials raining down on the heads of the Court. Fortunately for the principle of political equality, most of the other justices were willing to take the risk; only Justice John Harlan sided with Frankfurter. This willingness can be attributed in large part to the formidable negotiating and opinion-drafting skills of Justice William Brennan, who fashioned the majority coalition. In order to gain as strong a majority as he could (the vote was 6 to 2, with one justice not voting), Brennan insisted that the decision focus solely on the jurisdictional question—that is, whether the federal courts could hear malapportionment cases—rather than on the specific merits of the complaints of the Tennessee plaintiffs. He was after bigger fish. Brennan and his brethren knew that a jurisdictional decision would open the door to cases challenging states' failure to provide equal protection for their citizens.

The challenges did, indeed, flood in (36 in the year after *Baker*), and the Court moved quickly to construct the doctrine of "one person, one vote" as the basis for political representation in the United States. *Baker* was the opening salvo of a constitutional revolution that eventually transformed American politics and made it more democratic. Chief Justice Earl Warren later said that the decision was the most vital one made during his long tenure on the Supreme Court.

feet. The *Brown* decision is a good example. In a follow-up case meant to determine the timetable for desegregation (usually referred to as *Brown II*), the Court used the phrase "with all deliberate speed." President Eisenhower opposed the *Brown* decision and did little to encourage compliance by the southern states. Nor did President Kennedy put much pressure on recalcitrant states and school districts to desegregate. As Justice Hugo Black finally complained in 1964, "There has been entirely too much deliberation, and not enough speed."[26]

The president has certain constitutional powers that give them some degree of influence over the Court. In addition to the Court's dependence on the president to carry out its decisions (when the parties to a dispute do not do it voluntarily), the president influences the direction of the Court by his power of appointment. He can also file suits through the Justice Department, try to move public opinion against the Court (as Richard Nixon tried to do), and threaten to introduce legislation to alter the Court's organization or jurisdiction (as Franklin Roosevelt did with his "court-packing" proposal).

Congressional Influences Congress retains the power to change the size, organization, and appellate jurisdiction of the federal courts. The Jefferson-controlled Congress postponed a session of the Supreme Court in 1802 so that the Court would not be able to hear a suit that challenged the repeal by Congress of the Judiciary Act of 1801. Congress also "sent a message" to the Court when it instituted impeachment proceedings against Justice Samuel Chase, apparently for the sole crime of being a Federalist. During the Civil War, Congress removed the Court's jurisdiction over habeas corpus cases so that civilians could be tried in military courts. Congress can also bring pressure to bear by being unsympathetic to pleas from the justices for pay increases or for a suitable budget for clerks or office space. The Senate also plays a role in the appointment process, as we have learned, and can convey its views to the Court during the course of confirmation hearings. Finally, Congress can change statutes or pass new laws that specifically challenge Supreme Court decisions, as it did when it legislated the Civil Rights Act of 1991 to make it easier for people to file employment discrimination suits.

Political-Linkage-Level Influences on the Supreme Court

The Supreme Court is influenced not only by other government officials and institutions, but by what we have termed *political linkage factors,* such as social movements, interest groups, and elections.

Groups, Movements, and Test Cases Interest groups, social movements, and the public not only influence the Court indirectly through the president and Congress but often do so directly. An important political tactic of interest groups and social movements is the **test case.** A test case is an action brought by a group that is designed to challenge the constitutionality of a law or an action by government. Groups wishing to force a court determination on an issue that is important to them will try to find a person (called the *plaintiff*) on whose behalf they can bring a suit. When Thurgood Marshall was chief counsel for the NAACP in the 1950s, he spent a long time searching for the right plaintiff to bring a suit that would drive the last nail into the coffin of the *Plessy* "separate-but-equal" doctrine that was the legal basis for southern segregation. He settled on a fifth-grade girl named Linda Brown who was attending a segregated school in Topeka, Kansas. Several years later, Marshall's guest met success in *Brown v. Board of Education.*

test case A case brought to force a ruling on the constitutionality of some law or executive action.

Test cases can also be created by the purposeful breaking of a law that an individual or group believes to be unconstitutional, so that the law can be tested in the courts. This approach was one of the pillars of the nonviolent civil rights movement in the South during the 1960s. It is a strategy that has been used at various times by antidraft groups, antitax groups, and anti-abortion groups, such as Operation Rescue, which purposely breaks local ordinances and state laws to test their constitutionality in court.

Many test cases take the form of **class action suits.** These are suits brought by an individual on behalf of a class of people who are in a similar situation. A suit to prevent the dumping of toxic wastes in public waterways, to use an example, may be brought by an individual in the name of all the people living in the area who are adversely affected by the resulting pollution. Class action suits were invited by the Warren Court's expansion of the definition of *standing* in the 1960s. The Rehnquist Court later narrowed the definition of *standing,* making it harder to bring class action suits.

class action suit A suit brought on behalf of a group of people who are in a situation similar to that of the plaintiffs.

Social movements use test cases to challenge the constitutionality of laws and government actions. After a long search, NAACP attorney Thurgood Marshall selected Linda Brown, a fifth-grader from Topeka, Kansas, as the principal plaintiff in *Brown v. Board of Education,* the historic case that successfully challenged school segregation.

Interest groups often get involved in suits, even when they are not parties to the case, by filing amicus curiae briefs. Such briefs set out the group's position on the constitutional issues or talk about some of the most important consequences of deciding the case one way or the other. In a sense, this activity is a form of lobbying.

Elites The Supreme Court does not usually stray very far from the opinions of public and private sector leaders.[27] Social and economic elites use their influence in a number of ways. As we learned in previous chapters, their influence is substantial in the media, the interest group system, party politics, and elections at all levels. It follows, then, that elites play a substantial role in the thinking of presidents and the members of Congress as they, in turn, deal with the Court. In addition to this powerful but indirect influence, the Court is also shaped by developments on issues and doctrine within the legal profession as these are expressed by bar associations, law journals, and law schools.

Public Opinion Public opinion influences the Supreme Court, but the extent of its effects are unclear. Some research shows that the Court conforms to public opinion about as much as the president and Congress do (about three-fifths of the time). Other research shows public support for the Court's actions only about one-third of the time.[28] That public opinion is important, to some degree, should not be surprising. After all, Supreme Court justices read the same newspapers and watch the same news programs as other Washington, D.C., decision makers. And they must be attentive to the views of other government actors, as we have seen, who are themselves somewhat responsive to public opinion. Supreme Court justices, then, cannot help but be influenced by changes in the opinion climate of the nation.

Antidemocratic Aspects of the Supreme Court

Democracy requires popular sovereignty. We have seen that popular preferences play a larger role in the actions of the Supreme Court than might appear to be the case at first glance. Court decisions are consistent with the opinions of the public in a substantial proportion of cases. However, the fact that the relationship is far from perfect would not have displeased the framers. As Alexander Hamilton put it in *The Federalist,* No. 78, the Constitution established a judiciary that was to serve as "an excellent barrier [against public opinion] and the encroachments of the representative body."

The Court's relationship to public opinion is problematic in democratic terms. Not only does the Court fail to conform to public opinion much of the time, but it also often lags behind, even when it eventually comes into line with public opinion. If we believe in the adage "Justice delayed is justice denied," then this lag is a significant problem. During the Great Depression, the Court's strong commitment to laissez-faire economics in the midst of a national economic emergency almost led to a constitutional crisis.

The public influences the Court indirectly through such elected institutions as Congress and the president. However, two factors render public influence less than it might be. First, as we saw in earlier chapters, Congress and the president are themselves far from perfect as democratic instruments of the people. Second, though the president and Congress constrain its behavior, the Court is able to go its own way to a considerable degree.[29] The Court is a fully

The Supreme Court has sometimes rendered decisions detrimental to liberty. Here, a Japanese-American man waits with his children to be taken to an internment camp. The Court supported the federal government's plan to intern Americans of Japanese descent during World War II.

coequal branch of the federal government, able to give and take on equal terms with the other two branches.

Democracy also requires liberty and political equality. To many people, the protection of freedom and equality is the primary mission of the Court. The Court has indeed played an important role in the protection and extension of civil liberties and citizenship rights. Still, its actions over the long course of our history have not been entirely praiseworthy in this respect. By and large, the Court has gone along with government efforts to silence dissident voices and to keep political and racial minorities from enjoying the full protection of the law. For instance, it went along with local, state, and federal actions to punish dissident voices during the McCarthy era's anti-Communist hysteria during the 1950s. Its *Plessy* decision formed the basis of the Jim Crow system in the South for over half a century. It also approved the forced relocation and internment of Japanese-Americans during World War II. While the Warren Court changed much of this, the Rehnquist Court is more inclined to favor the authorities.[30]

Democracy and the Supreme Court Reconsidered

People disagree about what the role of the Supreme Court should be in our democracy. To the framers, who believed (unlike the authors of this text) that popular democracy and liberty are contradictory, the appropriate role of the Court was that of protector of liberty against public opinion and the elected branches. They had in mind a frankly antipopular, sovereign institution. Most Americans today think better of democracy than the framers did, so this openly antidemocratic conception of the Court's role is probably not as appealing as in the past. Americans no doubt want the Court to champion liberty, but in a broader context that includes an appreciation of popular sovereignty and political equality.

In the conception of democracy used throughout this book, the appropriate role of the Court is to encourage the play of popular sovereignty, political equality, and liberty in American politics. In the game of American politics, the role of the Court ought to be that of a referee ensuring that the rules of democracy will be followed. The rules of the game of democracy involve assurances that the majority will prevail in the determination of public policy, that all members of the society will be allowed to enter on an equal basis into the public dialogue about the public business, and that each individual will be allowed all of the rights of conscience and expression connected with human dignity. We have learned at various places in this book that the Court does not always live up to these standards, but that it must do so for the health of our democracy goes without saying.

Finally, some scholars believe that the Court can play a role in enriching democracy by bringing the most fundamental issues of our political life to public attention. Individual freedom, equality, and the role of government are highlighted in virtually all of their decisions, and to the degree that they stimulate public debate and deliberation, democracy may be enhanced.[31]

Summary

Article III of the Constitution is vague about the powers and responsibilities of the US. Supreme Court. Especially noteworthy is the Constitution's silence on the Court's most important power: judicial review. Nevertheless, the Court has fashioned a powerful position for itself in American politics, coequal to that of the executive and legislative branches.

The federal court system is made up of three parts. At the bottom are 94 federal district courts, in which most cases originate. In the middle are 13 circuit courts. At the top is a single Supreme Court, with both original and appellate jurisdictions.

The Supreme Court operates on the basis of several widely shared norms: secrecy, courtesy, seniority, and adherence to precedent. The Court controls its agenda by granting or not granting certiorari. Cases before the Court wend their way through the process in the following way: submission of briefs, oral argument, initial consideration in conference, opinion writing, and final conference consideration by the justices. Published opinions serve as precedents for other federal courts and future Supreme Court decisions.

The Supreme Court is a national policymaker of considerable importance. Its unelected, life-tenured justices cannot, however, do anything they please, for the Court is significantly influenced by other political linkage and governmental factors. As a result, Court decisions rarely drift very far from public and elite opinion.

Constitutional interpretation by the Supreme Court, heavily influenced by structural changes in American history, has progressed through three stages. In the first, the Court helped settle the question of the nature of the federal union. In the second, it helped define the role of the government in a free enterprise economy. In the third, the Court focused on issues of civil liberties and civil rights.

The relationship of the Court to American democracy is ambiguous. While popular sovereignty plays a role in determining what it does, this role is less than it might be. While the Court has been a significant factor in the protection of political equality and liberty, it has not been entirely or consistently supportive of these essential attributes of democracy during our history. It can often, however, help to expand democratic deliberation.

Suggested Readings

Ackerman, Bruce. *We the People: Foundations.* Cambridge: Harvard University Press, 1991.

A compelling interpretation of American constitutional history in which popular pressures are the prime cause for major transformations in the U.S. Supreme Court's approach to major issues.

Carp, Robert A., and Ronald Stidham. *Judicial Process in America,* 3rd ed. Washington, DC: Congressional Quarterly Press, 1996.

A detailed description of how the U.S. federal and state court systems work.

Hall, Kermit L. *The Oxford Companion to the Supreme Court of the United States.* New York: Oxford University Press, 1992.

Everything you ever wanted to know about the Supreme Court in a single volume. An indispensable reference work.

Lewis, Anthony. *Gideon's Trumpet.* New York: Random House, 1964.

The moving story of Clarence Earl Gideon's successful campaign from a Florida prison cell to persuade the Supreme Court that defendants have a right to a lawyer.

McCloskey, Robert G. *The American Supreme Court.* Chicago: University of Chicago Press, 1960. Revised edition, edited by Sanford Levinson, 1994.

A modern classic about the history of constitutional interpretation tied to changes in American society and politics.

O'Brien, David M. *Storm Center: The Supreme Court in American Politics,* 3rd ed. New York: Norton, 1993.
Fast becoming the standard textbook on the U.S. Supreme Court; combines the latest in social science research and compelling anecdotes.

Rosenberg, Gerald. *The Hollow Hope: Courts and Social Reform.* Chicago: University of Chicago Press, 1991.
A thorough documentation of the limited circumstances in which the courts can bring about social change.

Schwartz, Bernard. *A History of the Supreme Court.* New York: Oxford University Press, 1993.
A surprisingly comprehensive and well-written one-volume history of the Supreme Court.

Woodward, Bob, and Scott Armstrong. *The Brethren: Inside the Supreme Court.* New York: Simon & Schuster, 1979.
A painstaking investigative examination that manages to raise the curtain on the inside workings of the Supreme Court during the years 1969–1975.

Internet Sources

Federal Court Statistics http://teddy.law.cornell.edu:8090/questata.htm
Assorted statistics on federal district courts, federal circuit courts, and the Supreme Court.

Justices of the Supreme Court http://www.law.cornell.edu/supct/justices/fullcourt.html
Biographical sketches of all past and present justices of the Supreme Court.

Oyez.Oyez http://ayez.at.nwu.edu/oyez.html
Recordings of oral arguments before the Supreme Court.

Rules of the Supreme Court http://www.law.cornell.edu/rules/supct/overview.html
The rules of procedure of the Supreme Court.

Supreme Court Decisions http://www.law.cornell.edu/supct
Complete text of Supreme Court decisions, including opinions of the Court, concurring opinions, and dissenting opinions.

Notes

1. Connie Page, *The Right to Lifers: Who They Are, How They Operate, Where They Get Their Money* (New York: Summit Books, 1983), p. 151.
2. From Suzy Platt, ed., *Respectfully Quoted: A Dictionary of Quotations Requested from the Congressional Research Service* (Washington, DC: Library of Congress, 1989), p. 67.
3. J. M. Sosin, *The Aristocracy of the Long Robe: The Origins of Judicial Review in America* (Westport, CT: Greenwood Press, 1989).
4. Hamilton, *The Federalist,* No. 78.
5. Robert G. McCloskey, *The American Supreme Court* (Chicago: University of Chicago Press, 1960), pp. 12–13.
6. On *Marbury,* see Sylvia Snowmiss, *Judicial Review and the Law of the Constitution* (New Haven, CT: Yale University Press, 1990).
7. David M. O'Brien, *Storm Center: The Supreme Court in American Politics,* 3rd ed. (New York: Norton, 1993), p. 68.

8. Robert A. Carp and Ronald Stidham, *Judicial Process in America,* 3rd ed. (Washington, DC: Congressional Quarterly Press, 1996), Chap. 8; Sheldon Goldman, "Federal Judicial Recruitment," in John B. Gates and Charles Johnson, eds., *The American Courts* (Washington, DC: Congressional Quarterly Press, 1991), pp. 195, 199.

9. Carp and Stidham, *Judicial Process in America,* pp. 241–242; Herbert Jacob, *Law and Politics in the United States* (Boston: Little, Brown, 1986), p. 221.

10. Ronald Stidham and Robert A. Carp, "Judges, Presidents, and Policy Choices," *Social Science Quarterly,* Vol. 68, No. 2 (1987), pp. 395–404; Carp and Stidham, *Judicial Process in America,* Chap. 9.

11. For details see H. W. Perry, Jr., *Deciding to Decide: Agenda Setting in the United States Supreme Court* (Cambridge: Harvard University Press, 1991).

12. David Adamany, "The Supreme Court," in John B. Gates and Charles Johnson, eds., *The American Courts,* pp. 111–112; Glendon Schubert, *The Judicial Mind* (Evanston, IL: Northwestern University Press, 1965); John D. Sprague, *Voting Patterns of the United States Supreme Court* (Indianapolis: Bobbs-Merrill, 1968).

13. Walter Murphy, *Elements of Judicial Strategy* (Princeton: Princeton University Press, 1964).

14. Joel B. Grossman, "Social Backgrounds and Judicial Decision-Making," *Harvard Law Review,* Vol. 79 (1966), pp. 1551–1564; S. Sidney Ulmer, "Dissent Behavior and the Social Background of Supreme Court Justices," *Journal of Politics,* Vol. 32 (1970), pp. 580–589.

15. John Harlan, "A Glimpse of the Supreme Court at Work," *University of Chicago Law School Record,* Vol. 1, No. 7 (1963), pp. 35–52.

16. Bob Woodward and Scott Armstrong, *The Brethren: Inside the Supreme Court* (New York: Simon & Schuster, 1979).

17. Herbert Jacob, *Justice in America,* 3rd ed. (Boston: Little, Brown, 1978), p. 225.

18. Bernard Schwartz, *A History of the Supreme Court* (New York: Oxford University Press, 1993), p. 369.

19. Jacob, *Justice in America,* p. 245.

20. McCloskey, *American Supreme Court.*

21. Robert A. Carp and Ronald Stidham, *Judicial Process in America* (Washington, DC: Congressional Quarterly Press, 1996), p. 28.

22. McCloskey, *American Supreme Court,* p. 57.

23. Quoted in Elder Witt, ed., *The Supreme Court and Its Work* (Washington, DC: Congressional Quarterly Press, 1981), p. 12.

24. McCloskey, *American Supreme Court.* Also see H. W. Perry, Jr., *The Transformation of the Supreme Court's Agenda: From the New Deal to the Reagan Administration* (Boulder, CO: Westview, 1991).

25. O'Brien, *Storm Center,* p. 64.

26. *Griffin v. Prince Edwards County School Board,* 377 U.S. 218 (1964).

27. Robert Dahl, "Decision Making in a Democracy: The Supreme Court as a National Decision Maker," *Journal of Public Law,* Vol. 6 (1957), pp. 279–295; Thomas R. Marshall, "Public Opinion, Representation, and the Modern Supreme Court," *American*

Politics Quarterly, Vol. 16 (1988), pp. 296–316; McCloskey, *American Supreme Court,* p. 22; O'Brien, *Storm Center,* p. 325.

28. G. Caldeira, "Courts and Public Opinion," in J. Gates and C. Johnson, eds., *The Courts: A Critical Assessment* (Washington, DC: Congressional Quarterly Press, 1991); Jay Casper, "The Supreme Court and National Policy Making," *American Political Science Review,* Vol. 70 (1976), pp. 50–63; Marshall, "Public Opinion, Representation"; William Mishler and Reginald S. Sheehan, "The Supreme Court as Counter-Majoritarian Institution? The Impact of Public Opinion on Supreme Court Decisions," *American Political Science Review,* Vol. 87 (1993), pp. 87–101; Benjamin I. Page and Robert Y. Shapiro, "Effects of Public Opinion on Policy," *American Political Science Review,* Vol. 77 (1983), p. 183.

29. William Lasser, *The Limits of Judicial Power: The Supreme Court in American Politics* (Chapel Hill: University of North Carolina Press, 1988); Mark Silverstein and Benjamin Ginsberg, "The Supreme Court and the New Politics of Judicial Power," *Political Science Quarterly,* Vol. 102, No. 3 (Fall 1987), pp. 371–388.

30. Adamany, "Supreme Court," pp. 15–18; Lincoln Caplan, "The Reagan Challenge to the Rule of Law," in Sidney Blumenthal and Thomas Byrne Edsall, eds., *The Reagan Legacy* (New York: Pantheon Books, 1988); Linda Greenhouse, "The Court's Counterrevolution Comes in Fits and Starts," *New York Times* (July 4, 1993), Sec. 4, p. 1.

31. Lief Carter, *Contemporary Constitutional Lawmaking* (New York: Pergamon Press, 1985).

CHAPTER 15

State and Local Government

IN THIS CHAPTER

- ★ What mayors and governors do
- ★ How interest groups, the public, and economic factors influence state policies
- ★ The rise and decline of big cities
- ★ How democracy fares in state and local government

Gay Rights and State Politics

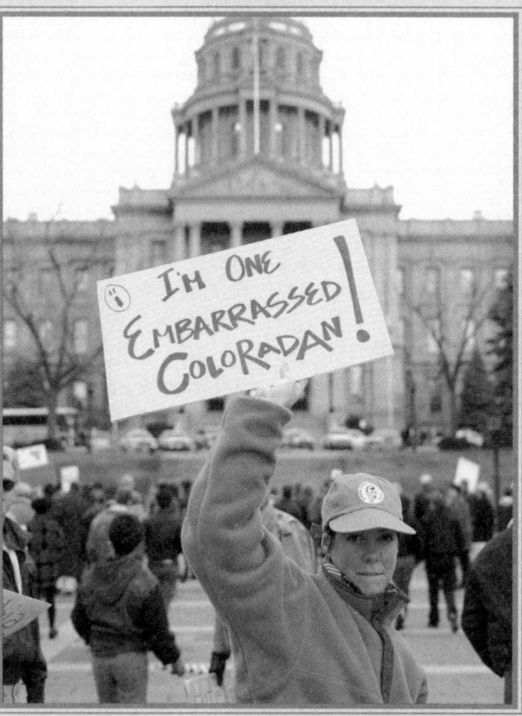

On November 3, 1992, Colorado voters—by a 53 to 47 percent majority—passed Constitutional Amendment 2, which declared that neither the State of Colorado nor its subdivisions could adopt or enforce any policy whereby homosexual orientation or conduct could be the basis of a protected status or claim of discrimination. This vote overturned the gay rights ordinances of Denver, Boulder, and Aspen, which had forbidden discrimination in housing, employment, or public accommodations on the basis of sexual orientation.[1]

Amendment 2 was put on the ballot by Colorado for Family Values (CFV), a conservative Christian organization formed in Colorado Springs. With help from the National Legal Foundation (a Pat Robertson–related conservative group located in Virginia), CFV crafted a ballot measure far more sophisticated and appealing than the crude condemnation of "perverts" that was soundly defeated by Oregon voters that same year. While gays and liberals in the urban Denver area were largely silent, CFV diligently organized eastern Colorado's Christian churches and conservative farmers, as well as the residents of Colorado Springs and Pueblo.[2]

CFV emphasized Amendment 2's prohibition of quotas or "special treatment" for gays, rather than its prohibition of ordinances forbidding discrimination. Thus, the group appealed to Americans' general dislike of affirmative action for minorities, rather than to their equally strong support for legal equality, tolerance, and sexual privacy. (Nationwide surveys have shown that most Americans—some 80 percent—consider homosexuality "immoral" or "wrong," but majorities feel that homosexual relations between consenting adults should not be illegal, and they oppose many kinds of antigay discrimination.[3]) Denying that homosexuality results from genetic or other factors beyond individuals' control, CFV argued that such lifestyle choices do not deserve protection of the kind given to racial minorities.

The campaign turned ugly. Besides citing biblical condemnations of homosexuality, Amendment 2 proponents fanned fears that gays were endangering children, breaking up traditional families, and exposing everyone to AIDS. A 20-minute campaign video, *The Gay Agenda,* featured scenes from a San Francisco gay-pride parade calculated to strike straight viewers as bizarre and disgusting (mock masturbation, sadomasochism, Man/Boy Love Association members), but omitting hundreds of ordinary-looking doctors, grocers, bank tellers, and other marchers. Brochures and tabloid news mailings spread false "medical evidence" (compiled by a defrocked psychologist) of dangers to heterosexuals from homosexual blood donors and food handlers. Cofounder Tony Marco quit CFV in disgust, saying, "It's easier to nauseate than educate."[4]

The passage of Amendment 2—which won in 52 low-population rural counties as well as in Colorado Springs and Pueblo, losing only in 11 densely populated counties—left gays, already demoralized by the AIDS epidemic, in shock and outrage. The cities of Denver, Boulder, and Aspen, along with half-a-dozen gay citizens, including tennis star Martina Navratilova, immediately sued to prevent enforcement of the amendment and won a temporary injunction. A nationwide boycott was called against the Denver airport, Coors beer, and other Colorado products, costing Colorado perhaps $100 million in lost conventions, tourism and other business.

But the boycott brought ugliness of its own. The owner of the nondiscriminatory Celestial Seasonings company charged that New York gay activists had tried to extort a $100,000 contribution to their cause. Wellington Webb, Denver's first black mayor and a strong supporter of gay rights, went on *the Arsenio Hall Show* to plead for mercy: the boycott, he said, was hurting the wrong people. Many Coloradans resented what they considered national bullying and judicial interference; polls showed no drop in support for Amendment 2—in fact, a slight rise.[5] Hate crimes against gays were rumored (though police denied it) to increase sharply.

Colorado courts ruled that Amendment 2 was void because it violated the equal protection clause of the Fourteenth Amendment to the U.S. Constitution: it denied gays the fundamental right "to participate equally in the political process." But legal arguments and appeals continued all the way to the U.S. Supreme Court, which finally ruled against Amendment 2 in 1996.[6] Meanwhile, antigay activists marched forward elsewhere. Antigay ordinances were passed at the city and county level in Oregon and several other states. In 1996 and 1997, the focus in Hawaii, California, and other states shifted to legislation banning state recognition of homosexual marriages. Indications are that gay rights will remain a contentious issue in state and local politics for years to come.

We will see that state and local politics often work much as national politics, with interest groups, election campaigns, and the like, as described in earlier chapters. But this story illustrates one feature that is unique to the state and local levels: direct votes by citizens to decide policy questions. It also illustrates that state and local governments, not just the national government, deal with important issues.

Politics of the States

In recent years, conservatives have worked to "devolve" many powers to the states, that is, to shift power from the federal to the state level. These efforts have made clear the great and growing political importance of the American states and their legal subdivisions—counties, cities, and various regional and local governments. State and local governments have broad responsibilities and spend enormous amounts of money: more than $900 *billion.* That amounts to about 14 percent of the gross national product, or nearly $3,600 for each American; it is more than one-half as much as the national government spends.[7]

Most of the contacts that ordinary Americans have with government are at the state and local levels. Public schools and colleges, welfare, roads, local parks, street cleaning, sewage treatment, recycling and garbage removal, water supplies, police and fire protection, traffic control, and court systems—all of these are primarily state and local responsibilities. In one fiscal year, for example, state and local governments spent about $312 billion on education (more than five times as much as the federal government), $236 billion on health and welfare, and $67 billion on highways[8] (see Figure 15.1).

At the top of a complicated system of subnational governments, with ultimate political power over all the rest, stand the governments of the 50 states. In many respects, state governments can be viewed as miniature versions of the national or federal government. They have similar written constitutions, which set up similar institutions of elected and appointed officials that work in similar ways. Often, their statehouses are architectural copies of the U.S. Capitol Building in Washington, D.C. Much of what we have said about the national government—about the functioning of legislators and executives; the influences of public opinion, interest groups, and the media; and the importance of

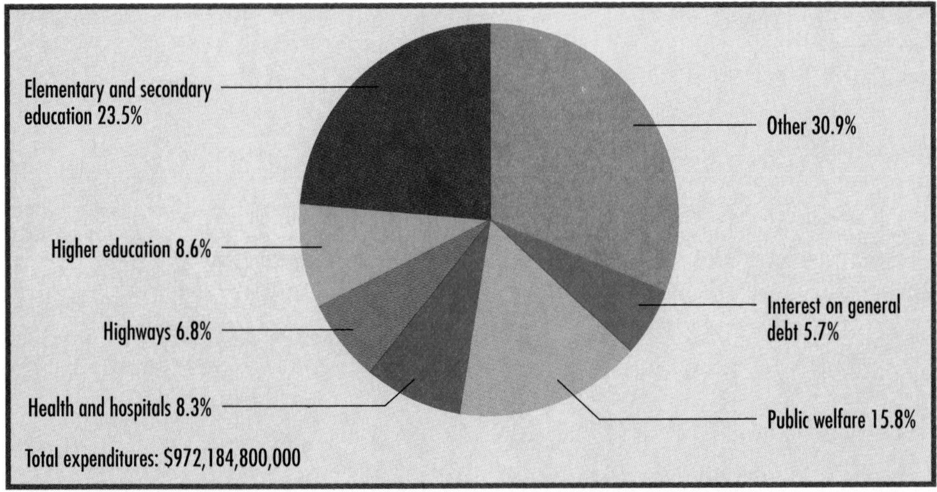

Figure 15.1 ■ How State and Local Governments Spend Their Money[a]

The largest shares of state and local budgets go to education, health and welfare, transportation, and interest on debt.

[a]Expenditures in 1992 as percentages of total expenditure.

Source: Advisory Commission on Intergovernmental Relations, Significant Features of Fiscal Federalism 1994 (Washington, D.C.: ACIR, 1994), pp. 120, 122.

structural factors—applies to state governments as well. But there are some important differences.

State Constitutions

All 50 states have written constitutions that establish three branches of government: legislative, executive, and judicial. They also enumerate certain limited powers for government and set forth the rights of citizens. The state constitutions are not as crisp and concise as the U.S. Constitution, however. Many of them go into specific, long-winded detail about particular matters of public policy and are very lengthy. Alabama's constitution, for example, is about 174,000 words long (including its 556 amendments since 1901), and New York's is about 80,000,[9] contrasted with the fewer than 5,000 words in the original U.S. Constitution and 3,000 or so words in its 27 amendments.

The main reason for this wordiness appears to be that organized interests of various sorts have worked hard to enshrine their aims in state constitutions, so they cannot easily be upset by the legislatures or courts and are insulated from the popular will. Even where the constitution can be amended fairly easily by popular vote, however—as in California, where ballot propositions to change the constitution by majority vote are routine—special interests apparently have a big advantage in getting and keeping the constitutional provisions they want. The legal language is complicated and difficult for voters to understand; special interests spend vast sums on media advertising that casts the question in favorable terms.

Governors

All state constitutions provide for a unitary chief executive, a governor, whose position resembles that of the president of the United States. Governors are

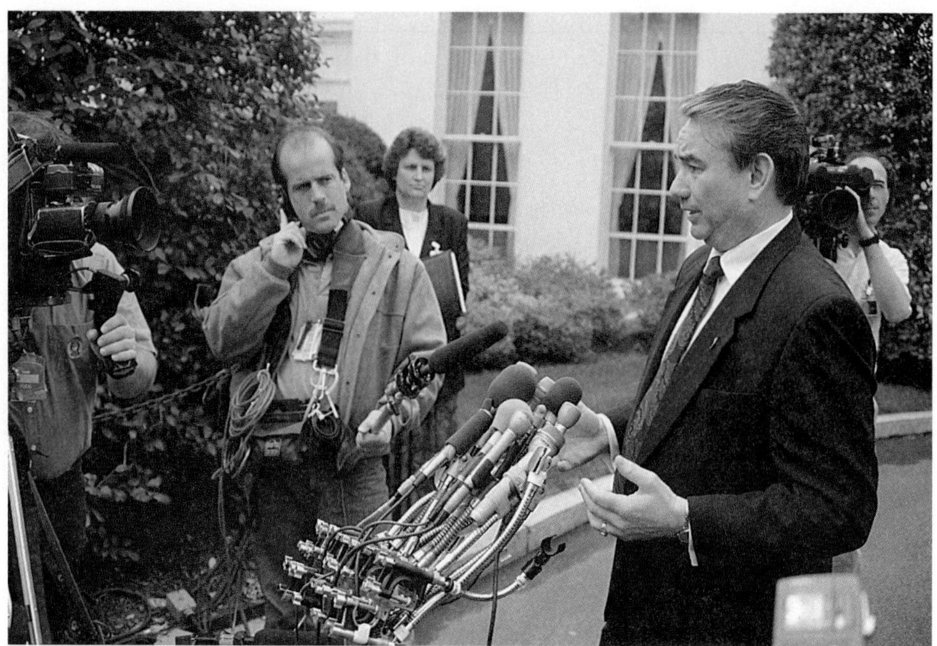

Governor Tommy Thompson of Wisconsin, a Republican, was an early leader in state-level efforts at welfare reform; President Clinton eventually endorsed his plan.

popularly elected, usually for 4 years at a time; only New Hampshire, Vermont, and Rhode Island have 2-year terms. Most states (29 of them) limit governors to one or two consecutive terms, but 21 states allow three or more terms in office. In Illinois, for example, Republican governor James Thompson (formerly a crusading U.S. attorney) served for 14 years, and in New York, Mario Cuomo served for 12. In an effort to insulate gubernatorial elections from national political tides (and perhaps to reduce voter turnout and increase the power of party leaders), most states hold elections for governor in federal "off years"—nonpresidential election years—or in odd-numbered years, when no federal elections are being held at all.[10]

Varying Powers Governors' legal powers vary from state to state. Some governors are strong, while others are relatively weak. Nearly all have president-like powers to appoint some top executive officials, propose legislation, and sign or veto bills passed by the legislature (though the governor of North Carolina, one of the weakest, has no veto power). Governors in 42 of the 50 states enjoy a power of **line-item veto,** which means that they can reject parts of bills or particular appropriations while accepting others; this veto power gives them a big advantage over the legislature.[11] Throughout the 1980s, until the voters banned the practice, Wisconsin governor Tommy Thompson even vetoed particular letters within words, saving up those letters to insert new words of his own into laws.[12]

line-item veto The executive's power to delete part of a bill while signing the rest.

But most governors are hindered by limitations on their appointment powers. Nearly all states have some separately elected top officials whom the governors cannot remove or control: secretary of state, state treasurer, attorney general, and the like. Some states have many independent officials. In Texas, for example, the governor has to deal with a very independent commissioner of agriculture, the Texas Railway Commission (which regulates the oil industry), and an unusually strong lieutenant governor, as well as a very powerful state senate. (For an international comparison, see the Resource Feature on state executives in Mexico, Canada, and the United States.)

Early in American history, state governors rivaled the president of the United States in power and prestige. As the federal government grew, however, the relative standing of state governors declined. More recently, tight financial pressure on the states, especially after federal funds dried up during the 1980s, has made it much harder to succeed as governor and has led to many single-term governorships. At the beginning of the 1990s, many states had billion-dollar shortfalls in their budgets. In the 1990 elections, incumbent governors won reelection in fewer than half (17) of the 36 gubernatorial races.[13] Things improved a bit as state economies recovered from recession, but many incumbent governors either decided not to run or were defeated in 1994 and 1996 as well.[14]

Party Balance The Democratic party dominated most state governments for decades after the New Deal of the 1930s, when many more Americans identified themselves as Democrats than as Republicans. Even during the period

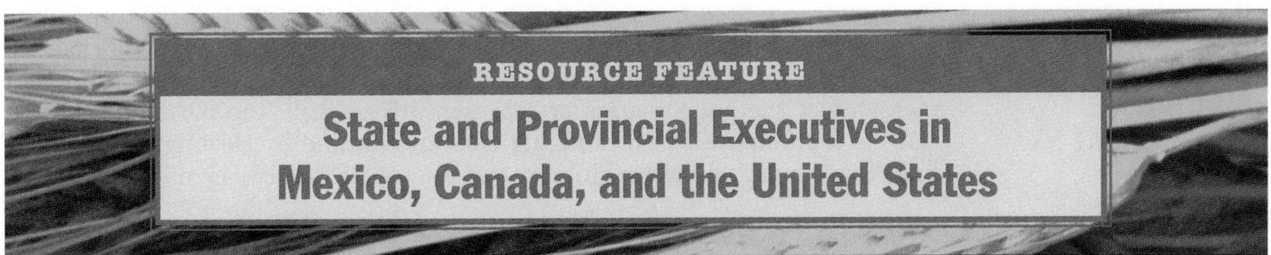

RESOURCE FEATURE

State and Provincial Executives in Mexico, Canada, and the United States

Like the United States, both Mexico and Canada have federal systems in which states or provinces, with their own chief executives, officially enjoy some independence. But their arrangements are actually quite different from each other and from our own.

In each of Mexico's 31 states, a governor is popularly elected for a single six-year term; reelection is prohibited. The governor is given strong authority over his one-chamber state legislature, which acts mostly as a rubber-stamp committee, formalizing the details of his program. But the governor himself is mostly a creature of the central government, which retains authority over most major policies and, in practice, generally picks the governor.

The vast majority of Mexican state governors since 1929 have been members of the Partido Institucional Revolucionario (PRI), whose top officials, especially the president of Mexico, choose state gubernatorial candidates. (Only very recently has the opposition PAN party become more competitive and captured 4 of the 31 governorships.) Under the Mexican constitution, the president of the country can have the Senate remove any state governor for failure to maintain law and order. These removals are no longer so frequent as they were between 1917 and 1964 (an average of one per year), but many governors have been pressured to resign "voluntarily."

Each of Canada's ten provinces and two territories, on the other hand, has an unusual degree of autonomy and self-direction in political matters. They control issues of education, health, social services, and civil justice. Each of the provinces is a classical parliamentary democracy, with free competition existing among several political parties. Canadian premiers, like British prime ministers, are chosen by the parliament and dismissed when their party loses its majority or is defeated in a vote of confidence. Canadian premiers have considerable influence over policy but are ultimately at the disposal of their parties.

Sources: George Delury, ed., World Encyclopedia of Political Systems and Parties, 2nd ed. (New York: Facts on File, 1987), pp. 158, 732, 734, 735; The Economist (October 28, 1995), p.16.

when four Republicans (Nixon, Ford, Reagan and Bush) and only one Democrat (Carter) served as president of the United States, most state governors were Democratic. In 1992, for example, 29 governors were Democrats, 19 were Republicans, and 2 were Independents.

The 1994 elections, however, brought a major switch to Republican dominance, perhaps reflecting voters' desire for efficient, lean budget management at a time of financial stringency. In 1996, Republican governors held office in 31 states with some 72 percent of the total U.S. population. These included several national stars of the Republican party—known for tax cuts, welfare reforms, and other policy innovations—such as Tommy Thompson of Wisconsin, William Weld of Massachusetts, Christine Todd Whitman of New Jersey, and John Engler of Michigan.

State Legislatures

bicameral Made up of two houses (for example, a legislative body).

Every U.S. state but one has a **bicameral** (two-chamber) legislature, consisting of a large assembly or house of representatives and a smaller state senate. (Nebraska has a unicameral, or single-chamber, nonpartisan legislature.)

For many years, state legislative districts, especially senate districts, were defined by counties or other geographical boundaries, regardless of population, so that people living in underpopulated rural areas got more legislative representation than those living in the growing cities and suburbs. Since the important U.S. Supreme Court decision in *Baker v. Carr* (1962), however, the states have been required to **reapportion** both chambers of their legislatures on a one-person–one-vote basis. Unlike the U.S. Senate, therefore, which has equal representation of large and small states, the state senates are now just smaller versions of the state houses of representatives. Still, the bicameral system makes a difference by encouraging deliberation and by slowing down policymaking,[15] especially when different parties control the two chambers.

reapportionment The redrawing of legislative district lines to account for population change.

Organization State legislatures are organized in much the same way as the U.S. Congress. The majority parties pick presiding officers (majority leader,

The New York State legislature and the legislative chambers of other states are organized much as is the United States Congress.

Willie Brown dominated the assembly in California until term limits forced him out. He was then elected mayor of San Francisco, and is shown celebrating his inauguration.

president, or speaker), who have varying degrees of influence over such matters as committee assignments, the legislative agenda, and the order of business. In California, for example, Speaker Willie Brown thoroughly dominated the state assembly for two decades, before term limits forced him out and he became mayor of San Francisco.

A great deal of work is done in specialized committees on education, public works, and so on, which resemble congressional committees. Just like committees of the U.S. Congress, they often develop close relationships with interest groups and bureaucrats who are involved in the same policy area. Since the general public usually cannot tell what goes on in such committees, they are an important entry point for interest group influence on state politics.

Party Control Even more than governorships, state legislatures tended, for many decades, to be controlled by the Democrats. In 1994, for example, the Democratic party had majorities in both the houses and the senates of 25 states, covering nearly all of the South and much of the East and West Coasts. The Republicans controlled only 8 states (4 of them in the Rocky Mountain area); in 14 states, the Republicans controlled one chamber and the Democrats dominated the other. Here, too, however, a Republican tide hit in the 1994 elections; for two years afterward party control was evenly split, with the Republicans and Democrats each controlling both legislative bodies in 20 states.[16] (See Figure 15.2.)

Professionalization Like the federal government, state governments have become more professional over the years as the size and responsibilities of government have increased.

During the nineteenth century, jobs in state government were part time. There was not much to do. Legislatures met only every two years or so, for brief sessions—usually during the winter, so that farmers would be free to attend. Most legislators relied on other jobs to make a living. As the country grew

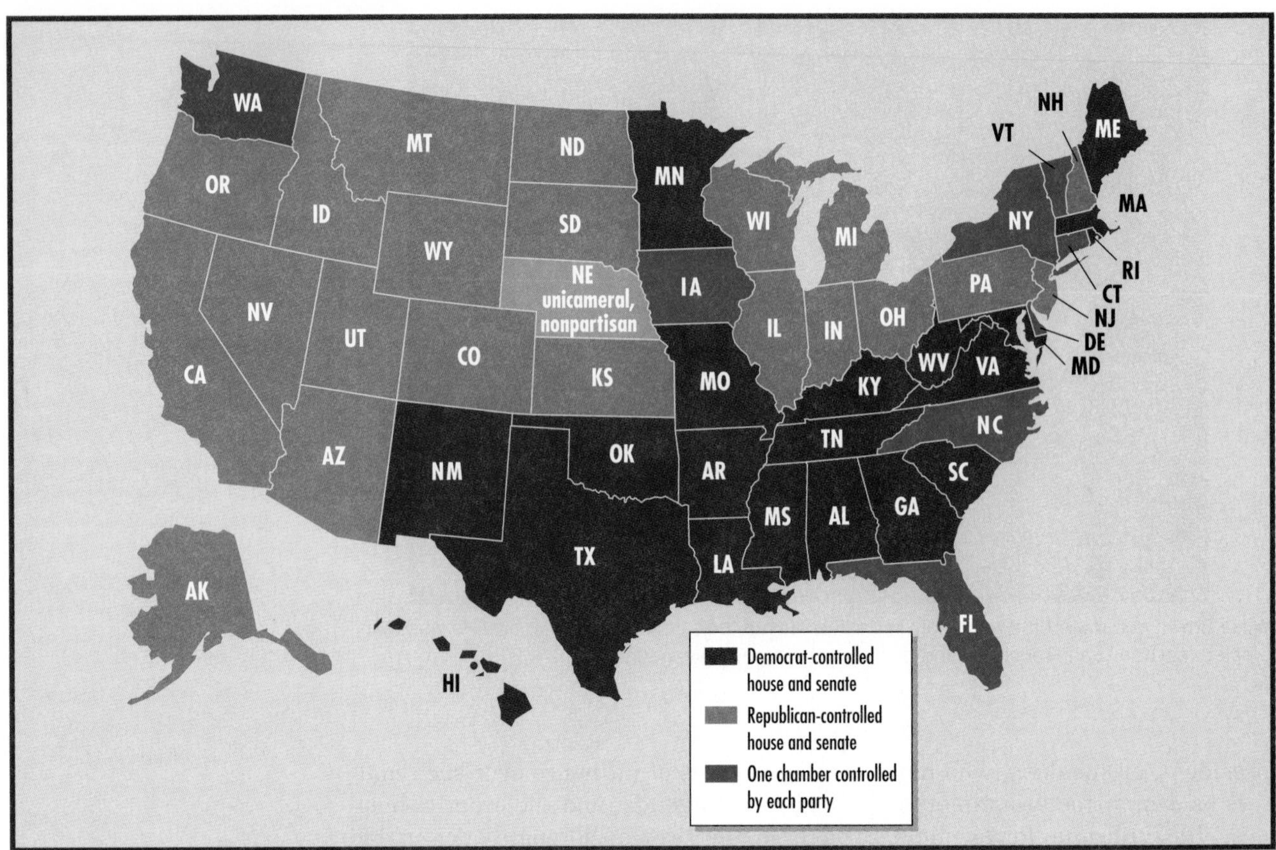

Figure 15.2 ▪ Party Control of State Legislatures

In 1995, the states were rather evenly balanced between Republican and Democratic control.

Source: State Elective Officials and Legislatures, 1995 (Lexington, KY: Council of State Governments, 1995).

and became industrialized, however, and as government took on more responsibility, state governments had more and more work to do, and the part-time system became clearly inadequate. Legislative sessions grew longer; most legislatures began to meet every year instead of every other year. (Texas, for example, still meets regularly only for a biennial session, but a "special session" has been held just about every nonregular year for as long as anyone can remember.) Legislating became a full-time job, requiring full-time salaries in order to attract talented people and large staffs of experts to deal with specialized legislation. There has been a strong trend, therefore, toward increased professionalization of the state legislatures, with higher salaries, stronger research staffs, and more efficient procedures.

Corruption At the same time, however, as the role of state government increased and the stakes grew higher, legislators—especially those who were still low-paid or part-time—became increasingly vulnerable to the growing numbers of corporate and other lobbyists, who could hire the legislators' law firms, pay speaking and "consulting" fees, and provide cash for campaigns, or even, in some cases, pay outright bribes. States like New York, California, and Wisconsin, which led the way in professionalizing their legislatures, seem mostly to have avoided large-scale corruption; those same states have also made many of the policy innovations discussed in Chapter 3. States that have lagged behind in professionalizing their legislatures, however, like Arizona and South Carolina, appear to have suffered some serious betrayals of the public trust.[17]

Early in 1991, for example, TV news programs showed videotapes of Arizona legislators, whose salaries barely exceeded the poverty line, pocketing many thousands of dollars in cash from gold-chained casino operator "J. Anthony Vincent," who was actually an undercover agent. (One legislator commented for the hidden camera, "I don't give a [expletive] about issues. . . . My favorite line is, 'What's in it for me?'") In this "sting," 7 legislators and 11 other people were indicted for bribery. After similar sting operations, 10 South Carolina state legislators were indicted for bribery.[18]

State legislatures have long been white, male bastions. Only in recent years have significant numbers of women broken in, and their numbers have increased very gradually; see the Struggle for Democracy box and Figure 15.3.

Direct Legislation

One aspect of state government that is quite different from national politics is the power of the citizens in 24 states (mostly in the West) to use an **initiative** in order to vote directly on legislation that they themselves propose, or to use a **referendum** in order to approve or overturn laws that the legislature has passed. When these ideas were championed by the Progressive movement at the beginning of the twentieth century, they were considered prodemocratic reforms: ways to let the people override corrupt or elitist legislatures. There is some evidence that they do work to increase popular influence; the mere existence of channels for direct legislation may force legislatures to be more responsive to the public.[19]

initiative Citizens' proposal of and direct voting on policy.

referendum Citizens' vote to approve or overturn legislation passed by the legislature.

But initiatives and referenda have turned out to be mixed blessings. Groups with a lot of money can pay on the "bounty system" to gather signatures and get measures on the ballot. Moreover, it is so difficult for ordinary voters to sort out ballot propositions that the wealthy and the well organized tend to prevail through media campaigns. California voters in one year, for example, faced a ballot with 17 different state initiatives and constitutional

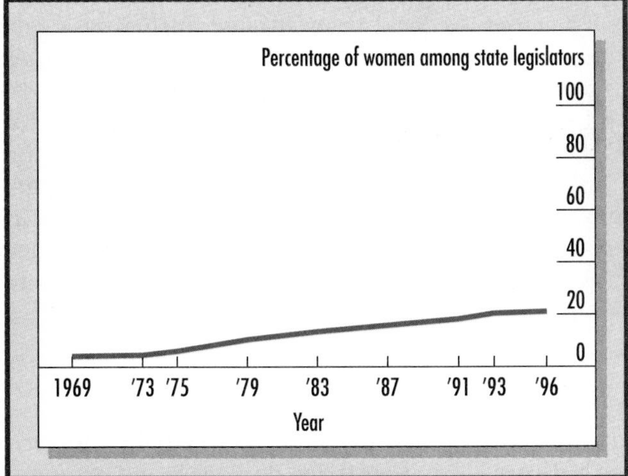

Figure 15.3 ▪ Women in State Legislatures

The proportion of state legislators who are women has risen slowly but steadily since 1969. However, women still make up less than a quarter of the legislative bodies.

Sources: Center for the American Woman and Politics, Rutgers University, reported in the New York Times (February 26, 1991), p. A13, and in a telephone interview, December 17, 1993. Rutger's Center Web page, December 1995.

Women in State and Local Politics

The Struggle for Democracy

Women won the right to vote in 1920, but they have only recently begun to move toward political equality in the sense of holding important political offices. Progress has been greatest in state and local governments.

Just after the 1990 elections—when Kansas, Oregon, and Texas inaugurated women as governors—only 31 women were serving in the U.S. Congress, accounting for just 6 percent of the seats there. But the Center for the American Woman and Politics at Rutgers University found that women constituted 18.1 percent of state legislators, up fairly steadily from the 4 percent of 1969. (see Figure 15.3). By 1995, the number of women in Congress had jumped to 55 (47 in the House plus 8 in the Senate), over 10 percent of the total membership. The proportion of women in state legislatures continued to rise, reaching 21 percent.

Some observers say that there is a long way to go and that progress is much too slow: at the present rate of increase (less than 1 percent per year), it would take a total of 64 years for women to win 50 percent of state legislative seats. But others, pleased that the trend is in the right direction, point out that state legislatures are traditional pipelines to higher office, state or national, and that they handle many important issues. Louisiana, for example, when it had a 97.9 percent male legislature, passed an extremely restrictive abortion law; with more women members, it might have acted differently.

States vary widely in their proportion of women legislators, from Alabama's 3.6 percent to Washington State's 39.5 percent. Most of the lowest proportions are found in the South; several of the highest are in states like Arizona and New Hampshire, with part-time (and low-paid) legislatures that are easier to get into. The proportion of women working outside the home, the power of political parties, their openness to women, and the extent of legislative turnover in each state also make a difference.

Even more women work in state and local government executive agencies, but they appear to face something of a glass ceiling. A Rutgers study found that women filled 43.5 percent of lower-level state and local jobs, but only 31.3 percent of high-level positions and only 19.8 percent of the very top (cabinet-level) state positions. States generally hire fewer women than localities, and the percentages of women in high positions varies greatly from state to state. Almost everywhere, however, the trend is up.

Sources: Rutgers Center for the American Woman and Politics, interview (December 17, 1993), Web page (January 1996); Robin Toner, "Women in Politics Gain, but Road Is a Long One," New York Times (February 25, 1991), p. A6; "Few Women Found in Top Public Jobs," New York Times (January 3, 1992), p. A8.

amendments (plus, in San Francisco, 11 local propositions), including a far-reaching Environmental Protection Act and an initiative called the Consumer Pesticide Enforcement Act that was sponsored by the agriculture industry to neutralize the environmental proposal. The state published a 250-page official pamphlet to explain voters' choices. "Most people can't even wade through the ballot pamphlet because of all the initiatives. It's all written in technical jargon," complained one citizen. "They're so long and involved and written in legalese," said another, "who knows what ramifications one phrase or sentence might have?"[20] Winning propositions have often proved disappointing to the public.

Courts

Most of the law courts that Americans encounter, from municipal traffic tribunals to courts dealing with divorces, civil suits for damages, and criminal charges, are part of state judicial systems.

These systems are headed by a court of last resort, usually called the state supreme court (New York calls it the court of appeals), which is elected by the voters. State supreme courts, like the U.S. Supreme Court, supervise their lower court systems and hear appeals from them; most also have the power to declare state laws invalid under the state constitution. But their independence is limited. In only four states do supreme court justices serve for life or until the age of 70; most state justices come up for periodic reelection or are subject to recall, or both.[21] Those who render unpopular decisions can be removed from office, as were three liberal justices, including Chief Justice Rose Bird, from the California Supreme Court during the mid–1980s.

In recent years, as the U.S. Supreme Court has pulled back from some of its earlier decisions protecting civil liberties, some state courts have become more activist in upholding rights under the U.S. Constitution or their own state constitutions. In certain cases, federal courts' interpretations of the U.S. constitution have subsequently been affected, in what one scholar calls a "dynamic judicial federalism."[22]

Structural and Political Influences on State Policy

Each state in the union is unique. Even next-door neighbors New Hampshire and Vermont are very different politically: New Hampshire has a long history of social conservatism and low-tax, low-spending fiscal conservatism, while Vermont has tended to be liberal about lifestyles and to provide more generous social programs. But the very differences among the states make it possible to study systematically why they differ. The federal system, with 50 state governments, provides a sort of laboratory for comparative research. We can examine exactly which characteristics of the states are associated with which differences in policy. A number of structural and political linkage factors are important.

Structural Factors Key structural factors include a state's level of economic development, the nature of its economy, and its political institutions.

Level of Economic Development Political science researchers have found that many of the sharpest political differences between states are related to their level of economic development. To put it simply, there are rich states and poor states. The rich ones have more tax money to spend, and they spend it on somewhat different things. For example, if you want to know how high or low the welfare benefits are likely to be in a particular state, you can make a good guess based on how rich or poor that state is in terms of per capita income (the average amount of money its citizens earn).[23] State spending policies are very different in New York, which in one year had a disposable per capita income of $18,631, and in Mississippi, which ranked last among the states, with a $11,528 per capita income. While New York's state and local governments were spending $5,021 per person, Mississippi's state and local governments were spending only about half as much: $2,562. While the average poor family participating in New York's social programs received $536 monthly in AFDC and SSI benefits (see Appendix II for definitions), the average poor family in Mississippi received only $119 per month.[24] (For related state-by-state comparisons, see Figure 15.4.)

Nature of the Economy Per capita income or wealth is not the only structural factor that affects states' politics and policies. The precise nature of the economy also makes a difference. The agricultural states of the Great Plains, for example, tend to have policies different from the old industrialized states of

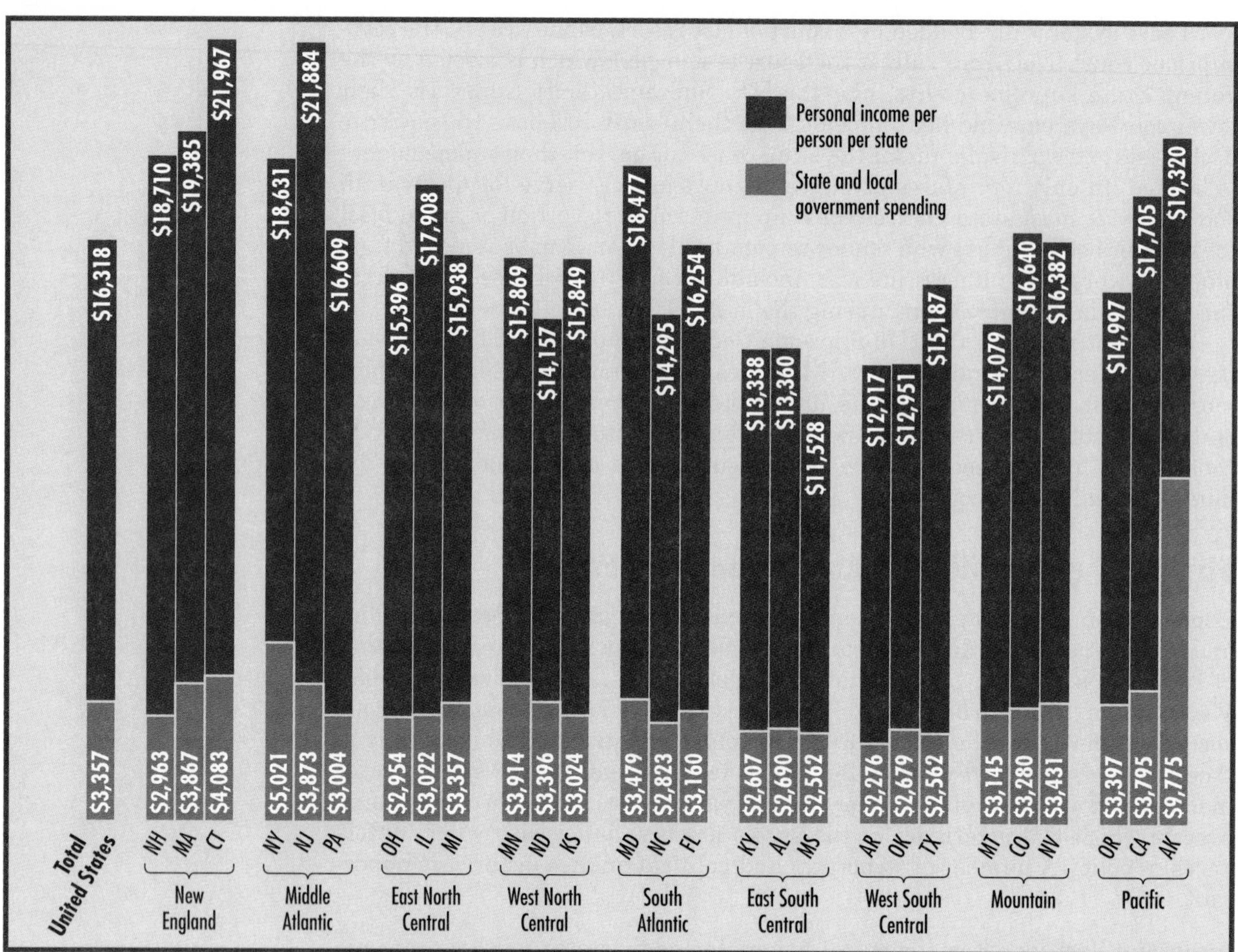

Figure 15.4 ▪ State Wealth and Government Spending

Some states have much more income than others. The richer states spend more on government programs and spend their money somewhat differently.

Source: Statistical Abstract of the United States, 1992, p. 437; U.S. Census Bureau, Government Finances, 1991, p. 107.

the Northeast or the newly industrializing Sun Belt. Population and culture matter, too. For example, several states of the old South, where slavery was once widespread, have noncompetitive political systems and very restricted social programs. The heavily Mormon, community-oriented population of Utah, on the other hand, has enacted much more generous social welfare programs than its low income level would predict.

Institutional Arrangements Certain political institutions and arrangements that have endured over many years and that can be thought of as structural factors also affect policymaking. The most important are those involving political competition and popular participation in politics—key ingredients of democracy. Before the civil rights movement, for example, most southern states made it extremely difficult for black people to vote, and the dominant position of a single white (Democratic) party prevented protest or dissent from getting a public hearing. The result was public policies that segregated and neglected blacks and, in many cases, poor whites as well. Today, African-Americans are enfranchised and two-party competition has increased in much of the South, but the southern states vary widely in this respect.[25] In the nation as a whole, the states with the most vigorous competition between parties tend to be the most generous with social benefits. A system of strong party competition seems to make more of a difference than which party—Republican or Democratic—actually holds power.[26]

Political Linkage Factors Political influences on state policies include public opinion and organized interest groups.

Public Opinion Research indicates that public opinion has substantial effects on state government policy. Gallup opinion surveys from the 1930s, for example, with unusually large samples that can be broken down by state, indicate that, when the people of a state favored or opposed capital punishment, child labor laws, or the inclusion of women on juries, the state tended to have policies in harmony with whatever its citizens wanted.[27] More recently, states' decisions about whether or not to ratify the Equal Rights Amendment depended partly on how their populations felt about it.[28]

In another leading study, a number of opinion surveys with large samples were used to rank the states according to how liberal or conservative (on the average) their populations were; state policies of many different sorts were also ranked according to their liberalism or conservatism. It turned out that the two things go together. States in which the public is more liberal tend to have more liberal policies, whereas states in which the public is more conservative have conservative policies. This is not just a coincidence, or a result of people endorsing whatever sorts of policies their states happen to have; a sophisticated statistical analysis indicates that public opinion genuinely influences policy.[29]

These results are illustrated in Figure 15.5, in which each state is located according to the liberal or conservative opinion of its public and the liberalism or conservatism of its policies. The clustering of states along the regression line rising upward to the right indicates that the more liberal the public is, the more liberal the policies tend to be. Economic development and other structural factors have much of their effect through the liberalism or conservatism of the public; people in poorer states tend to be more conservative. But additional factors are at work in the states above or below the trend line. Oregon, Wisconsin, and New York, for example, known for liberal political cultures among their elites, have enacted even more liberal policies than their public opinion would indicate. The same is true of Utah (presumably because of the Mormon church), whereas several southern and border states, including Arkansas, Alabama, Georgia, and West Virginia, have policies that are more conservative than their citizens would appear to want. The citizens of each state tend to get the kinds of policies they want, but not always.

Interest Groups It is impossible to be sure exactly how much influence interest groups have on state governments, but there is reason to believe that their impact is substantial. The conditions for interest group power are ripe. The states decide on policies that make a great deal of difference to groups and corporations—millions or even billions of dollars' worth of difference. Those groups are happy to invest money and effort in politics. State politicians, for their part, need outside money for campaigning and, in some cases, to make

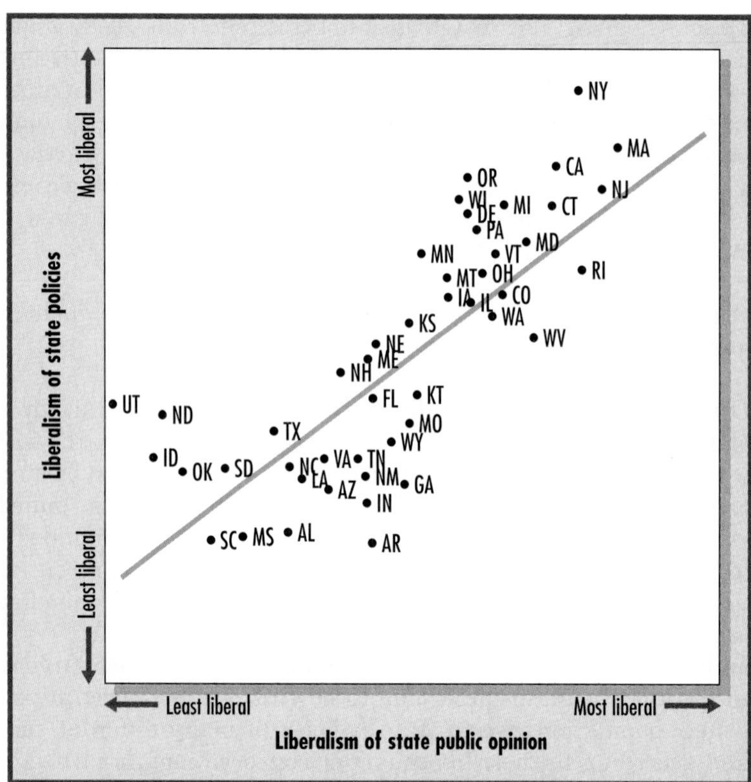

Figure 15.5 ■ **Public Opinion and the Liberalism or Conservativism of State Policies**

State policies tend to be in harmony with what their citizens want.

Source: Robert S. Erikson, Gerald C. Wright, and John P. McIver, *Statehouse Democracy: Public Opinion and Policy in the American States* (New York: Cambridge University Press, 1993), p. 79.

ends meet. Also, state policy decisions are often made without close public scrutiny.

In recent years, the gambling industry may have become the biggest single political influence in many states. Gambling casinos operate in 24 states, and 48 states have legalized gambling of some kind; total revenues exceed $39.9 billion. The gambling industry works hard to expand gambling, to get licenses, and to cut taxes and regulations, hiring lobbyists and spending millions of dollars on campaign contributions and referendum campaigns.[30]

In Missouri, for example, casino companies spent $4.2 million on a referendum to allow slot machines, outspending the opponents by 50 to 1; they lost narrowly but came back a few months later, spending $11.5 million and winning. In Texas, gambling interests hired 74 lobbyists, more than two for each state senator. Gambling lobbyists often include former high government officials: in Illinois, a governor, a state attorney general, a state police director, a mayor of Chicago, and dozens of state legislators. The governor of Mississippi got one third of all his campaign funds from casino interests; the president of the Louisiana Senate handed out $2,500 contributions from a casino owner to colleagues on the Senate floor. In the past few years, gambling-related bribery scandals have hit Louisiana, Missouri, Arizona, Kentucky, South Carolina, West Virginia, and Pennsylvania. There are signs of voter backlash, but gambling interests continue to pour money into politics, now at the federal as well as the state level.

Some state policies—perhaps including the state licensing of doctors, lawyers, opticians, liquor stores, taxicabs, and other businesses and services—may reflect not popular demand or experts' judgments, but the urging of organized interests. State regulation does sometimes protect the public from charlatans by providing helpful information, but often, its main effect is to limit the number of people engaged in regulated professions or businesses. This limitation drives up prices and pleases the lucky ones with licenses.[31] In some cases, the high value of licenses invites corruption.

Interest groups prevail even on some issues about which the public cares a good deal. In what was called a "resounding victory" for the National Rifle Association (NRA), for example, the Illinois State Senate defeated, by a tight 28–26 vote, a popular ban on large-capacity, semiautomatic weapons of the sort used by drug dealers. Some lawmakers said privately that they favored the ban but voted against it because they feared "retaliation." The chief Illinois lobbyist for the NRA called the bill "misdirected," having nothing to do with crime, and claimed to stand for "grass roots democracy": "The National Rifle Association is 100,000 dues-paying members in the state of Illinois who are constituents of every senator here."[32] (He did not mention that substantial NRA funding comes from gun manufacturers.) As popular agitation for gun control has increased in many parts of the country, the gun lobby has resisted fiercely at every step—and has often succeeded.

Interest groups invest a lot of money in state politics. The New York State Commission on Lobbying, for example, reported that, in one year, the 1,832 lobbyists that were registered with the state had been paid $38.5 million in fees and expenses—an amount that had risen 74 percent over five years. The top spender was Phillip Morris ($623,637), which had hired 9 lobbyists to resist proposals to increase the cigarette excise tax and to restrict smoking and tobacco advertising.[33] After a similar report three years earlier, a Common

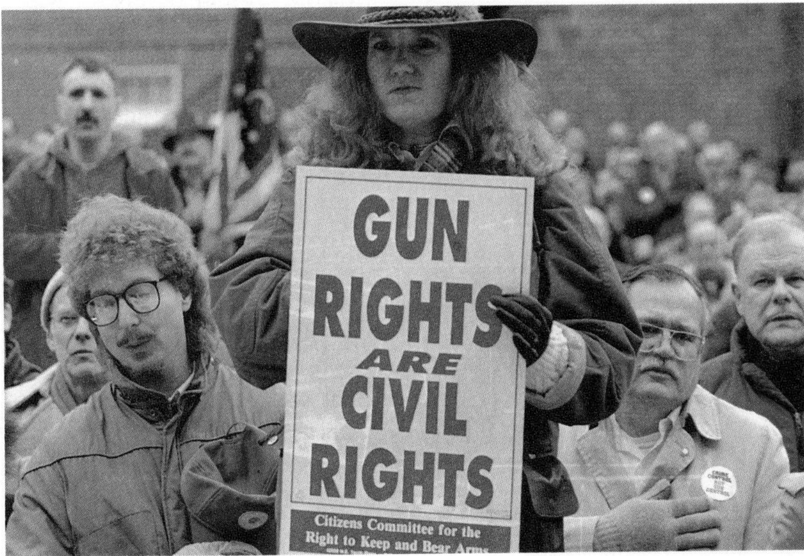

Popular support for gun control has made some headway at the state and local levels, but it has met fierce resistance from organized interests like the National Rifle Association.

Cause staffer remarked, "This [lobbying] is probably one of the few recession-proof industries left." The earlier report revealed that more than $1 million each was taken in by four lobbying firms, including one headed by the former chief counsel to the last two speakers of the state assembly. The biggest clients of the New York lobbying firms at that time included the tobacco industry, which was active in the defeat of then-governor Cuomo's proposal to restrict cigarette promotional schemes and vending machine sales (Philip Morris spent $566,223), and the New York State Soft Drink Association, which paid $430,224 to lobbyists in a successful effort to block Cuomo's plan to turn unclaimed 5-cent bottle deposits over to the state.[34]

Democracy in the States

We have suggested that state policy may be more susceptible to interest group influence and less subject to popular control than federal government policy is. Political scientists Grant McConnell and E. E. Schattschneider have spelled out some reasons. As McConnell put it, when the size of a political constituency is small, it is easier for wealthy and well-organized interests to dominate it. Decentralized state institutions "give very great advantages to structures of private power and to private interests generally." The multiplicity and obscurity of elective offices and agencies diminishes the public's interest in them and makes them "effectively accountable only to a narrow constituency consisting of the group or groups most directly and intimately affected by the agencies' activities."[35] Schattschneider analyzed the matter in a similar way: the smaller and more narrow the "scope of conflict"—that is, the number of people aware and involved—the more likely it is that well-organized and wealthy minorities will win. Information and visibility are crucial. What the public does not know about, it cannot control.[36]

State governments often operate with relatively narrow constituencies and low visibility. Television news programs on the national networks naturally devote much more attention to Congress and the president than to any particular state governor or legislature. Local newspapers mostly follow suit. Citizens seldom learn much about what their state governments are doing (few even know the names of their state senators or state representatives), whereas organized interests pay very close attention indeed.

On the other hand, we cannot be sure that there really is such a clear contrast between state and federal governments. Remember the substantial relationship between the public's ideology and the liberal or conservative thrust of states' policy, shown earlier. A different study of the effects of public opinion on policy turned up no significant state-national difference at all. It found that, when the public changed its preferences about state policies, the policies of the states tended to change accordingly, responding to public opinion, just as federal policies do.[37] (Many of the state policies that were studied, however, involved high-visibility matters, such as abortion and capital punishment; on more typical, mundane issues, states may be less responsive to the public.)

The increasing importance of state government over the years may have led to more public scrutiny and more public control, while the professionalization of state governments may have reduced their susceptibility to bribery or interest group pressure. In any case, the situation certainly varies from state to state.

Local Politics

America's cities, towns, and suburbs have a variety of governmental forms and face a variety of problems.

The Rise and Fall of Urban Machines

As we saw in Chapter 4, one of the great trends in American history has been the rise of big cities. Much of the growth of cities resulted from immigration. All told, some 57 million people immigrated to America between 1820 and 1990, about 1 million per year coming during the peak period between 1905 and 1914, mostly from southern and eastern Europe.[38]

Many of these people settled in ethnic enclaves in big cities on the East Coast. Remnants of their ethnic neighborhoods can still be seen today in such cities as Boston, New York, and New Haven, even though the waves of European immigration mostly stopped at the beginning of World War I. Later, especially after World War II, millions of southern blacks moved to northern cities.[39] From the 1960s to today, Latino and Asian immigration has been especially significant. Each wave of immigrants has changed the face of America's cities and has altered urban politics.

Development of Political Machines The rise of cities and the immigration of ethnic groups created a new kind of politics. They were responsible for the development of the urban **political machine,** a party organization staffed by city workers who owed their **patronage** jobs to the party and kept in close touch with their friends and neighbors in the precincts and wards, doing people favors and getting votes in return.

political machine A party organization staffed by city workers who owe their jobs to the party.

patronage Government offices and contracts distributed to the supporters of the winning party; same as *spoils.*

The first political machine emerged in pre–Civil War New York, built on Irish immigrants' fire companies, militia companies, gangs, and workingmen's clubs. Politicians used these class and ethnic organizations to dispense assistance and to organize voters.[40] Irish immigrants seem to have been particularly skillful in politics.

Later, as hundreds of thousands of non-English-speaking immigrants arrived on the East Coast, urban machines in New York, Boston, and elsewhere helped them with jobs, housing, applications for citizenship, and emergency relief, winning their loyalty at the polls. Thus, the urban machines were enabled to control the **spoils** of government: "honest graft," including lucrative contracts, bribes, and contributions from businesspeople seeking streetcar or utility monopolies.[41] Many of these party organizations (the Pendergast machine in Kansas City, for example, and William Green's in Philadelphia) persisted well into the twentieth century and formed important elements of the national Democratic party. Mayor Richard J. Daley's Chicago Democratic organization, one of the last of the breed, flourished from the 1950s to the 1970s, operating on the principle "Don't make no waves, don't back no losers."[42]

spoils The practice of distributing government offices and contracts to the supporters of the winning party; same as *patronage.*

The topic of political machines used to arouse strong emotions. Many immigrant and working-class Americans appreciated the help that political organizations gave them, particularly during the years when the federal government offered no social welfare programs. Some social scientists refer to the beneficial "functions" of urban machines, though others point out the uneven and sometimes skimpy or symbolic nature of the benefits delivered. But many middle- and upper-class Americans deplored the corruption and inefficiency associated with these machines. Some also disliked the political power that urban machines provided for foreign-born and working-class people.

Progressive Reforms After 1900 or so, the Progressive movement, largely energized by white Anglo-Saxon Protestant businesspeople and professionals, crusaded to "clean up" city governments and to destroy political machines, through a series of institutional changes: civil service laws that forbade political hiring or firing and kept city workers out of politics; secret ballots and poll watchers to prevent ballot-box stuffing; nonpartisan elections for city councils,

Richard J. Daley (center, with U.S. Senator Birch Bayh on the left and Polish supporters on the right), the leader of one of the last great urban political machines in the United States. Daley's son, Richard M. Daley, later served as a more reformist mayor.

often held at large in the entire city, rather than by machine-dominated ward; and, especially in smaller and middle-sized cities, appointive, nonpartisan **city manager** executives (rather than elected mayors), who were supposed to use businesslike management techniques and to be immune from political influence.[43]

city manager An appointed official who runs the day-to-day government of many towns and small cities.

city council–mayor system A system of local government in which an elected city council passes legislation and a mayor acts as chief executive.

The biggest cities tended to resist these reforms and to retain elected **city council–mayor systems.** Political parties remained active in such places as Chicago, even when the elections were supposedly "nonpartisan" and no party labels were allowed on the ballot. Party machines put up candidates, and precinct workers made clear to voters which candidates were the nonpartisan Democrats and which were the nonpartisan Republicans. Many big-city machines stayed strong until New Deal social welfare programs took over key functions that had been used to attract voters, and until court decisions clamped down on political hiring and further weakened patronage systems.

But the changes that resulted from the Progressive movement swept through much of America, including most small and middle-sized cities in the West, where city manager government remains the norm. These changes undoubtedly resulted in more honest and efficient government. City managers tend to be highly professional; they keep in touch with the latest policy ideas and management techniques through nationwide professional associations and journals. At the same time, however, the Progressives' measures probably reduced the popular control of city government and thereby impeded democracy. When political parties are weakened or eliminated, they are less able to alert people to government actions that might hurt them, and citizens have a harder time figuring out how to vote. At-large elections generally reduce the representation of minorities, who could win if they ran in their own communities. Also, nonpartisan elections generally show lower rates of citizen participation, particularly by the poor. Fewer people's voices are heard.[44]

Diverse Urban Governments

Our present city governments reflect this history of immigration, growth, and reform. There is a crazy quilt of different arrangements. Many cities have city manager governments with councils or commissions. Some cities elect city councils and **strong mayors,** who appoint other officials and veto council ordinances. Still others have city councils with **weak mayors,** who do little but preside over council meetings. There is every imaginable sort of electoral system, often mixing partisan and nonpartisan elections, district and at-large elections, within one city.

strong-mayor system A system of local government in which the mayor has extensive powers of appointment, budgeting, rule making, and the like.

weak mayor A local mayor who has few powers of appointment, budgeting, or rule making; the city council and/or independent boards and commissions exercise most powers.

The Impact of Institutions Institutional arrangements make a difference. The fiscal crises of expanding demands and shrinking revenues that beset America's cities from the 1970s through the 1990s had much more devastating effects in New York, where decisions were centralized and the mayor was beholden to city workers' unions, than in Chicago, where many government functions were insulated on independent boards with their own sources of revenue, and where the mayor could use his party machine to keep city workers under control.[45] In one year, for example, New York City had an enormous budget of $42.5 *billion,* of which about $8 billion went for education, $6.8 billion for public welfare, $4.7 billion for utilities, $3.6 billion for health and hospitals, and $2.6 billion for police and fire protection. The city governments of Los Angeles and Chicago, by contrast, had far smaller budgets of only $6.6 and $3.9 billion, respectively, most of which went for police and fire protection, highways, and, in the case of Los Angeles, utilities.[46] Many expensive functions that New York City paid for were farmed out by the Los Angeles and Chicago to counties, special districts, or other governmental units.

Many city mayors have been frustrated by the legal limitations on their powers and functions that can be traced back to the Progressive era. For example, after a bystander's videotape recorded the brutal beating of black motorist Rodney King by Los Angeles police officers, and transcripts of squad car communications suggested that such violence was routine for the Los Angeles Police Department, Mayor Tom Bradley could not fire Police Chief Daryl Gates, who had been chosen by an independent commission and was protected by civil service regulations. Gates stayed on for more than a year before resigning. Similarly, New York mayor Rudolph Guiliani struggled hard to exert some control over the huge New York school system, run by an independent board.

Privatization As financial pressures have increased, many cities have **privatized** public services, contracting them out to private entrepreneurs, who, it is hoped, will be more efficient and less expensive. Virtually all cities now contract out food services and construction; most use private janitorial services; and many contract out garbage collection, security services, and automobile towing (see Figure 15.6). Even park maintenance, data processing, and street repair, which only 15 to 20 percent of local governments contracted out ten years ago, are now privatized by about one-third of our cities and towns.[47]

privatization The process of turning over certain government functions to the private sector.

Seventy years after the city of Philadelphia led the nation in having public workers provide public services, it moved to privatize garbage collection and custodial services. Los Angeles County contracted out the management of five small airports; Chicago turned vehicle towing into a profit center; Fort Worth even transferred the operation of its zoo to a charitable organization.[48]

One problem with privatization, however, is that private firms can get fat and inefficient if they enjoy the same monopolies that city departments used to

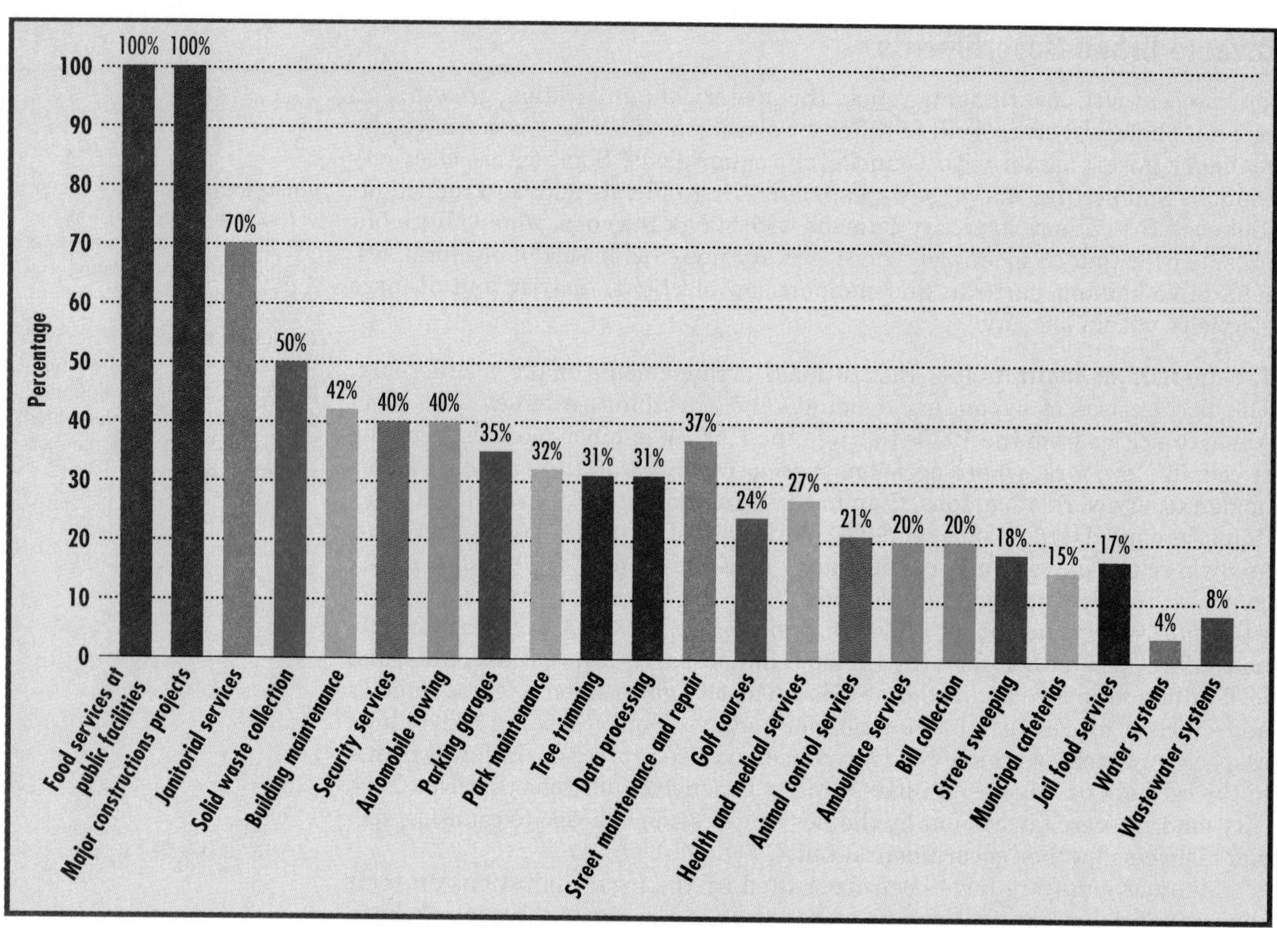

Figure 15.6 ▪ Percentages of Surveyed Local Governments That Contract Out Services

A wide range of government work is now done by private contractors.

Source: Data provided by the Mercer Group, Inc., January 6, 1996.

hold. Indianapolis, under Republican mayor Stephen Goldsmith, has taken the lead in a rather different, competition-based strategy in which city departments regularly bid against private businesses to perform services. Indianapolis has cut millions of dollars from its city budget and has reduced the number of city employees by a quarter, while it has also used the expertise of city workers to improve services and has avoided layoffs.[49]

This kind of experimentation with privatization and with mixed public-private arrangements, which is encouraged by our federal system, has fed back to influence the national government. Much of the Clinton administration's excitement about "reinventing government," for example, drew on ideas from state and local governments.[50]

Politics in Towns and Suburbs

The growth of suburbs, the decline of small towns and rural areas, and the rise of the Sun Belt are also important to an understanding of present-day local politics.

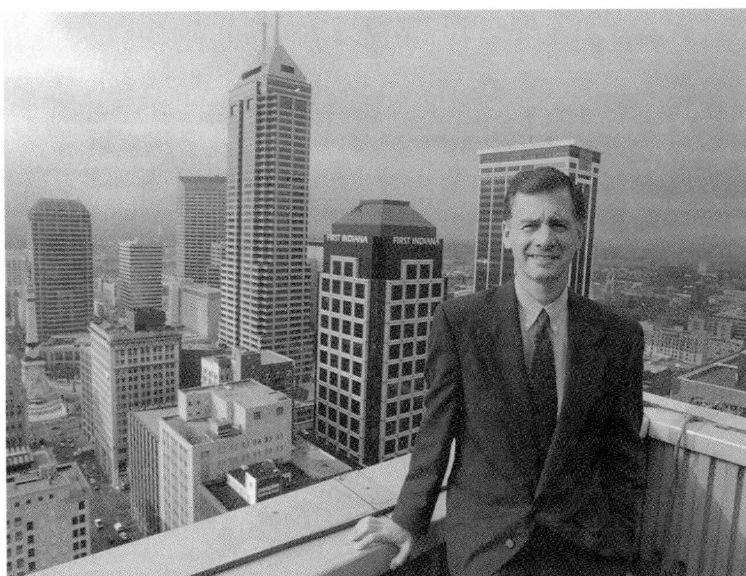

Mayor Stephen Goldsmith of Indianapolis established a system in which city departments compete against private businesses to see who can provide services most cheaply and efficiently.

Suburbs The concept of *suburb* is hard to define precisely. The Latin words *sub urbe* mean "under" or "next to" the city. We think of the English word *suburb* as meaning a bedroom community, a residential district on the outskirts of town from which most people commute to work in an inner city. But just how residential must it be, and just what proportion of its people must commute, for us to distinguish a suburb from a separate town or city? The U.S. Census has given up trying to answer these questions; it does not mention suburbs; instead, it talks about *cities* like Chicago (population 2.768 million), *primary metropolitan statistical areas* like "Chicago, IL PSMA" (population 7.561 million), and *consolidated metropolitan statistical areas* like "Chicago–Gary–Lake County (IL), IL-IN-WI CMSA" (population 8.410 million).[51]

Obviously, these metropolitan areas include many suburbs, even if we cannot be sure exactly how many. Residents of Santa Monica, Bethesda, or Evanston may firmly assert their towns' independence, but to much of the world, they look like suburbs of Los Angeles, Washington, D.C., and Chicago, respectively. The contrast between the city of Chicago's 3 million people and the Chicago CMSA's 8 million indicates that there are a lot of people living in suburbs.

Since the end of World War II, in fact, widespread ownership of automobiles and the building of freeways, along with federal home loans and mortgage tax deductions, have enabled many millions of Americans to settle in the suburbs and still go to work in the city. Attracted by large homes with spacious lawns and gardens, on quiet streets, with convenient shopping centers and good public schools and other facilities, many middle-class and upper-middle-class people have moved to suburbia (see Figure 15.7). Echoing earlier waves of immigration to the United States, ethnic groups that have prospered economically—first the Irish, Germans, and Scandinavians, and then the Italians, Poles, and Asians—have tended to move to the suburbs, leaving many black people and recent immigrants in the central cities.

Suburbs, with their relatively affluent and mostly white-collar populations, generally follow the Progressive model of nonpartisan, efficiency-

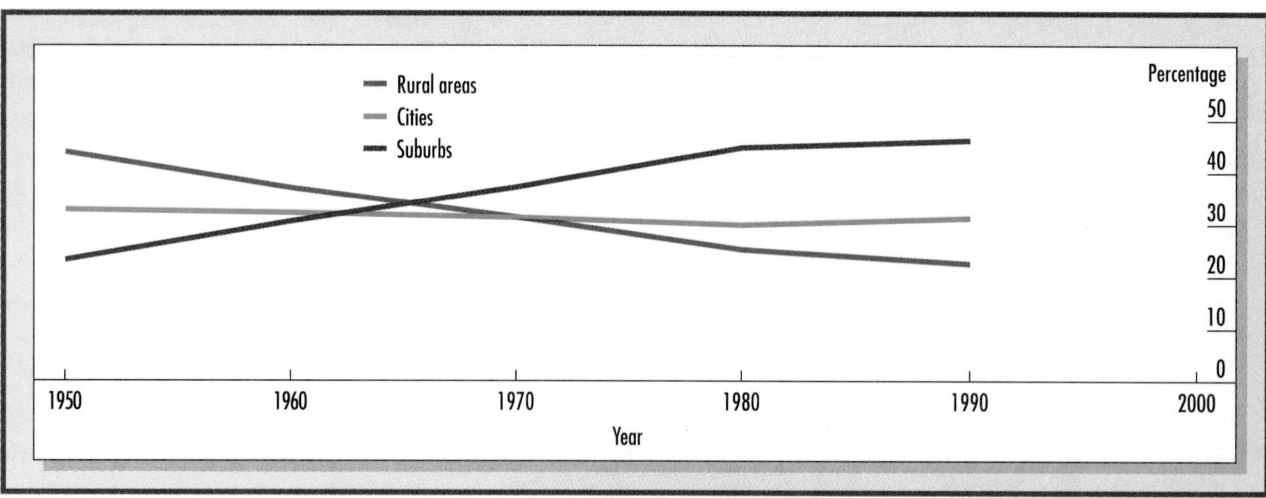

Figure 15.7 ■ Percentage of the U.S. Population Living in Cities, Suburbs, and Rural Areas, According to the Decennial National Census

Rural areas have shrunk, while suburbs have grown rapidly and cities have stayed about the same.

Source: U.S. Census Bureau, as reported in the *New York Times* (September 11, 1990), p. A20; (May 27, 1992), p. A17.

oriented, city-manager-style government. They tend to spend a great deal of money on schools and other public services but also try to keep property taxes low.

Small Towns At the same time that suburbs have grown, rural areas and small towns in America have shrunk, from about 44 percent of the U.S. population in 1950 to just 23 percent in 1990. (Big cities have declined slightly, too.) Tractors and mechanized farming have decreased the number of farmers needed. In Scranton, Iowa, for example, where the county population dropped between the 1980 and the 1990 census by 17 percent, to about 10,000, a visitor found Main Street deserted. The Scranton Cafe still had its daily specials scribbled on a chalkboard, and men in bib overalls still swapped stories over coffee, but the town's arcade, drugstore, and Friday-night high-school football games were just memories. One resident told a reporter, "It looks like a ghost town. I sure miss the people." In the nearby county seat, a poster proclaimed, "$1,000 Reward!" for anyone who could attract an employer providing at least 15 jobs, and the economic development officer spoke with pride of a planned Japanese factory where about 25 workers were going to make soyflake for instant tofu.[52]

Small towns often find it necessary to professionalize their governments, just as states and cities have done. As a retiring town official of Derby, Vermont (population 4,500), put it, it used to be that "a little bit of arithmetic, some good common sense and a sense of honesty" were all you needed to be a selectman. "Now it's preferable that you be a lawyer." A flood of federal and state directives pours in, concerning everything from solid-waste disposal to personnel management. Labor negotiations, budget planning, and applying for grants require technical skills. Volunteers are scarce. Many small towns have begun to hire professional managers.[53]

Throughout the United States, small towns have declined as suburbs have grown.

The Sun Belt In recent years, the movement toward suburbia has combined with a population shift toward the Sun Belt of the South and the Southwest, as the industries of the northern Rust Belt have declined and as those in the South have grown. Most of the biggest population increases evident in census figures have occurred in Sun Belt suburbs. For example, Moreno Valley, California, a suburb of Riverside, grew by 466 percent in 12 years, from a population of 28,309 to 132,000. Mesa, Arizona, a suburb of Phoenix, grew from 152,404 to 297,000. Rancho Cucamonga, California, a Los Angeles suburb, increased in population from 55,250 to 111,000. Plano, Texas, a suburb of Dallas, grew from 72,331 to 142,000. Other fast-growing cities include Irvine, Escondido, Oceanside, Santa Clarita, Chula Vista, and Ontario, California; Arlington and Mesquite, Texas; Glendale and Scottsdale, Arizona; and Virginia Beach, Virginia—all of them suburbs.[54] In many cases, however, these communities have developed major shopping areas and industries of their own, increasing their economic independence and changing what it means to be a suburb. In fact, many people now commute from one suburb to another.

The rise of suburbs in the Sun Belt and elsewhere has had two important effects on local politics. First, more and more people are living in places with political systems based on the Progressives' "good government" model, with city managers and professional staffs, but facing the great strains that come with rapid growth: pressure on schools and other services, and problems of traffic congestion and air pollution. Second, many inner cities have been left with poor people, decaying infrastructures, and very limited tax bases to pay for needed services.

The Plight of the Cities

Many older cities now have large minority populations and extensive poverty. These two things are connected. At the time of the 1990 census, when the total U.S. population was only about 12 percent black and 9 percent Hispanic, the population of New York City was 28.7 percent black and 24.4 percent Hispanic; Los Angeles was 14 percent black and 39.9 percent Hispanic; and Chicago was 39.1 percent black and 19.6 percent Hispanic. A number of cities were more

In parts of the growing Sun Belt, crowding and pollution have become problems.

than 50 percent black: Baltimore, Detroit, Gary, Inglewood, Newark, and Washington, D.C., in the North, as well as Atlanta, Birmingham, Richmond, and four other cities in the South. There were Hispanic majorities in Brownsville, Corpus Christi, El Paso, Laredo, and San Antonio, Texas, as well as in six California cities and Hialeah and Miami, Florida.[55]

Poverty Blacks and Hispanics tend to be poorer than other Americans. In one year, for example, the median family income of black Americans was only $21,161, compared with $38,909 for whites, and 33 percent of blacks, but only 12 percent of whites, fell below the poverty line. Hispanics are not much better off than blacks, with a median family income of $23,901 and with 29 percent below the poverty line.[56]

Many problems accompany poverty. Drug use is common and flagrant in most inner cities. Crime rates and gun use are high. According to FBI figures, violent crimes in major metropolitan areas occurred at the rate of 871 crimes per 100,000 population, about twice the rate for smaller cities and four times that for rural areas. Robbery in big cities was 6 times more frequent than in small cities and 20 times more common than in rural areas. The police in Miami, Newark, Atlanta, New York, Chicago, Baltimore, St. Louis, and Washington, D.C., each reported more than 1,200 robberies and more than 30 murders per 100,000 population, and many other cities were not far behind.[57] Young men in the United States are killed at more than 10 times the rate of these many other industrialized countries (see Figure 15.8). In fact, homicide is the leading cause of death among America's young black men, and young men in Harlem are less likely to survive to the age of 40 than are their counterparts in impoverished Bangladesh.[58]

Children One of the most unhappy aspects of life in the inner city is that children who are born there (through no choice of their own, of course) face severe

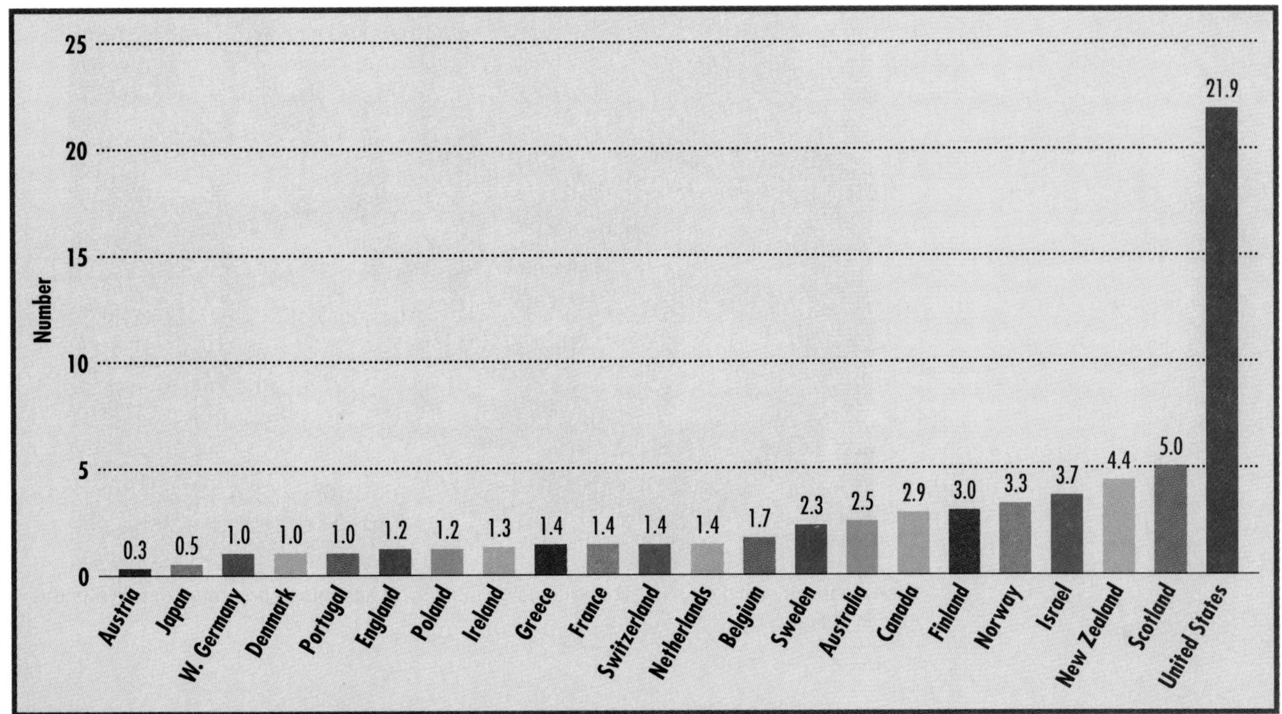

Figure 15.8 ■ Killings per 100,000 Men Aged 15–24 in 1986 and 1987

Young men in the United States are killed far more frequently than in other advanced countries.

Source: Journal of the American Medical Association, reported in the *New York Times* (June 27, 1990), p. A9.

disadvantages. A few begin life in crisis, born to drug-abusing mothers, and are rushed to neonatal intensive-care units with seizures, severe respiratory problems, or congenital infections. Others are born with AIDS. Many more find themselves living in poverty with a single parent (generally their mother), getting poor nutrition, poor health care, little inspiration from parent or peers, and inadequate schooling.

About 46 percent of all black children in the country and 39 percent of all Hispanic children are in families with incomes below the poverty level. Of all black children in the United States, 61.3 percent live with their mothers only, and more than 83 percent of those children are poor.[59] These rates are still higher in the inner cities. As they grow up, even young people who are determined to overcome all obstacles and who manage to avoid danger and resist the temptations of gang membership or drug dealing find stark limits on what they can accomplish. In some inner-city high schools, the very top graduating student often finds that her or his record is not sufficient for admission to a good college.

Of course, poverty is not found only in cities or among minorities; severe pockets of poverty also exist in Appalachia, the rural South, and rural areas generally. In fact, most poor people are white. But the high concentrations of poor people in the cities present a major problem for urban governments. They also create a stark contrast between impoverished ghettos and vibrant commercial, entertainment, and residential areas populated by young urban professionals.

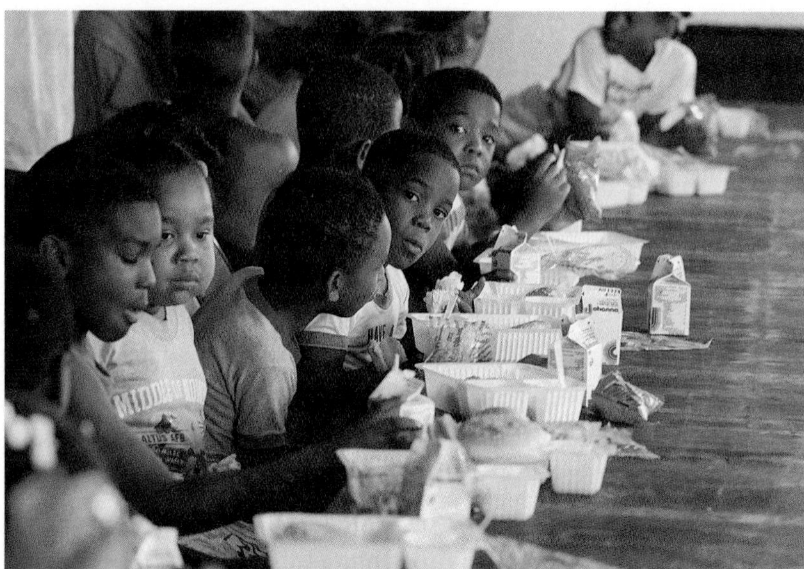

Many inner-city children can get nutritious meals only at schools or day care centers like this one in Philadelphia.

Minority Power The large minority populations in America's cities have gradually won political power and government representation. Cities with majority black populations, such as Gary, Detroit, and Newark, have had a number of black mayors. The largest cities, with substantial black minorities, have also elected black mayors from time to time, for example, Tom Bradley in Los Angeles, Harold Washington in Chicago, and David Dinkins in New York City. Racial and ethnic divisions have led to some bitter campaigns, though. Harold

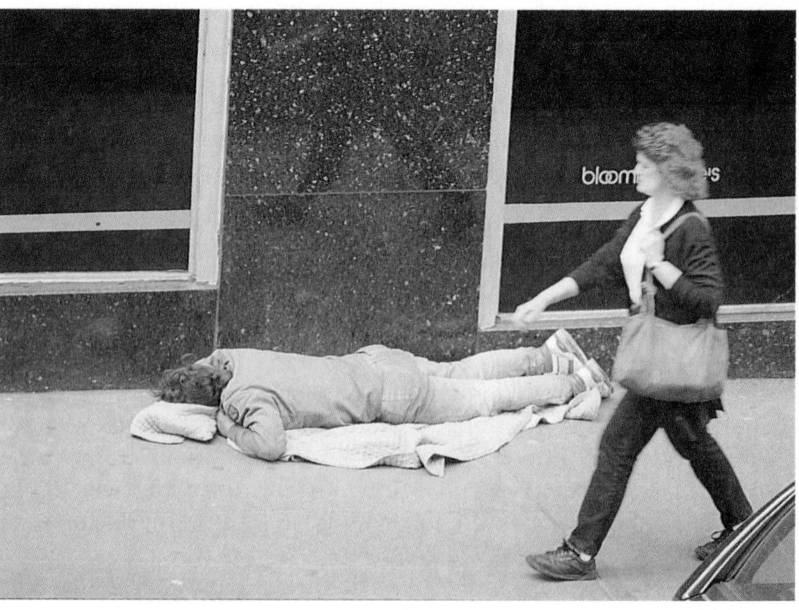

Many urban areas show stark contrast between rich and poor.

Washington was elected in Chicago in 1983 only because two white candidates divided the vote against him, and he faced stonewalling opposition and "Council Wars" from white ethnic aldermen; Bradley and Dinkins were both replaced by white mayors. Hispanic mayors have been elected, at one time or another, in San Antonio, Denver, Miami, and other cities. The makeup of city councils, city workers, and officials has also come to reflect the importance of minority populations.

Many city governments have made vigorous attempts to address urban problems. Detroit mayors Coleman Young and Dennis Archer, for example, have led major renovation efforts in their city's decaying downtown area. Chicago, once said to have the weakest public school system in the nation, pioneered in school reform and decentralized control to elected local boards that could hire and fire principals. Cities have tackled their drug problems with rehabilitation and strict law enforcement, and they have tried to provide shelter for the homeless and support for the poor.

City Limits The problems are vast, however, and the resources are sparse. Urban poverty not only creates many problems for city governments to solve but also means that city governments do not have much money with which to solve them. There is not a great deal of income or wealth to tax. Also, as we noted in Chapter 3, competition among political units creates "city limits," practical constraints on what any local government can do. If, for redistributive purposes, a city imposes taxes that are too heavy on businesses or wealthy people, those businesses and wealthy people may move out to the suburbs or the Sun Belt while more poor people move in, defeating what the government is trying to accomplish. Thus, local governments generally put more emphasis on policies for economic development than on fighting poverty.[60]

In order to attract businesses and to keep corporate headquarters and major enterprises from fleeing, many cities feel obliged to offer generous tax breaks and subsidies that then reduce the money available to solve urban problems. At the same time that New York faced a fiscal crisis, firing schoolteachers and leaving roads and bridges unrepaired, for example, it offered the commodity exchanges $145 million in cash and tax breaks for a new 43-story office tower so they would not move to New Jersey. Extended protests by the "Tribeca Task Force" and other neighborhood groups eventually forced the project to move to a less residential location, but it still cost the taxpayers millions.[61]

The tendency of city governments to subsidize development while cutting back on social programs is exacerbated by the political power of developers and corporations, which lobby city governments intensely and provide much of the money that urban politicians need to get elected. New York mayor Rudolph Giuliani, for example, when he was first elected, got $76,550 in contributions bundled together by landlord William Koeppel. In the city elections that year, 16,400 people made donations of $100 or less, but seven times as much money came from just 500 people who made the maximum contribution ($6,500) allowed by law.[62] Earlier, while David Dinkins was mayor, real estate developers, city contractors, unions, and other interest groups spent a total of $8.5 million on lobbyists in New York City. The top lobbying firm, which received more than $1.6 million in fees, was headed by Sid Davidoff, a longtime friend, tennis partner, and occasional adviser of Mayor Dinkins. Davidoff told the *New York Times* that his firm made the most money because it was "the best." Others explained that clients saw Davidoff as providing a high level of "access": "This guy is a phone call away from the top levels of City Hall."[63]

Federal Help?

Some analysts argue that the federal government should provide money to deal with urban problems, because only a national solution is possible. City governments cannot cope on their own; if they scrape up their own money to help the poor, more poor people will move in and rich people will move out. Moreover, the cities provide important commercial, financial, and cultural services to surrounding communities and the entire country, for which they are not fully compensated.

As we saw in Chapter 3, national grants-in-aid are a significant source of state and local government revenue. During the 1980s and early 1990s, however, the Reagan and Bush administrations cut rather than increased urban aid. In 1981, the federal government had spent a total of $27.4 billion on five urban-related programs: employment and training, general revenue sharing, community development block grants, urban mass transit, and urban development action grants. But ten years later, President Bush's budget allocated less than one-third as much—a total of $8.9 billion—to those same five programs. Bush also proposed to take control of many federal programs away from the cities and to give it to the states, which have tended to favor their suburban rather than urban areas. Mayors of both parties protested. Republican mayor Althaus of York, Pennsylvania, called Bush's proposal "entirely wrong," while Democratic mayor Flynn of Boston declared, "This isn't federalism; this is fraud." He complained that "the federal government has been walking away from America's cities" at a time of extraordinary problems.[64]

But even the subsequent Clinton administration, while expressing sympathy for the cities, was itself pressed for cash and did not hurry to provide more federal money. And the Republican-controlled 104th Congress cut back federal funds still further, while proposing to put most of the money into block grants controlled by the states rather than the cities. Many state governors were enthusiastic; city mayors were distressed.

Democracy in the Cities

We cannot easily assess how democratic city governments are, or compare them with state and national governments, because there are no comparable data on relationships between public opinion and policy. We can only hazard an informed guess. Cities may tend to stand in a middle position, more highly visible and more responsive to their citizens than most state governments, but less so than the national government. Undoubtedly, cities vary a great deal; among the large ones, we would expect that those with the most coherent, competitive party systems and the clearest and most centralized lines of governmental authority would respond most fully to the wishes of their citizens.

Summary

State and local governments spend a great deal of money—more than half as much as the federal government does—and provide most of the government services that we encounter in our daily lives.

State governments resemble miniature versions of the federal government, with written constitutions; governors who have varying powers of veto and appointment; legislatures that are generally organized into two chambers and do much of their business in committee; and court systems headed by a supreme court. State governments have become increasingly professionalized and increasingly open to women and minorities, but their low visibility probably reduces their democratic responsiveness. Some have been susceptible to corruption. State policies are affected by the state's level of economic development and its degree of political competition, and by public opinion and organized interest groups.

Big cities grew rapidly for more than a hundred years. Immigrants from abroad built urban political machines that provided patronage and some social services in return for votes, but Progressive reforms undercut the machines and produced weak-mayor and city manager systems, especially in the West.

Recent population growth has focused on the suburbs, particularly in the Sun Belt; population in small towns has declined. The cities have been left with many poor and minority citizens in need of social programs, which are limited by competition among localities for wealth and by declining federal aid.

City governments may tend to be more democratic than state governments but less so than the national government.

Suggested Readings

Beatty, Jack. *The Rascal King: The Life and Times of James Michael Curley, 1874–1958.* Reading, MA: Addison-Wesley, 1992.
An account of the intriguing political career of the famous political boss of Boston.

Dahl, Robert. *Who Governs?* New Haven: Yale University Press, 1961.
A classic and still compelling account of pluralistic politics in New Haven, Connecticut.

Erikson, Robert A., Gerald Wright, and John McIver. *Statehouse Democracy: Public Opinion and Democracy in the American States.* New York: Cambridge University Press, 1994.
A thorough, quantitative study.

Gray, Virginia, Herbert Jacob, and Robert B. Albritton, eds. *Politics in the American States: A Comparative Analysis,* 6th ed. Glenview, IL: Scott, Foresman, 1995.
Articles on many aspects of state government by leading scholars.

Judd, Dennis R., and Todd Swanston. *City Politics: Private Power and Public Policy.* New York: HarperCollins, 1993.
A thorough and critical account of urban politics.

Lemann, Nicolas. *The Promised Land: The Great Black Migration and How It Changed America.* New York: Knopf, 1991.
A gripping account of the lives of blacks who moved north and of how public policies affected their lives.

Osbourne, David, and Ted Gaebler. *Reinventing Government: How the Entrepreneurial Spirit Is Transforming the Public Sector.* New York: Penguin, 1993.
Packed with ideas for making government more efficient and effective.

Rakove, Milton L. *Don't Make No Waves, Don't Back No Losers: An Insider's Analysis of the Daley Machine.* Bloomington: Indiana University Press, 1975.
A lively account of one of the last strong urban political machines.

Internet Sources

National Conference of State Legislatures http://www.ncsl.org/
A vast collection of information on the legislatures of all of the states.

Political Science Resources: Local and Regional Governments http://www.keele.ac.uk/depts/po/local.htm
Comprehensive information on the demographics, economics, and politics of states and municipalities.

State Governments http://www.kentlaw.edu/lawlinks/stategov.html
In addition to a wide range of information about state governments, this site provides hot links to the home pages of each of the states.

Yahoo/States http://www.yahoo.com/Regional/U_S_States/
Information on the governments, politics, economics, and demographics of the states, as well as the text of their election laws and constitutions.

Notes

1. "Battle Ground: The Fight over Gay Rights," *Denver Post* (September 19, 1993), Section D, pp. 1–16; Bella Stumbo, "American Scene: The State of Hate," *Esquire* (September 1993), pp. 73–80.
2. "Battle Ground," *Denver Post;* Stumbo, "American Scene."
3. Benjamin I. Page and Robert Y. Shapiro, *The Rational Public* (Chicago: University of Chicago Press, 1992), pp. 98–100.
4. "Battle Ground," *Denver Post;* Stumbo, "American Scene."
5. *Denver Post* (October 25, 1993), p. 6A.
6. Howard Pankratz, "Amendment 2 Tossed Out," *Denver Post* (December 15, 1993), pp. A1, A16; "Judge Junks Colorado's Anti-Gay-Rights Law," *Chicago Tribune* (December 15, 1993), p. A2; Linda Greenhouse, "U.S. Justices Hear, and Also Debate, a Gay Rights Case," *New York Times* (October 11, 1995), p. 1; Linda Greenhouse, "Gay Rights Laws Can't be Banned, High Court Rules, *New York Times* (May 21, 1996), p. 1.
7. *U.S. Statistical Abstracts,* 1994, p. 297.
8. Advisory Commission on Intergovernmental Relations, *Significant Features of Fiscal Federalism 1994* (Washington, DC: ACIR, 1994), p. 120.
9. *The Book of the States* (Lexington, KY: Council of States Governments, 1994–1995), p. 19.
10. Ibid., p. 30.
11. Ibid., pp. 55–56.
12. Ibid., pp. 44-–45.
13. Calculated from data appearing in the *New York Times* (November 9, 1990), p. A13.
14. *Congressional Quarterly Almanac, 1994,* p. 579.
15. William K. Muir, Jr., *Legislature: California's School for Politics* (Chicago: University of Chicago Press, 1982).
16. *State Elective Officials and the Legislatures, 1995* (Lexington, KY: Council of State Governments, 1995); 1993–1994 edition, pp. viii–ix.
17. Alan Rosenthal, "The Legislative Institution—In Transition and at Risk," in Carl E. Van Horn, ed. *The State of the States,* 2nd ed. (Washington, DC: Congressional Quarterly Press, 1993), p. 119.

18. Seth Mydans, "Civics 101 on Tape in Arizona, or, 'We All Have Our Prices,'" *New York Times* (February 11, 1991), pp. A1, A10; *Washington Post,* Weekly Edition (March 4–10, 1991), p. 14.

19. Elisabeth R. Gerber, "Legislative Response to the Threat of Popular Initiatives," *American Journal of Political Science,* Vol. 40 (February 1996), pp. 99–128.

20. Robert Reinhold, "Complicated Ballot Is Becoming Burden to California Voters," *New York Times* (September 24, 1990), p. A1. See David Kehler and Robert M. Stern, "Initiatives in the 1980's and 1990's," in *The Book of the States, 1994,* pp. 279–293.

21. *Book of the States,* 1994–1995, pp. 184–185.

22. Stanley H. Friedelbaum, "Reactive Responses: The Complementary Role of Federal and State Courts," *Publius: The Journal of Federalism,* Vol. 17 (Winter 1987), pp. 33–50.

23. See Richard I. Hofferbert and Ira Sharkansky, eds., *State and Urban Politics: Readings in Comparative Public Policy* (Boston: Little, Brown, 1971).

24. *Statistical Abstract of the United States, 1992,* p. 437.

25. V. O. Key, Jr., *Southern Politics in State and Nation* (New York: Knopf, 1949); Merle Black and Earl Black, *Politics and Society in the South* (Cambridge: Harvard University Press, 1987).

26. Robert D. Plotnik and Richard D. Winters, "Party, Political Liberalism, and Redistribution: An Application to the American States," *American Politics Quarterly,* Vol. 18 (October 1990), pp. 430–458.

27. Robert S. Erikson, "The Relationship Between Public Opinion and State Policy: A New Look Based on Some Forgotten Data," *American Journal of Political Science,* Vol. 20 (February 1976), pp. 25–36.

28. Jane Mansbridge, *Why We Lost the ERA* (Chicago: University of Chicago Press, 1986).

29. Gerald C. Wright, Jr., Robert S. Erikson, and John P. McIver, "Public Opinion and Policy Liberalism in the American States," *American Journal of Political Science,* Vol. 31 (November 1987), pp. 980–1001; Robert A. Erikson, Gerald Wright, and John McIver, *Statehouse Democracy: Public Opinion and Policy in the American States* (New York: Cambridge University Press, 1993).

30. Kevin Sack, "Gambling's New Winnings," *New York Times* (December 18, 1995), p. B12.

31. George Stigler, "The Theory of Economic Regulation," *Bell Journal of Management Science,* Vol. 2, No. 1 (Spring 1978), pp. 3–21.

32. Rick Pearson, "Senate Cripples Gun Package," *Chicago Tribune* (May 25, 1991), pp. A1, A14.

33. Ian Fisher, "Philip Morris Tops List of Lobbying Spenders in New York," *New York Times* (March 16, 1994), p. B2.

34. Kevin Sack, "Report Says More Lobbyists in Albany Earn Record Fees," *New York Times* (March 19, 1991), p. A16.

35. Grant McConnell, *Private Power and American Democracy* (New York: Random House, 1966), Chaps. 4 and 6, pp. 168, 182–185.

36. E. E. Schattschneider, *The Semi-Sovereign People: A Realist's View of Democracy in America* (New York: Holt, 1960), Chaps. 1 and 2.

37. Benjamin I. Page and Robert Y. Shapiro, "Effects of Public Opinion on Policy," *American Political Science Review,* Vol. 77 (March 1983), pp. 182–185.

38. U.S. Department of Commerce, Bureau of the Census, *Historical Statistics of the United States: Colonial Times to 1970* (Washington, DC: U.S. Government Printing Office, 1989), pp. 105–109.
39. Nicolas Lemann, *The Promised Land: The Great Black Migration and How It Changed America* (New York: Knopf, 1991).
40. Amy Bridges, *A City in the Republic: Antebellum New York and the Origins of Machine Politics* (Cambridge: Harvard University Press, 1984).
41. William L. Riordan, *Plunkett of Tammany Hall* (New York: Dutton, 1963).
42. Milton Rakove, *Don't Make No Waves, Don't Back No Losers* (Bloomington: Indiana University Press, 1975), p. 11.
43. Dennis R. Judd, *The Politics of American Cities: Private Power and Public Policy*, 3rd ed. (Glenview, IL: Scott, Foresman, 1988), pp. 106–109.
44. William Crotty, *The Party Game* (New York: Freeman, 1985), p. 108.
45. Esther Fuchs, *Mayors and Money: Fiscal Policy in New York and Chicago* (Chicago: University of Chicago Press, 1991).
46. *Statistical Abstracts, 1994,* p. 318.
47. Data provided by the Mercer Group, Inc., January 6, 1996.
48. Michael deCourcy Hinds, "Cash-Strapped Cities Turn to Companies to Do What Government Once Did," *New York Times* (May 14, 1991), p. A8.
49. Dirk Johnson, "In Privatizing City Services, It's Now 'Indy-a-First-Place,'" *New York Times* (March 2, 1995), p. 8.
50. See David Osborne and Ted Gaebler, *Reinventing Government: How the Entrepreneurial Spirit Is Transforming the Public Sector* (New York: Penguin, 1993).
51. *Statistical Abstracts, 1994,* pp. 39, 44.
52. Dirk Johnson, "Population Decline in Rural America: A Product of Advances in Technology," *New York Times* (September 11, 1990), p. A12.
53. "Small-Town Governance: The Workers Are Fewer," *New York Times* (June 25, 1990), p. A10.
54. *Statistical Abstracts, 1994,* p. 45.
55. *Statistical Abstracts, 1992,* pp. 17, 35–37.
56. *Statistical Abstracts, 1994,* pp. 469, 475.
57. *Statistical Abstracts, 1994,* p. 200.
58. *New York Times* (June 27, 1990), p. A9.
59. *Statistical Abstracts, 1994,* pp. 475, 476.
60. Paul Peterson, *City Limits* (Chicago: University of Chicago Press, 1981).
61. Jill Dutt, "Trouble in Tribeca for Commodities Exchange Plan," *Newsday* (November 26, 1990); Beth Belton, "Moms Battle Skyscraper: Project a Threat to Urban Park," *USA Today* (December 20, 1990), p. 2B.
62. William Bunch, "Tighter Limits on Big Donors Urged," *Newsday* (September 2, 1994), p. A29
63. Josh Barbanel, "Lobbying List Led by Dinkins' Friend," *New York Times* (March 13, 1991), p. A6.
64. *New York Times* (May 21, 1990), p. A11.

PART V

What Government Does

Parts II and III of this book examined the structural and political linkage influences on government institutions and public officials. Part IV directly examined government institutions and public officials themselves, asking how and why they operate as they do. This part examines what government does, and how effective it is in tackling the most important problems facing the United States.

As such, this part represents a kind of summing up; it examines how well our political and governmental institutions operate to fulfill the expectations of the American people. Chapters in this part have a strong comparative aspect, because evaluating how well we are doing requires that we look at what governments in other countries are doing to address similar problems. These chapters also address the democracy theme, asking whether or not public policies are the outcome of a democratic process, and whether policies improve the health and vitality of democracy in the United States.

The chapters in this part do not, however, look at everything government does. Because government policies, decisions, and actions affect virtually every aspect of life in American society, and because government produces such a vast number of laws, regulations, rulings, findings, and decisions, only the most important and timely are addressed in the chapters in this section. Chapters 16 and 17 look at the status of civil liberties and civil rights in the United States, with special attention paid to decisions of the Supreme Court concerning our most cherished rights and liberties. Chapter 18 looks at American foreign and military policy; Chapter 19 examines economic policy, with particular attention paid to patterns of government expenditure, the tax system, and regulation of the economy, including regulation affecting the environment; Chapter 20 examines our relatively unique system of social welfare, with particular attention paid to programs of social insurance, such as Social Security and Medicare, and means-tested welfare programs.

CHAPTER 16

Freedom: The Struggle for Civil Liberties

IN THIS CHAPTER

- ★ Why liberty is so important in a democracy
- ★ How liberties were gradually applied to the states by the Supreme Court
- ★ How the U.S. Supreme Court's interpretation of the meaning of liberties has changed
- ★ How the struggle for democracy has increased the enjoyment of liberties in the United States

Campus Speech Codes and Free Speech

- Khalid Abdul Muhammad, at the time an aide to Nation of Islam leader Louis Farrakhan, ignites controversy at several universities with a series of fiery appearances. Frequently using anti-Semitic themes, Muhammad's speeches polarize campuses: some defend his First Amendment right to free speech; others denounce his inflammatory tone.
- At the University of Pennsylvania late one night, a white student shouts at noisy members of an African-American sorority, "Will you water buffaloes get out of here?" He is accused of racial harassment, and the university takes disciplinary action against him.
- During a class at the University of Michigan, a student argues that homosexuality could be treated with psychotherapy. He is accused of violating a campus rule against victimizing people on the basis of their sexual orientation.
- At Southern Methodist University, a student is sentenced to work with minority organizations for 30 hours because, among other things, he sang "We Shall Overcome" in a sarcastic manner.
- A University of Wisconsin student is suspended for telling an Asian-American, "It's people like you—that's the reason this country is screwed up."[1]
- At George Mason University, Professor Michael Krauss argues that racist speech may be so hurtful under certain circumstances that it might be "actionable" under tort doctrine, resulting in the award of damages to the aggrieved party. He uses two examples of such hurtful speech, one involving a Nazi march in a Jewish neighborhood, the other involving a Ku Klux Klan march in an African-American neighborhood. Krauss uses words in his examples that such demonstrators might use. Several offended students demand that Krauss be reprimanded and that the racial slur he used in the African-American example be banned from all classrooms at George Mason University. Several faculty members sign petitions against Krauss and write letters to local newspapers expressing their outrage.
- Stanford University enacts a speech code in 1990 that prohibits "personal vilification of students on the basis of their sex, race, color, handicap, religion, sexual orientation, or national and ethnic origin." The code is pressed by, among others, the African-American Law Students Association, the Asian-American Law Students Association, and the Jewish Law Students Association. It is strongly opposed by Stanford's eminent constitutional scholar Gerald Gunther, who claims that hate speech should not be banned but vigorously rejected "with more speech, with better speech, with repudiation and contempt." The California Superior Court in 1995 agrees with the Gunther position, saying that the Stanford code unconstitutionally restricts free speech rights under the First Amendment to the Constitution.[2]

The college campus has become one of the most visible battlegrounds in the continuing struggle over the meaning of free speech in the United States. Campus speech codes have been instituted at many colleges and universities across the country in an effort to rid campuses of speech that may offend members of minority groups. Many civil libertarians, like Gerald Gunther, though protective of the rights of minority students to a supportive learning environment, have fought hard against such codes in the service of free speech and a free society. By and large, the courts have sided with the civil libertarians, as in the Stanford case.

This chapter examines civil liberties in the United States. It shows that the meaning of each of our freedoms—whether of speech, of the press, of association, or of religion—is never settled, but is the subject of continuing disagreement and even, on occasion, of contentious political struggle. We shall see in this chapter how structural, political linkage, and governmental factors influence the meaning and practice of our civic freedoms. Especially important in this story is the role of the Supreme Court as interpreter of the Constitution. A second important theme is the struggle for democracy, exemplified by the efforts of many groups and individuals to protect and expand civil liberties.

Civil Liberties in the Constitution

We saw in Chapter 2 that the framers were particularly concerned about establishing a society in which liberty might flourish. While government was necessary to protect liberty from the threat of anarchy, the framers believed that government might threaten liberty if it became too powerful. **Civil liberties** are freedoms protected by constitutional provisions, laws, and practices, from certain types of government interference. As embodied in the Bill of Rights, civil liberties are protected by prohibitions against government actions that threaten the enjoyment of freedom.

civil liberties Freedoms protected from government interference.

In the Preamble to the Constitution, the framers wrote that they aimed to "secure the Blessings of Liberty to ourselves and our Posterity." But in the original Constitution, they protected few liberties from the national government they were creating and almost none from state governments. The safeguard against tyranny that the framers preferred was to give the national government little power with which to attack individual liberties. Rather than listing specific prohibitions against certain kinds of actions, they believed that liberty was best protected by a constitutional design that fragmented government power, a design that included separation of powers, checks and balances, and federalism. Still, the framers singled out certain freedoms as too crucial to be left unmentioned. The Constitution prohibits Congress and the states from suspending the **writ of habeas corpus,** except when public safety demands it because of rebellion or invasion, and from passing **bills of attainder** or **ex post facto laws** (see Table 16.1 for an enumeration).

habeas corpus The legal doctrine which holds that those who are arrested must have a timely hearing before a judge.

bills of attainder A governmental decree or announcement that a person is guilty of a crime that carries the death penalty, rendered without benefit of a trial.

ex post facto law A law that retroactively declares some action illegal.

As we saw in Chapter 2, many citizens found the proposed Constitution too stingy in its listing of liberties, so that the Federalists were led to promise a "bill of rights" as a condition for passing the Constitution. The Bill of Rights was passed by the 1st Congress in 1789 and was ratified by the required number of states by 1791. Passage of the Bill of Rights made the Constitution more democratic by specifying protections of political liberty and by guaranteeing a context of free political expression that makes popular sovereignty possible.

Looking at the liberties specified by the text of the Constitution and its amendments, however, emphasizes how few of our most cherished liberties are to be found in a reading of the bare words of the Constitution. Decisions by government officials and changes worked by political leaders and groups remade the Constitution in the long run, so many of the freedoms we expect today are not specifically mentioned there. Some extensions of protected liberties were introduced by judges and other officials. Others have evolved as the culture has grown accustomed to novel and even once-threatening ideas. Still

Table 16.1

Civil Liberties in the U.S. Constitution

The exact meaning and extent of civil liberties in the Constitution are matters of debate, but here are some freedoms from government spelled out in the text of the Constitution and its amendments, or clarified by early court decisions.

Constitution

Article I, Section 9

Congress may not suspend a writ of habeas corpus.

Congress may not pass bills of attainder or ex post facto laws.

Article I, Section 10

States may not pass bills of attainder or ex post facto laws.

States may not impair obligation of contracts.

Article III, Section 2

Criminal trials in national courts must be jury trials in the state in which the defendant is alleged to have committed the crime(s).

Article III, Section 3

No one may be convicted of treason unless there is a confession in open court or testimony of two witnesses to the same overt act.

Article IV, Section 2

Citizens of each state are entitled to all privileges and immunities of citizens in the several states.

The Bill of Rights

Amendment 1

Congress may not make any law with respect to the establishment of religion.

Congress may not abridge the free exercise of religion.

Congress may not abridge freedom of speech or of the press.

Congress may not abridge the right to assemble or to petition the government.

Amendment 2

Congress may not infringe the right to keep and bear arms.

Amendment 3

Congress may not station soldiers in houses against the owner's will, except in times of war.

Amendment 4

Citizens are to be free from unreasonable searches and seizures.

Federal courts may issue search warrants based only on probable cause and specifically describing the objects of search.

Amendment 5

Citizens are protected against double jeopardy and self-incrimination.

Citizens are guaranteed against deprivation of life, liberty, or property without due process of law.

Citizens are guaranteed just compensation for public use of their private property.

Amendment 6

Citizens have the right to a speedy and public trial before an impartial jury.

Citizens have the right to face their accuser and to cross-examine witnesses.

Amendment 8

Excessive bail and fines are prohibited.

Cruel and unusual punishments are prohibited.

Americans are often shocked when newspapers report stories of activists jailed without a public trial in other parts of the world, but it was a fairly common occurrence in the American colonies before the Revolution. It was the Founders' fear of such tyranny that led them to incorporate the right to due process of law into the Constitution; most other civil liberties are addressed in amendments to the Constitution or by Supreme Court decisions.

other liberties have secured a place in the Republic through partisan and ideological combat. The key to understanding civil liberties in the United States is to follow their evolution during the course of our history.

Rights and Liberties in the Nineteenth Century

During the nineteenth century, the range of protected civil liberties in the United States was somewhat different from their range today. Especially noteworthy were the special place of property rights as a freedom to be protected and the understanding that the Bill of Rights did not apply to state governments.

Property

Liberty may be understood as protection against government interference in certain kinds of activities. Among the few such protections mentioned in the original Constitution was one concerned the use and enjoyment of private property: "No State shall . . . pass any . . . Law impairing the Obligation of Contracts" (Article I, Section 10). The importance of property rights as a fundamental liberty in the body of the Constitution was reinforced by more than a century of judicial interpretation.

Property Rights in the Marshall Court (1801–1835) Though the Supreme Court ruled (in *Barron v. Baltimore,* 1833) that the Bill of Rights did not to apply to the states, it ruled on several occasions that the **contract clause** in the Constitution directly applied against unwarranted state action. In the hands of Chief Justice John Marshall, the clause became an important defense of property rights against interference by the states. In *Fletcher v. Peck* (1810), for example, the Marshall Court upheld a sale of public land, even though almost all of the legislators who had voted for the land sale had been bribed by the prospective purchasers. Chief Justice Marshall argued that even a fraudulent sale created a contract that the state could not void. In *Dartmouth College v. Woodward* (1819), Marshall argued that New Hampshire could not modify the charter of Dartmouth College, because the original charter constituted a contract, the terms of which could not be changed without impairing the obligations in the original contract. The Founders' attempt to protect the contractual agreements of private parties ballooned in the hands of the Marshall Court to bar virtually any and all changes by the states of established property relations.[3] This expansion of property rights protections made it almost impossible for states to regulate business activities.

contract clause In Article I, Section 10 of the Constitution: no state shall pass any "law impairing the obligation of contracts."

Property Rights in the Taney Court (1836–1864) Under the leadership of Chief Justice Roger Taney, the Court began to make a distinction between private property used in ways that encouraged economic growth and private property used for simple enjoyment rather than economic growth. In landmark cases, the Taney Court issued rulings favoring the former when the two concepts of property conflicted.[4] In his opinion in *Charles River Bridge v. Warren Bridge* (1837), Chief Justice Taney said that Massachusetts, in chartering the Charles River Bridge, had not agreed to create a monopoly that closed off competitors. He ruled that Massachusetts could charter the rival Warren River Bridge because the states should encourage economic competition and technological advances. It did not matter that, as a result, the stockholders in the Charles River Bridge would lose money. Taney argued that the "creative destruction" of established but idle property in a dynamic market economy was the price of economic and social progress.

Property Rights in Human Beings The defense of property rights was especially and tragically strong when it came to slavery. Until the Civil War, courts North and South consistently upheld the right of slaveholders to recapture fugitive slaves. In his opinion in *Dred Scott v. Sandford* (1857), Chief Justice Taney claimed that slaves were not citizens who possessed rights, but simply private property, no different from land or tools.

Property Rights After the Civil War The Fourteenth Amendment, passed after the Civil War, was designed to guarantee the citizenship rights of the newly freed slaves in the nation and in each of the states (we will have much more to say about the Fourteenth Amendment below and in the chapter on civil liberties). It included a clause—called the **due process clause**—stating that no state may "deprive a person of life, liberty, or property, without due process of law." Strangely enough, the Supreme Court in the late nineteenth century interpreted this clause as a protection for business against the regulatory efforts of the states.

due process clause The section of the Fourteenth Amendment that reads "no person shall be deprived of life, liberty, or property without due process of law," representing a guarantee against arbitrary or unfair government action.

The Court's most famous decision in this regard was *Lochner v. New York* (1905). Lochner ran a bakery in Utica, New York. He was convicted of requiring an employee to work more than 60 hours per week, contrary to a New York State maximum-hours statute. But Justice Rufus Peckham wrote for a 5–4 Supreme Court majority that the right of employer and employee to negotiate hours of work was part of the "liberty" of which, under the Fourteenth Amendment, no person could be deprived without due process of law. In other words, New York State had no right to regulate the hours of labor.

Justice Oliver Wendell Holmes, Jr., penned one of his most famous dissenting opinions in *Lochner.* Holmes exposed the Court's opinion as an unjustified defense of property rights against the will of the majority, without constitutional foundation:

> This case is decided upon an economic theory which a large part of the country does not entertain. If it were a question whether I agreed with that theory, I should desire to study it further and long before making up my mind. But I do not conceive that to be my duty, because I strongly believe that my agreement or disagreement has nothing to do with the right of the majority to embody their opinions in law. . . . But a constitution is not intended to embody a particular economic theory.

The nineteenth century was an era in which the rights of property were expanded, refined, and altered to become consistent with an emerging, dynamic industrial economy. The twentieth century would bring new approaches to property rights and to political liberties in general. These new approaches would be triggered by structural transformations in the economy and culture, the efforts of new political groups and movements, and the actions of government officials.

Nationalization of the Bill of Rights

Americans rightly understand the Bill of Rights to the be the foundation of American liberties. Until the twentieth century, however, the Bill of Rights did not apply to the states, only to the national government. The Supreme Court only gradually applied the Bill of Rights to the states through a process known as *selective incorporation.*

Selective Incorporation

The framers were worried more about national government intrusion on freedom than about state government intrusion. Most of the states, after all, had bills of rights in their own constitutions, and being closer to the people, state governments would be less likely to intrude on the people's freedom, or so the framers believed. This reading of the Bill of Rights as a prohibition of certain actions by the national government seems explicit in the language of many of the first ten Amendments. The first, for instance, starts with the words "Congress shall make no law. . . ." This understanding of the Bill of Rights was confirmed by John Marshall in *Barron v. Baltimore* (1833). It is apparent that Congress wanted to change the reach of the Bill of Rights, extending it to the states, however, when it approved the Fourteenth Amendment after the Civil War. Three clauses in this amendment specify that the states cannot violate the rights and liberties of the people living in them:

- The first specifies that all persons born or naturalized in the United States are citizens of both the United States and the states in which they reside.
- The **privileges and immunities clause** specifies that no *state* "shall make or enforce any law which shall abridge the privileges or immunities of citizens of the United States."

privileges and immunities clause That portion of Article IV, Section 2 which says that citizens from out of state have the same legal rights as local citizens in any state.

While the Second Amendment makes it difficult for Congress to pass laws restricting the sale and use of firearms, states can do so more easily because the Second Amendment has not yet been incorporated by the Supreme Court.

- The due process clause specifies that no *state* shall "deprive any person of life, *liberty,* or property, without due process of law."

Though Congress wrote the Fourteenth Amendment to guarantee that the states would protect all of U.S. citizens' rights and liberties, including those found in the Bill of Rights, the Supreme Court was very slow in **nationalizing** or **incorporating** the Bill of Rights (that is, in making it binding on the state governments). Indeed, the Supreme Court has not yet fully incorporated or nationalized the Bill of Rights. Rather, it has practiced what constitutional scholars term **selective incorporation,** only slowly adding, step by step, even traditional civil liberties to the constitutional obligations of the states. Table 16.2 reports which parts of the Bill of Rights have been incorporated (including the case establishing the precedent) and which have not.

nationalizing The process by which provisions of the Bill of Rights have been incorporated. See *incorporation.*

incorporation The gradual use of the Fourteenth Amendment by the Supreme Court to make the Bill of Rights and other constitutional protections relevant at the state level.

selective incorporation Refers to the fact that, rather than make the protections of the Bill of Rights relevant to the states all at one time, the Supreme Court has only gradually and selectively made constitutional protections relevant at the state level.

Standards for Incorporation

How does the Supreme Court decide whether or not to incorporate some portion of the Bill of Rights? That is, what standard does the Court use to protect a liberty specified in the Bill of Rights from violation by a state government? The answer is quite simple and is spelled out, as strange as it may seem, in footnote 4 of the opinion of the Court in *U.S. v. Carolene Products Company* (1938), written by Justice Harlan Fiske Stone. Stone suggested that most legislative enactments by states would be considered constitutional and subject only to **ordinary scrutiny** by the Court. However, the footnote declares, three classes of state actions would automatically be presumed unconstitutional, the burden being on the states to prove otherwise. When state actions are presumed to be unconstitutional, the Court is said to be exercising **strict scrutiny.** The three classes of suspect state actions that bring strict scrutiny are those that seem to:

- contradict specific prohibitions in the Constitution, including those of the Bill of Rights
- restrict the democratic process
- discriminate against racial, ethnic, or religious minorities

ordinary scrutiny The assumption that the actions of elected bodies and officials are legal under the Constitution.

strict scrutiny The assumption that the actions of elected bodies and officials that violate "equal protection" or other constitutional rights are unconstitutional.

The first of these is the subject matter of this chapter. The second has been addressed at several points in the text. The third will be the subject of Chapter 17, on civil rights.

In the remainder of this chapter, we focus on specific civil liberties, clarifying their present status in both constitutional law and political practice.

Table 16.2

Selective Incorporation of the Bill of Rights

First Amendment	Totally incorporated
Establishment clause	*Everson v. Board of Education* (1947)
Free exercise clause	*Cantwell v. Connecticut* (1940)
Free speech	*Gitlow v. New York* (1925)
Free press	*Near v. Minnesota* (1931)
Free assembly	*DeJonge v. Oregon* (1937)
Freedom of association	*NAACP v. Alabama* (1958)
Second Amendment	Not yet incorporated
Third Amendment	Not yet incorporated
Fourth Amendment	Totally incorporated
Searches and seizures	*Wolf v. Colorado* (1949)
Exclusionary rule	*Mapp v. Ohio* (1961)
Fifth Amendment	Partly incorporated
Grand jury indictment	Not yet incorporated
Double jeopardy	*Benton v. Maryland* (1969)
Self-incrimination	*Malloy v. Hogan* (1964)
Due process clause	Directly repealed in Fourteenth Amendment
Public use	*Missouri Pac. Rv. Co. v. Nebraska* (1896)
Just compensation	*Chicago, B. & O. Rv. v. Chicago* (1897)
Sixth Amendment	Totally incorporated
Speedy trial	*Klopfer v. North Carolina* (1967)
Public trial	*In re Oliver* (1948)
Impartial jury	*Parker v. Gladden* (1966)
Confront witnesses	*Pointer v. Texas* (1965)
Subpoena witnesses	*Washington v. Texas* (1967)
Right to counsel	*Powell v. Alabama* (1932) (capital cases)
	Gideon v. Wainwright (1963) (felony cases)
	Duncan v. Louisiana (1968) (serious cases)
	Argersinger v. Hamlin (1972) (jail involved)
Seventh Amendment	Not yet incorporated
Eighth Amendment	Partly incorporated
Excessive bail	Not yet incorporated
Excessive fines	Not yet incorporated
Cruel and unusual punishments	*Robinson v. California* (1962)

Source: Craig R. Ducat and Harold W. Chase, *Constitutional Interpretation* (St. Paul: West, 1988), pp. 845–846.

Freedom of Speech

> **Congress shall make no Law . . . abridging the freedom of speech.**
>
> —FIRST AMENDMENT

Speech can take many forms. The Court has had to consider which forms of speech are protected under the Constitution.

Political Speech For many, the right to speak one's mind is the first principle of a free and democratic society. It is not very surprising, then, that the first incorporation of the Bill of Rights (that is, making constitutional protections apply against the states) occurred with respect to free speech, in *Gitlow v. New York* (1925). Benjamin Gitlow had published "The Left Wing Manifesto," which embraced a militant, revolutionary socialism to mobilize the proletariat to destroy the existing order in favor of communism. Gitlow did not advocate specific action to break the law, but he was nonetheless convicted of a felony under the New York Criminal Anarchy Law (1902).

The Supreme Court majority held that New York State was bound by the First Amendment but then argued that even the First Amendment did not prohibit New York from incarcerating Gitlow for his pamphlet. Said Justice Edward Sanford, "A single revolutionary spark may kindle a fire that, smoldering for a time, may burst into a sweeping and destructive conflagration. It cannot be said that the State is acting . . . unreasonably when . . . it seeks to extinguish the spark without waiting until it has enkindled the flame or blazed into the conflagration." In his famous dissent, Justice Oliver Wendell Holmes said, "Every idea is an incitement. . . . Eloquence may set fire to reason. But whatever may be thought of the redundant discourse before us, it had no chance of starting a present conflagration."

While the *Gitlow* precedent proved to be an important advance for civil liberties in the United States, the Court was still willing to leave Gitlow in jail

Once "free speech" was incorporated by the Supreme Court, states were no longer at liberty to suppress unpopular speech as many of them had done with some frequency.

and allow the states very wide latitude in controlling what they considered dangerous speech. For many years, especially during the 1940s and 1950s, the Court deferred to political hysteria and allowed the widespread suppression of what we now consider acceptable speech and publication. The Court seldom moved far ahead of the political branches on free-speech issues during this period or later.[5]

This early stage of the nationalization of the Bill of Rights by the Court was helped along by a new force, the American Civil Liberties Union (ACLU), which brought the *Gitlow* appeal. Less than ten years old, the ACLU had little to show for its efforts until 1925, when *Gitlow* provided a spark of hope for civil libertarians. The Court's application of the First Amendment to the states provided the ACLU with opportunities to resist censorship and the strangulation of dissent by the states as well as by the national government. While victories remained rare, the Court's willingness to incorporate free speech encouraged and energized the ACLU.[6]

Freedom of speech has grown in the ensuing years so that far more speech is protected than is not. In general, no U.S. government today may regulate or interfere with the content of speech without a compelling reason. For a reason to be compelling, a government must show that the speech poses a "clear and present danger"—the standard formulated by Holmes in *Schenck v. United States* (1919)—that it has a duty to prevent. The danger must be very substantial, and the relationship between the speech and the danger must be direct, such as falsely yelling "Fire!" in a crowded theater. The danger must also be so immediate that those responsible for order cannot afford to tolerate the speech. Abstract advocacy of ideas, even ideas considered dangerous by police, politicians, or popular majorities, is protected unless it meets both conditions. Clearly, freedom of speech has grown, and with it, an important part of democracy in the United States.

Actions and Symbolic Speech Difficult questions about free expression persist, of course. Speech mixed with *conduct* may be restricted if the restrictions are narrowly and carefully tailored to curb the conduct while leaving the speech unmolested. Symbolic expressions (e.g., wearing armbands or picketing) may also receive less protection from the Court. The use of profanity or words that are likely to cause violence ("fighting words") may be regulated in some cases, as are symbolic actions that prevent others from carrying out legitimate activities. Thus, the Court has upheld state laws and municipal ordinances that keep antiabortion demonstrators some distance away from clinic entrances. Still, freedom of speech throughout the United States has grown to the point at which contenders wrestle with relatively peripheral issues, leaving a large sphere of expressive freedom. *Texas v. Johnson* (1989) shows just how far the protection of free speech has expanded. In this case, Mr. Gregory Johnson challenged a Texas state law against flag desecration under which he had been convicted for burning an American flag as part of a demonstration at the 1984 Republican convention. Though dominated by a conservative majority, the Rehnquist Court overturned the Texas law, saying that flag burning falls under the free expression protections of the Constitution unless imminent incitement or violence is likely.

Efforts have also been made to suppress speech that certain minorities find objectionable. The courts have generally found such repression unconstitutional. Thus, the regulation of student speech at the Universities of Wisconsin and Michigan has been disallowed, as has an ordinance against racially motivated cross burning (*R.A.V. v. St. Paul,* 1992). When regulations aim at

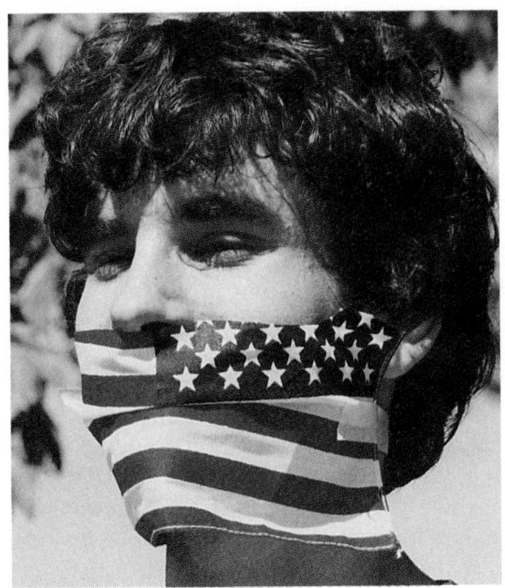

Can state legislatures pass laws prohibiting flag burning? The Supreme Court agreed with this demonstrator that such laws violate freedom of expression.

hateful *actions,* however, courts have approved them. In 1993, for example, the Court upheld a Wisconsin statute that increased punishment for certain offenses if the convicted defendant had chosen the victim(s) on racial grounds. Congress then passed a similar law.

Suppression of Free Expression A major exception to this story of the expansion of freedom of expression has been the periodic concern about "internal security." This century has witnessed several periods when dissenters and radicals were persecuted for their political speech and writings. Censorship of dissent and protests during World War I proved to be a portent of abuses after the war. At least 32 states enacted laws to suppress dangerous ideas and talk, and the Lusk Committee in New York State raided the offices of "radicals." Hoping to become president, New York State attorney general A. Mitchell Palmer conducted raids on the headquarters of suspect organizations in 1919 and 1920, setting a young J. Edgar Hoover to collect information on radicals and nonconformists.

A similar period of hysteria followed World War II. Its foundations were laid when the Democrat-controlled House of Representatives created the House Committee on Un-American Activities (generally referred to as HUAC). When the Republicans won control of Congress, they professed to see security risks in the Truman administration and Hollywood (see the Politics and Film box). The HUAC found no spies and contributed little to security, but it managed to ravage lives and reputations (see the Struggle for Democracy box on page 560). Soon Democrats and Republicans alike were exploiting the "red scare" for political gain. The greatest gain (and, subsequently, the hardest fall) was for Senator Joseph McCarthy (Republican of Wisconsin). McCarthy hid behind congressional immunity to promote himself and his friends by brandishing imaginary lists of communists and by denouncing all who opposed him as traitors. McCarthy and "McCarthyism" eventually fell victims, however, to the newest force in U.S. politics: television. Once ordinary Americans saw McCarthy and his tactics in their living rooms, they recognized that he was a liar and a bully. McCarthy's demise led to a slow retreat from this period of utter disregard for liberty.[7]

POLITICS AND FILM

Hollywood Enlists in the War Against Communism

Made anxious by several congressional loyalty probes during the HUAC, McCarthy, "red scare" era, the Hollywood studios were determined to demonstrate their good citizenship. During the early 1950s, the studios produced a stream of films affirming the American way of life and the rightness of American institutions, and warning of the danger of the communist enemy at home and abroad.

Several films in the form of lowbrow morality plays were so short on entertainment value that people stayed away in droves. Such films as *I Married a Communist* (1950) and *I Was a Communist for the FBI* (1951) were the worst of the lot. Their efforts to paint communists and so-called fellow travelers in the most villainous light and to affirm such government institutions as the FBI helped to convince public officials that Hollywood was no hotbed of communism, but their efforts were so crude that the studios reaped few financial rewards. Somewhat more successful was the Leo McCarey film *My Son John* (1952), about parents who turn their wayward son (a young man who is a little too smart for his own good and who consorts with university intellectuals and professors) in to the FBI after they learn that he is seeing a female Soviet spy. He escapes but relents after listening to pleas from his parents and an FBI agent to turn himself in and "name names." On his way to FBI headquarters, he is shot by the Communists, and he dies on the steps of the Lincoln Memorial. McCarey's screenplay was nominated for an Academy Award.

Films like these were so didactic and moralizing in tone that few people wanted to see them. Much more successful at the box office were movies that tied the communist threat to science fiction stories of alien invasion.

Them! (1954) is a story about giant ants, mutated by atomic testing, that threaten civilization. The first victim of the ants is an FBI agent, and the FBI is part of the team that eventually destroys the ants' nest in the storm sewers under Los Angeles. The insects (dronelike legions not much different from communists) are no match in the end for the alliance of science, the FBI, and the U.S. military.

Although there was some public and official concern about direct Soviet invasion, the animating fear during the McCarthy era was the enemy within—a conspiracy so insidious that it worked through friends, neighbors, and even relatives (*My Son John,* for instance). Hollywood captured this theme perfectly in such alien invasion movies as *Invaders from Mars* (1953) and *The Invasion of the Body Snatchers.* (1956) Both are stories of aliens who manage to take on human form so that we cannot see that we have been invaded. They bore gradually from within, just like communists. Appearances are deceptive and the seemingly normal has been subverted. In *The Invasion of the Body Snatchers,* alien plants clone and replace people as they sleep. When they awaken, the aliens look like the people whom they have replaced, but there is something slightly amiss: they all seem the same; they lack emotion and passion; they feel no need for love or affection; they have no ambition or faith. They want to conform and to work together in order to spread the pods far and wide. The hero escapes the small town where the invasion is centered when he discovers that the pod people are assembling truck convoys to spread the pods. The film ends when a sheriff, finally convinced that the hero is not crazy, lifts the phone and says, "Operator, get me the FBI." We are saved, and just in the nick of time.

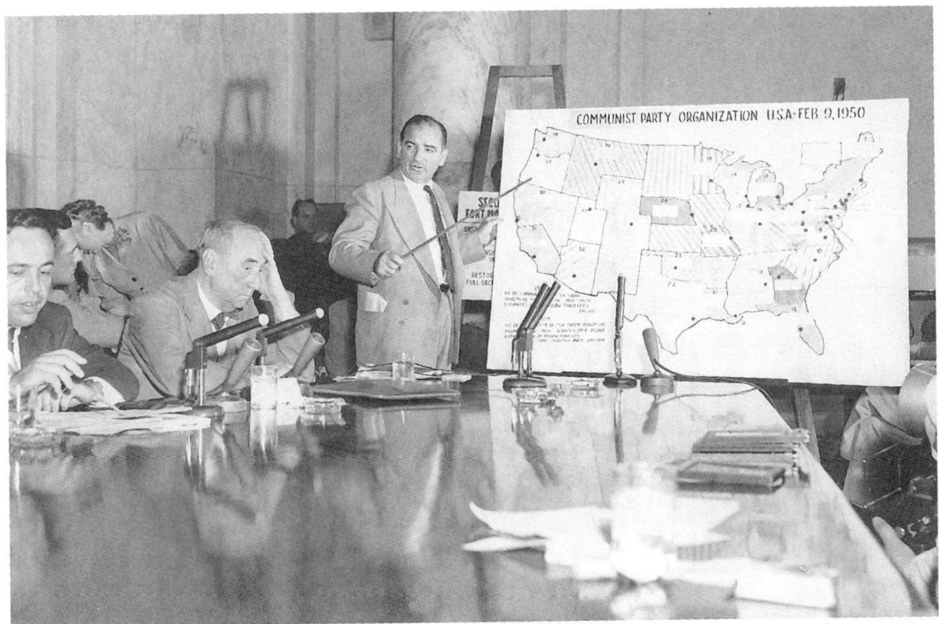

Senator Joseph McCarthy issues a warning about the "Red Tide" of Communism sweeping the nation. McCarthy discovered few communists but managed to wreck the lives of many innocent people and created an atmosphere that threatened liberty in the United States for many years.

Freedom of the Press

Congress shall make no law . . . abridging the freedom . . . of the press.

—FIRST AMENDMENT

In an aside in the opinion of the Court in *Gitlow v. New York* (1925), the Supreme Court included freedom of the press as a freedom guaranteed against state interference by the Fourteenth Amendment. Incorporation of this aspect of the Bill of Rights seems reasonable in light of the importance of the free flow of information in a society that aspires to freedom and democracy. In *Near v. Minnesota* (1931), the Court made good on the promise of *Gitlow* by invalidating the Minnesota Public Nuisance Law as a violation of freedom of the press.[8] Jay Near published the *Saturday Press,* a scandal sheet that attacked local crime, public officials, and a few other groups that he disliked: Jews, Catholics, blacks, and unions, for example. Near and his associates were ordered by a state court not to publish, sell, or possess the *Saturday Press.* This sort of state action is called **prior restraint,** because it prevents publication before it has occurred. Freedom of the press is not necessarily infringed if publishers are sued or punished for harming others after they have published, but Minnesota was trying to keep Near and his associates from publishing in the future.

prior restraint Government power to prevent publication, as opposed to punishment afterward.

Prior Restraint The prohibition of prior restraint on publication remains the core of freedom of the press. Freedom of the press and freedom of speech tend to be considered together as freedom of expression, so the general principles applicable to free speech apply to freedom of the press as well. Thus, the Court will countenance the repression of publication only if the state can show some "clear and present danger" that publication poses, similar to its position on free speech. Thus, in *New York Times Co. v. United States* (1971), the Court ruled that the U.S. government could not prevent newspapers from publishing portions of the "Pentagon Papers" revealing the sordid story of how the United

Saying No to HUAC

The Struggle for Democracy

The patience of Representative Harold Velde, current chairman of the House Committee on Un-American Activities, was at an end: "This is not a court of law. We make the rules." Lloyd Barenblatt, a psychology instructor recently fired from Vassar College, would not be allowed to read his opening statement questioning HUAC's right to inquire into the nature of his political beliefs and associations. All HUAC wanted to know of Mr. Barenblatt was "Are you now or have you ever been a member of the Communist party?"

HUAC was first created in 1938 by a House leadership trying to appease conservative Democrats who were worried about purported communist influence in the New Deal. It held few hearings and was not responsible for a single piece of legislation from 1938 to the end of World War II. HUAC became a standing committee of the House of Representatives in the increasingly anti-Soviet climate of 1945, under the chairmanship of John Rankin of Mississippi, one of the House's most openly antiblack, anti-Jewish, and anti–New Deal members. Its charter was broad: "To investigate the extent, character, and objects of un-American propaganda activities in the United States."

For the next 12 years, until 1957, HUAC hauled over 3,000 witnesses before it, focusing not on pending or proposed legislation or on the behavior of executive branch agencies—the only function of standing committees under the rules of the House—but on rooting out people with suspect ideas from the fields of education, religion, and entertainment. Its preferred mode of operation was to press for public recantations of past political beliefs and memberships, and for the naming of past associates. People named by witnesses almost always became the object of public scorn and lost their jobs. People who did not cooperate with HUAC, by refusing to name names (so-called unfriendly witnesses), were subject to contempt of Congress citations, with attendant jail terms.

Despite HUAC's formidable weapons, Lloyd Barenblatt was saying that his beliefs and associations were none of the committee's business: "I object," under the terms of the First Amendment, "to the power and jurisdiction of this committee to inquire into my political beliefs, my religious beliefs, and any other personal and private affairs." At the time, Barenblatt could have avoided a contempt citation had he rested his refusal to cooperate on Fifth Amendment protections against self-incrimination (later, HUAC would close this loophole). He was an extremely idealistic young man, however, who believed not only that he had done nothing wrong, but also that First Amendment freedoms had to be protected against government intrusions. The members of HUAC and the House were unimpressed and voted a contempt citation for Barenblatt in July 1954. After a series of failed court appeals, including two before the Supreme Court, Lloyd Barenblatt entered Danbury Federal Penitentiary in 1959.

Barenblatt later reflected on his experience:

> Would I do it over again? Yes . . . the experience was one that caused some damage and some enhancement to my life. I lost a lot of friends, and it cost me money and jobs. But I stood up at a time when many people kept quiet, or became informers, or left the country. I am still an American. I'm glad I took my stand. I don't regret it.

During the late 1950s, the Supreme Court began a slow process of reining in HUAC. Much later, the House, finally embarrassed by HUAC's roughshod tactics and the increasing willingness of witnesses (this time, anti–Vietnam war protesters) to defy it, abolished the committee in 1975. The bravery of Lloyd Barenblatt and others in resisting the committee on principled constitutional grounds contributed to the excising of what Representative Robert Drinan called "that self-inflicted wound called HUAC from the body politic."

Source: Peter Irons, *The Courage of Their Convictions* (New York: Free Press, 1988), pp. 81–104.

States had become involved in the Vietnam War (see the Struggle for Democracy: "The Pentagon Papers and Freedom of the Press" in Chapter 6). A major expansion of freedom of the press in *New York Times v. Sullivan* (1964) protects newspapers against punishment for trivial or incidental errors when they are reporting on public persons. This limits the use or threat of libel prosecutions by officials, because officials can recover damages only by showing that the medium has purposely reported untruths or has made no effort to find out if what they are reporting is true.

Offensive Mass Media The limits of freedom of expression are often tested by media publications that offend many Americans. Pornography, for example, has challenged the ability of citizens, legislatures, and courts to distinguish art from trash that degrades human beings. Typically, communities and legislators have tried to regulate or eliminate pornography, while civil liberties lawyers and courts have tried to leave choices up to consumers and the market.

Pornography is a nonlegal term for sexual materials. The legal term is **obscenity.** Although the courts have held that obscenity is unprotected by the First Amendment, the definition of obscenity has provoked constitutional struggles for half a century. Early disputes concerned the importation and mailing of works that we regard today as classics: James Joyce's *Ulysses* and D. H. Lawrence's *Lady Chatterley's Lover,* for example.[9] While justices admit that principled distinctions sometimes elude them (Justice Potter Stewart once said that he did not know how to define hard-core pornography but that he knew it when he saw it), a reasonably clear three-part test emerged from *Miller v. California* (1973):

obscenity As the Supreme Court understands it, the representation of sexually explicit materials in a manner that violates community standards and is without redeeming social importance or value.

1. The average person, applying contemporary community standards, must find that the work as a whole appeals to lust.
2. The state law must specifically define what sexual conduct is obscene.
3. The work as a whole must lack serious literary, artistic, political, or scientific value.

If the work survives even one part of this test, it is not legally obscene and cannot be regulated under the First Amendment. Community standards, applied by juries, are used to judge whether the work appeals to lust and whether

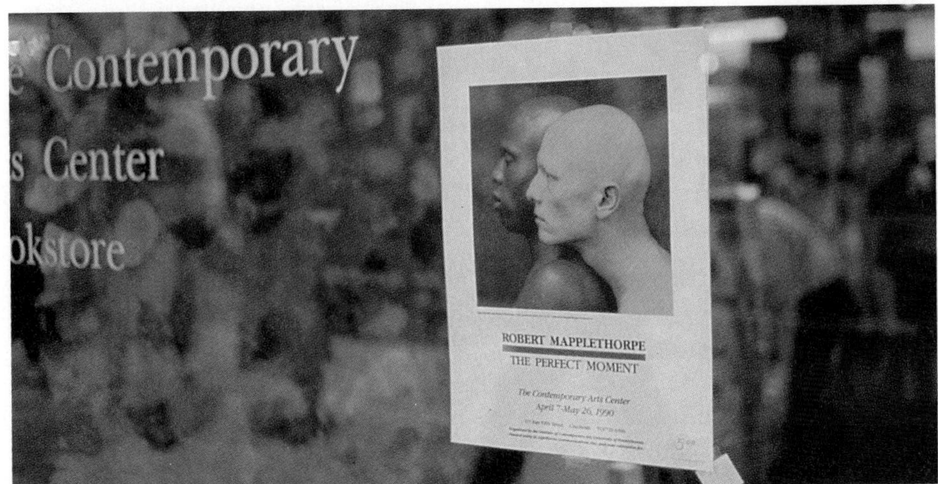

The distinction between art and obscenity can be very difficult to establish, and battles over the banning of controversial works, such as Robert Mapplethorpe's homoerotic photographs, are quite common in American communities.

WHAT ROLE FOR GOVERNMENT?

Should Government Censor the Internet?

On February 8, 1996, President Clinton signed the Telecommunications Act into law. The act includes provisions making it a crime to transmit or to allow to be transmitted indecent materials to which minors may have access. These provisions were immediately challenged in federal court by the American Civil Liberties Union as a violation of the First Amendment. Two federal district courts agreed with the ACLU on Internet censorship, declaring restrictions unconstitutional, in the summer of 1996. The issue remains on the public agenda, however, and the Supreme Court has yet to rule. The following statements from the debate in Congress on the Telecommunications Act nicely represent the contrasting positions on censoring the Internet.

Yes, the Government Should Censor the Internet[a]

[We urge that Congress] include in the final bill the strongest possible criminal law provisions to address the growing and immediate problem of computer pornography without any exemptions, defenses, or political favors of any kind accorded to those who knowingly participate in the distribution of obscenity to anyone or indecency to children. . . .

Thousands of individuals both in this country and abroad are regularly placing obscenity and indecency on the Internet. It is not possible to make anything more than a dent in the serious problem of computer pornography if Congress is willing to hold liable only those who place such material on the Internet while at the same time giving legal exemptions or (denies to service or access) providers who profit from and are instrumental to the distribution of such material. The Justice Department normally targets the major offenders of laws. In obscenity cases prosecuted to date, it has targeted large companies which have been responsible for the nationwide distribution of obscenity and who have made large profits by violating federal laws. Prosecution of such companies has made a substantial impact in curbing the distribution of obscenity, with many such offenders going out of business altogether. So too will prosecution of access providers which *knowingly* traffic in obscenity have a substantial impact, a far greater impact than just the prosecution of a person who places one or a few prohibited images on the Internet. Such a person could not traffic in pornography without the aid or facilitation of the service or access providers. Indeed, if Congress includes provisions protecting access or service providers in whatever bill is finally passed, it is likely that most in this country who are trafficking in indecency to children or obscenity would continue to do so since the threat of prosecution would be minuscule, given the numbers of those currently involved in this activity. . . . Thus, unless all who knowingly participate in such matters are subject to the law, the Internet will remain the same and Congress will have failed in its responsibilities to the children and families of America.

No, the Government Should Not Censor the Internet[b]

We should not underestimate the effect that the heavy hand of government regulation will have on the future growth of the Internet. The legislation has not even passed and we are seeing that just the threat of it is already having a chilling effect on the Internet. Last week, a Vermonter from Underhill, Vermont found that her personal profile on America Online had been deleted because she used vulgar words. In fact, she used AOL to communicate with other breast cancer survivors. What was the vulgar word she had

the work is clearly offensive. However, literary, artistic, political, and scientific value (called the *LAPS test,* after the first letter of each of the four values) is *not* judged by community standards but by the jury's assessment of the testimony of expert witnesses. If, and only if, all three standards are met, the Supreme Court will allow local committees to regulate the sale of pornographic materials.

used? BREAST. After many angry complaints, AOL apologized and again allowed the word to be used by its subscribers when "appropriate." One wonders if, in the future, recipes for Chicken Cacciatore sent online will only call for dark meat to avoid using the dreaded "B-"word.

While the proponents of the proposals claim that they do not "ban" indecency—only prohibit making it available to minors—the practical result of such a restriction on the Internet is the complete criminalization of all indecent speech. . . . Because indecency means very different things to different people, an unimaginable amount of valuable political, artistic, scientific, and other speech will disappear in this new medium. What about, for example, the university health service that posts information online about birth control and protections against the spread of AIDS? With many students in college under 18, this information would likely disappear under threat of prosecution. In bookstores and on library shelves the protection of indecent speech is clear, and the courts are unwavering. Why are some of our colleagues trying to alter the protection of the First Amendment here and cripple this new mode of communication?

In addition to effectively banning indecent speech, the conference is considering proposals to impose criminal liability on both the "speakers" of indecent content as well as online service providers. The result would be to draft the service providers into the role of "Net police." Service providers like America Online and Prodigy, telephone companies providing modem connections, and libraries and schools hooking our nation's children up to this brilliant new medium would face the risk of being fined and even jailed.

To avoid liability, service providers, libraries, and schools would bear the onus of asserting complicated defenses to prosecution. The implications of being hauled into court in the first place—especially for schools and libraries—should not go unnoticed. Many providers will seek to avoid the risk of litigation altogether by censoring all online speech to that appropriate for Kindergarten children, or refusing to serve children at all . . . .

[a]From a petition to Congress dated October 16, 1995, signed by Edwin Meese, III (former U.S. Attorney General), Ralph Reed (Christian Coalition), Donald E. Wildmon (American Family Association), Phyllis Schlafly (Eagle Forum), and nine others.

[b]From a floor speech by Senator Patrick J. Leahy (Democrat of Vermont), December 5, 1995.

Some feminist activists have attempted to broaden the term *obscenity* to include any communication that degrades women. Activists Andrea Dworkin and Catherine MacKinnon, for example, have composed feminist antipornography ordinances that were enacted in Minneapolis and Indianapolis. Such ordinances define pornography as a denial of women's equality, creating a clash between the civil rights of women and the freedom of sellers to sell and buyers

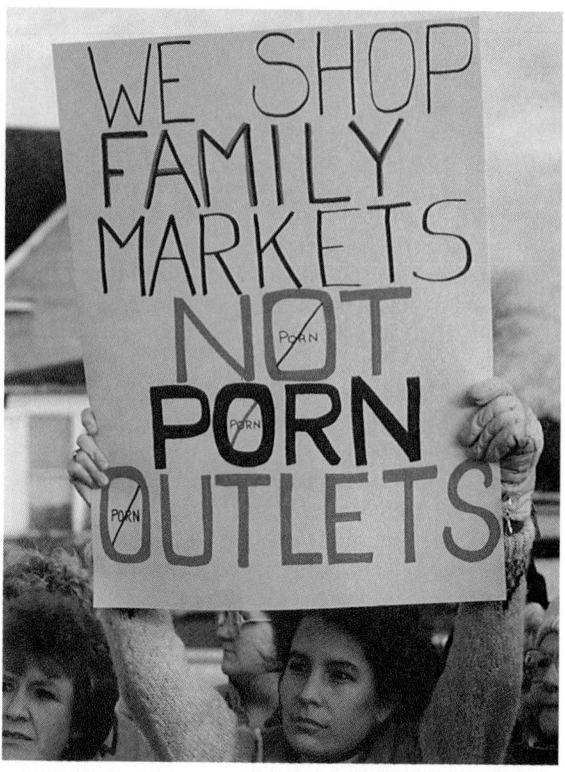

Americans disagree about whether the publication of sexually explicit material ought to be a protected right under the Constitution.

to buy pornography. In *American Booksellers Association v. Hudnut* (1985), U.S. Judge Sarah Evans Barker found the Indianapolis ordinance a clear violation of freedom of expression. Since the definition of *pornography* in the ordinance went far beyond the constitutional definition of *obscenity* in the *Miller* test, Judge Barker ruled that the ordinance was unconstitutional.

Efforts to regulate offensive mass media persist, however. MacKinnon has written a book, *Only Words* to persuade citizens that pornography keeps women frightened, victimized, and unequal.[10] Building on the efforts of Tipper Gore to get album liners to alert parents to raunchy lyrics, prosecutors have attacked 2 Live Crew and other rap groups for allegedly obscene lyrics. During his campaign for the Republican presidential nomination in 1996, Robert Dole attacked the ill effects of the film and music industries on American culture.

Free Exercise of Religion

Congress shall make no law . . . prohibiting the free exercise [of religion].

—First Amendment

For much of our history, Congress did not impede the exercise of religion because it did not legislate much on the subject. Since the states were not covered by the First Amendment, the free exercise of religion was protected by state constitutions or not at all. The Supreme Court was content to defer to the states on issues of religious freedom.

As late as 1940, in *Minersville School District v. Gobitis,* the Supreme Court upheld the expulsion of two schoolchildren who refused to salute the flag because it violated their faith as Jehovah's Witnesses. Justice Harlan Stone wrote a stinging dissent:

> The Constitution expresses more than the conviction of the people that democratic processes must be preserved at all costs. It is also an expression of faith and a command that freedom of mind and spirit must be preserved, which government must obey, if it is to adhere to that justice and moderation without which no free government can exist.

Stone's dissent, as well as a series of decisions deferring to state restrictions on Jehovah's Witnesses in 1941 and 1942, eventually moved other justices to Stone's side. In *West Virginia v. Barnette* (1943), the Court reversed *Gobitis* and firmly established free exercise of religion as protected against the states.

The core of the nationalized free exercise clause today is that government may not interfere with religious *beliefs.* This is one of the few absolutes in U.S. constitutional law. Religious *actions,* however, are not absolutely protected. The Court has upheld state laws, for instance, outlawing the use of peyote (a proscribed hallucinogen) in Native American religious ceremonies (*Employment Division v. Smith,* 1990). This decision was explicitly overturned when President Bill Clinton signed the Religious Freedom Restoration Act in 1993.

Establishment of Religion

> **Congress shall make no law respecting an establishment of religion.**
>
> —FIRST AMENDMENT

Freedom of conscience requires that government not favor one religion over another by granting it special favors, privileges, or status. It requires, in Jefferson's famous terms, "a wall of separation between church and state." Nevertheless, incorporation of the **establishment clause** proved to be a particularly messy matter. In *Everson v. Board of Education* (1947), Justice Hugo Black for the Supreme Court determined that no state could use revenues to support an institution that taught religion, thus incorporating the First Amendment ban into the Fourteenth Amendment. But the majority in that case upheld the New Jersey program that reimbursed parents for bus transportation to parochial schools. A year later, Justice Black wrote another opinion incorporating the establishment clause in *McCollum v. Board of Education* (1948). This time, a program for teaching religion in public schools was found unconstitutional. In *Zorach v. Clauson* (1952), however, the Court upheld a similar program in New York State that let students leave school premises early for religious instruction. The establishment clause had been incorporated, but the justices were having a difficult time determining what "separation of church and state" means in practice.

establishment clause The part of the First Amendment which prohibits Congress from establishing an official religion; the basis for the doctrine of "separation of church and state."

The Lemon Test The Warren Court (1953–1969) brought together a solid church-state separationist contingent whose decisions the early Burger Court (1969–1973) distilled into the major doctrine of the establishment clause: the "*Lemon* test." In *Lemon v. Kurtzman* (1971), Chief Justice Warren Burger specified three conditions that every law must meet to avoid "establishing" religion:

- First, the law must have a secular purpose. That secular *purpose* need not be the only or primary purpose behind the law. The Court requires merely some plausible, nonreligious reason for the law.
- Second, the *primary effect* of the law must be neither to advance nor to retard religion. The Court will assess the probable impact of a governmental action for religious neutrality.
- Third, government must never foster *excessive entanglements* between the state and religion.

While lawyers and judges frequently disagree about each of the three "prongs" of the *Lemon* test, the test has erected substantial walls that bar mixing church and state. The Rehnquist Court has been taking some of the bricks out of the walls, however. In *Rosenberger v. University of Virginia* (1995), it ruled that the university (a state-supported institution) must provide the same financial subsidy to a student religious publication that it provides to other student publications. In *Capital Square Review Board v. Pinette* (1995), it ruled that the Ku Klux Klan had a right to erect a cross in a state park in Columbus, Ohio.

School Prayer One of the most controversial aspects of constitutional law regarding the establishment of religion concerns school prayer. Though a majority of Americans support allowing a nondenominational prayer or a period of silent prayer in the schools—51 percent favor the former, 25 percent favor the latter[11]—the Court has consistently ruled against such practices since the early 1960s. In *Engel v. Vitale* (1962), the Court ordered the State of New York to suspend its requirement that all students in public schools recite a nondenominational prayer at the start of each school day. Writing for the majority, Justice Hugo Black found the prayer requirement to be a state-sponsored religious activity "wholly inconsistent with the establishment clause." In *Stone v. Graham* (1980), the Court ruled against posting the Ten Commandments in public school classrooms. In *Lee v. Weismann* (1992), it ruled against allowing school-sponsored prayer at graduation ceremonies. In these and other cases, the Court has consistently ruled against officially sponsored prayer in public schools as a violation of the separation of church and state. The Court has been willing, however, to allow religious groups to meet in public schools, and to allow students to pray on their own or in unofficial study groups while on public school premises.

Returning prayer to the public schools is very high on the agenda of Christian conservatives. Bills supporting voluntary classroom prayer (such as a moment of silent contemplation) are constantly being introduced into Congress and state legislatures, with little success so far. Christian conservatives have

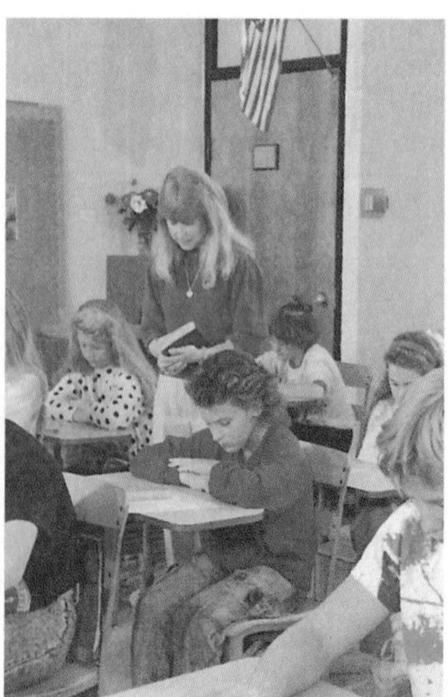

Many school districts still allow religious observations in classrooms, despite a long string of Supreme Court decisions defining such practices as a violation of the doctrine of the separation of church and state.

also tried without success to pass a school prayer constitutional amendment. Responding to religious voters, several legislatures in the South have mandated the teaching of "creation science" (as opposed to the theory of evolution), but the courts have not cooperated. Finally, in several very religious communities, school officials have simply ignored the Supreme Court and continue to allow prayer in public school classrooms.

With no sign that the tide of religious feeling is about to recede in the United States, school prayer in particular, and the question of where to draw the line between church and state in general, is likely to be with us for some time to come.

The Right to Privacy

The freedoms addressed so far—speech, press, and religion—are explicitly mentioned in the Bill of Rights. The freedom to be left alone in our private lives—what is usually referred to as the *right to privacy*—is nowhere mentioned. Nevertheless, most Americans consider the right to privacy one of our most precious freedoms; most believe we ought to be spared wiretapping, E-mail snooping, and the regulation of consensual sexual activities in our own homes, for instance. Many (though not all) constitutional scholars believe, moreover, that a right to privacy is *inherent* (not explicitly stated) in the Bill of Rights; note the prohibitions against illegal searches and seizures and against the quartering of troops in our homes, as well as the right to free expression and conscience. Such scholars also point to the Ninth Amendment as evidence that the framers believed in the existence of liberties not specifically mentioned in the Bill of Rights: "The enumeration in the Constitution of certain rights, shall not be construed to deny or disparage others retained by the people." The Supreme Court agreed with this position in *Griswold v. Connecticut* (1965), in which it ruled that a constitutional right to privacy exists when it struck down laws making birth control illegal.

Whether there is or ought to be a constitutionally protected right to privacy remains an issue of intense debate. First, scholars and jurists who take a **strict construction** position (see Chapter 14) believe that only liberties specifically mentioned in the Constitution are protected liberties and that the right to privacy, not mentioned in the document, is something that has been invented out of thin air is, by virtue of that fact, illegitimate. Second, the right to privacy was the constitutional basis for the *Roe v. Wade* (1973) abortion decision that has so inflamed the nation. As a consequence, the status of this liberty has been caught up in the passions surrounding the debate about abortion. We will return to this issue in Chapter 17 in the section on the civil rights of women.

strict construction The view among some legal scholars that the Supreme Court should interpret the Constitution narrowly and strictly.

Rights of the Accused

Most Americans treasure the constitutional rights and liberties that protect innocent individuals from wrongful prosecution and imprisonment. But most Americans also want to control crime as much as possible. Balancing the two sentiments is not easy. Those alarmed by lawlessness—actual or imagined—tend to support "whatever it takes" to reduce that lawlessness, even if the rights or liberties of others must be restricted. Others are more alarmed by the lawlessness—real or imagined—of police and prosecutors. These advocates of *due process* values see violations of rights and liberties as unnecessary and dangerous in a free society.

During the 1950s and 1960s, the Warren Court favored the due process approach and subjected the states' criminal procedures to rigorous interpretations of constitutional guarantees. Increased protections for criminal defendants, however, gave many political candidates an electorally useful explanation for rising crime: too much regard for "legal technicalities" was "coddling" the guilty and "handcuffing" the police. Republican presidential candidates Nixon, Ford, Reagan, and Bush all promised to appoint federal court judges who would be more sympathetic to crime control and less insistent on protecting the rights of suspects and defendants. One result of Republican domination of the White House between 1968 and 1993 is that a majority of federal judges have been appointed by presidents who "ran against the courts" on the issue of criminal procedure. A gradual but important shift to a higher regard for crime control than for due process has followed from electoral politics and has reshaped constitutional interpretation.

The shift is obvious in the decisions of the Supreme Court. The Warren Court (1953–1969) expanded due process, preferring constitutional guarantees to efficient law enforcement. The Burger Court (1969–1986) preserved most of the basic due process decisions that the Warren Court had crafted but limited the further growth of protections and introduced many exceptions. The Rehnquist Court (1986–present) has reversed many due process protections.

Unreasonable Searches and Seizures Consider, for example, the Fourth Amendment, which secures the right of all persons against unreasonable searches and seizures and allows the granting of search warrants only if the police can specify evidence of serious lawbreaking that they reasonably expect to find. Until the Warren Court compelled the states to abide by the Fourth Amendment in 1961, they had frequently used searches and seizures that the federal courts would consider "unreasonable" in an effort to control crime.

In *Mapp v. Ohio* (1961), the Supreme Court enunciated the "exclusionary rule" to prevent the police and prosecutors from using evidence to convict peo-

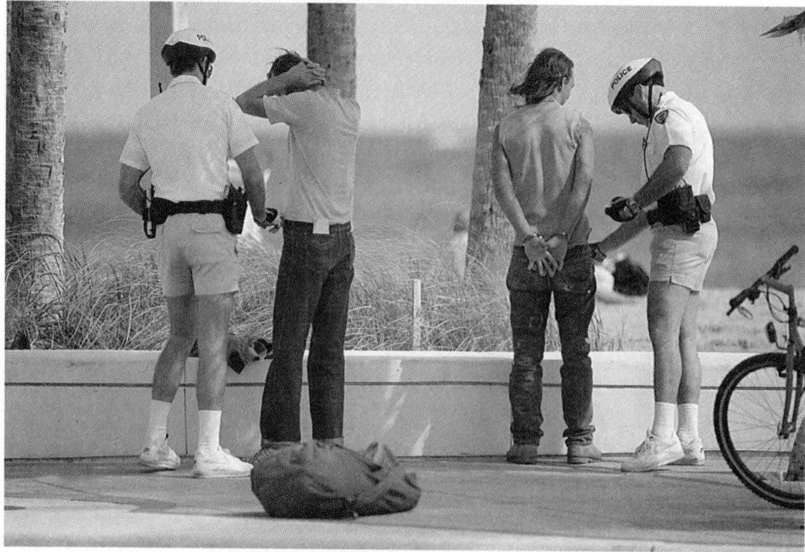

While the right to due process was incorporated into the Constitution, it was the Supreme Court's *Miranda* decision that required law enforcement officials, at arrest, to read the accused their rights.

ple that had been gained through warrantless and unreasonable searches. In this case, the police forcibly entered the apartment of Dollree Mapp looking for a fugitive. They found no fugitive but decided to search Dollree Mapp's apartment anyway, even though they had no search warrant. Finding what they considered obscene photos and books, they arrested Mapp under Ohio's law covering the possession of obscene materials. She was convicted, an action later supported by the Ohio Supreme Court. The conviction was overturned by the U.S. Supreme Court. A majority of the justices believed that the threat of perpetrators' being freed in cases like this would force the police to play by the constitutional rules. The justices did not believe that due process threatened crime control, because police lawlessness was not the only way to deal with crime.

The Warren Court demanded that the police get warrants whenever the person to be subjected to a search had a "reasonable expectation of privacy."[12] The Burger Court limited the places in which privacy could be reasonably expected, allowing searches of moving cars stopped even for routine traffic infractions, and of garbage cans set out for collection. The Burger Court authorized a "good faith" exception to the exclusionary rule, under which prosecutors may introduce evidence obtained illegally if they can show that the police had relied on a warrant that appeared valid but later proved to be invalid.[13] The Court allowed another exception for illegally gathered evidence that would have been discovered eventually without the illegal search.[14] The Rehnquist Court has gone well beyond these exceptions. In *Murray v. United States* (1988), it allowed prosecutors to use products of illegal searches if other evidence unrelated to the illegal evidence would have justified a search warrant. The combination of "good faith," "inevitable discovery," and "retroactive probable cause" has considerably narrowed the exclusionary rule.

Self-Incrimination Concerning the Fifth Amendment protection against self-incrimination, the Warren Court similarly waxed, the Burger Court waffled, and the Rehnquist Court waned. The Warren Court determined that the privilege not to be forced to incriminate oneself was useless at trial if the police coerced confessions long before the trial took place. To forestall "third-degree" tactics in the station house, the Court detailed a stringent set of procedural guarantees: the famous rights established in *Miranda v. Arizona* (1966). Once detained by authorities, all persons had to be informed of their right to remain silent and to consult with an attorney. While the Burger Court upheld *Miranda,* it allowed exceptions. Thus, it allowed the use of information obtained without "Mirandizing" suspects if the suspects took the stand in their own defense. It also allowed the use of information obtained without *Miranda* warnings if some immediate threat to public safety had justified immediate questioning and postponing the warnings.[15] The Rehnquist Court has gone beyond these exceptions in holding that a coerced confession may be "harmless error" that does not constitute self-incrimination.[16]

The Right to Counsel The Sixth Amendment's right to counsel was nationalized—that is, made binding on the states—in two landmark cases. In *Powell v. Alabama* (1932) the Court ruled that legal counsel must be supplied to all indigent defendants accused of a capital crime, that is, crimes in which the death penalty can be imposed. Before this decision, many poor people in the southern states, especially African-Americans, had been tried for and convicted of capital crimes without benefit of an attorney. Thirty-one years later, in *Gideon v. Wainwright* (1963), the Court ruled that defendants accused of any felony in state jurisdictions are entitled to a lawyer and that the states must supply a lawyer when a defendant cannot afford to do so on his or her own. In this case, Clarence Earl Gideon asked for but was denied a lawyer in a Florida court where he was being tried for having broken into a poolhall. He conducted his own defense and lost. After years of study in his Florida prison's law library and the submission of numerous handwritten appeals to the courts to overturn his conviction, the Supreme Court finally agreed to hear his case, assigning the prominent attorney Abe Fortas (later, a Supreme Court justice) to argue for Gideon. Justice Black wrote the following for a unanimous Court:

> Not only . . . precedents but also reason and reflection require us to recognize that in our adversary system of criminal justice, any person hauled into court, who is too poor to hire a lawyer, cannot be assured of a fair trial unless counsel is provided for him. This seems to be an obvious truth.

The Court ordered a new trial. This time, assisted by a public defender supplied by the State of Florida, Gideon was acquitted. By incorporating the Sixth Amendment's guarantee of legal counsel, the Court has ensured that every criminal defendant in the United States can mount a defense even if he or she cannot afford to pay for a lawyer.

Capital Punishment The Burger Court strenuously examined capital punishment under the Eighth Amendment's prohibition of "cruel and unusual punishment." In *Furman v. Georgia* (1972), a split Court found that the death penalty, as used, constituted "cruel and unusual punishment." Congress and 70 percent of the states passed new authorizations of the death penalty, most of which met the Court's objections with procedures to make the infliction of capital punishment less capricious. The Burger Court held that capital punishment was not inherently cruel or unusual in *Gregg v. Georgia* (1976). However, the Court tended to create an "obstacle course" of standards that the states had to meet if they wanted to use the death penalty. Basically, the Court insisted that defendants be given every opportunity to show mitigating circumstances, so that as few convicts as possible would be killed.

The Rehnquist Court has tried to expedite the use of the death penalty. In *McCleskey v. Kemp* (1987), the Court chose to ignore statistical evidence that blacks who kill whites are four times more likely to be sentenced to death than whites who kill blacks. The Court insisted that individual defendants must show that racism played a role in their specific cases. In *Penry v. Lynaugh* (1989), the Court allowed the execution of a convicted murderer who had the intelligence of a 7-year-old. In *Stanford v. Kentucky* (1989), the Court allowed the execution of a minor who had been convicted of murder.

Chief Justice Rehnquist and some of his colleagues have also worked hard to expedite executions by limiting avenues of appeal and delay. In *McCleskey v. Zant* (1991), the Court made delays much less likely by eliminating many means of challenging capital convictions. In its 6–3 decision, the majority reached out to eliminate delays even though no party to the case had requested the Court to do so. In *Keeney v. Tamayo-Reyes* (1992), the Court limited the right of "death row" inmates convicted in state courts to appeal to the Supreme Court. The Court is never entirely predictable, however. In *Wright v. West* (1992), it rejected Bush administration efforts to restrict sharply appeals by state prisoners to the federal courts.

In contrast to the curtailment of the rights of the accused that we have discussed, some other aspects of due process pioneered by the Warren Court have

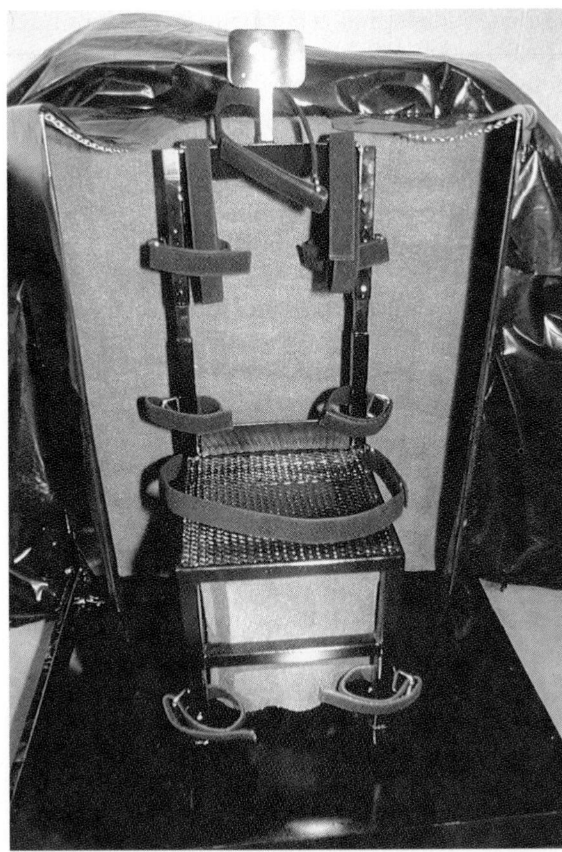

The United States stands almost alone among the rich democratic nations in the use of the death penalty. Some states continue to use the electric chair, as shown in this photo, though most have switched to the use of lethal injection.

been ratified by succeeding Courts. Poor people's right to counsel at trials and first appeals has long and continuously garnered support, for example. However, protections for criminal defendants may be rolled back if the fear of crime continues to pervade American society. As we have seen on numerous occasions, judges are not immune from the influence of the political and governmental contexts in which they operate.

Liberty and Democracy

We suggested in Chapter 1 that liberty is one of the constituent elements of a democratic society. Without liberty—the freedoms of conscience, expression, assembly, and petition, and the freedom from arbitrary arrest and punishment—democracy cannot be said to exist. Without liberty, popular sovereignty cannot function. We have been fortunate in this country, given the central place of liberty in a democratic society, that freedom has expanded greatly over the course of our history. It is, in our view, one of the great achievements of the American experience. What started as a set of protections against intrusions by the federal government has become a set of protections against state and local governments as well. Narrow interpretations of the range of protections of particular liberties have been broadened considerably. Liberties not explicitly mentioned in the Bill of Rights have been identified and elaborated.

Nevertheless, it is clear that civil liberties remain imperfectly realized, and that much remains to be accomplished. Much of what has been accomplished so far has been accomplished because judges and other political leaders have been pushed by popular pressures: elections, public opinion, civil liberties organizations, and social movements. Future progress on the civil liberties front will require a continuation of the struggle for democracy.

Summary

The formal foundation of American liberties is found in the Constitution and its amendments, particularly the Bill of Rights and the Fourteenth Amendment, but their actual enjoyment depends on the actions of the courts, the behavior of government officials, and the struggle for democracy. American history has witnessed an expansion of the boundaries of liberties, especially during the present century, though much remains to be achieved.

During the nineteenth century, the Supreme Court concerned itself mainly with rights to property. Somewhat belatedly, it nationalized the constitutional protection of civil liberties (i.e., made them applicable in the states), by using the Fourteenth Amendment as its main instrument. The familiar liberties of expression, association, press, and religion, as well as certain due process protections for the accused, were gradually incorporated and guaranteed throughout the nation. The expansion of the rights of the accused was always a hotly disputed political issue, and the conservative orientation of the present Court has resulted in the reversal of many of the due process innovations of the Warren and Burger Courts.

Suggested Readings

Abraham, Henry J. *Freedom and the Court,* 6th ed. New York: Oxford University Press, 1993.

Students have begun their study of civil rights and liberties with this textbook for 25 years.

Glasser, Ira. *Visions of Liberty: The Bill of Rights for All Americans.* Boston: Arcade/ Little Brown, 1991.

A book that describes and celebrates the Bill of Rights; rich in historical detail.

Hentoff, Nat. *Free Speech for Me . . . But Not for Thee: How the American Left and Right Relentlessly Censor Each Other.* New York: HarperPerennial, 1992.

A disturbing survey of efforts across the nation by both the right and the left to censor speech and publications they do not like.

Irons, Peter. *The Courage of Their Convictions.* New York: Free Press, 1988.

Brief histories of U.S. Supreme Court cases recount struggles for civil rights and civil liberties since 1940.

McCann, Michael W., and Gerald L. Houseman, eds. *Judging the Constitution.* Glenview, IL: Scott, Foresman, 1989.

A collection of many essays criticizing the status of civil rights and civil liberties in modern U.S. politics.

Walker, Samuel. *In Defense of American Liberties—A History of the ACLU.* New York: Oxford University Press, 1990.

A comprehensive review of the American Civil Liberties Union, highlighting most major battles for civil liberties in the twentieth century.

Internet Sources

ACLU Home Page http://www.aclu.org/
Home page of the American Civil Liberties Union; news about developments in government and American society that affect civil liberties, links to other organizations concerned with civil liberties, landmark civil liberties court cases, and more.

Electronic Frontier Foundation http://www.eff.org/
Information about free expression, privacy, and access to the Internet.

Human Rights Source http://www.gatech.edu/amnesty/source.html
Human rights news and information at home and abroad, with special attention to the death penalty and censorship issues.

Jefferson Project/Justice http://www.stardot.com/jefferson/issues/Justice/
The Jefferson Project's gateway to groups, news, and other information on civil liberties in the United States.

Notes

1. These examples were cited in George F. Will, "Compassion on Campus," *Newsweek* (May 31, 1993), p. 66.
2. Nat Hentoff, "Chilling Codes," *Washington Post,* Nexis: LEGI-SLATE Article No. 225/266.
3. Laurence H. Tribe, *American Constitutional Law,* 2nd ed. (Mineola, NY: Cornell Law Foundation, 1988), Chap. 9.
4. Morton J. Horwitz, *The Transformation of American Law, 1780–1860* (Cambridge: Harvard University Press, 1977); J. Willard Hurst, *Law and the Conditions of Freedom in the Nineteenth-Century United States* (Madison: University of Wisconsin Press, 1956).
5. Robert A. Dahl, "Decision-Making in a Democracy: The Supreme Court as National Policy-Maker," *Journal of Public Law,* Vol. 6 (1967), pp. 279–295.
6. Samuel Walker, *In Defense of American Liberties—A History of the ACLU* (New York: Oxford University Press, 1990).
7. See Stanley I. Kutler, *The American Inquisition: Justice and Injustice in the Cold War* (New York: Hill & Wang, 1982).
8. See Fred W. Friendly, *Minnesota Rag* (New York: Vintage, 1981).
9. See Charles Rembar, *The End of Obscenity* (New York: Harper & Row, 1968).
10. See Richard A. Posner's scathing review in the *New Republic,* Vol. 209, No. 16 (October 18, 1993), p. 31.
11. *American National Election Study, 1988,* University of Connecticut: Roper Center.
12. *Katz v. United States* (1967).
13. *United States v. Leon* (1984) and *Massachusetts v. Sheppard* (1984).
14. *Nix v. Williams* (1984).
15. *Harris v. New York* (1971) and *New York v. Quarles* (1984).
16. *Arizona v. Fulminate* (1991).

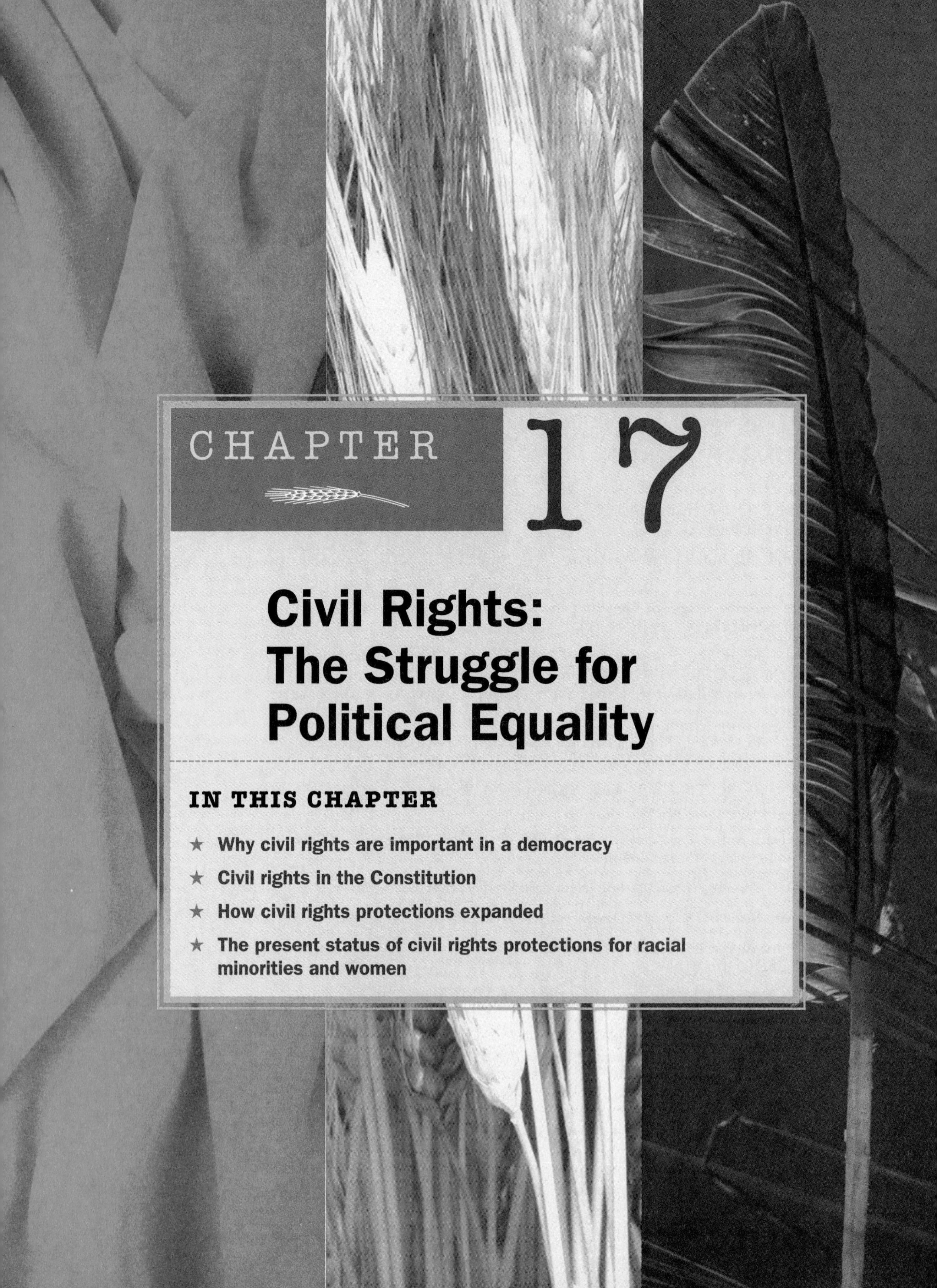

CHAPTER 17

Civil Rights: The Struggle for Political Equality

IN THIS CHAPTER

- ★ Why civil rights are important in a democracy
- ★ Civil rights in the Constitution
- ★ How civil rights protections expanded
- ★ The present status of civil rights protections for racial minorities and women

From Martin Luther King to Louis Farrakhan

On August 28, 1963, approximately 500,000 people converged on the Lincoln Memorial in Washington, D.C., to urge passage of the Civil Rights Act then being considered by Congress. The gathering was predominantly African-American, but a substantial number of whites were there, as well, to lend their support. In their large numbers, they had come to Washington to make a statement to the nation and to hear speeches by the leaders in the fight for civil rights, including Martin Luther King, Jr., of the Southern Christian Leadership Conference (SCLC), Roy Wilkins of the National Association for the Advancement of Colored People (NAACP), and John Lewis of the Student Nonviolent Coordinating Committee (SNCC). The crowd was festive and optimistic. Most who were there believed that Congress had no choice but to pass the civil rights bill because Americans were now ready to accept a fully integrated society without significant barriers to black and white cooperation, or to black advancement and equality. The mood of the historic "March on Washington" was perfectly captured by King in his memorable "I Have a Dream" speech.

A little more than 30 years later, approximately 600,000 African-American men gathered in front of the U.S. Capitol Building on a beautiful October day in 1995 in response to a call from Louis Farrakhan, the leader of the Nation of Islam. His "Million Man March" was designed, he said, to encourage self-reliance and responsibility among African-American men. Though few of the attendees said they supported Farrakhan's overall program of racial separatism, anti-Semitism, and hostility to gays and lesbians, it is striking that so many responded to the call of a man long regarded as being on the extreme "black nationalist" fringe of American politics, that traditional civil rights organizations had not displayed for many years an equivalent ability to mobilize the African-American population, and that women and white men were conspicuously absent on the speakers' platform and in the crowd.

The Million Man March, with its sometimes harsh separatist temper, reflected the uncertain climate for civil rights in the nation as a whole in the mid–1990s compared to the headier times of the mid–1960s. Long gone was the biracial political coalition that had achieved passage of the 1964 Civil Rights Act and the 1965 Voting Rights Act. Also gone was the optimism about the future of race relations and the possibilities for an integrated society that had propelled the Civil Rights Movement. In its place stood racial polarization and isolation, and competing visions of what civil rights policies might be most appropriate for the future.

That the racial climate had changed by the mid–1990s was not in question. In 1994, Republicans swept to a stunning victory in congressional elections, running on a "Contract with America" platform that was silent on the need to make further advances in the area of racial justice and filled with promises that most observers believed would adversely affect African-Americans: cuts in a wide range of social programs, punitive anticrime measures, and termination of federal entitlement programs such as Aid to Families with Dependent Children. In 1995, Governor Pete Wilson convinced the Regents of the University of California to end all affirmative action programs in the statewide university system. In 1996, California voters overwhelmingly approved a proposition initiated by two college professors to end all government affirmative action programs in the state. In that same year, anti-affirmative-action-initiative petition drives were under way in a dozen states, and similar proposals were introduced in Congress. President Clinton undertook a broad review of federal affirmative action programs after the Supreme Court

affirmative action Programs instituted by private and public institutions to overcome the effects of and to compensate for past discrimination.

strict scrutiny The presumption by the Supreme Court that a law, ordinance, or administrative ruling is unconstitutional because it violates fundamental constitutional rights.

ruled in *Adarand Construction v. Peña* (1995) that it would subject **affirmative action** to **strict scrutiny** (that is, presume such programs to be unconstitutional unless a compelling government interest could be demonstrated). Arguments for and against affirmative action may be found in the What Role for Government? box on page 584.

Civil rights are the equal treatment by government of all citizens, as well as guarantees of equal citizenship for all Americans. They are government guarantees, that is to say, of political equality. Civil rights became a more prominent part of the American agenda as democracy itself became more widely accepted in the United States. Because most formal barriers to equal participation in political life have been used to exclude groups of people (women, various ethnic groups, and racial minorities), civil rights initiatives over the years have been directed at removing group barriers and at helping groups overcome the disadvantages created by past discrimination.

The expansion of civil rights protections for African-Americans, as well as for other racial, ethnic, and religious minorities, and for women, is one of the great achievements of American history. This expansion did not come easily or quickly; it took the struggle of millions of Americans to force change from political leaders and government institutions. But change happened, and the result has been the enrichment of American democracy. As the opening story suggests, however, the expansion of civil rights protection in the United States is neither complete nor unproblematic. Passionate disagreements continue to exist on a wide range of civil rights issues, and these disagreements remain at the center of the American political debate. In this chapter, we will examine civil rights in detail, following the changing meaning of the concept over the years. In the course of telling this story, we shall make clear how structural, political linkage, and governmental influences have shaped the meaning of civil rights.

Civil Rights Before the Twentieth Century

Concern about civil rights protections for women and racial minorities was a comparatively late development in the United States, and most major advances were not evident until well into the twentieth century.

In the Beginning, an Absence of Civil Rights

Neither the original Constitution nor the Bill of Rights said anything about political equality beyond insisting that all are equally entitled to due process in the courts. Indeed, the word *equality* does not appear in the Constitution at all. Nor did state constitutions offer much in the way of guaranteeing citizenship equality other than equality before the law. Americans in the late eighteenth and early nineteenth centuries seemed more interested in protecting individuals against government (see Chapter 16) than in guaranteeing certain political rights through government.[1] For most racial or ethnic minorities and women, political equality eluded constitutional protection until the present century, though the groundwork was laid earlier.

The political inequality of African-Americans and women before the Civil War was apparent. In the South, African-Americans lived in slavery, with no rights at all. Outside the South, though a few states allowed African-Americans to vote, the number of states doing so actually declined as the Civil War

Slaves were regarded as property in the antebellum South and were bought and sold at auction like any other kind of property. The Supreme Court upheld this attitude in the infamous *Dred Scott* decision in 1857.

approached, even as universal white male suffrage was spreading. In many places outside the slave South, African-Americans were denied entry into certain occupations, were required to post bonds guaranteeing their good behavior, were denied the right to sit on juries, and were occasionally threatened and harassed with mob violence when they tried to vote or to petition the

Many African-Americans took an active role in fighting for their civil rights before emancipation. Free blacks helped organize the Underground Railroad to smuggle slaves out of the South.

government. Justice Roger Taney, in *Dred Scott v. Sandford* (1857), went so far as to claim that African-Americans had no rights that whites or government were bound to honor or respect. As for women, no state allowed them to vote, few allowed them to sit on juries, and a handful even denied them the right to own property or enter into contracts.

Many African-Americans and women refused to play a passive political role, however, even though the pre–Civil War period was not conducive to their participation in politics. African-Americans, for instance, voted in elections where they were allowed, helped organize the Underground Railroad to smuggle slaves out of the South, and were prominent in the Abolitionist movement against slavery. Both black and white women played an important role in the Abolitionist movement—the antislavery speaking tours of Angelina and Sarah Grimké caused something of a scandal in the 1840s when women's participation in public affairs was considered improper—and a few began to write extensively on the need for women's emancipation and legal and political equality. In 1848, Elizabeth Cady Stanton issued her call for a convention on women's rights to be held at the Village of Seneca Falls, New York. The Declaration of Sentiments and Resolutions issued by the delegates to the convention stands as one of the landmarks in women's struggle for political equality in the United States.

The Civil War Amendments

After the Civil War, the Thirteenth Amendment to the Constitution outlawed slavery throughout the United States, settling the most divisive issue of the nineteenth century. The Fourteenth Amendment reversed *Dred Scott* by making all people who are born or naturalized in the United States, black or white, citizens both of the United States and of the states in which they reside. To se-

White women played a strong role in the Abolitionist movement at a time when female participation in political arenas was considered improper, even scandalous. Female abolitionists such as Angelina and Sarah Grimké met with such harsh male objections to their antislavery activities that they soon found themselves fighting for women's rights as well as those of black Americans.

In 1848, Elizabeth Cady Stanton helped organize the Seneca Falls Convention on women's rights. The resulting Declaration of Sentiments and Resolutions was patterned after the Declaration of Independence, stating that "all men and women are created equal," and including a list of the injustices of men against women.

cure the rights and liberties of recently freed slaves, Article I of the amendment further provided that "No State shall make or enforce any law which shall abridge the privileges or immunities of citizens of the United States" (called the privileges and immunities clause); "nor shall any State deprive any person of life, liberty, or property, without due process of law" (called the due process clause); "nor deny to any person within its jurisdiction the equal protection of the laws" (called the **equal protection** clause). The Fifteenth Amendment guaranteed African-American men the right to vote. Imposing as this constitutional language sounds, the Supreme Court would soon transform it into a protection for property rights (as we saw in Chapter 16), but not for African-Americans or women.

equal protection That part of the Fourteenth Amendment to the constitution that enjoins the state to treat all of their citizens equally.

Undermining the Effectiveness of the Civil War Amendments The privileges and immunities clause was rendered virtually meaningless by *The Slaughterhouse Cases* (1873). Writing for the Court, Justice Samuel Miller found that the clause protected only the rights of citizens of the United States as citizens and not rights that were the responsibility of states. In these cases, the Court denied citizens protection against abuses by state governments, including African-Americans disenfranchised by state actions. Within five years of its passage, then, the Fourteenth Amendment had been seriously compromised by the Court, which foiled an attempt by the post–Civil War Radical Republican Congress to amend the Constitution in favor of equality.

The equal protection clause survived *The Slaughterhouse Cases* but soon lost all practical meaning. First, the Court said that the Fourteenth Amendment gave Congress no power to prohibit discrimination unless it was practiced by state government. "Equal protection of the laws" did not, therefore, preclude race discrimination by private owners or managers of restaurants, theaters, hotels, and other public accommodations, the Court said in *The Civil Rights Cases* (1883). Then, the Court made even state-sponsored discrimination constitutional in *Plessy v. Ferguson* (1896). The Court said that the states could separate the races in intrastate railways if they provided "equal" facilities for the races. This doctrine of "separate but equal" would provide the legal foundation for **Jim Crow** segregation in the South and would remain in force until it was overturned in *Brown v. Board of Education* over half a century later.

Jim Crow The popular term for the system of legal racial segregation that existed in the American South until the middle of the twentieth century.

poll tax A tax to be paid as a condition of voting.

literacy test A device used by the southern states to prevent blacks from voting before the passage of the Voting Rights Act of 1965, which banned its use; usually involved interpretation of a section of a state's constitution.

grandfather clause A device that allowed whites who had failed the literacy test to vote; it allowed all to vote whose grandfathers had voted in the past.

white primaries Primary elections open only to whites.

The Fifteenth Amendment's voting guarantees were rendered ineffectual by a variety of devices invented to prevent African-Americans from voting in the former states of the Confederacy. The **poll tax** was a tax required of all voters in many states, and it kept many African-Americans away from the polls. Even a small tax was a heavy burden for many to bear, given the desperate economic situation of African-Americans in the South in the late nineteenth and early twentieth centuries. Several states required voters to pass a **literacy test** devised and administered by local officials. The evaluation of test results was entirely up to local officials, who rarely passed blacks, including those with a college education or even a Ph.D. degree. If white voters failed the literacy test, many states allowed them to vote anyway under the **grandfather clause,** which provided that anyone whose grandfather had been a voter could vote as well. Since the grandfathers of African-Americans in the South had been slaves, the grandfather clause was no help to them at all. Several states instituted **white primaries** that excluded African-Americans from the process of nominating candidates for local, state, and national offices. The states based these primaries on the argument that political parties were private clubs that could define their own membership requirements, including skin color. For those African-Americans who might try to vote anyway in the face of the poll tax, the literacy test, and the white primary, there was always the use of terror as a deterrent; night riding, bombings, and lynchings were used with regularity, especially during times when blacks showed signs of assertiveness.

The statutory devices for keeping African-Americans away from the polls were consistently supported by state and federal courts until well into the twentieth century. Terror remained a factor until the 1960s, when the civil rights movement (described in detail in Chapter 10) and federal intervention finally put an end to it.

While we might be tempted to explain these interpretations of constitutional provisions simply as mistakes by the justices who happened to be on the Supreme Court at the time, it is far more persuasive to attribute them to the political, governmental, and structural contexts within which the justices decided cases: the presidents who appointed the justices; the senators who confirmed them; the voters who supported the presidents, senators, and other officials who tolerated attacks on African-Americans; the public and private elites that abandoned the newly freed people to states run by their former owners; and the intellectuals who formulated elaborate theories of white racial supremacy. To resolve the presidential election of 1876, for example, the Democrats agreed that Republican Rutherford B. Hayes would become president, even though he had received fewer popular votes than Samuel Tilden. In return, the Union Army was withdrawn from the Democratic South, ending even a minimal protection of black Americans. Reinforced politically and governmentally, racial discrimination easily reacquired constitutional status.

Although the Fifteenth Amendment expanded the right to vote to include all men born or naturalized in the United States, poll taxes, literacy tests, and intimidation at the polls kept African-American voting to a minimum. The amendment neglected to include women, fueling the suffragist movement that let to the Nineteenth Amendment, which granted women the right to vote in 1920.

Women and the Fifteenth Amendment Stung by the exclusion of women from the Fifteenth Amendment's extension of the right to vote to African-Americans—the amendment said only that no state could exclude people on the grounds of "race, color, or previous condition of servitude"—politically active women turned their attention to winning the vote for women. Once the Supreme Court had decided, in *Minor v. Happersett* (1874), that women's suffrage was not a right inherent in the national citizenship guarantees of the Fourteenth Amendment, women abandoned legal challenges based on their inferior political position and turned to more direct forms of political agitation: petitions, marches, and protests. After many years of struggle, the efforts of the women's suffrage movement bore fruit in the Nineteenth Amendment, ratified in 1920: "The right of citizens of the United States to vote shall not be denied or abridged by the United States or by any State on account of sex."

The Contemporary Status of Civil Rights

We saw in Chapter 16 how the Supreme Court, using the guidelines written by Justice Harlan Fiske Stone in *U.S. v. Carolene Products Company* (1938), gradually extended the protections of the Bill of Rights to the states, based on the Fourteenth Amendment. Recall that among the actions by the states that would trigger strict scrutiny were those that either "restricted the democratic process" or "discriminated against racial, ethnic, or religious minorities." It is this reading of the Fourteenth Amendment, particularly the equal protection clause, that lent judicial support to the gradual advance of civil rights guarantees for African-Americans and other minorities, and eventually (though less so) for women. In the following sections, we look at the extension of the civil rights of racial minorities and women. Here we concentrate mainly (though not exclusively) on Supreme Court decisions (see Chapter 10 for more information on the civil rights and women's movements).

Civil Rights for Racial Minorities

Two basic issues have dominated the story of the extension of civil rights since the mid–1960s: the ending of legal discrimination, separation, and exclusion, and the debate over affirmative actions to rectify past wrongs. We examine both in this section.

The End of "Separate but Equal" We reviewed earlier how the Constitution was long interpreted to condone slavery and segregation. In the twentieth century, however, the legal and political battles waged by the civil rights movement eventually pushed the Supreme Court, the president, and Congress to take seriously the equal protection clause of the Fourteenth Amendment.

In 1944, amid World War II (a war aimed in great part at bringing down the racist regime of Adolf Hitler) and the NAACP's campaign to rid the nation of segregation, the Supreme Court finally declared that race was a **suspect classification** that demanded strict judicial scrutiny. This meant that any state or national enactment using racial criteria was presumed to be unconstitutional. Having declared racial laws suspect, the Court nevertheless decided that the internment of more than 100,000 Japanese-Americans without any due process whatsoever survived strict scrutiny. In *Korematsu v. United States* (1944), Justice Hugo Black and the majority deferred to Executive Order 9066 on the basis of the war powers of Congress and the president's prerogative as commander in chief. Since the Supreme Court has often accepted military judgments uncritically, such extreme deference during wartime should perhaps not be very surprising.

suspect classification The designation of a group for special treatment by government that is invidious, arbitrary and/or irrational.

Pressed by the legal efforts of the NAACP, the Court gradually chipped away at *Plessy* and the edifice of segregation (see the Struggle for Democracy box for the story of the NAACP's most important attorney, Thurgood Marshall). In *Smith v. Allwright* (1944), the Court declared that the practice of excluding nonwhites from political-party primary elections was unconstitutional. Then, the Court ruled that the states' practice of providing separate all-white and all-black law schools was unacceptable.

The great breakthrough for racial equality came in *Brown v. Board of Education* (1954), in which a unanimous Court declared that "separate but equal" was inherently contradictory, and that segregation was constitutionally unacceptable in public schools. *Brown* was a constitutional revolution, destined to transform racial relations law and practices in the United States.

The white South did not react violently at first, but it did not desegregate either. Once recognition spread that the Court was going to enforce civil rights, however, massive resistance to racial progress gripped the South. This resistance was what Dr. Martin Luther King, Jr., and others had to work (and die) to overcome. The Court—even with many follow-up cases—was able to accomplish little before the president and Congress backed up the justices with the 1964 Civil Rights Act and the 1965 Voting Rights Act. These legislative actions were forced by the civil rights movement.

The drive to protect the rights of racial minorities has occupied the nation ever since. The main doctrine on racial discrimination is straightforward: Any use of race in law or government regulations will trigger strict scrutiny (a pre-

The Young Thurgood Marshall

The Struggle for Democracy

Thurgood Marshall became one of the nation's most prominent civil rights attorneys, representing Linda Brown and other plaintiffs in *Brown v. Board of Education,* and later a distinguished member of the U.S. Supreme Court. In the following selection, historian William Chafe tells the story of Marshall's early days as a civil rights lawyer in the South, during which he repeatedly risked his life in the struggle for democracy.

During the 1940s Marshall traveled throughout the South, organizing teachers to fight for equal pay, mobilizing parents to insist on equal bus transportation, and enlisting lawyers to risk their practices by standing up for equality. He lived with the people, rarely spending more than a dollar for a meal, never more than two dollars for a room. Wherever he went he built alliances, showing the people he worked with that here was someone they could "travel the river" with. "Everybody loved Thurgood," one NAACP staff officer said, "[he] had the common touch." While previous NAACP leaders had spoken down to the people, another black observed, "Thurgood Marshall was of the people. He knew how to get through to them. Out in Texas or Oklahoma or down the street here in Washington at the Baptist Church, he would make these rousing speeches that would have them all jumping out of their seats."

Marshall's own courage in the face of constant danger became legendary, inspiring others to follow his example. In Tennessee, in the aftermath of the Columbia riot, his car was stopped three times by police harassing him, trying to scare him away. But Marshall never wavered. As Herbert Hill of the NAACP observed, "he was a very courageous figure. He would travel to the court houses of the South, and folks would come from miles, some of them on muleback or horseback, to see the nigger lawyer' who stood up in white men's courtrooms." More to the point, when he got to those courtrooms he often won, demonstrating to local residents that a black man could stand up in the face of white intimidation and prevail.

Source: From William H. Chafe, *The Unfinished Journey* (New York: Oxford University Press, 1986), p. 149.

sumption of unconstitutionality) by the courts. Recall from our earlier discussion that a state or the federal government can defend its acts under strict scrutiny only if it can produce a *compelling* government interest for which the act in question is a *necessary* means. Almost no law survives this challenge; laws that discriminate on the basis of race are dead from the moment of passage. (See the Film and Politics box on page 588 for the story of how America's

WHAT ROLE FOR GOVERNMENT?

Should Government Insist on Racial Remedies in College Admission as a Way to Compensate for Past Discrimination?

Yes: Justice Thurgood Marshall, from his opinion in Regents of the University of California v. Bakke (1978)

The position of the Negro today in America is the tragic but inevitable consequence of centuries of unequal treatment. Measured by any benchmark of comfort or achievement, meaningful equality remains a distant dream for the Negro.

. . .

In light of the history of discrimination and its devastating impact on the lives of Negroes, bringing the Negro into the mainstream of American life should be a state interest of the highest order. To fail to do so is to ensure that America will forever remain a divided society.

. . .

It is plain that the Fourteenth Amendment was not intended to prohibit measures designed to remedy the effects of the nation's past treatment of Negroes. The Congress that passed the Fourteenth Amendment is the same Congress that passed the 1866 Freedmen's Bureau Act, an act that provided many of its benefits only to Negroes.

. . .

While I applaud the judgment of the Court that a university may consider race in its admissions process, it is more than a little ironic that, after several hundred years of class-based discrimination against Negroes, the Court is unwilling to hold that a class-based remedy for that discrimination is permissible. In declining to so hold, today's judgment ignores the fact that for several hundred years Negroes have been discriminated against, not as individuals, but rather solely because of the color of their skins. It is unnecessary in twentieth-century America to have individual Negroes demonstrate that they have been victims of racial discrimination: the racism of our society has been so pervasive that none, regardless of wealth or position, has managed to escape its impact. The experience of Negroes in America has been different in kind, not just in degree, from that of other ethnic groups. It is not merely the history of slavery alone but also that a whole people were marked as inferior by the law. And that mark has endured. The dream of America as the great melting pot has not been realized for the Negro: because of his skin color he never even made it into the pot.

These differences in the experience of the Negro make it difficult for me to accept that Negroes cannot be afforded greater protection under the Fourteenth Amendment where it is necessary to remedy the effects of past discrimination.

. . .

It is because of a legacy of unequal treatment that we now must permit the institutions of this society to give consideration to race in making decisions about who will hold the positions of influence, affluence, and prestige in America. For far too long, the doors to those positions have been shut to Negroes. If we are ever to become a fully integrated society, one in which the color of a person's skin will not determine the opportu-

changing racial attitudes have been reflected in Hollywood films.) Needless to say, other racial minority groups in addition to African-Americans—Latinos, Asian-Americans, and Native Americans—have benefited from the constitutional revolution that has occurred.

Affirmative Action Constitutional interpretation now protects racial minorities against discrimination that is sanctioned or protected by law or government action. The issues are not as clear-cut, however, in the area of government actions that *favor* racial minorities (and women) in affirmative action programs designed to rectify past wrongs.

nities available to him or her, we must be willing to take steps to open those doors. I do not believe that anyone can truly look into America's past and still find that a remedy for the effects of that past is impermissible.

No: Robert Sowell, from his article "Are Quotas Good for Blacks?" Commentary, Vol. 65 (June 1978), pp. 39–43

The past is a great unchangeable fact. *Nothing* is going to undo its sufferings and injustices, whatever their magnitude. Statistical categories and historic labels may seem real to those inspired by words, but only living flesh-and-blood people can feel joy or pain. Neither the sins nor the sufferings of those dead are within our power to change. Being honest and honorable with the people living in our own time is more than enough moral challenge, without indulging in illusions about rewriting moral history with numbers and categories.

. . .

Underlying the attempt to move people around and treat them like chess pieces on a board is a profound contempt for other human beings. To ignore or resent people's resistance—on behalf of their children or their livelihoods—is to deny our common humanity. To persist dogmatically in pursuit of some abstract goal, without regard to how it is reached, is to despise freedom and reduce three-dimensional life to cardboard pictures of numerical results. The false practicality of results-oriented people ignores the fact that the ultimate results are in the minds and hearts of human beings. Once personal choice becomes a mere inconvenience to be brushed aside by bureaucrats or judges, something precious will have been lost by all people from all backgrounds.

A multi-ethnic society like the United States can ill afford continually to build up stores of intergroup resentments about such powerful concerns as one's livelihood and one's children. It is a special madness when tensions are escalated between groups who are basically in accord in their opposition to numbers games, but whose legal establishments and "spokesmen" keep the fires fueled. We must never think that the disintegration and disaster that has hit other multi-ethnic societies "can't happen here." The mass internment of Japanese Americans just a generation ago is a sobering reminder of the tragic idiocy that stress can bring on. We are not made of different clay from the Germans, who were historically more enlightened and humane toward Jews than many other Europeans—until the generation of Hitler and the Holocaust.

The situation in America today is, of course, not like that of the Pearl Harbor period, nor of the Weimar Republic. History does not literally repeat, but it can warn us of what people are capable of, when the stage has been set for tragedy. We certainly do not need to let emotionally combustible materials accumulate from ill-conceived social experiments.

In *Regents v. Bakke* (1978), the Court authorized a compromise on such affirmative action programs. The Constitution and federal law prohibited employers and admissions committees from using strictly racial quotas, the Court said, but it saw no problem with the use of race as one factor among several in hiring or admissions. The Court later indicated that it would be very lenient with legislative programs that were intended to redress past discrimination. Recently, however, the Court has insisted that laws that are not colorblind be subject to strict scrutiny. In *Wygant v. Jackson Board of Education* (1986) and *Richmond v. Croson Co.* (1989), the Court said that programs that narrowly redress specific violations will be upheld but that broader

Martin Luther King waves to the "March on Washington" crowd at the Lincoln Memorial after delivering his "I Have a Dream" speech. This event, one of the high points of the Civil Rights movement, helped convince Congress to pass the Civil Rights Act of 1964.

affirmative action programs that address societal racism will be struck down. In *Adarand Constructors v. Peña* (1995), the Court ruled by a 5–4 majority that the federal government must abide by the strict standards for affirmative action programs imposed on the states in the *Richmond* case and could not award contracts using race as the main criterion. In *Miller v. Johnson* (1995), the Court ruled, again by a 5–4 majority, that race could not be used as the basis for drawing House district lines in an effort to increase the number of racial minority members in Congress. The Court also refused to overturn a 5th Circuit Court ruling that race cannot be considered at all in admissions decisions at the University of Texas law school, putting the *Bakke* principle in jeopardy. The Court was saying clearly that various programs whose aim is simply to increase racial diversity are no longer acceptable. Programs must be designed to redress past discrimination in a particular occupation, business sector, or institution and must not serve vague societywide goals of better minority representation. Such programs must also be temporary efforts to transcend past practices and not a permanent feature of hiring, contracting, or admissions.

The Court's direction on affirmative action seems to mirror the mood of the country, as indicated by the passage of an anti-affirmative action proposition in California in 1996, President Clinton's suspension of minority "set asides" in federal contracts, anti-affirmative-action initiatives in the states, and attempts in Congress to end federal affirmative action programs. Programs meant to overcome racial disadvantages by compensating an entire racial group for wrongs done to it in the past apparently seem unfair to many Americans and have generated a great deal of hostility. It is unlikely that such programs will survive in their present form (see Table 17.1 for a summary of government policies on affirmative action).

Table 17.1 A History of Federal Government Actions on Affirmative Action

Presidential Initiatives

1. *Lyndon Johnson* signs an executive order in 1964 requiring contractors doing business with the federal government to adopt affirmative action plans, complete with goals and timetables for minority hiring.
2. *Richard Nixon* in 1970 initiates the "Philadelphia plan" requiring minimum percentages of minority employees for all federal contractors.
3. *Ronald Reagan* weakens the enforcement of affirmative action guidelines in federal contracts and challenges many of them in the courts (with little success).
4. *Bill Clinton,* in the aftermath of *Adarand Constructors v. Peña* (1995), orders a review of all federal government affirmative action programs to determine which ones will and which ones will not pass constitutional muster. The Justice Department directive to all federal agencies says that all such programs must be justified by evidence of particularized discrimination and that programs simply designed to increase diversity are legally suspect.

Congressional Initiatives

1. Title VII of the 1964 Civil Rights Act specifies principles of employment nondiscrimination and ways to redress violations of such principles by a limited use of affirmative action.
2. In 1991, Congress endorses the principle of affirmative action when it passes amended civil rights legislation making it easier for workers to sue for job discrimination.
3. In 1996, Senate Majority Leader Robert Dole introduces a bill to end all federal preferences.

Court Initiatives

1. The courts generally support local, state, and federal affirmative action programs arising under Title VII of the 1964 Civil Rights Act.
2. In *Regents v. Bakke* (1978), the Supreme Court rules against strict numerical quotas but says that using race among several factors to be considered in hiring and admissions is acceptable.
3. In *Richmond v. Croson Co.* (1989), the Supreme Court subjects all state and local affirmative action policies to "strict scrutiny"; such programs may be used to redress past discrimination in a particular set of practices or institutions, but not societywide racism.
4. The U.S. Court of Appeals for the Fourth Circuit rules in 1994 that a University of Maryland scholarship program restricted to African-American students is unconstitutional. The court says that the University of Maryland has failed to prove that the program is designed to redress discrimination that the University of Maryland has practiced in the past.
5. In *Adarand Constructors v. Peña* (1995), the Supreme Court rules that federal government affirmative action programs must meet the same standards of acceptability as those set out for the states and localities in *Richmond.*
6. In *Miller v. Johnson* (1995), the Supreme Court rules that race cannot be used as the sole criterion for drawing House district lines even if the goal is to increase minority representation.
7. The U.S. Court of Appeals for the Fifth Circuit rules in 1996 that the University of Texas Law School is barred from using affirmative action admissions policies for the purpose of making its student body more diverse.

POLITICS AND FILM

Changing Portrayals of African-Americans in Film

Hollywood films tend to reflect the mood, attitudes, and outlooks of the times in which they are made. Those about African-Americans generally follow this pattern; their treatment in films tells us a great deal about the state of race relations in the United States at the time they were produced and screened for the public. Three classic American films about race show this close relationship between film and society: *The Birth of a Nation, Gone with the Wind,* and *Glory.*

D. W. Griffith's *Birth of a Nation* (1915) was America's first "blockbuster" film, drawing record-breaking crowds across the country, the adoration of critics and public figures, and a private showing in the White House (the first film ever screened there) for President Woodrow Wilson, whose book *A History of the American People* (1902) was cited at the end of the film to validate its authenticity.[a] Film historians estimate that 200 million people around the world saw the film between 1915, when it was first released, and the end of World War II in 1945. The *Birth of a Nation* was a technical and artistic achievement, introducing film techniques used by other film directors for decades after, justifying its selection by the Library of Congress to the National Film Registry. Unfortunately, it also is one of the most racist films ever made.

The Birth of a Nation celebrates and justifies the rise of the Ku Klux Klan (KKK) in the late nineteenth century as the defender of Western civilization and white women against the threat of the Black Peril. Griffith portrays the post–Civil War Reconstruction period—when federal troops provided order in the former states of the Confederacy and African-Americans played a prominent role in several state governments in the South—as a time of unrelieved insult and threat to white southerners. Not only were whites politically powerless in Griffith's telling, but they were beset by a lawless, bestial, sexually depraved, and violent black population protected by federal troops. The Klan is portrayed as the last resort of a desperate and long-suffering race attempting to restore honor, law, and a just social order. In the most vivid image in the film, the Klansmen dip the hems of their robes in the blood of a white, blond virgin, violated and killed by a black man, before they ride off to wreak revenge.

Few white Americans in 1915 were offended by *The Birth of a Nation* because its portrayal of African-Americans was close to the ways of thinking of the general public. During the late nineteenth and early twentieth centuries in the United States, after all, theories of white racial superiority were common in the culture. It was a time when social Darwinist philosophers celebrated the dominance of the white race as the outcome of "natural selection" and the "survival of the fittest," when imperial expansion and colonialism were justified in terms of civilizing the dark peoples of the planet, when the Jim Crow system of formal racial segregation was introduced throughout the South, and when lynching was so common that the newly formed NAACP kept a yearly tally. D. W. Griffith's justification for using whites in "blackface" to play all of the main black roles in the film—he said that he would not have "black blood among the principals"—gives a taste of the sensibilities of the time.

By the 1930s, the bestial African-American of *The Birth of a Nation* had been replaced in Hollywood films by the Stepin Fetchit type of happy-go-lucky, fun-loving, and irresponsible Negro. In several Shirley Temple films, for instance, the child star was shown as more intellectually and emotionally mature than the childlike Negroes in the films, who were always ready to break into song and dance. The childlike Negro, requiring the paternalistic help of whites, is one of the main themes of *Gone with the Wind,* one of the most popular and celebrated of American films.[b] The film paints the plantation system in the antebellum (before the Civil War) South as an idyllic world of order and chivalry, in which black slaves were well cared for, protected, and contented with their lot. Though African-American actors made their most prominent appearance to date in this film, they are shown as uniformly one-dimensional and inferior beings, ranging from the comic Pork to the imbecilic Prissy and the ever-faithful Mammy. During the Reconstruction period in *Gone With the Wind,* after Atlanta has been put to the torch and Tara has been devastated, the freed black slaves are shown as lost, shiftless, and unhappy souls, longing for the good old days.

Gone with the Wind (1939) was released at a time when American culture had moved away from the virulent racism that had prevailed at the turn of the century and when Americans were more concerned about the hard economic times of the Great Depression than

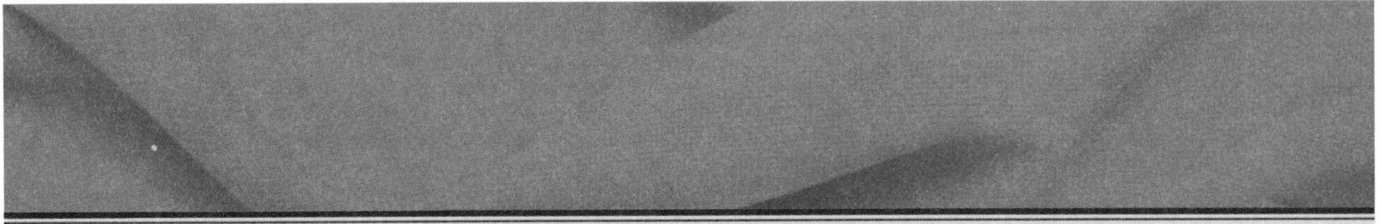

with the race issue. It was a time, moreover, when African-Americans posed no tangible political or social threat to white Americans, especially in the South, where African-Americans lived under the tyranny of Jim Crow. Though the American culture assumed blacks to be inferior, they were not necessarily a group to worry much about.

Glory (1989) is of a different order entirely and the product of a different time in American history. In this portrayal of the all-black Fifty-Fourth Massachusetts Volunteer Infantry, African-Americans are shown as disciplined and brave combat troops in the battle for Fort Wagner near Charleston, South Carolina, during the American Civil War. In the battle, the details of which are shown with unusual historical accuracy by the standards of Hollywood,[c] the Fifty-Fourth suffered nearly 50 percent casualties, fighting in near-hopeless conditions, yet never flinched. It is fair to say that this film could not have been made in 1915 or in 1939, when the most acceptable ways to portray African-Americans in popular culture were as bestial subhumans or childlike innocents. *Glory* was possible only at a time when the civil rights movement had already occurred, after legal forms of segregation and subjugation had been abolished in the United States, after African-Americans had distinguished themselves as combat soldiers in Korea and Vietnam, and when a black man, Colin Powell, was serving as the chairman of the Joint Chiefs of Staff. Though racial discrimination and racial tension had not (and still have not) disappeared from American society by 1989, it was no longer possible to treat African-Americans in the traditional ways in Hollywood.

[a]Material in this section on *The Birth of a Nation* is from Leon Litwack, "The Birth of a Nation," in Ted Mico, John Miller-Monzon, and David Rubel (eds.), *Past Imperfect: History According to the Movies* (New York: Holt, 1995).

[b]See Catherine Clinton, "*Gone with the Wind,*" in Mico et al., *Past Imperfect.*

[c]James M. McPherson, "*Glory,*" in Mico et al., *Past Imperfect.*

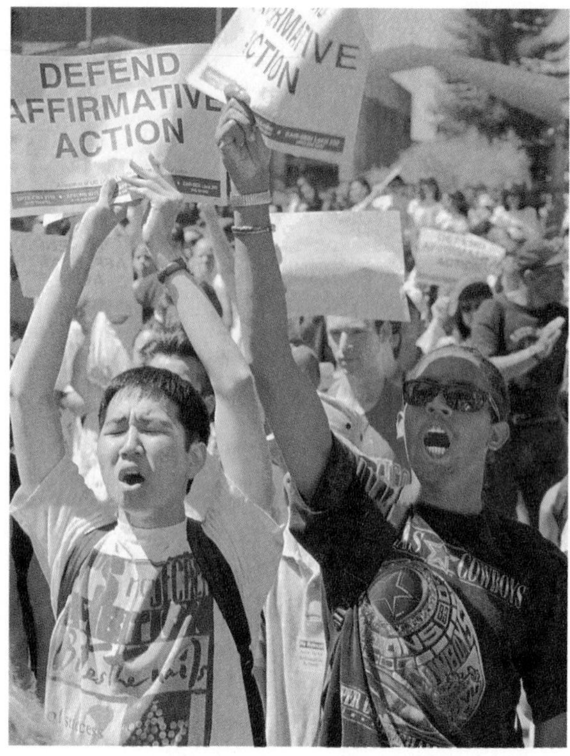

Affirmative action programs are increasingly in jeopardy in the United States. Here students protest the decision of the University of California Board of Regents to end affirmative action for admissions to the university.

Civil Rights for Women

The expansion of civil rights protections for women has taken a decidedly different path from that of racial minorities. We examine that story in this section.

Intermediate Scrutiny For all its egalitarian reputation, the Warren Court did not significantly advance the cause of women's rights. Once the Burger Court seriously looked at sex discrimination laws, it had to decide whether to apply "ordinary scrutiny" (the presumption of constitutionality that almost all laws survive) or "strict scrutiny" (the presumption of unconstitutionality that dooms almost all laws). The Burger Court opted for a new position, called **intermediate scrutiny,** but not before coming to the very brink of declaring gender a "suspect category" demanding strict scrutiny.

intermediate scrutiny A legal test falling between ordinary and strict scrutiny relevant to issues of gender; under this test, the Supreme Court will allow gender classifications in laws if they serve a *substantial* government objective.

Equal Rights Amendment (ERA) A proposed constitutional amendment that would have prohibited the U.S. or state governments from denying or abridging equal rights on the grounds of gender; the amendment passed Congress but failed because it did not win approval from the required number of states.

Sharon Frontiero, an air force lieutenant, had requested the benefits routinely provided married male officers. She was told that she could qualify only if she could prove that her husband received more than 50 percent of his income from her. The justices quickly concluded that such discrimination was unconstitutional. Justice Brennan's first draft of the majority opinion used only ordinary scrutiny to conclude that the air force regulations were too arbitrary to stand. In response to circulation of that draft, Justices Byron White and William Douglas pushed Justice Brennan to base the opinion on sex as a suspect category. Justice Brennan incorporated this suggestion into his second draft and began to lobby his colleagues to take the big step. Had he succeeded, *Frontiero v. Richardson* (1974) would have inaugurated a new era of constitutional equality, and there would have been no need for the women's movement to push for passage of the **Equal Rights Amendment (ERA)** to the Constitution to guarantee full legal equality for women.

By 1976, the ERA had been stalled, and there were still not five Supreme Court votes for a strict scrutiny of gender classification. There was support, however, for a new doctrine that came to be called *intermediate scrutiny.* In *Craig v. Boren* (1976), six justices supported Justice William Brennan's compromise, which created a more rigorous scrutiny of gender as a *somewhat* suspect category. This intermediate scrutiny provided a compromise solution to the problem of choosing between strict and ordinary scrutiny. In the view of the justices, the use of strict scrutiny would endanger traditional sex roles, while the use of ordinary scrutiny would allow blatant sex discrimination to survive. The Burger Court defined a test that it believed to be "just right." Under intermediate scrutiny, government enactments that relied on gender would be constitutional if the use of gender were *substantially related* to an *important objective.* Intermediate scrutiny defines a legal test, then, somewhere between strict and lax. Thus, for example, certain laws protecting pregnant women from dangerous chemicals in the workplace have passed this test.

The improvement of women's rights under the doctrine of intermediate scrutiny is less than what many in the women's movement wanted. While the new standard has allowed the courts to throw out some laws based on degrading stereotypes of women, it was used in *Craig v. Boren* to justify invalidating an Oklahoma law that discriminated against young *men.* Similarly, the beneficiaries of intermediate scrutiny decisions in *Wengler v. Druggists Mutual Insurance Company* (1980) and *Mississippi University for Women v. Hogan* (1982) were also men.

Thus, women's rights have not followed the path of other rights and liberties. The nation has not restructured civil rights for women. Instead, the definition of *rights* has hinged on coalition building on the Supreme Court and the tug of war of parties and interest groups. Civil rights for women are still more a subject for the political process than for the courts.

Abortion Rights One of the most controversial decisions of the Burger Court was *Roe v. Wade* (1973). Two recent graduates of the University of Texas Law School, Linda Coffee and Sarah Weddington, were looking for a client who would challenge a Texas statute that prohibited physicians from performing abortions except to save the life of the pregnant woman.[2] They found a client in Norma "Pixie" McCorvey, a 21-year-old divorcee who had already given birth to a child. McCorvey claimed that she had been gang-raped, but her attorneys doubted her story. They argued instead for a general constitutional right to decide not to complete a pregnancy. McCorvey gave birth before her case was decided by the Supreme Court, but her case yielded a qualified right for women to choose whether or not to complete a pregnancy.

For women's rights activists Coffee and Weddington, the federal courts offered an alternative to the Texas legislature. The case transformed abortion from a legislative issue into a constitutional issue, from a matter of policy into a matter of rights. Eleven states had reformed their statutes to allow women abortions when the woman's health, fetal abnormalities, or rape or incest were involved. Four more states (Alaska, Hawaii, Washington, and New York) went further and repealed prohibitions of abortion. In most states, however, progress was slow or nonexistent.

The litigation over abortion reflected changes in public opinion, pressure by interest groups, and persisting inequities against women. Disapproval of abortion decreased and discussion of abortion increased during the 1960s, even among Roman Catholics.[3] Numerous groups worked to reform or to eliminate abortion laws before *Roe* was decided.[4] Norma McCorvey's case relied greatly on the money of supporters of women's rights. The prochoice team benefited from 42 amicus curiae briefs. The medical profession, which had been instrumental in making abortion a crime in the nineteenth century,[5] supported reform in the 1960s. Justice Harry Blackmun's opinion for the majority prohibited the states from interfering with a woman's decision to have an abortion in the first two trimesters of her pregnancy. He based his opinion on the right to privacy, first given constitutional protection in *Griswold v. Connecticut* (1965), even though no such right is mentioned in the Constitution. As Blackmun put it in *Roe:*

> This right of privacy, whether it be founded in the Fourteenth Amendment's concept of personal liberty and restrictions upon state action, as we feel it is, or, as the District Court determined, in the Ninth Amendment's reservation of rights to the people, is broad enough to encompass a woman's decision whether or not to terminate her pregnancy.

The Court's decision hardly resolved matters. Antiabortion groups, energized by the repeal of abortion laws, struck back after *Roe.* Single-issue antiabortion politics surfaced in the 1976 and subsequent elections, and became an important pillar of the conservative Reagan movement. The prolife forces that helped elect Ronald Reagan insisted that he appoint antiabortion judges to the federal courts. He did so with great effectiveness. In the end, the Supreme Court responded to antiabortion politics by deciding two cases, *Webster v. Reproductive Health Services* (1989) and *Planned Parenthood v. Casey* (1992), that gave considerable latitude to the states in restricting abortions. To the surprise of many observers, however, the Court majority, despite the appointment of new justices by Presidents Reagan and Bush, affirmed its support of the basic principles of *Roe* in the *Planned Parenthood* opinion. Even more surprising was the Court's decision, in *National Organization for Women v. Scheidler* (1994), that abortion clinics could sue antiabortion groups for damages under the federal racketeering law.

Abortion has been an important issue[6] in recent confirmations of judges and Supreme Court justices. Judge Robert Bork has ascribed his own defeat in part to the issue, and hearings on Judge David Souter in 1990 raised the issue directly and repeatedly. Abortion was also an issue in the confirmation hearings for Clarence Thomas. Ruth Bader Ginsburg took a Solomonic position: like conservative prolifers, she opposed the reasoning of *Roe v. Wade,* but like liberal prochoicers, she insisted that some abortion rights are essential to women's equality.

Sexual Harassment Another issue of concern to many women (and men) is sexual harassment in the workplace. One poll reports that 21 percent of women say they have experienced sexual harassment at work, while 41 percent claim to know someone who has been the victim of such treatment.[7] The Equal Employment Opportunity Commission (EEOC) reports that 35 percent of female federal employees have been subjected to unwelcome sexual remarks, and that 26 percent have experienced unwelcome touching.[8]

People disagree, of course, about what kinds of behavior constitute sexual harassment, though the courts, regulatory agencies, and legislative bodies are gradually defining the law in this area. In 1980, the EEOC ruled that making sexual activity a condition of employment or promotion violates the 1964 Civil Rights Act, a ruling upheld by the Supreme Court in *Meritor Savings Bank v. Vinson* (1986). The EEOC also ruled that creating "an intimidating, hostile, or offensive working environment" is contrary to the law. State courts have begun to fill in the meaning of "intimidating, hostile, or offensive." The Florida Supreme Court ruled in 1991, for instance, that an open display of nude pin-ups in a mixed-gender workplace fits the definition. A California court ruled that unwelcome love letters from a supervisor constitute harassment. The U.S. Supreme Court took a major step in further defining sexual harassment when it ruled unanimously, in *Harris v. Forklift Systems, Inc.* (1993), that workers do not have to prove that offensive actions make them unable to do their jobs or cause them psychological harm, only that the work environment is hostile or abusive.

The dramatic testimony of law professor Anita Hill at the confirmation hearings of Supreme Court nominee Clarence Thomas raised awareness of sexual harassment among men and women nationwide and helped inject the issue into several electoral races in 1992. One development has been an increase in lawmaking by state legislatures to define and prohibit sexual harassment in the workplace. Many private companies have also begun to specify appropriate behavior on the job for their employees. It remains to be seen whether this new environment will have a significant effect on the prevalence of the problem.

Affirmative Action Affirmative action guidelines and laws passed by national, state, and local governments have been aimed at rectifying past discrimination against women as well as against racial minorities. The precarious legal and political status of these guidelines and laws, reviewed above in the section on racial minorities, means that affirmative action programs for women are in jeopardy across the nation. For this reason, many women's organizations have become increasingly engaged in the struggle over affirmative action. The fight in 1996 against California's proposition #187 ending all affirmative action programs in the state was spearheaded by women's groups.

Broadening the Civil Rights Umbrella

The expansion of civil rights protections for women and racial minorities has encouraged other groups to press for expanded rights.

The Elderly and the Disabled Interest groups for the elderly have pressed for laws barring age discrimination and have enjoyed some success in recent years. Several federal and state laws, for instance, now bar mandatory retirement. And the courts have begun to strike down hiring practices based on age unless a compelling reason for such age requirements can be demonstrated.

Disabled Americans have also pushed for civil rights and other protections and have won some notable victories, including passage of the Americans with Disabilities Act of 1990. The act prohibits employment discrimination against the disabled and requires that reasonable efforts be made to make places of employment and public facilities (such as concert halls, restaurants, retail shops, schools, and government offices) accessible to them. The proliferation of wheelchair ramps and wheelchair-accessible toilet facilities is a sign that the legislation is having an important impact. Several advocates for the disabled, however, claim that the act depends too much on voluntary compliance rather than mandatory penalties for noncompliance.

Gays and Lesbians Efforts to secure constitutional rights for gays and lesbians exemplify political exertions in the face of governmental wavering. When

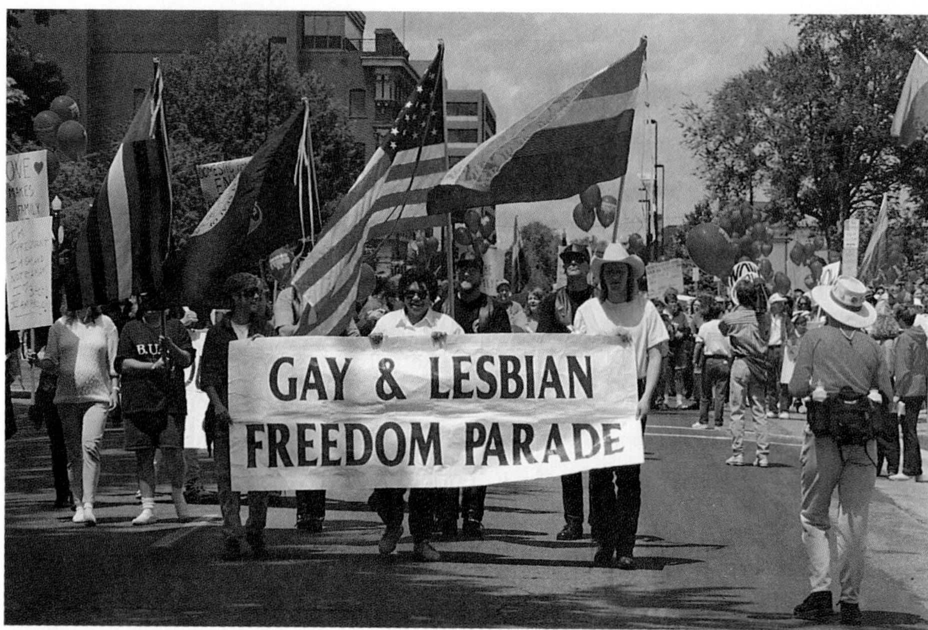

Gay and lesbian Americans have become much more assertive recently in pressing for civil rights protections.

the U.S. Supreme Court upheld Georgia's law against sodomy in *Bowers v. Hardwick* (1986), the majority opinion declared assertions of a constitutional right to homosexuality to be "facetious."[9] Gay activists and their opponents have now shifted the battle to other political arenas. In the electoral arena, candidate Bill Clinton promised to lift the ban on gay people in the military but was forced to reverse his course in light of the hostile reaction from Congress and the armed services. Clinton's efforts in 1993 embroiled the White House, the Congress, the Pentagon, and the media in a policy struggle that highlighted the strengths and weaknesses of gay political advocates and their opponents. Demonstrated gay strengths include victories in winning protections of privacy and sexual orientation in *state* laws: eight states and many localities ban discrimination against gay people, and seven other states operate under executive orders that prohibit such discrimination.[10] However, opposition to gay rights was strong in elections across the nation in 1993 and 1994, as several states and localities voted down protections for gay. Dozens of other cities and several states have rescinded protections for gay people or have refused to extend protections. A bill to prevent job discrimination against gays and lesbians was defeated in the 104th Congress. On the other hand, voters in Maine refused in 1995 to approve an initiative brought by Christian Coalition conservatives to rescind protections. And, in 1996, the Supreme Court ruled in *Romer v. Evans* that Colorado's constitutional provision (known as Amendment 2) prohibiting local communities from passing gay anti-discrimination ordiances is unconstitutional. As Justice Anthony Kennedy put it in his opinion of the Court, "a state cannot so deem a class of persons a stranger to its laws."

It is evident that the struggle over gay and lesbian rights will remain an important part of the American political agenda for a long time to come, the eventual outcome being very much in doubt.[11] Several important cases on gay and lesbian civil rights await action by the Supreme Court, including the "don't ask, don't tell" policy in the U.S. military.

The Supreme Court voided a Colorado law barring the singling out of homosexuals for civil rights protection (*Romer v. Evans,* 1996). Jean Dubofsky, right, the lead attorney in a suit against the law, hugged Priscilla Inkpen, a plaintiff.

Civil Rights and Democracy

Political equality is one of the three pillars of democracy, equal in importance to popular sovereignty and political liberty. For most of our history, political equality was not a very high priority in the United States, and the quality of democracy was less than it might have been.

The advance of civil rights protections since the end of World War II has enriched American democracy because it has helped make political equality a reality in the United States. It is no longer acceptable, for instance, to deny minorities and women the right to vote, to assemble, to petition the government, or to hold public office, practices widely enforced in this country for most of our history. This is not to say that racial minorities and women have attained full social or material equality; many areas of American life, from wealth holding to representation in the professions and in Congress, remain highly unequal and unrepresentative. Nevertheless, the attainment of formal political equality is real and something in which Americans may take great pride.

Summary

The Constitution and the Bill of Rights are relatively silent on political equality, other than providing for equality before the law. Important advances for civil rights were the passage of the Thirteenth, Fourteenth, and Fifteenth Amendments after the Civil War. The Fourteenth Amendment, with its specification that all persons born or naturalized in the United States are citizens of both the nation and the states in which they live, and that federal and state governments must provide for "equal protection of the laws," was a particularly important civil rights milestone, even though the Supreme Court was slow to act on its promise.

The Court paid little attention during the nineteenth century to the issue of political equality for racial minorities and women. Under the pressure of structural changes in society, the transformation of attitudes about race and gender, and the political efforts of racial and ethnic minority group members and women of all races, the Court slowly began to pay attention by the middle of the twentieth century. Important advances toward equality have been made by both racial minorities and women. Though constitutional law now fully protects both racial minorities and women against discrimination sanctioned by law or government action, the status of affirmative action programs meant to rectify past wrongs and to compensate for institutional barriers to equality remains unsettled. In the last decade of the twentieth century, the question of whether or not lesbians and gay men can be discriminated against in housing, employment, military service, and other areas of public life remains a subject of political debate.

Suggested Readings

Burns, James MacGregor, and Stewart Burns. *A People's Charter: The Pursuit of Rights in America.* New York: Knopf, 1991.
A magisterial survey of the history of civil rights and liberties in the United States.

Edsall, Thomas Byrne, and Mary D. Edsall. *Chain Reaction.* New York: Norton, 1991.
Suggests that the politics of race, the rapid advancement of the civil rights agenda, and new federal tax policies fueled the conservative revolution in American politics.

Greenberg, Stanley B. *Middle Class Dreams: The Politics and Power of the New American Majority.* New York: Times Books, 1995.
A controversial book about how the Democratic party's support of racial preferences and affirmative action broke apart the New Deal coalition and contributed to the decline of the Democrats.

Hall, Kermit L. (ed.). *The Oxford Companion to the Supreme Court of the United States.* New York: Oxford University Press, 1992.
Contains complete and vivid descriptions of all major Supreme Court rulings and opinions regarding civil rights.

Polenberg, Richard. *One Nation Divisible: Class, Race and Ethnicity in the United States Since 1938.* New York: Penguin, 1980.
A brief history of the civil rights struggles of a wide range of minority groups in the United States.

Internet Sources

Civil Rights Division, U.S. Department of Justice http://gopher.usdoj.gov/crt-home.html
Official documents and reports of action by the Civil Rights Division.

Human Rights Source http://www.gatech.edu/amnesty/source.html
Gateway to groups and information concerned with women's, African-American, Latino, Asian-American, Native American, and gay and lesbian civil rights.

National Civil Rights Museum http://www.magibox.net/~ncrm/struggle.html
Virtual tours of the civil rights movement.

Yahoo/Civil Rights http://www.yahoo.com/Society_and_Culture/Civil_Rights/
Linkages to a vast compendium of information on civil rights and to organizations devoted to the protection and expansion of rights.

Notes

1. James MacGregor Burns and Stewart Burns, *A People's Charter: The Pursuit of Rights in America* (New York: Knopf, 1991), p. 37.

2. See Marian Faux, *Roe v. Wade* (New York: Macmillan, 1988).
3. Faux, *Roe v. Wade,* p. 45.
4. Eva R. Rubin, *Abortion, Politics, and the Courts* (Westport, CT: Greenwood Press, 1982), Chap. 2.
5. Kristen Luker, *Abortion and the Politics of Motherhood* (Berkeley: University of California Press, 1984), Chap. 2.
6. Robert Bork, *The Tempting of America: The Political Seduction of the Law* (New York: Free Press, 1990), p. 281.
7. *Newsweek* (October 21, 1991), p. 34.
8. *Ibid.,* p. 36.
9. 106 S. Ct. 2841 (1986) at 2846.
10. Lisa Keen, "Referendums and Rights: Across the Country, Battles over Protection for Gays and Lesbians," *Washington Post,* Outlook Section (October 31, 1993), p. C3.
11. See Aart Hendriks, Rob Tielman, and Evert van der Veen, eds., *The Third Pink Book* (Buffalo, NY: Prometheus Books, 1993; Louis Diamant, ed., *Homosexual Issues in the Workplace* (Washington, DC: Taylor & Francis, 1993).

CHAPTER 18

Foreign Policy and National Defense

IN THIS CHAPTER

- ★ How the United States became the strongest world power
- ★ What the Cold War was about, and how it ended
- ★ Problems of the "new world order"
- ★ Who helps presidents make foreign policy
- ★ What part interest groups play in shaping foreign and defense policy
- ★ How democratic foreign policy is

U.S. Troops Go to Bosnia

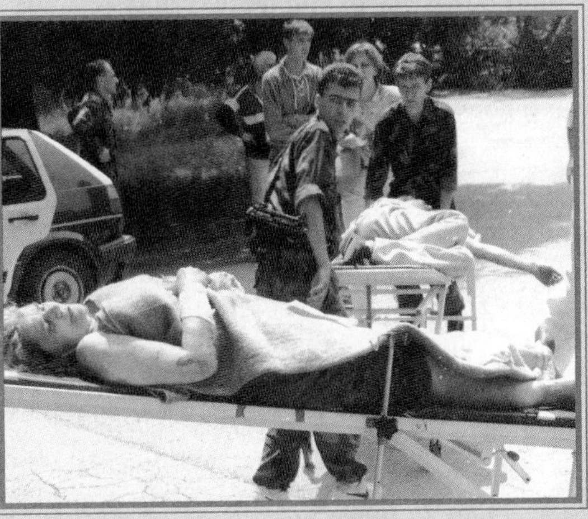

At the end of the Cold War, formerly Communist Yugoslavia disintegrated into a number of separate countries with different ethnic, linguistic, and religious orientations: in the north, Roman Catholic, Austria-like Slovenia; just below it, Catholic but ethnically distinct Croatia; in the middle, predominantly Muslim Bosnia; and to the south, the Eastern Orthodox, Serb-controlled remnant of Yugoslavia. But ethnic minorities were scattered through cities and villages everywhere, especially in Bosnia, which included many Serbs and Croatians as well as Bosnian Muslims.

Nationalist movements, particularly Yugoslav president Slobodan Milosevic's movement for a "Greater Serbia," stirred up ethnic fears and ambitions. The Bosnian Serbs, with arms and support from Yugoslavia, tried to declare independence from Bosnia and launched a civil war against the Muslim-dominated Bosnian government. They engaged in "ethnic cleansing," driving Muslim and Croat civilians out of their homes and sometimes slaughtering them, and they surrounded Bosnia's main city, Sarajevo, cutting off supplies and terrorizing the population with sniping and shelling.

The world was appalled by televised images of death and destruction. Western countries, distressed at such ugliness within the supposedly civilized confines of Europe, nonetheless resisted involvement. NATO and the United States dithered. The United Nations, lacking superior force or unified purpose (subject, for example, to Russian and Chinese vetoes in the Security Council), tried to make peace but was repeatedly humiliated by the Serbs. Lightly armed UN soldiers were taken hostage to prevent air strikes; the UN-proclaimed "safe haven" of Srebrenica was abandoned to the Serbs, who conducted one of the worst massacres of the war.

Only in 1995, after UN soldiers were pulled back from exposed positions, did NATO, under Clinton administration pressure, conduct devastating air strikes on Serb air defenses. The air strikes and economic sanctions helped coerce leaders of the warring parties to go to Dayton, Ohio, where the United States brokered a peace agreement to be enforced by 60,000 NATO troops—including 20,000 Americans. Everyone understood that the promise of American enforcement was crucial to making the agreement work.[1]

Polls showed that a large majority of the U.S. public opposed the deployment of U.S. troops to Bosnia, even after President Clinton made a televised speech strongly arguing for it. Most members of Congress opposed it as well. Leading Republicans had pushed for lifting the arms embargo, building up the Bosnian army, and perhaps launching air attacks—but not committing U.S. troops.

Still, Congress reluctantly went along—as it does in most cases when presidents use U.S. forces abroad—in order to let the president conduct a unified, credible foreign policy, and to support the soldiers already sent to Bosnia. Brent Scowcroft, former national security adviser to George Bush, told the Senate Armed Services Committee that "to turn our back now would be a catastrophe for U.S. reliability." Senate Majority Leader Bob Dole declared, "if we would try to cut off funds, we would harm the men and women in the military who have already begun to arrive in Bosnia." A leading House Republican acknowledged, "we have no choice but to go along."[2] The House and the Senate eventually passed resolutions that symbolically refused to endorse the deployment but supported the troops and did not cut off funds.[3]

This did not end the story, of course. Even though American forces' first months in Bosnia went quietly, the depth of destruction and ethnic hatred there made clear that it would not be easy to arrange a smooth U.S. exit within the promised one year. Detailed evidence about massacres turned up; conflicts arose over whether and how to arrest accused war criminals; refugees were barred from going home; and territorial lines of ethnic separation grew even sharper. Bosnian Serbs, for example, fled the Sarajevo suburbs that they were required to turn over to Bosnian government control, burning homes and businesses as they left. Neither Congress nor the American public appeared likely to stand for extensive U.S. casualties or for a long, messy stay.

The Bosnia story illustrates how the president and the executive branch generally take the lead, at least initially, in making U.S. foreign policy. It also illustrates how new problems like ethnic conflict now trouble the post–Cold War world. In this chapter, we will discuss how the United States came to be a superpower; the nature of the Cold War; current foreign policy problems; and the factors that influence foreign policy, including the role of domestic politics and public opinion.

Foreign Policy and Democracy: A Contradiction in Terms?

Foreign policy has traditionally been different from domestic policy, especially during wars or crises. For one thing, presidents and the executive branch tend to play a much more important part than they do on domestic issues. In the tug-of-war between presidents and Congress on international matters, presidents usually win. Also, the ordinary political factors, such as public opinion and interest groups, are sometimes set aside in favor of considerations of the **national interest,** as defined by a small number of national security advisers.

national interest What is in the interest of the nation as a whole.

Public opinion is sometimes reshaped or ignored. In crisis situations, the public often "rallies 'round the flag," accepting the president's actions, at least as long as the results seem good and there is little dissent among political leaders. (When things go wrong, however, domestic politics can return with a vengeance, as it did in the case of the Vietnam War; recall Chapter 5.) Also, much of foreign policy is influenced by *structural* factors, such as the power and resources of the United States, its economic interests abroad, and the nature and behavior of other nations.

By the same token, foreign policy is not always purely the result of democratic processes, as we understand democracy. Several features of foreign affairs tend to limit the role of ordinary citizens in policymaking. The sheer complexity of international matters, their remoteness from day-to-day life, and the unpredictability of other countries' actions all tend to make the public's convictions about foreign policy less certain and more subject to revision in the light of events. The need for speed, unity, and secrecy in decision making and the concentration of authority in the executive branch mean that the public may be excluded and that government policy sometimes shapes public opinion rather than being shaped by it.

At the same time, however, the exclusion of the public is far from total. The American public has probably always played a bigger part in the making of foreign policy than some observers have imagined, and its role appears to be increasing. Just how big that role should be is a matter of dispute, an object of the ongoing struggle for democracy.

The United States as Superpower: Structure and History

In the autumn of 1990, the United States sent more than a half million troops, 1,200 warplanes, and 6 aircraft carriers to the Persian Gulf region, in order to roll back Iraq's invasion of Kuwait. This deployment, even more than the later dispatch of troops to Bosnia, reflected the status of the United States as a **superpower,** that is, a nation armed with nuclear weapons, strong enough militarily and economically to project its power into any area of the globe. Indeed, since the collapse of the Soviet Union, the United States is the world's *only* superpower.

superpower A nation armed with nuclear weapons and able to project force anywhere on the globe.

U.S. Economic and Military Power

In the mid–1990s, the United States had a population of more than 250 million people—considerably fewer than China's 1.2 billion or India's 900 million, but enough to support the world's largest economy, with an annual gross domestic product (GDP) of more than $6 *trillion.* It is worth pausing to think about what $6 trillion means. It is $6,000 billion, or $6,000,000,000,000, or about $24,000 for each person in the country. The GDP of the United States is more than twice that of Japan or China (though Japanese production *per person* is similar to American production per person); five times that of Germany, India, or Britain; and nine times the GDP of Russia (see Table 18.1).

Table 18.1

Major World Powers

The United States has a larger economy and much stronger military than any other country.

Country	Population (Millions)	GDP ($ Billion)	Military Spending ($ Billion)	No. of Milit. Personnel (Thousands)	No. of Strat. Nuclear Warheads
U.S.	258	6,400	298	1,837	8,770
Russia	149	775	114	2,250	10,312 (CIS)
Japan	125	2,549	42	242	0
Germany	81	1,331	37	398	0
China	1,178	2,610	56	3,031	284
India	903	1,080	8	1,265	0
Britain	58	980	34	273	200
France	58	240	43	506	554

Sources: Population, military spending, number of active armed forces from U.S. Arms Control and Disarmament Agency, *World Military Expenditures and Arms Transfers 1993–1994* (Washington, DC: U.S. Government Printing Office, 1995); GDP figures from the Central Intelligence Agency and *The World Factbook, 1994, 1993;* strategic warheads from *World Armament and Disarmament: Stockholm International Peace Research Yearbook 1993.*

The F–117A Stealth fighter-bomber, a star of the Persian Gulf War, represents just a small part of U.S. military strength.

Military Power This enormous economic strength enables the United States to field the most powerful armed forces in the world. The United States now spends roughly $260 billion per year on the armed forces, about $1,000 for each person in the country. About 1.5 million men and women are on active military duty, while another 850,000 civilians work for the Department of Defense. According to official statistics (which may undercount U.S. nuclear arms in order not to appear too belligerent), the air force now boasts 585 intercontinental ballistic missiles and 140 strategic bombers, each carrying multiple nuclear warheads, along with thousands of tactical warplanes and 354 strategic airlift aircraft. The navy has 11 aircraft carriers, 16 nuclear missile submarines (armed with 384 multiple-warhead missiles), and many other warships, amphibious assault ships, and tactical aircraft. The army is organized into 12 active divisions, backed by large numbers of tanks, artillery, and tactical missiles with many tactical nuclear warheads. The U.S. armed forces have been downsized somewhat from their Cold War peak, but the force levels seem now to have mostly stabilized until at least the year 2000.[4]

Other Countries' Armed Forces No other country in the world comes close to matching the power of the U.S. armed forces. To be sure, for decades the Soviet Union squeezed its smaller economy hard in order to produce a military establishment roughly equal to that of the United States; it actually had more men and women in uniform (though they were not as well armed or equipped), and it had enough **intercontinental ballistic missiles (ICBMs)** and **submarine-launched ballistic missiles (SLBMs)** with nuclear warheads to bring about total mutual destruction in any major strategic conflict. This created a "balance of terror" in which neither side dared start a war.

After the 1991 collapse of the Soviet Union, a large part of its forces reverted to Russia. But Russia's population is only about half that of the former Soviet Union, and its economy is much smaller. Moreover, the Russians re-

intercontinental ballistic missiles (ICBMs) Guided missiles capable of carrying nuclear warheads across continents.

submarine-launched ballistic missiles (SLBMs) Guided missiles, capable of carrying nuclear warheads, launched from submarines.

nounced most foreign adventures and proceeded to cut their nuclear and conventional arms under international treaties. Their economy fell into disarray, and their once-proud armed forces suffered sharp drops in salaries and prestige. Russia's capability to use force abroad (except on its immediate periphery, in former Soviet republics), therefore, is now very much in doubt.

China has a fast-growing economy, millions of military personnel, and some strategic nuclear missiles, but it is much weaker than it looks on paper. Most of China's arms consist of old Soviet-style weapons that the Iraqis found inadequate when they were decisively defeated by U.S. airpower, **"smart" bombs,** and missiles in the Persian Gulf War. China's recent efforts at modernizing its weapons have not yet got very far. Indeed, U.S. military spending is nearly twice that of both erstwhile Cold War adversaries, China and Russia, put together. (Perhaps more to the point, U.S. military spending is more than 20 times that of the so-called "rogue states" of Iran, Iraq, Libya, and North Korea.)[5]

smart bombs Bombs capable of being guided precisely to their targets.

Japan and Germany have considerable economic strength but still have relatively small military establishments and no nuclear weapons. They exert influence mainly in their own spheres of influence in Asia and Europe.

The Only Superpower In terms of global influence, then, the United States stands alone. No other nation has anything like the scores of U.S. military bases abroad (with about 100,000 troops stationed in Europe and another 100,000 in Asia), the ports and ships that control the Atlantic and Pacific oceans, the high-tech attack aircraft and missiles, the satellite surveillance capabilities, or the rapid-deployment ships and planes that can project force anywhere on any continent.

The superpower status of the United States is a crucial *structural* fact about international relations and American foreign policy. American power and resources have been important not only in the Bosnia mission and the war against Iraq, but also in a whole series of U.S. actions abroad since World War II. Indeed, this superpower status may largely account for the main thrust of U.S. foreign policy: the exertion of influence all over the globe. Some scholars have argued that nearly all great powers, whatever their form of government and society—whether democracy, monarchy, or dictatorship; whether capitalist, socialist, or feudal—tend to behave in similar ways when they face similar world situations.[6]

The Growth of U.S. Power

The story of the gradual emergence of the United States as a superpower was outlined in Chapter 4. It involved American territorial expansion and settlement of the West; the industrialization of the economy; and the assertions of military power in the Spanish-American War and World War I. Especially important in that story was the impact of World War II.

When World War II ended with Japan's surrender on August 15, 1945, Germany and Japan, devastated by the bombing of their cities and industries, found themselves occupied by Allied forces. Britain and France, great powers of the past, had also suffered severe damage and were losing their world empires to nationalist revolutions. But the United States emerged with its homeland intact, its economy much larger than before the war (accounting for more than half the manufacturing production of the entire world), its military forces victorious around the globe, and—for a few years, at least—with monopoly control of nuclear weapons. As historian Paul Kennedy puts it, "among the

Figure 18.1 ▪ Growth of U.S. Exports, 1910–2000

Source: U.S. Department of Commerce, *Historical Statistics of the U.S.: Colonial Times to 1970,* p. 884; *Statistical Abstract of the United States, 1992,* p. 796; *Economic Report of the President, 1995,* p. 396.

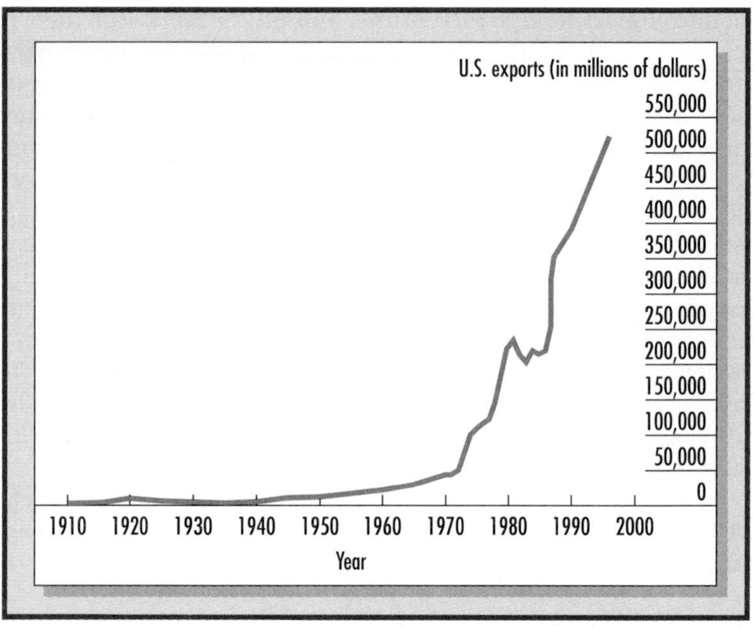

great powers, the United States was the only country which became richer—in fact, much richer—rather than poorer because of the war."[7]

There followed a remarkable period in which the United States thoroughly dominated the world economy. U.S. exports soared, from $4 billion in 1940 to $20.6 billion in 1960 and $42.5 billion in 1970 (see Figure 18.1). (U.S. exports have continued to surge, to $224.3 billion in 1980, and $456.9 billion in 1993, though they are no longer larger than other countries').[8] U.S. investments abroad jumped as well, from $34 billion in 1940 to $85.6 billion in 1960, $166.9 billion in 1970, and nearly $2 trillion in 1990.[9] American business flourished around the globe. But at the same time, U.S. foreign policy became entangled in a tense Cold War rivalry with the Soviet Union.

The Cold War with the Soviet Union

After World War II, the only serious challenge to the power of the United States came from the Soviet Union, which had been terribly damaged in the war (suffering perhaps 20 to 25 million deaths) but retained a large population, a substantial economy, and troops occupying most of Eastern Europe. The United States and the Soviet Union soon found themselves in a series of confrontations.

Scholars disagree about the exact causes of the Cold War. Some have argued that the Soviet Union was a strongly expansionist state, driven by Communist ideology and aiming for world domination; it had to be resisted and contained at every point on its periphery. Scholars of a revisionist perspective, on the other hand, have maintained that the Soviets behaved like any other great power, seeking friendly buffer states in Eastern Europe in order to protect themselves against new invasions from the West, like those of Napoleon, the Kaiser, and Hitler. Revisionists have claimed that the United States misunderstood or misstated Soviet aims, had expansionist plans of its own, and itself took some provocative actions.[10]

Both sides may have a point. Throughout history, powerful countries have tended to push up against each other's spheres of influence and to compete for influence and resources. Yet ideology also played a part in the Cold War. What is absolutely clear is that American foreign policy was focused, for more than 40 years, on the Cold War struggle against the Soviet Union.

The Beginnings of the Cold War

The Cold War began in Europe. When World War II left the Soviet army occupying many countries of eastern and central Europe, American policymakers formulated a doctrine of **containment:** Diplomatic, economic, and military means should be used to prevent the Soviet Union from extending its influence further. In March 1947, President Truman (somewhat overstating outside involvement in the Greek civil war) declared that "the very existence of the Greek state" was threatened by armed terrorist activities led by Communists; he proclaimed in the **Truman Doctrine** that the United States should help "free peoples" to resist "armed minorities or outside pressures." Substantial U.S. military aid followed.[11]

containment The policy that expansion of the Soviet Union's influence should be resisted by diplomatic, economic, and military means.

Truman Doctrine President Truman's policy that the United States should resist outside pressure against "free" countries.

In 1948, the Soviet occupiers imposed a Communist regime on Czechoslovakia. After the United States, Great Britain, and France merged their occupation zones of Germany and integrated them into the Western economy, the Soviets tried to eliminate the Western presence in Berlin (an enclave in the middle of their own occupation zone) by blockading all ground traffic, but the United States airlifted supplies and broke the blockade. The United States provided billions of dollars in aid under the **Marshall Plan** to rebuild the economies of its European allies.

Marshall Plan The program of U.S. economic aid set up to rebuild Europe after World War II.

This truckload of American flour, being blessed by a Greek Orthodox priest, arrived as part of the Marshall Plan, an extensive aid plan designed to rebuild the economies of U.S. European Allies in the early part of the Cold War.

North Atlantic Treaty Organization (NATO) The alliance of the United States, Canada, and Western European countries for defense against the Soviet Union.

Warsaw Pact An alliance of the Soviet Union and Eastern European Communist countries.

The Federal Republic of Germany was established; the Soviets set up various Communist-dominated regimes in Eastern Europe; the **North Atlantic Treaty Organization (NATO)** was established in 1949 as an anti-Soviet alliance, and the **Warsaw Pact** was eventually set up (1955) on the other side. Sharply drawn armed boundaries divided Eastern from Western Europe. Meanwhile, both the United States and the Soviets armed themselves with nuclear weapons—A-bombs and then H-bombs.[12]

The Korean War

The first major armed struggle of the Cold War occurred in Korea. Here, too, historians have disagreed about exactly what happened. Provoked or not, Communist North Korean troops poured across the thirty-eighth parallel on June 25, 1950, and drove south. President Truman, under color of a United Nations resolution authorizing the use of force, sent American troops, who engaged in a basically successful but increasingly unpopular war—first pushing North Korean forces out of South Korea, then marching up through North Korea toward China (where a Communist revolution had taken place in 1949), but finally being thrown back by Chinese armies to a stalemate in the middle of the country.[13]

Military Buildup The Korean War had many important consequences. Immediately after World War II, most U.S. armed forces had been demobilized and sent home. For the Korean War, the size of the remaining force more than doubled, to 3.6 million in 1952, and U.S. troop strength never fell much below 2.5 million before the Vietnam War.[14] The military budget nearly quadrupled, from $13 billion in 1950 to $50 billion in 1953, and it stayed close to that level until the Vietnam War.[15] (For those and subsequent trends in constant dollars, adjusting for inflation, see Figure 18.2.)

Globalization of the Cold War The Korean War also expanded the Cold War from Europe to the entire periphery of the Soviet Union and Communist China. The United States took on many new commitments around the world: protect-

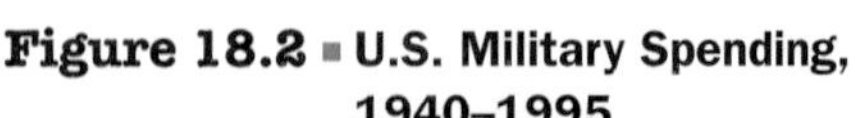

Figure 18.2 ■ **U.S. Military Spending, 1940–1995**

U.S. military spending, adjusted for inflation, dropped sharply from its World War II peak but then rose quickly for the Korean War. Since then, it has stayed fairly constant, except for temporary bulges during the Vietnam War and the Reagan military buildup.

Source: *The Budget of the United States, Fiscal 1994*, pp. 81–86.

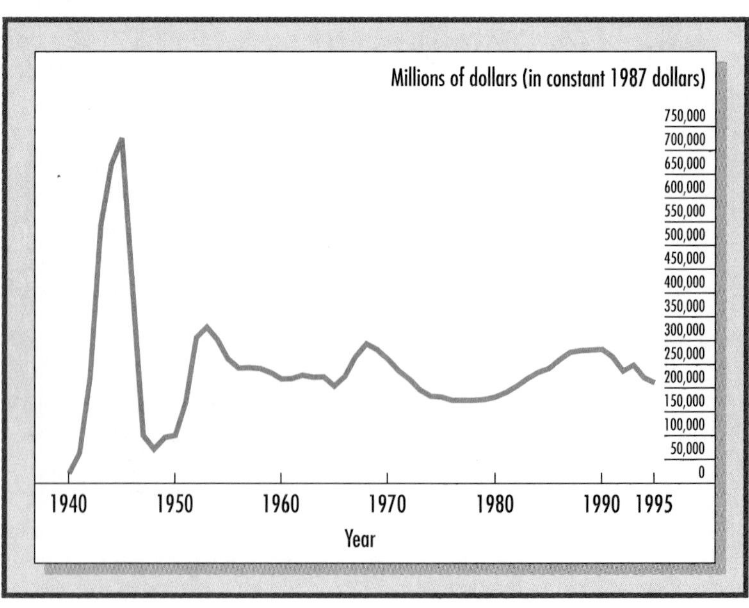

ing Taiwan from mainland China, aiding the French colonialists in Indochina, rearming Germany, organizing various NATO-like alliances against the Soviets and the Chinese, giving anti-Communist military and economic aid, and conducting covert operations. Historians have found that some of these moves were worked out well before the Korean War began, as part of a general plan for intensified anti-Communist policies embodied in a National Security Council document **(NSC–68).**[16] The resulting anti-Communist alliances are shown in Figure 18.3.

NSC–68 A 1950 National Security Council document planning for a military buildup and anti-Communist activities around the world.

Stalemate

The Korean War ended in 1953 with the boundaries between North and South Korea much the same as they had been before the war. During the eight years of the Eisenhower administration, relations between the United States and the Soviet Union were relatively peaceful. There were some skirmishes between the two major powers and their allies in such places as Iran, Guatemala, Lebanon, and Indonesia, but no fighting that involved U.S. troops, and no major changes in the boundaries of U.S. and Soviet influence. There were negotiations and talk of "peaceful coexistence" between the United States and the USSR.

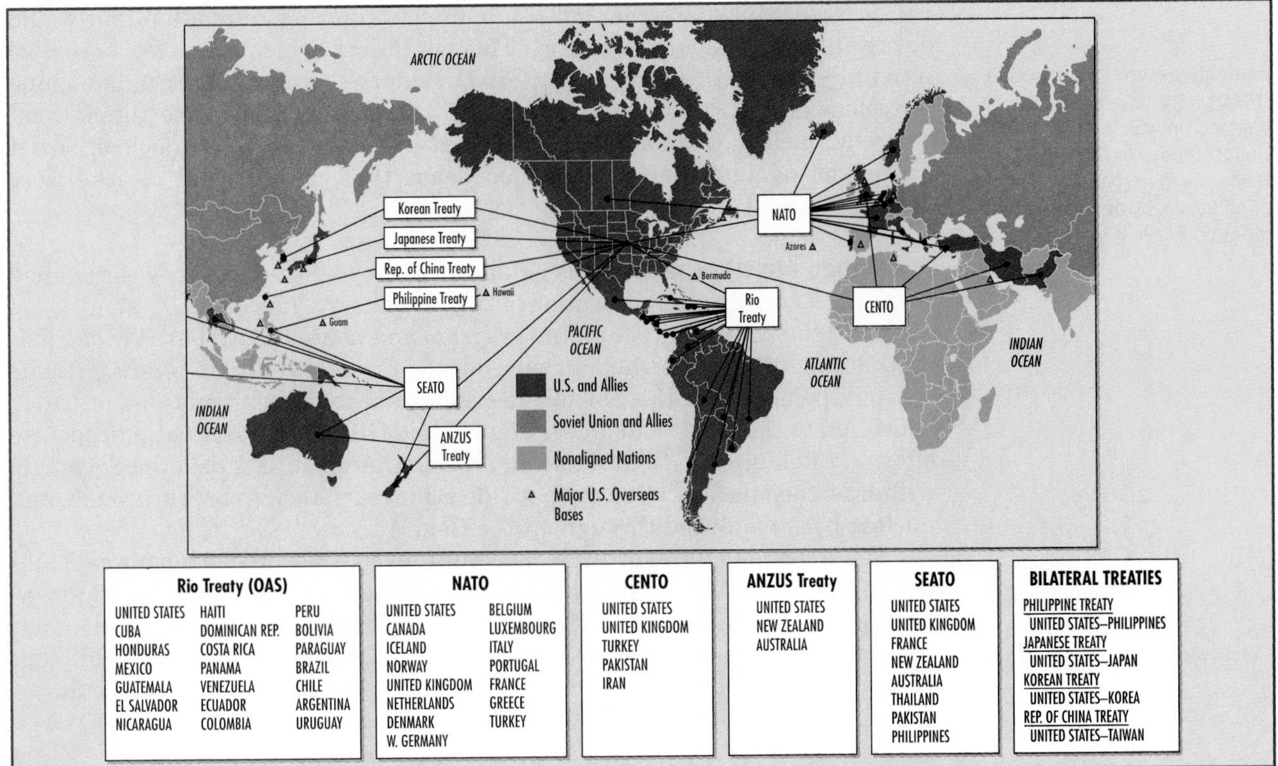

Figure 18.3 ■ **U.S. Alliances and Overseas Bases, 1959**

Many regional alliances against the Soviet Union and Communist China were established in the 1950s.

Source: Robert D. Schulzinger, *American Diplomacy in the Twentieth Century,* 2nd ed. (New York: Oxford University Press, 1990), p. 249.

In retrospect, we can see that the Cold War essentially stalemated or stabilized in the early 1950s, with most of the world divided into two opposing camps that had fairly fixed boundaries and a reasonably stable balance of power. One important sign of this stabilization came in 1956, when the United States refused to intervene in support of the Hungarians' rebellion against Soviet control. In effect, the United States decided to live with Soviet control of Eastern Europe.

For some 35 years afterward, both sides spent immense resources—perhaps $12 trillion—on huge armies that faced each other across the stable boundaries in Europe, never fighting but deterring attack and helping to control their own countries' allies. Elsewhere in the world, the many covert operations, skirmishes, and civil wars between pro- and anti-Communist forces had important (sometimes devastating) effects on the local people involved, but they had little real impact on the great powers or on the shape of the Cold War world.

Nuclear Parity One crucial reason for this stalemate was the presence on both sides of powerful nuclear weapons. Shortly after World War II, the Soviets had broken the U.S. monopoly and developed thermonuclear bombs. Both the United States and the Soviet Union built large numbers of strategic bombers that could drop nuclear warheads on the other country, and both began ballistic missile programs.

As a result, both sides attained a sort of nuclear "parity," or rough equality. No surprise attack by either side could prevent nuclear retaliation that would devastate the attacking country. This situation, which came to be called **mutually assured destruction (MAD),** deterred either side from launching a nuclear attack. Moreover, the 1954 U.S. doctrine of "massive retaliation," whereby nuclear weapons would be used in the event of nonnuclear Soviet aggression against Western Europe, meant that conventional attacks were deterred as well.

mutually assured destruction (MAD) A situation of nuclear balance, in which either the United States or the Soviet Union could respond to a surprise attack by destroying the other country.

The Cuban Missile Crisis This balance of terror was temporarily threatened when the Kennedy administration (citing an illusory "missile gap") sharply accelerated the U.S. missile-building program and neared a "first-strike" capability that might have been able to wipe out the Soviets' ability to retaliate. Some scholars believe that the Soviets' decision to base nuclear missiles in Cuba, which led to the tense Cuban Missile Crisis of 1962, represented a desperate effort to catch up.[17] (U.S. threats and an embargo of Cuba forced the Soviets to withdraw the missiles.) But neither side achieved a nuclear breakthrough, and nuclear parity endured throughout the Cold War.

The Kennedy administration also built up conventional weapons capabilities to fight "limited" or "brushfire" wars without nuclear weapons, and it intensified confrontations with the USSR in the Third World. It sponsored an unsuccessful Cuban-exile invasion of Cuba, intervened in Laos, and sent substantial numbers of military advisers to Vietnam, where United States troops eventually became engaged in a bloody war.

Vietnam and Détente

Vietnam was the great exception to the relative peace that Americans enjoyed for more than three decades after the Korean war. As we saw in Chapter 5, the Vietnam War, fought in an effort to prevent a Communist takeover of South Vietnam, was a major setback for American foreign policy. The war's costs in

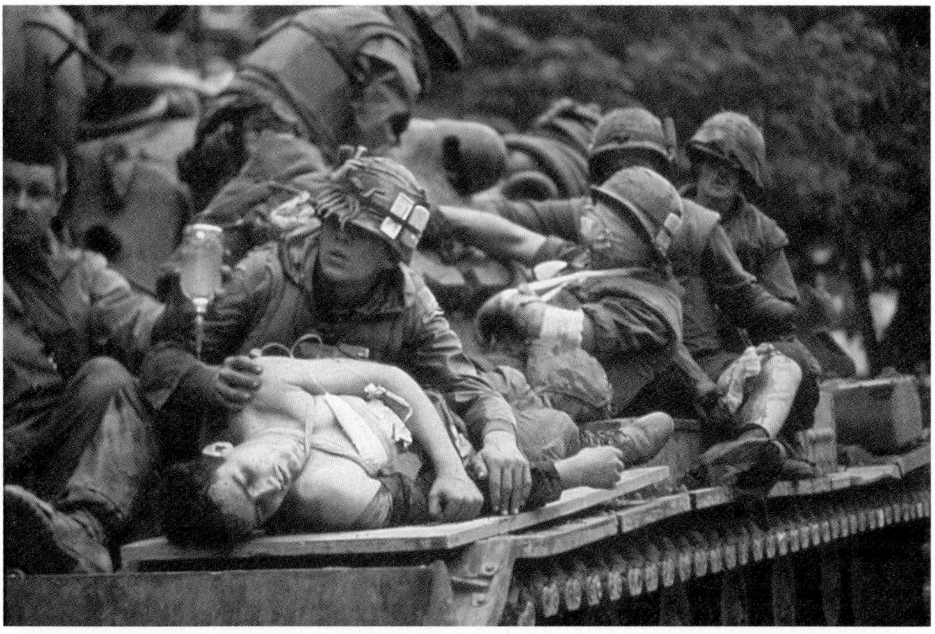

These casualties from the 1968 Tet offensive added to the total of more than 45,000 Americans killed and 150,000 wounded during the Vietnam War.

money (about $179 billion, in 1990 dollars) and casualties (47,355 battle dead, 153,303 wounded),[18] as well as the social disruption and moral unease that accompanied it, discouraged intervention abroad for a while.

The Nixon administration, slowly extricating itself from Vietnam, pursued a policy of rapprochement (closer relations) with China and **détente** (relaxation of tensions) with the Soviet Union. It negotiated trade and arms control agreements, including the first Strategic Arms Limitation Treaty (SALT I). Table tennis players and then many other Americans visited China; some U.S. businesspeople began to buy and sell in Russia.[19]

détente A relaxation of tensions, for example, between the United States and the Soviet Union in the early 1970s.

The "New" Cold War

During the 1970s, the United States faced increasing economic competition from Japan and Germany, sharp oil price increases, and inflation, all of which weakened the U.S. economy. At the same time, groups like the Committee on the Present Danger called for a U.S. military buildup, arguing that the Soviet Union was rapidly upgrading its military and expanding its influence in Africa and elsewhere. Although this alarm proved to be exaggerated, many Americans began to listen after the 1979 Soviet intervention in Afghanistan and the Iranian seizure of hostages from the U.S. embassy in Tehran. There was a tremendous upsurge in public support for military spending and for a strong foreign policy (see Figure 18.4).

The Carter administration reacted with higher defense budgets, a boycott of the 1980 Olympics (which were held in Moscow), and a halt in grain sales to the Soviet Union.

The Reagan Military Buildup The new Reagan administration that took office in 1981 went still further, more than doubling military outlays, from $134

Figure 18.4 ▪ Public Support for Increased Defense Spending, 1970–1996

Public support for increased defense spending rose sharply in 1979 and 1980, after U.S. hostages were taken in Iran and the Soviet Union invaded Afghanistan. But support soon fell and has remained at low levels ever since.

Source: GSS, Roper, and NBC surveys.

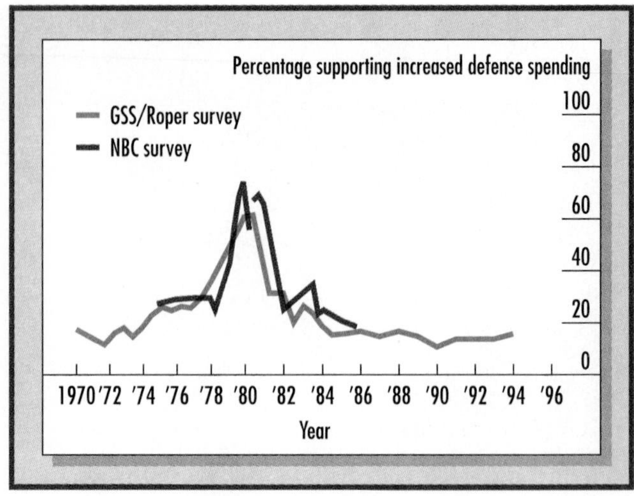

billion in 1980 to $282 billion in 1987,[20] investing heavily in naval ships and in sophisticated new weapons like the MX ("Peacemaker") ballistic missile, the Strategic Defense Initiative (Star Wars) missile defense system, and various Stealth radar-evading warplanes. Reagan warned of a U.S. "window of vulnerability" to Soviet missiles (which, however, never materialized),[21] and called the Soviet Union an "evil empire." He sought to roll back Soviet influence all around the world, particularly trying to overthrow Soviet-allied regimes by giving covert aid to rebels in Afghanistan, Angola, and Nicaragua. Resisting leftist rebels in El Salvador, the United States trained troops who committed a number of atrocities.[22]

Relaxing Tensions Very soon, however, most Americans became convinced that the United States was militarily strong and that no further boosts in defense spending were needed. A record-high 75 percent of the public had said in 1980 that the United States should increase the amount of money spent on defense, but this percentage dropped as sharply as it had risen, falling to about 20 percent by the end of 1981 (look again at Figure 18.4).

Moreover, after Mikhail Gorbachev took power in the Soviet Union in 1985, he made sweeping proposals for arms-control and other agreements with the United States. In a series of summit meetings, Reagan resisted Gorbachev's package deal, which would have maintained a strategic balance between the United States and the USSR; he insisted on an Intermediate-range Nuclear Forces (INF) treaty that would remove destabilizing Soviet medium-range missiles from Europe and leave the United States dominant there.[23] Gorbachev's Soviet Union, suffering from Brezhnev-era economic stagnation, the severe pressures of the arms race, and restiveness within its Eastern bloc, eventually agreed.

The End of the Cold War and the Collapse of the Soviet Union

Starting in 1989, when the Bush administration took office, a series of dramatic world events completely transformed international affairs. Eastern Europe broke away from Soviet domination, the Soviet Union itself collapsed, and the Cold War was over.

Independence for Eastern Europe First, a wave of demands for independence from the weakened and inward-turning Soviet Union swept through Eastern Europe. With Gorbachev's tacit approval, non-Communist regimes gained power in Poland, Czechoslovakia, and Hungary. In November 1989, the Berlin Wall—the harshest symbol of the Cold War—was breached, and shortly thereafter, East Germany gave up its sovereignty to join the West in a reunified Germany. The Soviets, Americans, and others agreed on a Conventional Forces in Europe (CFE) treaty, drastically reducing the number of conventional forces in Europe; the newly independent Eastern European countries pressed the Soviets to remove their forces entirely, and Western Europe showed much less interest in hosting American troops. Progress was made on Strategic Arms Reduction Talks (START).

The Soviet Retreat from World Politics As Eastern Europe turned toward democracy and capitalism, the Soviet Union cut its military budget, withdrew from Afghanistan, sought peaceful solutions in various Cold War trouble spots (Angola, Cambodia, and the Middle East), and struggled with proposals for its own democratic and market reforms (*perestroika* and *glasnost*), while its economy declined. By the summer of 1990, President Bush agreed that the Cold War was "over." That fall, a survey of U.S. public opinion found that substantial majorities favored arms control agreements, Middle East cooperation, trade, and scientific exchanges with the Soviets.[24] The large majorities that had once thought that "Russia seeks global domination" had nearly vanished (see Figure 18.5).

The Persian Gulf War One mark of the drastic change in relations among the world powers was the Persian Gulf War.

On August 2, 1990—following failed negotiations concerning oil prices, war debts, and boundaries—massed tanks and troops from Saddam Hussein's Iraq poured across their southern border into the tiny but oil-rich emirate of Kuwait, quickly conquering it. Outraged, President Bush declared that this aggression "will not stand." He dispatched an enormous U.S. military force to the Persian Gulf region, pushed supporting resolutions through the United Nations, and cajoled most of the world's nations to join an economic blockade (which began to strangle Iraq's economy) and a military buildup.

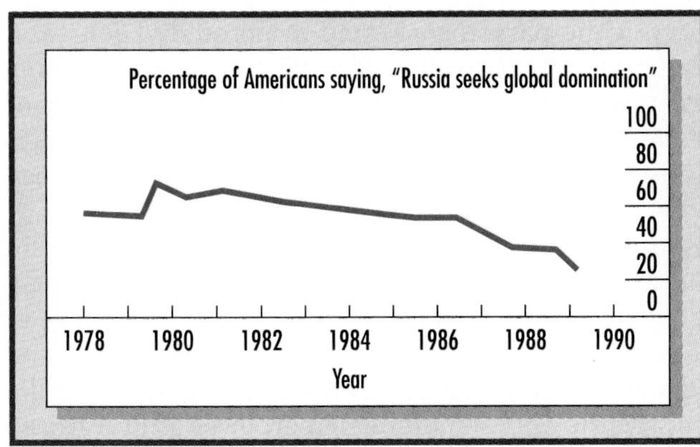

Figure 18.5 ▪ **Declining Perceptions of a Soviet Threat**

Source: Roper surveys.

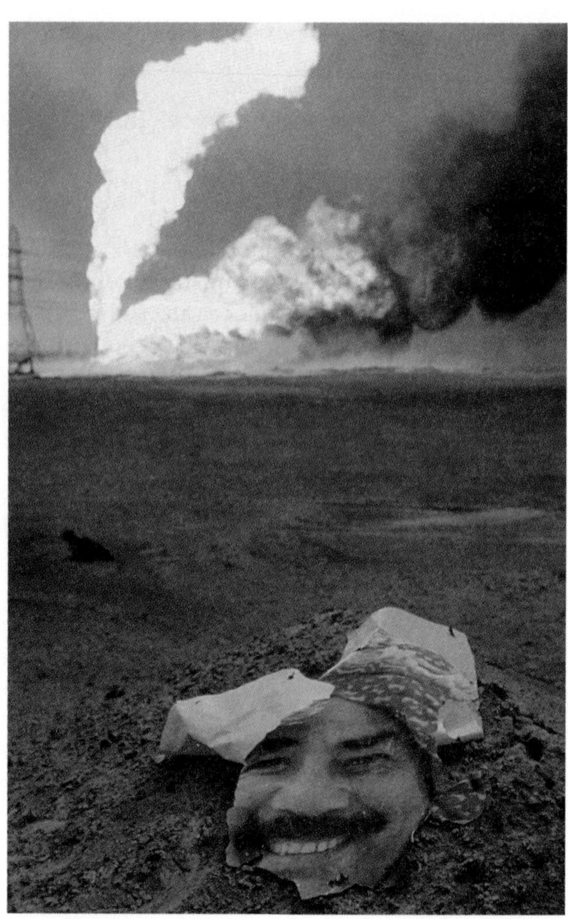

U.S. and allied military forces drove Saddam Hussein's troops out of Kuwait in the Gulf War. However, the retreating Iraqis left a wake of destruction, including field after field of burning oil wells.

But Hussein would not budge. On January 16, 1991, the United States launched a fierce air attack, in which U.S. Tomahawk missiles, Stealth fighters, and fighter-bombers (with laser-guided bombs that could pick their way through ventilation shafts) destroyed Iraqi air defenses and then pounded military installations and troops. After about five weeks of bombing, General Norman Schwarzkopf launched a major ground attack from Saudi Arabia. American M1A1 tanks, rocket launchers, and unopposed air strikes destroyed the Iraqis' Soviet-made T–72 tanks and slaughtered their troops. U.S. Marines pushed north to Kuwait City, while paratroopers and armored divisions executed an end run, sweeping rapidly northward west of Kuwait and turning eastward through southern Iraq, completely liberating Kuwait within about 48 hours. Only about 200 Americans were killed; the number of Iraqi deaths is unknown, but—including children who got sick because of destroyed sewage and water treatment plants—it may have reached a hundred thousand.[25]

Although the ultimate outcome of the Gulf War was ambiguous—Hussein remained in control of Iraq and continued to resist UN sanctions—it sent a strong signal to ambitious regional powers that they had better not engage in aggressive behavior. The Gulf War also marked the end of Soviet resistance to the U.S. use of force abroad, a complete change from the Cold War years and a sign that the United States was the only remaining superpower. And it raised questions about how peacekeeping would work in the future: whether or not the United States would take on responsibilities around the world, for example; whether multinational coalitions could again be assembled; and whether the United States, the United Nations, or some other body (perhaps NATO) would take the lead.

The Collapse of the Soviet Union Soviet cooperation was crucial to the effort led by the United States to drive Iraq out of Kuwait. After the war, Presidents Gorbachev and Bush signed the START nuclear arms reduction treaty at a summit meeting in Moscow, and Gorbachev met in London with leaders of the "G–7" (the seven largest industrialized countries: the United States, Japan, Canada, Germany, Great Britain, France, and Italy), seeking economic aid from the West to help in the Soviet transition to a market economy.

The final collapse of the Soviet Union followed a failed coup attempt in August 1991, when hard-line Communist party, military, and KGB (Soviet intelligence) officials tried to overthrow the vacationing President Gorbachev. Boris Yeltsin, president of the Russian Republic—the first popularly elected official in Russian history—led the resistance in Moscow and Leningrad. The coup plotters, winning little popular support and unwilling to slaughter their fellow citizens, quickly gave up. Gorbachev was restored to office. But the central government rapidly disintegrated. The Communist party, which Gorbachev had tried to reform, lost all legitimacy and was temporarily banned in most of the Soviet Union. The Soviet Union itself fell apart as the Baltic republics (Estonia, Latvia, and Lithuania) became completely independent, and virtually all the other 12 republics, even the crucial Ukraine and Russia, then insisted on independence. Power passed to Yeltsin and other leaders of the republics.

President Bush reacted by declaring large unilateral cuts in tactical nuclear weapons (hoping for reciprocity from the republics) and by authorizing

President Boris Yeltsin of Russia addresses a cheering crowd in Moscow following the failed Communist coup in 1991. Yeltsin led the popular resistance against the last-ditch coup attempt.

assistance with economic reform and food aid to stave off hunger and unrest. The Soviet adversary of the Cold War era was no more.

Problems of the Post–Cold War World

After the collapse of the Soviet Union, some spoke of a "New World Order," but others saw new *dis*order. In recent years, a whole series of new foreign policy problems has arisen, including the possible spread of nuclear weapons, ethnic strife, and the consequences of world poverty. There are disputes with other countries over economic competition, drugs, immigration, the environment, and human rights. At the same time, the U.S. economy has declined relative to those of other countries, and the costs of maintaining large military forces and carrying out an active foreign policy are more keenly felt.

New Security Issues

The most frightening possibility of the past—a Soviet-led invasion of Western Europe that could lead to a nuclear Armageddon between the superpowers—has completely vanished. Despite Americans' eagerness to focus on domestic matters, however, the end of the Cold War has not meant that all foreign policy problems have disappeared. Many difficult new questions remain, including how to define national security and how to pursue it in each of the regions of the world.

Russia and the Former Soviet Union The collapse of the centralized Communist regime threw into question the fate of the vast Russian and former Soviet armed forces, with their millions of troops and many nuclear weapons—more than ten thousand of them. Could these weapons fall into the hands of warring ethnic factions, criminal organizations, or aggressive Third World countries, creating new dangers and instability? The United States worked out agreements for drastic reductions in Russian, Ukrainian, and Kazakh nuclear weaponry. Ukraine and Kazakhstan have renounced nuclear weapons altogether, but their stockpiles of weapons remain large, and central control appears shaky. There is some evidence of Russian nuclear materials showing up on the international black market, raising dangers of **nuclear proliferation,** or the spread of nuclear weapons. A high priority task for American foreign policy has been to prevent proliferation.

nuclear proliferation The spread of nuclear weapons to new countries or to terrorist groups.

The United States has so far avoided entanglement in the bloody ethnic strife that broke out in the former Soviet republics of Armenia, Azerbaijan, and Georgia, and between Russians and rebels in Chechnya. But the long Chechen war and the economic decline in Russia undermined the Yeltsin government and inspired anti-Western nationalism in the elections of 1995 and 1996. Will this lead to military adventures, or to waves of refugees heading west? To what extent can or should the United States, amid its own economic troubles, help rebuild the Soviet economy on a free enterprise basis, or help prevent widespread hunger and suffering?

Eastern Europe What about the countries of Eastern Europe, newly freed from Soviet domination? Most have moved peacefully (if haltingly) to establish democracy and economic reforms. But bitter ethnic and national tensions have arisen in some areas, most notably among the Serbs, Croats, and Muslims of the former Yugoslavia, where the United States finally brokered a peace agree-

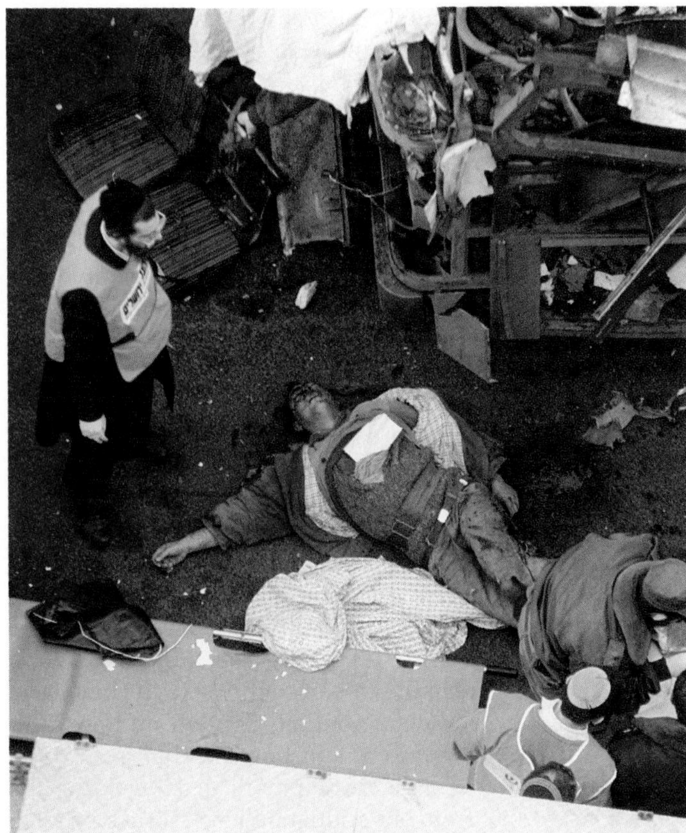

Terrorist bombings in Israel, the Israeli bombardment of Lebanon, and the election of the more conservative Netanyahu government slowed the U.S.-brokered peace process between Israel and the Palestinians.

ment and sent troops to help enforce it (recall the opening story of this chapter). Could some kind of collective peacekeeping, through NATO or the United Nations, prevent such strife in the future? Is the United States, as the world's greatest economic and military power, obliged to play a role?

Western Europe With the Soviet threat gone, how much of a "peace dividend" for domestic needs can or should be gained by withdrawing U.S. forces from Western Europe, where—during the Cold War—about 300,000 troops were stationed and many billions of dollars per year were spent? (So far, more than 100,000 U.S. troops—137,575 of them, as of the mid–1990s—have stayed on.)[26] What role, if any, remains for the NATO alliance? Should Eastern European countries be admitted to NATO, even over Russian objections? What can be done about economic competition from the increasingly unified European Union?

Japan, China, and the Pacific Similarly, how much reduction can or should there be in the vast U.S. naval forces in the Pacific Ocean or in the nearly 100,000 troops stationed in Japan and South Korea? The threat of a North Korean nuclear weapons program has apparently been averted by a deal involving Western help with energy resources, but border skirmishes between the Koreas threaten further trouble. What about China, with its huge population and fast-growing economy? Some Americans have warned of a great "clash of civilizations" between the West and "Confucian" China.[27] Disputes over fair trade, threats against Taiwan (including noisy military maneuvers), and human rights disputes periodically cloud U.S.-Chinese relations. Should democracy be encouraged in China? How?

What can be done to meet what some see as the biggest new security threat: vigorous economic competition from Japan, South Korea, and large, newly industrializing countries like Indonesia, India, and China? How can still-restricted markets like Japan's be opened more fully to American goods?

The Developing World Can regional conflicts be resolved, for example, between the Israelis and the Palestinians (where the United States has played an active diplomatic part), or between nuclear-armed India and Pakistan? Can or should regional powers like Iraq and Iran be restrained or disarmed and kept from acquiring nuclear weapons, as U.S. policy has sought to do? Will the United States have to keep sending troops abroad from time to time, or might the United Nations or regional alliances be strengthened for peacekeeping and humanitarian purposes? Closer to home, can drug shipments from Colombia, Peru, Mexico, and elsewhere be stopped?

Does the enormous gap between rich and poor nations pose a long-term security threat to the United States, in terms of illegal immigration, terrorism, or armed conflicts? How can or should the United States encourage economic growth and/or democracy in poor countries? (The Clinton administration's restoration of freely elected President Aristide to power in Haiti, in the face of military resistance, extreme poverty, and class conflict, pointed up how difficult such a task can be.) Can the world environment be protected from rapid Third World population growth and economic development (e.g., avoiding the destruction of rain forests), as well as from the industrialized world's production of pollution and global warming?

Military Spending Can some American spending on defense be reallocated to domestic investments, in order to meet needs at home? U.S. military spending has declined only slowly from its Cold War peak of $300 billion per year, to $280 and then $260 billion—still about $1,000 for each American. A "two-war" grand strategy (planning for fighting and winning two major regional wars at once with no help from allies) remains in place, though it is unclear who might start even one such war (Iraq? North Korea?). Should the United States more thoroughly rethink its military goals and policies? Can defense industries be helped to convert to production for domestic needs?[28] What should be done with excess nuclear weapons and with the radioactive waste from weapons plants, which the government has estimated may take 30 years to clean up, at a cost of perhaps $100 billion?[29] What can be done to strengthen U.S. industries and to improve the workforce to meet international economic competition, which has contributed to wage stagnation for many Americans?

Such questions as these make clear that attaining the exalted status of the world's only military superpower has not made U.S. foreign policy problems go away. In fact, national security has taken on new and broader meanings and encompasses new problems.

Economic and Social Dilemmas

Especially pressing are economic questions, as increasing numbers of Americans wonder whether America's superpower standing may eventually be undercut or hollowed out by relative economic decline.

International Trade At the peak of its economic dominance after World War II, the United States presided over a world regime of free trade in which many countries negotiated lower tariff barriers through the **General Agreement on Tariffs and Trade (GATT).** Tariffs, duties, quotas, and other means of keeping out foreign exports were reduced in much of the world (although agricultural goods were mostly exempted, and certain nontariff barriers grew). This reduction was very advantageous for U.S. exports and investments, which continued to grow. Also, under the 1944 **Bretton Woods agreement,** the U.S. dollar (fixed in value at $24 per ounce of gold) became the reserve currency for most of the world; that is, the value of other countries' money was pegged to the dollar, so that we had enormous power over other countries' economies.

General Agreement on Tariffs and Trade (GATT) An international agreement that requires the lowering of tariffs and other barriers to free trade.

Bretton Woods agreement The 1944 international agreement to set fixed exchange rates among currencies and to establish the International Monetary Fund (IMF) and the International Bank for Reconstruction and Development (IBRD, or World Bank).

Sharper International Competition By the late 1960s, however, the rebuilt economies of Germany and Japan began to turn out goods that challenged American products abroad and in the United States, beginning with automobiles and moving on to consumer electronics (recall Chapter 4). Additional competition came from newly industrialized countries (NICs), such as South Korea, Taiwan, Singapore, and Hong Kong, and from the increasingly integrated Economic Community (EC) of Europe.

In August 1970, with the dollar weakening, the United States led the way to abandoning permanently the Bretton Woods agreement on dollar-gold convertibility.[30] (Since then, the price of gold has soared to $300 per ounce and more.) The oil shocks of the 1970s, which twice doubled the prices of petroleum products, further damaged the U.S. economy. By the mid–1980s, Americans were importing many more goods than they were exporting, creating a multibillion-dollar **trade deficit.** Foreign companies bought American factories and real estate; as more investment flowed in than out, the United States switched from being the world's largest creditor nation to being the largest debtor nation.

trade deficit An excess of the value of the goods a country imports over the value of the goods it exports.

Free Trade Agreements Reacting to this competitive pressure, the United States during the 1980s unilaterally pressured other countries (especially Japan and the EC—now the **European Union,** or **EU**) to lower hidden barriers and subsidies that hurt American exports, while at the same time arranging voluntary quotas and other policies to control imports to the United States. Next, U.S. policymakers negotiated the **North American Free Trade Agreement (NAFTA)** with Canada and Mexico, which was finally implemented after a 1993 vote in Congress resolved a bitter political conflict over its implications for U.S. jobs.[31]

European Union (EU) The combination of Western European nations into a single market, with free trade and free population movement among them.

North American Free Trade Agreement (NAFTA) An agreement among the United States, Canada, and Mexico to eliminate nearly all barriers to trade and investment among the three countries.

The Clinton administration quickly moved on to conclude a comprehensive free trade agreement with 116 countries, under the Uruguay Round of GATT. The agreement—signed in 1994—set up a **World Trade Organization (WTO)** for enforcement. It cut already-low tariffs by about an additional one-third and, for the first time, reduced restrictions on trade in agricultural products and financial services. U.S. negotiator Mickey Kantor said this reduction would stop "the spiraling of self-defeating agricultural subsidies" (which impede U.S. exports) and would halt the piracy of patents and copyrights; he predicted a $6-*trillion* boost in world trade over ten years.[32]

World Trade Organization (WTO) An agency designed to enforce the provisions of the General Agreement on Tariffs and Trade and to resolve trade disputes among nations.

A crucial question about rapidly growing international trade, and about the increased ability of U.S. and other firms to produce goods cheaply abroad, is whether they bring prosperity to all Americans, or whether they tend to push American workers' wages down while wages in the newly industrializing countries rise toward equilibrium.[33] If free trade hurts U.S. wages, what can be done, short of inefficient protectionism? Could enforceable worldwide agreements on working conditions and environmental protection soften the pressure?

Foreign Aid The world is divided rather starkly into rich nations and poor nations, with totally different standards of living (see Figure 18.6). While the average American enjoys a comfortable home, car, television set, and so on, the average citizen of Ethiopia or Bangladesh struggles for food and shelter, and may at any time face a sudden famine or other disaster that will destroy her or his livelihood.

Limited Aid The United States has made some modest efforts to improve the lives of the world's poor, through such programs as Food for Peace, the Peace Corps (and providing technical and educational assistance), and World Bank developmental loans aimed at encouraging free enterprise (and often imposing stringent financial controls). But spending on foreign aid is very low and has been declining—to $12.1 billion, or less than 1 percent of the federal budget, in 1996. This amount is much lower, proportionally, than that of the aid given by such countries as Sweden and Japan. Moreover, only part of U.S. foreign aid goes for assistance with economic development—only 22 percent of it in 1996.[34] Much of U.S. foreign aid has always been linked to military and security aims.

At the beginning of the Cold War, for example, the huge Marshall Plan aid to Europe helped Europeans rebuild their economies (while opening markets for the United States), but its chief purpose was to resist Communism. Even

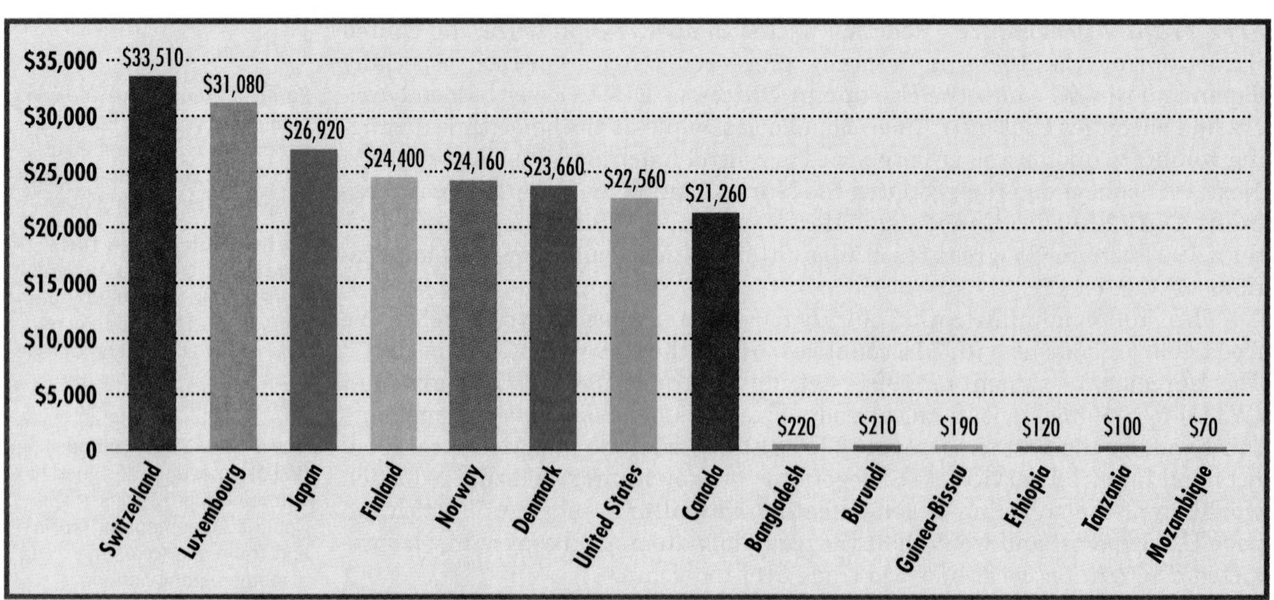

Figure 18.6 ▪ **Rich Nations and Poor Nations**

There is an enormous gap between the standards of living in rich nations and poor nations. The figures are for 1991 per capita GDP, in U.S. dollars.

Source: World Bank, *The World Bank Atlas, 1992* (Washington, DC: World Bank, 1992).

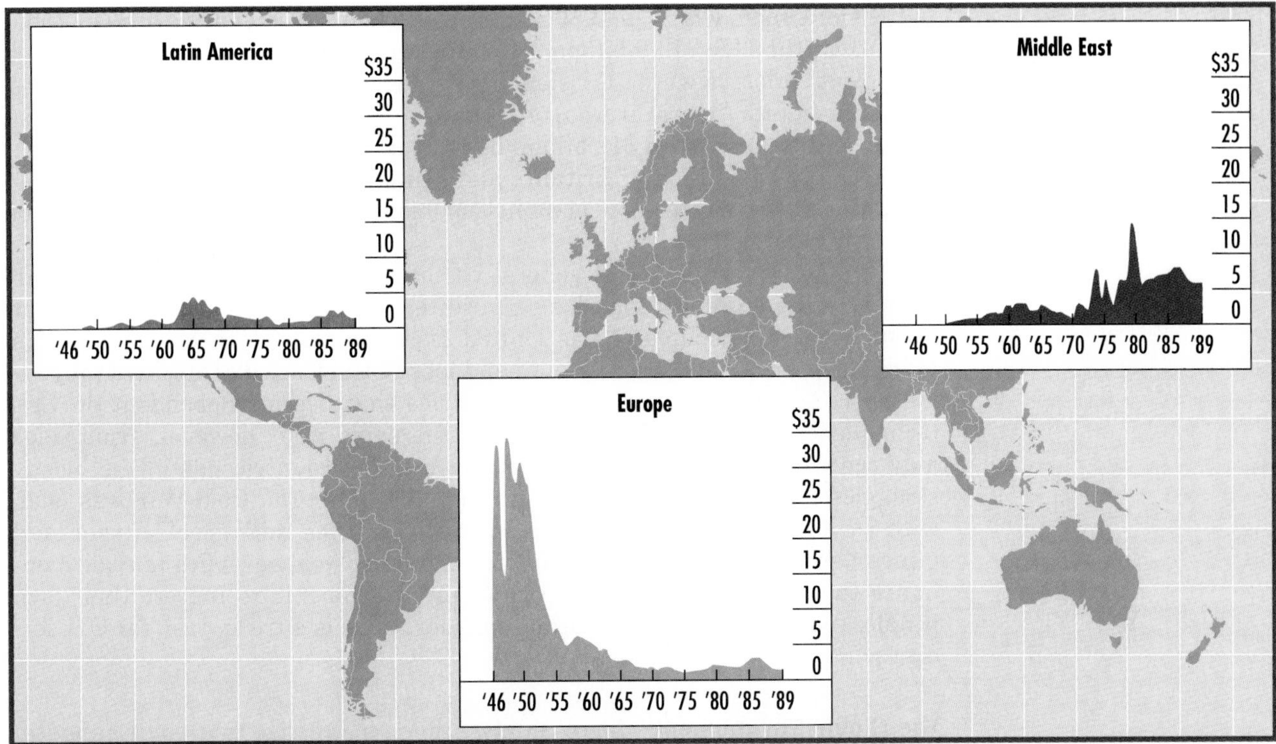

Figure 18.7 ▪ **U.S. Foreign Aid to Three Regions of the World, 1946–1989 (in Billions of Dollars)**

During the Cold War, U.S. foreign aid went predominantly to Western Europe under the Marshall Plan, and then to the Middle East and other areas on the periphery of the Soviet Union and China. The figures are in constant (1989) U.S. dollars.

Source: Congressional Research Service, in the *Washington Post,* National Edition (June 11–17, 1990), p. 7.

more pointedly anti-Communist were the large Cold War payments to South Korea, Taiwan, South Vietnam, Turkey, Pakistan, and other allies around the periphery of the Soviet Union and China. After the Camp David Middle East peace accords, Israel and Egypt became the top recipients of U.S. aid. (For the pattern of aid during the Cold War years, see Figure 18.7.)

Since the end of the Cold War, the total amount of U.S. aid and the portion devoted to military purposes have both declined, and the pattern of recipients has changed somewhat. Israel still tops the list, with about $3 billion of security assistance (loans and grants for weapons purchases, military assistance, and economic support) in 1996; Egypt got just over $2 billion. But now, substantial money is also given to Russia and Ukraine (largely for the destruction of armaments), and to the formerly Communist nations of Eastern Europe. Some funds for development, population programs, and the environment are disbursed through the World Bank, the United Nations, and other international agencies. And some money is always reserved for humanitarian crises like the Rwandan refugee disaster of 1994, to which the United States contributed $194 million.[35]

Arms Sales The United States sells many weapons to other countries. During the Cold War, we shared dominance of the international arms market with the Soviet Union, which in 1989 sold $11.7-billion worth of arms abroad, a bit more than the U.S. $10.8 billion. After the war with Iraq and the breakup of the Soviet Union, however, Russian arms sales fell sharply, and most countries clamored to buy American weapons. Now we are by far the biggest arms exporter in the world, with $12 billion in sales in 1994, much more than runner-up Germany's $3 billion or Britain's and China's roughly $1 billion apiece. Indeed, the United States now accounts for more than half the arms exports of the entire world.[36]

The U.S. government has generally tried to encourage arms sales abroad, through Export-Import Bank loan guarantees and other programs lobbied for by such weapons companies as United Technologies, Raytheon, and Martin Marietta.[37] Arms sales bring profits and jobs to the United States and may increase U.S. influence over foreign countries that become dependent on U.S. technologies and replacement parts. At the same time, however, arms sales may contribute to death and destruction in other countries, as in the bloody struggles fought in Afghanistan and Somalia, after the Cold War was over, with Soviet and American weapons. In some countries, millions of leftover land mines have killed or maimed countless civilians. Weapons sales may also enhance the ability of certain authoritarian governments to repress their own people. To sort out these conflicting considerations is a tricky task for U.S. foreign policy.

The Global Environment Increasingly, Americans realize that environmental problems cross national borders. The United States and Canada have worked out a joint approach to reduce acid rain; many nations have tried to negotiate agreements on oil spills, the exploitation of Antarctica, the protection of the ozone layer, and the prevention of global warming. In some of these cases, the United States initially took a go-slow attitude, insisting, for example, that the evidence of global warming was not yet sufficient to justify reducing the consumption of fossil fuels in order to cut carbon dioxide emissions. The Clinton administration, under Vice-President Gore's leadership, moved ahead somewhat more rapidly, agreeing to sign the biodiversity treaty and to plan to limit greenhouse gas emissions.

Environmentalists express particular concern about the rapid cutting and burning of tropical rain forests, which remove oxygen-producing trees and at the same time pour smoke and carbon dioxide into the atmosphere. However, such countries as Brazil strongly resist any restrictions on their economic development unless they get substantial compensation. Various possible solutions have been discussed, including land purchases or forgiveness of debts to U.S. banks in return for preservation of the rain forests.

The Drug Trade U.S. relations with nations south of the border are also complicated by the flow of enormous amounts of marijuana and cocaine from Peru, Bolivia, and Colombia through Mexico into the United States, and by the inability or unwillingness of those countries to stop the profitable drug trade. When Medellín drug lord Pablo Escobar was killed, for example, thousands of Colombians turned out for his funeral, and the rival Cali drug cartel continued to flourish; leading Colombian politicians may be on drug producers' payrolls. U.S. responses have included assistance with law enforcement (not always fully welcomed), crop eradication (bitterly resented), and crop replacement (very costly). Some military strategists have proposed using U.S. armed forces to seize drug shipments and eradicate production, but that would threaten

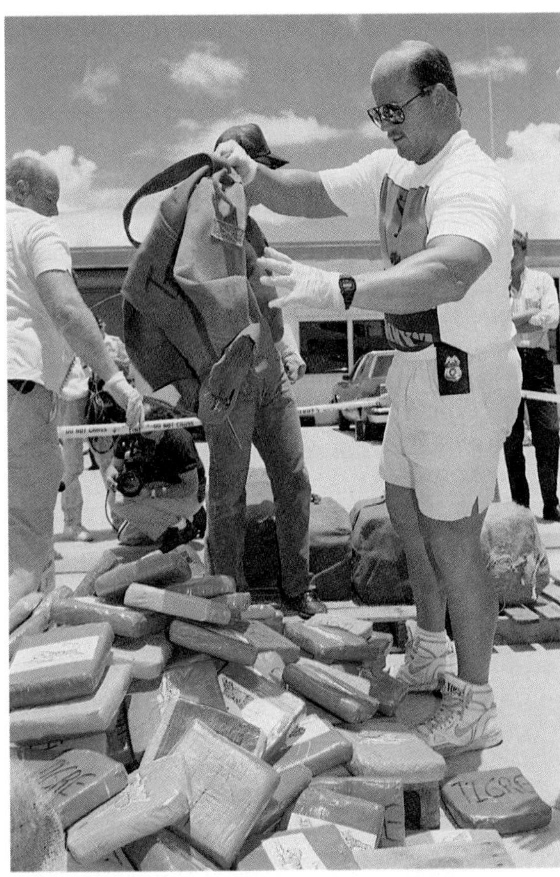

An official with cocaine seized on a freighter from Latin America. Stopping the flow of illegal drugs, which brings huge profits to exporting countries, is a major U.S. foreign policy challenge.

other countries' sovereignty and raise the specter of Vietnam-like drug wars in which the United States might be pitted against local populations.

Immigration In recent years, immigration from abroad—especially illegal immigration—has become a major political issue, as many Americans perceive pressure on their jobs, wages, and tax-supported social benefits, as well as worrying about cultural conflict. (In one poll, 62 percent of respondents said that immigrants "take the jobs of U.S. workers," and 59 percent said that many immigrants wind up on welfare and raise taxes, though large majorities also responded that many immigrants work hard and take jobs that Americans don't want, and that immigrants improve the country with their different cultures and talents.[38]) The policy trend has been toward tightening the borders and making it harder to hire illegal aliens.

Who Makes Foreign Policy?

The president and members of the executive branch are the chief governmental decision makers concerning most foreign policy issues, particularly those involving crisis situations or covert operations. But Congress is often involved in decisions about international trade, foreign aid, military spending, immigration, and other matters that clearly and directly touch constituents' local interests. Public opinion, the mass media, and organized interest groups affect what both Congress and the executive branch do. Moreover, certain aspects of *structure*—especially the economic and military strength of the United States and its position in the international system—have profound effects on foreign policy.

Types of Foreign Policy Decisions Different types of foreign policy are made in very different ways. *Crisis decision making,* for example, involving sudden threats, high stakes, and quick action, belongs mostly to the executive branch: often, just a small, unified group of top national security officials, like those George Bush relied on before and during the war with Iraq. Congress, the public, interest groups, and others usually do not play much part, except to the extent that executive decision makers consult a few key members of Congress and try to anticipate the public's reactions. **Covert operations**—that is, secret or semisecret actions abroad—are also usually governed by small groups of executive branch decision makers, with limited supervision by congressional committees.

covert operations Secret or semisecret activities abroad, often involving intelligence gathering, influence on other countries' politics, or the use of force.

Broader issues of *defense policy,* on the other hand—including treaties on arms control or military alliances, participation in major wars, the amount of money spent on defense, and so on—involve much more participation by Congress, the general public, interest groups, and others. Here, too, the executive branch ordinarily takes the lead, but it must either respond to domestic political forces or change those forces. Decisions about military bases and procurement contracts involve congressional committees and interest groups, especially local businesspeople dependent on bases and weapons-producing corporations. *Foreign trade,* international economic policy, and immigration also sometimes provoke substantial political conflict. The executive branch is generally authorized to negotiate trade agreements with other countries, but Congress has increasingly worried about protecting Americans' jobs and ensuring fair trade with Japan and other countries.

The Executive Branch

The president of the United States, as chief executive officer and commander in chief of the armed forces, is the top decision maker on foreign policy issues. To provide the expertise and information for making and carrying out foreign policy, he has help from many people and organizations.

The National Security Council As we saw in Chapter 12, one of the president's most important White House staff members is the national security adviser, head of the National Security Council (NSC) who meets with the president nearly every day on major matters of defense and foreign policy. Occasionally, advisers with strong intellects and powerful personalities, such as Henry Kissinger, have exerted a major influence on such matters as negotiating the end of the Vietnam War and opening diplomatic relations with China. More common, however, have been self-effacing advisers like Brent Scowcroft, who quietly helped George Bush work out strategy and tactics, and Bill Clinton's appointee, Anthony Lake.

The NSC itself, established in 1947, is the main formal body for coordinating the far-flung civilian and military agencies involved in foreign policy. In theory, the NSC includes the vice-president and the secretaries of state and defense, the director of the Central Intelligence Agency (CIA), and the chairman of the Joint Chiefs of Staff (as advisers), as well as various other high officials.[39] For the most part, however, the department secretaries stay at their agencies and send deputies to the NSC, which often works in committees to coordinate long-range planning, to oversee covert operations, and to make crisis decisions.

The NSC staff, headed by the national security adviser, constitutes a miniature State Department, CIA, and Pentagon combined, right in the basement of the White House. At a moment's notice, it can brief the president on any part of the world or on any military or intelligence matter. In times of crisis, the NSC's Situation Room becomes a command center for the president. It is in close touch with the State and Defense Departments and with embassies and military units around the globe.

The Department of State The State Department—located in "Foggy Bottom," a reclaimed marsh in Washington, D.C., just off the Potomac River—is the president's chief arm for getting day-to-day foreign policy information and for carrying out diplomatic activity.

The State Department is organized partly along functional lines, with bureaus or offices in charge of such matters as economic affairs, human rights, international organizations, narcotics, terrorism, and refugees. But it is mainly organized geographically, with bureaus for Europe and Canada, Africa, East Asia and the Pacific, Inter-American Affairs, and the Near East and South Asia. The geographic bureaus have "country desks" devoted to each nation of the world, where at least one foreign service officer is charged with keeping track of what is going on in that country. In the process of faithfully reporting each country's point of view, desk officers, like ambassadors abroad, tend to identify with the government of that country, sometimes provoking charges of excessive friendliness to regimes that mistreat their own citizens or thwart the interests of the United States. This is one reason that presidents and their political appointees have been known to complain that the State Department is "unresponsive," full of officials who have their own points of view and resist policy directions from the top.

Attached to the State Department are also the Arms Control and Disarmament Agency, the U.S. Information Agency, and the Agency for International Development, which oversees foreign economic aid. Recently, Senator Jesse Helms has worked, over objections by the Clinton administration, to abolish these partly independent agencies and to consolidate their functions in the Department of State. Another partly independent agency of particular interest to young people is the Peace Corps (see the Resource Feature).

Embassies Abroad Reporting back to the Department of State are about 270 embassies and missions in more than 170 countries around the world.[40] U.S. embassies help American travelers and businesspeople abroad, cultivate good relations with the host country, communicate U.S. policy, and—probably most important—gather political, economic, and military intelligence, which is conveyed by secure communications to Washington, D.C. The consulates make local contacts and offer on-the-spot assistance to American citizens.

Most ambassadors, about two-thirds of them, are career foreign service officers.[41] The rest are political appointees, usually heavy financial contributors to the president's party. These amateur diplomats sometimes concentrate on the social side of the job, leaving the heavy work to a professional who is deputy chief of mission. Ambassadors generally discover that they do not fully run their own embassies; they preside over officials who report to superiors in

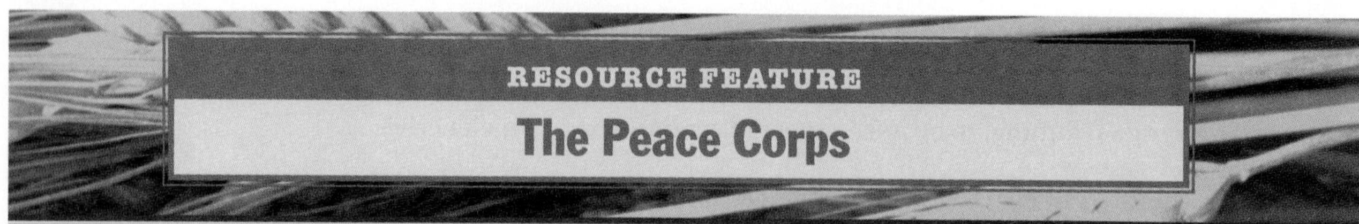

The Peace Corps, Senator Hubert H. Humphrey's brainchild which was brought to life in 1961 in the glow of John F. Kennedy's "New Frontier," has somehow managed to survive for more than 35 years despite much early criticism. Former President Eisenhower once called it a "juvenile experiment." "An extension of socialism," growled one member of Congress. Some liberals saw the Peace Corps as a tool of aggressive foreign policy; some countries feared U.S. imperialism and spying. Yet Republican and Democratic presidents alike have continued the program with little change. In a 1991 Rose Garden send-off of the first volunteers to Poland and Hungary, George Bush declared, "The men and women of America's Peace Corps have built bridges of understanding and goodwill between the people of the United States and . . . scores of other nations."

Since 1961, more than 125,000 young and not-so-young Americans have served in more than 100 nations, from Ghana to Guatemala, Togo to Tuvala, Belize to Botswana, and now Eastern Europe. They have taught English to more than 5 million people; improved agricultural techniques; taught nutrition; given vaccinations; and helped supply potable drinking water. Increasingly they focus on global environmental problems and on the world's children, nearly 100 million of whom are homeless, abandoned, or neglected.

"I don't regret for a second having been a Peace Corps Volunteer," said Joseph T. Banas, who lived for three years in Botswana, one of the poorest nations in Africa. As an engineer, Banas helped expand the program there to include drought relief, horticulture, marketing and research, and agricultural teaching. Volunteers don't earn more money than they need to live on, and they often endure primitive conditions, but they do earn a healthy respect for the problems of undeveloped nations. Many find their own lives transformed.

Source: *Peace Corps Times,* 30th Anniversary Edition (March 3, 1991).

many different Washington agencies: the CIA, the Department of Defense, and—increasingly, with the growing emphasis on economic matters—the Departments of Treasury, Agriculture, and Commerce.

The Department of Defense The titan of foreign and military policy is the Department of Defense (DOD), whose 926,583 civilian and 1,610,490 military employees in 1994 dwarfed the number in any other agency in the U.S. government.[42] (By contrast, the State Department has only about *one one-hundredth* that number of employees.) Defense spending now takes up a bit less than 20 percent of the federal budget. It constitutes by far the largest discretionary part of the budget, that is, the largest part that, unlike Social Security or other entitlements, requires annual appropriations by Congress.

Pentagon The enormous building in Arlington, Virginia, that holds military chiefs and top officials of the Defense Department.

The top echelons of the Defense Department are housed in the **Pentagon** in Arlington, Virginia, an enormous five-sided complex holding more than 23,000 employees. The Pentagon is reputed to have some 17.5 miles of corridors "running into and around 83 acres of offices, drafting rooms, tabulating sections, storerooms, laboratories, libraries, restaurants, auditoriums, dispensaries, banks, a shopping center, a printing plant, and even its own fire department."[43]

Organization of the DOD The organization of the Defense Department is quite complicated, because it tries to deal with two dilemmas: (1) how to en-

Economic matters have become central in U.S. foreign policy. Secretary of Commerce Ron Brown, before his death in an air crash in Bosnia, was a prime salesman for U.S. companies around the world and a chief negotiator in trade disputes with Japan and other countries.

sure a clear, hierarchical military command structure, while at the same time insisting on civilian control of the military, and (2) how to make the different services work together while maintaining their distinct identities.

A civilian **secretary of defense** (under Clinton, William J. Perry), who has authority over the entire department, reports directly to the president. Civilian secretaries are nominally in charge of the Departments of the Army, Navy (including the U.S. Marine Corps), and Air Force; they report to the secretary of defense. Each service also has a military command structure headed by people in uniform: the army and air force chiefs of staff, the chief of naval operations, the commandant of the marine corps, and their subordinates.

secretary of defense The civilian in charge of the Department of Defense and the military services.

At the same time, however, the uniformed chiefs of each branch serve together in a body called the **Joint Chiefs of Staff (JCS),** headed by the chairman of the Joint Chiefs, who reports not only to the secretary of defense but also directly to the president, and who has his own joint staff of officers. General Colin Powell was a particularly influential chairman during George Bush's presidency; John Shalikashvili replaced him in the Clinton administration. Under the Joint Chiefs are ten unified defense commands, which bring together all military units from all branches for a particular purpose or in a particular geographic region. The actual chain of command through which orders pass runs from the president through the secretary of defense and the chairman of the Joint Chiefs to the commanders in chief (CINCs) of these commands.

Joint Chiefs of Staff (JCS) The military officers in charge of each of the armed services.

The Persian Gulf War, for example, came under the authority of the Central Command (based in Tampa, Florida), which was headed by U.S. Army General Norman Schwarzkopf. Schwarzkopf became something of a television celebrity because of his blunt, confident talk. Under Schwarzkopf were many units, each of which had its own commander: the 400,000 or so U.S. Army troops; the 120 or so U.S. Navy ships; the tens of thousands of U.S. Marines; the almost 1,800 war planes; and many troops, ships, and planes from other nations.[44] It was Schwarzkopf's job to coordinate all these forces in a coherent air-land strategic plan. Schwarzkopf reported to Powell and to Secretary of Defense Dick Cheney, both of whom reported directly to Bush.

Interservice Rivalry The organization of the Defense Department represents a series of shifting compromises. There are inevitable tensions between civilian control and military hierarchy, and between the unity and the independence of the services. Interservice rivalry can be fierce. The air force struggled mightily before winning independence from the army, and it struggled again before gaining control of ground-to-ground intercontinental ballistic missiles. The navy, boasting its own airplanes and its own ground soldiers (marines), has resisted army plans for unification of the services. The navy has also argued that its hard-to-detect submarine missile forces provide a secure nuclear deterrent that makes the air force's bombers and land-based missiles largely unnecessary. The great successes of air force Stealth fighters and bombers in the war with Iraq, however, gave the air force a big boost, and the air force showed signs of adapting best to post–Cold War downsizing and the search for new missions.

At its best, interservice rivalry provides healthy competition that makes each service try harder and helps civilian outsiders make informed decisions about which weapons systems and strategies will be most effective. At its worst, however, such rivalry encourages expensive and unnecessary duplication of capabilities and results in log-rolling deals that help obsolete systems survive. The long-held strategic doctrine of the "triad," for example (maintaining that strategic nuclear weapons should be deliverable all three possible ways, from land, sea, and air), may have had as much to do with balance among the U.S. military services as with balance between the United States and the Soviet Union.

Defense Politics Defense politics are special because the Defense Department is so deeply intertwined with the American economy. In addition to its approximately 2.5 million military and civilian employees, another 2 million or so people have been employed in defense-oriented industries or have depended on military contracts. If we take into account the multiplier effect of government expenditures, the number of Americans directly or indirectly dependent on the peacetime military establishment may, at its Cold War peak, have reached beyond 10 million, or about 9 percent of the total U.S. labor force.[45] These people and their companies—which tend to give generous campaign contributions—are located in nearly every congressional district. They can mobilize strong pressures for military spending, even when the need is unclear or the same dollars spent on domestic programs would produce more jobs.

It should be no surprise, therefore, that members of Congress, especially members of the key congressional Armed Services and Appropriations committees, tend to be supportive of the military. So does the executive branch. The Clinton administration, for example, decided to continue the construction of a Seawolf missile submarine, even though its mission was murky, in order to keep General Dynamics' production line going in Connecticut. Similarly, congressional Republicans pushed the production of B–2 Stealth bombers, made by Grumman in southern California, even when Pentagon officials did not ask for them and even though there were strong pressures to cut the federal budget.[46]

Intelligence Agencies The exact size is secret, but the U.S. intelligence community is very large. It enjoyed especially rapid growth—about 17 percent per year—in the early years of the Reagan administration. Most estimates put its size at around 150,000 to 160,000 employees and its budget at around $10 to $13 billion during the late 1980s.[47]

The intelligence budget apparently rose to about $28 billion in the 1990s, and it shows no signs of declining. In fact, some have argued that *more* rather than less intelligence effort is needed in the confusing post–Cold War world, to deal with nuclear proliferation, commercial espionage, ethnic conflicts, and the like. One member of the House intelligence committee recently declared, "Good intelligence is even more important when we no longer face a monolithic opponent but rather several rogue states."[48]

Spy Technology The most expensive U.S. intelligence agencies, consuming 75 percent or more of the federal intelligence budget and providing most of the raw intelligence information, are technologically oriented and are located in the Defense Department. The **National Security Agency (NSA)** is headquartered in a 1.912-million-square-foot building at Fort George Meade, Maryland. It spends about $3.5 billion per year intercepting electronic messages from around the world (including, it is widely believed, Americans' personal telephone calls), analyzing messages, breaking foreign codes, and ensuring the security of U.S. government communications. The NSA's computers are said to be the most advanced in the world.[49]

National Security Agency (NSA) The federal government agency that intercepts and decodes electronic messages and secures U.S. communications around the world.

Even larger is the **National Reconnaissance Office (NRO),** which spends about $7 billion per year. The NRO was created in 1962, but its very existence remained officially secret until 1992. The NRO, closely tied to the air force, runs the satellite reconnaissance programs that provided such striking close-up photographs for the war with Iraq and the peacekeeping operation in Bosnia. The most advanced secret satellites are believed to be capable of taking clear-weather daytime photographs of virtually any spot on the earth, with

National Reconnaissance Organization (NRO) The government agency in charge of surveillance by satellite photography and other technological means.

These B–52 bombers, destroyed by the United States as part of the Strategic Arms Limitations Treaty, must be left in their dismembered state for 90 days so that Russia can confirm their destruction with satellite photos. Satellite photography is used by the United States and other nations to confirm arms control measures and as a strategic device to monitor activities around the world.

such fine resolution that vehicle license plates can be read. At night or in bad weather, radar and infrared images are nearly as good. Such photographs provide a tremendous strategic advantage in spotting targets; they have transformed the nature of warfare. They also makes arms control and other agreements feasible without a reliance on mutual trust: most cheating can be caught at once by satellite.[50]

Military Intelligence Each of the armed services has a separate tactical intelligence unit. The Office of Naval Intelligence, for example, used to keep track of exactly what the Soviet Navy was doing, and it continues to watch Russian submarines. Military intelligence organizations sometimes exaggerate the threats that their services face in order to maximize their own budgets: the air force reported worrisome "bomber gaps" and "missile gaps" that never materialized, and the navy and army often overestimated Soviet naval and land power.[51]

Defense Intelligence Agency (DIA) The organization in charge of coordinating the intelligence units of the different armed services.

The **Defense Intelligence Agency (DIA)** was established in 1961 in order to consolidate, and perhaps replace, the armed-service intelligence units, but it does not collect much information on its own and has not succeeded fully in its coordination function.

Central Intelligence Agency (CIA) The organization that coordinates all U.S. intelligence agencies; it also gathers and evaluates intelligence itself and carries out covert operations.

The Central Intelligence Agency The **Central Intelligence Agency (CIA)** was established in 1947 to advise the National Security Council, to coordinate all U.S. intelligence agencies, to gather and evaluate intelligence information, and to carry out such additional functions as the NSC directed. Soon, the additional functions came to include covert operations, which have brought the CIA considerable notoriety and have made the agency a more important part of the intelligence community than its approximately 15 percent share of the intelligence budget would indicate.

Intelligence Gathering The intelligence-gathering and analysis activities of the CIA, relying partly on secret agents within foreign governments, have brought some spectacular successes. Oleg Penkovsky, for example, fed the United States information on the Soviets from right within the Kremlin, between about 1952 and 1963, when he was caught and shot by the KGB (the Soviet counterpart of the CIA).

The CIA failed, however, to predict such momentous events as the Iraqi invasion of Kuwait and the collapse of the Soviet Union. Some recent failures, especially overestimates of Soviet strength, resulted when in the early 1980s high-ranking CIA official Aldrich Ames betrayed nearly all U.S. agents in Russia. For years afterward, the Soviets fed the United States disinformation through double agents it controlled. In some cases, the CIA apparently knew about the double agents but passed on the information to high U.S. officials anyhow, influencing how billions of dollars were spent on weapon systems. "It's just mind-boggling, the scope of what went on here," commented Senator Arlen Specter (Republican of Pennsylvania).[52]

The vast bulk of intelligence gathering does not involve spies. Much of it consists of the tedious work of evaluating thousands of foreign publications and personal observations by diplomats, attachés, and travelers. Using such material, CIA analysts write hundreds of reports not unlike high-quality college term papers. Electronic surveillance, too, is increasingly important. One of the CIA's early coups was to listen to East German and Soviet officials by tapping the main telephone exchanges from a tunnel under East Berlin. Now, much crucial intelligence is drawn from electronic intercepts by the NSA and satellite photographs taken by the NRO.

An important question is whether U.S. agencies should gather private economic information for the use of the U.S. government or U.S. companies. An international furor ensued when it was revealed that the United States had used the CIA to ferret out secret Japanese negotiating positions in crucial trade talks about automobile imports.[53]

Coordination The CIA's coordination function has always presented difficulties. The Director of Central Intelligence (DCI) is in a peculiar position, trying to coordinate other agencies while at the same time heading his own; he is bound to be suspected of favoring CIA views. Moreover, the DCI has very little actual control over other agencies; he cannot hire or fire their employees or control their budgets, which are much larger than his own.[54] **National intelligence estimates (NIEs),** which are supposed to summarize the best judgment of the intelligence community as a whole, remain collective products in which National Intelligence Council analysts piece together, but don't always reconcile, the views of separate agencies.

National Intelligence Estimates (NIEs) Official summaries of the best available intelligence information on major national security issues.

Covert Operations Covert operations, designed to influence or overthrow governments abroad, have become the most visible trademark of the CIA. CIA operations overthrew the Musaddiq government of Iran in 1953 and the Arbenz government of Guatemala in 1954 and, during the 1950s and 1960s, assisted revolts in Indonesia, Cuba, the Congo (now Zaire), the Dominican Republic, Vietnam, Cambodia, and other places. Some of these target governments were allied with the Soviet Union, but others were simply too leftist or too nationalistic to suit U.S. officials' tastes.[55] There was a brief post-Vietnam retrenchment in the 1970s; then, the Reagan administration launched or continued actions against the governments of Afghanistan, Angola, Mozambique, and Nicaragua, among others, under DCI William Casey, whom a biographer described as the last "great buccaneer."[56]

After the Cold War, these operations left behind considerable human wreckage. Some former "freedom fighters" kept on fighting; Islamic fundamentalists whom the United States had armed in Afghanistan, for example, continued to shell rival clans in the capital, Kabul, and may have organized terrorist groups in Egypt, Saudi Arabia, and the United States. Joseph Savimbi's UNITA forces, ignoring their election loss, pursued an extremely bloody civil war in Angola. CIA ties with the repressive, paramilitary "Fraph" organization in Haiti complicated U.S. efforts to help establish a legitimate democratic government there.

Covert operations are supposed to be secret, or at least officially "deniable." Direct supervision is confined to small groups of executive branch officials. Neither Congress nor the public is much involved; since 1980, only the two intelligence committees of the House and the Senate—with limited staffs, and bound by secrecy—must be informed of major operations.

Criticisms of Covert Action Critics have objected that covert operations infringe on the independence of foreign countries, especially when popular or freely elected governments are overthrown, and that secret alliances with unreliable people sometimes contaminate the CIA's intelligence gathering. Further, the very idea of covert operations may conflict with the idea of democracy. How can ordinary citizens control government actions they do not know about?

The Fraph organization in Haiti, which had ties with the military dictatorship and the U.S. C.I.A., killed a number of civilians and fiercely resisted U.S. efforts to restore the elected government of Bertrand Aristide.

The U.S. public is ambivalent about this question. Many Americans tell pollsters that the CIA *should* "work secretly inside other countries to try to weaken or overthrow governments unfriendly to the United States"; 48 percent said so in one recent survey, while 40 percent disagreed.[57] On the other hand, the public has expressed strong disapproval of some specific covert actions that have come to light, such as assassination plots against foreign officials, the placing of explosive mines in the Managua (Nicaragua) harbor, and the secret arms sales to Iran.

Congress

Congress has generally played a less active role in foreign than in domestic policy. Members of Congress believe that their constituents care more about policies that are close to home than those that are far away. Moreover, the executive branch, with its vast intelligence and national security apparatus, has far more information, expertise, and control of events. Still, Congress shows signs of more activity since the end of the Cold War.

Constitutional Powers The Constitution gives Congress the power to declare war and to decide about any spending of money. It also gives the Senate the power to approve or disapprove treaties and the appointment of ambassadors.

Each of these powers can make a difference. Many of President Clinton's appointments of ambassadors, for example, were held up for months as a result of his dispute with Senator Jesse Helms over the organization of the State Department. The United States was left with no ambassador in several important countries, including India and China. At times, Congress has used its treaty or spending powers to challenge the president on important issues: trying to force an end to the Vietnam War, creating difficulties over the Panama Canal treaty and the SALT II arms control treaty, resisting the Reagan administration's aid to the Nicaraguan contras, and sounding warnings against U.S. involvement in Bosnia.

Congressional Acquiescence More often, however, Congress has gone along with the executive branch or has been ignored. The power of Congress' to declare war, for example, loses some of its impact because most armed conflicts are initiated by the executive branch without a declaration of war. The treaty power means less because the executive branch relies heavily on **executive agreements,** like President Bush's agreement to defend Saudi Arabia against Iraq, that do not require Senate approval.

executive agreements Agreements with other countries that have the same legal force as treaties but do not require approval by the Senate.

Even when congressional approval has been needed, on major issues Congress has usually gone along with executive initiatives, for example, appropriating money for the Marshall Plan, defense buildups, and fighting the wars in Korea and Vietnam. The congressional vote approving presidential authority to use force against Iraq involved an unusually high level of congressional participation, but ultimately, it, too, fit this pattern of acquiescence—and President Bush made it clear he would fight Iraq with or without congressional approval. When President Clinton sent U.S. troops to Bosnia, Congress expressed symbolic opposition (refusing to endorse the policy) but went ahead and voted money to support the troops. Congress has accepted most overt and covert uses of force by the executive branch (see the Struggle for Democracy box).

The Senate has substantial power over foreign policy. Senator Jesse Helms (R-N.C.), chairman of the Foreign Relations Committee, blocked a number of Clinton administration ambassadorial appointments in a struggle over the organization of the State Department.

Control of War Powers

The Struggle for Democracy

A decision to go to war is one of the most important choices that a government can make, but Americans continue to struggle over whether and how such decisions can be subject to democratic control. Although the Constitution grants Congress the power to declare war (Article I, Section 8), presidents have insisted that the need for speed, secrecy, and decisiveness in foreign policy may justify the commander in chief's use of military force with little or no advance approval by Congress or the people.

During the Vietnam War, antiwar senators repeatedly sought to limit the president's power to use military force without explicit congressional authorization; the Senate approved one such bill in 1969 by a 70–16 vote. House resolutions, however, required only quick reporting by the president *after* committing troops. Provoked by President Nixon's sudden 1970 incursion into Cambodia and his 1972 Christmas bombing of North Vietnam, and emboldened by Nixon's deepening Watergate troubles, in October 1973 both chambers passed a compromise War Powers Resolution that required the president to report any combat involvement and to end it within 60 or 90 days unless Congress approved it. President Nixon vetoed the resolution, but the House and Senate overrode the veto and the resolution became law.

Senators Thomas Eagleton and Gaylord Nelson, who had sought tight restrictions on executive action, were not at all pleased by the reliance on after-the-fact congressional review. It is not easy to stop a president after American troops are committed to battle, they pointed out. Eagleton called the resolution a "congressional surrender," passed only because the Democratic leadership, hungry for a symbolic victory over President Nixon, pressured liberals to keep quiet and compromise. He quoted one senator as saying, "I love the Constitution, but I hate Nixon more."[a]

In practice, the War Powers Resolution has made little difference. All subsequent presidents have declared it to be unconstitutional or have ignored it, in such cases as Jimmy Carter's attempted rescue of hostages in Iran, Ronald Reagan's dispatch of troops to Lebanon and invasion of Grenada, and George Bush's invasion of Panama. Bush claimed that he had the power to attack Iraq even without a congressional vote; Clinton said the same about sending troops to Haiti and Bosnia. The struggle continues.

[a]Thomas Eagleton, *War and Presidential Power* (New York: Liveright, 1974), pp. 215–216, 220.

Source: Thomas Eagleton, *War and Presidential Power* (New York: Liveright, 1974); W. Taylor Reveley, *War Powers of the President and Congress* (Charlottesville: University Press of Virginia, 1981), pp. 229–234; Carroll J. Doherty and Mark T. Kehoe, "The Balance of War Powers," *Congressional Quarterly Weekly Report* (December 2, 1995), p. 3670.

Appropriating Money for Defense and Foreign Policy Congress has probably exerted its greatest influence on issues that involve spending money, which must pass through the regular congressional appropriations process. Foreign aid appropriations, for example, tend to be cut in Congress, except for aid to Israel, which is sometimes increased.

Military bases and contracts are a special focus of attention. Many members of Congress, especially members of the Senate and House Armed Services Committees and defense appropriations subcommittees, are very concerned about "real estate" (military bases) and defense contracts, both of which can have great economic impact on congressional districts and powerful interest groups. Despite defense downsizing after the end of the Cold War, for example, expensive weapon systems like the Seawolf submarine and the B–2 bomber

The purchase of certain expensive weapon systems, like the B–2 bomber, continued even during post–Cold War downsizing because of political pressure exerted by manufacturers and local congressional districts.

kept surviving, with energetic backing by members of Congress in the states where they were made. Under congressional pressure, the commission on base closings and the Clinton administration decided to keep open some bases that the military said it did not need.

Trade and Immigration Money is not the only thing Congress cares about, however. In recent years, Congress has pushed for more restrictive or retaliatory trade policies toward Japan and other international competitors. Winning approval to implement NAFTA (by just a 234–200 vote in the House of Representatives) required a maximum effort by Clinton, including special protection for Louisiana sugar and Florida orange growers, as well as side agreements on environmental and workplace regulation.[58] Disputes over restricting legal immigration into the United States have also become very contentious, though curbs on *illegal* immigration have been popular with both parties and the public.

Public Opinion and the Mass Media

Public opinion has some influence on foreign policy, though it is sometimes ignored and may sometimes be manipulated.

Responsiveness to the Public It was once thought that public opinion on foreign policy was so uninformed, unstable, and weak that it could not possibly have much effect on policymaking. As we saw in Chapter 5, however, this picture is not correct. It is now clear that public opinion does, in fact, have substantial effects. Historical studies of such issues as arms control and foreign aid have indicated that policymakers have often taken public opinion into account in making their decisions.[59] Looking at many different foreign policy cases, scholars have found that, most of the time, policy has corresponded with what a majority of the public wants. About two-thirds of the time, too, *changes* in public opinion on foreign policy are followed within a year or so by policy changes moving in the same direction.[60] The State Department has a special office to keep track of what the public is thinking. And as we saw in Chapter 12, the White House listens even more carefully to the public, doing extensive polling of its own.

Leeway for Policymakers Still, the executive branch has considerable leeway. Seldom does public opinion demand that particular actions be taken abroad. More often, the public more or less goes along with what the president does, at least until the results begin to come in. If the results look bad (e.g., in the Vietnam War: see the Politics and Film box on page 638), the public tends to punish the administration with low popularity ratings and rejection at the polls. If the results look good (e.g., the Persian Gulf War, at least initially), the public rewards the administration.

electoral reward and punishment Voting for the incumbents when times are good and against them when times are bad.

As indicated in Chapter 9, this system of **electoral reward and punishment** creates incentives for presidents to do things that will please the public in the long run, but there is leeway in the short run, and presidents sometimes miscalculate how things will work out. Moreover, with many foreign policies that are secret or barely visible, the moment for reward or punishment never comes, and the administration can act without being called to account.

Shaping Opinion Furthermore, the executive branch can sometimes shape public opinion to its own ends, by putting its own interpretation on world events and especially by creating or encouraging events that will alter the public's thinking. Franklin Roosevelt's secret naval policies in the Atlantic and his economic squeeze on Japan, for example, helped provoke hostile actions that led to the public acceptance of U.S. involvement in World War II.[61] In this and other cases like the Tonkin incident in Vietnam (see Chapter 5), the mass media have tended to convey the government's point of view to the public. The antiwar Vietnam films were the exception.

For all these reasons, political scientist V. O. Key, Jr., may have been correct—at least, concerning foreign policy—when he argued that public opinion mainly just sets up "dikes" that confine policy to certain broad channels.[62] Within those channels, the president and the executive branch largely determine the flow.

Corporations and Interest Groups

The role of corporations and interest groups in American foreign policy is a matter of controversy. Some observers maintain that executive branch officials are motivated chiefly by concern for a "national interest" that transcends the selfish interests of any particular group.[63] Others say that conceptions of the national interest are actually determined, in large part, by the narrow interests of wealthy and well-organized individuals and corporations with links to executive decision makers. The truth may lie somewhere in between.

Interest Group Influence? There are indications, for example, that the United States may have adopted free trade and internationalist policies as part of the New Deal of the 1930s because of the rise of large corporations with operations abroad, especially multinational oil companies and investment bankers. It has been argued that some of these multinational firms made a deal with the Democratic party, getting the free trade laws they wanted in return for supporting the Democrats' social welfare policies, which were not very costly to capital-intensive firms.[64]

According to this line of argument, the great arms buildup and anti-Communist policies of the late 1970s and early 1980s (together with the clampdown on social spending and the decline of the Democratic party) were sparked by U.S. corporations that faced sharper foreign competition, turned against government taxation and regulation, and insisted on military protection for their markets in the Third World. Similarly, the big push for free trade agreements and deficit cutting in the 1990s may have been fueled by multinational corporations and investment bankers.[65]

There is also some historical evidence of interest group involvement in foreign policy decisions that seemed, on the surface, quite remote from domestic political considerations. A study of U.S. involvement in the Congo (now Zaire) during the 1950s and 1960s, for example, indicates that the U.S. switch from Eisenhower's backing of the Belgian colonialists to Kennedy's support for Congolese independence reflected differing, administration-linked U.S. financial interests in that mineral-rich country. Many prominent American officials had ties, through law firms, stock holdings, and the like, to companies with large sums of money at stake in the Congo.[66]

The Stakes for Business American businesses have good reasons to care about U.S. foreign policy. As Table 18.2 indicates, in 1994, each of 20 large American corporations had more than $8 billion in sales abroad. The top three—Exxon, General Motors, and Mobil—together took in more than $160 billion in foreign revenues that year; IBM, Ford, and Texaco were not far behind.[67] Many multinational firms seek free trade policies and diplomatic or military protection abroad. Other firms, especially those relying on U.S. markets but threatened by foreign competition (e.g., in automobiles, steel, clothing, and consumer electronics) have sought government subsidies, tariffs, or quotas against foreign goods.

The defense budget involves big money, as well. In 1993, McDonnell Douglas, Lockheed, Martin Marietta, and General Motors each got more than $4 billion in prime military contracts.[68] Arms manufacturers play a significant part in decisions about weapons systems. The air force's selection of the Lockheed, General Dynamics, and Boeing corporations to build $95-billion worth of F–15 Eagle fighters, for example, followed a five-year technical and political battle in which the winners and the losers (Northrop and McDonnell Douglas) brought every kind of pressure to bear; Senator Sam Nunn of Georgia (Lockheed's home state) was thought to be pivotal in the choice.[69]

Some corporations' efforts have crossed over into the illegal; former assistant secretary of the navy Melvyn Paisley, once in charge of all navy procurement, pleaded guilty to charges of bribery and conspiracy in a long-running scheme in which such companies as Martin Marietta, Unisys, and United Technologies apparently paid for confidential information in order to rig their weapons bids.[70]

Besides business corporations and trade associations, certain ethnic groups sometimes affect U.S. foreign policy. This is most obvious in the case of U.S. policy toward Israel, in which widespread public sympathy toward that country is reinforced by the efforts of the American-Israel Public Affairs Committee (AIPAC) and by various organized groups representing Jewish Ameri-

Table 18.2

Foreign Revenues of U.S. Corporations

Many American firms do a great deal of business abroad and therefore have high stakes in U.S. foreign policy, especially in its effects on trade and investment.

		Foreign Revenue (Millions)	Foreign as Percentage of Total Revenue
1	Exxon	77,125	77.4
2	General Motors	44,041	28.4
3	Mobil	40,318	67.6
4	IBM	39,934	62.3
5	Ford Motor	38,075	29.6
6	Texaco	24,760	55.9
7	Citicorp	19,703	62.3
8	Chevron	16,533	42.9
9	Philip Morris Cos.	16,329	30.4
10	Procter & Gamble	15,650E	51.7
11	El du Pont de Nemours	14,322	42.1
12	Hewlett-Packard	13,522	54.1
13	General Electric	11,872	19.8
14	American Intl. Group	11,636	51.8
15	Coca-Cola	11,048	68.3
16	Dow Chemical	10,073	50.3
17	Motorola	9,770E	43.9
18	Xerox	9,678	47.8
19	United Technologies	8,300	39.2
20	Digital Equipment	8,274	61.5

Source: *Forbes* (July 17, 1995), pp. 274–275.

cans.[71] Similarly, African-American groups strongly opposed apartheid in South Africa and military rule in Haiti, and Cuban-American groups have insisted on tough policies against Fidel Castro's Cuba.

Structural Factors

Certain important factors that affect U.S. foreign policy operate in the *structural* sphere. These include U.S. economic and military power, as well as features of the international system.

Economic and Military Power One structural factor is the enormous economic and military might of the United States. The strength of the U.S. economy is what makes it possible to produce war planes, ships, and ground forces that can operate virtually anywhere in the world, giving the United States the capacity to intervene where it chooses. Countries with the capacity to act as great powers tend to do so.

By the same token, the size of the U.S. economy and its deep involvement in world trade and investment have created U.S. interests almost everywhere.

Ethnic groups sometimes affect U.S. foreign policy. President Clinton's triumphal 1995 tour of Northern Ireland, where he helped to encourage peace between Protestants and Catholics, helped him win support from Irish-Americans.

Any country where Americans might want to sell something, buy something, or build factories may become a target of foreign policy objectives: lowered tariff barriers, political stability, or a sound business climate for U.S. investments. These structural facts produce foreign policy goals.

The International System The place of the United States in the international system also affects U.S. foreign policy. During the nineteenth century, for example, when the growing U.S. economy remained considerably smaller than that of Great Britain, the United States could take a free ride on the order-producing and free-trade-enforcing efforts of the British. However, when the United States became the greatest industrial power and then the biggest world trader, it took over the responsibilities of a world leader, or **hegemon.**[72]

More broadly, the overall shape of the international system makes a great difference. A **multipolar** world, with many different nations of roughly equivalent power, would call for very different U.S. foreign policies than did the **bipolar** world of the U.S.–Soviet Cold War or would a **unipolar** world of U.S. dominance. And international actors themselves are changing, as multinational corporations, nongovernmental organizations, and even cities or states pursue their own foreign policies—to some degree displacing the nation-state.[73]

hegemon A dominant power: for example, the dominant nation in the world.

multipolar system A world system in which many powerful nations divide up influence.

bipolar system An international system with two great powers.

unipolar system A world system in which a single superpower dominates all other nations.

Foreign Policy and Democracy

Democratic control over foreign policy is incomplete. In this respect, the American political system tends to fall short of the ideals of popular sovereignty and political equality.

POLITICS AND FILM

Hollywood Against the Vietnam War

Hollywood films about World War II were almost always positive and celebratory, instruments of cohesion that helped the American people pull together for the struggle against Nazi Germany and Imperial Japan. Not so with the Vietnam War. Americans felt conflicted about that war, and many were downright opposed. This attitude among the public was reflected in the movies Hollywood made about Vietnam.

The only major studio film supportive of the Vietnam War was *The Green Berets* (1968), directed by and starring John Wayne. The story revolves around a liberal reporter, played by David Janssen, who first opposes the war but then passionately approves of it after witnessing Viet Cong atrocities and the good deeds of American soldiers. The film was a flop at the box office.

Other films focused on the moral dilemmas at the center of the Vietnam conflict. In *Apocalypse Now* (1979), director Francis Ford Coppola adapted his story from Joseph Conrad's great novel *Heart of Darkness* (1902), about a journey into a moral quagmire. Coppola's film is an unrelenting picture of violence, corruption, horror, madness, and despair, alternating with brief moments of humor and humanity. The journey we follow is that of Captain Willard, played by Martin Sheen. Moviegoers are unlikely to forget the madmen he encounters: Colonel Kilgore (Robert Duvall), whose helicopter gunships assault a hostile Vietnamese hamlet in order to secure a beachhead where the surfing is unsurpassed, and Green Beret Colonel Kurtz (Marlon Brando), who lives as a violent demigod among the Montagnard tribespeople.

Other films suggest that, in the midst of the moral quagmire and confusion about the purposes of the war, all one can depend on are one's buddies. In Michael Cimino's Academy Award–winning movie, *The Deerhunter* (1978), the tight bonds linking a group of men from a small industrial town are shattered forever by the Vietnam War, though the central figure in the film (Robert DeNiro) struggles to the end to salvage some remnants of their previous lives together. Oliver Stone, a former combat soldier in Vietnam, won an Academy Award as best director for his hair-raising depiction of war on the ground in *Platoon* (1986). Amid the horror of the war, in a world of mixed-up moral values, all that counts is survival, and all one can count on is the person sharing one's foxhole.

Several movies make their antiwar point through the stories of soldiers disabled in a war that makes no sense to them. In Hal Ashby's *Coming Home* (1978), Jane Fonda plays the wife of a gung-ho and slightly manic marine officer (Bruce Dern). Her views on the war are transformed by her love affair with a wheelchair-bound combat veteran, played by Jon Voight. Oliver Stone's *Born on the Fourth of July* (1989) is based on the book of the same name written by paraplegic antiwar activist, Ron Kovic. Tom Cruise plays the title role in this film, which follows Kovic from all-American boy and believer in the Vietnam War to the confusions and hell of the Vietnam battlefields on which he is wounded, the grim veterans' hospital where he begins his rehabilitation, and finally, his agonizing journey to self-realization and political activism against the war.

Hollywood also produced a number of films whose theme was the purported betrayal of the American fighting man. In Sylvester Stallone's *First Blood* (1982), a Vietnam vet (Rambo) is forced into a war of

To a substantial extent, public opinion is taken into account, through the public's elected representatives in Congress and through the executive branch's responsiveness to what the public wants and its anticipation of electoral punishment if it fails to deliver. Still, the centralization of decisions in the executive branch means that popular participation is quite limited. Secrecy means that the public often does not know what the government is doing and hence cannot hold it responsible. Government control of information means that the public is sometimes deceived or misled, acquiescing in policies that it

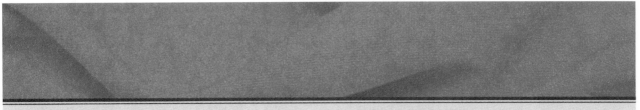

revenge against a small Pacific Northwest town after the local police unjustly harass and jail him. Stallone, who wrote the screenplay and played the leading role, wanted to show how unwelcome vets felt back home, aliens in a country that was ashamed of the war it had sent them to fight. Rambo's final speech is a passionate summary of often-heard complaints: resentment at being called "baby killers" by antiwar activists, anger at being trained for tasks of destruction and mayhem that make them unable to reintegrate into society, and rage at being asked to fight a war that politicians would not allow the military to win. The ultimate betrayal of the American soldier, abandoning him to the enemy, is the theme of *Rambo: First Blood Part II* (1985), in which Stallone is launched on a mission to rescue Americans held as prisoners of war in Vietnam, and *Uncommon Valor* (1983), in which Gene Hackman plays a father who must buck the U.S. government itself in order to rescue his son from a prison camp.

The Vietnam War, like no other war in American history, is almost universally cast in negative terms in Hollywood films. Though filmmakers disagreed wildly among themselves concerning what was amiss about that war, almost none saw anything of positive value in it.

would resist if it were fully informed. And interest groups sometimes push policy in unpopular directions.

The domestic impacts of foreign policy are becoming stronger and more obvious, however. As more and more Americans become aware of international affairs, insist on knowing what their government is doing, and demand government responsiveness to the popular will, democratic control of foreign policy may increase.[74] This is particularly likely to happen if the political parties reject bipartisanship on foreign affairs, and if the opposition party vigorously criticizes government policy. But there is no guarantee they will do so. In this area, the struggle for democracy continues.

Summary

The United States has become the world's only superpower, with a much larger economy and much more powerful armed forces than any other nation. It grew into this role during roughly 200 years of westward expansion and settlement, industrialization, and then active involvement in World War I and World War II.

For more than 40 years, American foreign policy focused on the tense Cold War confrontation with the Soviet Union, competing for influence in Europe, fighting Soviet allies in Korea and Vietnam, and skirmishing over the Third World. When the Soviet Union collapsed, attention turned to other issues, including regional conflicts (e.g., Iraq's invasion of Kuwait and the civil war in Bosnia), international economic competition, efforts at transition to democracy and free markets in Russia and Eastern Europe, problems of world poverty, and the global environment.

Foreign policy has traditionally been made mostly in the executive branch, where the president is assisted by a large national security bureaucracy, including the National Security Council, the Department of Defense, the Department of State, and various intelligence agencies. Congress has been little involved in crises or covert actions and has generally gone along with major decisions on defense policy; it has asserted itself chiefly on matters of foreign trade and aid, military bases, and procurement contracts. Public opinion affects policy, perhaps increasingly so, but this influence is limited by the executive branch's centralization of decision making, secrecy, and control of information. How large a part interest groups and corporations play is disputed but probably substantial. Structural factors, including U.S. economic and military strength and the nature of the international system, strongly affect what policies seem feasible or desirable.

Democratic control, though it may be increasing, is more difficult and less complete in foreign than in domestic policy.

Suggested Readings

Barnet, Richard J., and John Cavanagh. *Global Dreams: Imperial Corporations and New World Order.* New York: Simon & Schuster, 1994.
A hard-hitting, controversial critique of the role of multinational corporations in the world economy.

Kegley, Charles W., Jr., and Eugene R. Wittkopf. *American Foreign Policy, Pattern and Process,* 5th ed. New York: St. Martin's Press, 1995.
Thoroughly describes the institutions and processes of foreign policymaking.

LaFeber, Walter. *America, Russia, and the Cold War, 1945–1990.* New York: McGraw-Hill, 1991.
A clear, brief history of the Cold War.

Markusen, Ann, and Joel Yudken. *Dismantling the Cold War Economy.* New York: HarperCollins, 1992.
The nature of U.S. military industries and how to convert them to peaceful production.

Russett, Bruce M. *Controlling the Sword: The Democratic Governance of National Security.* Cambridge: Harvard University Press, 1990.
Argues that public opinion is much more important in making foreign policy than was previously thought.

Internet Sources

Amnesty International http://www.organic.com/Non.profits/Amnesty/Info/what.html
Reports and documents from the international human rights organization.

The CIA's World Factbook http://www.odci.gov/publications/95Fact/index.html
Detailed information on the countries of the world from the Central Intelligence Agency.

Defense Link http://www.dtic.dla.mil/defenselink/
The home page of the Department of Defense.

The Global Politics Home Page http://www.yorku.ca/research/crs/mills/GP_Home.html
A cornucopia of linkages to information on global politics and issues, academic associations, global organizations, and journals.

IMF http://www.unicc.org/Welcome.html/
The home page of the International Monetary Fund, complete with studies, statistical information, and IMF policy documents.

Peacenet http://www.peacenet.apc.org/peacenet/
A web site devoted to peace, social and economic justice, and human rights; information on all of these subjects as well as links to organizations working in these fields.

United Nations http://www.un.org/
Home page of the United Nations; links to a wealth of statistics, documents and reports, UN departments and conferences, information on reaching UN officials.

United States Department of State gopher://marvel.loc.gov/11/federal/fedinfo/byagency/executive/state
This gopher site makes available a wealth of documents on international affairs from the State Department.

Notes

1. Craig R. Whitney, "Balkan Foes Sign Peace Pact, Dividing an Unpacified Bosnia," *New York Times* (December 15, 1995), pp. 1, 8.
2. "Congress Reluctantly Acquiesces in Peacekeeping Mission," *Congressional Quarterly Weekly Report* (December 2, 1995), pp. 3668–3671.
3. "Congress Takes Symbolic Stand on Troop Deployment," *Congressional Quarterly Weekly Report* (December 16, 1995), pp. 3817–3818.
4. United States, *Budget for Fiscal Year 1996,* Tables 10–1 and 10–2, pp. 123–124.
5. William D. Hartung, "Notes from the Underground: An Outsider's Guide to the Defense Budget Debate," *World Policy Journal,* Vol. 12 (Fall 1995), pp. 15–16; Nicholas D. Kristof, "The Real Chinese Threat," *New York Times* (August 27, 1995), Sec. 6, p. 50.
6. Kenneth Waltz, *Theory of International Politics* (Reading, MA: Addison-Wesley, 1979).

7. Paul Kennedy, *The Rise and Fall of the Great Powers* (New York: Random House, 1987), p. 358.

8. *Historical Statistics of the United States: Colonial Times to 1970,* Part 2, p. 884; *Economic Report of the President 1995,* p. 396.

9. *Historical Statistics,* pp. 868–869; *Statistical Abstracts, 1994,* p. 807.

10. Melvin P. Leffler, "The Interpretive Wars over the Cold War, 1945–60," in Gordon Martel, ed., *American Foreign Relations Reconsidered 1890–1993* (London: Routledge, 1996), pp. 106–124.

11. "X" (George F. Kennan), "The Sources of Soviet Conduct," *Foreign Affairs,* Vol. 25 (July 1947), pp. 566–582; Lawrence S. Wittner, *American Intervention in Greece, 1943–1949* (New York: Columbia University Press, 1982).

12. Walter LaFeber, *America, Russia, and the Cold War, 1945–1990* (New York: McGraw-Hill, 1991); gives a good brief history of the Cold War.

13. Bruce Cumings, *The Origins of the Korean War, Vol. 2: The Roaring of the Cataract, 1947–1950* (Princeton: Princeton University Press, 1990); David Rees, *Korea: The Limited War* (New York: St. Martin's Press, 1964).

14. *Historical Statistics,* p. 1141.

15. *Historical Statistics,* p. 1116.

16. Samuel Wells, "Sounding the Tocsin: NSC 68 and the Soviet Threat," *International Security* (Fall 1979), pp. 116–158.

17. Raymond L. Garthoff, *Reflections on the Cuban Missile Crisis,* rev. ed. (Washington, DC: Brookings Institution, 1989); James A. Nathan, ed., *The Cuban Missile Crisis Revisited* (New York: St. Martin's Press, 1992).

18. *Statistical Abstracts, 1992,* pp. 341, 344. Some give a figure of 58,000 for total U.S. *war-related* deaths in Vietnam.

19. Robert S. Litwak, *Detente and the Nixon Doctrine: American Foreign Policy and the Pursuit of Stability, 1969–1976* (New York: Cambridge University Press, 1984).

20. *Statistical Abstracts, 1994,* p. 352. In constant (1987) dollars, spending increased from $187 billion to $282 billion.

21. Tom Gervasi, *The Myth of Soviet Military Superiority* (New York: Harper & Row, 1986); Robert H. Johnson, *Improbable Dangers: U.S. Conceptions of Threat in the Cold War and After* (New York: St. Martin's, 1994).

22. Robert J. McMahon, "Making Sense of American Foreign Policy During the Reagan Years," *Diplomatic History,* Vol. 19, No. 2, (Spring 1995), pp. 367–384; David E. Kyvig, ed., *Reagan and the World* (Westport, CT: Praeger, 1990); Tim Weiner, "Documents Assert U.S. Trained Salvadorans Tied to Death Squads," *New York Times* (December 14, 1993), pp. A1, A4.

23. Richard Smoke, *National Security and the Nuclear Dilemma: An Introduction to the American Experience in the Cold War* (New York: McGraw-Hill, 1993).

24. John E. Rielly, ed., *American Public Opinion and U.S. Foreign Policy 1991* (Chicago: Chicago Council on Foreign Relations, 1991). Even in 1994, however, close to half of the American public (43 percent) saw Russia as a significant military threat to the United States. *The Gallup Poll Monthly,* No. 340 (January 1994), p. 39.

25. Lawrence Freedman and Efraim Karsh, *The Gulf Conflict 1990–1991: Diplomacy and War in the New World Order* (Princeton: Princeton University Press, 1993); Michael R. Gordon and General Bernard E. Trainor, *The Generals' War: The Inside*

Story of the Conflict in the Gulf (New York: Little, Brown, 1995); John O'Loughlin, Tom Mayer, and Edward S. Greenberg, eds., *War and Its Consequences: Lessons from the Persian Gulf Conflict* (New York: HarperCollins, 1994), esp. Chap. 4.

26. U.S. Department of Defense, *Selected Manpower Statistics 1994,* p. 37.

27. Samuel P. Huntington, "The Clash of Civilizations," *Foreign Affairs* (Summer 1993).

28. Ann Markusen and Joel Yudken, *Dismantling the Cold War Economy* (New York: Basic Books, 1992).

29. Michael Arndt, "Study: Cleaning Up Nuclear Arms Plants Will Take Years, Cost Billions," *Chicago Tribune* (February 12, 1991), p. 4.

30. Fred Block, *The Origins of International Economic Disorder* (Berkeley: University of California Press, 1977).

31. Mario F. Bognanno and Kthryn J. Ready, eds., *The North American Free Trade Agreement: Labor, Industry, and Government Perspectives* (Westport, CT: Praeger, 1993).

32. Ray Moseley, "Deal Struck on Historic World Trade Pact," *Chicago Tribune* (December 15, 1993), pp. A1–A18.

33. Bognanno and Ready, *The North American Free Trade Agreement.*

34. George Moffett, "Skeptical Congress Accelerates Foreign-Aid Cuts," *Christian Science Monitor* (November 30, 1995), p. 4.

35. United States, *Budget for Fiscal Year 1996,* pp. 115–118.

36. *Stockholm International Peace Research Yearbook, 1993,* p. 447; *1995,* p. 493. Russian arms sales, mostly to China, caught up with U.S. sales in 1995.

37. For example, Clyde H. Farnsworth, "White House Seeks to Revive Credits for Arms Exports," *New York Times* (March 18, 1991), pp. A1, C8.

38. *The Public Perspective* (January–February 1994), p. 98.

39. Charles W. Kegley, Jr., and Eugene R. Wittkopf, *American Foreign Policy, Pattern and Process,* 4th ed. (New York: St. Martin's Press, 1991), p. 387.

40. State Department Web page, January 1996.

41. Donald M. Snow and Eugene Brown, *Puzzle Palaces and Foggy Bottom: U.S. Foreign and Defense Policy-Making in the 1990s* (New York: St. Martin's Press, 1994), p. 96.

42. U.S. Department of Defense, *Selected Manpower Statistics, 1994.*

43. W. Borklund, *The Department of Defense* (New York: Praeger, 1968), pp. 95–97; *World Almanac 1994* (Mahwah, NJ: Funk & Wagnalls, 1993), p. 661.

44. *Chicago Tribune* (February 13, 1991), p. 4.

45. Charles W. Kegley, Jr., and Eugene R. Wittkopf, *American Foreign Policy, Pattern and Process,* 3rd ed. (New York: St. Martin's Press, 1987), p. 389.

46. Eric Schmitt, "G.O.P. Would Give Pentagon Money It Didn't Request," *New York Times* (July 5, 1995), p. 1; David Maraniss and Michael Weisskopf, "In Test of Strength, Stealth Survives; Defense Sponsors Clip Budget-Cutting Wing of G.O.P," *Washington Post* (September 24, 1995), p. 1.

47. Kegley and Wittkopf, *American Foreign Policy,* pp. 383–384; Victor Marchetti and John D. Marks, *The CIA and the Cult of Intelligence* (New York: Knopf, 1974).

48. "House Backs Increased Budget for CIA, Other Spy Activity," *Congressional Quarterly Weekly Report* (September 16, 1995), p. 2824.

49. Jeffrey T. Richelson, *The U.S. Intelligence Community,* 3rd ed. (Boulder, CO: Westview Press, 1995), pp. 24–29; James Bamford, *The Puzzle Palace* (New York: Penguin, 1983).

50. *New York Times* (September 29, 1995); Richelson, *U.S. Intelligence Community,* p. 31.

51. Harry Rowe Ransom, *The Intelligence Establishment* (Cambridge: Harvard University Press, 1970), pp. 103–104.

52. Nathan Miller, *Spying for America* (New York: Paragon, 1989), pp. 329, 375, 380, 390; "Drive to Reform CIA Intensifies as Ames Case Fallout Worsens," *Congressional Quarterly Weekly Report* (November 4, 1995), p. 3392.

53. David E. Sanger and Tim Weiner, "Emerging Role for the C.I.A.: Economic Spy," *New York Times* (October 15, 1995), p. 1.

54. Steven J. Flanagan, "Managing the Intelligence Community," *International Security,* Vol. 10 (Summer 1985), pp. 58–95.

55. David Wise and Thomas B. Ross, *The Invisible Government* (New York: Random House, 1964); *The Need to Know: The Report of the Twentieth Century Fund Task Force on Covert Action and American Democracy* (New York: Twentieth Century Fund, 1992).

56. Joseph E. Persico, *Casey: From the OSS to the CIA* (New York: Viking Press, 1990), p. 572.

57. Rielly, ed., *American Public Opinion,* p. 37.

58. "Congress OKs North American Trade Pact," *Congressional Quarterly Almanac, 1993,* pp. 171–181.

59. Bruce M. Russett, *Controlling the Sword: The Democratic Governance of National Security* (Cambridge: Harvard University Press, 1990); Richard Sobel, ed., *Public Opinion in U.S. Foreign Policy: The Controversy over Contra Aid* (Lanham, MD: Rowman & Littlefield, 1993).

60. Alan D. Monroe, "Consistency Between Public Preferences and National Policy Decisions," *American Politics Quarterly,* Vol. 7 (January 1979), pp. 3–19; Benjamin I. Page and Robert Y. Shapiro, "Effects of Public Opinion on Policy," *American Political Science Review,* Vol. 77 (March 1983), pp. 175–190.

61. Robert Dallek, *Franklin D. Roosevelt and American Foreign Policy, 1932–1945* (New York: Oxford University Press, 1979).

62. V. O. Key, Jr., *Public Opinion and American Democracy* (New York: Knopf, 1961), p. 552.

63. Stephen D. Krasner, *Defending the National Interest: Raw Materials Investments and U.S. Foreign Policy* (Princeton: Princeton University Press, 1978).

64. Thomas Ferguson, "From Normalcy to New Deal: Industrial Structure, Party Competition, and American Public Policy in the Great Depression," *International Organization,* Vol. 38 (1984), pp. 41–94.

65. Thomas Ferguson and Joel Rogers, *Right Turn: The Decline of the Democrats and the Future of American Politics* (New York: Farrar, Straus & Giroux, 1986); Thomas Ferguson, *Golden Rule* (Chicago: University of Chicago Press, 1995).

66. David N. Gibbs, *The Political Economy of Third World Intervention: Mines, Money, and U.S. Policy in the Congo Crisis* (Chicago: University of Chicago Press, 1991).

67. *Forbes* (July 17, 1995), pp. 274–275.

68. *World Almanac 1995* (Mahwah, NJ: Funk & Wagnalls, 1994), p. 159.

69. *New York Times* (April 24, 1991), pp. A1, C5.

70. Neil A. Lewis, "Ex-Naval Official Makes Guilty Plea in Bid-Rigging Case," *New York Times* (June 15, 1991), pp. A1, A18.

71. Edward Tivnan, *The Lobby* (New York: Simon & Schuster, 1987).

72. David Lake, *Power, Protection, and Free Trade* (Ithaca, NY: Cornell University Press, 1988).

73. Richard Stubbs and Geoffrey R. D. Undershill, eds., *Political Economy and the Changing Global Order* (New York: St. Martin's Press, 1994).

74. David A. Deese, ed., *The New Politics of American Foreign Policy* (New York: St. Martin's Press, 1994); Russett, *Controlling the Sword.*

CHAPTER 19

Economic Policy and the Budget

IN THIS CHAPTER

★ Why government is involved in the economy
★ What tools government uses to manage the economy
★ How interest groups, parties, social movements, and public opinion affect economic policy
★ What the federal government spends money on
★ How the federal tax system works
★ The deficit and the national debt
★ Government subsidies for business: what and why
★ Government regulation and deregulation

The Budget Train Wreck in the 104th Congress

House Republicans were feeling quite confident in Fall 1995. Under the leadership of Newt Gingrich, bolstered by the presence of 53 freshman conservatives, and emboldened by their success in passing virtually all of the provisions of their "Contract with America" (most of the provisions failed to become law because of opposition by the Senate and President Clinton, however), they were eager to take on the task of cutting the federal government down to what they considered its proper size and appropriate role. Some talked of rolling back Lyndon Johnson's Great Society programs; some dreamed aloud about undoing the New Deal. Their tool would be the federal budget. The budget revolutionaries, as they came to be called, were willing to go to the brink to force President Clinton to accept the heart of their conservative agenda, vowing to shut down the government if the president refused to sign on the dotted line.

The budget bill fashioned in the House of Representatives was unprecedented in several respects. Normally, budget bills simply decide what the overall level of government spending will be for a single year. The 1995 bill was far more ambitious. It not only aimed for a balanced budget over the course of seven years but also included many provisions about specific federal programs normally left to the congressional committees. These provisions included drastic cutbacks in the regulatory responsibilities of the federal government (especially in banking and securities, environmental protection, consumer protection, and workplace safety), a slowdown in Medicare funding, a tax cut (including a capital gains tax cut), and the transformation of welfare and Medicaid into block grants run by the states. Senate Republicans, not quite as single-minded as their House counterparts, forced some changes in the bill, including a smaller tax cut and less stringent cutbacks in environmental regulation. In the end, however, they went along with most of what the budget revolutionaries were trying to achieve.

Congressional leaders apparently believed that they could achieve their larger goals by forcing the president to sign a politically popular bill to balance the budget. Having seen Bill Clinton waiver and fold on important issues in the past, they were confident that the threat to close down the government in the absence of a budget—and the additional threat of forcing the government to default on its debts by not raising the debt ceiling—would be too much for the president to resist. Much to their surprise, Clinton refused to be intimidated, vetoing temporary budget measures (loaded with provisions unacceptable to Clinton) in November and the full budget bill in December. After each veto, the federal government shut down, with only "essential" services, such as national defense and air traffic control, permitted to operate under temporary funding measures.

For a week in November and three weeks in December and January, the government shutdown dominated the news. Stories of people turned away at passport and Social Security offices, national parks, and national museums filled the airwaves. News broadcasts showed government workers on picket lines asking to go back to work or with their families trying to cope without paychecks. Newscasts also reported air- and water-polluting activities going unregulated, meat inspections not being carried out, and the cleanup of toxic waste sites being suspended. Behind the scenes, members of Congress were hearing complaints from large government contractors about their inability to finish their work or to collect for work already completed. High-tech companies in Houston, for instance, were forced to lay off workers when the National Aeronautics and Space Administration (NASA) stopped operations at the Johnson Space Center. Exporting companies were stymied by the absence of federal inspectors to certify cargoes. By the end of December, the Veterans Administration had over 400,000 compensation claims awaiting action. The National Institutes of Health had stopped processing applications for biomedical research grants. Financial leaders were angry about the mere mention of the possibility of default for fear of sparking economic chaos.[1]

Republican leaders were unprepared for the firestorm of criticism. Much to their chagrin, they and not the president were taking most of the public blame. Almost desperate, congressional leaders announced in early January that a budget deal that would reopen the government was possible if the president would agree to a balanced budget in seven years using economic and budget assumptions supplied by the Congressional Budget Office. Clinton called their bluff, producing just such a balanced budget, but without the fundamental changes in the role of the federal government envisioned by the budget revolutionaries. Clinton claimed that he, too, favored a balanced budget but one that would not be damaging to the environment, education, or the elderly.

Congressional leaders, realizing that their most conservative members would never agree to the Clinton plan (because they wanted much more than a balanced budget), and sensing the rising public anger at the government shutdown, abandoned their effort to pass a radical budget bill. The House and the Senate voted, instead, for a resolution to reopen the government with slightly reduced budgets for most federal programs. Somewhat dispiritedly, House and Senate Republicans turned their attention to other legislative matters, many of them feeling that a historic opportunity had been lost.

Federal budget decisions are only one of many sources of direct and indirect federal government effects on the U.S economy and the well-being of U.S. citizens. In this chapter, we will see how economic and budget policies are made and how these policies affect us. We will focus our attention on the changing role of the federal government in economic affairs, the debate over the proper role of government in this domain, and the kinds of tools government uses to try to manage the economic health of the nation. We will look at some of the most pressing issues of contemporary American politics, including the deficit and the national debt, taxes, and regulation. Because of space limitations, the discussion of agricultural, trade, and labor policies will be limited, though much of what is covered is relevant to these policy areas as well. We will see not only how government policies affect the economy but also how the structure of the economy shapes what government does. We will also pay attention to how government economic policies reflect and influence the quality of democracy in the United States.

Why Government Is Involved in Economic Policymaking

Governments in all modern capitalist societies play a substantial role in managing their national economies. No government today would dare leave problems like stagnant economic growth, unemployment, international trade imbalances, or inflation to work themselves out "naturally." Citizens and leaders in the Western democracies have learned that free market economies, left to themselves, are subject to periodic bouts of **inflation** and unemployment, as well as occasional collapses of employment and economic output (called **depressions**). The trauma of the worldwide Great Depression in the 1930s was

inflation A period of generally rising prices.

depression A severe and persistent drop in economic activity.

the crucial event that etched this lesson into the minds of virtually everyone, and that forever changed the role of government in economic affairs.

The American public's inclination to use the federal government to manage the national economy has been enhanced by the relative success of this endeavor since the end of World War II. While many economic troubles are still with us, our government has proved surprisingly effective in easing the swings of the business cycle (see Figure 19.1) and stimulating economic growth. It has been less successful recently, however, in helping to ensure that economic growth is accompanied by growth in the number of good-paying and secure jobs.

The federal government must pay attention to economic policy, moreover, because its purchases of goods and services are so substantial (the federal government is the largest customer in the United States, the biggest borrower, and the biggest employer) that its actions inevitably have an impact on the economy. Given this presence, it would be difficult for government leaders to deny responsibility for what is happening in the national economy.[2]

Government responsibility for the state of the national economy is now so widely accepted that national elections are often decided by the voters' judgment of how well the party in power is carrying out this responsibility. When times are good, the party in power is very likely to be reelected; when times are bad, the party in power has an uphill battle staying in office. Most analysts believe that it was the very poor performance of the U.S. economy that cost George Bush the presidency in the 1992 election.

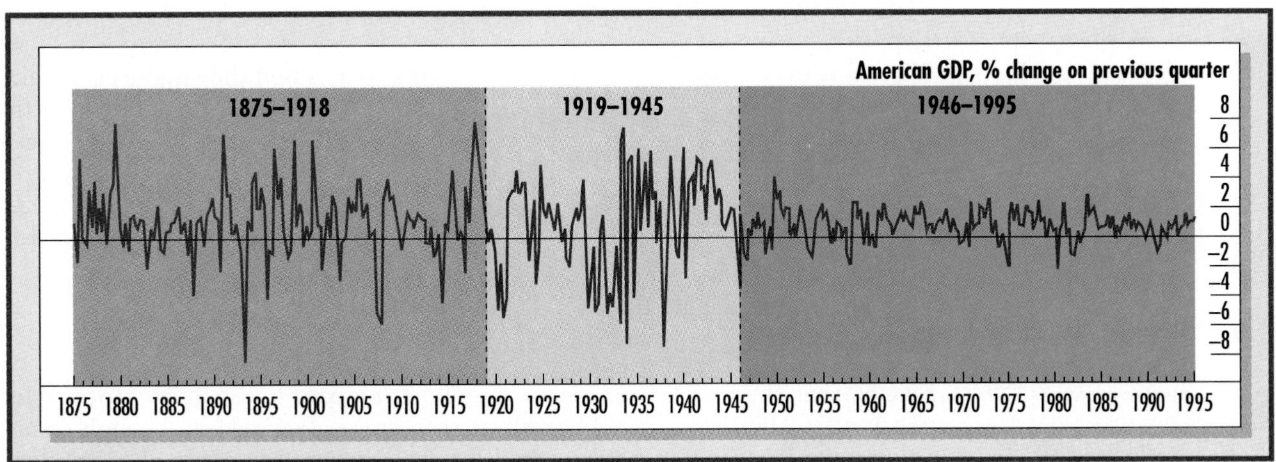

Figure 19.1 ■ **Gaining Control of the Business Cycle**

This graph shows changes in the American Gross Domestic Product (GDP) from the previous quarter. Several things are immediately apparent. First, there are frequent deep plunges in GDP—representing depressions—before the early 1940s, and there are none after that. Particularly noteworthy are the economic collapses in 1893, 1907, 1915, 1920, and 1921 and the Depression years of the 1930s; the postwar years have periods of economic slowdown, but not crises. Second, the earlier period is characterized by a wild roller-coaster, boom-and-bust pattern; this pattern disappears in the later period. Third, the earlier period shows as many "down" years as "up" years; after World War II, there are more up than down years. These suggest that government fiscal and monetary management of the economy, which began only after World War II, has had an important stabilizing effect on the U.S. economy.

Source: "Taking the Business Cycle's Pulse," *The Economist* (October 28, 1995), p. 89.

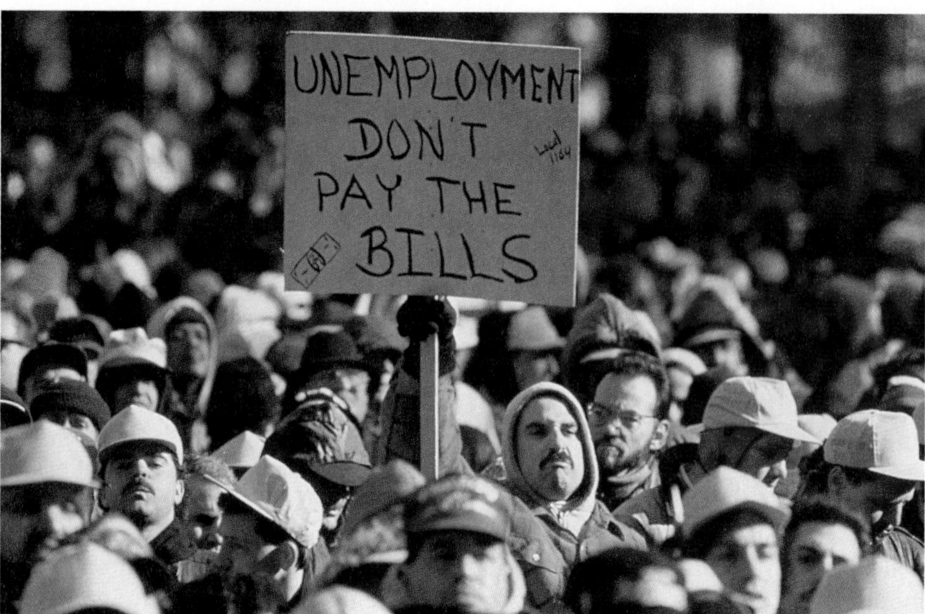

The government is regularly held accountable for economic hardships like inflation and unemployment. Here, demonstrators protest what they believed to be President George Bush's unwillingness to take strong fiscal measures to stimulate the economy. Many analysts believe that these economic difficulties cost Bush his reelection bid in 1992.

The Goals of Economic Policy

What is it that government officials are trying to do when they make economic policies? In this section, we review what political leaders have been trying to accomplish.[3] It will become evident that economic policy goals sometimes conflict and that important trade-offs are involved whenever economic policies are selected. We will see later in this chapter, moreover, that serious disagreements exist among political leaders, economic scholars, and the public about which policies are most likely to achieve the desired goals.

Economic Growth

gross domestic product (GDP) Same as the gross national product, except that income residents earn abroad is excluded.

Economic growth—defined here as an annual increase in the **gross domestic product (GDP)**—is the "holy grail" of economic policymakers. Though some environmental thinkers have argued for the long-term benefits of a smaller, less technologically driven economy, Americans generally want an economy where each year brings more jobs, more products, and higher incomes. Economic growth is also the basis for increased profits, so business tends to support this goal. For political leaders, economic growth, accompanied by rising standards of living, brings public popularity and heightened prospects for reelection, as well as more revenues for government programs. It is generally understood, finally, that economic growth is essential to the solution of many social problems, including poverty.

Increasingly in recent years, however, some delinking has occurred between economic growth and rising living standards in the United States. As we demonstrated in Chapter 4, GDP increased substantially during the 1990s, even while the living standards of a vast majority of American families stagnated.

Low Unemployment

Like most people everywhere, Americans want to be working. They want to use their talents in a job, gain a pay check, and be self-supporting. To a very great extent, all of this depends on a growing economy. Historically, economic growth has been associated with increases in the number of Americans working and a decline in the unemployment rate. Economic **recessions** bring slower job growth and rising unemployment rates. Depressions bring a collapse of the job market (during the Great Depression, the U.S. unemployment rate twice reached 33 percent) and potential and actual social and political instability. It is no wonder, then, that public officials try to keep unemployment levels from becoming too high.

recession A period of decline in overall economic activity.

A number of problems are associated with the low-unemployment goal, however. First, because low unemployment usually leads to rising wages and salaries (since labor is scarce under such conditions, it costs more), the profits of corporations and other businesses tend to suffer, all other things being equal. Second, because profit margins begin to suffer, policies designed to achieve low unemployment sometimes lead to inflation, putting political leaders in the position of having to choose between two undesirable outcomes. As a result, business leaders tend to pressure political leaders to change course when the unemployment rate threatens to fall too low.

Stable Prices

Most people want to avoid inflation, an increase in the cost of goods and services or, put another way, a decline in the buying power of money. With serious inflation, people's wages, salaries, savings accounts, and retirement pensions are worth less. So, too, are the holdings of banks and the value of their loans. Economists point out that inflation also brings uncertainty and irrational economic behavior as consumers and businesses try to shape their behavior to protect themselves from the effects of future price changes. To nobody's surprise, political leaders seek policies that dampen inflation and provide stable prices. Their problem is that such policies often require slower economic growth, with its lower wages and higher levels of unemployment (as we saw above). Setting economic policy is therefore a delicate balancing act.

A Positive Balance of Payments

The **balance of payments** is the difference between the value of a nation's imports and exports. All nations, including the United States, strive to keep the balance positive, that is, to export more than they import. They do so because sustained negative trade balances lead to a decline in the value of a nation's currency in international markets, as more money leaves the country than is brought in. In such a situation, businesses and consumers find that their dollars buy less, and they must either do without or borrow to make up the difference. The U.S. trade deficit has been in the red for many years now, despite several efforts by presidents and Congresses (see Chapter 18 for more details on U.S. trade policy).

balance of payments The annual difference between payments and receipts between a country and its trading partners.

Minimizing "Diseconomies"

A growing free enterprise economy always produces, in addition to rising living standards, a range of adverse consequences, such as air and water pollution, toxic wastes, and workplace injuries and health hazards. These adverse

Before government regulation, industries were allowed to dump hazardous wastes into the environment without threat of financial or legal repercussions.

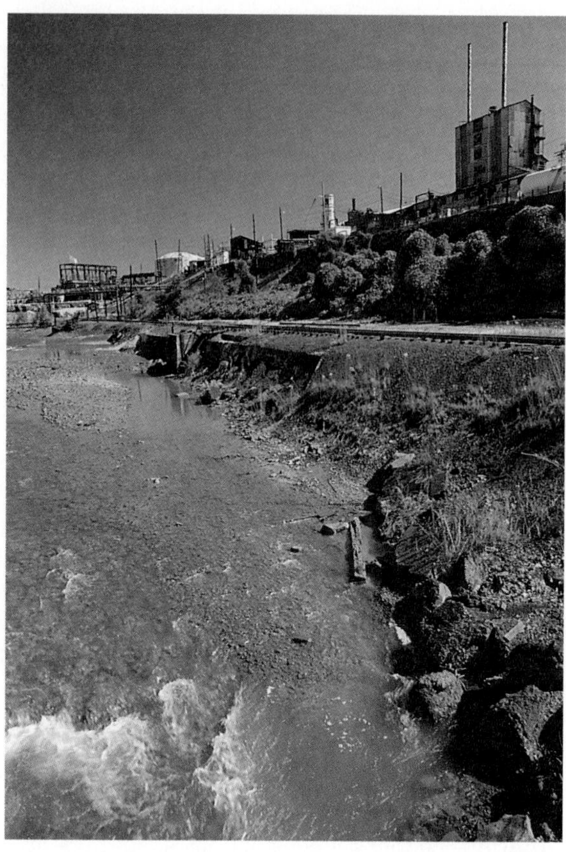

diseconomies The positive and negative effects of economic activities on third parties.

side effects of economic activity—called **diseconomies**—have generated enormous public pressure for compensatory government action. Much of the regulatory activity of the federal government is designed to decrease the incidence of diseconomies. The problem is that too much regulation of corporations may adversely affect other prized economic policy goals, such as economic growth and low unemployment.

Supporting Key Economic Sectors

Certain economic activities are important for the general health of the national economy; yet they are unlikely to be provided by private firms. Almost without exception, governments in the Western democracies, including the United States, have stepped into the breach and provided support for such vital activities and services, either by direct subsidy and tax incentives or by public ownership (though not in the United States). In an effort to win back commercial aviation business from Boeing, for instance, several European countries created a consortium that finances Airbus Ltd. All European countries and the United States, moreover, subsidize farmers. The federal government tries to encourage business activity in America's inner cities by using enterprise-zone tax incentives, supports the defense industry by direct purchases of weapons systems and subsidization of research, and pays for essential infrastructure such as airports, harbors, and highways.

The federal government often pays for essential infrastructure such as airports and highways. Here, construction moves forward on the Denver International Airport.

The Tools of Macroeconomic Policy

Government actions affect (but don't, by themselves, determine) the rate of inflation, the level of unemployment, and the growth of income and output in the national economy. This always has been so. What is new since World War II is that government leaders, economists, and citizens know this to be true and insist that government use whatever means it has available to ensure good economic outcomes.

Government efforts to encourage economic growth, low unemployment, and stable prices fall under the heading of **macroeconomic** policy. The term *macroeconomic* refers to the fact that the object of the attention of policymakers is the performance of the economy as a whole. The main tools of macroeconomic policy are **fiscal policies** (having to do with government spending and taxes) and **monetary policies** (having to do with the supply and cost of money). What government leaders try to do when fashioning macroeconomic policy is to adjust the money supply, government spending, and taxes in such a way that **aggregate demand**—the total of what is spent by government, consumers, and business—is consistent with the full use of the productive capacity of the economy.[4] Government can alter aggregate demand by raising or lowering its own spending, by leaving more or less money in the pockets of individuals and companies by raising or lowering taxes, and by adjusting interest rates so that money is easier or more difficult to get.

macroeconomic Having to do with the performance of the economy as a whole.

fiscal policies The government's overall policies on spending and taxing levels; affect overall output and income in the economy.

monetary policies Government policies designed to affect the supply of money and the level of interest rates in the economy.

aggregate demand The total of purchases of a country's output by consumers, government, businesses, and foreigners.

Fiscal Policy

In theory, fiscal policy is a flexible tool for stimulating the economy when there is high unemployment and low use of productive capacity, and for slowing the economy down when things are getting too hot. Government leaders can increase government spending and/or decrease taxes when economic stimulation is required; they can cut spending and/or increase taxes when the economy needs a cooling-off period.

Fiscal tools are not easy to use, however. Decisions about how much government should spend or what level and kinds of taxes ought to be levied are not made simply on the basis of their potential effects on economic stability and growth. Many other issues come into play.

Federal spending, for instance, cannot be easily adjusted up or down as economic conditions change. Farmers want federal crop subsidies to continue, regardless of macroeconomic effects. The elderly want Social Security and Medicare benefits to keep pace with inflation. Nor is it easy to adjust tax rates in response to changing economic conditions, because both total tax levels and the distribution of the tax burden (that is, who pays) are among the most contentious issues in American politics, with many interests involved. As a result, tax policy cannot be changed annually, whatever may be the fiscal policy needs.

Moreover, changes in spending and taxing take so long to bring about that they may very well be inappropriate by the time they filter into the economy. A tax cut meant to stimulate a sluggish economy, for instance, may kick in just as the economy is entering a period of inflation.

Monetary Policy

Fiscal policy is made by the president and Congress when they determine the annual federal government budget. The Federal Reserve Board (commonly known as the Fed) is responsible for monetary policy, that is, those decisions which affect how much money is available to businesses and individuals from banks, savings and loans, and credit unions. The more money that is available and the lower the interest rates at which money can be borrowed, the higher overall consumer and business spending are likely to be. If the Fed wants to increase aggregate demand in the economy, it increases the money supply and lowers interest rates. If it wants to slow the economy down, it decreases the money supply and increases interest rates.

The Fed controls the money supply in three ways. First, its "open-market" committee buys federal government securities from private brokers or dealers or sells government securities to them. When it buys, it injects money into the economy; when it sells, it in effect takes money from financial institutions and lowers the amount of money in private circulation. This kind of buying and selling is the Fed's most commonly used approach. Second, the Fed can make it easier or more difficult for banks who are members of the Federal Reserve to borrow from the Reserve to cover their short-term deficits by changing the **discount rate** (the interest rate that it charges member banks). If the discount rate is high, the member banks must pay more to borrow, and the amount of money in circulation increases; if the rate is low, the member banks must pay less, and the amount of money in circulation increases. Third, the Fed can change the rule on how much banks must have on hand to cover outstanding loans (called **reserve requirements**). If the Fed buys government securities, lowers the discount rate, and lowers the reserve requirement, inter-

discount rate The interest rate charged to member banks by the Federal Reserve to cover short-term loans.

reserve requirements The proportion of its total deposits that a bank must keep in reserve.

est rates in the economy will decline because money is plentiful. Interest rates will rise if the Fed moves in the other direction in these three areas.

Political leaders and economists now believe that effective macroeconomic policy requires that attention be given to both fiscal and monetary tools, and that they be used in ways that do not work at cross-purposes.[5] It would not do, for instance, to have fiscal policy encouraging economic expansion and monetary policy choking it off.

Other Economic Policy Tools

Fiscal and monetary policies are the main instruments by which government leaders try to manage economic growth, to ensure rising living standards and to manage price levels. We learned earlier, however, that other important economic policy goals exist, including supporting particular industries, minimizing diseconomies, and managing the balance of trade. We will see later in this chapter how government leaders attempt to achieve these goals.

The Debate About the Proper Role of Government in the Economy

People may agree that government must play an important role in managing the economy, but they disagree about how it should be done. Debate revolves around four main alternatives: Keynesianism, monetarism, supply side economic policy, and industrial policy.

Keynesianism

In his classic work, *The General Theory of Employment, Interest, and Money,* English economist John Maynard Keynes showed that capitalist economies do not consistently operate at a level that fully employs a nation's workers or keeps its factories and businesses operating at full capacity. The reason is that aggregate demand is rarely high enough. The solution, he suggested, is for government to fill the gap during slack times by increasing its own spending or cutting taxes so that businesses and consumers may increase theirs. When demand is too high and triggers inflation (too many dollars chasing few goods), the Keynesian formula is for government to cut spending or increase taxes.

The Keynesian approach dominated economic policy in the United States and Western Europe for three decades following World War II.[6] The Kennedy tax cut of 1964 (passed after his assassination) was sold to the public, Congress, and the business community by Presidents Kennedy and Johnson in explicitly Keynesian terms.[7] Even Republican president Richard Nixon joined the bandwagon, proclaiming in a *Newsweek* cover story in 1971 that "we are all Keynesians now." Economic growth during the Reagan years in the 1980s was fueled by substantial government deficits in the Keynesian mode.

Keynesianism is consistent with an activist government role. Since the economy is almost always operating at less than full capacity, it justifies expansive government programs. Keynes offered no advice on which programs to expand; his theory is indifferent to what government spends its money on. His theory requires only that government fill the demand gap. From the end of World War II to the end of the 1980s, Keynesian expansions in the United States were fueled mostly by defense spending. What Keynes failed to

The economic theory of English economist John Maynard Keynes dominated American economic policy for three decades following World War II. Keynesian theory dictates that governments design spending and tax policies to stimulate the economy when demand is too low and slow the economy when demand is too high.

appreciate, however, was the political difficulty of slashing government spending once groups in the population, ranging from military contractors to farmers, came to look at federal money as their right, even when people agreed that government spending needed to be cut. There is a tendency for what some have called *one-eyed Keynesianism* to hold sway, that is, heeding only those parts of the Keynesian doctrine that call for deficits in bad economic times to stimulate the economy, and ignoring advice about running budget surpluses in good economic times.[8] The resistance to military base closings and cutbacks in defense contracts at the end of the Cold War is an example of this tendency.

Monetarism

Monetarists like economist Milton Friedman argue that the key to a healthy economy is the proper management of the supply of money and credit by central banks (the Federal Reserve Board in the United States). Monetarists believe that the main objective of a central bank should be setting and enforcing long-range targets for a growth in the money supply that matches the rate of growth in productivity. Such a policy, monetarists claim, encourages steady growth and price stability.

Monetarists claim that their approach is more consistent with American values than is Keynesianism, because it does not depend on an expansive government. Government need only set and enforce money targets so that individuals and businesses can operate in a stable economic environment that permits long-range planning and investment, leaving the free market to do the rest. Balanced federal budgets are an essential ingredient of the monetarist position. Unbalanced budgets, in their view, not only shift scarce resources from productive to unproductive activities (such as paying interest on government debt) but make it difficult for central banks to properly control the money supply.

Keynesianism, they suggest, is the economic philosophy of big government; monetarism is the economic philosophy of small government. It is hardly surprising, then, that monetarism is the approach favored by many conservatives and was an important feature of economic policy during the Reagan and Bush years.[9]

Supply Side Economic Policy

According to supply side theory, government should help increase the supply of goods and services in the economy by removing barriers to individual investment and entrepreneurship.[10] In particular, supply-siders advocate substantial reductions in taxes, welfare, and Social Security and the removal of all but the most essential regulations on business. While tax cuts may temporarily unbalance the budget, government revenues are supposed to increase in the long run because of economic growth, this increase bringing the budget into balance.

Supply side thinking strongly influenced the Reagan administration's economic policy. Most important were the Kemp-Roth tax cuts of 1981, cuts in government programs for the poor, and deregulation. The problems in the economy at the end of the Reagan years, especially the massive budget deficit and the deterioration of the U.S. position in the international economy, have dramatically reduced the appeal of the supply side approach among economists, political leaders, and the public. However, supply side proposals came to public attention again during the 1996 presidential race when Bob Dole added Jack Kemp to his ticket and incorporated some of Kemp's economic ideas into his campaign.

Industrial Policy

Industrial policy advocates argue that broad macroeconomic fiscal and monetary policies are too blunt to help the United States remain competitive in international markets.[11] What is needed, they say, is national strategic planning that follows the Japanese and European models. Strategic planning should guide investment to high-technology sectors (microchips, for example) and away from outmoded industries, should remedy the painful social dislocations of a reoriented economy, and should encourage a vigorous American export trade, using instruments such as the Japanese government's Ministry of International Trade and Industry (MITI). Advocates point to the success of MITI in planning the steel, automobile, and electronics surge in Japan and to its present efforts to help the microchip, supercomputer, and biotechnology industries. The Clinton administration has included several prominent advocates for such policies, for example, Labor Secretary Robert Reich. Industrial policy has made little headway in the United States because of traditional American concerns about big government.

Making Economic Policy: Factors and Players

Why do we have the kinds of economic policies that we do? In this section, we examine the many influences that shape American economic policy.

Structural Factors

The shape, operation, and health of the national *economy* is the obvious starting point for understanding the economic policies of the federal government.

Strategic planning by Japan's Ministry of International Trade and Industry has powered the surge in Japanese exports over the past few decades. Traditional concerns about big government have prevented the United States from using such strategic economic planning on a national level; the result is a huge trade deficit, as we continue to import more goods than we export.

Economic policy is a product, first of all, of the stage of development of a free enterprise economy. A simple market economy, like the one in existence at the founding of the United States, requires little government coordination. An industrial, corporate, and transnational economy like the one America has today, most believe, cannot be left strictly to its own devices. The swings of the business cycle in such an economy, for instance, are broad and deeply felt, and the failure of a firm or a set of firms (such as the savings-and-loans institutions) affects a broad range of businesses, investors, lenders, and consumers.

Economic policy is also affected by the health of the economy at any particular time. During periods of prosperity, when growth is happily joined to low rates of inflation, opinion generally favors loosening the grip of the government on the economy and allowing market forces to take over. The "go-go 1920s" are a good example of such a time. When things turn sour, however, as they did during the Great Depression of the 1930s, pressure mounts from all quarters for the government to take decisive action.

incomes policy The government regulation of wages and salaries used to control inflation.

Economic policy is also shaped by the *political culture* of the United States. Though Americans have gradually come to believe that the government has an important role to play in the management of the economy, we are still very much taken with the free market ideal and remain uneasy about the idea of an activist government. This is one reason why we have so little government ownership of our basic economic infrastructure (transportation, power, banking, and communications, in particular) compared to other countries and only rarely resort to planning and **incomes policies** (government control of wages and prices), which have been commonly used in Europe in years past.

The *constitutional rules* also matter. Economic policy, like most other policies in the United States, tends to be fairly incoherent, contradictory, and inconsistent when compared to that of other capitalist nations, primarily because of our checks and balances, separation of powers, and federalism. As the budget impasse in late 1995 and early 1996 between President Clinton and the Republican 104th Congress shows, America's constitutional design sometimes makes it extremely difficult to make economic policy at all.

Political Linkage Factors

Interest groups, particularly those representing business, take a keen interest in economic policy, and their permanent representatives in Washington, D.C., are a constant presence in the halls of Congress and at regulatory agencies. While business tends to speak with a single voice on such issues as deregulation and balanced budgets, it is not always united on what kind of overall economic policy it wants from the government. Tight money policies, with their associated high interest rates, for instance, are attractive to financial institutions but very unattractive to manufacturing firms, which often must borrow to modernize and expand their operations. Nor do business interests have the field to themselves; labor, consumer, and public interest groups are also important players in the economic policy game.

Business interest groups are attentive especially to the regulatory activities of the federal government. Changes in the regulatory climate—new laws or new interpretations of existing laws—may have profound effects on the viability and profitability of business enterprises, so their lobbyists stay in touch with executive and congressional actors. All major telecommunications companies were fully represented, for instance, when the 104th Congress considered the 1996 Telecommunications Act.

Voters and *public opinion* are also important. The public is attuned to overall economic conditions and generally pays attention to what its elected leaders are doing to curb inflation and unemployment and to stimulate growth. We saw in Chapter 9 that the general state of the economy is one of the most important factors in the outcome of national elections. Knowing this, elected leaders do what they can to ensure steady economic growth with low inflation and to prevent economic downturns at election time. Some social scientists believe that there is a **political business cycle,** in which elected leaders stimulate economic growth before elections and postpone economic pain (taxes, for instance) until after elections.[12] Frequently cited examples are the Johnson and Reagan economic stimulation before the 1964 and 1984 presidential elections and Nixon's wage and price freeze (to dampen inflation) imposed in time for the 1972 election. Recent research, however, suggests that the political business cycle may not be as common as these examples suggest.[13]

political business cycle The practice in which elected officials intentionally stimulate growth before elections and postpone economic pain until after elections.

Political parties also play a role in economic policymaking. Because each has its own electoral and financial constituency, made up of groups with identifiable economic interests, the two parties tend to support different economic policies. The Democratic party has traditionally been supported by labor unions, racial minorities, and lower-income Americans and tends to favor these groups in the course of governing. The Republican party has always attracted the support of business and upper-income Americans and tries to look out for its core constituency. Democrats talk more about "fairness" when they are making economic policy; Republicans talk more about financial stability, economic efficiency, and government waste. Over many decades, Democrats in office have tended to favor economic policies that decrease unemployment and disparities in income and to worry less about inflation, whereas Republicans

Under the full glare of television lights, Budget Director Alice Rivlin watches a Government Printing Office employee pack copies of President Clinton's 1997 Budget Report for delivery to Congress.

have tended to favor policies that control inflation, despite the resulting higher unemployment and greater inequality. The policies matter. Inequality decreases slightly when Democrats control the presidency and increases slightly when Republicans control it.[14]

Governmental Factors

The President When things go wrong in the economy, it is the president to whom we usually turn for action. This role is recognized formally in the Employment Act of 1946, which requires that the president report on the state of the economy and recommend action to ensure full employment and economic stability. At the center of every modern president's legislative program are proposals for spending, taxing, and regulation that usually have broad macroeconomic effects. The president is advised on economic matters by the Council of Economic Advisors, the director of the Office of Management and Budget (OMB), and the secretary of the treasury.

Bill Clinton came to office with aspirations for an activist government role in stimulating economic growth and reinvigorating American competitiveness in the international economy. Most of his efforts, however, ran into difficulties in Congress, a demonstration that Congress is a full partner in economic policymaking. Presidents must always attend to their relations with Congress, therefore, if they are to be successful on the economic policy front.

They must also be skillful at affecting the behavior of the Federal Reserve Board if they want the Fed to regulate the money supply and interest rates in a way that is consistent with the presidential program. This isn't always easy, for after the president nominates someone for the Fed's board of governors, he has virtually no control over that person.

Congress Nearly everything that Congress does has macroeconomic consequences, especially its decisions about the annual federal budget. The decisions it makes about the overall balance of government spending and taxes are, as we have seen, a powerful fiscal instrument, either stimulating or retarding the economy. Taxes levied by Congress shape the incentives for individual and company economic decision making: laws that regulate, grant subsidies, or supply loan guarantees influence private-sector economic behavior, and Trade bills and treaties affect the fortunes of American consumers and many companies. Congress is helped in its economic policymaking by the research activities and reports of the Congressional Budget Office (CBO).

Congress also plays a powerful economic oversight role. The heads of independent regulatory agencies and federal departments, as well as the chair of the Federal Reserve Board, frequently testify before congressional committees, in which the legislative point of view and the concerns of constituents are conveyed to those who fashion economic policies in the executive branch.

The Federal Reserve Board The Federal Reserve Board makes monetary policy for the nation. Its original role, back in 1913, when it was created, was to provide funds for member banks that found themselves short of cash with which to pay panicky depositors. In the mid–1950s, however, the Fed also took on broad macroeconomic responsibilities in an effort to control interest rates and the money supply. By doing so, it began to act like central banks in other modern capitalist democracies.[15] Representative Henry Gonzalez (Democrat of Texas) believes that the Fed is too secretive, too responsive to the interests of the nation's big banks, and unduly enamored of restricting economic growth as a way to fight inflation. In taking on the Fed in a series of hearings before his House Banking Committee in 1993 to publicize his concerns, he was carrying on the work of former Texas populist Wright Patman (see the Struggle for Democracy box).

The Federal Reserve Board is made up of seven members (called governors) and a chair, who serve overlapping and very long (14-year) terms. Each is appointed by the president. The Fed is closely connected with, and very solicitous of, the needs of commercial and investment bankers and generally prefers to control inflation as a first order of business in order to protect the value of financial assets.

The Fed sometimes takes very harsh action to control inflation. It is generally credited with bringing on the 1957 and 1981 recessions by severely contracting the nation's money supply. Under the leadership of Allen Greenspan, the Fed has maintained tight money policies during the 1990s and kept inflation in check. Many political leaders, including President Clinton, believe that the hand of the Fed has been too heavy under Greenspan, dampening economic growth.

The Fed is relatively independent. It was designed this way to insulate the central bank from direct political influence. Though presidents and Congress sometimes try to apply pressure by threatening to change the Fed's powers and organization, they have never actually done so. Punitive actions would surely trigger adverse reactions on Wall Street and in the financial community in general—reactions that neither presidents nor Congress are eager to contend with.

Our System Compared

Our system of separation of powers and checks and balances allows many groups, institutions, and political actors to be involved in economic policymaking. Policy decisions are the outcome of conflicts and bargaining among the president, the Fed, the OMB, the Treasury Department, regulatory agencies,

Two Texas Populists Try to Democratize the Fed

The Struggle for Democracy

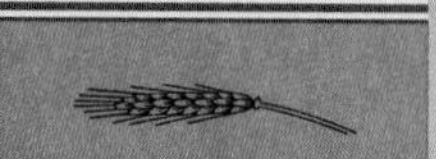

"A slight acquaintance with American constitutional theory and practice demonstrates that, constitutionally, the Federal Reserve is a pretty queer duck." So said Texas populist Wright Patman, a lifelong opponent of the Fed, on the floor of the House of Representatives in 1962. "The Fed," he once concluded, "is a dictatorship on money matters by a bankers' club."

Patman was not entirely off base. The Federal Reserve Board is a strikingly undemocratic institution. Like the Supreme Court, it makes enormously consequential decisions, but its members are not elected by the people. Like the Supreme Court, moreover, it must take account, in the long run, of the wishes of the president and Congress, but not too slavishly. It has substantial room for the exercise of independent judgment. It meets in secret and is not obligated to give reasons for its actions; unlike those of the Supreme Court, its decisions are not accompanied by opinions. The Fed is under less democratic control, in fact, than the central bank in Great Britain, France, Italy, Japan, and other such countries, where bank policies must be approved by elected officials.

This arrangement never seemed right to Patman, and he spent his career trying to rein in the Fed. Patman's most important achievements were the hearings he chaired in 1964 as head of the House Banking Committee. The hearings placed the Fed under more scrutiny than it had ever before experienced and forced some changes in Federal Reserve practices.

Patman's efforts have been carried on in recent years by another Texas representative in the populist mold, Henry Gonzalez. His campaign in 1993 to open up Fed proceedings to public scrutiny is described in the following portrait:

> Often colorful and always outspoken, House Banking Committee Chairman Henry Gonzalez from Texas loves a good fight, and that's what he faces with his plan to reform the way the Fed works.
>
> . . .
>
> Gonzalez . . . has been a burr under the Federal Reserve's saddle since taking over the reins of the House Banking Committee in 1989. As chairman of one of the most powerful committees on Capitol Hill, and a Democrat who bided his time during 12 years of Republicans in the White House, Gonzalez has used the opportunity of Bill Clinton's 1992 Presidential victory to wage war on the Fed and how it conducts monetary policy.
>
> In February, his perseverance yielded an unprecedented concession from the Fed—a public pronouncement of its intent to shift to a restrictive monetary policy. This, on the heels of a Fed agreement in 1993 for the more immediate release of monetary policy proceedings. . . . Others in the Congress share Gonzalez's goal of greater Fed transparency and have bills of their own, but none can match his passion or tenacity.
>
> "He is relentless, and I think that was totally underestimated," Gerald O'Driscoll, a senior fellow with the Cato Institute, says of Gonzalez. O'Driscoll, who until May 1 served as a vice president and senior economic advisor at the Federal Reserve Bank of Dallas, confirms the Fed's unprecedented openness in 1994 regarding monetary policy operations is a direct result of Gonzalez's tireless campaign.

Though his Federal Reserve System Accountability Act failed to win approval in the 103rd Congress, Gonzalez's crusade for greater democratic control of the Fed bore some fruit.

Source: William Greider, *Secrets of the Temple* (New York: Simon & Schuster, 1987), pp. 48–51; Susan Stawick, "Regarding Henry," *Futures* (July 1994), pp. 8–9.

and Congress (especially the budget and tax-writing committees). In Great Britain, in contrast, economic policymaking is centered in the Treasury under the leadership of the chancellor of the exchequer, who works closely with the prime minister. The prime minister's control over Parliament, in turn, allows the government to implement its economic policies in a reasonably rapid and straightforward fashion. Because of this system, former prime minister

Margaret Thatcher was able to make her monetarist views the basis of British economic policy during most of the 1980s without much parliamentary opposition. By the same token, her successor, John Major, was able to abandon that policy without a big fight in the House of Commons.

Values and Economic Policy

Debates about economic policy are spirited because the stakes are so high in terms of our personal beliefs and values. Decisions about spending, taxing, and regulation affect not only the lives and well-being of all Americans, for instance, but also our deepest beliefs about the kind of government we want to have and the kind of society we want to live in. Often, no consensus exists among us about these fundamental questions.

Take debates about government spending. They inescapably involve conceptions about the proper role of the federal government. Many who oppose specific spending programs often do so because of their broader concerns about the problem of big government. For many conservatives, increased government spending is, by its very nature, a threat to liberty and economic efficiency.[16]

Debates about taxes concern not only the size of government, but also the question of who will bear the tax burden and, ultimately, how much inequality we are willing to tolerate. **Progressive taxes** require that the most well-off pay the highest percentages of their incomes in taxes, the result being, all other things being equal, a downward redistribution of income. **Flat taxes** levy the same percentage rate on all income earners and leave income distribution untouched. **Regressive taxes** impose a heavier relative burden on the lowest-income earners and cause an upward redistribution of income, increasing the level of inequality in society.

progressive taxes Taxes that take a larger percentage of the income of those at the upper end of the income scale rather than those at the bottom.

flat taxes Taxes that take the same percentage of the income of all persons.

regressive taxes Taxes that take a larger percentage of the income of those at the bottom of the income scale rather than of those at top.

Regulatory policies reflect not only technical and scientific issues but also our confidence in the ability of private markets to solve their own problems. To regulate is to admit that the market is imperfect and requires remedial action by government. That is why those who believe that market economies work best when they are left alone are so vehemently opposed to government regulation.

The Federal Budget and Fiscal Policy

The size and shape of the federal budget, as well as the issue of mounting deficits in the budget, are among the most pressing political issues before the American people. In this section, we examine the elements of the federal budget, some of the implications of the spending and taxing choices our elected officials have made, and the debate over the deficit and balanced budgets.

Government Spending

The federal government spent a little more than $1.6 trillion in 1996. This amount represents a fourfold increase since 1960 (in constant dollars) and an expansion of federal outlays as a proportion of GDP from about 18 percent to about 22 percent. (The high-water mark for the post–World War II years was 24.4 percent in 1983). Figure 19.2 shows the change over time in federal outlays as a percentage of GDP. Several things are immediately apparent.

First, the most dramatic increases in federal government spending are associated with involvement in major wars; note the big spikes in the graph for the years associated with World War I, World War II, and the Korean War.

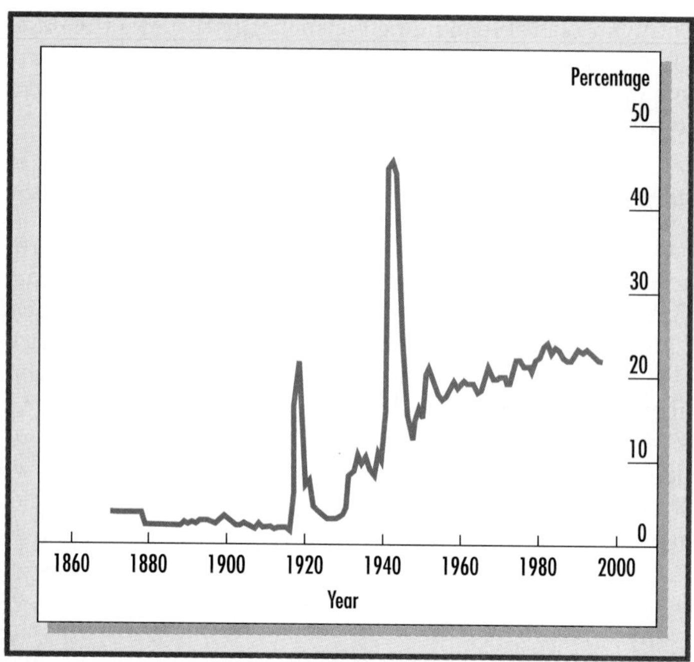

Figure 19.2 ▪ Federal Government Spending as a Percentage of GDP, 1869–1996

This graph shows the scale of federal government spending relative to the size of the American economy. We see that the increase in the relative size of the federal government is a twentieth-century phenomenon. We also see that involvement in major wars has been an important factor in the growth in federal spending, with the major spikes coming during World Wars I and II. The permanent change in the role of the federal government in American society is also seen in the steady rise in spending triggered by the Great Depression during the 1930s. Also noteworthy is the recent leveling off of federal spending as a proportion of U.S. economic activity.

Source: 1869–1993, U.S. Census Bureau, *Historical Statistics of the United States* (Washington, DC: U.S. Government Printing Office, 1975), pp. 224, 1, 114; 1934–1991, Office of Management and Budget, *Budget Baselines, Historical Data, and Alternatives for the Future* (Washington, DC: U.S. Government Printing Office, 1993), pp. 280–281; 1992–1998, Office of Management and Budget, *Budget of the U.S. Government, Fiscal Year 1994* (Washington, DC: U.S. Government Printing Office, 1993), pp. 6, A–6 and from Harold W. Stanley and Richard G. Niemi, *Vital Statistics on American Politics* (Washington, DC: Congressional Quarterly Press, 1994), p. 424.

These increases are to be expected; modern wars mobilize society and governments and are costly in human and financial terms. Second, the relative spending level of the federal government increased steadily from the early 1930s to the early 1980s. This increase bespeaks a gradual yet persistent transformation of the role of the federal government in American society. Third, and finally, from the early 1980s to the present, the relative size of federal spending first leveled off and then declined. This decrease in spending reflects the conservative presidencies of Ronald Reagan and George Bush and the effects of Bill Clinton's first two budgets, along with the slowdown in federal spending forced by the Republican-dominated 104th Congress.

It may surprise many to learn that government spending relative to the overall wealth of the United States has been stable or declining at the very same time that the rhetoric of antigovernment spending has reached fever pitch in American politics. Federal government spending relative to GDP is likely to decline even further, given the public mood. Figure 19.3 shows that a majority of Americans seems to want a smaller, less expensive government.

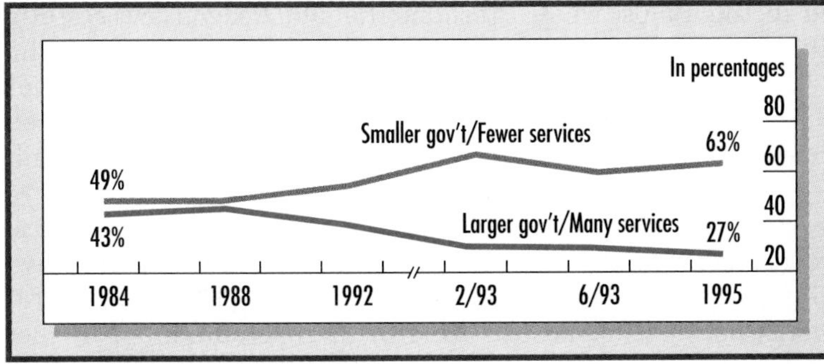

Figure 19.3 ▪ **What Kind of Government Do the American People Want?**

Since the mid–1980s, there has been a growing mood among the American people in favor of less government. When asked about their support for particular programs, however, Americans show little inclination to make substantial cuts.

Sources: 1984, 1988, 1992, and February 1993 surveys by ABC News/*Washington Post;* June 1993 and January 1995 surveys by the *Los Angeles Times.*

What Do We Spend Money On? Figure 19.4 shows how tax revenue is divided among major functions and how federal government commitments have changed since the last year of the Carter administration in 1980. A little more than 16 percent of federal government expenditures is for *national defense.* Defense spending is actually somewhat higher than this, because national defense-related expenditures are scattered throughout the budgets of other government agencies. Two-thirds of the budget of the Department of Energy, for instance, is for nuclear weapons development. However measured, U.S. expenditures for national defense are substantial and much higher than those of other rich democracies. By the same token, our spending is much lower than it was in 1980, when it officially accounted for almost 23 percent of federal spending (in 1960 it accounted for over one-half of all federal government spending!). This steady downward trend in national defense outlays was tem-

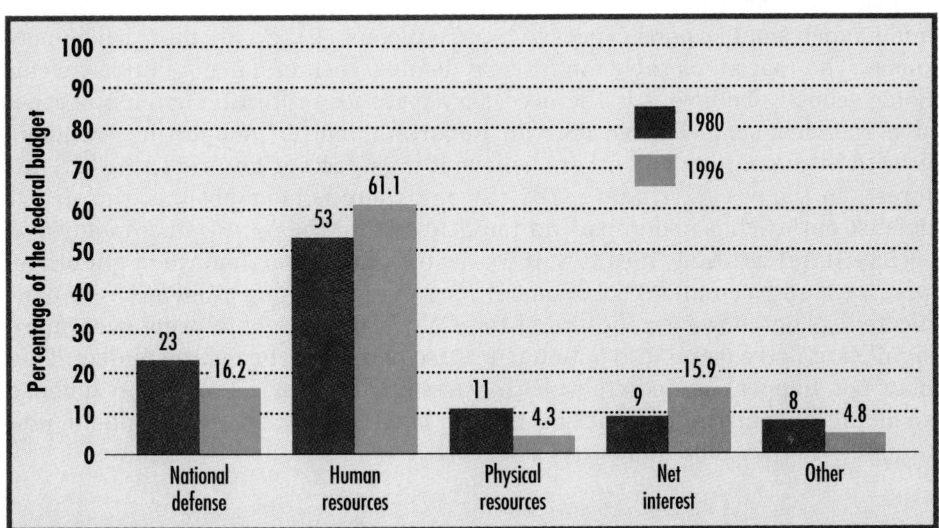

Figure 19.4 ▪ **Major Categories of Federal Government Spending, 1980 and 1996**

Over the past two-and-a-half decades, how the federal government spending pie is divided up has changed substantially. Most notable is the shift from national defense spending to human resources spending, mainly for Social Security, Medicare, and Medicaid.

Source: *The budget of the United States, Fiscal 1996* (Washington, DC: U.S. Government Printing Office).

porarily reversed in the 1980s, when President Ronald Reagan successfully pushed for a military buildup, but it resumed its downward course with the end of the Cold War during the early 1990s. With the collapse of the Soviet Union, and the resulting decrease in direct military danger to the United States, there is reason to believe that spending for national defense will shrink even more.

Outlays as a proportion of total federal expenditures for *human resources,* including welfare, health, veterans' benefits, and education and training, have grown considerably since 1980 and now account for over 60 percent of federal spending. It is worth noting that most of the growth is accounted for by just two programs, each of which has a predominantly middle-class constituency: Social Security and Medicare. As we shall see in Chapter 20, federal spending on many other social programs, particularly those that benefit the poor, has actually declined since 1980. Outlays for *physical resources,* including transportation, energy, and the environment, account for about 4.3 percent of federal dollars, a drastic drop from 1980. *Other federal nondefense outlays,* which support programs ranging from housing to agriculture, national parks, science and technology, international affairs, and the administration of justice, now attract less than 5 cents of every federal dollar spent. A significant development is the increase in the level of payments to cover interest on the national debt. In 1996, it accounted for 15.9 percent of federal expenditures, an increase of 77 percent since 1980. We will have more to say about the national debt later.

How Do We Compare with Other Nations? It is sometimes said that government spending in America is "out of control." Your opinion about this matter is related to your own values, of course; any level of spending for programs that you don't like would be considered "too much." But the data show that, compared to the other modern nations, the United States ranks *very low* on total government spending relative to GDP (see Figure 19.5).

The *pattern* of expenditures is also of considerable interest. A much larger proportion of government outlays in the United States goes to national defense and a much smaller portion goes to human resources than in other rich democracies. The reason for this emphasis on defense spending is not entirely clear. Some scholars believe it is the necessary price for protection against aggressive enemies; some believe it is an important tool for supporting economic growth in the nation; and others believe it is important for protecting U.S. interests in the world. Whatever the reasons, there is no doubt that the size of defense outlays has had important implications for the American economy and society. It has certainly meant that we have higher taxes than we might otherwise have and a smaller pool of money for solving pressing problems. As we indicated earlier, however, the end of the Cold War is likely to bring even more significant decreases in the national defense portion of the federal budget. This may not happen immediately: both parties called for increases in defense spending during the contentious budget battles between the president and Congress in late 1995 and early 1996.

Taxes

Nothing raises the dander of Americans more than taxes. One of the fateful steps leading to the revolutionary break with England was, of course, the Boston Tea Party, protesting what many New Englanders believed to be an unjust tax on their favorite beverage. Shays's Rebellion (Chapter 2) over the seizure of farms for the nonpayment of taxes helped call into being the Consti-

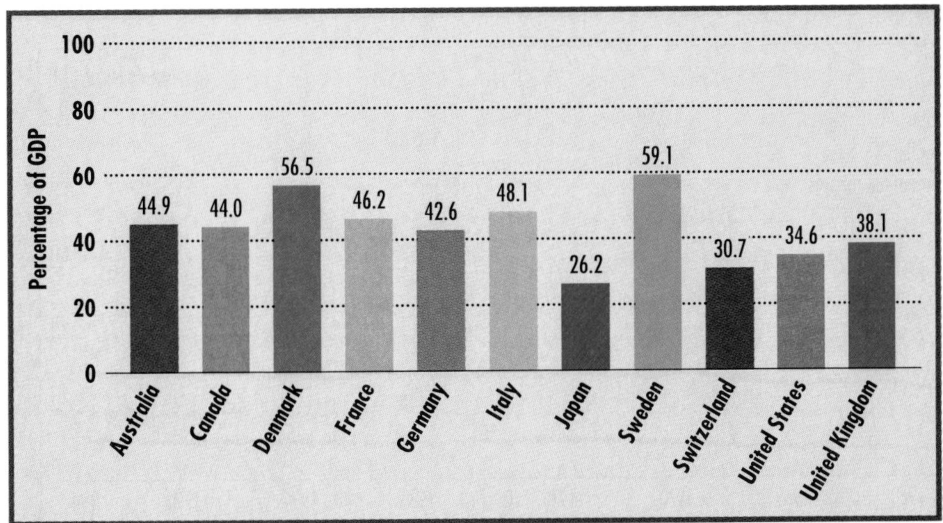

Figure 19.5 ▪ Comparing Total Government Spending in the United States to Government Spending in Other Rich Democracies: Spending as a Percentage of GDP in 1990

Compared to the spending in other rich democracies, government spending by all levels of government in the United States is quite low. Only Japan and Switzerland have lower public-sector spending than the United States.

Source: *Organization of Economic Cooperation Development Economic Surveys 1992–1993* (Paris: OECD Publications, 1995).

tutional Convention. Federal troops were used for the first time to "insure domestic tranquillity" in 1794 in order to quell the Whiskey Rebellion against a tax on whiskey and other commodities.

Public discontent with taxes continues to be an important feature of American politics. Many states and localities have passed tax limitation proposals in recent years. Steven Forbes gained attention during the 1996 Republican presidential nomination fight because he proposed a simple flat tax. Presidential candidate Ross Perot called for the abolition of the Internal Revenue Service during the 1996 campaign. Proposals for a balanced-budget amendment to the Constitution are regularly introduced in state legislatures and the Congress (it failed in the Senate in 1995 by only one vote). Presidential candidates find that pledges of "read my lips; no new taxes" are useful in winning office, as are promises of middle-class tax cuts.

Features of the American Tax System Though the American tax system shares some features with those of other countries, ours is unique in many important respects.

The Size of the Tax Bite Though Americans from all walks of life report feeling squeezed by taxes, the total of all taxes levied in the United States as a proportion of GDP (Figure 19.6) has remained virtually constant since 1969, at around 30 percent (though it had jumped from that of 25 percent in the mid–1950s). By the mid–1990s, the federal share of tax revenues had fallen slightly from that of 1969 to around 19 percent of GDP, while state and local governments took in about 11 percent. When all federal taxes, including pay-

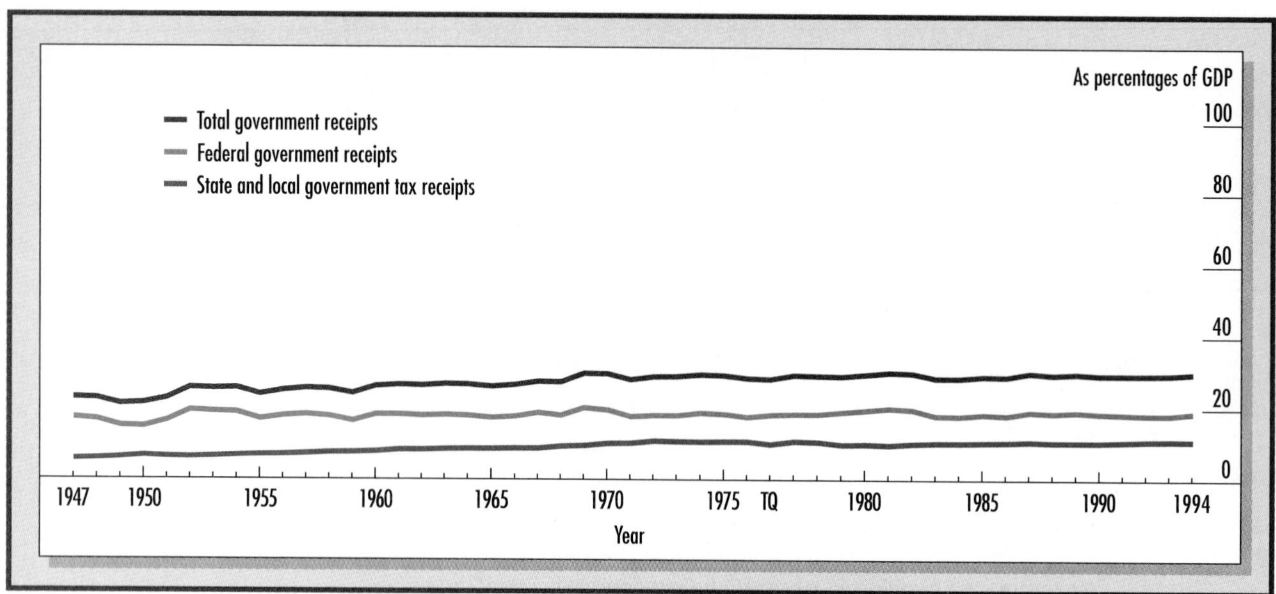

Figure 19.6 ■ **The Size of the Tax Bite: Total Federal, State, and Local Tax Receipts as a Percentage of the GDP**

Though the relative burden of taxes on the economy grew between 1947 and 1969, it has not changed since 1969. One important change in the postwar years has been the relative increase in the burden of state and local taxes compared to federal taxes.

Source: *The Budget of the United States, Fiscal 1996* (Washington, DC: U.S. Government Printing Office).

roll taxes for Social Security and Medicare, are combined, Americans paid 23.2 percent of their income in taxes in 1992, about the same as they did in 1980.[17]

Although substantial, the American tax burden relative to GDP is *significantly lighter* than that in all of the other rich democracies. We can see this difference in Figure 19.7, which compares the United States to the countries of the OECD (Organization of Economic Cooperation and Development). Even countries considered very low-tax countries—namely, Japan and Switzerland—take a larger share of GDP in taxes than the United States. It is fascinating that the "tax revolt" of recent years has been most evident in our own country, where the total tax burden is comparatively light.

Forms of Taxation Our tax system is also different from others in the kinds of taxes we impose. In our federal system, states and localities levy their own taxes. The federal government in the United States depends primarily on income taxes (personal and corporate) and payroll taxes to fund its activities (see Figure 19.8); other industrial democracies depend more on a mix of payroll and national sales and consumption taxes. In Norway, for instance, the **value-added tax**—a form of national sales tax—accounted for over 17 percent of government revenue, while social security taxes accounted for 25 percent. In the United States, the states get most of their revenues from sales taxes, though many have income taxes, as well. Local governments depend most heavily on property taxes. In recent decades, state and local taxes have risen faster than federal taxes. This trend is likely to continue as states and localities are forced to pick up the tab for programs abandoned by the federal government in its effort to solve the deficit problem.

value-added tax A national sales tax levied on intermediate goods (between raw materials and the final product); used mainly in Europe.

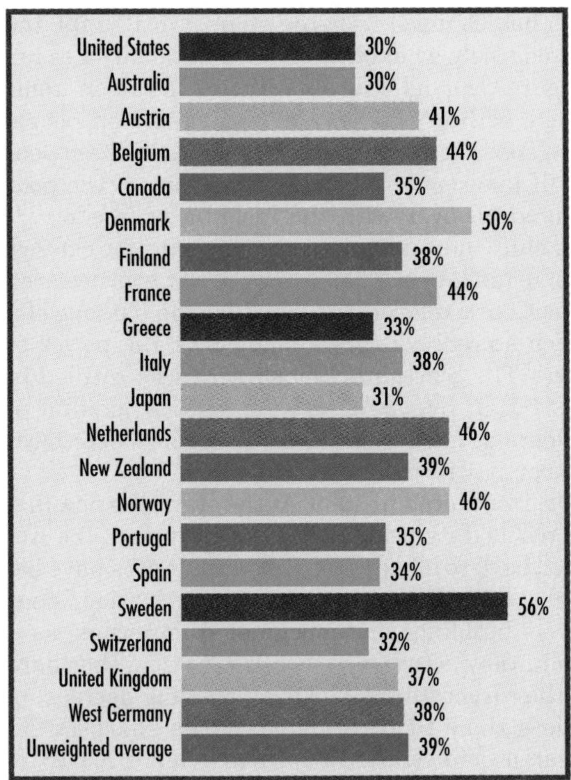

Figure 19.7 ▪ How the Tax Burden in the United States Compares: Tax Receipts as a Percentage of GDP, the United States and the OECD Countries, 1991

The tax burden of the United States is lighter than that of any other rich democratic nation, except Australia.

Source: *Statistical Abstracts of the United States 1994–1995,* Table No. 1376, p. 867 (Washington, DC: U.S. Bureau of the Census, 1996).

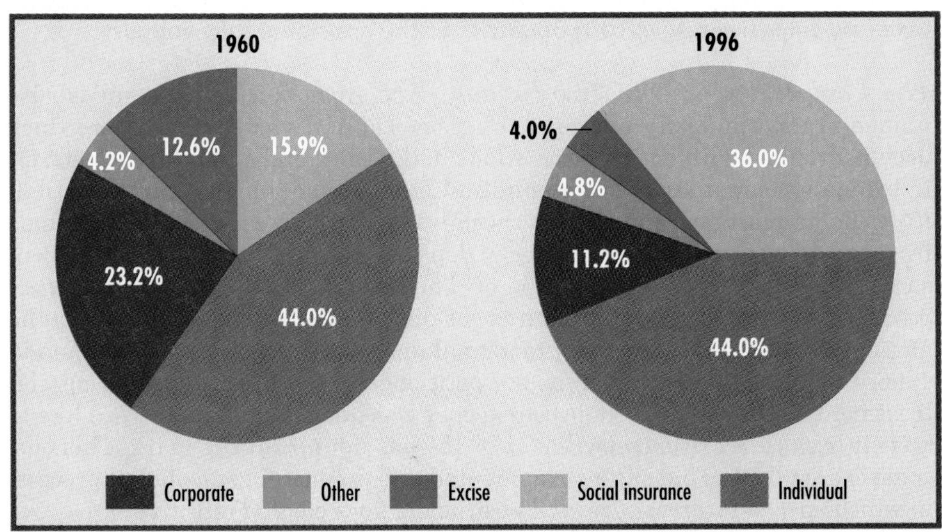

Figure 19.8 ▪ Sources of Federal Tax Revenues, 1960 and 1996

The source of federal tax receipts has shifted over the years. Most notable have been the increase in the share of taxes accounted for by payroll and social insurance taxes and the shrinking share shouldered by corporations.

Source: *Budget of the United States, Fiscal 1996* (Washington, DC: U.S. Government Printing Office).

excise tax A tax on some specific good, such as alcohol or cigarettes.

customs duties Taxes levied on imports.

The mix of tax instruments has changed over the years. Until 1909, the federal government was supported solely by **excise taxes** (a national sales tax on such items as alcohol and cigarettes) and **customs duties** (a tax on items imported into the United States), both of which fall most heavily on people with lower incomes. Noting this, Populist presidential candidate William Jennings Bryan once complained, "If taxation is a badge of freedom . . . the poor people of this country are covered all over with the insignia of freedom."[18] Pressed by popular demands to shift the tax burden to the wealthier classes, Congress passed a national income tax law in 1894. After the law was declared unconstitutional by the Supreme Court, reformers pushed for the passage of a constitutional amendment, which stated: "Congress shall have the power to lay and collect taxes on incomes." The Sixteenth Amendment was ratified in 1913. The personal income tax began by taxing only a relative handful of wealthy individuals. Over the years, it has expanded to the point where most Americans, excepting the very poor, pay income tax.

The corporate income tax was introduced in 1909. At the start, the nominal tax rate was only 1 percent. It reached its peak of 52 percent during the Korean War. By 1990, it had dropped back to 33 percent. But actual rates have become much lower because of rules that allow "accelerated depreciation," that is, subtracting part of the value of buildings and machines from income as if they were wearing out faster than they actually do. For this reason, the share of total taxes accounted for by the corporate tax has been steadily decreasing from 23.2 percent in 1960 to less than 10 percent today. The sharpest decreases resulted from the Reagan administration's 1981 tax cuts.[19] A part of these cuts was restored in the 1980s, and the Clinton budget for fiscal 1994 increased corporate taxes by another percentage point.

Social insurance programs for the elderly, such as Social Security and Medicare, are the largest and fastest-growing federal programs. Accordingly, payroll taxes to pay for these programs are now second only to the personal income tax as a source of government revenues, and the fastest growing. Working Americans have been slower to object to these taxes compared to income taxes, perhaps because of the popularity of the programs they support.

The Complexity of Our Tax System The American tax system is also unique in its complexity and particularism. The U.S. tax code is a very thick document, filled with endless exceptions to the rules and special treatment for individuals, companies, and communities. These range from the tax deductibility of home mortgage interest to special treatment of capital gains (income from the sale of property) and energy depletion allowances (a tax to compensate oil companies for the depletion of their oil reserves). Often called *tax expenditures,* these shortfalls in what government would collect on income in the absence of these devices amount to a great deal of money, about $270 billion in 1996. When Oregon Trappist monks petitioned Congress in 1984 for special treatment of their profits, their bookkeeper was quoted as saying, "We'd like to have it because everyone else has it."[20] He was not far off the mark. This outcome is a product of our highly fragmented and decentralized political process, in which special interests are well positioned, favored, and effective.[21]

Who Bears the Tax Burden? To understand the distribution of the tax burden among Americans, it is important to understand the effects of each kind of tax and how much government revenue comes from each. The personal income tax is *progressive;* that is, higher-income earners pay a higher percentage of their income in taxes (the actual percentage paid is called the **effective tax rate**). Payroll taxes (such as those for Social Security and Medicare) and sales

effective tax rate The percentage of income actually paid in taxes.

taxes are *regressive;* that is, lower-income earners pay a higher percentage of their incomes in these taxes. The effects of the corporate income tax are not entirely clear. It is progressive if one assumes that it is a burden borne only by corporations. It is regressive if one assumes, as most economists do, that corporations pass on the cost of their taxes to the consumer in the prices of their goods and services.

Needless to say, the calculation of the total distributive effect of all of these taxes is extremely complex. Nevertheless, scholars generally agree on the overall outline:[22]

- The poor, especially the working poor, pay taxes at a higher effective rate than the average for all Americans.
- The rich pay taxes at a higher effective rate then the average for all Americans.
- Almost all other Americans pay at roughly the same effective rate.

These findings may surprise some readers, especially those concerning the poor, but the reasons for the observed patterns make sense on reflection. While the poor pay less than others in federal and state income taxes, they are hit hard by regressive sales and excise taxes and are subject to Social Security taxes as well.

Those who are not poor are able to save some of their income rather than spend all of it on daily necessities, as the poor must do, so sales and excise

While the poor pay less than other groups in federal and state income taxes, they are hit harder by regressive sales, excise and Social Security taxes.

taxes take a smaller bite. Social Security taxes, moreover, are not imposed above a certain threshold, so people above the threshold pay such taxes as a smaller percentage of their income. Finally, capital gains income is not subject to Social Security taxes at all, a tax advantage not readily available to the poor.

The overall tax system, including state and local as well as federal taxes, has become less progressive in recent years. The reason is the decline in the progressivity of the federal income tax (for both individuals and corporations), the rapid increase in the share of taxes accounted for by regressive payroll taxes, and increases in the burden of regressive taxes at the state and local levels (mainly sales taxes and an expanded list of user fees).[23] The extraordinary deterioration of progressivity at the federal level can be seen in Figure 19.9. The graph shows that, between 1977 and 1992, the richest Americans experienced substantial cuts in their effective tax rates and substantial increases in their after-tax income. In real dollar terms, according to the Congressional Budget Office, families in the top 1 percent saw a reduction in their annual tax bill of about $40,000, while those at the median level of income paid about $400 more in federal taxes.[24]

The Perennial Debate About Taxes Debate about taxes usually focuses on questions of economic efficiency, fairness, and the deficit.

Efficiency Concerns about efficiency take several forms. Many conservatives and supply side economists believe that a progressive system with high tax rates at the top acts as a disincentive for the industrious, because it penalizes high incomes and profits. Also, the very complexity of the tax code and the enormous energy devoted to mastering and getting around it (thus, the legion of tax lawyers and accountants) can undermine efficiency. Industrial policy advocates believe that our tax system damages our international competitive-

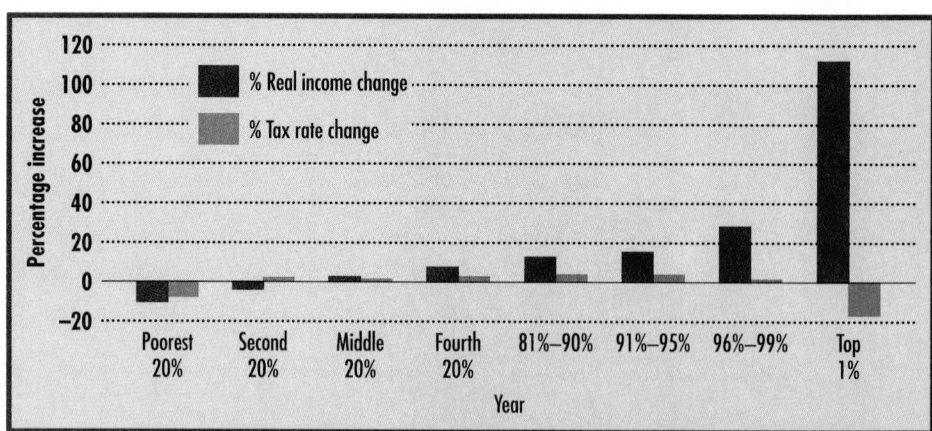

Figure 19.9 ▪ **Changes in Effective Federal Tax Rates and Changes in After-Tax Income for Various Income Groups, 1977–1992**

Since the late 1970s, the tax burden on the very wealthiest (and the very poorest) Americans has fallen. One result has been huge gains in the after-tax income of the wealthiest Americans. For reasons explored in detail in Chapter 4, the after-tax income of the poorest Americans has declined, despite a lightening of their tax burden.

Source: *The 1991 Green Book,* U.S. House of Representatives, Ways and Means Committee, Charts 1 and 2.

ness by rewarding unproductive economic activities. During the 1980s, for instance, investment in new plant and equipment lagged behind real estate development because of the latter's favorable treatment in the tax code.

The incredible complexity of our tax code has led to many proposals over the years for a radical simplification of our system. One attempt was made in the 1986 Tax Reform Act that shrank the number of tax brackets and eliminated a range of tax deductions and preferences, but complexity remained. In the mid–1990s, several Republican presidential candidates—most notably Steven Forbes—proposed a flat tax, and congressional committees considered similar proposals. Critics claimed that a flat tax, by abandoning "progressivity," would decrease the taxes of the wealthy and increase the tax burden on the middle class.

Fairness Many Americans are concerned about the fairness of our tax system. The idea of "ability to pay" has long supported a progressive income tax as the centerpiece of the system. The system, however, has become less progressive over time. The top **nominal tax rate** was 91 percent from the late 1950s to 1964, 70 percent from 1965 to 1980, 50 percent from 1982 to 1986, 38.5 percent in 1987, 28 percent in 1988, back up to 31 percent in 1990, and 33 percent in 1993. In 1994, the top rate reached 36 percent. Effective rates are never as progressive as nominal rates, however, because of the generosity of Congress in fashioning deductions, exemptions, and special tax breaks, especially for businesses and high-income individuals. Given this history, tax reforms with the announced intention of improving tax fairness are usually met with skepticism by the public.

nominal tax rate The percentage of income paid in taxes by each income class according to the income tax tables; differs from the actual percentages paid (known as the *effective rate*) by each income class.

Shortfalls Finally, almost everyone is now concerned about tax revenues falling short of government outlays, creating annual budget deficits and a mounting public debt. We turn to this subject in the next section.

The Deficit and the National Debt

Few issues get more attention than the annual federal budget deficit and the national debt. The **budget deficit** is the annual difference between what the government spends and what it receives in revenues. Like any other person, organization, or institution that spends more than it makes, the federal government must borrow from others to cover the shortfall and must pay interest to those from whom it borrows. The total of what government owes in the form of treasury bonds, bills, and notes to American citizens and institutions (financial institutions, insurance companies, corporations, etc.), foreign individuals and institutions (including foreign governments and banks), and even to itself (that is, to units such as the Social Security Trust Fund) is the **national debt.** Interest on the national debt has become an important component of annual federal outlays, amounting to almost 16 percent in 1996.

budget deficit The amount by which annual government expenditures exceed revenues.

national debt The total outstanding debt of the federal government.

The Size of the Debt and the Deficit The national debt is in the news because persistent annual budget deficits over the past two decades have caused the debt to increase significantly over a very short period of time. Most of the national debt before the 1980s was accumulated during major wars. After each war, the debt, relative to GDP, gradually declined. Despite increased government spending during the Great Depression, World War I, World War II, the Korean War, and the Vietnam War, our debt as a percentage of GDP in 1980 was about the same as it was in 1920.[25] Interest on the national debt as a percentage of GDP followed the same pattern. This pattern changed dramatically during the 1980s, however, when the size of annual federal budget deficits escalated dramatically, reversing the long, gradual decline in the size of the federal debt relative to the total wealth of the economy. The changes are illustrated in Figure 19.10. Note, however, that the national debt as a percentage of GDP has leveled off, primarily because of better news on the size of recent deficits (see Figure 19.11).

The growth of the debt during the 1980s occurred because of persistent deficits. Deficits occurred for two simple reasons:

1. Government spending increased, especially for national defense, Social Security, and Medicare, at a rate considerably faster than annual tax receipts.

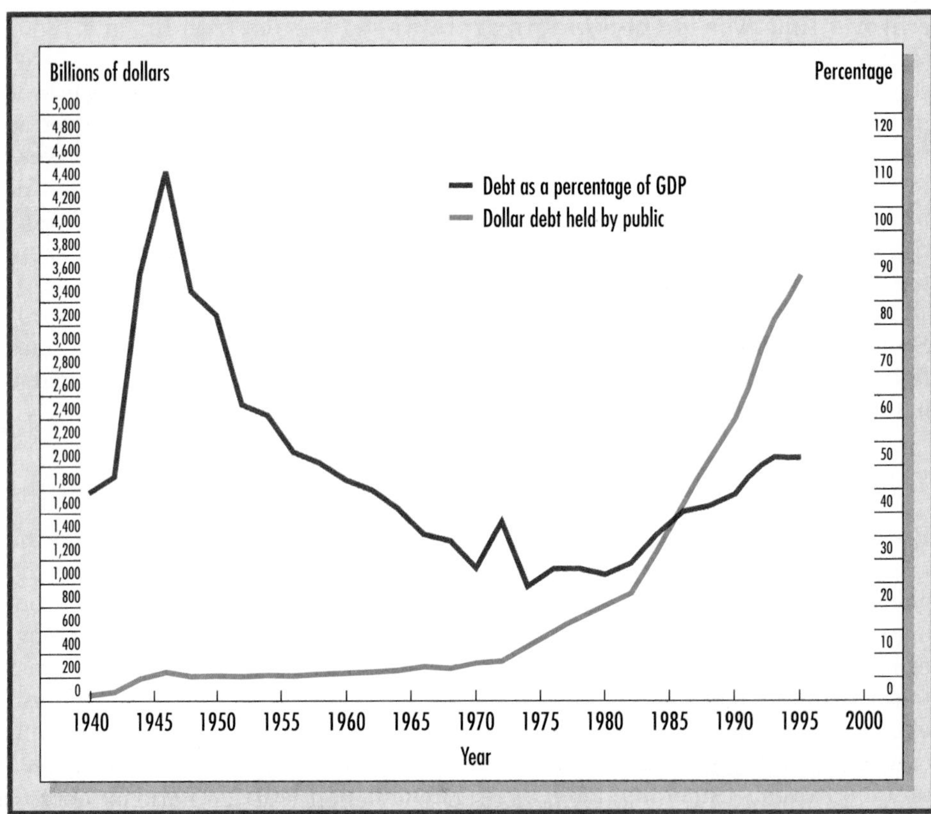

Figure 19.10 ▪ The National Debt, in Total Dollars and as a Percentage of the GDP

In dollar terms, the national debt has been escalating precipitously since the mid–1970s. A different story emerges if we look at the national debt as a percentage of the total wealth of the nation, measured as GDP. What we might call the relative national debt has increased, to be sure, but not as steeply as it seems. Nor is it anywhere near the historic high point it reached during World War II. Finally, the relative national debt has been leveling off recently, an effect suggesting that efforts to control the federal budget have been having an impact.

Sources: 1940–1992, Office of Management and Budget, *Budget Baselines, Historical Data, and Alternatives for the Future* (Washington, DC: U.S. Government Printing Office, 1993), p. 346; 1993–1998, Office of Management and Budget, *Budget of the U.S. Government, Fiscal Year 1994* (Washington, DC: U.S. Government Printing Office, 1993), p. 32; and from Harold W. Stanley and Richard G. Niemi, *Vital Statistics on American Politics* (Washington, DC: Congressional Quarterly Press, 1994), pp. 426–427; *Budget of the United States, Fiscal 1996* (Washington, DC: U.S. Government Printing Office), Historical Tables, p. 90.

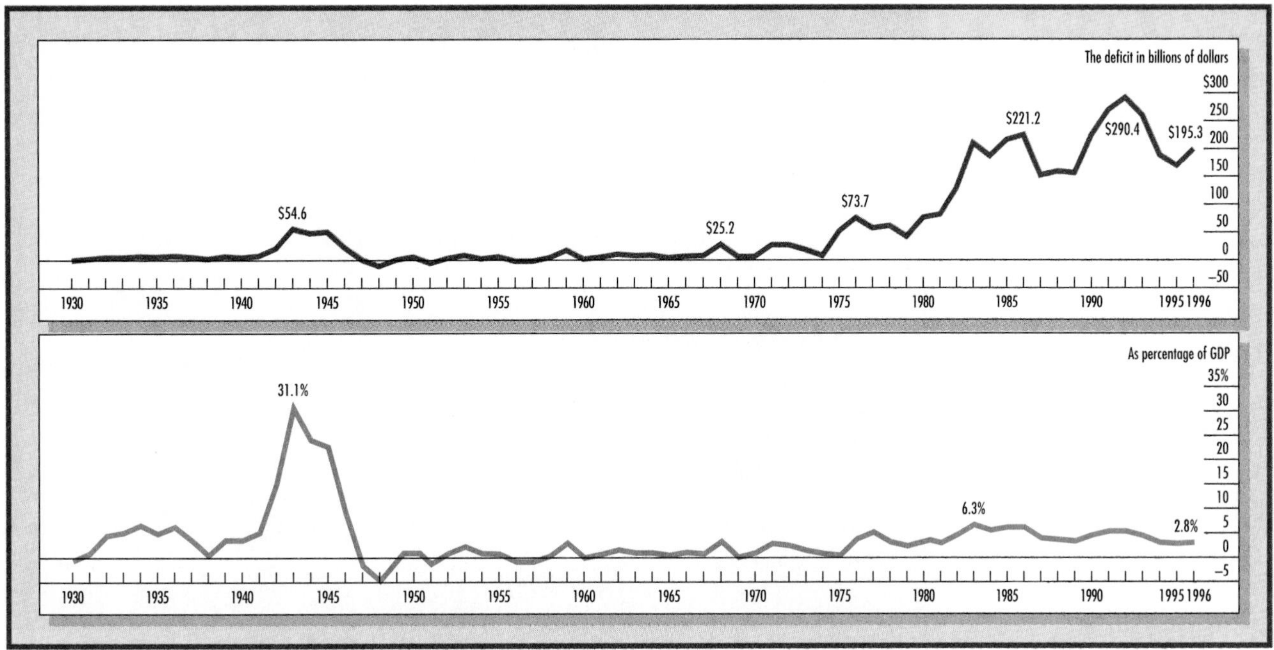

Figure 19.11 ■ **The Deficit over the Years**

In total dollar terms, annual federal budget deficits increased substantially and steadily from 1975 (with a brief dip in the late 1980s) until reaching their peak in 1992, then began to shrink in size. Even with this change of direction, the deficits remain much higher than historical norms. When annual deficits are measured in terms of GDP, however, the record is not very alarming. Since 1983, relative deficits have actually been declining.

Source: *Budget of the United States, Fiscal 1996* (Washington, DC: U.S. Government Printing Office); Alice Rivlin, Director, Office of Management and Budget, *Midsession Review of the 1996 Budget* (July 28, 1995).

2. Government revenues lagged because of the 1981 tax cuts, the deep economic recession of 1981–1982, and the reduction of the top tax rates in 1986.

Increased welfare and other domestic spending had little to do with the increase in the national debt during this period,[26] despite the great attention they received from politicians and the public.

Does the National Debt Matter? As strange as it may seem, economists do not agree about the long-term effects of the deficit and the national debt. To one group, it is the basis of national decline; to another, it is a relatively trivial problem.

The pessimists make the following case:[27]

- The national debt, relative to GDP, rose during the 1980s and the early 1990s at a rate that was unprecedented in our *peacetime* history. If deficits are not brought under better control, a sharp rise in the rate of growth of the national debt is certain to begin again.
- The enormous increase in the national debt during the 1980s coincided with the general stagnation of the American economy and the decline of American competitiveness. This stagnation at decline of competitiveness may have been caused by the drag on private investment that is produced by government borrowing.

Concern over the size and growth of the national debt is high among many Americans, as symbolized by this debt clock in New York. Scholars do not agree, however, about the social and economic effects of the national debt.

- Much of our national debt is funded by borrowing from abroad, which puts increasing shares of the American economy in the hands of non-Americans.
- The federal government has not put borrowed money to good use (e.g., for programs in education, research and development, and infrastructure to spur long-term economic growth) but has squandered it on such noneconomically productive activities as the military, corporate subsidies and bailouts, and failed social programs.
- Because the national debt is owed mostly to large banks, financial institutions, and wealthy individuals, it contributes to increasing inequality in the United States.

The optimists argue that the threat is greatly exaggerated. They make the following points:[28]

- The national debt is not as big as it seems because we measure it incorrectly. We do not, for instance, include the considerable assets of the government (buildings, land, equipment, natural resources, etc.) in our calculations, as any conventional business would do when calculating its debt.
- The national debt, even as normally measured, is no higher relative to GDP than it was during the late 1940s and the early 1950s.

- There is no evidence of "crowding out." Other modern capitalist countries with larger relative national debts had no trouble sustaining investment and productivity growth during the 1980s. There was plenty of money around in the United States at reasonable interest rates, but individuals and business enterprises didn't use it productively.

- Eighty-seven percent of the interest paid on the national debt goes to Americans.
- Government deficits are useful for spurring economic activity when labor and productive capacity are being used at less than full capacity, which is most of the time. The key to long-term growth and international competitiveness is that the deficit be used to fund such programs as education, research, and infrastructure that strengthen the economy.
- Making reduction of the national debt a central tenet of public policy in bad economic times would put the economy into a tailspin, increasing unemployment and decreasing overall economic activity. The cure would be worse than the disease.
- The U.S. national debt as a percentage of its GDP is smaller than the debt among any of the other G–7 nations (Japan, Germany, Canada, France, Britain, and Italy).[29]

The Deficit Issue in American Politics Despite disagreement about the effects of the national debt, the issue is an important one in our political life and has been so since the beginning of the Republic.[30] Apparently, enough voters, politicians, and business leaders today worry about deficits and the national debt to make them persistently hot issues. Ross Perot made a balanced budget the main theme of his efforts to win the presidency. Republicans won both houses of Congress in the 1994 national elections on the same theme, and as we saw in the story that opens this chapter, the struggle over how to balance the federal budget dominated relations between President Clinton and the Republican 104th Congress, and led to several federal government shutdowns.

Despite the apparent power of the deficit issue in American politics, the public is deeply conflicted about its support of a balanced budget. When asked directly whether Congress and the president should balance the budget, Americans answer yes in overwhelming numbers; polls in the mid–1990s routinely reported support of between 70 and 80 percent. However, when asked if they would favor a balanced budget if it meant raising taxes or cutting popular programs like Medicare, Social Security, and environmental protection, support dropped into the 30 to 40 percent range. The trade-offs Americans seem willing to make to achieve a balanced budget are shown in Figure 19.12.

Deficit Management For most of our history, taxes and spending were considered separately by Congress, and little consideration was given to their relationship and to the overall fiscal situation of the nation. In 1974, however, the Congressional Budget and Impoundment Act set up procedures for Congress to consider the budget as a whole, in relation to overall national fiscal goals. The act required that no action be taken on individual spending or taxing until a resolution in both houses set spending and taxing targets, and it specified an amount of surplus or deficit that is "appropriate in the light of economic conditions." Congress was not permitted to adjourn, moreover, until the spending and taxing programs were reconciled (made consistent) with the overall targets.

In 1985, fiscal conservatives who were worried about the growing national debt successfully pushed enactment of the Balanced Budget and Emergency Deficit Control Act (popularly known as Gramm-Rudman, after its Senate

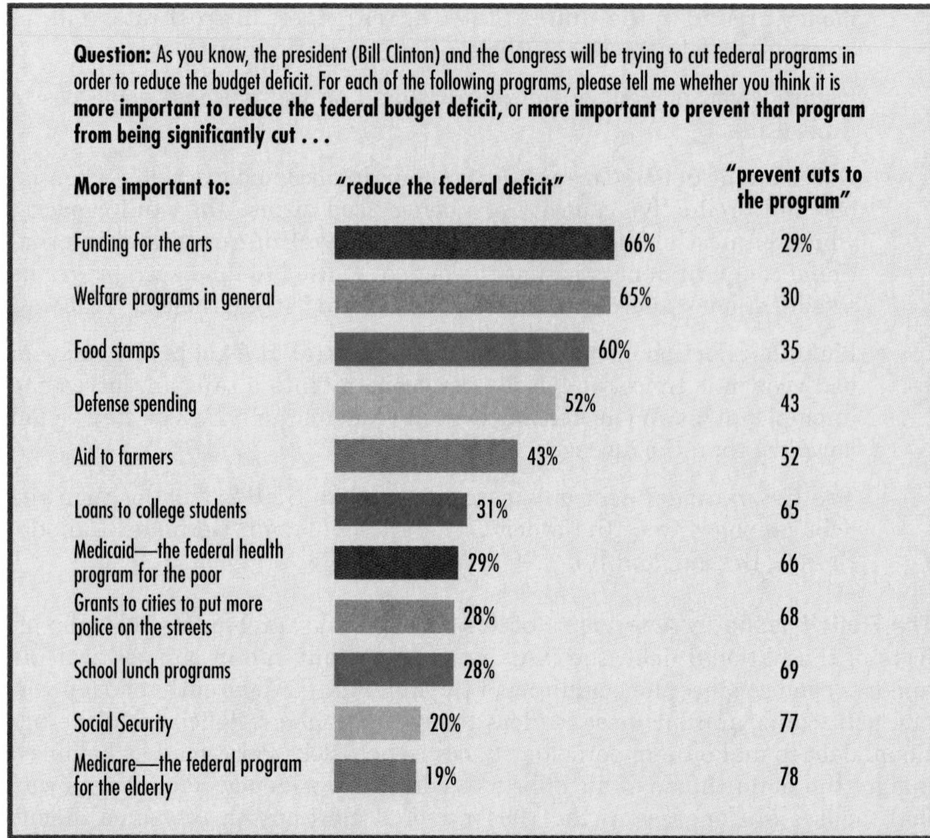

Question: As you know, the president (Bill Clinton) and the Congress will be trying to cut federal programs in order to reduce the budget deficit. For each of the following programs, please tell me whether you think it is **more important to reduce the federal budget deficit,** or **more important to prevent that program from being significantly cut . . .**
More important to:
"reduce the federal deficit"
"prevent cuts to the program"
Funding for the arts 66% 29%
Welfare programs in general 65% 30
Food stamps 60% 35
Defense spending 52% 43
Aid to farmers 43% 52
Loans to college students 31% 65
Medicaid—the federal health program for the poor 29% 66
Grants to cities to put more police on the streets 28% 68
School lunch programs 28% 69
Social Security 20% 77
Medicare—the federal program for the elderly 19% 78

Figure 19.12 ▪ **What Americans Say They Are Willing to Do to Balance the Federal Budget**

While Americans tend to support a balanced federal budget in the abstract, they do not want to cut the most popular and expensive programs in order to meet that goal. The only large program that a majority of Americans is willing to cut is national defense.

Source: Survey by the Gallup Organization for CNN/*USA Today,* February 24–26, 1995.

sponsors, Phil Gramm of Texas and Warren Rudman of New Hampshire). Gramm-Rudman specified amounts by which the annual deficit would have to be cut each year over a period of six years in order to balance the budget by 1991. Failure to meet annual targets was to trigger automatic cuts in federal spending (half in defense, half in nondefense programs, excluding Social Security). Because of difficulties in reaching these targets, a bill was enacted in 1987 postponing a balanced budget until 1993.

In 1990, faced with the threat that the automatic budget cut ax might fall on a wide range of cherished programs, President Bush and the Congress agreed to suspend Gramm-Rudman until at least 1994 (and eventually beyond) and to raise taxes and cut spending, making a small dent in what otherwise would have been an astonishingly high deficit. In 1993, President Clinton proposed a budget with deep spending cuts and large tax increases whose central goal was to get the mounting deficit under control. In late 1995 and 1996, as we saw in the story opening this chapter, the deficit issue came to a head in the fierce conflict between President Clinton and the Republican Congress.

Subsidizing Business

All governments in the rich democracies support a variety of economic activities considered important to society, but unlikely to occur at optimum levels without taxpayer help. *Public ownership* is the most fully developed form and is common in Western Europe, though not in the United States. In Europe, airlines, railroads, and telephone systems are more likely than not to be owned and operated by government. In the United States, government support for business enterprises is much more likely to take the form of *tax incentives.* Thus, homeowners and the building industry reap large benefits from the tax deductibility of interest on mortgage loans; manufacturing firms benefit from accelerated depreciation on new plants and equipment; oil and mining interests pay lower taxes because of "energy depletion allowances"; and companies that locate in inner-city "enterprise zones" are rewarded with generous tax breaks. The federal government also provides *loan guarantees* to troubled but important firms when the need arises, as it did for the Chrysler Corporation in the 1980s.

Programs that pay direct *subsidies* to private businesses are also an important part of the economic policy environment in the United States. Much of this subsidizing goes on at the state and local level. Thus, many states pay for such essential services as roads and utilities for corporations that agree to build manufacturing plants that will provide much needed jobs in the state. This was an important factor in Toyota's decision to build a manufacturing plant in Kentucky, and in BMW's decision to build in South Carolina. Many cities have attracted major league baseball teams and National Football League franchises by paying for new stadiums with taxpayer money.

The federal government also directly subsidizes private enterprises. The examples are legion:[31]

- The Agricultural Marketing Promotion Program encourages exports of American agricultural commodities and finished foods. Campbell Soup Company receives $500,000 annually to help advertise its products abroad. Pet Foods receives about $1 million a year to, among other things, win Japanese consumers to Friskies. Washington State apple growers receive help in their efforts to penetrate the Japanese market.
- Over $31 billion a year goes to support American farmers in the form of wheat, rice, peanut, cotton, milk, and other commodity price-support subsidies to guarantee farmers a certain price regardless of market fluctuations. A recent farm bill will gradually phase out most of these subsidies.
- The Forest Service spent over $150 million in 1995 building roads and trails for companies that log in national forests.
- The Rural Electrification Administration has provided low-interest loans to help expand ski resorts in Colorado and other states.
- Texas Instruments and the Chrysler Corporation received $13 million and $6 million, respectively, in 1994 under a program designed to help defense contractors develop products for the civilian market.
- American auto companies have received almost $350 million to help develop a less polluting car.

The Cato Institute, a conservative, free-market-oriented think tank, estimated that the federal government made payments in 1994 of over $86 billion to private business enterprises or private trade associations.[32] People disagree, of course, about whether such expenditures are necessary for national economic health, or are a waste of taxpayer money, or are cynical examples of "corporate welfare" at a time when welfare payments to the poor are being cut. Strangely enough, positions on the issue of government subsidies do not follow the usual partisan lines. Thus, the Cato Institute and House Budget Committee Chair John Kasich (Republican of Ohio) have called for an end of corporate welfare, while their conservative Republican colleagues in the 104th Congress refused to touch any of the business subsidy programs.

Regulation

regulations Rules issued by government agencies.

Regulation is one of the most visible and important things the federal government does. By **regulation,** we mean the issuing by federal agencies of rules and regulations that private businesses must follow. These rules and regulations may involve how a company treats its toxic wastes, or what hiring procedures it practices, or how it reports its profits and losses. Regulations are issued by federal agencies, such as the Environmental Protection Agency (EPA) or the Securities and Exchange Commission (SEC) under the authority of laws passed by Congress and signed by the president.

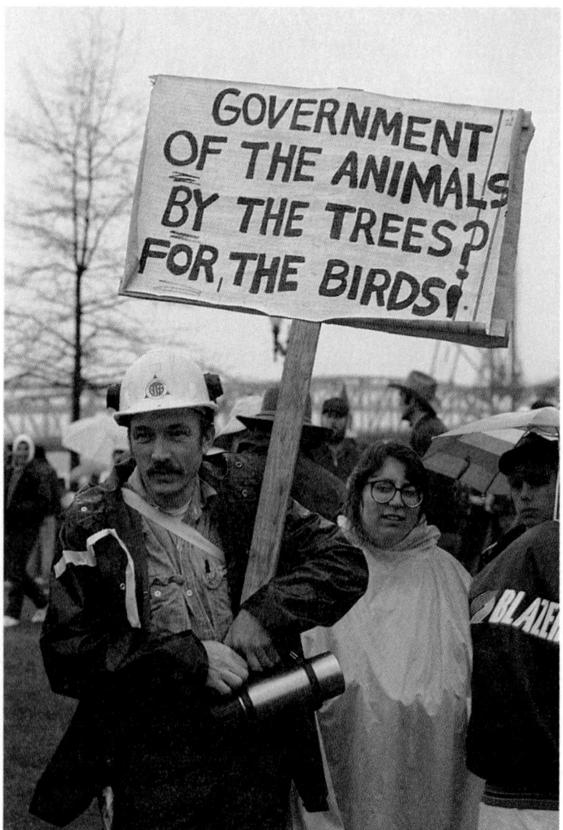

While strong environmental policies are supported by a majority of Americans, business and industry as well as their employees, often exert strong pressure to reduce government action in this area.

Why Government Regulates

The level of the government regulation of private business activities has grown substantially in this century, particularly since the 1960s. Scholars disagree on why this has happened.

The Democratic Explanation A free market economy, even when it is working optimally, produces a range of problems that cannot be or are unlikely to be solved by private businesses on their own. These problems include, among others, air and water pollution, inadequate information for investors, unsafe products, unsafe and unwholesome workplaces, toxic wastes, and reckless financial practices. The American people have demonstrated on a number of occasions that they want government to do something about these problems. In a democracy, of course, politicians must respond to such popular pressures on pain of losing office. Democracy, then, is one reason why government regulates.

The Business Power Explanation Not all scholars are convinced, however, that regulation is solely the product of democratic politics. *The economic theory of regulation* holds that regulation is caused by the political efforts of powerful business firms that turn to government for protection against competitors. Regulation allows firms, it is argued, to restrict overall output, to deny entry to business competitors, and to maintain above-market prices.[33]

A History of American Regulation

A brief review of the history of regulation[34] illustrates how the interaction of democratic and nondemocratic factors has produced the regulatory agencies and policies that we have today.

Progressive Era Regulation Between 1900 and World War I, (the "Progressive Era"), laws were passed to regulate some of the activities of powerful new corporations and to break up the "trusts." Reform was spurred by labor unions, the women's movement, the Populists, and middle-class Americans anxious about the conditions reported by the muckrakers, that is, journalists and novelists, such as Upton Sinclair (*The Jungle*), Frank Norris (*The Octopus*), and Ida Tarbell (*A History of the Standard Oil Company*), who exposed current dangerous and unethical business practices.

Landmark regulatory measures included the Federal Trade Commission Act, the Meat Inspection Act, the Pure Food and Drug Administration Act, and the Federal Reserve Act, as well as new uses for the previously enacted Sherman Anti-Trust Act and the Interstate Commerce Act. These measures dealt with such problems as monopolies, unstable financial institutions, unwholesome products, and unsafe working conditions.

Some scholars believe, however, that major corporations were themselves the beneficiaries of many of the regulatory enactments of the period and were major players in the conception, formulation, and enactment of regulatory legislation.[35] For example, the Federal Reserve Act was not simply the result of popular concerns about bank instability, but a government response to the entreaties of the American Bankers Association and its large member banks, who were worried about their inability to mobilize reserves in a financial emergency.

New Deal Regulation The next wave of regulatory reform occurred during the New Deal in the 1930s. The regulatory innovations of this period aimed squarely at speculative and unsafe practices in the banking and securities industries that had contributed to the onset of the Great Depression. Legislation included federal bank inspection, federal deposit insurance, the prohibition of speculative investments by banks, enhanced capacities for the Federal Reserve to coordinate the supply of money and credit, and the creation of the Securities and Exchange Commission to regulate stock market operations. Also, the new airline industry was brought under the wing of the Civil Aeronautics Board (CAB).

Again, the political sources of New Deal regulation were mixed. The principal impetus for the New Deal came from popular discontent with the status quo and pressure on the government to solve the many problems of the Great Depression.[36] But powerful interest groups were also at work. Important segments of the corporate community were intimately involved in the formulation of reform legislation and benefited greatly from it. Much of the financial community, for instance, pressed for legislation to bring stability to financial markets.[37] Other corporations eventually came to dominate and control regulatory policy, protecting themselves against competitors and ensuring above-market profits.[38]

The New Social Regulation Progressive Era and New Deal regulation was aimed at the problems of a particular industry (e.g., the railroads, banking, and securities) rather than the corporate economy as a whole. In addition, it was mainly of the "economic" variety, designed to regulate pricing patterns and the conditions of entry and production in a particular industry.[39] Finally, regulators during these eras welcomed the involvement of the regulated industry in setting standards, providing information, and lending personnel to regulatory agencies.

What has been called the *new social regulation* of the 1970s was different. For one thing, the sheer volume of regulatory legislation passed during these years was unprecedented (see Table 19.1). Regulation in this period, moreover, was directed at corporate practices in general rather than at the problems of particular industries. Thus, antipollution and antidiscrimination regulations covered all businesses, not just particular ones.

More important, perhaps, an entirely new approach to regulation was initiated during this period. Conscious of the degree to which older regulatory agencies had become captives of the industries they regulated and the number of "iron triangles" and "subgovernments" at the core of the governing process in Washington, D.C. (see Chapter 7), reformers convinced elected officials to encourage broad public participation and accountability.[40] The new social regulation encouraged citizen lawsuits, for instance, by granting automatic "standing" in regulatory proceedings to "interested parties." In practice, these citizens were usually public interest lobbies, such as Common Cause, Citizen Action, and the Sierra Club. The push for citizen involvement was a product of the rising tide of social movements during the late 1960s and early 1970s (see Chapter 10) and a loss of confidence in the nation's business corporations, tied to a troubled economy and the general deterioration in confidence in all established institutions brought on by the Vietnam War and Watergate.[41] It was one of the only times in our history when business was almost entirely on the defensive, unable to halt the imposition of laws and regulations to which it was strongly opposed.[42]

Deregulation By the end of the 1970s, the mood of opinion leaders both inside and outside the government had turned against regulation. Many blamed ex-

Table 19.1

The High Tide of the New Social Regulation

This table indicates the tremendous growth in federal government regulatory activity during the 1970s.

Federal Regulatory Agencies Created During the 1970s

Environmental Protection Agency (1970)
National Highway Safety Commission (1970)
Consumer Product Safety Commission (1970)
Mine Safety and Health Administration (1973)
Occupational Safety and Health Administration (1973)
Nuclear Regulatory Commission (1975)

Regulatory Enactments (Selected) of the 1970s

Cigarette Advertising Act
Clean Air Act (amendments)
Consumer Product Safety Act
Federal Water Pollution Control Act
Hazardous Materials Transportation Act
Medical Devices Safety Act
Mine Safety and Health Act
Noise Pollution and Control Act
Ocean Dumping Act
Pesticide Regulation Act
Poison Prevention Packaging Act
Railroad Safety Act
Saccharin Study and Labeling Act
Safe Drinking Water Act
Seat Belt and School Bus Standards
Toxic Substances Control Act
Warranty Improvement Act
Water Quality Improvement Act

Source: *The 1991 Green Book,* U.S. House of Representatives, Ways and Means Committee, Charts 1 and 2.

cessive regulation for forcing inefficient practices on American companies, and thus hastening the decline of the United States in the world economy. Many began to find fault with government imposition on companies of uniform national standards, strict deadlines for compliance with regulations and detailed instructions.[43] Some economists wanted to substitute "cost-benefit" analysis in place of rigid rules and regulations to evaluate regulations and more market-oriented forms of regulations (such as taxing damaging activities or granting tax breaks for meeting standards). The deregulatory mood was spurred by a business political offensive that took the form of funding for think tanks, journals of opinion, and foundations favorable to the business point of view, as well as funding for the electoral campaigns of sympathetic candidates.[44]

The change in climate was first apparent in the deregulation of the airline, banking, railroad, and trucking industries under President Jimmy Carter. The deregulation momentum increased under President Ronald Reagan's program of "regulatory relief." This program slowed the regulation-writing process, cut the investigatory and research capabilities of regulatory agencies, and appointed heads of regulatory units who were hostile to the legislated missions of their agencies. The deregulation offensive was continued by George Bush, who appointed Vice-President Dan Quayle to head the Competitiveness Council, a body created by the president to slow the writing and implementation of regulations by federal agencies. President Bill Clinton reversed many Reagan-Bush era policies, especially those related to the environment. One of Clinton's first acts was to abolish the Competitiveness Council, which had been used to block many environmental regulations. The president also ordered the OMB to release 26 Environmental Protection Agency rules that it had been "reviewing" for years. However, Clinton continued to use much of the antiregulatory rhetoric of the times.

The Republican landslide victory in the 1994 elections brought to power a strong antiregulatory majority in the House of Representatives. Under the leadership of Speaker Newt Gingrich, House Republicans set out to deliver on the antiregulatory promises of the Contract with America. Within the first 100 days, as promised, the House voted to diminish the power of the federal government to regulate air and water pollution, toxic sites, oil drilling, workplace safety, product safety, and wetlands and endangered species protections. Opposed by the Senate and President Clinton, most of these deregulatory efforts came to naught. Opinion polls showed that the public overwhelmingly sided with the Senate and the president.

The Future of Regulation

While especially egregious, unfair, and inefficient regulations may be erased from the books (or at least we can hope so), it is likely that the regulatory state is here to stay. There are a number of reasons to think this may be true:

First, little permanent deregulation was achieved during the 1980s, an era dominated by conservative ideas, business values, and an extremely popular president (Ronald Reagan) committed to deregulation. Nor was much accomplished by the strongly conservative, Republican-controlled 104th Congress. If fundamental change in government regulation could not be achieved in such favorable environments, it seems unlikely that it will happen any time soon.

Second, most regulatory policies are supported by the public. Even at the height of President Reagan's popularity, polls continued to show overwhelming support for most regulatory programs. The Roper Poll reported in 1982, for instance, that only 21 percent of Americans believed that "environmental protection laws and regulations have gone too far," while 69 percent believed that "they are about right or haven't gone far enough."[45] Polls conducted in the mid–1990s continued to show strong public support for most regulatory programs, especially those aimed at environmental protection.

Third, deregulation has created so many problems that many people are having second thoughts. Deregulation of the savings-and-loan industry (S & Ls) and its subsequent collapse in various states is only the most glaring example. Nonenforcement of the antitrust laws and lax supervision of the securities industry contributed to a decade of leveraged buyouts, junk-bond financial shell games, and unprecedented levels of corporate debt in the 1980s. Many Americans worry that the nation's banks and insurance companies may follow the disastrous path of the S & Ls if they are not subject to more stringent regulation.

Finally, new problems are beginning to appear that are likely to stimulate public demands for government intervention. Pornography on the Internet has triggered efforts by Christian conservatives and others to regulate its content. Environmental disasters such as the Exxon *Valdez* oil spill in Alaska led to calls for the government to do something to prevent their recurrence. The problems of such long-range threats to the environment as acid rain and the "greenhouse effect" seem beyond the capacities of the free market to solve and will presumably require government action of some kind.

Economic Policy and Democracy

Like most of what the federal government does, economic policy in the United States is the product of a political process that reflects both democratic and nondemocratic factors. With respect to spending, for instance, Americans strongly support those programs that account for the most federal government spending, namely, Social Security, Medicare, Medicaid, and national defense, though there is some support for slightly decreasing the latter two. The public reserves its ire for government "waste" (which is hard to define or measure; see Chapter 13), foreign aid, welfare, and subsidies to business, which together account for a very small share of federal expenditures. In sum, while Americans like to complain about the size of the government, they generally support those programs that make it so big.

Though complaining about taxes is as common as complaining about the weather, it seems that Americans generally get what they want in terms of tax policy. To be sure, they are exasperated by the complexity of our tax system; there is concern about its fairness; and many worry about its overall economic effects. Yet the message that the American people want low taxes is conveyed quite clearly to elected officials, and they respond, as shown by how low our taxes are when they are compared with those of other modern capitalist countries. When combined with Americans' support for most federal spending programs, this penchant for low taxes helps explain why the deficit problem is so intractable.

We have also seen that the American people generally support the overall outlines of the regulatory state. Though there are many complaints about an overly obtrusive government, when asked about specific regulatory programs, ranging from those covering the banking industry to pollution control, strong majorities not only accept what is in place but would also like to see even more regulation.

While popular sovereignty is served in the general outlines of economic policy, the details are the stuff of special interests. This is the case for spending, where commitments to specific priorities and projects, from weapons systems procurement to direct business subsidies, are hammered out in a legislative process in which special interests dominate; in the area of taxation, where the detailed provisions of the tax code are the outcome of the efforts of special interests—which are also the main beneficiaries; and in regulatory policy, where such arrangements as "captured" agencies and "iron triangles" have not yet disappeared.

Summary

Governments play an important role in the management of the economy in all of the industrialized democracies. Governments have been successful in easing many, though by no means all, of the problems generated by dynamic market economies.

The federal government's macroeconomic responsibilities entail policies that affect economic growth, inflation, and employment in the economy. The goal of macroeconomic policy is a growing economy, with low unemployment and stable prices. Government officials try to meet this goal by using fiscal tools, such as government spending and taxing, and monetary tools that attempt to affect the money supply and interest rates.

There is no consensus among Keynesian, monetarist, supply side, and industrial policy economists on how to meet government's economic responsibilities. Each approach embodies a conception of the proper role of government. The Keynesian and industrial policy approaches favor a large and interventionist government; monetarist and supply side theorists favor a small and noninterventionist one.

Structural, political-linkage, and governmental factors affect economic policy. Problems arising from the economy itself are crucial. The Constitution structures the rules of the game of the economic policymaking process, and the political culture affects what we believe to be appropriate policy. Interest groups play a particularly central role. Political parties are also important: Democrats and Republicans take different approaches to economic questions.

Federal government spending and taxing have grown during the twentieth century but remain significantly below the levels common in other Western democratic countries. Spending is mainly for social insurance programs and national defense. The tax system is slightly progressive but is becoming less so. The annual imbalance between spending and taxing has contributed to a worsening national debt, but economists cannot agree on the debt's effects or the best way to diminish its size.

The federal government also plays an important regulatory role. The origins of this role lay in market failures and diseconomies that triggered popular and business pressures on government. Despite the deregulation efforts of recent years, the regulatory responsibilities of the federal government are likely to remain substantial, especially as the government has begun to tackle difficult problems such as environmental protection.

Suggested Readings

Friedman, Benjamin. Day of Reckoning: *The Consequences of American Economic Policy Under Reagan and After.* New York: Random House, 1988.

A book that rings the alarm about the potentially disastrous effects of our growing national debt.

Harris, Richard, and Sidney Milkis. *The Politics of Regulatory Change.* New York: Oxford University Press, 1989.

A history of regulation organized around the idea that different kinds of "regulatory regimes" follow one another.

Heilbroner, Robert, and Peter Bernstein. *The Debt and the Deficit: False Alarm/Real Possibilities.* New York: Norton, 1989.

Swimming very much against the mainstream, these two economists argue that the problem of the debt is greatly exaggerated and misunderstood.

Hibbs, Douglas. *The American Political Economy.* Cambridge: Harvard University Press, 1987.

A sophisticated historical and statistical analysis of the relationship between American politics and the formation of economic policies, and of the effects of such policies.

Peters, Guy B. *American Public Policy: Promise and Performance,* 4th ed. Chatham, NJ: Chatham House, 1996.

The leading textbook on U.S. economic and social policy.

Phillips, Kevin. *Boiling Point: Democrats, Republicans, and the Decline of Middle Class Prosperity.* New York: Random House, 1993.
Argues that the rising burden of taxes, mainly federal payroll and state and local taxes, has helped diminish the middle class's standard of living and fueled populist anger in American politics.

Savage, James D. *Balanced Budgets and American Politics.* Ithaca, NY: Cornell University Press, 1988.
A fascinating look at the long history of the politics of the balanced budget in the United States.

Vogel, David. *Fluctuating Fortunes: The Political Power of Business in the United States.* New York: Basic Books, 1989.
A detailed description and analysis of how the "new social regulation" came to burden business during the 1970s and how business successfully fought back during the 1980s.

Internet Sources

The Budget of the United States, Fiscal Year 1997 http://www.doc.gov/inquery/BudgetFY97/BudgetFY97.html
The budget of the United States, with numbers and documentation.

The Concord Coalition Homepage http://sunsite.unc.edu/concord/info/cc_crfb.html
Lots of budget statistics and position papers from the Committee for a Responsible Federal Budget.

Environmental Issues on Jefferson http://www.stardot.com/jefferson/issues/Environment/
A gateway to a broad range of groups, agencies, and information related to environmental issues.

Income Tax Information on the Internet http://www2.best.com/ftmexpat/html/taxsites.html
A gateway to other web sites and Gopher locations devoted to the issue of taxes; links to sites as varied as the Internal Revenue Service and tax protest groups.

National Budget Simulator http://garnet.berkeley.edu:3333/budget/budget.html
An interactive site that allows you to make your own federal budget and examine the consequences of your choices.

The National Debt Clock http://www.brillig.com/debt_clock/
The national debt, up to the minute.

Statistical Abstracts of the United States http://www.census/gov:80/stat_abstract/
Historical data on government expenditures and revenues.

Notes

1. Michael Weisskopt and David Maraniss, "Endgame: The Revolution Stalls," *Washington Post,* National Edition (January 29–February 4, 1996), p. 6.

2. Arnold J. Heidenheimer, Hugh Heclo, and Carolyn Teich Adams, *Comparative Public Policy: The Politics of Social Choice in America, Europe, and Japan,* 3rd ed. (New York: St. Martin's Press, 1990), p. 137.

3. This section owes a great deal to B. Guy Peters, *American Public Policy: Promise and Performance,* 4th ed. (Chatham, NJ: Chatham House, 1996), pp. 197–205.

4. Joseph A. Pechman, *Federal Tax Policy,* 5th ed. (Washington, DC: Brookings Institution, 1987), p. 28.

5. Ibid., p. 8.
6. Heidenheimer et al., *Comparative Public Policy,* p. 137.
7. Kim McQuaid, *Big Business and Presidential Power* (New York: Morrow, 1982).
8. Peters, *American Public Policy,* p. 206.
9. William A. Niskanen, *Reaganomics: An Insider's Account of the Policies and the People* (New York: Oxford University Press, 1988), p. 155.
10. Jude Wanniski, *The Way the World Works* (New York: Basic Books, 1978).
11. Robert Reich and Ira Magaziner, *Minding America's Business: The Decline and Rise of the American Economy* (New York: Harcourt Brace Jovanovich, 1982).
12. William Nordhaus, "The Political Business Cycle," *Review of Economic Studies,* Vol. 42 (April 1975), pp. 169–190; Edward Tufte, *Political Control of the Economy* (Princeton: Princeton University Press, 1978).
13. Douglas Hibbs, *The American Political Economy* (Cambridge: Harvard University Press, 1987), Chap. 8.
14. Ibid., Chap. 7.
15. Benjamin Friedman, *Day of Reckoning: The Consequences of American Economic Policy Under Reagan and After* (New York: Random House, 1988), p. 144.
16. Milton Friedman, *Capitalism and Freedom* (Chicago: University of Chicago Press, 1962).
17. Joseph Pechman *Federal Tax Policy* (Washington, DC: Brookings, 1987), p. 3 and *The Economic Report of the President, 1993* (Washington, DC: Government Printing Office, 1993).
18. Quoted in Jeffrey H. Birnbaum and Alan S. Murray, *Showdown at Gucci Gulch* (New York: Vintage, 1988), p. 6.
19. See Cathie J. Martin, *Shifting the Burden* (Chicago: University of Chicago Press, 1991).
20. Birnbaum and Murray, *Showdown at Gucci Gulch,* p. 7.
21. Ibid., p. 6; Sven Steinmo, "Political Institutions and Tax Policy in the United States, Sweden, and Britain," *World Politics,* Vol. 41 (July 1989), pp. 510–515.
22. Joseph A. Pechman, *Who Paid the Taxes, 1966–1985?* (Washington, DC: Brookings Institution, 1985), p. 10.
23. Kevin Phillips, *Boiling Point: Democrats, Republicans, and the Decline of Middle Class Prosperity* (New York: Random House, 1993), Chap. 2.
24. Congressional Budget Office, "The Changing Distribution of Federal Taxes: 1975–1990" (Washington, DC: CBO, 1987).
25. Friedman, *Day of Reckoning,* p. 90.
26. Ibid., p. 272.
27. Ibid.
28. Robert Heilbroner and Peter Bernstein, *The Debt and the Deficit: False Alarm / Real Possibilities* (New York: Norton, 1989).
29. "Balancing the Government's Books," *The Economist* (February 12, 1994), p. 73.
30. James D. Savage, *Balanced Budgets and American Politics* (Ithaca, NY: Cornell University Press, 1988).
31. Robert D. Hershey, Jr., "A Hard Look at Corporate Welfare," *New York Times* (March 7, 1995), p. C2.

32. Ibid.
33. George J. Stigler, "The Theory of Economic Regulation," *Bell Journal,* Vol. 2 (Spring 1971), pp. 3–21. Also see Gabriel Kolko, *The Triumph of Conservatism* (Chicago: Quadrangle, 1967); James Weinstein, *The Corporate Ideal in the Liberal State* (Boston: Beacon Press, 1968).
34. See Richard Harris and Sidney Milkis, *The Politics of Regulatory Change* (New York: Oxford University Press, 1989).
35. See G. William Domhoff, *The Higher Circles* (New York: Random House, 1970); Edward S. Greenberg, *Capitalism and the American Political Ideal* (Armonk, NY: M. E. Sharpe, 1985); Kolko, *The Triumph of Conservatism;* Weinstein, *The Corporate Ideal.*
36. Frances Fox Piven and Richard A. Cloward, *Poor People's Movements* (New York: Vintage, 1979).
37. Greenberg, *Capitalism and the American Political Ideal.*
38. Marver Bernstein, *Regulation by Independent Commission* (Princeton: Princeton University Press, 1955); Grant McConnell, *Private Power and American Democracy* (New York: Vintage, 1966); Theodore J. Lowi, *The End of Liberalism,* 2nd ed. (New York: Norton, 1979).
39. See Eugene Bardach, "Social Regulation as a Generic Policy Instrument," in Lester M. Salamon, ed., *Beyond Privatization* (Washington, DC: Urban Institute, 1989), p. 198, for the distinction between economic and social regulation.
40. Harris and Milkis, *The Politics of Regulatory Change.*
41. Seymour Martin Lipset and William Schneider, *The Confidence Gap: Business, Labor, and Government in the Public Mind* (New York: Free Press, 1983).
42. David Vogel, *Fluctuating Fortunes: The Political Power of Business in the United States* (New York: Basic Books, 1989), pp. 59, 112.
43. James Buchanan and Gordon Tullock, "Polluters, Profits and Political Responses: Direct Control Versus Taxes," *American Economic Review,* Vol. 65 (March 1975), pp. 139–147); L. Lave, *The Strategy of Social Regulation* (Washington, DC: Brookings Institution, 1981); Murray Weidenbaum, *The Costs of Government Regulation of Business* (Washington, DC: Joint Economic Committee of Congress, 1978).
44. See Thomas Edsall, *The New Politics of Inequality* (New York: Norton, 1984); David Vogel, *Fluctuating Fortunes* (New York: Basic Books, 1989); and Kevin Phillips *The Politics of Rich and Poor* (New York: Random House, 1990); Thomas Ferguson and Joel Rogers *Right Turn* (New York: Hill and Wang 1986).
45. As reported in Vogel, *Fluctuating Fortunes,* pp. 262–263, 278–279.

CHAPTER 20

Social Welfare

IN THIS CHAPTER

- ★ Why all rich industrial democracies are welfare states
- ★ How and why the American welfare state is different
- ★ How Social Security and other social insurance programs work
- ★ How public assistance and other means-tested programs work
- ★ How the social welfare state is changing
- ★ On the relationship between the welfare state and democracy

Touching the Third Rail: Social Security

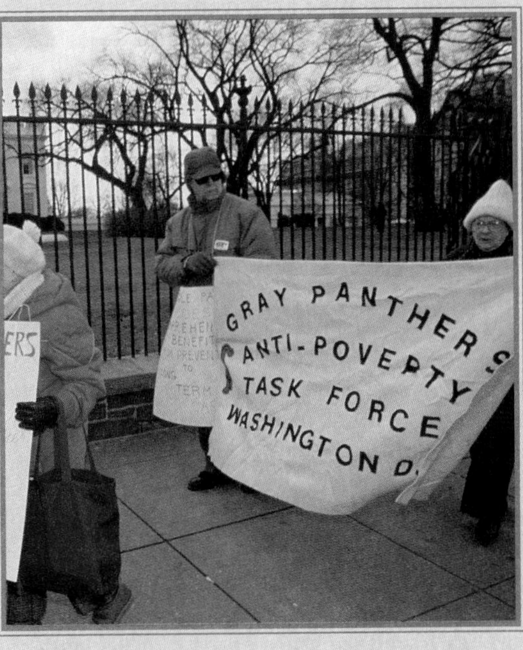

"Danger, do not touch!" Signs in subway tunnels warn workers to stand clear of the electrified "third rail" that powers subway cars. Although there is no such sign in Washington, D.C., warning politicians to stand clear of Social Security—called the third rail of American politics—most politicians know that tampering with Social Security is dangerous to political life and limb. Ronald Reagan forgot this central truth of American politics and saw his 1981 proposal to slash Social Security benefits defeated in Congress.

The president's budget director, David Stockman, flushed with confidence after the president's decisive victory in Congress on the budget, wanted to go after Social Security as the next step in the "Reagan Revolution." As Stockman described his objectives, "A frontal assault on the inner fortress of the American welfare state [Social Security] . . . was now in order." Marginal tinkering seemed out of the question: "What was needed was something far more radical, . . . a once-in-a-century opportunity. . . . Our job is to shrink the Social Security monster."[1]

Stockman focused on two features of Social Security that he found particularly troublesome. First, he believed the definition of *disabled* to be too lax, allowing many undeserving people to receive disability benefits. Second, he believed that giving 80 percent of the maximum old age benefit to those retiring early at age 62 rather than age 65 was damaging to both the economy and the Social Security system. With nearly three-quarters of Americans retiring early, not only was the economy being deprived of their labor, but the treasury was being deprived of needed Social Security payroll taxes.

Stockman's plan was worked out with Health and Human Services Secretary Richard Schweiker and was presented to the president at a meeting on May 11, 1981. The plan called for a significant tightening of disability requirements and an increase in the early retirement penalty from a 20 percent to a 45 percent loss of benefits. The changes, moreover, were to happen immediately rather than phasing in over several years—the usual practice for painful policy changes. The president loved it. He thought it would permanently fix the Social Security problem without raising taxes. "Our people on the Hill want this," he said. "It represents exactly what we have always said should be done. Let's go forward with it."[2]

The president was wrong. His people on Capitol Hill were furious. One very angry Republican member of Congress cornered Stockman at a meeting: "You absolutely blind-sided us with this Social Security plan. My phones are ringing off the hook. I've got thousands of sixty-year-old textile workers who think it's the end of the world. What am I supposed to tell them? How can I explain to the person who was planning to retire two years from now at age sixty-two that he will have to make do with $450 a month rather than $650?"[3] White House Chief of Staff James Baker believed that the plan would do great damage to the president and quickly began to put distance between him and the new approach to Social Security. He first called it a plan of the Department of Health and Human Services, then implied that it was only a minor response to a request from a congressional committee, and finally disclaimed any presidential involvement at all. By the end, White House operatives were calling the plan "Schweiker's Folly."[4]

Senate Republican leaders knew when to concede defeat. They withdrew the plan and substituted a mild resolution, pledging fiscal reform of Social Security. The substitute passed 96–0. David Stockman was appalled by this abandonment of a key element of the Reagan Revolution. The president, however, was anxious to cut his losses. A few months after the fiasco, he was persuaded by key

Republican leaders in Congress and his advisers in the White House to insulate himself and his party from the "third rail" by appointing a bipartisan committee of distinguished Americans to study problems in the Social Security system and to recommend solutions. The president bent with the prevailing winds and announced the formation of the commission as a way "to remove Social Security once and for all from politics." The commission eventually presented its plan for changes in Social Security in a report made public after the 1982 elections, much to the relief of Republicans and Democrats alike. The bipartisan commission's modest package was eventually passed by Congress and signed by the president.

Social Security is the largest part of the American welfare state. It is dear to the hearts of most Americans and virtually immune from criticism and tampering. It is noteworthy that Social Security was not "on the table" during the contentious budget battle between President Clinton and the Republican 104th Congress (see Chapter 19); neither side wanted to touch it. Public assistance (commonly called *welfare*), on the other hand, is almost universally disliked,[5] and was fundamentally refashioned by President Clinton and Congress in 1966. In this chapter, we explore the differences between public assistance and social insurance programs like Social Security. We also examine why a society that believes so strongly in the benefits of the free market and individualism has a welfare state at all. Finally, we shall enter the debate about the reform of the American welfare state. Answering these questions requires that we take account of structural, political-linkage, and governmental influences.

Why Welfare States Exist

welfare state A society in which a set of government programs protects the minimum standards of living of families and individuals against loss of income.

A social **welfare state** is a society in which a set of government programs protects the minimum standards of living of families and individuals against loss of income due to economic instability, old age, illness and disability, or family disintegration.[6] All rich industrial democracies are also social welfare states. Though the details of their programs differ, all provide social welfare for their citizens.

But why do we have social welfare? Why not simply leave the welfare of the people to the operations of the market economy? We suggest that the existence of a welfare state represents a recognition by the people in a democracy that a market economy, even when it is working at peak efficiency, does not guarantee a minimum decency of living for all of its citizens or offer protection against economic dislocations.[7]

The Making of the Welfare State: Structural Factors

Industrialization has produced unprecedented levels of wealth and improved living standards in the Western countries over the past century, but it has also produced disruptions and hardships. Industrialized market societies are places of rapid economic growth and transformation. They are places where factories open and close, where some regions become prosperous while others languish, and where one technology supersedes another. We saw in Chapter 4, for instance, that the American economy is now changing from one characterized by the factory and blue-collar work to one characterized by high technology, information processing, and white-collar workers. Market industrial soci-

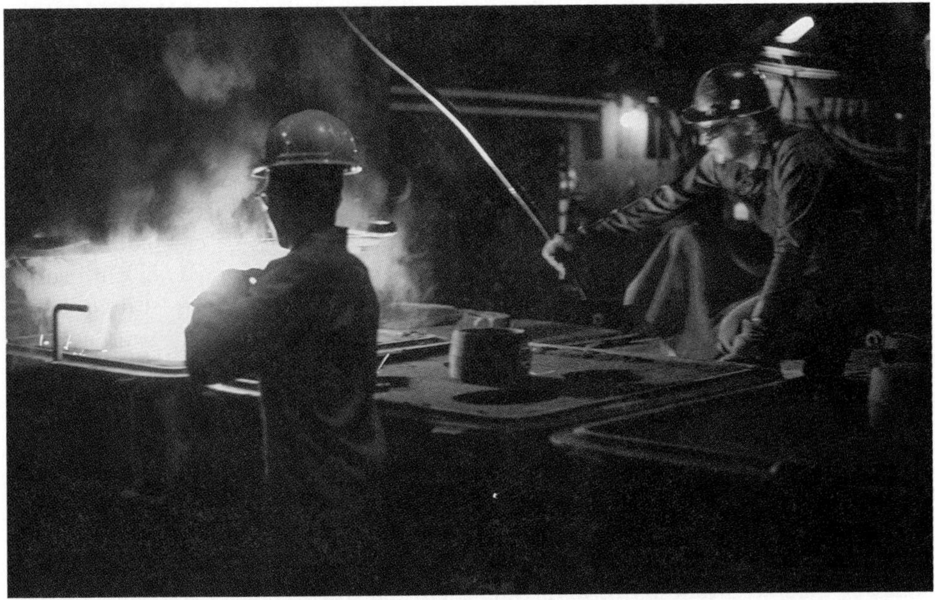

Industrial work is often dangerous to life and limb. To cope with industrial illness, disability, and death, most industrial societies have created government medical and financial support programs to help victims and their families.

eties are also places where the business cycle and periods of high unemployment are a part of life.

In industrialized societies, people also live longer because of advances in medical care and public health practices. But old age brings increased health care needs at the same time that people's separation from the workforce makes them less able to pay for those needs on their own. Work in the mines, factories, and transportation systems of industrial societies is not without risk, moreover, and occupational illness and disability are a problem. Industrial societies are also urban societies, in which people of widely varying backgrounds and economic circumstances live in close proximity. Poverty is more concentrated and visible in urban settings than in rural ones, and the possibilities for social conflict are greater.[8]

Industrialization also undermines the family, which provided welfare and caring in traditional, preindustrial societies.[9] Industrial and postindustrial societies are mobile; people must move to follow jobs. In such societies, families are not only smaller but also less likely to stay intact (note the high divorce rate in all industrial societies).

Industrial and postindustrial market societies, then, are places where the normal operations of the economy create many social problems that individuals and families cannot solve on their own.

The Making of the Welfare State: Political Linkage Factors

Though scholars generally agree that economic change and industrialization provide the preconditions for the social welfare state, they do not agree on why political leaders create and expand them. Presumably, in a democracy, people generally get what they want from government because their elected officials depend on their support to gain and maintain public office. The citizens of the

Western democracies have made it clear in public opinion polls and elections that they want government to do something to help them cope with the problems and dislocations resulting from industrialization.[10] We have welfare states, that is, because people want them.

There are several variants of the "democracy-as-cause-of-the-welfare-state" theme. One argues that the industrial *working class* is the main catalyst. In Europe, powerful labor and socialist parties introduced social welfare measures when they were in control of the government or caused sufficient anxiety so that other parties introduced such measures as a way of undermining the political popularity of the political left.[11] In the United States, it was the rising militancy and political influence of workers and labor unions, after all, that helped make the New Deal possible, including such landmark measures as Social Security and the beginnings of the federal role in public assistance.

Others believe that the proliferation of *interest groups* in democracies is the most important factor in the creation and expansion of the social welfare state. The elderly in the United States, for instance, are well represented by interest groups, vote in high numbers, and make substantial political contributions, so elected officials are favorably disposed toward programs that benefit them, such as Social Security and Medicare. Some conservative commentators believe that middle-class interests that depend on welfare state expenditures—the so-called "new class" of teachers, welfare workers, doctors, hospital administrators, and the like—are another important force in sustaining social welfare.[12]

Still other scholars argue that social welfare is designed by political and business leaders to forestall popular discontent and to undermine radical movements for social change. These scholars point to the significant role played by corporate and banking leaders in the creation of the social welfare state in the United States.[13]

An Outline of the American Welfare State

Before we turn our attention to current debates about social welfare in the United States, it is important that we have a clear picture of the basic forms and costs of the American welfare state.

Types of Programs

social insurance Government programs that provide services or income support in proportion to the amount of mandatory contributions made by individuals into a government trust fund.

means-tested Meeting the criteria of demonstrable need.

There are two basic kinds of welfare state programs in the United States. The first kind is **social insurance**, in which individuals contribute to an insurance trust fund by way of a payroll tax on their earnings and receive benefits based on their lifetime contributions. Social Security is an example. The second kind is **means-tested**, in which benefits are distributed on the basis of need to those who can prove that their income is low enough to qualify them. These programs are funded by general income tax revenues, rather than by payroll taxes. The food stamp program is an example.

There are other ways to categorize social welfare programs. A distinction can be drawn, for instance, between social welfare programs that pay people directly—cash transfer programs, such as unemployment insurance—and those that provide a service, such as job training or Medicare (which pays hospitals on behalf of recipients).

A distinction can be drawn, as well, between social welfare programs that are administered directly from Washington, D.C., and those that are jointly administered by federal and state governments. Social Security is an example of a program run from the nation's capital. Taxes for Social Security are levied directly on wages and salaries by the federal government, and benefit checks are issued to the elderly and the disabled by the Social Security Administration. Medicaid, and food stamps, on the other hand, are jointly funded and administered. One result of such mixed programs is wide variation in benefit levels across the states (see Figure 20.1).

Many welfare state programs are **entitlement** programs; that is, payments are made automatically to people who meet certain eligibility requirements. Thus, all Americans over the age of 65 are covered by Medicare, while most of those whose income is under a certain limit are entitled to food stamps. Because payments are made automatically, much of the federal budget is locked in, and Congress can only tinker around the margins of the budget. In

entitlements Program benefits that go automatically to individuals, groups, or businesses that meet criteria set out in law.

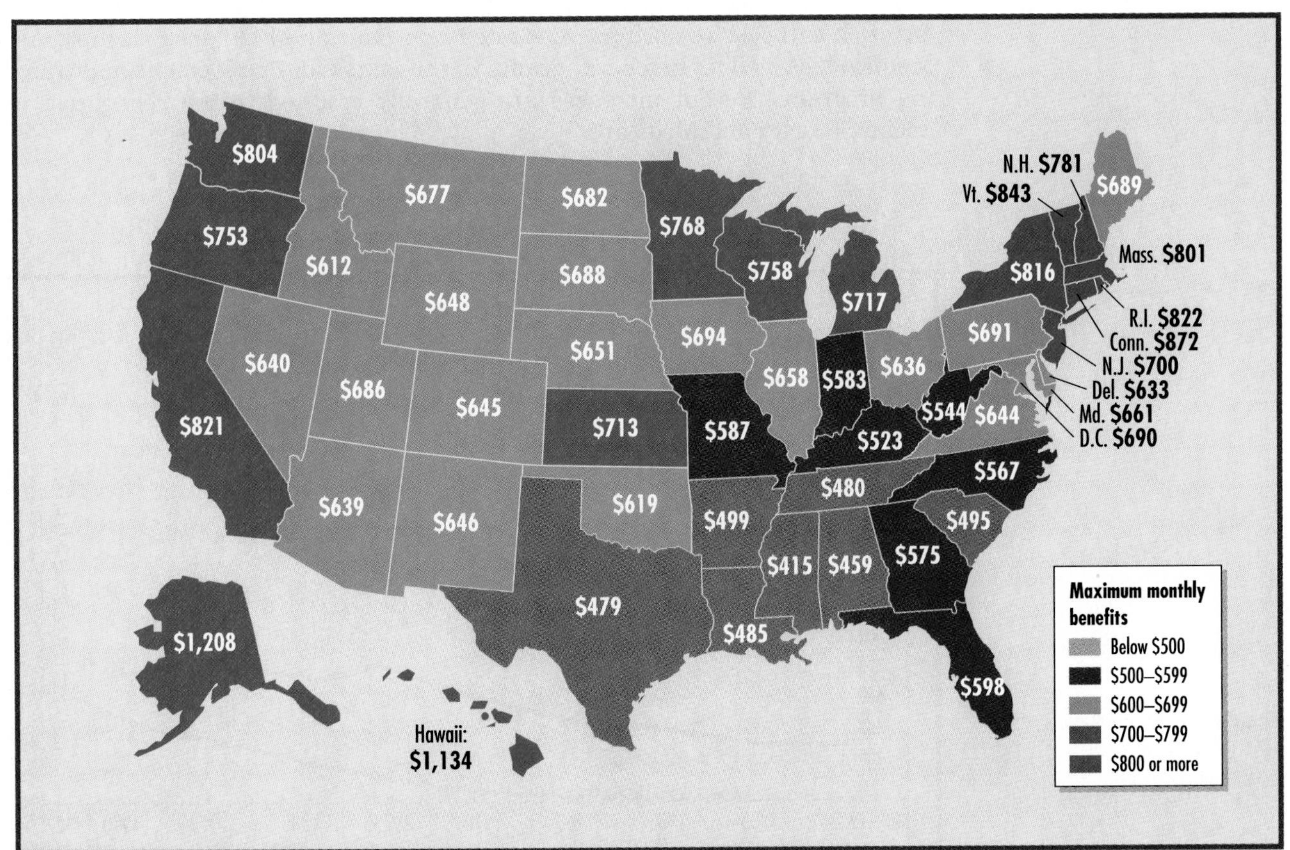

Figure 20.1 ■ **State Variations in AFDC and Food Stamp Maximum Monthly Benefits**

The states vary considerably in the maximum level of benefits they have provided to recipients covered by the Aid to Families with Dependent Children (now ended) and the food stamp programs. The most generous states are in the Northeast and the West; the least generous ones are in the Deep South.

Source: *Washington Post,* National Edition (September 18, 1995), p. 31.

1995, fully 50 percent of the federal budget went to various entitlements (including farm subsidy programs). Increasingly, policymakers are talking about controlling entitlements as the only way to gain control over the federal budget.

The Cost of the Social Welfare State

We spend a substantial amount of money in the United States on what the federal budget calls human resources (which includes spending not only for means-tested and social insurance programs, but for college loans, education, job training, medical research, and military pensions). In 1995, the total was $1,543 billion, of which the federal government's share was 60 percent, or over $900 billion. As a proportion of the gross domestic product (GDP), human resources spending was 22 percent in 1995—up from only 8.2 percent in 1950—considerably outstripping spending in any other area of government responsibility, including national defense. As a proportion of total federal spending, social welfare reached its peak in 1976, leveled off until the early 1980s, declined during the Reagan years, and has risen again in recent years (see Figure 20.2). The decline during the 1980s was caused mainly by Reagan administration cutbacks in such means-tested programs as AFDC, food stamps, and Medicaid, as well as in federal grants to the states for employment and training programs. Recent increases are generally credited to the rising cost of Social Security and Medicare.

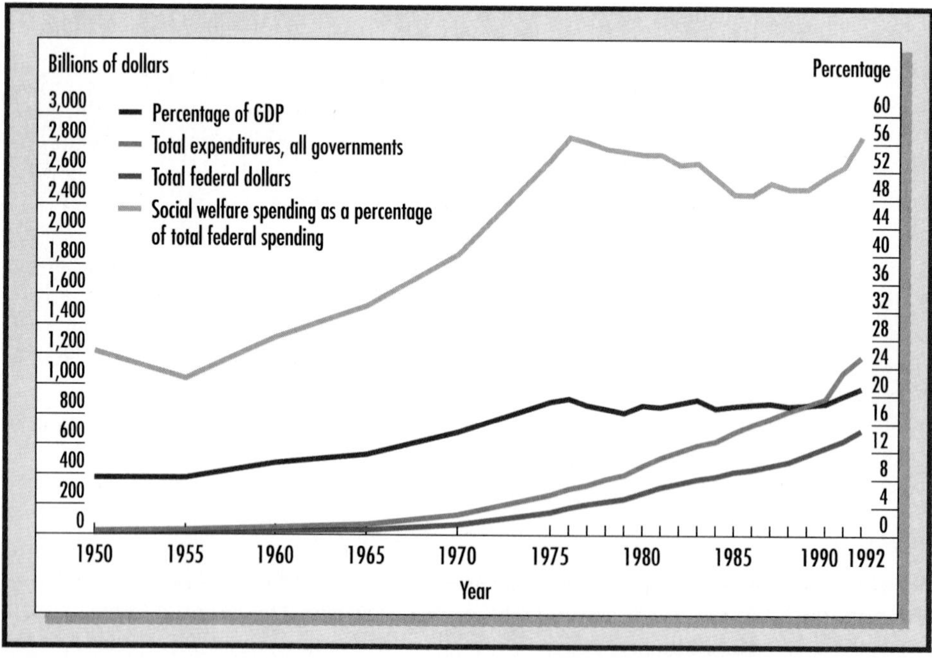

Figure 20.2 ▪ Social Welfare Expenditures in the United States, 1960–1992

The social welfare commitment of federal, state, and local governments in the United States is considerable. Relative to the size of the American economy—considered as a proportion of the GDP—social welfare spending in the United States has been fairly stable since the mid-1970s.

Source: *Statistical Abstracts of the United States, 1995* (Washington, DC: U.S. Census Bureau, 1996).

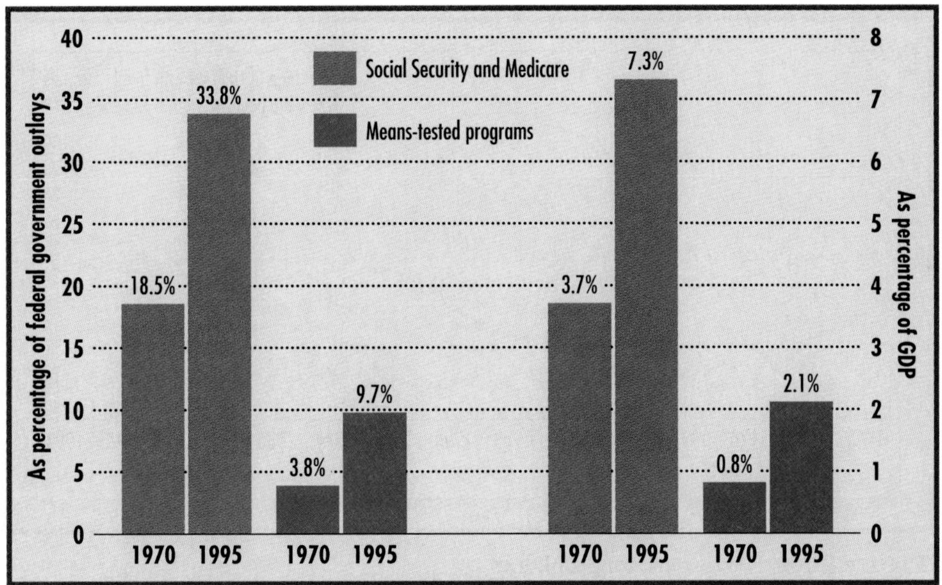

Figure 20.3 ■ Comparing the Size of Social Insurance and Means-Tested Programs

Social insurance programs, such as Social Security and Medicare, receive many more federal dollars than do means-tested programs, such as public assistance, food stamps, and Medicaid. Recently, the relative advantage of social insurance over means-tested programs has become even more pronounced.

Source: U.S. House of Representatives, Committee on Ways and Means, *The 1995 Green Book* (Washington, DC).

Social insurance represents the largest single federal expenditure. Social Security and Medicare, taken together, cost American taxpayers $512.2 billion in 1995, about one-third of all federal government expenditures (see Figure 20.3). By way of contrast, spending on national defense in 1995 accounted for 18 percent of the federal budget. Moreover, Social Security and Medicare have grown substantially, both in terms of the federal budget and as a percentage of GDP. Means-tested programs (including Medicaid and AFDC), on the other hand, despite all of the complaints about them by politicians and citizens, did not account for a very large proportion of federal expenditures, amounting to only 9.7 percent in 1995.

The implications of this pattern are significant. First, most benefits of the American welfare state go not to the poor but to the nonpoor. Those who receive the most benefits from social insurance programs such as Social Security and Medicare are those who were fully employed during their working lives, had the highest incomes, and paid the maximum level of Social Security taxes. Second, because social insurance benefits go mainly to those who are retired, the elderly fare much better than the young. One result is a significant decrease in the poverty rate among the elderly over the past two decades and a dramatic increase in the poverty rate among children.[14] Roughly one in five children now lives below the poverty line in the United States (see Figure 20.4). Because Social Security remained untouched in the recent efforts to balance the budget, and Medicare took only minor hits, while Medicaid and other means-tested programs suffered serious cuts, the disproportionality in

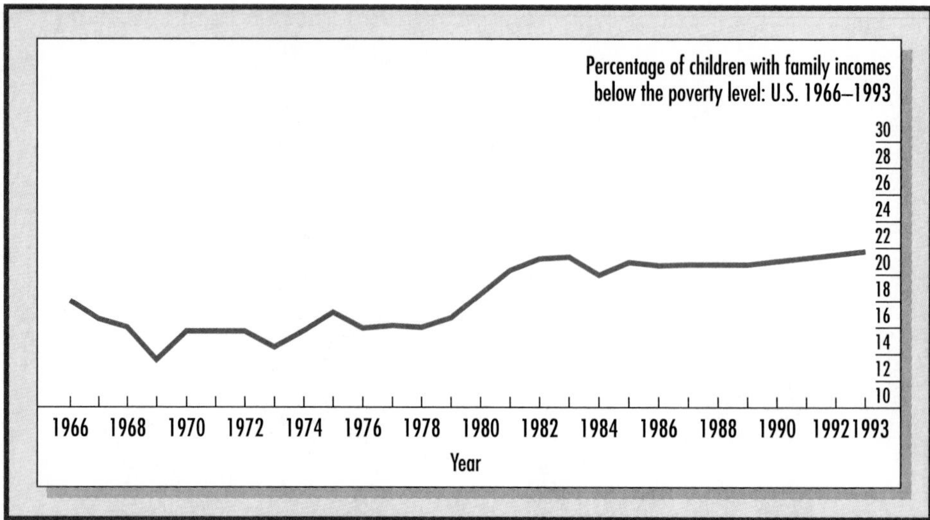

Figure 20.4 ■ Poverty Among Children

Social welfare spending in the United States goes disproportionately to those over 65, and the spending gap has been widening between programs that help the elderly and those that help children under the age of 18. One result has been a decline in poverty among the elderly and an increase in poverty among children.

Source: *Statistical Abstracts of the United States, 1995* (Washington, DC: U.S. Census Bureau).

poverty rates between the elderly and children is likely to become even more pronounced. Many believe that the wholesale refashioning of AFDC in 1996 from an entitlement program to a block grant program will make these disparities even more serious.

Social Security and Other Social Insurance Programs

Social insurance programs that guard against loss of income due to old age, disability, illness, and unemployment are the largest, most popular, and fastest-growing parts of the American welfare state.[15]

Components of Social Insurance

There are a number of social insurance programs designed to meet different contingencies.

Old Age, Survivors, and Disability Insurance (OASDI) This is the largest of the social insurance programs and the full, technical name of Social Security. When Social Security was created in 1935, it was designed to provide benefits to the elderly. Within a year, however, benefits were added for survivors (popularly referred to as the "widows-and-orphans program"). Coverage for the disabled was added in 1956. Today, almost all employed Americans are covered by Social Security, the main exception being the employees of many state and local governments.

OASDI is funded by a payroll tax on employees and employers under the Federal Insurance Contributions Act (the familiar FICA on your weekly or

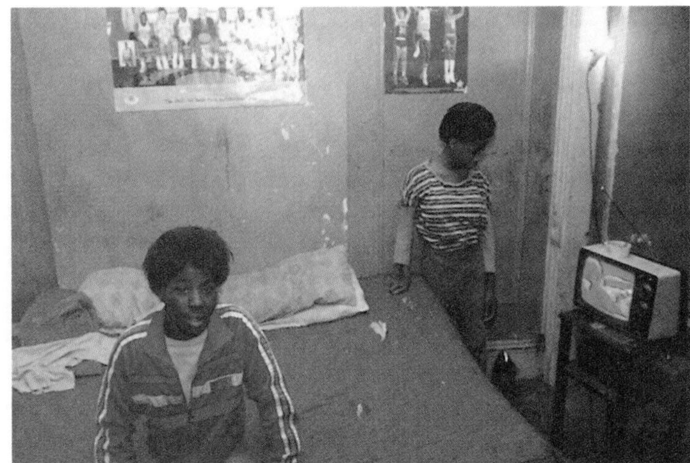

Social welfare spending in the United States favors the old over the young. One result has been an increase in poverty among children since 1980.

monthly pay stub); these tax revenues are deposited in a Social Security trust fund. The self-employed pay into a similar trust fund. Unlike private insurance premiums, the premiums paid into the fund over a person's lifetime are not sufficient to pay for the level of benefits actually received. That is, retirees receive more than they actually pay in, and more than they would receive had they put their payroll taxes in a savings account or paid premiums for private insurance. As a result, and because the program is paid for to a substantial degree by those who are currently working, the net effect is to redistribute income across generations.

Because inflation tends to undermine the purchasing power of benefits over time, Congress added automatic annual cost-of-living adjustments (COLAs) to OASDI in 1975. Alarm at the rising cost of COLAs during the Reagan years led the National Commission on Social Security to recommend and Congress to legislate a provision for a cutback in COLAs if the Social Security trust fund reserves ever fell to dangerously low levels. Bill Clinton asked Congress in 1993 to cut COLAs as part of his deficit-reduction package, but a firestorm of protest from organizations representing the elderly forced him to withdraw the proposal.

Many Americans worry that Social Security funds will run out before they can begin collecting benefits. There are some grounds for this fear, even though Social Security now takes in more than it pays out each year and its trust fund shows a strong positive balance. The problem is that this pleasant state of affairs will not last very much longer, as the proportion of Americans receiving benefits grows, while the proportion of Americans paying taxes to support Social Security declines (see Chapter 4). Especially troublesome is the sizable baby-boom generation whose first members will reach retirement age in 2010. Recent estimates suggest that the Social Security trust fund will move into the red by the year 2020. Of course, Americans can decide long before then to solve the trust fund problem by raising OASDI payroll taxes or by cutting back benefit levels. Both options, needless to say, involve considerable risk for elected political leaders. One thing is certain, however: given the great popularity of the Social Security program (see Figure 20.5), political leaders are unlikely to allow it to "go bankrupt."[16]

Medicare Medicare pays for a substantial portion of the hospital and doctor bills of retirees and the disabled. It has two main parts. Part A, funded by a

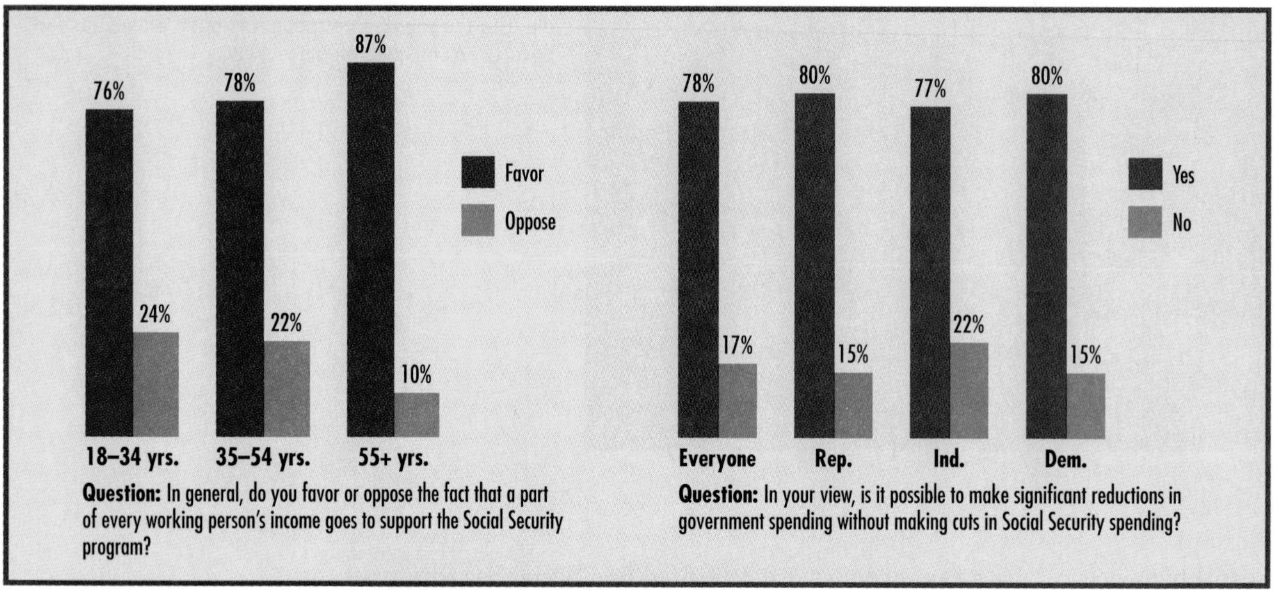

Figure 20.5 ▪ **Popular Support for Social Security**

Social Security enjoys widespread, across-the-board public support. This support is not affected at all by partisanship. Age has a slight effect, though even the very youngest voting-age Americans, who support Social Security the least, favor the program by a 3:1 margin.

Source: Survey by the Gallup Organization for the Employee Benefit Research Institute (January/February 1994); survey by Yankelovich Partners for *Time*/CNN (December 7–8, 1994).

payroll tax on employees and employers, pays hospital bills (though not in total). Part B is a supplementary and voluntary insurance program, financed by premiums from enrollees, to cover doctor bills.

Since Medicare was created in 1964, it has grown into one of the largest federal programs in total dollar expenditures; over $177 billion was spent in 1995, or almost 12 percent of the federal budget.

The problem of paying for Medicare is becoming ever more acute. Outlays have been growing at about 10 percent a year, much faster than those for other federal programs, and much faster than Medicare revenues are coming in. And waiting in the wings, again, is the baby-boom generation. One recent report suggests that Medicare Part A will be in deficit by the year 2001 unless steps are taken to rectify the problem. One estimate holds that 70 million retirees will be eligible for Medicare in 2030, compared to 37 million today, with each retiree being supported by the taxes of two working people, compared to three today.[17] It is no wonder, then, that the issue of controlling Medicare costs has become one of the constants of recent American politics. Bill Clinton's deficit reduction legislation in 1993 targeted Medicare, and Congress went along with his plan to decrease Medicare payments to doctors and hospitals. Clinton's health-care-reform proposals were also designed to help slow the rapid rise of Medicare expenditures, but the plan did not win approval from Congress. A slowdown in the rate of growth in Medicare spending was one of the key provisions in the Republicans' 1995 plan, unveiled in the 104th Congress, to balance the federal budget in seven years.

Unemployment Insurance Unemployment insurance is administered by the states under federal guidelines, assisted by federal subsidies. It is financed by

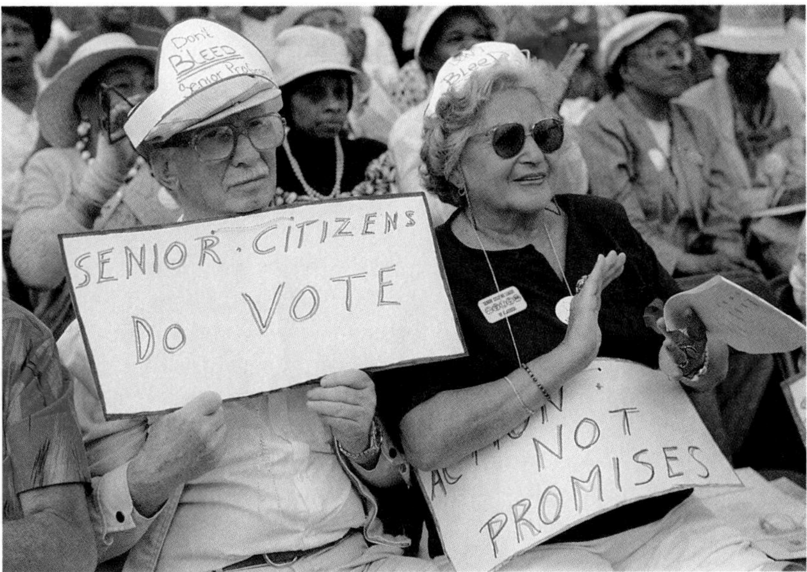

Organizations representing senior citizens have been influential in shaping the kinds of social welfare programs found in the United States.

federal and state taxes on employers for each of their employees. Studies show that the program is not very popular with Americans (unlike other social insurance programs, such as Medicare), perhaps because employees do not contribute to the fund, and perhaps because of the importance of work in American culture. Physically able people who are not working do not seem "deserving" to many Americans.[18] The level of unemployment benefits is set by the states, and wide variations are evident among them. Because of strict eligibility requirements and limited funds, fewer than half of those who are unemployed are covered by the program,[19] and the extent of coverage is diminishing year by year. In 1990, only four in ten unemployed workers were covered, compared to seven in ten in 1976.[20]

Do Social Insurance Programs Work?

In an era when it is fashionable to deride the ability of government to do anything well, it is important to know about the relative success of America's social insurance programs. Though they are not without problems, most people believe they do a fairly good job of delivering on their promises at a reasonable cost.

Successes Social Security and Medicare work beyond the wildest dreams of their founders. Though the benefits do not allow people to live luxuriously (over 60 percent of the elderly in 1993 had annual family incomes of less than $20,000),[21] they provide an income floor for the retired and pay for costly medical services that, before 1965, were as likely as not to impoverish those who had serious illnesses and long hospital stays. The improvement in the living standards of the elderly is evident in the decline in their official poverty rate. The Office of Management and Budget once estimated that the poverty rate for Americans over the age of 65 would be about 55 percent if Social Security did not exist;[22] the current figure is about 12 percent.

The effectiveness of social insurance programs is shown by a massive study reported in 1989 by the U.S. Census Bureau on the effects of all government taxing and spending programs on income inequality and poverty. The principal finding was that Social Security (including Medicare) "is the Federal government's most effective weapon against poverty and reduces the inequality of Americans' income more than the tax system and more than recent social welfare [means-tested] programs."[23]

Problems Despite these successes, many problems remain. Social Security and Medicare have remained viable, for instance, only because Congress has steadily raised payroll taxes to pay for them. FICA and Medicare taxes now take a larger bite out of the paychecks of a majority of Americans, than the personal income tax. For those who generally oppose taxes, this trend is cause for concern. Whether taxes are too high cannot be answered objectively or scientifically, of course, though it is worth repeating the point that our overall effective tax rates remain well below those of most other Western countries.

Some critics also worry about the overall *regressive* effects of social insurance. In many respects, the well-off do better than the not-so-well-off. The main reason is that Social Security benefits are tied to one's lifetime earnings. The higher one's income has been, the higher the payroll taxes paid and the higher the benefits received. Moreover, income earned in wages and salaries beyond a certain ceiling causes a retiree to lose old age benefits; this is not the case for the more wealthy retiree who receives income from investments (stock, real estate, etc.). The middle-class elderly also seem better able to take advantage of the medical care provided by Medicare and to participate in the heavily subsidized Supplemental Medical Insurance program (Part B) to cover doctor costs. Some of the regressivity of social insurance was rectified in 1984, however, when 50 percent of Social Security income for those annually earning more than $25,000 ($32,000 for married couples) became taxable.

Another problem is the political tension that seems to be building between the elderly who receive benefits and those who are still working and paying payroll taxes to support the programs. As the population ages, there are fewer workers to pay taxes to support those who receive benefits. Because the elderly are well organized and politically active, moreover, their needs are attended to by elected officials and are likely to receive even more attention in the future. The effect is likely to be a further accentuating of the tendency of the American social welfare state to favor the elderly at the expense of others in need, particularly the very young and the poor. As Senator Daniel Patrick Moynihan says, "Old people vote. Children don't. That much is a simple fact. For people with the franchise, this is a tremendously responsive system."[24] Whether younger voters will continue to support this arrangement remains to be seen; interest organizations representing younger workers and professionals (such as "Lead . . . or Leave," founded in the early 1990s) have already appeared on the political scene.

There is also concern that Medicare, while vastly improving the health care of the elderly, has introduced significant adverse distortions into the American health care system. Complaints have been heard about the steadily escalating costs of Medicare because of increases in the number of Americans over the age of 65, the steady introduction of high-technology (and expensive) medical care, and loose controls over doctor and hospital costs. Others worry that the inflation in health care costs introduced by this massive influx of government money has put first-class doctor and hospital services out of the reach of the nonelderly and the nonpoor (the very poor are assisted by Medicaid).

These persistent problems are why the issue of national health insurance is being talked about so much. If and when a national health program is implemented in the United States, Medicare is likely to change substantially.

Public Assistance (Welfare)

Public assistance (more commonly known as *welfare*) accounts for only a small part of the annual federal budget but has attracted more popular discontent than virtually anything else government does. While Social Security and Medicare are politically sacrosanct and largely immune from criticism, welfare has long been the target of widespread criticism and the object of scores of reform proposals.

It is probably fair to say that, while most Americans want government to help the poor, almost everybody dislikes welfare in its traditional AFDC form (see Figure 20.6): not just conservatives, but liberals as well; not just the average citizen, but also welfare recipients; and not just voters and political leaders, but people who work for welfare agencies. A general consensus has long existed among very strange bedfellows that something is wrong with the way we have traditionally organized public assistance. As one student of welfare put it, "The general pattern has varied little since the New Deal: since 1935 a majority of Americans have never wanted to spend more on welfare."[25]

It's no great mystery why people have not liked welfare. For most Americans, welfare seems to contradict such cherished cultural values as independence, hard work, stable families, and responsibility for one's own actions. Public opinion polls consistently show that Americans believe that welfare keeps

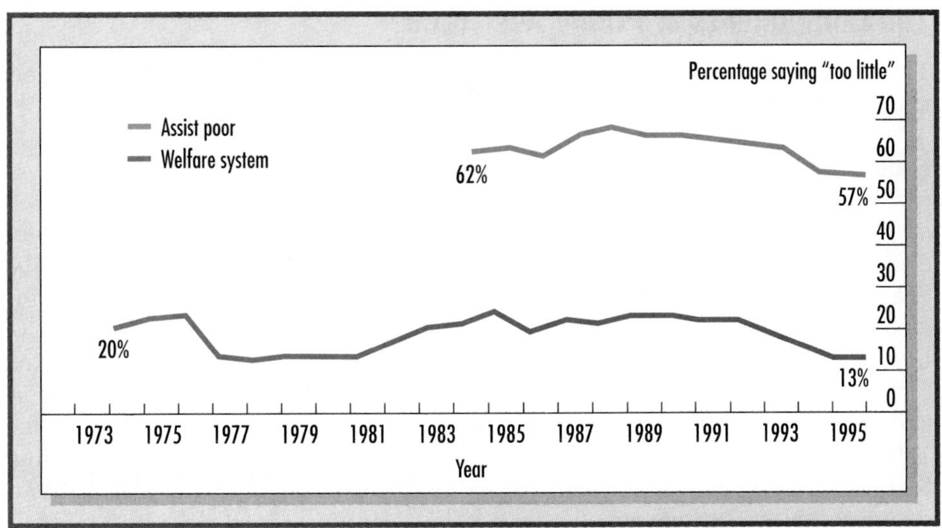

Figure 20.6 ■ **"Helping the Poor" and Support for Welfare Are Not the Same Thing**

Americans consistently say that government is spending too little to help the poor, but few say government should be paying more for welfare. This discrepancy suggests that a majority of Americans have been dissatisfied with the welfare system in its AFDC form but do not reject the general principle of help for the poor.

Source: Surveys by the National Opinion Research Center, General Social Surveys.

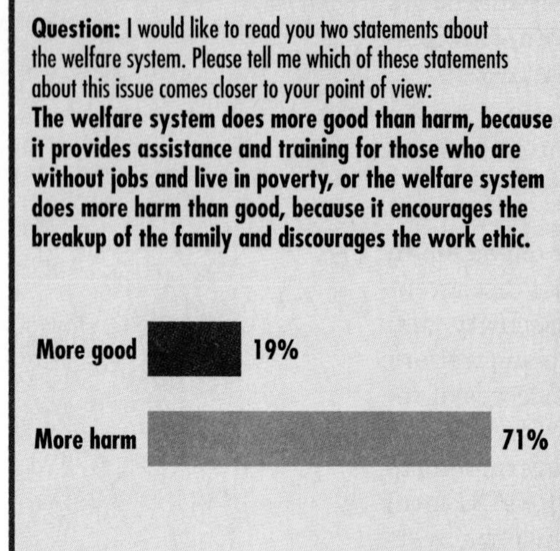

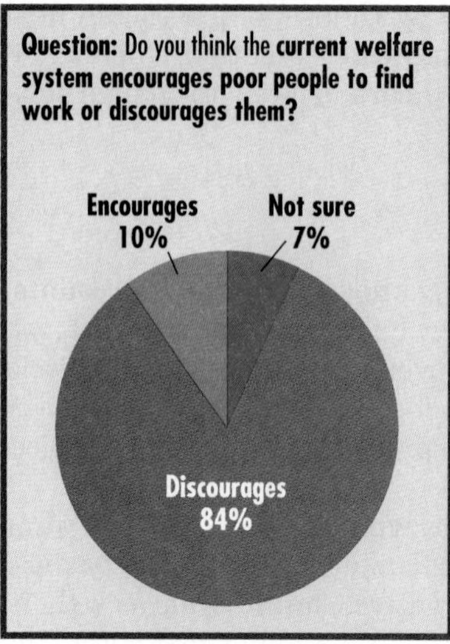

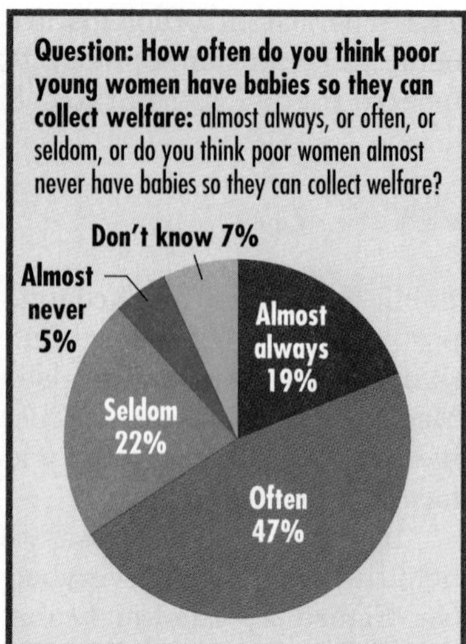

Figure 20.7 ■ **Why Americans Are Dissatisfied with Welfare**

American disaffection for welfare programs seems to be based on the public's assessment of the purported negative impact of welfare on families and the work ethic, as these opinion poll results demonstrate.

Source: Survey by Hart & Teeter Research Companies for NBC News/*Wall Street Journal* (January 15–18, 1994); survey by Yankelovich Partners for *Time*/CNN (May 18–19, 1994); survey by the *Los Angeles Times* (April 16–19, 1994).

people dependent, doesn't do a good job of helping people stand on their own two feet, and encourages divorce and family disintegration (see Figure 20.7).[26]

The Components of Public Assistance

There are several means-tested programs designed to assist low-income Americans. They are described in this section.

Food Stamps This program is available to most Americans who fall below a certain income line. About 8 percent of Americans presently receive food stamps. Food stamp benefit levels are set by the individual states under general federal guidelines, and states vary substantially in their generosity. Stamps can only be used for food and basic necessities; they cannot be used for alcohol or gambling, despite rumors to the contrary. The program seems to have made a significant dent in the prevalence of malnutrition in the United States, even though the average benefit has never exceeded 80 cents per person per meal.[27] Federal support for food stamps was cut substantially in the 1996 legislation that overhauled the nation's welfare system. Cuts, totaling $25 billion over six years, come mainly at the expense of poor people without young children in the home.

Medicaid The federal government allocates matching funds to the states to provide medical assistance for their indigent citizens in this rapidly growing program (expenditures grew from $30 billion in 1988 to $96.2 billion in 1995). Except for the requirement that they provide Medicaid for all public assistance recipients, the states formulate their own eligibility requirements and set their own benefit levels. The eligibility rules are complex and tend to exclude those who are not extremely poor, blind, disabled, or children of out-of-work parents. Furthermore, as states try to contain Medicaid costs in the face of rising taxpayer discontent and budgetary problems, they have made access even more difficult. The problem of noninclusion is serious; only about 40 percent of the nation's officially designated poor are covered by Medicaid,[28] and the remainder are without medical benefits or protection. On the other hand, the inability to contain Medicaid costs is one of the main reasons that the states have run into fiscal difficulties (Figure 20.8). States can choose not to be a part of the Medicaid program. Two presently are not; several others are considering leaving. A bill passed by the Republican-dominated 104th Congress to make Medicaid a block grant program and to remove its federal entitlement status failed to win approval from President Clinton.

Other Means-Tested Programs

- Supplemental Security Income (SSI) is a program created in 1974 that provides cash benefits to the elderly, blind, and disabled poor whom social insurance programs are insufficient to elevate above the poverty line. The program is a relatively small one and getting smaller.
- Housing-assistance programs come in a dizzying number of forms, including subsidies to states and local communities to build public housing, tax incentives for developers to build in low-income areas, and rent supplement payments to poor families to help them pay rent.
- Job training was a major part of the federal antipoverty programs during the 1960s and 1970s—with apparent success, according to most studies[29]—but was cut back to almost nothing during the 1980s. The Clinton administration, under the leadership of Labor Secretary Robert Reich, began in 1993 to put more emphasis on job-training programs, but a hostile Congress refused to fund many of them after 1995.

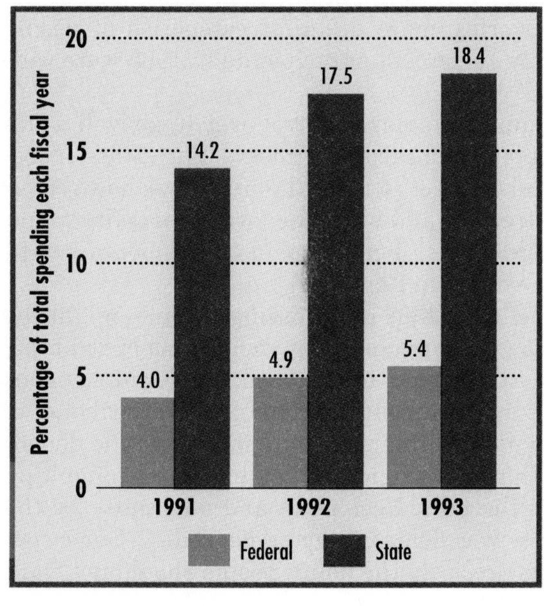

Figure 20.8 ■ **The Growing Medicaid Burden on the States**

Medicaid is a federally mandated program for which the states pick up most of the bill. The growing burden of Medicaid on state budgets is one of the factors leading to calls for reform of this entitlement program.

Source: Office of Management and Budget and National Association of State Budget Officers, reported in Rodney Smith, "The Growing Medicaid Bill" (*The New York Times,* September 5, 1995, p. 1).

- Head Start, by far the most popular means-tested social welfare program, reaches about 300,000 children per year (only about 20 percent of those who are technically eligible) in its effort to prepare poor preschool children for entrance into public schools.
- While technically not a "program," the Earned Income Tax Credit, which reduces taxes for the families of low-income workers, is a highly effective way to give modest support to the "working poor." Republican President Gerald Ford signed the bill into law in 1975. President Reagan voiced his support on a number of occasions during his administration, once calling it "our most effective antipoverty program." The tax credit cost $28 billion in 1995; over 90 percent of the benefits went to working families making under $20,000 per year.

Welfare Block Grants The United States' way of providing public assistance to the needy changed dramatically with passage of a new welfare block grant program in 1996. From the time of the New Deal until recently, the largest, most visible, and least popular public assistance program was Aid to Families with Dependent Children, or AFDC. Before addressing the new block grant welfare system, and as preparation for understanding it, we describe AFDC and the many criticisms leveled against it.

How AFDC Worked AFDC distributed cash benefits directly to the poor, primarily to single-parent households with children (about $17 billion in 1995). Most went to female-headed single-parent households, among whom poverty is most pronounced.

AFDC was created in 1935 as part of the original Social Security Act. The act specified that the federal government would contribute to state and locally administered programs of assistance to low-income families with children, as long as the states were willing to operate under general federal guidelines. At the time, government officials thought these measures would be temporary instruments to ease some of the suffering of families made destitute by the death or incapacitation of fathers, destined to wither away after the Great Depression eased, the economy revived, and the Social Security system reached maturity.[30] Instead, the program became a permanent and significant part of the nation's social welfare system covering more different categories of people than originally intended. Thus, only 15 percent of recipients in 1995 were widows or wives of disabled men.[31]

Administratively, AFDC was quite complex. Control over it, as well as its funding, was shared by federal, state, and local governments. Each state, moreover, decided who would receive aid (subject to federal guidelines), how recipient income and assets were to be treated, and what the level of benefits would be. Because of the large role of the states, benefits paid to recipients varied dramatically across the states, as we saw in Figure 20.1.

Because many Americans believe that undeserving people might be tempted to "go on the dole," AFDC was surrounded by mountains of red tape. Welfare workers spent much of their time investigating the employment records of applicants, their assets and sources of income, the whereabouts of spouses who might be expected to make a financial contribution to the dependent family, and the possibility that the single mother might be cohabiting with a male who might help pay the bills. Recipients and advocates for the poor insisted that the entire process was demeaning and degrading. Some conservatives responded that this was precisely the point; people should not want

RESOURCE FEATURE

How Well Do Welfare Mothers Live?

These welfare mothers did not live extravagantly. The typical mother spent only $954 a month to support a family of four, which is slightly less than the federal poverty line. The poverty line is an arbitrary threshold, set 25 years ago as a matter of political convenience, but surveys suggest that most Americans think the threshold is too low, not too high. . . .

In 1986 the typical Gallup respondent said that a family of four needed $349 a week (roughly $1,500 a month) to get along. Poorer families set the threshold lower, but even the heads of families with incomes below $10,000 said that a family of four needed $1,200 a month to get along. Allowing for inflation, the 1988 figure would be about $1,300. Using this standard, Edin's welfare families were getting along on three-quarters of what low-income Americans thought a family needed. . . .

None of the 22 mothers reported expenditures totaling more than 133 percent of the poverty line, even when we include Food Stamps. Half lived in very bad neighborhoods. Half lived in badly run-down apartments, where the heat and hot water were frequently out of order, the roof leaked, plaster was falling off the walls, or windows fit so badly that the wind blew through the apartment in the winter. One in three did without a telephone, and one in three reported spending nothing whatever on entertainment. Many said their food budgets were too tight for fresh fruit or vegetables. Only one had a working car.

It is true that all these welfare mothers had color television sets, and that a third had video recorders—"extravagances" that often offend intellectuals who rely on books for entertainment. But because both TV sets and video recorders last a long time, they cost only a few dollars a month. Since they provided both the mothers and their children with free entertainment, the mothers were willing to forgo almost any other comfort (such as reliable hot water or fresh vegetables) to ensure that they had a working television. Without one, their lives would have been unimaginably bleak.

Source: From a study by Kathryn Edin, reported in Christopher Jencks and Kathryn Edin, "The Real Welfare Problem," *American Prospect* (Spring 1990), pp. 84–85.

to be on welfare and should not feel comfortable being there. Whether intended or not, this kind of treatment kept many poor people who were eligible for AFDC from applying for it.

The Cost of AFDC Though the size of AFDC grew steadily until its termination in 1996, it never amounted to much as a proportion of federal government spending or of GDP (see Figure 20.9). Nor did it provide very much money to poor families. From 1950 until 1995, the average annual AFDC payment never provided more than 70 percent of what the government considered the minimum a family needs to no longer be considered poor (the **poverty line**). In 1996, the average payment hovered at slightly below 40 percent of the poverty line. Even when noncash programs, such as food stamps and Medicaid, were added, welfare did not lift recipient families above the official government poverty line. It is important to note, moreover, that the value of welfare benefits going to poor families with dependent children had been declining steadily since the early 1970s (see Figure 20.10). The average AFDC payment to a family in 1993 ($373) was only 55 percent of what it was in 1990.[32] Despite stereotypes to the contrary, life on welfare was no picnic (see the Resource Feature on how welfare mothers live).

poverty line The federal government's annual calculation of the dividing line between the poor and nonpoor; there is a different line for individuals and families according to their size.

Although AFDC had long been declining as a share of the federal budget and as a proportion of GDP, many Americans were alarmed by the rate of increase in the number of people who depended on it (see Figure 20.11), and the extraordinary number of people who had been in the program over the years. A University of Michigan study showed, for instance, that 22 percent of all American children had spent at least one year on AFDC before they are 18, and that 72 percent of all African-American children had done so.[33] The impact of the program, then, was all out of proportion to the actual dollars spent on it.

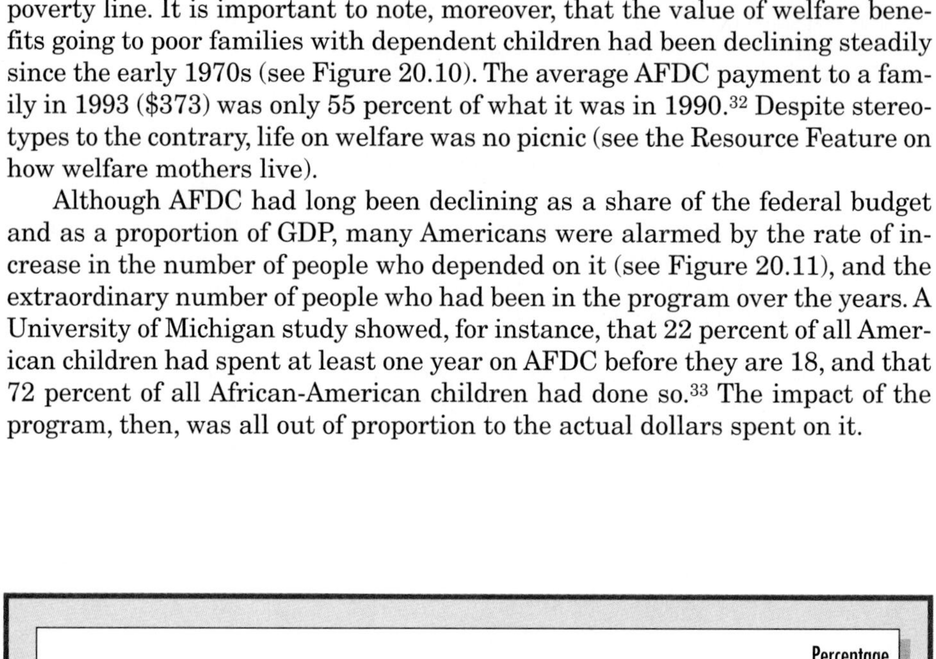

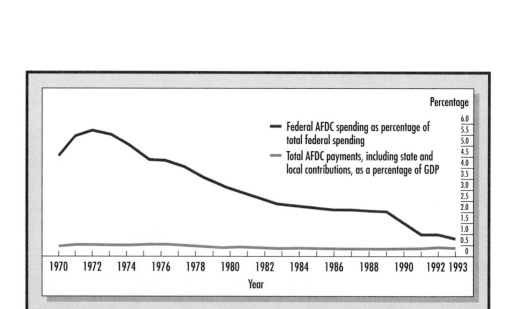

Figure 20.9 ■ **Trends in AFDC Benefits**

Spending for AFDC never amounted to much, either as a proportion of federal expenditures or as a proportion of GDP. Since the early 1980s, the financial burden grew steadily lighter even as disaffection with the program increased.

Source: *Statistical Abstracts of the United States, 1995* (Washington, DC: U.S. Census Bureau, 1995).

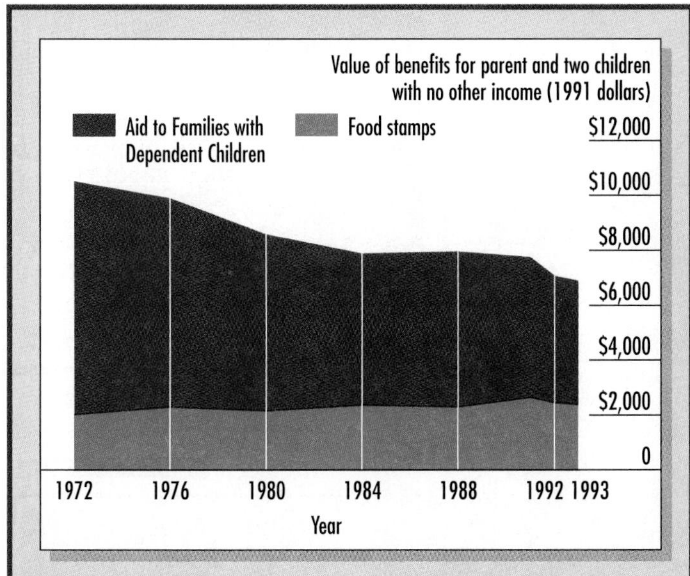

Figure 20.10 ■ **The Declining Value of Welfare Benefits**

The real dollar value of AFDC and food stamp benefits going to poor families fell significantly over the last two decades.

Source: *Statistical Abstracts of the United States,* 1995 (Washington, DC: U.S. Census Bureau, 1995).

Criticisms of AFDC By the 1990s, a virtual consensus had developed that something was terribly amiss with the Aid to Families with Dependent Children program.[34] We outline here the main criticisms of AFDC before describing the new block grant system that is taking its place.

- *AFDC Undermined the Work Ethic:* If people can live reasonably well "on the dole" without working, it was argued, they will lose the incentive to work. Opponents of AFDC argued that benefits were so generous

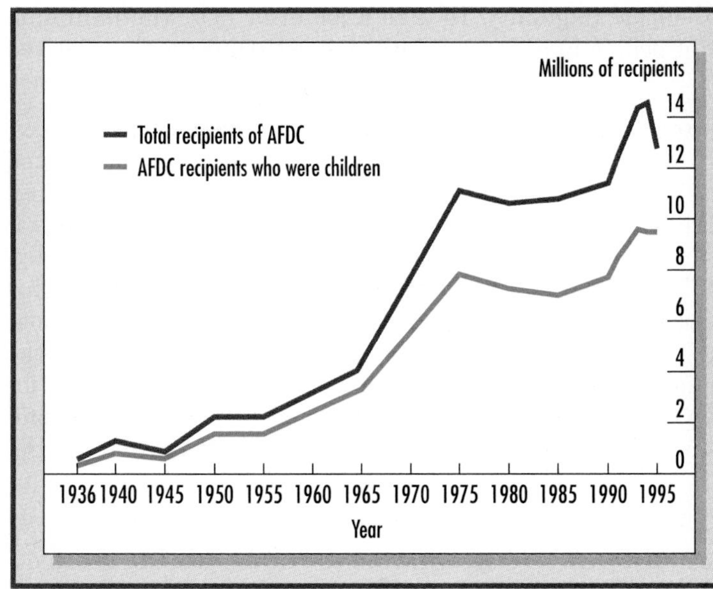

Figure 20.11 ■ **Numbers of AFDC Recipients**

Over the years, the number of Americans on welfare (AFDC) rose considerably. The number increased sharply in the late 1960s, leveled off in the 1980s, and began to increase again in the early 1990s.

Source: U.S. House of Representatives, Committee on Ways and Means, *The 1994 Green Book* (Washington, DC: 1994) and *The Budget of the United States, Fiscal Year 1997* (Washington, DC: Government Printing Office, 1996).

Borgman, with permission of King Features.

that many people saw no reason to work. As economists Milton and Rose Friedman put it, "Those on relief have little incentive to earn income."[35]

Even many of those who supported AFDC in principle complained that it encouraged welfare dependency because it penalized poor people who took jobs by radically reducing their levels of assistance and taking away their Medicaid eligibility. To take a job at or near the minimum wage, then, put people in a worse circumstance than if they had stayed on welfare.

- *AFDC Encouraged Family Disintegration:* Prominent conservatives, such as Lawrence Mead, Charles Murray, and George Gilder, claimed that the AFDC welfare program contributed to the breakup of families. As evidence, they pointed to the fact that the rate of family disintegration and the level of welfare spending increased at the same time, starting in the late 1960s. A number of factors are said to have produced this effect. First, because AFDC went only to single-parent families, poor couples were financially better off if they did not marry or if they broke up their marriages when a baby was born. Second, AFDC gave more independence to women with children who no longer felt financially compelled to enter into, or stay in, a marriage they did not want to be in. Depending on your point of view, of course, this might be a positive or negative development.
- *AFDC Created a Permanent Dependent Class:* Life on welfare became a habit, many argued. People remained recipients for long stretches of

time. Their children, knowing no other model of how life might be lived, eventually came to see life on welfare as normal. This life of dependency, in turn, contributed to a syndrome of problem behavior that made escape from dependency unlikely. While recent research shows that lifelong dependency on welfare was not as common as most Americans think (see Figure 20.12), it is true that roughly 25 percent of recipients had been on the welfare rolls for more than 10 years (though not necessarily continuously).[36] Many social scientists believe that blaming AFDC for the creation of what has come to be known as the "urban underclass" is unfair, however.[37] Slow growth in the American economy and job migration from central cities, in their view, have been the main causes of dependency and family breakup.[38]

- *AFDC Did Not Do Enough to Help the Poor:* One criticism of welfare that did not get much play in the press was that it did not reach all of the poor who needed benefits. Approximately one-fourth of those who were eligible for AFDC did not take part in the program, for example. [39] The stigma attached to being on welfare apparently kept many people away.

  Nor did AFDC do much for the *working poor.* Most welfare programs—whether AFDC, food stamps, or Medicaid—traditionally distribute benefits to those poor people who cannot be expected to work: children, the elderly and disabled, and mothers of young children. Poor people, who are in two-parent families where one or both parents work full or part time, have rarely been covered by welfare. This group includes about 60 percent of the poor. The working poor are overwhelmingly white and of prime working age. They suffer high rates of unemployment or are stuck in low-wage, part-time jobs without benefits. The number of Americans who fit into this category has increased since 1978.[40] The Earned Income Tax Credit helps the working poor, but efforts are underway to cut it back.

The New System In 1996, the Republican-controlled 104th Congress passed a bill to fundamentally refashion welfare in the United States. Having run in the 1992 presidential on a pledge to "change welfare as we know it," and

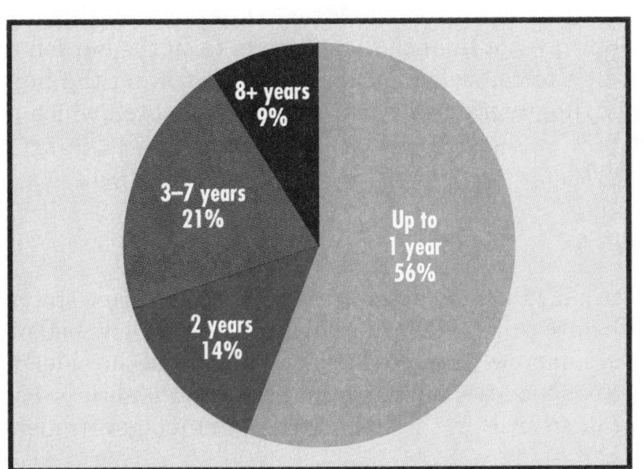

Figure 20.12 ■ **Average Continuous Time on Welfare**

Contrary to popular opinion, the average welfare recipient did not spend a lifetime on the welfare rolls. Indeed, recent research shows that more than half were on the rolls on a continuous basis for a year or less; only 9 percent were there for more than eight continuous years.

Source: U.S. House of Representatives, Committee on Ways and Means, *The 1994 Green Book* (Washington, DC: 1994).

having vetoed two previous welfare bills, President Clinton felt compelled to sign the bill, though he had many reservations about it. He promised that if he were reelected in 1996, he would ask Congress to rescind the steep cuts in food stamps and the prohibition of welfare benefits for legal immigrants.

The new welfare system is extremely complex and only in its earliest stages, so how it will eventually develop or how effective it will prove to be is unknown at this time. Its major features are as follows:

- The status of welfare assistance as a federal entitlement has been ended. The families of poor children are no longer guaranteed assistance by the federal government.
- The design and administration of welfare programs have been turned over to the individual states. In the end, the United States will have fifty different welfare systems.
- States will receive block grants from the federal government to help them finance the welfare systems they devise.
- The head of every family receiving welfare is required to work within two years of receiving benefits and is limited to a total of five years of benefits. States are allowed to impose even more stringent time requirements. States are also allowed to use their own funds (not federal block grant money) to extend the two-year and five-year limits.
- Unmarried teenage parents can receive welfare benefits only if they stay in school and live with an adult.
- Future legal immigrants are ineligible for benefits during their first five years in the United States.
- States must provide Medicaid to all who qualify under current law.
- The eligibility of poor people who are not raising children to receive food stamps is severely restricted.

Proponents of the legislation suggest that the new welfare system will end welfare dependency, reestablish the primacy of the family, improve the income situation of the poor as they enter the job market, and help balance the federal budget. Opponents of the legislation, who point to the paucity of high wage jobs in poor neighborhoods and the absence of child care and job training in the new system, believe that the new welfare system will result in rising poverty, homelessness, and hunger, especially among children. Others worry that the states are not prepared for or are not financially able to take on the burden of running their own welfare systems, or are incapable of generating the high number of jobs required for the program to work. Only time will tell which of these scenarios is correct.

How the American Welfare State Is Different

Although all of the industrialized democracies are also social welfare states, not all social welfare states are alike. Welfare states range from low-benefit types where beneficiaries are narrowly targeted (e.g., the poor and the elderly) to high-benefit types where beneficiaries include most people in the society. The former are called *minimal* or *liberal* (in the free-market, limited-government sense of the word *liberal*) *welfare states;* the latter are called *developed* or *social democratic* welfare states.[41] The United States is very close to the minimal end of the spectrum. How you feel about where the United States fits on the spectrum depends on your values. For those who believe that small government is always better than big government, it is a very good thing. Others may disagree, believing that government should play a more significant role in protecting and sustaining its citizens.

How the United States Compares

How do we compare to other social welfare states? In what ways is the United States different from the other rich democracies? The comparisons that follow are to the nations of the Organization of Economic Cooperation and Development (OECD): Western Europe, Japan, Australia, and New Zealand.

- *The U.S. welfare state developed later than the others.* The term *laggard* has been used to characterize the American welfare state.[42] With rare exceptions, social insurance programs were introduced in America much later than elsewhere (see Table 20.1). National health insurance was introduced in Germany in the late nineteenth century; it was available in almost all Western European nations by 1950. Medicare for the elderly and Medicaid for the indigent didn't happen in the United States until the 1960s.
- *The American welfare state is smaller than most.* Despite complaints about its size and cost, ours is one of the smallest of the social welfare states.[43] Among the OECD countries, only Japan and Australia spend relatively less (that is, less, relative to their GDP) than we do on social welfare, and the former is well known for the generosity of company benefits to workers, including lifetime employment in many of its largest corporations.
- *The American welfare state covers fewer people than other welfare states.* Welfare states near the developed end of the spectrum blanket their entire populations with benefits. Family allowances in such places as Austria, the Netherlands, Norway, and Sweden, for instance, go to all

Table 20.1

Introduction of Welfare State Programs

Country	Disability Insurance	Pension Insurance	Unemployment Insurance
Germany	1884	1889	1927
Great Britain	1887	1908	1911
United States	1930	1935	1935

Source: Adapted from R. T. Kudrle and T. R. Marmor, "The Development of Welfare States in North America," in P. Flora and A. J. Heindenheimer, eds., *The Development of Welfare States in Europe and America* (London: Transaction, 1981), p. 83.

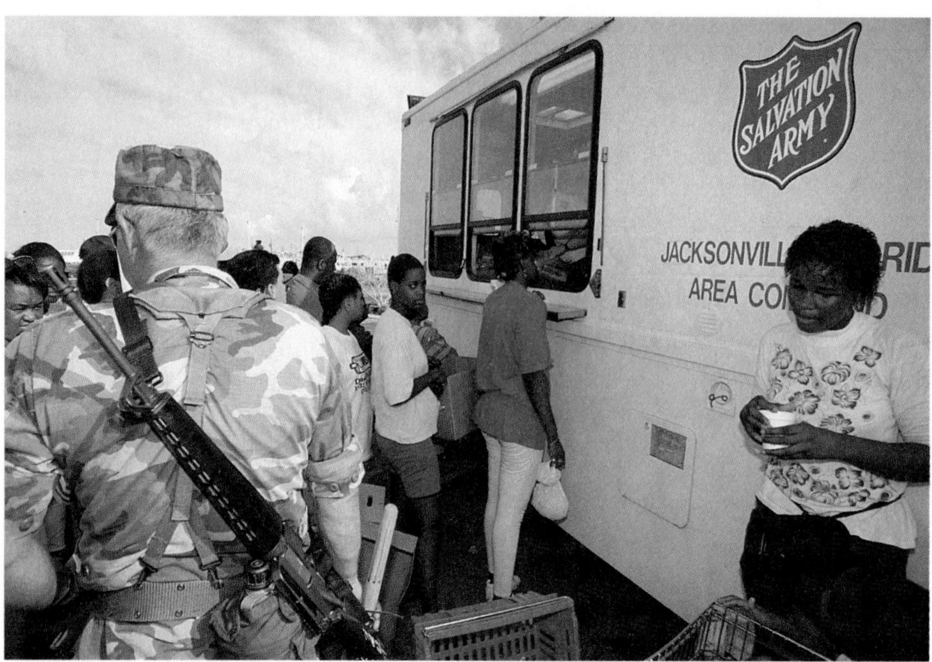

Americans have a long tradition of voluntarism and charitable giving, somewhat reducing the pressure for the kinds of social services provided by governments in other countries.

citizens who have children. Medical coverage is universal in most of the OECD nations. In the United States, in contrast, social welfare provision is a patchwork, and many citizens are not protected or covered. Thus, children in AFDC families received more generous benefits than did poor children in two-parent families. Many poor Americans receive Medicaid, while others do not.

- *The elderly do considerably better than the young in the American welfare state.* Medicare and Social Security, already the largest parts of social welfare in the United States, continue to outstrip the rate of growth of programs that benefit the nonelderly poor, especially children.[44] In most other welfare states, family allowances and universal medical coverage make benefit distributions more balanced.[45]
- *The American welfare state is less redistributive.* The degree of income equality in the OECD nations (with the exception of Japan) is a function of the amount of money they spend on social welfare programs and the degree to which program coverage is universal. The United States ranks very low on both, so our social welfare state does not make much of a dent in the degree of income and wealth inequality in comparison with those of other nations.[46] Table 20.2 shows the share of national income going to the bottom 20 percent of the population in several countries, before and after government benefits and taxes are taken into account. The lag in U.S. performance is obvious. If you believe that inequality is a natural and just outcome of a free market system that must not be tampered with, then you will not be bothered much by such findings. If you believe otherwise, however, you may think some changes are in order.

Table 20.2

Share of National Income Received by Bottom 20 Percent of Families

Country	Share of National Income, Not Taking Government Benefits or Taxes into Account	Share of National Income, Taking Government Benefits and Taxes into Account
Canada	4.6	5.3
Israel	4.5	6.0
Norway	4.9	6.3
Sweden	6.6	8.0
United Kingdom	4.9	5.8
United States	3.8	4.5
West Germany	4.4	5.0

Source: From Timothy M. Smeeding, Michael O'Higgins, and Lee Rainwater, *Poverty, Inequality and Income Distribution in Comparative Perspective* (Washington, DC: Urban Institute, 1990), p. 34.

- *The American welfare state requires less of private employers.* All Western European welfare states require that employers help employees with their parenting obligations. All require employers to offer maternity and parenting leaves (now required for workers in firms with 50 or more employees in the United States under the Family and Medical Leave Act), with pay (not required here); all require that work schedules be adjusted for parenting needs. German mothers receive six weeks' paid leave before giving birth, and eight weeks' after. All Western European governments mandate four to six weeks of paid vacation. All insist on employer participation in employee pension programs. U.S. employers are not so obligated.

- *The American welfare state does not include universal health care.* The OECD countries either provide health services directly (the National Health Service in Great Britain is an example), universal health insurance coverage (the Canadian system, for example), or some combination of the two. In the United States, Medicare has provided health insurance coverage for the elderly, while Medicaid has provided coverage for the poor. Other Americans must depend on private insurance or do without. Today, over 40 million Americans have no insurance coverage at all. To make matters worse, the American system is also the most costly (the United States spends roughly 13 percent of its GDP on health and medical expenses; Canada, the next most costly nation among the industrial democracies, spends about 9.5 percent) and the least effective, according to a number of standard medical measures (the United States ranks below every industrial democracy in the world, except Spain, on infant mortality and life expectancy).

This combination of uneven coverage, escalating costs, and poor health outcomes has convinced a rapidly growing majority of Americans that something must be done to fix the system. A 1990 Harvard University survey of ten industrial democracies showed that Americans were the least satisfied with their system of health care; only 10 percent of Americans said they were happy with their system, compared to 56 percent of Canadians.[47] Even the American Medical Association, long opposed to any tampering with private enterprise medicine, announced in 1993 that something must be done to fix our present system.

The consensus breaks down, of course, when it comes to finding solutions. President Clinton's proposal, put together in 1993 by a number of expert working committees chaired by his wife, Hillary Rodham Clinton, called for a nationally mandated, decentralized system of health insurance, financed mainly by employers, providing coverage of a basic package of services for all, and depending on managed competition to control costs. One Republican plan proposed tax-deductible medical savings accounts that people could use to buy insurance and pay medical bills. Many liberals have favored what is called a *single-payer system,* similar to that of Canada.[48] The Republican plan failed to gain much support. The single-payer approach was opposed not only by Republicans but by President Clinton, so it never received serious consideration. Clinton's plan, opposed strongly by the medical insurance industries and by small business (see Chapter 7), never made it to the floor of the Senate. A bill mandating the portability of health insurance coverage for those who have insurance became law in 1996, however.

It remains to be seen whether the nation will be able to reform its health care system. Honest disagreement among members of Congress about the proper path to take and interest group opposition to nearly every proposed alternative mean that the obstacles to change are significant.

Are the Western European Welfare States Becoming More Like Us?

Competitive pressures in the global economy are forcing major companies in every country to become "lean and mean," as the saying goes. Similar pressures are forcing even very rich nations to become more concerned about the high taxes and budget deficits that seem to be associated with highly developed welfare states. These conditions adversely affect the international competitiveness of countries and their business enterprises. In response, several nations with highly developed welfare states, such as France, Finland, and the Netherlands, have stopped the growth of social welfare spending as a proportion of their GDP. Germany, Belgium, and Ireland have actually cut back the relative size of social welfare spending. Great Britain has subjected more of its programs to means testing. Many of these countries have increased the retirement age, and most of the rest are currently considering doing so.[49]

Despite recent changes, Western European political leaders have not been able to do much more than chip away at the edges of the welfare state. The reason is that the vast majority of people in Western Europe, including powerful labor unions, support the welfare state and are willing to fight to keep it. Few European leaders, therefore, have tried wholesale reform. Those who have, paid the price. When French prime minister Jacques Chirac attempted to make major cuts in welfare state benefits in 1995, massive demonstrations and prolonged public employee strikes forced him to withdraw his proposals. Conservative prime ministers in Finland and Sweden tried systematic reform and were driven from office. The upshot is that the welfare states of most of the other rich democracies, even if they are scaled back, are unlikely to look anything like the American welfare state. They are likely to remain more generous, universal in coverage, and redistributive in their effects than ours.

Why the American Welfare State Is the Way It Is: Structural and Political Linkage Factors

How do we explain the special character of the American welfare state? In this section, we identify structural and political linkage factors that influence the kind of social welfare state we have.

Constitutional Rules

Federalism is one of the reasons why social welfare programs were introduced here so late. Until the 1930s, it was not clear where the main responsibility for social welfare was lodged constitutionally. It was not generally accepted that the national government had any authority at all on social welfare matters until the U.S. Supreme Court belatedly relented and accepted the New Deal. It was only in 1935, with the passage of the Social Security Act, that our nation took the first step toward building the kind of social insurance safety net that had already been in place in Germany since 1889.

Federalism is also responsible for the incredible administrative complexity of our social welfare state: Some programs are run as national programs from Washington, D.C.; some are jointly funded and administered by federal and state governments; and some are mainly local but operate under federal guidelines. This divided and shared authority, of course, characterizes many government programs.

Federalism also causes the great unevenness in program coverage. Rather than being a universal and uniform national system that covers all citizens, our system takes into account the needs and interests of each of the states.[50] The result is great variation among the states in benefits, eligibility requirements, and rules. The only programs that are universal in the European sense (uniform, comprehensive, and administered and funded by the national government) are Social Security and Medicare.

Racial and Ethnic Diversity

It is often argued that Europe's greater propensity toward welfare states with universal coverage is a result of the ethnic and racial homogeneity of their societies. In homogeneous societies, the argument goes, voters are willing to support generous welfare programs, because recipients are felt to be very much like themselves. Recipients are considered neighbors, down on their luck, perhaps, but not strangers. Recipients are looked on as "us" rather than "them."[51]

Whether or not this argument is valid, it is apparent that racial and ethnic tensions influence the shape of the American welfare state. Some of the hostility toward AFDC, for instance, was probably related to the fact that African-Americans made up a disproportionately large share of AFDC recipients (though less than a majority of all recipients). Politicians such as David Duke in Louisiana and Jesse Helms in North Carolina demonstrated considerable skill in weaving together the racial and welfare themes in their electoral campaigns.

Political Culture

Almost every aspect of the American political culture works against a generous and comprehensive welfare state. The belief in individualism is especially important—that part of the American creed that emphasizes independence, responsibility, and autonomy. Voters who believe that people should stand on their own two feet and take responsibility for their lives are not likely to be sympathetic to welfare claims. Voters who believe that people generally get what they deserve are not likely to take kindly to appeals for help from able-bodied, working-age people.[52]

Antigovernment themes in the political culture also play a role. Generous and comprehensive welfare states, such as those in Europe, are almost always large and centralized states supported by high taxes. Being deeply suspicious of politicians, centralized government, and taxes, Americans are strongly resistant to welfare state appeals.

In addition, our political culture supports more voluntary efforts in welfare matters than other nations do, leaving government with less to do. Such organizations as the United Way and the Salvation Army take on many responsibilities that governments shoulder in other Western democracies. Because people believe that there are inevitable inefficiencies in government and efficiencies in the private sector, many aspects of social welfare are turned over to private insurance companies, nursing homes, and hospitals.

Business Power

Business plays a disproportionately powerful role in American politics (see Chapter 7). Almost without exception, the business community has opposed the creation of a welfare state along European lines. It has been a voice for low taxes and limited benefits, voluntary efforts over government responsibility, and profit-making welfare providers over government agencies. We can see this stance in the area of medical care. Ours is a patchwork quilt that combines social insurance for the elderly (Medicare), a means-tested program (Medicaid) for *some* of the poor, private insurance (Blue Cross/Blue Shield, Prudential, etc.) for many Americans, and a multitude of "for-profit" hospitals and nursing homes. Doctors, hospital corporations, insurance companies, and nursing-home owners are major players in the American system of interest group politics, and they continuously press politicians to maintain this system of mixed government–private-enterprise medical care.

Labor Union Weakness

Those countries in which the working class is organized and exercises significant political power have extensive welfare states; those countries in which the working class is not well organized and fails to exercise significant political power have minimal welfare states.[53] The political power of the working class is usually measured by scholars in terms of the percentage of workers in labor unions and the relative success of parties that are closely associated with unions (such as the Socialist, Social Democratic, and Labor parties). American labor unions have never been very strong or influential when compared with labor unions in other Western capitalist societies. The proportion of American workers who join labor unions has always been lower in the United States than in other capitalist countries and is steadily declining. Moreover, neither of our political parties defines itself as a working-class or a labor party committed to using government as an instrument of equality. We have no party equivalent, for example, to the labor-backed Social Democratic party that has dominated Swedish politics since the mid–1930s.

Interest Groups

American interest groups, as we saw in Chapter 7, speak with a strong "upper-class accent," overrepresenting business, the well-to-do, and the professions. By and large, these groups are not among those that push for the expansion of the welfare state.

A particularly important interest group in defining the character of the American welfare state is the elderly, who are well organized and active as an electorate. The U.S. elderly are probably more influential in politics than the elderly in other countries, where strong political parties dissipate the power of interest groups.[54] The poor, on the other hand, have little political influence given their low voting turnout and their relative lack of resources to form interest groups. The "Motor Voter" bill may slightly increase the political voice of the poor, however. See the Struggle for Democracy box.

Social Welfare and Democracy

Democratic politics played an important role in the formation of the American social welfare state. The main elements of social welfare in the United States—namely, Social Security and public assistance—happened only because of strong popular pressures on political and economic leaders. The Great Depression and the popular movements for economic justice that it spawned during the 1930s were the catalysts for the United States to institute a range

The enormously popular Townsend movement, with its call for financial payments to elderly Americans, was an important factor in the passage of the Social Security Act.

The Motor Voter Bill Increases Registration Among Welfare Recipients

The Struggle for Democracy

Voting turnout in the United States is lower than the voting turnout in other democratic countries, barely exceeding 50 percent in presidential elections and 35 percent in non-presidential-year congressional elections. Political scientists have identified a number of factors to explain low voting turnout (see Chapter 9), but barriers to voter registration are among the most important. To be sure, barriers to registration affect all groups in the American population, but the young, the poor, and racial minorities seem to be the most adversely affected. This clear violation of the principle of political equality, however, may finally be on its way to amelioration. After years of lobbying by "public interest" and "good government" advocacy groups, Congress passed the National Voter Registration Act of 1993 (known popularly as the motor voter bill) requiring that the states allow registration by mail and at motor vehicle, welfare, and other government offices. Before the new law was passed, registration typically took place in scattered registrar offices, often with odd and inconvenient hours. The hope of the bill's advocates was that making registration easier and more accessible would increase registration (and, ultimately, voting) by Americans in general and by underrepresented groups in particular.

The evidence to date is that the motor voter bill has served its purpose. Indeed, some political experts say we are currently experiencing "the greatest expansion of voter rolls in the nation's history," with over 5 million Americans newly registered in the first eight months after the bill went into effect on January 1, 1995. Never before in the United States has there been such a significant surge in registration in so short a time; when women and 18-year-olds gained the vote, for instance, they joined the voter rolls at a much slower pace. For the past three or four decades, roughly 63 percent of eligible Americans have been registered. By the end of 1995, the figure stood at 66 percent. Some believe that almost 80 percent of eligible voters will be registered by the year 2000.

It also appears that the new law is making inroads on political inequality. Preliminary figures show that roughly one-third of new registrants are under the age of 28, while another one-third are members of a minority racial group. Roughly one in five, moreover, have registered at state and county welfare offices (50 percent registered at motor vehicle offices), and one must presume that most of these registrants are poor. In some states, the proportion registering at welfare offices is even higher: in West Virginia, welfare offices accounted for 58 percent of newly registered voters.

Not everyone is happy about the new law. Republicans almost held up the bill in Congress because of fears that motor voter registration would work to the long-run benefit of Democrats; they apparently were afraid that the provision for registration at welfare offices would increase registration among those most likely to vote for Democrats. Moreover, a number of states with Republican governors—Illinois, California, Pennsylvania, Virginia, Michigan, and South Carolina—have brought suits in the federal courts to block implementation of the new law (so far, without success), claiming that it represents undue federal interference in legitimate state activities and that it also requires the states to spend money on a federal program for which they are not reimbursed (called *unfunded mandates*). It is not unreasonable to assume that concerns about giving an advantage to their electoral opponents also were a factor in these state suits. Their concerns may be unfounded; early evidence does not support the hopes of Democrats and the fears of Republicans that the law would favor the Democrats. Indeed, among those added to the voter rolls under the motor voter provisions, the largest proportion registered as independents, and the remainder was split about evenly between the two parties.

Whatever the partisan fallout may be in the long run, there is no doubt that the motor voter legislation has added considerably to democracy in the United States. It has done so by increasing the likelihood of higher voting turnout and by enhancing the potential for the representation of groups whose voices have not been very loud in electoral politics, particularly the poor. If this potential becomes reality, we may well see the day when the poor have a seat at the table where American welfare policy is decided.

Sources: Drummond Ayres, Jr., "Law to Ease Voter Registration Has Added 5 Million to the Rolls," *New York Times* (September 3, 1995), p. 1; Jamie Cooper, "Center for Policy Alternatives Shows Welfare Agencies Are New Home for New Voters," *U.S. Newswire* (November 6, 1995), p. 1.

of social insurance programs that were already widely available in Europe. The steady expansion of Social Security, furthermore, was carried out during the postwar decades with strong support from the American people. Moreover, the most significant expansion of public assistance took place from the mid–1960s to the mid–1970s, at least in part as a response to the civil rights and antipoverty movements that represented a significant new involvement in politics by Americans who had long been excluded from politics. Finally, public opinion polls show strong public support for almost every program of the American welfare state, though most Americans would like to see a larger federal role in providing health insurance and something done to fix the so-called welfare mess.

On the other hand, the kind of welfare state that we have is also attributable to the prominent role played by business and by interest groups representing the professions and the elderly. It may be that the catalyst for the creation of social welfare programs is provided by democratic politics, while program details are often worked out by those who have the resources to be significant players in the political game.

The effects of social welfare on democracy are also mixed. Social insurance, especially Social Security and Medicare, has surely enhanced the health and well-being of the elderly and has enabled them to become more active citizens. By making a dent in the prevalence of poverty among the elderly, social insurance has made the elderly more equal among themselves and more equal in relation to other groups in American society. Thus, social insurance has played a significant role in enhancing popular sovereignty and political equality in the United States. On the other hand, those on public assistance have not been so fortunate. Most important, welfare does not appear to leave much room for the development of dignity, independence, and self-confidence among its recipients, characteristic essential to democratic citizenship. The health of democracy in the United States may depend, in part, on what we choose to do about this problem. Only time will tell if the 1996 transformation of the welfare system will help or hurt.

Summary

All of the industrial democracies are also social welfare states. The main catalyst for the development of welfare states was industrialization, which created many social and economic problems, and which undermined institutions that had traditionally provided for the welfare of the population. Industrialization also produced the economic and organizational resources that make the social welfare state possible. The political impetus for the creation of social welfare programs has come from both the business community and the public.

The social welfare commitment of the federal government has grown substantially since the 1930s, though the Reagan Revolution slowed the growth considerably, even reversing the trend in means-tested programs for the poor. Recently, however, political leaders in Washington and in the states have acted to reverse these historical growth trends.

Social insurance is the largest and most popular part of the American social welfare state. Social Security and Medicare are universal entitlement programs, funded by payroll taxes. Social Security and Medicare have worked, in the sense that those who have retired are less likely to live in poverty than the elderly before the programs were introduced and are more likely to receive adequate medical care.

Means-tested programs, such as AFDC, food stamps, and Medicaid, have long been the least popular and least well funded parts of the American social welfare state. Conservative critics believe that welfare has hurt the economy, undermined work incentives and the family, and created dependency rather than self-reliance. Liberal critics think that welfare has not done enough to help the poor because of spotty coverage and low benefits, and that it has failed to treat recipients with dignity. It also has done very little to help the working poor. In 1996, President Clinton and Congress transformed the largest and most popular means-tested program—AFDC—from a federal entitlement program to a block grant program run by the states.

The American welfare state is very different from others. Ours is smaller, less comprehensive, less redistributive, and more tilted toward the benefit of the elderly. Structural and political linkage factors explain most of the differences.

Suggested Readings

Glazer, Nathan. *The Limits of Social Policy.* Cambridge: Harvard University Press, 1988.

An eloquent neoconservative critique of welfare and an argument for why it is so difficult for government to solve social problems.

Jencks, Christopher. *Rethinking Social Policy: Race, Poverty, and the Underclass.* Cambridge: Harvard University Press, 1992.

An unconventional, stimulating, and controversial argument which claims that both liberal and conservative positions on race, poverty, and social policy are misdirected.

Jencks, Christopher, and Paul E. Peterson, eds. *The Urban Underclass.* Washington, DC: Brookings Institution, 1991.

A series of research reports on the extent of the urban underclass and how it was created, and how it might be eliminated.

Marmor, Theodore R. K., Jerry L. Mashaw, and Philip L. Harvey. *America's Misunderstood Welfare State.* New York: HarperCollins, 1990.

This book examines the most persistent myths about American social welfare.

Murray, Charles. *Losing Ground: American Social Policy, 1950–1980.* New York: Basic Books, 1984.

The most popular and widely discussed book of the 1980s on what is wrong with welfare; Murray's central point is that welfare makes poverty worse.

Peters, Guy B. *American Public Policy: Promise and Performance,* 4th ed. Chatham, NJ: Chatham House, 1996.

A comprehensive description of social welfare state programs in the United States and how they work.

Ringen, Stein. *The Possibility of Politics: A Study in the Political Economy of the Welfare State.* New York: Clarendon Press, 1987.

The most exhaustive compilation and analysis of the research literature on the effects of the welfare state; demonstrates that welfare state programs in the capitalist nations are, in the main, effective and legitimate.

Schwarz, John E. *America's Hidden Success: A Reassessment of Public Policy from Kennedy to Reagan.* New York: Norton, 1988.

A careful look at most social insurance and means-tested programs in the United States and a compilation of evidence about how they work; he concludes that most work better than most Americans imagine.

Wilensky, Harold. *The Welfare State and Equality.* Berkeley: University of California Press, 1975.
The classic exposition of the view that Western welfare states are the product of industrialization and the aging of populations.

Internet Sources

The Electronic Policy Network http://epn.org/
A gateway to reports, studies, statistics and articles on welfare and health policy from the Twentieth Century Fund, the Russell Sage Foundation, American Prospect Magazine, the Center for Budget and Policy Priorities, the Economic Policy Institute, and more.

EDIN Fast Stats http://garnet.berkeley.edu.3333/faststats/faststats.html
Fifty surprising facts about poverty and welfare in the United States.

The Green Book http://www.os.dhhs.gov/progorg/aspe/green_book/gbpage.html
The annual report of the House Committee on Ways and Means on the social insurance and means-tested programs of the federal government; an essential statistical source.

The Social Security Administration Online http://www.ssa.gov/
Almost everything there is to know about Social Security: rulings, history, benefit information, statistics, and policy debates.

Statistical Abstracts of the United States http://www.census.gov:80/stat_abstract/
Statistical compendium that includes comprehensive information on government spending on social insurance and means-tested programs, the number of recipients of such programs, and the average benefits received by individuals and households.

Notes

1. David Stockman, *The Triumph of Politics: Why the Reagan Revolution Failed* (New York: Harper & Row, 1986), pp. 181, 183, 185.
2. Ibid., p. 188.
3. Ibid., p. 190.
4. Hedrick Smith, *The Power Game: How Washington Works* (New York: Random House, 1988), p. 359.
5. See Fay Lomax Cook and Edith J. Barrett, *Support for the American Welfare State: The Views of Congress and the Public* (New York: Columbia University Press, 1992).
6. Fred C. Pampel, *Age, Class, Politics, and the Welfare State* (New York: Cambridge University Press, 1989), p. 16; Harold Wilensky, *The Welfare State and Equality* (Berkeley: University of California Press, 1975); International Labor Organization, *The Cost of Social Security* (Geneva, Switzerland: International Labor Organization, 1985).
7. Robert E. Goodin, "Reasons for Welfare," in J. Donald Moon, ed., *Responsibility, Rights, and Welfare: The Theory of the Welfare State* (Boulder, CO: Westview Press, 1988).
8. Wilensky, *Welfare State.* Also see Clark Kerr, John T. Dunlop, Fredrick H. Harbison, and Charles A. Myers, *Industrialism and Industrial Man* (New York: Oxford University Press, 1964).

9. Wilensky, *Welfare State;* Kerr et al., *Industrialism and Industrial Man.*

10. Reinhold Bendix, *Nation-Building and Citizenship* (New York: Wiley, 1964); Stein Rokkan, *Citizens, Elections, and Parties* (Oslo: Universitetsforlaget, 1970).

11. Gosta Esping-Andersen, *Politics Against Markets* (Princeton: Princeton University Press, 1985); Walter Korpi, *The Democratic Class Struggle* (New York: Routledge & Kegan Paul, 1983); John Stephens, *The Transition from Capitalism to Socialism* (London: Macmillan, 1979).

12. Irving Kristol, *Two Cheers for Capitalism* (New York: New American Library, Mentor, 1979).

13. Paul Conkin, *The New Deal* (New York: Crowell, 1967); G. William Domhoff, *The Higher Circles* (New York: Vintage, 1971); Gabriel Kolko, *The Triumph of Conservatism* (Chicago: Quadrangle, 1967); James Weinstein, *The Corporate Ideal in the Liberal State* (Boston: Beacon Press, 1968).

14. Eugene Smolensky, Sheldon Danziger, and Peter Gottschalk, "The Declining Significance of Age in the United States: Trends in the Well-Being of Children and the Elderly Since 1939," in John L. Palmer, Timothy Smeedling, and Barbara Boyle Torrey, eds., *The Vulnerable* (Washington, DC: Urban Institute, 1988).

15. See Merton C. Bernstein and Joan Brodshaug Bernstein, *Social Security: The System That Works* (New York: Basic Books, 1988), pp. 13–14; Alvin Schorr, *Common Decency: Domestic Politics After Reagan* (New Haven: Yale University Press, 1986), pp. 49–50.

16. G. Guy Peters, *American Public Policy,* 4th ed. (Chatham, NJ: Chatham House, 1996), p. 283.

17. Spencer Rich, "Saving Medicare," *Washington Post,* National Edition (November 6, 1995), p. 9.

18. Cook and Barrett, *Support for the American Welfare State,* Chap. 7.

19. Schorr, *Common Decency,* p. 74.

20. Hobart Rowan, "A Safety Net Is Missing," *Washington Post,* National Edition (May 27, 1991), p. 5.

21. Jason DeParle, "Complexity of a Fiscal Giant: A Primer on Social Security," *New York Times* (February 11, 1993), p. 1.

22. Bernstein and Bernstein, *Social Security,* p. 208.

23. "U.S. Pensions Found to Lift Many of the Poor," *New York Times* (December 28, 1989), p. A1. Also see Theodore R. K. Marmor, Jerry L. Mashaw, and Philip L. Harvey, *America's Misunderstood Welfare State* (New York: HarperCollins, 1990), Chap. 4.

24. "Furor on Medicare Cuts Offers Political Lesson," *New York Times* (October 12, 1990), p. A11.

25. Hugh Heclo, "The Political Foundations of Anti-Poverty Policy," in Sheldon Danziger and Daniel Weinberg, eds., *Fighting Poverty: What Works and What Doesn't?* (Cambridge: Harvard University Press, 1986), p. 330. Also see Cook and Barrett, *Support for the American Welfare State.*

26. David T. Ellwood, *Poor Support: Poverty in the American Family* (New York: Basic Books, 1988).

27. John E. Schwarz, *America's Hidden Success: A Reassessment of Public Policy from Kennedy to Reagan* (New York: Norton, 1988), p. 37.

28. Schorr, *Common Decency,* p. 169.

29. Schwarz, *America's Hidden Success,* pp. 42–46.

30. Gilbert Steiner, *Social Insecurity: The Politics of Welfare* (Chicago: Rand McNally, 1966), p. 34.

31. Peters, *American Public Policy,* p. 298.

32. U.S. House of Representatives, Committee on Ways and Means, *The 1994 Green Book* (Washington, DC, 1994).

33. Robin Toner, "Politics of Welfare: Focusing on the Problems," *New York Times* (July 5, 1992), p. 1.

34. See Charles Murray, *Losing Ground: American Social Policy, 1950–1980* (New York: Basic Books, 1984); Martin Anderson, *Welfare* (Stanford, CA: Hoover, 1978); Roger A. Freeman, *The Growth of American Government* (Stanford, CA: Hoover, 1975); Lawrence M. Mead, *Beyond Entitlement* (New York: Free Press, 1986); George Gilder, *Wealth and Poverty* (New York: Basic Books, 1981). Also see Paul E. Peterson, "The Urban Underclass and the Poverty Paradox," in Christopher Jencks and Paul E. Peterson, eds., *The Urban Underclass* (Washington, DC: Brookings Institution, 1991); Christopher Jencks, *Rethinking Social Policy* (Cambridge: Harvard University Press, 1992).

35. Milton Friedman and Rose Friedman, *Free to Choose* (New York: Avon, 1981), p. 98.

36. Research of David T. Ellwood, Harvard University, reported in Erik Eckholm, "Solutions on Welfare: They All Cost," *New York Times* (July 26, 1992), p. 1.

37. See Fred Block, Richard A. Cloward, Barbara Ehrenreich, and Frances Fox Piven, eds., *The Mean Season* (New York: Pantheon, 1987); Danziger and Weinberg, *Fighting Poverty;* Ellwood, *Poor Support;* Robert Havemann, ed., *A Decade of Federal Anti-Poverty Programs* (New York: Academic Press, 1977); Christopher Jencks and Paul E. Peterson, eds., *The Urban Underclass* (Washington, DC: Brookings Institution, 1991); Marmor et al., *America's Misunderstood Welfare State;* Peterson, "The Urban Underclass"; Stein Ringen, *The Possibility of Politics: A Study in the Political Economy of the Welfare State* (New York: Clarendon Press, 1987); Schorr, *Common Decency;* Schwarz, *America's Hidden Success;* Shirley Zimmerman, "The Welfare State and Family Breakup," *Family Relations,* Vol. 40, No. 2 (April 1991), pp. 45–59.

38. Christopher Jencks, *Rethinking Social Policy* (Cambridge: Harvard University Press, 1992); William Julius Wilson, *The Truly Disadvantaged* (Chicago: University of Chicago Press, 1987).

39. Spencer Rich, "Missing Out on Welfare," *Washington Post,* National Edition (July 10–16, 1989), p. 6.

40. Sar A. Levitan and Isaac Shapiro, *Working but Poor* (Baltimore: Johns Hopkins University Press, 1987), Chap. 2.

41. Gosta Esping-Andersen, "The Three Political Economies of the Welfare State," *Canadian Review of Sociology and Anthropology,* Vol. 26, No. 1 (1989), pp. 10–36; Norman Furniss and Timothy Tilton, *The Case for the Welfare State* (Bloomington: Indiana University Press, 1977); and Korpi, *Democratic Class Struggle.*

42. Christopher Pierson, "The 'Exceptional' United States: First New Nation or Last Welfare State," *Social Policy and Administration,* Vol. 24, No. 3 (November 1990), p. 188.

43. Vincent A. Mahler and Claudio J. Katz, "Social Benefits in Advanced Capitalist Countries: A Cross-National Assessment," *Comparative Politics,* Vol. 21, No. 1

(1988), pp. 37–50. Also see Arnold Heidenheimer, Hugh Heclo, and Carolyn Teich Adams, *Comparative Public Policy,* 3rd ed. (New York: St. Martin's Press, 1990); Ringen, *Possibility of Politics.*

44. Eugene Smolensky, Sheldon Danziger, and Peter Gottschalk, "The Declining Significance of Age in the United States: Trends in the Well-Being of Children and the Elderly Since 1939," in Palmer et al., eds., *The Vulnerable.*

45. Fred Pampel and Paul Adams, "Demographic Change and Public Support for Children: Family Allowance Expenditures in Advanced Industrial Democracies," Boulder, Colorado, 1990.

46. Mahler and Katz, "Social Benefits"; John Freeman, *Democracy and Markets* (Ithaca, NY: Cornell University Press, 1989); Ringen, *Possibility of Politics,* Chap. 7.

47. Ted Marmor, "U.S. Medical-Care System: Why Not the Worst?" *Wall Street Journal* (June 20, 1991), p. A15.

48. Theodore R. Marmor and Jerry L. Mashaw, "Canada's Health Insurance and Ours," *American Prospect* (Fall 1990), pp. 12–16.

49. "The Changing Face of the Welfare State," *The Economist* (August 26, 1995), p. 41.

50. Norman Furniss and Timothy Tilton, *The Case for the Welfare State;* Jill Quadagno, *The Transformation of Old Age Security: Class and Politics in the American Welfare State* (Chicago: University of Chicago Press, 1988).

51. Nathan Glazer, *The Limits of Social Policy* (Cambridge: Harvard University Press, 1988), pp. 187–188. Also see W. Sombart, *Why There Is No Socialism in the United States* (Armonk, NY: M. E. Sharpe, 1976).

52. See Louis Hartz, *The Liberal Tradition in America* (New York: Harcourt Brace Jovanovich, 1955); G. V. Rimlinger, *Welfare Policy and Industrialization in Europe, America and Russia* (New York: Wiley, 1971); Marmor et al., *America's Misunderstood Welfare State;* Wilensky, *The Welfare State and Equality.*

53. See David Cameron, "Social Democracy, Corporatism, Labor Quiescence, and the Representation of Interests in Advanced Capitalist Society," in John H. Goldthorpe, ed., *Order and Conflict in Contemporary Capitalism* (New York: Clarendon Press, 1984); Francis G. Castles, *The Impact of Parties: Politics and Policies in Democratic Capitalist States* (Newbury Park, CA: Sage, 1982); Esping-Andersen, *Politics Against Markets;* Korpi, *Democratic Class Struggle;* Stephens, *Transition from Capitalism.*

54. Pampel and Adams, "Demographic Change."

Afterword

The United States is more democratic than many of its critics believe, but less democratic than it could be.

As people around the world struggle to make their societies more democratic, we have much to be proud of. We aspire to democracy and have made considerable advances along the democratic road. Yet democracy is still incomplete and may be facing new dangers in the United States. There remain serious obstacles to government of the people, by the people, and for the people.

What can be done to make our nation more democratic? What can you, personally, do? We will not attempt to spell out the details of specific policy proposals, about which people can (and should) disagree, but we will suggest some general directions of change to enhance popular sovereignty, political equality, and political liberty.

Enhance Popular Sovereignty

Many things can be done to strengthen the linkage between what the people want and what government does. One crucial step is to increase the extent to which the American people participate in politics. The low level of voting turnout in the United States is not consistent with a fully functioning democracy. Exhortation alone will not do the trick. Improvements in parties, election campaigns, and political information can play an important role (we will discuss these matters further, below), but the biggest, most immediate gains would come from simply lowering the barriers that make voting unnecessarily difficult. Must we force people to vote at inconvenient times or to skip work? Why not declare a holiday on election days, as is done in much of the world? Furthermore, research shows that our system of personal voting registration substantially decreases participation, especially among the least well-off Americans, thus harming political equality as well as popular sovereignty. The "Motor Voter" law, which allows registration at motor vehicle departments and other government offices, was a step in the right direction, but the burden on citizens could be further reduced by allowing registration and/or voting by mail (as is now done in several states) or by having registration automatically carried out by the government (as in European countries).

Improving our political parties may be the single most important thing we could do to improve democracy in the United States. Strong, coherent, and internally democratic parties, we have seen, are the linchpins of democracy. Experience shows that they are the best instruments for clarifying electoral and policy choices, transmitting popular preferences to government, and keeping political leaders accountable. Yet our major parties tend to be diffuse, disorganized, and dependent on special interest money. To enhance democracy, therefore, we should make our parties more powerful and coherent as organizations, better able to discipline elected officials who carry the party label, and more responsive to ordinary citizens rather than interest groups or activists. Much in our Constitution and our culture work against centralized parties of the European sort, but several reforms (reviewed in Chapter 8) could strengthen U.S. parties or at least halt their disintegration.

It would also enhance democracy and help citizens to form intelligent preferences and make wise political choices, if the quality of public discourse and deliberation were improved. Negativity and triviality might be curbed, and more substantive information provided, if citizens insisted upon it. It is especially important to diversify news sources and broaden the range of views available, both in the mainstream media and through alternative media. Regulating or breaking up media monopolies might be considered. Government secrecy about important policy matters needs to be minimized and the Freedom of Information Act strengthened. Stronger and more internally democratic political parties would undoubtedly provide better political information. Campaigns might be improved by providing public funding for debates and substantive ads or by requiring broadcasters to make time slots available for those purposes.

Make American Politics More Equal

We have seen that inequalities of income and wealth are often translated into political inequality. Individuals and organizations (e.g., business corporations) that have a lot of money and other resources tend to get their way in politics, even against the wishes or interests of ordinary citizens. Money power is a major threat to political equality.

Some Americans believe that the only way to eliminate this problem would be to make our society and economy more equal, with smaller gaps between the rich and the poor. In a free enterprise system, economic equality is extremely difficult to achieve, but several European democracies have public policies (such as family allowances, progressive taxes, and universal social insurance programs) that move in this direction. Our constitutional rules, political institutions, and political culture make it hard to enact such policies in the United States, but it is not impossible to do so. Some of you may believe that a strong effort in this direction is called for.

Others of you, however, may believe that policies to redistribute income and wealth would threaten liberty and undermine economic efficiency. For those who think this way, but who also believe that extensive inequality of income and wealth endanger democracy, it is important to devise means to prevent the translation of social and economic advantages into political advantages. Many reform proposals are designed to do so. The impact of private and interest-group money might be decreased, for example, by more thoroughly documenting and publicizing the sources of funds; by more seriously limiting campaign contributions and expenditures; by broadening the public financing of electoral campaigns; and by subsidizing radio and television appearances by candidates. History suggests, however, that politicians often resist efforts to limit the private financing that got them elected. Even when reforms are enacted, those with money often figure out clever loopholes like "soft money" that defeat the purpose of the legislation.

Direct restrictions on interest group activity are probably neither possible nor desirable because they tend to intrude on the constitutional liberties of individuals and groups to speak freely, assemble, and petition the government. Even indirect controls on the effects of political money may have become more difficult to enact because of economic globalization. Business corporations, prospering and free to move practically anywhere in the world to find low-wage workers, low taxes, and lax regulations, are in a powerful bargaining position with the U.S. (or any other) government: if they do not get their way politically—if, for example, they do not get low taxes, lenient regulation, and limited social spending—they may simply take their money and jobs to some friendlier country. Organizations that might counter business power, like labor unions, have been severely weakened. We believe that economic globalization poses great potential threats to democracy, and we expect that many political struggles will be fought over it.

Be Vigilant in the Protection of Liberty

While certain other democratic countries probably do better than the United States at promoting popular sovereignty and political equality, we undoubtedly lead the world in political liberty. Our constitutional protections for the essential rights of freedom of assembly, of speech, and of the press are unmatched elsewhere.

At the same time, we have seen that formal liberties are sometimes infringed on or made meaningless, especially in times of war or crisis. During cold wars, shooting wars, crusades against pornography, wars on drugs, and the like, those who differ or dissent may be labeled dangerous to the public welfare, and some Americans seem willing to turn their heads and ignore violations of basic freedoms. Such violations rarely stop with their initial victims but often spread to hurt many innocent people and to stifle unpopular (but perhaps valuable) ideas. This can poison the democratic process for years to come. We urge that you practice tolerance in your own life and insist that public officials do the same.

Does It Matter?

Does it matter that democracy remains incomplete? That depends on what you think is important. If you believe, as the authors of this book do, that democracy is the optimal way for a society to make decisions about its public business, and that democracy is the method of decision making that best develops the capacities and capabilities of human beings, then it matters. It surely matters to the millions of people in Eastern Europe, South Africa, China, and elsewhere, who in recent years have put their lives on the line for democracy. It surely mattered to the many people, both famous and not so famous, who struggled to enrich and advance democracy here in the United States. We hope and trust that it matters to you as well. We have seen that ordinary people have played an important part in determining what government does in the United States. You, too, can make a difference. That is the point of the struggle for democracy.

The basis of a democratic state is liberty . . .
—Aristotle, *The Politics*

. . . and that government of the people, by the people, for the people, shall not perish from the earth.
—Abraham Lincoln, *Gettysburg Address*

Suffrage is the protected right.
—Susan B. Anthony, *The Arena*

I have cherished the ideal of a democratic and free society in which all persons live together in harmony and with equal opportunities. It is an ideal I hope to live for and achieve. But if needs be, it is an ideal for which I am prepared to die.
—Nelson Mandela, *Statement at the Rivonia Trial*

Free at last, free at last; Thank God Almighty, we are free at last.
—Martin Luther King, Jr., *I Have a Dream*

We have awakened the people
We have seeded democracy
We will win
Our next generation
Will continue
It doesn't matter
If we don't succeed
—Anonymous, *Poems from Tiananmen Square*

Freedom and democracy, after all, require everyone to participate and thus to share responsibility.
—Vaclav Havel, *New Year's Address*

Appendix

- ★ The Declaration of Independence
- ★ The Constitution of the United States
- ★ Federalist Papers Nos. 10, 51, and 78
- ★ Presidents and Congresses, 1789–1996

The Declaration of Independence

When in the Course of human events, it becomes necessary for one people to dissolve the political bands which have connected them with another, and to assume among the Powers of the earth, the separate and equal station to which the Laws of Nature and of Nature's God entitle them, a decent respect to the opinions of mankind requires that they should declare the causes which impel them to the separation.

We hold these truths to be self-evident, that all men are created equal, that they are endowed by their Creator with certain unalienable Rights, that among these are Life, Liberty and the pursuit of Happiness. That to secure these rights, Governments are instituted among Men, deriving their just powers from the consent of the governed, That whenever any Form of Government becomes destructive of these ends, it is the Right of the People to alter or to abolish it, and to institute new Government, laying its foundation on such principles and organizing its powers in such form, as to them shall seem most likely to effect their Safety and Happiness. Prudence, indeed, will dictate that Governments long established should not be changed for light and transient causes; and accordingly all experience hath shown, that mankind are more disposed to suffer, while evils are sufferable, than to right themselves by abolishing the forms to which they are accustomed. But when a long train of abuses and usurpations, pursuing invariably the same Object evinces a design to reduce them under absolute Despotism, it is their right, it is their duty, to throw off such Government, and to provide new Guards for their future security.—Such has been the patient sufferance of these Colonies; and such is now the necessity which constrains them to alter their former Systems of Government. The history of the present King of Great Britain is a history of repeated injuries and usurpations, all having in direct object the establishment of an absolute Tyranny over these States. To prove this, let Facts be submitted to a candid world.

He has refused his Assent to Laws, the most wholesome and necessary for the public good.

He has forbidden his Governors to pass Laws of immediate and pressing importance, unless suspended in their operation till his Assent should be obtained; and when so suspended, he has utterly neglected to attend to them.

He has refused to pass other Laws for the accommodation of large districts of people, unless those people would relinquish the right of Representation in the Legislature, a right inestimable to them and formidable to tyrants only.

He has called together legislative bodies at places unusual, uncomfortable, and distant from the depository of their Public Records, for the sole purpose of fatiguing them into compliance with his measures.

He has dissolved Representative Houses repeatedly, for opposing with manly firmness his invasions on the rights of the people.

He has refused for a long time, after such dissolutions, to cause others to be elected; whereby the Legislative Powers, incapable of Annihilation, have returned to the People at large for their exercise; the State remaining in the mean time exposed to all the dangers of invasion from without, and convulsions within.

He has endeavoured to prevent the population of these States; for that purpose obstructing the Laws of Naturalization of Foreigners; refusing to pass others to encourage their migration hither, and raising the conditions of new Appropriations of Lands.

He has obstructed the Administration of Justice, by refusing his Assent to Laws for establishing Judiciary Powers.

He has made Judges dependent on his Will alone, for the tenure of their offices, and the amount and payment of their salaries.

He has erected a multitude of New Offices, and sent hither swarms of Officers to harass our People, and eat out their substance.

He has kept among us, in times of peace, Standing Armies without the Consent of our legislature.

He has affected to render the Military independent of and superior to the Civil Power.

He has combined with others to subject us to a jurisdiction foreign to our constitution, and unacknowledged by our laws; giving his Assent to their acts of pretended legislation:

For quartering large bodies of armed troops among us:

For protecting them, by a mock Trial, from Punishment for any Murders which they should commit on the Inhabitants of these States:

For cutting off our Trade with all parts of the world:

For imposing taxes on us without our Consent:

For depriving us in many cases, of the benefits of Trial by Jury:

For transporting us beyond Seas to be tried for pretended offences:

For abolishing the free System of English Laws in a neighbouring Province, establishing therein an Arbitrary government, and enlarging its Boundaries so as to render it at once an example and fit instrument for introducing the same absolute rule into these Colonies:

For taking away our Charters, abolishing our most valuable Laws, and altering fundamentally the Forms of our Governments:

For suspending our own Legislature, and declaring themselves invested with Power to legislate for us in all cases whatsoever.

He has abdicated Government here, by declaring us out of his Protection and waging War against us.

He has plundered our seas, ravaged our Coasts, burnt our towns, and destroyed the lives of our people.

He is at this time transporting large armies of foreign mercenaries to compleat the works of death, desolation and tyranny, already begun with circumstances of Cruelty & perfidy scarcely paralleled in the most barbarous ages, and totally unworthy the Head of a civilized nation.

He has constrained our fellow Citizens taken Captive on the high Seas to bear Arms against their Country, to become the executioners of their friends and Brethren, or to fall themselves by their Hands.

He has excited domestic insurrections amongst us, and has endeavoured to bring on the inhabitants of our frontiers, the merciless Indian Savages, whose known rule of warfare, is an undistinguished destruction of all ages, sexes and conditions.

In every stage of these Oppressions We have Petitioned for Redress in the most humble terms: Our repeated Petitions have been answered only by repeated injury. A Prince, whose character is thus marked by every act which may define a Tyrant, is unfit to be the ruler of a free People.

Nor have We been wanting in attention to our British brethren. We have warned them from time to time of attempts by their legislature to extend an unwarrantable jurisdiction over us. We have reminded them of the circumstances of our emigration and settlement here. We have appealed to their native justice and magnanimity, and we have conjured them by the ties of our common kindred to disavow these usurpations, which, would inevitably interrupt our connections and correspondence. They too have been deaf to the voice of justice and of consanguinity. We must, therefore, acquiesce in the necessity, which denounces our Separation, and hold them, as we hold the rest of mankind, Enemies in War, in Peace Friends.

We, therefore, the Representatives of the united States of America, in General Congress, Assembled, appealing to the Supreme Judge of the world for the rectitude of our intentions, do, in the Name, and by Authority of the good People of these Colonies, solemnly publish and declare, That these United Colonies are, and of Right ought to be Free and Independent States; that they are Absolved from all Allegiance to the British Crown, and that all political connection between them and the State of Great Britain, is and ought to be totally dissolved; and that as Free and Independent States, they have full Power to levy War, conclude Peace, contract Alliances, establish Commerce, and to do all other Acts and Things which Independent States may of right do. And for the support of this Declaration, with a firm reliance of the Protection of Divine Providence, we mutually pledge to each other our Lives, our Fortunes and our sacred Honor.

John Hancock,

Josiah Bartlett, Wm Whipple, Saml Adams, John Adams, Robt Treat Paine, Elbridge Gerry, Steph. Hopkins, William Ellery, Roger Sherman, Samel Huntington, Wm Williams, Oliver Wolcott, Matthew Thornton, Wm Floyd, Phil Livingston, Frans Lewis, Lewis Morris, Richd Stockton, Jno Witherspoon, Fras Hopkinson, John Hart, Abra Clark, Robt Morris, Benjamin Rush, Benja Franklin, John Morton, Geo Clymer, Jas Smith, Geo. Taylor, James Wilson, Geo. Ross, Caesar Rodney, Geo Read, Thos M:Kean, Samuel Chase, Wm Paca, Thos Stone, Charles Carroll of Carrollton, George Wythe, Richard Henry Lee, Th. Jefferson, Benja Harrison, Thos Nelson, Jr., Francis Lightfoot Lee, Carter Braxton, Wm Hooper, Joseph Hewes, John Penn, Edward Rutledge, Thos Heyward, Junr., Thomas Lynch, Junor., Arthur Middleton, Button Gwinnett, Lyman Hall, Geo Walton.

The Constitution of the United States

We the people of the United States, in Order to form a more perfect Union, establish Justice, insure domestic Tranquility, provide for the common defence, promote the general Welfare, and secure the Blessings of Liberty to ourselves and our Posterity, do ordain and establish this constitution for the United States of America.

Article I

Section 1 All legislative Powers herein granted shall be vested in a Congress of the United States, which shall consist of a Senate and House of Representatives.

Section 2 The House of Representatives shall be composed of Members chosen every second Year by the People of the several States, and the Electors in each State shall have the Qualifications requisite for Electors of the most numerous Branch of the State Legislature.

No person shall be a Representative who shall not have attained to the Age of twenty-five Years, and been seven Years a Citizen of the United States, and who shall not, when elected, be an Inhabitant of that State in which he shall be chosen.

Representatives and direct Taxes shall be apportioned among the several States which may be included within this Union, according to their respective Numbers, which shall be determined by adding to the whole Number of free Persons, including those bound to Service for a Term of Years, and excluding Indians not taxed, three fifths of all other Persons. The actual Enumeration shall be made within three Years after the first Meeting of the Congress of the United States, and within every subsequent Term of ten Years, in such Manner as they shall by Law direct. The Number of Representatives shall not exceed one for every thirty Thousand, but each State shall have at Least one Representative; and until such enumeration shall be made, the State of New Hampshire shall be entitled to chuse three, Massachusetts eight, Rhode-Island and Providence Plantations one, Connecticut five, New-York six, New Jersey four, Pennsylvania eight, Delaware one, Maryland six, Virginia ten, North Carolina five, South Carolina five, and Georgia three.

When vacancies happen in the Representation from any State, the Executive Authority thereof shall issue Writs of Election to fill such Vacancies.

The House of Representatives shall chuse their Speaker and other Officers; and shall have the sole Power of Impeachment.

Section 3 The Senate of the United States shall be composed of two Senators from each State, chosen by the Legislature thereof, for six Years; and each Senator shall have one Vote.

Immediately after they shall be assembled in Consequence of the first Election, they shall be divided as equally as may be into three Classes. The

Seats of the Senators of the first Class shall be vacated at the Expiration of the second Year, of the second Class at the Expiration of the fourth Year, and of the third Class at the Expiration of the sixth Year, so that one-third may be chosen every second Year; and if Vacancies happen by Resignation, or otherwise, during the Recess of the Legislature of any State, the Executive thereof may make temporary Appointments until the next Meeting of the Legislature, which shall then fill such Vacancies.

No Person shall be a Senator who shall not have attained to the Age of thirty Years, and been nine Years a Citizen of the United States, and who shall not, when elected, be an Inhabitant of that State in which he shall be chosen.

The Vice President of the United States shall be President of the Senate, but shall have no vote, unless they be equally divided.

The Senate shall chuse their other Officers, and also a President pro tempore, in the absence of the Vice President, or when he shall exercise the Office of the President of the United States.

The Senate shall have the sole Power to try all Impeachments. When sitting for that purpose, they shall be on Oath or Affirmation. When the President of the United States is tried, the Chief Justice shall preside: And no person shall be convicted without the Concurrence of two thirds of the Members present.

Judgment in Cases of Impeachment shall not extend further than to removal from Office, and disqualification to hold and enjoy any Office of honor, Trust, or Profit under the United States: but the Party convicted shall nevertheless be liable and subject to Indictment, Trial, Judgment, and Punishment, according to Law.

Section 4 The Times, Places and Manner of holding Elections for Senators and Representatives, shall be prescribed in each state by the Legislature thereof; but the Congress may at any time by Law make or alter such Regulations, except as to the Places of Chusing Senators.

The Congress shall assemble at least once in every Year, and such Meeting shall be on the first Monday in December, unless they shall by Law appoint a different Day.

Section 5 Each House shall be the Judge of the Elections, Returns and Qualifications of its own Members, and a Majority of each shall constitute a Quorum to do Business; but a smaller number may adjourn from day to day, and may be authorized to compel the Attendance of absent Members, in such Manner, and under such Penalties, as each House may provide.

Each House may determine the Rules of its Proceedings, punish its Members for disorderly Behavior, and, with the Concurrence of two thirds, expel a Member.

Each House shall keep a Journal of its Proceedings, and from time to time publish the same, excepting such Parts as may in their Judgment require Secrecy; and the Yeas and Nays of the Members of either House on any question shall, at the Desire of one fifth of those Present, be entered on the Journal.

Neither House, during the Session of Congress, shall, without the Consent of the other, adjourn for more than three days, nor to any other Place than that in which the two Houses shall be sitting.

Section 6 The Senators and Representatives shall receive a Compensation for their Services, to be ascertained by Law, and paid out of the Treasury of the United States. They shall in all Cases, except Treason, Felony, and Breach of the Peace, be privileged from arrest during their Attendance at the Session of their respective Houses, and in going to and returning from the same; and for any Speech or Debate in either House, they shall not be questioned in any other Place.

No Senator or Representative shall, during the Time for which he was elected, be appointed to any civil Office under the Authority of the United States, which shall have been created, or the Emoluments whereof shall have been increased, during such time; and no Person holding any Office under the United States shall be a Member of either House during his continuance in Office.

Section 7 All Bills for raising Revenue shall originate in the House of Representatives; but the Senate may propose or concur with Amendments as on other bills.

Every Bill which shall have passed the House of Representatives and the Senate, shall, before it become a Law, be presented to the President of the United States; If he approve he shall sign it, but if not he shall return it, with his Objections, to that House in which it shall have originated, who shall enter the Objections at large on their Journal, and proceed to reconsider it. If after such Reconsideration two thirds of that House shall agree to pass the bill, it shall be sent, together with the objections, to the other House, by which it shall likewise be reconsidered, and if approved by two thirds of that House, it shall become a Law. But in all such Cases the Votes of both Houses shall be determined by Yeas and Nays, and the Names of the Persons voting for and against the Bill shall be entered on the Journal of each House respectively. If any Bill shall not be returned by the President within ten Days (Sundays excepted) after it shall have been presented to him, the Same shall be a Law, in like Manner as if he had signed it, unless the Congress by their Adjournment prevent its Return, in which Case it shall not be a Law.

Every Order, Resolution, or Vote to which the Concurrence of the Senate and House of Representatives may be necessary (except on a question of Adjournment) shall be presented to the President of the United States; and before the Same shall take Effect, shall be approved by him, or being disapproved by him, shall be repassed by two thirds of the Senate and House of Representatives, according to the Rules and Limitations prescribed in the Case of a Bill.

Section 8 The Congress shall have Power To lay and collect Taxes, Duties, Imposts and Excises, to pay the Debts and provide for the common Defence and general Welfare of the United States; but all Duties, Imposts and Excises shall be uniform throughout the United States;

To borrow money on the credit of the United States;

To regulate Commerce with foreign Nations, and among the several States, and with the Indian Tribes;

To establish a uniform Rule of Naturalization, and uniform Laws on the subject of Bankruptcies throughout the United States;

To coin Money, regulate the Value thereof, and of foreign Coin, and fix the Standard of Weights and Measures;

To provide for the Punishment of counterfeiting the Securities and current Coin of the United States;

To establish Post offices and post Roads;

To promote the Progress of Science and useful Arts, by securing for limited Times to Authors and Inventors the exclusive Right to their respective Writings and Discoveries;

To constitute Tribunals inferior to the Supreme Court;

To define and punish Piracies and Felonies committed on the high Seas, and Offences against the Law of Nations;

To declare War, grant Letters of Marque and Reprisal, and make Rules concerning Captures on Land and Water;

To raise and support Armies, but no Appropriation of Money to that Use shall be for a longer Term than two Years;

To provide and maintain a Navy;

To make Rules for the Government and Regulation of the land and naval forces;

To provide for calling forth the Militia to execute the Laws of the Union, suppress Insurrections and repel Invasions;

To provide for organizing, arming, and disciplining the Militia, and for governing such Part of them as may be employed in the Service of the United States, reserving to the States respectively, the Appointment of the Officers, and the Authority of training the Militia according to the discipline prescribed by Congress;

To exercise exclusive Legislation in all Cases whatsoever, over such District (not exceeding ten Miles square) as may, by Cession of particular States, and the acceptance of Congress, become the Seat of Government of the United States, and to exercise like Authority over all Places purchased by the Consent of the Legislature of the State in which the Same shall be, for the Erection of Forts, Magazines, Arsenals, dock-Yards, and other needful Buildings;—And

To make all Laws which shall be necessary and proper for carrying into Execution the foregoing Powers, and all other Powers vested by this Constitution in the government of the United States, or in any Department or Officer thereof.

Section 9 The Migration or Importation of such Persons as any of the States now existing shall think proper to admit, shall not be prohibited by the Congress prior to the Year one thousand eight hundred and eight, but a tax or duty may be imposed on such Importation, not exceeding ten dollars for each Person.

The privilege of the Writ of Habeas Corpus shall not be suspended, unless when in Cases of Rebellion or Invasion the public Safety may require it.

No Bill of Attainder or ex post facto Law shall be passed.

No capitation, or other direct, Tax shall be laid unless in Proportion to the Census or Enumeration herein before directed to be taken.

No Tax or Duty shall be laid on Articles exported from any State.

No Preference shall be given by any Regulation of Revenue to the Ports of one State over those of another: nor shall Vessels bound to, or from, one state, be obliged to enter, clear, or pay Duties in another.

No Money shall be drawn from the Treasury, but in Consequence of Appropriations made by Law; and a regular Statement and Account of the Receipts and Expenditures of all public Money shall be published from time to time.

No Title of Nobility shall be granted by the United States: And no Person holding any Office of Profit or Trust under them, shall, without the Consent of the Congress, accept of any present, Emolument, Office, or Title, of any kind whatever, from any King, Prince, or Foreign State.

Section 10 No state shall enter into any Treaty, Alliance, or Confederation; grant Letters of Marque and Reprisal; coin Money; emit Bills of Credit; make any Thing but gold and silver Coin a Tender in Payment of Debts; pass any Bill of Attainder, ex post facto Law, or Law impairing the Obligation of Contracts, or grant any Title of Nobility.

No State shall, without the Consent of the Congress, lay any Imposts or Duties on Imports or Exports, except what may be absolutely necessary for executing its inspection Laws: and the net Produce of all Duties and Imposts, laid by any State on Imports or Exports, shall be for the Use of the Treasury of the United States; and all such Laws shall be subject to the Revision and Control of the Congress.

No State shall, without the Consent of Congress, lay any duty of Tonnage, keep Troops, or Ships of War in time of Peace, enter into any Agreement or Compact with another State, or with a foreign Power, or engage in War, unless actually invaded, or in such imminent Danger as will not admit of delay.

Article II

Section 1 The executive Power shall be vested in a President of the United States of America. He shall hold his Office during the Term of four years, and, together with the Vice President, chosen for the same Term, be elected, as follows:

Each State shall appoint, in such Manner as the Legislature thereof may direct, a Number of Electors, equal to the whole Number of Senators and Representatives to which the State may be entitled in the Congress; but no Senator or Representative, or Person holding an Office of Trust or Profit under the United States, shall be appointed an Elector.

The Electors shall meet in their respective States, and vote by Ballot for two persons, of whom one at least shall not be an Inhabitant of the same State with themselves. And they shall make a List of all the Persons voted for, and of the Number of Votes for each; which List they shall sign and certify, and transmit sealed to the Seat of the Government of the United States, directed to the President of the Senate. The President of the Senate shall, in the Presence of the Senate and House of Representatives, open all the Certificates, and the Votes shall then be counted. The Person having the greatest Number of Votes shall be the President, if such Number be a Majority of the whole Number of Electors appointed; and if there be more than one who have such Majority, and have an equal Number of Votes, then the House of Representatives shall immediately chuse by Ballot one of them for President; and if no Person have a Majority, then from the five highest on the List the said House shall in like Manner chuse the President. But in chusing the President, the votes shall be taken by States, the Representation from each State having one Vote; a quorum for this Purpose shall consist of a Member or Members from two-thirds of the States, and a Majority of all the States shall be necessary to a Choice. In every Case, after the Choice of the President, the Person having the greatest Number of Votes of the Electors shall be the Vice President. But if there should remain two or more who have equal votes, the Senate shall chuse from them by Ballot the Vice President.

The Congress may determine the time of chusing the Electors, and the Day on which they shall give their Votes; which Day shall be the same throughout the United States.

No person except a natural-born Citizen, or a Citizen of the United States, at the time of the Adoption of this Constitution, shall be eligible to the Office of President; neither shall any Person be eligible to that Office who shall not have attained to the Age of thirty-five years, and been fourteen Years a Resident within the United States.

In Case of the Removal of the President from Office, or of his Death, Resignation, or Inability to discharge the Powers and Duties of the said Office, the same shall devolve on the Vice President, and the Congress may by Law provide for the Case of Removal, Death, Resignation, or Inability, both of the President and Vice President, declaring what Officer shall then act as President, and such Officer shall act accordingly, until the disability be removed, or a President shall be elected.

The President shall, at stated Times, receive for his Services a Compensation, which shall neither be increased nor diminished during the Period for which he shall have been elected, and he shall not receive within that Period any other Emolument from the United States, or any of them.

Before he enter on the execution of his Office, he shall take the following Oath or Affirmation:—"I do solemnly swear (or affirm) that I will faithfully execute the Office of President of the United States, and will, to the best of my Ability, preserve, protect, and defend the Constitution of the United States."

Section 2 The President shall be Commander in Chief of the Army and Navy of the United States, and of the Militia of the several States, when called into the actual Service of the United States; he may require the Opinion, in writing, of the principal Officer in each of the executive Departments, upon any subject relating to the Duties of their respective Offices, and he shall have Power to Grant Reprieves and Pardons for Offences against the United States, except in Cases of Impeachment.

He shall have Power, by and with the Advice and Consent of the Senate, to make Treaties, provided two thirds of the Senators present concur; and he shall nominate, and by and with the Advice and Consent of the Senate, shall appoint Ambassadors, other public Ministers and Consuls, Judges of the supreme Court, and all other Officers of the United States, whose Appointments are not herein otherwise provided for, and which shall be established by Law: but the Congress may by Law vest the Appointment of such inferior Officers, as they think proper, in the President alone, in the Courts of Law, or in the Heads of Departments.

The President shall have Power to fill up all Vacancies that may happen during the Recess of the Senate, by granting Commissions which shall expire at the End of their next Session.

Section 3 He shall from time to time give to the Congress Information of the State of the Union, and recommend to their Consideration such Measures as he shall judge necessary and expedient; he may, on extraordinary occasions, convene both Houses, or either of them, and in Case of Disagreement between them, with respect to the Time of Adjournment, he may adjourn them to such Time as he shall think proper; he shall receive Ambassadors and other public Ministers; he shall take Care that the Laws be faithfully executed, and shall Commission all the Officers of the United States.

Section 4 The President, Vice President and all civil Officers of the United States, shall be removed from Office on Impeachment for, and Conviction of, Treason, Bribery, or other high Crimes and Misdemeanors.

Article III

Section 1 The judicial Power of the United States, shall be vested in one supreme Court, and in such inferior Courts as the Congress may from time to time ordain and establish. The Judges, both of the supreme and inferior Courts, shall hold their Offices during good Behaviour, and shall, at stated Times, receive for their Services, a Compensation, which shall not be diminished during their Continuance in Office.

Section 2 The judicial Power shall extend to all Cases, in Law and Equity, arising under this Constitution, the Laws of the United States, and treaties made, or which shall be made, under their Authority;—to all Cases affecting ambassadors, other public ministers and consuls;—to all cases of admiralty and maritime Jurisdiction;—to Controversies to which the United States shall be a Party;—to Controversies between two or more States;—between a State and Citizens of another State;—between Citizens of different States,—between Citizens of the same State claiming Lands under Grants of different States, and between a State, or the Citizens thereof, and foreign States, Citizens or Subjects.

In all Cases affecting Ambassadors, other public Ministers and Consuls, and those in which a State shall be Party, the supreme Court shall have original Jurisdiction. In all the other Cases before mentioned, the supreme Court shall have appellate Jurisdiction, both as to Law and Fact, with such Exceptions, and under such Regulations as the Congress shall make.

The trial of all Crimes, except in Cases of Impeachment, shall be by Jury; and such Trial shall be held in the State where the said Crimes shall have been committed; but when not committed within any State, the Trial shall be at such Place or Places as the Congress may by Law have directed.

Section 3 Treason against the United States, shall consist only in levying War against them, or in adhering to their Enemies, giving them Aid and Comfort. No Person shall be convicted of Treason unless on the testimony of two Witnesses to the same overt Act, or on Confession in open Court.

The Congress shall have power to declare the Punishment of Treason, but no Attainder of Treason shall work Corruption of Blood, or Forfeiture except during the Life of the Person attained.

Article IV

Section 1 Full Faith and Credit shall be given in each State to the public Acts, Records, and judicial Proceedings of every other State. And the Congress may by general Laws prescribe the Manner in which such Acts, Records and Proceedings shall be proved, and the Effect thereof.

Section 2 The Citizens of each State shall be entitled to all Privileges and Immunities of Citizens in the several States.

A Person charged in any State with Treason, Felony, or other Crime, who shall flee from Justice, and be found in another State, shall on demand of the executive Authority of the State from which he fled, be delivered up, to be removed to the State having Jurisdiction of the crime.

No Person held to Service or Labour in one State, under the Laws thereof, escaping into another, shall, in Consequence of any Law or Regulation therein, be discharged from such Service or Labour, but shall be delivered up on Claim of the Party to whom such Service or Labour may be due.

Section 3 New States may be admitted by the Congress into this Union; but no new State shall be formed or erected within the Jurisdiction of any other State; nor any State be formed by the Junction of two or more States, or parts of States, without the Consent of the Legislatures of the States concerned as well as of the Congress.

The Congress shall have Power to dispose of and make all needful Rules and Regulations respecting the Territory or other Property belonging to the United States; and nothing in this Constitution shall be so construed as to Prejudice any Claims of the United States, or of any particular State.

Section 4 The United States shall guarantee to every State in this Union a Republican Form of Government, and shall protect each of them against Invasion; and on Application of the Legislature, or the Executive (when the Legislature cannot be convened) against domestic Violence.

Article V

The Congress, whenever two-thirds of both Houses shall deem it necessary, shall propose Amendments to this Constitution, or, on the Application of the Legislatures of two-thirds of the several States, shall call a Convention for proposing Amendments, which, in either Case, shall be valid to all Intents and Purposes, as part of this Constitution, when ratified by the Legislatures of three-fourths of the several States, or by Conventions in three-fourths thereof, as the one or the other Mode of Ratification may be proposed by the Congress; Provided that no Amendment which may be made prior to the Year One thousand eight hundred and eight shall in any Manner affect the first and fourth Clauses in the Ninth Section of the first Article; and that no State, without its Consent, shall be deprived of its equal Suffrage in the Senate.

Article VI

All Debts contracted and Engagements entered into, before the Adoption of this Constitution, shall be as valid against the United States under this Constitution, as under the Confederation.

This Constitution, and the Laws of the United States which shall be made in Pursuance thereof; and all Treaties made, or which shall be made, under the Authority of the United States, shall be the supreme Law of the Land; and the Judges in every State shall be bound thereby, any Thing in the Constitution or Laws of any State to the Contrary notwithstanding.

The Senators and Representatives before mentioned, and the Members of the several State Legislatures and all executive and judicial Officers, both of the United States and of the several States, shall be bound by Oath or Affirmation to support this Constitution; but no religious Test shall ever be required as a qualification to any Office or public Trust under the United States.

Article VII

The Ratification of the Conventions of nine States shall be sufficient for the Establishment of this Constitution between the States so ratifying the same.

Done in Convention by the Unanimous Consent of the States present the Seventeenth Day of September in the Year of our Lord one thousand seven hundred and Eighty seven, and of the Independence of the United States of America the Twelfth. In Witness whereof We have hereunto subscribed our Names.

Go. Washington, *President and deputy from Virginia; Attest* William Jackson, *Secretary; Delaware:* Geo. Read,* Gunning Bedford, Jr., John Dickinson, Richard Basset, Jaco. Broom; *Maryland:* James McHenry, Daniel of St. Thomas' Jenifer, Danl. Carroll; *Virginia:* John Blair, James Madison, Jr.; *North Carolina:* Wm. Blount, Richd. Dobbs Spaight, Hu Williamson; *South Carolina:* J. Rutledge, Charles Cotesworth Pinckney, Charles Pinckney, Pierce Butler; *Georgia:* William Few, Abr. Baldwin; *New Hampshire:* John Langdon, Nicholas Gilman; *Massachusetts:* Nathaniel Gorham, Rufus King; *Connecticut:* Wm. Saml. Johnson, Roger Sherman,* *New York:* Alexander Hamilton; *New Jersey:* Wil. Livingston, David Brearley, Wm. Paterson, Jona. Dayton; *Pennsylvania:* B. Franklin,* Thomas Mifflin, Robt. Morris,* Geo. Clymer,* Thos. FitzSimons, Jared Ingersoll, James Wilson, Gouv. Morris.

Articles in Addition to, and Amendment of, the Constitution of the United States of America, Proposed by Congress, and Ratified by the Legislatures of the Several States, Pursuant to the Fifth Article of the Original Constitution.

Amendment I [1791]

Congress shall make no law respecting an establishment of religion, or prohibiting the free exercise thereof; or abridging the freedom of speech, or of the press; or the right of the people peaceably to assemble, and to petition the Government for a redress of grievances.

Amendment II [1791]

A well regulated Militia, being necessary to the security of a free State, the right of the people to keep and bear Arms shall not be infringed.

Amendment III [1791]

No Soldier shall, in time of peace, be quartered in any house, without the consent of the Owner, nor in time of war, but in a manner to be prescribed by law.

Amendment IV [1791]

The right of the people to be secure in their persons, houses, papers, and effects, against unreasonable searches and seizures, shall not be violated, and no Warrants shall issue, but upon probable cause, supported by Oath or affirmation, and particularly describing the place to be searched, and the persons or things to be seized.

Amendment V [1791]

No person shall be held to answer for a capital or otherwise infamous crime, unless on a presentment or indictment of a Grand Jury, except in cases arising in the land or naval forces, or in the Militia, when in actual service in time of War or public danger; nor shall any person be subject for the same offence to be twice put in jeopardy of life or limb; nor shall be compelled in any criminal case to be a witness against himself, nor be deprived of life, liberty, or property, without due process of law; nor shall private property be taken for public use, without just compensation.

Amendment VI [1791]

In all criminal prosecutions, the accused shall enjoy the right to a speedy and public trial, by an impartial jury of the State and district wherein the crime shall have been committed, which district shall have been previously ascertained by law, and to be informed of the nature and cause of the accusation; to be confronted with the witnesses against him; to have compulsory process for obtaining witnesses in his favor, and to have the Assistance of Counsel for his defence.

Amendment VII [1791]

In suits at common law, where the value in controversy shall exceed twenty dollars, the right of trial by jury shall be preserved, and no fact tried by a jury, shall be otherwise reexamined in any Court of the United States, than according to the rules of the common law.

Amendment VIII [1791]

Excessive bail shall not be required, nor excessive fines imposed, nor cruel and unusual punishments inflicted.

* Also signed the Declaration of Independence

Amendment IX [1791]

The enumeration in the Constitution, of certain rights, shall not be construed to deny or disparage others retained by the people.

Amendment X [1791]

The powers not delegated to the United States by the Constitution, nor prohibited by it to the States, are reserved to the States respectively, or to the people.

Amendment XI [1798]

The Judicial power of the United States shall not be construed to extend to any suit in law or equity, commenced or prosecuted against one of the United States by Citizens of another State, or by Citizens or Subjects of any Foreign State.

Amendment XII [1804]

The Electors shall meet in their respective States and vote by ballot for President and Vice President, one of whom, at least, shall not be an inhabitant of the same State with themselves; they shall name in their ballots the person voted for as President, and in distinct ballots the person voted for as Vice President, and they shall make distinct lists of all persons voted for as President, and of all persons voted for as Vice President, and of the number of votes for each, which lists they shall sign and certify, and transmit sealed to the seat of the government of the United States, directed to the President of the Senate;—The President of the Senate shall, in the presence of the Senate and House of Representatives, open all the certificates and the votes shall then be counted;—The person having the greatest number of votes for President, shall be the President, if such number be a majority of the whole number of Electors appointed; and if no person have such majority, then from the persons having the highest numbers not exceeding three on the list of those voted for as President, the House of Representatives shall choose immediately, by ballot, the President. But in choosing the President, the votes shall be taken by states, the representation from each state having one vote; a quorum for this purpose shall consist of a member or members from two-thirds of the states, and a majority of all the states shall be necessary to a choice. And if the House of Representatives shall not choose a President whenever the right of choice shall devolve upon them, before the fourth day of March next following, then the Vice President shall act as President, as in the case of the death or other constitutional disability of the President.—The person having the greatest number of votes as Vice President, shall be the Vice President, if such number be a majority of the whole number of Electors appointed, and if no person have a majority, then from the two highest numbers on the list, the Senate shall choose the Vice President; a quorum for the purpose shall consist of two-thirds of the whole number of Senators, and a majority of the whole number shall be necessary to a choice. But no person constitutionally ineligible to the office of President shall be eligible to that of Vice President of the United States.

Amendment XIII [1865]

Section 1 Neither slavery nor involuntary servitude, except as a punishment for crime whereof the party shall have been duly convicted, shall exist within the United States, or any place subject to their jurisdiction.

Section 2 Congress shall have power to enforce this article by appropriate legislation.

Amendment XIV [1868]

Section 1 All persons born or naturalized in the United States, and subject to the jurisdiction thereof, are citizens of the United States and of the State wherein they reside. No State shall make or enforce any law which shall abridge the privileges or immunities of citizens of the United States; nor shall any State deprive any person of life, liberty, or property, without due process of law; nor deny to any person within its jurisdiction the equal protection of the laws.

Section 2 Representatives shall be apportioned among the several States according to their respective numbers, counting the whole number of persons in each State, excluding Indians not taxed. But when the right to vote at any election for the choice of electors for President and Vice President of the United States, Representatives in Congress, the Executive and Judicial officers of a State, or the members of the Legislature thereof, is denied to any of the male inhabitants of such State, being twenty-one years of age, and citizens of the United States or in any way abridged, except for participation in rebellion, or other crime, the basis of representation therein shall be reduced in the proportion which the number of such male citizens shall bear to the whole number of male citizens twenty-one years of age in such State.

Section 3 No person shall be a Senator or Representative in Congress, or elector of President and Vice President, or hold any office, civil or military, under the United States, or under any State, who, having previously taken an oath, as a member of Congress, or as an officer of the United States, or as a member of any State legislature, or as an executive or judicial officer of any State, to support the Constitution of the United States, shall have engaged in insurrection or rebellion against the same, or given aid or comfort to the enemies thereof. But Congress may by a vote of two-thirds of each House, remove such disability.

Section 4 The validity of the public debt of the United States, authorized by law, including debts incurred for payment of pensions and bounties for services in suppressing insurrection or rebellion, shall not be questioned. But neither the United States nor any State shall assume or pay any debt or obligation incurred in aid of insurrection or rebellion against the United States, or any claim for the loss or emancipation of any slave; but all such debts, obligations, and claims shall be held illegal and void.

Section 5 The Congress shall have the power to enforce, by appropriate legislation, the provisions of this article.

Amendment XV [1870]

Section 1 The right of citizens of the United States to vote shall not be denied or abridged by the United States or by any State on account of race, color, or previous condition of servitude—

Section 2 The Congress shall have power to enforce this article by appropriate legislation.

Amendment XVI [1913]

The Congress shall have power to lay and collect taxes on incomes, from whatever source derived, without apportionment among the several States, and without regard to any census or enumeration.

Amendment XVII [1913]

The Senate of the United States shall be composed of two Senators from each State, elected by the people thereof, for six years; and each Senator shall have one vote. The electors in each State shall have the qualifications requisite for electors of the most numerous branch of the State legislatures.

When vacancies happen in the representation of any State in the Senate, the executive authority of such State shall issue writs of election to fill such vacancies: *Provided,* That the legislature of any State may empower the executive thereof to make temporary appointments until the people fill the vacancies by election as the legislature may direct. This amendment shall not be so construed as to affect the election or term of any Senator chosen before it becomes valid as part of the Constitution.

Amendment XVIII [1919]

Section 1 After one year from the ratification of this article the manufacture, sale, or transportation of intoxicating liquors within, the importation thereof into, or the exportation thereof from the United States and all territory subject to the jurisdiction thereof for beverage purposes is hereby prohibited.

Section 2 The Congress and the several States shall have concurrent power to enforce this article by appropriate legislation.

Section 3 This article shall be inoperative unless it shall have been ratified as an amendment to the Constitution by the legislatures of the several States, as provided in the Constitution, within seven years from the date of the submission hereof to the States by the Congress.

Amendment XIX [1920]

The right of citizens of the United States to vote shall not be denied or abridged by the United States or by any State on account of sex.

Congress shall have power to enforce this article by appropriate legislation.

Amendment XX [1933]

Section 1 The terms of the President and Vice President shall end at noon on the 20th day of January, and the terms of Senators and Representatives at noon on the 3d day of January, of the years in which such terms would have ended if this article had not been ratified; and the terms of their successors shall then begin.

Section 2 The Congress shall assemble at least once in every year, and such meeting shall begin at noon on the 3d day of January, unless they shall by law appoint a different day.

Section 3 If, at the time fixed for the beginning of the term of the President, the President elect shall have died, the Vice President elect shall become President. If a President shall not have been chosen before the time fixed for the beginning of his term, or if the President elect shall have failed to qualify, then the Vice President elect shall act as President until a President shall have qualified; and the Congress may by law provide for the case wherein neither a President elect nor a Vice President elect shall have qualified, declaring who shall then act as President, or the manner in which one who is to act shall be selected, and such person shall act accordingly until a President or Vice President shall have qualified.

Section 4 The Congress may by law provide for the case of the death of any of the persons from whom the House of Representatives may choose a President whenever the right of choice shall have devolved upon them, and for the case of the death of any of the persons from whom the Senate may choose a Vice President whenever the right of choice shall have devolved upon them.

Section 5 Sections 1 and 2 shall take effect on the 15th day of October following the ratification of this article.

Section 6 This article shall be inoperative unless it shall have been ratified as an amendment to the Constitution by the legislatures of three-fourths of the several States within seven years from the date of its submission.

Amendment XXI [1933]

Section 1 The eighteenth article of amendment to the Constitution of the United States is hereby repealed.

Section 2 The transportation or importation into any State, Territory, or possession of the United States for delivery or use therein of intoxicating liquors, in violation of the laws thereof, is hereby prohibited.

Section 3 This article shall be inoperative unless it shall have been ratified as an amendment to the Constitution by conventions in the several States, as provided in the Constitution, within seven years from the date of the submission hereof to the States by the Congress.

Amendment XXII [1951]

No person shall be elected to the office of the President more than twice, and no person who has held the office of President, or acted as President, for more than two years of a term to which some other person was elected President shall be elected to the office of the President more than once.

But this Article shall not apply to any person holding the office of President when this Article was proposed by the Congress, and shall not prevent any person who may be holding the office of President or acting as President, during the term within which this Article becomes operative from holding the office of President or acting as President during the remainder of such term.

Amendment XXIII [1961]

Section 1 The District constituting the seat of Government of the United States shall appoint in such manner as the Congress may direct:

A number of electors of President and Vice President equal to the whole number of Senators and Representatives in Congress to which the District would be entitled if it were a State, but in no event more than the least populous State; they shall be in addition to those appointed by the States, but they shall be considered, for the purposes of the election of President and Vice President, to be electors appointed by a State; and they shall meet in the District and perform such duties as provided by the twelfth article of amendment.

Section 2 The Congress shall have power to enforce this article by appropriate legislation.

Amendment XXIV [1964]

Section 1 The right of citizens of the United States to vote in any primary or other election for President or Vice President, for electors for President or Vice President, or for Senator or Representative in Congress, shall not be denied or abridged by the United States or any State by reason of failure to pay any poll tax or other tax.

Section 2 The Congress shall have the power to enforce this article by appropriate legislation.

Amendment XXV [1967]

Section 1 In case of the removal of the President from office or his death or resignation, the Vice President shall become President.

Section 2 Whenever there is a vacancy in the office of the Vice President, the President shall nominate a Vice President who shall take the office upon confirmation by a majority vote of both houses of Congress.

Section 3 Whenever the President transmits to the President pro tempore of the Senate and the Speaker of the House of Representatives his written declaration that he is unable to discharge the powers and duties of his office, and until he transmits to them a written declaration to the contrary, such powers and duties shall be discharged by the Vice President as Acting President.

Section 4 Whenever the Vice President and a majority of either the principal officers of the executive departments, or of such other body as Congress may by law provide, transmit to the President pro tempore of the Senate and the Speaker of the House of Representatives their written declaration that the President is unable to discharge the powers and duties of his office, the Vice President shall immediately assume the powers and duties of the office as Acting President.

Thereafter, when the President transmits to the President pro tempore of the Senate and the Speaker of the House of Representatives his written declaration that no inability exists, he shall resume the powers and duties of his office unless the Vice President and a majority of either the principal officers of the executive departments, or of such other body as Congress may by law provide, transmit within four days to the President pro tempore of the Senate and the Speaker of the House of Representatives their written declaration that the President is unable to discharge the powers and duties of his office. Thereupon Congress shall decide the issue, assembling within 48 hours for that purpose if not in session. If the Congress, within 21 days after receipt of the latter written declaration, or, if Congress is not in session, within 21 days after Congress is required to assemble, determines by two-thirds vote of both houses that the President is unable to discharge the powers and duties of his office, the Vice President shall continue to discharge the same as Acting President; otherwise, the President shall resume the powers and duties of his office.

Amendment XXVI [1971]

Section 1 The right of citizens of the United States, who are 18 years of age or older, to vote shall not be denied or abridged by the United States or any state on account of age.

Section 2 The Congress shall have the power to enforce this article by appropriate legislation.

Amendment XXVII [1992]

No law varying the compensation for the service of Senators and Representatives shall take effect until an election of Representatives shall have intervened.

The Federalist Papers

The Federalist Papers *is a collection of 85 essays written by Alexander Hamilton, John Jay, and James Madison under the pen name Publius. They were published in New York newspapers in 1787 and 1788 to support ratification of the Constitution. Excerpts from Federalist Nos. 10, 51, and 78 are reprinted here.*

JAMES MADISON: Federalist No. 10

Among the numerous advantages promised by a well constructed Union, none deserves to be more accurately developed than its tendency to break and control the violence of faction. The friend of popular governments never finds himself so much alarmed for their character and fate as when he contemplates their propensity to this dangerous vice. He will not fail, therefore, to set a due value on any plan which, without violating the principles to which he is attached, provides a proper cure for it. The instability, injustice, and confusion, introduced into the public councils, have, in truth been the mortal diseases under which popular governments have everywhere perished; as they continue to be the favorite and fruitful topics from which the adversaries to liberty derive their most specious declamations. The valuable improvements made by the American constitutions on the popular models, both ancient and modern, cannot certainly be too much admired; but it would be an unwarrantable partiality, to contend that they have as effectually obviated the danger on this side, as was wished and expected. Complaints are everywhere heard from our most considerate and virtuous citizens, equally the friends of public and private faith, and of public and personal liberty, that our governments are too unstable; that the public good is disregarded in the conflicts of rival parties; and that measures are too often decided, not according to the rules of justice, and the rights of the minor party, but by the superior force of an interested and overbearing majority. However anxiously we may wish that these complaints had no foundation, the evidence of known facts will not permit us to deny that they are in some degree true. It will be found, indeed, on a candid review of our situation, that some of the distresses under which we labor, have been erroneously charged on the operation of our governments; but it will be found, at the same time, that other causes will not alone account for many of our heaviest misfortunes; and, particularly, for the prevailing and increasing distrust of public engagements, and alarm for private rights, which are echoed from one end of the continent to the other. These must be chiefly, if not wholly, effects of the unsteadiness and injustice, with which a factious spirit has tainted our public administrations.

By a faction, I understand a number of citizens, whether amounting to a majority or minority of the whole, who are united and actuated by some common impulse of passion, or of interest, adverse to the rights of other citizens, or to the permanent and aggregate interests of the community.

There are two methods of curing the mischiefs of faction: The one, by removing its causes; the other, by controlling its effects.

There are again two methods of removing the causes of faction: the one, by destroying the liberty which is essential to its existence; the other, by giving to every citizen the same opinions, the same passions, and the same interests.

It could never be more truly said, than of the first remedy, that it was worse than the disease. Liberty is to faction what air is to fire, an aliment, without which it instantly expires. But it could not be a less folly to abolish liberty, which is essential to political life because it nourishes faction, than it would be to wish the annihilation of air, which is essential to animal life, because it imparts to fire its destructive agency.

The second expedient is as impracticable, as the first would be unwise. As long as the reason of man continues fallible, and he is at liberty to exercise it, different opinions will be formed. As long as the connection subsists between his reason and his self-love, his opinions and his passions will have a reciprocal influence on each other; and the former will be objects to which the latter will attach themselves. The diversity in the faculties of men, from which the rights of property originate, is not less an insuperable obstacle to a uniformity of interests. The protection of those faculties is the first object of government. From the protection of different and unequal faculties of acquiring property, the possession of different degrees and kinds of property immediately results; and from the influence of these on the sentiments and views of the respective proprietors, ensues a division of the society into different interests and parties.

The latent causes of faction are thus sown in the nature of man; and we see them everywhere brought into different degrees of activity, according to the different circumstances of civil society. A zeal for different opinions concerning religion, concerning government, and many other points, as well of speculation as of practice; an attachment to different leaders, ambitiously contending for preeminence and power; or to persons of other descriptions, whose fortunes have been interesting to the human passions, have, in turn, divided mankind into parties, inflamed them with mutual animosity, and rendered them much more disposed to vex and oppress each other, than to cooperate for their common good. So strong is this propensity of mankind, to fall into mutual animosities, that where no substantial occasion presents itself, the most frivolous and fanciful distinctions have been sufficient to kindle their unfriendly passions, and excite their most violent conflicts. But the most common and durable source of factions has been the various and unequal distribution of property. Those who hold, and those who are without property, have ever formed distinct interests in society. Those who are creditors, and those who are debtors, fall under a like discrimination. A landed interest, a manufacturing interest, a mercantile interest, a moneyed interest, with many lesser interests, grow up of necessity in civilized nations, and divide them into different classes, actuated by different sentiments and views. The regulation of these various and interfering interests forms the principle task of modern legislation, and involves the spirit of party and faction in the necessary and ordinary operations of government.

No man is allowed to be a judge in his own cause; because his interest will certainly bias his judgment, and, not improbably, corrupt his integrity. With equal, nay, with greater reason, a body of men are unfit to be both judges and parties at the same time; yet what are many of the most important acts of legislation, but so many judicial determinations, not indeed concerning the rights of single persons, but concerning the rights of large bodies of citizens? And what are the different classes of legislators, but advocates and parties to the cause which they determine? Is a law proposed concerning private debts? It is a question to which the creditors are parties on one side, and the debtors on the other. Justice ought to hold the balance between them. Yet the parties are, and must be, themselves the judges; and the most numerous party, or, in other words, the most powerful faction, must be expected to prevail. Shall domestic manufactures be encouraged, and in what degree, by restrictions on foreign manufactures? are questions which would be differently decided by the landed and the manufacturing classes; and probably by neither with a sole regard to justice and the public good. . . .

It is in vain to say, that enlightened statesmen will be able to adjust these clashing interests, and render them all subservient to the public good. Enlightened statesmen will not always be at the helm; nor, in many cases, can such an adjustment be made at all, without taking into view indirect and remote considerations, which will rarely prevail over the immediate interest which one party may find in disregarding the rights of another, or the good of the whole.

The inference to which we are brought is, that the causes of faction cannot be removed; and that relief is only to be sought in the means of controlling its *effects.*

If a faction consists of less than a majority, relief is supplied by the republican principle, which enables the majority to defeat its sinister views, by regular vote. It may clog the administration, it may convulse the society; but it will be unable to execute and mask its violence under the forms of the constitution. When a majority is included in a faction, the form of popular government, on the other hand, enables it to sacrifice to its ruling passion or interest, both the public good and the rights of other citizens. To secure the public good, and private rights, against the danger of such a faction, and at the same time to preserve the spirit and the form of popular government, is then the great object to which our inquiries are directed. Let me add, that it is the great desideratum, by which alone this form of government can be rescued from the opprobrium under which it has so long labored, and be recommended to the esteem and adoption of mankind.

By what means is this object attainable? Evidently by one of two only. Either the existence of the same passion or interest in a majority, at the same time must be prevented; or the majority, having such coexistent passion or interest, must be rendered, by their number and local situation, unable to concert and carry into effect schemes of oppression. If the impulse and the opportunity be suffered to coincide, we well know, that neither moral nor religious motives can be relied on as an adequate control. They are not found to be such on the injustice and violence of individuals, and lose their efficacy in proportion to the number combined together; that is in proportion as their efficacy becomes needful.

From this view of the subject, it may be concluded, that a pure democracy, by which I mean a society consisting of a small number of citizens, who assemble and administer the government in person, can admit of no cure from the mischiefs of faction. A common passion or interest will, in almost every case, be felt by a majority of the whole; a communication and concert, results from the form of government itself; and there is nothing to check the inducements to sacrifice the weaker party, or an obnoxious individual. Hence it is, that such democracies have ever been spectacles of turbulence and contention; have ever been found incompatible with personal security, or the rights of property; and have, in general been as short in their lives, as they have been violent in their deaths. Theoretic politicians, who have patronized this species of government, have erroneously supposed that by reducing mankind to a perfect equality in their political rights, they would, at the same time, be perfectly equalized and assimilated in their possessions, their opinions, and their passions.

A republic, by which I mean a government in which the scheme of representation takes place, opens a different prospect, and promises the cure for which we are seeking. Let us examine the points in which it varies from pure democracy, and we shall comprehend both the nature of the cure and the efficacy which it must derive from the union.

The two great points of difference, between a democracy and a republic, are, first, the delegation of the government, in the latter, to a small number of citizens elected by the rest; secondly, the greater number of citizens, and greater sphere of country, over which the latter may be extended.

The effect of the first difference is on the one hand, to refine and enlarge the public views, by passing them through the medium of a chosen body of citizens, whose wisdom may best discern the true interest in their country, and whose patriotism and love of justice, will be least likely to sacrifice it to temporary or partial considerations. Under such a regulation, it may well happen, that the public voice, pronounced by the representatives of the people, will be more consonant to the public good, than if pronounced by the people themselves, convened for the purpose. On the other hand, the effect may be inverted. Men of factious tempers, of local prejudices, or of sinister designs, may by intrigue, by corruption, or by other means, first obtain the suffrages, and then betray the interests, of the people. The question resulting is, whether small or extensive republics are most favorable to the election of proper guardians of the public weal; and it is clearly decided in favor of the latter by two obvious considerations.

In the first place, it is to be remarked, that however small the republic may be, the representatives must be raised to a certain number, in order to guard against the cabals of a few; and that however large it may be, they must be limited to a certain number, in order to guard against the confusion of a multitude. Hence, the number of representatives in the two cases not being in proportion to that of the constituents, and being proportionally greatest in the small republic, it follows that if the proportion of fit characters be not less in the large than in the small republic, the former will present a greater option, and consequently a greater probability of a fit choice.

In the next place, as each representative will be chosen by a greater number of citizens in the large than in the small republic, it will be more difficult for unworthy candidates to practice with success the vicious arts, by which elections are too often carried; and the suffrages of the people being more free, will be more likely to center in men who possess the most attractive merit, and the most diffusive and established characters. . . .

The other point of difference is, the greater number of citizens, and extent of territory, which may be brought within the compass of republican, than of democratic government; and it is this circumstance principally which renders factious combinations less to be dreaded in the former, than in the latter. The smaller the society, the fewer probably will be the distinct parties and interests composing it; the fewer the distinct parties and interests, the more frequently will a majority be found of the same party; and the smaller the number of individuals composing a majority, and the smaller the compass within which they are placed, the more easily they will concert and execute their plans of oppression. Extend the sphere, and you take in a greater variety of parties and interests; you make it less probable that a majority of the whole will have a common motive to invade the rights of other citizens; or if such a common motive exists, it will be more difficult for all who feel it to discover their own strength, and to act in unison with each other. . . .

Hence, it clearly appears, that the same advantage, which a republic has over a democracy, in controlling the effects of faction, is enjoyed by a large over a small republic—is enjoyed by the union over the states composing it. Does this advantage consist in the substitution of representatives, whose enlightened views and virtuous sentiments render them superior to local prejudices, and to schemes of injustice? It will not be denied, that the representation of the union will be most likely to possess these requisite endowments. Does it consist in the greater security afforded by a greater variety of parties, against the event of any one party being able to outnumber and oppress the rest? In an equal degree does the increased variety of parties, comprised within the union, increase this security? Does it, in fine, consist in the greater obstacles opposed to the concert and accomplishment of the secret wishes of an unjust and interested majority? Here, again, the extent of the union gives it the most palpable advantage. The influence of factious leaders may kindle a flame within their particular states, but will be unable to spread a general conflagration through the other states; a religious sect may degenerate into a political faction in a part of the confederacy; but the variety of sects dispersed over the entire face of it, must secure the national councils against any danger from that source; a rage for paper money, for an abolition of debts, for an equal division of property, or for any other improper or wicked project, will be less apt to pervade the whole body of the union, than a particular member of it; in the same proportion as such a malady is more likely to taint a particular country or district, than an entire state.

In the extent and proper structure of the union, therefore, we behold a republican remedy for the diseases most incident to republican government. And according to the degree of pleasure and pride we feel in being republicans, ought to be our zeal in cherishing the spirit, and supporting the character of Federalists.

JAMES MADISON: Federalist No. 51

To what expedient then shall we finally resort, for maintaining in practice the necessary partition of power among the several departments, as laid down in the constitution? The only answer that can be given is, that as all these exterior provisions are found to be inadequate, the defect must be supplied, by so contriving the interior structure of the government, as that its several constituent parts may, by their mutual relations, be the means of keeping each other in their proper places. . . .

In order to lay a due foundation for that separate and distinct exercise of the different powers of government, which, to a certain extent, is admitted on all hands to be essential to the preservation of liberty, it is evident that each department should have a will of its own; and consequently should be so constituted, that the members of each should have as little agency as possible in the appointment of the members of the others. . . .

It is equally evident, that the members of each department should be as little dependent as possible on those of the others, for the emoluments annexed to their offices. Were the executive magistrate, or the judges, not independent of the legislature in this particular, their independence in every other would be merely nominal.

But the great security against a gradual concentration of the several powers in the same department, consists in giving to those who administer each department, the necessary constitutional means, and personal motives, to resist encroachments of the others. The provision for defense must in this, as in all other cases, be made commensurate to the danger of attack. Ambition must be made to counteract ambition. The interest of the man must be connected with the constitutional rights of the place. It may be a reflection on human nature, that such devices should be necessary to control the abuses of government. But what is government itself, but the greatest of all reflections on human nature? If men were angels, no government would be necessary. If angels were to govern men, neither external nor internal controls on government would be necessary. In framing a government, which is to be administered by men over men, the great difficulty lies in this: You must first enable the government to control the governed; and in the next place, oblige it to control itself. A dependence on the people is, no doubt, the primary control on the government; but experience has taught mankind the necessity of auxiliary precautions.

This policy of supplying by opposite and rival interests, the defect of better motives, might be traced through the whole system of human affairs, private as well as public. We see it particularly displayed in all the subordinate distributions of power; where the constant aim is, to divide and arrange the several offices in such a manner, as that each may be a check on the other; that the private interest of every individual, may be a sentinel over the public rights. These interventions of prudence cannot be less requisite to the distribution of the supreme powers of the state.

But it is not possible to give to each department an equal power of self-defense. In republican government, the legislative authority necessarily predominates. The remedy for this inconvenience is, to divide the legislature into different branches; and to render them by different modes of election, and different principles of action, as little connected with each other, as the nature of their common functions, and their common dependence on the society will admit. It may even be necessary to guard against dangerous encroachments, by still further precautions. As the weight of the legislative authority requires that it should be thus divided, the weakness of the executive may require, on the other hand, that it should be fortified. An absolute negative on the legislature, appears, at first view, to be the natural defense with which the executive magistrate should be armed. But perhaps it would be neither altogether safe, nor alone sufficient. On ordinary occasions, it might not be exerted with the requisite firmness; and on extraordinary occasions, it might be perfidiously abused. May not this defect of an absolute negative be supplied by some qualified connection between this weaker department, and the weaker branch of the stronger department, by which the latter may be led to support the constitutional rights of the former, without being too much detached from the rights of its own department?

There are, moreover, two considerations particularly applicable to the federal system of America, which place that system in a very interesting point of view.

First. In a single republic, all the power surrendered by the people is submitted to the administration of a single government, and the usurpations are guarded against by a division of the government into distinct and separate departments. In the compound republic of America, the power surrendered by the people is first divided between two distinct governments, and then the portion allotted to each subdivided among distinct and separate departments. Hence a double security arises to the rights of the people. The different governments will control each other, at the same time that each will be controlled by itself.

Second. It is of great importance in a republic not only to guard the society against the oppression of its rulers, but to guard one part of the society against the injustice of the other part. Different interests necessarily exist in different classes of citizens. If a majority be united by a common interest, the rights of the minority will be insecure. There are but two methods of providing against this evil: the one by creating a will in the community independent of the majority—that is, of the society itself; the other, by comprehending in the society so many separate descriptions of citizens as will render an unjust combination of a majority of the whole very probable, if not impracticable. The first method prevails in all governments possessing an hereditary or self-appointed authority. This, at best, is but a precarious security; because a power independent of the society may as well espouse the unjust views of the major, as the rightful interests of the minor party, and may possibly be turned against both parties. The second method will be exemplified in the federal republic of the United States. Whilst all authority in it will be derived from and dependent on the society, the society itself will be broken into so many parts, interests and classes of citizens, that the rights of individuals, or of the minority, will be in little danger from interested combinations of the minority. In a free government the security for civil rights must be the same as that for religious rights. It consists in the one case in the multiplicity of interests, and in the other in the multiplicity of sects. The degree of security in both cases will depend on the number of interests and sects; and this may be presumed to depend on the extent of country and number of people comprehended under the same government. This view of the subject must particularly recommend a proper federal system to all the sincere and considerate friends of republican government, since it shows that in exact proportion as the territory of the Union may be formed into more circumscribed Confederacies, or States, oppressive combinations of a majority will be facilitated; the best security, under the republican forms, for the rights of every class of citizens, will be diminished; and consequently the stability and independence of some member of the government, the only other security, must be proportionately increased. Justice is the end of the government. It is the end of civil society. It ever has been and ever will be pursued until it be obtained, or until liberty be lost in the pursuit. In a society under the forms of which the stronger faction can readily unite and oppress the weaker, anarchy may as truly be said to reign as in a state of nature, where the weaker individual is not secured against the violence of the stronger; and as, in the latter state, even the stronger individuals are prompted, by the uncertainty of their condition, to submit to a government which may protect the weak as well as themselves; so, in the former state, will the more powerful factions or parties be gradually induced, by a like motive, to wish for a government which will protect all parties, the weaker as well as the more powerful. It can be little doubted that if the State of Rhode Island was separated from the Confederacy and left to itself, the insecurity of rights under the popular form of government within such narrow limits would be displayed by such reiterated oppressions of factious majorities that some power altogether independent of the people would soon be called for by the voice of the very factions whose misrule had proved the necessity of it. In the extended republic of the United States, and among the great variety of interests, parties, and sects which it embraces, a coalition of a majority of the whole society could seldom take place on any other principles than those of justice and the general good; whilst there being thus less danger to a minor from the will of a major party, there must be less pretext, also, to provide for the security of the former, by introducing into the government a will not dependent on the latter, or, in other words, a will independent of the society itself. It is no less certain than it is important, notwithstanding the contrary opinions which have been entertained, that the larger the society, provided it lie within a practical sphere, the more duly capable it will be of self-government. And happily for the *republican cause,* the practicable sphere may be carried to a very great extent, by a judicious modification and mixture of the *federal principle.*

ALEXANDER HAMILTON: Federalist No. 78

We proceed now to an examination of the judiciary department of the proposed government.

In unfolding the defects of the existing confederation, the utility and necessity of a federal judicature have been clearly pointed out. It is the less necessary to recapitulate the considerations there urged; as the propriety of the institution in the abstract is not disputed; the only questions which have been raised being relative to the manner of constituting it, and to its extent. To these points, therefore, our observations shall be confined.

The manner of constituting it seems to embrace these several objects: 1st. The mode of appointing the judges; 2nd. The tenure by which they are to hold their places; 3rd. The partition of the judiciary authority between courts, and their relations to each other.

First. As to the mode of appointing the judges: This is the same with that of appointing the officers of the union in general, and has been so fully discussed . . . that nothing can be said here which would not be useless repetition.

Second. As to the tenure by which the judges are to hold their places: This chiefly concerns their duration in office; the provisions for their support; the precautions for their responsibility.

According to the plan of the convention, all the judges who may be appointed by the United States are to hold their offices *during good behavior;* which is conformable to the most approved of the state constitutions. . . . The standard of good behavior for the continuance in office of the judicial magistracy is certainly one of the most valuable of the modern improvements in the practice of government. In a monarchy, it is an excellent barrier to the despotism of the prince; in a republic, it is a no less excellent barrier to the encroachments and oppressions of the representative body. And it is the best expedient which can be devised in any government, to secure a steady, upright, and impartial administration of the laws.

Whoever attentively considers the different departments of power must perceive, that, in a government in which they are separated from each other, the judiciary, from the nature of its functions, will always be the least dangerous to the political rights of the constitution; because it will be at least in a capacity to annoy or injure them. The executive not only dispenses the honors, but holds the sword of the community. The legislature not only commands the purse, but prescribes the rules by which the duties and rights of every citizen are to be regulated. The judiciary, on the contrary, has no influence over either the sword or the purse; no direction either of the strength or of the wealth of the society; and can take no active resolution whatever. It may truly be said to have neither force nor will, but merely judgment; and must ultimately depend upon the aid of the executive arm for the efficacious exercise even of this faculty.

This simple view of the matter suggests several important consequences: It proves incontestably, that the judiciary is beyond comparison, the weakest of the three departments of power, that it can never attack with success either of the other two: and that all possible care is requisite to enable it to defend itself against their attacks. It equally proves, that, though individual oppression may now and then proceed from the courts of justice, the general liberty of the people can never be endangered from that quarter; I mean so long as the judiciary remains truly distinct from both the legislature and executive. For I agree, that "there is no liberty, if the power of judging be not separated from the legislative and executive powers." It proves, in the last place, that as liberty can have nothing to fear from the judiciary alone, but would have everything to fear from its union with either of the other departments; that, as all the effects of such a union must ensue from a dependence of the former on the latter, notwithstanding a nominal and apparent separation; that as, from the natural feebleness of the judiciary, it is in continual jeopardy of being overpowered, awed or influenced by its coordinate branches; that, as nothing can contribute so much to its firmness and independence as permanency in office, this quality may therefore be justly regarded as an indispensable ingredient in its constitution; and, in a great measure, as the citadel of the public justice and the public security.

The complete independence of the courts of justice is peculiarly essential in a limited constitution. By a limited constitution, I understand one which contains certain specified exceptions to the legislative authority; such, for instance, as that it shall pass no bills of attainder, no *ex post facto* laws, and the like. Limitations of this kind can be preserved in practice no other way than through the medium of the courts of justice, whose duty it must be to declare all acts contrary to the manifest tenor of the constitution void. Without this, all the reservations of particular rights or privileges would amount to nothing.

Some perplexity respecting the right of the courts to pronounce legislative acts void, because contrary to the constitution, has arisen from an imagination that the doctrine would imply a superiority of the judiciary to the legislative power. It is urged that the authority which can declare the acts of another void, must necessarily be superior to the one whose acts may be declared void. As this doctrine is of great importance in all the American constitutions, a brief discussion of the grounds on which it rests cannot be unacceptable.

There is no position which depends on clearer principles than that every act of a delegated authority, contrary to the tenor of the commission under which it is exercised, is void. No legislative act, therefore, contrary to the constitution, can be valid. To deny this would be to affirm, that the deputy is greater then his principal; that the servant is above his master; that the representatives of the people are superior to the people themselves; that men, acting by virtue of powers, may do not only what their powers do not authorize, but what they forbid.

If it be said that the legislative body are themselves the constitutional judges of their own powers, and that the construction they put upon them is conclusive upon the other departments, it may be answered, that this cannot be the natural presumption, where it is not to be collected from any particular provisions in the constitution. It is not otherwise to be supposed that the constitution could intend to enable the representatives of the people to substitute their *will* to that of their constituents. It is far more rational to suppose that the courts were designed to be an intermediate body between the people and the legislature, in order, among other things, to keep the latter within the limits assigned to their authority. The interpretation of the laws is the proper and peculiar province of the courts. A constitution is, in fact, and must be, regarded by the judges as a fundamental law. It must therefore belong to them to ascertain its meaning, as well as the meaning of any particular act proceeding from the legislative body. If there should happen to be an irreconcilable variance between the two, that which has the superior obligation and validity ought, of course, to be preferred; in other words, the constitution ought to be preferred to the statute, the intention of the people to the intention of their agents.

Nor does this conclusion by any means suppose a superiority of the judicial to the legislative power. It only supposes that the power of the people is superior to both; and that where the will of the legislature declared in its statutes, stands in opposition to that of the people declared in the constitution, the judges ought to be governed by the latter, rather than the former. They ought to regulate their decisions by the fundamental laws, rather than by those which are not fundamental. . . .

It can be of no weight to say, that the courts, on the pretense of a repugnancy, may substitute their own pleasure to the constitutional intentions of the legislature. This might as well happen in the case of two contradictory statutes; or it might as well happen in every adjudication upon any single statute. The courts must declare the sense of the law; and if they should be disposed to exercise will instead of judgment, the consequence would equally be the substitution of their pleasure to that of the legislative body. The observation, if it proved anything, would prove that there ought to be no judges distinct from the body.

If then the courts of justice are to be considered as the bulwarks of a limited constitution, against legislative encroachments, this consideration will afford a strong argument for the permanent tenure of judicial officers, since nothing will contribute so much as this to that independent spirit in the judges, which must be essential to the faithful performance of so arduous a duty.

This independence of the judges is equally requisite to guard the constitution and the rights of individuals, from the effects of those ill-humors which are the arts of designing men, or the influence of particular conjunctures, sometimes disseminate among the people themselves, and which, though they speedily give place to better information, and more deliberate reflection, have a tendency, in the meantime, to occasion dangerous innovations in the government, and serious oppressions of the minor party in the community. . . . Until the people have, by some solemn and authoritative act, annulled or changed the established form, it is binding upon themselves collectively, as well as individually; and no presumption, or even knowledge of their sentiments, can warrant their representatives in a departure from it, prior to such an act. But it is easy to see, that it would require an uncommon portion of fortitude in the judges to do their duty as faithful guardians of the constitution, where legislative invasions of it had been instigated by the major voice of the community.

But it is not with a view to infractions of the constitution only, that the independence of the judges may be an essential safeguard against the effects of occasional ill-humors in the society. These sometimes extend no farther than to the injury of the private rights of particular classes of citizens, by unjust and partial laws. Here also the firmness of the judicial magistracy is of vast importance in mitigating the severity, and confining the operation of such laws. It not only serves to moderate the immediate mischiefs of those which may have been passed, but it operates as a check upon the legislative body in passing them; who, perceiving that obstacles to the success of an iniquitous intention are to be expected from the scruples of the courts, are in a manner compelled by the very motives of the injustice they meditate, to qualify their attempts. . . .

That inflexible and uniform adherence to the rights of the constitution, and of individuals, which we perceive to be indispensable in the courts of justice, can certainly not be expected from judges who hold their offices by a temporary commission. Periodical appointments, however regulated, or by whomsoever made, would, in some way or other, be fatal to their necessary independence. If the power of making them was committed either to the executive or legislature, there would be danger of an improper compliance to the branch which possessed it; if to both, there would be an unwillingness to hazard the displeasure of either; if to the people, or to persons chosen by them for the special purpose, there would be too great a disposition to consult popularity to justify a reliance that nothing would be consulted but the constitution and the laws.

There is yet a further and a weighty reason for the permanency of judicial offices, which is deducible from the nature of the qualifications they require. It has been frequently remarked, with great propriety, that a voluminous code of laws is one of the inconveniences necessarily connected with the advantages of a free government. To avoid an arbitrary discretion in the courts, it is indispensable that they should be bound down by strict rules and precedents, which serve to define and point out their duty in every particular case that comes before them; and it will readily be conceived, from the variety of controversies which grow out of the folly and wickedness of mankind, that the records of those precedents must unavoidably swell to a very considerable bulk, and must demand long and laborious study to acquire a competent knowledge of them. Hence it is, that there can be but few men in the society, who will have sufficient skill in the laws to qualify them for the stations of judges. And making the proper deductions for the ordinary depravity of human nature, the number must be still smaller, of those who unite the requisite integrity with the requisite knowledge. . . .

Presidents and Congresses, 1789–1996

Year	President and Vice-President	Party of President	Congress	Majority Party: House	Majority Party: Senate
1789–1797	**George Washington**	None	1st	Admin. Supporters	Admin. Supporters
	John Adams		2nd	Federalist	Federalist
			3rd	Democratic-Republican	Federalist
			4th	Federalist	Federalist
1797–1801	**John Adams**	Federalist	5th	Federalist	Federalist
	Thomas Jefferson		6th	Federalist	Federalist
1801–1809	**Thomas Jefferson**		7th	Democratic-Republican	Democratic-Republican
	Aaron Burr (to 1805)		8th	Democratic-Republican	Democratic-Republican
	George Clinton (to 1809)		9th	Democratic-Republican	Democratic-Republican
			10th	Democratic-Republican	Democratic-Republican
1809–1817	**James Madison**	Democratic-Republican	11th	Democratic-Republican	Democratic-Republican
	George Clinton (to 1813)		12th	Democratic-Republican	Democratic-Republican
	Elbridge Gerry (to 1817)		13th	Democratic-Republican	Democratic-Republican
			14th	Democratic-Republican	Democratic-Republican
1817–1825	**James Monroe**	Democratic-Republican	15th	Democratic-Republican	Democratic-Republican
	Daniel D. Tompkins		16th	Democratic-Republican	Democratic-Republican
			17th	Democratic-Republican	Democratic-Republican
			18th	Democratic-Republican	Democratic-Republican
1825–1829	**John Quincy Adams**	National-Republican	19th	Admin. Supporters	Admin. Supporters
	John C. Calhoun		20th	Jacksonian Democrats	Jacksonian Democrats
1829–1837	**Andrew Jackson**	Democratic	21st	Democratic	Democratic
	John C. Calhoun (to 1833)		22nd	Democratic	Democratic
	Martin Van Buren (to 1837)		23rd	Democratic	Democratic
			24th	Democratic	Democratic

Year	President and Vice-President	Party of President	Congress	Majority Party	
				House	Senate
1837–1841	**Martin Van Buren** Richard M. Johnson	Democratic	25th 26th	Democratic Democratic	Democratic Democratic
1841	**William H. Harrison** (died a month after inauguration) John Tyler	Whig			
1841–1845	**John Tyler** (VP vacant)	Whig	27th 28th	Whig Democratic	Whig Whig
1845–1849	**James K. Polk** George M. Dallas	Democratic	29th 30th	Democratic Whig	Democratic Democratic
1849–1850	**Zachary Taylor** (died in office) Millard Fillmore	Whig	31st	Democratic	Democratic
1850–1853	**Millard Fillmore** (VP vacant)	Whig	32nd	Democratic	Democratic
1853–1857	**Franklin Pierce** William R. King	Democratic	33rd 34th	Democratic Republican	Democratic Democratic
1857–1861	**James Buchanan** John C. Breckinridge	Democratic	35th 36th	Democratic Republican	Democratic Democratic
1861–1865	**Abraham Lincoln** (died in office) Hannibal Hamlin (to 1865) Andrew Johnson (1865)	Republican	37th 38th	Republican Republican	Republican Republican
1865–1869	**Andrew Johnson** (VP vacant)	Republican	39th 40th	Unionist Republican	Unionist Republican
1869–1877	**Ulysses S. Grant** Schuyler Colfax (to 1873) Henry Wilson (to 1877)	Republican	41st 42nd 43rd 44th	Republican Republican Republican Democratic	Republican Republican Republican Republican
1877–1881	**Rutherford B. Hayes** William A. Wheeler	Republican	45th 46th	Democratic Democratic	Republican Democratic
1881	**James A. Garfield** (died in office) Chester A. Arthur	Republican	47th	Republican	Republican
1881–1885	**Chester A. Arthur** (VP vacant)	Republican	48th	Democratic	Republican
1885–1889	**Grover Cleveland** Thomas A. Hendricks	Democratic	49th 50th	Democratic Democratic	Republican Republican
1889–1893	**Benjamin Harrison** Levi P. Morton	Republican	51st 52nd	Republican Democratic	Republican Republican
1893–1897	**Grover Cleveland** Adlai E. Stevenson	Democratic	53rd 54th	Democratic Republican	Democratic Republican

Year	President and Vice-President	Party of President	Congress	Majority Party House	Majority Party Senate
1897–1901	**William McKinley** (died in office)	Republican	55th	Republican	Republican
	Garret A. Hobart (to 1901)		56th	Republican	Republican
	Theodore Roosevelt (1901)				
1901–1909	**Theodore Roosevelt**	Republican	57th	Republican	Republican
	(VP vacant, 1901–1905)		58th	Republican	Republican
	Charles W. Fairbanks (1905–1909)		59th	Republican	Republican
			60th	Republican	Republican
1909–1913	**William Howard Taft**	Republican	61st	Republican	Republican
	James S. Sherman		62nd	Democratic	Republican
1913–1921	**Woodrow Wilson**	Democratic	63rd	Democratic	Democratic
	Thomas R. Marshall		64th	Democratic	Democratic
			65th	Democratic	Democratic
			66th	Republican	Republican
1921–1923	**Warren G. Harding** (died in office)	Republican	67th	Republican	Republican
	Calvin Coolidge				
1923–1929	**Calvin Coolidge**	Republican	68th	Republican	Republican
	(VP vacant, 1923–1925)		69th	Republican	Republican
	Charles G. Dawes (1925–1929)		70th	Republican	Republican
1929–1933	**Herbert Hoover**	Republican	71st	Republican	Republican
	Charles Curtis		72nd	Democratic	Republican
1933–1945	**Franklin D. Roosevelt**	Democratic	73rd	Democratic	Democratic
	(died in office)		74th	Democratic	Democratic
	John N. Garner (1933–1941)		75th	Democratic	Democratic
	Henry A. Wallace (1941–1945)		76th	Democratic	Democratic
	Harry S Truman (1945)		77th	Democratic	Democratic
			78th	Democratic	Democratic
1945–1953	**Harry S Truman**	Democratic	79th	Democratic	Democratic
	(VP vacant, 1945–1949)		80th	Republican	Republican
	Alben W. Barkley (1949–1953)		81st	Democratic	Democratic
			82nd	Democratic	Democratic
1953–1961	**Dwight D. Eisenhower**	Republican	83rd	Republican	Republican
	Richard M. Nixon		84th	Democratic	Democratic
			85th	Democratic	Democratic
			86th	Democratic	Democratic
1961–1963	**John F. Kennedy** (died in office)	Democratic	87th	Democratic	Democratic
	Lyndon B. Johnson				
1963–1969	**Lyndon B. Johnson**	Democratic	88th	Democratic	Democratic
	(VP vacant, 1963–1965)		89th	Democratic	Democratic
	Hubert H. Humphrey (1965–1969)		90th	Democratic	Democratic

Year	President and Vice-President	Party of President	Congress	Majority Party	
				House	Senate
1969–1974	**Richard M. Nixon** (resigned office) Spiro T. Agnew (resigned office) Gerald R. Ford (appointed vice-president)	Republican	91st 92nd	Democratic Democratic	Democratic Democratic
1974–1977	**Gerald R. Ford** Nelson A. Rockefeller (appointed vice-president)	Republican	93rd 94th	Democratic Democratic	Democratic Democratic
1977–1981	**Jimmy Carter** Walter Mondale	Democratic	95th 96th	Democratic Democratic	Democratic Democratic
1981–1989	**Ronald Reagan** George Bush	Republican	97th 98th 99th 100th	Democratic Democratic Democratic Democratic	Republican Republican Republican Democratic
1989–1993	**George Bush** J. Danforth Quayle	Republican	101st 102nd	Democratic Democratic	Democratic Democratic
1993–	**Bill Clinton** Albert Gore, Jr.	Democratic	103rd 104th 105th	Democratic Republican Republican	Democratic Republican Republican

NOTES

1. During the entire administration of George Washington and part of the administration of John Quincy Adams, Congress was not organized in terms of parties. This table shows that during these periods the supporters of the respective administrations maintained control of the Congress.
2. This table shows only the two dominant parties in Congress. Independents, members of minor parties, and vacancies have been omitted.

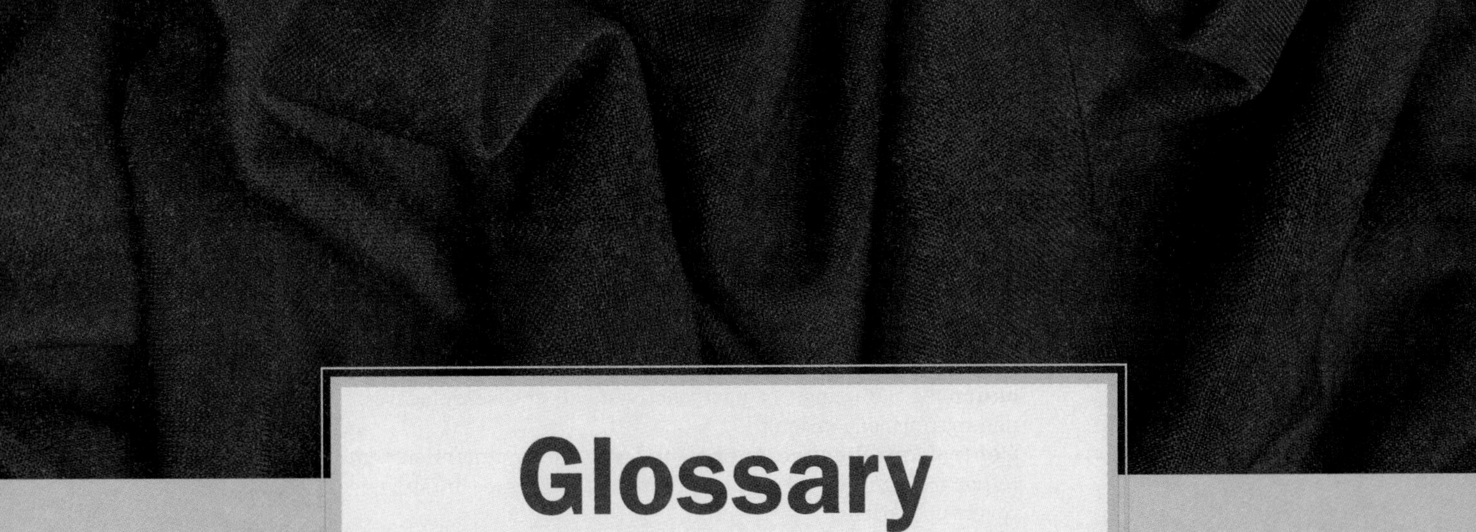

Glossary

affirmative action Programs instituted by private and public institutions to overcome the effects of and to compensate for past discrimination.
agenda setting Influencing what people consider important.
aggregate demand The total of purchases of a country's output by consumers, government, businesses, and foreigners.
amicus curiae Literally, a friend of the court; describing a brief in which those not directly a party to a suit may have their views heard.
Anti-Federalists Opponents of the Constitution during the fight over ratification.
appellate courts Courts that hear cases on appeal from other courts.
appropriation Legal authority for a federal agency to spend money from the U.S. Treasury.
balance of payments The annual difference between payments and receipts between a country and its trading partners.
beat The assigned location where a reporter regularly gathers news stories.
bias Deviation from some ideal standard, such as representativeness or objectivity.
bicameral A legislative body made up of two houses.
bill of attainder A governmental decree or announcement that a person is guilty of a crime that carries the death penalty, rendered without benefit of a trial.
Bill of Rights The first ten amendments to the Constitution, concerned with basic liberties.
bipolar system An international system with two great powers.
block grants Federal grants to the states to be used for general types of activities.
blue-collar workers Industrial workers; may be skilled, semiskilled, or unskilled.
Bretton Woods agreement The 1944 international agreement to set fixed exchange rates among currencies and to establish the International Monetary Fund (IMF) and the International Bank for Reconstruction and Development (IBRD, or World Bank).
briefs Documents prepared by attorneys and presented to courts; these documents set out the arguments in cases.
budget deficit The amount by which annual government expenditures exceed revenues.
bureaucracy A form of large organization characterized by a chain of command, a hierarchy of offices with specified missions, formal rules of behavior, and appointment on the basis of merit and specialized knowledge.
bureaucrat One who works in a bureaucratic organization.
capitalism An economic system based on the private ownership of property and the existence of markets to coordinate most economic activities.
capture A situation in which a regulated industry exercises substantial influence on the government agency regulating it.

casework Services performed by members of Congress for constituents.
categorical grants Federal aid to states and localities clearly specifying what the money can be used for.
caucus, congressional party Members of a single party in one of the houses of Congress who meet to elect leaders, approve committee assignments, and debate party positions on policies.
caucuses Meetings of party activists to choose delegates to national presidential nominating conventions.
Central Intelligence Agency (CIA) The organization that coordinates all U.S. intelligence agencies; it also gathers and evaluates intelligence itself and carries out covert operations.
checks and balances The constitutional principle that government power shall be divided, and that the fragments should balance or check one another to prevent tyranny.
chief of staff A top adviser to the president who also manages the White House staff.
Circuit courts, U.S. The 11 geographical jurisdictions and 2 special courts that hear appeals from the federal district courts.
city council–mayor system A system of local government in which an elected city council passes legislation and a mayor acts as chief executive.
city manager An appointed official who runs the day-to-day government of many towns and small cities.
civil disobedience The act of purposely breaking a law and accepting the consequences of the action, as a way to publicize its unjust nature.
civil liberties Freedoms protected from government interference.
civil rights Guarantees of equal citizenship to all social groups.
civil servants Government workers employed under the merit system; not political appointees.
civil service Federal government civilian employees, excluding political appointees.
class action suit A suit brought on behalf of a group of people who are in a situation similar to that of the plaintiffs.
cloture A vote to end a filibuster or a debate; requires the votes of three-fifths of the membership of the Senate.
coattails The ability of a popular, high-level official to win votes for lower-level officials of the same party.
Cold War A term used for the period of tense relations between the United States and the Soviet Union, stretching from the late 1940s to the late 1980s.
collective public opinion The political attitudes and beliefs of the public as a whole, expressed as averages, percentages, or other summaries of many individuals' opinions.
commerce clause The section of Article I, Section 8, of the Constitution which says "Congress shall have the power . . . To regulate Commerce with foreign Nations, and among the several States."
concurring opinion The opinion of a judge or judges who vote with the majority on a case but wish to set out different reasons for their decision from those of the majority.
conditions Provisions in federal assistance requiring that state and local governments follow certain policies in order to obtain the money.
confederation A loose association of states or units bound together for limited purposes.
conference committees Ad hoc committees, made up of members of both the Senate and the House of Representatives, set up to reconcile differences in the provisions of bills.
Connecticut Compromise Also called the *Great Compromise;* the compromise between the New Jersey and Virginia Plans put forth by the Connecticut delegates at the constitutional convention; called for a lower legislative house based on population and an upper house based on equal representation of the states.
conservatives Those who favor private enterprise and oppose government regulations or spending; the term sometimes also refers to those who favor military strength or the enforcement of traditional social values.

constituency The district of a legislator.
constituent One who lives in the district of an elected official.
constitutional courts Federal courts created by Congress under the authority of Article III of the Constitution.
containment The policy that expansion of the Soviet Union's influence should be resisted by diplomatic, economic, and military means.
contract clause In Article I, Section 10, of the Constitution: No state shall pass any "Law impairing the Obligation of Contracts."
conventional participation Political activity related to elections (voting, persuading, and campaigning) or to contacting public officials.
conventions Gatherings of delegates who nominate a party's presidential candidate.
cooperative federalism Federalism in which the powers of the states and the national government are intertwined like the swirls in a marble cake.
cost-benefit analysis A method of evaluating rules and regulations which weighs their potential costs against their potential benefits to society.
Council of Economic Advisers (CEA) An organization in the Executive Office of the President made up of a small group of economists who advise on economic policy.
covert operations Secret or semisecret activities abroad, often involving intelligence gathering, influence on other countries' politics, or the use of force.
customs duties Taxes levied on imports.
dealignment A process by which the superiority of a dominant political party diminishes without another party's supplanting it.
Defense Intelligence Agency (DIA) The organization in charge of coordinating the intelligence units of the different armed services.
delegate The doctrine, best articulated by Edmund Burke, that elected representatives ought to act in perfect accord with the wishes of their constituents.
democracy A system of rule by the people, defined by the existence of popular sovereignty, political equality, and political liberty.
depression A severe and persistent drop in economic activity.
détente A relaxation of tensions, for example, between the United States and the Soviet Union in the early 1970s.
deviating elections Elections in which the party with only a minority of identifiers wins.
devolution The delegation of power by the central government to state or local bodies.
discharge petition A bill before a committee for at least 30 days while the House is in session may be forced out of the committee and brought to the floor for consideration if a petition with the signatures of 218 House members is secured.
discount rate The interest rate charged to member banks by the Federal Reserve to cover short-term loans.
diseconomies The positive and negative effects of economic activities on third parties.
dissenting opinion The opinion of the judges who are in the minority in any particular case before the Supreme Court.
disturbance theory A theory that locates the origins of interest groups in changes in the economic, social, or political environment that threaten the well-being of some segment of the population.
divided government Control of the executive and the legislative branches by different political parties.
dual federalism Federalism in which the powers of the states and the national government are neatly separated like the sections of a layer cake.
due process; due process clause The section of the Fourteenth Amendment that reads "nor shall any State deprive any person of life, liberty, or property, without due process of law"; a guarantee against arbitrary or unfair government action.
earmarked A budget expenditure tied to a particular program or purpose.
effective tax rate The percentage of income actually paid in taxes.
elastic clause Article I, Section 8; also called the "necessary and proper" clause; gives Congress the authority to make whatever laws are necessary and proper to carry out its enumerated responsibilities.

electoral college Representatives of the states who formally elect the president; the number of electors in each state is equal to its total number of its senators and representatives.
electoral competition A process by which parties seeking votes move toward the center of the political spectrum.
electoral reward and punishment Voting for the incumbents when times are good and against them when times are bad.
electors Those who are elected in the states to formally choose the U.S. president.
entitlements Government benefits that are distributed automatically to citizens who qualify on the basis of a set of guidelines set by law.
enumerated powers Powers of the federal government specifically mentioned in the Constitution.
equal protection clause The section of the Fourteenth Amendment that reads "nor deny to any person within its jurisdiction the equal protection of the laws."
equal protection That part of the Fourteenth Amendment to the constitution that enjoins the state to treat all of their citizens equally.
Equal Rights Amendment (ERA) A proposed constitutional amendment that would have prohibited the U.S. or state governments from denying or abridging equal rights on the grounds of gender; the amendment passed Congress but failed because it did not win approval from the required number of states.
equal time provision A past requirement that television stations give or sell the same amount of time to all competing candidates.
equality of opportunity An equal chance to get ahead economically and socially.
establishment clause The part of the First Amendment which prohibits Congress from establishing an official religion; the basis for the doctrine of "separation of church and state."
European Union (EU) The combination of Western European nations into a single market, with free trade and free population movement among them.
ex post facto law A law that retroactively declares some action illegal.
excise tax A tax on some specific good, such as alcohol or cigarettes.
executive agreements Agreements with other countries that have the same legal force as treaties but do not require approval by the Senate.
executive branch The part of government responsible for executing or carrying out the laws passed by a legislative body or the decisions rendered by a court.
Executive Office of the President (EOP) A group of organizations that advise the president on a wide range of issues; includes the Office of Management and Budget, the National Security Council, and the Council of Economic Advisers.
executive privilege A presidential claim that certain communications with subordinates may be withheld from Congress and the courts.
faction Madison's term for groups or parties that try to advance their own interests at the expense of the public good.
fairness doctrine A past requirement that television stations present contrasting points of view.
federalism A system in which significant governmental powers are divided between a central government and smaller units, such as states.
Federalists Proponents of the Constitution during the ratification fight; also the political party of Hamilton, Washington, and Adams.
filibuster A parliamentary device used in the Senate to prevent a bill from coming to a vote by "talking it to death"; made possible by the norm of unlimited debate.
fiscal policies The government's overall policies on spending and taxing levels; affect overall output and income in the economy.
flat tax A tax that takes the same percentage of the income of all persons.
framing Providing a context for interpreting, for example, in news stories.
franchise The right to vote.
franking, franking privilege Public subsidization of mail from the members of Congress to their constituents.
free rider One who gains a benefit without contributing; a term used to explain why it is so difficult to form social movements and noneconomic interest groups.

General Agreement on Tariffs and Trade (GATT) An international agreement that requires the lowering of tariffs and other barriers to free trade.
general revenue sharing Federal aid to the states without any controls on how the money is spent.
gerrymander Redrawing electoral district lines to give an advantage to a particular party or candidate.
globalization The decentralization and distribution of corporate design, production, marketing, and sales activities around the world.
grand juries Groups of citizens who decide whether there is sufficient evidence to bring an indictment against accused persons.
grandfather clause A device that allowed whites who had failed the literacy test to vote; it allowed all to vote whose grandfathers had voted in the past.
grassroots Referring to constituents, voters, or the rank and file of a party.
Great Compromise *See* Connecticut Compromise.
Great Depression The period of economic crisis in the United States stretching from the stock market crash of 1929 to the entry of America into World War II.
gross domestic product (GDP) Same as the gross national product, except that income residents earn abroad is excluded.
habeas corpus The legal doctrine which holds that those who are arrested must have a timely hearing before a judge.
hearings The process of a congressional committee or subcommittee's taking testimony from witnesses.
hegemon A dominant power: for example, the dominant nation in the world.
hopper The box in the House of Representatives in which proposed bills are placed.
ideology A system of interrelated attitudes and beliefs.
impoundment Refusal by the president to spend money appropriated by Congress.
in forma pauperis Describing a process by which indigents may file a suit with the Supreme Court, free of charge.
incomes policy The government regulation of wages and salaries used to control inflation.
incorporation The gradual use of the Fourteenth Amendment by the Supreme Court to make the Bill of Rights and other constitutional protections relevant at the state level.
incumbent One who holds office.
Industrial Revolution The period of transition from predominantly agricultural to predominantly industrial societies in the Western nations in the nineteenth century.
inflation A period of generally rising prices.
initiative Citizens' proposal of and direct voting on policy.
integration Policies encouraging the interaction of different races, as in schools or public facilities.
intercontinental ballistic missiles (ICBMs) Guided missiles capable of carrying nuclear warheads across continents.
interest group liberalism A political regime in which interest groups help formulate and carry out government policies.
interest group Private organizations and associations that try to influence public policy as a way to protect or advance some interest.
intermediate scrutiny A legal test falling between ordinary and strict scrutiny relevant to issues of gender; under this test, the Supreme Court will allow gender classifications in laws if they serve a *substantial* government objective.
iron triangle An enduring alliance of common interest between an interest group, a congressional committees, and a bureaucratic agency.
isolationism The policy of avoiding involvement in foreign affairs.
Jim Crow The popular term for the system of legal racial segregation that existed in the American South until the middle of the twentieth century.
Joint Chiefs of Staff (JCS) The military officers in charge of each of the armed services.
joint committees Congressional committees with members from the House and the Senate.

judicial activism Actions by the courts which, according to critics, go beyond the role of the judiciary as interpreter of the law and adjudicator of disputes.
judicial review The power of the Supreme Court to declare unconstitutional the actions of other branches and levels of government.
lame-duck Ones who serve out terms after being defeated in an election or after deciding not to run again.
legislative branch The elected lawmaking part of government.
legislative courts Highly specialized federal courts created by Congress under the authority of Article I of the Constitution.
liberal The political position that holds that the federal government has a substantial role to play in economic regulation, social welfare, and overcoming racial inequality.
liberals Those who favor government regulation of business and government spending for social programs; the term sometimes also refers to those who favor international cooperation or favor civil liberties and diverse lifestyles.
libertarians Those who are conservative on economic issues but liberal on social issues.
line-item veto The executive's power to delete part of a bill while signing the rest.
literacy test A device used by the southern states to prevent blacks from voting before the passage of the Voting Rights Act of 1965, which banned its use; usually involved interpretation of a section of the state constitution.
lobbies Another name for interest or pressure groups; also, acts of conveying groups' interest to government decision makers.
macroeconomic Having to do with the performance of the economy as a whole.
majority rule The form of political decision making in which policies are decided on the basis of what a majority of the people want.
majority tyranny Suppression of the rights and liberties of a minority by the majority.
majority-minority districts Districts drawn purposely so that a racial minority is in the majority.
mandate A demand; for example, a demand that the states carry out certain policies.
markup The process of revising a bill in committee.
Marshall Plan The program of U.S. economic aid set up to rebuild Europe after World War II.
mass mobilization The process of involving large numbers of people in a social movement.
means-tested Meeting the criteria of demonstrable need.
monetary policies Government policies designed to affect the supply of money and the level of interest rates in the economy.
multipolar system An international system with more than two great powers.
mutually assured destruction (MAD) A situation of nuclear balance, in which either the United States or the Soviet Union could respond to a surprise attack by destroying the other country.
national debt The total outstanding debt of the federal government.
National Intelligence Estimates (NIEs) Official summaries of the best available intelligence information on major national security issues.
national interest What is in the interest of the nation as a whole.
National Reconnaisance Organization (NRO) The government agency in charge of surveillance by satellite photography and other technological means.
national security adviser A top foreign policy and defense adviser to the president who heads the National Security Council.
National Security Agency (NSA) The federal government agency that intercepts and decodes electronic messages and secures U.S. communications around the world.
National Security Council (NSC) An organization in the Executive Office of the President made up of officials from the State and Defense Departments, the CIA, and the military, advising on foreign and security affairs.
nationalizing The process by which provisions of the Bill of Rights have been incorporated. See *incorporation.*
nativist Antiforeign; referring to political movements active in the nineteenth century.

necessary and proper clause Article I, Section 8, of the Constitution: "The Congress shall have Power . . . To make all Laws which shall be necessary and proper for carrying into Execution the foregoing powers." Also known as the *elastic clause.*

New Deal Coalition The informal electoral alliance of working-class ethnic groups, Catholics, urban dwellers, Jews, racial minorities, and the South that was the basis of the Democratic party dominance of American politics from the New Deal to the early 1970s.

New Deal The programs of the administration of President Franklin D. Roosevelt.

New Jersey Plan Proposal of the smaller states at the Constitutional Convention to create a government based on the equal representation of the states in a unicameral legislature.

newsworthy Worth printing or broadcasting as news, according to editors' judgments.

nominal tax rate The percentage of income paid in taxes by each income class according to the income tax tables; differs from the actual percentages paid (known as the *effective rate*) by each income class.

normal vote The proportion of the votes that each party would win if party identification and nothing else affected voting decisions.

North American Free Trade Agreement (NAFTA) An agreement among the United States, Canada, and Mexico to eliminate nearly all barriers to trade and investment among the three countries.

North Atlantic Treaty Organization (NATO) The alliance of the United States, Canada, and Western European countries for defense against the Soviet Union.

NSC–68 A 1950 National Security Council document planning for a military buildup and anti-Communist activities around the world.

nuclear proliferation The spread of nuclear weapons to new countries or to terrorist groups.

nullification An attempt by states to declare national laws or actions null and void.

objective news News reported with no evaluative language and with any opinions quoted or attributed to a specific source.

obscenity As the Supreme Court understands it, the representation of sexually explicit materials in a manner that violates community standards and is without redeeming social importance or value.

Office of Management and Budget (OMB) An organization within the Executive Office of the President that advises on the federal budget, domestic legislation, and regulations.

open seat election An election in which there is no incumbent officeholder.

opinion (of the court) The majority opinion that accompanies a Supreme Court decision.

ordinary scrutiny The assumption that the actions of elected bodies and officials are legal under the Constitution.

original intention The doctrine that the courts must interpret the Constitution in ways consistent with the intentions of the framers rather than in light of contemporary conditions and needs.

original jurisdiction The location where a particular kind of case is initially heard in court.

PAC (political action committee) A private organization whose purpose is to raise and distribute funds to candidates in political campaigns.

parallel campaign A device used to bypass campaign-spending-limits laws; a campaign that helps a particular candidate without mentioning the name of the candidate.

participation Political activity, including voting, campaign activity, contacting officials, and demonstrating.

party caucus (caucus system) A meeting of party activists to choose delegates to presidential nominating conventions.

party identification The sense of belonging to one or another political party.

patronage Government offices and contracts distributed to the supporters of the winning party; same as *spoils.*

Pentagon The enormous building in Arlington, Virginia, that holds military chiefs and top officials of the Defense Department.
petit (trial) juries Trial juries; they hear evidence and sit in judgment on charges brought in civil or criminal cases.
plaintiff One who brings suit in a court.
platform A party's statement of its positions on the issues of the day.
pluralist A political scientist who views American politics as best understood in terms of the interaction, conflict, and bargaining of groups.
plurality More votes than other candidates, but not necessarily a majority.
pocket veto A bill is vetoed if the president does not act on it before 10 days have passed and, in the meantime, Congress adjourns.
policy implementation. The execution, or actual carrying out, of policy.
policy preferences Citizens' preferences concerning what policies they want government to pursue.
political action committee (PAC) A private organization whose purpose is to raise and distribute funds to candidates in political campaigns.
political agenda The menu of issues of peak concern to citizens and public officials.
political business cycle The practice in which elected officials intentionally stimulate growth before elections and postpone economic pain until after elections.
political efficacy The sense that one can affect what government does.
political equality The principle that says that each person in a democracy must carry equal weight in the conduct of the public business.
political liberty The principle that citizens in a democracy are protected from government interference in the exercise of a range of basic freedoms, such as the freedoms of speech, association, and conscience.
political machine A party organization staffed by city workers who owe their jobs to the party.
political socialization Teaching and learning about politics.
poll tax A tax to be paid as a condition of voting.
popular sovereignty A basic principle of democracy; means that the people ultimately rule.
populists Those who are liberal on economic issues but conservative on social issues.
pork Also called pork barrel; projects designed to bring to the constituency jobs and public money for which the members of Congress can claim credit.
poverty line The federal government's calculation of the amount of income families of various sizes need to stay out of poverty.
precedents Rulings by courts that guide judicial reasoning in subsequent cases.
preemption Exclusion of the states from actions that might interfere with federal legislation.
presidential approval rating A president's standing with the public, indicated by the percentage of Americans who tell survey interviewers that they approve a president's "handling of the job."
presidential popularity Conventionally indicated by the percentage of Americans who approve a president's "handling" of the job.
pressure group Another name for *interest group* or *lobby;* implies a group that brings pressure to bear on government decision makers.
primary elections State elections in which delegates to national presidential nominating conventions are chosen.
prior restraint The government's power to prevent publication, as opposed to punishment afterward.
privatization The process of turning over certain government functions to the private sector.
privileges and immunities; privileges and immunities clause That portion of Article IV, Section 2 which says that citizens from out of state have the same legal rights as local citizens in any state.
progressive taxes Taxes that take the largest percentage of the income of those at the upper end of the income scale.

proportional representation A type of electoral system in which legislative seats are apportioned to political parties in proportion to the popular vote that each party receives.
public opinion Political attitudes and beliefs expressed by ordinary citizens.
rally 'round the flag A temporary rise in presidential popularity due to solidarity during a crisis.
random sampling The selection of survey respondents by chance, with equal probability, in order to ensure their representativeness of the whole population.
ranking minority member The minority party member with the greatest seniority on a committee.
real and adverse A Supreme Court rule stating that cases must involve a genuine dispute between two parties. This requirement helps the Court screen out a number of requests for appeal, thus reducing the number of cases it will consider hearing.
realignment The process by which one party supplants another as the dominant party in a political system.
reapportionment The redrawing of congressional district lines to account for population change.
recession A period of decline in overall economic activity.
reciprocity A congressional norm in which members of Congress defer to the judgment of subject-matter specialists, mainly on minor technical bills.
red tape Popular term for overbearing bureaucratic rules and procedures.
referendum Citizens' vote to approve or overturn legislation passed by the legislature.
regressive taxes Taxes that take a larger percentage of the income of those at the bottom of the income scale rather than of those at top.
regulations Rules issued by government agencies.
remedy An action that a court determines must be taken to rectify a wrong.
representative democracy Indirect democracy, in which the people rule through elected representatives.
republicanism A political doctrine advocating limited government based on popular consent, protected against majority tyranny.
reservation clause The Tenth Amendment to the Constitution, reserving powers to the states or the people.
reserve requirements The proportion of its total deposits that a bank must keep in reserve.
responsible party A political party that takes clear, distinct, stands on the issues and enacts them as policy.
retrospective voting Voting on the basis of the past performance of a government.
ripeness A condition a case must meet before the Supreme Court will hear it; the condition is that all other avenues of appeal have been exhausted and the injury has already occurred.
rule of four An *unwritten* practice that requires at least four justices of the Supreme Court to agree that a case warrants review by the Court before it will hear the case.
Rust Belt States of the upper Midwest that have lost manufacturing jobs.
sample survey An interview study asking questions of a set of people who are chosen as representative of the whole population.
scope of conflict Referring to the number of groups involved in a political conflict; few groups mean a narrow scope of conflict, and many groups mean a wide scope of conflict.
secretary of defense The civilian in charge of the Department of Defense and the military services.
secularization The spread of nonreligious values and outlooks.
segregation A social order characterized by the legal separation of the races; common in the southern states from the late nineteenth century until the 1960s.
select committees Temporary committees in Congress created to conduct studies or investigations. They have no power to report bills.

selective incorporation Refers to the fact that, rather than make the protections of the Bill of Rights relevant to the states all at one time, the Supreme Court has only gradually and selectively made constitutional protections relevant at the state level.
senatorial courtesy The tradition which holds that the president's nominations must be cleared with the senior senator of the president's party from the appointee's state.
seniority Length of service, on which most assignments are based.
separate but equal The constitutional doctrine articulated in *Plessy v. Ferguson* (1896) that laws separating the races are permissible if equal public facilities and services are provided.
separation of powers The distribution of government legislative, executive, and judicial powers to separate branches of government.
sit-down strike A form of labor action in which workers stop production but do not leave their place of employment.
smart bombs Bombs capable of being guided precisely to their targets.
social insurance Government programs that provide services or income support in proportion to the amount of mandatory contributions made by individuals into a government trust fund.
soft money Expenditures by political parties on general public education, voter registration, and voter mobilization.
spillover effects Policy effects that go outside the boundaries of the governmental unit making the policy.
spoils The practice of distributing government offices and contracts to the supporters of the winning party; same as patronage.
stagflation A combination of economic stagnation and inflation.
standing A legal term meaning that one may bring legal action because one is affected by the issues raised.
standing committees Relatively permanent congressional committees that address specific areas of legislation. Examples are the House Appropriations, Budget, Rules, and Ways and Means Committees.
stare decisis The legal doctrine that says precedent should guide judicial decision making.
"stay" acts Enactments postponing the collection of taxes and/or mortgage payments.
strict construction Associated with *original intention;* the doctrine that the provisions of the Constitution have a clear meaning and that judges must stick closely to this meaning when rendering decisions.
strict scrutiny The presumption by the Supreme Court that a law, ordinance, or administrative ruling is unconstitutional because it violates fundamental constitutional rights.
strong-mayor system A system of local government in which the mayor has extensive powers of appointment, budgeting, rule making, and the like.
submarine-launched ballistic missiles (SLBMs) Guided missiles, capable of carrying nuclear warheads, launched from submarines.
suffrage The right to vote.
Sun Belt States of the lower South, Southwest, and West where sunny weather and often conservative politics prevail.
superpower A nation armed with nuclear weapons and able to project force anywhere on the globe.
supremacy clause The provision of Article VI of the Constitution that the Constitution itself and the laws and treaties of the United States are the supreme law of the land, taking precedence over state laws.
suspect classification The designation of a group for special treatment by government that is invidious, arbitrary, and/or irrational.
test case A case brought to force a ruling on the constitutionality of some law or executive action.
trade deficit An excess of the value of the goods a country imports over the value of the goods it exports.

Truman Doctrine President Truman's policy that the United States should resist outside pressure against "free" countries.
trustee Edmund Burke's term for representatives who believe they ought to use their best judgment, rather than instructions from their constituents, in making legislative decisions.
trusts Popular term used around the turn of the century to refer to large combinations of business corporations.
turnout The proportion of eligible people who vote.
tyranny The abuse of power by a ruler or government.
unanimous consent Legislative action taken "without objection" as a way to expedite business; used to conduct much of the business of the Senate.
unconventional participation Political activity through demonstrations or protests, rather than taking part in elections or contacting officials.
unipolar system A world system in which a single superpower dominates all other nations.
unitary system A system in which a central government has complete power over its constituent units or states.
value-added tax A national sales tax levied on intermediate goods (between raw materials and the final product); used mainly in Europe.
veto The presidential power to disapprove a bill that has been passed by both houses of Congress. The president's veto can be overridden by a two-thirds vote in each house.
Virginia Plan Proposal by the large states at the Constitutional Convention to create a strong central government with power apportioned to the states on the basis of population.
Warsaw Pact An alliance of the Soviet Union and Eastern European Communist countries.
watchdog The role of the media in scrutinizing the actions of government officials.
weak mayor A local mayor who has few powers of appointment, budgeting, or rule making; the city council and/or independent boards and commissions exercise most powers.
welfare state A society in which a set of government programs protects the minimum standards of living of families and individuals against loss of income.
whip A political party member in Congress charged with keeping members informed of the plans of the party leadership, counting votes before action on important issues, and rounding up party members for votes on bills.
whistleblowers People who bring official misconduct in their agencies to public attention.
white primaries Primary elections open only to whites.
white-collar workers Those who work in service, sales, and office jobs.
winner-take-all An electoral system in which the party or candidate winning the most votes gets all the representatives.
World Trade Organization (WTO) An agency designed to enforce the provisions of the General Agreement on Tariffs and Trade and to resolve trade disputes among nations.
writ of certiorari An announcement that the Supreme Court will hear a case on appeal from a lower court; its issuance requires the vote of four of the nine justices.
writ of mandamus A court order that forces an official to act.
yellow journalism Sensational newspaper stories with large headlines and, in some cases, color cartoons.

Credits

Literary, Figures, and Tables

77 Figure 3.3 (a and b) From *Vital Statistics on American Politics,* 4th ed. by Harold Stanley and Richard G. Niemi. Reprinted by permission of Congressional Quarterly Inc. **94** Figure 4.1 "Productivity vs. Real Compensation" from *The New York Times,* January 2, 1996. Copyright © 1996 by The New York Times Co. Reprinted by permission. **96** Figure 4.3 "The Racial Composition of the U.S. Population" from *The Washington Post,* September 1991. Copyright © 1991, Washington Post Writers Group. Reprinted with permission. **96** Figure 4.3 "The Racial Composition of the U.S. Population" from *The Washington Post,* September 23, 1991, p. 7. Copyright © 1994 The Washington Post. Reprinted with permission. **98** Figure 4.4 "Population Shift from Rural to Urban to Suburban" from *The New York Times,* September 11, 1990. Copyright © 1990 by The New York Times Co. Reprinted by permission. **108–109** From "Europe Jobless, America Penniless" by Paul Krugman reprinted with permission from *Foreign Policy 95* (Summer 1994). Copyright © 1994 by the Carnegie Endowment for International Peace. **105** Figure 4.9 "GDP and Income" from "The Survey of American Business" in *The Economist,* September 16, 1995, p. 12. Copyright © 1995 The Economist Newspaper Group, Inc. Reprinted with permission. Further reproduction prohibited. **106** Figure 4.11 "Comparative Income Distribution" from *The New York Times,* April 17, 1995. Copyright © 1995 by The New York Times Co. Reprinted by permission. **119** Figure 4.15 © The Public Perspective, a publication of the Roper Center for Public Opinion Research, University of CT, Storrs. Reprinted by permission. **123** Figure 4.16 Adapted from "Percentage of People Who Say They Draw Comfort from Religion," Social Surveys, The Gallup Organization, 1981. Reprinted with permission. **147** Figure 5.4 Adapted from *The American Ethos Public Attitudes Toward Capitalism and Democracy* by Herbert M. McClosky and John Zaller (Cambridge, MA Harvard University Press). Copyright © 1984 by Twentieth Century Fund Inc. Reprinted by permission of Harvard University Press. **183** Table 6.1 From *The Wall Street Journal,* August 1, 1995, p. B-1. Reprinted by permission of The Wall Street Journal; copyright © 1995 Dow Jones & Company, Inc. All rights reserved worldwide. **212** Figure 7.1 From Edward S. Greenberg. *The American Political System: A Radical Approach,* 5th ed. (Glenview, IL: Scott, Foresman, 1989). **254** Table 8.2 "State Requirements for Ballot Access" from *The New York Times,* September 28, 1995. Copyright © 1995 by The New York Times Co. Reprinted by permission. **299** Figure 9.6 "Opinions and Views Convention Delegates Versus the Public" from *The New York Times,* August 14, 1988. Copyright © 1988 by The New York Times Co. Reprinted by permission. **308** Figure 9.8 "Portrait of the Electorate: How Groups Voted" from *The New York Times,* November 5, 1992. Copyright © 1992 by The New York Times Co. Reprinted by permission. **326** "Mary Beth Tinker Protests the War" reprinted with the permission of The Free Press, a division of Simon & Schuster from *The Courage of Their Convictions* by Peter Irons. Copyright © 1988 by Peter Irons. **360** Figure 11.5 "Where congressional campaign money comes from, comparing 1974 and 1994" from *Congress and Its Members,* 4th ed. by Robert Davidson and Walter J. Oleszek. Reprinted by permission of Congressional Quarterly Press. **361** Figure 11.6 "Incumbent Reelection Rates, 1964–1992" from *The Congressional Quarterly,* November 1992. Reprinted by permission of Congressional Quarterly Press. **362** Figure 11.7 Adapted from *The Congressional Quar-*

terly, November 10, 1990, p. 3797. Reprinted by permission. **363** Figure 11.8 From "Democracy in America: How Are We Doing?" by Burns W. Roper, *The Public Perspective,* March/April 1994, p. 4. Reprinted by permission of The Roper Center. **455** Figure 13.2 "Percentage of presidential appointees who are women" adapted from "Women Appointees in Percent of Appointees" by Pat Carr from *Knight-Ridder Tribune,* September 27, 1993. Reprinted by permission of Tribune Media Services. **486** Figure 14.3 From *Storm Center: The Supreme Court in American Politics,* 3rd ed. by David M. O'Brien. Copyright © 1993 by David M. O'Brien. Reprinted by permission of W. W. Norton & Company, Inc. **515** Figure 15.1 "How States Spend Their Money" from *The New York Times,* December 30, 1990. Copyright © 1990 by The New York Times Co. Reprinted by permission. **526** Figure 15.5 From Erikson, Robert, and John McIver. "Public Opinion and Policy Liberalism in the American States." *American Journal of Political Science,* Volume 31 (November, 1987). Reprinted by permission of The University of Wisconsin Press. **607** Figure 18.3 From *American Diplomacy in the Twentieth Century,* 2nd ed. by Robert D. Schulzinger. Copyright © 1984 by Robert D. Schulzinger. Used by permission of Oxford University Press, Inc. **636** Table 18.2 From *Forbes* magazine, 07/17/95, pp. 274–275. Reprinted by permission of *Forbes* magazine © Forbes Inc., 1995. **695** Figure 20.1 Graph from *The Washington Post,* September 18, 1995. Copyright © 1995, The Washington Post. Reprinted with permission. **698** Figure 20.4 Graph from *The Washington Post,* March 4, 1991. Copyright © 1991, The Washington Post. Reprinted with permission.

Photo

1 Bill Weems/Woodfin Camp, Inc. **3** © Michael Heron/Woodfin Camp. 4 AP/Wide World. **5** © A. Ramey/Unicorn. **6** AP/Wide World. **8** Granger. **11** Granger. **14** Granger. **18** © M. Schwarz/The Image Works. **23** Tony Stone Images. **25** Granger. **28 left** Granger. **28 right** Library of Congress. **29** Trumbull Collection/Copyright Yale University Art Gallery. **33** Joe Marquette/Philadelphia Enquirer/Woodfin Camp. **39** The Illustrated London News/February 16, 1861. **42** Independence National Historic Park Collection/Eastern National Parks and Monuments Association . **45 top** David Scull/NYT Pictures. **45 bottom** Reuters/Win McNamee/Archive Photos. **53** Art Resource. **54** © Bob Strong/The Image Works. **59** Win McNamee/Reuters/Archive Photos. **60** AP/Wide World. **63** Reuters/Peter Jones/Archive Photos. **68** Alan Reininger/Contact Press Images. **71** Bob Daemmrich/The Image Works. **73** Bart Bartholomew/Black Star. **75** Scott, Foresman & Company. **78** Courtesy Lyndon Baines Johnson Library, Austin, TX. **81** P. Jorden/Sygma. **83** By Lorenz; © The New Yorker Magazine, Inc. **84** Ira Wyman/Sygma. **85** AP/Wide World. **86** Anneal Vohra/Unicorn. **93** © James Wilson/Woodfin Camp. **97** S. Kelly © San Diego Union-Tribune, Copley News Service. **99** P. F. Bentley/Black Star. **102** © Spencer Grant/Photobank. **107** Drawing by D. Fradon; © 1993 The New Yorker Magazine, Inc. **110** © 1992 Chromosohm/Joe Sohm/Unicorn. **113** © Lee Snider/The Image Works. **114** Reuters/Win McNamee/Archive Photos. **116** AP/Wide World. **121** Special Collections/New York Public Library, Astor, Lenox and Tilden Foundations. **125** PhotoFest. **131** Crandall/The Image Works. **133** © J. P. Fizet/Sygma. **137** Bob Daemmrich/The Image Works. **138** UPI/Bettmann. **143** © Liaison/Gamma-Liaison. **144** Reuters/Bettmann. **146** Mark Peterson. **153** By Lorenz; © The New Yorker Magazine, Inc. **154** Scott, Foresman & Company. **156** Regis Bossu/Sygma. **157** Harvard University Portrait Collection. **160** Tony Freeman/Photo Edit. **163 left** Naoki Okamoto/Black Star. **163 right** David Frazier. **173** Jason Laure. **174** The Kobal Collection. **175** Reprinted by permission Tribune Media Services. **176** Scott, Foresman & Company. **178 left** *New York Journal,* February 7, 1898. **178 right** The State Historical Society of Colorado. **180** Charles Steiner/JB Pictures, Ltd. **181** Chenet/Gamma-Liaison. **182** Reuters/Corbis/Bettmann. **185** Lee Snider/The Image Works. **187** Reuters/Bettmann. **190** © Cynthia Johnson/Gamma-Liaison. **194 left** Lisa Quinones/Black Star. **194 right** Reuters/Luc Novovitch/Archive Photos. **196** P. Forden/Sygma. **197** Charles Steiner/JB Pictures Ltd. **201** Dennis Brack/Black Star. **209** Mark Burnett. **212** Library of Congress. **215** Library of Congress. **218** Jeffrey Markowitz/Sygma. **219** Paul Conklin/PhotoEdit. **221** PhotoFest. **226** © Jeffrey Markowitz/Sygma. **230** AP/Wide World. **234** AP/Wide World. **243** AP/Wide World. **245** Tony Freeman/PhotoEdit. **248** Scott, Foresman & Company. **251** Reuters/Peter Morgann/Archive Photos. **255** Les Stone/Sygma. **259** AP/Wide World. **260** UPI/Bettmann. **261** © Mathieu Polak/Sygma. **262** AP/Wide World. **264** Wally McNamee/Sygma. **266** © Steve Barrett/Contact Press Images. **268** Reuters/Reed Schumann/Archive Photos. **275** AP/Wide World. **282** From the Art Collection of the Boatmen's National Bank of St. Louis. **285** UPI/Bettmann. **288** AP/Wide World. **291** Lisa Quinones/Black Star. **294** © Markel/Gamma-Liaison. **295** PhotoFest. **296** Gifford/Gamma-Liaison. **300** UPI/Bettmann. **301** AP/Wide World. **302** Scott, Foresman. **310 left** UPI/Bettmann. **310 right** UPI/Bettmann. **310 bottom** © 1995,

Chip Bok, Akron Beacon Journal. Reprinted with permission by Creators Syndicate. **319** AP/Wide World. **322** © 1994 ChromoSohm/Sohm/Photo Researchers. **323** Sylvia Johnson/Woodfin Camp, Inc. **327** McCartney/Photo Researchers. **329** Donna Binder/Impact Photos. **330** UPI/Corbis-Bettmann. **331** © Bruce Roberts/Photo Researchers. **333** Rob Nelson. **337** The Kobal Collection. **339** Larry Fisher/Quad City Times/Sygma. **343** Morris Best/Uniphoto. **345** AP/Wide World. **351** Scott, Foresman and Company. **356** © Mark Richards/PhotoEdit. **358** UPI/Bettmann. **362** © 1991 Seattle Post-Intelligencer, North America Syndicate; cartoon by David Horsey. **364** J. Barr/Gamma-Liaison. **370** Reuters/Bettmann. **371** © Brad Markel/Gamma-Liaison. **375** AP/Wide World. **377** AP/Wide World. **383** © Paul Conklin/PhotoEdit. **386** AP/Wide World. **393** Dennis Brack/Black Star. **395 left** Gift of Edgar William, Chrysler & Bernice Garbish/The Metropolitan Museum of Art. **395 right** AP/Wide World. **397** The New York Historical Society, New York City. **398** Library of Congress. **399** AP/Wide World. **403** © Sygma. **404** UPI/Bettmann. **405** Arthur Grace/Sygma. **409** Bettmann. **410** AP/Wide World. **412** Dennis Brack/Black Star. **415** Sygma. **422** © Cynthia Johnson/Gamma-Liaison. **425** George Tames/NYT Pictures. **427** Brown Brothers. **428** UPI/Bettmann. **432** The Record, New Jersey/Jimmy Margulies. **441** AP/Wide World. **446** UPI/Corbis-Bettmann. **448** © J. Langevin/Sygma. **450** © 1995 Alex Webb/Magnum Photos. **451** © Ramey/Reuters/Archive Photos. **466** © Margot Granitsas/Photo Researchers. **467** Reuters/Gary Cameron/Archive Photos. **470** Cameron Davidson/Folio. **471** PhotoFest. **477** © Diana Walker/Gamma Liaison. **479 left** Superstock. **479 right** Washington & Lee University. **489** Shepard Sherbell/SABA. **490** © Reinstein/The Image Works. **491** Jeffrey Markowitz/Sygma. **496** © 1986 Ken Heinen. **498** Granger. **499** Everett CCU Archives. **505** Carl Iwasaki/Life Magazine/Time Warner Inc. **506** Dorothea Lange Collection/The National Archives. **513** James Cook/Stock Boston. **516** © Brad Markel/Gamma-Liaison. **518** Joe Traver/Gamma Liaison. **519** © Alex Tehrani/Gamma-Liaison. **527** AP/Wide World. **530** Jean-Claude LeJeune. **533** AP/Wide World. **535** Scott, Foresman and Company. **536** © Mike Yamashita/Woodfin Camp. **538 top** Lester Sloan/Woodfin Camp & Associates. **538 bottom** © Robert Brenner/PhotoEdit. **545** Terry Vine/Tony Stone Images. **547** Joe Traver/Gamma-Liaison. **550** © Radhika Chalasani/Gamma-Liaison. **553** © Yvonne Hensey/Gamma-Liaison. **555** Culver. **557** AP/Wide World. **558** Kobal Collection. **559** UPI/Bettmann. **561** N. Tully/Sygma. **563** Archive Photos/AMW Pressedienst GMBH. **564** © M. Douglas/The Image Works. **566** Mike Clemmer/Picture Group. **568** G. Ronald Lopez/Unicorn. **571** © Tom Smart/Gamma-Liaison. **575** AFP/Bettmann. **577 top** Chicago Historical Society. **577 bottom** Granger. **578** Granger. **579** Granger. **581** Granger. **583** UPI/Bettmann. **586** Archive Photos. **589** © Gamma/Gamma-Liaison. **590** AP/Wide World. **594** © David R. Frazier/Photobank. **595** AP/Wide World. **599** AP/Wide World. **602** Harley Dod/SABA. **605** AP/Wide World. **609** John Olson © 1973 Time Magazine. **612** Abbas/Magnum Photos. **613** Alexander Auokian/Contact Press Images. **615** AP/Wide World. **621** C. Brown/SIPA Press. **625** AP/Wide World. **627** © 1994 Alex S. MacLean. **630** © Chantal Regnault/Gamma-Liaison. **631** © Bruce Hoertel/Gamma-Liaison. **633** © Universal Press Syndicate. Reprinted with permission. All rights reserved. **637** AP/Wide World. **639** Liaison/Gamma-Liaison. **647** © Porter Gifford/Gamma-Liaison. **650** Les Stone/Sygma. **652** © 1993 Andrew Jenny/Unicorn. **653** AP/Wide World. **656** UPI/Corbis-Bettmann. **658** Rick Maiman/Sygma. **660** AP/Wide World. **671** Bernard Wolf/Monkmeyer. **676** Evan Agostini/Gamma Liaison. **680** Robert Trippett/SIPA Press. **691** Jeffrey Markovitz/Sygma. **693** Mark Antman/The Image Works. **699** Eli Reed/Magnum Photo. **701** John Ficoio/Sygma. **707** Robert Brenner/Photo Edit. **710** Borgman, with permission of King Features. **714** Tony Sairni/Gamma Liaison. **719** AP/Wide World. **730** S. Franklin/Magnum.

Index